Far From Unworkable

A Comprehensive Reference on the History, Rules and Impact of Intercolonial and Interstate Conventions Leading to the Fears, Facts, FAQs, the Fight Over and the Findings of State and Federal Court Decisions Relating to the United States Constitution's Provision for an **Article V Amendatory Convention**

TIMOTHY J. DAKE

Libertas Books • Franklin, Wisconsin

Copyright © 2017 by Timothy J. Dake

All rights are reserved. No part of this book shall be reproduced or transmitted in any form or by any means, electronic, mechanical, magnetic, photographic including photocopying, recording or by any information storage and retrieval system, without prior written permission from the author except in the case of brief quotations embodied in critical articles and reviews. No patent liability is assumed with respect to the use of the information contained herein. Although every precaution has been taken in the preparation of this book, the author and publisher assume no responsibility for any errors or omissions. Nor is there any liability assumed for damages resulting from the use of the information herein.

Published by:
Libertas Books
3286 W. Plaza Dr.
Franklin, Wisconsin 53132

To Contact: libertasbooks@wi.rr.com

Cover Art and Interior Design: Lori B. Lang

Library of Congress Control Number: 2016917780

ISBN: **978-0-9982109-1-9 (Paperback)**

ISBN: **978-0-9982109-0-2 (Hardback)**

ISBN: **978-0-9982109-2-6 (eBook)**

Printed in the United States of America

Dedication

This book was inspired by the fifty-five men who came from all corners of the young United States to boldly and calmly assess, discuss and address the problems facing the new nation. In doing so they overcame regional, religious, political, economic and philosophical differences to create the greatest political charter ever conceived. They exhibited, in varying degrees, vision, hope, non-partisanship, statesmanship, and in terms of Article V, humility enough to publicly recognize their own fallibility and to possess deference to the needs and desires of the future generations. Their inclusion of the convention method of amendment demonstrates their wisdom and their grasp of human nature and history. We cannot ever repay them.

This book is dedicated to that most exquisite of creatures, my beautiful, beloved wife, Michele: sounding board, critic, grammatician, devil's advocate, gentle prodder, dose of reality, editor, facilitator, fearless expositor of truth, rejecter of dubious data, dispenser of incredulous glances at unsupportable conclusions, calm suggestor of alternative and therefore more probable explanations, muse and exemplar of patience. I cannot ever repay her.

Contents

Article V of the United States Constitution	i
Acknowledgments	ii
State Legislators' 15-Minute Executive Summary	**VII**
Purpose:	vii
Definitions:	viii
Central Premises (Myths):	viii
Most Common Objections (Taken from Excursus 2):	ix
Introduction: THE FRAMERS' FORESIGHT	**XV**

Part I - From Contiones to Constitutions

ONE: Defining an Article V Convention Exactly	**1**
The Roman Republic	2
Great Britain	5
What Do We Mean When We Say "Convention"?	10
The Many Types and Forms of Political Conventions	15
The Powers of Conventions	28
The Limitations of Conventions	48
The Procedures of Conventions	62
TWO: An All Too Brief Overview of the History of Intercolonial and Interstate Conventions	**73**
The History of American Conventions	75
The Development of the Amending Process	101
Post-Revolutionary American Conventions	106
THREE: Pivotal Philadelphia, 1787	**123**
The Push to Philadelphia	131
The Development of Article V	136

The Battle Over a Second General Convention, Part I	152
Ratification	155
The Battle Over a Second General Convention, Part II	162

FOUR: An All Too Brief History of the Attempts to Call an Article V Convention — 179

Early Efforts at an Amendatory Convention	181
The Advent of the Organized Convention Campaign	188
Modern Campaigns	197
The Impact of Legislation of the Proposal of an Article V Convention	208

Part II - Put on Parchment, Set in Stone

FIVE: Holding Court on Article V — 217

The Judiciary's Power and Requirements	223
The Political Question Doctrine	223
Standing	232
Ripeness	244
Congress's Powers and Requirements	247
Homogeneity	250
Contemporaneity	253
Validity	256
The Necessary and Proper Clause	258
The Tenth Amendment	261
The States' Power and Requirements	265
Rescission	266
Control of Delegate Selection and Qualifications	270
Determination of the Subject and the Extent of the Application	272
The Executive's Power and Requirements	275
The Report of The American Bar Association	277
The Impact of the State Experience and State Courts on Amendatory Conventions	278

EXCURSUS 1: Cases and Court Findings Relating to Article V — 287

    United States Supreme Court — 288

    Federal District and Appeals Courts — 328

    State Supreme and Appeals Courts — 349

    Court Decisions Listed by Year of Rendering — 395

SIX: Seeking and Establishing the Rules of an Article V Convention — 401

    The Congress Acts — 403

    The Grassroots Act — 409

    A Comparison of the Rules Proposals — 412

    Can a Convention be Called that Merely Approves a Pre-written Amendment? — 414

    Can a Continuity Clause be Applied to a Convention? — 416

    Can the Content of the Convention Call be Controlled, and by Whom? — 424

    A Summary of the Rules as Gleaned from Article V, Court Decisions, Traditions and Customs — 432

    Powers Prohibited to the Amendatory Convention — 436

Part III - Questioning Everything

SEVEN: So Many Questions and the Search for Answers — 441

    Perpetuating Uncertainty — 443

    The Evolution of Scholarly Thought on Article V — 452

    The Issues of the Article V Convention Academic Debate — 462

    Major Issues: — 463

    Minor Issues: — 465

    The Origins of the Opposition — 466

EXCURSUS 2: Article V Convention FAQs — 473

Defining an Article V Convention (AVC)	479
Powers of the Convention and Delegates	502
Congress' Role in an AVC	517
States' Role in an AVC	530
Operation of the AVC	540
Legal Aspects of the AVC	547
Views of the Founding Fathers on a Second General Convention	552
Miscellaneous Questions	557

EIGHT: Arguing *The Federalist* Essays, "Publius" Speaks — 571

The Impact of the Essays	571
The Federalist Essays by the Numbers	578
The Prelude and Postscript to The Federalist	592

Part IV: Constitutional Déjà Vu

NINE: The Argument Against an Article V Convention — 599

Caution versus Constitutionalism	600
The Potential for a "Runaway" Convention	611
Could a Convention be Controlled?	625
Congress Will Take Control of the Convention	630
Congress Cannot Take Control of the Convention	632
Could the Constitution and/or Bill of Rights be Eliminated?	633
There are No Rules to Govern the Convention	637
The Limited versus Unlimited Convention Debate	640
The Delegates May Be Controlled by Special Interests	651
No Restraining or Reversing of the Actions of a Convention is Possible	654
The States Will Not Have an Equal Vote	655
The Convention Can Enact a New Ratification Process	655
No Washington, Franklin, Jefferson or Madison, etc., Exists Today	658
A Convention would Cause a Confrontation Between the	

Branches of the Federal Government, the States and the Convention		662
The Past is Not Necessarily Prologue		665

TEN: And the Argument In Favor... 673

Circumvention of Congress		676
Limitability of the Convention		678
Cooling Effect of the Convention		681
Prodding Effect of the Convention		682
Leveling Effect of a Convention		691
Difficulty in Obtaining a Convention		693
Public Scrutiny		694
Ratification Threshold		695
Delegate Scrutiny		696
Restoring Federalism		697
The Necessity of Action		699
The Necessity of Change		701
The Familiarity of Convention Practices		702
Constitutionality of Article V		706

CONCLUSION: The Framers' Eminently Workable Solution 709

Appendices

Appendix A: Relation of All Powers 729

Appendix A.1- Relation of All Powers		732

Appendix B: Tables of Intercolonial, Interstate and Constitution Related Conventions 735

Appendix B.1 - All State Constitutional Conventions		740
Appendix B.2 - All State Non-constitutional Conventions		752

Appendix B.3 - All Territorial Constitutional Conventions   755

Appendix B.4 - Provisional State and Territory Conventions   756

Appendix B.5 - All National Constitutional Conventions (Non-US Govt)   757

Appendix B.6 - All Article V Federal Conventions   759

Appendix B.7 - All Article VII Federal Conventions   761

Appendix B.8 - Select Intercolonial and Interstate Conventions   762

Appendix B.9 - All Amendatory Conventions   764

Appendix C: 1787 Delegate Commissions   767

Appendix D: Glossary of Terms   773

Bibliography   781

   CITED MATERIALS   781

      Books   781

      Government Documents   788

      Articles   791

      Reports   804

   SURVEYED MATERIALS   805

      Books   805

      Articles   806

Index   811

Article V of the United States Constitution

"The Congress, whenever two thirds of both Houses shall deem it necessary, shall propose Amendments to this Constitution, or, on the Application of the Legislatures of two thirds of the several States, shall call a Convention for proposing Amendments, which, in either Case, shall be valid to all Intents and Purposes, as Part of this Constitution, when ratified by the Legislatures of three fourths of the several States, or by Conventions in three fourths thereof, as the one or the other Mode of Ratification may be proposed by the Congress; Provided that no Amendment which may be made prior to the Year One thousand eight hundred and eight shall in any Manner affect the first and fourth Clauses in the Ninth Section of the first Article; and that no State, without its Consent, shall be deprived of its equal Suffrage in the Senate."

Acknowledgments

Many hands have had a part in creating this work. The road to this book began with a conversation with Professor Kevin Gutzman of Western Connecticut State University. In a discussion concerning the abuse of the federal constitution and of the decay of constitutionality in general, he suggested and then argued persuasively that the Article V convention was the only remaining viable solution. At that time, I was firmly in the camp of the convention opponents. Kevin got me thinking and he recommended a number of books. Over the next couple of years, he answered questions and expanded on points that led me to believe that my position was untenable. As a member of the Wisconsin Grand*Sons of Liberty*, it fell to me to conduct an Issue Analysis for the group and then to present the case to the group. We concluded that the facts dictated that we were on the wrong side of the amendatory convention issue and our Position Statement now endorses an Article V Amendatory Convention as the logical step to righting a number of constitutional wrongs. Thank you, Kevin.

Because so much of the topic of an amendatory convention rests on the legal issues and I am not an attorney, I had to turn to members of the legal community for assistance in understanding and interpreting the legal issues and sources. I am deeply, deeply, indebted to constitutional attorney Michael L. Stern for review, guidance, and suggestions for this work. I extend to Mike the credit for what is correct; but the mistakes are all my own.

The sourcing of material, reviewing of drafts, checking of footnotes and generally arguing about the finer points were carried out by a number of people in the Wisconsin Grand*Sons of Liberty*: Jim Bartkowski, Norm Reynolds, Larry Gamble, Kathy Mueller, Lori Lang, Bob Fischer and Michele Dake. Other group members served as sounding boards. Many of these people read the successive drafts from the perspective of being an activist. They provided feedback and constructive criticism that helped to shape a more coherent – and balanced – argument for the convention. They also provided many of the questions in the FAQs that are echoed throughout the book.

Reviewers outside of the group contributed by standing in for the state legislators and critiquing the drafts from the state legislators' perspective: Dr.

Anthony Bowman and Dr. Vikram Cariapa, both of Marquette University, Dr. David Stein, and Ross Brown. Dr. Bowman was instrumental in securing a good portion of the harder to obtain articles, books and legal materials used in research.

Many others contributed answers to questions, opinions and ideas that helped to flesh out answers: Dr. Peverill Squire of the University of Missouri, Dr. Mary Sarah Bilder of Boston College, former Chief Justice of the Michigan Supreme Court Thomas Brennan, graciously addressed specific questions that I posed to them. I am beholden to a number of wonderful state and territorial archivists: Steve Murray of the Alabama Department of Archives & History; Chris Heib of Alaska State Archives; Lauren Jarvis of the Arkansas History Commission; Elizabeth Behnam of the California State Archives; Elena Cline of the Colorado State Archives; Mel Smith of the Connecticut State Library; Joshua Goodman of the State Archives of Florida; Kayla Barrett of The Georgia Archives; Alice Tran of the Hawaii State Archives; Rachel Hollis of the Idaho State Archives; Dave Joens of the Illinois State Archives; Jim Corridan of the Indiana Archives and Records Administration; Jeffery Dawson of the Iowa State Historical Library & Archives; Sara Keckeisen of the Kansas Historical Society; the Kentucky Department for Libraries and Archives; Dave Cheever of the Maine State Archives; Jennifer Hafner of the Maryland State Archives; Jennifer Fauxsmith of the Massachusetts Archives; Jessica Harden of the Archives of Michigan; Sarah Quimby of the Minnesota Historical Society; Katie Blount of the Mississippi Department of Archives and History; Jodie Foley of the Montana Historical Society; Gayla Koerting of the Nebraska State Historical Society; Jeffery Kintop of the Nevada State Library, Archives and Public Records; Brian Burford of the New Hampshire Division of Archives and Records Management; Bette Epstein of the New Jersey State Archives; Rick Hendricks of the New Mexico Commission of Public Records; the New York State Archives Reference Services Office; Ansley Wegner of the North Carolina Office of Archives and History; Jim Davis of the State Historical Society of North Dakota; Tom Rieder of the Ohio History Connection; Carol Guilliams of the Oklahoma State Archives; Austin Schulz of the Oregon State Archives; Jonathan Stayer of the Pennsylvania State Archives; Kenneth Carlson of the Rhode Island Department of State; Steve Tuttle of the South Carolina Department of Archives and History; Ken Stewart of the South Dakota State Historical Society; Allison Griffey of the Tennessee

State Library & Archives; the Texas State Library and Archives Commission; Heidi Stringham of the Research Center of the Utah State Archives & Utah State History; Mariessa Dobrick of the Vermont State Archives & Records Administration; William Luebke of the Library of Virginia; Lupita Lopez of the Washington State Archives Research Services; Joe Geiger of the West Virginia Archives and History; Lee Grady of the Wisconsin Historical Society; Michael Strom of the Wyoming State Archives; James Himphill of the Office of Archives and Records Management of the American Samoa Government; Rebecca Katz of the Office of Public Records of the Government of the District of Columbia; and Christopher Todd of the Northern Marianas College (Territorial Archivist).

I have had the great pleasure of working with some phenomenal people in the Article V Convention movement. I extend my thanks for conversations, ideas and review of pieces of the work to Loren Enns, Bill Fruth, Tom Llewellyn, Lou Marin and Lew Uhler, all of the Balanced Budget Amendment Task Force; Arthur Taylor; Steven Gillespie of I Am American; Kyle Maichle formerly of the Heartland Institute; Wisconsin State Senator and Assembly of State Legislatures member and committee chair David Craig and Wisconsin State Senator and Assembly of State Legislatures co-president Chris Kapenga and their respective staffs, especially Kaleb Vander Wiele and Nik Rettinger.

Also, educators Mrs. Miriam Long, Dr. Joseph Majdalani and Dr. Hyunjae Park.

I would be remiss if I failed to acknowledge that there were many people that have adamantly argued with me against the Article V amendatory convention – they helped me to recognize points of contention that needed to be fully addressed to do the topic justice. These people include state legislators and their staffs, John Birch Society members, some of whom I engaged in a formal debate, and grassroots and Tea Party activists. It was all great fun.

State Legislators' 15-Minute Executive Summary

> *"No intelligent American will gainsay the proposition that voting to amend the Constitution of the United States is the most crucial task a state legislator can perform. This is true because an amendment to the federal Constitution will control the lives of all generations of Americans as long as time shall last unless it is sooner removed from that instrument by another Amendment."*
>
> –Statement of US Senator Sam Ervin, Jr.[1]

Purpose:

The amendatory convention option was included in Article V by the Framers to provide a method of going around an obstructionist federal government (specifically Congress) that refused to heed the will of the people. The Framers expected that the day would come when Congress began to act like Parliament and they deliberately planned for the people to assert and protect their constitutional rights. The amendatory convention is the ultimate in the system of checks and balances as it is the only check on the ENTIRE federal government by the people and the States. The power of an amendatory convention is equivalent and identical to that of Congress in the amendment process.

---

[1] Statement of US Senator Sam Ervin, Jr., Concerning the Bizarre and Specious Claim of Supporters of the Equal Rights Amendment That a State Which Has Rejected the Amendment Can Change Its Mind and Vote to Ratify, Whereas a State Which Has Ratified the Amendment Cannot Change its Mind and Vote to Rescind or Withdraw its Ratification. 5 April 1977

Definitions:

- ***Constitutional Convention*** – a plenary (fully powered) convention called to write a constitution. It is empowered to deal with all facets of government.

- ***Amendatory Convention*** – a non-plenary (limited power) convention called to discuss, draft and propose an amendment to a constitution. It does <u>not</u> have the power to write or rewrite a constitution, nor to change the ratification process, nor to enact any amendment of new constitution. It can only propose.

- ***Ratification Convention*** – a non-plenary (limited power) convention called to discuss and vote on whether to accept a proposed amendment to a constitution. It can only vote up or down, it cannot change or rewrite the proposed amendment.

- An amendatory convention is NOT the same as a constitutional convention.

- A summary of all of the numerous types of conventions and their powers and limitations is found in Chapter 1.

Central Premises (Myths):

- ***There has never been an Article V convention before*** - Article V covers both amendatory conventions and ratificatory conventions. There were 39 ratificatory conventions held under Article V for the 21st Amendment. The States and Territories have held more than 80 strictly limited power amendatory conventions. None ran away or attempted to rewrite the Constitution. (Covered in depth in Chapters 1-4.)

- ***There are no rules for an amendatory convention*** - All conventions have rules and this is proven by examining the proceedings of the hundreds of constitutional, amendatory, ratificatory and other political conventions held since the settling of America. Establishment of the rules is usually the second action taken in a convention after the selection of the conventions officers and the Rules Committee. Generally, the rules are similar from one convention to another. There have been hundreds of court decisions at the state, federal and Supreme Court levels that cover the operations of an amendatory convention. Summaries of the 105 examined cases are found in Excursus 1. (Covered in depth in Chapters 5 & 6.)

- *We don't know what will happen in a convention so it is dangerous* - The States and their predecessor colonies have been meeting in conventions since the early 1600s. To this day, the States participate in regular interstate compact meetings that are synonymous with conventions. The average state is a party to 25 compacts. Because convention delegates do not require re-election, delegates are insulated from special interests and donors making, according to university studies, conventions more honest and moderate. (Covered in depth in Chapters 7 and 8.)

Most Common Objections (Taken from Excursus 2):

- *An amendatory convention can run away and write a new constitution, or repeal the bill of rights, or reinstate slavery, etc.* – an amendatory convention can do none of those things as it is not empowered to do anything other than propose an amendment. And then, it cannot enact anything, including that proposed amendment, as Congress must specify the method of ratification and the States are the only parties authorized to ratify/amend the Constitution. (Details are found in Chapter 1.)

- *The 1787 Philadelphia Convention ran away* – the convention delegates acted according to the commissions issued to them by their respective states. Ten of the 12 attending states intended for their delegates to address the problem of the ineffective Articles of Confederation by either improving or replacing the federal government. Eighteen of the 55 delegates were sitting members of the Confederation Congress and all but one of them served in their states' respective ratification conventions as well; if the convention ran away, then they ran away from themselves. (Details are found in Chapter 3 and Appendix C.)

- *There are no safeguards existing to prevent a runaway convention* - The States retain the power to instruct their delegations. Since Congress does not make the rules for the AVC, the States are free to restrain their respective delegates as they see fit. This power includes recalling the delegate(s) as needed or limiting their capabilities. The States and the convention itself can limit the agenda of the AVC to a single issue prohibiting introduction, or even discussion, of any other issue or proposed amendment. Anything proposed by the convention requires a supermajority of three-quarters (or currently 38) of the States to ratify separately from the convention. The States limit the convention by the topic specified in their resolutions to Congress. (Details are found in Chapters 9 and 10.)

- *Congress selects the delegates to the convention* – The States are empowered to select their own delegates according to their own respective criteria. This has been the practice of intercolonial and interstate conventions for hundreds of years. The delegates to the Philadelphia Convention of 1787 were selected by the States without any input from Congress. The delegates to the 1933-34 Article V ratification conventions for the Twenty-first Amendment were elected in the States. (Details are found in Chapters 5, 6 and 10.)

- *Congress makes the rules for the convention* – Congress does not make the rules as the historical practice has been to allow the convention to develop and implement its own rules. Over the last few years, state legislators have worked through the Assembly of State Legislatures to develop a set of proposed convention rules that are agreeable to all of the States. During the late 1970s and into the 1990s, 41 separate bills were introduced in Congress for the purpose of defining and codifying the AVC process. None passed. (Details are found in Chapters 6, 9 and 10.)

- *Congress controls (or cannot control) the convention* - Congress is more of a "processor" of the applications. Its role is "ministerial" and not legislative. Ironically, people argue that both sides of this issue are problems. Those that see control by Congress as necessary will argue that the convention is a bad idea because Congress cannot control the convention and therefore it will run away. Those that see control by Congress as a disaster will argue that Congress will assert control and the convention will not be able to complete its task. Constitutionally, Congress has only the power to call the convention and set the date and place of the convention. By precedent, history, tradition and law, Congress may not control a convention that is designed to circumvent Congress. (Details are found in Chapters 6, 9 and 10.)

- **The convention cannot be limited to just one or a few topics** – The content of the call to convention issued by Congress is determined by the topic(s) stated in the aggregated applications of the States. In order to avoid the concerns of contemporaneity, validity and homogeneity, the States have instituted a practice of copying the wording of the States that have preceded each in passing a resolution for a convention and also by including in the resolution, the names of the preceding States. Each state specifically states the purpose of the desired convention making certain that the purpose is clearly discernible from the resolution so that the resolution is counted with the other States' submittals. If the States name a single topic, for example, a balanced budget amendment, then the convention is limited to that topic only. (Details are found in Chapters 6, 9 and 10.)

- **The larger states will have more votes than the smaller states** – The historical practice of intercolonial and interstate conventions has been for hundreds of years to use unit voting, or voting by the "one-State, one-vote" method. In this manner, every state is equal in the application of federalism. Although there have been many proposals to emulate the Electoral College method, this method has not been used in the history of federal conventions. The application process is made state-by-state; the ratification is done state-by-state; the 1787 Constitutional Convention operated on a state-by-state basis; the Constitution was ratified and therefore adopted state-by-state; so it stands to reason that we would adhere to this circumscription of a state-by-state unit vote within the amendatory convention itself. The process is not an exercise of democracy, but one of exercising federalism. (Details are found in Chapters 6, 9 and 10.)

- **Special interests will control the convention** – Since the delegates will not need to consider the implications of their vote in terms of re-election or campaign donations, special interests will find little ground for asserting influence on the convention. (Details are found in Chapters 6, 9 and 10.)

- **If Congress does not follow the Constitution now, a new amendment won't help** – The purpose of an amendatory convention is to secure those amendments that Congress will not pass, that is, those that threaten to reduce or eliminate a power of Congress. Typically, an enabling act is passed that grants the federal government the power to enforce the new constitutional power granted in an amendment. In this instance, the wording of the amendment should include enforcement provisions or mechanisms. To be effective, the States should reserve the power to enforce the amendment themselves – even against the federal government. The fact the federal government and all of its components are still working, such as electing senators, the Supreme Court convening, we change presidents regularly, shows that the Constitution is still being followed. (Details are found in Excursus 2 and Chapter 10.)

For greater detail,

- The summaries of all of the 105 cited court cases are found in Excursus 1.
- The 106 Frequently Asked Questions are found in Excursus 2.
- A summary of the known laws and rules are found at the end of Chapter 6.
- Graphical depictions of the powers of government and a convention are found in Appendix A.
- Tables of all known American constitutional, amendatory, ratificatory, statehood and planning conventions are found in Appendix B.
- 1787 Convention delegate commissions are found in Appendix C.
- A glossary of terminology is found in Appendix D.

Introduction
THE FRAMERS' FORESIGHT

> *"The formal amendment process set forth in Article V represents a domestication of the right of revolution. Article V maintains the spirit of '76 – the right of the people to alter or abolish an inadequate government."*
> – *Walter Dellinger III, Duke University Professor of Law and former Acting Solicitor General of the United States*

The ancient Greek mathematical genius Archimedes is reputed to have said, in reference to using a lever, "Give me a place to stand and I will move the Earth."[1] Over the late spring and summer of 1787, a total of fifty-five generally successful, professional, well-educated men from twelve states gathered in Philadelphia at the Pennsylvania State House, now called Independence Hall, and crafted their own lever, the United States Constitution. The delegates grasped their new lever on the seventeenth of September and in presenting it to the nation, the Framers of the Constitution moved the world - politically. Their action ushered in two centuries of liberty, political self-determination and economic freedom. Today, we find that lever under strain from, depending on the source of complaint, an over-bearing and intrusive national government, fiscal irresponsibility, political elitism, attempts at economic central planning and excessive regulation, and perhaps most important of all, a judiciary that seems unable to understand the meaning of the very document that it is entrusted to protect and administer. This great American lever has developed

---

[1] Quoted by Pappus of Alexandria, *Collection*, Book VIII, c.340 A.D.

cracks and is bending due to abuse in some parts and neglect in others. Providentially, the delegates to the 1787 Grand Federal Convention in Philadelphia had the brilliant foresight to include within the Constitution a method to repair their great lever. That all-important repair kit is found in Article V of the United States Constitution. It is the limited-power amendatory convention convened by the States for the purpose of proposing amendment(s) to correct deficiencies and omissions.

This work explores the questions – and the answers – associated with calling and operating an Article V amendatory convention. It addresses long standing questions by examining academic and legal arguments, detailing the relevant court decisions that have shaped the body of law governing amendatory conventions. Its goal is to fill in the history that so few in the American public are even aware exists. On this journey we will meet numerous fascinating individuals. Along the way, we are going to hear from many people: legal scholars and professors, lawyers and jurists, political leaders and politicians, philosophers, Founders, Framers, Ratifiers, historians, a wide assortment of influential characters. We are indebted to these past writers and thinkers for their contributions to the understanding of Article V and the convention method of amendment. The sources cited come from all parts of the political spectrum, left, right, and center. Amendatory conventions are not intended to be partisan events.

This book is intended, primarily, for state legislators and their staffs and for Article V convention activists, and secondarily, the media and those members of the general public that have a deeper interest in the subject of amending the United States Constitution by the "state-application-and-convention" method. The people who have been involved over the last several decades in the various campaigns to secure an Article V amendatory convention are aware of the paucity of sourced material that is presented in a manner which assists in dispelling the misinformation and half-truths that dominate this controversial topic. It has only been in the last few decades that non-academic material written for the general public on the topic of Article V conventions has become widely available. It is the intent of this work to comprehensively answer the many questions that people ask about Article V conventions and to address and, hopefully, refute the falsehoods and fears associated with Article V amendatory conventions.

Many people are currently hard at work to bring about an Article V amendatory convention, and as of the fall of 2016, there are twenty-eight states with pending convention applications, or resolutions as they are often termed, focused on a balanced budget amendment to rein in federal spending. Others are working to call a convention to address reform of campaign finance laws. According to a 2016 report by the Congressional Research Service, there have been campaigns for single-subject amendments covering forty-seven issue areas.[2] The people working for a convention include the aforementioned political activists, state legislators and their staffs. They are all striving to deal in *facts,* which is the ultimate purpose of this book. The amendatory convention has been termed unworkable and impossible to control. A long, hard look at the facts is sorely needed to judge this claim.

The book is not intended to be a strictly academic work written for university scholars, although the research and documentation was meant to make this book of some interest and utility to academics, students and researchers. The book is structured as two books in one. For the less academically, but more pragmatically, inclined legislators and activists, the excursus on the Frequently Asked Questions (FAQs) and the Court Decisions will be of greater interest, as might be the descriptions in Chapters 9 and 10 of the opposing positions on a convention. For the more scholarly user, the earlier chapters that detail the history of constitutional conventions and the operational details are the repository of detail along with the footnotes. Taken together, these two approaches should provide a comprehensive view of a little known, barely understood and predominantly misunderstood and misrepresented process.

It is assumed that the general public may have a greater interest in the FAQs and that in accessing those questions, some may not wish to read each FAQ in order, perhaps some may read only select questions. To better accommodate such readers, each FAQ is treated as a stand-alone proposition with the full information of the answer included. This approach may be cumbersome to those readers who will sequentially read all the FAQs and find much information repeated from question to question. In the interest of both being thorough and satisfying the reader's curiosity, it is thought better to treat each question as a separate entity and give it the full measure of attention that the question deserves.

---

[2] Thomas N. Neale, Library of Congress, Congressional Research Service Report R44435, *The Article V Convention to Propose Constitutional Amendments: Current Developments,* (29 March 2016), 1

The amendatory convention is called by many names, some correct, others not. It is often called an Article V convention, an amendments convention, a convention for proposing amendments, a convention of the States; and is pejoratively called a constitutional convention or colloquially a "con-con." Technically speaking, the correct term is an *amendatory convention* since a state ratifying convention[3] is also an Article V convention and a convention of the States may be convened to simply discuss issues in common with no intent to issue a document or pronouncement such as a proposed amendment.[4] In Article V of the Constitution, the Framers specifically referred to an amendatory convention as a "Convention for proposing Amendments." As early as 1831, the phrase "convention of the States" began to appear in the judicial records.[5] Earlier than that, in the very first application from a state for an amendatory convention under Article V, the State of Virginia wrote in 1789,

> "[t]he anxiety with which our countrymen press for the accomplishment of this important end, will ill admit of delay. The slow forms of Congressional discussion and recommendation, if, indeed, they should ever agree to any change, would, we fear, be less certain of success. Happily for their wishes, the Constitution hath presented an alternative, by admitting the submission to a **convention of the States**. To this, therefore, we resort as the source from whence they are to derive relief from their present apprehensions."[6]

The path to using an Article V convention first begins with an explanation of what an Article V convention is exactly. Traditionally, amendments to the United States Constitution have originated in the Congress. Some federal senator or representative will introduce a bill proposing an amendment and then that bill will be assigned to a committee where it will receive a hearing. If successful, the bill will then be brought to a vote of the full chamber where it will require a two-thirds approval to move to the other chamber. The process is repeated in the other chamber and, if again successful, the proposed amendment is then sent to the States for ratification. This is how all but one of the twenty-seven current amendments

---

[3] Actually, there are two kinds of state ratifying conventions mentioned in the Constitution: one for ratifying the Constitution itself (in Article VII) and one for ratifying amendments to the Constitution (in Article V).

[4] Robert G. Natelson, "Proposing Constitutional Amendments by Convention: Rules Governing the Process," *Tennessee Law Review*, 78 (2011): 696

[5] *Smith v. Union Bank*, 30 U.S. 518 at 528 (1831)

[6] *Annals of Cong.*, 5 May 1789, Application of the State of Virginia, at 259 – author's emphasis added in italics.

to our Constitution were added to our fundamental law.[7]

But what if a particular idea for an amendment cannot get a sponsor for a bill in the Congress? What if that certain idea involves limiting the power of the federal government? What if the Congress does not want to surrender any of its power? What if the topic is something that is overwhelmingly supported by the people and the States but Congress does not support the idea because it reduces their power? Recent examples that come to mind are a balanced federal budget or campaign finance reform. What then can the people or the States do?

Fortunately, the amendatory convention is a constitutional mechanism designed for just such a scenario. The Framers of the United States Constitution foresaw an obdurate, recalcitrant, stubborn Congress refusing to heed the voice and will of the people and the States. The Framers predicted a future where Congress became tyrannical or oppressive and treated the people as subjects and not citizens.[8] This was how the people and the Framers had looked at Parliament just a little over a decade earlier. Remember that one of the first catch phrases to come out of the American Revolution was the complaint of "no taxation without representation." While taxation was indeed a major concern, it was the lack of respect for their constitutional rights as Englishmen and the absence of colonial representation in the form of an American voice in Parliament that really irritated the colonial peoples.[9,10] The colonists relied on their colonial legislatures to be their voice and Parliament had begun to shut down that voice.

The Framers did not just think that such a situation was possible; they believed that it was probable - to the extent that they fully expected that future to be inevitable. They had studied the histories of prior republics over the centuries and around the world.[11] All republics had at some point been

---

[7] The singular exception being the Twenty-first Amendment.
[8] Max Farrand, *The Records of the Federal Convention of 1787, Vol. I* (New Haven: Yale University Press, 1911 rev. 1937), 629 - George Mason: "since no amendments of the proper kind would ever be obtained by the people, if the Government should become oppressive."
[9] Gordon S. Wood, *The Creation of the American Republic, 1776-1787* (Chapel Hill: University of North Carolina Press, 1998), 177. Published for the Omohundro Institute of Early American History and Culture.
[10] Leonard Levy, *Origins of the Bill of Rights* (New Haven, CT: Yale University Press, 1999), 150
[11] Gordon S. Wood, *The Creation of the American Republic, 1776-1787* (Chapel Hill: University of North Carolina Press, 1998), 6, 92, 472. Published for the Omohundro Institute of Early American History and Culture.

subjected to the extreme pressures of unresponsive assemblies, dictatorial leaders, authoritarian movements and severe economic downturns. True problems began when, in response to these pressures, the people caved to the forces assaulting their principles and institutions. The people violated or permitted the violation of their constitutions, laws and political institutions most often for the sake of a quick fix. A republic once lost, was rarely regained.[12] This is a rule of history.[13]

Our constitutional drafters debated this point and acted to provide a method for circumventing the force of government run amok. The Article V amendatory convention is a key, although unused to date, feature of federalism. The Article V convention was included as a means of maintaining constitutional rule and stability in the face of a *national* government that does not and will not observe constitutionality. Whether the threat be from a Congress that ignores its own laws, or an executive who fancies himself or herself above the law, or a judiciary that takes to making up the law as it goes along, the people and the States are empowered to identify and redress the cause of the constitutional infirmity or deficiency and to emplace the proper remedy. Article V is, herein paraphrasing so many who have spoken before on the subject, the peaceful alternative to the necessary use of the force of arms to restore the constitutional balance. It is a safety valve, or a reset button, or the emergency brake, or in its simplest, a warning to the national government that it has moved dangerously close to the limits of the people's and the States' tolerance.

Few have described the purpose of Article V so articulately as Professor Henry N. Butler,

> *"The convention method of Article V is merely another example of the brilliance of the Framers at identifying political decision makers' incentives to act in an undesirable manner and then creating institutional constraints to reduce the occurrence of such behavior."*[14]

It is then a check on the ambitions of those in power. There are other

---

[12] Carl J. Richard, *The Founders and the Classics, Greece, Rome, and the American Enlightenment* (Cambridge, MA: Harvard University Press, 1994), 113-4

[13] The counter-argument is often made that nations have had multiple republics and will include the citation of France's five republics, but that example omits that each republic was different, and no particular French republic, once lost, was fully restored.

[14] James E. Bond, David E. Engdahl and Henry N. Butler, *The Constitutional Convention* (Washington, D.C.: National Legal Center for the Public Interest, 1987), 28

checks and balances in our Constitution. They perform different tasks for different facets of government. Most are for the purpose of one branch of the federal government to restrain another branch. Impeachment is found in Article I, Section 3 and assigns the power of trying government officials to the Senate. Thus a check by the Legislative branch is made on the Executive and Judicial branches.[15] Per Article I, Section 7, the president may veto legislation allowing the Executive branch to check the Legislative branch. The Supreme Court may strike down legislation permitting the Judicial branch to check the Legislative. But Article V amendatory conventions are a check on the ENTIRE federal government by the people and the States making the Article V amendatory convention the most powerful check in the Constitution.

In the process of carrying out an Article V convention, the convention mechanism simply replaces the Congress in the role of suggesting, drafting, debating, voting on and proposing an amendment to our Constitution. Congress is not entirely eliminated from the process, but the most important and powerful aspects are removed from Congress and placed in the hands of the people, represented in the form of their delegates to the convention. The shape of the amendment is developed in the convention and thus so is the shape of the modified Constitution. If any part of the national government is, by necessity, to ever be reined in, it will be done here in a convention of the States – the Congress will not do it. The Executive cannot do it. The Judiciary has proven that they have rarely, and of late, will even more rarely, do it.

Any correction of errant government, any restraint of government power, any limitation of governmental authority, any redefinition or clarification of constitutional interpretation, any enactment of constitutional principle that is perceptible as a threat to the national government, any rollback of actions taken by any part of the national government, will of necessity, more likely than not, have to be done in an Article V convention. Lord Acton famously noted that, "Power tends to corrupt, and absolute power corrupts absolutely. Great men are almost always bad men."[16] That is the fundamental principle all too often at work in our national government.

---

[15] To date, two presidents have been impeached: Andrew Johnson and William Jefferson Clinton. The Senate has impeached fifteen federal judges including one Supreme Court Associate Justice, Samuel Chase. It has also impeached one Cabinet secretary, Joseph Belknap and a US senator, William Blount of Tennessee.

[16] John Emerich Edward Dahlberg, Lord Acton to Archbishop Mandell Creighton, letter of 5 April 1887

Of course, many, if not most, of our great men were not bad men, but the lure of power is a difficult siren song to ignore. The term "beltway mentality" did not come into use for nothing.

The system of federalism is highly dependent on the use of checks and balances. Keeping the balance between the federal government and States has proven to be increasingly problematic over time. Since the Progressive Era, the size and scope of the federal government has grown – at the expense of the States' powers and the people's liberties. Thomas Jefferson astutely observed, "The natural progress of things is for liberty to yeild,[17] and government to gain ground."[18]

Compare this sentiment to the First Article of the Massachusetts Constitution of 1780,

> *"Article I. All men are born free and equal, and have certain natural, essential, and unalienable rights; among which may be reckoned the right of enjoying and defending their lives and liberties;"*[19]

It becomes clear that the Founders, Framers and Ratifiers of the Revolutionary and Federal Eras recognized the ominous threat of an ever-growing-in-power national government. Having shed their blood over stopping the British government's abuse of their [British] constitutional rights, it would be ridiculous to assume that an American national government would be ever-respectful of the rights of its citizens without some measure of induced restraint. Moreover, it would be a farce if some form of rectification of an abusive government was not included in the new national charter. An Article V amendatory convention is that ultimate tool in the checks and balances on the burgeoning power of the federal government. It is not a stretch or even a long path to take to reach the conclusion that Article V was, and is, the intended solution of the Framers. Our federal constitution is littered with checks and balances. Every power has a check

---

[17] http://www.monticello.org/site/jefferson/natural-progress-things-quotation. As noted on the Monticello website: "Yeild" is Thomas Jefferson's original spelling, and one that he used with a fair degree of frequency: there are approximately seventy usages of "yeild" in letters authored by Jefferson in the *Papers of Thomas Jefferson* in the years 1760-1802 vs. approximately 200 usages of "yield."

[18] Thomas Jefferson to Edward Carrington, letter from Paris, 27 May 1788, may be found quoted in Adrienne Koch & William Peden, *The Life and Selected Writings of Thomas Jefferson* (New York: Random House, 1944), 412 – the original is found in the Library of Congress.

[19] Constitution of the Commonwealth of Massachusetts, (1780)

or two; every responsibility has a balance or two; every potential problem, every potential abuse, every potential excess has an integral solution or two. When we look back to the Framing at the Philadelphia Convention and read the notes of delegates James Madison or Robert Yates or John Lansing or the compilation of Professor Max Farrand, one can view the ebb and flow of ideas. One can follow the train of thought of the delegates as they discuss and debate the what-ifs and the maybes and watch the development of their provisions for the contingencies to maintain the Republic. Near the end of the convention on September 15th, we find George Mason of Virginia warning of the impending inevitability of the federal government becoming oppressive and echoing Roger Sherman of Connecticut and Elbridge Gerry of Massachusetts on their concerns for the dangers of an all-powerful consolidation.[20] Article V was destined to be devised and included; what other option was there for resolving all the various dangers and threats to the States' and the people's liberties and rights? What other method remained from <u>outside</u> of the national government?

At the beginning of this introductory chapter, there is a quote from Duke University law professor Walter Dellinger. He refers to the "domestication of the right of revolution." This is not hyperbole; the Declaration of Independence directly refers to our right "to alter or to abolish" government that does not protect our rights. If the United States federal government does not meet our needs or fails to respect our rights, then the people and the States should, and have a right to, alter it. Article V conventions are included in our Constitution not just as a check and balance but as a method of "revolution" that is far less bloody and far more focused on achieving the exact changes that we need. It is a surgical solution to the cancer of unconstitutionality spreading through the body and form of our federal government.

An Article V amendatory convention originates with the States; its purpose and agenda are initially determined by the States; its delegates come from the people of the States; it is operated by the delegates of the people of the States; it answers to the legislatures and the peoples of the States; its product is debated, considered, and approved or rejected by the legislatures, or ratificatory conventions, of the States. It is a last line of defense for the

---

[20] William Montgomery Meigs, *The Growth of the Constitution in the Federal Convention of 1787: An Effort to Trace the Origin and Development of Each Separate Clause from Its First Suggestion in That Body to the Form Finally Approved – Primary Source Edition* (Philadelphia: J. P. Lippincott, 1900), 276-7

people and the States against a federal government which has forgotten its place and assumed powers beyond its station.

With the passage of time, the inevitability of the calling of an Article V amendatory convention increases just as the Framers expected. There is a certain urgency to perfecting our understanding of the workings of such an amendatory convention. The political convention, of any type, is a tool not to be handled lightly and indiscriminately. It can be a powerful weapon with the ability to do great damage if not wielded carefully and with an eye to a clear and proper purpose. The federal amendatory convention, a subset of the category of political conventions, is a specialty tool of limited power, used for a specific purpose and is to be rarely taken out of the political tool box.

At the heart of the controversy surrounding calling an Article V amendatory convention are three premises, proclaimed in their usual order, that,

- There has never been an Article V convention before…
- There are no rules for an Article V convention…
- A convention is too dangerous because we just don't know what will happen…

These premises lead opponents to a general conclusion that such a convention will inevitably runaway and cause a host of horrors. The response to these statements depends entirely on how one interprets the statements. As to the first, if one is contending that there has never been a federal, national, convention limited strictly to discussing amendments to the US Constitution, then yes, that is true. If however, one takes the statement as written, then no, it is not true as there have been many Article V conventions in the form of the thirty-nine state ratification conventions for the Twenty-first Amendment. Also, there have been many, over eighty, amendatory conventions by the States and territories for their respective constitutions. The States and their predecessor colonies held numerous conventions between the colonies or States – and continue to do so – since the earliest immigrants arrived and contemplated governance. This is an important point as the existence of prior conventions provides prior rules and procedures.

If one takes the second statement to mean that there are no fully written out (and formally adopted)[21] rules strictly for a national, federal, amendatory convention under Article V, then again we must say yes, that is true. If one means that there are no rules for an interstate convention, then we must firmly conclude no, it is not true as such conventions have been held for centuries and are still held today. We have the rules of the aforementioned thirty-nine Article V amendment ratifying conventions to draw upon. The rules of conventions are well known and codified and have been for centuries. We have the rules of the fifteen Article VII Constitution ratifying conventions held during 1787-91. We have the rules found in the proceedings of the hundreds of state constitutional conventions. We have the rules found in the proceedings of the over eighty state and territorial amendatory conventions. Every year, dozens of conventions are held between the States to discuss a multitude of issues and some to create or maintain formal compacts between the States.

For the third statement, we cannot look at this point in two ways, for we do know exactly what will happen based on the experience of the uncountable number of intercolonial and interstate conventions over the last four centuries in North America. Similarly, we have the prior experience of our forebears in Great Britain and the other European countries extending back to the Roman Republic and the democracies of ancient Greece.

Without exaggeration, one can argue that the debate over whether to call an Article V convention has been waged since the ink was still wet on the first draft of the Constitution. Over the last couple of centuries, the reasons for both calling and preventing a convention have changed but the consistent thread has been the use, or misuse, of the well-known historical and legal facts to advance either side's case.

To address the three premises just given, the history of political conventions and the development and evolution into the many forms of conventions that we know today are laid out in Part I. To lay the groundwork for the establishment of the rules for such a convention, the legal basis is presented along with the detailing of case histories in Part II. That section of the book concerns the body of law generated over the more than two

---

[21] With the successful conclusion of the Assembly of State Legislatures' efforts in June 2016, there are now a set of formal rules, although these rules are not formally adopted by any states and would still need to be adopted by an Article V Convention. Additionally, the Convention of States Project conducted a "dry run" or simulated convention in September 2016 employing their proposed rules and experienced no problems with those rules.

centuries of court decisions since the Constitution was ratified. All too often it is claimed that there is no law or precedent that covers an Article V convention. Nothing, in regard to an Article V convention, could be further from the truth. We have much to draw on and many rules have been codified through numerous court decisions and rulings. State, federal district, federal appellate and US Supreme Court decisions were surveyed and summarized. To make the information more accessible and useful, Part III presents Frequently Asked Questions with corresponding answers. The FAQs are grouped by topic. The academic treatment of Article V and the ubiquitous referral to *The Federalist* essays wherein the amending process is mentioned are also treated in Part III. Finally, in Part IV the two sides of the Article V convention debate are presented with a refutation of the objections.

Lastly, there are appendices which cover supporting documentation. Appendix A provides a graphical representation of the types and separation of government powers. Of major importance is Appendix B that details all of the known constitutional conventions of all types within the United States and associated statehood or territorial conventions. Paramount among these is the table, B.9, of all the known amendatory conventions. Appendix C focuses on the delegate commissions to the Philadelphia Convention and why they refute the contention that the 1787 convention was a runaway. There is a glossary of the terminology in Appendix D and finally a list of sources. This glossary refers, wherever possible, to the dictionary usage at the time of the Ratification so that the understanding of what the Framers thought that they were framing and the Ratifiers thought they were ratifying is understood.

As an aside, it should be noted here that this book does not seek to rehash the whole 1787 convention. There are plenty of books to cover that topic in great depth. What is covered herein is intended to provide background and grounding on the subject in support of the relevant and key points made. The amendment process is discussed in terms of the development in the convention option.

While there have been – seriously – tens of thousands of books[22] written on the subjects of the Constitution, the Constitutional Convention

---

[22] Go to Amazon.com and place "constitution" or "constitutional convention" in the search field and note the number of listings that it generates – the number returned is in excess of 100,000 for the first term.

of 1787, the delegates[23] to the 1787 convention, and to a lesser extent, the amendments themselves, there have been few books written that focus on addressing the concept of the Article V amendatory convention and its operation. Most books written on amendatory conventions are skewed to justifying a call for a convention and more likely a proposal for a specific amendment or set of amendments. This book looks primarily at the HISTORY, RULES and PROCEDURES for the operation of an amendatory convention. No proposal for an amendment is made although this work admittedly takes a decidedly pro-convention stance.

Few books have been written on the operation of an Article V convention and those which have been were written in just two waves of scholarship/publication. In the 1980s and early 1990s, the drive to secure a balanced budget amendment generated interest in the subject resulting in three key works: Russell L. Caplan's *"Constitutional Brinkmanship – Amending the Constitution by National Convention"* in 1988; Paul J. Weber and Barbara A. Perry's *"Unfounded Fears – Myths and Realities of a Constitutional Convention"* in 1989; and John R. Vile's *"Contemporary Questions Surrounding the Constitutional Amending Process"* in 1993. All three of these works were, for the most part, academic and scholarly but definitely not beyond the understanding of the non-attorney or non-political scientist. A private citizen with an interest in Article V conventions would find these books easily readable and informative. In addition to these books, the same period yielded three important monographs: Wilbur Edel's *"A Constitutional Convention – Threat or Challenge?"* and Kermit Hall, Harold Hyman and Leon Sigal's *"The Constitutional Convention as an Amending Device,"* both released in 1981 and lastly, James E. Bond, David E. Engdahl and Henry N. Butler's *"The Constitutional Convention"* issued in 1987.

Since the recent turn of the century, there has been another pique in interest in an amendatory convention, and this new surge has produced many more books, alas, few of which are of a scholarly nature or focused on the convention process itself. Most are concerned with promoting specific amendment proposals. Four important works in the last few years have been dedicated to the Article V amendatory convention: Professor Darren Patrick Guerra published his *"Perfecting the Constitution – The Case for the*

---

[23] In 1787, the representatives of the States at the convention in Philadelphia were called either "deputies" or "commissioners" by their respective states. Today, the vernacular uses the word "delegate." For the sake of convenience, this book will use the modern terminology of "delegate."

Article V Amendment Process" in 2013 and former Michigan Supreme Court Chief Justice Thomas E. Brennan produced his *"The Article V Amendatory Constitutional Convention – Keeping the Republic in the Twenty-first Century"* released in 2014. Arizona State Senator Andy Biggs published *"The Con of the Con-Con"* in 2015 as the first book intended to explain the objections to an amendatory convention. Finally in 2016, John R. Vile issued his *"Conventional Wisdom"* which sought to address many of the issues in a thorough manner. In between these two waves of publication, a highly honorable mention goes to historian David E. Kyvig's *"Explicit and Authentic Acts – Amending the U.S. Constitution 1776-1995"* which includes sections on the Article V convention process and appeared in 1996.

Earlier than these two peaks of book publishing, there were some works printed that address the constitutional convention first and foremost but include some mention of the amendatory convention process. Although these books appear somewhat dated, they still contain much historical information that frames the development of the process as we now consider it. Four works stand out: John Alexander Jameson's *"A Treatise on Constitutional Conventions – Their History, Powers and Modes of Proceeding,"* first published in 1867; Walter Farleigh Dodd's 1910 work *"The Revision and Amendment of State Constitutions"*; followed by Roger Sherman Hoar's *"Constitutional Conventions – Their Natures, Powers and Limitations,"* issued in 1917 and Lester Bernhardt Orfield's *"Amending the Federal Constitution,"* first printed in 1942. Other works made minimal mention of the convention method typically limiting their commentary to cite the method's existence and non-use and then to often condemn the method as an historical anachronism.

The books by Judge Jameson and State Senator Hoar are the foundational works for the field of study of constitutional conventions and cannot be overlooked despite their ages. These works fixated primarily on state constitutional conventions, but the material is often applicable to a federal convention. Their emphasis on the state conventions is understandable when we consider that the United States has experienced a single constitutional convention (for drafting) at the federal level, although there have been hundreds of constitutional conventions at the state level.[24]

---

[24] The *Articles of Confederation and Perpetual Union* were not drafted by a formal constitutional convention but by a committee of the Second Continental Congress.

Jameson and Hoar, writing exactly a half century apart and published a century and a half ago and a century ago, respectively, still dominate much of the thought on the legal issues of an amendatory convention. Polar opposites with regard to the source of power – and therefore the limitation – of a convention, the argument over whether an amendatory convention can be limited or must be unlimited lies, in large part, at their feet. We will get to know these two authors and come to understand why their early writing has deeply influenced several generations of political scientists and legal scholars working on the issue of amendatory convention operations.

John Alexander Jameson was a judge in Chicago during the Civil War and the period following it. At that time, the infamous "Copperhead Convention" to revise the Illinois state constitution took place in 1862. As an abolitionist and a co-founder of the Illinois branch of the Republican Party, Jameson was incensed by the liberties taken in the convention and set out to write the authoritative standard work on constitutional conventions – he had an axe to grind.

Roger Sherman Hoar was an equally fascinating man for different reasons. He was a Harvard educated attorney, Massachusetts state senator and assistant Massachusetts attorney general, prolific science fiction writer and, although not an engineer or scientist, a founding member of the Marquette University College of Engineering faculty. He was as dispassionate as Jameson was passionate. Hoar sought to grind no axe; rather he worked to set out only the facts.

These twelve books and three monographs comprise the bulk of academic or scholarly expertise on the subject of constitutional conventions and Article V amendatory conventions. Just eleven of these works focus directly and primarily on the amendatory convention method and all where published in the one-third of a century since 1981. Much of the rest of what we know is drawn from such recognized secondary sources as "*The Federalist Papers*," the "*Anti-Federalist Papers*," Max Farrand's "*The Records of the Federal Convention of 1787*," Jonathan Elliot's "*The Debates in the Several State Conventions on the Adoption of the Federal Constitution*," William Montgomery Meigs' "*The Growth of the Constitution in the Federal Convention of 1787: An Effort to Trace the Origin and Development of Each Separate Clause from its First Suggestion in That Body to the Form Finally Approved*," and Phillip B. Kurland and Ralph Kerner's "*The Founders' Constitution*." Additional sources include the notes of the 1787 delegates themselves. Most people are aware of James Madison's *"Notes of the Constitutional Convention"* initially published posthumously in 1840, but few are aware that twelve other delegates kept records as well.[25] The notes of 1787 Constitutional Convention delegates Attorney General Gunning Bedford, Jr. of Delaware; Maj. Pierce Butler of South Carolina; Col. Alexander Hamilton of New York; Maj. Rufus King of Massachusetts; John Lansing, Jr. of New York; Luther Martin of Maryland; Col. George Mason of Virginia; Dr. James McHenry of Maryland; former Attorney General William Paterson of New Jersey; Capt. William Pierce of Georgia, Gov. Edmund Randolph of Virginia,[26] and Judge Robert Yates of New York were all surveyed.[27] Additionally, the 1787 Constitutional Convention Secretary, Maj. William Jackson, kept some notes and these were also reviewed. The notes of John Dickinson of Delaware are also helpful although they tend more towards his idea of the structure of the national government than a chronological record of the events of the convention.[28] These gentlemen comprise fully one quarter of the attending delegates.

Founding Era dictionaries provided insight into the changed meaning and interpretation of the wording in documents over time. Tertiary sources that include hundreds of academic papers and books from the Framing through the present form much of the rest of the sourcing. Papers cited were preferably peer-reviewed and published in reputable journals, especially law reviews. On occasion, the blog of a prominent legal or academic expert may be referenced where no other source is available for citation, but this is the extreme exception and not the rule. The website of an historical repository or a government agency is occasionally given to source a document.

Providing the color and context of the respective times comes from the works of several historians without whom the reasoning of the amending process and its development would be confusing and perhaps more difficult to understand. The works of John Andrew Doyle, Ralph Ketcham, David Kyvig, Richard Labunski, David Lefer, Pauline Maier, Drew McCoy, Forrest

---

[25] After Madison's passing in 1836, his widow, Dolley, needed to raise funds. She offered his notes to the Congress for the sum of $30,000 in 1837. She sold additional documents to the federal government in 1848 for $25,000.

[26] For the Committee on Detail

[27] Mary Sarah Bilder, *Madison's Hand, Revising the Constitutional Convention* (Cambridge: Harvard University Press, 2015), 267, n.2

[28] James H. Hutson, "John Dickinson at the Federal Constitutional Convention," *The William and Mary Quarterly* 40, no. 2 (Apr. 1983)

McDonald, Alan Taylor and Gordon S. Wood cast much needed light on the times, people and political machinations at work in the events that led us to the state of constitutional amending today.

A deeper note on the quality of the sources is necessary. Much of the records of the Constitutional Convention of 1787 are considered negatively by many in the academic community of historians and legal scholars. The reasons vary. Madison made corrections to his notes at least twice; once after the 1819 publication of the *"Journal of the Proceedings"* by Congress and again in his last years when he was refining his notes for posthumous publication. Scholars have speculated for years on the cause of his revisions when time has proven that, in some instances, he was right to begin with and there was no need to change his notes. But Madison is not without critics of his notes.[29] Professor Mary Sarah Bilder warns of "the danger of applying twenty-first century assumptions to eighteenth-century legal records" and states that "None of us can entirely escape Madison's version."[30]

Major William Jackson has been criticized for the brevity of his records– he focused on recording the motions and the votes of the delegates more than on the substance and details of the deliberations.[31,32,33,34] Seated in the same room, James Madison was recording details of the debates and discussions. Perhaps Jackson was aware of this and consciously decided to focus on recording the votes? Whether or not this is the case, we are the richer for it. Other delegates came and went during the convention and made notes of varying quantity and quality. None were expected to take notes. What we have, in terms of historical records, we should be thankful for having at all! The Convention voted to extend the secrecy of the deliberations indefinitely. It was many years before any of the delegate notes were made public. The delegates were not even aware of who all had taken notes. The last complete set of notes discovered and published were those of

---

[29] Mary Sarah Bilder, *Madison's Hand, Revising the Constitutional Convention* (Cambridge: Harvard University Press 2015), generally

[30] Mary Sarah Bilder, "How Bad Were the Official Records of the Federal Convention?," *The George Washington Law Review* 80, no. 6 (2012): 1624

[31] Ibid., 1620-82

[32] Abraham C. Weinfeld, "Power of Congress Over State Ratifying Conventions," *Harvard Law Review* 51, no.3 (Jan. 1938): 496

[33] Drew R. McCoy, *The Last of the Fathers, James Madison & The Republican Legacy* (New York: Cambridge University Press, 1989), 85-6, – McCoy discusses Robert Yates' notes and how they were "mutilated" by Edward Genêt in an effort to embarrass Madison.

[34] Gregory E. Maggs, "A Concise Guide to the Records of the Federal Constitutional Convention of 1787 as a Source of the Original Meaning of the U.S. Constitution," *George Washington Law Review* 81 (2012): 1724

New York delegate John Lansing, Jr., found by his grandchildren in 1901.[35] A fragment of Robert Yates' notes were found in 1978. Pierce Butler's notes were first published in 1980.[36] Might other sets of delegate notes remain undiscovered? The fact that so many of the note taking delegates adhered to their agreement to maintain secrecy is a credit to their honor and integrity as the public would surely have forgiven the delegates their indiscretion for the publication in exchange for the satisfaction of the public's curiosity and the clear benefit to the legal community. For the most comprehensive treatment on the accuracy and completeness of the various sets of notes, there is probably no better commentary than that of Professor Max Farrand in the introduction to his multi-volume set of *Records of the Federal Convention of 1787.* Similarly, Elliot's notes on the ratification debates have come under the same scrutiny and derision.[37]

Numerous government documents were also perused. A very deliberate and concerted effort was made to identify and use sources as contemporaneous to the 1787 convention as is possible. Over time, the academic community based in the nation's law schools have vigorously debated and debunked ideas on the Article V convention. The author studied academic papers and law review or journal articles relating to either amending the Constitution, Article V conventions or both. Papers from history journals were also surveyed. The subject has been well discussed within the academic and legal communities.

It is extremely important to recognize those sources that are credible and authoritative as to the meaning, intent and interpretation of how Article V works. Primary sources involve the delegates themselves and are indispensable to determining what they meant by the wording of Article V. The Framers of the Constitution had an intent that it is imperative to identify and comprehend. The Ratifiers of the Constitution in the state ratification conventions had their ideas of what they thought that Article V meant. Hopefully, the Framers and the Ratifiers agreed on the meaning,

---

[35] Joseph Reese Strayer, *The Delegate from New York or Proceedings from the Federal Convention of 1787 from the Notes of John Lansing, Jr.* (Princeton: Princeton University Press, 1939) - reprinted by The Lawbook Exchange, (2002)

[36] James H. Hutson, "John Dickinson at the Federal Constitutional Convention," *The William and Mary Quarterly* 40, no. 2 (Apr. 1983): 256-7

[37] James H. Hutson, "Riddles of the Federal Constitutional Convention," *William and Mary Quarterly* 3d ser., 44, no.3 (July 1987): 411-2

powers and limitations of Article V.[38] Many of the Framers were also Ratifiers and this made interpretation less necessary as some of the Framers were present in the state ratification conventions as delegates to say, more or less: "We mean this."[39,40,41,42] In fact, Philadelphia convention delegates from every state except Rhode Island served in their respective state ratification conventions and many made explicit statements on the meanings of various provisions.[43] As an example, in Connecticut, all three of her delegates to the Federal Convention, served as ratification convention delegates.[44] Gregory Maggs notes that,

> *"They were seen as Framers, and they spoke as Framers. They did not need to preface their remarks by saying that they were representing the views of the federal convention because that was likely taken for granted."*[45]

The writings of the Framers, Ratifiers and leading legal thinkers of the Federal Period were consulted. Key jurists and legal minds of the

---

[38] Article V was a point of conciliation during the ratification debates. Federalists directed attention to Article V to prove that any deficiencies or omissions were correctable and to prove that the Constitution was better than the Articles of Confederation, in part, because the amending process was more useful than that under the Articles.

[39] Drew R. McCoy, *The Last of the Fathers, James Madison & The Republican Legacy* (New York: Cambridge University Press, 1989), 75-80

[40] Without going to deeply into the woods here, there are at least three recognized meanings that could apply: the "original intent" of the Framers who drafted the Constitution in the convention; the "original understanding" of the Ratifiers in the ratification conventions; and the "original objective meaning" that a person of 1787 would understand – per Gregory E. Maggs, "A Concise Guide to the Federalist Papers as a Source of the Original Meaning of the United States Constitution," *Boston University Law Review* 87 (2007): 805-6

[41] To the extent that they did not violate the secrecy requirement that remained in effect after the convention, -again, see Maggs, (2007), *supra* n.19, 837 – contrast with Mary Sarah Bilder who states that the delegates did not believe that the bar on discussing the convention extended past the end of the convention, *Madison's Hand*, 57

[42] Elbridge Gerry lost election to the Massachusetts ratifying convention but was invited to attend and give insight on the intention and meaning of parts of the Constitution.

[43] Gregory E. Maggs, "A Concise Guide to the Records of the State Ratifying Conventions as a Source of the Original Meaning of the U.S. Constitution," *University of Illinois Law Review* 2009, no.2 (2009): 481-3, – state ratification convention delegates that had also served as Philadelphia convention delegates, by state: Connecticut: Oliver Ellsworth, William Samuel Johnson and Roger Sherman; Delaware: Richard Bassett and Gunning Bedford, Jr.; Georgia: William Few; Maryland: Luther Martin, James McHenry and John F. Mercer; Massachusetts: Nathaniel Gorham, Rufus King and Caleb Strong. Elbridge Gerry was invited to address the ratifying convention.; New Hampshire: Nicholas Gilman and John Langdon; New Jersey: David Brearly; New York: Alexander Hamilton, John Lansing, Jr. and Robert Yates; North Carolina: William Blount, William R. Davie and Richard Dobbs Spaight; Pennsylvania: James Wilson; South Carolina: Charles Pinckney, Charles Cotesworth Pinckney and John Rutledge; Virginia: John Blair, James Madison, Jr., George Mason, Edmund J. Randolph and George Wythe

[44] Pauline Maier, *Ratification, The People Debate the Constitution, 1787-1788* (New York: Simon & Schuster, 2010), 137

[45] Gregory E. Maggs, "A Concise Guide to the Records of the State Ratifying Conventions as a Source of the Original Meaning of the U.S. Constitution," *University of Illinois Law Review* 2009, no.2 (2009): 483

Federal Era were read including Supreme Court Justice Joseph Story, John Taylor of Caroline, and St. George Tucker, whom all produced early legal commentaries on the Constitution.

With the eventual passing of the Framers, the legal and academic worlds were left to interpretation of the meaning and intent of Article V. Little research was done in the area of Article V conventions between the beginning of the Republic and the Reconstruction Period after the Civil War. By the late nineteenth century, with the rise of the Populist Movement and its successor in the Progressive Movement, a new interest in constitutional change had risen. From then, interpretation meant re-interpretation as the meaning has been slowly coerced under a "living constitution" theory of evolving constitutional purpose. Many university law schools began to publish regular journals and reviews during the last third of the nineteenth century and the early twentieth century. The articles printed explored "more democratic" methods of amending the Constitution as the national charter was seen as too difficult to amend. The early progressives began to look for alternatives to the usual rigid congressional amendment process. The "informal" court decision amendment method that is in vogue today was still a few years in the future.[46]

Without the benefit of the recall, referenda and initiative processes that were successfully introduced in many states during the early twentieth century, progressive activists had to look elsewhere for methods to introduce reforms at the federal level. They found the Article V amendatory convention and set to work. The law journals of the Progressive Era are dotted with articles on the limitations of the amending process and the powers of conventions. It was in this time that the details of the operation of an Article V amendatory convention first became a topic of serious debate and scholarly research.

Although the Progressive Era produced four amendments[47] to the Constitution, none were achieved through the state-application-and-convention method although the threat of a convention prompted the Congress to pass amendments – the more frequently cited example being the Seventeenth Amendment. The first major works of research were completed

---

[46] This work takes no wide interest in the "informal" amending theory other to note its definition as Article V is clearly formal and the informal method is beyond the already extremely ambitious scope of this project.

[47] The Sixteenth, Seventeenth, Eighteenth and Nineteenth are all typically cited as the "Progressive Amendments."

in this timeframe. The dominant writer of this time was Professor Lester B. Orfield. The event of the Constitutional Revolution of 1937[48] and the occurrence of World War II diminished interest in Article V amendatory conventions as evidenced by the sharp decline in the number of papers in legal journals. Then again, several controversial US Supreme Court decisions in the 1950s and 1960s led to a revival of interest in the utility of Article V conventions. In the post-WW II period, scholarship increased in terms of academic papers.

Ultimately, there have been attempts by Congress to formulate rules to govern operation of an Article V convention, although no such bill has yet to pass. All this activity has led to a frenzy of research and writing on the topic. Professor Robert G. Natelson is probably the most prolific and detail oriented researcher on the subject of Article V conventions - ever. He divides the post-war scholarship into three waves.[49] The first wave occurred in the 1960s and 1970s terminating in 1978 and was most often characterized by a view of the amendatory convention as an unpredictable and dangerous unknown quantity. It was this general opinion that led Congress to delve into attempting to regulate the convention's operation. Walter Dellinger and Charles Black dominated the scholarly writing in this era.

The second wave coincided with the period from 1979 to 2000. It is in this time that the scholarship deepened and the academics turned from speculation to researching the Federal Era records. Debate arose over the limits and powers of the amendatory convention. Akhil Reed Amar, William Van Alstyne and Brendon Ishikawa were very active and each produced a number of papers in this timeframe. The third and last period as denoted by Natelson began about 2010 with the current push for both a balanced budget amendment and a restraint on campaign money from corporations. Robert Natelson, Michael Rappaport, and Michael Stokes Paulsen are currently high producers. This period is characterized by examining the most obscure

---

[48] This term refers to the "Switch in Time that Saved Nine" as the abrupt about face in the general tenor of the US Supreme Court's views has been known. In response to President Franklin Roosevelt's attempt to "pack" the Supreme Court with new, younger – and decidedly more progressive – justices, the Court changed its philosophy to be more accommodating of FDR's agenda in an effort to avoid the forced diminution of the Court's power. The conservative jurisprudence that had predominated over the first century and a half was not just thrown out but blatantly reversed. It is ironic that the New Deal Era justice most associated with this flip-flop is Associate Justice Owen Roberts. Today's major flip-flop, on the Affordable Care Act related cases, is attributed to Chief Justice John Roberts providing an interesting, albeit very minor, historical aside.

[49] Robert G. Natelson, *A Compendium for Lawyers and Legislative Drafters* (Purcellville, VA: Convention of States, 2014): 13

resources and attempting to define the intent of the Framers. The greatest outcome of this research is the attention to the operational details of an amendatory convention. For the first time, the emphasis has been on the fact-based response to the questions posed by the opponents of an Article V convention.

A number of current scholars have distinguished themselves with the quality and quantity of publications and research that they have produced on both the topics of the amending process and Article V conventions. Beginning in the 1970s, Professor John R. Vile of Middle Tennessee State University has excelled on the topic of constitutional conventions and amendments in general. He has deftly picked up the torch from Jameson, Dodd, Hoar, Orfield and Herman V. Ames and produced not only a large number of scholarly papers published in law journals but also several authoritative books including the definitive work on all of the proposed amendments to the Constitution introduced since the ratification.

More recent scholars, particularly Natelson, lately of the University of Montana and now the Independence Institute, have worked tirelessly to examine the records of the dozens of intercolonial and interstate conventions held in the Colonial and Federal periods to determine how those conventions operated. The rules of the hundreds of state constitutional conventions, and the ratification conventions for the state and federal constitutions and amendments have been studied to find how they developed as well as worked (and continue to work). The workings of the 1787 convention and the anticipated workings of a modern Article V convention would most assuredly be based on the customary operations of past intercolonial and interstate conventions.

The result of this recent flood of research is to return to the roots of the matter and begin by defining exactly what an Article V convention is and for what it is intended. In addition, the current scholars are turning to the legal realm to determine the extent, and the development, of the body of law in existence regarding Article V conventions. This long overlooked area is the key to the successful operation of an amendatory convention. It has also permitted us to take this journey into examining and understanding the Article V amendatory convention and how it can help us today.

In fairness, it must be admitted that not every question can be answered. Opponents often say that there are _no_ answers to the questions concerning Article V amendatory conventions.[50] They are for the greater part incorrect. But for some questions, there are indeed presently no answers and the research will just have to continue. This is the case with many things in life so we should be neither surprised nor deterred by the lack of an answer to a particular question. It is merely another challenge to which we should, and shall, rise.

---

[50] This is the common refrain from the Eagle Forum. They have published a list of "20 Unanswerable Questions" since the 1980s. Most organizations that promote or support an Article V convention have responded and published their answers/refutations to the twenty unanswerable questions.

Part I - From Contiones to Constitutions

The Forgotten History of Conventions

Addressing the premise: "We have never had an Article V convention before...

ONE
DEFINING AN ARTICLE V CONVENTION EXACTLY

> "*A Convention is the provided machinery of peaceful revolution. It is the civilized substitute for intestine war.*"[1]
> - George Mifflin Dallas, 11th Vice-President of the United States

Long before the delegates gathered in Philadelphia in 1787 to draft our Constitution – and Article V - the colonies, and after the Revolution, the States, had been convening with some regularity to discuss issues held in common. Englishmen had been meeting in conventions to work out large-scale, societal problems for centuries before the establishment of the United States and even earlier, prior to the establishment of the individual colonies. The Continental Congresses, and their successor, the Confederation Congress, and in turn its successor, the United States Congress, are, in a manner, just on-going examples of such a gathering. More precisely, Congress was a revolutionary convention that eventually evolved into a permanent government.

These extra-legal, extra-governmental formal meetings of the citizens have their roots at least as far back as the noblemen of England convening to draw up a plan for extorting a form of a "bill of rights" out

---
[1] From a letter published in "*The Pennsylvanian*" on 5 September 1836.

2 Far From Unworkable

of King John.² The meeting known as the "Convention of the Barons," at Runnymede on the banks of the Thames in 1215, culminated in the *Magna Carta Libertatum*.³ History provides numerous examples of local meetings, or conventions of a sort, pre-dating Runnymede.⁴ In Saxon England, freeholders would gather to discuss and vote on issues directly.[5,6] Judge Jameson mentions that early English histories spoke of "*conventus publicos propria authoritate*" or " voluntary meetings of the people, under the protection of the common law."⁷ It has been theorized in the works of early English historians that the roots of the English convention lay in the earliest northern European nations. The northern proto-Germans had filled the void left by the collapse of the Roman Empire in the fifth century and their early Germanic conventions were perhaps modeled on the Roman practices.

The Roman Republic

We can look back more than two and a half millennia to the ancient Greeks and Romans for the oldest recorded versions of a convention as we now think of the word. Of course, what we think of as a convention bears little resemblance to an ancient convention, which would probably look more like a restrained public argument to modern eyes. Without question the original roots of a convention lay somewhere far, far back in time at a point that preceded written history; what we are able to find are the already refined versions of the convention's roots. Current scholars of antiquity point to the works of second-century Roman author Aulus Gellius⁸ writing of

---

[2] Dan Jones, *Magna Carta, The Birth of Liberty* (New York: Viking, 2015), generally - The drafting of the Magna Carta could indeed be viewed as a convention. It occurred over several days and numerous people were there to represent those living on their lands. In the six months run-up to the meeting, the rebels produced the "Unknown Charter" and the "Articles of the Barons" as rough drafts or working papers that would lead to the Magna Carta, 127.

[3] Allen Caperton Braxton, "Powers of Conventions," *Virginia Law Register* 7, no.2 (1901): 82

[4] Francis Palgrave, *The Rise and Progress of the English Commonwealth, Vol. I* (London: John Murray, 1832), generally – lists many examples of Middle Ages conventions not only in Great Britain but also Western Europe back into the period of Roman rule.

[5] Kris W. Kobach, "May "We the People" Speak?: The Forgotten Role of Constituent Instructions in Amending the Constitution," *University of California-Davis Law Review* 33, no.1 (Fall 1999): 27-8, n.106, This work, copyright 1999 by Kris W. Kobach, was originally published in the *UC Davis Law Review*, vol. 33, pp.1-94, copyright 1999 by The Regents of the University of California. All rights reserved. Reprinted with permission. – citing also Marc Kruman, *Between Authority and Liberty: State Constitution Making in Revolutionary America* (1997).

[6] Gordon S. Wood, *The Creation of the American Republic, 1776-1787* (Chapel Hill: University of North Carolina Press, 1969), 310. Published for the Omohundro Institute of Early American History and Culture.

[7] John Alexander Jameson, *A Treatise on Constitutional Conventions – Their History, Powers, and Modes of Proceeding* (New York: Scribner, 1867, 4ᵗʰ ed., 1887), §5, 4, - reprint by The Lawbook Exchange, (2013)

[8] Aulus Gellius, *Noctes Atticae*

the mostly lost works of Favorinus who wondered whether the Latin word *contio*, or "official public meeting of the populous," is equivalent to the Greek, δημηγορία, "a speech in the public assembly."[9]

Contio[10] was derived from the Latin words *conventio, conventus* and *convenire*, the roots of our modern English word "convention" and meant "a coming together." A *contio* was a public meeting during the Roman Republic officially called by a magistrate for some public purpose. The topic could be anything from pending legislation to a court decision to an execution for treason to election season magisterial puffery.[11] Usually, the magistrate calling the *contio* gave a speech on some pressing matter of public importance and then the issue was openly debated, somewhat. *Contiones* were open to all and served as the first public step in the Roman legislative process. After the *contio*, the people would proceed to then gather in their *comitia*[12] where they voted by tribes.[13] Both the *contio* and the *comitia* were forms of *concilium*, or political gatherings that were, to one degree or another, deliberative assemblies with defined rules.[14] These were the earliest forms of Roman public assemblies.[15] According to Cicero, the *contio* was one of the three methods by which the people of Rome could express their sentiments to the Senate and the magistrates.[16] It is also described as providing "the only official setting for political leaders to meet the people."[17]

It has been speculated that the violence and the breakdown in civility during the last century of the Roman Republic led to the decline of the *contiones*.[18,19] In the Roman Republic, the Senate proposed, debated and refined bills but the people had the final say – the people, gathered in their

---

[9] Roman M. Frolov, "Public Meetings in Ancient Rome: Definitions of the *Contiones* in the Sources," *Graeco-Latina Brunensia* 18 (2013): 76 – δημηγορία = *demegoria*.

[10] Pronounced "KOHN-shee-oh"

[11] James Tan, "*Contiones* in the Age of Cicero," *Classical Antiquity* 27, no.1 (April 2008): 170 – the paper includes an Appendix listing known *contiones* of the Ciceronian period

[12] Pronounced "koh-MISH-ee-ah"

[13] Fotini Metaxaki-Mitrou, "Violence in the *Contio* During the Ciceronian Age," *L'Antiquité Classique* 54 (1985): 180

[14] Andrew Lintott, *The Constitution of the Roman Republic* (New York: Clarendon Press, 1999), 42

[15] George Willis Botsford, *The Roman Assemblies From Their Origin to the End of the Republic* (New York: Macmillan, 1909), generally, Chapter VII, 139-51

[16] *Contiones*, assemblies, or plays and gladiatorial displays – per citation of Metaxaki-Mitrou

[17] Henrik Mouritsen, *Plebes and Politics in the Late Roman Republic* (New York: Cambridge University Press, 2004), 38

[18] Marcus Tullius Cicero, *Pro Sestio*, (56 BC)

[19] Fotini Metaxaki-Mitrou, "Violence in the *Contio* During the Ciceronian Age," *L'Antiquité Classique* 54 (1985): 184

civilian *comitia*,[20] voted directly on the passage of laws.[21] The process was then two part: the *contio* was the loose, informal public discussion open to any and all; the *comitia* was a regimented, second assembly using voice votes and later using ballots to finalize passage. *Comitia* meant "going together" and is derived from the Latin *committere* which is also the source of our English word, "committee."[22] The *comitiatus* took place in a *comitium*, a specially constructed meeting place.[23]

This arrangement is loosely analogous to our Article V **amendatory** convention proposing a constitutional amendment, and then being followed by an Article V ***ratification*** convention which formally adopts the amendment. The *contio* debated but did not vote and it enacted nothing; the *comitia* was more restricted as to attendance and debated and voted – and enacted.[24] One might make the error of comparing the two-part Roman process to the bicameral American state and national legislatures but this is erroneous as in our modern legislatures both houses vote. A truer comparison is found in the American constitutional amendment process wherein the amendatory convention plays the role of the *contio* in debating and referring but not enacting and the state legislatures or state ratification conventions are analogous to the *comitia* in their final debate and voting to enact. The *comitia* was organized by tribe similarly to our segregation among states for ratification. The Roman Senate appears most similar to the Article V convention in that it conducts debate and makes a proposal but cannot pass or ratify legislation. Also, like our Electoral College, the electors of the *comitia* voted popularly to obtain a majority in each tribe which then gave one single vote per tribe without regard to the number of electors per any given tribe.[25] One must wonder whether the Framers in Philadelphia were deliberately following the Roman example. It is well known that the Framers of the United States Constitution were "obsessed with ancient Rome."[26]

---

[20] There were two comitia: The Comitia Tributa for the civilian public and the Comitia Centuriata for the soldiers.

[21] Robert Morstein-Marx, *Mass Oratory and Political Power in the Late Roman Republic* (New York: Cambridge Press, 2004), 8

[22] Eric A. Posner, "The Constitution of the Roman Republic: A Political Economy Perspective," *University of Chicago Law School*, Working Paper No. 540, (Nov. 2010): 11-3

[23] Andrew Lintott, *The Constitution of the Roman Republic* (New York: Clarendon Press, 1999), 42

[24] Robert Morstein-Marx, *Mass Oratory and Political Power in the Late Roman Republic* (New York: Cambridge Press, 2004), 35 – quoting Aulus Gellius, "to hold a *contio* is to speak to the People without taking a vote."

[25] At the height of the Roman Republic (~241 B.C.), there were 35 tribes.

[26] Eric A. Posner, "The Constitution of the Roman Republic: A Political Economy Perspective," *University of Chicago Law School*, Working Paper No. 540, (Nov. 2010): 3

The Founders and Framers looked at the nation that they were designing and building as "a rebirth of the ancient Roman republic." The use and the construction of "mixed constitutions" was intended to copy Rome and with it, the idea of Roman-style citizenship.[27]

The descriptions given here of the *contio* and the *comitia* are simplistic at best. The *concilium* process is a complex subject and is given a more thorough treatment elsewhere and in many works. That the Romans established a framework for a social tool that evolved into our present forms of political conventions is hopefully sufficiently argued by the detail presented herein. It is the practices and the concept that are passed down through the last two and a half millennia of history that matter.[28]

Great Britain

It is conceivable that the Germanic tribes had learned the Roman convention method and adopted it, with modifications, into their public decision making practices after watching Roman habits over the many years that they were in contact with the Roman military, which also practiced *contiones* and *comitia* in the field.[29] The tribes spread the Germanic practices across northern Europe and seeded their methods in the places that they conquered such as England, Holland, northern France and Normandy. The Teutonic Saxons flowed into England as *foederati*, or mercenaries, for the Romans and stayed after the Romans retreated in the fifth century. The local British people would have recognized the similarity of the decision making habits shared by the Romans and the Saxons. It is possible that after four centuries of Roman occupation, the familiarity of the Roman traditions evidenced in the Saxons made the assimilation, in a small way, of the Saxons amongst the native Britons easier.

The Framers looked to the Saxon model of the "small republics" that had been created by the Saxons and that were governed through "voluntary

---

[27] Gordon S. Wood, *The Idea of America, Reflections on the Birth of the United States* (New York: Penguin Books, 2011), 72
[28] For greater detail on the *contio* and *comitia* assemblies, see:
  • George Willis Botsford, *The Roman Assemblies From Their Origin to the End of the Republic*
  • Andrew Lintott, *The Constitution of the Roman Republic*
  • Robert Morstein-Marx, *Mass Oratory and Political Power in the Late Roman Republic*
  • Henrik Mouritsen, *Plebes and Politics in the Late Roman Republic*
[29] Robert Morstein-Marx, *Mass Oratory and Political Power in the Late Roman Republic* (New York: Cambridge Press, 2004), 34, n.1

6 Far From Unworkable

delegations of the whole People."[30] Among the earliest English examples are the "conventions" called by West Saxon, or Wessex, King Ine in 720 to promulgate his laws and settle disputes "done by the advice and counsel of all his aldermen and senior wisemen,"[31] the convention of King Edgar, of Mercia and the Danelaw, convening "all of his nobles" at Salisbury in 970,[32] and the convention of King Canute, of all England, at Oxford in 1030. These conventions, as they are termed in the early English histories, all pre-date the Norman Conquest of England by William in 1066.[33,34]

Post-Norman Conquest, the use of the convention method of problem solution was expanded. The Normans quickly took to using the English convention, or assembly, as the pre-eminent form of non-violent, political dispute resolution and as a political consensus building mechanism. The conventions employed are often found in the oldest English records as a "convention of the estates" or "convention of the nobles," occasionally the clergy are enumerated among those in attendance. We can find an "assembly of barons," an "assembly of peers," a "general assembly" or a "meeting of barons" given as the descriptor of many of the assemblages. It is not until the reign of Henry II[35] that the word "parliament" becomes the normal term for a legislative gathering. Convention is thereafter used to distinguish a temporary and unofficial meeting from a parliament, which was an officially called and eventually permanent assemblage. The writings of early historians make this distinction when discussing the period from Richard I onward.[36] One early nineteenth-century, multivolume history of English parliamentary action lists at least seventeen conventions or political meetings held between 1107 and 1254 while also cataloguing many separate but contemporaneous parliaments, taking the pains to distinguish between the two.[37]

These conventions used the force of numbers and the display of armed

---

[30] Gordon S. Wood, *The Creation of the American Republic, 1776-1787* (Chapel Hill: University of North Carolina Press, 1998), 227. Published for the Omohundro Institute of Early American History and Culture. Used by permission of the publisher.

[31] William Corbett, John Wright, & Thomas Curson Hansard, *The Parliamentary History of England, from the Earliest Period to the Year 1803* (London: R. Bagshaw, Oct. 1806), col.1

[32] Ibid., col.2

[33] Ibid., cols.5-6.

[34] *The Parliamentary or Constitutional History of England, From the Earliest Times, to the Restoration of King Charles II* (London: J. & R. Tonson, April 1751), 3

[35] Reigned 19 December 1154 – 6 July 1189

[36] Reigned 6 July 1189 – 6 April 1199

[37] William Corbett, John Wright, & Thomas Curson Hansard, *The Parliamentary History of England, from the Earliest Period to the Year 1803* (London: R. Bagshaw, Oct. 1806), col.5-27

troops and the united will of the people, the gentry and the nobility to demonstrate to the Crown the resolve of the English people to acquire and maintain civil liberties. Issuing a written charter sought to assure clear and continued observance of the terms agreed upon in convention without the obfuscation of semantic games over the passage of time. On 13 January 1223, Henry III hosted a convention in London wherein the barons "requested the King that he would confirm the liberties and free customs for which a war was made with his father" and stressing that "both the King and all the nobility had sworn to observe, and cause to be observed, those liberties, and, therefore, could not refuse to do it."[38]

This convening aspect of political life was a well-established practice by the time that the first Englishmen emigrated to the New World. Being located so far from the seat of British government situated in London, the North American colonies were forced to take it upon themselves to solve their own problems.[39] And, so they did. The famously democratic New England Town Hall Meeting is the direct descendant of the English town meeting which itself has medieval roots; in America it was created by both English habit and colonial necessity. Over time and along the way, the colonists developed a taste for conventions as an effective method of quickly debating and resolving overarching and shared issues. Permanent assemblies or parliaments are well suited to attend to the daily internal issues and the financial aspects of a given geographic political entity. But those problems that cross political borders or address matters that formal assemblies ignore or seek to oppress call for a different instrument of resolution. These early conventions were often spontaneous gatherings. They were clearly most often unauthorized by the Crown. As such, they were free to consider and decide whatever they chose to do. The rules, although concretized over time and usage, were initially fluid. The authority to carry out their decisions however was often another matter.

The next step in the English evolution of conventions was the revolutionary convention model called to sort out what to do about the absence of government. The very early "Convention of the Estates" addressed the change in government in 1327 when Edward II abdicated

---

[38] Ibid., col.10
[39] David E. Kyvig, *Explicit and Authentic Acts, Amending the U.S. Constitution 1776-1995* (Lawrence: University Press of Kansas, 1996), 12

and in 1399 when Henry IV took the throne.[40] In 1660, in the wake of the conclusion of the English Civil Wars and the death of Oliver Cromwell, the restored Royalists found themselves without a monarch. They called an elected convention to decide who should rule. They had few recent guides or traditions relating to this exact matter to govern their convention necessitating that they "make it up as they went along." The result of the "Convention Parliament"[41] was the recall of Charles II to England, and the re-establishment of the monarchy.[42,43] A generation later, the English repeated the experiment from 29 December 1688 to 22 January 1689 when they needed to resolve, again, who would reign.[44] Once more, an elected Convention Parliament was called that established the English Bill of Rights and ended in the conditional offer of the crown to William and Mary.[45] Until 1689, the word "convention" had a negative connotation in England, afterward it was associated with the concept of "liberty."[46] These two seventeenth-century English conventions were the prototypes for the American conventions to establish governments in the thirteen colonies during the American Revolution.[47] In all of these examples, the same political situation existed: the formal government had collapsed and only local control remained, if that.[48]

In North America, that was about to change. With the publication of the Declaration of Independence in 1776 and its pronouncement that,

> "[I]t is the Right of the People to alter or to abolish it [the government], and to institute new Government,..."

the dictate of the Divine Right of Kings to rule,[49] dating back to the

---

[40] Gordon S. Wood, *The Creation of the American Republic, 1776-1787* (Chapel Hill: University of North Carolina Press, 1969), 310. Published for the Omohundro Institute of Early American History and Culture.
[41] 25 April – 29 December 1660
[42] Russell B. Caplan, *Constitutional Brinkmanship* (New York: Oxford University Press, 1988), 5
[43] The Convention Parliament went on to declare itself the true parliament and govern.
[44] Russell B. Caplan, *Constitutional Brinkmanship* (New York: Oxford University Press, 1988), 5
[45] This second Convention Parliament also declared itself a legal parliament and governed, continuing to do so to this day.
[46] Russell B. Caplan, *Constitutional Brinkmanship* (New York: Oxford University Press, 1988), 5
[47] Technically fourteen colonies as Vermont also asserted its right to exist and established a constitutional government.
[48] Allen Caperton Braxton, "Powers of Conventions," *Virginia Law Register* 7, no.2 (1901): 83
[49] The fully developed theory of the Divine Right of Kings is ascribed to French jurist Jean Bodin in his 1576 work *Six Livres de la République* and was embraced by James I of England thereby setting in motion the problems to come.

Middle Ages, was forever gone in the United States.[50] This evolution in political thinking spawned new problems. In the motherland of England, the aristocracy of the nobles and the landed gentry along with the church hierarchy had held the reins of power, but in the newly independent colonies, the formal and rigid aristocracy was gone, henceforth forbidden. And the plethora of religions and churches had no dominant sect nationwide. Who would populate and lead these nascent conventions? What now were the powers and limitations of these conventions? Americans responded by electing their representatives and having their state legislatures and provincial congresses define the powers and limits of the constitutional conventions beyond the traditions and customs that had developed to date. Each of these conventions was limited in powers to one degree or another and their product was often subject to the approval of the people. That is to say, for the first time, the people were sovereign and the conventions were called in the name of and under the authority of the people.

To understand the promise, or specter, depending on one's point of view, of an Article V Convention, it is necessary to define the evolved meaning of a "convention" and the genesis of the amendatory convention. The American experience with political conventions extends far beyond that of just the 1787 Constitutional Convention and the quadrennial nominating conventions of the political parties that most readily come to the modern American mind. The powers, limitations, procedures and history of these hundreds of American political conventions are varied and, for some time in our past, were well known and understood. Today, we think of only the political party nominating conventions of every four years with their apparent chaos and we recoil in fear of the potential result of applying such a spectacle to our federal Constitution. We imagine such a convention to be confused, chaotic, unstructured and…unworkable.

This was not always the perception. Once upon a time, as we have seen and will see, conventions were the go-to solution to our large-scale political problems. Conventions were the preferred option to out and out warfare, especially a civil war. They provided a democratic method of venting the public's frustrations and for discussing the possible solutions absent the usual constraints and the messiness of the daily parliamentary process. That parliamentary process is too well known for its unseemly wheeling

---

[50] Michael Kammen, *People of Paradox* (Ithaca, NY: Cornell University Press, 1972), 26

and dealing, secret quid pro quo, and the all-important preservation of the elite driven status quo with its pre-eminent goal of the reinforcement of the divide between the governing establishment and the taxpaying governed. To make the most of employing an Article V amendatory convention today, it is incumbent on the present to fully understand the complexity of the convention. It is useful that we begin by exploring the history of the wide variety of conventions and the semantics of the wording to better understand the situation of the Article V amendatory convention of today. Distinguishing between the many forms, powers, limitations and standard procedures of conventions is the starting point for utilizing this tool.

What Do We Mean When We Say "Convention"?

The meaning of the word "convention" has changed over the centuries. What we think of today as a convention is far from that of the medieval meaning or even from the meaning of as recent as just three hundred years ago. The structure of a convention with delegates acting on behalf of and in representation of others; of producing some sort of output, typically documentary; and of debate and deliberation of a topic describes the convention of the medieval period just as today. The formal parliamentary procedures governing who speaks and when; the regimented order of business; the clearly defined legality of the actions and the limitations of those actions are all products of the last few centuries.

There is a difference in the historical meaning of the term "convention" in comparison to that of a "parliament" or a "congress" or even an ordinary assembly. Initially, the words "congress" and "convention" were interchangeable.[51] In England, prior to the Glorious Revolution of 1688, convention had become a sparsely employed word but it did have a distinct meaning politically. It meant an unofficial meeting, with a specific purpose – an "irregular assembly."[52] It was refined to mean a political meeting that was NOT summoned by the King's writ. A parliament was summoned by the King; if it was not, then it was a convention. To the north in Scotland, the Convention of Estates was a constitutional legal institution with powers

---

[51] Robert G. Natelson, *A Compendium for Lawyers and Legislative Drafters* (Purcellville, VA: Convention of States, 2014): 22
[52] Gordon S. Wood, *The Creation of the American Republic, 1776-1787* (Chapel Hill: University of North Carolina Press, 1969), 311. Published for the Omohundro Institute of Early American History and Culture. Used by permission of the publisher.

less than that of the Scottish Parliament. Alongside that body was the Convention of the Royal Burghs, which convened to discuss matters of interest to the merchants and trades. This convention has its roots back to at least the twelfth century. Starting in the seventeenth century, the "Royal" was dropped and it was called simply the Convention of the Burghs.[53] These bodies were often called in parallel to the Scottish Parliament in order to render a second opinion or to gauge the collective state of mind of the Scottish people. What makes these bodies conventions instead of parliamentary bodies is the irregular calling and meeting of the bodies. The Convention of the Burghs persisted in Scotland until 1975, long after the dissolution of the Scottish Parliament nearly three centuries earlier.[54] In some instances, a convention was called in lieu of consulting Parliament so as to provide a less biased assessment of a given situation. The common products of these early conventions were opinions, recommendations and in some instances a plan of action – similar to what one might expect from an Article V amendatory convention of today. Conventions were an integral part of the government, albeit initially informal, and therefore a common occurrence in Scotland and thus their existence was well-known, and often emulated, in bordering England.[55] After the establishment of Parliament as a formal and semi-permanent, semi-regular body in the thirteenth century, the use of the convention did fade in England; but it did not fade away.[56]

The early English and Scottish conventions were characterized by their spontaneous occurrence in response to a specific issue or event that had roiled the political waters of the day. They were, as constitutional convention historian Roger Sherman Hoar described them, echoing the Latin, a simple "comings-together" and the meetings lacked the quality of being truly representative of the whole people.[57] The citizens who were most incensed by the prevailing situation were the ones who were willing to leave their families, fields, mills and shops, and thus, the representation in the early conventions was decidedly skewed toward to a singular, common opinion.

---

[53] The Convention of the Burghs was replaced by the Convention of Scottish Local Authorities.
[54] J. D. Mackie, *A History of Scotland* (London: Penguin Books, 1964), generally
[55] John Franklin Jameson, "The Early Political Uses of the Word Convention," *American Historical Review* 3, no.3 (1898): 480-5
[56] Henry III is most responsible for the establishment of a permanent, more or less, Parliament about 1326. http://www.historyofparliamentonline.org/periods/medieval
[57] Roger Sherman Hoar, *Constitutional Conventions – Their Nature, Powers, and Limitations* (Boston: Little, Brown, 1917), 2

12 Far From Unworkable

Allen Braxton defined more than a century ago that,

> *"The first and crudest conventions were in no sense representative bodies; but were mere voluntary, irregular, illegitimate assemblies of individuals, acting in their own motion and on their own behalf, who felt themselves sufficiently powerful to resort to the ultimate right of Revolution, and wrest, by violence, from their sovereigns, such governmental concessions as they desired. The existence of such bodies was neither provided for, nor recognized, by the laws or existing social system."*[58]

These early British Isles conventions lacked a number of the practices and procedures of today's conventions, but they set the precedent for today and provided the original practices that have transformed into today's traditions. Early delegate selection was nothing like today. Those attendees in the Middle Age convention were determined more by whom was affected by the issue at hand. English nobility attended Runnymede; Scottish tradesmen attended the Convention of the Burghs; commoners attended the English town meetings; and landed gentry and the aristocracy attended the conventions for filling the throne.

For the English and Scottish peasants of a thousand years ago, living in a feudal society, how else might they communicate their frustration and growing impatience to the powers that be? They were observing the time-honored adage that there is strength in numbers and adding to that their articulation of grievances in remonstrance to those in power. Our English and Scottish ancestors a millennium past found themselves in the same situation as the Romans a millennium or more prior. It wasn't until 1689 that the law concerning the change of the unwritten English constitution was modified to allow for constitutional change only by Parliament, thereby shutting the people out of the process directly.[59] But by that time, the colonists in North America had already cemented roughly seven decades of convention usage firmly into place.

These early colonial American conventions morphed into several variants, including constitutional conventions, nominating conventions, amendatory conventions and a "revolutionary convention." What then in the Colonial Era best describes the convention as the people of that time knew it? Certain aspects had to be common to all conventions and to distinguish a

---

[58] Allen Caperton Braxton, "Powers of Conventions," *Virginia Law Register* 7, no.2 (1901): 82
[59] Ibid.

convention from a legislature. Historian John Franklin Jameson highlighted the differences in 1898, noting that,

> *"It is well known that they usually consisted of, or closely resembled, a colonial legislature minus the governor and council, and not summoned by the governor, and that they were called conventions because, of all words denoting a political assemblage, convention was held to be the fit and technical term by which to designate such bodies as these."*[60]

Since the convention is doing similar work to a legislature, it is logical to expect it to look like a legislature. What made these American conventions distinct from their British counterparts can be found in a key phrase which appeared in the notes from an early eighteenth-century convention in South Carolina, stating, "That we cannot Act as an Assembly, but as a Convention, delegated by the People,…"[61] Note the use of that distinctive turn of phrase, "*delegated by the People.*" American conventions have been said to draw their legitimacy from the sovereign power delegated to the convention by the people and not by a regent or a royal decree. Furthermore, this grant of power is also NOT from the colonial or state legislature, who, likewise draw their legitimacy from a grant of power from the people. In England, the convention is unauthorized and certainly not by royal consent as the people lack sovereignty. In England, the sovereign is, well, sovereign and the people are mere subjects.

In the United States, the definitive difference between the legislature and a convention was articulated in 1933 in a decision of the Maine Supreme Court where they wrote that, "The principle distinction between a convention and a Legislature is that the former is called for a specific purpose, the latter for general purposes."[62] It is "designed to serve an ad hoc governmental function."[63]

It has been noted that the Framers of the federal constitution were not very fond of democracy or of the uninformed or ill-informed having the

---

[60] John Franklin Jameson, "The Early Political Uses of the Word Convention," *American Historical Review* 3, no.3 (1898): 478

[61] Ibid., 477-8 - referring to a South Carolina convention held in 1719 and citing *A Narrative of the People of South Carolina*, in Bartholomew Carroll's *Historical Collections of South Carolina, Vol. II*, (1836), 189

[62] *In Re Opinion of the Justices*, 167 A. 176 at 179, 132 Me. 491 (1933)

[63] Robert G. Natelson, "Proposing Constitutional Amendments by Convention: Rules Governing the Process," *Tennessee Law Review* 78 (2011):706 . The full text of this Article was published originally by the Tennessee Law Review Association, Inc. at 78 Tenn. L. Rev. 693 (2011), and this version, approved by the Author, appears by their permission.

voting franchise. The structure of the federal constitution is such that any direct action by the public is precluded. The Article V convention system is the closest real measure of direct action by the public. The convention process uses representative bodies to act in and speak on behalf of the people. The convention is termed as "in a special manner the epitome of the People." Kris Kobach stresses that "'The people' were thought to speak in such conventions, but only through their elected delegates."[64]

A look at the system of amendment production embedded in the federal constitution shows that the doctrines of federalism and the separation of powers are not just words or intangible concepts; they are carried through in the amending process itself. The convention mechanism is dependent on the execution and the support of those doctrines. The States and the Congress each have roles in both amendment processes. The distribution of the powers between the States and the Congress exemplifies the distribution of power in federalism.[65]

Conventions have certain attributes that make them preferable to state legislatures for drafting, revising or amending constitutions. At the top of the list is that the temporary nature of the convention removes much of the political influence and "horse-trading" that goes on in a legislature. Since the convention is of a short duration and there is no need for the re-election of the delegates, there is less potential for influence by lobbyists, parties, factions and donors. The view of the work is presumably more non-partisan. This theory is proven out in studies that show that constitutional conventions have produced less radical innovations in government than normal legislative bodies.[66]

The use of separate conventions and separate types of conventions to propose amendments and also to ratify amendments – and to ratify the Constitution itself distinct from the 1787 Constitutional Convention to draft the document - is a perfect example of the application of the doctrine of the separation of powers. Deliberative conventions with limited powers and duties exemplify the need to avoid concentration of power in too few hands or in a single body. Additionally, extending the separation of powers

---

[64] Kris W. Kobach, "Rethinking Article V: Term Limits and the Seventeenth and Nineteenth Amendments," *Yale Law Journal* 103, no.7 (May 1994): 1985-6
[65] Abraham C. Weinfeld, "Power of Congress Over State Ratifying Conventions," *Harvard Law Review* 51, no.3 (1938): 487
[66] Dale A. Kimball, "The Constitutional Convention, Its Nature and Powers – And the Amending Procedure," *Utah Law Review* (Sept. 1966): 391

to include the divergence between the state and federal exercise of powers is an application of the doctrine of federalism. Two for one.[67]

The Many Types and Forms of Political Conventions

The proliferation of the many types of American political conventions all stem predominantly from the early English conventions, but Americans have taken the political convention to heart and created the diversity that we know today. It has been said of the constitutional convention that it is "America's basic institution."[68] There is more than one type of *"constitutional convention."* We can think of both state and federal constitutional conventions and without much effort define the difference between them. Both types create constitutions, in the American system - the *federal constitutional convention* created a limited or enumerated power government; but the *state constitutional convention* creates a plenary, or widely powered government.

The state constitutional convention differs from the federal constitutional convention in that the state conventions are subject to the oversight and judicial review of the federal judiciary. State constitutions are also limited in what provisions they may incorporate to the extent that they may not interfere with federal constitutional provisions. The US Supreme Court has made great use, in the last century, of the Supremacy Clause and the incorporation doctrine to modify the state constitutions and the state powers.[69]

Both types of constitutional conventions are considered "constitutional bodies"; that is, they are based upon already existing constitutional provisions. As assemblies, their constitutionality is derived from adherence to the prevailing constitutional structure. Since many states require, by a provision of their state constitutions, that periodic state constitutional conventions be held to revise or amend their state constitution, these events are held under the authority of the currently in force state constitution. The constitutionality of that document extends to cover the convention called under its auspices. These conventions are most often called by an existing

---

[67] Abraham C. Weinfeld, "Power of Congress Over State Ratifying Conventions," *Harvard Law Review* 51, no.3 (Jan. 1938): 487

[68] Merrill D. Peterson, ed., *Democracy, Liberty, and Property - The State Constitutional Conventions of the 1820s* (Indianapolis: The Liberty Fund, 2010. Originally published by Bobbs Merrill Co., 1966), xxi

[69] John A. Eidsmoe, "A New Constitutional Convention? Critical Look at Questions Answered, and Not Answered, by Article Five of the United States Constitution," *United States Air Force Academy Journal of Legal Studies* 3 (1992): 10

government in order to create reform or constitutional reorganization. Unlike the revolutionary convention, the constitutional convention does not replace or supplant the existing government as a governing body – to act as a government would be to morph into a revolutionary convention.

There is a third form of the constitutional convention that is very rare and will probably not appear again, but still warrants mention. It is a *"hybrid"* of the constitutional, legislative and ratification conventions all wrapped up into one form. The ***"Reconstruction conventions"*** used in the southern states after the Civil War were intended to return the southern states to a form of government that complemented the federal constitution. This intention meant the ratification of the Thirteenth and Fourteenth Amendments, legislative repeal of secession acts and ordinances along with the repudiation of Confederate war debt and the drafting of a new conforming state constitution. These specialized conventions were anomalies unique to their time.[70]

These three constitutional convention scenarios are very different from a *"revolutionary convention"* that is designed to step in where there is no existing government or where there is widespread opposition to the prevailing - and technically legitimate - government. The Continental Congress that eventually drafted and put in place the Articles of Confederation was a revolutionary convention since the British system had collapsed in parts of North America.[71] It acted on behalf of all of the colonies then in rebellion in place of the rejected Parliament in London. The Philadelphia Federal Convention of 1787 was a constitutional convention because it sought to reform and replace the existing Confederation government which was already operating under the Articles of Confederation.[72,73] The 1787 convention was not operating

---

[70] Roger Sherman Hoar, *Constitutional Conventions – Their Nature, Powers, and Limitations* (Boston: Little, Brown, (1917), 129-30

[71] The Second Continental Congress drafted the *Articles of Confederation and Perpetual Union* in 1776-77.

[72] Allen Caperton Braxton, "Powers of Conventions," *Virginia Law Register* 7, no.2 (1901): 79

[73] In contrast, the secessionary conventions of 1861 in the Confederate States were all revolutionary because they were convened in the revolt against the United States government and therefore against the United States Constitution. See Homer Hendricks, "Some Legal Aspects of Constitutional Conventions," *Texas Law Review* 2 (1924): 196, n.6. Hendricks argues that the reconstruction conventions would have been revolutionary as well, but since one of the requirements of readmission to the United States was the ratification of the Thirteenth and Fourteenth Amendments, it could be argued that the reconstruction conventions were held under the United States Constitution in the same manner that new states have always had to affirm their acceptance of the US Constitution in their territorial and later state constitutional conventions.

under the authority of the Articles of Confederation because that charter contained no provision for such a convention. An invitation to the States to attend and address the problems of the nation was eventually issued by the Confederation Congress making it an authorized convention and not a revolutionary convention. Note that it was an invitation and not a command from the Confederation Congress. The revolutionary convention is unlimited in power and without a guide for the law. It fills a political and social vacuum. It has been termed as a "provisional government" and is beyond similarity to any other convention, in particular, a constitutional convention. Braxton draws the distinction between the constitutional and the revolutionary conventions,

> "*The Constitutional Convention co-exists with the former government, which continues to perform its functions, by virtue of the old Constitution and laws, until the new Constitution is adopted; the Revolutionary Convention is the Government itself, the co-existence with which of any other government is impossible. The Constitutional Convention repairs and improves the Government, the Revolutionary Convention rebuilds it de novo after it has been pulled down and destroyed.*"[74]

In his classic 1867 work, *A Treatise on Constitutional Conventions*, Judge Jameson differentiated four types of conventions: the aforementioned constitutional convention, the revolutionary convention, the legislative convention and the spontaneous convention.[75] This distinction between the various types of conventions is often lost on people – and it is continuously and deliberately used by those who oppose an Article V amendatory convention to purposely confuse people for the sake of fear-mongering. A century ago, Braxton said of these two convention types,

> "*[I]n many respects, Constitutional and Revolutionary Conventions are the antitheses of each other. So essentially different are the two bodies and their functions, powers and purposes, that it is to be regretted that we have but one word – 'Convention' – by which to designate them both; but that they should both have come to be recognized, in the minds of some public men, not only as Conventions, but as* **Constitutional Conventions***, is both lamentable and dangerous.*"[76]

---

[74] Allen Caperton Braxton, "Powers of Conventions," *Virginia Law Register* 7, no.2 (1901): 80
[75] John Alexander Jameson, *A Treatise on Constitutional Conventions – Their History, Powers, and Modes of Proceeding* (New York: Scribner, 1867, 4th ed., 1887), §§ 4-13, 3-12, - reprint by The Lawbook Exchange, (2013)
[76] Allen Caperton Braxton, "Powers of Conventions," *Virginia Law Register* 7, no.2 (1901): 80

It is that very confusion that has proven so valuable to amendatory convention opponents as they intentionally obscure and misrepresent the difference for political gain. Noting the division drawn by Jameson between the two types of conventions, Professor John R. Vile has condensed Jameson's distinction between the revolutionary and constitutional conventions and defined that whatever issues or "irregularities" could be found to be associated with the first kind of convention, they could not be cited as justifying the second kind.[77]

Today's Article V convention opponents go to great lengths to assert that an amendatory convention called under Article V is not an amendatory convention, but is actually a constitutional convention. They use the term "constitutional convention" but when they describe the powers and limitations of that particular convention, they will give the description that most describes a revolutionary convention - not a constitutional convention, let alone an amendatory convention. These opponents will never say, or admit, that they are, in fact, describing a revolutionary convention. The fear of the power of the unregulated, unlimited, plenary, all-powerful revolutionary convention serves well to dissuade the average person, or state legislator, from not only considering the possibility of an amendatory convention but from considering almost all forms of constitutional change at the federal level.

Modern constitutional conventions are heavily regulated and legally structured. They have become commonplace as the States have held, depending on the source consulted, approximately 236 such conventions since the founding of the Republic.[78] Many states have made provisions within their state constitutions for holding constitutional conventions on a regular basis. Because the modern constitutional convention is designed to accommodate change by a process that is non-violent and without the usual and attendant social upheaval, it has been called an "Anti-revolutionary Convention" and is considered an American invention.[79]

The revolutionary convention is sometimes referred to as a "*spontaneous convention*" by later historians but Jameson would clearly

---

[77] John R. Vile, "American Views of the Constitutional Amending Process: An Intellectual History of Article V," *American Journal of Legal History* 35, no.1 (Jan. 1991): 57

[78] John J. Dinan, *The American State Constitutional Tradition* (Lawrence: University Press of Kansas, 2006), 7-9 – Dinan lists 233 state conventions, but records show that there are at least three more.

[79] Allen Caperton Braxton, "Powers of Conventions," *Virginia Law Register* 7, no.2 (1901): 81-2

disagree with this classification.[80] Sometimes this type of convention can be found referred to as a "factional convention."[81] The spontaneous convention is more of a "public meeting" called without a fixed agenda or any real preparations. Jameson characterized this type of convention as the oldest, with its roots at least as far back as the twelfth century, and protected by the common law of England.[82] This idea makes sense as we see this happening still today, where citizens are angered by some event, or proposed bill, or an act of a legislature, and one or more citizens call for an open meeting. That meeting then produces a public pronouncement, in our age it is usually a press release or a press conference, maybe some printed declaration is issued, where the public sentiment is measured and declared. Recent examples that follow the pattern of convening after an open call, then deliberating and issuing a resolution, or a public statement of demands or proposed social and/or legal changes include conventions and conferences of the Tea Party and Occupy grassroots movements.

These spontaneous conventions serve a number of purposes: they allow the public to vent their dissatisfaction, they communicate the public's desires for change, they initiate the determination of consensus, and they foster the generation of ideas. Such conventions are distinguished by a lack of rules or protocol, more often than not they are tumultuous and raucous, they incite some level of excitement or panic in society (without which the spontaneous convention would be rather pointless), and they frequently signal a change in the political direction of our society. Jameson noted that these spontaneous conventions are "wholly unofficial," necessary to "the continued healthy life of a commonwealth" and "a common and most invaluable provision of our constitutions, State and Federal." He is suggesting that these spontaneous conventions are perhaps what are being referenced in the First Amendment to our federal Constitution where it guarantees "the right of the people peaceably to assemble, and to petition the Government for a redress of grievances." Obviously, the spontaneous convention is the necessary and often first step in the cumulative American political process that occasionally and eventually results in amendment of the state and/or

---

[80] Roger Sherman Hoar, *Constitutional Conventions – Their Nature, Powers, and Limitations* (Boston: Little, Brown, 1917), 34

[81] Ibid., 19-21

[82] John Alexander Jameson, *A Treatise on Constitutional Conventions – Their History, Powers, and Modes of Proceeding* (New York: Scribner, 1867, 4th ed., 1887), §5, 4-5, - reprint by The Lawbook Exchange, (2013)

federal Constitutions.[83]

The last of Jameson's designated conventions is that of the "*legislative convention.*" As noted previously, this is nothing more than the legislative bodies that today are found in Congress, state legislatures, municipal common councils, county boards and any other political division with a controlling body. They are not normally considered conventions in the sense that we think of a convention today, but to Jameson and early researchers, it seemed logical to include them since many had evolved from revolutionary conventions. They share generally the same rules and procedures and function in the same manner as the other types of conventions. They are the legitimate, civilized and refined children of the constitutional conventions and the grandchildren of the revolutionary conventions.

From these four major types of political conventions, almost all other minor political conventions have descended as either a subaltern convention, such as an amendatory or a ratification convention, or as a distinctly different convention, such as a nominating or secessionary convention. Occasionally we see the development of a new or unusual convention, such as the hybrid reconstruction convention in the late 1860s and 1870s or the latest incarnation, the twenty-first century's "convention of the States" that actually resurrects the deliberative discussion purpose of the original conventions of hundreds of years ago. This last example is exemplified by the Assembly of State Legislatures that meets to discuss how to resolve the problems with operating an Article V amendatory convention.

A sub-group of conventions is the authorized convention – this is the convention that is often provided for in the existing, currently-in-effect constitution and is called by either the legislature or by the constitution itself, typically at a regular interval. Many state constitutions require periodic state constitutional conventions for updating their charter. These regularly scheduled conventions act as safety valves for the release of any pent up frustration with government or as idea generators for dealing with recalcitrant problems that the usual political solutions have proven inadequate at solving.[84] Roger Sherman Hoar stated that the authorized convention can be found as a subaltern to each of the revolutionary,

---

[83] Ibid.
[84] Roger Sherman Hoar, Constitutional Conventions – Their Nature, Powers, and Limitations (Boston: Little, Brown, 1917), 51-2

constitutional and legislative conventions.[85]

Another sub-group is the *popular convention* – this is a convention that is not mentioned in the state or federal constitution but is called by the electors in a regular and legally authorized election. It is an expression of the popular will. If a state constitution called for a regularly scheduled convention and the electors call a convention at a time not scheduled by the state constitution, then that is also a popular convention. If a legislature calls an unscheduled convention without first obtaining the approval of the people, then such a convention is popular but supra-constitutional. The people are recognized to be the sole possessors of the sovereign power to call a convention despite the legislative prerogative to do so as that permission is conditional upon the explicit approval of the people.[86]

There is yet another set of convention types. These are not typically grouped together in the academic literature but they are a distinctive subset and could be termed *specialized conventions*. These are all limited in power and they are each called to perform a specific political function. They have evolved to address narrow issues and needs that cannot be handled within the usual political processes or conventions without some conflict or compromise.

First, of the specialized conventions, we come to the *ratification convention*. It is convened solely under the authority of a constitution or in response to the proposal of a new constitution or amendment. Like the constitutional convention itself, the ratification convention comes in different styles. It may be for the ratification of a new constitution or the ratification of a proposed amendment(s). Its power is strictly constrained to the consideration of an amendment or of a new constitution. It does not possess the power to alter or amend the considered object in any way. It debates and it votes, nothing more. It is an American innovation.[87]

Another specialized convention is the *secessionary convention*. While this is not a usual convention type regularly encountered, it does fit the category as a limited power, action specific convention. Most would think of the secession conventions of 1860-61 of the southern states as the only

---

[85] Ibid., 38
[86] Ibid., 61 – Hoar points to a very explicit ruling of the New York Supreme Court on the matter. He goes on to cite more state supreme court decisions from several states.
[87] England's 1649 *Agreement of the People* called for popular ratification although it was not implemented. The ratification convention was an American improvement on the idea of popular ratification.

examples, but we can find secessionary conventions in the Revolutionary Era as well. Some colonies, counties, towns, militias, grand juries and trade guilds called such a convention, without terming it a secession convention, for the purpose of debating and then avowedly leaving the authority of the British Crown by declaring their independence. Historian Pauline Maier catalogued more than ninety such conventions and declarations that preceded the 4 July 1776 national declaration.[88] North Carolina led the States on 12 April 1776. Even Rhode Island got a jump on the Continental Congress by declaring the colony's independence on 4 May 1776. Throughout American history, there have been many, usually small and inconsequential, secession movements and those that have been taken seriously are few and far between, such as the southern states in the early 1860s and the Hartford Convention of 1814. Hartford may not even qualify as the discussion of secession was brought up as a suggestion and was not the original or sole express purpose of the convention. Even today, there are secession movements that hold conventions such as those sponsored in the first decade of the twenty-first century by the Middlebury Institute and the League of the South. South Carolina's history of secession conventions is extensive as the state called for secession in 1822, 1828-32, 1850 and 1860. It could be argued that the secessionary convention is also a subset of the revolutionary convention.

Although not called to act on government itself or on a political charter, another convention type that deals with the part of the political process is the *nominating convention*. Like the other specialized conventions, it is limited in purpose and specific as to function. Nominating conventions follow many of the rules of other political conventions and are a distinct part of the political process. They most resemble in purpose the amendatory convention as they both propose but do not ratify or conclude. Nominating conventions have been a long established part of the American political process. Most states held nominating conventions at the town or county level to select their delegates to the state ratifying conventions for the Constitution.[89]

Finally, we arrive at the *amendatory convention*. This specialized type of convention is another truly American invention. Professor Lester Orfield,

---

[88] Pauline Maier, *American Scripture: Making the Declaration of Independence* (New York: Vintage Books, 1997), 48, Appendix A, 217-223 and Appendix B, 225-34

[89] Pauline Maier, *Ratification, The People Debate the Constitution, 1787-1788* (New York: Simon & Schuster, 2010), 329

the first to publish a book dedicated solely to the topic of the amending power, said of this matter,

> "The idea of amending the organic instrument of a state is peculiarly American. Although many of our political and legal institutions take their origin from English and occasionally Continental conceptions, such is not the case in the fundamental matter of altering the constitution."[90]

The purpose of the amendatory convention is strictly, explicitly and expressly limited to the drafting, debate and proposition of new constitutional amendments. It is NOT for the purpose of drafting a new constitution. It may be for a single amendment or a finite set of amendments or for an unlimited number of amendments. The restriction is dependent on whether the amendatory convention agenda is limited or unlimited and that all-important attribute depends on the act of the legislature that calls the amendatory convention.

An amendatory convention is always constitutional in nature as it is called under the authority of the existing constitution. It may be a limited convention in terms of the subject matter or it may be unlimited as an open or general (in modern terms) convention. Traditionally, amendatory conventions set their own rules and select their own officers. It is independent of the legislature but may be controlled by enabling legislation.

The authority to propose amendments is conditional upon the instructions from the legislature. Jameson noted as early as 1867 that unless an amendatory convention is given carte blanche in its enabling act to propose amendments at will and without limits, then it is under the limitations set by the specific mandate imposed.[91] That permission to examine any subject would have to be also explicitly laid out to be a valid exercise of authority.[92]

Professor John R. Vile went a step further in his 2016 book, *Conventional Wisdom*, and described four types of amendatory convention. The **sovereign-delegate** convention model was most espoused during the Civil War era and involved the convention assuming any and all powers that the delegates chose to take up. Vile assigns much of the fear of a runaway convention to the advent of this model. While Vile thinks that the model

---

[90] Lester Bernhardt Orfield, *The Amending of the Federal Constitution* (Ann Arbor: The University of Michigan Press, 1942), 1
[91] John Alexander Jameson, *A Treatise on Constitutional Conventions, Their History, Powers, and Modes of Proceeding* (New York: Scribner, 1867, 4th ed., 1887), §409e, 412, - reprint by The Lawbook Exchange, (2013)
[92] Thomas A. Gilliam, "Constitutional Conventions: Precedents, Problems, and Proposals," *St. Louis University Law Review* 16 (1971): 49

is "inconsistent" with part of Article V, he thinks that it may be valid with regard to creating convention rules. The **state-dominated** convention model assumes that the States handle all of the preparations and operations of the convention. Vile states that the roots of this convention type are found in the Articles of Confederation and in *The Federalist* and gives rise to the modern convention of States model. Vile cites the issue of representation as the weakness of this model. The **congressionally-dominated** convention model harkens back to the model promoted in the 1970s and 1980s. It would, in the words of Professor Vile, "leave the fox in charge of the henhouse." The **mixed, or federal**, convention model is a model that Professor Vile most comports with the federal constitution. A flaw of this model is that it does not use unit voting among the States.[93] It is this last model that Professor Vile endorses as "most consistent with the Framers' wishes."[94]

It is necessary to note that all of these definitions of the types of conventions are not neat and clean. That is, they sometimes overlap and they do not always provide for easy classification of conventions. Hoar pointed out in comparing the "People's Convention" held in Rhode Island in 1842 and the West Virginia state constitutional convention during the Civil War that both were revolutionary and factional, but the Rhode Island convention was considered illegitimate by the federal government whereas the West Virginia convention was not only considered legitimate but supported by the federal government. We can conclude that the acquiescence and acceptance of the product of a convention is extremely dependent on the benefit it proposes or provides to the powers that be! The constitutionality of the convention is really a function of the impact on the status quo and stands in deference to the legal definition.[95] Hoar summarized the impact and acceptance of the types of conventions, referring to them by the movements that push for the conventions, as,

> *"Thus authorized movements depend upon either constitutional or congressional authority; popular movements depend upon the power of the people; spontaneous movements depend upon force, or at least upon acquiescence."*[96]

---

[93] John R. Vile, *Conventional Wisdom* (Athens, GA: University of Georgia Press, 2016), 122
[94] Ibid., xiv
[95] Roger Sherman Hoar, *Constitutional Conventions – Their Nature, Powers, and Limitations* (Boston: Little, Brown, 1917), 21-5
[96] Ibid., 24

The last distinction concerns the scope of the convention. With respect to the agenda of a convention, there are two types. The ***open*** or ***unlimited*** convention is free to consider all topics brought before it. The ***limited*** convention is restricted to the topic(s) or issue(s) named in the call to the convention. This subject is of immense importance today as the possibility of an amendatory convention is debated. All questions focused on the operation and outcome of such a convention depend on the scope given to the convention. An unlimited convention was assumed to be "plenary" or "plenipotentiary."[97,98]

Specialized conventions, such as a ratification conventions for the Constitution held in the late eighteenth century, and ratification conventions held for a proposed constitutional amendment, such as those held in the early 1930s, are ***intrastate*** or ***in-state*** as they are designed for operation within a given state. An amendatory convention which draws delegates from several or all states is an ***interstate*** or ***general*** convention. A ***partial*** convention is a regional convention. General and partial are geographic terms and have been for centuries.[99] It is helpful to note that during the Colonial and Federal Eras, a "general" convention referred to the attendance and not the agenda. The usage of the word "general" has been changed over time. In that earlier period, if a convention was not general in attendance, it was "partial" or today we would call it "regional."

We can now categorize the aforementioned convention types and sub-types according to not just their function, but their chronological appearance on the historical stage. We can also separate the types by the authority which the convention possesses and that authority under which the convention is called.

- Spontaneous Convention - (plenary) (unauthorized)
  - Spontaneous Town Meeting
- Revolutionary Convention - (plenary) (unauthorized)
- Legislative Convention -(semi-plenary/plenary) (authorized)
- Constitutional Convention - (plenary) (authorized)
  - State Constitution Convention

---

[97] Russell B. Caplan, *Constitutional Brinkmanship* (New York: Oxford University Press, 1988), xx
[98] Michael B. Rappaport, "The Constitutionality of a Limited Convention: An Originalist Analysis," *Constitutional Commentary* 81 (2012). 87, n.78
[99] Generally, Robert G. Natelson, "Founding-Era Conventions and the Meaning of the Constitution's "Convention For Proposing Amendments," *Florida Law Review* 65 (2013): 7, 15

- Federal Constitutional Convention
- Hybrid "Reconstruction" Convention
- Specialized Convention - (non-plenary) (authorized)
  - Secessionary Convention
  - Amendatory Convention
  - Ratificatory Convention
  - Nominatory Convention
  - Convention or Assembly of the States
  - Planning (Statehood) Convention

As a final note on the types of conventions, it is prudent to observe that although there are numerous similarities between state and federal conventions of all types, the dissimilarities are enough that we must be extremely careful in making comparisons between and generalizations on the conventions of both levels of government. There are many, many more court decisions involving the state conventions, in part, due to the outlandishly large number of state conventions of all types in comparison with the number of federal conventions. Any comparison made must be carefully constructed, and in great detail to avoid making a purported connection that does not truly exist.[100]

The differences in the source of power for each convention type; the ability to impose and reinforce limitations on each; the variation in the methods of initiation, authorization, call, and ratification; and most importantly, the purpose of each convention type, create questions as to the validity of comparison. However, the state and federal conventions are closely tied together through the same types of problems and potential resolutions. The history of the state conventions starts with the revolutionary state constitution drafting conventions. Then came the federally called conventions for ratification of the proposed federal constitution. Those conventions led to the constitutional drafting conventions for the admission of new states. Finally, the genesis of the state conventions morphed into their own amendatory and ratificatory conventions.

When we consider an Article V convention, we must be very specific as to what type of convention we are making reference. There are four types of conventions enumerated in the Constitution and although two of those may not ever happen again (under this constitution legally, that is,

---

[100] Francis H. Heller, "Article V: Changing Dimensions In Constitutional Change," *University of Michigan Journal of Law Reform* 7 (Fall 1973): 85

the 1787 Constitutional Convention for drafting and the state ratification conventions for the Constitution), the other two types may happen, and in the case of one of those types – the 1933-34 Twenty-first Amendment ratification state conventions - it has happened in the past. The complexity of proposing and ratifying amendments to the Constitution by constitutional bodies is demonstrated by Raymond Uhl's 1936 explanation of these types of conventions and bodies,

> *"Four governmental bodies are provided for in the Fifth Article of the Federal Constitution: a Congress, a national [amendatory] convention, state legislatures and state [ratifying] conventions. Two of these agencies, Congress and the national convention, can only propose amendments, while the state legislatures and state conventions have only the power to ratify proposed amendments."*[101]

The ratifying convention is also an Article V convention and must be considered when discussing an Article V convention if for no more reason than to check the claims made against the amendatory convention. Imagine the claim that an amendatory convention can assume powers and re-write the Constitution now applied to the ratifying convention. It is similar to the amendatory convention in limitations and powers as it is prescribed by the same article of the federal constitution. It has a history, although not as numerous, at the state level that also shows that it does not runaway or usurp other branches of government.[102] In the ratification of the Twenty-first Amendment, nearly forty such conventions were held and not a single one ran away or had mention of addressing rewriting the federal constitution. No more detail is given to the ratificatory convention in the text of the Constitution than is given to the amendatory convention, yet, one is feared and the other is not.

We can see that the evolution of conventions from simple, spontaneous gatherings in a medieval field through planned, ordered meetings in large halls to discuss the state and governance of the kingdom, to designing and implementing a new government, past establishing a permanent civil legislature, into determining the wording of amendments to a governmental charter, through the debate and ratification of that charter or amendment,

---

[101] Raymond Uhl, "Sovereignty and the Fifth Article," *Southwestern Social Science Quarterly* XVI, no.4 (1936): 2
[102] Robert G. Natelson, "Proposing Constitutional Amendments by Convention: Rules Governing the Process," *Tennessee Law Review* 78 (2011): 724

to finally how best to select our potential political leaders has led us to the point today where we find ourselves weighing the necessity and outcome of a potential Article V amendatory convention. It has been through the imposition of limitations on the powers of the convention that we have arrived at a point where the specialized conventions now exist. The spontaneous convention was restricted somewhat and led to or became the revolutionary convention which acts as a provisional government. The revolutionary convention was limited by the need to only do a few regular actions and this became the legislative convention. That legislative convention was further restricted by the need to only form a constitution and that gave us the constitutional convention. Finally, the need to only amend the constitution or to ratify that proposed constitution gave us the specialized convention in the forms of the amendatory and ratificatory conventions. It has been the need to accomplish more refined tasks in a public but limited manner that has forced the diversification of the types of conventions. Fears of a runaway convention that has no limits, which is a plenary convention, are unfounded when we look at the broader picture of the developmental trend of conventions. Having learned how we arrived here, let us turn to where "here" finds us.

The Powers of Conventions

Conventions have varied powers, many of them and of several types. To better understand those powers, and their corresponding limitations detailed in the next section, it is imperative to look at the types and separations of powers between the state and federal governments. The state and federal governments and their respective constitutions are quite different – the States are not "clones" of the federal government. The set of powers that each government enjoys and exercises overlaps only to an extent. The federal government has, through the federal Constitution, limited and specific powers. As James Madison famously noted in *The Federalist*, "The powers delegated by the proposed Constitution to the federal government, are few and defined. Those which are to remain in the State governments are numerous and indefinite."[103]

Mason Kalfus has neatly defined the relative powers of the States and

---

[103] James Madison, "Federalist Paper No. 45," in *The Federalist Papers: Hamilton, Madison, Jay*, ed. Clinton Rossiter (New York: Mentor, 1961), 292

federal government and how Article V fits with these powers,

> "The Constitution created two versions of separation of powers. Horizontal separation divides power among the three equal branches of the federal government: Congress, the Executive, and the Judiciary. Vertical separation, also known as federalism, divides power between the Federal Government and the States. Under the latter, power is not equal, for federal law is supreme (yet limited in scope) whereas state law is inferior (yet unlimited in scope). Article V does not neatly fit within this framework, because it combines both the power balance of horizontal separation of powers with the traditional players of federalism."[104]

The federal government's powers are defined, for the most part, in the Constitution in Article I, Section 8, but these eighteen powers are just more than half of the **enumerated** powers in the Constitution – the rest are scattered about in the original body and in the amendments. Enumerated powers are those that are clearly named and often defined – in writing. These are also known as **delegated, expressed** or **explicit** powers because they have expressly, explicitly been enumerated and delegated to the federal government. Simplistic as that sounds, it is an extremely important distinction. In granting these powers to the federal government, the States and the people have surrendered these powers. We can easily name and explain these powers. Examples include: laying duties, imposts and excises; operating the Navy; printing money; fixing weights, measures and standards; granting patents; and operating post offices, to name just a few.

In terms of a hierarchy of powers, the next category of powers is that of the **implied** powers. These powers are not as easy to name but with a little thought and reasoning they come to mind. The implied powers are those that are needed to carry out the execution of the enumerated powers. The Necessary and Proper Clause is most often the source of this broad grant of power. While a rational argument can be made for the existence and the granting of the implied powers to the federal government, creating the Necessary and Proper Clause simply solidified their grant. Implied powers

---

[104] Republished with permission of the University of Chicago Law School, from Mason Kalfus, "Why Time Limits on the Ratification of Constitutional Amendments Violate Article V," *University of Chicago Law Review* 66, no.2 (Spring 1999): 458; permission conveyed through Copyright Clearance Center, Inc. – Kalfus references Edward Levi's "Some Aspects of Separation of Powers," *Columbia Law Review* 76 (1976): 376

are sometimes referred to as ***incidental*** powers.[105] Examples are: oversight; conscription; approval of appointees; and establishing agencies, to cite just a few.

There are also ***inherent*** powers. These are the powers that all nations have by virtue of being a nation. These powers are analogous to the unalienable rights of individuals; they are naturally occurring powers. Examples include: wage war, extend diplomatic recognition, and conclude treaties, again, to note just a few.

Lower still in the hierarchy are ***concurrent*** powers. The States and the federal government share some duties. The division between the States and the federal government is not always clear. This type of powers is characterized by a significant overlap in responsibility. One of the more disturbing aspects of concurrent powers is that the federal government has usurped many of these ***shared*** powers. Examples include: chartering corporations and banks; operating schools; building and maintaining roads and highways; and enforcing the laws and operating courts, once more, to name just a few.

The federal government thus enjoys these four types of powers: enumerated, implied, inherent and concurrent. But there are other types of powers which the federal government does not possess. These powers are left in the hands of either the States or the people. In addition to the concurrent, or shared, powers, the States have other powers including their own implied, inherent and in some instances, enumerated powers.

The States exercise the ***reserved*** powers. These are the powers which are denied to the federal government and are the province of the States or the people. Examples include: regulating intrastate trade; arbitrating contracts; validating marriages; conducting elections and determining the qualifications of voters; issuing licenses; and ratifying amendments to the

---

[105] There is a distinction to be made between implied and incidental. It is a fine difference that has a test which can be applied. It appears in the literature that incidental seems to draw from the second half, or as it is often called, the "horizontal half," of the Necessary and Proper Clause. The distinction involves whether the power in question is considered "indispensable" and subservient to the execution of the main, or enumerated, power. A deeper discussion of incidental powers can be found in several places, but two in particular address the issue succinctly:
- The amicus brief of "Authors of *The Necessary and Proper Clause* (Gary Lawson, Robert G. Natelson & Guy Seidman) and the Independence Institute as Amici Curiae in Support of Respondents (Minimum Coverage Provision) for *Dept. of Health and Human Services, et al., v. State of Florida, et al.*", No.11-398, specifically 2-4
-Walter F. Dodd, "Implied Powers and Implied Limitations in Constitutional Law," *Yale Law Journal* 29, no.2 (Dec. 1919)

federal Constitution, to name just a few. These are sometimes referred to as residual powers. These powers are guaranteed by the Tenth Amendment.

Finally, there are the ***prohibited*** powers. These are exactly as they sound; the powers that are prohibited to government, however, these powers come in two distinct flavors, those that are prohibited to the federal government and those that are prohibited to the state governments.[106] The reservation of the prohibited powers depends on who is making the prohibition. The prohibition on the federal government is made by the United States Constitution. Examples include: no ex-post facto laws; no bills of attainder; and no conferring of titles of nobility, to name some examples. The States have their own prohibited powers. They have prohibitions made by the federal Constitution and by their own state constitutions. Examples include: no treaties; no letters of marque; no coinage of money; and no duties on imports/exports without the approval of Congress, to name just a few at the federal level. There are also prohibitions on infringing on speech and of imprisonment for debt to cite just a couple.

A visual or graphical representation of the relationship between all these types of powers, state, federal and personal, can be found in Appendix A. The graphs in Appendix A depict both the distribution of powers between the governments and the people and the same distribution with the convention imposed.

When contemplating an Article V convention, we must look at the powers ascribed to it as well to understand its utility. There are clearly *delegated*, and hence, *enumerated*, powers – the proposing aspect of the amending power has been delegated by the States and the people to the convention. This is more than just the proposing of an amendment; it is the suggestion, debate, voting upon and eventually proposition of the amendment. It is the all-important and supremely crucial part of determining the purpose, and the exact wording of the amendment proposal. The future form of the Constitution rests on the output of this phase of the process. Another way of looking at the proposing power is to consider it a *concurrent*, or shared, power with Congress since both can, as stipulated in Article V, propose amendments.

---

[106] Another related set of prohibited powers are those that are denied to county and municipal governments. These are typically categorized with the state prohibited powers since in most states, the county and municipal governments are considered to be extensions of the state government. In some states with "local control" the state's power is separate from the municipal power.

The amendatory convention has *implied* powers in the operational aspect of the convention.[107] Internal rules must be set, officers must be elected, committees appointed, and funds expended. The day-to-day details of the housekeeping of the convention would fall under this category. Neither Congress nor the States have control over these matters; it is in the discretion of the convention itself. This view has been reasserted in the federal courts as recently as 1975 in *Dyer v. Blair*.[108] Hoar spent an entire chapter on the internal powers of a convention in his 1917 book, summarizing,

> *"Thus we see that a convention ordinarily has full control over its internal affairs, including its own membership, the filling of vacancies, the obtaining of quarters, the election of officers and employees, the establishment of rules, the purchasing of supplies, the printing of records, etc., the maintenance of internal order, and even the disciplining of strangers; but these powers may be enlarged or curtailed by popular vote."*[109]

There are also *inherent* powers of an amendatory convention. All conventions, amendatory and otherwise, are expected to be able to determine the qualifications of the credentials and to regulate the behavior of their delegates or commissioners, to create its own internal agenda or schedule and establish its procedures.[110] Every convention enjoys the "parliamentary privileges and immunities" for the delegates. They cannot be harassed or delayed when going about their business. This is a tradition long established in England and then in America for hundreds of years. These same privileges were carried over into Congress and are found in the Constitution.[111,112] It has been held in some cases that conventions possess no inherent powers; but it would appear that those decisions did not consider the examples found herein.[113]

A *reserved* power of the amendatory convention is the guaranteed unit suffrage or the ability of the convention to speak for the constituents.

---

[107] Robert G. Natelson, "Proposing Constitutional Amendments by Convention: Rules Governing the Process," *Tennessee Law Review* 78 (2011): 706
[108] *Dyer v. Blair*, 390 F. Supp. 1291 (N.D. Ill. 1975)
[109] Roger Sherman Hoar, *Constitutional Conventions – Their Nature, Powers, and Limitations* (Boston: Little, Brown, 1917), 184
[110] Note, "Constitutional Revision by a Restricted Convention," *Minnesota Law Review* 35 (1951): 290
[111] Russell B. Caplan, *Constitutional Brinkmanship* (New York: Oxford University Press, 1988),123
[112] United States Constitution, Article I, §6
[113] As an example, see *Wells v. Bain*, 75 Pa. St. 39, 15 Am. Rep. 563 (1875)

A *shared* power associated with an amendatory convention is that of deliberation. That power is reserved to the amendatory and ratification conventions only. No other bodies may conduct the deliberation of the subject matter under the convention mode. This power is analogous to the Speech and Debate Clause of the Constitution. It is also the express purpose of these conventions. Congress may deliberate under the congressional amendment mode and in that aspect, the deliberation power is then shared or is concurrent with Congress.

Last to be considered are the *prohibited* powers to the amendatory convention. Ratification and promulgation are denied to the convention. Another prohibited power for the Article V amendatory convention is that of making the call for the convention. Also, setting the beginning date and the location of the convention are reserved to the Congress. These small, but important, details are beyond the power of the States and the convention. The Congress is delegated the power to promulgate a proposed amendment and the States retain the power of ratification for any proposed amendment. Most important to opponents of an Article V amendatory convention is the prohibition of writing or promulgating or ratifying any new constitution – this is simply not permitted under any circumstances. In the case of a limited convention, the selection of the topics for debate and proposal are severely restricted to those in the convention call. Those topic(s) included in the call for the convention are express, enumerated and explicit and are therefore an example of a delegated power. Any other topics are prohibited and therefore the debate or proposition of any amendment concerning those topics are prohibited powers of the convention.

The convention delegates themselves enjoy certain privileges and immunities by virtue of their position. The exact status of the delegates is something that has been debated for centuries. Jameson and Hoar actually agreed upon the role of the delegates. The consensus devised a century ago was that the convention delegates were neither public officers nor *constitutional* officials. This idea was predicated on the fact that the convention was not a regular feature of the state or federal governments and as such the delegates were not named in the constitutions of either. They are endowed with the same privileges as members of the state or federal legislatures or jurors. They are not to be harassed or arrested in the comings and goings to their offices or convention; they are exempt from legal process; their debate and speech is not to be infringed; and they may not be compelled to other service such as for a jury or the military during their convention activities. The body itself possesses other privileges such as being able to summon witnesses or experts, to demand records and even services; and to place its requirements above that of other agencies or bodies.[114]

Having looked at the various types of powers and provided examples of each power that the Article V amendatory convention possesses, it is obvious that the amendatory convention is extremely and deliberately limited in powers. Let us then list exactly what powers the <u>amendatory</u> convention is empowered to exercise:

The amendatory convention holds the power to judge the credentials and the behavior of the delegates but not their appointment or election. That power remains in the hands of the respective states. Jameson held that the legislature dictates the criteria and selection of the delegates and points to the examples of the Convention Acts passed by the territorial conventions seeking statehood and those of the states calling state constitutional conventions to revise or replace their state constitutions. These acts not only specified the requirements of who may serve but also, occasionally, who may not be a delegate as some discrimination has occurred over the last couple of centuries. As a corollary, Congress passed enabling acts for the territories identifying who may serve. This creates the issue of whether Congress may do the same for an Article V amendatory convention. The answer rests in who controls the convention – the States or Congress or the delegates.[115] Historically then, it has been the States that determined,

> *"the time and mode of electing the delegates, the qualifications of the electors, the time of assembling of the Convention, and such other particulars as either fall more naturally within the scope of legislative authority, or as require to be definitively settled before the body meets. Such, on the other hand, are as incidental to the exercise of the functions of the Convention, as such, are commonly left to discretion of the body itself."*[116]

In the above quote, the section pertaining to setting the time, that is the actual date, of assembling would clearly not be within the purview

---

[114] Roger Sherman Hoar, *Constitutional Conventions – Their Nature, Powers, and Limitations* (Boston: Little, Brown, 1917), 185-92

[115] John Alexander Jameson, *A Treatise on Constitutional Conventions, Their History, Powers, and Modes of Proceeding* (New York: Scribner, 1867, 4th ed., 1887), §§267-9, 271-4, - reprint by The Lawbook Exchange, (2013)

[116] Ibid., §272, 275

of the States as the Constitution grants that power to the Congress for an amendatory convention. Instead, the rest of the decisions are in the hands of the States or of the convention itself. For many of the procedural practices employed, most early conventions turned to one or another manual of codified parliamentary procedure such as the 1689 *"Lex Parliamentaria,"* Henry Scobell's 1689 *"Remembrances of Methods, Orders, and Proceedings, Heretofore Used and Observed in the House of Lords"* or John Hatsell's 1780 *"Precedents of Proceedings in the House of Commons."*[117] More recent conventions often used Thomas Jefferson's 1801 *"Manual of Parliamentary Practice,"* Luther Stearns Cushing's 1856 *"Lex Parliamentaria Americana,"* Paul Mason's 2010 *"Mason's Manual of Legislative Procedure"* or a state government document drafted to govern its own state conventions. An example is Hawaii's *"Constitutional Convention Organization and Procedures"* published by the state's Legislative Reference Bureau. Even the mundane, arcane, trivial minutiae of the day-to-day operation of the convention has been defined to the smallest detail and recorded in almost every state.

For the 1787 Grand Federal Convention, all of the preceding discussion was common knowledge. The convention benefited from the presence of parliamentarians such as Charles Thomson, Secretary of the Confederation Congress, and George Wythe, who was an expert in parliamentary practice and a member of the Virginia legislature and in Congress. Wythe had written a book on parliamentary practices.[118] Mary Sarah Bilder outlined the practices of the 1787 Philadelphia convention in her 2012 paper, *"How Bad Were the Official Records of the Federal Convention?"* and gives us a picture of a carefully organized, constrained and regimented convention which could possibly be considered even rigid.

James E. Bond and David E. Engdahl made a most salient point in their 1987 work. They argued that the Necessary and Proper Clause is <u>not</u> relevant to the discussion of the powers of an Article V convention. They set up the argument and then stress the obvious, that Article V is separate and distinct from the rest of the Constitution because it operates in an area beyond the normal realm of the federal government. It is found in a separate article of the Constitution because it covers a separate activity and it is derived from a different power than the rest of the Constitution. Although

---

[117] Mary Sarah Bilder, "How Bad Were the Official Records of the Federal Convention?," *George Washington Law Review* 80, no.6 (Oct. 2012): 1633-4
[118] Ibid., 1640-1

an amendatory convention is considered a "federal function" according to a Supreme Court decision, it is not a "federal power" but a distinct power derived from the people and the States.[119] The difference between the amending power, incidental powers and federal power was covered by Bond and Engdahl.

> "'Incidental powers' is one of those unfortunate, imprecise and misleading idioms commonly associated with the 'necessary and proper' clause. This clause enables Congress to pass laws 'for carrying into Execution' its Article V power, no less than for carrying into execution every other federal power, whether of Congress or of another branch, But the 'necessary and proper' clause helps Congress only to implement **federal** powers; and most questions about how an Article V convention for proposing amendments would function are not within **federal** power!"[120]

Bond and Engdahl stressed that federalism is the controlling aspect of Article V. No single branch of the federal government has the authority to control or dictate to the convention. Those powers that the convention possess and require are inherently part of the concept of an amendatory convention. So while we use the Necessary and Proper Clause to draw parallels and analogies we are limited to doing only that as the balance of the power remains in the hands of the conventioneers to do as they see fit to accomplish their mission.

Professor Robert Natelson groups the "Article V assemblies" referred to in the Article as four types: Congress, state legislatures, state ratifying conventions and conventions for proposing amendments. He goes on to enumerate the powers ascribed to these assemblies and to separate them into two groups: the four powers in the proposal stage and the four powers in the ratification stage:

> "At the proposal stage, Article V:
> 1. grants to two thirds of each house of Congress authority to 'propose' amendments,
> 2. grants to two thirds of the state legislatures power to make 'Application' for a convention for proposing amendments,
> 3. grants to Congress power to 'call' that convention, and

---

[119] *Leser v. Garnett*, 258 U.S. 130 (1922)

[120] James E. Bond, David E. Engdahl, and Henry N. Butler, *The Constitutional Convention* (Washington, D.C.: National Legal Center for the Public Interest, 1987), 11

4. grants to the convention authority 'for proposing' amendments.

In the ratification stage, Article V:
1. authorizes Congress to 'propose' whether ratification shall be by state legislatures or state conventions;
2. if Congress selects the former method, authorizes three fourths of state legislatures to ratify;
3. if Congress selects the latter method, impliedly empowers, and requires, each state to call a ratifying convention; and
4. empowers three fourths of those conventions to ratify."[121]

The powers of a convention are dictated by the type of convention. Obviously, a constitutional convention is *plenipotentiary* or *plenary* and therefore unlimited in its power. It could draft a new constitution or rewrite the existing constitution. There are two prevailing theories as to the powers of conventions: the first argues that the convention is the representative of the people, who are sovereign in their own right and that their political sovereignty devolves on the convention and as such, is unlimited. The second theory claims that the powers are commensurate with the limits placed in the application of the States and the subsequent call from Congress.[122] Such a convention is then limited in power.

The source and limited exercise of the convention's power is a theme that has resonated throughout the academic debate over amendatory conventions. It can be distilled down to two opposing views or doctrines: the **supremacy of the legislature** and its ability to limit, define and control the convention versus the **sovereignty of the convention** as a separate political entity on an equal footing with the legislature and the arbiter of its own power. This has been the contention since Jameson took the legislature's position and a half century later Hoar took the side of the convention. These two early giants of convention theory are both partly right and partly wrong. Jameson argued that the legislature could and should limit the amendatory convention through restrictions in the enabling act that authorizes the convention. He contended that the legislature must first ask the people for permission to exercise their power to call a convention. He argued that the

---

[121] Robert G. Natelson, "Proposing Constitutional Amendments by Convention: Rules Governing the Process," *Tennessee Law Review* 78 (2011): 702. The full text of this Article was published originally by the Tennessee Law Review Association, Inc. at 78 **Tenn. L. Rev.** 693 (2011), and this version, approved by the Author, appears by their permission.

[122] Wayne B. Wheeler, "Is a Constitutional Convention Impending?," *Illinois Law Review* 21 (1927): 797

individual states must win the vote of their citizens to call a state convention and then restrict the agenda to the limits imposed by the people.

The federal analogy to Jameson's position is that the States are acting on behalf of their respective citizens when they submit their applications for a convention to Congress. In a similar vein then, the restriction of the agenda is found in the applications themselves which define the agenda of the amendatory convention. The enabling legislation is not ordinary legislation but is special legislation as the state legislatures are acting in their federal function and are creating a temporary "fourth branch" of the federal government, independent of both the States and Congress.

Where Jameson goes wrong is in his assertion that the amendatory convention is endowed with <u>all</u> of the people's sovereignty and with unlimited power and that the convention is subservient to Congress. The amendatory convention is endowed with only the people's sovereign powers of debate and the proposal of amendments. The convention is not subservient to, but is equal in standing to the Congress, albeit on a temporary basis. The consent to convene and propose is given by the people and not by the Congress.[123] With the conclusion of the convention's business, those "loaned" powers and the consent to exercise them return to the people.

Hoar argued strenuously against the position of Jameson and took him to task point-by-point. Hoar cited passages within state constitutions to refute that the state legislature may control the convention or even dictate its operation. Hoar conceded that many state legislatures retain the right to call conventions and to control the amending process. A convention that is controlled by the legislature loses much of its usefulness to the people if it becomes the servant of the legislature.[124]

While Jameson and Walter F. Dodd,[125] writing contemporaneously

---

[123] Some may argue that the people are not really giving the consent to convene, that the state legislature is giving the consent, but it must be remembered that the ability to do so by the state legislature is only through its role as acting on behalf of the people. Additionally, the argument might be made that Congress is giving consent because the States must make "application" to Congress for an amendatory convention, but Congress's role is purely ministerial in that it decides only the location and date of convening. Congress has NO discretion in calling the convention and therefore makes no consent.

[124] Roger Sherman Hoar, *Constitutional Conventions – Their Nature, Powers, And Limitations* (Boston: Little, Brown, 1917), 107

[125] Walter Fairleigh Dodd, *The Revision and Amendment of State Constitutions* (Baltimore: Johns Hopkins Press, 1910), 76

with Hoar, argue for the ability of a legislature to restrict a convention,[126] Hoar points out that at the time of his writing in 1917, there were few examples of a state legislature successfully constraining a state constitutional convention.[127] This point at first would give us pause about an Article V amendatory convention, but then we have to realize that, once again, a constitutional convention is different from an amendatory convention which is limited by definition. Jameson and Hoar represent the extremes of the swing of the pendulum through the range of convention powers. When the people of a particular state vote to hold a constitutional convention, they are extending their sovereignty to that convention, though it is in a limited sense. The act which is generated by the state legislature in response to the successful result of the election referendum to call the convention, can stipulate the limits of the convention in terms of the purpose to be addressed. This popular control at the state level has a corollary at the federal level. When the States make an application to Congress for an amendatory convention, that convention, likewise, may be limited in purpose based on the express purpose given in the aggregated state applications.[128]

Where Jameson and Hoar also disagree is with respect to the acceptability of the people, acting through the legislature, to instruct the convention delegates. Hoar sees this instruction as a form of limited popular control of the convention.[129,130] Hoar goes a step further and contends that the convention delegate has a moral responsibility to seek out the popular opinion of his constituents and act accordingly. The state legislature that drafts, debates, passes and forwards to the Congress an application for an Article V convention is doing exactly the same action of measuring the desire and will of the people of its state.

Contrary to the modern assertion that such conventions are solely unlimited in power, we can look back throughout the legal literature and see that these powers were always understood. In 1930, during the push for a convention to repeal Prohibition, Professor Lester Orfield discussed the

---

[126] John Alexander Jameson, *A Treatise on Constitutional Conventions, Their History, Powers, and Modes of Proceeding* (New York: Scribner, 1867, 4th ed., 1887), §§381-2b, - reprint by The Lawbook Exchange, (2013)

[127] Roger Sherman Hoar, *Constitutional Conventions – Their Nature, Powers, And Limitations* (Boston: Little, Brown, 1917), 111

[128] Ibid., 122-3

[129] John Alexander Jameson, *A Treatise on Constitutional Conventions, Their History, Powers, and Modes of Proceeding* (New York: Scribner, 1867, 4th ed., 1887), §§363-4, - reprint by The Lawbook Exchange, (2013)

[130] Roger Sherman Hoar, *Constitutional Conventions – Their Nature, Powers, And Limitations* (Boston: Little, Brown and Co., 1917), 126-7

powers of an amendatory convention. He believed the powers to be unlimited – except where the Congress had stipulated the powers of the convention in the call. He states that "the primary and in fact the sole business of the Convention would be to propose changes in the Constitution."[131]

Similarly, Jameson said, more than a half century earlier, that conventions have strictly limited powers and are subject to the conditions placed upon them by the Congress in the call.[132] Orfield echoes this belief,

> *After all it seems that there need be no fear of usurpation by a convention. In the first place, it is limited to the business of altering the Constitution. In the second place, its power in this respect is further limited, for it may merely propose, and not adopt changes. Article V confers on it simply a right to propose, and makes specific provision for adoption in another mode. In the third place, the convention not only has no power to adopt, but also has no power to provide for ratification."*[133]

The distinction between the Congress and the federal amendatory convention is narrow with respect to the amendment process. Congress can create, introduce, debate and submit proposed amendments without any limit other than that found within Article V. There is no need for a predetermined or provisional consensus among the members of Congress. The amendatory convention is hampered only by any limitation placed on it, first by the applications of the States, and second, by the Congressional call that reflects the position of the States. Of course, the same two subject matter limitations found in Article V constrain the States. "There is no distinction made between the kinds of amendments Congress might propose and the kinds a convention ought to propose. The power of each mode thus seems to be co-extensive. Whatever Congress may propose, a convention may propose; inherent constitutional limits on Congress would seem to be equally binding on a convention."[134]

The internal management of the convention is in the hands of the convention itself. All authorities consulted agree that the selection of officers, establishment of rules of procedure, schedule, determination of credentials

---

[131] Lester B. Orfield, "The Procedure of the Federal Amending Power," *Illinois Law Review* 25 (1930): 424

[132] John Alexander Jameson, *A Treatise on Constitutional Conventions, Their History, Powers, and Modes of Proceeding* (New York: Scribner, 1867, 4th ed., 1887), §§382-9, - reprint by The Lawbook Exchange, (2013)

[133] Lester B. Orfield, "The Procedure of the Federal Amending Power," *Illinois Law Review* 25 (1930): 425

[134] Frank Balog, "Popular Sovereignty and the Question of the Limited Constitutional Convention," *Cooley Law Review* 1 (1982), 111

and qualifications, and other "housekeeping" are internal matters and the province of the convention. It is curious that so much modern attention is given to the perceived lack of rules to govern an Article V amendatory convention and this is seen as a justification for avoiding holding such a convention. The ratification conventions permitted by Article V lack the same governing rules, yet there is no similar outcry against holding this type of convention. This is said in the context of the 1933-34 ratification conventions held to consider the Twenty-first Amendment. These ratification conventions were held without issues or glitches – can we not reasonably expect the same behavior from an amendatory convention held today?

In 1933, Professor Herman Ames looked at the source of the amending power and its execution. He took note of the apparent inconsistency in the 1787 convention's concerns over the rules governing the various conventions mentioned in Article V and wondered how this misunderstanding could take place. He pointed out that in the records of the 1787 convention, Madison brought up his issue with the "constitutional regulations" of a convention to propose amendments, but he made no mention of the ratification conventions – both for the Constitution and for amendments!

> *"In discussing this proposal Madison declared he 'did not see why Congress would not be as much bound to propose amendments applied for by two-thirds of the state as to call a convention on the like application. He saw no objection, however, against providing for a convention for the purpose of amendments, except only that difficulties might arise as to the form, the quorum, etc., which in constitutional regulations ought to be as much as possible avoided.' This amendment to Article V was accepted by general consent, the only other changes were, excepting from amendments the two well-known provisions of the constitution. In view of Madison's reference to difficulties that might arise in regard to 'constitutional regulations,' it is rather remarkable that neither he nor any other member of the Convention, as far as the Records show, raised a similar query to regulating the details of the procedure of ratifying conventions in the states. Is it not reasonable to conclude, in the absence of such considerations, that the framers expected that the State Legislatures would make all necessary provisions relative to such matters, just as they expected the Legislatures of the respective state to attend to the details of the state conventions to which they desired the draft of the Constitution to be submitted?"*[135]

---

[135] Herman V. Ames, "Recent Development of the Amending Power as Applied to the Federal Constitution," *Proceedings of the American Philosophical Society* 72, no.2 (1933): 92-3

Here, Ames is making one of the most important points affecting us today as we contemplate an Article V convention. He is stressing that all of the discussion in 1787 focused on the permissibility and the responsibility for operation of the future amendatory conventions. But where was the discussion of the operation and rules for both the immediately impending Article VII ratification conventions for the proposed Constitution and the future ratification conventions for future amendments? To explore a little deeper in order to answer Madison's questions, let us ask who had planned, convened, and conducted the very same convention in which Madison was posing his questions. The obvious answers to those three acts – the States, the States and the States. Who, reasonably, would then be responsible for planning, convening and conducting the Constitution ratification conventions, the future amendatory conventions (if any) and the future amendment ratification conventions (if any)? The obvious answers remain the same – the States, the States and to a limited extent the States.

How can we be so sure that the Framers intended that the States and the People would be the operators of these future conventions? First, a look at the history of the conventions that preceded the 1787 Philadelphia convention gives us the answer. Professor Natelson has extensively researched the intercolonial and the early inter-state conventions and found over thirty examples to study.[136] In every case, without exception, the conventions were called, planned, convened and conducted by the colonies themselves and the later conventions by their successor states. Ames stated more than four score years ago, and is echoed today by Natelson, that it is American tradition that the States possess and exercise the powers to conduct these conventions. Second, if the Framers had any other intention than to follow the well-established tradition, would they have not said and done so during the 1787 convention considering the enormity of the breach in eighteenth century practice which that deviation entailed?

Most sources tell us that the limitation of the powers is on the part of the Congress. The amendatory convention needs to be able to carry out its duties without infringement or restriction by Congress. One of the purposes of an amendatory convention is to modify the powers of Congress when necessary. The amendatory convention must be unencumbered to perform

---

[136] Generally, Robert G. Natelson, "Founding-Era Conventions and the Meaning of the Constitution's 'Convention For Proposing Amendments'," *Florida Law Review* 65 (2013)

this act.

> "Nor is Congress empowered to limit the authority of the convention, for the latter ought to be independent of a body whose powers it may find it necessary to alter. It should be remembered that provision for conventions was made **intentionally**[137] to avoid complete Congressional control over the amending process."[138]

Grover Rees notes that the convention must be free of the control of Congress, even a bare minimum of control, to work properly. If Congress can control any aspect of the convention, then Congress's role is no longer ministerial, and the convention is no longer truly independent and a work-around to the obstinacy of Congress. He states,

> "The central purpose of the convention method was to make it possible to amend the constitution over the opposition of Congress, this purpose would be defeated by the concession to Congress of absolute power to regulate, which is effectively the power to destroy."[139]

What of a constitution that lacks the ability to be amended? History is replete with such documents – and their failures. Examples can be given of the dangers of an unamendable constitution, a too difficult to amend constitution and a too easy to amend constitution. For one that was too difficult to amend we can look to the Articles of Confederation as the most obvious and relevant example since its failure led to the Constitution. For those that are too easy to amend, we can look to numerous state constitutions that proved so facile to amend that the constitution quickly lost relevance as it was loaded up with amendments that hindered the legal system and society. The States have frequently replaced their state constitutions when they have proven irrelevant, anachronistic or no longer serviceable. As to length and amendment count, we can look to the example of Alabama, though in use and working well,[140] their 1901 state constitution has 340,136 words and 856 amendments comprising 90% of its length.[141] In comparison, the federal constitution, before amendments, contains a mere 4,543 words

---

[137] Author's emphasis added.
[138] William A. Platz, "Article Five of the Federal Constitution," *George Washington Law Review* 3 (1934): 46
[139] Grover Rees III, "The Amendment Process and Limited Constitutional Conventions," *Benchmark* II, no.2 (March-April 1986): 84
[140] A group of citizens are working to call a new commission to replace the 1901 Alabama state constitution. http://www.constitutionalreform.org/
[141] http://alisondb.legislature.state.al.us/alison/codeofalabama/constitution/1901/constitution1901_toc.htm

and after including the twenty-seven amendments, it has only 7,818 words.

For the unamendable, we have the example of the Rhode Island constitution in the form of the 1663 colonial charter that extended voting enfranchisement to only men who owned real property and to their eldest sons.[142] By 1830, more than 60% of the state's free white men were excluded from voting – as were all women and minorities.[143] The public's resentment came to a head in 1841 when Thomas Wilson Dorr led a movement that resulted in the People's Convention in October which drafted a new state constitution while at the same time, the Rhode Island General Assembly called a competing convention that produced the Freemen's or Landholder's Constitution.[144] The Rhode Island electorate took up a vote on both proposed constitutions with the People's Constitution prevailing.[145] The two competing factions then held separate elections and each elected a new governor. Samuel Ward King, leading the General Assembly faction, claimed the governorship but did not implement the new constitution; instead he declared martial law. The state legislature appealed to the federal government to invoke the Constitution's Guarantee Clause and requested that President John Tyler provide federal troops which he considered but ultimately and judiciously decided not to send. On 19 May 1842, violence broke out in Providence. Badly outnumbered and outgunned, the "Dorrite" cause quickly collapsed. In September of 1842, the state legislature drafted a new constitution – with an amendment provision – and order was restored. The inability to amend the colonial/state charter to address society's ills and changes, led, predictably and sadly, to Dorr's Rebellion, a lesson so well learned that the Rhode Island "civil war" has become, fortunately, a little known footnote to our history.[146]

We note that both sides in Rhode Island chose to use a constitutional convention to address their complaints and to provide for a permanent solution. One convention, the People's Convention as it was named, was clearly extra-legal although not revolutionary. The other, called by the state

---

[142] Henry Paul Monaghan, "We the People[s], Original Understanding, and Constitutional Amendment," *Columbia Law Review* 96, no.1 (Jan.1996): 163

[143] Presaging by more than a century the state legislature apportionment issue of the 1960s.

[144] John R. Vile, *Conventional Wisdom* (Athens, GA: University of Georgia Press, 2016), 67

[145] Christian G. Fritz, "Recovering the Lost Worlds of America's Written Constitutions," *Albany Law Review* 68, no.2 (2005): 285

[146] Eric J. Chaput, *The People's Martyr: Thomas Wilson Dorr and His 1842 Rhode Island Rebellion* (Lawrence: University Press of Kansas, 2013), generally

legislature, was legal and also not revolutionary. The state legislature did have the authority, under the 1663 charter, to consider a new constitution and thus acted not in an *ultra vires* manner, but, nonetheless, acted in, arguably, the proper manner to solve the problem facing the state. The state had turned at least three times to calling a convention before the November 1841 convention. The constitution produced was rejected by the electorate. The new governor, Samuel Ward King, created the problem with his refusal to implement the constitution adopted. All of this turbulence turned on the questions of who had the power to enact the constitution and what limitations existed on that power. As Walter Dellinger has stated, , "An unamendable constitution, adopted by a generation long since dead, could hardly be viewed as a manifestation of the consent of the governed."[147]

All of the turmoil that the state of Rhode Island experienced could have been avoided had the state turned to the example of sister state Maryland just five years prior and four hundred miles to the southwest. Under similar circumstances, Marylanders found themselves unable to secure the desired changes from their state legislature. They called an amendatory convention in June of 1837 and drafted proposed amendments to the state constitution. The Maryland state legislature had the good sense to read the political tea leaves and successfully enacted the proposed amendments through a formal process. Their crisis was averted, but the Rhode Islanders failed to observe the lesson of Maryland and pressed their issue more forcefully which led them to fall into rebellion. What makes the Maryland example so intriguing is that the people, recognizing that they had the mechanism with which to affect their desired changes, but could not secure the support of the state legislature, first called an *ultra vires* spontaneous convention in Baltimore in June 1836 for the purpose of planning how to call and operate an amendatory constitutional convention and to determine how to select delegates for that convention.[148] They also sought to select a slate of candidates for the fall election in order to secure the necessary numbers in the state legislature to carry out their scheme. Then, they held a second "reform" convention in November of 1836, following their success in the elections, to draft proposed amendments to recommend to the General

---

[147] Republished with permission of the Harvard Law Review Association, from Walter Dellinger, "The Legitimacy of Constitutional Change: Rethinking the Amendment Process," *Harvard Law Review* 97 (1983): 387; permission conveyed through Copyright Clearance Center, Inc.

[148] James McSherry, *History of Maryland* (Baltimore: Baltimore Book, 1904), 313-20.

Assembly. These proposed amendments were in turn suggested to the General Assembly which directed that they be taken up for consideration at the constitutional convention called in June of 1837.[149] The people of Maryland resorted to a convention thrice in rapid succession to peacefully resolve their problem. It cannot be stressed enough that the 1837 convention in Maryland was not a constitutional convention but was an authorized amendatory convention.[150] While the process may have been tedious and meticulous, the methodology assured that it was peaceful in what could have been a volatile situation – as proven in a few short years distant in Rhode Island.

The examples of Rhode Island and Maryland were merely later versions of the havoc that the unamendability of a constitution could wreak. The situation in the newly independent United States in the mid-1780s demonstrated that just because a political charter contains an amendment provision does not mean that it is amendable. The Articles of Confederation had an amending provision in Article XIII, but were never once amended. The States tried many times to amend the Articles to provide taxing authority so that the federal government could fund itself but every time, at least one state stood in the way and prevented the required unanimous consent. Interestingly, that state was usually Rhode Island. The cause of the problem was widely known and it was for that reason that the new Constitution did not repeat the same mistake in a too stringent amendment approval threshold.[151] Philadelphia delegate Charles Pinckney of South Carolina made it clear that "it is to this unanimous consent, the depressed situation of the Union is undoubtedly owed."[152]

The precedents of the many state constitutional and amendatory conventions would seem to provide some guidance as to how a federal amendatory convention might be operated and as to the powers and limitations thereof. But the difference in the source of powers between the state and federal governments is widely divergent, so much so that we cannot

---

[149] Charles A. Rees, "Remarkable Evolution: The Early Constitutional History of Maryland," *Baltimore Law Review* 3, no.2 (2007): 238

[150] Marylanders had become incensed about the level of public debt that the state had accumulated. The state was guaranteeing loans to private corporations and extending them lines of credit to build railroads and canals. This was the on-going equivalent of the modern drives for government stimulus and green energy programs.

[151] Paul J. Scheips, "Significance and Adoption of Article V of the Constitution," *Notre Dame Lawyer* 26, no.1 (1950): 48

[152] Max Farrand, *The Records of the Federal Convention of 1787, Vol. III* (New Haven: Yale University Press, 1911 rev. 1937), 120

always easily use the States' experiences as a guide. Francis Heller studied the issue and concluded that there are two reasons for this lack of comparability. First, an Article V convention is created through federalism and the separation of powers. The States do not have such concerns at the state level. In the Article V design, the States are an integral part of the mechanism and the States' and convention's powers are in balance with that of the federal government. Second, popular vote approval of both the convention call and the output is typically an integral part of the state scheme of constitutional amendment. There is no fully corresponding facet to popular approval of the convention call in the federal amendment process.[153] But one of the most important lessons that can be learned from the States' experience with constitutional and amendatory conventions does clearly apply – that of the body of rules and procedures employed. The rules have become homogenized over the centuries making the States the experts on American convention practices and rules.

One of the key powers of the amendatory convention, if not THE key power, is that of deliberation. The convention must be able to consider a proposal in its entirety and not be forced to simply vote in an up or down manner. The Framers saw the convention as a method of resolving problems. The diverse regions of the nation bring different perspectives to the problem under consideration. Arthur Bonfield notes, "All the alternatives should be carefully explored and debated on a national level, and the details of any proposed amendments fully worked out on a national level, before they are sent to the states for their more locally oriented action of ratification."[154]

A smaller issue of no less importance is that of whether a convention may make expenditures or appropriations of the public monies. While a federal amendatory convention will undoubtedly be located and scheduled by the Congress, the funds for the operating expenses, such as printing, security, catering, office supplies, recording, staffing, consultation and legal advising will need to be met on a timely basis. One cannot easily predict the duration of the convention beforehand. The federal government may very well dispatch personnel from the General Services Administration to handle such provisioning or the States themselves may decide to bear the cost in an

---

[153] Francis H. Heller, "Limiting a Constitutional Convention: The State Precedents," *Cardozo Law Review* 3 (1982): **579**

[154] Arthur Earl Bonfield, "Proposing Constitutional Amendments by Convention: Some Problems," *Notre Dame Lawyer* 39, no.6 (Sept. 1964): 662

effort to reduce the weight of the federal hand on the convention's shoulder. It would seem that financial control would come under the heading of an inherent power of the convention.

The delegates themselves may be considered as employees of their respective states and be compensated by those states. Leaving the control of the purse strings in Congress's power may prove to be too influential if the convention is called to address a topic that involves reducing the power of Congress. The 1787 Convention was funded by Congress directly.[155] With this auspicious example in mind, it would seem logical and prudent for Congress to allocate a fixed amount from the Treasury for the convention's operation and to appoint a Government Services Administration official to oversee and facilitate the financial operation of the convention should the States decline to bear the burden. The States must weigh the potential savings of the cost to themselves against the possibility of congressional influence on the convention.

Additional powers, if they can be called that, are the extension of the typical legislative privileges and immunities extended to all members of any American legislature. That is, prevention of any detention or holding of a delegate in travel to the convention or being detained during the convention, any restriction of free speech, protection from any legal process or jury duty, and from harassment or undue influence.[156]

The division of powers between the federal government, the States and the convention itself is for the most part clear. Where there is still some ambiguity, it may behoove the States to assume both the powers and the expense of exercising those powers in order to prevent undue influence or conflict over the convention operation.

The Limitations of Conventions

All legal conventions must have *some* limitations on their powers. Even a plenipotentiary constitutional convention has some limitations – it cannot just order summary executions! If one thinks of the French Revolution's

---

[155] By a resolution of Congress on 5 September 1787, found in John Alexander Jameson, *A Treatise on Constitutional Conventions – Their History, Powers, and Modes of Proceeding* (New York: Scribner, 1867, 4th ed., 1887), §436, 436, - reprint by The Lawbook Exchange, (2013)

[156] John Alexander Jameson, *A Treatise on Constitutional Conventions – Their History, Powers, and Modes of Proceeding* (New York: Scribner, 1867, 4th ed., 1887), §§471-2a, 473-5, - reprint by The Lawbook Exchange, (2013)

National Assembly doing just that as a counter-example, that would be in error as that convention was a revolutionary convention without rules or legal guidelines. A convention must follow some rules to operate effectively. The extreme and completely hypothetical example made of executions is intended to show dramatically that even a convention which is reputed to be without any external controls cannot do whatever it wants – contrary to the assertions and protestations of opponents to amendatory conventions that insist such conventions are without any limits. By definition, a constitutional convention has more power and less limitation than an amendatory convention. Similarly, ratification conventions rank below amendatory conventions in their allotted power. The revolutionary convention has become almost unheard of in the United States today.

The Article V amendatory convention has been established to be of limited power and purpose. There is good reason to limit the convention. The discussion begins with acknowledging that there are constitutional limits on the amending power: two are named directly in Article V. The lapsed, due to the passage of time, prohibitions on interfering with slavery and the still in effect protection of the equal suffrage of the States within the US Senate, are set in stone.

The amending power itself is more complex than it may appear on the surface. The source of that power, the potential for its abuse, and the partition and/or delegation of its power are all aspects of this complexity. The power to amend comes from the sovereignty of the people. Sovereignty means that there is no one or nothing above the people as a polity. Legislatures, conventions and elected officials are mere agents of the people. Perhaps the best explanation of these concepts to be found all in one passage was given in 1932 by Hugh Willis,

> "*The amending power, it should be noted, is not a power delegated to the federal government, nor a power delegated to the states, in either of which cases limitations on the power might be presumed, but the amending power is an independent and absolute power granted to different branches of both governments, free from any limitations in other parts of the Constitution upon the branches of the federal government as such or the branches of the state government as such, and unlimited except for the limits upon the procedure of amendment set forth in Article V. The possibility of abuse of the amending power is not a test of its existence. Sovereignty certainly has such a power. If sovereignty desired to delegate the power, it certainly could do*

> so, and if sovereignty desired directly to exercise the power, it certainly could do so. The 5th Article has not only delegated such a broad power as this, but has provided for direct action by sovereignty itself. Abuse by a principal is a different thing from abuse by an agent, and an agent cannot be guilty of abuse when he exercises only a power which has been given to him. There is no power above the people, and the amending power of the Constitution does not recognize any power above them. Sovereignty certainly does not."[157]

It is important to understand why we must limit the power of amending conventions, but is there any reason, or right, to also limit the amending power? Before we can begin to examine the limitations of an amendatory convention, we must examine the limitations of the amending power exercised, in part, by the amendatory convention. The impact of the amendment proposed is not always immediately apparent. The consequences of our actions are often obscured for years to come. Other times, the unintended consequences are instantly felt.[158]

This notion of unspecified, unnamed implicit limitations on the amending power was dubbed the "***implied limitations of amending power***." This theory has raised its head several times over the last century whenever some group wanted to prevent an amendment.[159] Thus, an Article V convention may find itself dealing with the issue of limitations on the subject matter before it even convenes.[160]

A number of theories have been advanced over the years as to how the amending power is actually limited and that in terms of these limitations, various legal arguments have been made that a number of the successful amendments are neither legal nor binding. A somewhat long, but thought-provoking argument was laid out by William L. Marbury in 1919,

> "…the language with which the taxing power is conferred upon Congress, … is no less broad and unqualified than the language in which the power to adopt amendments is conferred upon the legislatures … of the states by Article V, … Both of these powers are **delegated** powers, pure and simple.

---

[157] Hugh Evander Willis, "The Doctrine of the Amendability of the United States Constitution," *Indiana Law Journal* 7, no.8 (1932): 466

[158] For a deeper analysis of this issue, see generally, David E. Kyvig's *Unintended Consequences of Constitutional Amendment* (Athens: University of Georgia Press, 2000)

[159] Everett P. Wheeler, "Limit of Power to Amend Constitution," *American Bar Association Journal* 7, no.2 (1921): 75-9

[160] Walter F. Dodd, "Amending the Federal Constitution," *Yale Law Journal* 30, no.4 (1921): 329-39

If the grant, ... of the power to levy taxes does not confer upon Congress the power to levy any taxes which would impair the integrity, the autonomy and independent existence of the states, and thereby destroy the Union, ... it would seem clear, ... that the grant of the power to amend the Constitution cannot be deemed to have been intended to confer the right upon Congress, ... to adopt any amendment, or any measure under the guise of an amendment, which would have the same tendency, ... to destroy the states, by taking from them, directly, any branch of their legislative powers.

The result would be same in both cases. As was said by Chief Justice Marshall, in **McCulloch v. Maryland***: 'The power to tax involves the power to destroy.'*

A right to tax would do little harm, ... if the tax were light, but there is no definite point at which the line can be drawn.

So with the amending power. A so-called amendment which takes from a state the right to legislate with reference to the drinking habits of its people might not seriously interfere with the state's autonomy.

But it would be the beginning of the end. The next thing to be taken away might be the right to regulate domestic relations, the right to fix the devolution of estates, the right to dispose of property by will, the right to determine the kinds of property which the people of the states might be permitted to own, etc., **ad infinitum,** *until the state would cease to exist; certainly in the sense in which the word 'state' is used in the Constitution of the United States."*[161]

Marbury has, almost a century into the past, predicted the problems that we are facing today. In his comment regarding "domestic relations," we see today a federal judiciary that acts like a legislature amending the Constitution or creating federal law with regard to marriage, a traditional province of the States. In his comment regarding "the kinds of property which the people might be permitted to own," we see today attempts to regulate the ownership of firearms, even the use of property as evidenced by the EPA's regulation of navigable waterways to include puddles after a light

---

[161] William L. Marbury, "The Limitations Upon the Amending Power," *Harvard Law Review* 33, no.2 (1919): 228-9, – Marbury makes some "interesting" claims about the validity of the Eighteenth and Nineteenth Amendments. Citation of his points regarding the limitations and the impact of amending powers does not constitute endorsement of his opinions of the Prohibition and Suffrage Amendments or the imposition of limits on the amending power.

rain. Marbury is referring to, at the time of his writing in 1919, the recently enacted Eighteenth Amendment in his comment regarding drinking habits, but this could just as well refer to the attempts by government, explicitly New York City government, to regulate the soda intake of Americans today.[162] It is for this reason that the States, in supplying the delegates to an Article V convention, are well suited to decide such questions in light of the impact upon the States. Where issues concerning the constitutional limitation of the federal powers are to be determined, it is in the interest of restored federalism that the States have a greater say in the division of powers in recognition of the disproportionate power already held by the federal government.

Of course, the necessary rebuttal to this argument is that States hold the ratification power thereby prohibiting the addition of any constitutional amendment that is beyond the will of the majority of the people and therefore the majority of the States. All powers granted to the federal government were surrendered, willingly, by the States and the people.[163] Somewhere in between the extremes of what Mr. Marbury and his respondent, Mr. Frierson, each have to say, lay the key point. Yes, anything outside of the prohibition on infringing on the equal suffrage of the States in the Senate can be proposed and even amended. But the prudent course is to carefully and fully debate the issue, both before and during the Article V convention. It is for this reason, that the courts have held that a pre-worded proposed amendment may not be dictated and that deliberations must occur.[164] An amendment may not be "railroaded" through the convention. These are very important points - in our time, there are organizations that wish to draft their proposed amendment and then push it through in a manner that avoids debate or modification.

The strongest refutation of the implicit limitations theory may be that of the textual legal canon of construction of "*Expressio unius est exclusio alterius*" or "the express mention of one thing excludes all others."[165] In this

---

[162] In fairness, the States and municipal governments are not as restricted in such powers as the federal government, but the sentiment that any government could restrict a personal decision such as what to drink is still, for most people, a stretch.

[163] William L. Frierson, "Amending the Constitution of the United States: A Reply to Mr. Marbury," *Harvard Law Review* 33, no.5 (1920): 659-60

[164] *Gralike v. Cooke*, 191 F. 3d. 911 (8th Cir. 1999); *Donovan v. Priest*, 931 S.W. 2d. 119 (Ark. 1996)

[165] Antonin Scalia & Bryan A. Garner, *Reading Law: The Interpretation of Legal Texts* (St. Paul, Minnesota: Thomson/West, 2012), 107-11 – Chap. 10: The Negative-Implication Canon

statutory interpretation, the fact that the 1787 convention listed specific exclusions to the amending power means that the list of unamendable clauses is finite. If it isn't listed, it isn't implied. The Court spoke to this issue very early in the landmark *Gibbons v. Ogden* decision in 1824 wherein Chief Justice John Marshall addressed limitations on a constitutional power with,

> "*It is a rule of construction, acknowledged by all, that the exceptions from a power mark its extent; for it would be absurd, as well as useless, to except from a granted power, that which was not granted.*"[166]

The Supreme Court, speaking on the exclusions made to the amending power in Article V in the 1787 Convention, held in 1920 that,

> "*The rejection of most of the proposed limitations on this power and the inclusion of but one permanent disability is strong evidence that, save as to the included exception, it was intended that the legislative departments of the governments of both the United States and the several states, acting in a special capacity for such purpose, should be practically unlimited in their power to propose and adopt amendments.*"[167]

Orfield posited that the amending power was the paramount power in the Constitution, and that the amount of thought and deliberation was commensurate with that importance of that power,

> "*Certainly no power conferred in the Constitution is ultimately of more importance than the amending power. If the fathers were careful in the drafting of any clause of the Constitution, it would seem that certainly nothing would be left to implication as to the bounds of the amending power.*"[168]

The federal courts, and in particular, the US Supreme Court, have rejected every attempt to assert the implied limitations theory. The first case to directly take on the issue of the scope of the amending power was the *Leser v. Garnett* decision in 1922. The Court held that there are no restrictions outside of those enumerated in Article V.[169] It is interesting to note that the state courts have not accepted the implied limitations on

---

[166] *Gibbons v. Ogden*, 9 Wheat. 1, at 191 (1824)
[167] *Feigenspan v. Bodine*, (D.C. N.J. 1920), 264 Fed. 186 (1920)
[168] Lester B. Orfield, "The Scope of the Federal Amending Power," *Michigan Law Review* 28, no.5 (1930): 554
[169] *Leser v. Garnett*, 258 U.S. 130 (1922), 42 Sup. Ct. 217

the amending power as doctrine.[170] Orfield lays out a substantial list of the publicized predictions of what could not be done – and therefore, which amendments are theoretically not legal – in Footnote 4 of his paper "The Scope of the Federal Amending Power."[171]

A century ago, many of the political scientists and legal professors of the day took a different view of the amendment power than we do today. They saw the slow encroachment of the federal government on the historical powers of the States as a threat. Specifically, the police powers of the States were at risk as more and more federal agencies and programs were launched – Prohibition would be used to attempt to prove this claim true in very short order. One Princeton professor pointed out,

> *"If the Ninth and Tenth Amendments are to be given any significance at all, they must be considered as limitations on the amending power as specific as any other grant or power in the same instrument upon which the essential form of our government depends."*[172]

Today, the Ninth and Tenth Amendments are, sadly, anathema to law professors and considered antiquated and useless anachronisms.[173] Although incorrectly quoted, it is frequently claimed that Judge Robert Bork called the Ninth Amendment an "inkblot" during hearings on his nomination to the US Supreme Court.[174] This idea has, most unfortunately, gained some acceptance today.[175]

A second theory of the limitation of the amending power was developed wherein the Tenth Amendment was construed to be a deliberate and intentional limit on the amending power in order to define what was limited. Originated by a group of New York lawyers concerned with the

---

[170] Lester B. Orfield, "The Federal Amending Power: Genesis and Justiciability," *Minnesota Law Review* 14 (1930): 382

[171] Lester B. Orfield, "The Scope of the Federal Amending Power," *Michigan Law Review* 28, no.5 (1930): 553

[172] George D. Skinner, "Intrinsic Limitations on the Power of Constitutional Amendment," *Michigan Law Review* 18, no.3 (1920): 221-4

[173] Constitutional lawyer, scholar, professor and author Kevin Gutzman noted in a book review which he wrote in 2012 and which was published in *The American Conservative* that when he studied for the bar exam, the review course instructor advised that when faced with the Tenth Amendment as a possible answer, always choose anything else since the Tenth Amendment was always wrong. http://www.theamericanconservative.com/articles/misjudging-rehnquist/

[174] *The Nomination of Robert H. Bork to Be Associate Justice of the Supreme Court of the United States*, Hearing before the Committee on the Judiciary, 100th Cong., 1st sess. at 249 (1987) (statement of Robert H. Bork) – Bork later expanded on his understanding of the Ninth Amendment in his book, *The Tempting of America*.

[175] Kurt T. Lash, "Inkblot: The Ninth Amendment as Textual Justification for Judicial Enforcement of the Right to Privacy," *University of Chicago Law Review Dialogue* 80 (2013): 220

recent adoption of several amendments, they foresaw the possibility of the extinguishment of all civil liberties unless the amending power was recognized as severely limited. In this *"Tenth Amendment modifies Article V"* theory, the amending power is the sole reserved power under the Tenth Amendment and was not delegated to the United States, prompting the question, if Congress were to have unlimited amendment powers, then, what rights were reserved to the people?[176]

Under this theory, Article V "gave a loop-hole of power" which effectually eliminated the reserved liberties completely and that the only way that the federal government can be granted additional powers is through appeal to the people. The authors of the theory argued that the States and the people have very different abilities to grant power to the federal government based on whose power is being granted. Therefore, the States cannot act to bestow the power on the federal government if the power to be granted belongs not to the States but to the people. The difference, according to the theory, lies in the ratification method. This exposition was argued, primarily, in the context of the Seventeenth and Eighteenth Amendments.[177]

The contention was vigorously debated as to whether the States may act on behalf of their people as the "recognized agents" of the people. The entire amending power was called into question. The argument was made that the States, as represented by their respective legislatures, could surrender powers and rights of their people to the federal government under the Constitution but lacked the power to do so prior to the ratification of the Constitution.[178]

The theory of the Tenth Amendment limiting the amending power was quickly attacked and refuted by Henry Taft. Citing the notes of the 1787 Convention and a recent Supreme Court decision, Taft stressed that Article V delegated the power of proposal to the United States and ratification to the States. He saw no limitation or impairment by the Tenth Amendment and the Supreme Court had repeatedly affirmed that fact.[179,180]

---

[176] Selden Bacon, "How the 10th Amendment Affected the Fifth Article of the Constitution," *Virginia Law Review* 16, no.8 (1930): 778 – emphasis from the original of Bacon.

[177] Ibid., 780-4

[178] Ibid., 791.

[179] Henry W. Taft, "Amendment of the Federal Constitution. Is the Power Conferred by Article V Limited by the 10th Amendment?," *Virginia Law Review* 16, no.7 (1930): 652-3, - brother of US President and US Supreme Court Chief Justice William Howard Taft.

[180] Referencing the US Supreme Court decision in *Hawke v. Smith, No.1*, 253 U.S. 221 (1920)

Taft argued that if the Tenth Amendment was actually intended for limiting Article V, would not this limiting be explicitly stated in the Tenth Amendment and the extent of the limits be defined so as to provide clarity? This theory of Tenth Amendment limitation lived on for a while until finally falling out of favor due to a dwindling lack of adherents. Hugh Evander Willis concisely negated the argument,

> "*The Tenth Amendment did not reserve the amending power which had already been delegated, but only the non-delegated powers, and hence, it must be held, as it has been held, that the Tenth Amendment is not an amendment of Article V.*"[181]

Orfield took a different approach to refute the Tenth Amendment modification theory. He pointed out that the limitation on the amending power, if it truly existed, was a limitation on the power of the States and not the federal government as the theorists claimed. He pointed out that the States "perform the most important part of the amending process, namely, ratification." He should have added that under the Article V amendatory convention process, the States carry out nearly all of the process. Taking this argument to its extreme, he showed that if the power to amend was limited to its exercise by the States, the impact would be felt by the States. Under this *reductio ad absurdum* experiment, no new powers could be conferred on the federal government and in fact, federal powers could only be removed.[182] Clearly, this view runs counter to the course of history. But a more time focused analysis would note that if the Framers intended for the power to amend be limited by the Tenth Amendment in 1789, then it should have said so directly. Since not explicit limitation was made in the drafting of the Bill of Rights, the amending power remained unchanged from what was first laid down in 1787.

A third theory of limitation rests on the assumption that an amendment must be somehow germane to some other existing part of the Constitution.[183] Under the ***"alterations only"*** theory, a proposed amendment must be directly affecting some clause or doctrine already recognized. As an example, the first twelve amendments all would be safe as they are

---

[181] Hugh Evander Willis, "The Doctrine of the Amendability of the United States Constitution," *Indiana Law Journal* 7, no.8 (1932): 465

[182] Lester B. Orfield, "The Scope of the Federal Amending Power," *Michigan Law Review* 28, no.5 (1930): 569

[183] Hugh Evander Willis, "The Doctrine of the Amendability of the United States Constitution," *Indiana Law Journal* 7, no.8 (1932): 464-5

modifications of the existing Constitution or reflect issues discussed during the 1787 convention or the ratification debates. The Fourteenth and Fifteenth Amendments would not apply. The Sixteenth and Seventeenth apply but the Eighteenth and Nineteenth do not. What then is the test for germaneness?

The definition of the word "amendment" as it was in used in 1787 was assumed to dictate whether an amendment was germane. This is an intriguing look at an originalist or perhaps even textualist view of an amendment. The argument is that "amendment" – in the legal sense – meant that only an alteration or an "improvement" of the Constitution was permissible.[184] Using this premise, the earlier examples of the Fourteenth, Fifteenth, Eighteenth and Nineteenth Amendments not qualifying become clear. The extension of enfranchisement to minorities is not discussed in the national charter. Removing the liberty of persons to use alcohol was not discussed – and in all likelihood, would have been extremely appalling to the Framers.[185]

Like the Tenth Amendment theory, the federal courts stomped on this notion fairly hard:

> *"Words in the Constitution of the United States do not ordinarily receive a narrow and contracted meaning, but are presumed to have been used in a broad sense with a view to covering all emergencies.... The definition of the word 'amendment' includes additions to, as well as correction of, matters already treated; and there is nothing in the immediate context which suggests that it was used in a restricted sense."*[186]

> *"The Constitution is the organic and fundamental law, but that law may be changed, added to, or repealed, if that is done by the states and the people themselves in the way provided. Their power to better it, as they think, is not to be hamstrung by mere rigidity of definition of words. Adding something new to the organic law is an amendment of the organic law, in the judgment of this court."*[187]

> *"The Constitution is a mere grant of power to the federal government by*

---

[184] William A. Platz, "Article Five of the Federal Constitution," *George Washington Law Review* 3 (1934): 23-4 – citing the definition in the 1797 Jacob's *Dictionary of English Law* and the *Bouvier Law Dictionary*.
[185] Lester B. Orfield, "The Scope of the Federal Amending Power," *Michigan Law Review* 28, no.5 (1930): 574-5
[186] *Feigenspan v. Bodine*, 264 Fed. 186 (1920)
[187] *State v. Cox*, 257 Fed. 334 (1919)

> *the several states and any amendment which adds to or in any manner changes the powers thus granted comes within the legal and even within the technical definition of that term."*[188]

Each time that counsel has attempted in a case before the US Supreme Court to introduce the idea of "intrinsic limitations" on the amending power, the Court has seen fit to reject the idea. Frequently, the lawyers will seek to use the records of the 1787 convention debates to prove that the Framers intended some measure of federal control over the amendatory and ratification conventions.[189] It is worth noting that William Platz looked specifically at this contention and found that, "No such limitation can be inferred from the debates in the Convention, and in theory the amending power ought to extend to any change made necessary by an alteration of circumstances."[190]

The amending power is thus widely seen as nearly unlimited by legal scholars and has been so throughout the history of the Republic. If the Framers of our Constitution had intended for the amending power to be constrained beyond the provisos enumerated in Article V, they obviously would have done so by explicitly detailing how it was to be limited; this being the practice that they repeated with all such grants of power and their attendant limitations throughout the Constitution and the subsequent Bill of Rights. To assume otherwise, we turn to Frederick Stimson, a constitutional scholar of a century ago,

> *"Such an event to their labors would make the framers turn in their graves. Never for one moment did the idea occur to them that the Fifth Article of the Constitution, providing for its future amendment, might open the door to the destruction of all its principles by changes sacrificing those elemental rights which they all believed no government might take away and which they had fought the Revolution to secure; by amendments* **qualitative** *or what I have termed substantive in nature, controlling or overriding those very rights which it was framed to protect, and losing sight of their own vision that this Constitution was being made to protect the people from the government even, as to these essential human liberties, never to further*

---

[188] *Ex parte Dillon*, 262 Fed. 563 (1920)
[189] William A. Platz, "Article Five of the Federal Constitution," *George Washington Law Review* 3 (1934): 22
[190] Ibid., 39

bind them, albeit it had a majority behind it."[191]

We can easily define the limitations of the powers of the convention, in fact, writers and scholars have been doing so for a century and a half. Jameson listed a number of actions that some conventions had attempted or considered which were beyond the realm of its powers:[192]

- Removing state officers from their positions
- Appointing people to state positions
- Instructing state officers as to how to perform their duties

To be clear, Hoar notes that Jameson, publishing in 1867 and 1887, Braxton in 1901 and Dodd in 1910, can point to no known usurpations of executive power by a convention after the mid-1860s. The matter of convention interference with the legislative branch is another story. Such actions are widely found throughout the body of state constitutions. The state constitutional convention is occasionally a legislative body meant to undertake legislative functions according to its instructions. These legislative acts are often knocked down by courts on the grounds that the people have the right to approve the acts before they are put into effect. All such actions have been performed by constitutional conventions and not amendatory conventions. The same limitations on power of a constitutional convention to pass ordinances or statutes would be inherent on an amendatory convention.[193]

The question remains as to whether a convention can amend its own enabling act and increase its own powers. Hoar maintains that a constitutional convention could do so as long as it had a significant amount of sovereignty already.[194] As a corollary, would the same apply to an amendatory convention? Not at all, as the amendatory convention is strictly limited by the definition of an amendatory convention. Because the plenary constitutional convention is so powerful and able to do so much, it makes the argument for us that the amendatory convention be limited. If

---

[191] Frederick J. Stimson, *The American Constitution As It Protects Private Rights* (New York: Scribner, 1923), 216 - quoted in Taft, *supra*.

[192] John Alexander Jameson, *A Treatise on Constitutional Conventions, Their History, Powers, and Modes of Proceeding* (New York: Scribner, 1867, 4th ed., 1887), §§325-30, 320-5, - reprint by The Lawbook Exchange, (2013)

[193] Roger Sherman Hoar, *Constitutional Conventions - Their Nature, Powers, And Limitations* (Boston: Little, Brown, 1917), 139-47

[194] Ibid., 147

the amendatory convention were not limited, what would distinguish it from the plenary constitutional convention? There is clearly a need for a limited power convention to do a limited amount of change without throwing the whole system into chaos. By the time that Hoar was publishing in 1917, the States had found that they could limit the convention to the matters at hand through the enabling acts for the conventions.

An additional limitation is that of the ability of a state to restrict the activities of either a state constitutional convention or, acting as one of the states applying for an Article V amendatory convention, a national amendatory convention by the explicit instructions included in the convention call. This argument dates back before Jameson and Hoar spoke on it. Jameson concluded that the state could not limit the state convention.[195] But he also concluded, conversely, that the states could limit the federal convention.[196] Indeed, many states do include such prohibition in their own state statutes. But does this state limitation extend to the federal convention? Jameson pointed out that this again is the convention sovereignty/legislative supremacy debate. Those who argue for the unlimited ability of a convention to do as it sees fit are pushing convention sovereignty and will recognize no limits on the convention's authority. Those who see the legislature as supreme will see no limits on the ability of the legislature to restrict, and inevitably control, the convention.[197] These two views are, as previously stated, merely the two opposing poles of the debate. The reality is somewhere in between and is a function of the purpose of the convention. Jameson went on to note that the application of state restrictions were often employed for amendatory conventions and sometimes included in the legislation the stipulation of such punishments as imprisonment.[198] The determination of who could limit the convention depended on the "locus of sovereignty" according to Paul Weber and Barbara Perry.[199]

Professors Weber and Perry get to the heart of this issue in their comparison of the state and federal conventions. They looked to the ability

---

[195] John Alexander Jameson, *A Treatise on Constitutional Conventions, Their History, Powers, and Modes of Proceeding* (New York: Scribner, 1867, 4th ed., 1887), §§362-4, 352-4, - reprint by The Lawbook Exchange, (2013)

[196] Ibid., §61, 64

[197] Ibid., §§376-9, 362-4

[198] Ibid., §382, 370

[199] Paul J. Weber & Barbara A. Perry, *Unfounded Fears, The Myths and Realities of a Constitutional Convention* (New York: Praeger, 1989), 88

of the States to limit their own conventions and then sought to determine if the same limitations existed on the federal level. They concluded that, the States are to be the final arbiters of limits for a federal convention under Article V as the people are for state conventions. Analogously, the States then, like the people, may delegate a measure of their sovereignty to limit the convention.[200]

A second major limitation of an amendatory convention is that it may not pass ordinary legislation. It is convened for the purpose of recommendations for amendments to the fundamental law and not to take upon itself the power of addressing those items and issues that are the traditional province of the state or federal legislatures. The amendatory convention is, by definition precluded from passing any legislation of any type. All of our state and federal constitutions observe the legal canon of the Non-delegation Doctrine that prohibits the surrender of legislative power to another body not expressly created and designated for that purpose. Once we allow conventions, constitutional, amendatory, ratificatory, or any other form to act as a normal legislature, the need for the legislature is exhausted and the limitations on the convention cease to exist. The convention becomes revolutionary and a higher power unto itself. The temporary convention will have morphed into a permanent legislature.[201]

After all of this discussion of legal and constitutional limitations, there are still the psychological and societal limitations that are imposed on the convention. These are as strong, sometimes stronger, than the imposition of the legal constraints. People are conditioned to think and act in a particular way and they are driven to promote and protect societal institutions and practices. In discussing the safety of an amendatory convention, Weber and Perry, stressed that,

> "A number of well-accepted political inferences are relevant to the present discussion. For example, barring cataclysmic events, the political culture and values of a society are stable over time and change only slightly. The behavior of most citizens and most institutions in a stable society is highly predictable, even in times of stress and change, and whenever possible, citizens and institutions will handle new problems by following patterns

---

[200] Ibid., 88
[201] John Alexander Jameson, *A Treatise on Constitutional Conventions – Their History, Powers, and Modes of Proceeding* (New York: Scribner, 1867, 4th ed., 1887), §§423-5, 425-7, - reprint by The Lawbook Exchange, (2013)

> they established to handle old problems. In the United States, mass voting patterns and political ideologies are relatively stable over time. Political elites rarely reject the political values or destroy the political and societal institutions within which they rose to success.
>
> When established political institutions function within what the public perceives to be their normal parameters, they retain their legitimacy, whereas new institutions strive to function as much as possible in traditional patterns in order to establish their legitimacy. New issues are either added to the political agenda when established elites see them as a significant means to retain or regain political power, or added by non-elites only to be co-opted by established elites. No established political groups or elites will stand aside and allow their power bases to be reduced or destroyed without attempting to defend against such attacks."[202]

The nature of an amendatory convention is such that those in power will seek to moderate the proceedings as much as possible to prevent too much change or too radical an innovation. The convention will be a platform for the careful, though speedy, deliberation of a topic and the proposal of resolutions. The output will need to be carefully considered and picked apart before formally incorporating it into the political fabric of the nation. The convention does nothing more than say, this is now the pre-eminent issue, the discussion begins now and the most likely solution is this. The conformance with the established societal norms for the greatest number of the citizens is the outcome with the highest probability.

The Procedures of Conventions

The powers and limitations of a convention are not the only point of contention between Article V amendatory convention advocates and opponents. The procedures of a convention are often the focus of argument as opponents decry the apparent or perceived lack of rules to govern the convention. While it is a well-known fact that each convention is free to set its own rules, custom has evolved over time to select certain habits that have proven to be the most conducive to the efficient and fair operation of a convention. We can see in the examination of the records of the dozens of intercolonial and interstate conventions held since the seventeenth century

---

[202] Republished with permission of ABC-CLIO Inc., from Paul J. Weber & Barbara A. Perry, *Unfounded Fears, The Myths and Realities of a Constitutional Convention* (New York: Praeger, 1989), 108; permission conveyed through Copyright Clearance Center, Inc.

that certain practices have predominated and we can expect that future conventions will appeal to those same practices.

Albert Sturm documented the state constitutional convention process and believed that it will apply equally to the federal level amendatory convention. Looking at the state conventions held between 1938 and 1968, he found that they followed the following format:

- Organizational Phase: seating delegates, adopting the rules, electing officers, appointing the committees and any other activities needed to commence the convention
- Committee Phase: receive proposals, conduct hearings, reach decisions, draft recommendations
- Debate Phase: hold debates, vote for proposals, make final recommendations and issue documents[203,204]

The process of operating a convention was so well known at the time of the nation's founding that the necessity of inclusion of the rules for operating an amendatory or a ratification convention was considered pointless. Everyone knew the rules as conventions were commonplace. Each step in the process was well known and obvious. Both the powers and limitations of the convention were taken as givens. Natelson outlined the situation,

"Universally-accepted protocols determined multi-government convention procedures. These protocols fixed the acceptable ways of calling such conventions, selecting and instructing delegates, adopting convention rules, and conducting convention proceedings. The actors involved in the process – state legislatures and executives, the Continental and Confederation Congresses, and the delegates themselves – each had recognized prerogatives and duties, and were subject to recognized limits."[205]

Historian Pauline Maier noted this fact in her work on the ratification of the Constitution. In describing the Pennsylvania ratification convention of November of 1787, she states that, "To regulate its proceedings it adopted a set of rules that provoked no controversy, probably because the rules were

---

[203] Albert L. Sturm, *Thirty Years of State Constitution-Making: 1938-68* (New York: National Municipal League, 1970), 69

[204] Paul J. Weber & Barbara A. Perry, *Unfounded Fears, The Myths and Realities of a Constitutional Convention* (New York: Praeger, 1989), 98

[205] Generally, Robert G. Natelson, "Founding-Era Conventions and the Meaning of the Constitution's "Convention For Proposing Amendments," *Florida Law Review* 65 (2013): 6

fairly standard."[206]

The efforts over the 1960s through 1990s to successfully pass a bill in Congress to establish convention procedures were often criticized as too cumbersome and difficult to manage. Predictions that it would take too long to develop rules, in part, prompted the initiation of the bills. This prediction seems suspect in retrospect when one considers that a more dire situation faced the States in 1933 when they needed to prepare for the ratification conventions for the Twenty-first Amendment. Ratification was anticipated to take as much as two years due to the recess of state legislatures. Historian David Kyvig relates the story of the Voluntary Committee of Lawyers which took only two months to create model legislation for the States to organize ratification conventions in 1933.[207]

Topping the list of procedural concerns is the issue of **delegate voting or suffrage**. Opponents are quick to point out that the less populous states are at a disadvantage in terms of representation if the convention is staffed by the method of allotting delegates by population. This argument is as old as the 1787 convention itself where the delegates had to devise a method of equating the smaller states to the larger.[208] They settled on the two houses with the Senate representation comprised of two senators per state. In this manner, each state has two votes. This is termed "unit voting" and in this particular example, it is double unit voting. The US House representation is comprised per population. Modern convention opponents have long argued that a convention might choose to use a method of allocating delegates by the states' electoral vote count – often referred to as the "electoral voting" method. Thus California would have fifty-five delegates and Wyoming would have three in a modern convention apportioned by electoral voting.

The difference between the unit-vote and the electoral-vote camps in the Article V Convention debate can be defined by the appeal to experience. The history of unit voting by the States is long and varied. The colonies in the seventeenth century first organized into a confederation briefly as the *United Colonies of New England* or the New England Confederation in

---

[206] Pauline Maier, *Ratification, The People Debate the Constitution, 1787-1788* (New York: Simon & Schuster, 2010), 102
[207] David E. Kyvig, *Explicit and Authentic Acts, Amending the U.S. Constitution 1776-1995* (Lawrence: University Press of Kansas, 1996), 284
[208] Sara R. Ellis, Yusuf Z. Malik, Heather G. Parker, Benjamin C. Signer & Al'Reco L. Yancy, "Article V Constitutional Conventions: A Primer," *Tennessee Law Review* 78 (2011): 681

1643.²⁰⁹ In this confederation, each colony possessed two votes.²¹⁰ Next came the *Dominion of New England*. While governed by a single governor, the colonies each had a vote on issues during the short duration of the Dominion in the late 1680s.²¹¹ In the first major intercolonial convention in 1754, known as the *Albany Congress*, Benjamin Franklin proposed the Albany Plan of Union. Thirteen colonies discussed uniting to share common defense. While the Albany Congress did not necessarily use unit voting, it did set the precedent for colonial cooperation.²¹² It was a limited power convention.²¹³

The next attempt at continental cooperation involved the limited power *Stamp Act Congress* of 1765. Nine of the eighteen British colonies in North America sent representatives to New York to discuss how best to respond to the new taxes. Voting was by a single vote per colony.²¹⁴,²¹⁵ The result of this collaboration was the willingness to convene the First and Second *Continental Congresses*. They drafted and ratified the *Articles of Confederation and Perpetual Union* that prescribed unit-voting by States.²¹⁶ These led to the *Confederation Congress*. The Continental Congresses voted by states according to unit-voting. The Confederation Congress allowed each state to seat between two and seven delegates but each state delegation voted as a whole with a single unit-vote for the state.²¹⁷ While the Confederation Congress was in recess, the functions of the government were carried out by the *Committee of the States* according to unit voting.²¹⁸ After the Revolutionary War came the *Annapolis Convention* in 1786 and the *Federal*

---

²⁰⁹ John Andrew Doyle, *English Colonies in America – The Puritan Colonies, Vol. II* (New York: Henry Holt, 1886), generally Chapter VIII, 220-67
²¹⁰ Articles of Confederation of the United Colonies of New England, (1643), http://avalon.law.yale.edu/17th_century/art1613.asp
²¹¹ Alan Taylor, *American Colonies: The Settling of North America* (New York: Penguin Books, 2001), 276-8
²¹² Albany Convention, (1754), http://avalon.law.yale.edu/18th_century/albany.asp
²¹³ Robert G. Natelson, "Founding-Era Conventions and the Meaning of the Constitution's "Conventions For Proposing Amendments," *Florida Law Review* 65 (2013): 19
²¹⁴ In town after town across the colonies, people came together as voters, tradesmen, churchgoers, etc., to protest the Stamp Act and to draft resolutions in protest and defiance of the Act.
²¹⁵ Clinton Alfred Weslager, *The Stamp Act Congress* (Newark: University of Delaware Press, 1976), 126
²¹⁶ Bruce M. Van Sickle and Lynn M. Boughey, "Lawful and Peaceful Revolution: Article V and Congress' Present Duty to Call a Convention for Proposing Amendments," *Hamline Law Review* 14, no.1 (Fall 1990): 5
²¹⁷ Thomas E. Brennan, "Return To Philadelphia," *Cooley Law Review* I (1982): 62
²¹⁸ Bruce M. Van Sickle and Lynn M. Boughey, "Lawful and Peaceful Revolution: Article V and Congress' Present Duty to Call a Convention for Proposing Amendments," *Hamline Law Review* 14, no.1 (Fall 1990): 5

Constitutional Convention in Philadelphia in 1787.[219] The ratification of the Constitution, done by unit voting of the States created the *United States Congress* in which the States vote in the Senate by double unit voting.

Nearly all of the more than thirty intercolonial and interstate conventions and conferences that Natelson has identified operated on a unit vote basis.[220] Since the Constitution was ratified, roughly two hundred interstate compacts have been adopted. Within the interstate compacts, each state has equal standing. Post-ratification conventions such as the *1814 Hartford Convention*, the *Nashville Convention* of 1850 and the *Washington Peace Conference* of 1861 operated on the unit voting basis. As a case in point, in the *Nashville Convention*, the host state of Tennessee sent 101 delegates to the convention while the rest of the nine attending states sent a combined seventy-five delegates.[221,222] The convention's officers wisely decided to uphold the time-honored convention rule of one-state, one-vote lest Tennessee dominate the convention.[223]

The Constitution was drafted by the States sharing equal standing and unit voting. The Constitution was ratified by the States through unit voting. All twenty-seven amendments added to the Constitution were ratified by the States through unit voting. The six amendments that were unsuccessful in ratification were considered and voted upon by the States using unit voting.[224,225]

It is demonstrative to note that on May 25, the first day of the 1787 Convention in which there was a sufficient quorum to do business, one of the acts was the reading of the deputies' (delegates) credentials. In Madison's Notes it was recorded that,

---

[219] On the opening day of the Constitutional Convention of 1787, the Delaware delegation emphasized that they were restrained from agreeing to any vote other than one vote per state as per the 5th Article of Confederation- Joseph Reese Strayer, *The Delegate from New York* (Princeton: Princeton University Press, 1939), 22, - reprint by The Lawbook Exchange, (2002)

[220] Generally, Robert G. Natelson, "Founding-Era Conventions and the Meaning of the Constitution's 'Convention For Proposing Amendments'," *Florida Law Review* 65 (2013): 6

[221] St. George K. Sioussat, "Tennessee, the Compromise of 1850, and the Nashville Convention," *Mississippi Valley Historical Review* 2, no.3 (Dec. 1915): 313-47

[222] Thelma Jennings, *The Nashville Convention: Southern Movement for Unity, 1848-1850* (Memphis, TN: Memphis State University Press, 1980), generally

[223] http://tennesseeencyclopedia.net/entry.php?rec=968 Accessed 29 August 2014

[224] Max Farrand, *The Records of the Federal Convention of 1787, Vol. I* (New Haven: Yale University Press, 1911 and rev. 1937), 8-10

[225] Bruce M. Van Sickle and Lynn M. Boughey, "Lawful and Peaceful Revolution: Article V and Congress' Present Duty to Call a Convention for Proposing Amendments," *Hamline Law Review* 14, no.1 (Fall 1990): 5

> "On reading the Credentials of the deputies it was noticed that those from Delaware were prohibited from changing the Article in the Confederation establishing an equality of votes among the States."[226]

Madison's notes for Monday, the 28th of May included a detailed note on the debate over unit voting with the larger states wanting population based voting.[227] Yates commented similarly in his notes for the first day,

> "After which, the respective credentials of the seven states were read. N.B. That of Delaware restrained its delegates from assenting to an abolition of the fifth article of the confederation, by which it is declared that each state shall have one vote."[228]

The significance of these two brief notes from attending deputies is two-fold: first, the unit vote is mandated by the convention and sets a precedent for any future convention operating under the Constitution. Any future convention would be considered as a product of the 1787 Convention. Second, that the states may, by precedent, restrict or limit their delegates to a convention operated under the Constitution. The Delaware stipulation is not coincidental. Delegate George Read had requested that the Delaware legislature include the binding instruction to provide leverage against the larger states.[229] Nothing in the Constitution withstanding to the contrary, these two points are still worthy of application to a modern amendatory convention. It is understandable that the delegates to the 1787 convention would expect that any future Article V convention would do as they themselves had done, and look backward to see what had worked in the past conventions involving the colonies/States, and adopt the same practice. In this manner, the States have an equal say not only in both the application and ratification stages, but in the convention voting as well.[230]

If the States were no longer afforded their equal vote in an amendatory convention, then the large deviation among the States due to population will result in an extremely disproportionate allocation of votes and the more

---

[226] Max Farrand, *The Records of the Federal Convention of 1787, Vol. I* (New Haven: Yale University Press, 1911 and rev. 1937), 4
[227] Ibid., 10-1
[228] Ibid., 6, – the condition of the Delaware delegation's constraints were re-examined more than once and the convention remained mindful of the situation for the deputies from Delaware.
[229] Christopher Collier & James S. Collier, *Decision at Philadelphia* (New York: Ballantine Books, 1986, 2007 ed.), 111-2
[230] Douglas G. Voegler, "Amending the Constitution by the Article V Convention Method," *North Dakota Law Review* 55 (1979): 379-80

populous states will dominate the convention. States with several large cities would be the most influential and dominant players.

To date, the only electoral voting system employed by a convention, conference or legislative body of the States is that employed by the US House of Representatives. Even the voting in the US House is not limited to proportional voting as the Constitution's Article II, Section 1 stipulates that in the event of a tie for the office of president, the House will vote for the president, by state with each state having a single unit vote.[231] For the majority of the states, even their Electoral College allocation is made by unit voting.

All five of our founding charters were adopted through unit voting: the *Continental Association*, the *Declaration of Independence*, the *Articles of Confederation*, the *Constitution* and the *Bill of Rights*. Thus by tradition, unit voting is the usual and accepted manner of voting for conventions between the States. Unit voting equalizes the States without regard to population and tax contribution. Smaller states are on an equal footing with their more populous sister states. Electoral voting is beneficial to special interests and regional factions.

During the 1787 convention, the method of debate provided for consideration of an issue more than once based on the resolution of the convention into committees. In their prefatory notes to Madison's Notes on the convention, Larson and Winship provided this detailed explanation,

> *"The delegates, when meeting in Convention, were bound to follow established rules of parliamentary procedure and decision-making much like those that still govern formal legislative assemblies in the United States… Utilizing this procedure for the proposed Constitution gave delegates the opportunity to consider each element of it at least twice – once in the Committee of the Whole and then in Convention – and allowed for them to experiment with new ideas, especially at the committee stage. Both in the Committee of the Whole and in Convention, state delegations vote by majority rule as a single unit either for or against a proposition, with one vote per state. If the delegates from a state split evenly on a proposition, that state's vote would be "divided."*[232]

---

[231] US Constitution, Article II, §1, Cl.3 and as modified by the Twelfth Amendment.
[232] Edward J. Larson and Michael P. Winship, *The Constitutional Convention, A Narrative History from the Notes of James Madison* (New York: The Modern Library, 2005), 15

The final word on the unit voting tradition is given to former Michigan Supreme Court Chief Justice Thomas Brennan, who summarized the process of constitutional amendment from the perspective of the states,

> *"Whether a constitutional amendment begins with a congressional proposal, or with a convention devised proposal, it must receive the approval of the people of three-fourths of the states, in order to become a part of the Constitution. The approval of the people is expressed either by the state legislatures or by conventions in each of the states as one or the other mode of ratification shall be proposed by the Congress. It is therefore, a concurrence of the people* **by states** *that works a change of the Federal Constitution."*[233]

Brennan has highlighted that the process is driven by the states; it is begun by being proposed in the convention method by the states – voting as units – and it is ended by being ratified by the states – voting as units – so it stands to reason that the middle portion of the process is conducted for debate, adoption and proposal at the convention by the states – voting as units.

A necessary corollary to the voting apportionment is the establishment of a quorum for passage. The sufficient number of votes may be a simple majority of a supermajority. Tradition is for a supermajority. The text of Article V is silent on the matter regarding a convention but requires a two-thirds supermajority for the congressional method. Adopting the two-thirds rule would make the convention analogous to the congressional method.[234] Finally, Article V includes the entrenched clause concerning the preservation of the equal suffrage of the States in the US Senate. An examination of the debate on 15 September 1787 shows that the Convention's concern with preserving unit voting among the States points to the inclusion of equal suffrage in an Article V convention as the intention of the Framers.

The issue of the **establishment of rules** for a convention is traditionally among the first major acts of any convention. At the Philadelphia Convention, the convention convened on Friday, 25 May 1787 and its first act was to select George Washington as the convention chair; its second act was to name the three-man Rules Committee and then immediately adjourn to allow that committee to do its work. The third major

---

[233] Thomas E. Brennan, "Return to Philadelphia," *Cooley Law Review* 1 (1982): 64
[234] Sara R. Ellis, Yusuf Z. Malik, Heather G. Parker, Benjamin C. Signer & Al'Reco L. Yancy, "Article V Constitutional Conventions: A Primer," *Tennessee Law Review* 78 (2011): 690

action was the reporting and adoption of the rules on Monday, 28 May to the whole convention.[235]

The amendatory convention is a "virtual fourth branch" of government. If Congress were able to define the rules and the procedures of the convention, the convention's function would be severely curtailed. Remember that the convention method was included, in large part, to provide a method of circumventing a recalcitrant Congress.[236] The convention method was designed to provide a safeguard when the federal government, particularly the Congress became corrupted and unresponsive. The Framers anticipated that at some point, perhaps several times, the people and the States would need to redirect the focus and actions of Congress through constitutional amendment – the ONLY legitimate, non-violent and legal means of changing the course of the nation through the fundamental law. "The convention mechanism was designed to come in to existence in response to congressional insensitivity to public demands for a constitutional amendment."[237]

The ability of Congress to determine, or even to influence, issues such as the voting method, the officer selection, the credential acceptance or any other aspect of the convention's operation is a license to direct and derail the convention – particularly when the topic involves anything that may restrict or restrain the power of Congress. The convention itself should select and police its own rules. The price of that responsibility is that the delegates will spend a significant amount of time debating and discerning exactly what those rules will be.[238]

Every convention has exercised the power and right to **select its own officers**. It is an inherent power of a convention. At no time has any convention been subject to the designation of a temporary officer by Congress.[239]

---

[235] Col. Alexander Hamilton of New York, Lt. Charles Pinckney of South Carolina, and George Wythe of Virginia - Joseph Reese Strayer, *The Delegate from New York* (Princeton: Princeton University Press, 1939), 22, - reprint by The Lawbook Exchange, (2002)
[236] Patricia A. Brannan, David L. Lillehaug, Robert P. Reznick, "Critical Details: Amending the United States Constitution," *Harvard Journal on Legislation* 16 (1979): 802
[237] Ibid.
[238] Sara R. Ellis, Yusuf Z. Malik, Heather G. Parker, Benjamin C. Signer & Al'Reco L. Yancy, "Article V Constitutional Conventions: A Primer," *Tennessee Law Review* 78 (2011): 689
[239] Robert G. Natelson, *A Compendium for Lawyers and Legislative Drafters*, (Purcellville, VA: Convention of States, 2014), 59

A number of people over the decades have advocated for the creation of rules and procedures for an amendatory convention before one is called. From the bills that Senator Sam Ervin, Jr., and later Senator Orrin Hatch attempted to pass in the 1970s and 1980s to the calls by academics in the last decade, such as Mary Margaret Penrose[240] and the response to Dr. Penrose by Michael Stern,[241] there has been a consistent plea for and suggestions for a codified plan. Finally a number of state legislators took up the challenge in 2013 and began to do exactly that. And it is entirely appropriate that the States are the party to take on these tasks. Should the Congress attempt to do so, as it has done several times in the past, there is every possibility that the process will be devalued if not destroyed.[242]

Natelson noted in his 2014 *Compendium* that it was suggested that a pre-convention meeting be held to determine and agree among the States as to the rules of an amendatory convention. In this manner, the basic outline of the rules, at the least, would be already constructed and allow for the convention's Rules Committee to work more expeditiously to emplace rules and provide structure.[243] This is exactly what the Assembly of State Legislatures has done – convening a "Convention of the States" to develop and agree upon the rules for operating an Article V amendatory convention before one is called.

The work of the Assembly of State Legislatures concludes the last aspect of the purpose of this chapter: to define an amendatory convention by establishing its English and European roots, demonstrating the source of its practices, powers and limitations, spelling out the traditional early actions of the convention and pointing to the reason for the inclusion of the Article V amendatory convention in our Constitution. We should all be aware of and concerned about the debate regarding the potential of an amendatory convention. The Article V amendatory convention, in partnership with the Tenth Amendment, are the constitutionally specified remedies provided to the States and the people for bringing an out-of-control federal government back within constitutional limits.

---

[240] Mary Margaret Penrose, "Conventional Wisdom: Acknowledging Uncertainty in the Unknown," *Tennessee Law Review* 78 (2011): 793-4
[241] Michael Stern, "A Brief Reply to Professor Penrose," *Tennessee Law Review* 78 (2011): 808
[242] Ibid., 809
[243] Robert G. Natelson, *A Compendium for Lawyers and Legislative Drafters*, (Purcellville, VA: Convention of States, 2014), 60

Now that we have been able to define an amendatory convention, its forms, its powers, its limitations, its procedures and its purpose distinct from other conventions, we can turn to the history of how such conventions were developed in America and how they have been used – or attempted to be used. The arguments that an amendatory convention "has never been done before" or that "we just don't know what will happen" require closer examination. We can trace the evolution of the amendatory convention from the first colonial conventions to draft charters organizing colonial governance to the eventual conventions to modify and amend those charters. To make that study, it is necessary to travel back through time and see the development of North American convention practice and history.

TWO

AN ALL TOO BRIEF OVERVIEW OF THE HISTORY OF INTERCOLONIAL AND INTERSTATE CONVENTIONS

> *"As one who loves constitutional government, I must confess that I am abhorred by the proposition that Congress has complete and unreviewable power to control the amending process in all its stages. This proposition would permit a false decision by a partisan or radical Congress to rob the people, the states, and the courts of their power to enforce constitutional government in our land."*[1]
>
> -Senator Sam J. Ervin, Jr.

It is imperative that we understand where the amendatory convention came from and why it developed as it did so that we can employ that tool properly. With an understanding of what constitutes a convention and of the powers and limitations that they hold, we are now well equipped to look to the development of the amendatory convention. Although the political convention did not originate in North America, like so many other great inventions, it was refined, perfected and spread to the masses here. As the colonists began to arrive from the Old World, the diversification of political conventions had already begun. From the conventions of nobility such as Runnymede and the 1660 and 1689 English

---

[1] "Statement of Sam J. Ervin, Jr. Concerning the Bizarre and Specious Claim of Supporters of the Equal Rights Amendment that a State Which Has Rejected the Amendment Can Change Its Mind and Vote to Ratify, Whereas a State Which Has Ratified the Amendment Cannot Change Its Mind and Vote To Rescind or Withdraw Its Ratification," at p.6 – quoted in Judith L. Elder, "Article V, Justiciability, and the Equal Rights Amendment," *Oklahoma Law Review* 31 (1978): 94, n.103

conventions to the English version of town meetings to the Scottish conventions of trades and nobles, the people of the British Isles brought a tool box full of conventions and their operational practices to the colonies and immediately began to deploy them for use in self-governance. But these conventions were just the beginning of the transformation of the traditional English Isles convention as Americans would adapt, modify and create new types of conventions as the need arose.

By the time that the 1787 Grand Convention met in Philadelphia, conventions were so ingrained into the British and American cultures that the need to codify their practices and define their operations seemed like a waste of time. Conventions were commonplace and their procedures were obvious to all in politics and to the public at large as well. Most of the Revolutionary Era political leaders whose names we recognize today were seasoned veterans of colonial and intercolonial conventions as well as members or past members of the various colonial legislatures.[2] The many conventions held to discuss the undertaking of the Revolutionary War and the construction of the colonial, state and later national governments provided the education of convention practices. Russell Caplan noted that,

> *"Once the underlying decisions were made the choice of words at Philadelphia was second nature, and one reason article V is so terse is because the salient features of conventions were generally well understood. In his* **Manual of Parliamentary Practice**, *composed for his own use as presiding officer of the Senate during his vice presidency, Thomas Jefferson remarked that for the most familiar rules of British practice 'no written authority is or can be quoted, no writer having supposed it necessary to repeat what all were presumed to know.'"*[3]

We can segregate the history of American conventions into distinct periods based on the usage of the convention tool. In the earliest period, the colonists used conventions to establish colonial government and provide order. The first few decades of North American settlement were punctuated by conventions that were almost solely purposed for the foundation of government at all levels. By the mid-1600s, the emphasis had shifted to include a mix of governmental functions and military issues. In the latter

---

[2] Robert G. Natelson, "Appendix - Delegates to Founding-Era Conventions," *Florida Law Review* (2013), generally
[3] Russell B. Caplan, *Constitutional Brinkmanship* (New York: Oxford University Press, 1988), x

half of the seventeenth century, conventions focused on the shuffling of colonies among governmental bodies and various widely shared issues, often economic. The military aspect was due to both the ever present conflict with the Native Americans and the influence of European wars such as the War of the League of Augsburg (King William's War to the colonists),[4] the War of the Spanish Succession (Queen Anne's War),[5] the War of the Austrian Succession (King George's War)[6] and the Seven Years' War (French and Indian War).[7,8] The eighteenth-century conventions were dedicated primarily to military and economic issues until the end of the French and Indian Wars which led slowly, but decidedly, to the American Revolution. In the just over a decade following French and Indian War, the convention mechanism morphed dramatically and became focused on, initially the restoration of constitutional rights, and when that did not occur, independence. The next decade, during the Revolutionary War itself, saw conventions concentrating on managing the war and establishing the States. The decade post-Revolution reached the convention climax with the establishment of the United States under the 1787 Constitution. Beginning in the Federal Era, convention types began to increase to the more than a dozen configurations that we know today. The evolution of American conventions can be traced in an arc from the establishment of colonial government to those of the modern governments at all levels and, in between, through the issues that defined the particulars that form the principles of American government.

The History of American Conventions

The earliest form of an American "convention" may have been the drafting of the *Mayflower Compact*, or as the people of that day called it, the "*Plimouth Combination*" of 11 November 1620.[9,10] It is the oldest surviving compact that is based on popular consent.[11] The gentlemen that drafted and agreed to it were indeed convening politically. Their convention could

---

[4] 1688-97
[5] 1702-13
[6] 1744-48
[7] 1754-63
[8] John R. Galvin, *The Minute Men, The First Fight: Myths and Realities of the American Revolution* (Washington, D.C.: Brassey's, 1989, 1996 ed.), 19
[9] John R. Vile, "Three Kinds of Constitutional Founding and Change: The Convention Model and Its Alternatives," *Political Research Quarterly* 46, no.4 (Dec. 1993): 887
[10] The name of "The Mayflower Compact" was not bestowed until 1793 by a New York historian.
[11] Donald S. Lutz, *Colonial Origins of the American Constitution: A Documentary History* (Indianapolis: Liberty Fund, 1998), 31

be considered a crude prototype of a "constitutional convention" and not a revolutionary convention under the aforementioned definitions. Clearly, the Compact was drafted under the aegis of the British Crown and not in the total absence of any government. There may have not been any government in the Plymouth Colony at that exact moment in time, but they were still looking to Britain for protection, supplies and some fundamental rules from which to draw inspiration and to create civil order.[12,13] The Pilgrims also fully expected that their compact and their community would comport with English law.

The Mayflower Compact was soon after complemented by the *Agreement at Cambridge* drafted 26 August 1629 in Cambridge, England by the colonists who were about to embark to the Massachusetts Bay Colony. Although the Agreement was written and signed in England and not in America, it was, nonetheless, an American charter as it was forged by those who would live under it and not the company directors as had happened and would continue to happen in other colonies.[14] Of course, like the Mayflower Compact, the Cambridge drafters comprised all of those (adult male) colonists who expected to be subject to the agreement. They were not representative of anyone else other than their wives, children and in some rare instances, servants. The Cambridge Agreement was supplemented in 1632, 1634 and 1652.[15] The 3 February 1634 agreement was significant in that it moved the colony from the prevailing direct democracy to a more representative form of government.

After little more than a decade in existence, Massachusetts Colony had already experimented with a number of principles that we now take today as mandatory. The *Massachusetts Election Agreement* of 18 May 1631, approved by a majority of the people present, assured the electorate the voting franchise, popular sovereignty, representation in the legislature, and

---

[12] There is some irony to citing the Mayflower Compact as America's first convention and constitution of sorts. Technically, the Compact was NOT convened and drafted in America. The "convention" and the drafting of the Compact took place aboard the Mayflower on 11 November 1620 in Provincetown Harbor meaning that the convention took place offshore and not ON America. It is a small but amusing historical note.

[13] John Alexander Jameson, *A Treatise on Constitutional Conventions – Their History, Powers, and Modes of Proceeding* (New York: Scribner, 1867, 4th ed., 1887), §138, 125, note 1, reprint by The Lawbook Exchange, (2013)

[14] Donald S. Lutz, *Colonial Origins of the American Constitution: A Documentary History* (Indianapolis: Liberty Fund, 1998), 54-5

[15] Ibid., 45, 48, 141

majority rule.¹⁶ Several Massachusetts settlements convened and drafted their own documents to regulate their new societies. The *Dorchester Agreement* of 8 October 1633,¹⁷ the *Watertown Agreement* of 23 August 1634,¹⁸ and the *Plymouth Agreement* of 15 November 1636.¹⁹ But the earliest real approximation to a constitution was the *Pilgrim Code of Law* adopted 15 November 1636.²⁰ It was a consolidation of prior works and it introduced a truly federal system among the independent towns of Plymouth Colony.²¹ The Code was adopted by a majority of the men selected to represent each of the townships.

After the Mayflower Compact, the Agreement at Cambridge and the Pilgrim Code of Law came the next major document in the *Fundamental Orders of Connecticut* drafted at the 14 January 1639 Hartford Convention. This convention established what has been recognized by historians the first true "constitution" in the New World.²² The document produced the first governing rules that ascribed the power to enact the charter to the people through what would be called popular sovereignty, and not through a monarch. The three major towns of Connecticut each sent representatives to the convention to contribute their thoughts and requirements for the new colony that was seeking to break away from the Massachusetts colony. The pattern was set for the New England colonies first, and then for the rest of the North American colonies for using conventions to address the creation of political charters.²³ The alternative methods of charter creation included drafting by company directors, parliamentary acts, and royal grants and decrees. Concurrent with the development of the Fundamental Orders, towns in Connecticut were also convening individually to draft their own charters of municipal or town government. Like mini-constitutional conventions, they had representatives meeting to suggest, debate and then put on parchment their agreed upon form of government, albeit local.²⁴

At nearly the same time, dissidents from the Massachusetts colonies

---

¹⁶ Ibid., 40
¹⁷ Ibid., 46
¹⁸ Ibid., 56
¹⁹ Ibid., 60
²⁰ Ibid., xviii
²¹ Ibid., 61
²² Hence, Connecticut's claim to be the "Constitution State."
²³ Wilbur Edel, *A Constitutional Convention – Threat or Challenge?* (New York: Praeger, 1981), 1-4
²⁴ Surviving examples are the Guilford and New Haven covenants of 1639.

branched off and settled in Rhode Island and Connecticut. They followed the now established, two decades old, custom of creating a compact. At Quinnipiack, now New Haven, Connecticut, "In June, 1639, the whole body of settlers came together to frame a constitution. A tradition, seemingly well founded, says that the meeting was held in a large barn."[25,26] The convention produced the *Fundamental Articles of New Haven*.[27] This same colony held, in 1643, what may possibly have been the first ever "amendatory" convention when they decided to change their four-year-old constitution by the addition of the *New Haven Fundamentals* – 144 years before the drafting of Article V![28] The existence of this convention throws into question the claims of modern opponents of Article V conventions that there are no precedents for an amendatory convention. It appears that this first of the many precedents was a mere quarter century after the settling of New England. It is reasonable to assume that the New England delegates meeting in Philadelphia in 1787 would have known of the earliest amendatory conventions and may have even suggested their examples for inclusion in the Constitution. Examination of the extensive 1643 constitutional changes show that the New Haven colonists were responding to the influx of new settlers with varying religious beliefs and making accommodations for the newcomers' civil liberties.

Rhode Island saw its first convention and document with the *Providence Agreement* of 20 August 1637. That document was the first to establish the separation of church and state, something unusual in New England.[29] A year later, at Pocasset, a group of Antinomians drew up a government charter and founded a new town. They followed the now established procedure, "They too drew up a formal agreement, and declaring themselves a body politik."[30] Pocasset in turn saw a group of settlers break

---

[25] John Andrew Doyle, *English Colonies in America – The Puritan Colonies, Vol. II* (New York: Henry Holt, 1886), 194

[26] The New Haven settlers were actually modifying an agreement made a year earlier, the *Plantation Covenant of Quinnipiack* of 1638.

[27] Donald S. Lutz, *Colonial Origins of the American Constitution: A Documentary History* (Indianapolis: Liberty Fund, 1998), 221

[28] John Andrew Doyle, *English Colonies in America – The Puritan Colonies, Vol. II* (New York: Henry Holt, 1886), 197

[29] Donald S. Lutz, *Colonial Origins of the American Constitution: A Documentary History* (Indianapolis: Liberty Fund, 1998), 161, 163-4

[30] John Andrew Doyle, *English Colonies in America – The Puritan Colonies, Vol. II* (New York: Henry Holt, 1886), 184-8

off and form a government under a compact at Newport the next year.[31] Another group convened and the *Portsmouth Compact* was drafted in March 1638 and has been called the first document to begin to sever political ties with England.[32] The Portsmouth settlers took the extra step of also drafting a *Compact of Loyalty* on 30 April 1639.[33] Nearby in Patuxet, in what soon became Rhode Island, the settlers seeking to separate from the Providence colony selected four arbitrators to draft a constitution.[34] The agreement that the arbitrators drafted is among the first in which a form of government was proposed by representatives selected by the people who would be governed by the document. The produced the *Plantation Agreement of Providence* on 27 August 1640.[35] By May of 1647, the colonists of the various independent townships had decided to hold a convention at Providence and draft a constitution for most of what we now know as the state of Rhode Island.[36,37] The product of that convention was a document called the *Acts and Orders of 1647* which would govern Rhode Island until the granting of a royal charter in 1663.[38]

Just two years after the Connecticut Fundamental Orders, on 22 October 1641, the people who had settled along the Piscataqua River, at now Portsmouth, New Hampshire and Kittery, Maine, came together to draft a compact similar to that of the Mayflower Compact. This charter, *The Combination Of The Inhabitants Upon The Piscataqua River For Government*, is important for the distinction of being the first charter which states that it is not done with the approval of the regent, thereby establishing the concept of explicit popular sovereignty for the first time.[39] The Piscataqua Combination is significant not only for its establishment of popular sovereignty, but for the

---

[31] Donald S. Lutz, *Colonial Origins of the American Constitution: A Documentary History* (Indianapolis: Liberty Fund, 1998), 161, 165

[32] http://www.portsmouthhistorycenter.org/items/show/155 accessed 25 February 2015

[33] Donald S. Lutz, *Colonial Origins of the American Constitution: A Documentary History* (Indianapolis: Liberty Fund, 1998), 166-7

[34] John Andrew Doyle, *English Colonies in America – The Puritan Colonies, Vol. II* (New York: Henry Holt, 1886), 183-4

[35] Donald S. Lutz, *Colonial Origins of the American Constitution: A Documentary History* (Indianapolis: Liberty Fund, 1998), 168-71

[36] John Andrew Doyle, *English Colonies in America – The Puritan Colonies, Vol. II* (New York: Henry Holt, 1886), 247

[37] David E. Kyvig, *Explicit and Authentic Acts, Amending the U.S. Constitution 1776-1995* (Lawrence: University Press of Kansas, 1996), 12

[38] Donald S. Lutz, *Colonial Origins of the American Constitution: A Documentary History* (Indianapolis: Liberty Fund, 1998), 178

[39] Ibid., 96

exercise of it. By this time, the settlers and colonists had firmly established a practice of documenting their political rules by consensus as peers. They specifically state that they, "have voluntarily agreed to combine ourselves into a body Politik."[40] Piscataqua just eight years later in July of 1649 formed a federal form of government with two of its neighboring towns, Wells and Gorgiana, in the turmoil of the Cromwellian disruption thereby establishing another American political element.[41]

While the colonies did not necessarily set out to create what we consider today to be a genuine, modern constitution, they followed many of the same convention practices of today. Generally, the colonies and settlements were creating either a compact, a combination or a covenant. These covenants were a mixture of political, church and social pacts. Technically, neither compacts nor covenants nor combinations are constitutions, but for the establishment of constitutional government during the early colonial period, the process is what is important as the use of the convention and later representatives as delegates or commissioners leads to our first constitutional conventions. Many of the covenants, both religious and political, were established by meetings or conventions including: Salem, Massachusetts (1629); Watertown, Massachusetts (1630); Enlarged Salem, Massachusetts (1636); Dedham, Massachusetts (1636); Quinnipiack, Connecticut (April 1638); Guilford, Connecticut (June 1639); and Exeter, New Hampshire (1639).[42] This tradition of covenant and compact making was concentrated in New England, in part due to the homogeneity of the settlers. The practices used in this covenants and compacts explain the rise of constitutional conventions and their variants in New England and the Middle Atlantic colonies.

There are other factors involved in the proliferation of American colonial constitution making. At the time that the colonies and towns were going about creating their political charters, England was having a very turbulent century. When Charles I came to the throne in 1625, he sought to suppress dissent and conducted a campaign of rampant religious persecution. The 1630s and 1640s saw the Great Migration wherein 80,000 people left the British Isles for elsewhere; 20,000 of those emigrants went to New England. Adding to the religious reasons to leave, the emigrants found little

---

[40] Ibid., 88
[41] Ibid., 139 – Lutz points out that other locales had also exercised federalism prior to Piscataqua.
[42] Ibid., generally

peace in England. Charles undertook a number of wars with the Spanish, the French, the Scots, the Irish and even the Bishops. The English Civil Wars both disrupted the continuation of government from London and increased the migration of displaced and distraught people to the colonies. From 1639 to 1651, the British Isles were wracked by a series of internal wars. This period was immediately followed by the brief English Commonwealth, and then, the equally brief English Republic and the three Dutch Wars spread over 1652 through 1674.

Leading up to the Civil Wars was a period in which Charles I prorogued, or suspended, Parliament and conducted the "Personal Rule," otherwise known as the "Eleven Years' Tyranny" which covered the years from 1629 to 1640. With so much chaos, persecution, uncertainty and distraction occurring in England for a full half century, the colonists were forced to fend for themselves politically.[43] Consistent, politically stable government in the British Isles was simply untenable. Compounding this problem with the unbelievably long time for the transmission of news and government direction (by twenty-first-century standards), and it is all too easy to imagine the natural progression of the colonies towards self-government through conventions to determine consensus.[44] And, consensus was the key to maintaining peace and stable government. With competing factions present and the possibility of outside assistance remote, stability came only through agreement by the majority of citizens. What better method existed in the seventeenth century to assess and direct the political winds than a convention of all eligible electors or their representatives?

But the English were not unique in their use of conventions in the New World. The Dutch had founded and settled New Amsterdam, now New York City, and made ample use of the convention mechanism while they briefly possessed the colony. Like their English counterparts, Dutch settlers needed consensus for their society to grow and function smoothly. There is no surprise here; the Pilgrims lived temporarily in the Netherlands at Amsterdam and then Leiden for a dozen years before leaving for the New World. The proximity of the two countries did engender the sharing of ideas and practices. At that time, the English and the Dutch societies shared much in common, making not only the proximity to England, but the familiarity

---

[43] Norman Davies, *The Isles – A History* (New York: Oxford University Press, 1999), 581-97, 703
[44] Donald S. Lutz, *Colonial Origins of the American Constitution: A Documentary History* (Indianapolis: Liberty Fund, 1998), xxi

attractive to the religious dissidents. For matters of defense, taxation, public works, sanitation, economic issues and every other governance matter, the Dutch called regular conventions of their towns and in varying places. These pre-war conventions, or *Landtag*, under the Dutch included: 28 August 1641 at New Amsterdam; and again in 1643; and 21 February 1648. The regularity of these conventions increased with the rising tensions with the English due to the Anglo-Dutch Wars and included: September 1653 at New Amsterdam; October 1653 at New Amsterdam; 25-26 November 1653; 8-14 December 1653 at New Amsterdam; 10 December 1663 at New Amsterdam; 6 July 1663 at New Amsterdam; 27 February 1664 at Flatbush; and a general convention on 10 April 1664 at New Amsterdam City Hall.[45] The Dutch conventions concluded when the English seized New Amsterdam in late August of 1664 and renamed it New York.

On 25 February 1665, the colony of New York held a convention in Hempstead, or Heemstede to the Dutch settlers, that proved pivotal in our history. The first English governor of the colony, since acquiring New York from the Dutch, sought to integrate the local laws into the English judicial system. It was in this convention that the first expression of the desire for "no taxation without representation" was made. The judiciary of the colony was laid out during this convention.[46] The Hempstead Convention was one part listening session on the English Governor's behalf and one part lecture for the colonists. What distinguishes the Hempstead Convention is that the population was a mix of predominantly English, Dutch, Walloon, French, Flemish, Native American (Lenape) and African colonists as New Amsterdam was already an international port. The solution achieved was an integration of all into New York life and government – setting a precedent for the rest of the nation to be. The proverbial American melting pot was forged in New Amsterdam. It wasn't an easy transition as it happened in fits and starts, but the employment of the convention method made change possible and easier. The colony of mixed settlers continued its practice of conventions after the English assimilation holding more on 4 September

---

[45] Stephen C. Hutchins & Edgar Albert Varner, *Civil List and Constitutional History of the Colony and State of New York* (Albany: Weed, Parsons, 1891 ed.), 62-3
[46] Martha Bockée Flint, *Early Long Island: A Colonial Study* (New Rochelle: Knickerbocker Press, 1896), 299-303

1673 at Jamaica on Long Island and 26 March 1674 at New Orange.⁴⁷,⁴⁸

In the many attempts to tinker with the colonial governments, the English Crown undertook to combine or divide several of the colonies. First, the New England colonies of Connecticut, Massachusetts, New Haven and Plymouth met in Boston in a convention to discuss mutual military assistance against the Dutch, French and Native Americans. That meeting of nine representatives resulted in the drafting of the *Articles of Confederation of the United Colonies of New England* on 19 May 1643. This meeting is probably the <u>earliest</u> example of an intercolonial convention as we may term it. The participating colonies each sent two delegates to the annual meeting providing the earliest example of unit voting – in this instance, double unit voting as is found in the United States Senate today. For a measure to pass, six of the eight delegates had to vote in favor requiring a supermajority. The General Court in each of the colonies had to ratify any measure adopted. The Confederation lasted until 1684.⁴⁹

Next, New Jersey was divided nearly equally in half and split between two groups of proprietors, i.e., investors, in 1674.⁵⁰ The experiment in government differed in the two new colonies.⁵¹ In West Jersey, the colonists called a convention at Burlington on 25 November 1681 and drafted a governing document.⁵² East Jersey followed the Dutch model and had a constitution handed down by the colonial proprietors. Then in 1686, James II sought to assert control over all of the northern colonies and tried to unite the colonies of Massachusetts Bay, Plymouth, Connecticut, Rhode Island, New Hampshire, New York and East and West New Jersey into the Dominion of New England.⁵³ That experiment lasted a mere three years. One of the reasons for the failure was the governing style of the ever-unpopular last governor-general, Sir Edmond Andros, who worked to

---

⁴⁷ Stephen C. Hutchins & Edgar Albert Varner, *Civil List and Constitutional History of the Colony and State of New York* (Albany: Weed, Parsons, 1891 ed.), 62-3
⁴⁸ Alden Chester & Edwin Melvin Williams, *Courts and Lawyers of New York: A History 1609-1925, Vol. I* (New York: American Historical Society, 1925), 167
⁴⁹ Donald S. Lutz, *Colonial Origins of the American Constitution: A Documentary History* (Indianapolis: Liberty Fund, 1998), 365
⁵⁰ Peverill Squire, *The Evolution of American Legislatures, Colonies, Territories, and States, 1619-2009* (Ann Arbor: University of Michigan Press, 2014), 21
⁵¹ Alan Taylor, *American Colonies, The Settling of North America* (New York: Penguin Books, 2001), 262
⁵² Donald S. Lutz, *Colonial Origins of the American Constitution: A Documentary History* (Indianapolis: Liberty Fund, 1998), 263
⁵³ David E. Kyvig, *Explicit and Authentic Acts, Amending the U.S. Constitution 1776-1995* (Lawrence: University Press of Kansas, 1996), 13

extend the Dominion beyond the original boundaries. He had an attitude of both arrogance and spite for the colonists. He once remarked that the colonists had no rights as they had left those rights in England when they emigrated. Among the most onerous of Andros' actions was to restrict the traditional New England town meetings to once a year and for the sole purpose of elections. Thus, Andros deprived the people of a large measure of the colonial political independence established - and relished - over the preceding two-thirds of a century.[54,55]

By 1689, England was once again experiencing upheaval due to the lack of a monarch and to the simmering religious differences. Some in the colonies saw this political vacuum as a threat to the peace and sought to fill the void. A group of men, calling themselves the Massachusetts Council of Safety, opposing Governor-General Andros declared their opposition in print, rounded up the governor-general, the magistrates and all officials of the Dominion government and imprisoned them. The rebels knew that their actions were undoubtedly illegal – and if they failed, it would surely result in their all being hung – so they immediately called a convention for May 9 to draft a new government and hurriedly put it in place. The rebels were unsuccessful in their initial convention attempt so they quickly convened a second convention. This more successful second effort drew representatives from fifty-four towns who voted to cast off the Dominion and resume governing under the old royal charter.[56] These were both clearly revolutionary conventions acting not so much in the wake of an absent government (the Crown government was still operating in Massachusetts despite James II having fled England) as they were seizing an opportunity locally. Fortune was in their favor as they declared the old royal charter was once again in effect, and the elected Massachusetts officials solemnly re-pledged to uphold it. Two days after the new government took over a ship arrived from London with the news of William and Mary assuming the throne.[57] With this act, New England had settled on the path of using revolutionary conventions

---

[54] In one instance in 1687, Andros prosecuted a minister who spoke out against the actions of Andros and upon the man's conviction his official reminded the Rev. John Wise that, "Mr. Wise, you have no more priviledges Left you then not to be Sould for Slaves." - Alan Taylor, American Colonies: The Settling of North America (New York: Penguin Books, 2001), 277

[55] John Andrew Doyle, *English Colonies in America – The Puritan Colonies, Vol. III* (New York: Henry Holt, 1887), 227-69

[56] Russell B. Caplan, *Constitutional Brinkmanship* (New York: Oxford University Press, 1988), 6-7

[57] John Alexander Jameson, *A Treatise on Constitutional Conventions – Their History, Powers, and Modes of Proceeding* (New York: Scribner, 1867, 4th ed., 1887), §9, 8-9, reprint by The Lawbook Exchange, (2013)

– albeit backed in this instance by the force of arms - which would lead inevitably to the colonial and provincial revolutionary conventions less than a century later during the American Revolution.

This "Boston Revolt of 1689" in Massachusetts was just one of several that occurred during the void created by the Glorious Revolution of 1688 in England. With the colonies receiving no instruction from London, the people did what they had always done – called conventions and decided for and amongst themselves. Concurrent with the Boston Revolt, the New York colony saw Jacob Leisler's Rebellion which also led to an intercolonial convention in New York on 1 May 1690 and a pledge of loyalty to William and Mary. The opposition to Leisler apparently read the same book and called a convention of their own in Albany. In Maryland that summer, Coode's Rebellion did the same; revolting, calling a convention and expressing fealty to the new King and Queen. John Coode went a step further and called a second convention to formulate a permanent government.[58] The pattern of the people of the colonies resorting to their own independent administration repeated itself over the next century as necessary until the American Revolution.[59]

Yet, another important example of the use of the convention in the colonial era is that of the South Carolina revolt against the colony's owners in December of 1719. South Carolina was a proprietary colony, that is, it was like Pennsylvania, the Jerseys and Maryland, owned by a consortium of investors. By the early eighteenth century, the colony's inhabitants, particularly the planter elite, were displeased by the actions of the proprietors and seeking a governance change. The South Carolina Commons House of Assembly elected to declare itself "a Convention, delegated by the People, to prevent the Ruin of this Government" and proceeded to carry out a series of actions that displaced the Lords Proprietors.[60] The convention seized power with the consent and assistance of the South Carolina militia. The rebels promptly and shrewdly dispatched an emissary to London to inform the King and to obtain the King's orders. Surprisingly, King George I gave his consent to the revolt and the convention reverted back to being the colonial Assembly. The king decreed that South Carolina had changed from a proprietary colony to a royal or crown colony. All in all, it was a highly

---

[58] Russell B. Caplan, *Constitutional Brinkmanship* (New York: Oxford University Press, 1988), 7
[59] Michael Kammen, *People of Paradox* (Ithaca, NY: Cornell University Press, 1972), 36-7
[60] Alan Taylor, *American Colonies, The Settling of North America* (New York: Penguin Books, 2001), 226

unusual turn of events. This convention example is not easily classified as to the type of convention employed. Clearly, the convention spurred by the revolt was revolutionary, and, at the same time constitutional. It was, however, authorized by the Assembly in as far as the Assembly could authorize such a convention. It was spontaneous in the sense that the public participated since the Assemblymen were also the convention delegates. The convention was popular in the sense that it possessed public support from all but the Governor and the Proprietors themselves. It was a legislative convention obviously. This example ran the gamut of all convention types at once.[61]

It is beneficial to observe at this point that the types of colonies differed and played a role in the amount of self-government and therefore the tendency of the people to experiment with their government. Nineteenth-century progressive historian Frederick Jackson Turner described the types of government as,

> *"Three types of colonial government are usually mentioned as having flourished on the Atlantic coast: the charter colonies, outgrowths of the trading company organization; the proprietary, modelled on the English palatinate; and the provincial colonies, which, having been established under one of the forms just mentioned, were taken under the government of the crown, and obliged to seek the constitutional law of their organization in the instructions and commissions given to the royal governor."*[62]

No matter the type of colony, they all employed conventions. These colonial era conventions had many purposes and agendas, but foremost among these may have been shared defense. Robert Natelson has painstakingly detailed the history of the early conventions. He has accounted for many of these defense conventions. He has provided a list that enumerates defense conventions among varying colonies in 1689, 1690, 1693, 1704, 1711, 1744, 1745, 1747 and 1757. He lists additional conventions focused on meeting and treating with Indian tribes in 1677, 1684, 1689, 1694, 1722, 1744, 1745, 1746, 1751, 1754 and 1768.[63] Historian Robert

---

[61] Edward McCrady, *The History of South Carolina Under the Proprietary Government 1670-1719* (New York: MacMillan, 1897), generally Chapter XXIX, 645-64

[62] Frederick Jackson Turner, "Western State-Making in the Revolutionary Era," *American Historical Review* 1, no.1 (Oct. 1895): 71

[63] Robert G. Natelson, "Founding-Era Conventions and the Meaning of the Constitution's "Conventions For Proposing Amendments'," *Florida Law Review* 65 (2013): 13

Gough details that New York convened with her New England neighbors at least seven times between 1690 and 1755. New York and New Jersey met together in that period no less than three times. New York and Pennsylvania met with some of the New England colonies and occasionally some southern colonies after 1709 on at least eight occasions. Pennsylvania and her immediate southern neighbors convened regularly including at least twice in 1757 alone.[64] Conventions were popping up in colonial America like weeds.

One of the most famous of the early intercolonial conventions was that of the Albany Congress of June and July 1754 that attracted seven colonies. Although the purpose was to treat with the Iroquois, a youthful Benjamin Franklin used the convocation to introduce his idea of a Plan of Union for eleven of the British colonies. Franklin's plan was approved by the convention but rejected by the colonial legislatures. It planted the seed for the eventual Stamp Act Congress and the Continental Congresses.[65]

Many of the colonies used conventions during the early days of the American Revolution to draft their first state constitutions when the British colonial governments collapsed in the wake of open warfare in Massachusetts and the proclamation of the Declaration of Independence. In all but three of the colonies were the new state constitutions prepared by conventions; in the three exceptions, the colonial legislatures drafted the new charters.[66] During the early part of the Revolution, the States were administered by a series of *Provincial Conventions* in each state. These conventions were often the outgrowth of and successors to *Councils of Safety*, *Committees of Safety* or *Committees of Correspondence*, a few of which had been formed by the independent, semi-secret Sons of Liberty organizations.[67,68,69] The Provincial Conventions were often restyled as the *Provincial Congress* and constituted a revolving government by an ever-changing and somewhat regular convention

---

[64] Robert J. Gough, "The Myth of the "Middle Colonies," An Analysis of Regionalization in Early America," *Pennsylvania Magazine of History and Biography* 107, no.3 (1 July 1983): 413-4

[65] Donald S. Lutz, *Colonial Origins of the American Constitution: A Documentary History* (Indianapolis: Liberty Fund, 1998), 370

[66] Connecticut, South Carolina and Virginia. Per Wilbur Edel, *A Constitutional Convention – Threat or Challenge?* (New York: Praeger, 1981), 3

[67] Roger Sherman Hoar, *Constitutional Conventions – Their Nature, Powers, and Limitations* (Boston: Little, Brown, 1917), 3

[68] Another early use of the "Committee of Safety" appears to have been in the 1689-91 Jacob Leisler's Rebellion in New York which functioned as the government "till orders shall come from their majesties" and at the direction of a convention, the Inter-colonial Congress or the Albany Convention, called to address the situation.

[69] Pauline Maier, *From Resistance to Revolution* (New York: W. W. Norton, 1972, 1991 ed.), viii-ix

until the States adopted "permanent" constitutions as urged by the Continental Congress in 1776.[70] In some instances, the Committees of Safety were designated by the Provincial Congress or Convention to act in their name during recesses.[71] The First Continental Congress had "resolved" that the States form a Committee of Safety in "every county, city and town" to enforce Congress's ban on trade with England.[72] The Provincial Congresses and Conventions were both deliberative and legislative bodies.[73] Once the Declaration of Independence was proclaimed, some of the Provincial Congresses morphed once again and became the original state legislatures upon the adoption of their respective individual state constitutions.[74,75] In other states, as the provincial convention or congress finished its work, it disbanded and a formal state legislature was elected to take its place.[76] Russell Caplan points out that there is often confusion today as to the nature of these conventions because they acted as not only conventions, but also legislatures – so there was a mix of the limited and the unlimited in terms of powers within a single body.[77,78]

As an example, Maryland convened its Annapolis Convention, formally called the Assembly of Freemen, nine times between June 1774 and November 1776.[79] The convention was called in response to colonial governor Robert Eden proroguing the Maryland colonial Assembly on 19 April 1774 – one year to the day before the battles of Lexington and

---

[70] Jameson noted that, "The organizations provided were of the simplest character, consisting of *Provincial Conventions* or *Congresses*, modelled on the same plan as the general Congress at Philadelphia, comprising a single chamber, in which was vested all the powers of government." - §126, 113

[71] Agnes Hunt, *The Provincial Committees of Safety of the American Revolution* (Cleveland: Winn & Judson, 1904), 158 - republished contemporarily by the University of Michigan Libraries.

[72] Ralph Ketcham, *James Madison, A Biography* (Charlottesville, VA: University of Virginia Press, 1990), 63

[73] Agnes Hunt, *The Provincial Committees of Safety of the American Revolution* (Cleveland: Winn & Judson, 1904), 9 - republished contemporarily by the University of Michigan Libraries.

[74] John Alexander Jameson, *A Treatise on Constitutional Conventions – Their History, Powers, and Modes of Proceeding* (New York: Scribner, 1867, 4th ed., 1887), §§124-58, 112-45, reprint by The Lawbook Exchange, (2013)

[75] Peverill Squire, *The Evolution of the American Legislatures, Colonies, Territories, and States, 1619-2009* (Ann Arbor: University of Michigan Press, 2014), 72-83

[76] Ibid., 82

[77] Russell B. Caplan, *Constitutional Brinkmanship* (New York: Oxford University Press, 1988), xi

[78] Forrest McDonald, *E Pluribus Unum, The Formation of the American Republic 1776-1790* (Indianapolis: Liberty Fund, 1979, 2d ed.), 27

[79] June 22-25, 1774; November 21-25, 1774; December 8-12, 1774; April 24-May 3, 1775; July 26-August 14, 1775; December 7, 1775-January 18, 1776; May 8-25, 1776; June 21-July 6, 1776; August 14-November 11, 1776

Concord.⁸⁰ In their final meeting, the convention drafted the first Maryland state constitution.⁸¹ In some states, the Provincial Congresses met several times and in successive congresses. Eventually, most of the congresses replaced the colonial assemblies and in South Carolina, the Provincial Congress even took over the statehouse, as the royal government had more or less ceased effective operation after 1771.⁸² The South Carolina Provincial Congress had succeeded the Committee of Ninety-Nine that had been formed by the delegates of a colony-wide General Meeting held 6 July 1774 in Charleston.⁸³ Not to be outdone by their neighbors, the North Carolina Provincial Congress convened in the "same room, with the same person presiding, and with largely the same personnel as the legal Assembly" in April 1775.⁸⁴ In Massachusetts, the General Court, by and large, became the new Provincial Congress.⁸⁵ To the British government, all of these congresses and conventions were illegal, unconstitutional and subversive.⁸⁶

The size of the provincial congresses and their lack of a permanent standing caused administrative problems. The colonies/states solved the infrequency of the provincial congresses meeting by designating the Committee of Safety to execute the edicts and orders of the congress. The committees were the executive branches of the alternative colonial governments during the period of transition and administered the government during the congress or convention recesses. While most committees of safety were appointed, some were elected but nearly all were overseen by the elected Provincial Congress or Convention.⁸⁷

The Committee of Safety appears to have its earliest roots in the English Civil Wars.⁸⁸ The Parliamentarians set up a Committee of Safety

---

⁸⁰ Winton U. Solberg, *The Constitutional Convention and the Formation of the Union* (Urbana: University of Illinois Press, 2d ed., 1990), lxv

⁸¹ http://msa.maryland.gov/megafile/msa/speccol/sc2900/sc2908/html/convention1776.html Archives of Maryland Online

⁸² Walter Edgar, *Partisans & Redcoats, The Southern Conflict That Turned the Tide of the American Revolution* (New York: Perennial, 2003), xiii

⁸³ Ibid., 28

⁸⁴ Gordon S. Wood, *The Creation of the American Republic, 1776-1787* (Chapel Hill: University of North Carolina Press, 1969), 315. Published for the Omohundro Institute of Early American History and Culture. Used by permission of the publisher.

⁸⁵ Arthur B. Tourtellot, *Lexington and Concord* (New York: W. W. Norton, 1959, 2000 ed.), 85

⁸⁶ Peverill Squire, *The Evolution of the American Legislatures, Colonies, Territories, and States, 1619-2009* (Ann Arbor: University of Michigan Press, 2014), 73-5

⁸⁷ Agnes Hunt, *The Provincial Committees of Safety of the American Revolution* (Cleveland: Winn & Judson, 1904), 20 - republished contemporarily by the University of Michigan Libraries.

⁸⁸ Generally, Lotte Glow, "The Committee of Safety," *English Historical Review* 80, no.315 (Apr. 1965)

in July of 1642 to organize and carry out governance and the prosecution of the wars. This committee sponsored local county level committees that were charged with the recruitment of men to the Parliamentarian army, to raise funds through tax collection, to secure horses and supplies, and to reform the churches. We can see this idea carried over into the American structure of resistance during the Stamp Act period and the subsequent early Revolutionary War period where American counties adopted the idea for a committee of safety. Like their English ancestors, they used the committees to further the revolutionary cause and to punish the Loyalists in the same manner that their predecessors of the prior century punished the Royalists.[89] Historian Agnes Hunt noted in 1904 that,

> "The resemblance between the English Committee and the American Committees of Safety is marked. Both acted as the chief advisor of the legislature. Both were concerned in raising and distributing men and supplies, in order to put the territory under their supervision in a state of defense and maintain it there effectively."[90]

A common ancestor, although by no means the earliest example, in North America of the Committees of Safety and Correspondence was the Stamp Act Congress of 7-25 October 1765. Called in New York by the Sons of Liberty, this convention was the first <u>successful</u> joint political action by the colonies. It was patterned on the Conference of Albany held just eleven years prior. Historian Pauline Maier noted that this should be expected as the Sons of Liberty were a very highly organized body; they had, as early as 1765, "carefully drafted articles of association that defined their organizational structures and rules of proceeding."[91] Calling a "nationwide" convention would have been right up the Sons of Liberty alley; their appeal and power lay "in reliance upon mass meetings."[92] The Stamp Act Congress was also styled as "The First Congress of the American Colonies."[93] In the buildup to the continental Stamp Act Congress in October, there

---

[89] www.nationalarchives.gov.uk/education/civilwar/g4/key/
[90] Agnes Hunt, *The Provincial Committees of Safety of the American Revolution* (Cleveland: Winn & Judson, 1904), 161, - republished contemporarily by the University of Michigan Libraries.
[91] Pauline Maier, *From Resistance to Revolution, Colonial radicals and the development of American opposition to Britain, 1765-1776* (New York: W. W. Norton , 1972, 1991 ed.), viii
[92] Ibid., 88
[93] In Cruger's Journal (see next note *infra*), the congress is also named as "First Convention of the American Colonies" (iii), "The First American Congress" (v), the "Continental Congress of 1765" (7), and the "Congress of Delegates" (vi) – it is interesting to note the plethora of names but of greatest interest is the use of the term "convention."

were many other local and colonial conventions called, both before and after the continental convention, to discuss the impact of the new tax and to issue a public declaration of opposition to Parliament.⁹⁴ To cite just two examples that include a local variant, the Essex County, New Jersey meeting in Elizabeth on 25 October 1765 that issued the *Essex County, New Jersey Resolutions on the Stamp Act*, and a colonial variant, the *Connecticut Resolutions on the Stamp Act of 1765*, drafted at a meeting in New London on 10 December 1765.⁹⁵ These lesser conventions were repeated all across the colonies and exemplified the grassroots nature of the opposition to the stamp tax. The meetings were also a continuation and a rejuvenation of the colonial tradition of the people to assemble, to discuss and jointly resolve to action on an issue. The revolutionary twist comes in the form of non-governmental groups, such as the Sons of Liberty, being the drivers behind the movement. As the earlier, local conventions met, the people discussed and worked out potential actions. The ideas generated were repeated and discussed in the colonial conventions. Then, the most useful ideas made their way to the continental Stamp Act Convention. Thus, the best ideas were filtered and shared. After the October convention in New York, the outcome of the continental convention was disseminated back down to the local level through more colonial and local conventions. An informal system was now in place to complement, or to supplant, the formal, authorized colonial legislatures. In a sense, we can see the formation of a parallel government.

In the run-up to the Revolution, a number of instances where conventions were called points to a new development – in place of meetings led by the aristocracy or the gentry or the political elite, the common people of the trades, farming and mercantile classes instigated conventions in response to the legislation passed in London. The Townshend Revenue Act of 1768 prompted Massachusetts to call meetings at the township level. The royal governor, Francis Bernard, responded by dismissing the colonial House and proclaimed that the "Calling of an Assembly by private persons only" was a challenge to the legal authority.⁹⁶ Sons of Liberty (and General Court House Clerk) Sam Adams and (and General Court House Speaker) Thomas Cushing then called a colony-wide convention of the towns attracting

---

⁹⁴ Lewis Cruger, *Journal of the First Congress of the American Colonies* (New York: E. Winchester, 1845), generally
⁹⁵ The *Massachusetts Gazette*, 19 December 1765
⁹⁶ Gordon S. Wood, *The Creation of the American Republic, 1776-1787* (Chapel Hill: University of North Carolina Press, 1969), 312-3. Published for the Omohundro Institute of Early American History and Culture. Used by permission of the publisher.

representatives from about one hundred of the 250 towns.⁹⁷ This distinct, carefully orchestrated convention was instigated by the public's opposition and ire to the landing of British troops, taxation, and the dissolution of the General Court.⁹⁸

Massachusetts provides the most stirring example of the use of the convention to first resolve the issues and then to build the consensus that led to independence. In popular history taught today, the prelude to the Revolution is sparsely covered. The Boston Massacre and the Tea Party are covered. The passage of the Intolerable Acts is cited. But the intervening period between the 16 December 1773 Boston Tea Party and the 19 April 1775 battles at Lexington and Concord is rarely detailed. It is in this interim that the convention tool was widely leveraged and used to lead to Revolution. Massachusetts provides a study in microcosm of the employment of conventions to produce the political change. The foundational level of political engagement in 1770s Massachusetts was the town meeting. Called to address local issues and to promote discussion, the meetings became the foci of agitation in the years preceding the Revolution.⁹⁹ Between the sermons given in the day long Sunday services and the political caucuses that the town meetings had evolved into, Massachusetts colonists were experiencing a steady stream of political information (and disinformation) that caused the political power to move downward from the colonial assembly in Boston to the township level. The Committees of Correspondence and Safety were first organized at the town level.¹⁰⁰

As the tensions grew in the colony and with the arrival of British General Thomas Gage as military governor, the resistance worked its way up to the county and then the provincial levels. The Coercive Acts (Intolerable Acts to the colonials) closed the Boston harbor and cut off trade. The Massachusetts Government Act of 1774 put the hands of colonial government solely in Gage's power. Concurrent with these actions, the people of the colonies were already thinking on a national scale and, as always, of a convention. Ralph Ketcham wrote in his biography of Madison that

---

[97] Russell B. Caplan, *Constitutional Brinkmanship* (New York: Oxford University Press, 1988), 8

[98] Richard D. Brown, "The Massachusetts Convention of Towns of 1768," *William and Mary Quarterly*, 3d Series, 26, no.1 (Jan. 1969): 99

[99] Willi Paul Adams, *The First American Constitutions, Republican Ideology and the Making of the State Constitutions in the Revolutionary Era* (Lanham, MD: Rowman & Littlefield, 2001), 28-9

[100] John R. Galvin, *The Minute Men, The First Fight: Myths and Realities of the American Revolution* (Washington, D.C.: Brassey's, 1989, 1996 ed.), 35-6

in Philadelphia on 20 May 1774, a meeting at the City Tavern resulted in a call for a, as termed by the *Pennsylvania Journal*, "Congress of deputies of all the colonies" to "confront Lord North."[101] The 1691 Charter granted to the Massachusetts colonists the ability to choose the governor's council, which in turn selected the judges, sheriffs, justices of the peace, to summon juries, and to call town meetings was revoked and these rights were taken from the people and placed at Gage's prerogative. The response of the towns was immediate – they called their meetings anyway and right away. Samuel Adams had produced a plan for calling county conventions with the intention of leading to a provincial convention that would function as an alternate provincial government. The county Committees of Correspondence called their conventions in early August.[102] The committees employed tools such as economic boycotts, disrupting trials and mass protests to publicly display the colonists' displeasure. The county conventions were the true base of the revolutionary spirit in New England. Middlesex County, typical of all counties in Massachusetts, held its convention on 30 August 1774 in Concord and from that point on, the county was on a war footing following a plan of "well-ordered resistance."[103] All of these county level actions culminated in the Suffolk Resolves in late 1774.[104]

One Massachusetts county stands out for its resistance and its use of conventions: Worcester. Each of the counties held a convention and then issued its own set of resolves.[105] The conventions reorganized their militia units and expanded them. But, Worcester went farther than most and became the example and model for not only the rest of Massachusetts but for all of New England and in some cases, for other southern colonies. Worcester held an August 1774 convention on the 9th and 10th. Then others on August 30-31, September 6-8 and 20-21, December 6, and in 1775, January 26, March 28 and May 31. The 6-8 September 1774 convention held at Mary Stearn's tavern came in response to the rumor that General Gage was going

---

[101] The *Pennsylvania Journal*, May 4, 11, and 18, 1774 as quoted in Ralph Ketcham, *James Madison, A Biography* (Charlottesville, VA: University of Virginia Press, 1990), 60

[102] John R. Galvin, *The Minute Men, The First Fight: Myths and Realities of the American Revolution* (Washington, D.C.: Brassey's, 1989, 1996 ed.), 43-5

[103] Robert A. Gross, *The Minutemen and Their World* (New York: Hill and Wang, 1976), 53, 68

[104] Willi Paul Adams, *The First American Constitutions, Republican Ideology and the Making of the State Constitutions in the Revolutionary Era* (Lanham, MD: Rowman & Littlefield, 2001), 32-3

[105] Berkshire July 6, Bristol September 28-29, Cumberland September 21-22, Essex September 6-9, Hampshire September 22-23, Middlesex August 30-31, Plymouth September 26-27, and Suffolk September 6-13, per William Lincoln, *The Journals of Each Provincial Congress of Massachusetts in 1774 and 1775 and of the Committee of Safety* (Boston: Dutton & Wentworth, Printers to the State, 1838), 601-60

to send troops to Worcester. The Worcester convention drew in 4,622 militia men from thirty-seven towns across western and central Massachusetts. The militia forced the closure of the courts and ordered the crown officials to renounce their positions, forcing them to parade up and down the main street and to publicly proclaim their renunciations of loyalty to the Crown no less than thirty-two times each.[106] The convention also made on 4 October 1774 what, historian Ray Raphael argues, is the first official declaration of independence. The militia and colonists did this all without firing a single shot.[107] Despite the show of force, the leaders of the now decade-old movement had been following an extremely, carefully scripted plan of non-violence. They had realized very early that the colonists were not ready for violent confrontation with the mother country. The goal had remained to regain their English constitutional rights and rejoin the British Empire. All of the Sons of Liberty actions were geared toward political and not military force. The Sons of Liberty sought to work closely with the local town governments.[108] Pauline Maier states,

> *"The county conventions that sprung up in Massachusetts from July 1774 similarly sought 'the discouragement of all licentiousness, and suppression of all mobs and riots,' encouraging citizens 'to observe the most strict obedience to all constitutional laws and authority.'"*[109]

On September 5, the day prior to the Worcester convention opening, the First Continental Congress began convening in Philadelphia. On the 8th of September, the Worcester rebellion continued with forty-three blacksmiths holding their own convention. They published a list of Tories for whom they would do no work. They met again on November 8 to expand their list and their resolves.[110] What was done in Worcester was then emulated in other Massachusetts, Connecticut, Rhode Island and New Hampshire counties. These local conventions led, as Samuel Adams had planned, to the Massachusetts Provincial Congress meeting on 7 October 1774 in Salem, then again on the 11th in Concord and then once more on the

---

[106] John R. Galvin, *The Minute Men, The First Fight: Myths and Realities of the American Revolution* (Washington, D.C.: Brassey's, 1989, 1996 ed.), 42-9
[107] Generally, Ray Raphael, *The First American Revolution: Before Lexington and Concord* (New York: New Press, 2003)
[108] Pauline Maier, From Resistance to Revolution (New York: W. W. Norton, 1972, 1991 ed.), 98
[109] Ibid., 280
[110] *Boston Gazette*, 28 November 1774, p.1

17th in Cambridge.[111]

In several of the colonies, during the early days of the Revolution, the colonial military governors dismissed the colonial legislatures and assumed personal rule.[112] The pressing internal matters of the colonies went unanswered. As had happened during the English Civil Wars and the Glorious Revolution, a vacuum formed that needed prompt attention. Tradition dictated the calling of conventions to form governments – even shadow governments as they were. The conventions that were called and convened in the beginning days of the American Revolution were indeed revolutionary conventions in the sense discussed in Chapter 1. Roger Sherman Hoar clarifies that,

> "*The dissolution of the constitutional assemblies, by the governors appointed by the crown, obliged the people to resort to other methods of deliberating for the common good. Hence the first introduction of convention: bodies neither authorized by, or known to the then constitutional government; bodies, on the contrary, which the constitutional officers of the then existing governments considered illegal, and treated as such. Nevertheless, they met, deliberated, and resolved for the common good.*"[113]

The acceptance of these governments was made, generally, by the people. The issue of the conventions' legality, and that of the bodies that they created to govern, was not given much consideration in light of the accompanying military force and the potential for societal chaos in the absence of civil government.[114] The people desired stability and the revolutionary conventions and the constitutions that they generated provided more stability and a less harsh treatment than a transient British military force. Acquiescence by the people to the constitutions and the governments that those constitutions established and supported as time went by gave legitimacy to the constitutions and the state governments. The governments of the new states have been termed, by one writer, as "anti-parliaments."[115] Of course, some colonies had an easier time of implementing new government than others; New Hampshire had less of a Tory presence and no real military

---

[111] John R. Galvin, *The Minute Men, The First Fight: Myths and Realities of the American Revolution* (Washington, D.C.: Brassey's, 1989, 1996 ed.), 53-8.
[112] Excepting Connecticut, Delaware and Rhode Island which could not be prorogued.
[113] Roger Sherman Hoar, *Constitutional Conventions – Their Nature, Powers, and Limitations* (Boston: Little, Brown, 1917), 3
[114] Ibid.
[115] Michael Kammen, *People of Paradox* (Ithaca, NY: Cornell University Press, 1972), 50

operations to speak of within its territory. This relative calm made for an easier and quicker transition; they were the first colony to deploy the constitutional convention mechanism. To better facilitate the transition, the New Hampshire Provincial Congress called a convention for 21 December 1775 and that body adopted a *temporary* constitution on 5 January 1776 that was intended to carry it through until the convention of the towns met in June of 1777 to draft the permanent constitution – this was the first written constitution for an English colony that was implemented without the approval or even the consultation of Parliament.[116] Hoar points out that the colony of New Hampshire was actually copying (roughly) the action of the town of Concord, Massachusetts.[117,118] The people of New Hampshire took the constitution making process very seriously. They followed the example and pattern set by their English ancestors in the Convention Parliament of 1689. They collected feedback from the people and made modifications, so many so, that over the two year period covering 1783-1784, they held a total of nine convention sessions to revise – that is, to *amend* - their state constitution in the post-war period. Jameson pointed out that the last two sessions were called and operated under the existing state constitution, making these sessions true amendatory conventions and not revolutionary conventions.[119] The amending provision of the 1784 New Hampshire constitution required the use of a convention comprised of elected delegates to propose amendments, and then, that proposal had to be ratified by two-thirds of the voters.[120]

Next door in Vermont, or the New Hampshire Grants as it was called in the early days of the Revolution, the convention script was again followed. Despite the claim to the colony by New York, the people of Vermont were determined to stand on their own and forged ahead in defiance of New York. With the British occupying Massachusetts initially and New York focused on keeping the British out of the city of New York, Vermont found itself of little

---

[116] Willi Paul Adams, *The First American Constitutions, Republican Ideology and the Making of the State Constitutions in the Revolutionary Era* (Lanham, MD: Rowman & Littlefield, 2001), 3

[117] Roger Sherman Hoar, *Constitutional Conventions – Their Nature, Powers, and Limitations* (Boston: Little, Brown, 1917), 4-7

[118] John Alexander Jameson, *A Treatise on Constitutional Conventions – Their History, Powers, and Modes of Proceeding* (New York: Scribner, 1867, 4th ed., 1887), §§131-3, 113-22, reprint by The Lawbook Exchange, (2013)

[119] Ibid., §132, 121-2,

[120] Michael B. Rappaport, "The Constitutionality of a Limited Convention: An Originalist Analysis," *Constitutional Commentary* 81 (2012): 94-5

regard and therefore able to move forward with its bid for independence, not only of Britain but of New York as well. They called the Convention of the New Hampshire Grants in January 1777 and declared their independence. In June, another convention drafted a constitution and in July a third convention ratified the constitution. Because Vermont had no history of self-government, it had little experience with the machinations of government at a colonial or state level. The various town and county committees of safety were occasionally called by local conventions for input.[121] A last convention was held to amend the new constitution in December 1777 and then turned governance over to the new Assembly.[122] Thus, Vermont followed the usual chain of conventional events and progressed from a revolutionary convention, through a constitutional, then a ratificatory and finally an amendatory convention to complete the process. Vermont has the further distinction of continuously operating Committees of Safety from 1764 and the Stamp Act period through the Revolution. The reason for their operation was the on-going dispute with New York over the ownership of the New Hampshire Grants. They periodically employed conventions to ascertain and assess public sentiment and to decide on actions.[123]

The arrival of the Revolution brought with it a rash of conventions at all levels. Historian Gordon S. Wood details how the local Committees of Safety and Correspondence took upon themselves the duties of governing towns, then counties, then whole colonies and eventually establishing the Continental Congress. He tells of the royal governors' dismissals of the provincial and colonial assemblies instigating the formation – and acceptance – of these conventions and standing replacement assemblies. The void created required something to fill it.[124] Over time, the conventions took on every issue of importance and moved progressively more and more into every aspect of life. The point came where the provincial and state conventions were concerned about the local and regional conventions' actions.[125] The conventions did overstep their bounds on occasion and use "coercion and

---

[121] Agnes Hunt, *The Provincial Committees of Safety of the American Revolution* (Cleveland: Winn & Judson, 1904), 34-5, - republished contemporarily by the University of Michigan Libraries.
[122] Ibid., 41
[123] Ibid., 167-8
[124] Gordon S. Wood, *The Creation of the American Republic, 1776-1787* (Chapel Hill: University of North Carolina Press, 1969), 313-6, 130, 85. Published for the Omohundro Institute of Early American History and Culture.
[125] Ibid., 323-5

intimidation" to achieve their wartime goals.[126] By that time, the local committees and conventions had become established governments. Many of these local units had been recognized or created under the Continental Association of 1774.[127]

Rhode Island, by virtue of her position on the coast, received additional attention from the British and faced occupation of the central island. The Assembly remained in power and swung to the Patriot side as a whole and the need for conventions was not realized. The Assembly did recognize that the colony was too small and underpowered to wage an individual war and sought to ally with her neighbors. From 25 December 1776 to 2 January 1777, Rhode Island hosted a convention in Providence of the New England states to plan a combined defense of the region and to address inflation.[128,129] The efforts of the convention were thwarted by the swift overrun of the colony by the British military.[130,131]

The Colony of Virginia's use of conventions in the months just before the outbreak of the Revolution and in its initial days is a perfect example of the deployment of the different types of conventions. Virginia had the foresight to see what was coming before the majority of the colonies and this helps to explain her leadership among the colonies. The pressure against the Crown began to rise in Virginia early on. As soon as 1763, Virginia began to agitate against the British government. Governor John Murray, Lord Dunmore, dissolved the Assembly in 1773 and ruled by decree after the House of Burgesses passed a resolution for establishing the "Inter-Colonial Committee of Correspondence."[132]

After Dunmore again dissolved the Assembly in 1774, the Burgesses called the first of what would be a total of five conventions between 1 August 1774 and 6 May 1776. The August 1774 convention and the March 1775

---

[126] Ibid., 63
[127] Pauline Maier, *American Scripture, Making the Declaration of Independence* (New York: Vintage Books, 1997), 14, 281
[128] Rhode Island, Massachusetts, Connecticut and New Hampshire.
[129] Agnes Hunt, *The Provincial Committees of Safety of the American Revolution* (Cleveland: Winn & Judson, 1904), 47 - republished contemporarily by the University of Michigan Libraries.
[130] William Read Staples, *Rhode Island in the Continental Congress, Council of War to President of Congress, 26 April 1779* (Providence, RI: Providence Press, 1870)
[131] Charles J. Hoadly, *The Public Records of the State of Connecticut, From October 1776 to February 1778, Inclusive* (Hartford, CT: Case, Lockwood & Brainard, 1894), 585
[132] Wayland F. Dunaway, Jr., "The Virginia Conventions of the Revolution," *Virginia Law Register* 10, no.7 (Nov.1904): 567-9

convention were typical deliberative conventions issuing proclamations and resolutions. The second convention was more forceful than the first, resolving – unanimously, after strenuous debate – to arm Virginia and prepare for war.[133] It was during the second convention in Richmond that Patrick Henry delivered his famously inspiring "Liberty or Death" speech. The third convention went a step farther than the previous conventions and began issuing ordnances – that is, they acted legislatively and made actual *laws*. With the collapse of Dunmore's government and his fleeing the capital at Williamsburg, a void existed and the convention created and appointed a Committee of Safety to govern in Dunmore's stead.[134] The fourth convention convened in December of 1775 and took on all the aspects of a government, including actively waging war.[135] The fifth and final convention met in May of 1776. The foremost act was to decide that independence was necessary and to urge the rest of the colonies to reach the same conclusion. On May 15, Virginia, acting through the convention, declared itself independent, seven weeks before the Second Continental Congress did the same for the colonies as a whole. Then it proceeded to form a permanent government and draft a state constitution. The five conventions moved through the spectrum from a spontaneous, unauthorized convention to a revolutionary convention to a plenary constitutional convention and when it formed a government, it became a legislative convention.[136]

The transition by Virginia from a colony to a self-governing state was predicted by Dunmore himself. In 1775, he wrote to the secretary of state in London with concern about the conventions taking place in the colony. He foresaw that the March 1775 convention had the opportunity to become the de facto government in Virginia. The planning and execution of the Virginians had been carried out in the open and the public went along leaving Dunmore and the royal government out-maneuvered.[137]

On 10 May 1776, less than two months prior to the Declaration of Independence's issuance, the Continental Congress voted to issue a

---

[133] Ibid., 570-7

[134] For a thorough analysis of how the Virginia Committees of Safety operated, see generally, Larry Bowman, "The Virginia County Committees of Safety, 1774-1776," *Virginia Magazine of History and Biography* 79, no.3 (Jul. 1971)

[135] Wayland F. Dunaway, Jr., "The Virginia Conventions of the Revolution," *Virginia Law Register* 10, no.7 (Nov.1904): 579-80

[136] Ibid., 581-5

[137] Willi Paul Adams, *The First American Constitutions, Republican Ideology and the Making of the State Constitutions in the Revolutionary Era* (Lanham, MD: Rowman & Littlefield, 2001), 27

resolution which it promulgated on the 15th to the colonies and ended with,

> *"Resolved, That it be recommended to the several Assemblies and Conventions of the united colonies, where no government, sufficient to the exigencies of their affairs, hath been hitherto established, to adopt such government as shall, in the opinion of the representatives of the people, best conduce to the happiness and safety of their constituents in particular, and America in general."*[138]

The phrasing of the just-over-the-horizon Declaration of Independence is hinted at in this resolution. It cannot be emphasized enough that the colonists participating in the conventions and committees ardently believed that they were acting in the most constitutional of manners. The Congress claimed that its actions were in concert with the English constitution and taken to protect the constitutional rights of Englishmen in North America.[139] Congress pointed to the actions of their English forefathers at Runnymede, at the conventions in the seventeenth century and, as always, stated that the actions were taken in hopes of a reconciliation.[140,141] The role of conventions in our early history as precursors to our legislatures, state and federal, is of greater importance than we are usually taught. They have been the glue that has bound the permanent and more settled periods of our history together at the cracks which mark our sometimes violent, transitional periods. We can see some of the future structure of American government coming into view in the late colonial period. Americans had come to expect a significant degree of self-administration and along with that benefit they had developed an equally significant degree of distrust in standing governmental institutions as entrenchments of cronyism and privilege. Special conventions provided a manner of control for the non-aristocratic segment of society. Changes to government were best worked

---

[138] *Journal of the Continental Congress, Vol. II*, 158, 166 as quoted by Jameson, §128, 116

[139] The argument over whether the colonists enjoyed British constitutional rights was new at the time of the Revolution. Concurrent to the establishment of the first English colonies, the London Company charter, drafted in 1606, for Virginia, stated "that each and every the persons being our subjects, which shall dwell and inhabit within every and any of the said colonies and plantations, and every of their children which happen to be born in any of the limits and precincts of the several colonies and plantations, shall have and enjoy all Liberties, Franchises, and Immunities within any of our other dominions as if they had been abiding and born, within this our Realm of England." – William C. Morey, "The Genesis of a Written Constitution," *The Annals of the American Academy of Political and Social Science* 1 (Apr. 1891): 532, 538

[140] Willi Paul Adams, *The First American Constitutions, Republican Ideology and the Making of the State Constitutions in the Revolutionary Era* (Lanham, MD: Rowman & Littlefield, 2001), 57-8

[141] G. Alan Tarr, *Understanding State Constitutions* (Princeton: Princeton University Press, 1998), 61

out in conventions and then submitted to the people for ratification.[142] These earliest of state constitutional conventions varied in structure and how they interacted with the Continental Congress, if at all. Some evidence exists of the state conventions reporting on their progress to Congress.[143]

Massachusetts is most often given the credit for developing the constitutional convention and the subsequent ratification convention process. More specifically, the honor goes to Concord in October 1776. They had pointed out that the legislature that has the power to change a constitution which it had itself created does not protect the individual from the arbitrary acts of the legislature. The Massachusetts General Court had sought the permission of the people to draft a new state constitution. Concord insisted that only the people could draft a constitution and in a town meeting the citizens of Concord voted unanimously that "the Present House of Representatives is not a proper Body to form a Constitution for this State."[144] In the town meeting resolves of 21 October 1776, the people demanded "a Convention, or Congress… to form and establish a Constitution." The council that reviewed the replies from the towns then advised the General Court to hold a constitutional convention. At the same time, the towns of Lexington and Pittsfield also demanded that the ratification of the proposed constitution then be done by a second convention.[145] The people had come to realize that the legislative and constitutional drafting powers were separate steps in the political process and should be treated as such, each with its own representative body. In Massachusetts, the distrust by the rural people of the governing bodies meeting in Boston led to the demand for the ratification conventions.[146] From this, the first true, modern constitutional convention – as we define it today, and that is supremely key – met in Cambridge to draft a state constitution for Massachusetts on 1 September 1779.[147]

The Development of the Amending Process

Perhaps one of the most important developments to come out of

---

[142] John R. Vile, "Three Kinds of Constitutional Founding and Change: The Convention Model and Its Alternatives," *Political Research Quarterly* 46, no.4 (Dec. 1993): 887
[143] David Lefer, *The Founding Conservatives* (New York: Sentinel, 2013), 115
[144] Robert A. Gross, *The Minutemen and Their World* (New York: Hill and Wang, 1976), 154
[145] Willi Paul Adams, *The First American Constitutions, Republican Ideology and the Making of the State Constitutions in the Revolutionary Era* (Lanham, MD: Rowman & Littlefield, 2001), 86-7
[146] Ibid., 62-3, 85-7
[147] Ibid., 89

the Massachusetts experiment with conventions is the necessity of the amendment process. The people fully recognized that the inability of amending the British Constitution by the colonists had contributed to the inevitability of the war. Historian Willi Paul Adams treats this topic in depth in his *The First American Constitutions*. He observes that the voters of Lexington rejected the 1778 state constitution because it did not provide for amendment by majority vote. The townspeople referred to the result of "Commotions, Mobs, Bloodshed and Civil War." Adams points to Roxbury and Essex County echoing Lexington.[148]

The earliest known charters or colonial constitutions that included a provision for amendment were those of the Pennsylvania colony. The Pennsylvania colonial charter, the *Frame of Government of Pennsylvania of 1682*, granted by William Penn, was the only one to initially provide for amendment in Article XXIII.[149] A Council of Censors was convened every seven years and they would decide if amendments to the Pennsylvania constitution were needed.[150] That charter was ratified by a special convention called for that specific purpose in 1683.[151] The Continental Congress had recommended to the state legislatures, following the issuance of the Declaration of Independence, that they produce new state constitutions early in the Revolutionary War to separate them from Great Britain. Initially, the first state constitutions contained no amendment provisions. Massachusetts created a new state constitution in 1780 that used the convention method of amendment.[152] When Pennsylvania adopted a new revolutionary state constitution in 1776, an amending provision employing the Council of Censors in convention was retained.[153] Vermont made the same allowance

---

[148] Ibid., 138-9

[149] The Frames of Government of 1683 and 1696 also included amendment provisions as did the 1701 *Charter of Delaware* that was also granted by William Penn.

[150] Abraham C. Weinfeld, "Power of Congress Over State Ratifying Conventions," *Harvard Law Review* 51, no.3 (1938): 485

[151] John Andrew Doyle, *English Colonies in America – The Puritan Colonies, Vol. II* (New York: Henry Holt, 1886), 505

[152] Massachusetts Constitution, Part II, Chapter VI, Article X, (1780)
"And if it shall appear, by the returns made, that two-thirds of the qualified voters throughout the State, who shall assemble and vote in consequence of the said precepts, are in favor of such revision of amendment, the general court shall issue precepts, or direct them to be issued from the secretary's office, to the several towns to elect delegates to meet in convention for the purpose aforesaid."

[153] Pennsylvania Constitution, §47, (1776)
"The said council of censors shall also have power to call a convention, to meet within too years after their sitting, if there appear to them an absolute necessity of amending any article of the constitution…"

in its constitution of 1786 for a regular meeting every seven years of a Council of Censors.[154,155,156] By 1787, eight of the states had constitutions that included amendment provisions.[157] Amending a constitution is then a very old and very American doctrine.[158]

It is useful to recognize that the amending process was a small but integral part of the impetus to revolution in the 1770s. In the wake of the repeated issuance of legislation from Parliament that incensed and inflamed the colonies, the American colonists had to conclude that they lacked any recourse to preserve their rights as "Englishmen." The traditional view of the colonists as Englishmen equivalent to their peers in the British Isles was a one-sided proposition.[159] London and Parliament didn't see it that way. The power to alter the unwritten British constitution was firmly and solely in the hands of Parliament. Professor Darren Patrick Guerra argues in his 2013 book, *Perfecting the Constitution*, that many Acts of Parliament constituted a deliberate "intent to tyrannize over the colonies and enslave America." A written constitution with an amending proviso was utterly essential to the provision and protection of liberty. Guerra states,

> "By the time political wrangling morphed into armed conflict many Americans believed that there were no longer any practical constitutional restraints on Parliament and no means of altering the constitution peaceably; thus leaving them no choice but to take up arms."[160]

The primitive, Revolutionary War era state constitutions with amending provisos were a mix of methodologies. Three states left the process to the state legislature; five gave the power to conventions composed of the people. Interestingly, nine of the twelve state constitutions in use during

---

[154] John Alexander Jameson, *A Treatise on Constitutional Conventions – Their History, Powers, and Modes of Proceeding* (New York: Scribner, 1867, 4th ed., 1887), §155, 141-2 - reprint by The Lawbook Exchange, (2013)

[155] The Vermont Council of Censors met every seven years through 1869.

[156] Vermont Constitution, Chapter II, §XL, (1786)

[157] Ralph R. Martig, "Amending the Constitution Article V: The Keystone of the Arch," *Michigan Law Review* 35, no.8 (1937): 1254

[158] Hugh Evander Willis, "The Doctrine of Amendability of the United States Constitution," *Indiana Law Journal* 7, no.8 (1932): 462

[159] The colonies began to reaffirm the unchanged, unwavering, uninterrupted constitutional rights as Englishmen as early as Maryland in 1639. Leonard Levy, *Origins of the Bill of Rights* (New Haven, CT: Yale University Press, 1999), 205

[160] Darren Patrick Guerra, *Perfecting the Constitution, The Case for the Article V Amendment Process* (Lanham, MD: Lexington Books, 2013), 31

the Revolution were adopted by conventions.[161,162] The types of amendment processes included, in addition to the convention and the state legislature, the mechanisms of councils, special elections and petitions.[163] By the late 1780s, the amendment method had become somewhat standardized. The legislative method was beginning to be shunned in favor of the convention method. Five states had "explicitly prohibited" legislative amendment of state constitutions.[164] Jameson stated that the reason many of the states did not make an amending provision was probably due to the temporary nature of those first state constitutions. Many states expected that peace would soon be restored and with it, the states would rejoin the British Empire.[165] Proof of this is found in the 1776 New Jersey state constitution wherein it states in closing that,

> "it is the true intent and meaning of this Congress, that if a reconciliation between Great-Britain and these Colonies should take place and the latter be taken again under the protection and government of the crown of Britain, this Charter shall be null and void – otherwise to remain firm and inviolable."[166]

South Carolina did the same in her 26 March 1776 state constitution that was to serve "till a reconciliation between the colonies and Great Britain should take place."[167] Even Congress itself was unsure of the course that history would take and cautioned the colonies about the permanence of the breach with Great Britain, telling Massachusetts to elect a new legislature which would "exercise the powers of Government, until a Governor, of his Majesty's appointment, will consent to govern the colony according to its charter."[168] The early delegate instructions to the Continental Congress

---

[161] John Alexander Jameson, *A Treatise on Constitutional Conventions, Their History, Powers, and Modes of Proceeding* (New York: Scribner, 1867, § 171, 4th ed., 1887), reprint by The Lawbook Exchange, (2013)

[162] Abraham C. Weinfeld, "Power of Congress Over State Ratifying Conventions," *Harvard Law Review* 51, no.3 (1938): 478

[163] Darren Patrick Guerra, *Perfecting the Constitution, The Case for the Article V Amendment Process* (Lanham, MD: Lexington Books, 2013), 53

[164] Marc W. Kruman, *Between Authority and Liberty* (Chapel Hill: University of North Carolina Press, 2006), 57 – Georgia, Massachusetts, New Hampshire, Pennsylvania and Vermont.

[165] John Alexander Jameson, *A Treatise on Constitutional Conventions, Their History, Powers, and Modes of Proceeding* (New York: Scribner, 1867, 4th ed., 1887), §§ 548-9, and §527, 548 - reprint by The Lawbook Exchange, (2013)

[166] Benjamin Poore, *The Federal and State Constitutions* (Washington, D.C.: Government Printing Office, 2d ed., 1878), 1314

[167] John Alexander Jameson, *A Treatise on Constitutional Conventions – Their History, Powers, and Modes of Proceeding* (New York: Scribner, 1867, 4th ed., 1887), §133, 122 reprint by The Lawbook Exchange, (2013)

[168] Russell B. Caplan, *Constitutional Brinkmanship* (New York: Oxford University Press, 1988), 9

included admonitions to seek reconciliation and the colonial papers were full of stories and letters asking for the King to intervene and control his errant ministers.[169] Obviously, at least some of the colonists were hedging their bets and providing for a "Plan B." Their intent in the interim was to "secure civil order and foster independence."[170]

During the post-revolutionary period, most of the States replaced their original, hastily drafted, war-time state constitutions with better thought out, more well-constructed and more adaptable documents. The revolutionary constitutions had been tried and found wanting. South Carolina went first in October of 1776.[171] As an example, the experience of Georgia is instructive of how the States experimented with the convention process and the amendatory convention concept. The Georgia state constitution of 1777 was very explicit in the amendment process,

> *"No alteration shall be made in this constitution without petitions from a majority of the counties, and the petitions from each county to be signed by a majority of voters in each county within this State; at which time the assembly shall order a convention to be called for that purpose, specifying the alterations to be made, according to the petitions preferred to the assembly by the majority of the counties as aforesaid."*[172]

Note that the 1777 Georgia constitution required: 1) a convention for "alterations;" 2) the convention is specified to be "for that purpose;" and 3) limited to "specifying the alterations to be made." The Georgia constitution pre-dates Article V by a full decade but has the same features of a limited power amendatory convention very much in accordance with the definition of today. The Georgia convention was constrained from ratifying; it could only propose – much as our Article V amendatory convention operates today.

In November of 1788, Georgia held a convention and drafted a new state constitution. That constitution was to be proposed to another body for consideration of ratification. The second convention was held on 4 January 1789 and instead of ratification, upon examination, that convention proposed a series of amendments and alterations. It is coincidental that the First

---

[169] Pauline Maier, *American Scripture, Making the Declaration of Independence* (New York: Vintage Books, 1997), 7-9
[170] Marc W. Kruman, *Between Authority and Liberty* (Chapel Hill: University of North Carolina Press, 1997), 1
[171] Willi Paul Adams, *The First American Constitutions, Republican Ideology and the Making of the State Constitutions in the Revolutionary Era* (Lanham, MD: Rowman & Littlefield, 2001), 69
[172] Georgia Constitution, Article LXIII, (1777)

United States Congress, operating under the authority of the newly ratified United States Constitution, convened for the first time on that same exact day as the first state amendatory convention was itself convening. Finally, a third convention was called in May 1789 for the consideration of the original proposed constitution, the amendments and alterations from the second convention and lastly, the ratification of the results. The culmination of this tri-partite convention process was the second state constitution of Georgia. Georgia repeated the amendatory convention in 1795, 1833 and 1839.[173]

Post-Revolutionary American Conventions

So important and well-established had conventions become, that by 1800, Congress was requiring new states to hold an elected convention to draft their proposed state constitution as a requirement for statehood. Each of these proposed state constitutions had to have provisions for amendment. By the mid-to-late nineteenth century, the convention requirement was extended to include ratification of the state constitution as well.[174] Additionally, in some instances the States would convene a second convention after Congress had studied the proposed state constitution and made recommendations for changes as a condition of statehood. Some states called new conventions; others simply reconvened their previous drafting conventions with the same slate of delegates.[175] The petitioning states' conventions then transformed from a drafting constitutional convention to an amendatory convention in order to incorporate the changes desired and/or required by Congress.

The process of holding a state constitutional convention and perhaps a ratification convention was not immediately perfected. The first state to successfully join the union after the original thirteen and Vermont (which is really a Revolutionary Era state) was Kentucky. She provided the experiment for developing not only the process for the admission of new states, and the development of a state constitution, but also the model for

---

[173] John Alexander Jameson, *A Treatise on Constitutional Conventions – Their History, Powers, and Modes of Proceeding* (New York: Scribner, 1867, 4th ed., 1887), §148, 135-6 and §382, 369 - reprint by The Lawbook Exchange, (2013).

[174] Wilbur Edel, *A Constitutional Convention – Threat or Challenge?* (New York: Praeger1981), 8-9

[175] John Alexander Jameson, *A Treatise on Constitutional Conventions – Their History, Powers, and Modes of Proceeding* (New York: Scribner, 1867, 4th ed., 1887), §167, 153-4 - reprint by The Lawbook Exchange, (2013)

separating a piece of one state to form a new state.[176] Kentucky held a total of eleven conventions between 1784[177] and 1792[178] to measure the will of the people to separate and finally to draft their own state constitution.[179,180] The unusually large number of conventions in Kentucky can be attributed to the negotiation that had to take place between Kentucky and parent state Virginia.[181] Without the provision for separation of part of the one state to form a new state that would be included in the Constitution in 1787, the process was undefined.[182] In one known incident of frontier settlers unilaterally seeking autonomy, the people of the self-designated "State of Franklin,"[183] also found as Frankland, arranged in what was then western North Carolina and what is now northeast Tennessee, called four conventions. The first, for the discussion of whether the settlers should seek their own state, on 23 August 1784 in Jonesborough,[184] and the second, for drafting a proposed state constitution on 14 December 1784, held again in Jonesborough.[185] A third constitutional convention was held on 14 November 1785 in Greenville.[186] Finally, Franklin completed the process by holding a ratification convention at Greenville in May of 1787 – at which amendments were proposed and made.[187] With the Revolution now completed, the people of the "Commonwealth of Franklin" or the "Free State

---

[176] George L. Willis, Sr., "History Kentucky Constitutions and Constitutional Conventions," *Register of the Kentucky State Historical Society* 28, no.85 (Oct. 1930), generally

[177] Frederick Jackson Turner, "Western State-Making in the Revolutionary Era II," *American Historical Review* 1, no.2 (Jan. 1896): 263

[178] 7/8 November 1784, 27 December 1784, 23 May 1785, 8 August 1785, 25 September 1786, 17 September 1787, 28 July 1788, 3 November 1788, 20 July 1789, 26 July 1790 and 2/19 April 1792.

[179] John Alexander Jameson, *A Treatise on Constitutional Conventions – Their History, Powers, and Modes of Proceeding* (New York: Scribner, 1867, 4th ed., 1887), §§173-4, 158-9 - reprint by The Lawbook Exchange, (2013)

[180] Kentucky in no way holds the record after taking eight years to separate from Virginia and become a state – that is, eight years between first and final conventions. The District of Maine took nearly 35 years to separate from the State of Massachusetts and achieve statehood between initial and final conventions. West Virginia took even longer with its first rumblings toward statehood occurring before the Revolution and eventual statehood having been finally achieved in 1863.

[181] Pauline Maier, *Ratification, The People Debate the Constitution, 1787-1788* (New York: Simon & Schuster, 2010), 239

[182] Article IV, §3

[183] Edwin R. Keedy, "The Constitutions of the State of Franklin, the Indian Stream Republic and the State of Deseret," *University of Pennsylvania Law Review* 101 (1953): 516-21

[184] Frederick Jackson Turner, "Western State-Making in the Revolutionary Era II," *American Historical Review* 1, no.2 (Jan. 1896): 257-8

[185] Peverill Squire, *The Evolution of the American Legislatures, Colonies, Territories, and States, 1619-2009* (Ann Arbor: University of Michigan Press, 2014), 182

[186] Samuel Cole Williams, *History of the Lost State of Franklin* (New York: Press of the Pioneers, 1933), Chapter XIII

[187] Ibid., Chapter XX

of Franklin"[188] were seeking to be recognized as a state alongside the thirteen other states in existence.[189] The state constitutional convention process was now becoming firmly established. But even the "Frankliners" were not the first attempted state to follow the process and seek admission to the state club. Nearly a decade prior in 1775, the settlers in the Monongahela River valley formed a committee of correspondence and unsuccessfully asked the Continental Congress to acknowledge them as the state of "Westsylvania." While Congress did not take up action on their plea, due to the more pressing matter of the Revolution, the foundation was set for the eventual formation, nearly a century later, of the state of West Virginia.[190] Prior to the Westsylvania project, an attempt to organize the area had been made under the name of "Vandalia."[191]

The process that took place over the Allegheny Mountains was reminiscent of that of the earliest colonists. The small populations, long distances between settlements, lack of existing political structure provided by the governing colony, lack of a legal system and the ever present threat of fighting led the settlers to form local governments as soon as possible. The methodology resembled the New England form of calling together the leading members of the electorate and composing more of a compact than a constitution although this too was done. Historian Frederick Jackson Turner studied the frontier in detail. In the period immediately preceding the American Revolution, settlers have moved into the trans-mountain frontier from Georgia to upper New York. Turner noted the proliferation of "claim associations" that wrote "articles for their conduct" and "found it necessary to 'associate' in written agreements for the purpose of 'regulating' the horse thieves by summary methods in the absence of efficient courts, or of resisting fees of colonial officers when they deemed them illegal or extortionate."[192]

These governments, if they may be called as such, were all intended to

---

[188] David S. Shields, "'We declare you independent whether you wish it or not': The Print Culture of Early Filibusterism," paper delivered at the 24th Annual James Russel Wiggins Lecture in the History of the American Culture, 16 June 2006, *American Antiquarian Society*, 257

[189] Walter Fairleigh Dodd, *The Revision and Amendment of State Constitutions* (Baltimore: Johns Hopkins Press, 1910), 21

[190] Willi Paul Adams, *The First American Constitutions, Republican Ideology and the Making of the State Constitutions in the Revolutionary Era* (Lanham, MD: Rowman & Littlefield, 2001), 91-2

[191] Frederick Jackson Turner, "Western State-Making in the Revolutionary Era II," *American Historical Review* 1, no.2 (Jan. 1896): 265

[192] Frederick Jackson Turner, "Western State-Making in the Revolutionary Era," *American Historical Review* 1, no.1 (Oct. 1895): 76

be temporary until the colony, and later the state, could extend its protection over the settlers. As an example, the Watauga Association of North Carolina directly and formerly petitioned the North Carolina Provincial Council to extend government to the region in 1776, after establishing their Articles. The Cumberland Association held a convention of delegates on 13 May 1780 to create a compact for governance. The Clarksville settlement held a convention on 27 January 1785 that sought "to make laws not repugnant to the Constitution of the United States, or to the resolves of Congress." In perhaps one of the more famous experiments in frontier self-governance, Daniel Boone's settlers in Powell's Valley in eastern Tennessee took part in the establishment of the Transylvania Company. They convened outdoors on 23 May 1775 drafting laws and a working compact.[193]

Other examples of failed states, territories and countries that did not survive but produced constitutions by the convention method include the Republic of West Florida,[194] the Republic of East Florida, the Republic of Indian Stream,[195] the Republic of the Rio Grande, and the Confederate States of America, and the proposed states of Sequoyah, Jefferson (there were at least four by that name), Lincoln (at least two), Deseret[196,197] and Superior. These details of the dates and locations for these conventions are found in Appendix B.

The experience of the Floridas provides a look at early American expansionism and the use of conventions in that effort. West Florida in the early 1800s was composed of that territory east of New Orleans extending, depending on the year and which nation was in control of the area, to the Perdido River under France, and to the Apalachicola River under Spain. East Florida lay in the present day State of Florida and in the early 1800s was under Spanish control. The tug of war over the territories was not limited to France, Spain and the United States; Great Britain was also attempting

---

[193] Ibid., 76-9

[194] David S. Shields, "'We declare you independent whether you wish it or not': The Print Culture of Early Filibusterism," paper delivered at the 24th Annual James Russel Wiggins Lecture in the History of the American Culture, 16 June 2006, *American Antiquarian Society*, 237

[195] Edwin R. Keedy, "The Constitutions of the State of Franklin, the Indian Stream Republic and the State of Deseret," *University of Pennsylvania Law Review* 101 (1953): 521-5

[196] Ibid., 526-8

[197] Deseret provides an interesting historical aside in the form of a "faked" constitutional convention. In the rush to achieve statehood, the leaders of Deseret more or less copied the Iowa state constitution, drafting fake convention and legislative proceedings, along with fake election results and sent them to Washington, D.C. to impress Congress!

to exert influence and control over the Gulf Coast region as well.[198] The situation came to head in West Florida in 1810 while Madison was president. Spain was losing its grip on West Florida; the United States claimed it as part of the Louisiana Purchase; France and Great Britain each saw it as theirs to occupy. In June of 1810, Madison came up with the idea of having William Claiborne, the governor of the Orleans Territory, suggest to the 80% of the West Florida population that was American, to hold a convention in which they would resolve to "request" that the United States occupy and then assimilate West Florida. In this way, he could forego sending in American troops and avoid provoking a war with France, Great Britain or both.[199] But the West Floridians went a step further and held a constitutional convention in St. Francisville (now in Louisiana) between 22 September and 28 October 1810 and declared the Republic of West Florida. Madison responded by sending troops and deposed the Republic of West Florida. Madison then upped the ante and secured passage of a law that gave him permission to also seize East Florida. Madison acted by executive order and sent the "Patriot Army" assembled from Georgia settlers and attempted to seize East Florida. The Patriot Army held its own constitutional convention in March of 1812 in Fernandina and announced the constitution and Republic of East Florida.[200,201] Its life was brief.

In one of the most interesting and thought provoking books on state constitutional conventions, David M. Gold lays out in *The Great Tea Party in the Old Northwest* a theory of state constitution making that links to the modern, twenty-first-century Tea Party Movement. He describes the frustration and anger of the common American in the early 1840s with the state governments' disastrous experiment with financing corporations for canals, turnpikes, railroads and other speculation that did not pay off. The increasing tax burden is theorized to have contributed to the Panic of 1837 which led to a grassroots movement to rewrite state constitutions as a means to prevent such public fiscal irresponsibility. In 1837 alone, nine states defaulted on their debt.[202] While Gold focuses on the states formed in the upper Midwest of the old Northwest Territory, he uses examples of rewritten

---

[198] Ralph Ketcham, *James Madison, A Biography* (Charlottesville, VA: University of Virginia Press, 1990), 422-424
[199] Ibid., 500-502
[200] Office of the State Historian, State Archives of Florida
[201] Ralph Ketcham, *James Madison, A Biography* (Charlottesville, VA: University of Virginia Press, 1990), 500-502
[202] G. Alan Tarr, *Understanding State Constitutions* (Princeton: Princeton University Press, 1998), 111-2

constitutions of other states as well making a case for limiting the "enormous public debt" brought on by government financing of "internal improvements." Then, as now, the grassroots were clamoring for greater accountability in public officials. The people saw that the path led through state constitutional conventions, as organic law was more difficult to undo than statutory law.[203] It is not difficult to see how the experiences of the Midwesterners in the late 1840s and early 1850s with constitutional conventions as a method of reforming society could have inspired the later flurry of post-Civil War state constitutional conventions.

The state constitutional convention process got a workout in the 1860s, mostly in the southern states. Prior to the commencement of the Civil War nineteen states had joined the original thirteen and Vermont for a total of thirty-three states, all employing the process laid out by Kentucky. But then history took a twist. With the Civil War looming, the southern states conducted first, secession conventions, most often without first appealing to the voters for permission to call a convention,[204] then constitution drafting conventions for new Confederate state constitutions, and in some cases, ratification conventions. While these secessionary conventions were occurring early in the war in 1861-62, Union troops occupied some states or parts of states and the Lincoln administration encouraged competing pro-Union conventions for side-by-side governments reminiscent of the Rhode Island debacle just two decades earlier. Though the example of West Virginia and the Wheeling Conventions that angled for statehood is famous, there are many other conventions which have gone unnoticed. East Tennessee Unionists sought to take the same road as West Virginia and separate to form a new state – almost within the same boundaries as the failed state of Franklin nearly a century earlier. Three conventions were held to debate and plan separation in Knoxville on 30-31 May 1861; in Greeneville on 17-20 June 1861; and in Knoxville again on 15-16 April 1864.[205] The Confederates successfully suppressed the Unionists' effort but the region remained a thorn in the Confederacy's side for the duration of the Civil War.[206] Following

---

[203] David M. Gold, *The Great Tea Party in the Old Northwest, State Constitutional Conventions, 1847-1851* (New Orleans: Quid Pro Books, 2015), 13-5

[204] Jameson noted that only Tennessee and North Carolina submitted the question to the voters and in both states, the measure did NOT pass. Jameson, 244

[205] Oliver Perry Temple, *East Tennessee and the Civil War* (Cincinnati: Robert Clarke Company, 1899), 340-65

[206] Charles F. Bryan, "A Gathering of Tories: The East Tennessee Convention of 1861," *Tennessee Historical Quarterly* 39, no. 1 (Spring 1980): 27-48

the conclusion of the war, the bitter feelings remained and several counties in western Kentucky and Tennessee and in northern Mississippi held an unsuccessful convention on 29-30 May 1873 in Jackson, Mississippi to plan and promote the secession of those parts and the establishment of a proposed State of Jackson.[207]

When the war concluded, the southern states started the cycle over and produced new, Reconstruction state constitutions through conventions.[208] As an historical aside, the one time that a President was involved in the Article V process was during the Reconstruction period when Andrew Johnson used his power as commander-in-chief of the military to order, by presidential proclamation, the calling of constitutional conventions in the formerly Confederate southern states.

The State of Georgia is typical of the post-war experience. Georgia held a secession convention from 16 January to 23 March 1861, then, she held a Reconstruction convention during Presidential Reconstruction in October of 1865. Because Georgia surrendered so late after the war, the dominant Radical Republicans in Congress deemed that she did not qualify for the terms of President Abraham Lincoln's and President Andrew Johnson's reconstruction plan and was forced to hold a second Reconstruction convention in December of 1867 under Congressional Reconstruction with more punitive terms.[209] After all that drama, over the next two decades the southern states then repeated the constitutional convention process and enacted "Redemption" state constitutions that re-established as much of the ante-bellum social and political structure as the federal government would tolerate.[210] Georgia held its Redemption convention in July of 1877.

Mississippi took a similar path. Provisional Governor William Sharkey called the first of the reconstruction state constitutional conventions to be held in August 1865. The existing 1817 state constitution was amended to end slavery in this convention. Because the Mississippi state legislature

---

[207] *The Weekly-Intelligencer*, "The Proposed Creation of the New State of Jackson," (Paris, Tennessee), 7 August 1873, and *The Whig-Tribune*, "The Convention and Its Work," (Jackson, Tennessee), 7 August 1873,

[208] Kermit Hall, Harold Hyman, Leon Sigal, *The Constitutional Convention as an Amending Device* (Washington, D.C.: American Historical Association and American Political Science Association, 1981), vii

[209] George Justice, "Reconstruction Conventions," *New Georgia Encyclopedia*, (17 Dec. 2013), accessed 3 June 2015

[210] Morton Keller, *The Constitutional Convention as an Amending Device* (Washington, D.C.: American Historical Association and American Political Science Association, 1981), 73

refused to ratify the Thirteenth and Fourteenth Amendments, Congress put Mississippi under the Fourth Military District and a new constitutional convention was called for 1868 by the commanding general. This second convention was a "Black and Tan Convention," so-called derogatorily because of the mix of Negro and Caucasian delegates. Some were termed by the media of the day by the equally derisive "Bones and Banjo Conventions."[211] The proposed new state constitution produced was rejected by the state's voters. President Ulysses Grant intervened and ordered the proposed state constitution resubmitted to the electorate and on the second try it was adopted which allowed Mississippi to be readmitted to the Union. What followed was an extended period of bitter political acrimony that did not cease until the state called a redeemer constitutional convention and adopted a new state constitution in 1890.[212] The tactics developed in the Mississippi redeemer convention were adopted by other former slave states and dubbed the "Second Mississippi Plan."[213]

Looked at differently, the reconstruction process had actually started earlier than usually defined and took on the structure of a feedback loop. In the first round of conventions, the seceding states reconstructed their state government to be out from under the United States federal constitution and eventually took their place under the Confederate States confederal constitution. These secessionary conventions varied in form. Some simply passed a secession ordinance or statute. Other states wrote new state constitutions in addition to passing the secession bill. Still other states merely amended their state constitution and passed their secession bill. These processes made the secessionary conventions part legislative convention, part constitutional convention or part amendatory convention. Then in the second round of conventions, when the war began to wind down, these same states then reconstructed their governments to be under the federal constitution again during Presidential Reconstruction. The states were required to revoke or repeal their secession ordinances or statutes or state constitutional amendments. These actions made the Restoration conventions of 1864-65 legislative, or constitutional, or amendatory depending on the

---

[211] Robert F. Williams, *The Law of American State Constitutions* (New York: Oxford University Press, 2009), 91

[212] The Works Progress Administration and Robert S. McElvaine, *Mississippi: The WPA Guide to the Magnolia State* (New York: Viking Press 1938), republished by the University of Mississippi Press, Jackson, Mississippi, (1988), 73

[213] Eric Biber, "The Price of Admission: Causes, Effects, and Patterns of Conditions Imposed on States Entering the Union," *American Journal of Legal History* XLVI (2004): 189

prior action of the state's previous 1861 convention. The conventions were also required to repudiate Confederate debts, abolish slavery and disavow secession.[214] These restoration conventions produced minor changes to the ante-bellum state constitutions.[215] In the third group of conventions, the Reconstruction conventions held in 1867-68, some of the states had not met the requirements of Congress when, with congressional disapproval of President Johnson's policy, Congress took over the management of Reconstruction and launched the period of Congressional, or Radical, Reconstruction. Congress placed the states under military control in accordance with the Reconstruction Acts. The states were required to conduct a third set of conventions for further reconstruction that would assure black suffrage, and demonstrate acceptance of and compliance with the Thirteenth and Fourteenth Amendments. In the fourth series of conventions, with the end of Congressional Reconstruction, they once again reconstructed to be, in a manner of speaking, out from under the federal constitution again – but in a limited fashion – with the redeemer, or Redemption convention state constitutions.[216] This Bourbon Era (1877-90) set of conventions sought to re-establish, as much as possible, and in the face of the Fifteenth Amendment's passage, the ante-bellum social relations by tying the blacks to the land through sharecropping and the enforcement of the Black Codes and passage of Jim Crow laws by the restored Democrat Party majorities.[217] All of this reconstruction was done under the aegis of constitutional conventions. Of course, Judge Jameson considered all of these reconstruction conventions to be constitutionally *extra legem* and he called them "irregular and illegitimate."[218] He was writing as these events unfolded and these conventions probably had the impact of causing him to periodically revise his treatise. Finally, in the fifth set of conventions, a new type of convention was held during the Straight-Out Era (1890-1915) that made no bones about the intent of the southern states to disenfranchise their black voters.[219] The other major aim of these conventions was the introduction of

---

[214] Eric Foner, *A Short History of Reconstruction, 1863-1877* (New York: Harper & Row, 1990), 90

[215] Joseph A. Ranney, *In the Wake of Slavery, Civil War, Civil Rights, and the Reconstruction of Southern Law* (Westport, CT: Praeger, 2006), 6

[216] Eric Foner, *A Short History of Reconstruction, 1863-1877* (New York: Harper & Row, 1990), 248

[217] Joseph A. Ranney, *In the Wake of Slavery, Civil War, Civil Rights, and the Reconstruction of Southern Law* (Westport, CT: Praeger, 2006), 8-9

[218] John Alexander Jameson, *A Treatise on Constitutional Conventions – Their History, Powers, and Modes of Proceeding* (New York: Scribner, 1867, 4th ed., 1887), §258, 254 - reprint by The Lawbook Exchange, (2013)

[219] Joseph A. Ranney, *In the Wake of Slavery, Civil War, Civil Rights, and the Reconstruction of Southern Law* (Westport, CT: Praeger, 2006), 9-11

institutionalized segregation.[220]

Thus, the southern states went through a process of secession, restoration, reconstruction, redemption and disenfranchisement conventions.[221] The frequency of the conventions is indicative of the shifts in political power. Democrats held power in every southern state in 1861; every governorship, every statehouse chamber, every state supreme court. By 1864-65, Republicans held sway. In 1867-68, the Radical Republicans had overtaken the party and imposed their view of a more retributive reconstruction. By 1877-90, with the end of Reconstruction, the Democrats were back in power and asserting their vision of the South once again. The hybridization of the early secession and restoration conventions may be due to the sense of a need to hurry in the volatile political climate of the early 1860s. Every constitutional convention is an exercise in reconstruction. Sometimes it is a convention for the reaffirmation of our fundamental and revolutionary principles; other times it is for a peaceful revolution of those principles to maintain the organic law with the times; and still other times, as in the post-Civil War half century, it is for a mob-driven, greed-based, self-centered revolution against our founding principles.

There is one last type of convention experience that the States have undertaken that deserves mention before moving on to the amendatory convention. The authorized convention has remained a persistent but irregular tool of the people. Reserved for those instances when government has refused to hear the complaints of the public, this tool has been employed to bring a voice of popular warning to the government. It is used neither for organizing government nor changing government, but for making government aware of the complaints of the people and for remonstrance. It is similar to the purpose of the Roman *contio*. A perfect example of this is the 1871 Tax-Payers' Convention held in the Texas Capitol at Austin. Republicans and Democrats fed up with the taxation policy of Governor Edmund Davis called for the election of delegates statewide. They met in September and the delegates included former governors, senators and other political leaders who emphasized that the convention was non-partisan. The convention formed the requisite committees to study the problems and issue

---

[220] Michael Perman, *The Road to Redemption, Southern Politics, 1869-1879* (Chapel Hill: University of North Carolina Press, 1984), 181-2

[221] As an example of a detailed study of the process, see Wayne Flynt, "Alabama's Shame: The Historical Origins of the 1901 Constitution," *Alabama Law Review* 53, no.1 (2001)

a report and recommendations. According to the Texas State Historical Association,

> "This group concluded that Davis had imposed a despotic government upon the state and catalogued twenty-one incidents it believed illustrated the governor's illegal behavior. Among the incidents cited by the subcommittee were the governor's school law and school tax, a law prohibiting the carrying of arms, the use of the state police in elections, and a redistricting of the state's legislative districts. A second report from the subcommittees on taxes and statistics, chaired by Christopher C. Upson, investigated charges that Davis and the legislature had wasted taxpayers' money and imposed excessive taxes on the state. The committee reported that taxes had risen between 1866 and 1871 from $956,850 to $2,120,605 and that possible railroad subsidies might increase the latter figure by $14 million."[222]

The people of Texas followed the recommendations of the convention and refused to pay the taxes or to support the Davis administration. Despite the explicit approval of the Texas Supreme Court for Davis' actions, the public ignored the Court's edicts and pressed on with overt civil disobedience. Davis earned the stain of corruption and his support evaporated. The Grant administration refused to lend its aid. The convention's effort was successful and effectively ended the Davis administration.[223]

These Taxpayers' Conventions were widespread across the post-Civil War south – partly because they provided a means of rebelling against the Reconstruction governments, and partly because they were a backlash against the excessive taxing and spending of the southern state governments. The convention delegates also complained about the corruption, extravagance and the expansion of government – state and federal. Northerners sympathized with the Taxpayer conventioneers because they were paying off their own state government debt incurred during the prosecution of the war.[224]

South Carolina, Texas, Louisiana and Mississippi held the most virulent taxpayer conventions.[225] But in the north, New York Gov. Samuel

---

[222] Carl H. Moneyhon, "TAX-PAYERS' CONVENTION," *Handbook of Texas Online* (http://www.tshaonline.org/handbook/online/articles/vft01), accessed 6 June 2015
[223] Ibid.
[224] Eric Foner, *A Short History of Reconstruction, 1863-1877* (New York: Harper & Row, 1990), 181-182
[225] Columbia, South Carolina hosted taxpayer conventions on 9-12 May 1871 and 17-20 February 1874. Jackson, Mississippi saw conventions on 2 August 1874 and in 4 January and August of 1875 and Greenville held one in November 1873. Baltimore saw a taxpayer convention on 12 August 1879.

Tilden rode his leadership of the New York City Taxpayers' convention to the Democrat Party presidential nomination in 1876. Some of the claims of the conventions were unrealistic; in South Carolina the conventioneers professed that they would pay off the state's debt.[226] The conventions also had the issue of an alleged association with the Ku Klux Klan with which to contend.[227] The connection between the grassroots taxpayer conventions and the state constitutional conventions is that these same taxpayer conventioneers were the people that pressed for the Redemption conventions just two or three years later after the Democrats returned to power.

Almost a century prior to Texas' Taxpayer Convention, the State of Connecticut experienced a series of four extralegal "general conventions" in Middletown.[228] Between September 1783 and April 1784, the people of approximately fifty of the towns convened to vent their disgust with the Confederation Congress for proposing a plan to commute the pensions of Continental Army officers. The Congress had the idea of giving five years' pay all at once in lieu of half-pay for life.[229,230] With the pressing economic downturn bearing on the people, the notion of handing over a pension before its time irritated the general public. The issue of increasing the power of government also was a common theme. The "Commutation Conventions" had the result of leading to the formation of political parties in Connecticut, particularly the Democratic-Republican Party composed of the small government Anti-federalists.[231] The result of the "convention movement" was not successful as they quickly turned unpopular and lost the support of the people.

Lastly, we have the States' experience with amendatory conventions to consider. Jameson listed a number of examples of additional post-ratification, state amending conventions: New York in 1801 and 1867, California in 1878, Massachusetts in 1820, 1853 and 1917-1919, North Carolina

---

[226] Michael Perman, *The Road to Redemption, Southern Politics, 1869-1879* (Chapel Hill: University of North Carolina Press, 1984), 215-6

[227] W. Scott Poole, *Never Surrender: Confederate Memory and Conservatism in the South Carolina Upcountry* (Athens: University of Georgia Press, 2004), 77-9

[228] Pauline Maier, *Ratification, The People Debate the Constitution, 1787-1788* (New York: Simon & Schuster, 2010), 129

[229] John Clark Ridpath, *The New Complete History of the United States of America* (Chicago: Elliot, Madison, 1912), 3217-8

[230] James Hammond Trumbull, *Historical Notes on the Constitutions of Connecticut, 1639-1818* (Hartford, CT: Hartford Press, 1901), 19-20

[231] Christopher Grasso, *A Speaking Aristocracy: Public Discourse in Eighteenth Century Connecticut* (Chapel Hill: University of North Carolina Press, 1999), 423-8

in 1835 and 1875, Pennsylvania in 1837 and 1872-73, to list just a few. Appendix B lists all known constitutional conventions that have occurred within the boundaries of the present United States. The compilation includes constitution drafting conventions, amendatory, ratificatory, secessionary, reconstruction and legislative constitutional conventions. When the territories, federal ratification and drafting conventions and the conventions of failed provisional states and other countries that existed at one time or another within the United States borders are counted, the number of constitutional conventions is close to 400 with over eighty strictly amendatory conventions held to date. It is clear that the idea of a *limited* power state constitutional convention for the *expressed* purpose of proposing, debating and referring amendments only is as old as the federal Constitution itself. It is, according to Professor Robert F. Williams, a deliberate invention of the States and in some cases, the state constitution has a provision for the calling of a limited agenda convention. He cites as examples, Kansas, North Carolina and Tennessee.[232] What distinguishes these amendatory conventions from their constitution drafting relatives have been the very explicit restrictions as to powers, topics for consideration and methodology of application.[233] The limited power amending convention was not just an early-Republic idea; it persists today. The difficulty of securing state constitutional amendments legislatively has been circumvented by the amendatory convention process. As a singular example, Professor John Dinan studied state constitutional conventions and points to Tennessee holding five limited conventions in the latter half of the twentieth century.[234] From these examples, we can conclude that an amendatory convention is not only permissibly restricted, but is wisely restricted. One of the pre-eminent complaints of our time is that an amendatory convention is unlimited in power, and therefore, the delegates can do anything, including scrapping the Bill of Rights. It is worthwhile to mention that Jameson documented the restrictions that state legislatures placed on state amendatory conventions. Among these restrictions is a prohibition on any alteration of the state Bill

---

[232] Robert F. Williams, *The Law of American State Constitutions* (New York: Oxford University Press, 2009), 392-3 – interestingly, Alaska prohibits a limited convention: Article 13, §4.

[233] John Alexander Jameson, *A Treatise on Constitutional Conventions – Their History, Powers, and Modes of Proceeding* (New York: Scribner, 1867, 4th ed., 1887), §§382a-b, 371-5, reprint by The Lawbook Exchange, (2013)

[234] John J. Dinan, *The American State Constitutional Tradition* (Lawrence: University Press of Kansas, 2006), 11

of Rights.[235] And note that these restrictions were documented by Jameson in 1867!

Conventions were de rigueur for not only drafting and adopting state constitutions, but for about half the states, they were used for amending as well. Abraham Weinfeld laid out the details of the amending process of the early state constitutions in 1938. He showed that conventions were de rigueur for not only drafting and adopting state constitutions, but for about half the states, they were used for amending as well,

> *"As to amending the state constitutions, four of them, namely, those of New Jersey, New York, North Carolina, and Virginia contained no provision for amendment; three, namely, those Delaware, Maryland, and South Carolina provided for methods of amendment which did not involve conventions; and five, those of Georgia, Massachusetts, New Hampshire, Pennsylvania, and Vermont provided for amendment by conventions. In these five states where provision was made for amendment by conventions, the prevailing procedural pattern included (1) a method of proposing amendments, (2) elections of delegates to conventions by voters presumably familiar with the nature of the proposed changes, and (3) conventions, which either adopted or rejected the amendments. Subsequent ratification by the people was not required. This pattern prevailed in four out of the five states mentioned, the exception being New Hampshire, where the first formulation of the proposed amendments took place in a convention and subsequently the decisions of the convention were submitted to the people for ratification."*[236]

Natelson detailed at least ten interstate, or "federal" as they were often called at that time, conventions in addition to the Continental Congresses during the Revolutionary War Era. He pointed out that sometimes the conventions were termed "convention of States" and other times "convention of committees" depending on the composition of the delegations:

> *"The initial interstate convention of the Founding Era was the First Continental Congress (1774), which despite being denoted a 'Congress,' qualified as a convention and was understood to be one. There were at least ten other interstate conventions held after the Declaration of Independence*

---

[235] As an example, Jameson cites the 1872 convention act in Pennsylvania: John Alexander Jameson, *A Treatise on Constitutional Conventions – Their History, Powers, and Modes of Proceeding* (New York: Scribner, 1867, 4th ed., 1887), §382c, 376, reprint by The Lawbook Exchange, (2013)

[236] Republished with permission of the Harvard Law Review Association, from Abraham C. Weinfeld, "Power of Congress Over State Ratifying Conventions," *Harvard Law Review* 51, no.3 (1938): 479; permission conveyed through Copyright Clearance Center, Inc.

> and before the meeting of the Constitutional Convention in 1787: two in Providence, Rhode Island (1776-77 and 1781); one in Springfield, Massachusetts (1777); one in York, Pennsylvania (1777); one in New Haven, Connecticut (1778); two in Hartford, Connecticut (1779 and 1780); one in Philadelphia (1780), one in Boston (1780), and one in Annapolis (1786)."[237]

All of these conventions were limited in powers and none were plenary. They were tasked with deliberating and then making recommendations to the colonial and later state legislatures. This did not include the First Continental Congress of 1774 which was plenary in power. These early interstate conventions were handling such issues as currency, price stabilization, trade and shipping regulation, debt, defense and supplying war matériel. Not one of these conventions exceeded its mandate and "ran away."[238] These commercial conventions met often to the chagrin of the state and national governments.[239] They also proved to be a training ground for the newly involved generation of up-and-coming politicians. In fact, the accumulated convention experience of the Philadelphia delegates was prodigious; at least seventeen of the delegates had served in one or more prior intercolonial or interstate conventions.[240] Robert F. Williams notes that another early scholar estimated that "one-third to one-half of the members of the [Philadelphia] federal convention had been members of the conventions which framed the several state constitutions and a very large number of the members of the various ratifying conventions had also had a part in the formation of the respective state constitutions." Williams points out the overwhelmingly important fact that these members of the Philadelphia convention had the experience of shaping about twenty state constitutions prior to the 1787 convention.[241] Their accumulated knowledge of convention procedure and operations was unparalleled. At least forty-four

---

[237] Robert G. Natelson, "Proposing Constitutional Amendments by Convention: Rules Governing the Process," *Tennessee Law Review* 78 (2011): 707-8. The full text of this Article was published originally by the Tennessee Law Review Association, Inc. at 78 **Tenn. L. Rev.** 693 (2011), and this version, approved by the Author, appears by their permission.

[238] Ibid., 717-8

[239] Gordon S. Wood, *The Creation of the American Republic, 1776-1787* (Chapel Hill: University of North Carolina Press, 1969), 323-4. Published for the Omohundro Institute of Early American History and Culture.

[240] Robert G. Natelson, "Founding-Era Conventions and the Meaning of the Constitution's "Conventions For Proposing Amendments," *Florida Law Review* 65 (2013): 65

[241] Robert F. Williams, *The Law of American State Constitutions* (New York: Oxford University Press, 2009), 38-9 – citing W.C. Webster, "Comparative Study of the State Constitutions of the American Revolution," *Annals American Academy Politics & Social Science* 9 (1897): 417

of the fifty-five delegates had served in Congress.[242] It is ludicrous to think that they would include an amendment provision that could prove harmful, let alone prove fatal, to the Constitution bearing in mind the extensive body of convention procedural experience that they possessed. Had they believed that the process of operating an amendatory convention was so obscure or imperceptible, they would have obviously opted to include those details in the Constitution itself. The fact that the delegates did not do so makes clear their belief that it was simply not necessary to restate the obvious.

The colonists and early Americans were very familiar with the convention mechanism and its operation in the political process. Their knowledge and acceptance of conventions clearly contributed to the expansion of the American system of federalism. We can see a proclivity on the part of the States to employ conventions for many of the political processes that required public deliberation. The States used conventions for drafting charters, proposing amendments, ratifying charters and amendments, for working out trade agreements and resolving economic differences, for strategizing defense, for settling border disputes, for really just about anything that involved two or more states. The occurrence of a convention on the moving frontier indicated that a milestone had been reached in that location where a certain level of self-government has been reached. It is difficult to imagine that the Framers would have held the same fears of an amendatory convention that we have seen develop over the last century. One can imagine that they would look to us today in utter disbelief while asking why we do not utilize interstate conventions *more*.

---

[242] David Lefer, *The Founding Conservatives* (New York: Sentinel, 2013), 297

THREE
PIVOTAL PHILADELPHIA, 1787

> *"The plans now to be formed will certainly be defective, as the Confederation has been found on trial to be. Amendments therefore will be necessary and it will be better to provide for them in an easy, regular, and constitutional way, than to trust to chance and violence."*[1]
>
> -George Mason, delegate from Virginia to the 1787 Philadelphia Convention

All of this discussion of conventions so far has focused on either drafting, amending or ratifying a constitution; before moving any further, it is essential to define what we mean by a constitution. Like the words for convention, the meaning has changed over time and we must put an historical reference in the proper contemporary context. Today's twenty-first-century Americans are conditioned to think of a constitution as a written charter that follows a somewhat familiar or expected format. This was not always the case, and in the United Kingdom of today, it is still not the case and rarely has been. The English constitution, as previously mentioned is an unwritten, uncodified charter of the United Kingdom government. A written constitution has its roots firmly in the documentary history of the United Kingdom and before that, in many of the European proto-states including the Germanic Visigoths, Burgundians, Lombards, Saxons, Alamanni, Frisians and Salic Franks between the fifth and ninth centuries and all generally drafted in Latin, a Russian constitution in the eleventh century and a Welsh constitution in the tenth, middle eastern states,

---

[1] Max Farrand, *The Records of the Federal Convention of 1787, Vol. I* (New Haven: Yale University Press, 1911 rev. 1937), 202

in Asia, the Chinese constitution of the late fourteenth century, Japan's proto-constitution written by Prince Shotoku in 604, even India back to the third century B.C., and ultimately as far back as the Republic of Rome and the ancient Greek city-states. The oldest continuously functioning document is the *Leges Statutae Republicae Sancti Marini* of San Marino dating to 1600. Professor William Morey characterized a written constitution in 1891 as, "any positive organic law, or body of statutory provisions established by a competent political authority defining the powers and branches of government and securing the political and civil rights of the subject."[2] This definition is a step beyond and much more specific than what was done initially during the establishment of most of the earliest colonies.

Aristotle and his students collected and were credited with drafting about 158 constitutions for the Greek city-states.[3] Aristotle is said to have been the first to distinguish between constitutional law and ordinary or statutory law about 350 B.C. Aristotle undertook the first attempt to identify and classify the types of constitutions and their features. Written constitutions were known at least as far removed in time as 594 B.C when Solon drafted a constitution for the Athenian state. The Romans put their governmental structure, literally, in stone about 450 B.C. with *The Twelve Tables*.[4] Before these men, laws had been codified and scribed since the Sumerians but the structure of government itself was not usually written down.

In England, even the famous and vaunted *Magna Carta* was preceded by *The Charter of Liberties* handed down more than a century earlier by Henry I in 1100.[5] Both of these documents addressed the guarantees of liberties for the English people rather than the form of English government. What makes those documents relevant are the formal documentation of the agreed upon principles and rights. The English experiment with constitutionalism did briefly include written constitutions – twice. First in 1653 during the Commonwealth Period, *The Instrument of Government* was drafted as the first codified, written English constitution. It incorporated

---

[2] William C. Morey, "The Genesis of a Written Constitution," *The Annals of the American Academy of Political and Social Science* 1 (Apr. 1891): 534

[3] P. J. Rhodes, *A Commentary on the Aristotelian Athenaion Politeia* (New York: Oxford University Press, 1993), 1-2

[4] http://avalon.law.yale.edu/ancient/twelve_tables.asp

[5] Henry L. Cannon, "The Character and Antecedents of the Charter of Liberties of Henry I," *American Historical Review* 15, no.1 (Oct. 1909), generally

elements of the prior, unadopted manifestos of the *Agreement of the People* of 1647 and the competing *Heads of Proposals* of 1647 and 1649.[6] The second written English constitution was the 1657 *Humble Petition and Advice*. This document lasted a short three years until Charles II took the throne.[7] Both English "constitutions" were only nominally constitutions and not what we would consider a formal constitution today. All of these documents led to the eventual drafting of a codified, regimented, structured form of American government, first in the form of *The Articles of Confederation and Perpetual Union* of 1777 and subsequently in *The Constitution of the United States* of 1787.[8] Historian Gordon S. Wood explained,

> "The most obvious difference between eighteenth-century English and American constitutionalism was the American Revolutionaries' conception of a constitution as a written document, as a fundamental law circumscribing the government. Before the American Revolution, a constitution was rarely distinguished from the government and its operations. Traditionally in English culture, a constitution referred both to the way the government was put together, or constituted, and to the fundamental rights the government was supposed to protect. The eighteenth-century English constitution was an unwritten mixture of laws, customs, principles, and institutions.
>
> By the end of the Revolutionary era, however, the Americans' idea of a constitution had become very different. A constitution was now seen to be no part of the government at all; it was a written document distinct from and superior to all the operations of government. A constitution was, as Thomas Paine said in 1791, 'a thing **antecedent** to a government; and a government is only the creature of a constitution.'"[9]

Wood states that putting the form of government in writing made the American government seem, to Americans at least, "something fundamental" and more tangible or permanent than the English form. For the newly independent former colonists, it was all about preserving their rights and in that regard they were, as Wood quoted a Connecticut clergyman, "anxious

---

[6] George D. Heath III, "Making the Instrument of Government" *Journal of British Studies* 6, no.2 (May 1967), 15

[7] Ralph C. H. Catterall, "The Failure of the Humble Petition and Advice," *American Historical Review* 9, no.1 (Oct. 1903), generally

[8] Charles Borgeaud, "The Origin and Development of Written Constitutions," *Political Science Quarterly* 7, no.4, (Dec. 1892): 614

[9] Gordon S. Wood, *The Idea of America, Reflections on the Birth of the United States* (New York: Penguin Books, 2011), 173-4. Used by permission of Penguin Press, an imprint of Penguin Publishing Group, a division of Penguin Random House LLC. All rights reserved.

to preserve and transmit" those rights "unimpaired to posterity."[10] A written constitution could more ably preserve those newly established and hard-won rights and the sovereignty of the people. Leonard Levy succinctly stated,

> *"Over a period of a century and a half America had become accustomed to the idea that government existed by a consent of the governed, that people created government, that they did it by written compact, that the compact constituted fundamental law, that the government must be subject to such limitations as are necessary for the security of the rights of the people, and, usually, that the reserved rights of the people were enumerated in bills of rights."[11]*

But with time, there would obviously be new rights for the people and the granting of new powers to the government, and these changes would require either a wholly new constitution or a remaking of the existing one. In some cases, that action meant an addition to the constitution in the form of a formal amendment. The people, to be clear, are only loaning their law making power to a legislature; the people retain the permanent ownership of that power and would, on rare occasions, exercise that law-making power directly through the amendment process. The American notion of constitution making was deeply ingrained by the time that the Revolution commenced. As shown, American constitution making had its roots in New England and extended not just to political life but also to social life. Not only were governments formed under constitutions but churches, schools and other social institutions were governed by constitutions. Professor Robert Gross noted in 1976 that, "New Englanders thus operated on the unspoken assumption that later generations of Americans would take to extremes: every institution must have its charter."[12] Sooner or later, that charter would require amendment.

The amendment process is so important because it gives the rest of the constitution its permanence and stability. Today we are faced with the concept of the "living constitution" that changes meaning over time and with no attribution to whomever has supposedly changed the charter. This notion was anathema to the Framers and to most of those that followed. Legal giant Thomas McIntyre Cooley explained crisply that,

---

[10] Ibid., 175
[11] Leonard Levy, *Origins of the Bill of Rights*, (New Haven, CT: Yale University Press, 1999), 24
[12] Robert A. Gross, *The Minutemen and Their World* (New York: Hill and Wang, 1976), 36

> *"The constitution, when expressed in writing and put in force by a people whose theory of government is that the sovereign power is in their hands, must stand always as written except as changes are made according to the method as provided for it. There is no such thing as imperceptible change in such a constitution."*[13]

Those rare occasions for remaking and amending constitutions most often came in the form of conventions.[14] With so many new governments forming and reforming during the Revolutionary era, it is no surprise that conventions were commonplace and that eventually the largest of the interstate problems would inevitably lead to an interstate, that is, a <u>national</u>, convention endowed with the plenary powers to address and propose a solution to those interstate problems.

The final impetus for the Philadelphia Convention in 1787 was the failure of the Annapolis Convention of 1786, which was formally titled the "Meeting of Commissioners to Remedy Defects of the Federal Government." Only twelve delegates from five states met at Mann's Tavern on 11-14 September 1786 to discuss trade issues.[15] Nine had selected delegates.[16] The poor turnout underscored to the delegates in attendance the true cause of the economic problems facing the American Confederation. The commissioners prepared a report and forwarded it to all the state legislatures and the Congress. The report of the Annapolis Convention commissioners unanimously recommended that all of the states meet in Philadelphia the next May to take up the more pressing issues of a financial, commercial and foreign affairs nature.[17] The Annapolis delegates' motivation to act which prompted them to issue their own convention call was simply that the Congress had, repeatedly, failed to act successfully.[18] If the delegates failed to accomplish anything in Annapolis, it would appear that the effort to save the young nation was a failure. Inspired by a clause in the delegate instructions

---

[13] Thomas M. Cooley, "The Power to Amend the Federal Constitution," *Michigan Law Journal*, Vol.2, no.4 (April 1893): 110

[14] Gordon S. Wood, *The Idea of America, Reflections on the Birth of the United States* (New York: Penguin Books, 2011), 185

[15] Jonathan Elliot, *The Debates in the Several State Conventions on the Adoption of the Federal Constitution* (Philadelphia: J.B. Lippincott, 2d ed., 1836), 116 - Delaware, New Jersey, New York, Pennsylvania and Virginia attended. The topic was the coordinated regulation of foreign and interstate commerce.

[16] Robert A. Feer, "Shays' Rebellion and the Constitution: A Study in Causation," *New England Quarterly* 42, no.3 (Sep. 1969): 391

[17] http://avalon.law.yale.edu/18th_century/annapoli.asp

[18] Thomas E. Brennan, "Return To Philadelphia," *Cooley Law Review* I (1982): 67

for the New Jersey delegation, the delegates adopted the wording of the clause to support their call to another convention in Philadelphia. That wording referred to the "rendering of the federal constitution as adequate to the exigencies of the Union." This phrase would prove crucial.[19] Prior to the Annapolis Convention, other conventions had been proposed or discussed for repairing the Articles of Confederation. Proposals to amend the Articles of Confederation were submitted almost monthly as were suggestions for a convention.[20] Alexander Hamilton had been urging a convention "vested with plenipotentiary authority" to rework the Articles as early as September of 1780 – before Maryland had even ratified the Articles and thereby putting them into effect![21,22] Hamilton was not alone in this regard, historian Robert Feer has pointed out that William Grayson, a Continental Congress member from Virginia, had said that any partial amending of the Articles would forestall the need to make "extensive revisions and would therefore be worse than nothing." Grayson wanted the Annapolis Convention to fail and prompt Virginia to call a convention "to comprehend all the grievances of the Union."[23] Grayson got his wish. Virginia's James Monroe was in New York serving in the Confederation Congress and wrote that the men in Congress from the eastern States were scheming to use the Annapolis convention to do more "than the object originally comprehended."[24] It is meaningful to highlight that Annapolis was not a convention "vested with plenipotentiary authority" – it was a limited convention.[25]

Hamilton was undoubtedly aware before making his convention suggestion in September of 1780 that delegates from three states had met a month earlier in Boston to undertake just such a task. In November of 1780, more delegates met in Hartford to continue the discussion. In July of 1782, the New York legislature issued a resolution to call another convention to modify the Articles. In 1784, Virginia and Maryland met to

---

[19] Jack N. Rakove, *Original Meanings, Politics and Ideas in the Making of the Constitution* (New York: Vintage Books, 1996), 32
[20] Robert A. Feer, "Shays' Rebellion and the Constitution: A Study in Causation," *New England Quarterly* 42, no.3 (Sep. 1969): 389
[21] Russell B. Caplan, *Constitutional Brinkmanship* (New York: Oxford University Press, 1988), 20
[22] Letter of Alexander Hamilton to James Duane, 3 September 1780
[23] Robert A. Feer, "Shays' Rebellion and the Constitution: A Study in Causation," *New England Quarterly* 42, no.3 (Sep. 1969): 391
[24] Ibid.
[25] Michael B. Rappaport, "The Constitutionality of a Limited Convention: An Originalist Analysis," *Constitutional Commentary* 81 (2012): 68

discuss their boundary and the joint use of the Potomac River and the two states concluded that a convention of the States was necessary and debated inviting other states to meet.[26] The dissatisfaction with the Articles of Confederation existed as long as the Articles themselves.[27] Convention after convention took up the debate over what to do about the Articles and no state was unaware of the need to reform – or to replace - them.[28] There is an absurdity in considering that conventions sought to reform the Articles of Confederation in that the Articles were drafted by the Continental Congress – not a constitutional convention - they were ratified by state legislatures – not state ratificatory conventions - the people had no input in the development, drafting, ratification or attempted amendment of the Articles: it was an organ for the States and not the people. Gordon Wood points to this distinction and asks, "Indeed, what did it matter if the Constitution were a violation of the Articles, since the Confederation had been 'adopted and confirmed without being submitted to the great body of the people for their approbation.'"[29]

The Massachusetts General Court had entertained the notion of issuing a legislative call for a nationwide convention to revise the Articles of Confederation in 1785 but the Confederation Congress representatives from Massachusetts thought it unwise.[30] The General Court sought to consider "how far it may be necessary, in their opinion, to alter or enlarge" the Articles.[31] The Annapolis Convention was also not authorized by the Confederation Congress since, like the subsequent Philadelphia Convention, the Confederation Congress held no power under the Articles of Confederation with which to call a convention.[32] In both instances, the States had initiated the call to convention. Article V is then an anomaly when compared to other interstate or federal conventions. The inclusion of

---

[26] James Stasny, "The Constitutional Convention Provision of Article V: Historical Perspective," *Cooley Law Review*, I (1982): 76

[27] Paul J. Weber & Barbara A. Perry, *Unfounded Fears, The Myths and Realities of a Constitutional Convention* (New York: Praeger, 1989), 23

[28] Russell B. Caplan, *Constitutional Brinkmanship* (New York: Oxford University Press, 1988), 21

[29] Gordon S. Wood, *The Creation of the American Republic, 1776-1787* (Chapel Hill: University of North Carolina Press, 1969), 534. Published for the Omohundro Institute of Early American History and Culture. Used by permission of the publisher.

[30] Letter of 17 September 1785 from Rufus King to Nathan Dane - http://www.loc.gov/exhibits/creating-the-united-states/ext/transcription37.html -

[31] Robert A. Feer, "Shays' Rebellion and the Constitution: A Study in Causation," *New England Quarterly* 42, no.3 (Sep. 1969): 389 – citing the General Court records.

[32] Robert G. Natelson, "A Compendium for Lawyers and Legislative Drafters," Convention of States (2014), 27

Congress in the process diverges from the previous conventions. Following the Annapolis convention, Virginia took the lead and sent the invitations to the other states to meet in Philadelphia. In that invitation, Virginia suggested that all the States provide "the powers of their deputies to other objects than those of Commerce."[33] A survey of the commissions of the delegates from the twelve states that attended shows that all, to one degree or another, understood the severity of the situation and provided the necessary authority to their respective delegates to make major changes to the federal government. Only two states restricted their delegations. Appendix C addresses this issue in depth.

The Congress understood very well the situation facing the nation and a majority agreed with the necessity for a convention of the States. South Carolina's Charles Pinckney had been leading the push for a reformation of the Confederation within the Congress since at least 1784. In May of 1786, Pinckney had chaired a congressional committee that reported seven proposed amendments to the Congress.[34] Seconding Virginia's call was New Jersey; then, finally, Congress issued an invitation to the States in February 1787. The sentiment of doing more and having the authority to act was found at the state level as New Jersey had authorized its delegates to Annapolis to take up not only commercial matters but also "other important matters…necessary to the common interest and permanent harmony of the several States."[35] When the Congress eventually got around to issuing their call, it was at the insistence of New York and Massachusetts – strongly Anti-Federalist states - that the convention, and the delegates, be given limitations.[36] The fact that all but one of the States sent delegations to Philadelphia, but eight states did not attend the Annapolis convention demonstrates the degree of seriousness which they gave to the necessity to undertake a major reform of the national government instead of just a modification of the economic matters which was on the limited agenda

---

[33] Robert A. Feer, "Shays' Rebellion and the Constitution: A Study in Causation," *New England Quarterly* 42, no.3 (Sep. 1969): 392

[34] Christopher Collier & James S. Collier, *Decision at Philadelphia* (New York: Ballantine Books, 1986, 2007 ed.), 93-4

[35] Robert A. Feer, "Shays' Rebellion and the Constitution: A Study in Causation," *New England Quarterly* 42, no.3 (Sep. 1969): 391

[36] Robert G. Natelson, "A Response to the "Runaway Scenario"," (2013), 7 - independently published on the website of the Independence Institute at http://constitution.i2i.org/2013/02/15/a-response-to-the-"runaway-scenario"/

for Annapolis.[37] Congress's 21 February 1787 convention call was nothing more than an attempt to save face in light of the States' decisions to go forward with the Philadelphia convention. This historical anecdote is also a lesson for current advocates and activists for an amendatory convention: the States must act together to force the calling of the convention or Congress will procrastinate as long as possible, as they have done for over a century already.[38]

The Push to Philadelphia

There were many causes for calling a convention in 1787, but at least two directly involved conventions. First, the state legislatures were viewed as abusing their powers and creating a corrupt environment in which the States were competing with and taxing each other's citizens. Madison cited this as one of his reasons to reform the national government.[39] The proliferation of conventions that addressed, and absorbed, every possible issue had impinged on the ability of the state legislatures to carry out their work. People had become frustrated once again with government and turned to taking matters into their own hands. Even Madison's Virginia had to endure the outbreak of the burning of court houses and protesting that led to conventions organized to resist tax collections and the convening of the courts.[40]

Second, the economic picture of the nation in the mid-1780s was bleak. Debt, both governmental and personal, was high. Currency was being steadily devalued and inflation was increasing. The lack of hard money was forcing small farmers into bankruptcy. In Massachusetts, these conditions prompted the rise of Shays' Rebellion.[41] In 1786, the militias repeated their actions of a dozen years earlier and forced the closing of the county courts to prevent foreclosures.[42,43] The farmers and the militias called county conventions as they had done in 1774 and set out to force the state government to listen to their grievances. The populist rebellion began to

---

[37] Wilbur Edel, *A Constitutional Convention – Threat or Challenge?* (New York: Praeger, 1981), 20-1
[38] Thomas E. Brennan, *The Article V Amendatory Constitutional Convention* (Lanham, MD: Lexington Books, 2014), 24
[39] Gordon S. Wood, *The Creation of the American Republic, 1776-1787* (Chapel Hill: University of North Carolina Press, 1969), 404-9, 467. Published for the Omohundro Institute of Early American History and Culture.
[40] Ibid., 325-6
[41] Michael Kammen, *People of Paradox* (Ithaca, NY: Cornell University Press, 1972), 240
[42] Ray Raphael, *The First American Revolution, Before Lexington and Concord* (New York: New Press, 2002), 214
[43] Maryland and South Carolina also experienced such uprisings and courthouse closings.

cause similar stirrings in neighboring states. The same western counties led the way as they had done so in 1774. The state was able to suppress the rebellion in early 1787 but the effect nationwide was to lend some credibility to the idea of the convention in Philadelphia that the Annapolis convention delegates had recommended in September of 1786.[44,45] As Shays' Rebellion played out and then wound down, state after state decided that the Articles had been a dismal enough failure to warrant trying something new – and so another interstate or federal convention was in order.[46,47] There is an irony in that the same people in the state legislatures who were incensed at the actions of the county conventions also realized that the answer to the national problem was that there had to be a higher authority which could impose on the state legislatures a solution to the persistent problems, and that solution was a national convention.[48]

 The political leaders of the day were keenly aware of the state of chaos in which the Confederation was falling. Future essayist of *The Federalist* and first Chief Justice of the United States Supreme Court John Jay wrote to Thomas Jefferson in mid-1786 that, "I have long thought and become daily more convinced; that the construction of our Federal Government is fundamentally wrong."[49] Jay had been equally concerned in an exchange with George Washington earlier in the year, stating that, "Experience has pointed out errors in our National Government which call for correction, and which threaten to blast the fruit we expected from our tree of liberty."[50] Washington shared Jay's view, writing back later in the exchange, "Your sentiments, that our affairs are drawing rapidly to a crisis, accord with my own."[51] Washington has been aware of and concerned by the diminishing effects of the Articles. He wrote that, "No day ever dawned more favorably than ours did; and no day was ever more clouded than the present...We are fast verging to anarchy and confusion!" Robert Feer points out that Washington had been

---

[44] John R. Vile, *Conventional Wisdom* (Athens, GA: University of Georgia Press, 2016), 21

[45] For a counterargument on the impact of Shays' Rebellion, see, Robert A. Feer, "Shays' Rebellion and the Constitution: A Study in Causation," *New England Quarterly* 42, no.3 (Sep. 1969): 388-410

[46] Forrest McDonald, *E Pluribus Unum, The Formation of the American Republic 1776-1790* (Indianapolis: Liberty Fund, 2d ed., 1979), 241-57

[47] Winton U. Solberg, *The Constitutional Convention and the Formation of the Union* (Urbana: University of Illinois Press, 2d ed., 1990), lxxxvi

[48] Gordon S. Wood, *The Creation of the American Republic, 1776-1787* (Chapel Hill: University of North Carolina Press, 1969), 532. Published for the Omohundro Institute of Early American History and Culture.

[49] John Jay to Thomas Jefferson, letter of 18 August 1786

[50] John Jay to George Washington, letter of 16 January 1786

[51] George Washington to John Jay, letter of 18 May 1786

writing letters from Mount Vernon to anyone that would listen cautioning that the Articles must be amended else the government would collapse.[52] With the failure of the Annapolis Convention and the call going out from the Virginia legislature on 16 October 1786 to meet in Philadelphia the next May, the lesson learned at Annapolis that severely restricting the convention's powers would not solve the problems made the necessity for plenary power in Philadelphia obvious. James Madison wrote to Thomas Jefferson in between the Virginia legislature's convention call and that of the Confederation Congress, "The recommendation from the meeting at Annapolis of a ***plenipotentiary*** Convention in Philadelphia in May next has been well received by the [Virginia] Assembly here. Indeed the evidence of dangerous defects in the Confederation has at length proselyted the most obstinate adversaries to a reform."[53,54] On the very same February day that the Confederation Congress issued its resolution in support of the Philadelphia Convention, James Madison wrote in his diary, "All [members of Congress] agreed and owned that the Federal Government in its existing shape was inefficient and could not last. The members from the Southern and Middle States seemed generally anxious for some republican organization of the system which should preserve the Union and give due energy to the Government of it."[55] Even the Congress which had reluctantly endorsed the 1787 convention could not just see, but agree, that drastic change was not only necessary but imminent.

Among the reasons for replacing the Articles of Confederation was the extreme difficulty in obtaining an amendment to the Articles. The most pressing issue had been the ability of the national government to secure the necessary cash flow with which to operate. The Congress had been dependent on the charity – and that is the correct term – of the States. Congress could not compel payment from anyone, especially the States. It had to rely on the goodwill of the States to make "donations" to Congress. The requirement of Article XIII for unanimity to approve any amendment was the undoing of the amendment process.[56] Little Rhode Island stood

---

[52] Robert A. Feer, "Shays' Rebellion and the Constitution: A Study in Causation," *New England Quarterly* 42, no.3 (Sep. 1969): 395-6

[53] James Madison to Thomas Jefferson, letter of 4 December 1786

[54] Author's emphasis added to 'plenipotentiary.'

[55] Diary of James Madison, entry for 21 February 1787

[56] The unanimity requirement was objected to from the inception of the Articles. South Carolina objected to the requirement when it ratified the Articles and sought to have the requirement changed to eleven states.

firmly against any and all amendment proposals.⁵⁷ The Rhode Islanders had profited from the American and French troops during the Revolution and were highly averse to paying taxes to any government body. The smallest state had earned the enmity of her sister states and become labeled "Rogue Island" for her unwillingness to follow the course of the rest of the Confederation. In 1782, a proposed amendment to allow Congress to apply import duties of 5% was quashed by Rhode Island's lone stand against the proposal.⁵⁸,⁵⁹ That proposal involved paying the import duty into the federal treasury. Hamilton and Madison worked out the wording of a rebuke of Rhode Island for her offense of non-support of the amendment proposal in the Confederation Congress.⁶⁰ By 1786, the onus has shifted from Rhode Island to New York as the lone obstructer on the impost amendment.⁶¹

Madison specifically addressed the matter of the recalcitrance of Rhode Island to permit and accede to the granting of a taxing power to the Confederation and the impact of that refusal in *The Federalist*, No.40,

> "[W]as it not an acknowledged object of the convention and the universal expectation of the people that the regulation of trade should be submitted to the general government in such a form as would render it an immediate source of general revenue? Had not Congress repeatedly recommended this measure as not inconsistent with the fundamental principles of the Confederation? **Had not every State but one**, had not New York herself, so far complied with the plan of Congress as to recognize the principle of the innovation?"⁶²

And he continued in the same *The Federalist* essay that,

> "In one particular it is admitted that the convention have departed from the tenor of their commission. Instead of reporting a plan requiring the confirmation of all the States, they have reported a plan which is to

---

57 Michael B. Rappaport, "The Constitutionality of a Limited Convention: An Originalist Analysis," *Constitutional Commentary* 81 (2012): 99-100
58 Forrest McDonald, *Novus Ordo Seclorum, The Intellectual Origins of the Constitution* (Lawrence: University of Kansas Press, 1985), 175
59 Forrest McDonald, *E Pluribus Unum, The Formation of the American Republic 1776-1790* (Indianapolis: Liberty Fund, 1979, 2d ed.), 55-7
60 James Schouler, *History of the United States of America, Under the Constitution, 1783-1801, Vol. I, Rule of Federalism* (New York: Dodd, Mead & Co., 1880, 1908 ed.), 31
61 Winton U. Solberg, *The Constitutional Convention and the Formation of the Union* (Urbana: University of Illinois Press, 2d ed., 1990), lxxiv
62 James Madison, "Federalist Paper No.40," in *The Federalist Papers: Hamilton, Madison, Jay*, ed. Clinton Rossiter (New York: Mentor, 1961) – author's emphasis added to denote Rhode Island reference.

be confirmed and maybe carried into effect by nine States only....The forbearance can only have proceeded from an irresistible conviction of the absurdity of subjecting the fate of twelve States to **the perverseness or corruption of a thirteenth***; from the example of inflexible opposition given by a majority of one sixtieth of the people of America to a measure approved and called for by the voice of twelve States...*"[63]

Add the obstinacy of avoiding taxes to the folly of Rhode Island printing fiat currency which flooded the state's economy with nearly worthless script in 1786, and that humiliated the state nationwide. It is easy to see why the rest of the States were fed up with Rhode Island.[64] It had become the national capital of fiscal irresponsibility.[65,66] The on-going collapse of the public credit had killed all hopes of Congress securing any revenue stream and this was one of the main reasons for the 1787 convention. Much of the funding for the government came through European loans. Congress had been forced to pay some of its debts in western land grants.[67] In 1783, another attempt was made to amend the Articles and allow for taxation based on the population of the states instead of on the land values. This effort too was stymied by the requirement of unanimity.[68] As an aside, one of the unfounded rumors swirling about Philadelphia in the summer of 1787 was that in the closed door sessions of the Grand Convention, the debate had centered on expelling Rhode Island from the Union.[69]

Had the proposed amendment to the Articles been successfully passed, Congress could have managed the public debt (which for both the States and the Congress had grown to about $100 million) and the whole fiasco avoided. In the Virginia ratifying convention, on 5 June 1788, Madison referred to Rhode Island as "the most trifling minority" which sought to "obstruct every attempt to reform the government" and he asked of Patrick

---

[63] James Madison, "Federalist Paper No.40," in *The Federalist Papers: Hamilton, Madison, Jay*, ed. Clinton Rossiter (New York: Mentor, 1961) – again referring to Rhode Island.

[64] Christopher Collier & James S. Collier, *Decision at Philadelphia* (New York: Ballantine Books, 1986, 2007 ed.), 260

[65] Forrest McDonald, *Novus Ordo Seclorum, The Intellectual Origins of the Constitution* (Lawrence: University of Kansas Press, 1985), 175-6

[66] North Carolina had also issued paper money, twice, but with less depreciation.

[67] Forrest McDonald, *Novus Ordo Seclorum, The Intellectual Origins of the Constitution* (Lawrence: University of Kansas Press, 1985), 94-6

[68] Richard Albert, "The Next Constitutional Revolution," *University of Detroit Mercy Law Review* 88, no.4 (Summer 2011): 712

[69] John P. Kaminski, *Secrecy and the Constitutional Convention* (Madison: The Center for the Study of the American Constitution, University of Wisconsin-Madison 2005), 17

Henry, his political nemesis and prime antagonist in the Virginia ratifying convention, if Henry wanted "to continue the most radical defects in the old system, because the petty state of Rhode Island would not agree to remove them?"[70] Madison had laid the dire situation of the national government on the doorsteps of Rhode Island and Article XIII.[71] The necessity of ending the unanimity for amendment was considered a *given* by the time that the Philadelphia Convention met.[72] So much so was Rhode Island blamed that her declination to attend was warmly received by some of the political leaders of the day. Edward Carrington of Virginia expressed his disgust in a letter to Thomas Jefferson just three weeks before the Philadelphia Convention opened, "Rhode Island is at all points so antifederal and contemptible that her neglecting the invitation will probably occasion no demur whatever in the proceedings."[73]

The Development of Article V

The development of the Article V convention concept in the Constitution was not, as is often portrayed today by its opponents, a sudden and last minute addition. In fact, the idea of the States holding the amending power was part of the original design proposals and actually preceded the inclusion of Congress in the amending power.[74] The intent of the States amending what became the Constitution was part of the Virginia plan developed prior to the Constitutional Convention taking place. The competing plan of Charles Pinckney of South Carolina also included a provision for amendment by the States in its sixteenth article.[75] The Philadelphia Convention lasted roughly four months and it was not until the last few of weeks of the convention that the congressional amendment process was included. Until that time, the state convention model has been

---

[70] Philip B. Kurland and Ralph Lerner, *The Founders' Constitution, Vol.4* (Indianapolis: Liberty Fund, 1987), 580-1 – pointing towards Elliott's Debates as their source.

[71] Sanford Levinson, "'Veneration" and Constitutional Change: James Madison Confronts the Possibility of Constitutional Amendment," *Texas Tech Law Review* 21 (1990): 2448-9

[72] Bruce M. Van Sickle and Lynn M. Boughey, "Lawful and Peaceful Revolution: Article V and Congress' Present Duty to Call a Convention for Proposing Amendments," *Hamline Law Review* 14, no.1 (Fall 1990): 8

[73] Edward Carrington to Thomas Jefferson, letter of 24 April 1787

[74] Walter Dellinger, "The Recurring Question of the "Limited" Constitutional Convention," *Yale Law Journal* 88 (1979): 1626

[75] Lester Bernhardt Orfield, *The Amending of the Federal Constitution* (Ann Arbor: The University of Michigan Press, 1942), 2 - No copy of Pinckney's plan survives to the present but the notes of other delegates detail some of the provisions of the plan. Lansing's notebook contains a detail in the endnotes.

the primary method under consideration.⁷⁶

The process of developing Article V was slow and deliberate with some reversals and with modifications galore. The allegation that it was a hasty addition is inaccurate and intentional. Note the derogatory language and the unsubstantiated claims in one writer's perspective,

> *"[I]n contrast to the meticulous care the Framers exercised in deliberating on various other provisions of the Constitution, the Concon provision of Article V was added rather hastily, at a time when the delegates were preparing to close their deliberations; and this provision did not receive the careful attention given to most other provisions of the Constitution."*⁷⁷

It is worth reviewing the development of the amendment process in the 1787 convention to understand why the state-application-and-convention process is, although unused to date, still vitally important. Consulting the notes of the 1787 delegates and Professor Max Farrand, we can construct a timeline that leads to the wording of Article V as it was fixed in the Constitution. We begin by noting that Edmund Randolph opened the Philadelphia Convention by examining in great detail the long list of defects and negatives of the Confederation. He laid a foundation for the justification for abandoning the Confederation in favor of a more solidly constructed federal government. Lacking that indictment of the Confederation, the convention would have had a difficult time in explaining to the state legislatures, the public and the Congress why they chose to undertake from the outset to demolish and then rebuild the national government. Many delegates came expecting to repair the Confederation and the experience of each State had varied. Randolph had to declare the Confederation dead, else, all that the convention did from that point forward was suspect.⁷⁸

The problems that Randolph detailed had been painstakingly studied and listed by Madison the previous year. Thomas Jefferson had shipped from Paris a trunk of books on history, politics and commerce to Madison. In their correspondence, the trunk was referred to as the "literary cargo" and provided the basis for the material that eventually became Madison's paper titled "*Of*

---

[76] Wilbur Edel, *A Constitutional Convention – Threat or Challenge?* (New York: Praeger, 1981), 24
[77] John A. Eidsmoe, "A New Constitutional Convention? Critical Look at Questions Answered, and Not Answered, by Article Five of the United States Constitution," *United States Air Force Academy Journal of Legal Studies* 3 (1992): 7
[78] Pauline Maier, *Ratification, The People Debate the Constitution, 1787-1788* (New York: Simon & Schuster, 2010), 260-1

Ancient and Modern Confederacies." He made special note of the constitutions of the various leagues and confederacies and of their components, failings and successes.[79] That research formed the basis of the "Virginia Plan."

Focusing strictly on the discussion of the amending process and the convention options for amendment and ratification, we begin with the first day of actual work by the Philadelphia Convention:

Friday, 25 May 1787:

The convention opened with a sufficient quorum. It was supposed to have convened on May 14 but not enough states were present to begin. Seven states are represented initially. In its first action, General George Washington of Virginia was unanimously chosen as the convention chair.

Tuesday, 29 May 1787:

Virginia governor Edmund Randolph submitted his "Virginia Plan" to the Philadelphia Convention. It included fifteen resolutions, and a specific allowance, Resolution 13, for amendment that, "Res[olve]d., provision ought to be made for the amendment of the Articles of Union whensoever it shall seem necessary, and that the assent of the National Legislature ought not to be required thereto."[80] Randolph's Resolution 15 covering ratification augmented the prior amendment resolution. On this same day, Charles Pinckney of South Carolina proposed his plan as well. It contained Article XVI that stated, "The assent of the Legislature of States shall be sufficient to invest future additional Powers in U.S. in C.ass. and shall bind the whole confederacy."[81,82] Not much was given in terms of how the amendments were to be made according to Pinckney's Plan.[83] But according to the version published by then Secretary of State John Quincy Adams in 1818, Article XVI read, "If two-thirds of the Legislatures of the States apply for the same, the Legislature of the United States shall call a convention for the purpose

---

[79] Gordon S. Wood, *The Creation of the American Republic, 1776-1787* (Chapel Hill: University of North Carolina Press, 1969), 183-4. Published for the Omohundro Institute of Early American History and Culture.

[80] Max Farrand, *The Records of the Federal Convention of 1787, Vol. I* (New Haven: Yale University Press, 1911 rev. 1937), 22, 121

[81] Max Farrand, *The Records of the Federal Convention of 1787, Vol. III* (New Haven: Yale University Press, 1911 rev. 1937), Appendix D, 609

[82] 'in C. ass.' is short hand for "in Congress assembled."

[83] Bruce M. Van Sickle and Lynn M. Boughey, "Lawful and Peaceful Revolution: Article V and Congress' Present Duty to Call a Convention for Proposing Amendments," *Hamline Law Review* 14, no.1 (Fall 1990): 10

of amending the Constitution; or should Congress, with the consent of two-thirds of each House, propose to the States amendments to the same, the agreement of two-thirds of the Legislatures of the States shall be sufficient to make the said amendments parts of the Constitution."[84,85] This phrasing sounds so familiar...and occurred so early in the convention. From the beginning, a convention of the States for the proposition of amendments was included in the plan with a supermajority required for any action. In these early drafts, the States are the repositories of the power to amend and the convention is the vehicle preferred. The Congress is denied the power to amend.

Tuesday, 5 June 1787:

The matter of amendment was deferred for a week and when it was taken up again by the Committee of the Whole, the Randolph amendment clause was adopted, but the delegates held back on leaving the legislature out of the amendment process and postponed that part for review later.[86] In his notes for the day, New York delegate John Lansing has the notation that Rufus King of Massachusetts argued the state legislatures "have a Right to confirm any alterations" to the new constitution.[87]

Madison placed in his notes, "that provision ought to be made for [hereafter] amending the system now to be established, without requiring the assent of the Natl. Legislature." And that "Mr. Pinckney doubted the propriety and necessity of it." Elbridge Gerry of Massachusetts favored it. He noted that several of the states possessed, in comparison to the Articles of Confederation, a more lax method of amendment and that no problems with their systems had yet to be found. He said that, "The novelty & difficulty of the experiment requires periodical revision. The prospect of such a revision would also give intermediate stability to the Govt."[88]

For the 15th Resolution concerning using ratification conventions,

---

[84] Jonathan Elliot, *The Debates in the Several State Conventions on the Adoption of the Federal Constitution, Vol. I* (Philadelphia: J.P. Lippincott, 2d ed., 1836), 149 – punctuation and capitalization varies from Farrand.

[85] Max Farrand, *The Records of the Federal Convention of 1787, Vol. III* (New Haven: Yale University Press, 1911 rev. 1937), Appendix D, 601

[86] Max Farrand, *The Records of the Federal Convention of 1787, Vol. I* (New Haven: Yale University Press, 1911 rev. 1937), 117

[87] Joseph Reese Strayer, *The Delegate from New York* (Princeton: Princeton University Press, 1939), 34 - reprint by The Lawbook Exchange, (2002)

[88] Max Farrand, *The Records of the Federal Convention of 1787, Vol. I* (New Haven: Yale University Press, 1911 rev. 1937), 121-2

Rufus King commented that using a convention was easier than a state legislature because its traditional construction of a single house versus a bicameral legislature. James Wilson of Pennsylvania expressed the opinion that a convention by the people was the appropriate method of ratification.[89] Madison had intended for ratification conventions from the beginning.[90] The use of conventions was being proposed for most aspects of the process; it was becoming obvious that the intent for amending by convention is the natural course in the Framers' view. It was the best method of measuring the popular will.[91]

Prof. Walter Dellinger has commented that the central issue, was "the propriety of making the consent of the Natl. Legisl. unnecessary," and this underscores the entire debate – whether or not Congress or the States would control the amending process, put in a more exact form, control the amending *power*.[92] Professor William Van Alstyne contrasted this view with the idea that Madison was, in the August 6th session, looking to "leave the national legislature no room to manipulate the amendment process, but since the principal purpose was to provide a means of checking untoward congressional usurpations, to involve Congress at all, even in this presumably ministerial role, might be vexing." Van Alstyne argues that Madison clearly was willing to compromise as long as he could successfully limit the influence and participation of Congress in the amending process to an absolute minimum, what Van Alstyne termed "a manageable one."[93] Concisely, Congress could play a part – but only a small part.

Monday, 11 June 1787:

Randolph's plan was revisited, especially the 13th resolution.[94] Some of the delegates thought it "improper to dispense" with Congress's consent to the amending process. Col. George Mason of Virginia remarked that

---

[89] Ibid., 127 – Yates notes, Pierce recorded this point with the opposite conclusion.
[90] Christopher Collier & James S. Collier, *Decision at Philadelphia* (New York: Ballantine Books, 1986, 2007 ed.), 72
[91] Winton U. Solberg, *The Constitutional Convention and the Formation of the Union* (Urbana: University of Illinois Press, 2d ed., 1990), xc
[92] Walter Dellinger, "The Recurring Question of the "Limited" Constitutional Convention," *Yale Law Journal* 88 (1979): 1626
[93] William Van Alstyne, "The Limited Constitutional Convention – The Recurring Answer," *Duke Law Journal* 1979 (1979): 988
[94] Jonathan Elliot, *The Debates in the Several State Conventions on the Adoption of the Federal Constitution, Vol. V* (Philadelphia: J.P. Lippincott, 2d ed., 1836), 182

the Constitution, like its predecessor, the Articles of Confederation would eventually prove defective and that Congress need not be involved.[95,96] Mason noted,

> "*The plan now to be formed will certainly be defective, as the Confederation has been found on trial to be. Amendments therefore will be necessary, and it will be better to provide for them, in an easy, regular and Constitutional way than to trust to chance and violence. It would be improper to require the consent of the Natl. Legislature, because they may abuse their power, and refuse their consent on that very account. The opportunity for such an abuse, may be the fault of the Constitution calling for amentmt.*"[97]

Mason was putting into words the concerns of several of the delegates that the future Congress would not be trust-worthy – to the point of being tyrannical. Providing for Congress to have control of, or even just a "first right of refusal" over, proposing amendments would create a situation where nothing would be approved by Congress. There would always be some new impediment in the applications, in the proposed amendments, in the ratifications. This is the situation that the States find themselves in for the last half century regarding their Article V convention applications. Congress is exercising a form of veto that Mason and Randolph predicted more than two centuries in the past. One writer, seeing the need to a body independent of Congress, put it as,

> "*[their concerns] were, in short, that Congress would not always be trusted to do what was best for the country, and that when it was a practice of Congress itself that gave rise to the need for amendments, some other body should be made available to the people to initiate changes to the Constitution.*"[98]

But, Madison also noted that several members of the convention did not see the need of the resolution and they felt that the national legislature should be involved. Mason and Randolph reiterated their desire, and the

---

[95] Lester Bernhardt Orfield, *The Amending of the Federal Constitution* (Ann Arbor: The University of Michigan Press, 1942), 2 – Orfield has this as June 9th.

[96] Jonathan Elliot, *The Debates in the Several State Conventions on the Adoption of the Federal Constitution, Vol. V* (Philadelphia: J.P. Lippincott, 2d ed., 1836), 182

[97] Max Farrand, *The Records of the Federal Convention of 1787, Vol. I* (New Haven: Yale University Press, 1911 rev. 1937), 202-3

[98] E. Donald Elliott, "Constitutional Conventions and the Deficit," *Duke Law Journal* 1985, no.6 (Dec. 1985): 1085

need, for amendment capability.[99] Lansing made note of the 13th Resolve being agreed to, but other delegates' notes include that the first clause, wherein the need for amendment is recognized, was agreed to but the second clause that negated the assent of the national legislature was postponed.[100,101]

Wednesday, 13 June 1787:

The 15th Resolve was voted upon favorably for the consideration of amendments by a convention.[102] The Committee of the Detail reported back to the convention and had set down all the approved resolutions with the amendment resolution now numbered as XVII. It was in this report that the proviso against requiring the assent of the national legislature was removed.[103] It now read,

> "Resolved, that provision ought to be made for the amendment of the Articles of Union whensoever it shall seem necessary."[104]

Resolution XIX addressed how the proposed amendments would be made by a [ratification] convention of representatives chosen by the people.[105]

Friday, 15 June 1787:

New Jersey Attorney General William Paterson proposed the "New Jersey Plan." Whereas the Virginia Plan was considered to be the "large-states" plan, Paterson's proposal was geared toward the "small-states" and kept much of the current structure. After five days of debate, Paterson's plan was set aside permanently.[106] The plan was generally a modification of the

---

[99] William Montgomery Meigs, *The Growth of the Constitution in the Federal Convention of 1787: An Effort to Trace the Origin and Development of Each Separate Clause from Its First Suggestion in That Body to the Form Finally Approved* (Philadelphia: J. B. Lippincott, 1899), 273
[100] Joseph Reese Strayer, *The Delegate from New York* (Princeton: Princeton University Press, 1939), 47 - reprinted by The Lawbook Exchange, (2002)
[101] Max Farrand, *The Records of the Federal Convention of 1787, Vol. I* (New Haven: Yale University Press, 1911 rev. 1937), 194
[102] Joseph Reese Strayer, *The Delegate from New York* (Princeton: Princeton University Press, 1939), 47 - reprinted by The Lawbook Exchange, (2002) – Lansing has this occurring on Monday, the 11th – all other delegates' notes say the 13th.
[103] Jonathan Elliot, *The Debates in the Several State Conventions on the Adoption of the Federal Constitution, Vol. V* (Philadelphia: J.P. Lippincott, 2d ed., 1836), 189-90
[104] Max Farrand, *The Records of the Federal Convention of 1787, Vol. I* (New Haven: Yale University Press, 1911 rev. 1937), 227, 231 and 237
[105] Ibid., 227-8, 232 and 237
[106] Ibid., 240-5

Articles of Confederation and left the Article XIII amending provision unchanged.

Monday, 18 June 1787:

New York delegate Alexander Hamilton late in the game proposed his plan for the new government. It included ten articles and Article IX, §12 read,

> "*This Constitution may receive such alterations and amendments as may be proposed by the Legislature of the United States, with the concurrence of two thirds of the members of both Houses, and ratified by the Legislatures of, or by Conventions of deputies chosen by the people in, two thirds of the States composing the Union.*"[107]

Hamilton was seeking a strong national government and that included a national legislature that controlled the amendment process. Hamilton's plan was politely debated and then rejected although parts were later incorporated in the final scheme.[108]

Friday, 29 June 1787:

The process of amendment was brought up in the context of the discussion on the senate voting. Oliver Ellsworth of Connecticut was comfortable with the idea that late amendments will repair what is not done well at the Philadelphia convention. Madison warned against relying on the amendment process to correct deficiencies.[109] Ironically, that is exactly the path later taken but the Anti-Federalists to obtain the Bill of Rights, and by the Federalists to acquiesce to the Bill of Rights.

Monday, 2 July 1787:

Elbridge Gerry commented that, "Accommodation is absolutely necessary, and defects may be amended by a future convention."[110]

---

[107] Max Farrand, *The Records of the Federal Convention of 1787, Vol. III* (New Haven: Yale University Press, 1911 rev. 1937), Appendix F, 630

[108] Bruce M. Van Sickle and Lynn M. Boughey, "Lawful and Peaceful Revolution: Article V and Congress' Present Duty to Call a Convention for Proposing Amendments," *Hamline Law Review* 14, no.1 (Fall 1990): 10

[109] Max Farrand, *The Records of the Federal Convention of 1787, Vol. I* (New Haven: Yale University Press, 1911 rev. 1937), 475-8

[110] Ibid., 519

Monday, 23 July 1787:

The convention gave its unanimous approval to Resolution XVII as presented and as one of twenty-three approved resolutions. These resolutions were referred to the Committee of Detail to "prepare and report the Constitution."[111] The debate centered on whether the amendments should be unanimous as under the Articles of Confederation. Oliver Ellsworth thought that the amendment process should remain unanimous and the Constitution itself should require unanimous adoption but Pennsylvanian Gouverneur Morris reminded the convention that,

> "The amendmt. moved by Mr. Elseworth erroneously supposes that we are proceeding on the basis of the Confederation. This Convention is unknown to the Confederation."[112]

Three important points are to be made here: First, that the issue of the amendment process was proposed to be patterned after the Articles of Confederation, but the amendment process was part of the problem as no amendment was ever successfully made to the Articles, no matter how badly needed.[113] Second, the convention was clearly recognized by, at least some of, the delegates as not authorized by the Articles. Although not revolutionary, the convention was indeed constitutional. Third, the ratification issue, that is, the procedure itself, was tightly tied to that of the amendment process. Morris went so far as to propose that a general convention be held for the peoples' representatives to "consider, amend & establish" the Constitution. The motion was not given a seconding.[114] James Wilson questioned whether an oath should be required and what effect it would have on Resolution XVII; Massachusetts delegate Nathaniel Gorham agreed, but saw no impact of oaths on amendments. Elbridge Gerry concurred.[115]

In the records prepared by Professor Max Farrand, there are numerous copies of drafts for the Committee of Detail. These are all similar but the variations give some idea as to how the individual concepts developed.

---

[111] Max Farrand, *The Records of the Federal Convention of 1787, Vol. II* (New Haven: Yale University Press, 1911 rev. 1937), 84, 87

[112] Ibid., 92

[113] Jack N. Rakove, *Original Meanings, Politics and Ideas in the Making of the Constitution* (New York: Vintage Books, 1996), 31

[114] Max Farrand, *The Records of the Federal Convention of 1787, Vol. II* (New Haven: Yale University Press, 1911 rev. 1937), 93

[115] Ibid., 87-8

Somewhere in this period, the convention concept was fully fleshed out. The Committee of Detail was conducting its work during a hiatus in the convention overall.

Between the dates of July 26 and August 4, Farrand's Records give a series of versions of the Reports of the Proceedings of the Committee of Detail. These were the reports given to the Committee for consideration.[116]

- Version I: "That Provision ought to be made for the Amendment of the Articles of Union, whensoever is shall seem necessary."[117] – Proceedings of the Convention, June 19 – July 23

- Version IV: "(An alteration may be effected in the articles of union, on the applications of two thirds *nine* (2/3d) of the State legislatures (by a Convn. [added apparently by Rutledge]))" replaced with "(on appln. of 2/3ds of the State Legislatures to the Natl. Leg. they call a Convn. to revise or alter ye Articles of Union)[Rutledge making the change]."[118,119]

- Version VI: "This Constitution ought to be amended whenever such Amendment shall become necessary; and on the Application of the Legislatures of two thirds of the States in the Union, the Legislature of the United States shall call a Convention for that Purpose."[120]

- Version IX: "This Constitution ought to be amended whenever such amendment shall become necessary; and on the Application of (two thirds) the Legislatures of two thirds of the States of the Union, the Legislature of the United States shall call a Convention for that Purpose."[121]

South Carolinian John Rutledge's modifications in Version IV show the evolution of the amendment by convention concept. Judge Bruce Van

---

[116] Bruce M. Van Sickle and Lynn M. Boughey, "Lawful and Peaceful Revolution: Article V and Congress' Present Duty to Call a Convention for Proposing Amendments," *Hamline Law Review* 14, no.1 (Fall 1990): 15-6

[117] Max Farrand, *The Records of the Federal Convention of 1787, Vol. II* (New Haven: Yale University Press, 1911 rev. 1937),133, Report I

[118] Ibid., 148, Report IV – the "nine" is a replacement for the two thirds.

[119] William Montgomery Meigs, *The Growth of the Constitution in the Federal Convention of 1787: An Effort to Trace the Origin and Development of Each Separate Clause from Its First Suggestion in That Body to the Form Finally Approved* (Philadelphia: J. B. Lippincott, 1900), 273-4

[120] Max Farrand, *The Records of the Federal Convention of 1787, Vol. II* (New Haven: Yale University Press, 1911 rev. 1937), 159, Report VI

[121] Ibid., 174, Report IX

Sickle and Lynn Boughey point to this set of modifications as the origin of the application and call provision. The last version given in Version IX, found in the handwriting of James Wilson, suggests that the singular amendment proposal was expected. This would clearly imply a limited amendatory convention.[122] It also proves that the convention concept was not a late addition to the Constitution.

Monday, 6 August 1787:

The amendment process as proposed remained in the first report of the Committee of the Whole, including the omission of the national legislature's participation in or approval of amendments and was once again approved by the convention. After two months, the draft was referred to the Committee of Detail which refined the wording of now Article XIX to read,

> "On the application of the Legislatures of two thirds of the States in the Union, **for an amendment** of this Constitution, the Legislature of the United States shall call a Convention **for that purpose.**"[123]

The amendment process has barely changed, but more importantly, it remained in the hands of the States and not the national legislature. The italics added are to emphasize the meaning of the latest draft. It is this emphasis that Robert Rhodes highlighted in 1973 and suggested that the significance of the clause, "*for that purpose*," refers to the convention itself and that the convention must then be limited to that proposed topic for amendment consideration. Rhodes said that,

> "by employing the specific language "an amendment," the draftsmen of the Constitution demonstrated a clear intention to enable state legislatures to request a convention for consideration of **limited**[124] constitutional change."[125]

The intention of the delegates, and especially those on the Committee of Detail, was clearly to provide for a limited convention for the purpose of

---

[122] Bruce M. Van Sickle and Lynn M. Boughey, "Lawful and Peaceful Revolution: Article V and Congress' Present Duty to Call a Convention for Proposing Amendments," *Hamline Law Review* 14, no.1 (Fall 1990): 16

[123] Max Farrand, *The Records of the Federal Convention of 1787, Vol. II* (New Haven: Yale University Press, 1911 rev. 1937), 188

[124] This author's bold italics added for emphasis.

[125] Robert M. Rhodes, "A Limited Federal Constitutional Convention," *University of Florida Law Review* XXVI, no.1 (Fall 1973): 3-5

considering specific amendments – and it appears from the records of the 1787 convention, that it always was the delegates' intention! Furthermore, Rhodes argued that the subsequent revisions to the amending article were consistent in this position.[126] The revised draft was submitted to the convention and the amendment process would be brought up for discussion again on September 10th. The Article XIX version occurred a full six weeks before the end of the convention.

Thursday, 30 August 1787:

The long gap between actions is due to the consideration of the proposed articles one-by-one over the intervening period. This day, the Committee of Detail report was discussed and the amendment power was given in Article XIX. Gouverneur Morris suggested "that the [national] Legislature should be left at liberty to call a Convention, whenever they pleased." That comment was accepted without objection.[127] As it stood on this day, only the States may initiate the amendment process. Of equal interest is that there is no mention of the ratification method.[128]

Wednesday, 5 September 1787:

Elbridge Gerry made a motion to reconsider proposed Article XIX.[129] No action was taken.

Monday, 10 September 1787:

This day proved the most important for the development of Article V and the convention method. The delegates began by reading Article XIX as "On the application of the legislatures of two-thirds of the states in the Union for an amendment of this Constitution, the legislature of the United States shall call a convention for that purpose." Now the delegates began to voice serious concerns. Elbridge Gerry worried that the state constitutions could be subverted by the national government and made a motion to reconsider. Alexander Hamilton worried just the opposite – that the States would use the amendment process to increase their powers, so he seconded

---

[126] Ibid., 5-8

[127] Max Farrand, *The Records of the Federal Convention of 1787, Vol. II* (New Haven: Yale University Press, 1911 rev. 1937), 468

[128] Opinion 79-75 of the Office of Legal Counsel, (10 Oct 1979), 399

[129] Max Farrand, *The Records of the Federal Convention of 1787, Vol. II* (New Haven: Yale University Press, 1911 rev. 1937), 511

Gerry's motion. Hamilton proposed that the Congress instead be vested with the power to propose amendments. Hamilton theorized that the majority could force amendments on the whole union so amendments should be easier to make. He believed that the national legislature was better equipped to discern when an amendment was needed and that the two chambers should each be able to call a convention when two-thirds of each chamber voted to do so. Here, "Madison remarked on the vagueness of the terms, 'call a Convention for the purpose' as sufficient reason for reconsidering the article. How was a Convention to be formed? by what rule decide? what the force of its acts?"[130] Perhaps Madison was seeking only to codify the procedure for calling a convention – if so, that was prescient of today's difficulties. More likely, he was distinguishing between the plenary power of a constitutional convention and the limited and restrained powers of an amendatory convention.

Now, Gerry's motion was passed.

With this motion, the horse trading began. Connecticut's Roger Sherman moved to place the power to propose amendments in the hands of Congress, but leaving the ratification to the States. He suggested the wording,

> "or the Legislature may propose amendments to the several States for their approbation, but no amendments shall be binding until consented to by the several States."[131]

Gerry seconded. Sensing that this development put the nation back to the very problem that precipitated the crisis, that of unanimous approval of amendments, James Wilson suggested changing this requirement to two-thirds of the States. When that was rejected, he then suggested three-quarters of the States to ratify. There was no objection.[132] Now the wording went as follows,

> "On the application of the Legislatures of two thirds of the States in the Union, for an amendment of this Constitution, the Legislature of the United States shall call a Convention for that purpose or the Legislature may propose amendments to the several States for their approbation, but no amendments shall be binding until consented to by three fourths of the

---

[130] Ibid., 558
[131] Ibid.
[132] Ibid., 559

*several States."*¹³³

In this version, the wording for both singular and multiple amendments are found. Then, Madison joined the bidding and proposed that two thirds of either the Congress or the States could propose amendments and that three-quarters of the state legislatures or conventions could ratify. The new wording read,

> *"The Legislature of the U- S- whenever two thirds of both Houses shall deem necessary, or on the application of two thirds of the Legislatures of the several States, shall propose amendments to this Constitution, which shall be valid to all intents and purposes as part thereof, when the same shall have been ratified by three fourths at least of the Legislatures of the several States, or by Conventions in three fourths thereof, as one or the other mode of ratification may be proposed by the Legislature of the U.S."*¹³⁴

Although Hamilton seconded the motion, John Rutledge objected to the threat to slavery and the compromise of protection until 1808 was added. The new phrasing passed decisively, nine states to one.

The finalized version, the Madison-Hamilton proposal, was given to the Committee of Style and Arrangement to put the Constitution into a final draft. In this finalized form, the Madison-Hamilton proposal did not hinder or prohibit the state legislatures from initiating specific amendments.¹³⁵ Each antecedent of Article V consistently permitted the States to initiate amendments and allowed for a limited convention. Two days later, the draft was given to the delegates to consider.

The final wording through September 10th of Article XIX now read as,

> *"The Legislature of the United States, whenever two thirds of both Houses shall deem necessary, or on the application of two thirds of the Legislatures of the several States, shall propose amendments to this Constitution which shall be valid to all intents and purposes as parts thereof, when the same shall have been ratified by three fourths at least of the Legislatures of the several States, or by Conventions in three fourths thereof, as one or the*

---

¹³³ Bruce M. Van Sickle and Lynn M. Boughey, "Lawful and Peaceful Revolution: Article V and Congress' Present Duty to Call a Convention for Proposing Amendments," *Hamline Law Review* 14, no.1 (Fall 1990): 19

¹³⁴ Max Farrand, *The Records of the Federal Convention of 1787, Vol. II* (New Haven. Yale University Press, 1911 rev. 1937), 559

¹³⁵ Ibid., 558-9

other mode of ratification may be proposed by the Legislature of the United-States: Provided that no amendments which may be made prior to the year 1808, shall in any manner affect the 4th and 5th Sections of article the 7th."[136]

Wednesday, 12 September 1787:

The Committee of Style and Arrangement finished its work and submitted the completed draft to the Convention. The article was renumbered as V after cleaning up the changes.[137]

Saturday, 15 September 1787:

The final debate took place on the last day of official discussion, September 15. By now, the amendment provision was known as Article V. Roger Sherman brought up the danger to the smaller states and the threat to their equality in the Senate. He made suggestion of a clause to protect their suffrage and internal police powers. George Mason still thought the congressional role to be "excessive."[138] Mason now expressed his worry over the process, predicting the oppressive nature of a future federal government. He called the amendment process "exceptional and dangerous." He noted that the process in both modes was, "in the first immediately, and in the second, ultimately" dependent on Congress.[139] Mason was displeased and insisted that the States be able to propose amendments independent of Congress. Mason expressly gave his reason that he expected that the national "Government should become oppressive, as he verily believed would be the case." At this point Gouverneur Morris and Elbridge Gerry proposed the "convention of the States for proposing amendments."[140] They suggested that two thirds of the states be necessary to successfully apply for a convention. This is very crucial – Gerry had proposed a *limited* convention mechanism as he was insisting that the States retain a role in ratifying and not leave it to a future convention to conduct the entire amendment process without oversight and approval. The role left to Congress was now ministerial and the States were again equal to Congress in the amendment power.

---

[136] Ibid., 578
[137] Ibid., 578, 602
[138] William Van Alstyne, "The Limited Constitutional Convention – The Recurring Answer," *Duke Law Journal* 1979, (1979): 988
[139] Max Farrand, *The Records of the Federal Convention of 1787, Vol. II* (New Haven: Yale University Press, 1911 rev. 1937), 629
[140] Ibid.

At this point, Madison injected his remarks about the ambiguity of the process. He,

> "did not see why Congress would not be as much bound to propose amendments applied for by two-thirds of the States as to call a Convention on the like application. He saw no objection, however, against providing for a Convention for the purpose of amendments, except only that difficulties might arise as to the form, the quorum, etc., which in Constitutional regulations ought to be as much as possible avoided."[141]

Madison's observations on the difficulties have proved to be somewhat prophetic in light of the debate today.[142] But then, Madison did not fight the proposition; rather, he acquiesced quickly. The reason for his swift agreement is most likely that he already knew the answers to his questions. The composition and operation of the convention to propose amendments would undoubtedly operate on the same rules of the current convention and all those prior intercolonial and interstate conventions – some of which Madison had participated in, such as the Annapolis convention in 1786.[143]

At this suggestion, Madison stated that he saw the Congress and the States proposing amendments as equal propositions. He would expand on this point in *The Federalist* No.43 during the ratification campaigns.[144] Although the motion of Morris and Gerry was agreed to, Sherman and Gerry began proposing that parts of Article V be struck out until Sherman asked for the complete removal of Article V. Sherman stated that he feared that "amendments might be made fatal to particular States, such as abolishing them altogether or depriving them of their equality in the Senate."[145] Sherman suggested that Article V be modified to read so that it would be interpreted, "to leave future conventions to act like the present Convention, according to circumstances."[146] This action would have

---

[141] Ibid., 629-30
[142] Henry D. Levine, "Limited Federal Constitutional Conventions: Implications of the State Experience," *Harvard Journal on Legislation* 11 (1973): 128
[143] Robert G. Natelson, "James Madison and the Constitution's "Convention For Proposing Amendments"," *Akron Law Review* 45 (2012): 440
[144] Michael Stern, "Reopening the Constitutional Road to Reform: Toward a Safeguarded Article V Convention," *Tennessee Law Review* 78 (2011): 771
[145] William Montgomery Meigs, *The Growth of the Constitution in the Federal Convention of 1787 An Effort to Trace the Origin and Development of Each Separate Clause from Its First Suggestion in That Body to the Form Finally Approved* (Philadelphia: J. B. Lippincott, 1900), 276
[146] Max Farrand, *The Records of the Federal Convention of 1787, Vol. II* (New Haven: Yale University Press, 1911 rev. 1937), 629-30

permitted future Article V conventions to be plenary and do as they saw fit – including the modern concern of replacing the Constitution. The motion was voted down by a vote of 3 ayes, 7 noes, 1 divided. Then Elbridge Gerry made a motion to remove the convention option and that was crushed decisively: 1 aye, 10 noes.[147]

Roger Sherman wanted to add another clause to protect the States' internal police power. This also was rejected. Then Sherman made a motion to strike Article V in its entirety and that was seconded by David Brearly of New Jersey. The convention continued its streak of squashing changes. But then Gouverneur Morris suggested the clause for equal suffrage in the Senate and that was accepted without either debate or opposition. At this time, Col. Mason proposed a change to the clause to protect the slave trade but it was refused.[148]

Gov. Randolph made a similar request "that amendments to the plan might be offered by the State Conventions, which should be submitted to and finally decided on by another general Convention." Col. Mason seconded Randolph's motion. Gerry concurred. Both of these ideas were refused by the delegates of the convention. The vote against a second general convention was…unanimous.[149] No provision was then made for either another general convention to refine the Constitution as proposed or for any other future plenary constitutional conventions.[150,151] All states had voted against the proposals for another general convention and for any future plenary conventions. The equal senate suffrage was added without debate and the matter closed.

The Battle Over a Second General Convention, Part I

The brief exchange on the last day of the convention has proven crucial over time. The call for a second general convention became a major issue that roared throughout the debates of the ratification conventions. George Mason, Elbridge Gerry and Edmund Randolph worked strenuously

---

[147] Ibid.

[148] Ibid., 630-1

[149] Edward Larson and Michael Winship, *The Constitutional Convention, A Narrative History from the Notes of James Madison* (New York: The Modern Library, 2005), 153

[150] Robert M. Rhodes, "A Limited Federal Constitutional Convention," *University of Florida Law Review* XXVI, no.1 (Fall 1973): 7-8

[151] Max Farrand, *The Records of the Federal Convention of 1787, Vol. II* (New Haven: Yale University Press, 1911 rev. 1937), 631-2

during the final days of the Philadelphia convention to secure a second fully plenary convention to consider changes and amendments to the proposed constitution. Randolph wanted the ratification to be made by the state legislatures and not the ratification conventions that Article VII required. He knew that the desired amendments stood a greater chance of success with the wily state legislators than with the mix of legislators and the public expected to be present in the ratification conventions.[152]

It was theorized that if the States, through either their legislatures or ratification conventions, were allowed to propose amendments, that the whole process would bog down indefinitely and that the proposed constitution would be so radically altered by amendments that it would bear little semblance to the document submitted. Richard Labunski succinctly summarizes the inevitable result, "When Congress eventually met, it would have to sort out hundreds of amendments, knowing that the failure to give them sufficient attention would permit a state to withdraw its conditional ratification."[153]

And, the States did ultimately submit hundreds of amendment proposals. While many overlapped from state-to-state, some states submitted dozens, such as Virginia which submitted the most proposed amendments. The allowance of a conditional ratification was another issue that Madison sought to avoid. But, once the submission of proposed amendments started, there would be no way to stop it. Those states that did not submit early amendment proposals with their ratifications might well decide to revisit the matter and submit their own amendment proposals and the process would soon escalate. What bothered Madison most is that the powers that the States were delegating to the new federal government would be brought back to the States and just leave the nation where it started – with a dysfunctional national government. The issue of taxation – which was the central issue of curing the lack of funding for the national government - was already being attacked. On 23 August 1788, Madison wrote to Jefferson that the second convention would be, "composed of men who will essentially mutilate the system, particularly in the article of taxation."[154]

---

[152] Richard Labunski, *James Madison and the Struggle for the Bill of Rights* (New York: Oxford University Press, 2006), 10-1
[153] Ibid., 51
[154] Letter of James Madison to Thomas Jefferson, 23 August 1788

Charles Pinckney had said of the ideas, in an oft quoted, but usually shortened form,

> "The Deputies to a second Convention coming together under the discordant impressions of their Constituents, will never agree. Conventions are serious things, and ought not to be repeated..."[155]

James Madison tried to define the limits and powers of the convention, but no one joined in the debate. The intent then of the delegates remained unknown. To get a better grasp of the thinking of the delegates, one has to look to the ratification debates for more detail. In the Virginia ratification convention, Madison spoke little on the subject of Article V. A fellow Virginia ratification convention delegate, Wilson Nicholas, offered this rationale for supporting Article V,

> "The conventions which shall be so called will have their deliberations confined to a few points; no local interest to divert their attention; nothing but the necessary alterations. They will have many advantages over the last convention. No experiments to devise; the general and fundamental regulations being already laid down."[156]

We can see in this comment the idea of the application of the traditional convention rules and regulations that had prevailed over the last century and a half in British North America being the expected course of action. The concept of the limited convention with defined powers is implicit in Nicholas' comment.[157] More importantly, it shows that the Founding Era leaders expected future conventions to follow the same rules as they had used in the Philadelphia Constitutional Convention, and in the subsequent ratification conventions in the several states.

The final product of the amending process was a parallel path system that was not necessarily intended to be used equally in terms of the number of times employed, but for all contingencies. The real utility lay in the problems that it solved rather than in the potential that the process holds. Walter Dellinger summed it up as a method of solving both the problem of a

---

[155] Max Farrand, *The Records of the Federal Convention of 1787, Vol. II* (New Haven: Yale University Press, 1911 rev. 1937), 632

[156] Jonathan Elliot, *The Debates in the Several State Conventions on the Adoption of the Federal Constitution, Vol. III* (Philadelphia: J.P. Lippincott, 1836), 102

[157] Wilbur Edel, *A Constitutional Convention – Threat or Challenge?* (New York: Praeger, 1981), 31

recalcitrant Congress and the States following their self-interest.[158]

Upon reflection, we find two ways to look at the events in Philadelphia. The first is that a great compromise was reached where both the staunch defenders of the States and the visionary proponents of a stronger, more effective national government prevailed. The system of checks and balances was expanded to include dual paths to amendment. From the other perspective, we see that a deception was perpetuated on the States. The state-application-and convention method has been described as, "the clumsy and uncertain method of a constitutional convention…a more harmless sop to Mason and his followers…the practical result has been to deprive the states of any effective role in proposing constitutional amendments."[159] Until we try the state convention method, we will not know which is the correct assessment.

Ratification

The Philadelphia Convention was not the heroic, popular event at the time that we imagine today. It was controversial from the beginning as the delegates met in secrecy. The nature of the work and the possibility of the incomplete and on-going deliberations being misconstrued by the public made secrecy necessary.[160] As it were, the rumor mill in 1787 Philadelphia was working overtime attempting to discern what could be happening behind the closed doors of the State House. Alexander Hamilton spent time in August writing to associates in New York in an effort to determine who had started a rumor that the Convention had been negotiating with a nephew of George III to become king of the United States.[161,162] Even after the Convention concluded, rumors circulated that the real goal of the Constitution was to

---

[158] Walter Dellinger, "The Recurring Question of the "Limited" Constitutional Convention," *Yale Law Journal* 88 (1979): 1626

[159] Fred P. Graham, "The Role of the States in Proposing Constitutional Amendments," *American Bar Association Journal* 49, no.12 (Dec. 1963): 1176

[160] John P. Kaminski, *Secrecy and the Constitutional Convention* (Madison: The Center for the Study of the American Constitution, University of Wisconsin-Madison, 2005), generally

[161] Forrest McDonald, *Novus Ordo Seclorum, The Intellectual Origins of the Constitution* (Lawrence: University of Kansas Press, 1985), 79

[162] There is an analogy to be drawn to today in this aspect of the convention history. Eventually, proto-Antifederalists were determined to be behind the effort to derail the convention for "revising" the Articles. This is similar to today's efforts by national organizations to derail an Article V convention effort.

install an aristocracy.[163] Key and influential patriot leaders, such as Sam Adams, John Hancock and Patrick Henry sat out the proceedings as well as the entire state of Rhode Island.[164] When the Constitution was done, the Convention Secretary, Major William Jackson, forwarded it to the Confederation Congress for review and promulgation to the States. Congress reviewed, and debated, the proposed Constitution for two days. More than anything else, they were surprised at the anticipated "alterations" made to the Articles of Confederation. The Congress was shocked and annoyed at the "liberties" taken by the delegates with their instructions from their state legislatures. Eventually Congress realized that the Convention had not operated under the authority of the Articles of Confederation because there was no provision in the Articles for a convention. Congress passed a resolution on 28 September 1787 to transmit the Constitution to the state legislatures, "in order to be submitted to a Convention of delegates chosen in each state, by the people thereof, in conformity to the resolves of the Convention made and provided in that case."[165]

The choice of requiring the States to hold ratification conventions was intentional. After holding the people's attention hostage for the summer and the press speculating on what was transpiring in the Pennsylvania State House the delegates were aware that their actions would be under intense scrutiny and the results of their work would be judged suspiciously and with the closest inspection for errors. The men who met for over one hundred days to reshape the young nation were almost all from the upper crust of colonial society. They were predominantly lawyers and land owners. In the new post-colonial America, they were the new aristocracy of landed gentry. They were, on the whole, wealthy and well connected. It was understandable and even expected that their actions would be treated with apprehension. Madison had urged in the convention that the new constitution be ratified by state conventions since "he thought it indispensable that the new Constitution should be ratified in the most unexceptionable form, and by the supreme authority of the people themselves."[166] Connecticut delegate

---

[163] Stephen B. Presser, "Constitutional Amendments: Dangerous Threat or Democracy in Action," *Texas Review of Law & Policy* 5, no.1 (2000): 212 – referring to Letters from a "Federal Farmer" in *The Republican*, 8 November 1787

[164] Patrick Henry was selected as a delegate from Virginia but declined because he said that "I smelt a Rat."

[165] Jonathan Elliot, *The Debates in the Several State Conventions on the Adoption of the Federal Constitution* (Philadelphia: J.B. Lippincott, 2d ed., 1836), 319

[166] Max Farrand, *The Records of the Federal Convention of 1787, Vol. I* (New Haven: Yale University Press, 1911 rev. 1937), 123

and future US Supreme Court Chief Justice Oliver Ellsworth anticipated the potential for public mistrust of the delegates and penned a public letter published in the newspapers under the name "A Landholder" which explained the decision of leaving the ratification to the people in state conventions:

> *"It proves the honesty and patriotism of the gentlemen who composed the general Convention, that they chose to submit their system to the people rather than the legislatures, whose decisions are often influenced by men in the higher departments of government, who have provided well for themselves and dread any change lest they should be injured by its operation... This danger was foreseen by the Federal Convention, and they have wisely avoided it by appealing directly to the people."*[167]

For a group that despised democracy – and the words "democracy" and "democratic" appear NOWHERE in the Constitution – this was a most democratic as well as politically shrewd move.[168] The inevitable reverence that the people adopted toward the Constitution began with the people's choice to ratify THEIR Constitution.

Consequently, the next phase of American conventions began as the ratification conventions got underway in the States. Once again, Americans had produced political innovations in the form of the constitutional convention and the amendatory convention. And then another...as the state ratification conventions did their work of debating the proposed Constitution, point by point and clause by clause, the ratification convention delegates took note of what was missing – a bill of rights to protect the hard won liberties of the people.[169] The ratification conventions worked as planned and went off almost without a hitch. The conventions were often contentious and the latter ones were in doubt until the end, but the methodology prevailed. The only unexpected occurrences being the rejection by North Carolina and that the ratification notices from the conventions which were returned to Congress were accompanied by lists of recommended changes – 189 in total from five states that held ratification conventions.

---

[167] Max Farrand, *The Records of the Federal Convention of 1787, Vol. III* (New Haven: Yale University Press, 1911 rev. 1937), 137.

[168] Nonetheless, there are and have been those that are incensed by this idea. For example, see Walter Clark, "The Next Constitutional Convention of the United States," *Yale Law Journal* 16, no.2 (Dec. 1906): 70

[169] Charles Pinckney had submitted a partial bill of rights to the Committee of Detail on August 18 during the Philadelphia Convention.

Three more added their recommendations later.[170,171] Surprisingly, none of the 189 proposed amendments affected or addressed Article V – the process seemed to have passed muster with the States and the people.[172,173] So the later ratification conventions have another interpretation: they were a new hybridization of the ratifying convention and the amendatory convention. They operated as back-to-back conventions, first ratifying the Constitution and then proposing, debating and sending to Congress amendment proposals. The proposal of amendments, although not done by all the States, together and at once, proved the feasibility of the amendatory convention for the federal constitution.

Take a moment to consider the gravity of this observation. The States convened to ratify the Constitution, which they did. They had objections – some quite significant, as evidenced by North Carolina's rejection of the Constitution in its first ratifying convention – but they dealt with the objections through the submission of proposed amendments. The eight states that proposed, debated and drafted proposed amendments were acting, although individually, in the same exact manner and procedure as an amendatory convention. They did not "runaway" and attempt to rewrite the Constitution. They did not pass legislation. They did not impose a new ratification process. They did act to redress their grievances by directing those in a written form to the Congress. They assumed the additional function of an amendatory convention in order to complete the ratification process for which they were called. Should Congress have chosen to reject or ignore the submissions from the five states, nothing would have come of that action, or inaction. Caplan highlighted that Thomas Jefferson himself went from "skeptic to supporter" of the Constitution, based on the tactic introduced in Massachusetts of ratifying and then recommending amendments, providing that a proposed bill of rights accompanied the

---

[170] Jonathan Elliot, *The Debates in the Several State Conventions on the Adoption of the Federal Constitution* (Philadelphia: J.B. Lippincott, 2d ed., 1836), 319-24 - Massachusetts, New Hampshire, New York, South Carolina, and Virginia.

[171] In total, eight of the thirteen original States submitted proposed amendments: Pennsylvania, Massachusetts, South Carolina, New Hampshire, Virginia, New York, North Carolina and Rhode Island, some after the fact of ratification.

[172] Henry Paul Monaghan, "We the People[s], Original Understanding, and Constitutional Amendment," *Columbia Law Review* 96, no.1 (Jan.1996): 160

[173] When Rhode Island did finally get around to considering the Constitution, they did include proposed amendments and the suggestion that the amendment process be made MORE DIFFICULT. See, William F. Swindler, "Current Challenge to Federalism: The Confederating Proposals," *The Georgetown Law Journal* 52, no. 1 (Fall 1963): 19

ratification resolution.[174,175] Thus, the ratification conventions for the Constitution were themselves, in a manner, our first Article V amendatory conventions.

The ratification conventions had done exactly what they were designed to do: they appealed to and convinced the people of the value of the proposed Constitution. The people took to the Constitution enough to immediately begin using the Article V provision and suggest amendments before the Constitution was even ratified and carried into effect!

These ratification conventions were no mere rubber stamps. North Carolina outright rejected the Constitution for the lack of a bill of rights. But once the Congress was prodded into passing a bill of rights, North Carolina called another ratification convention and ratified the Constitution and rejoined the Union proving the efficacy of not just the Constitution, and in particular Article V, but of conventions as effective vehicles of constitutional change.[176] New Hampshire recessed its initial convention and waited to see what the other states would do before reconvening to ratify.

The use of the convention method of amendment ratification has also been tried by opponents of proposed amendments as a way of appealing to popular dislike of the amendment proposal in order to secure the proposed amendment's defeat. Opponents had suggested that the Thirteenth and Fifteenth Amendments be sent to ratification conventions in the States. They hoped to use the unpopularity of the proposed amendment to protect state legislators from having to vote on what was considered a repugnant issue.[177] The opponents of the Sixteenth Amendment took the same tack of suggesting state ratification conventions counting on the sensibilities of state legislators to want to avoid a vote on the proposal. The opponents even accused the amendment's proposers of intentionally planning to defeat the bill just to claim the moral high ground.[178] Similarly, for the Eighteenth Amendment, it was proposed in the US House that state ratification conventions be used. The idea was to sidestep the powerful influence of the

---

[174] Russell B. Caplan, *Constitutional Brinkmanship* (New York: Oxford University Press, 1988), 35

[175] Letter of Thomas Jefferson to James Madison of 18 November 1788

[176] Ralph R. Martig, "Amending the Constitution Article V: The Keystone of the Arch," *Michigan Law Review* 35, no.8 (1937): 1264

[177] David E. Kyvig, *Explicit and Authentic Acts, Amending the U.S. Constitution 1776-1995* (Lawrence: University Press of Kansas, 1996), 180-1

[178] Ibid., 203

"dry" lobbyists.[179] The use of conventions for the ratification of the Twenty-first Amendment was a plank in the platforms of both the Democratic and Republican parties in the 1932 election.[180] The publicly stated argument of the parties was that the people should be able to have as direct a voice as possible on the issue.[181] The not-so-publicly stated reason was that the power of the prohibitionists had not yet politically waned and there could be electoral ramifications for legislators who vote for repeal as the "drys" would surely target pro-repeal voting incumbents in the 1934 elections.[182]

The impact of the Twenty-first Amendment ratification conventions – still Article V conventions by definition – on the Article V process was tremendous. The same questions as today were raised: who would organize the conventions; who would select the delegates; who would set the rules, etc.? Ethan Davis summarized,

> "A [third] view was for Congress to call and prescribe the form of the state conventions directly. This suggestion triggered ire in the House. Representative Celler argued that "by reasonable interpretation the word 'convention' as used in Article V of the Constitution precludes and repels the idea that the convention shall be called, elected, organized, or governed by congressional fiat. I incline to the belief that that must and shall be a State matter exclusively."[183] Representative Garber insisted that "[t]he State legislatures will fix the time and place of holding the conventions, the number of delegates, the apportionment of delegates, the qualifications of delegates, and the voters."[184] Representative McSwain, during a long speech, lambasted the idea of allowing Congress to construct the conventions as "unconstitutional, un-American, undemocratic, and unwise."[185] Since the state legislatures acted rapidly, Congress never had the opportunity to test its power to prescribe state constitutional conventions directly. An important constitutional question was left for another day–a question that

---

[179] Ibid., 223

[180] Herman V. Ames, "Recent Development of the Amending Power as Applied to the Federal Constitution," *Proceedings of the American Philosophical Society* 72, no.2 (1933): 93-5

[181] In 1930, Justice Clark of the Federal Circuit Court had stated in *U.S. v. Sprague*, 44 Fed. 2d. 982 that the Eighteenth Amendment had been unconstitutionally ratified since the people had not been given the opportunity to pass on the amendment in a convention. The Supreme Court rejected this in *U.S. v. Sprague*, 282 U.S. 716. Taken from Ames, supra 95.

[182] Ethan P. Davis, "Liquor Laws and Constitutional Conventions: A Legal History of the Twenty-first Amendment," *Yale Law School Student Scholarship Papers*, Paper 65 (2008): 19

[183] 76 Cong. Rec. 4515 (statement of Rep. Celler)

[184] 76 Cong. Rec. 4519 (statement of Rep. Garber)

[185] 76 Cong. Rec. 4524 (statement of Rep. McSwain)

remains unanswered."[186]

As a corollary, proponents of the Seventeenth Amendment, in the form of state legislatures in thirty-one states, had asked for a state ratification convention because they feared that the state legislators might be susceptible to influence.[187] They viewed the probability for passage higher if tried in a state convention than a state legislature. It has been surmised that if the Equal Rights Amendment had gone to state ratification conventions instead of the state legislatures, the high popular support would have quickly secured passage.[188]

Herman Ames related an anecdote where a debate of sorts took place, in 1932-33 just prior to the ratification conventions for the Twenty-first Amendment, between former Attorney General A. Mitchell Palmer and former Solicitor General and Congressman James Beck on the issue of whether Congress could take control of the ratification convention function. Palmer argued that the Congress could assume the powers to "create and maintain" a convention and to determine how it might operate as the Supreme Court had recognized a convention as a federal function. Palmer asserted that "either Congress has the necessary power or no one has it."[189] Palmer, according to Ames, "argues in favor of a broad construction of the implied powers of Congress" and relies on the Necessary and Proper Clause to justify a congressional takeover of the convention process where the Constitution makes no such provision.

Beck, in turn, relies on a simple view that if the Framers meant for Congress to have these powers, they would have explicitly delegated them to Congress in the Constitution. Beck cites the Tenth Amendment as the source of the States' power to convene and operate the Article V conventions.[190] The outcome of this exchange was the introduction in Congress of a bill to federalize the operation of the ratification conventions.[191] An immediate backlash resulted from the more constitutionally minded members of

---

[186] Ethan P. Davis, "Liquor Laws and Constitutional Conventions: A Legal History of the Twenty-first Amendment," *Yale Law School Student Scholarship Papers*, Paper 65 (2008): 22

[187] David E. Kyvig, *Explicit and Authentic Acts, Amending the U.S. Constitution 1776-1995* (Lawrence: University Press of Kansas, 1996), 213

[188] Ibid., 418

[189] 76 Cong. Rec. (Daily) at 138 (1932)

[190] 76 Cong. Rec. (Daily) at 113 (1932)

[191] Cong. Rec., 72nd Cong., 2d sess., at 4584, H.R.14728

both houses of Congress. They expressed doubt as to the "validity of the ratification of the amendment" should this federalization process proceed. The front-running candidate for the open Attorney General appointment called it "questionable." In the end, Congress chose to leave the operation of the ratification conventions to the States thus setting today's precedent.[192]

The most important lesson to be learned, according to Ames, was that, "It has been demonstrated that 'the cumbrous machinery of Article V,' as it was once described by President Woodrow Wilson, can be made to work when public opinion is sufficiently aroused"[193] proving that the people remain the driving force behind constitutional amendment. In recognition of this fact, it must be conceded that the power of amendment is still in the hands of the people if, and only if, they will act to set the priorities of the political agenda and to launch the process. The public pushed for the Twenty-first Amendment by launching a public relations campaign almost immediately after the passage of the Eighteenth Amendment. Their actions at the polls demonstrated their resolve to the elected officials. Finally, their actions in approving the Twenty-first Amendment in ratification conventions independent of the state legislatures culminated the effort to repeal and end Prohibition. The system worked exactly as the Framers had intended – according to the will of the people and despite the political consequences that were so fervently feared by the legislators.

The Battle Over a Second General Convention, Part II

The constitutional convention story has one more episode to relate before moving on to the experience of pursuing an Article V convention. While some of the states were compiling a list of proposed amendments during their ratification conventions in 1787-91, other states were echoing Philadelphia convention delegate George Mason in calling for a second constitutional convention to re-examine and rewrite the proposed constitution. This effort was being led by the Anti-Federalists. Madison recognized this attempt for what it was worth – a wholesale scrapping of the constitution and the imposition of the Anti-Federalist agenda in a new constitution. Much has been made over the last half century of Madison's rejection of a second convention. Opponents of an Article V convention

---

[192] Herman V. Ames, "Recent Development of the Amending Power as Applied to the Federal Constitution," *Proceedings of the American Philosophical Society* 72, no.2 (1933): 96-8
[193] Ibid., 100

claim that Madison thought that the 1787 convention a stroke of luck – a fluke – that could not be repeated. They posit that the Philadelphia experience was lightening in a bottle and term it a miracle.

The truth is less dramatic, but no less interesting. Madison realized that the patience of the public and the state legislatures was at end; any attempt at a new or second constitutional convention would result in a public spectacle, most likely with no new charter produced in the end. The States would end up either with each going their own way or in smaller, regional – and therefore competing - confederacies. Any delegates to a second convention would come prepared with their list of demands and the foreknowledge of what had been produced by the first convention. Using this knowledge, the States would each seek to manipulate the debate to their own advantage. Over the course of a single year, Madison's view changed, prompted by the ratification of the Constitution. Initially, he opposed amendments let alone a second convention. Mason, Gerry and Randolph had continued their campaign to secure a second general, plenary convention without let up since leaving Philadelphia.[194] In January of 1788 Madison wrote to Edmund Randolph advising that,

> *"In this State the party adverse to the Constitution notoriously meditate either a dissolution of the Union, or protracting it by patching up the Articles of Confederation…You are better acquainted with Mr. [Patrick] Henry's politics than I be, but I have for some time considered him as driving at a Southern Confederacy and not further concurring in the plan of amendments than as he hopes to render it subservient to his real designs. Viewing the matter in this light, the inference with me is unavoidable that were a second trial to be made, the friends of a good constitution for the Union would not only find themselves not a little differing from each other as to the proper amendments; but perplexed and frustrated by men who had objects totally different. A second Convention would, of course, be formed under the influence, and composed in a great measure of the members of the opposition in the several States. But were the first difficulties overcome, and the Constitution re-edited with amendments, the event would still be infinitely precarious… The very attempt at a second Convention strikes at the confidence in the first; and the existence of a second, by opposing influence to influence would in a manner destroy an effectual confidence in either, and give a loose rein to human opinions; which must be as various and*

---

[194] Ralph Ketcham, *James Madison, A Biography* (Charlottesville: University of Virginia Press, 1990), 234

> *irreconcilable concerning theories of Government, as doctrines of Religion; and give opportunities to designing men which it might be impossible to counteract."*[195]

Madison sees neither a second convention nor amendments as appropriate. He recognizes that the opposition has an objective of perpetuating the weak federal government of the Articles of Confederation as opposed to the strengthened government of the Constitution designed to resolve the weaknesses that were driving the United States to ruin. By April of 1788 he was writing to George Nicholas that,

> *"Conditional amendments or a second general Convention will be fatal… It is a fact, of which though probably not a great number may be apprized, that the late Convention were in one stage of the business for several days under the strongest apprehensions of an abortive issue to their deliberations. There were moments during this period at which despair seemed with many to predominate. I can ascribe the final success to nothing but the temper with which many Members assembled, and their ignorance of the opinions & confidence in the liberality of their respective constituents. The circumstances under which a second Convention composed even wiser individuals, would meet, must extinguish every hope of an equal spirit of accommodation; and if it should happen to contain men who secretly aimed at disunion, (and such I believe would be found from more than one State) the game would be as easy as it would be obvious, to insist on points popular in some parts, but known to be inadmissible in others of the Union. Should it happen otherwise, and another plan be agreed on, it must now be evident from a view of the objection prevailing in the different States among the advocates for amendments, that the opponents in this State who are attached to the Union and sensible of the necessity of a nervous Government for it, would be more dissatisfied with the result of the second than of the first experiment."*[196]

Madison doubts that the men who would serve in the second convention would be as dedicated to the national service and free of personal gain as the men who set aside differences in the first convention. He knows that the convention will be a show, a farce, put on for the purpose of justifying the breakup of the young nation and manipulated to push the southern states into a southern nation. Just two days later, Madison tells Edmund Randolph that he may be ready to consider amendments,

---

[195] Letter of James Madison to Edmund Randolph, 10 January 1788
[196] Letter of James Madison to George Nicholas, 8 April 1788

> "*Recommendatory amendments are the only ground that occurs to me. A conditional ratification or a second convention appears to me utterly irreconcilable in the present state of things with the dictates of prudence and safety. I am confirmed, by a comparative view of the publications on the subject, and still more of the debates in the several conventions, that a second experiment would be either wholly abortive, or would end in something much more remote from your ideas and those of others who wish a salutary Government, than the plan now before the public.*"[197]

Similarly to his writings to Nicholas and Randolph, Madison writes on April 22 to Thomas Jefferson, warning that,

> "*The preliminary question will be whether previous alterations shall be insisted on or not? Should this be carried in the affirmative, either a conditional ratification, or a proposal for a new Constitution will ensue. In either event, I think the Constitution and the Union will be both endangered... And if a second Convention should be formed, it is as little to be expected that the same spirit of compromise will prevail in it as produced amicable result to the first. It will be easy also for those who have latent views of disunion, to carry them on under a mask of contending for alterations popular in some but inadmissible in other parts of the U. States.*"[198]

By previous alterations, Madison is speaking of those demands that were not accommodated during the Philadelphia convention. He expects that the rejected demands will be, once again, unacceptable to the delegates of a second convention and force the failure of the convention. It is not a stretch to imagine that the Three-Fifths Compromise over the representation in the House of Representatives of "all other persons" than those who were free would be fertile ground for a battle which would culminate in the southern states leaving the Union.

Next came the Virginia ratification convention. Madison verbally sparred with Patrick Henry and the issue of amendments was a point of contention. Henry thought that amendments or corrections to the Constitution, once ratified, would be impossible. Madison sought to assure the convention that nothing could be more incorrect. He cautioned all that a second convention would not be the genial gathering of statesman that they were being led to expect. He thought that the Philadelphia convention had

---

[197] Letter of James Madison to Edmund Randolph, 10 April 1788
[198] Letter of James Madison to Thomas Jefferson, 22 April 1788

the benefit of "calm and dispassionate discussion" and a shared desire for crafting a truly agreeable charter. Madison warned of the men who would attend and their intentions.[199] The Virginia convention opened on 2 June 1788. On 21 June New Hampshire becomes the ninth state to ratify the Constitution putting it into operative effect. Four days later, Virginia ratified as the tenth state.

This brings us to the oft quoted and usually grossly misinterpreted Madison letter of 2 November 1788 to George Lee Turberville which is so frequently submitted as the pivotal evidence of Madison's fear of a second convention which Madison allegedly believed would destroy the Constitution. This letter is cited with just the fewest lines possible, and in doing so, significantly changes the meaning of the quotation. By this time, a full third of a year after the event, the Constitution had already been ratified. A second convention is now moot, but the Constitution, and therefore Article V, is in effect although there are Anti-Federalists still pushing for a second general convention. It is advisable, due to the great importance that the opponents of an Article V convention place on the document, to recreate the letter in its entirety. The emphasis in italics is that of this author. The emphasis in bold is that of the section most frequently quoted in support of the argument against an Article V convention.

> Dear Sir,
>
> Your favor of the 20th. Ult: not having got into my hands in time to be acknowledged by the last mail, I have now the additional pleasure of acknowledging along with it your favor of the 24. which I recd. yesterday.
>
> *You wish to know my sentiments on the project of another general Convention as suggested by New York.* I shall give them to you with great frankness, though I am aware they may not coincide with those in fashion at Richmond or even with your own. *I am not of the number if there be any such, who think the Constitution, lately adopted, a faultless work. On the Contrary there are amendments wch. I wished it to have received before it issued from the place in which it was formed.* These amendments I still think ought to be made according to the apparent sense of America and some of them at least I presume will be made. There are others, concerning which doubts are entertained by many, and which have both advocates and opponents on each

---

[199] Ralph Ketcham, *James Madison, A Biography* (Charlottesville: University of Virginia Press, 1990), 263

side of the main question. These I think ought to receive the light of actual experiment, before it would be prudent to admit them into the Constitution. With respect to the first class, the only question is which of the two modes provided be most eligible for the discussion and adoption of them. *The objections agst. a Convention which give a preference to the other mode in my judgment are the following. 1. It will add to the difference among the States on the merits, another and an unnecessary difference concerning the mode.* There are amendments which in themselves will probably be agreed to by all the States, and pretty certainly by the requisite proportion of them. If they be contended for in the mode of a Convention, there are unquestionably a number of States who will be so averse and apprehensive as to the mode, that they will reject the merits rather than agree to the mode. *A convention therefore does not appear to be the most convenient or probable channel for getting to the object. 2. A convention cannot be called without the unanimous consent of the parties who are to be bound by it, if first principles are to be recurred to; or without the previous application of ⅔ of the State legislatures, if the forms of the Constitution are to be pursued. The difficulties in either of these cases must evidently be much greater than will attend the origination of amendments in Congress, which may be done at the instance of a single State Legislature, or even without a single instruction on the subject. 3. If a General Convention were to take place for the avowed and sole purpose of revising the Constitution, it would naturally consider itself as having a greater latitude than the Congress appointed to administer and support as well as to amend the system; it would consequently give greater agitation to the public mind; an election into it would be courted by the most violent partizans on both sides; it wd. probably consist of the most heterogeneous characters; would be the very focus of that flame which has already too much heated men of all parties; would no doubt contain individuals of insidious views, who under the mask of seeking alterations popular in some parts but inadmissible in other parts of the Union might have a dangerous opportunity of sapping the very foundations of the fabric. Under all these circumstances it seems scarcely to be presumeable that the deliberations of the body could be conducted in harmony, or terminate in the general good.* **Having witnessed the difficulties and dangers experienced by the first Convention which assembled under every propitious circumstance, I should tremble for the result of a Second,** *meeting in the present temper of America and under all the disadvantages I have mentioned. 4. It is not unworthy of consideration that the prospect of a second Convention would be viewed by all Europe as a dark and threatening Cloud hanging over the Constitution just established, and*

> *perhaps over the Union itself*; and wd. therefore suspend at least the advantages this great event has promised us on that side. It is a well known fact that this event has filled that quarter of the Globe with equal wonder and veneration, that its influence is already secretly but powerfully working in favor of liberty in France, and it is fairly to be inferred that the final event there may be materially affected by the prospect of things here. We are not sufficiently sensible of the importance of the example which this Country may give to the world; nor sufficiently attentive to the advantages we may reap from the late reform, if we avoid bringg. it into danger. The last loan in Holland and that alone, saved the U. S. from Bankruptcy in Europe; and that loan was obtained from a belief that the Constitution then depending wd. be certainly speedily, quietly, and finally established, & by that means put America into a permanent capacity to discharge with honor & punctuality all her engagements. I am Dr. Sir, Yours[200]

The extent of the letter taken altogether radically changes the meaning of the oft-cited yet incomplete sentence. Madison is making several important points in this short letter. We can see that Madison's concerns were not that a second **general** constitutional convention would runaway as modern opponents claim, but that he saw the need for letting the new system try itself. Firstly, he felt a pressing urgency to bring the issue of the addition of a bill of rights to a speedy conclusion and that the most efficacious manner of doing so was to introduce a proposed bill of rights in the upcoming first session of the federal Congress just two months into the future. Madison stated that he believed that it would take too long to call a convention and to debate, propose, promulgate and ratify any amendments. He had an understanding of what the States wanted from the submitted lists of proposed changes that the States included with their ratifications of the Constitution. He was able to draw from those and produce the proposed twelve amendments that he (after several attempts) finally succeeded in getting introduced into Congress on 8 June 1789.[201] Madison had made the "gentlemen's agreement" of promising to introduce legislation to amend as soon as the new Congress convened.[202] He agreed that he would sponsor the bill and explicitly include a guarantee for religious liberty to Baptist

---

[200] Letter of James Madison to George Lee Turberville, 2 November 1788
[201] Paul J. Weber, "Madison's Opposition to a Second Convention," *Polity* 20, no.3 (Spring 1988): 516
[202] Philip L. Martin, "The Application Clause of Article Five," *Political Science Quarterly* 85, no.4 (Dec. 1970): 617-9

preacher John Leland whose support was needed by Madison to win election as a delegate to the Virginia ratification convention.[203] Secondly, Madison is making a clear distinction between a "General Convention" of presumably unlimited plenary power in his Point #3 and an amendatory convention in his Points #1 and #2. He states that the rules must be observed, as he says, "*if the forms of the Constitution are to be pursued.*" Madison uses the word "amendments" in Points #1 and #2 but not in Point #3 where he uses the words "revising" and "alterations." He uses the word "amend" only once in Point #3 and that is in reference to the congressional method of amendment. He is obviously choosing his words carefully as they mean clearly different actions. Madison was by this time convinced of the need for amendments, as opposed to alterations, and says so directly prior to his enumeration of his points with the line, "*These amendments I still think ought to be made…*" Thirdly, Madison notes in Point #3 that the General Convention will "*naturally consider itself as having a greater latitude than the Congress,*" that is, have more power than Congress. He lists the expected offenses of a second convention and concludes the point by noting that the times and "*present temper of America*" were not conducive to another convention especially "*under all the disadvantages I have mentioned.*" His remarks were conditional and specific to a plenary convention. Lastly, Madison knew that the people would not be confident in the new government if there was any chance of failure on the part of the amendatory convention to draft and propose the bill of rights. Of the three options that Madison saw open, the congressional method of amendment, an Article V amendatory convention, and a second general convention, he considered the congressional method the most expeditious in terms of time, effort and minimization of both the potentials for failure and public upheaval. It was simply quicker, easier, less problematic and devoid of any political shenanigans to draft and propose a bill of rights in Congress himself.

Madison knew what the Anti-Federalists, such as Gerry, Henry, Mason and Randolph, were up to in calling a second convention. He knew that they wished to weaken the newly proposed government. But, they were not the only ones looking to take a second bite at the apple. On the other side of the political spectrum were others that wanted to further increase the power of the proposed central government. Gouverneur Morris expressed that

---

[203] Ralph Ketcham, *James Madison, A Biography*, University of Virginia Press, Charlottesville, (1990), p.251

"He had long wished for another Convention, that will have the firmness to provide for a vigorous Government, which we are afraid to do."[204] Russell Caplan explains Madison's apprehension that the Convention agreeing to a second convention could be taken by the public as a "self-proclaimed lack of confidence in their own work."[205] Madison said this himself to Edmund Randolph in April of 1788, "The very attempt at a second Convention strikes at the confidence in the first and the existence of a second opposing influence to influence, would in a manner destroy an effectual confidence in either."[206]

Professor Paul Weber concisely summarized the four points that he sees Madison giving as the basis of his opposition to a second convention,

- First, a second convention would "add to the difference among the States."

- Second, that calling a second convention was inefficient and time-consuming.

- Third, that the safety of the republic from the "undue public agitation."

- Fourth, a second convention would send the wrong message to Europe.[207]

Finally, Madison did not fear a second constitutional convention because of what it may propose – as today's Article V convention opponents claim; he feared that a nation weary of the debate over the Constitution and the form and failure of the national government under the Articles of Confederation would lead to the individual states to simply washing their hands of the Confederation and each state choosing to go their own way.[208] At the time that Madison was replying to Turberville, eleven states had already ratified the Constitution thereby putting the charter into effect. A second convention was not just improbable but moot. Just six months later, Madison would be arguing on the floor of Congress in response to Virginia's application for an amendatory convention. He made no opposition to that convention, rather he argued that the application must be kept pending

---

[204] Max Farrand, *The Records of the Federal Convention of 1787, Vol. II* (New Haven: Yale University Press, 1911 rev. 1937), 479
[205] Russell B. Caplan, *Constitutional Brinkmanship* (New York: Oxford University Press, 1988), 33
[206] Letter of James Madison to Edmund Randolph, 10 April 1788
[207] Paul J. Weber, "Madison's Opposition to a Second Convention," *Polity* 20, no.3 (Spring 1988): 515-6
[208] Madison and Hamilton addressed their concerns in this regard at length in *The Federalist, Nos. 6-10*.

before Congress.

A month after his letter to Turberville, Madison wrote to Thomas Jefferson again and with a new tone stating,

> "*The questions which divide the public at the present related 1. to the extent of the amendments that ought to be made to the Constitution. 2. to the mode in which they ought to be made. The friends of the Constitution, some from approbation of particular amendments, others from a spirit of conciliation, are generally agreed that the System should be revised. But they wish the revisal to be carried no farther than to supply additional guards for liberty, without abridging the sum of power transferred from the State to the general Government or altering previous to trial, the particular structure of the latter and are fixed in opposition to the risk of another Convention whilst the purpose can be well answered, by the other mode provided for introducing amendments. Those who have opposed the Constitution, are on the other hand, zealous for a second Convention, and for a revisal which may either not be restrained at all, or extend at least as far as alterations have been proposed by any States.*"[209]

Madison had come around fully to the necessity of amendments and even given serious thought as to how best to make them happen. He weighed the political cost to the nation of convening a second convention and found it too high a price to pay. He was convinced that the proponents of a second convention did not have the nation's best interests in mind and would most assuredly go beyond the mandate of any second convention. And just two days after the Jefferson letter, Madison wrote to Philip Mazzei[210] in Europe and brought him up to date on recent developments,

> "*The object of the antifederalists is to bring about another General Convention, which would either agree on nothing as would be agreeable to some, and throw every thing into confusion; or expunge from the Constitution parts which are held by its friends to be essential to it. The latter party are willing to gr[atify their] opponents with every supplemental provision for gua[ranteeing their] rights, but insist that this can be better done in the [congressional?] mode provided for amendments.*"[211]

---

[209] Letter of James Madison to Thomas Jefferson, 8 December 1788

[210] Philip Mazzei is a fascinating character of colonial history. He was an Italian by birth who had moved to London, whereupon he met Benjamin Franklin and John Adams who convinced Mazzei to move to Virginia, where he became a neighbor and friend of Jefferson and Madison. He later served in the Prussian court.

[211] Letter of James Madison to Philip Mazzei, 10 December 1788

Far From Unworkable

Madison was almost a full convert at this point. There was one last step in Madison's year-long transformation from his no-convention, no-amendments stance to one of employing the new Article V process effectively and without fear. At the urging of Madison's brother William, he wrote to a Baptist leader to recommit to his word to introduce a bill of rights with support for religious liberty before he left for New York and the convening of the First United States Congress.[212] His letter of 2 January 1789 to Reverend George Eve contains this,

> "*Circumstances are now changed: The Constitution is established on the ratifications of eleven States and a very great majority of the people of America; and amendments, if pursued with a proper moderation and in a proper mode, will be not only safe, but may serve the double purpose of satisfying the minds of well meaning opponents, and of providing additional guards in favour of liberty. Under this change of circumstances, it is my sincere opinion that the Constitution ought to be revised, and that the first Congress meeting under it, ought to prepare and recommend to the States for ratification, the most satisfactory provisions for all essential rights, particularly the rights of Conscience in the fullest latitude, the freedom of the press, trials by jury, security against general warrants &c... I have intimated that the amendments ought to be proposed by the first Congress. I prefer this mode to that of a General Convention, 1st. because it is the most expeditious mode. A convention must be delayed, until 2/3 of the State Legislatures shall have applied for one; and afterwards the amendments must be submitted to the States; whereas if the business be undertaken by Congress the amendments may be prepared and submitted in March next. 2dly. because it is the most certain mode. There are not a few States who will absolutely reject the proposal of a Convention, and yet not be averse to amendments in the other mode. Lastly, it is the safest mode. The Congress, who will be appointed to execute as well as to amend the Government, will probably be careful not to destroy or endanger it. A convention, on the other hand, meeting in the present ferment of parties, and containing perhaps insidious characters from different parts of America, would at least spread a general alarm, and be but too likely to turn every thing into confusion and uncertainty. It is to be observed however that the question concerning a General Convention, will not belong to the federal Legislature. If 2/3 of the States apply for one, Congress can not refuse to call it: if not, the other mode of amendments must be pursued.*"[213]

---

[212] Ralph Ketcham, *James Madison, A Biography* (Charlottesville: University of Virginia Press, 1990), 276
[213] Letter of James Madison to Rev. George Eve, 2 January 1789

It is so important to note that not only does Madison not fear an Article V limited amendatory convention - he just sees it as not politically expedient at this time - but that Madison already understands the workings of the Article V process and is successfully navigating the process to mitigate a serious constitutional crisis in the form of the publicly demanded but lacking Bill of Rights. Madison speaks specifically of a General Convention because the opponents to the new Constitution, we must remember, were not seeking a limited-power amendatory convention but a general, or open and unlimited, plenary convention starting with the proverbial blank sheet of paper (or parchment in this case!). A final letter, this one public,[214] secures the evidence of Madison's conversion to an amendment supporter. He writes to Thomas Mann Randolph[215] on 13 January 1789 that,

"The change of situation produced by the establishment of the Constitution, leaves me in common with other friends of the Constitution, free, and consistent in espousing such a revisal of it, as will either make it better in itself; or without making it worse, will make it appear better to those, who now dislike it.

It is accordingly, my sincere opinion, and wish, that in order to effect these purposes, the Congress, which is to meet in March, should undertake the salutary work. It is particularly, my opinion, that the clearest, and strongest provision ought to be made, for all those essential rights, which have been thought in danger, such as the rights of conscience, the freedom of the press, trials by jury, exemption from general warrants, &c.

I think also, that the periodical increase of the House of Representatives, until it attains a certain number, ought to be expressly provided for, instead of being left to the discretion of the government. There is room likewise in the Judiciary department for amendment. It ought to be so regulated, as to render vexatious, and superfluous appeals, impossible. In a number of other particulars, alterations are eligible either on their own account, or on account of those, who wish for them."[216]

In this reviewed series of letters dating from 10 January 1788 to 13 January 1789, Madison has "evolved" in his thinking over the course of just one year and both gained and exhibited confidence in the new constitution.

---

[214] Ralph Ketcham, *James Madison, A Biography* (Charlottesville: University of Virginia Press, 1990), 276
[215] The then, soon to be son-in-law of Thomas Jefferson, marrying Martha Washington Jefferson in 1790.
[216] Letter of James Madison to Thomas Mann Randolph, 13 January 1789

In his effort to resolve the problem and to avoid a convention, be it a general convention or an amendatory convention, Madison has discovered what will eventually be called the "prodding effect." For the American citizens, they had quickly seen and proved the utility and ease of operation of the new Constitution's amending process and successfully exercised one of its most important features. It is ironic that today's opponents of an Article V convention use Madison's letter to Turberville as an example of the dangers of the convention amending process when in actuality, the cited example shows both the efficacy and the safety of the process to achieve constitutional change with a modicum of, albeit appropriately and strategically applied, public pressure.

Kevin Gutzman has explored the push by Virginia Governor Edmund Randolph for a second General Convention and the resistance by Madison in his *James Madison and the Making of America*. He notes that Randolph wanted the state ratification conventions to propose amendments and these would be taken up in the second general convention. He made his resolution for the second convention in the Philadelphia Convention on 10 September 1787 and was seconded by Benjamin Franklin.[217] As a leading Anti-Federalist in Virginia – a position that Gutzman states Randolph did not relish – Randolph worked to secure a second convention because he thought that once ratification was achieved, the potential of obtaining a bill of rights would die. Madison told Randolph in the 10 January 1788 letter that those Virginians who wanted disunion were dropping Randolph's name liberally. Madison was seeking to persuade Randolph to just dump the whole second convention idea. Gutzman concludes that the name recognition of Randolph and Patrick Henry and some of the other prominent Virginians who were supporting the call for a second convention would give it weight and also devalue the proposed Constitution.[218]

It wasn't just Madison that was reluctant to take on another convention. The Federalists overall saw no good coming out of a second convention. They knew what was going to be debated and argued. They were acutely aware that the next convention, if held, would be driven by "faction and demagoguery" predominantly.[219] They had their concerns over

---

[217] Kevin R. C. Gutzman, *James Madison and the Making of America* (New York: St. Martin's Press, 2012), 126
[218] Ibid., 157-9
[219] Kurt T. Lash, "Rejecting Conventional Wisdom: Federalist Ambivalence in the Framing and Implementation of Article V," *American Journal of Legal History* 38, no.2 (April 1994): 221-31

who would be serving in the convention. They knew that the critiques of the Federalist views were already written. They expected that there would be bargaining over the already settled points with the result being worse that the compromises in the Philadelphia product. The Federalists knew that the States would have studied the proposed Constitution and sought ways to leverage their position so that the end looked like the beginning, that is, like the Articles of Confederation.

The interaction between Madison and Jefferson deserves further examination. They were close on so many issues but they diverged on the topic of not just a second constitutional convention, but further, even regular constitutional conventions altogether. While this divergence did not cause a breach between the friends (and neighbors in a fashion) it did lead to some interesting public debate in the written form. It is important to observe that their perspectives were far apart in the aspect that Madison had been a delegate to the 1787 convention and an architect of the Virginia Plan while Jefferson had been in France as the American ambassador. Jefferson's knowledge of the convention's operations, debates and compromises was all second hand through the correspondence that he received from delegates – who were under an obligation to divulge nothing – and third hand from those that were speculating on events occurring within the Pennsylvania State House. In the wake of the convention, Jefferson took time to study the proposed document and reached his conclusions as to the deficiencies of the work. He lamented the lack of a bill of rights and term limits. He was bothered by the secrecy of the proceedings and deliberations.[220] Jefferson's objections were strong enough that he expressed his recommendation that four states should withhold ratification unless the changes were made.[221,222]

But, it was an idea that had appeared in Jefferson's *Notes on the State of Virginia* that Madison saw as the most troubling, so much so that he directly challenged that notion in *The Federalist No.49*. Jefferson had advocated for frequent popular conventions to address issues such as the constitutionality of laws and court decisions. His suggestion that differences between the co-equal branches of government could be resolved through this turning

---

[220] Adrienne Koch and William Peden, *The Life and Selected Writings of Thomas Jefferson* (New York: Random House, 1944, 1993 ed.), 76

[221] Drew R. McCoy, *Last of the Fathers, James Madison & The Republican Legacy* (New York: Cambridge University Press, 1989), 45-6

[222] Adrienne Koch and William Peden, *The Life and Selected Writings of Thomas Jefferson* (New York: Random House, 1944, 1993 ed.), 574-5, Letter to John Adams of 27 June 1813

to public plenary conventions to settle who is right did not sit well with Madison. Frequent conventions were, in Madison's opinion, risky and would lead to mob rule with a constant spectacle of trying constitutionality. He was just a few years ahead in prediction of the show trials of Revolutionary France. Drew McCoy summarizes Madison's view of Jefferson's idea,

> "But Jefferson's scheme was unsatisfactory – indeed, profoundly dangerous – for even more fundamental reasons. By mandating regular and probably frequent recurrences to the people, it promised to erode confidence in the government and to unleash the perilous juggernaut of public passion."[223]

McCoy points out that Madison recognized that this perpetual trial of the Constitution would "jeopardize popular faith in the Constitution" and inevitably cause the people to fail to develop that "veneration" that is so necessary to inculcating the respect for the fundamental law which provides political stability and order.[224] Madison warned that if the recourse to frequent conventions was allowed, then the people's passions would rule over their reason.[225] Jefferson represented the view that public input through conventions was appropriate and that the society would only be the better; Madison saw the situation in the opposite, the convention was to be an infrequent and extraordinary event to be calmly and judiciously applied.

Finally, Madison convinced Jefferson of the correctness of using an Article V amendatory convention in lieu of other less constitutional means, such as nullification, to repair the problems between the States and the federal government. He wrote that,

> "Should the provisions of the Constitution as here reviewed be found not to secure the Govt. & rights of the States agst. usurpations & abuses on the part of the U.S. the final resort within the purview of the Constn. lies in an amendment of the Constn. according to a process applicable by the States."[226]

The ratification experience should have established for all time the efficacy, utility and operational characteristics of the convention system. The high profile of the proposed constitution was a curiosity to the people; they

---

[223] Drew R. McCoy, *Last of the Fathers, James Madison & The Republican Legacy* (New York: Cambridge University Press, 1989), 47-8.

[224] Ibid., 48

[225] James Madison, "Federalist Paper No. 49" in *The Federalist Papers: Hamilton, Madison, Jay*, ed. Clinton Rossiter (New York: Mentor, 1961)

[226] Galliard Hunt, ed., *James Madison, The Writings of James Madison*, Vol.9, (New York: G.P. Putnam's Sons, 1900), 398

flocked to the conventions to watch the deliberations as the great orators of the day expounded on the most pressing questions outside of the separation from Great Britain. The convention events were the eighteenth-century versions of modern prize fights. In the case of Virginia, the potential thrill of seeing Patrick Henry and James Madison verbally spar drew so many people that the convention had to be moved to a larger venue.[227] Similarly, in Massachusetts, the site had to be moved several times due to the burgeoning crowds.[228] The towns and counties held conventions for the selection of delegates to the state ratification conventions. They debated not just who, but sometimes how the delegates would be expected vote. Some towns and counties issued delegate instructions. All of these impositions of rules created a complicated spectacle of cerebral brawling. Add the high stakes of constitutional determination and we have the makings of the highest form of eighteenth-century drama and entertainment.

With the ratification of the Constitution, and the ratification conventions, behind the nation, the experience with political conventions for other than nominations did not end, it merely morphed. New states began joining the union less than a year after the last of the original thirteen states ratified. Vermont joined in 1791 and more came regularly every few years on average. Congress began requiring of the territories applying for statehood that they hold a convention for drafting a state constitution as part of the application process.[229] Beginning with the seventeenth state, Ohio, in 1802 Congress mandated this step.[230] With the admission of Louisiana, in 1811 Congress stipulated more from the applying territory; it required specific items in the proposed state constitution.[231] For thence forward, Congress usually passed an enabling act for admission which spelled out the requirements for admission and it varied by the state.[232] To plan for these provisions, the territories began to hold statehood conventions as precursors to their constitutional conventions to draft a state constitution. Prior to drafting, the territories sought to develop consensus and settle

---

[227] Pauline Maier, *Ratification, The People Debate the Constitution, 1787-1788* (New York: Simon & Schuster, 2010), 256

[228] Ibid., 166

[229] Henry D. Levine, "Limited Federal Constitutional Conventions: Implications of the State Experience," *Harvard Journal of Legislation* 11 (1973): 142

[230] Act of April 30, 1802; Ch.40, 1 Stat. 173

[231] Act of February 20, 1811; Ch.21, 2 Stat. 641

[232] As an example of the specialized requirements by state, Utah was required to constitutionally renounce polygamous marriage.

issues such as boundaries, representation and policy issues like slavery and banking. Even after holding numerous statehood and planning conventions – detailed in Appendix B – many of the states still needed multiple constitutional conventions to secure an acceptable initial state constitution.[233] After achieving the goal of statehood, many states continued to hold non-constitutional conventions that involved the quality and effectiveness of the state constitution. That is, these extra-legal constitutional conventions were called to discuss the dysfunction or the missing elements needed for the state constitution to perform as necessary. These planning conventions, also found in Appendix B, were used to focus attention on issues and to rally for a state constitutional convention to change either the existing state constitution or to amend it or to replace it.[234] The statehood process had begun to be refined and the convention mechanism was integral to statehood. The States would go on to hold hundreds of constitutional conventions for drafting, amending, revising and replacing their state constitutions as well as to ratify the Twenty-first Amendment to the federal constitution. The only facet of the experiment that has not been tried is the federal amendatory convention. Although the States have not held an amendatory convention for the federal constitution – it has not been for a lack of trying.

---

[233] Robert F. Williams, *The Law of American State Constitutions* (New York: Oxford University Press, 2009), 81
[234] Ibid., 88-9

FOUR
AN ALL TOO BRIEF HISTORY OF THE ATTEMPTS TO CALL AN ARTICLE V CONVENTION

> *"The one remedy specifically provided for in the Constitution is the amendment process that bypasses the Congress. I would like to see that amendment process used just once. I do not much care what it is used for the first time, but using it once will exert an enormous influence on both the Congress and the Supreme Court. It will establish the parameters of what can be done and how, and after that the Congress and the Court will behave much better."*[1]
>
> –Antonin Scalia, Associate Justice, United States Supreme Court

Throughout the history of the almost uncountable number of attempts to convene an Article V amendatory convention, a common thread running through the proposals has been the "unseriousness" of most of the applications. They have, as one writer put in 1963, "amounted to little more than state legislators blowing off political steam."[2] This misuse of a very serious process and power has given the Article V amendatory convention a bad name and tended to make it a *brutum fulmen* politically by the end of the twentieth century. The saber-rattling of threatening an amendatory convention has reduced the utility of the convention to a nearly

---

[1] Cited in, *A Constitutional Convention: How Well Would It Work?* (Washington, D.C.: American Enterprise Institute for Public Policy Research 1979), 36 – In the same forum, Scalia clarified his meaning of "I do not much care what it is used for the first time."

[2] Fred P. Graham, "The Role of the States in Proposing Constitutional Amendments," *American Bar Association Journal* 49, no.12 (Dec.1963): 1176 – Former Chief Counsel of the Senate Subcommittee on Constitutional Amendments

comical stance. That was not always the case as the Article V convention was not pursued with such regularity until the twentieth century. The result has been that Congress, and the people, had just about stopped taking Article V campaigns seriously. Of course, that problem can be, and is being, repaired with the proper due diligence of a bona fide campaign conducted for a genuine constitutional change that has widespread public support. The public's endorsement is everything to make that campaign happen as the last century has proven.

The issue of whether a convention could be called or should have been called is dependent on how one – that is, Congress - counts the applications. Congress has, through simple inaction, successfully managed to avoid having to call a convention for over a century although plenty of scholars have claimed that the threshold of applications has been met at one time or another. This apprehension on the part of the members of Congress is nothing new. Congress has deftly sidestepped the issue of calling a convention from the beginning of the First United States Congress in 1789. The individual members of Congress have exhibited a fear of leaving the control of drafting and proposing any amendment to any other body.[3]

The most commonly claimed reason, by members of Congress and by writers, for not calling a convention is that the applications received are not for the same subject, more accurately, a lack of *homogeneity*, and that Congress has no obligation to aggregate the applications. The second most commonly used reasoning is that the wording, or *specificity*, differs – slightly, and therefore, the intent of the States is not clear. Some applications may have petitioned for a convention on the direct election of US senators while other applications may have only suggested that Congress call a convention for the direct election of US senators. In the view of some members of Congress, these are two entirely different and unrelated requests.[4] The third issue is that of the *contemporaneity*, or the spread in the timing, of submission of the applications.

There are two competing theories as to the duty of Congress to call a convention. The "*mandatory theory*" holds that the use of the word

---

[3] David E. Kyvig, *Explicit and Authentic Acts, Amending the U.S. Constitution 1776-1995* (Lawrence: University Press of Kansas, 1996), 98

[4] Wayne B. Wheeler, "Is a Constitutional Convention Impending?," *Illinois Law Review* 21 (1927): 786-91 – Wheeler details not only the machinations of Congress to avoid making the convention call, but gives the details of the state applications by Congressional Record citation.

"shall" in the convention clause of Article V requires Congress to act and allows no leeway on congressional action. The *"discretionary theory"* posits that the deliberative aspect of the legislative function of Congress must be allowed for in considering whether to call a convention. If the discretionary theory were correct, then Congress would be carrying out a legislative and not a ministerial function.[5] This position, of course, is contrary to the stated opinions of the Framers expressed during the 1787-91 ratification campaigns. If indeed, Congress is mandated to call a convention upon the receipt of a sufficient number of applications from the States, then Congress is, and has been, in the opinion of many people, derelict in its duty for some time now.[6] The Friends Of the Article V Convention (FOAVC) have tallied well over seven hundred applications from the States.[7] It is the contention of the FOAVC that Congress is overdue in its obligation to call a convention. They argue that the stated reasons for a convention, as differing in each application, are irrelevant since the Constitution dictates that Congress call a convention when two-thirds of the States, in total, have applied – clearly a situation that has existed for an extended period of time. Let us examine the record.

Early Efforts at an Amendatory Convention

With the success of the constitutional and ratification conventions completed in the late 1780s, the States wasted no time in seeking to try their hand at yet another innovation in the form of the Article V amendatory convention. Shortly after filing the ratification notices to Congress from Virginia and New York, these states submitted applications for an amendatory convention to discuss and propose what would, by another route, become the Bill of Rights, recorded on 14 November 1788[8] and on 6 May 1789[9] respectively.[10] These attempts were contemporaneous with the prodding of Congress by the other states for the incorporation of individual

---

[5] Ibid., 790
[6] http://foavc.org/
[7] http://foavc.org/file.php/1/Amendments
[8] *Annals of Cong.*, 248
[9] H.R. Jour., 1st Cong., at 29 30 (1789)
[10] Edwin S. Corwin & Mary Louise Ramsey, "The Constitutional Law of Constitutional Amendment," *Notre Dame Lawyer* XXVI, no.2 (1951): 194

rights into the Constitution.[11] Virginia made clear her dissatisfaction, impatience and distrust of Congress in her application (some things never change),

> "The anxiety with which our countrymen press for the accomplishment of this important end, will ill admit of delay. The slow forms of congressional discussion and recommendation, if, indeed, they should ever agree to any change, would, we fear, be less certain of success. Happily for their wishes, the Constitution hath presented an alternative, by admitting the submission to a convention of the States. To this therefore we resort, as the source from whence they are to derive relief from their present apprehensions."[12]

When the Virginia Article V amendatory convention petition was received and placed before the Congress, James Madison was present to speak to the procedure for handling the application. The *Annals of Congress* records the action of Madison,

> "Mr. Madison said, he had no doubt but the House was inclined to treat the present application with respect, but he doubted the propriety of committing it [to a committee], because it would seem to imply that the House had a right to deliberate upon the subject. This he believed was not the case until two-thirds of the State Legislatures concurred in such application, and then it is out of the power of Congress to decline complying, the words of the Constitution being express and positive relative to the agency Congress may have in case of applications of this nature. 'The Congress, whenever two-thirds of both Houses shall deem it necessary, shall propose amendments to this Constitution; or, on the applications of the Legislatures of two-thirds of the several States, shall call a convention for proposing amendments.' From hence it must appear, that Congress has no deliberative power on this occasion. The most respectful and constitutional mode of performing our duty will be, to let it be entered on the minutes, and remain upon the files of the House until similar applications come to hand from two-thirds of the States."[13]

It is an interesting historical aside that the date of the record of the discussion of the Virginia petition on the floor of the House is 5 May 1789.

---

[11] Technically, the push for the Bill of Rights preceded the ratification and the amendment process. Leonard Levy detailed that just ten days after the conclusion of the Philadelphia Convention in 1787, Richard Henry Lee of Virginia, tried to derail the ratification process by introducing a Bill of Rights in the Confederation Congress.
[12] H.R. Jour. 1ˢᵗ Cong., at 35 (1789).
[13] *Annals of Cong.*, 259-60 - on the "Application of Virginia".

As noted earlier, the very first United States Congress convened under the Constitution on 4 May 1789 and the first amendatory convention held by a state, following the ratification of the Constitution, was also convening in Georgia. Amendatorily, it was a very significant week.

New York, ratifying after Virginia, went a step beyond the other states with regard to amendments. While many states were sending in requested amendments with their ratification notifications, New York decided that applying directly for an amendatory convention would be more plausible. A motion was made by Melancton Smith in the New York ratification convention to modify a previous motion by John Jay that called for a conditional ratification dependent on Congress not exercising certain powers "until a Convention shall be called and convened for proposing amendments to the said Constitution."[14] With the number of ratifying states at ten, the Constitution was now in effect, and the only legitimate road open to amendment and modification was through Article V. Despite this, several states still attempted to pursue a second constitutional convention outside of the Constitution. New York's governor, George Clinton, and forty-six New York delegates circulated a letter calling for a coordinated effort among the States to press for a second convention and forwarded it to the governors of the other states.[15] However, the majority of the States saw clearly that the path lay within the Constitution and not without.

The state of Pennsylvania went so far as to hold an intrastate amendatory convention on 3 September 1788 in Harrisburg for the purpose of drafting a set of proposed amendments to the federal constitution to be submitted to Congress. By that time, the Constitution had been ratified by eleven states and was technically in effect in those states. Calling a convention publicly highlighted Pennsylvania's concern for a bill of rights more than just submitting a list of proposed amendments would have.

The appeal to an Article V convention contributed to saving the nation from the call for a second constitutional convention that the Anti-Federalists so badly wanted and pressed for during the ratification campaigns. As noted in Chapter 3, the Federalists foresaw that either the Articles of Confederation would be retained or, that a new constitution

---

[14] Pauline Maier, *Ratification, The People Debate the Constitution, 1787-1788* (New York: Simon & Schuster, 2010), 386 - citing Jansen and Kaminski's *The Documentary History of the Ratification of the Constitution*, XXIII, 2177-8

[15] Ibid., 397

would be drafted, or more than likely, that the States would separate. A second proposed constitution, would, in Madison's opinion, be inferior to that currently being considered and that the most probable outcome was the fracturing of the United States – permanently.[16] Madison astutely heeded the concerns of the Anti-Federalists and promised the introduction of a Bill of Rights in the First Congress and the calls for the second convention abated.[17] After the election of 1789, Madison kept his word and formulated a bill that incorporated ideas taken, not just from the submitted requests for specific amendments, but as Professor John R. Vile points out, in large part from the state constitutions.[18] Thus, we have the very first incident of the prodding effect leading to amending the federal constitution.[19] Here, without being carried to its potential convention clause conclusion, Article V had succeeded in amending the Constitution. Today's opponents of an Article V Convention are deliberately confusing a constitutional convention with an amendatory convention when they reference Madison's apprehensions of a second convention.

Rhode Island proverbially saw the handwriting on the wall and faced isolation (and economic boycott) as the only one of the original thirteen colonies not to join the new United States under the Constitution and performed an about face, ratifying the Constitution on 29 May 1790. She included with her resolution of ratification, a petition for an amendatory convention to discuss a bill of rights.[20] Kyvig makes the argument that Rhode Island saw the stirrings in Congress of the imposition on non-member state Rhode Island of "high tariffs and immediate payment of its Revolutionary War debt." Including a list of desired amendments lent some plausible explanation to the state's reticence to ratify allowing her to save face.[21] This made three petitions within the first year of the federal Constitution's operation.

---

[16] Richard Labunski, *James Madison and the Struggle for the Bill of Rights* (New York: Oxford University Press, 2006), 51-3
[17] Leonard Levy, *Origins of the Bill of Rights*, (New Haven, CT: Yale University Press, 1999), 38 – Levy noted that Madison referred to the amendment proposals as "the nauseous project of amendments." Also, at 90, where Levy noted the 8-7 passage of the Bill of Rights in the Virginia Senate.
[18] Vile cites Donald Lutz's *A Preface to American Political Theory* (Lawrence: University of Kansas Press, 1992), 49-88, n.28.
[19] John R. Vile, *Contemporary Questions Surrounding the Constitutional Amending Process* (Westport, CT: Praeger, 1993), p.3
[20] H.R. Jour. 148, 1st & 2nd Cong.
[21] David E. Kyvig, *Explicit and Authentic Acts, Amending the U.S. Constitution 1776-1995* (Lawrence: University Press of Kansas, 1996), 106

The appeal to an amendatory convention then died down for quite a while. During the War of 1812, an attempt to amend the Constitution through a convention was tried although it nowhere near resembled anything that we would today consider an Article V amendatory convention. From mid-December of 1814 to early January of 1815, representatives of five New England states met in Hartford, Connecticut to discuss the issues involved in the effect of the War of 1812 on the region. New England was a Federalist enclave at the time and the Federalist Party attempted to use the unpopularity of the war to strengthen its political fortunes as the expense of the Democratic-Republican Party in power. The economic impact of the war had borne disproportionately on New England and the convention made use of the idea of secession as a rally point for the party.[22] Among the complaints were that the "federal ratio," or the Three-fifths Clause is it is usually referred to today, was giving too much congressional representation to the South; that the admission of new states was destabilizing New England's economy; that the economic policies such as embargoes were hurting New England more than the rest of the States; and that the Madison Administration was too militarily aggressive. Historians today agree that the secession talk was simply a ruse to gain favorable treatment from Washington.

The Hartford convention and the governmental pronouncements made prior to the convention by the New England state governments were the first mentions of "interposition" by government and are seen as having drawn on the *Kentucky Resolution of 1798* and the *Virginia Resolution of 1799*, written anonymously by Jefferson and Madison, respectively. The final report issued by the Hartford Convention recommended five proposed amendments.[23] None of these proposals were submitted to Congress. The end of the war in February 1815 made the convention moot and the Federalist Party national pariahs. The Federalists' legacy became secession, treason and a form of nullification until the Civil War passed that mantle to another political party.

---

[22] Ralph Ketcham, *James Madison, A Biography* (Charlottesville, VA: University of Virginia Press, 1990), 591-595
[23] 1. Requiring a two-thirds majority to declare war, admit a new state, or interfere with foreign trade
2. Conduct an embargo for more than 60 days
3. Limit presidents to a single term
4. Repeal the three-fifths clause
5. Require that a new president not be from the same state as his predecessor

The Federalist Party ceased to be a political force by the end of the decade.[24]

The next time that actual applications for an Article V convention were received by the Congress was in 1832. The argument over the Tariff of 1832 that led to the Nullification Crisis in South Carolina and the attempt by Georgia to expropriate the lands of the Cherokee and Creek Indians prompted Georgia to submit an application for an Article V convention.[25] South Carolina, while not actually formally applying, slyly appealed to her sister states, and expressed its desire that,

> "a convention of the States be called as early as practicable to consider and determine such questions of disputed powers as have arisen between the States of this Confederacy and the General Government."[26,27,28]

The other states did not respond to South Carolina in a supportive manner.[29] Concurrently, Alabama submitted an Article V convention application to discuss the protective tariff, but did not side with South Carolina in her nullification exploration.[30] The States saw South Carolina's tact as unconstitutional and divisive; they chose to try the constitutional methods first. They succeeded in reducing the tariff although they did not succeed in calling an amendatory convention. Once again, the prodding effect had successfully come in to play.

The next episode of attempting to call an amendatory convention came in the last days just before the Civil War. In 1860, Arkansas, Delaware and Tennessee all made applications for a convention.[31] Illinois,[32] Indiana,[33] Kentucky,[34] New Jersey,[35] Ohio[36] and Virginia[37] made each a request in 1861

---

[24] Samuel Eliot Morison, "Our Most Unpopular War," *Massachusetts Historical Society Proceedings* 80 (1968): 38-54.
[25] 23 S. Jour.65
[26] Wilbur Edel, *A Constitutional Convention – Threat or Challenge?* (New York: Praeger, 1981), 9
[27] S. Jour., 22nd Cong., 2d sess., at 83 (1833)
[28] H. Jour., 22d Cong., 2d sess., at 219-20 (1833)
[29] Ralph R. Martig, "Amending the Constitution Article V: The Keystone of the Arch," *Michigan Law Review* 35, no.8 (1937): 1268, ns. 70, 71
[30] 23 S. Jour. 194 and H. Jour., 22d Cong., 2d sess., at 361-2 (1833)
[31] Russell B. Caplan, *Constitutional Brinkmanship* (New York: Oxford University Press, 1988), 53
[32] Law of Illinois (1861)
[33] S. Jour. 420, 421, 36th Cong. 2d sess.
[34] S. Jour. 189, 190, 36th Cong. 2d sess.
[35] Cong. Globe, 36th Cong., 2d sess., at 751 (1861)
[36] Vol.58, Laws of Ohio 181 (1861)
[37] S. Jour. 149

as did a Missouri state convention.[38] Desperate to prevent civil war, these states made application to Congress for an amendatory convention. Virginia took the lead in calling a convention without waiting for the rest of the States and Congress to act, as she had done in 1786 for the Annapolis and Philadelphia conventions. Additionally, nine members of Congress submitted resolutions for a convention.

With the nation careening toward war, some felt that following procedure would take too long and that action was needed at once. The General Assembly of the State of Virginia convened what was labeled the Washington Peace Conference of 1861 but became known as the "Old Gentlemen's Convention"[39] on February 4, 1861 at the Willard's Hall in Washington, D.C. Fourteen free and seven slave states sent a total of 136 delegates to the convention. The convention was named for the distinguished character of its delegates. Former President John Tyler of Virginia was named to chair the convention. By the date of convening, seven southern states had already seceded and during the convention, the Confederate States of America declared itself a nation with the issuance of the provisional Confederate Constitution at a revolutionary constitutional convention in Montgomery, Alabama.[40]

The Old Gentlemen's Convention adopted the same rules that had governed the 1787 convention. The delegates met daily for three weeks with the exception of a single day when they broke for the funeral of a delegate. Ohio congressman Thomas Corwin had been working on a compromise plan in Congress but held off on presenting it in order to give the Peace Conference a chance. They proposed amendment that would have protected slavery and, they hoped, reconciled the nation. The seven point amendment much resembled the Crittenden Compromise then waiting in the Senate. The convention finished business on February 27 and then sent the proposition over to Congress. The House refused to consider the proposal. The Senate finally took up a vote on March 4, the last day of session business and Inauguration Day for President Lincoln. The convention had failed and

---

[38] Paul J. Weber & Barbara A. Perry, *Unfounded Fears, The Myths and Realities of a Constitutional Convention* (New York: Praeger, 1989), 59

[39] The convention earned its sobriquet due to the social status and governmental service of the delegates including: one former president, nineteen former governors, six former cabinet members, fourteen former US senators, fifty former US representatives, and twelve state supreme court justices.

[40] John R. Vile, *Conventional Wisdom* (Athens, GA: University of Georgia Press, 2016), 71 – Vile gives a good treatment of the Confederate amending process and history.

Virginia left the Union a month later and joined the Confederacy.[41]

What the Peace Conference had succeeded in was proving that the States could still conduct, at least something resembling, a convention of the States, and discuss issues which led to a proposed agreement. A precedent or template was laid down that could be used again. The questions being asked today had all been answered in 1861 – and very quickly. The failure to produce an amendment that was eventually adopted is insignificant to the present task at hand, which is determining how to operate a convention which leads to an amendment proposal.

The first century of the Republic saw few applications for an amendatory convention, but most of those that were submitted were for "general (open and to include all states) conventions" and not limited subject conventions, exceptions were for the tariff debate and an 1864 application from Oregon concerning slavery.[42] In fact, the total number of applications from the States in the first one hundred years of the Republic amounted to only ten.[43] Perhaps this is a result of the experience of the States with having a list of grievances culminating in the Bill of Rights; the States were merely following the examples of the ratification conventions.[44] Twice the States had pushed for change and twice the prodding effect had worked. The failure of a convention to prevent the Civil War was more a matter of the timing and the fact that events had already progressed too far to stop by the time the Washington Peace Conference had convened. That realization may have had something to do with the dearth of applications for an Article V convention for the next thirty years.

The Advent of the Organized Convention Campaign

Decades passed, and in 1893 Nebraska became the first state to apply for a convention for the purpose of proposing an amendment for the direct election of US senators, and with that action the modern amending race

---

[41] Robert Gray Gunderson, *Old Gentlemen's Convention* (Madison: University of Wisconsin Press, 1961), generally

[42] Robert G. Natelson, "Proposing Constitutional Amendments by Convention: Rules Governing the Process," *Tennessee Law Review* 78 (2011): 731-2

[43] Cyril Brickfield, *Problems Relating To A Federal Constitutional Convention*, Staff of the House Committee on the Judiciary, 85th Cong., 1st sess., at 7 (Comm. Print 1957)

[44] John R. Vile, *Contemporary Questions Surrounding the Constitutional Amending Process* (Westport, CT,: Praeger 1993), 57 – Vile cites Caplan explaining that by "general" the States may have meant that all states be included and not necessarily referring to topic.

was on.[45] The drive for what became the Seventeenth Amendment did not seriously take off until 1901 when seventeen states applied for either direct election of the senators and president; direct election of the senators; or a general convention that included focusing on the direct election of senators. Until the amendment for the direct election of senators was ratified in 1913, the States continued to apply for a convention to take up the subject with applications being received every year between 1901 and 1911 with exceptions for 1906 and 1910. Although it is difficult to count the applications due to the mix of reasons given in the applications, it appears that between 1893 and 1911 approximately a total of seventy-three applications were submitted on the topic with some states submitting obviously multiple times.[46,47,48]

The effort to land the Seventeenth Amendment was actually orchestrated by the States. They had become concerned over extremely long vacancies due to state legislatures being deadlocked over candidates, the susceptibility of senators to influence buying, and the impact of special interests on the Senate.[49] Several states saw the need for the amendment and took it upon themselves to devise and direct a coordinated effort. In 1900, Pennsylvania's legislature formed a standing committee to investigate the best method of achieving the goal. The committee accurately predicted that the threat of a convention would force the hand of Congress.[50] The Pennsylvania legislature then sent their resolution to all of the other state legislatures to use as a model and exhorted the other states to pass parallel resolutions.[51] Iowa then stepped up in 1906, when Governor Albert Cummins called an interstate meeting of the representatives of several states to devise a strategy to force a convention. This led to formation of a lobbying group that focused on the singular issue of direct election of the

---

[45] The application does not appear in the Cong. Rec. but was mentioned in S. Doc.78, 71ˢᵗ Cong., 2d sess. (1930)
[46] Fred P. Graham, "The Role of the States in Proposing Constitutional Amendments," *American Bar Association Journal* 49, no.12 (Dec. 1963): 1179-81
[47] Montana seems to have held the record on this drive with 6 applications for direct election of senators.
[48] Cyril Brickfield, *Problems Relating To A Federal Constitutional Convention*, Staff of the House Committee on the Judiciary, 85ᵗʰ Cong., 1ˢᵗ sess., (Comm. Print 1957)
[49] Thomas N. Neale, Library of Congress, Congressional Research Service Report R42589, *The Article V Convention to Propose Constitutional Amendments: Contemporary Issues for Congress*, (11 April 2014), 9-10
[50] Russell B. Caplan, *Constitutional Brinkmanship* (New York: Oxford University Press, 1988), 63, n.7
[51] Gerard N. Magliocca, "State Calls for an Article V Convention: Mobilization and Interpretation," *Cardozo Law Review De Novo* (2009): 79-80 – referring to Christopher Henry Hoebeke's *The Road to Mass Democracy: Original Intent and the Seventeenth Amendment* (1995), 149 and Caplan: 63-4, n.7 and Ralph A. Rossum's *Federalism, The Supreme Court, and the Seventeenth Amendment: The Irony of Constitutional Democracy* (2001), 193

US Senators.[52] Cummins' effort was the forerunner of the modern Assembly of State Legislatures.

Much of the effort to enact the Seventeenth Amendment was attributed to the media of the day. The "progressive muckrakers" capitalized on the negative image of Congress and in particular, that the Senate had become a "millionaire's club." Between 16 January 1893 and 13 February 1902, the US House had voted five times for the direct election of senators but the Senate refused to consider the amendment bills.[53,54] The Senate's Committee on Privileges and Elections had issued a report in 1896 recommending the bill, but warned that the Senate would not take up such as bill unless an amendatory convention threatened. The report included a model application that the States used. Caplan noted that the language employed by the States went from "most respectfully request" that Congress propose an amendment to a more forceful insistence that Congress "shall call a Convention."[55] It is doubtful that Congress would behave any differently today.

Simply, the Senate took the position of refusing to do anything that might compromise its power until it had absolutely no options left except to pass the amendment bill. Even then, the prodding effect left the Senate with the decision of, more or less, passing a bill to its liking, versus watching an amendatory convention pass a bill very much to the Senate's displeasure. In the end, it is really the States that lost power, more so due to the passage of the bill which Congress wrote than if the writing of the amendment had been left to the States in convention. After all that drama, it still took until 1912 to pass the bill. As the bill that eventually became the Seventeenth Amendment was winding its way through the process, the States continued to press for a convention, not trusting Congress to get the job done. By the end of the drive for the bill's passage in Congress, thirty of the thirty-one necessary states had submitted applications specifically for a convention for drafting an amendment for the direct election of federal senators.[56]

---

[52] Ibid., 80 – referring again to Hoebeke, 149
[53] Paul J. Weber & Barbara A. Perry, *Unfounded Fears, The Myths and Realities of a Constitutional Convention* (New York: Praeger, 1989), 61
[54] James Stasny, "The Constitutional Convention Provision of Article V: Historical Perspective," *Cooley Law Review* I (1982): 82
[55] Russell B. Caplan, *Constitutional Brinkmanship* (New York: Oxford University Press, 1988), 63
[56] Paul J. Weber & Barbara A. Perry, *Unfounded Fears, The Myths and Realities of a Constitutional Convention* (New York: Praeger, 1989), 61

The situation with respect to Congress, and more directly the Senate, was summed up quite well by Fred Graham and provides a guide for future campaigns with,

> "So, in 1908, when twenty-three legislatures had adopted applications, Congress proposed its own direct-election amendment.[57]
>
> Here the states were able to play a significant role in the amending process, because the applications were concurrent in time, valid in form and enjoyed sufficient public support to be approved by a convention. Since congressional opposition was obviously self-serving, no Congressman could have afforded to oppose the convention, once the required number of applications was received. So Congress was forced to act, despite the fact that the amendment was contrary to the personal interests of many of the senators."[58]

Assuming that the aggregation of applications would have been acceptable and legal, Congress has failed to make the convention call numerous times. The requisite number was technically reached in 1909 for a convention on the subject of the direct election of US senators. Since 1901, a total of thirty-two states had requested a convention but for divergent reasons. Of these, twenty-six states requested a convention to discuss a proposed amendment for the direct election of US senators.[59] Congressional leaders refused to act on calling a convention claiming that they believed that the requirements had not been met.[60] The lack of constitutional integrity in Congress is, regrettably, not a recent innovation.

Fatefully, the Seventeenth Amendment has done damage to the people's options with regard to calling an amendatory convention as well as to the States' ability to control or regulate the federal government. Jay Bybee noted in 1997 on the impact of the Seventeenth Amendment,

> "In sum, the Seventeenth Amendment affected Article V directly, but not formally. It took from the states a means of defending themselves against unwise amendments, and it severely limited the power of the states to amend the Constitution without a state call for a convention. It has thus made constitutional conventions more likely since states cannot instruct senators

---

[57] By 3 February 1913 when the ratification was complete, Congress had received applications from 32 states. Two-thirds had been reached, albeit late.

[58] Fred P. Graham, "The Role of the States in Proposing Constitutional Amendments," *American Bar Association Journal* 49, no.12 (Dec. 1963): 1178

[59] William A. Platz, "Article Five of the Federal Constitution," *George Washington Law Review* 3 (1934): 44

[60] Lester B. Orfield, "The Procedure of the Federal Amending Power," *Illinois Law Review* 25 (1930): 422

> to propose and support amendments. Just as instruction by the people "displace[d] representation in ordinary government with direct action of the People themselves", so instruction of senators displaced the senators with the direct action of state governments themselves, but in a manner that fell short of constitutional convention. A subtle, but important change."[61]

The proper method of making the count has been argued for almost a century since the Seventeenth Amendment's ratification. If the count is for <u>all</u> types of applications – but for each state allowed to have just one pending application at a time - and considered to be pending indefinitely, then the number for the count reached the requisite thirty-three states again by 1929.[62] The number rose to thirty-five by September of 1929 at which point the legislature of the State of Wisconsin admonished the Congress for ignoring the States' applications insisting that Congress "perform the mandatory duty… and forthwith call a convention to propose amendments to the constitution of the United States."[63] Congress ignored the request, since the count submitted by Wisconsin included every type of petition ever submitted for all causes – including those that dated back to the original applications in the late 1780s.[64] Wisconsin was requesting that an open, unlimited convention be called. The Senate issued a report on a compilation of all of the submitted applications from the state legislatures. The opening statement of the Senate report reads,

> "*States Ask for Federal Constitutional Convention*
>
> *A joint resolution of the Wisconsin Legislature has been received by the United States Senate, asking that a constitutional convention be called to consider proposing to Congress such amendments to the Federal Constitution as may be agreed upon, in accordance with Article V of the Constitution. Wisconsin is the thirty-fifth State whose legislature has requested such a convention to be called, and the Wisconsin resolution cites the mandatory provision of Article V that Congress 'on the application of the legislatures of two-thirds of the several States, shall call a convention for proposing*

---

[61] Jay S. Bybee, "Ulysses at the Mast: Democracy, Federalism, and the Sirens' Song of the Seventeenth Amendment," *Northwestern University Law Review* 91, no.2 (1997): 567. Reprinted by special permission of Northwestern University School of Law, *Northwestern University Law Review.*

[62] S. Doc. 78, 71st Cong., 2d sess. (1930)

[63] 71 Cong. Rec. at 3369, 3856 (1929) – to be fair, eleven of those applications were for the direct election of US senators which were then discharged by the passage of the Seventeenth Amendment in 1913.

[64] Edwin S. Corwin & Mary Louise Ramsey, "The Constitutional Law of Constitutional Amendment," *Notre Dame Lawyer* XXVI, no.2 (1951): 195-6

amendments.'

The 35 States which have filed formal application with Congress are: Alabama, Arkansas, California, Colorado, Delaware, Georgia, Idaho, Illinois, Indiana, Kansas, Kentucky, Louisiana, Maine, Michigan, Minnesota, Missouri, Montana, Nebraska, Nevada, New Jersey, New York, North Carolina, Ohio, Oklahoma, Oregon, Pennsylvania, South Dakota, Tennessee, Texas, Utah, Vermont, Virginia, Washington, and Wisconsin.

The Wisconsin resolution does not cite any particular subject for amendment."[65]

This document previews another tool that the States would come to employ, that of the aggregated list of states that had preceded the petitioning state's application. Today, this tactic is de rigueur to prevent Congress from claiming that a particular application is not to be counted with those that it is intended to be counted among.

Almost concurrent with the push for a convention to take up direct election of federal senators, the success of the prodding effect seems to have encouraged the States to pursue another goal: the constitutional prohibition of polygamy. Beginning in 1906, this topic attracted the interest of eighteen states which requested a convention or that Congress introduce a proposed amendment to ban polygamy.[66] Eventually, there were applications for a total of twenty-seven states in all.[67] The interest in banning polygamy continued through 1916 when it appeared to become overshadowed by the war in Europe and the push died. Although the state legislatures were pressing for the amendment, this issue was never one that the public embraced widely. What makes the anti-polygamy drive an important part of the Article V convention movement history is that the high number of applications was, at the time, added to those for the direct election of senators and counted as sufficient by convention proponents to call a general convention. Once the Seventeenth Amendment was sent to the States for ratification, those applications were discharged and lost to the anti-polygamy petitioners as valid to their application tally.

---

[65] S. Doc. 78, 71ˢᵗ Cong., 2d sess. (1930) - dated calendar day,1 February 1930
[66] Wayne B. Wheeler, "Is A Constitutional Convention Impending?," *Illinois Law Review* 21 (1927): 787
[67] Philip L. Martin, "The Application Clause of Article Five," *Political Science Quarterly* 85, no.4 (Dec. 1970): 622

The anti-polygamy convention drive had a problem that would appear later – that of attempting to make a federal issue out of a concern that was the traditionally an interest of the States. Marriage is not mentioned anywhere in the federal Constitution and has always been, due to the proliferation of religions and ethnic traditions, handled by the States alone. To move to make this issue a subject of national interest and federal policy was setting a dangerous precedent that continues to exist to this day. Weber and Perry defined the problem as, even in Mormon communities, the potential reduction of traditional state police power in civil law as marriage has been a traditional province of the States. For others, the issue was the inclusion of a state based civil matter in the organic law.[68]

Surprisingly, through the 1920s and early 1930s there were only a small handful of states that requested a convention to cover repeal of the Eighteenth Amendment: Nevada (1925); Massachusetts, New York and Wisconsin (1931); and New Jersey (1932). There was sufficient public opinion against the Eighteenth Amendment that the usual method of congressional amendment (repeal) already had sufficient traction at the federal level.

Beginning in 1938, the first modern movement for an Article V convention to limit federal government power began. The movement to pass the Seventeenth Amendment was not really designed to limit federal power; rather it removed a power from the States. From 1938 through the early 1960s, the income tax rates in the United States continued to rise until they reached a sustained top nominal rate of 91% for the years 1947 to 1963. Within that period there was a short window of time where the top nominal rate was higher, namely 1952-53, when it was 92%. During WWII it had peaked during 1944-45 at the top nominal rate of 94%. Along came the American Taxpayers Association which wanted to cap the federal income tax top rate at 25%, repeal the Sixteenth Amendment and to restrict the federal government from collecting taxes on gifts and inheritances.[69]

Maryland and Wyoming got the ball rolling with their applications for a convention in 1939 and were eventually joined by twenty-six other states before the movement petered out in the early 1960s. The amendment had

---

[68] Paul J. Weber & Barbara A. Perry, *Unfounded Fears, The Myths and Realities of a Constitutional Convention* (New York: Praeger, 1989), 61-2
[69] Russell B. Caplan, *Constitutional Brinkmanship* (New York: Oxford University Press, 1988), 68-9

grown out of the frustration with the spending and taxation resulting from the Roosevelt Administration's New Deal. The spending peaks of the Second World War and the Korean War sustained the movement. Historian David E. Kyvig states bluntly that the rationale behind the movement was that, "Tax limitation advocates hoped to 'put the fear of God,' or at least concern about an uncontrollable constitutional convention, in Congress and thus compel it to propose the amendment."[70]

And that it did. The genie of misinformation and fear-mongering was let out of the bottle. The bill was introduced in 1951 and hearings were held in 1953.[71] Illinois U.S. Representative Chauncey Reed and Illinois Senator Everett Dirksen sponsored the joint resolution. Yet again, the prodding effect was in motion. This time however, the opposition was equally up to the challenge and began a campaign of disinformation. Representative Wright Patman of Texas called it the "Millionaire's Amendment" and alarmed all with his warning that the convention had the ability to "rewrite the whole Constitution."[72] The high water mark was hit in 1963 with Colorado's application, but Congressional leaders dismissed the applications due to "irregularities" and the rescissions of twelve applications.[73]

The claim that the convention would runaway was not the only charge lobbed against the Article V convention movement. The campaign marked the first real attempts to derail an amendatory convention effort through disinformation and unsubstantiated claims. Representative Patman labeled the campaign as "fascist" and slandered the leaders of the convention effort personally.[74]

Another proposal for limiting taxes was called the Liberty Amendment and is of note because of who supported it. One of its strongest proponents was the John Birch Society which has, despite the printed evidence, presently denied that their organization ever endorsed or worked for a convention to secure this or any other amendment. The Liberty Amendment proposal

---

[70] David E. Kyvig, *Explicit and Authentic Acts, Amending the U.S. Constitution 1776-1995* (Lawrence: University Press of Kansas, 1996), 336

[71] David E. Kyvig, "Everett Dirksen's Constitutional Crusades," *Journal of the Illinois State Historical Society* 95 (Spring 2002): 72

[72] David E. Kyvig, *Explicit and Authentic Acts, Amending the U.S. Constitution 1776-1995* (Lawrence: University Press of Kansas, 1996), 336

[73] Russell B. Caplan, *Constitutional Brinkmanship* (New York: Oxford University Press, 1988), p.69

[74] Paul J. Weber & Barbara A. Perry, *Unfounded Fears, The Myths and Realities of a Constitutional Convention* (New York: Praeger, 1989), 63

successfully garnered nine convention applications from states between 1959 and 1982.[75]

The post-war period covering the 1940s, 1950s, 1960s and 1970s brought a whole new list of reasons for applications from the States: limiting presidential tenure (five states);[76] presidential succession (three states);[77] tideland regulations; world federal government (six states); federal gasoline tax sharing; public education; oil and mineral rights; revising Article V to make amendment easier; executive treaty making (three states);[78] selecting federal judges; busing of school children (twelve states); school prayer (five states); electoral reform (eight states) and States' rights among others.[79] The 1970s, 1980s and 1990s brought other topics: nuclear power; defense spending; the exclusionary rule; and mandatory health insurance.[80] Excepting presidential tenure and succession, none of these subjects caught fire with the public. For the best, in-depth treatment of those individual campaigns the reader is referred to David E. Kyvig's *Explicit and Authentic Acts, Amending the U.S. Constitution, 1775-1996* and Paul J. Weber and Barbara A. Perry's *Unfounded Fears, Myths and Realities of a Constitutional Convention*.

Several of the issues that arose in the late 1950s were interrelated. The school busing,[81] selection of federal judges, state control of schools and states' rights issues were all the result of the backlash against the US Supreme Court's *Brown v. Board of Education of Topeka*[82] decision in 1954. Added to these were petitions for a review of the Fourteenth Amendment and for limiting the powers of the US Supreme Court.[83] Many of the applications in this era starting after 1900 mark a sharp turn from redefining the federal government to defining the social structure through the organic law. This is

---

[75] http://www.libertyamendment.com/
[76] Eventually, this effort led to the Twenty-second Amendment in 1951.
[77] This effort prompted the Twenty-fifth Amendment in 1967.
[78] It is of great interest to note that the effort to restrain the executive from concluding treaties by circumventing the Senate's constitutionally required approval in the late 1940s and the 1950s is shadowed today by the same complaints about the Obama administration.
[79] Fred P. Graham, "The Role of the States in Proposing Constitutional Amendments," *American Bar Association Journal* 49, no.12 (Dec. 1963): 1181
[80] Michael J. Molloy, "Confusion and a Constitutional Convention," *Western State University Law Review* 12 (1985): 794
[81] The school busing issue did succeed in prompting a proposed amendment, but it did not attract a majority of votes let alone the necessary two-thirds required to pass either chamber.
[82] 347 U.S. 483 (1954)
[83] Paul J. Weber & Barbara A. Perry, *Unfounded Fears, The Myths and Realities of a Constitutional Convention* (New York: Praeger, 1989), 64

a widely divergent intent from that of the Framers of the Constitution.

Modern Campaigns

Illinois Senator Everett Dirksen was extremely proactive in seeking constitutional amendments. He championed a couple of attempts at calling an Article V convention including one in the 1960s that would have removed the ability of the federal government to control the apportionment of state legislatures in the aftermath of the US Supreme Court's decisions in the *Baker v. Carr*,[84] *Reynolds v. Sims*[85] and the *Wesberry v. Sanders*[86] cases. The so-called "Reapportionment Revolution" was intended to rebalance the rural and urban interests within the state legislatures.[87] The Court decided that the state legislatures needed to adopt the "one person, one vote" method of determining the representation within districts for the houses of each chamber. This position is paradoxical when one considers that the state legislatures are most often patterned after the federal legislature and the US Senate clearly is not structured on such a rule. This point was aptly made at the time by US Senator Roman Hruska of Nebraska. The push for an Article V convention to address this subject came within just one state of calling an amendatory convention; it represents the high water mark among all post-World War II convention campaigns. The Senate responded to this effort with a collective fit. The leadership attacked the validity of the States' petitions – long standing court rulings on the matter to the contrary. Some in the Senate went so far as to declare that the state legislatures were illegitimate and that once a new legislature was elected the previously submitted petition was no longer valid![88] One senator, Paul H. Douglas of Illinois, was unabashed in proclaiming that Congress would not honor the applications from thirty-two states (at that time) and would not make a convention call. He boasted that he doubted whether Congress could be forced to make the call.[89] At this time, the effort to codify the process began and serious, voluminous academic and scholarly study started. The law reviews and journals of the time were filled with papers on Article V

---

[84] 369 U.S. 186 (1962)
[85] 377 U.S. 533 (1964)
[86] 376 U.S. 1 (1963)
[87] John J. Dinan, *The American State Constitutional Tradition* (Lawrence: University of Kansas Press, 2006), 10
[88] Wilbur Edel, *A Constitutional Convention – Threat or Challenge?* (New York: Praeger, 1981), 87-91
[89] Robert G. Dixon, Jr., "Article V: The Comatose Article of Our Living Constitution," *Michigan Law Review* 66, no.5 (Mar.1968): 944

conventions and law schools held symposia on the subject.[90]

For all the Senate's posturing, they did recognize the threat that the issue posed and they responded by taking up a resolution for an amendment – twice. Both times the vote fell short of the requisite two-thirds of the chamber by just seven votes.[91] The opposition to the reapportionment campaign was led by Senators Millard Tydings of Maryland, Robert Kennedy of Massachusetts, William Proxmire of Wisconsin and Jacob Javits of New York. They took the lead in trotting out the claim that the convention would be unlimited and uncontrollable. By 1969, a total of thirty-three states were on board and the movement was a single state short of meeting the required number of petitioning states. It had taken only five years to reach the point of being one state short of the requirement. Unlike the drive for the Seventeenth Amendment, the proponents of the convention were not seeking to use the prodding effect; they honestly, actually meant to hold an amendatory convention.[92] Then unexpectedly Sen. Dirksen died and the reapportionment convention movement died with him.[93] It has been theorized that the failure of this drive – which has come closer than any other drive in our history with the exception of the drive for the Seventeenth Amendment – can be attributed to, primarily, two causes: First, that the proponents came to recognize that the "traditional rural interests" with which they were concerned would not be affected by reapportionment. Second, that they feared that a "runaway convention" was a distinctly real possibility.[94]

The effort to fight reapportionment was instructive of how to properly conduct such a campaign. The proponents hired a public relations firm, raised money, and lobbied hard. With the application from Iowa in April 1969, the campaign was a single state short of the thirty-four state threshold, but failed when the Wisconsin Legislature voted down their resolution in

---

[90] As an example, one can still find copies of the March 1968 publication of the Michigan Law Review's *Symposium on the Article V Convention Process.*
[91] Paul J. Weber & Barbara A. Perry, *Unfounded Fears, The Myths and Realities of a Constitutional Convention* (New York: Praeger, 1989), p66
[92] James Stasny, "The Constitutional Convention Provision of Article V: Historical Perspective," *Cooley Law Review* I (1982): 85
[93] Paul J. Weber & Barbara A. Perry, *Unfounded Fears, The Myths and Realities of a Constitutional Convention* (New York: Praeger, 1989), 66-7
[94] Sara R. Ellis, Yusuf Z. Malik, Heather G. Parker, Benjamin C. Signer & Al'Reco L. Yancy, "Article V Constitutional Conventions: A Primer," *Tennessee Law Review* 78 (2011): 667

November 1969.[95,96] Even the federal courts got into the fight in 1969 when a Utah federal district court declared the Utah application invalid due to the malapportionment of the Utah legislature.[97]

The Senate took up the task of attempting to draft rules[98] for future Article V conventions when it became apparent that the reapportionment issue was now within a single state of calling a convention. A good point was made that if the States knew the rules ahead of time, before launching a campaign for an amendatory convention, they would not diffuse their efforts and omit key actions – the drives would go more smoothly and effectively.[99] A half century later, this is the driving premise behind such organizations as the Assembly of State Legislatures. All of the usual fears were paraded out in front of the nation. Hearings were held and expert witnesses called to give their predictions for the outcome of any convention. The testimony ranged from the extreme of stating that Congress controls all and that the States are narrowly limited in their abilities to the other extreme of the States having no limits and Congress is a mere servant to the States. Much of the testimony is error riddled and ignored the past Court decisions. A significant portion of time was spent covering issues settled as much as two centuries past, such as whether the president must sign an amendment. A certain measure of hypocrisy was evident in that testifiers argued that Congress was claiming the right and power to regulate amendatory conventions when it was pointed out that just three decades earlier, Congress refused to provide any guidance or legislation in relation to the about-to-be-tried-for-the-first-time ratification conventions made at the request of the States.[100]

Two other small but significant drives were undertaken in the 1950s and 1960s. These two efforts were low key and one did succeed in attracting enough support to prod for legislation. The first was a push by the States to call a convention for revising the Article V process itself. As a result of the legislative effort to regulate the constitutional convention process,

---

[95] Philip L. Martin, "The Application Clause of Article Five," *Political Science Quarterly* 85, no.4 (Dec. 1970): 624-7

[96] Russell B. Caplan, *Constitutional Brinkmanship* (New York: Oxford University Press, 1988), 76

[97] *Petuskey v. Rampton*, 307 Fed. Supp. 235 (1969)

[98] Edel notes that Congress attempted to pass a convention rules bill in 1953, 1957, 1961 and 1967 through 1974 in each successive Congress – all unsuccessfully.

[99] "Proposed Legislation on the Convention Method of Amending the United States Constitution," *Harvard Law Review* 85, no.8 (June 1972): 1616

[100] Wilbur Edel, *A Constitutional Convention – Threat or Challenge?* (New York: Praeger, 1981), 91-7

thirteen states submitted applications between 1953 and 1965 to abolish the convention option and permit the States to propose and ratify amendments directly and without any federal control or intervention. The second obscure attempt at a convention involved exploring federal-state revenue sharing. The growing state and federal budgets were outstripping the tax revenues leading the States to look for a new source of funds to balance their state budgets. They wanted to get in on the federal revenues and to shift some of that funding to the States and municipalities to help relieve the States' budget deficits.[101] This drive began in 1965 and secured the applications of fifteen states.[102] This campaign used a model application designed to counter the usual congressional objections. Several national organizations were behind the effort.[103] The campaign ended with Congress passing the State and Local Fiscal Assistance Act of 1972.[104] Once again, the prodding effect had succeeded, although this time it resulted in ordinary statute legislation and not a constitutional amendment.

The drive to pass the Equal Rights Amendment (ERA) peaked with the ratification by thirty-five of the requisite thirty-eight states before some states began to rescind their ratifications. Although the ERA was not the result of an amendatory convention drive, it impacted the convention method significantly. Two controversies came out of that effort. First, the rescission of the ratifications was contested and debated in the same manner as those rescissions from the 1924 proposed Child Labor Amendment.[105] Second, since Congress had stipulated a seven year window for ratification and that time had expired without enough states' approval, Congress debated and held hearings on the constitutionality of extending the ratification period. This piece of constitutional and legal legerdemain resulted in Congress passing a three year and three month extension which ultimately proved fruitless when the ratification did not garner enough states. The price of that extension was a constitutional argument over the permissibility and acceptability of limits on the ratification phase and some cries of bias when the amendment did not achieve passage within the seven year window. While this effort

---

[101] Robert M. Rhodes, "A Limited Federal Constitutional Convention," *University of Florida Law Review* XXVI, no.1 (Fall 1973): 2-3
[102] 117 Cong. Rec. S. 16, at 519 (Oct. 19, 1971)
[103] The National Legislative Conference, the National Society of State Legislators and the National Conference of State Legislative Leaders.
[104] Pub. L. No. 92-512
[105] The rescinding states were Idaho, Kentucky, Nebraska, South Dakota and Tennessee.

did not involve attempting to call an amendatory convention, the issues of ratification rescission and extensions of the window for ratification were compared to the state applications for an amendatory convention. Scholars speculated on the effect of these actions to efforts to call amendatory conventions. Since the questions of a time limit and the permissibility of rescission were open ended for state applications for a convention, some legal analogy in the form of the ratification process was attractive to convention proponents. These questions persisted for decades. It is only now that we can conclusively give answers to these questions. All of the major drives for a convention over the last third of a century have been affected by the outcome of the ERA drive and its treatment of rescissions and time limits.

Just after the Supreme Court's ruling in the *Roe v. Wade*[106] case, a dozen states applied to Congress within five months for a convention to discuss amending the federal Constitution to define a "person" and ensuring the right to life.[107] The establishment of a constitutional right to privacy and to abortion by the high court was preceded by debate in the state houses and the Congress. At least thirty-two proposed constitutional amendments were introduced in Congress in 1973 alone. Eventually, twenty states submitted petitions to defend the right to life.[108,109] Like so many other drives, these petitions are considered as remaining pending without a time limit on their viability.

The greatest drive in the last few decades has been that of the proposed Balanced Budget Amendment. It remains today still forging ahead with another attempt to rein in federal spending and to eliminate the national debt. The first submission of an application for a convention to focus on the balanced budget issue was that of Indiana in 1957. In the 1970s and early 1980s the campaign for the Balanced Budget Amendment attracted not only the support, in the form of a convention petition, of thirty-two of the requisite thirty-four state legislatures but that of luminaries such as economists like Milton Friedman and political leaders such as President Ronald Reagan and California Governor Edmund G. Brown. Their desire echoes that of one of Reagan's predecessors, Thomas Jefferson, who lamented

---

[106] 410 U.S. 113 (1973) and its companion case, *Doe v. Bolton*, 410 U.S. 179 (1973)

[107] Francis H. Heller, "Article V: Changing Dimensions In Constitutional Change," *University of Michigan Journal of Law Reform* 7 (Fall 1973): 88, n.108

[108] Russell B. Caplan, *Constitutional Brinkmanship* (New York. Oxford University Press, 1988), 72-3

[109] David E. Kyvig, *Explicit and Authentic Acts, Amending the U.S. Constitution 1776-1995* (Lawrence: University Press of Kansas, 1996), 449

in 1798 when he was Vice-President, that,

> "*I wish it were possible to obtain a single amendment to our constitution...I mean an additional article, taking from the federal government the power of borrowing.*"[110]

In the late 1970s, the National Taxpayers' Union[111] (NTU) and the American Farm Bureau Federation were the major forces behind the effort to secure the amendatory convention.[112] The NTU had openly predicted that it would secure the necessary number of state applications by 1981. The NTU had learned well from the reapportionment amendment campaign; they hired a PR firm, networked with other fiscal responsibility groups to share mailing lists, created model legislation and hired staff and lobbyists. One of the members of the coalition working to secure the amendment, the National Tax Limitation Committee (NTLC), stated in 1982 in its publicity effort when it divulged its plan, that it had been really to provoke the Congress into proposing an amendment of its own in order to avoid the potential of a convention that would both curtail the power of Congress and establish a precedent.[113] The NTLC's public admission of preferring the prodding effect is theorized to have helped to slow the campaign. The NTU maintained that its goal was still a convention.[114] Add to that the determination by Congress to produce a balanced budget by 1981 and the drive's momentum deteriorated quickly.[115] That was not the only admission though, as the NTU's founder James Clark also showed his cards: "This is just a way of getting attention – something akin to batting a mule with a board."[116] No admissions or public statements have done more harm to the convention method than these. Since these drives were not only high profile but also immensely popular, the damage done to the feasibility of an amendatory convention was severe.

---

[110] Letter of Thomas Jefferson to John Taylor, 26 November 1798

[111] The NTU is a public affairs and lobbying group that focuses on tax policy. They were the driving force behind California's Propositions 4 and 13. They worked to convince the States to adopt balanced budget provisions in state law or state constitutions.

[112] Maryanne R. Rackoff, "The Monster Approaching the Capital: The Effort to Write Economic Policy Into the United States Constitution," *Akron Law Review* 15 (Spring 1982): 735

[113] *New York Times*, 19 January 1982, at A18, statement made by the president of the National Tax Limitation Committee.

[114] Russell B. Caplan, *Constitutional Brinkmanship*, (New York: Oxford University Press, 1988), pp.78-89

[115] Frank J. Sorauf, *The Constitutional Convention as an Amending Device* (Washington, D.C.: American Historical Association and American Political Science Association, 1981), 115-7

[116] James Clark quoted in the *Baltimore Evening Sun* on 11 March 1983

The high water mark of the drive was 1979 when eight states passed resolutions for a convention. When Congress passed the Balanced Budget and Emergency Deficit Control Act of 1985, known as Gramm-Rudman-Hollings,[117] the momentum was stopped and the Senate failed by a single vote to pass a balanced budget amendment.[118,119,120] The organization of the opposition to the campaign was complete by then and they began a multi-faceted effort to stop the drive. They sought to educate state legislators to vote against the resolutions while educating federal legislators to act to pre-empt the need for a balanced budget amendment. They created a disinformation campaign to discredit the convention method and enlisted the support of political notables such as Vice-President Walter Mondale and President Jimmy Carter to speak out against the convention. Carter remarked,

> *"I think the convening of a constitutional convention to pass such an amendment would be very ill-advised and contrary to the best interest of our country. It would be a radical departure from the historical procedures that we have always used to amend our Constitution and might result in unlimited amendments which would change the basic thrust, the philosophy and the structure of our government."*[121]

President Carter wrote to the Speaker of the Ohio House to urge reconsideration of a resolution for a convention. He warned that a convention "might do serious, irrevocable damage to the Constitution." Carter thought it "flawed and harmful" and a "radical and unprecedented action."[122]

The campaign to dissuade the States from pursuing the balance budget amendment was not limited to liberals and Democrats only; they sought out and publicized the opinions of conservatives and Republicans who also opposed such a drastic move. Conservative icon Sen. Barry Goldwater stated

---

[117] Balanced Budget and Emergency Deficit Control Act of 1985, Pub. L. 99-177, 99 Stat. 1038 - intended to balance the federal budget by 1991.
[118] Russell B. Caplan, *Constitutional Brinkmanship* (New York: Oxford University Press, 1988), 85
[119] Ruled unconstitutional by the US Supreme Court in *Bowsher v. Synar*, 478 U.S. 714 (1986)
[120] S.J. Res. 58, 97th Cong.
[121] Frank J. Sorauf, *The Constitutional Convention as an Amending Device* (Washington, D.C.: American Historical Association and American Political Science Association, 1981), 117
[122] Russell B. Caplan, *Constitutional Brinkmanship* (New York: Oxford University Press, 1988), 81-2

that he thought a convention to be "very foolhardy" and a "tragic mistake."[123] Goldwater prophesized that,

> "[I]f we hold a constitutional convention, every group in the country – majority, minority, middle-of-the-road, left, right, up, down – is going to get its two bits in and we are going to wind up with a Constitution that will be so far different from the one we have lived under for 200 years that I doubt that the Republic could continue."[124]

Most important of all is that the opponents of the convention created this greater enhanced mythology of the runaway convention without limits or controls run by unassailable special interests and that the lack of precedent guaranteed a disaster despite the best efforts of politicians and citizens to do the right thing. The Reagan administration referred to this position of imagining constitutional disasters as the "wild beasts theory."[125] The last activity that the opponents undertook was a counter-drive to get the petitioning states to rescind their application resolutions. This effort was successful in about a dozen states by 2010.

With the explosion in spending again during the Gulf Wars and the recession that started in 2007, the states once more looked to the balanced budget amendment as a way to forestall the inevitable fiscal collapse. They began a new convention drive in the latter half of the first decade of the 2000s and began securing both new states and the reissuance of applications from the states that had rescinded. Proponents had studied the failure of the previous campaign and now have countered with new tactics such as detailed education materials for state legislators including personalized seminars and professional videos. At least twenty-two of the submitted state applications were for a limited convention and contained language that specifically restricted the application to a limited convention and cancelled the application should Congress fail to call a convention which is strictly limited.[126]

Special interest groups have responded with pressure campaigns to

---

[123] Gerard N. Magliocca, "State Calls for an Article V Convention: Mobilization and Interpretation," *Cardozo Law Review De Novo* (2009): 80, n.43: referring to the Cong. Rec., 125 (1979): 3159. Reprinted with permission.

[124] Russell B. Caplan, *Constitutional Brinkmanship* (New York: Oxford University Press, 1988), 81 - citing Cong. Rec., 125 at 3159 (1979)

[125] Ibid., 87 – not to be confused with the "starve-the-beast theory."

[126] Frank J. Sorauf, *The Constitutional Convention as an Amending Device* (Washington, D.C.: American Historical Association and American Political Science Association, 1981), 122

urge Congress to call a convention absent the requisite number of petitions. It should be noted that, no matter how unlikely it may seem right now, Congress does not possess the power to call a convention absent the petitions of the States.[127] Thus, one more power rests with the States outside of federal control.

There is one last important episode in the history of Article V convention attempts that deserves to be remembered, because it has, in part, seen some repetition today. In the early 1960s, Senator Everett Dirksen got involved with another constitutional convention drive. This one was launched at the behest of an organization called the Council of State Governments, a large policy making group that was not happy about a number of events including some US Supreme Court decisions. Following the Supreme Court decisions over reapportionment, the Council recommended, at their biennial meeting of the General Assembly of the States in 1962, to the state legislatures that they call for an amendatory convention.

The Council concocted one of the most clever campaigns ever for amending the Constitution through the alternative amending clause, for not one, but <u>three</u> proposed amendments simultaneously! These propositions were referred to as either the "States' Rights" or the "Confederating" Amendments.[128] The purported idea behind the proposals was to strengthen federalism. The Council worked out a plan wherein all fifty state legislatures would be presented with the uniform proposed amendments on 16 January 1963 and votes would be taken relatively concurrently so that the issue of contemporaneity would be decisively dispatched.

Their proposals addressed not just state legislative reapportionment but also two other related issues. They asked for,

- A reversal of the *Baker v. Carr* decision that would limit the jurisdiction of the federal courts on the issue of

---

[127] Lester B. Orfield, "The Procedure of the Federal Amending Power," *Illinois Law Review* 25 (1930): 420
[128] A number of articles appeared in law reviews that address the topic of the 3 proposals:
  • Charles L. Black, Jr., "The Proposed Amendment of Article V: A Threatened Disaster," *Yale Law Journal* 72 (1963)
  • Frank E. Shanahan, Jr., "Proposed Constitutional Amendments: They Will Strengthen Federal- State Relations," *American Bar Association Journal* 49, no.7 (July 1963)
  • William F. Swindler, "The Current Challenge to Federalism: The Confederating Proposals," *Georgetown Law Journal* 52, no.1 (Fall 1963)
  • Paul Oberst, "Genesis of the Three States-Rights Amendments of 1963," *Notre Dame Lawyer* 39, no.6 (Sept. 1963)

reapportionment of state legislatures.[129]

- Establishment of a "Court of the Union" that would be comprised of the chief justices from the fifty states and give them the ability to overrule US Supreme Court decisions.[130]
- A revision to Article V that would eliminate both the convention method of amendment proposal and the congressional method of proposal and replace them with a provision whereby the two-thirds of the States submit identically worded resolutions that are then ratified by the States.[131]

The language of the petitions was identical, but this requirement potentially ran afoul of the necessity for deliberation in a convention, else the proposing convention becomes merely a de facto ratifying convention. In 1963, a total of twelve applications regarding the proposal were received by Congress – the most ever received in a single year on the same subject. In 1964, twenty-two states submitted applications, including a few repeated applications, the total reached thirty-two quickly.[132] The *New York Times* ran an exposé on 18 March 1967 that sensationalized the story as a secret scandal. A counter-campaign immediately formed and flooded the airwaves with dire predictions. By late 1967, states began rescinding their applications and organizations as diverse as the ACLU and the U.S. Conference of Mayors announced their opposition. Finally, units of the Council of State Governments began to rebel – especially the Conference of Chief Justices. By 1968, the project was as good as dead, although it left a lasting impression for an aggressive manner of organizing a campaign, introducing and securing applications and more importantly, dealing with the questions of the subject decisively.[133]

The US House, angered over the 1964 *Reynolds v. Sims*[134] decision of the US Supreme Court, responded by passing a resolution adopting the elimination of the jurisdiction of the Supreme Court over reapportionment.

---

[129] Twelve states specifically petitioned on this issue.
[130] Five states specifically petitioned on this issue.
[131] Eleven states specifically petitioned on this issue.
[132] Sen. Sam Ervin, Jr., "Proposed Legislation to Implement the Convention Method of Amending the Constitution," *Michigan Law Review* 66, no.5 (Mar. 1968): 876-7
[133] Paul Oberst, "Genesis of the Three States-Rights Amendments of 1963," *Notre Dame Lawyer* 39, no.6 (Sept. 1963), generally
[134] 377 U.S. 533 (1964)

The Senate held hearings. However, Congress was deeply divided on the issue and the convention prospect posed a dilemma to Congress. Following the *Reynolds* decision, twenty-eight states submitted applications for a convention to address the subject of reapportionment explicitly and led to Sen. Everett Dirksen's aforementioned campaign for a convention.[135] These applications wanted to submit the question to a public referendum over reapportionment. The anti-convention faction of Congress looked for a way to avoid what it saw as an impending disaster. The mood of the nation in the late 1960s was, to make an understatement, volatile and the impact that the national disposition could have on a "constitutional convention" terrified many, acutely in the government. The apparent lack of restrictions on a convention led many to believe that a constitutional crisis was upon the nation. Former counsellor to President Kennedy, Theodore Sorenson, wrote several articles opposing the convention and testified before the Senate, remarking, "Even a convention dominated by liberals, could not be expected to adjourn without trying its hand at improving on the classic work of 1787 – and that, too, could only lead to catastrophe."[136]

Eventually, Senator Sam Ervin, Jr.,[137] of North Carolina realized that with thirty-two states applying in two short years and just two more states needed, the possibility of an Article V convention was close to becoming a reality – closer possibly than at any time in our history. He introduced the first bill to institute procedures for an amendatory convention.[138] Hearings were held but the bill could not pass. Ervin's bill, or some variation thereof, was introduced, and in some cases passed by one house, a total of forty-one times. Ervin, in a paper given at a symposium on Article V at the University of Michigan in 1967, explained the response within the Congress after the *New York Times* story broke,

> *"Those senators that agreed with the Supreme Court's ruling [in* Baker v. Carr*] were now contending that some or all of the petitions were invalid for a variety of reasons and should be discounted, and that, in any case, Congress did not have to call a convention if it did not want to. Most distressing of all was the apparent readiness of everyone to concede that any convention, once convened, would be unlimited in the scope of its*

---

[135] Eight of the petitions were reissues of the previous Council of State Governments amendment petitions.
[136] Theodore Sorenson, "A New Federal Constitutional Convention?," Cong. Rec., 113 (June 12, 1967): 7967-8 and in the *Saturday Review*, July 15, 1967, 19
[137] Ervin was a Harvard educated lawyer and recognized as a constitutional expert within the Senate.
[138] The Ervin bill was a much modified version of a bill originally suggested by Cyril Brickfield a decade earlier.

authority and empowered to run rampant over the Constitution, proposing any amendment or amendments that happened to strike its fancy. That interpretation, supported neither by logic nor constitutional history, served the convenience of both sides in the apportionment controversy."[139]

All of the usual objections were brought out by the convention opponents, but this time they were in the employ of a Congressional leadership determined to avoid, should the drive reach thirty-four states, having to comply with its constitutional duty.[140] A new disqualification was used in the form of claiming that the state legislatures which were malapportioned could not submit an application – although those legislatures could do all other forms of legislative and ministerial duties – because the state legislatures themselves were unconstitutional! When pressed as to whether this meant that all acts completed in the past by the state legislatures were null and void, Congressional opponents responded with a negative that only the applications to call a convention for this specific issue were nullities.

Although the Reapportionment Revolution and the Confederating Amendments drive failed to call an amendatory convention, they had succeeded in setting the standard for how all future amendatory convention campaigns would operate.[141]

The Impact of Legislation of the Proposal of an Article V Convention

Despite the fact that we have never completed the carrying out of the calling and convening of an Article V convention, the motion of its machinery has on a few occasions brought about the desired effect. It is doubtful that the threat of an Article V convention sparking the process of change was the intention of the Framers, but its reality is nevertheless a powerful tool. The brief wording in Article V has frustrated scholars and jurists for two centuries but that same brevity has given us some flexibility. The lack of defining language has also made possible the discussions that scholars have had for nearly a century and a half. Part of the process of

---

[139] Sen. Sam Ervin, Jr., "Proposed Legislation to Implement the Convention Method of Amending the Constitution," *Michigan Law Review* 66, no.5 (Mar. 1968): 878
[140] Carl Brent Swisher & Patricia Nelson, "In Convention Assembled," *Villanova Law Review* 13, no.4 (1968): 719
[141] James Stasny, "The Constitutional Convention Provision of Article V: Historical Perspective," *Cooley Law Review* I (1982): 89

amending is that national conversation over the necessity of amending, the proposed wording, the method of amending, and the goals of an amendment. We have to talk ourselves through the process before carrying it out. John Vile states,

> "Consistent with eighteenth-century notions of constitutional elegance, the language of Article V is sparse. This has left a number of important issues in doubt. Nowhere perhaps are questions more pronounced than in the matter of the still unused constitutional convention mechanism. These ambiguities have not, however, prevented the amending process from serving at some critical times in American history as the alternative to revolution that it was intended to be."[142]

The prodding effect is the most noticeable effect of an Article V convention campaign on legislation. Several times throughout our history, the threat of an impending Article V convention has prompted Congress to act.

As previously stated, between 1901 and 1909, the Congressional records show that twenty-six states had submitted applications specifically for the purpose of calling a convention to propose an amendment for the direct election of US senators.[143] As the number of applying states moved closer to the two-thirds total, Congress slowly took note. The US House of Representatives had passed the bill five times, but the US Senate refused to take up a bill that would clearly impact its composition, and therefore, its power.[144] The Senate leadership believed that they could control, or at least obfuscate, the process. History had shown that the Congress could simply "process" an issue or movement to a quiet death. Technically, the prodding effect means that the amendatory convention campaign succeeded in its mission to amend the Constitution; although it was not by the method planned, but it was a success nonetheless.

The effort to codify and create a comprehensive procedure for an Article V amendatory convention was seriously undertaken by Sen. Ervin

---

[142] Republished with permission of ABC-CLIO Inc., from John R. Vile, *Contemporary Questions Surrounding the Constitutional Amending Process* (Westport CT, Praeger 1993), 3; permission conveyed through Copyright Clearance Center, Inc.

[143] Wayne B. Wheeler, "Is A Constitutional Convention Impending?," *Illinois Law Review* 21 (1927): 786-7 for complete list and reference to resolutions by state.

[144] Ibid., Per the Cong. Rec., 21 July 1894 – House votes 141-50, Cong. Rec., 26: 7783; 11 May 1898 – House votes 185-11, Cong. Rec., 31: 4825; 13 April 1900 – House votes 242-15, Cong. Rec., 33: 4128; 13 February 1902 – House votes viva voce, Cong. Rec., 35: 1722

and carried through to the end of his career.¹⁴⁵ Ervin saw the problems created by the States' Rights Amendments drive and sought to impose a sense of order on the process. It was clear that over the preceding half century, an Article V campaign was started in just about every decade and that since the end of the Second World War, there were often several campaigns going at once. The hodge-podge of court rulings, sometimes conflicting, and the incessant debate among scholars left no firm ground on which to build such a campaign. Ervin believed that sooner or later, a convention campaign would succeed in securing the necessary number of state applications.¹⁴⁶ Arthur Bonfield summarized the situation in 1968,

> *"Because of the uniquely fundamental nature of a constitutional amendment, attempts to alter our Constitution should not be filled with questionable procedures which could reasonably cast doubt on the ultimate validity of the provision produced. The procedure followed in any effort to amend the Constitution should be so perfect that it renders unequivocal to all reasonable men the binding nature of the product."*¹⁴⁷

Members of Congress have attempted several times to extend its influence over an Article V convention by working to pass legislation that would give Congress control over the procedures of not just the convention, but the entire process of applying, calling, convening and operating an amendatory convention. Senator Ervin had recognized both the importance of the Article V amendatory convention as a legislative tool/option and the uncertainty that was associated with the convention. He was well acquainted with fellow Senator Everett Dirksen who had led a couple of amendatory convention drives. Ervin actually backed Dirksen's labors and introduced his bill in 1967 in an effort to support Dirksen by creating a formal process for the convention from beginning to end. Dirksen was championing the drive to call a convention to discuss the reapportionment issue that was raging at the time. Ervin had the wisdom to see that the opponents of a convention were using the anticipated confusion and uncertainty to stop the campaigns. The fear of a runaway convention is the most potent weapon in the opponents' arsenal and although Ervin did not think that such an outcome was possible,

---

¹⁴⁵ S.2307, 90th Cong., 1st sess. (1967)
¹⁴⁶ Sam J. Ervin, Jr., "Proposed Legislation to Implement the Convention Method of Amending the Constitution," *Michigan Law Review* 66, no.5 (Mar.1968), generally
¹⁴⁷ Arthur Earl Bonfield, "The Dirksen Amendment and the Article V Convention Process," *Michigan Law Review* 66, no.5 (Mar.1968): 952

he took the lead in working to dispel the notion.[148] He introduced the Federal Constitutional Convention Procedures Act.[149]

No action was taken on the bill and the reapportionment issue faded. But by 1971, the new issue of federal revenue sharing had enticed nine states to submit applications for a convention on that topic. Ervin sensed the direction of the political wind and pushed his bill again.[150] The Senate passed the new version of the bill by an 84-0 vote but the House did not take it up. He tried again in 1973 and once again the Senate passed the bill and the House did not. Ervin resigned office in December of 1974. Other senators and representatives saw the need for a convention regulation bill and submitted another bill in 1977. This time the issue was overturning *Roe v. Wade* and stopping abortion.[151] This bill also failed to pass.[152] No matter how Ervin and his supporters finessed their bill, they could not get past the entrenched portion of the Congress that did not want to share, let alone surrender, the power of amendment.

A number of provisions of the bills were controversial. Other provisions finally answered key questions. Among the more important aspects of the bills:[153]

- Limited conventions were permissible.

- Applications had a shelf life of seven years.

- Rescission was possible until the requisite two-thirds of the States were reached.

- The number of delegates was equal to the total of a state's number of senators and representatives. Two delegates were elected statewide and at large while the rest were elected by congressional district.

- The federal government financed the entire convention and delegates.

---

[148] C. Herman Pritchett, "Congress and Article V Conventions," *Western Political Quarterly* 35, no.2 (June 1982): 223
[149] S.2307, 90th Cong., 1st sess. (1967)
[150] S.215, 92nd Cong.
[151] S.1880, Senators Jesse Helms, Barry Goldwater and Richard Schweiker and HR7008, Representative Henry Hyde, 95th Cong.
[152] C. Herman Pritchett, "Congress and Article V Conventions," *Western Political Quarterly* 35, no.2 (June 1982): 223
[153] Ibid., 224

- The convention must be called by Congress and the start date had to be within a year of the required number of states having been reached.

- Electoral voting was used in place of unit voting.

- The Congress and not the Supreme Court decided all legal questions.

- Congress may disapprove of any proposed amendment if it believed the amendment proposal was not related to the purpose of the convention.

The work to get a procedures bill passed was then picked up by Sen. Orrin Hatch of Utah in 1981 when he got on the balanced budget amendment bandwagon.[154] Concurrent with these procedure bills were the submission of applications from the States for an amendatory convention concerning a balanced budget amendment. These applications were employing a delimiting provision that specified that an application was for a certain topic, to be invalid if Congress proposed such an amendment. The Hatch bill was significantly different from the previous Ervin bills in that the Hatch bill limited the power of the Congress to invalidate applications. The most important facet of these bills may have been the inclusion of the requirement that if the convention "ran away," the Congress would not promulgate the proposed amendments to the States for ratification consideration.[155]

An argument has been made for a century that the States should push for the amendatory convention even though they differ on the reasons that they desire the convention. It is part a matter of principle and part a matter of political strategy. The cost to the States is that they sacrifice the limited convention for an unlimited or open convention. Orfield explained,

> *"The better view would seem to be that the ground of the applications would be immaterial, and that a demand by two-thirds of the states would conclusively show a widespread desire for constitutional changes."*[156]

Orfield is suggesting that the States should just push Congress and take their chances. From his viewpoint, Congress is betting that the States

---

[154] S.817, 97th Cong. 1st sess., "The Constitutional Implementation Act of 1981"
[155] Kenneth Ripple, "Article V and the Proposed Federal Constitutional Convention Procedures Bills," *Cardozo Law Review* 3 (1982): 533
[156] Lester B. Orfield, "The Procedure of the Federal Amending Power," *Illinois Law Review* 25 (1930): 422

lack the political will to challenge Congress on its incessant power grabs.

But the failure of the States to exercise a responsible use of the convention clause has diminished the value of their efforts. Congress knows that most efforts to start a convention drive are merely diversions intended to force the passage of a bill in Congress. They also know that these efforts are easily deflected by submittal of a weak and often meaningless bill. Alternatively, Congress passes amendment bills that they expect the States would refuse to ratify. Congress's repertoire of tactics eclipses that of the convention proponents. Thus, the prodding effect has worn thin. Modern convention proponents should to take a page from the tactical playbook of President Abraham Lincoln. On 7 April 1865, he sent a telegram to General Ulysses Grant advising that,

> "Gen. Sheridan says 'If the thing is pressed I think that Lee will surrender.' Let the _thing_ be pressed. A. LINCOLN"

Proponents launching a modern convention drive should be well prepared for the fight - and let the thing be pressed - else Congress will find myriad ways to dismiss and dissolve the campaigns. Setting the goal of convening an amendatory convention and not merely prodding the Congress is the best manner of convincing those necessary last few states that the effort is real and an end game is in mind. Today's convention campaign is part politics, part marketing and part new product development.

Part II - Put on Parchment, Set in Stone

The Court Findings

Addressing the premise: "There are no rules for an Article V convention..."

FIVE
HOLDING COURT ON ARTICLE V

> *"But when so large a majority as three-fourths has finally expressed its will in the highest possible form outside of revolution, it becomes perilous for the judiciary to intervene."*[1]
>
> -Lester B. Orfield, Professor of Law, University of Nebraska

Imagine that you are a state legislator. Specifically, you are a member of the Assembly of Delegates of the Great State of East Somewhere. More specifically, you have a bill on your desk that is coming up for a vote in a week or so and you are trying to decide whether the bill makes sense and is worthy of your vote. The bill is a resolution applying to the Congress for an Article V convention. If you, like so many of your peers, know little about the topic you would have a difficult time reaching a decision as to how to vote. Clearly, you will need more information before casting your vote on the bill.

We could expect that the typical state legislator would employ a thought process something like the following. Let us assume that our state legislator does not have a legal background. So, what criteria would the legislator consider and by what process would that legislator reach his/her conclusions? Such a problem is one of politics first and foremost. The condensed version is simply that, first, Article V is extremely vague and lacking in any sufficient detail, and second, the evolution of the judicial

---

[1] Lester B. Orfield, "The Scope of the Federal Amending Power," *Michigan Law Review* 28, no.5 (Mar. 1930): 558

system has left the courts in a difficult situation where the courts could be expected to take a role in deciding the particulars of the process, much to their great reluctance and chagrin. Any state legislator will be concerned with the product of the bill. Will the legislation accomplish the desired purpose? Is the product sufficiently well-constructed enough to withstand a legal challenge? This scenario prompts a number of questions:

- What is the purpose of Article V and an amendatory convention?
- What does the Constitution – more to the point, Article V – actually say about an amendatory convention?
- What does the Constitution NOT say about the process?
- Which powers are reserved to the States and which are given to the federal government?
- What details are left to be filled in and by whom?
- As this process is really a complex legal matter, what have the courts (state, federal, appellate, and the US Supreme Court) said and decided about the process?

Answering the first question is by far the easiest. We have already firmly established in Chapter 3 that Article V is intended to provide both a means of change to the Constitution and a method of going around the federal government, especially Congress, when it is unresponsive to the people and the States. The amendatory convention empowers the state legislatures, through their applications and a convention, to restrain Congress, correct Supreme Court errors, limit the executive and establish rights under certain conditions. The power, or duty to be more exact, on the part of Congress to call a convention when the requisite two-thirds of the States have made applications has been found to be "purely ministerial" and without discretion on Congress' part.

The next consideration that our state legislator would undertake is that of determining what exactly the Constitution says about an amendatory convention. The lack of explanation and definition within Article V is the root of our problem and is traceable to the brief and somewhat vague wording of the article itself which has necessitated some judicial interpretation. It has been said of Article V that "its deceptively plain language conceals an array of ambiguities."[2] We are forced to weigh this sentiment against that of US Supreme Court Justice Hugo Black, who said, famously, that, "It was never meant that this Court have such power, which in effect would make us a continuously functioning constitutional convention."[3] The Constitution states that whenever two-thirds of the legislatures of the several States shall apply to the Congress for a convention, one shall be called for the purpose of proposing amendments. That is the sum total of the mention of the amendatory convention, leaving our state legislator with more questions than answers at this point.

As to what the Constitution does not say about the amendatory convention, well, we have this book. The vague generality of Article V leaves much to be determined by those who play a role in the amendment process. Those actors, that is, Congress, the state legislatures, the amendatory convention, and possibly ratifying conventions and the courts all have a potential role in the drama of the amendment process. As noted in Chapter 1, the convention is the arbiter of its own rules. Chapter 2 detailed that history and customs have set the limits of the convention's powers and defined many of its procedures. Congress has few powers or authority over the convention. The same can be said for the state legislatures. That leaves, potentially, the courts to fill in the blanks. Many of the steps in the amendatory convention process are analogous to the steps in the congressional method of amendment production.

Our state legislator would then most likely explore the division of the powers between the various entities in order to determine who can, and should, answer the remaining questions. The debate within the legal community can be distilled down to a set of principles that "highlight the constitutional dynamics involved in the amending process in general,"

> *"First Principle: The powers conferred by Article V are federal in character and are authoritative upon being executed by the appropriate political unit.*
>
> *Second Principle: The amending process consists of separate steps within each of which a distinct political unit exercises an independent power."*[4]

---

[2] Clifton McCleskey, "Along the Midway: Some Thoughts on Democratic Constitution-Amending," *Michigan Law Review* 66, no.5 (Mar. 1968): 1003

[3] *Katz v. United States*, 389 U.S. 347 at 373, (1967) – dissenting opinion of Justice Hugo Black.

[4] Republished with permission of SAGE Publications, Inc. Journals, from Bill Gaugush, "Principles Governing the Interpretation and Exercise of Article V Powers," *Western Political Quarterly* 35, no.2 (June 1982): 215; permission conveyed through Copyright Clearance Center, Inc.

This conclusion would appear to concur with the opinion of Professor Laurence Tribe who has summarized the Article V convention process as consisting of only three facts that are "known or knowable,"

1. Congress has a duty to call the convention,
2. Amendments proposed and ratified will become part of the Constitution,
3. The President has no role to play in the amendment process.[5]

However, this is a little simplistic and the truth is that a large body of law has developed around Article V and that includes the convention clause. But the law, as regarding Article V, is hardly settled and leaves much to interpretation. Between the decisions of the courts at multiple levels, the written positions of various governmental entities, such as the Attorney General and the Department of Justice, and the expositions of many constitutional law scholars over the last couple of centuries, we can discern much of the legal terrain of Article V. Each branch of government plays a part and has differing requirements and powers.

At this point, it becomes necessary to make a list of those remaining, as yet to be undetermined details and who should probably be addressing those details. We have ruled out Congress as having any discretion in their actions or in addressing any aspect other than those specifically assigned to Congress by the Constitution. We have similarly limited the authority of the state legislatures. Our state legislator would conclude that his/her legislature, at the outset of the process, is limited to preparing, voting on, and submitting the application prior to the calling of the convention. Prior to the convention being convened, the state legislature is empowered to determine the selection and number of its delegates and their powers. They would reserve the right to recall their delegates and to potentially instruct those delegates. Most other questions would fall to either the convention itself – as detailed in Chapter 1, and the convention does indeed have limitations on its exercise of authority – or to the courts. Among the details still unaddressed we find:

- What is to be done if any one of the constitutional actors fails, either willfully or unintentionally, to fulfill their obligation(s)? That is, as an example, what if Congress refuses to call a convention after receiving the necessary thirty-four

---

[5] Laurence Tribe, "Issues Raised by Requesting Congress to Call a Constitutional Convention to Propose a Balanced Budget Amendment," *Pacific Law Journal* 10 (1979): 634

states' applications? Who is empowered to resolve the issue and force action?

- Who may decide if a state's application resolution is invalid? The courts have addressed the validity of the state applications but there is, and always has been, a strong chorus of voices (particularly within Congress) in opposition to accepting the applications and calling a convention.

- Does the Congress have the latitude to vote on whether to convene a convention once the 34th state submits its application resolution? If not, who is responsible for executing the call to convention and making the determination of when and where?

- Do the state legislatures have any recourse, in terms of a power of their own, to a recalcitrant Congress that will not perform its mandatory duty? What course of action holds the highest likelihood of success from both standpoints of potential litigation and of politics?

- If no one body or branch of government will act to resolve an issue, what is the appropriate solution? If, for example, the federal courts refuse to take up the matter as a "political question" then where do the States turn – do they, by default, possess the power, or the right, to act on their own initiative?

In our effort to answer the first list of questions, we have generated a second list of questions, some of which must be answered so that we can return to and continue to answer the first list of questions. The one conclusion that has come to the foreground is that the courts are probably going to have to be involved in some way or another. That conclusion will create a new, high-profile host of issues.

Before we can tackle the last question from the first list that our state legislator faced and consider the judiciary's involvement, we have to assess the judicial situation. Our state legislator would prudently question how best to approach the problem. Does the legislature assume that all – or some – aspects of the amendment process are justiciable? This is not a simple assumption as there are both positive and negative results from pursuing this path. If the legislature assumes justiciability, then under what conditions and circumstances is a given issue justiciable? The legislature must realize that any assumption of justiciability may lead to extensive litigation. If the intent is (obviously) to obtain an amendment or a convention, then the litigation route will have associated costs and problems. Similarly, the political situation will also have costs and these two strategies may not necessarily be compatible.

To answer these questions, significant detail is needed on the powers and requirements of each actor. The following amount of information is undoubtedly more than any state legislator would expect to need, but we are being thorough here in describing the facets to the problem, and the weight of the seriousness of the matter deserves this level of detail. Nonetheless, some of the following is, despite the length, a mere overview as a few of these topics are of a complexity that merits an entire book to address – and many such books do exist.

The involvement of the courts, state and federal, in deciding the rules and procedures of an Article V amendatory convention has been inconsistent at best. The United States Supreme Court and the lower federal courts established a history of deciding a few points of the amending and convention processes early in the history of the Republic, but they began to back off in the last half of the nineteenth century. Then they turned around and began taking a heavier role again in the first half of the twentieth century. During this on-again, off-again approach to Article V, the courts have managed to decide conclusively a number of the major questions previously detailed. While Article V itself names only the States and Congress as participants in the amending process, the Judiciary, the States and the Congress are now a triune balance of powers with respect to Article V conventions and the amending process in general. Each has a distinct role to play and accompanying that role, they have expectations and exertions that must be met.

The issue with Article V and the court(s) is not a question of whether the judiciary is infringing on some other department's or branch's territory as has often been said but whether the court can cleanly inject itself between the litigants. One commentator described the situation as, "It seems unnecessary to add that adjudication of conflicts between state and federal interests under the Constitution should not present political questions. The difficult issues under Article V pose precisely such conflicts."[6]

---

[6] William H. White, "Article V: Political Questions and Sensible Answers," *Texas Law Review* 57 (1979): 1268

The Judiciary's Power and Requirements

Despite the numerous court decisions involving Article V or the amending process, the courts do take a hard look at whether they should even be involved in the issues concerning the process. And they should as they are enabled to reject or undo any action that they or the legislatures have taken. Thomas Millet pointed out that, "allowing the least republican branch to review cases involving amendments intended to overrule that branch's opinions gives the Court the unchecked power to thwart those efforts."[7] In other words, the litigation risk in that when resorting to the courts, the probability of an unfavorable outcome which not only stops a state legislature from securing its objective, but may actually place that objective permanently out of reach under the prevailing circumstances and actually sets the effort back significantly, is high. It is a gamble. As such a gamble, it may prove difficult to convince a court to consider a case and its merits involving an amendatory convention. It is, as Mike Stern has wisely cautioned, that the insistence on judicial review could prove to remove from "the States the autonomy that Article V guarantees."[8] He counsels that such judicial intervention might best be properly limited to those occasions when the Congress fails to perform its ministerial duty to issue a convention call.

The Political Question Doctrine

One of the over-arching concerns is referred to as "*the political question doctrine.*" The decision to take up a case involving the amending process concerns, and perhaps turns on, whether the court is considering a political question or a judicial question. This is a central issue of *"justiciability"* and is currently the one of most important judicial aspects of the amending process. For example, the validity of an application for a convention or an amendment might be called a political question (it is not addressed directly by the Constitution and who has the authority to make the resolution of the question is unknown or at least unspecified); the ability of Congress to stipulate the ratification method of a proposed amendment is a legal or judicial question (it is addressed directly by the Constitution). In 1993, Professor John Vile nailed the definition of justiciability in the amending

---

[7] Thomas Millet, "The Supreme Court, Political Questions, and Article V – A Case for Judicial Restraint," *Santa Clara Law Review* 23, no.3 (Jan. 1983): 764

[8] *Point of Order*, "The Justiciability of Controversies Related to the Article V Convention," blog by Mike Stern, 7 September 2016

process with the title of a book chapter as, "*The Question of Justiciability – Which Branch of Government Should Have the Ultimate Say Over Issues Involving the Amending Process.*"[9]

A "political question" would deal with the execution of powers, that is, in whose political sphere does it lay, more specifically, to which branch is it assigned – legislative or executive? At its simplest, it is then a matter of observing the separation of powers.[10] Even this split is not always clear. The earliest example of a US Supreme Court case involving the amending process was the 1798 decision of *Hollingsworth v. Virginia* in which the Court considered whether the Constitution required the signature of the President on the approval of a new amendment.[11] In that instance, the Court ruled that the Eleventh Amendment stood without the signature of President Washington. The US Attorney General, Charles Lee, did not attempt to argue as to the issue being a political question although today such a case, absent the prior precedent, might revolve around the point that this is a political question of whether the legislative branch is to be overruled by the executive branch since the Constitution makes no mention of it in Article V.[12] The point of the case was that proposal of an amendment to the States was in the sphere of the legislative branch as assigned by the Constitution. Of course, at the time of *Hollingsworth*, the political question doctrine was not yet a consideration.

A half century later in 1849, the US Supreme Court established the first details of the political question doctrine in the dictum written in the decision for the *Luther v. Borden* case.[13] The Court, speaking through Chief Justice Roger B. Taney, declared that an amendment was an act of the people and the ratification was also by the people so that the judicial power is bowing to the people.[14] Constitutional scholar Lester B. Orfield explained,

> "Last of all, inasmuch as the courts have not assumed to pass on the constitutionality of the constitution itself, there is some logic in arguing that since an amendment becomes as much a part of the constitution as any

---

[9] John R. Vile, *Contemporary Questions Surrounding the Constitutional Amending Process* (Westport, CT: Praeger, 1993), 23 – Vile devotes a significant portion of the book to the political question doctrine.
[10] Thomas Millet, "The Supreme Court, Political Questions, and Article V – A Case for Judicial Restraint," *Santa Clara Law Review* 23, no.3 (Jan. 1983): 759
[11] 3 Dall. 378 (1798), 1 L. Ed. 644
[12] Lester B. Orfield, "The Federal Amending Power: Genesis and Justiciability," *Minnesota Law Review* 14 (1930): 374
[13] 7 U.S. (How.) 1 (1849) at 39
[14] 7 U.S. (How.) 1 (1849), 12 L. Ed. 581 – relating to the Dorr Rebellion in Rhode Island case.

other part of it, in fact repeals any part inconsistent with it, as a result, the legality of an amendment is no more open to attack than that of the constitution itself."[15,16]

The phrase "political question" itself had been originally used in the *Marbury v. Madison* decision in 1803, a mandamus action against an executive branch official, but was not defined until the *Luther* decision nearly five decades later.[17] The issue is really a moving target. Alexis de Tocqueville famously noted that, "scarcely any political question arises in the United States that is not resolved, sooner or later, into a judicial question."

Orfield states that the same validity that is given the Constitution is due any amendment to that document. Both drafting the Constitution and amending it are an exercise of the "highest sovereign power of the state." Courts will most likely limit themselves to questions concerning interpretation for constitutionality, procedure or substance and avoid issues involving the separation of powers. With regard to procedure, the courts could probably declare null and void all those amendments that failed to follow the prescribed modes of amendments.[18] Orfield distinguishes two considerations for a court that is reviewing an amendment,

> *"First, was the procedure prescribed in the amendment clause of the constitution regularly followed? Second, granted that the procedure was regular, is the amendment valid in its substance? The vast majority of cases have involved the first point, and have regarded it as unquestionably a judicial question. The number of cases dealing with the second issue has been small and the outcome not so decisive."*[19]

So, to look at the amending process, and in particular, an Article V convention, from a legal perspective, we then have to begin with a two part

---

[15] Lester B. Orfield, "The Federal Amending Power: Genesis and Justiciability," *Minnesota Law Review* 14 (1930): 374 – Orfield goes on to discuss the constitutionality of the Constitution and the argument that has gone with that discussion for a couple of centuries. He concludes with the position that the Constitution is constitutional and no court, at any level, will entertain a challenge to that assertion. The same assumption is made in this work. This assertion is, surprisingly, not as obvious as one would expect in the literature. See for example, Richard S. Kay, "The Illegality of the Constitution," *Constitutional Commentary* 4:57 (1987) and Sebastian De Grazia, *A Country With No Name, Tales From The Constitution* (New York: Vintage Books, 1997)

[16] Lester B. Orfield, *The Amending of the Federal Constitution* (Ann Arbor: The University of Michigan Press, 1942), 8

[17] 5 U.S. (1 Cranch) 137 (1803)

[18] Lester B. Orfield, "The Federal Amending Power: Genesis and Justiciability," *Minnesota Law Review* 14 (1930): 377-8

[19] Ibid., 380

question: Will the courts even consider the issue and if they will, in what way will they approach the issue? Put another way, when are the complaints justiciable?

The pivotal case in this regard is *Coleman v. Miller*.[20] And here the first of several major diversions concerning the details and minutiae of law begins. The US Supreme Court took on a number of issues in deciding this case in 1939. The major focus of this decision can be watered down to a determination of the validity of an amendment on procedural terms by the federal courts.[21] In a decision that is still considered controversial by some, the Court took up a case involving the ratification by the legislature of the State of Kansas of the proposed Child Labor Amendment and in that case addressed whether the plaintiffs had standing; whether the Court had jurisdiction; whether the time limit requirement was valid and justiciable; whether the prior rejection by the state legislature and subsequent ratification was a true conflict; and whether the state's executive branch had a legitimate role in the ratification process.[22] The results were disappointing in that the Court decided one of the five points, deferred to Congress on two points as political, divided on another point and waffled on the remaining point. The decision was not unanimous, in fact, it wasn't even a majority – only four of eight justices voted that all aspects of the amendment process were within the political question doctrine. The bottom line: the Court generally deferred to Congress from beginning to end of the amending process,[23] with Justice Hugo Black writing in his concurrence with the decision stating, first that,

> "Undivided control of that [the amending] process has been given by the Article [V] exclusively and completely to Congress. The process itself is 'political' in its entirety, from submission until an amendment becomes part of the Constitution, and is not subject to judicial guidance, control or interference at any point."[24]

---

[20] 307 U.S. 433 (1939)

[21] Homer Clark, "The Supreme Court and the Amending Process," *Virginia Law Review* 39, no. 5 (June 1953): 622

[22] The result was completely predictable considering the history of judicial review going back over a century. Even in the years just prior to *Coleman*, lawyers and law professors saw the political question doctrine as settled. For example, see, Milton Yawitz, "The Legal Effect Under American Decisions of an Alleged Irregularity in the Adoption of a Constitution or Constitutional Amendment," *St. Louis Law Review* 10, no. 4 (1925): 280

[23] John R. Vile, *Contemporary Questions Surrounding the Constitutional Amending Process* (Westport, CT: Praeger, 1993), 27

[24] *Coleman v. Miller*, 307 U.S. 433 (1939), at 458-9

and more succinctly, "The Constitution grants Congress exclusive power to control submission of constitutional amendments."[25] This assertion is more than a little hard to swallow. If that were truly the case, there would be no provision for the convention method. Prof. Vile summarizes the *Coleman* decision thusly, that three arguments had been made for assuming that Article V was a political question. These arguments include: (1) the necessity of finality; (2) no provision of judicial criteria; and (3) the Constitution has allocated all discretion to Congress.[26]

Herewith inserting this book's conclusions on the Court's handling of the matter: With regard to the first point, is not the whole purpose of appealing to the Court to get resolution or "finality" where no other body could provide it? The Court, in taking up the case, is accepting, at least initially, that there is ground for the Court to intervene and to provide finality. Having conclusively dealt with only one of the five questions does not really provide the sought after finality.

Addressing the second point, the courts, especially the US Supreme Court, frequently concoct two-part, three-part, six-part, eight-hundred-and-twelve-part (intentional exaggeration for effect) tests for just such purposes, raising the question of why were this case and the subject of constitutional amendment any different? The criteria seem for the most part, obvious. That is, that the Constitution may not spell out in detail who is make such determinations as to the points of the Kansas action, but it also *implies* that the courts exist for such a purpose, since we must ask what other body exists that can perform that function? The Court later produced criteria in *Baker* so why not here? Had the Court done so, it could have perhaps decided a couple of additional points and aided future actions.

As to Vile's enumeration of the Court's third point, this is more easily refuted by pointing out that the ratification is solely the realm of the States and the proposition of amendments can be the territory of the States as well thereby invalidating the argument. It is paramount to point out that it is the Constitution that makes that distinction in favor of the States – and not in favor of the Congress. It is an interesting decision in that there are some facets lacking to substantiate it and this has been argued over by

---

[25] *Coleman v. Miller*, 307 U.S. 433 (1939), at 457
[26] John R. Vile, *Contemporary Questions Surrounding the Constitutional Amending Process* (Westport, CT: Praeger, 1993), 27

constitutional scholars ever since.[27] Nonetheless, *Coleman* still stands and the limits of its applicability remain as not completely defined despite the decision in *Baker*.[28] Not everything is barred by *Coleman* and following that decision, a number of issues have been taken up by the courts. The Court may not be able to disown *Coleman* without equally and simultaneously disowning the political question doctrine unless issuing a new ruling that clearly defined and elucidates the new boundaries of the redefined political question doctrine. The political question doctrine is a *necessary* doctrine as it preserves the independence of the other branches but in the matter of *Coleman*, it is clear that some additional definition was needed in terms of a discrete, quantifiable basis for applying the doctrine.

Future Supreme Court Justice John Paul Stevens took the *Coleman* criteria apart in 1975 ruling in a federal district court case, *Dyer v. Blair*, that it is indeed the States to which the Constitution assigns many aspects of the ratification procedure.[29] Stevens wrote that the courts would be avoiding their constitutional responsibility if they neglected to address a case where Congress might be in conflict with the opinion of the Court. It is because an Article V convention is meant to be an answer to conflict with the Congress that the power to initiate amendments was given to the convention – and the courts have to uphold that balance of power. And that was just the beginning of the reconsideration of *Coleman*.

In *Dyer*, a majority in the Illinois General Assembly ratified the ERA but not by the three-fifths of each house that the state constitution and the House rules required. Members of the General Assembly sought to force the ratification contending that, "first, that Congress has sole and complete control over the entire amending process, subject to no judicial review; and second, that even if every aspect of the amending process is not controlled by Congress, the specific issue raised in these cases is."[30] *Dyer* distinguishes that the Court found a slim exception in *Coleman* for a political question. The conclusion was that the state could impose a stringent supermajority requirement for the ratification of a federal amendment in the absence of

---

[27] For example, see Michael Stokes Paulsen, "A General Theory of Article V: The Constitutional Lessons of the Twenty-Seventh Amendment," *Yale Law Journal* 103, no.3 (Dec. 1993): 713-21

[28] The Court did make an effort to narrow the scope of the type of cases that come under the political question doctrine in *Zivotofsky v. Clinton* in 2012. 566 U.S. ___ (2012) Case 10-699, 571 F. 3d 1227, 132 S. Ct. 1421, 182 L. Ed. 2d 423

[29] 390 F. Supp. 1291 (1975), p.1304

[30] 390 F. Supp. 1291 (1975), p.1299

one required by Article V itself. The most important result of this ruling is that the relief requested by the plaintiffs, that of the federal district court ordering the Illinois legislature to ratify the amendment, was not possible. Mike Stern points out that to have done so would have prompted numerous questions involving "separation of powers, federalism and legislative immunity."[31]

The political question doctrine got a makeover in 1981 with the *Idaho v. Freeman* decision.[32] In a decision concerning the rescission of Idaho's ratification of the proposed Equal Rights Amendment, the federal district court decided that they rejected much of the *Coleman* and the 1962 *Baker v. Carr*[33] criteria for determining justiciability. Federal District Judge Marion Callister asserted that the Framers had not given complete control to Congress but believed it to be shared by Congress and the States thereby creating a situation where the courts had a role in adjudicating any disputes.[34] The failure of the ERA to achieve ratification within the allotted period of time allowed the Supreme Court to sidestep the issue and avoid taking up the case thereby rendering it moot.[35] This is a shame since no Article V case has been decided by the US Supreme Court since the *Coleman* decision three quarters of a century ago. It would have been interesting to see if the Court continued its practice of deferring to Congress. This tack has been taken through looking at the past actions of Congress as equivalent to a judicial precedent.[36] The possibility of the Court taking a different course than its past deference to Congress may come about due to the observance of the "present conflict" view wherein the Court looks to applying the political question doctrine only for the narrow segment of Article V cases where the amendment in question might overturn a previous Supreme Court decision.[37] This scenario is also one of the reasons for Article V. The power to overturn a US Supreme Court decision cannot be limited by the same Supreme Court

---

[31] *Point of Order*, "More on Article V Justiciability: Dyer v. Blair," blog by Mike Stern, 13 October 2016 – also, it is very important to note Stern's conclusion that post-*Raines v. Byrd*, such a conclusion is not possible.
[32] 529 F. Supp. 1107 (D. Idaho 1981)
[33] 369 U.S. 186 (1962)
[34] John R. Vile, *Contemporary Questions Surrounding the Constitutional Amending Process* (Westport, CT: Praeger, 1993), 31-3
[35] Mason Kalfus, "Why Time Limits on the Ratification of Constitutional Amendments Violate Article V," *University of Chicago Law Review* 66, no.2 (Spring 1999): 444
[36] Thomas Millet, "The Supreme Court, Political Questions, and Article V – A Case for Judicial Restraint," *Santa Clara Law Review* 23, no.3 (Jan. 1983): 751
[37] Ibid., 758

without making the court's motivation suspect.[38]

Having referenced *Baker v. Carr*, this is a good point at which to include a listing of the criteria of *Baker* for a political question. Finally getting around to attempting to outline the characteristics of the political question in 1962, the Court stipulated these six factors must be present to comprise a political question:

- A "textually demonstrable constitutional commitment of the issue to a coordinate political department." – Meaning that at some place within the Constitution, there is, in writing, an assignment of that particular issue to one of the branches of the government.

- A "lack of judicially discoverable and manageable standards for resolving it." – Here we are looking for an omission of a method for the courts to approach and dispatch with the problem. How would these standards apply?

- The "impossibility for a court's independent resolution without expressing a lack of respect for a coordinate branch of the government." – The court is seeking to avoid stepping on the toes of another branch of the federal government and interfering in that other branch's business.

- The "impossibility of deciding the issue without an initial policy decision, which is beyond the discretion of the court." – The executive or legislative branch needs to have first determined and implemented a policy with regard to the issue and then, after a controversy has arisen, the court may become involved.

- An "unusual need for unquestioning adherence to a political decision already made." – There is a division of opinion that forces the issue into a controversy over execution of policy.

- The "potentiality of embarrassment from multifarious pronouncements by various departments on one question." – On this point, the potential exists for differing government agencies or departments to be in conflict over how best to handle the issue possibly at the same point in time.[39]

---

[38] Ibid., 747
[39] Jared P. Cole, Library of Congress, Congressional Research Service Report R43834, *The Political Question Doctrine: Justiciability and the Separation of Powers*, (23 April 2014), 5

The political question doctrine probably should not even apply to congressional control of a convention; James Kenneth Rogers argued in 2007 that it fails the first part of the Court's *Coleman* test: the issue, according to Article V, is not constitutionally assigned to the Congress but to the States. He contends that the language in Article V leaves it clearly to the States to control the convention process. He points back to the Philadelphia convention of 1787 as the guide for the future conventions; the States organized and executed the 1787 convention in addition to dozens of other interstate conventions both prior to and following the 1787 convention.[40]

Before moving on, there is another extremely important major facet to justiciability, that of the difference between the States, the federal government and Article V in terms of the source of their respective powers and how those powers bear on an amendatory convention. The amending power is not a single prospect but a melding of a tripartite source and execution of powers. The separate character and operation of Article V has been covered already but the source of constitutional powers and performance is worthy of additional note. The federal constitution is, of course, a limited and enumerated powers charter that derives those powers from grants from both the people and the States. It is inelastic in its amending process. It is supreme over the States' constitutions. The state constitutions are derived from grants from the people and are often more normative in adherence. The combined state and federal exercise of the Article V amending power is something different than just an extension of the state and federal constitutional powers. It is, as Jameson described it, not a power belonging to the States "originally by virtue of rights reserved or otherwise."[41] When the state and federal governments act to amend the federal constitution, they are not acting in their individual capacities and under their usual powers but in, what the Supreme Court has termed in the *Leser v. Garnett*[42] decision, a *federal function*, under a special power found only in Article V.[43] Therefore, it is difficult to apply other parts of the Constitution or of law to the Article V process without an extremely elevated

---

[40] James Kenneth Rogers, "The Other Way to Amend the Constitution: The Article V Constitutional Convention Amendment Process," *Harvard Journal of Law & Public Policy* 30, no.3 (Summer 2007): 1014-5
[41] John Alexander Jameson, *A Treatise on Constitutional Conventions: Their History, Powers and Modes of Proceedings* (New York: Scribner, 1867, 4th ed., 1887), §§ 579-581
[42] 258 U.S. 130 (1922)
[43] Frank E. Packard, "Notes and Comments – Rescinding Memorialization Resolutions," *Chicago-Kent Law Review* 30, no.4 (Jan. 1952): 341

level of consideration. The bulk of the body of law does not necessarily apply to the deliberately separate amendment process so we must be careful in attempting to apply any other point of law to the amendment process.

There are lesser issues involved in bringing a case regarding Article V that merit mention. Specifically, the issue of justiciability has five components[44] to assess:

- Is there a request for an *advisory opinion* from the Court?
- Does the plaintiff have *standing* to bring suit?
- Is the issue *ripe* for adjudication?
- Is the issue *moot* – that is, has it been resolved already?
- Is the matter a *political or a judicial question*?

In regard to an advisory opinion, the US Supreme Court does not issue opinions without a case or controversy to address.[45] Likewise, if a solution to the conflict has presented itself and been implemented, then the intervention of the Court is moot and therefore unnecessary.[46] We have already addressed the determination of whether the issue is political or judicial. That leaves just two components to resolve. These are the issues of *"standing"* and of *"ripeness."* Just getting through the courthouse door to, proverbially speaking, have your day in court requires that you have standing. That is, to show that you are in some way injured and not just as a member of society. For ripeness, the issue must have an impending issue or controversy to resolve. The idea behind the determination of ripeness is to avoid clogging the courts with cases that have no immediate or near-term impact.

Standing

The question of *"standing"* with regard to challenging any aspect of the amending process is complicated by rulings of the US Supreme Court. The

---

[44] There are two other issues that sometimes come into play: abstention (avoiding intrusion into matters currently being addressed by another court) and Eleventh Amendment cases wherein a citizen attempts to sue a state. Also, constitutional attorney Mike Stern notes that there are other factors such as, the type of relief sought by the plaintiffs, the makeup of the judiciary at the time of the case, the identities of the parties, and whether or not the political climate is one that is favorable to the intervention of the courts. See generally, Stern's *Point of Order* blog, 7 September 2016: "*The Justiciability of Controversies Related to the Article V Convention.*"

[45] The prohibition on advisory opinions is based on Article III, §2, Cl.1 of the US Constitution and the doctrine of the separation of powers. For advisory opinions, the Chief Justice John Jay, in a letter dated 8 August 1793, directed President Washington to turn to the Attorney General.

[46] Issuing a decision on an issue that has already been resolved is equivalent to issuing an advisory opinion.

ratification process is considered a federal function, and therefore, is beyond the scope of the Court's power to address, a la *Coleman*.[47] The proposing aspect of the amending process is logically similar to the ratification process and most likely subject to the same limitations in the courts.[48] It has been observed by the Court that a private citizen does not necessarily have a right to challenge a federal law or a constitutional amendment simply because it hits the citizen in the pocketbook.[49] Also, the Court has alluded that a citizen does not have the right to participate directly in the amending process through referendum or popular vote.[50] The absolute bottom line has been that the US Supreme Court has consistently stated that Congress has the sole discretion over the amending process.[51] The Court has not, however, directly addressed the issue of controlling an Article V Convention.

To bring an action involving an Article V amendatory convention will necessitate the claimant to show that some harm has been done to him or her – that they have a personal, legal interest in the matter.[52] Also, that the injury was done to either an interest or a right that is protected by law and that the injury was performed by the defendant. We have two ways to approach this: the States clearly have an interest as they are an integral part of the amending process and have a well-defined, if not major, role to play in the whole affair. Individuals have the greater burden in demonstrating how they have been harmed, or in the terms of the Court, that they have "private damage." Using the example of going through the courts to force Congress to call an amendatory convention, an individual would most likely run into the brick wall of the courts declaring that the States are the petitioners for a convention and not the people or individuals. This would leave the States' attorneys-general to argue on behalf of the aggregated people while individuals and grassroots groups would be entirely shut out of the courts on this topic. But then, in *Coleman v. Miller* and several other precedents, the courts held that public officials could bring suits where they were harmed

---

[47] *Leser v. Garnett*, 258 U.S. 130 at 137 (1922)
[48] Wilbur Edel, *A Constitutional Convention – Threat or Challenge?* (New York: Praeger, 1981), 54
[49] *Fairchild v. Hughes*, 258 U.S. 130 (1922)
[50] *United States v. Sprague*, 282 U.S. 716 (1931) at 731
[51] Wilbur Edel, *A Constitutional Convention – Threat or Challenge?* (New York: Praeger, 1981), 55
[52] It must be an "injury in fact," it must be "individuated" and "concrete" and the federal action must be the "cause in fact" of the injury. There is more, always more…but one must turn to a law reference text for greater detail. See in particular, *United States v. Richardson*, 418 U.S. 166 (1974) at 177

in their official capacities but not their private capacities.[53] This has been relaxed over the years but it was a key reason for the dissatisfaction with *Coleman*. Homer Clark sharply opined that *Coleman v. Miller* is unsupported by any precedent.[54]

As a corollary, members of Congress do not have individual standing either. They might be able to act in unison although they would still be limited in their capacity to sue, especially in the case of a conflict between branches of the government.[55] State legislatures however, do as an entity, have standing.[56] A minor question remains whether both houses of the legislature must have experienced the same injury to have that standing.

So what role might the Court find itself asked to play in the Article V convention process, principally with respect to the issue of standing? Most likely, the first issue to arise will be whether the Congress can be pressed to call a convention. The Court will probably be the first institution to which the States will turn in their attempt at securing their constitutional right to a convention.

Even if all the previously listed criteria are met, the problem remains of how to compel Congress to act and call a convention when the requisite number of state petitions has been received. Constitutional scholars have debated whether there is any viable method of compelling Congress for at least the last century. In most instances, the conclusion reached is that the only constitutional method of punishing the Congress for its refusal is at the polls in the next election. As nice and simple as that sounds, it has consistently proven toothless. Still others maintain that there are additional methods. For example, William Barker states clearly that,

> "*the only 'sanction' imposed for Congressional refusal to propose an*

---

[53] See, for example, all (somewhat) contemporary to *Coleman*: *Smith v. Indiana*, 191 U.S. 138 (1903); *Braxton County Court v. West Virginia ex rel. Dillon*, 208 U.S. 192 (1908); *Stewart v. Kansas City*, 239 U.S. 14 (1915); *Columbus & Greenville Railway. v. Miller*, 283 U.S. 96 (1931); *Boynton v. Hutchinson Gas Co.*, 291 U.S. 656 (1934); *Morehead v. New York ex rel. Tipaldo*, 298 U.S. 587 (1936); *Blodgett v. Silberman*, 277 U.S. 1 (1928); *Kelly v. Washington ex rel. Foss Co.*, 302 U.S. 1 (1937); *FTC v. Curtis Publishing Co.*, 260 U.S. 568 (1923); *ICC v. Oregon-Washington R. & N. Co.*, 288 U.S. 14 (1933); *NLRB v. Jones & Laughlin Steel Corp.*, 301 U.S. 1 (1937)

[54] Homer Clark, "The Supreme Court and the Amending Process," *Virginia Law Review* 39, no.5 (June 1953): 636-43

[55] *Raines v. Byrd*, 521 U.S. 811 (1997)

[56] *Arizona State Legislature v. Arizona Independent Redistricting Commission, et al.*, 576 U.S. __ (2015), 997 F. Supp. 2d 1047 – "the Legislature has shown injury that is 'concrete and particularized' and 'actual or imminent'."

amendment is the convening of an equally representative convention through which the People of the United States might propose amendments if they wish to do so. Since the very purpose of the convention method of amendment is to allow the People of the United States to bypass an unresponsive Congress which refuses to propose amendments they desire, this degree of constraint on Congressional freedom in the amending process is entirely proper."[57]

It would appear that Barker is advocating that the people can call a convention directly circumventing Congress, and the States, if need be. This tactic would be...undoubtedly legally and constitutionally problematic but Barker has his adherents and there are people today attempting to do exactly that, and in the end, it may come down to exactly that course of action. Among the questions this tact will raise are: would the proposed amendment be valid? That is, without the constitutionally mandated step taken of Congress calling the convention, is the product of the convention even constitutional? The answer might be that if a series of escalating steps are taken and in each instance Congress has refused to carry out its constitutionally required actions, then by default, the States have, by implication, a recourse to calling and executing their own convention.

Attorney Walter Tuller argued a century ago that Congress could indeed be forced to act by an average citizen utilizing the federal courts stating unequivocally, "The form of remedy for compelling Congress to act would seem clearly to be a writ of mandamus, that is, a court order to compel a certain action. It is believed that such a proceeding may be instituted by any citizen."[58] But this assertion was ostensibly quashed by the *Coleman* decision. Constitutional scholars have argued that attempting to force Congress is more than pitting co-equal branches of the government against each other, as one states, "this position distorts and exaggerates the power of the federal judiciary and brutalizes the doctrine of the separation of powers."[59] Obviously a price will be paid either way that the legal fight would go. Sooner or later the Court must decide whether it has the right, power and obligation to uphold the Constitution or if it is limited only

---

[57] William T. Barker, "A Status Report on the 'Balanced Budget' Constitutional Convention," *John Marshall Law Review* 20 (1986): 36

[58] Walter K. Tuller, "A Convention to Amend the Constitution - Why Needed - How It May Be Obtained," *North American Review* 193, no.664 (Mar. 1911): 383 3

[59] Michael A. Almond, "Amendment by Convention: Our Next Constitutional Crisis?," *North Carolina Law Review* 53 (1975): 522. Reprinted with permission of the North Carolina Law Review.

to expressing an opinion as interpretation of the Constitution. Even if the Congress refused to call a convention after the required thirty-four state applications were received, or after having held a convention, the Congress refused to promulgate the proposed amendment, the Court may claim that it had no power or jurisdiction over an Article V case.[60] But in doing so, it risks great damage to its own prestige and credibility and it might spark an uproar of public demands for reform of the Court itself!

The issue of a federal court, including the US Supreme Court, ordering a governmental action is not that far-fetched. The earliest decisions that invoked the separation of powers as inviolable still had their exceptions. From 1813 to 1946, only the Federal District Court in the District of Columbia could issue a writ of mandamus to order a federal official to perform a ministerial act. That action has its roots in the famous *Marbury v. Madison*[61] decision of 1803. That decision inevitably led to *Kendall v. United States*[62] in 1838 and a mandamus order against the US Postmaster General.[63] Between 1946 and 1962, The Administrative Procedures Act of 1946[64] allowed for judicial review and limited the defenses to a suit against the United States or a federal officer. In 1962, Congress corrected the deficiencies of the mandamus option by passing the Mandamus and Venue Act of 1962[65] which now permits any federal district court to entertain a mandamus action against a federal official under original jurisdiction. But the 1976 amendment to this law still allows for refusal to consider a case due to the political question doctrine among others.[66] In 1925, the US Supreme Court spelled out the three conditions that apply to the mandamus law, herein quoting Howard Brill,[67]

> "*the* **Rives** *decision indicated that the writ of mandamus may be granted against a public official: (1) if the statute imposes a purely ministerial duty*

---

[60] Richard W. Hemstad, "Constitutional Amendment by Convention – a Risky Business," *Washington State Bar News* 36 (Feb. 1982): 20

[61] 5 U.S. (1 Cranch) 137 (1803)

[62] 37 U.S. (12 Pet.) 524 (1838)

[63] Howard W. Brill, "The Citizen's Relief Against Inactive Federal Officials: Case Studies In Mandamus, Actions 'In The Nature Of Mandamus,' And Mandatory Injunctions," *Akron Law Review* 16 (Winter 1983): 352

[64] Pub. L. No.79-404, 60 Stat. 237 (1946)

[65] Pub. L. No. 87-748, 76 Stat. 744 (1962) – codified as Chapter 28 U.S.C. §1361 (1976)

[66] Howard W. Brill, "The Citizen's Relief Against Inactive Federal Officials: Case Studies In Mandamus, Actions "In The Nature Of Mandamus," And Mandatory Injunctions," *Akron Law Review* 16 (Winter 1983): 348 - Referencing *Work v. United States ex rel. Rives*, 267 U.S. 175 (1925)

[67] Chief Justice of the Arkansas Supreme Court and University of Arkansas School of Law professor.

on the defendant; (2) if the officer having the discretionary duty has refused to act at all; and (3) if the officer having the discretionary duty has acted in an arbitrary or capricious fashion."[68]

From this we can see the immediate application as we have already established that the congressional duty to call an amendatory convention is purely ministerial and there is no discretion thereby presumably ruling out the second and third scenarios. Section 1361 of the US Code states,

> *"the district courts shall have original jurisdiction of any action in the nature of mandamus to compel an officer or employee of the United States or any agency thereof to perform a duty owed to the plaintiff."*[69]

Based on this description, we can possibly, tentatively, envision a situation where the Congress could be compelled to act on the purely ministerial duty to perform the action of calling an amendatory convention as owed to the States, represented in an action by their Attorneys-General. But this would apply only if the recipient of the notice was a federal official and not a chamber of Congress or Congress as a whole. Could the Clerk of the House or the Sergeant-at-Arms of the US House of Representatives or, equally, the Secretary of the Senate or the Sergeant-at-Arms of the US Senate be then legally compelled to perform a purely ministerial duty? Do they even have that authority in their offices? These officers of the legislative chambers do not possess the same immunity under the Speech and Debate Clause as the elected officials. Interestingly, it was the US Department of Justice that recommended the language of Section 1361.

More current scholars have turned back to the ideas presented a century ago and compared those to the decisions of the federal courts over the intervening century. Some argue that because the obligation of Congress is to call a convention when presented with thirty-four valid applications, that the mandatory duty is judicially enforceable. They cite a US Supreme Court suit involving Congress as evidence of the viability of a declaratory judgement against Congress.[70] Professor Francis Heller noted in 1973 that in one instance, the US Supreme Court did issue a writ of mandamus on the

---

[68] Howard W. Brill, "The Citizen's Relief Against Inactive Federal Officials: Case Studies In Mandamus, Actions "In The Nature Of Mandamus," And Mandatory Injunctions," *Akron Law Review* 16 (Winter 1983): 354

[69] 28 U.S.C. §1361 (1976)

[70] Robert G. Natelson, "Proposing Constitutional Amendments by Convention: Rules Governing the Process," *Tennessee Law Review* 78 (2011): 738

legislature of West Virginia but it was under special circumstances.[71]

The courts may surprise everyone and decide that they have the jurisdiction to interpret the meaning of the term "application"[72] or to define where the Congress's authority ends and that of the States' begins. It has happened before. In the Court's 1969 decision for the *Powell v. McCormack*[73] suit, it decided that it could address what everyone else thought to be a purely "political question" and took up the issue of the application of a US House rule concerning the seating of an elected candidate. The House denied a seat to Adam Clayton Powell, a congressman who had become deeply embroiled in a scandal involving numerous charges. The Speaker of the House, John William McCormack, sought to prevent Powell from retaking his seat in the new Congress. The Court ruled in Powell's favor and stated that it was not a case of pitting one branch of the federal government against another to have the Court intercede. The *Harvard Law Review* argued this very point in 1972 and then pointed to other examples of where the Court has used its authority to compel the other branches, including FDR's New Deal legislation and Truman's wartime seizure of the steel mills.[74] But the real issue in the case was whether a federal official, the Sergeant-at-Arms of the House, could be compelled to pay Rep. Powell – so *Powell* is not really the precedent that we are looking to use. The literature shows that most writers predict that the Court will try to have it both ways and claim that there is a difference between the Court telling Congress what it can do in *Coleman* and in the Court telling Congress what it has to do in *Powell*.[75] Between *Baker v. Carr* and *Powell v. McCormack*, the Court has rewritten the standards on justiciability, to the point where some, but not all, legal scholars now view *Coleman* as a dead issue.[76]

The other side of this coin is that Congress holds many of the cards and will probably be able to manipulate the process. In terms of standing,

---

[71] Francis H. Heller, "Article V: Changing Dimensions in Constitutional Change," *University of Michigan Journal of Law Reform* 7 (Fall 1973): 81 – citing *Virginia v. West Virginia* 246 U.S. 565 (1918).

[72] Morris B. Forkosch, "The Alternative Amending Clause in Article V: Reflections and Suggestions," *Minnesota Law Review* 51 (1967): 1065-6

[73] 395 U.S. 486 (1969); 89 S. Ct. 1944; 23 L. Ed. 2d 491; 1969 U.S. LEXIS 3103

[74] "Proposed Legislation on the Convention Method of Amending the United States Constitution," *Harvard Law Review* 85, no.8 (June 1972): 1638-40

[75] Thomas A. Gilliam, "Constitutional Conventions: Precedents, Problems, and Proposals," *St. Louis University Law Review* 16 (1971): 58

[76] Mason Kalfus, "Why Time Limits on the Ratification of Constitutional Amendments Violate Article V," *University of Chicago Law Review* 66, no.2 (Spring 1999): 444-5, - see note 56 for detail on those scholars who advocate for discounting *Coleman*.

this crucial aspect could prove the hindrance at each step. As the push for the proposed Reed-Dirksen Amendment, capping the federal income tax rate at 25%, among other issues, picked up momentum in the 1950s the public debate inevitably turned to the feasibility of the convention method to secure the proposal. The discourse turned to dispute as the method of counting the number of states which had applied for an Article V convention got heated. But preceding that debate, the issue of standing came first. In 1957, the *Harvard Law Review* argued that the courts will most likely stay out of the fray as they would not see where anyone had standing. In the determination of whether enough states had indeed filed an application with Congress, the *Harvard Law Review* believed that no individual could contest Congress's count as they would not be able to show harm. The amendment itself would have to be ratified and in effect before any single person could claim to have had his or her constitutional rights violated.[77]

The standing issue that would naturally occur earlier in the process, that of the States seeking to force Congress to make the convention call, would also be impacted. We find ourselves engaging in the proverbial Catch-22 scenario where we need standing, that is, to be harmed, to challenge the Congress but, we first need to challenge Congress in order for our legally protected interest to be harmed and thereby achieve standing. The *Harvard Law Review* theorized that,

> *"If Congress should determine that the prerequisites of a convention had not been met, it might be argued that a state would have standing to contest this determination on the theory that a constitutional right to use the convention method for the proposal of amendments has been denied. However, even if standing were found, a judicial decision that the congressional determination was erroneous would be without effect, since it would seem improper for the court either to order action by a coequal branch of the Government or to assume for itself the power to call the convention."*[78]

This view, naturally, returns us to the "political question" and justiciability issues. In the end, the Supreme Court may simply punt and refuse to get involved. Remember, the standing issue was one of the key

---

[77] "Proposing Amendments to the United States Constitution by Convention," *Harvard Law Review* 70, no.6 (Apr.1957): 1068

[78] Republished with permission of the Harvard Law Review Association, from "Proposing Amendments to the United States Constitution by Convention," *Harvard Law Review* 70, no.6 (Apr.1957): 1068; permission conveyed through Copyright Clearance Center, Inc.

points – and divided over – during the *Coleman v. Miller* case.⁷⁹ The rosy picture that the *Harvard Law Review* painted of the courts' involvement pales in comparison to the prediction of the reaction by Congress to the pressure to do its ministerial duty,

> "But Congress must of necessity decide whether the conditions exist which give rise to this duty, and, to the extent that this power to decide is subject to abuse, the intention of the framers may be frustrated. Because the courts are unwilling to intervene in the amending process, improper interference with the right of the states to propose amendments by convention can be avoided only by self-restraint of Congress and the force of public opinion."⁸⁰

Here we are brought back to recognizing the need for a definite and coherent legal strategy to force a Congress that will, in all probability, be an uncooperative, obstructive, self-protecting impediment to the States' and the people's efforts to right the wrongs which are, more often than not, of Congress's making. Orfield noted this problem in 1930 stating that we cannot assume that Congress will see their constitutionally mandated action as purely ministerial; that they will in all likelihood aggressively resist the encroachment on their powers. Orfield specifically cited the example of Congress's refusal to redistrict after the 1920 census although required by the Constitution to do so.⁸¹ Ever the pessimist, Walter Dodd echoed Orfield in claiming that there is no legal mechanism for compelling Congress to act.⁸²

The contention that the federal courts, and specifically the US Supreme Court, have no ability to compel Congress to take action and call an Article V convention is disturbing on a deeper level than that of just respecting the separation of powers doctrine. The claim that any judicial review of the non-performance of a constitutional duty by the Congress is a violation of the separation of powers and is not possible because one co-equal branch of the government cannot force another to act leaves only two possible remedies. Remember that any right must have a remedy to be upheld

---

⁷⁹ "Proposed Legislation on the Convention Method of Amending the United States Constitution," *Harvard Law Review* 85, no.8 (June 1972): 1643-4

⁸⁰ Republished with permission of the Harvard Law Review Association, from "Proposing Amendments to the United States Constitution by Convention," *Harvard Law Review* 70, no.6 (Apr.1957): 1071; permission conveyed through Copyright Clearance Center, Inc.

⁸¹ Lester B. Orfield, *The Amending of the Federal Constitution* (Ann Arbor: The University of Michigan Press, 1942), 41-2 – includes the 1930 paper.

⁸² Walter F. Dodd, "Judicially Non-Enforcible Provisions of Constitutions," *University of Pennsylvania Law Review* 80 (1932): 82

by the courts. The first avenue of recourse is the retaliation at the polls. This is more difficult than it appears and would take an unbelievable amount of time to secure as it would take at least three elections, or six years, to completely clean out the Senate. With the combined congressional rate of retention at roughly 95%, and the senatorial retention rate at roughly 82% for the 2014 election, this option is dead on arrival.[83] Then we are left with only the recourse for which Article V was designed to prevent.

Let us look to an imaginary scenario for clarification and demonstration. Let us say that, for the sake of example, the American public has, over time, become extremely angry with the abuse of the per diem expense reimbursement privilege. In our hypothetical scenario, congressmen and women are submitting grossly padded expense reports and taking blatant advantage of the public purse. The average congressman is, in our fabricated example, now collecting each year more in expense reimbursement than his annual salary. The practice has become widespread and is unquestionably out of control.

No amount of effort on the part of the people to restrain the Congress through electing new members has made a difference. Once the newly elected congressmen and women arrive in Washington, they are quickly infected with this pernicious "disease." Petitions are compiled and submitted, internet blogs are written, talk shows and political pundits devote hours to the topic, protests are held throughout the nation, state legislatures pass resolutions of condemnation, and good people run in each election promising to not take part and to stop the practice when they get to Washington. All to no avail.

The pleadings of the people go not only disregarded in the national capitol but they are laughed at with scorn and derision by Congress. Then one day, Mr. John Q. Public, an ordinary citizen of the Great State of East Somewhere, approaches his state senator, a man of great conviction, and Mr. Public implores State Senator Al L. Bluster to get a resolution passed in the state legislature for an application for an Article V amendatory convention. The good state senator is enamored with the prospect of reining in the Congress and excitedly agrees. He writes and files the bill and immediately begins to work on passage of the resolution for the purpose of amending the federal Constitution to limit the amount of per diem and to eliminate many

---

[83] https://www.opensecrets.org/bigpicture/reelect.php

other types of congressional reimbursement and largesse.

The media, sensing that the public will respond favorably and always seeking a cause célèbre to trumpet, seizes on the topic and begins promoting the idea of the amendatory convention. The legislators of the state legislature of East Somewhere also astutely feel the pulse of the public and rapidly get on board with State Senator Bluster's bill. The resolution is quickly passed and all of the state legislators are applauded for their courage and statesmanship by both the media and the public. The chorus of adulation is so strong that the legislatures of other states decide to emulate the efforts of East Somewhere and draft and pass their own, very similarly worded, resolutions for applications for an amendatory convention. Before long, let us say in less than two years, a little more than two-thirds of the States have applied for an amendatory convention exclusively for the topic of drafting an amendment to curtail the ability of Congress to determine its own reimbursement and pay policies.

The ball is now in the court of the Congress. At first, both houses refuse to discuss the accumulated applications from the States alluding to "problems and deficiencies" with the applications. No elected federal official will speak on the record with respect to the count or the status of the applications. The media, however, takes great delight in chronicling the abuses of the per diem and every other day or so has a new, tawdry story about an individual federal representative or a senator that is allegedly bilking the public treasury. Public protests increase; the media fixates on the topic; the new crop of candidates make pledging to reform the per diem the central focus of their campaign platforms; and the state legislatures adopt an "Us vs. Them" mentality with respect to the federal government. High drama ensues.

A year goes by without any congressional action on the convention and, surprisingly, the public does not tire of the news coverage but actually gets angrier. The grassroots takes up the cause and begins organizing more public pressure on the state legislatures. Petition drives and mass rallies in the state capitals and in Washington, D.C. occur. Finally, a number of state governors, led by Governor Vernon "Very" Slick of the State of East Somewhere, announce that they have directed their state attorneys-general to file a suit in the US Supreme Court to compel the Congress to issue the call for an amendatory convention.

The Supreme Court responds by refusing to hear the case on the grounds that this is a "political question" and that under *Coleman v. Miller* the Court has deferred to Congress believing that Congress has all authority to deal with the convention issue as it sees fit. Congress gleefully spikes the ball by announcing that there will be no convention as it does not "deem it necessary" to call a convention thereby alluding to the exact wording of Article V. Concurrent with the States' attorneys-general filing their suit, Mr. John Q. Public, that much irritated taxpaying citizen from the State of East Somewhere, had filed his own suit against Congress in a federal district court. His suit is immediately dismissed with the justification that he lacks standing as he cannot prove that he has experienced any direct and personal harm from the refusal of Congress to call a convention.

Meanwhile, the States respond in turn by returning to the Supreme Court and point out that the constitutional rights of the States are being violated and that there must be a remedy. They implore the Supreme Court to take up the case and order a writ issued to Congress or, if the Court cannot perform this action, to order the convening of the convention itself. The Court refuses and answers that per *Mississippi v. Johnson*,[84] Congress is accountable to no one and to no other body.[85,86]

Mr. John Q. Public, the Great State of East Somewhere, all of her sister states, and the American public at large find themselves in quite the proverbial legal pickle. They are clearly being harmed by the violation of their shared constitutional rights but they have, according to the federal courts and finally the US Supreme Court, no recourse and therefore no manner of redressability is available to them. If there is no remedy, then there is no right; if there is no right, then the Constitution is not being enforced and could be considered as no longer in effect. Our bottom line is then, that we apparently have no functioning Constitution and the Congress acts according to its whim as it has, arguably, no obligation to obey the Constitution. We are, at that point, theoretically in the realm of tyranny and oppression – the very situation which the Framers labored arduously to avoid. What then do we do?

---

[84] 71 U.S. (4 Wall.) 475 at 500 (1867).
[85] Arthur Earl Bonfield, "Proposing Constitutional Amendments by Convention: Some Problems," *Notre Dame Lawyer* 39, no.6 (Sept. 1964): 672.
[86] Douglas Voegler argues that the actions of President Truman and the Supreme Court in the seizure of the nation's steel mills resulting in the *Youngstown Sheet & Tube Co. v. Sawyer*, 343 U.S. 579 (1952) case negate, or at least seriously diminish, the legal effect of *Mississippi v. Johnson*, 71 U.S. 475 (1867).

We can turn to an early authority for a clear summary of our hypothetical situation, Aristotle, from his *Politics*, "Such a democracy is fairly open to the objection that it is not a constitution at all; for where the laws have no authority, there is no constitution."[87] Our intrepid state legislator would be wondering, after this example, whether her state legislature would quickly find itself in this situation of lacking standing after voting for the pending bill. If her state had no recourse, what would be the point of undertaking all of this effort?

Ripeness

The issue of ***ripeness*** is simply, much like the reverse of mootness. For an issue to be ripe, it must have a developed controversy or a situation that has defined, concrete, "precise acts" to consider. It is for this reason that the court cases involving Article V appear to come in waves, such as in the 1920s (federal courts) and 1980s (state courts). Whenever an Article V convention appeared to be imminent due to the number of applications pending – by closing in on the magic two-thirds of the States requirement – the issues involved became ripe for adjudication. In some instances, lawsuits were brought to address specific points in the process, although the courts have yet to reach a decision in a case on an amendatory convention. Without such a situation existing, bringing a suit, or suits, on a hypothetical would result in clogging the court system and delaying other pending matters that require a timely resolution.[88]

The final analysis of the effect of the Court on an amendatory convention will come down to reviewing and, mayhaps, supplanting *Coleman*. It may well be that part of the strategy of the next campaign for an amendatory convention will include a deliberate effort to bring these issues in front of the US Supreme Court. If the Court will not intercede then there are but four ways to correct the problems: rely on the polls – we have already examined the inefficacy of that route; rely on Congress to act constitutionally – we live with the results of that choice every day; to undertake a coordinated, nationwide program of mass civil disobedience and disruption; and to the final option that no one wants. Michael Almond pontificated on this situation in 1975,

---

[87] Aristotle, *Politics*, Book 4, Chapter 4, (~fourth century B.C.), - Benjamin Jowett translation of 1885
[88] The argument can be made that the inevitability of an Article V convention at some point in the nation's future invalidates the mootness of the scenario and implies ripeness.

> "*The powers of Congress must be considered in light of the justiciability of issues arising under article V, for it is in the courts that the issue of congressional authority will finally be decided. Should the courts find these issues justiciable, any attempt by Congress to control the convention will most surely be made in anticipation of how the Supreme Court will react. On the other hand, if these problems are found non-justiciable, the only check upon congressional power will be the good faith of Congress itself.*"[89]

Beyond the issue of whether the federal courts would take up a case involving Article V is the question of whether the courts may in any other way interfere with the convention. This interference may take the form of contributing advisory opinions (many state supreme courts have done so from their beginnings and in some states are required constitutionally to do so) or of assessing the validity of a proposed or even a recently adopted amendment. Prior cases at the state level have shown that courts will inject themselves into the workings of a convention but often at the expense of being overruled. At the federal level, the courts have been more circumspect about the effect of the involvement of the courts and taken a hands-off approach. The courts have carefully limited their actions to assisting "the conventions to prevent the encroachment of any other branches of government upon it."[90] Of course, all of those cases have involved state conventions only.

Douglas Voegler made an interesting claim in 1979 that still resonates. He argued that although the Supreme Court has decided that Article V questions are political, the Constitution may have the answer. Since the Constitution states that, "In all Cases affecting Ambassadors, other public Ministers and Consuls, and those in which a State shall be a Party, the supreme Court shall have original Jurisdiction."[91] Here, Voegler notes that the States will be the party to a lawsuit with Congress, but we have seen that this scenario may not be possible. He contends that the Court could stop the attempts by Congress to halt or hinder the convention.

Voegler has another very prominent point to make on the amendment process. He discriminates between the congressional and convention methods of amendment proposal by stating that *Coleman* was directed strictly at the

---

[89] Michael A. Almond, "Amendment by Convention: Our Next Constitutional Crisis?," *North Carolina Law Review* 53 (1975): 514. Reprinted with permission of the North Carolina Law Review.
[90] Roger Sherman Hoar, *Constitutional Conventions – Their Nature, Powers, And Limitations* (Boston: Little, Brown, 1917), 164
[91] United States Constitution, Article III, § 2

congressional method. The non-justiciable character of the congressional method does not apply to the convention method in Voegler's opinion. He believes this to be the case because the convention method is, to use the Supreme Court's phrase, not "committed" to the Congress but to the convention. He summarizes that,

> "It is the Court's responsibility to insure that this method be kept available to the states to use, something which would not occur were the Court to treat Article V convention method issues as nonjusticiable political questions. Were the Court to treat these issues as political, it would, in effect, be surrendering the convention method to Congressional control and dominance, clearly hostile and contrary to the reasons for placing it in the Constitution."[92]

In the *Idaho v. Freeman* decision, Judge Callister noted something significant as it relates to the claim by Article V convention opponents that there are just too many unknowns, stating that "the judiciary, while only dealing with Article V in a handful of cases, has nevertheless dealt with virtually all the significant portions of that article."[93] What remains then are the minor details and the minutiae. It is for that reason that the Ervin and Hatch bills addressed the regulation of the convention procedures and included in all bills provision for the limiting of or removing the jurisdiction of the federal courts in regard to Article V.[94]

When considering the role of the judiciary in the Article V convention process, it is important to keep in mind that the judicial restraint of the political question doctrine is self-imposed.[95] It could just as easily be self-lifted.

At this juncture, our state legislator could conclude that the courts are not necessarily a reliable arbiter of the issues involving Article V conventions. For her state legislature to pursue an amendatory convention will require a measure of commitment to seeing the convention through in spite of the refusal of Congress and the reluctance of the US Supreme Court to honor her state's resolution/application. That commitment would include

---

[92] Douglas G. Voegler, "Amending the Constitution by the Article V Convention Method," *North Dakota Law Review* 55 (1979): 403-4

[93] *Idaho v. Freeman*, 529 F. Supp. 1107 (D. Idaho 1981), at 1126

[94] James W. Lucas, "To Originate The Amendment Of Errors: Reforming Article V to Facilitate State and Popular Engagement in Constitutional Amendment," (2013): 18 - independently published, available at: http://papers.ssrn.com/sol3/papers.cfm?abstract_is=2275124

[95] Sara R. Ellis, Yusuf Z. Malik, Heather G. Parker, Benjamin C. Signer & Al'Reco L. Yancy, "Article V Constitutional Conventions: A Primer," *Tennessee Law Review* 78 (2011): 680

consumption of a significant portion the state's resources. A scenario such as that described will probably be of no more probability of litigation than any other controversial topic, such as legislation for Voter ID or federalized health care. But, as more states join the campaign, the cost sharing and legal resource sharing aspects become more attractive. The additional delay in the campaign to secure passage of a resolution and a convention can be rationalized as an amendatory convention is a long-term prospect to begin with and should not be viewed as a detriment but as another reality check built into the process.

Congress's Powers and Requirements

Our thoughtful state legislator will naturally wonder about the extent of Congress's power and the limitations of that power before considering her vote on the resolution for an amendatory convention. Her concern would be over the relative stature of each legislature in the amendment process – does the state legislature have an equal footing with the national legislature or does the state have a distinct disadvantage in this contest? And contest is the appropriate word since the situation of the States believing that they need to go around Congress to enact needed constitutional reform is undoubtedly a political contest of the highest order.

Before looking at the powers of Congress with respect to an amendatory convention, it is beneficial to reflect that Congress is, by virtue of its ability to propose, debate and pass a constitutional amendment at any time, a <u>permanent</u> constitutional convention.[96] It need not make application to any other body; it need not pass a resolution just to begin the process; it does not have to arrange a consensus of a majority to talk about the matter at hand. It needs merely to have a single member draft a proposal and submit it to the chamber. It can, and does, receive hundreds of amendment proposals in every biennial Congress. It has the States at a significant disadvantage as they do not enjoy the same power – and ease - of amendment proposal.[97] In this instance, a single Congressman or woman has the same power as thirty-four states acting in concert.

How has Congress come to wield so much authority in the amendment

---

[96] Douglas G. Voegler, "Amending the Constitution by the Article V Convention Method," *North Dakota Law Review* 55 (1979): 395-6

[97] Paul G. Kauper, "The Alternative Amendment Process: Some Observations," *Michigan Law Review* 66, no.5 (Mar. 1968): 913

process? In the *Dillon v. Gloss* decision in 1921, the United States Supreme Court looked at the power of Congress to set a time period for the ratification of a promulgated amendment proposal. The Court made the assertion that Congress was best suited to answer the questions concerning Article V. The Court said,

> *"An examination of Article V discloses that it is intended to invest Congress with a wide range of power in proposing amendments…As a rule the Constitution speaks in general terms, leaving Congress to deal with subsidiary matters of detail as the public interests and changing conditions may require; and Article V is no exception to the rule."*[98]

But this interpretation leaves the door wide open and almost anything can walk through. Moreover, the first sentence speaks of proposing amendments and not convening amendatory conventions. Tradition makes it clear that Congress has only "housekeeping duties" and any effort to control the convention, even minute matters such as the delegate qualifications or setting a time limit for deliberations, casts the appearance of undue influence. Most importantly, it circumvents the purpose of providing an alternative to the congressional process. Any other interpretation leads to Congress's manipulation of the proceedings.

Congress is expected to call the convention upon receipt of the number of state applications that reaches two-thirds of the States – presently thirty-four states. The wording is definite at "shall" and there has been almost no question as to the meaning of that term since the ratification debates.[99] The "mandatory" theory of Congress's duty to call a convention holds sway among legal academics and jurists. This point has been taken as a constitutional surety since the ratification debates. Alexander Hamilton famously declared in *The Federalist, No. 85*, that,

> *"The words of this article are peremptory. The Congress 'shall' call a convention. Nothing in this particular is left to the discretion of that body. And of consequence all the declamation about their disinclination to change, vanishes in air."*[100]

The unambiguity of the phrasing around the word "shall" was

---

[98] 256 U.S. 368 (1921) at 376
[99] Morris B. Forkosch, "The Alternative Amending Clause in Article V: Reflections and Suggestions," *Minnesota Law Review* 51 (1967): 1065-6
[100] Clinton Rossiter, ed., *The Federalist Papers: Hamilton, Madison, Jay* (New York: Mentor, 1961), 526

established by the US Supreme Court in 1816 with regard to its use in the Constitution.[101] As if the opinions of Madison and Hamilton – drafters of the final version of Article V – were not enough, their writings in *The Federalist*, speeches in the ratification convention debates and correspondence should convince everyone of their intent. The amendatory convention was intended to be a last measure of constitutional observance on the part of the people. It has, by design, an air of finality that implies and requires clear meaning.

Senator Sam Ervin, Jr. wrote, "To concede to the Congress any discretion to consider the wisdom and necessity of a particular convention call would in effect destroy the role of the states."[102] Ervin went on to point out that if Congress had the power to reject applications, by whatever criteria they chose, and if the power was not circumscribed, then Congress could arbitrarily reject all applications and we would have a single amending method.[103] What are less certain are the repercussions of Congress's lack of action or its refusal to act to call a convention. Legal theories have been worked out and published but none have been tried. Supposedly, the magic number of two-thirds of the States was hit in 1926 and again in 1957 but Congress did not act and various members of Congress independently claimed that the applications were not all for the identical purpose and therefore Congress had no obligation to call the convention. In 1926, the total received reflected the accumulation of applications from states that were applying for a convention to address the issue of the direct election of federal senators <u>and</u> for a general convention. At that time, twenty-six states had applied since 1901 for varying reasons for a total of thirty-two states. Since nothing was in writing that said the applications had to be for the same issue, it was put forth that the requirement could be seen as having been met.[104] But the Seventeenth Amendment had cancelled the need and the basis of the applications calling for a convention to propose an amendment for the direct election of federal senators, so those applications were now dead and should have not been counted in the total pending.

In 1957, the proposed Reed-Dirksen amendment capping the top

---

[101] *Martin v. Hunter's Lessee*, 14 U.S. (1 Wheat.) 304 (1816) at 327

[102] Sen. Sam Ervin, Jr., "Proposed Legislation to Implement the Convention Method of Amending the Constitution," *Michigan Law Review* 66, no 5 (Mar. 1968): 885

[103] Ibid., 887

[104] Lester B. Orfield, "The Procedure of the Federal Amending Power," *Illinois Law Review* 25 (1930): 422

federal income tax rate had reached thirty-three states applying.¹⁰⁵ This was one more state than necessary. Once again, the Congress was silent. Why Congress would refuse to act or, more accurately, simply refuse to acknowledge that the number has been reached is dependent on several requirements – all congressionally imposed, or more accurately stated, congressionally *implied*, as no one has spoken officially on the matter.

Congress looks at several factors when considering the applications from the States:

Homogeneity

First, is the ***homogeneity*** of the subject matter of the applications and the aforementioned congruence of the wording in the applications. This is sometimes referred to as "specificity."¹⁰⁶ Congress has demonstrated an unwillingness to discuss counting applications. Individual members of Congress have argued to not aggregate applications unless the subject matter is identical. This attitude extends to the wording as well. Congress seems to have indicated that it expects the States to collaborate in defining the need and purpose of an amendatory convention.¹⁰⁷ Scholars have argued that the differences in the subject matter or the wording are indicative of the lack of a consensus among the States for a constitutional revision. But the lack of defined wording has created an inability on the part of Congress to discern the "exact intent and the legality" of the applications from the States.¹⁰⁸ Clearly, Congress would be going a bit too far in requiring near unanimity of wording to "dispel any misinterpretation" but it has a point in that a divergence among the States as to topic does not point to a "general dissatisfaction" with the Constitution as it stands.¹⁰⁹ Congress itself conceded this point in 1952 in a report of the House Committee on the Judiciary,

---

[105] Frank E. Packard, "Constitutional Law: The States and the Amending Power," *American Bar Association Journal* 45, no.2 (Feb.1959): 161 – Tennessee became the 33rd applying state on March 30, 1957, the article notes that seven of the applying states had rescinded their applications and that this point was in contention.

[106] Walker Hanson, "The States' Power to Effectuate Constitutional Change: Is Congress Currently Required to Convene a National Convention for the Proposing of Amendments to the United States Constitution?," *Georgetown Journal of Law & Public Policy* 9 (2011): 252-5

[107] Sara R. Ellis, Yusuf Z. Malik, Heather G. Parker, Benjamin C. Signer & Al'Reco L. Yancy, "Article V Constitutional Conventions: A Primer," *Tennessee Law Review* 78 (2011): 674

[108] Doyle W. Buckwalter, "Constitutional Conventions and State Legislators," *Chicago-Kent Law Review* 48, no.1 (1971): 27

[109] "Proposing Amendments to the United States Constitution by Convention," *Harvard Law Review* 70, no.6 (Apr.1957): 1072

> *"[T]here appears no valid reason to suppose that the language of the amendments requested in State applications must be identical with one another in wording. It should be enough that the suggested amendments be of the same general subject matter in order to be included in a congressional count of applications for a constitutional convention..."*[110]

Writers have noted that by requiring specific language in the application, Congress would be going outside the normal practice of what is found in the Constitution. When the Framers wanted specific language used, they clearly said so. An example of which is the oath of office for the President found in Article II, Section 1, Clause 8. No such requirement for exact of mandatory wording is given in Article V, so we may safely conclude that it was not the intention of the Framers to require that the States use mandatory wording in their application resolutions.[111]

An example of the problem as viewed from the perspective of Congress is that of the wording found in the thirty-two applications for an amendatory convention submitted in the period of 1975 to 1983 for drafting a balanced budget amendment. In the 1995 Congressional Research Service report on amending the Constitution, the topic was examined and the applications were segregated into four groups:

- Petitions that propose that the appropriations do not exceed revenues
- Petitions which require that the federal budget be balanced
- Petitions which would prohibit any deficit spending
- Petitions that would require that the expenditures not exceed receipts[112]

Separating and counting the applications by <u>precise</u> wording defeats the purpose of calling the convention. Expecting the States to submit identical, or nearly identical, wording in the applications so strictly limits the convention topic – beyond even that of a limited convention – that it may

---

[110] House Committee on the Judiciary, *Problems Relating to State Applications for a Convention to Propose Constitutional Limitations on Federal Tax Rates*, 82nd Cong., 2d sess., at 11-2 (1952)

[111] Ronald D. Rotunda & Stephen J. Safranek, "An Essay on Term Limits and a Call for a Constitutional Convention," *Marquette Law Review* 80, no.1 (Fall 1996): 237-8

[112] Thomas M. Durbin, Library of Congress, Congressional Research Service Report CRS 95-589A, *Amending the U.S. Constitution: by Congress or by Constitutional Convention*, at CRS-15 (10 May 1995) - citing David C. Huckabee, *Constitutional Convention Applications of States Relating To Federal Spending*, Library of Congress, Congressional Research Service Report, at CRS-2 (22 April 1980)

be impossible to distinguish the amendatory convention from a ratificatory convention. Such an action would reduce the deliberative aspect required of a convention.

The consensus requirement can be thought of as the first step in the deliberation of the issue, pre-convention. If there is no consensus among the States as to whether a problem exists, then no reason exists for a convention. If the two-thirds of the States requirement is looked at as the lower limit for consensus, then we have conclusively determined what qualifies as a real problem. A campaign for an Article V convention that falls short of the two-thirds level in state support has not demonstrated its wide-spread conviction and commitment to the resolution of the problem. History has shown that as the number of applying states crosses the thirty-state threshold, the momentum slows as the remaining states much more carefully consider the consequences of their action. This reaction is a necessary and proper part of the process. As the drive for the direct election of senators reached the two-thirds threshold, the Senate was forced to act – this is not a failure of the Article V convention movement; it is proof of the power of the constitutional tool.[113]

The ability to apply for a convention for a single issue or just a limited set of issues is still debated although the evidence extending back to the Colonial and Federal Eras clearly indicate that the limitation was a common and accepted practice for conventions. Our Revolutionary Period history and our most recent state constitutional convention history possess far more examples of limited conventions. As a corollary to that assertion, Congress may also take the input from the state applications and specify the nature and purpose of the convention.[114]

A final note on homogeneity involves the discharge of an application. If Congress issues a call for an amendatory convention to address the specific issue of, say, campaign finance reform only, then what becomes of the other outstanding applications for other subjects or for a general convention? Logic would seem to dictate that any other non-campaign finance reform based application would remain valid and pending. The only applications that would be cancelled out are those that ask for the convention just called

---

[113] Paul J. Weber & Barbara A. Perry, *Unfounded Fears, The Myths and Realities of a Constitutional Convention* (New York: Praeger, 1989), 109-10

[114] Russell B. Caplan, *Constitutional Brinkmanship* (New York: Oxford University Press, 1988), 100

or convened.[115]

Contemporaneity

Second among the congressional criteria, is the ***contemporaneity*** of the applications.[116] Are applications "time-limited?"[117] Although there is nothing in the Constitution to specify how old – or "stale" – an application can be before Congress will no longer consider it valid, on the issue of twenty or thirty or forty year-old applications, even for the same subject as other more recent applications, Congress has made rumblings that it will not entertain old applications. Much debate has raged over this issue of application vitality for more than a century. During the drive for a convention to discuss an amendment on direct election of federal senators, members of Congress cited that applications going back to the 1830s were being unduly included in the tally and that those applications were for other subjects. What Congress is looking for is a current "meaningful debate and significant agreement" on the same question and concern. For those applications which Congress might reject as "stale" or void in terms of the subject, it has been suggested that the legislatures of those states can prove their commitment to the convention by a reissuance of the application.[118]

Such a requirement may appear to be reasonable, especially to our pensive state legislator. By pressing for a limited timeframe in which to evaluate the applications, Congress is assuring that the subject matter and the degree of concern is shared across the nation. As to what is "relatively contemporaneous" no one has yet to make a successful argument. Bonfield argued that those who invoke the Article V convention process bear the burden of proving that the issue in question is shared by the nation – at least two-thirds of it.[119,120] Jameson recognized this same limitation on a time to ratify more than a century ago. His reasoning could be just as easily applied

---

[115] Douglas G. Voegler, "Amending the Constitution by the Article V Convention Method," *North Dakota Law Review* 55 (1979): 373

[116] David Kyvig attributes this idea to Warren Harding; 468

[117] Thomas N. Neale, Library of Congress, Congressional Research Service Report R42589, *The Article V Convention to Propose Constitutional Amendments: Contemporary Issues for Congress*, (11 April 2014), 7-8

[118] "Proposing Amendments to the United States Constitution by Convention," *Harvard Law Review* 70, no.6 (Apr.1957): 1073

[119] Arthur Earl Bonfield, "Proposing Constitutional Amendments by Convention: Some Problems," *Notre Dame Lawyer* 39, no.6 (Sept. 1964): 666-9

[120] Staff of House Comm. on the Judiciary, 82nd Cong., 2d sess., "Problems Relating to State Applications for a Convention to Propose Constitutional Limitations of Federal Tax Rates" (Comm. Print 1952)

to the States' applications. He concluded that a ratification, and by extension an application, "has relation to the sentiment and the felt needs of to-day."[121] To bolster such an argument, one need merely look to the issue of rescission. Any state legislature that believes that its prior application is now unneeded or unwarranted is free to vote to rescind that prior application. In 2016, as the Balanced Budget Amendment campaign continued to close in on its goal, a 29th application was passed by West Virginia in March, this may have contributed to the decision by Delaware in May to rescind their application which dated to 1979.

At one point, the argument could convincingly be made that the application phase is but one part of the whole process and that the process itself must be contemporaneous overall. One writer pointed out that the US Supreme Court stated in dictum in *Dillon v. Gloss*[122] that "a textually demonstrable requirement of contemporaneity pervades article V."[123] With the Court looking at the process components as "succeeding steps in a single endeavor,"[124] it is rational to conclude that the application phase would need to exhibit a nationwide consensus within a definable time period. When the comparison of the convention method is made to the congressional method, it is noted that the Congress votes on an amendment proposal at the same time thus assuring contemporaneity in that method.[125]

Douglas Voegler made the case that if *Dillon* were used to justify setting a time limit on the ratification of an amendment, then the same logic could be applied to the application phase. He states that by applying a time limit, the "political, social and economical conditions prevailing" would be removed.[126] But this is not a wholly appropriate analogy. In ratification, Congress promulgates the proposed amendment to the States on a given day and asks for an answer. In the application-by-the-States process, some state decides to submit an application, typically without any consultation of either Congress or its sister states. That action may inspire other states

---

[121] John Alexander Jameson, *A Treatise on Constitutional Conventions: Their History, Powers and Modes of Proceedings* (New York: Scribner, 1867, 4th ed., 1887) § 418, 421 – reprint by the Law Book Exchange, (2013)

[122] 256 U.S. 368 (1921)

[123] Neal S. Manne, "Good Intentions, New Inventions and Article V Constitutional Conventions," *Texas Law Review* 58 (1979): 137. Reprinted with permission.

[124] 256 U.S. 368 (1921) at 374-5

[125] Neal S. Manne, "Good Intentions, New Inventions and Article V Constitutional Conventions," *Texas Law Review* 58 (1979): 137

[126] Douglas G. Voegler, "Amending the Constitution by the Article V Convention Method," *North Dakota Law Review* 55 (1979): 369-72

to act, or perhaps some states were already planning an application of their own. The application phase is somewhat individual and spontaneous in its initiation and growth. The ratification phase is more national and culminating. There is much more invested and dependent on the ratification than on the application, hence the application phase is more forgiving on the consumption of time.

Mason Kalfus takes the argument for a contemporaneous consensus apart. First, he cites that there is nothing, written or implied, in Article V that requires contemporaneity. Second, there is "no level of necessity" for proposing an amendment so no threshold exists to determine the consensus sought and the States are the arbiters of need for a given amendment not Congress. Third, history has proven that consensus builds over time and not always at the same pace. Fourth, the consensus requirement is the creation of the *Dillon* court and not any previous development. Fifth, the Framers clearly did not see the need to specify either a requirement for consensus or a time limit during the drafting of Article V and if they felt the need then they would have explicitly said so. Finally, the Constitution itself continues to be respected because of an "intergenerational consensus" and the present generation does not get to bind the future generations who are reserved the right to determine their own measure of consensus.[127] The historical records show that once a given state feels that its application for a convention is no longer needed, that state will usually rescind the application, and that action indicates the lack of consent and consensus by the States on the topic.

The ratification of the Twenty-seventh Amendment would seem to invalidate the *Dillon* based argument that there is a shelf-life to an application, after all, if a proposed amendment can sit dormant for over two hundred years before being ratified then why not an application?[128] The real issue is whether the circumstances that led to the application – analogous to the amendment proposal – are still a contemporary concern. Michael Stokes Paulsen asks the question of why can an amendment take centuries to ratify cannot the consensus for a convention grow over decades?[129]

The argument for "staleness" gets no support from Natelson. He

---

[127] Mason Kalfus, "Why Time Limits on the Ratification of Constitutional Amendments Violate Article V," *University of Chicago Law Review* 66, no.2 (Spring 1999): 447-9
[128] 74,003 days to be exact!
[129] Michael Stokes Paulsen, "A General Theory of Article V: The Constitutional Lessons of the Twenty-seventh Amendment," *Yale Law Journal* 103, no.3 (Dec. 1993): 734

contends that his research has turned up no support for either a natural aging and staleness of an application or of the power of Congress to declare an application stale. He believes that only the issuing state may declare the application to be of no further value. He argues that Congress may indeed set an expiration date on ratifications as Congress is constitutionally empowered to select the ratification method, but it is the States alone that are empowered to pass applications and therefore the States alone can judge the liveliness of their applications.[130] Natelson warns that allowing Congress to possess the power to determine or to declare that an application from a state legislature is "stale" grants Congress the power to interfere in – and to end - a process that was designed to clearly and specifically bypass Congress.[131]

As a last note on contemporaneity, a few of the States have approached this issue by including in their balanced budget amendment applications wording that states that the application is "continuing" until such time as either Congress passes a balanced budget amendment or an amendatory convention is called to address that particular issue.[132] Any state can rightly argue that the existence of that state's application is proof of its consent to a convention based on the continued existence of the problem that the application intends to address in a convention.

Validity

Third on the criteria list, is the *validity* of the States' applications. This aspect should be the colloquial "no-brainer" as the courts have looked at the applications in the distant past and decided that the validity is beyond question by anyone.[133] Though some academics will still make the claim that it is within the power of Congress to devise a "test" for validity.[134] What Congress is looking for in terms of validity concerns the process – did the state ask for a convention or just ask Congress to propose an amendment? Did the state follow its own legislative process? Did the state submit the application to the correct personnel in Congress? Did the state

---

[130] Robert G. Natelson, "Proposing Constitutional Amendments by Convention: Rules Governing the Process," *Tennessee Law Review* 78 (2011): 712-4

[131] Robert G. Natelson, *A Compendium for Lawyers and Legislative Drafters,* Convention of States (2014), 46

[132] Russell B. Caplan, *Constitutional Brinkmanship* (New York: Oxford University Press, 1988), 112

[133] *Prigg v. Commonwealth of Pennsylvania*, 41 U.S. 539 (1842); and *Jarrolt v. Moberly*, 103 U.S. 580 (1880)

[134] Morris B. Forkosch, "The Alternative Amending Clause in Article V: Reflections and Suggestions," *Minnesota Law Review* 51 (1967): 1060

ask for something unconstitutional or otherwise impermissible? Leaving Congress the option of reviewing and deciding on the validity of the States' applications and, presumably, to reject those applications, coupled with the assumption that any applications calling for a convention to propose an amendment that would curtail the power of Congress would be met with hostility, could give Congress a justification for refusing to call a convention.[135]

Bond and Engdahl find delineation between how the courts view Congress's power over the amending process in the way that the initiation of the convention call and amendment ratification facets are treated by Congress and the extent of that power. This difference defines a limit of the power of Congress in favor of the States,

> *"Therefore, even if Congress may exercise an unreviewable discretion to determine whether amendments have been ratified, it does not necessarily follow that it must possess a similar unreviewable discretion to determine whether sufficient States have applied for a convention. Indeed, the stronger argument seems to the contrary. Incontrollable congressional discretion at either the initiation or the ratification stage of a convention amendment would make it possible for Congress to frustrate the States' efforts to amend the Constitution. That would contravene the Framers' intent to give the States a way to amend the Constitution free of congressional control."*[136]

As positive as that distinction sounds today, Bond and Engdahl in the very next paragraph remind us of the reality of American constitutional politics,

> *"While a blatant attempt by Congress to block an apparently successful effort by the States to amend the Constitution would probably generate a heated political battle, the States could not necessarily protect their interests in that battle through the political process. The direct election of the senators has weakened the States' ability to discipline senators who ignore or frustrate their applications for a convention. When state legislatures elected senators, the senators ignored requests from state legislatures at their peril. Thus, the States could influence a senator's behavior through the political process. Since States no longer enjoy that political leverage, courts should not blithely*

---

[135] Sara R. Ellis, Yusuf Z. Malik, Heather G. Parker, Benjamin C. Signer & Al'Reco L. Yancy, "Article V Constitutional Conventions: A Primer," *Tennessee Law Review* 78 (2011). 675

[136] James E. Bond, David E. Engdahl and Henry N. Butler, *The Constitutional Convention* (Washington, D.C.: National Legal Center for the Public Interest, 1987), 7

assume that States can protect their interests through the political process, and therefore should be more willing to review serious questions of alleged congressional disregard of the duty to issue a convention call."[137]

It is therefore shown that the decision of a century ago for the States to give up the right and power of selection of their federal senators has created the unintended consequence of reducing the States' ability to go around the obstinate Congress when needed. When that time comes, the States will, paradoxically, need to argue hard for the judicial review that they occasionally argue against. Our state legislator contemplating a convention resolution will have to consider in her cost and benefit calculations not just whether her state, and the sister states, will be in a position to prevail but if they will have the stomach for the fight. Assuring the validity of the application, per the demands of Congress, is an acquiescence, that however distasteful, may be necessary from the outset.

The Necessary and Proper Clause

One of the most debated aspects of the power of Congress in regard to Article V focuses on the application of Congress's other powers to the amending power. Contention over the limits of Congress's authority has been explored in many theories as to the source of such power. Many scholars have argued that the other parts of the Constitution, and more precisely other grants of power to Congress, also apply to Article V. Still other constitutional scholars will argue just as effusively that the amending power is separate, distinct and deliberately segregated from the rest of the Constitution's articles because it is such an important power and because it is shared with the States in a nuanced hybrid form. It is the predominant power in the Constitution as it can affect all others.

A claim is often made that the grant of power found in the "Necessary and Proper Clause" is applicable to Article V and the amendatory convention, thereby which Congress can set the rules of a convention and make decisions as questions arise.[138,139,140] This has been called a dangerous

---

[137] Ibid.

[138] "Proposed Legislation on the Convention Method of Amending the United States Constitution," *Harvard Law Review* 85, no.8 (June 1972): 1617

[139] Patricia A. Brannan, David L. Lillehaug, Robert P. Reznick, "Critical Details: Amending the United States Constitution," *Harvard Journal on Legislation* 16 (1979): 801-2

[140] Charles L. Black, Jr., "The Proposed Amendment of Article V: A Threatened Disaster," *Yale Law Journal* 72 (1963): 964

assumption by other academics. Bond and Engdahl cautiously acknowledge this argument while carefully making their case in favor of this position,

> "Fortunately, it is permissible for Congress to establish rules in advance on such matters, to help everyone in planning and Congress itself in deciding such questions if they arise. Congress can do so by virtue of the 'necessary and proper' clause, which gives it power to make laws for carrying all the other federal powers into execution. Eliminating uncertainty on such matters as the similarity and specificity Congress will require in applications, the effect it will give to rescissions, and the time bounds of 'contemporaneity' in Congress's view, reasonably should help in fulfilling Congress obligation under Article V. But the 'necessary and proper' clause is a one-way rachet; it only authorizes laws that help effectuate federal duties and powers, not laws that hinder. In other words, statutory provisions apt to frustrate or preclude the calling of a convention, even though two-thirds of the States had contemporaneously requested it, would be invalid."[141]

The notion that the Necessary and Proper Clause empowered Congress to set the rules, select the delegates, determine the agenda, etc., was initially raised in the 1960s in response to the effort to secure a convention for the reapportionment battle. The historical expansion of the clause provides a basis for the fear of the clause being applied to an Article V convention in the form of another enlargement of federal powers. Also called the "Elastic" or "Sweeping" Clause, it has become almost unrestrained in its interpretation until the last couple of decades. This was not always the case, as James Madison stated in 1791, "Whatever meaning this clause may have, none can be admitted, that would give an unlimited discretion to Congress."[142]

The issue with the Necessary and Proper Clause, as argued by Bond and Engdahl, is that it covers *federal* powers delegated to Congress and not the distinctly *shared* amending power segregated in Article V from the rest of the Constitution.[143] More specifically, the Necessary and Proper Clause applies primarily to acts of legislative power and in those cases only to the extent required to carry out the enumerated powers. The actions of

---

[141] James E. Bond, David E. Engdahl and Henry N. Butler, *The Constitutional Convention* (Washington, D.C.: National Legal Center for the Public Interest, 1987), 5

[142] James Madison, "The Bank Bill", 2 Feb 1791, quoted in Philip B. Kurland & Ralph Lerner, *The Founders' Constitution, Vol. 3* (Indianapolis: Liberty Fund, 1987), 244 – referring to the First Charter of the Bank of the United States.

[143] James E. Bond, David E. Engdahl and Henry N. Butler, *The Constitutional Convention* (Washington, D.C.: National Legal Center for the Public Interest, 1987), supra, make precisely this point on page 11.

the executive branch in operating the various departments of the federal government are necessary and proper to fulfilling the mandates delegated to those departments. Article V is *not* a grant of ordinary, statutory, legislative power hence its segregation from the other powers; it is a reservation of existing powers. The implied power of discretion in Congress's action is lacking due to the "shall" requirement in Article V. The power granted to Congress in Article I is for the passage of ordinary legislation; the power reserved in Article V is for the proposal of a constitutional amendment.[144] Fundamental, or organic, law ranks higher than ordinary statutory law. Article I covers legislative powers leading to acts of statutory law; Article V covers acts of amendment for organic or fundamental law. The power of amendment is not a *delegated* power. Only the aspect of proposal is delegated to Congress, and then, it is a *shared* power with the States. The power of ratification – which completes the amendment process – is a *reserved* power to the States. The distribution of powers, as depicted in Appendix A, demonstrates that the amendment process is separate from the enumerated powers of Article I for good reason. If the powers of Article V were intended to be part of the powers of and under the authority of Congress, then the Framers would have included the amending power in Article I.

The matter of whether the convention is a federal *entity* is crucial. If the convention is considered an extension of the federal government, it means that the Congress obviously has a role in regulating the convention. If the convention is not a federal entity and is an entity of the States or an "*agent*" or a "*cooperative venture*" of the States, then the matter of control falls to the States or to the convention itself.[145] If the convention is under neither the Congress nor the States exclusively, then it is either a hybrid or a fully independent body. An Article V convention is more analogous to the Electoral College. The Electoral College is named and defined in the Constitution but is not a permanent body. The Electoral College meets as needed once every four years and then disbands. It is not part of any other branch of the federal government. It exists for a specific purpose and carries out a specific act, then dissolves. The Electoral College is not under the control of any branch of the federal government and there is no need for review of its processes and procedures. Congress must perform certain

---

[144] Russell B. Caplan, *Constitutional Brinkmanship* (New York: Oxford University Press, 1988), 118
[145] Michael B. Rappaport, "Reforming Article V: The Problems Created By The National Convention Amendment Method And How To Fix Them," *Virginia Law Review* 96, no.7 (Nov. 2010): 1524-5

actions to support the Electoral College – allocate funds for its functions, for instance – but no other interference is allowed.[146]

Professor Michael Stokes Paulsen nicely sums up the non-relationship between the Necessary and Proper Clause and Article V,

> *"Article V simply does not grant Congress power to judge the validity of state ratifications but clearly delimits Congress's role in the amendment process to* **proposing** *amendments and specifying their mode of ratification. Nothing in Article V suggests any further role. Nor does the Necessary and Proper Clause grant such power, since it cannot be 'necessary and proper' to Article V for Congress to take action that renders invalid that which Article V says is valid."*[147]

Paulsen can be taken a step further to explain that while there are actions that could be labeled as necessary and proper to the function of an Article V convention and that might be required to be executed by Congress to be carried out by the convention, those actions are ancillary to the function of the convention but do not exert an influence on the direction or performance of the convention nor are they contrary to the purpose of the convention. Finally, it needs to be stated that the Anti-Federalists that sought a bill of rights were, according to Leonard Levy, "enraged" by the Necessary and Proper Clause. In that clause, they saw a fountainhead of "undefined and unlimited" powers for the federal government that would be used against the people unless the limits were firmly defined.[148]

The Tenth Amendment

The Tenth Amendment has been termed the "flipside of the Necessary and Proper Clause" and it has been argued that the implied powers therein are subject to interpretation due to the States' possession of the reserved powers.[149] The Tenth Amendment and the Necessary and Proper Clause are seen as offsetting each other; if the Tenth is a powerful source of unnumbered and potentially unlimited state reserved powers, then the Necessary and Proper Clause must also be a powerful source of nearly equal unnumbered and unlimited congressional powers. For that reason,

---

[146] Thank you to Michael Stern for the suggestion of this analogy.
[147] Michael Stokes Paulsen, "A General Theory of Article V: The Constitutional Lessons of the Twenty-Seventh Amendment," *Yale Law Journal* 103, no.3 (Dec. 1993): 716-7
[148] Leonard Levy, *Origins of the Bill of Rights*, (New Haven, CT: Yale University Press, 1999), 28
[149] William Baude, "Sharing the Necessary and Proper Clause," *Harvard Law Review Forum* 128 (2014): 45

the Necessary and Proper Clause is often cited by convention opponents as grounds for Congress taking control of the convention process. This division is sourced in the difference in opinions of Madison – who sought a more restrained interpretation thereby protecting federalism – and Hamilton – who sought an expanded view of federal powers open to meet any situation.[150] Time has shown that Hamilton appears to be winning.

Despite the early twentieth-century, curious assertions of Selden Bacon as to the purpose of the Tenth Amendment and its impact on Article V, the much maligned Tenth does seem to play a role in the convention process. All of those powers required to carry out the convention and to empower the States to perform their federal function under Article V must be sourced from somewhere. It is a potentially sensible conclusion that the source of these powers is the Tenth Amendment, albeit that the Tenth came after the original Constitution, so the Tenth as a source of amending powers must be viewed as only the effort to make certain what was assumed to be understood at the time of the 1787 Convention. Bond and Engdahl make this clear,

> "As such, the convention is host to a residuum of powers confirmed by the Tenth Amendment: powers uncatalogued but ample to enable it to carry out fully its function. It is limited in function by Article V: it is a "Convention for proposing Amendments" to the existing Constitution, and nothing more. But because it partakes, so far as is needed, of the sovereign's reserved powers, no constraints sought to be placed upon its operations by legislatures or other government entities – federal or state – can have any more than a hortatory effect."[151]

The powers of the Congress, in the opinion of many constitutional scholars, extend beyond just the authority to make the call for a convention. Some argue that Congress may make the determination as to who makes the convention rules, how to select delegates and prescribe their qualifications, order and set the timing for delegate elections, among others powers.[152] One scholar makes his case that the omission of any mention in the Constitution is proof of an implicit grant to Congress – although this would clearly fly in

---

[150] J. Randy Beck, "The New Jurisprudence of the Necessary and Proper Clause," *University of Illinois Law Review* 2002, no.3 (2002): 586-8

[151] James E. Bond, David E. Engdahl and Henry N. Butler, *The Constitutional Convention*, National Legal Center for the Public Interest, Washington, D.C., (1987), 20

[152] Morris B. Forkosch, "The Alternative Amending Clause in Article V: Reflections and Suggestions," *Minnesota Law Review* 51 (1967): 1067-74

the face of the enumerated powers doctrine,

> "The initial question is whether Congress has the power to prescribe qualifications for the Convention delegates. The Constitution's silence allows one to argue that by omitting qualifying language the 1787 Convention intended to give Congress such a discretionary substantive power."[153]

The same writer chose to clarify the possibility by stating that Congress did exactly this in 1787 but "chose to leave the matter with the states" and to predict that it is easier to simply do so again today. All of this is contrary to tradition and precedent with regard to past intercolonial and interstate conventions. Using the experience of the States in ratifying the Twenty-first Amendment by ratificatory conventions, we see that the delegates were elected, qualified and seated per the rules adopted by the individual states.[154] In fact, the States moved so quickly to pass legislation for conducting elections and subsequently ratification conventions that Congress could not act fast enough and eventually decided that it was best to leave it to the States.[155] Forty-three of the forty-eight states passed legislation and thirty-nine carried out their task in less than a year.[156]

There is but another point to be made in regard to limiting the powers of Congress with respect to an amendatory convention. Does it make any sense to provide for and permit the States a method of initiating constitutional amendments by convention only to also endow Congress with the means to stifle the effort at every step?[157] Giving Congress control or even a veto over the convention process completely negates the purpose of the convention method and clearly is counter to the intent, as expressed by so many at Philadelphia, of the Framers. If Congress can selectively block amendment propositions it has become superior to the States and the convention method is been reduced to a "constitutional inkblot."[158] Congress becomes the final arbiter of what passes constitutional muster

---

[153] Ibid., 1069

[154] Ibid., 1070

[155] A bill was introduced into Congress for the purpose of setting such rules for the ratification conventions but it did not make it through the process before the States had acted.

[156] Edwin S. Corwin & Mary Louise Ramsey, "The Constitutional Law of Constitutional Amendment," *Notre Dame Lawyer* XXVI, no.2 (Winter 1951): 198

[157] Clifton McCleskey, "Along the Midway: Some Thoughts on Democratic Constitution Amending," *Michigan Law Review* 66, no.5 (Mar. 1968): 1005

[158] To borrow the phrase of Robert Bork.

for amendment material.[159] Allowing Congress to reject any application for requesting a limited convention or for specifying the topic would grant more power to Congress than the Framers had allotted. It would be an unwarranted expansion of congressional power.[160]

When contemplating Congress not acting, or refusing to act, in accordance with the Constitution, one should remember that such action is not without precedent. History provides another disappointing precedent of Congress refusing to fulfill its constitutional duties. Congress is required to reapportion after every census is taken. In 1920, Congress failed to do so and did not reapportion until after the 1930 census.[161] Nothing was done about this transgression – and those in Congress know it. That incident has become a nearly century old precedent in congressional discretion now.

Take note of the fact that Congress's powers and responsibilities connected to the amendatory convention are not unlimited just because we accept and acknowledge that there are indeed implied powers of Congress in this matter. It is not an all-or-none proposition as some argue.

> *"The mere fact that the Constitution gives Congress the duty to call a convention and the power to choose the mode of ratification should not be considered a textual commitment of unlimited discretionary power over the entire amendment process.*
>
> *To be sure, the duty imposed on Congress by article V implies certain powers incident to fulfilling that duty. However, the Constitution commits numerous powers to the political branches without committing absolute and unreviewable discretion in the exercise of those powers."*[162]

There is one last restriction on Congress's ability to play a part in the amendment process. Because Article V is not Article I, "the authority of Congress under the Supremacy Clause does not apply" to the ratifying conventions of the States acting in their authority under Article V.[163] Could

---

[159] "Proposed Legislation on the Convention Method of Amending the United States Constitution," *Harvard Law Review* 85, no.8 (June 1972): 1618

[160] Michael Stern, "Reopening the Constitutional Road to Reform: Toward a Safeguarded Article V Convention," *Tennessee Law Review* 78 (2011): 777

[161] Lester B. Orfield, "The Procedure of the Federal Amending Power," *Illinois Law Review* 25 (1930): 421

[162] Republished with permission of the Harvard Law Review Association, from "Proposed Legislation on the Convention Method of Amending the United States Constitution," *Harvard Law Review* 85, no.8 (June 1972): 1637-8; permission conveyed through Copyright Clearance Center, Inc.

[163] Brendon Troy Ishikawa, "Everything You Always Wanted to Know About How Amendments Are Made, but Were Afraid to Ask*," *Hastings Constitutional Law Quarterly* 24 (Winter 1997): 557

this same argument be applied to an amendatory convention of the States? That is, as the amendatory convention is, albeit temporarily, a fourth, and co-equal, branch of the federal government in a hybrid fashion, can we argue that Congress has little, or even no, say in the operations of the amendatory convention despite any reference back to the Supremacy Clause? As Article V is distinguished by its separation from the other articles, which individually define the powers and limitations of the co-equal branches of the federal government, we can make the case that the amendatory convention is, by design, intended to be separate and distinct as well as co-equal to the other branches and immune from the interference and influence of those branches with regard to the operation of the convention.

Congress is vested with the powers to propose amendments, determine when and where an amendatory convention will be held, the method to ratify any amendment, promulgation of proposed amendments, and there is one other power with which Congress can impact the convention: the power of the purse. Congress cannot constitutionally disburse funds without an appropriation. They could refuse or provide very little funding thus forcing the convention to bend to the will of Congress. Unless the States recognize and circumvent this situation by making their own appropriations, there might be a funding related standoff. If the topic of the convention is fiscal restraint and a balanced budget amendment, the irony would be at least waist deep.[164]

The States' Power and Requirements

Now we come to the topic that would matter most to our contemplative state legislator weighing the convention resolution. Although the judiciary and the Congress appear to hold, between them, all the cards in the game of convention poker, there are actually still quite a few cards remaining in the hands of the States. It is, after all, the States that precipitate the convention process with their applications, or petitions.[165]

---

[164] Russell B. Caplan, *Constitutional Brinkmanship* (New York: Oxford University Press, 1988), 122

[165] State applications are often found in the literature of the historical and legal professions described as "petitions," "resolutions," "memorials" or "memorializations." Specifically, memorials state a grievance and petitions request a specific action – per Caplan, p. xix - For greater detail on the differences, see Norman J. Small, "Procedures for Amending the United States Constitution," *Library of Congress Legislative Reference Service* (1965)

Rescission

One of the questions most bandied about has been whether the States may withdraw, or rescind, their applications, as many have attempted to do over the last couple of centuries.[166] Nothing in the Constitution addresses rescission of applications or amendments – it is all speculation.[167] Once again we are faced with the argument that if the Framers intended for rescission, they would have explicitly included it in the text of the Constitution.[168] For a brief period in the late 1950s, this battle was waged between attorneys writing in the *American Bar Association Journal* as they argued that rescission of a convention application was analogous to rescinding an amendment ratification by a state, an amendment proposal by Congress, or participation in an interstate compact by a state. An amendment proposal submitted within the Congress can be withdrawn at any time; on this basis and by analogy, a state application should be equally possible to rescind.[169] The long list of court decisions and erudite academic opinions have indicated that such rescissions are not legally permissible.[170] It is interesting to note that many of the state courts have long held that the amendment power – at the state level – in its entirety is justiciable.[171] The only stipulation on rescission should be that the same procedure must be followed by the state as that undertaken to pass the application originally.[172]

The rescission issue came to the forefront again during the campaign

---

[166] A story of the ratification of the Fourteenth Amendment pointedly involves rescission. In 1868, Secretary of State William Seward believed that he had enough state ratifications to declare the amendment ratified. Ohio and New Jersey had rescinded their ratifications and Seward stated this in his notice. Notes from the debates in Congress show that the Republican majority ignored the rescission issue. A resolution was passed announcing that the Fourteenth Amendment was now a valid part of the Constitution without debate or a roll-call vote. The total number was based on the Speaker of the House claiming to have a telegram from Georgia ratifying the amendment. Several congressmen wanted the resolution sent to a committee for study first but the Speaker wanted it passed that day. Grover Rees noted that the list of congressmen who voted that Ohio and New Jersey could not rescind was identical to those who had voted to impeach President Johnson five months before.

[167] Sara R. Ellis, Yusuf Z. Malik, Heather G. Parker, Benjamin C. Signer & Al'Reco L. Yancy, "Article V Constitutional Conventions: A Primer," *Tennessee Law Review* 78 (2011): 677

[168] Samuel S. Freeman & Pamela J. Naughton, *ERA, May a State Change Its Vote?* (Detroit, MI: Wayne State University Press, 1978), 6

[169] Dwight Connely, "Amending the Constitution: Is This Any Way to Call for a Constitutional Convention?," *Arizona Law Review* 22 (1980): 1034

[170] Frank E. Packard, "Constitutional Law: The States and the Amending Process," *American Bar Association Journal* 45, no.2 (Feb.1959): 161-3

[171] Leo Kanowitz & Marilyn Klinger, "Can a State Rescind Its Equal Rights Amendment Ratification: Who Decides and How?," *Hastings Law Journal* 28 (Mar. 1977): 984, n.29

[172] Dwight Connely, "Amending the Constitution: Is This Any Way to Call for a Constitutional Convention?," *Arizona Law Review* 22 (1980): 1036

to ratify the Equal Rights Amendment in the 1970s. Although both houses of Congress had overwhelmingly approved the amendment bill,[173] and the States began to ratify quickly, the last few states were not forthcoming and then the rescissions started. A number of states which had ratified in short order had begun to rethink their actions and wanted to reverse their ratifications.[174] While the Court had treated the matter as settled prior to *Coleman* in 1939, after that decision, all was thrown in to flux due to the Court calling it a political question in *Coleman*. What confuses the issue today is that commenters have declared that the *Coleman* references to the justiciability of rescission are mere dictum, that is, not an official opinion, but only a legal "aside."[175] In *Coleman*, the Court was clear,

> *"We find no basis in either constitution or statute for such judicial action. Article V, speaking solely of ratification, contains no provision as to rejection. Nor has the Congress enacted a statute relating to rejection."*[176]

It is claimed that the ability of a state to rescind is considered to be a prerogative of the States embedded in the Tenth Amendment, the *Leser* decision to the contrary,[177] and qualified by the caveat that as long as the magic number of three-quarters of the States has not been reached, then rescission of a ratification is permissible as a state power.[178] By extension, rescission of a state application for an Article V convention is also potentially held to be a state power. Since a federal district court held in *Dyer v. Blair*[179] that state legislatures are performing a federal function and can make their own rules, even in defiance of their own state constitutions, the rescission power would seem to be within a state legislature's power. But a century earlier Jameson said otherwise,

> *"Passage by a legislature or a ratifying resolution is, in this view, a sort of sacramental act, which may take only a moment to consummate but which*

---

[173] The US Senate approved by a vote of 84 to 8 on 22 March 1972 and the US House approved by a vote of 354 to 24 on 12 October 1973.

[174] Idaho, Nebraska and Tennessee passed resolutions to rescind. Kansas contemplated rescission.

[175] Leo Kanowitz & Marilyn Klinger, "Can a State Rescind Its Equal Rights Amendment Ratification: Who Decides and How?," *Hastings Law Journal* 28 (Mar.1977): 984-8

[176] 307 U.S. 433 (1939), 450

[177] *Leser v. Garnitz*, 258 U.S. 130 at 136-137 (1922) and similarly *Hawke v. Smith*, 253 U.S. 221 (1920)

[178] Grover Rees III, "Rescinding Ratification of Proposed Constitutional Amendments – A Question for the Court," *Louisiana Law Review* 37, no.4 (Spring 1977): 896

[179] 390 F. Supp. 1291 (N.D. Ill. 1975)

is forever binding on the legislature (and on the whole nation)."[180]

While opponents of an amendatory convention will point out that neither the Congress nor the Court has given a definitive statement on the ability of a state to rescind either a ratification of a constitutional amendment or an application for a convention, it is important to recognize that the Senate twice voted to reject a bill which would have declared that no state could rescind a ratification.[181] At the same time, another bill passed by the House would have allowed rescission.[182] Instead, the Court held in *Coleman* that the issue was a political question and that the Court recognized the "historic precedent."[183] Caplan details the history of colonial rescission under the Confederation and provides examples of state rescissions of amendments to the Articles of Confederation. The idea of refusing a rescission appears to have begun with the Reconstruction Amendments.[184]

The sole mention of rescission, of either a ratification or an application, by any of the Founders and Framers is found in a letter from James Madison to Alexander Hamilton,

> "My opinion is that a reservation of a right to withdraw, if amendments [the Bill of Rights] be not decided on...within a certain time, is a **conditional** ratification...In short any **condition** whatever must viciate [vitiate] the ratification... This idea of reserving the right to withdraw was started at Richmd. and was considered as a conditional ratification which was itself considered as worse than a rejection."[185]

This comment is significant as Madison and Hamilton are responsible for the final version of Article V. Of course, Madison is making reference to ratification, but by extension, rescission of an application might be reasonable when subject to the same restrictions.[186] One camp argues that rescissions are

---

[180] John Alexander Jameson, *A Treatise on Constitutional Conventions: Their History, Powers and Modes of Proceedings* (New York: Scribner, 1867, 4th ed., 1887), § 628

[181] Cong. Globe, 41st Cong., 2d sess., at 3971 (1870) and 3d sess., at 1381 (1871)

[182] Samuel S. Freeman & Pamela J. Naughton, *ERA, May a State Change Its Vote?* (Detroit, MI: Wayne State University Press, 1978), 8

[183] 307 U.S. at 449-50

[184] Russell B. Caplan, *Constitutional Brinkmanship* (New York: Oxford University Press, 1988), 108-10

[185] Letter of James Madison to Alexander Hamilton of 20 July 1788

[186] Patricia A. Brannan, David L. Lillehaug, Robert P. Reznick, "Critical Details: Amending the United States Constitution," *Harvard Journal on Legislation* 16 (1979): 784

not irrevocable because they are not "final acts."[187] Another camp argues back that no one will take the States seriously unless the applications are final and therefore no rescission is permissible.[188] The difference may be found in the location of the act within the process. Applications occur earlier with less consequence than ratifications that are at the tail end of the amendment process.[189]

It is claimed that the final word on rescission could be determined by the history of Congress appearing to accept rescissions when it was in their favor: More than enough states have applied for an amendatory convention to reform or limit the taxing authority of Congress, but there have been enough rescissions to drop the total below that of the requisite two-thirds.[190] The proponents of this line of argument believe that the final analysis is this: if Congress will acknowledge rescissions, then historical situations have existed where amendments, specifically, the Fourteenth and the Fifteenth, were not properly ratified; and if Congress will not acknowledge rescissions, then past and current situations exist where enough applications have been submitted that Congress is overdue for calling a convention.[191,192] The Congress are damned if they do and damned if they don't – entirely by their own doing. This is speculation at best; the problem is that none of this is conclusive and not of precedential value since Congress' sole course of action has been to take no action. This argument also mixes the examples of amendment ratifications with application resolutions.

Finally, if a state is to exert the will of its people, then it must have the ability to rescind a ratification or an application.[193] If we must make a firm decision, and constitutional consistency says that we should, then the acceptance of rescissions of ratifications before reaching the three-quarters of the States mark is the most appropriate choice. Similarly, acceptance of

---

[187] Bernard Fensterwald, Jr., "Constitutional Law: The States and the Amending Power – A Reply," *American Bar Association Journal* 46, no.7 (July 1960)

[188] Frank E. Packard, "Constitutional Law: The States and the Amending Process," *American Bar Association Journal* 45, no.2 (Feb.1959): 196-7

[189] Patricia A. Brannan, David L. Lillehaug, Robert P. Reznick, "Critical Details: Amending the United States Constitution," *Harvard Journal on Legislation* 16 (1979): 791

[190] Ibid., p.791, n.106

[191] Michael Stokes Paulsen, "A General Theory of Article V: The Constitutional Lessons of the Twenty-seventh Amendment," *Yale Law Journal* 103, no.3 (Dec. 1993): 764

[192] James Kenneth Rogers, "The Other Way to Amend the Constitution: The Article V Constitutional Convention Amendment Process," *Harvard Journal of Law & Public Policy* 30, no.3 (Summer 2007): 1018

[193] Brendon Troy Ishikawa, "Everything You Always Wanted to Know About How Amendments Are Made, but Were Afraid to Ask*," *Hastings Constitutional Law Quarterly* 24 (Winter 1997): 556

rescissions of applications for a convention before reaching the two-thirds of the States mark is also the most appropriate choice. "A state can hardly be said to be part of a consensus to call a convention after it has rescinded its application."[194]

Returning to Madison's comment about a conditional application, several states have used a conditional application to apply for a convention for decades. During the early push for a balanced budget amendment convention, some states wrote their applications to first, ask to apply for a convention, and second, ask that Congress propose an amendment upon which the application would be null and void if Congress did pass an amendment proposal. This type of application is often viewed as an invalid application, a mere request for an amendment from the States and not a bona fide application for an amendatory convention.[195] Because Congress has not formally counted applications, they have not formally sorted applications rendering this aspect unsettled.

A last view of rescission is introduced here: that ratification and application as such different animals that one cannot be used as an analogy for the other. That ratification as an act of finality in amendment is of such seriousness that rescission is not permissible since it would cheapen and degrade the decision to ratify. But rescission of an application is nowhere so serious as it could always be reintroduced – and has in many states for many subjects – without damaging the fundamental law of the nation. Application is the introduction of the topic whereas ratification is the conclusive word on the topic. This is the practice that best mirrors history.

We can easily envision state legislators finding rescission as an attractive aspect of voting in favor of a convention resolution since it would mean that there exists a mechanism for addressing the situation where the public's support of the convention may deteriorate or in the event that new information is found or a turn of events occurs.

Control of Delegate Selection and Qualifications

Additional powers that the States possess are the powers of selecting

---

[194] Douglas G. Voegler, "Amending the Constitution by the Article V Convention Method," *North Dakota Law Review* 55 (1979): 372-3.

[195] Thomas N. Neale, Library of Congress, Congressional Research Service Report R42592, *The Article V Convention to Propose Constitutional Amendments: Historical Perspectives for Congress* at 17-8 (22 October 2012)

their delegates and the manner in which the selection is made. Congress may well try to establish the requirements for delegates but the States would be within their rights to reject such an action and insist on drafting their own qualifications and commissions, state-by-state. This is the long-standing historical precedent. Conversely, the States would also be able to exclude from delegate service anyone they choose – such as federal officials, particularly sitting congressmen and women.

The selection and credentialing of delegates is, and always has been, in the hands of the States. This has been true since before the establishment of the United States. During the Colonial Period, the many intercolonial conventions left the determination of the delegates to the colonies. The 1787 Philadelphia Convention did the same, leaving it up to the States. At the time of this writing, many states have either passed or are currently considering legislation that would stipulate the requirements for a delegate to a "constitutional convention" – some states have already codified the criteria in their state constitution.[196] No one knows better than the people of a particular state, the situation and circumstances within their state, and therefore, who best could serve its interests in a convention. That includes the calculation of the number of delegates, their backgrounds, their professions, their residence within the state and their political affiliations.

The definition of "delegates" or "commissioners," like many other terms, is reserved to the States.[197] There is no federal definition, therefore it devolves to the States to individually set the criteria. Inherent in the States' setting their individual definition of "delegates" is the ability to define the powers and credentials of those delegates.

Remember that we previously noted that there are not one, but two precedents for the state control over the delegate selection process. Article V names two types of conventions and Article VII names one more type: Article V names federal amendment proposal conventions and federal amendment ratification conventions; Article VII names conventions for the ratification of the federal constitution. Two of the three types have already occurred. When the States held ratification conventions for the

---

[196] Paul J. Weber & Barbara A. Perry, *Unfounded Fears, The Myths and Realities of a Constitutional Convention* (New York: Praeger, 1989), 89 – the example is given of Illinois.

[197] Vikram David Amar, "The People Made Me Do It: Can the People of the States Instruct and Coerce Their State Legislatures in the Article V Constitutional Amendment Process?," *William and Mary Law Review* 41, no.3 (2000): 1053, and specifically note 68 – citing *Board of Regents v. Roth* 408 U.S. 564 (1972)

federal constitution in 1787-91, the selection, requirements, discipline and credentialing of delegates were left entirely to the States as there is no mention of such criteria in Article VII. When the state ratification conventions for the Twenty-first Amendment were held by thirty-nine states in 1933-34, the selection, requirements, discipline and credentialing of the delegates were left entirely to the States as there are no such criteria mentioned in Article V. The interpretation of the federal constitution's fifth and seventh articles then was conclusively determined to be that the States controlled the delegate process. Why would the delegate process for the third type of named convention in Article V be different now? If that were indeed the case, then Article V would have to say exactly that in order to reach a different conclusion than those reached in 1787-91 and 1933-34.

Determination of the Subject and the Extent of the Application

The States alone have the power, by virtue of the action of their legislatures, to determine the subject and the breadth of the subject for a convention. For example, the States could assert in their application resolutions that the subject matter is campaign finance reform and it could be limited to the proposal to prohibit the making of campaign donations by corporations or businesses. Or the subject may be specified as fiscal responsibility and the proposals limited to the deliberation and consideration of spending caps and tax hike limits.

Congress has not formally sought over the years to control the attempts to force a convention by rejecting applications. But individual members of Congress have stated that they refuse to consider a convention and the majority of those seem to hinge on the homogeneity of the applications. The States have found a work-around in making certain that the succeeding applications both use nearly identical wording and list the states which preceded the new application so that the applications are aggregated as applying for the same reason.

The issue of the selection of the subject matter is sometimes conflated with that of limiting the States' applications to a pre-worded text for a single amendment proposal, a situation underway today involving the proposal of an interstate compact for calling a convention. While many scholars have argued both for and against the idea of a pre-worded amendment and the scales seem to tip in favor of those who advocate against a pre-worded amendment, the impact of such an act is what is important. By restricting the debate to a simple up or down vote, the States may be depriving themselves of the opportunity for a better solution that the deliberation would potentially present. If the single pre-worded amendment proposal were the limitation on the convention and that proposal was rejected, then a new convention would have to be called to consider another proposal. Alternatively, deliberation of the pre-worded text may be just as productive in finding the errors in the proposal. This situation could lead to a better worded proposal, even if that outcome meant a new convention.[198] Applying the looser wording in the application circumvents that unsatisfactory outcome. It is potentially in the States' best interest to define the subject matter broadly.

One of the strongest arguments for the States to exert control over the federal amendatory convention comes from Henry Levine,

> *"If a federal convention is to be a device for circumventing Congress, it would be uncontrollable in the absence of state controls... To deny the states the power to limit a federal convention is to argue that the framers intended that the states be compelled to risk the entire structure of government whenever they sought to make a minor constitutional adjustment over the objections of Congress."*[199]

Levine goes in depth to study the issue of state control and contrasts it with the problems of sharing control with Congress. In a lengthy article, he looks at each facet of the debate and concludes that the original purpose of Article V's alternative amendment clause places an unresolvable point of contention between Congress and the States,

> *"Indeed, both the inherent conflict of interest between Congress and an article V convention and analogy to the state experience with legislative limitations imposed after electoral authorization suggest that only the state may limit an article V convention and that the contemplated congressional role in enforcing limitations is singularly inappropriate, perhaps even unconstitutional."*[200]

---

[198] Michael Stern, "Reopening the Constitutional Road to Reform: Toward a Safeguarded Article V Convention," *Tennessee Law Review* 78 (2011): 784-5.
[199] Republished with permission of the Harvard University/Law School, from Henry D. Levine, "Limited Federal Constitutional Conventions. Implications of the State Experience," *Harvard Journal on Legislation* 11 (1973): 150; permission conveyed through Copyright Clearance Center, Inc.
[200] Ibid., 157

Levine also points out some interesting statistics on limited state constitutional conventions. First, about 15% of all state constitutional conventions through his writing in 1973 were limited. This amounts to about thirty-five conventions per his count of 233 state conventions. He notes that the percentage was increasing in the post-WWII period.[201] Robert F. Williams commented in his 2009 book that states could limit a convention by both stating what may be discussed as well as what may NOT be discussed in the convention. He gave the example of the New Jersey convention of 1947 being forbidden to take up the issue of reapportionment and, ironically, the 1966 New Jersey convention was allowed to discuss only reapportionment.[202] Considering that the 15% of state constitutional conventions held were limited and that none of these limited conventions ran away, it would seem logical that the fear of a federal amendatory convention to runaway is, in the States' experience, wholly unfounded.

Of course, it must be stated here that there is a significant difference between state and federal constitutionalism and that what is appropriate for one is not necessarily appropriate, or legal, for the other. The experience of the States does not always translate to applicable to the federal situation. What is instructive is that the States' experience provides a starting point for consideration of a solution to a problem of a federal amendatory convention.[203] As a comparison, the American Bar Association noted in its 1974 study of the Article V Convention process that until the time of its study, only eighteen of the 356 studied convention applications submitted by the States were for a general, or open, convention.[204] Since the issuance of that ABA report, only six more applications for a general convention have been submitted in the last forty years.[205]

Weber and Perry go a step further and point to the history of limited state conventions as an example of how well the imposed limitations have worked. At the time of their publication in 1989, there were 233 state constitutional conventions chronicled. Of those, six had runaway or deviated from their mandates, but these were not limited conventions. The last of

---

[201] Ibid., 133, n.32
[202] Robert F. Williams, *The Law of American State Constitutions* (New York: Oxford University Press, 2009), 392
[203] Ibid., 393
[204] American Bar Association, Special Constitutional Convention Study Committee, (1974): 59-61
[205] http://foavc.org/file.php/1/Amendments Friends of Article V Convention website, listing of all state Article V convention applications to date – accessed 22 March 2015.

these had occurred in 1908.[206] Since that time, states had revamped how they wrote their convention enabling acts and in the eighty succeeding years up to the time of Weber and Perry's work, not one single state convention had gone astray.[207] Michael Stern makes the recommendation that one way that the States can assure that the convention does not stray from the topic in the call is for the States to require that their delegates vote at the early part of the convention when the rules are proposed to reject any rules that do not strictly limit the subject matter.[208] A state could go further in that regard and may potentially punish delegates that go rogue.

The Executive's Power and Requirements

The President, and his counterparts at the state level, the governors, play no role in the amendment process, with some states having a contrary requirement.[209] Although many have tried to claim that the two presentment clauses[210] require that the President's signature be affixed to the call from Congress, this was refuted permanently, by analogy, by the Supreme Court in 1798 in *Hollingsworth v. Virginia*.[211,212] In that decision, the Eleventh Amendment's validity was challenged for not bearing the signature of President Washington. Unfortunately, the actual reasoning of the Court has not survived, all that we have is the notice of the decision and the statement from oral argument of Justice Samuel Chase. That decision was reaffirmed in 1920 in the *Hawke v. Smith, No.1* ruling.[213] Numerous state court decisions have held that state governors have no role in the application process. In the aforementioned *Coleman* decision, the lieutenant governor of Kansas acting in his official role as the state Senate president voted to ratify the proposed Child Labor Amendment and this point was divided on by the US Supreme Court.[214]

---

[206] Weber & Perry cite Hoar, 111-115: Georgia (1789), Minnesota (1857), Pennsylvania (1872), Alabama (1901), Virginia (1901) and Michigan (1908) – but to this we should add the 1862 Illinois "Copperhead" convention.

[207] Paul J. Weber & Barbara A. Perry, *Unfounded Fears, The Myths and Realities of a Constitutional Convention* (New York: Praeger, 1989), 97

[208] Michael Stern, "Reopening the Constitutional Road to Reform: Toward a Safeguarded Article V Convention," *Tennessee Law Review* 78 (2011): 779

[209] As examples, Montana and Wyoming.

[210] United States Constitution, Article I, §7

[211] 3 U.S. (3 Dall.) 378 (1798)

[212] Russell B. Caplan, *Constitutional Brinkmanship* (New York: Oxford University Press, 1988), 134-7

[213] 253 U.S. 221 (1920) at 229

[214] *Coleman v. Miller*, 307 U.S. 433, 59 S. Ct. 972, 83 L. Ed. 1385

Allowing the executive to veto or to partially restrain the convention would circumvent the process and obstruct the express purpose of providing the people with a method of constitutionally correcting the government. We have several examples from history to examine. The first ten amendments, the Bill of Rights, were voted on by Congress and then promulgated to the States without President Washington's signature. The Twelfth Amendment was added without President's Jefferson's signature and in that instance, the Senate took up and defeated a motion to submit the bill to Jefferson for his approval. A proposed amendment was given to President Buchanan which he signed – that amendment was not a precedent as it did not gain the ratification of the States. President Lincoln inadvertently signed the Thirteenth Amendment and quickly sent an apology to the Congress for having unintentionally breached tradition. The Senate responded by passing a resolution that confirmed that the presidential signature was unnecessary. Finally, President Andrew Johnson sent a report to Congress stating that any action taken in regard to a proposed amendment was merely ministerial and not part of the official process.[215]

Analogously, the state governors, with some states excepted, have no role due to the nature of the action being taken and this point has been formalized through numerous state supreme court decisions. Any Article V related action on the part of the state legislature is not a normal legislative action – it is a special federal function carried out not under the authority of the state constitution that normally governs the actions of the state legislature but strictly under Article V of the federal constitution. The governor of any given state plays no role in the federal scheme of the execution of the federal amending power.

Related to the situation of the state governors, the Vice-President has no role to play even though he is the President of the US Senate. Since an action taken under Article V is not a normal legislative action under Article I, but is a special action taken under Article V, the Vice-President is exempted from the action and has no role. The Vice-President's role as a tiebreaker is not applicable since two-thirds of the vote is needed to pass in the Senate. This point was confirmed in 1803 by US Senator Pierce Butler, who had served as a delegate from South Carolina to the 1787 Philadelphia

---

[215] Douglas G. Voegler, "Amending the Constitution by the Article V Convention Method," *North Dakota Law Review* 55 (1979): 376

Convention, when he spoke on the US Senate floor and said that, "It was never intended by the Constitution that the Vice-President, should have a vote in altering the Constitution."[216]

The Report of The American Bar Association

The American Bar Association spent more than two years studying the Article V convention process in the mid-1970s and issued a report that generated significant attention and discussion.[217] The report is significant because if marks the first time that a professional legal association has taken a formal stance on the issue. Their conclusions were that Congress did indeed have the power to control and legislate the procedures of an amendatory convention. The ABA also found that a limited convention was permissible; that Congress could call a convention specifying the subject matter; that Congress could refuse to send the "unconstitutional" amendment proposals to the States; that Congress could judge the validity of state applications; that Congress could determine the contemporaneity of state applications; and that rescissions were also permissible. The ABA recommended some measure of judicial review be allowed.[218]

The ABA concluded that the practice of the state conventions in 1787 was to limit their conventions so that would have been a natural habit of the delegates to expect to do the same for any federal convention. Moreover, the practice of limiting a convention provides a benefit to the voters who must select delegates as knowing the agenda beforehand permits the voter to make an intelligent and informed choice.[219]

Also of importance is that the report examined the nearly four hundred applications to date and found that nearly every state had submitted an application at one point or another.[220] Even when we acknowledge that there is a great variety of reasons for the States to apply for a convention, it is readily apparent that the States are showing a consensus for discussing

---

[216] Ibid., n. 121

[217] *Amendment of the Constitution by the Convention Method Under Article V (Special Committee Report)*, American Bar Association, (1974)

[218] Kenneth Ripple, "Article V and the Proposed Federal Constitutional Convention Procedures Bills," *Cardozo Law Review* 3 (1982): 534

[219] Ronald D. Rotunda & Stephen J. Safranek, "An Essay on Term Limits and a Call for a Constitutional Convention," *Marquette Law Review* 80, no.1 (Fall 1996): 237

[220] Dwight W. Connely, "Amending the Constitution: Is This Any Way to Call for a Constitutional Convention?," *Arizona Law Review* 22 (1980): 1011-2

potential changes. The importance of the ABA Report is that it is the first major endorsement of the idea of the limited amendatory convention from the legal community. The period in which the ABA made its report coincides with Natelson's "first wave" and is therefore limited in its utility by the lack of applied resources characteristic of the period.

The Impact of the State Experience and State Courts on Amendatory Conventions

In the excursus following this chapter, the court cases are segregated by federal and state court jurisdiction. It is essential to demonstrate that there are significant differences between the state and federal constitutions. They differ in objective, powers and especially in the amendment processes. The allocation of powers and the spheres of influence are shown in Appendix A. The federal amendment process found in Article V is rigid and difficult to complete by either the congressional or the convention method. The state constitutions, by and large, are extremely easy to amend as evidenced by the high numbers of amendments per constitution. John Dinan has argued that this facility of amendment for the state constitutions is one of their points of success as the state constitutions are a mode of trying out variations of ideas that may eventually make its way in to the federal constitution.[221]

Dinan points to the 233 state constitutional conventions (by the time of his publication in 2009 – 2nd printing) and over 6,000 state constitution amendments made as proof of this experimentation.[222] He does not break out the number of amendatory or limited power conventions separately but he does address the issue in a later paper.[223] Dinan also points out that there are separate but distinct amendment and revision processes as some states will forego writing a new constitution and just overhaul, or revise, their existing constitution when an amendment or amendments are not enough to effect the structural change desired or needed. State conventions have more methods of amendment than the federal constitution – in addition to the convention and legislative methods are constitutional commissions, initiatives

---

[221] John J. Dinan, *The American State Constitutional Tradition* (Lawrence: University of Kansas Press, 2006), 3
[222] Ibid., 1
[223] John Dinan, "The Political Dynamics of Mandatory State Constitutional Convention Referendums: Lessons from the 2000s Regarding Obstacles and Pathways to their Passage," *Montana Law Review*, Vol.71, Iss.2, (Summer 2010), pp.396-7

and referendums.²²⁴

Vladimir Kogan notes that between 1930 and 2010, the States held forty state constitutional conventions and of those, seventeen were limited and/or amendatory.²²⁵ Those numbers can be found in Appendix B of this work. In the pursuit of the research for this book, many, many more state and territorial constitutional conventions were uncovered along with constitutional conventions for provisional (failed) states and territories as well as national constitutional conventions for nations that once existed within the borders of the present United States. The results of that research are presented in Appendix B but for the sake of making the point within the context of this chapter, we have identified 442 constitutional conventions of which eighty-two were amendatory/limited.

We can add to these the estimated at over two hundred constitutional conventions held by the Native American nations resulting in currently more than one hundred operating constitutions for the 567 federally recognized Native American nations and communities.²²⁶,²²⁷ These constitutions date back as far, in the southeast, as the 1827 convention with the earliest constitution created by the Cherokee nation and by the Choctaw nation holding a convention and adopting a constitution in 1838.²²⁸ The Cherokee held additional conventions in 1839, 1976, and 1999.²²⁹ The Choctaw have held additional conventions in 1842, 1852, 1858, 1860, 1979 and 1983. In the northeast, the Seneca adopted a constitution in 1848.²³⁰ Also among the earliest Native American constitutions were those of the Chickasaw and the Creek.²³¹ The Stockbridge-Munsee of Connecticut and New York and later of Wisconsin were the first to draft a constitution in English in 1837.²³² The Indian Reorganization Act of 1934 (IRA) instigated the creation of nearly one hundred modern native constitutions, most through conventions.

---

²²⁴ John J. Dinan, *The American State Constitutional Tradition* (Lawrence: University of Kansas Press, 2006), 29, and Chapter 2 generally

²²⁵ Vladimir Kogan, "Lessons from Recent State Constitutional Conventions," *California Journal of Politics & Policy* 2, no.2 (2010): 4

²²⁶ http://www.tribal-institute.org/lists/constitutions.htm

²²⁷ http://thorpe.ou.edu/const.html

²²⁸ Eric Lemont, "Developing Effective Processes of American Indian Constitutional and Governmental Reform: Lessons from the Cherokee Nation of Oklahoma, Hualapai Nation, Navajo Nation and Northern Cheyenne Tribe," *American Indian Law Review* 26, no.2 (2002), generally

²²⁹ http://thorpe.ou.edu/IRA.html

²³⁰ http://www.loc.gov/law/help/american-indian-consts/index.php

²³¹ http://blogs.loc.gov/law/2013/11/american-indian-constitutions/

²³² Robert J. Miller, "Tribal Constitutions and Native Sovereignty," SSRN-id1802890, (2011): 3

An estimated 35-40% of the federally recognized Native American nations operate under a constitution presently, but the number of conventions held is not known at present.[233] Add these to the numbers that Dinan cites and the number of constitutional conventions, or all types, held within the current boundaries of the present United States exceeds six hundred conventions.

The plethora of state constitutional conventions has generated an equally large number of state court cases involving the powers and limitations of the state constitutional conventions. These state level decisions are occasionally the beginning of legal theories and ideas that eventually migrate to the federal constitutional theatre. The state court decisions have several significant differences from the federal decisions. Foremost, the state courts have held that, almost without exception, contrary to the federal position found in *Coleman,* the state constitutional issues are justiciable and not political questions. This is important as that means that the States hold constitutional issues to be of such importance that the state courts will seek to address directly and not deflect the issues.[234]

In his seminal work, *The Law of American State Constitutions*, Robert F. Williams goes into great detail on the differences between not just the written state and federal constitutions, but the ideology behind each. He points out that the two types are deeply interrelated as he contends that the state constitutions *complete* the federal constitution.[235] Williams credits Professor James Gardner for the idea that the two forms compose the interrelated federal constitutional structure of the nation's governments. Williams states,

> "State constitutions, in addition to a variety of policy-based provisions, often contain positive or affirmative rights, or even mandates, while federal constitutional rights are primarily negative in nature. State courts interpreting state constitutions are therefore thrust more deeply and more often into the affairs of the coordinate branches of government than when they or federal courts are interpreting the federal constitution."[236]

It is for this reason that we must consider the body of state

---

[233] Ibid., 5

[234] "Proposing Amendments to the United States Constitution by Convention," *Harvard Law Review* 70, no.6 (Apr.1957): 1070, and Edwin S. Corwin & Mary Louise Ramsey, "The Constitutional Law of Constitutional Amendment," *Notre Dame Lawyer* XXVI, no.2 (Winter 1951): 185-6

[235] Robert F. Williams, *The Law of American State Constitutions* (New York: Oxford University Press, 2009), 18

[236] Ibid., 25

constitutional law with regard to the amendment process. Since many of the ideas that impact or pertain to the amendment process were shaped by or perfected in the state constitutions. The legal reasoning brought or expounded in the hundreds of state decisions is often elevated to the federal level and then extrapolated and expanded in later federal decisions. The hundreds of state constitutional conventions – drafting, amendatory, ratificatory, and revisory – permitted the exploration of ideas in the context of the changing times and political situations. The States have averaged more than one state constitutional convention per year providing a continuous evolution of political thought and experiment over the life of the nation. This view is an application of Justice Louis Brandeis' admonition that "It is one of the happy incidents of the federal system that a single, courageous state may, if its citizens choose, serve as a laboratory; and try novel social and economic experiments without risk to the rest of the country."[237]

The argument that a limited state constitutional convention is not, at least in part, analogous to a federal amendatory convention has been refuted repeatedly, beginning in earnest in the 1970s. Henry Levine wrote on the subject in 1973 pointing out that the limitations come in two types: procedural and substantive. The procedural limitations are usually denied but the substantive limitations are of many types (constitutional, executive, judicial, legislative and popular) and are usually spelled out in the enabling act for the convention.[238] This position makes sense as the convention is entitled to set its own procedures as an inherent power of a convention (Jameson's contention otherwise not withstanding). But it is the procedural issues that cause the problems at the federal level.[239] The involvement of Congress would be almost entirely procedural. It is for that reason that disallowing Congress any involvement beyond that stipulated by the text of Article V is the least problematic approach.[240]

The US Supreme Court has ruled <u>directly</u> on Article V in just a handful of cases although they issued decisions that impact Article V and the amendment process in many more. The decisions regarding Article V are, interestingly, grouped very closely together in time, with all but one of

---

[237] *New State Ice Co. v. Liebmann*, 285 U.S. 262 at 311 (1932)
[238] Henry D. Levine, "Limited Federal Constitutional Conventions: Implications of the State Experience," *Harvard Journal on Legislation* 11 (1973): 133-5
[239] Michael A. Almond, "Amendment By Convention: Our Next Constitutional Crisis?," *North Carolina Law Review* 53 (1975): 504, n.67.
[240] Ibid., 505

the major rulings being handed down within two decades and five of those coming within a two year period:

- *Hollingsworth v. Virginia* (1798)
- *Hawke v. Smith I* (1920)
- *Hawke v. Smith II* (1920)
- *National Prohibition Cases* (1920)
- *Dillon v. Gloss* (1921)
- *Leser v. Garnett* (1922)
- *United States v. Sprague* (1931)
- *Coleman v. Miller* (1939)

These decisions, along with all of the other Supreme Court and federal court decisions, are mandatory authority. The included, select state court decisions, almost all state supreme court decisions, are persuasive authority to the extent that the legal reasoning employed may be at some point used to crossover in a federal case. Those state decisions are included herein and interpreted as to how they might apply to any future Article V amendatory convention.

Now that the division of powers and duties between the States, Congress, the judiciary and the executive has been delineated, and the criteria required for consideration of the state applications has been considered, the impact of the decisions of the courts can be examined in context.

Following such a mental exercise, our careful state legislator could, and probably would, conclude that the amendatory convention is indeed constitutional, that is it the proper and intended vehicle for obtaining the desired constitutional change that Congress will not provide, and that an amendatory convention has the highest probability of successfully securing the amendment, but the prudent legislator would question whether this method would withstand the legal challenges presented by any attendant litigation.

Our state legislator would undoubtedly reach the conclusion that the Framers of the federal Constitution included Article V's state-application-and-convention method for those situations where Congress will not perform their duty. It is an irrefutable fact that the purpose of the convention method is to circumvent the Congress. The vague generality of Article V poses problems for our legislator in determining the boundaries of the convention method but that history, custom, tradition, and legal precedents have firmly established who should control which aspects of the convention process. What remains undecided could and possibly should be decided by the courts.

Having reached this conclusion, a state legislator would have assessed the probability of the matter ending up in the courts and considered whether the convention topic is justiciable. The costs of doing so include the time, talent and treasure that the State(s) will need to expend in pursuing resolution of the open questions. This process could take years, consuming the work of many lawyers and researchers, and eat up a significant portion of the state's budget. The benefits include a finality to the questions posed but at the expense of losing in the courts and closing off the method for perhaps decades or possibly permanently.

The circumstances for pursuing the path of litigation over a political solution would include, preferably, a favorably aligned judiciary, including the US Supreme Court; sufficient legal and academic research to support the states' position; a belief that the greater public will support the position of the States; and most importantly, a narrowly defined issue(s) for the courts that is perceived as manageable and winnable without expanding the case to include issues of which the States are less certain. The political environment must be such that the resort to a judicial solution is viewed as correct and preferable to other outcomes. Looking at the writings and past decisions of the judges and justices at the various levels of the judiciary along the chosen path for adjudication may give some insight into the probability of success. The legal climate might be ascertained from the recent topics in the legal community's literature. The court of public opinion weighs in on the perception of the Congress as the source of the problem. Should the majority of the American public view the federal government as the instigator and/or perpetuator of society's maladies, it will bolster the state legislatures' argument for a convention. We are making a very large assumption in this instance that the political path to a solution is closed due to the intractability of Congress. If Congress were responding in the normal of sensing that the public demand constitutional change and then Congress makes a priority of passing a proposed amendment, there would be no need for the States to consider the justiciability of a convention method solution. This scenario assumes that the prodding effect is not at work. At this point, our cautious state legislator is making a potentially career damaging decision: challenge the federal government and the good relations that state legislator may have with federal officials – even within her own party – thereby destroying the possibility of political advancement versus garnering the support of the public for bold reforms. For those state legislators who choose to lead in pushing the matter in the courts to secure a convention, the stakes are hypothetically heightened. It is a weighty decision.

The most likely issue to be brought before the courts is that of forcing a convention call. The impetus for an action might come in the form of Congress refusing to count the applications, or Congress refusing to consider the applications, or Congress invalidating the applications on allegedly spurious or indefensible grounds, or Congress requiring a passing vote to "approve" a convention call, or Congress referring the applications to a committee (indefinitely) for study or for determination of the intent of the Framers, or Congress proposing new criteria for a convention, such as requiring that hearings be held, or Congress simply declining to call a convention without any consideration or reason provided, as has be done in the past. At this stage, the State(s) have to have a response in the form of a plan of action for countering congressional resistance or subterfuge.

That plan would probably take the shape of an escalating set of responses. First, the state legislatures take to the court of public opinion and try their case with the people and lay their claim on the Constitution, urging the public to apply pressure to their federal officials. Then the States may begin a program of state officials showing solidarity against the federal overreach and refusal to heed the people and the States. They might turn to friendly media to highlight the impasse and present the States' side in a positive light. All of this culminates in the appeal to the judiciary for relief. In each of these actions, the States are seeking to appear as the aggrieved party who has acted in compliance with the law. These actions would be most supportive of the States from a litigation standpoint as they give the appearance of comporting with the federal Constitution.

Should the judiciary not respond in support of the States or simply not respond at all, the States might then take to acts of state-level civil disobedience. The States may openly refuse to comply with federal mandates on the States. They may conduct deliberate slow-downs of federal tax collection remittances, of fulfilling federal program requirements, of cooperating in servicing federal warrants and court orders. The States may then decide to up the ante and carry out more aggressive acts including forcing a federal government shut down, or to call a convention themselves without the call from Congress. These political options come at the expense of alienating any future court actions; they border on rebellion and would appear to challenge the authority of the Congress, the Supreme Court and the Executive – they might be perceived as defying the Constitution. The political and judicial options are then, in most instances, in opposition to each other.

Regardless of the path undertaken, the state legislatures must remain cognizant of the public's perception and their attendant support of the States to be effective. A lesson to be followed is that of the colonies in their struggle with the Stamp, Townshend and Intolerable Acts. The colonial legislatures and the Continental Congress had to follow a careful, escalating series of actions in order to maintain public support that eventually culminated in Independence. Had the Olive Branch Petition not been submitted, the argument that everything that could be done to maintain the peace had been tried would have rung hollow and much of the public may not have supported the patriot cause. Our state legislator in the Great State of East Somewhere must then follow a narrow and carefully laid path to first build consensus before acting and subsequently maintain the moral high ground while working toward a convention. The judicial recourse is then not so much an option as a requisite step in the process, no matter how aggravating and fruitless it may be.

The preceding lays out a worst case scenario for a state legislator. When considering whether to support a bill for a convention resolution, our legislator should keep in mind that in voting for a convention, the state legislator is acting in a very important capacity, that of helping to maintain constitutional fidelity and to keep the federal government on track. Those are the goals for any effort to secure an amendatory convention. Among all the duties of a state legislator, this may be the most important as it works to determine the future of not just her state but the nation as a whole. The legal history, precedents, ramifications and future legal actions are central to that vote.

EXCURSUS 1
CASES AND COURT FINDINGS RELATING TO ARTICLE V

> *"One precedent in favor of power is stronger than a hundred against it."*[1]
> *-Thomas Jefferson, Notes on the State of Virginia*

This excursus provides insight and an historical look at the relevant US Supreme Court, federal district court and appellate court, and state supreme court and appeals court cases that either involved or may apply to Article V of the United States Constitution. This section has been written, as much as possible, in laymen's language for the general public and includes the key findings in each case as it relates to an Article V Convention. The name and reference of the case itself is the citation while the footnotes provide additional information pertinent to the case reference. Cases are listed first by highest deciding court, then case name alphabetically. A chronological listing follows the descriptions with the date determined by the final decision. The synopsis of each case includes the:

- *Background of the Case:*
- *Constitutionally Related Issue:*
- *Court's Decision:*
- *Conclusions from the Court's Decision:*
- *Potential Applicability to an Article V Convention:*

---

[1] Thomas Jefferson, *Notes on the State of Virginia*, (Paris: 1785; Charles Wynne, Richmond, VA: 1853 ed.), 135

United States Supreme Court

Considered mandatory authority, the federal supreme court decisions are the ultimate authority on the interpretation of the federal constitution with regard to an Article V convention. The federal decisions that directly affect an amendatory convention are few but those that indirectly and potentially affect a convention are more numerous. It is because there is a scarcity of these definitive federal decisions that the state level decisions are included in this excursus. The federal rulings serve as the broad brush strokes in the constitutional picture while the supporting state rulings are the often the fine strokes that fill in the details.

A number of themes are present in the cases presented here. Overwhelmingly, the Eighteenth Amendment has figured in the US Supreme Court's caseload involving Article V. There are very good reasons for emphasis on that particular amendment. The Eighteenth Amendment relieved the States of a sizable portion of its police power and prompted a large expansion of federal government power. Even in its day, this action was recognized as having a transformative effect on American society. The amendment infringed on personal liberty, prompted the creation of national police units, helped to establish crime families, and disturbed the tax structure of the nation and how our government was financed. The people and the States responded with a ceaseless and dogged determination to fight the amendment that provides lessons for today on responding to unpopular legislation. Similarly, the Nineteenth Amendment caused much consternation and resulted in many cases. The change to American social structure was difficult for some to take as women were extended the voting franchise nationwide and the obvious implications that other facets of federal law may also see such an expansion of participation led to resistance. Among the major issues that run repeatedly through the cases are the ability of the people to participate directly in the amendment process through initiatives and referendums, term limits, and defining and refining the limits of the amendment process.

Much of this FAQ material has been published previously by the Wisconsin Grand*Sons of Liberty*.

1.

Board of Liquidation, et al, v. Henry S. McComb, 92 U.S. 531 (1875)[2]

Background: "The decree appealed from in this case was for a perpetual injunction to restrain the Board of Liquidation of the State of Louisiana from using the bonds known as the consolidated bonds of the State, for the liquidation of a certain debt claimed to be due from the State to the Louisiana Levee Company, and from issuing any other State bonds in payment of said pretended debt. Henry S. McComb, a citizen of Delaware, alleges that he is a holder of some of these consolidated bonds, and that the employment of the bonds for the purpose proposed, namely, the payment of the claim of the Levee Company, will be a violation of the pledges given by the act creating the bonds, and will greatly depreciate their value."

Issue: "In a clear case, of course, an unconstitutional enactment will be treated as void, as against the rights of an individual. But there are many constitutional provisions mandatory upon the legislature which cannot be directly enforced, — the duty, for example, when creating a debt, to provide adequate ways and means for its payment. It affects the public generally, but no individual in particular, in such manner as to give him a legal remedy. So the State debt may be increased beyond the prescribed limit, without admitting of judicial redress." The increase in indebtedness will harm not only McComb but all bond holders whether they are citizens of Louisiana or not. The state was invoking a claim of immunity under the Eleventh Amendment.

Court Decision: Written by Justice Joseph Philo Bradley. "The objections to proceeding against State officers by mandamus or injunction are: first, that it is, in effect, proceeding against the State itself; and, secondly, that it interferes with the official discretion vested in the officers. It is conceded that neither of these things can be done. A State, without its consent, cannot be sued by an individual; and a court cannot substitute its own discretion for that of executive officers in matters belonging to the proper jurisdiction of the latter. But it has been well settled, that, when a plain official duty, requiring no exercise of discretion, is to be performed, and performance is refused, any person who will sustain personal injury by such refusal may have a mandamus to

---

[2] https://supreme.justia.com/cases/federal/us/92/531/

compel its performance; and when such duty is threatened to be violated by some positive official act, any person who will sustain personal injury thereby, for which adequate compensation cannot be had at law, may have an injunction to prevent it. In such cases, the writs of mandamus and injunction are somewhat correlative to each other. In either case, if the officer plead the authority of an unconstitutional law for the non-performance or violation of his duty, it will not prevent the issuing of the writ. An unconstitutional law will be treated by the courts as null and void."

Conclusions: The levee funding was upheld as was the injunction against the state.

Applicability: A writ of mandamus may be used to force compliance with a constitutional requirement. Albeit in this instance against a state government.

2.

Albert B. Chandler, Governor of Kentucky, et al. v. James E. Wise, et al., 307 U.S. 474, 59 S. Ct. 992, (1939)[3], *originally 271 Ky. 252, 111 S.W.2d 633, 270 Ky. 1, 108 S.W.2d 1024*

-As *Chandler v. Wise*

Background: This case is considered a companion case to the concurrent and more oft cited *Coleman v. Miller* case. The majority of the people of the State of Kentucky had opposed the proposed Child Labor Amendment because an earlier state legislature in 1926 had originally rejected the proposed amendment. When the General Assembly of the Commonwealth passed the second ratification attempt in January 1937, plaintiffs (residents, taxpayers, voters and citizens) filed suit. After the filing, a restraining order was granted and summons was issued. But the Governor of Kentucky was unaware of the recently filed suit and went ahead and certified the ratification and notified the US Secretary of State. The defendants obtained a demurrer from the Circuit Court but that was reversed by the Appeals Court.[4]

Issue: The plaintiffs sought that the US Supreme Court order the Kentucky Secretary of State to set aside the ratification as it was already

---

[3] https://supreme.justia.com/cases/federal/us/307/474/case.html
[4] Edwin S. Corwin & Mary Louise Ramsey, The Constitutional Law of Constitutional Amendment," *Notre Dame Lawyer* XXVI, no.2 (Winter 1951): 210

being challenged at the time of the formal notification.

Secondarily, the plaintiffs claimed that the time limit for consideration had expired based on the *Dillion v. Gloss* decision of 1921.

Court Decision: 7-2, Written by Chief Justice Charles Evans Hughes. The US Supreme Court voted not to grant the plaintiff's request. They believed that the lower courts had acted correctly based on the *Coleman* decision. The Supreme Court dismissed the suit. Quoting from *Idaho v. Freeman* regarding *Chandler v. Wise*, "[T]he power of a state legislature to ratify cannot be any greater than its alternative, the state convention. Since a convention exhausts its authority by its initial action, whatever that action may be, it would be consistent to view a legislature as having only the same amount of authority."

Conclusions: Consistent with *Coleman*, the Court decided that once the ratification notification was sent, the issue was decided. With that first finding, the second issue of the time limit for ratification was moot.[5] There is a problem here that the decision states that "a convention exhausts its authority by its initial action, whatever that action may be." It would seem to mean that a rejection of a proposed amendment ends the opportunity to revisit the amendment in the future – a situation that was faced in the companion *Coleman* case.

Applicability: Concurrent with *Coleman* so dismissed without consideration.

3.

Rolla W. Coleman, et al. v. Clarence W. Miller, Secretary of the Senate of State of Kansas, et al., 307 U.S. 433 (1939)[6], 59 S. Ct. 972; 83 L. Ed. 1385, originally 146 Kan. 390; 71 P.2d 518.

–As ***Coleman v. Miller***

Background: Similar to the *Chandler* case, Kansas initially rejected the proposed Child Labor Amendment in January 1925 but in a later state legislature, reconsidered the amendment in January 1937 in Senate Concurrent Resolution No. 3. The Kansas Senate split evenly on the matter and the tie vote had to be broken by the Lt. Governor acting in the capacity of presiding officer of the state Senate. The Kansas House

---

[5] Lester B. Orfield & Henry M. Bates, *The Amending of the Federal Constitution* (Ann Arbor: University of Michigan Press, 1942), 19-20
[6] https://supreme.justia.com/cases/federal/us/307/433/

voted in favor of the resolution. Twenty-four members of the Kansas House and Senate brought an action before the Kansas Supreme Court to force the Kansas Secretary of State to change the endorsement from "adopted" to "did not pass." This action would restrict the Governor of Kansas from notifying the US Secretary of State of a Kansas ratification.[7]

Issue: The primary contention was that the Lt. Governor did not possess the authority to vote on the resolution as the Lt. Gov. was a member of the executive branch and a ratification of a federal constitutional amendment is strictly a prerogative of the legislative branch of the state. The second issue was that the deadline had passed for the ratification by the time that the vote had been taken. The third issue was that the prior rejection was conclusive and therefore the Kansas legislature had no business taking up the issue of ratification of the amendment again.[8]

Court Decision: 7-2, Written by Chief Justice Charles Evans Hughes. An amendment will remain pending before the States indefinitely unless Congress stipulates a ratification deadline. The Court equally divided on the role of the Lt. Gov. and therefore was unable to render a decision on that point.[9] "The argument in support of that view is that Article V says nothing of rejection but speaks only of ratification and provides that a proposed amendment shall be valid as part of the Constitution when ratified by three-fourths of the States; that the power to ratify is thus conferred upon the State by the Constitution and, as a ratifying power, persists despite a previous rejection."

With regard to the establishment by the Court of a set period of time for ratification when the Congress has not done so, the Court held that, "But it does not follow that, whenever Congress has not exercised that power, the Court should take upon itself the responsibility of deciding what constitutes a reasonable time and determine accordingly the validity of ratifications." The ruling later continued, "these conditions are appropriate for the consideration of the political departments of the Government. The questions they involve are essentially political and not

---

[7] Homer Clark, "The Supreme Court and the Amending Process," *Virginia Law Review* 39, no.5 (June 1953): 631-6

[8] Kermit L. Hall, ed., *The Oxford Companion to the Supreme Court of the United States* (New York: Oxford University Press, 2d ed., 2005), 190

[9] How a nine justice court split *equally* on a point is something that has perplexed people for three quarters of a century. – See generally, Note, "Sawing a Justice in Half," *Yale Law Review* 48, no. 8 (June 1939)

justiciable."[10]

Conclusions: This case has been considered the most important Article V related case for the last three quarters of a century but it has been called "an aberration" by law professors and constitutional scholars.[11] Dictum in this case **supported the "political question doctrine"** wherein the Supreme Court will not address an issue that the Court sees as of a political nature and not one of a constitutional law nature and is therefore not justiciable. The political question doctrine has been applied erratically. This decision also included the topic of the time limitation for ratification. Also, the Court **disavowed the "staleness" language of the prior *Dillon* decision**. And, once a ratification is made, it cannot be unmade, "It is also premised, in accordance with views expressed by text-writers, that ratification if once given cannot afterwards be rescinded and the amendment rejected, and it is urged that the same effect in the exhaustion of the State's power to act should be ascribed to rejection; that a State can act 'but once, either by convention or through its legislature.'" (Text-writers referring to Jameson, Willoughby and Ames)

Applicability: There are four amendment proposals still considered pending due to the holding of *Coleman*: Congressional Apportionment (1789 from the original Bill of Rights proposal); Titles of Nobility (1810); Corwin (1861);[12] and Child Labor (1924). The ratification of the Twenty-seventh Amendment in 1992 settled conclusively the issue of how long a proposed amendment may remain before the States without a time limit by Congress. It has become **congressional policy to set a time limit of seven years for pending ratification proposals** before the States. Decision issued concurrent with *Chandler v. Wise*.

The political question doctrine has undergone a reevaluation that is still on-going. Later Court decisions modified and narrowed the scope of the doctrine. Only a future challenge on Article V grounds will more fully clarify the extent or limitations of the political question doctrine as it relates to Article V.

---

[10] John R. Vile, *Contemporary Questions Surrounding the Constitutional Amending Process* (Westport, CT: Praeger, 1993), 24-7

[11] Walter Dellinger, "The Legitimacy of Constitutional Change: Rethinking the Amendment Process," *Harvard Law Review* 97 (1983). 389

[12] With respect to the Corwin Amendment proposal, the later ratification of the Thirteenth Amendment in 1865 negates the majority of the Corwin Amendment making it moot.

4. _____

Rebecca McDowell Cook v. Donald James Gralike and Mike Harman, et al., 531 U.S. 510 (2001),[13] 121 S. Ct. 1029; 149 L. Ed. 2d 44

-As *Cook v. Gralike*

Background: Appeal of three earlier lower federal court cases – see *Gralike v. Cook* for details.

Issue: The State of Missouri's new state constitutional amendment forced candidates to publicly declare their position on term limits resulting in compelled – and therefore, controlled - speech. Such action violates the federal constitution's Speech and Debate Clause and Article V.

Court Decision: 9-0, Written by Justice John Paul Stevens. "This evidence falls short of demonstrating that either the people or the States had a right to give legally binding, *i.e.*, non-advisory, instructions to their representatives that the Tenth Amendment reserved, much less that such a right would apply to federal representatives." Continuing, the decision noted that, "Indeed, contrary evidence is provided by the fact that the First Congress rejected a proposal to insert a right of the people "to instruct their representatives" into what would become the First Amendment.[14] The fact that the proposal was made suggests that its proponents thought it necessary, and the fact that it was rejected by a vote of 41-10,[15] suggests that we should give weight to the views of those who opposed the proposal. It was their view that binding instructions would undermine an essential attribute of Congress by eviscerating the deliberative nature of that National Assembly."

Conclusions: Any attempt by a state to regulate political speech is unconstitutional. The amendment is an effort by the State of Missouri to influence and control an election's outcome.

Applicability: A delegate to an amendatory convention cannot be subject to controls by his/her home state as to their political speech in the convention. They **cannot be forced to declare their positions** on the issues prior to the convention and election. However, they may willingly, as a campaign strategy, voice their opinions and positions.

---

[13] https://www.law.cornell.edu/supct/html/99-929.ZO.html
[14] 1 *Annals of Cong.* 732 (1789)
[15] *id.*, at 747

5.
___

George C. Dempsey v. Thomas J. Boynton, United States Attorney for Massachusetts, and Andrew J. Casey, Acting Collector of Internal Revenue for Massachusetts, 253 U.S. 350, 40 Sup. Ct. Rep. 486 (1920)– *A National Prohibition Case*

-as *Dempsey v. Boynton*

Background: Patrick Henry Kelley argued that the Eighteenth Amendment was not "self-executing" and therefore not actually in effect at the time of his arrest for liquor trafficking. The liquor laws of the States remained in effect until Congress passed corresponding enabling legislation.

Issue: Does Congress need to pass additional enabling legislation to make an amendment become effective?

Court Decision: 7-2, Written by Justice Willis Van Devanter. Ruling to be found under the National Prohibition Cases.

Conclusions: **An amendment can be augmented by enabling legislation to "give the amendment teeth"** for enforcement. Once the amendment is ratified, it is fundamental law.

Applicability: The lower court's decision was affirmed. An amendment proposed by an Article V convention will most likely require enabling legislation to carry out the operative effects of the amendment.

6.
___

John J. Dillon v. R. W. Gloss, Deputy Collector of United States Internal Revenue, 256 U.S. 368 (1921)[16], 41 S. Ct. 510, 65 L. Ed. 994

-As *Dillon v. Gloss*

Background: Dillon claimed at the time of his arrest for transporting illegal liquor, that the Eighteenth Amendment had not yet gone into effect and that the time limit of seven years for ratification was not constitutional.[17] He was arrested on 17 January 1920. The last (three) states to ratify did so on 16 January 1919. The Secretary of State certified the amendment on 29 January 1919. The amendment called for the ban

---

[16] https://supreme.justia.com/cases/federal/us/256/368/case.html
[17] John R. Vile, *Essential Supreme Court Decisions, Summaries of Leading Cases in U.S. Constitutional Law* (Lanham, MD: Rowman & Littlefield, 15th ed., 2010), 165-6

on alcohol to take effect one year after the ratification. As Dillon saw it, that day would have been 29 January 1920 – twelve days after his arrest.[18] He sought a writ of habeas corpus.

Issue: Does Congress control the time limit for an amendment proposal? When does an amendment take effect?

Court Decision: 9-0, Written by Justice Willis Van Devanter. Congress may set a time limit at its discretion. Dillon's conviction was upheld. "We do not find anything in the article which suggests that an amendment once proposed is to be open to ratification for all time, or that ratification in some of the states may be separated from that in others by many years and yet be effective. We do find that which strongly suggests the contrary. First, proposal and ratification are not treated as unrelated acts, but as succeeding steps in a single endeavor, the natural inference being that they are not to be widely separated in time." And further, "[A]s a rule the Constitution speaks in general terms, leaving Congress to deal with subsidiary matters of detail as the public interests and changing conditions may require, and article 5 is no exception to the rule."[19] The Court implied that the Necessary and Proper Clause authorizes Congress to set time limits for ratification.[20]

Conclusions: **Ratifications, to be valid, must occur within the time frame that Congress has specified.**[21] This stipulation, called "contemporaneous consensus," however, appears to apply only to those proposed amendments that Congress has made and sent to the States and not to those proposed amendments that originate in an Article V Convention.[22] The day that the last required state ratifies the proposed amendment, that amendment becomes part of the Constitution and takes effect. Also, that Congress has wide discretion and latitude in determining the details and particulars of implementation.

Applicability: The Twenty-seventh Amendment settled that a pending amendment proposal is still viable unless it has within

---

[18] Walter Dellinger, "The Legitimacy of Constitutional Change: Rethinking the Amendment Process," *Harvard Law Review* 97 (1983): 402

[19] Russell Caplan, *Constitutional Brinkmanship, Amending the Constitution by National Convention* (New York: Oxford University Press, 1988), 111

[20] Michael A. Almond, "Amendment by Convention: Our Next Constitutional Crisis?," *North Carolina Law Review* 53 (1975): 511-2.

[21] Lester B. Orfield & Henry M. Bates, *The Amending of the Federal Constitution* (Ann Arbor: University of Michigan Press, 1942), 17

[22] Robert G. Natelson, *Amending the Constitution by Convention: Practical Guidance for Citizens and Policymakers* (Part 3 of 3), Goldwater Institute Report No. 11-02, (22 Feb 2011): 19

the wording or the proposal resolution a time limit. All amendment proposals since have included a time limit for ratification, In one instance, for the proposed Equal Rights Amendment, the time limit was extended, itself a constitutional issue for the legitimacy of the extension. There is still an academic question as to whether Article V implies a time limit.[23]

7.

George C. Dodge v. John M. Woolsey, 59 U.S. (18 How.) 331 (1855)[24]
-As *Dodge v. Woolsey*

Background: John W. Woolsey was a resident of Connecticut that invested in an Ohio bank. That bank, through its state charter, paid 6% of profits to the State of Ohio as a tax. A new state constitution substantially increased the taxes owed. Dodge believed, as did the bank's directors, that the new tax provision did not apply to the bank as the charter was a contract with the state. When the bank's directors declined to file suit, Dodge did so as an individual investor.[25]

Issue: Was the Contracts Clause of the federal constitution violated by the application of the taxing provisions of the new 1852 Ohio state constitution?

Court Decision: 6-3, Written by Justice James Moore Wayne. The new taxing provision and law conflicted with the US Constitution. Wayne wrote that the power to amend the Constitution is actuated by agents and not the people or the States, therefore the amending power is a delegated power and is then constitutionally limited.[26]

Conclusions: In an expository section, Justice Wayne holds forth at great length on the nature and construction of the federal government. The Court determined that the amendment process was an act not by the people, who are represented by the delegates and/or commissioners or by the Congress depending on the mode of consideration and passage.[27]

---

[23] Michael Stokes Paulsen, "A General Theory of Article V: The Constitutional Lessons of the Twenty-Seventh Amendment," *Yale Law Journal* 103, no.3 (Dec.1993), generally
[24] https://supreme.justia.com/cases/federal/us/59/331/
[25] Kermit L. Hall, ed., *The Oxford Companion to the Supreme Court of the United States* (New York: Oxford University Press, 2d ed., 2005), 268
[26] Edwin S. Corwin & Mary Louise Ramsey, The Constitutional Law of Constitutional Amendment," *Notre Dame Lawyer* XXVI, no.2 (Winter 1951): 189
[27] Found at p.348

Dodge is often cited as an early proof of the inviolable validity of state applications as **no branch is empowered to overrule the Constitution.** The usual interpretation of the ruling is that **the States and/or the people cannot dictate the amendments** as that power rests in the hands of either Congress or the convention delegates; the electorate has no direct role in the amending process. Therefore, **a state application is valid solely because it was made by the state.**[28]

Applicability: More as an examination of the nature of government than a direct impact on the amendment process.

8.

Terry Druggan v. Palmer E. Anderson, U.S. Marshal, et al., 269 U.S. 36, 46 S. Ct. 14, 70 L. Ed. 151 (1925)[29]

-As ***Druggan v. Anderson***

Background: Petitioner, a former aide to Al Capone and one of the leaders of the Valley Gang, was caught transporting liquor in violation of the Prohibition Act and made the claim that the Eighteenth Amendment had not yet gone into effect.

Issue: When exactly did a ratified amendment go into effect?

Court Decision: Written by Justice Oliver Wendell Holmes. The amendment goes into effect immediately upon ratification by the state which makes three-quarters of the states.

Conclusions: "It is not correct to say that the Amendment did not exist until its prohibition went into effect -- in other words, that there was no Amendment until January 16, 1920, although one had been ratified a year before. The moment that the Amendment was ratified, it became effective as a law." "Congress was held to have power to legislate in anticipation of enforcement of the amendment and was not obliged to wait until the year had expired."[30]

Applicability: Concurs with *Dillon v. Gloss.*

---

[28] James Madison, *The Federalist*, No. 85.
[29] https://supreme.justia.com/cases/federal/us/269/36/case.html
[30] Michael A. Almond, "Amendment By Convention: Our Next Constitutional Crisis?," *North Carolina Law Review* 53 (1975): 517, n.143. Reprinted with permission of the North Carolina Law Review.

9.

Charles S. Fairchild v. Charles Evans Hughes, Secretary of State,
258 U.S. 126 (1922)[31]

-As *Fairchild v. Hughes*

Background: A private citizen sued to prevent proclamation of the ratification of the Nineteenth Amendment. He claimed that the states with male only voting privilege would be injured by the amendment. But the Secretary has declared that he is without power to examine into the validity of alleged acts of ratification, and that, upon receiving from one additional state the customary certificate, he will issue a proclamation declaring that the Suffrage Amendment has been adopted. Furthermore, 'a force bill' has been introduced in the Senate, which provides for a fine and imprisonment for any person who refuses to allow women to vote, and, if the bill is enacted, the Attorney General will be required to enforce its provisions.

Issue: Does a proposed amendment have a test for validity?

Court Decision: 9-0, Written by Justice Louis Dembitz Brandeis. Fairchild lacked standing due to the Case or Controversy Clause to sue. Since Fairchild lived in a state that already allowed women to vote, he was in no danger of being harmed.

Conclusions: "This case may not be heard under Article III, Section 2 of the Constitution, which allows the courts to hear a claim in equity. The plaintiff fails to present any claims that courts can evaluate through their regular proceedings, established by law or custom to protect rights and punish wrongs. No concrete harm has been shown, since the allegedly wrongful acts of the Secretary of State and the Attorney General are merely speculative at this stage. Citizens do not have a right to bring a claim to challenge the validity of statutes or constitutional amendments that have not yet been adopted. Standing is not conferred by a general right to ensure that the government lawfully administers its laws."

Applicability: The decision overturned prior rulings that private citizens had the standing to sue to preserve a public right. There is no standing for an individual bringing a generalized grievance based on taxpayer status, except for some situations involving the Establishment

---

[31] https://supreme.justia.com/cases/federal/us/258/126/

Clause.[32] An individual seeking to prevent an amendatory convention or the forwarding for ratification of a proposed amendment generated by an amendatory convention would not have standing to sue.

10.

James Rudolph Garfield, Secretary of the Interior v. United States, ex rel. John E. Goldsby, 211 U.S. 249 (1908)[33]
 -As *Garfield v. Goldsby*

Background: "This action was brought in the Supreme Court of the District of Columbia for a writ of mandamus against the Secretary of the Interior, in his official capacity, to require him to erase certain marks and notations theretofore made by his predecessor in office upon the rolls, striking therefrom the name of the relator, Goldsby, as an approved member of the Chickasaw Nation, and to restore him to enrollment as a member of the nation.

Goldsby, in his petition, claimed that he was a recognized citizen of the Chickasaw Nation, and entitled to an equal, undivided interest in the lands of the Choctaw and Chickasaw Nations; that he was an owner of an allotment of land which had been made to him as hereinafter stated, and that he was entitled to an equal, undivided, distributive share of the funds and other lands of the nation."

Issue: While acts of public officials which require the exercise of discretion may not be subject to review in the courts, if such acts are purely ministerial or are undertaken without authority, the courts have jurisdiction, and mandamus is the proper remedy.

Court Decision: Written by Justice William Rufus Day. "Since *Marbury v. Madison*, 1 Cranch 137, it has been held that there is a distinction between those acts which require the exercise of discretion or judgment and those which are purely ministerial, or are undertaken entirely without authority, which may become the subject of review in the courts."

Conclusions: "But, as has been affirmed by this Court in former decisions, there is no place in our constitutional system for the exercise of

---

[32] Lester B. Orfield & Henry M. Bates, *The Amending of the Federal Constitution* (Ann Arbor: University of Michigan Press, 1942), 31
[33] https://supreme.justia.com/cases/federal/us/211/249/case.html

arbitrary power, and if the Secretary has exceeded the authority conferred upon him by law, then there is power in the courts to restore the status of the parties aggrieved by such unwarranted action." Goldsby received his certificate of tribal membership and the right to keep his land.

Applicability: As Article V is already considered a "purely ministerial function" so the ability to argue for a mandamus action of an injunction is potentially implied here. This case, like all others, involved a federal official and not a suit against Congress.

11.

George S. Hawke v. Harvey C. Smith, Secretary of State of Ohio,
(I) 253 U.S. 221 (1920), 40 S. Ct. 495, 64 L. Ed. 87134

-As *Hawke v. Smith (I)*

Background: A 1918 amendment to the Ohio state constitution called for a public referendum for the approval of any amendment to the federal constitution. George S. Hawke sought to prevent the Ohio Secretary of State from expending public monies on a referendum for the ratification of the Eighteenth Amendment. The Ohio state legislature had successfully ratified the Eighteenth Amendment in January 1919.[35]

Issue: Does Article V permit only state legislatures or state ratification conventions to approve a proposed amendment? What does Article V refer to when using the term "legislature?"

Court Decision: 9-0, Written by Justice William Rufus Day. A legislature is the duly organized deliberative body of the representatives of the people and that a legislature and a state ratification convention are the sole bodies authorized to approve a proposed federal constitutional amendment. The choice of the method of ratification is the singular domain of Congress. No referendum is permissible.

Conclusions: Article V is a bestowal of power on the state legislature for ratification and for the selection of delegates. **The legislative ratification method cannot be replaced by public referendum. No legislature or convention itself has the power to alter**

---

[34] https://supreme.justia.com/cases/federal/us/253/221/case.html
[35] John R. Vile, *Essential Supreme Court Decisions, Summaries of Leading Cases in U.S. Constitutional Law* (Lanham, MD: Rowman & Littlefield, 15th ed., 2010), 164-5

the ratification procedure – that is fixed by Article V.[36] The meaning of the words and terms in the Constitution are fixed at the meaning understood at the time of the drafting of the Constitution and the respective amendments. The function of a state legislature or convention in ratifying a proposed amendment is a federal function at the time of its execution.

Applicability: The decision remains in effect and has been reiterated several times. **A public referendum may not replace, ratify or revise any portion of the federal Constitution.** To do so, requires that Article V itself be amended through the method laid out in Article V.

12.

George S. Hawke v. Harvey C. Smith, Secretary of State of Ohio, (II) 253 U.S. 231 (1920)[37]
-As *Hawke v. Smith (II)*

Background: This case is nearly identical to Hawke v. Smith (I) except for the concerned amendment is the Nineteenth in lieu of the Eighteenth. A 1918 amendment to the Ohio state constitution called for a public referendum for the approval of any amendment to the federal constitution. George S. Hawke sought to prevent the Ohio Secretary of State from expending public monies on a referendum for the ratification of the Nineteenth Amendment.

Issue: Does Article V permit only state legislatures or state ratification conventions to approve a proposed amendment? What does Article V refer to when using the term "legislature?"

Court Decision: 9-0, Written by Justice William Rufus Day. A legislature is the duly organized deliberative body of the representatives of the people and that a legislature and a state ratification convention are the sole bodies authorized to approve a proposed federal constitutional amendment. The choice of the method of ratification is the singular domain of Congress. No referendum is permissible.

Conclusions: Article V is a bestowal of power on the state legislature for ratification and for the selection of delegates. **The**

---

[36] Lester B. Orfield & Henry M. Bates, *The Amending of the Federal Constitution* (Ann Arbor: University of Michigan Press, 1942), 17
[37] https://supreme.justia.com/cases/federal/us/253/231/case.html

legislative ratification method cannot be replaced by public referendum. No legislature or convention itself has the power to alter the ratification procedure – that is fixed by Article V. The meaning of the words and terms in the Constitution are fixed at the meaning understood at the time of the drafting of the Constitution and the respective amendments. The function of a state legislature or convention in ratifying a proposed amendment is a federal function at the time of its execution.

Applicability: The decision remains in effect and has been reiterated several times.

13.

Levi Hollingsworth, et al. v. Virginia, 3 U.S. (3 Dall.) 378, 1 L. Ed. 344, (1798)[38]

-As ***Hollingsworth v. Virginia***

Background: Pennsylvanian Levi Hollingsworth bought shares in the Indiana Company, a land speculation company that was contesting with the State of Virginia for land in what is now West Virginia. He became a party to a lawsuit, as a non-Virginia resident, to sue the State of Virginia over the land in question. The Eleventh Amendment prohibited the suing of state without its permission. The Eleventh Amendment was passed and sent to the States for ratification without presentment to President Washington for his signature per Article I, § 7.[39]

Issue: The Eleventh Amendment was not properly ratified and is therefore not in effect without the approbation of the President. The grammatical tense of the words "commenced or prosecuted" was considered problematic; they should read "commenced and prosecuted."

Court Decision: 6-0, Written by Justice Samuel Chase. "The negative of the President applies only to the ordinary cases of legislation. He has nothing to do with the proposition, or adoption, of amendments to the Constitution."

Conclusions: Since the Constitution does not specify a role for the executive in the amendment process, the Presentment Clause does not

---

[38] http://caselaw.findlaw.com/us-supreme-court/3/378.html
[39] John R. Vile, *Essential Supreme Court Decisions, Summaries of Leading Cases in U.S. Constitutional Law* (Lanham, MD: Rowman & Littlefield, 15th ed., 2010), 162-3

apply. **No signature of the President is required for a constitutional amendment to be valid and complete.** The precedent was established with the passage and ratification of the Bill of Rights in 1791.[40]

Applicability: Still in effect.

Note: This issue has been raised in many state level cases with the same result each time. See: *Green v. Weller* 32 Miss. 50; *Koehler v. Hill* 60 Ia. 543; *Hatch v. Stoneman*, 66 Cal. 632, 6 Pac. 734; *Warfield v. Vandiver* 101 Md. 78; *In re Senate File 31*, 25 Neb. 864, 41 N.W. 981; *Oakland Paving Co. v. Hilton* 69 Cal. 514; *State ex rel. Morris v. Mason* 43 La. Ann. 590; *Commonwealth ex rel. Atty. Gen. v. Griest* 196 Pa. St. 396; *State v. Timme* 54 Wis. 333; *State v. Tuffly* 19 Nev. 391; *Edwards v. LeSueur* 132 Mo. 443; *People v. Sours* 31 Colo. 378; *Bott v. Secretary of State* 62 N.J.L 121

14.

Vital Jarrolt v. Town of Moberly, 103 U.S. 580, 26 L. Ed. 492, (1880)[41] – As *Jarrolt v. Moberly*

Background: The town of Moberly, Missouri decided to issue bonds to buy land for donation to a railroad in exchange for the railroad locating their repair facility in the town. A non-Missouri resident owned some of the bonds and brought suit to be paid interest on the bonds.

Issue: The bond scheme ran afoul of the Missouri state constitution's prohibition on a municipality taking on indebtedness for a railroad or private corporation.

Court Decision: Written by Justice Stephen Johnson Field. The Court held that the statute and the subsequent bonding scheme were unconstitutional.

Conclusions: "A constitutional provision should not be construed so as to defeat its evident purpose, but rather so as to give it effective operation and suppress the mischief at which it was aimed." **By extension: Any attempt to suppress a state convention application due to its timeliness, age, subject matter, or any other reason is in violation**

---

[40] Robert G. Natelson, *Learning from Experience: How the States Used Article V Applications in America's First Century* (Part 2 of 3), Goldwater Institute Report No. 11-02, (4 Nov 2010), 7
[41] https://supreme.justia.com/cases/federal/us/103/580/

of Article V.

Applicability: Remains in effect. The purpose of an amendatory convention application cannot be misconstrued or negated.

15.
___

Amos Kendall, United States Postmaster v. United States ex Rel. William B. Stokes 37 U.S. (12 Pet.) 524 (1838)[42]
-As *Kendall v. US*

Background: S & S had a contract to carry mail for the US Post Office under William T. Barry as Postmaster General. Certain credits and allowances were made in the contract to cover expenses. The new Postmaster General, Amos Kendall, disallowed the credits and allowances. S & S sought reimbursement by submitting a memorial to Congress which was passed on 2 July 1836 and the Treasury was ordered to pay S & S. The postmaster paid only about three-quarters of the amount owed. S & S applied for a writ of mandamus which was granted. The postmaster countered that the suit was an infringement on the executive branch and did not have to comply.

Issue: Can a part of the federal government, specifically the executive branch, be compelled by a writ of mandamus to perform a "purely ministerial duty"?

Court Decision: Written by Justice Smith Thompson. The Court held that the mandamus was the correct response. "The act required by the law to be done by the Postmaster General is simply to credit S. & S. with the full amount of the award of the Solicitor of the Treasury. This is a precise, definite act, purely ministerial, and about which the Postmaster General has no discretion whatever." And continued "There is no room for the exercise of discretion, official or otherwise. All that is shut out by the direct and positive command of the law, and the act required to be done is in every just sense a mere ministerial act." The Court found that the remedy was appropriate, "The right claimed is just and established by positive law, and the duty required to be performed is clear and specific, and there is no other adequate remedy." The Court cited previous instances of such action: "The result of the cases of *McIntire v. Wood* and *McCluny v. Silliman* clearly is that the authority to issue the

___
[42] https://supreme.justia.com/cases/federal/us/37/524/case.html

writ of mandamus to an officer of the United States commanding him to perform a specific act required by a law of the United States is within the scope of the judicial powers of the United States under the Constitution, but that the whole of that power has not been communicated by law to the circuit courts of the United States in the several states. It is a dormant power, not yet called into action and vested in those courts. And there is nothing growing out of the official character of a party that will exempt him from this writ if the act to be performed is merely ministerial."

Conclusions: "But the obvious inference from the case of *McIntire v. Wood* is that under the Constitution, **the power to issue a mandamus to an executive officer of the United States may be vested in the inferior courts of the United States, and that it is the appropriate writ, and proper to be employed, agreeably to the principles and usages of law, to compel the performance of a ministerial act, necessary to the completion of an individual right arising under the laws of the United States.** And the case now before the Court is precisely one of that description. And if the Circuit Court of this District has the power to issue it, all objection arising either from the character of the party, as an officer in the Executive Department of the government, or from the nature of the act commanded to be done, must be abandoned." The majority opinion includes, "The result of these cases, then, clearly is that the authority to issue the writ of mandamus to an officer of the United States commanding him to perform a specific act required by a law of the United States is within the scope of the judicial powers of the United States under the Constitution." And finally, "**there is nothing growing out of the official character of the party that will exempt him from this writ if the act to be performed is purely ministerial.**" The "purely ministerial" nature of the action requested is not "discretionary" making the action not political.

Applicability: An argument can made based on the history of *Kendall* and its predecessors that a writ of mandamus may be served on a co-equal branch of the federal government, specifically a federal official, to compel a "purely ministerial duty."

16.
___

Kentucky Distilleries & Warehouse Company v. W. V. Gregory, District Attorney for the United States for the Western District of Kentucky, and Elwood Hamilton, Collector of Internal Revenue for the Collection District of Kentucky
 – A *National Prohibition Case as Kentucky Distilleries & Warehouse Co. v. Gregory*

 Background: Levy Mayer and William M. Bullitt argued that the Eighteenth Amendment amounted to an invasion of the sovereignty of the States under the Ninth and Tenth Amendments. Additionally, the infringement on the sovereignty of the States must be consented to by ALL of the states.

 Issue: The Eighteenth Amendment was not properly proposed or voted on by the Congress as the number of votes cast in favor was less than the prescribed two-thirds of each chamber. The use of a referendum was argued for in twelve states.

 Court Decision: 7-2, Written by Justice Willis Van Devanter. The Court held that the decree refusing an injunction was affirmed.

 Conclusions: The Eighteenth Amendment had delegated formerly reserved police powers to the national government by the people. That sovereignty previously held by the States and the people was now given to the federal government.

 Applicability: The lower court's decision was affirmed.

17.
___

Isabel Kimble, Bruce Blackadar, Mary Frazzini, Theodore Oleson, Jr., and Majorie da Costa Eastman v. William D. Swackhamer, Secretary of State of the State of Nevada, and Legislative Commission of the State of Nevada, 439 U.S. 1385, *appeal dismissed* 439 U.S. 1041 (1978), 94 Nev. 600, 584 P.2d 16143
 -As *Kimble v. Swackhamer*

 Background: The Nevada Supreme Court considered a ballot initiative advising the state legislature whether to ratify the Equal Rights Amendment. The court distinguished *Hawke* v. *Smith, supra,* 253 U.S. 221, and *Leser v. Garnett, infra,* 258 U.S. 130 on the ground that the proposal "does not concern a binding referendum, nor does it impose a limitation upon the legislature.... [T]he legislature may vote for or against ratification, or refrain from voting on ratification at all, without regard to the advisory vote.

Issue: "At issue is the constitutionality of chapter 174, 1977 Nev. Stats., which requires the submission of an advisory question to the registered voters of this state on the ratification of the proposed amendment to the Constitution of the United States commonly known as the Equal Rights Amendment."

Court Decision: Written by Chief Justice William Hubbs Rehnquist; 4-1, Nevada Supreme Court decision written by Justice Gordon R. Thompson. When opponents of the Nevada initiative sought a stay from the United States Supreme Court, Justice Rehnquist, sitting as circuit justice, denied the stay with the following order: "Appellants' ... contention ... is in my opinion not substantial because of the nonbinding character of the referendum.... Under these circumstances ... reliance [on] ... *Leser* v. *Garnett* ... and *Hawke* v. *Smith* ... is obviously misplaced.... I can see no constitutional obstacle to a nonbinding advisory referendum of this sort."

Conclusions: Held that **any public referendum which was advisory only and could not dictate to the legislature was permissible**. (See also *AFL-CIO v. March Fong Eu*.)

Applicability: A referendum that determines a consensus on a public issue and then dictates to the convention delegates is not permissible unless the intent is advisory only.

18.
___

Oscar Leser, et al v. J. Mercer Garnett, et al, 258 U.S. 130 (1922),[43] 42 S. Ct. 217, 66 L. Ed. 505

-As ***Leser v. Garnett***

Background: Cecelia Streett Waters and Mary D. Randolph registered to vote in Baltimore in October 1920. Maryland Judge Oscar Leser and others objected since the Nineteenth Amendment had not been ratified by the State of Maryland and the Maryland state constitution did not extend the voting franchise to women. Leser brought suit to prevent women from voting and to stop ratification of the

___
[43] https://supreme.justia.com/cases/federal/us/258/130/case.html

Nineteenth Amendment by Maryland.

Issue: The Nineteenth Amendment is argued to be unconstitutional as no provision of this type was intended by the Framers. Such an amendment would "destroy the political autonomy of Maryland" by drastically changing the composition of the electorate. Several of the ratifying states (Missouri, Tennessee, West Virginia, Texas and Rhode Island) had constitutional provisions that did not permit women to vote making those states unqualified to ratify. Tennessee and West Virginia did not follow their respective ratification procedures making their ratifications flawed and void. The Nineteenth Amendment was patterned after the Fifteenth which opponents claimed was not officially ratified.

Court Decision: 9-0, Written by Justice Louis Dembitz Brandeis. He wrote,

> "[T]he function of a state Legislature in ratifying a proposed amendment to the federal Constitution, like the function of Congress in proposing the amendment, is a **federal function** derived from the federal Constitution; and it transcends any limitation sought to be imposed by the people of a state."

The Supreme Court held that the ratification of the Fifteenth Amendment was no longer open to question.[44] This was addressed in relation to the validity of the Nineteenth Amendment which was then equally valid. Since states were operating in a federal function when ratifying, their state provisions are immaterial to the process. Connecticut and Vermont's ratifications offset the questioned ratifications of Tennessee and West Virginia making the claim moot. Also, once the US Secretary of State accepted the Tennessee and West Virginia ratifications, those became valid and the matter became non-justiciable.[45] The Court affirmed the ratification and the right of women to vote.

Conclusions: Additionally, **the state legislature's discretion could not be supplanted by the rules imposed by a third party.** When a convention acts under Article V, it performs a **"federal function"** and this transcends any state limitations.

Applicability: The standard for ratification acceptance was

---

[44] Mary Margaret Penrose, "Conventional Wisdom: Acknowledging Uncertainty In The Unknown," *Tennessee Law Review* 78 (2011): 801

[45] Lester B. Orfield & Henry M. Bates, *The Amending of the Federal Constitution* (Ann Arbor: University of Michigan Press, 1942), 18

expanded and clarified and remains in effect.

19.

Charles L. Maxwell v. George N. Dow 176 U.S. 581, 20 Sup. Ct. Rep. 448, 44 L. Ed. 597 (1900)[46]
-As *Maxwell v. Dow*

Background: Maxwell was tried and convicted of burglary in Utah in 1898. The prosecutor used Utah's alternative to a grand jury, called "information," to bring the charges against Maxwell. Also, the jury had only eight jurors instead of the usual twelve.

Issue: Maxwell claimed that his Fourteenth Amendment rights to Due Process, and specifically the Privileges and Immunities Clause, were violated.

Court Decision: 8-1, Written by Justice Rufus Wheeler Peckham. The Court cited the Slaughter-House Cases as precedent and determined that Maxwell's rights under the Bill of Rights were not violated. The incorporation doctrine was expounded upon in the majority opinion and in the lone dissenting opinion.

Conclusions: "The Constitutions of the United States may be altered only by constitutional amendments duly submitted to and ratified by three-fourths of the states. Any attempt to revise or adopt a new constitution in any other manner than the one provided in the existing instrument is almost invariably treated as extra-constitutional and revolutionary."

Applicability: The Constitution cannot be replaced by an Article V amendatory convention.

20.

Missouri Pacific Railway Company v. State of Kansas, 248 U.S. 276 (1919)[47]
-As *Missouri Pacific Railway v. Kansas*

Background: The railroad sought to avoid penalties for transporting

---

[46] https://supreme.justia.com/cases/federal/us/176/581/case.html
[47] https://supreme.justia.com/cases/federal/us/248/276/case.html

intoxicating liquors into Kansas as proscribed by the Webb-Kenyon Act of 1913.

Issue: The railroad claimed that the Eighteenth Amendment was not constitutionally enacted as there was an insufficient quorum for voting on a constitutional amendment. They contended that the two-thirds requirement of both houses meant that all members of both chambers must be present and voting, not that a sufficient quorum is two-thirds of the members present. In this instance, the Webb-Kenyon bill had been originally vetoed by the President and his veto was overturned by a two-thirds vote of both chambers according to the constitutionally dictated provision.

Court Decision: Written by Chief Justice Edward Douglass White. The Court cited the journal of the First Congress with regard to the adoption by the Senate of the House's resolution for the Bill of Rights, stating, "Resolved: That the Senate do concur in the resolve of the House of Representatives on 'articles to be proposed to the Legislatures of the states as amendments to the Constitution of the United States,' with amendments; two-thirds of the Senators present concurring therein.' 1st Cong. (1st Sess.) September 9, 1789, Senate Journal, 77." Thereby, the precedent was set that **a two-thirds majority of the quorum of the members present will suffice to pass a constitutional amendment.**

Conclusions: A quorum according to the individual House or Senate rules is enough to vote on a constitutional amendment. Not all members need to be present and voting.

Applicability: The case is cited in one of the National Prohibition Cases as grounds for accepting the Eighteenth Amendment.

21.

Montanans for A Balanced Federal Budget Committee and Jim Waltermire, Secretary of State of Montana v. Steve Harper et al., 469 U.S. 1301, (105 S. Ct. 13, 83 L. Ed.2d 1) (1984)[48]

-As *Montanans for A Balanced Budget v. Waltermire*

Background: Similar to *Uhler*. Petitioners asked the SCOTUS to override the Montana Supreme Court's prohibition on the placement of a ballot initiative to compel the Montana Legislature to submit

---

[48] https://supreme.justia.com/cases/federal/us/469/1301/case.html

an application to Congress for a federal amendatory convention for a balanced budget amendment.

Issue: Whether a ballot initiative may be used to compel a state legislature to petition for an amendatory convention on behalf of the people.

Court Decision: Written By Chief Justice William Hubbs Rehnquist. "In addition to holding the initiative unconstitutional on its face, in violation of Article V, the Montana Supreme Court held it to be "independently and separately facially invalid under the Montana Constitution." The Montana Court's *per curiam* order stated that an opinion would follow—an opinion which apparently has not yet been issued—but the order is sufficient to indicate an adequate and independent state law ground for the decision. I am not persuaded by petitioners' attempt to distinguish *Uhler v. American Federation of Labor-Congress of Industrial Organizations*. The Montana Supreme Court has rested its decision on the Montana Constitution, and it is the final authority as to the meaning of that instrument. Accordingly, for the same reasons given in *Uhler*, the application for a stay is denied."

Conclusions: As held in other cases contemporary to this one, the ballot initiative was held to be in violation of Article V and not permissible.

Applicability: Remains in effect.

22.

National Prohibition Cases, 253 U.S. 350, 40 S. Ct. 486, 64 L. Ed. 946 (1920)[49]

Background: Several cases were brought in challenge to the validity of the Eighteenth Amendment regarding prohibition of alcohol consumption and production. The SCOTUS consolidated those that were similar. A number of issues relating to the amendment process and amendment validity were raised and dealt with accordingly and also with the constitutionality of the enabling Volstead Act. In each case, the plaintiff sought relief in the form of an injunction to prevent execution of the law. The consolidated cases, defined separately in this work, include:

- State of Rhode Island v. A. Mitchell Palmer, Attorney General,

---

[49] https://supreme.justia.com/cases/federal/us/253/350/

and Daniel C. Roper, Commissioner of Internal Revenue

- State of New Jersey v. A. Mitchell Palmer, Attorney General, and Daniel C. Roper, Commissioner of Internal Revenue
- George C. Dempsey v. Thomas J. Boynton, United States Attorney for Massachusetts, and Andrew J. Casey, Acting Collector of Internal Revenue for Massachusetts
- Kentucky Distilleries & Warehouse Company v. W. V. Gregory, District Attorney for the United States for the Western District of Kentucky, and Elwood Hamilton, Collector of Internal Revenue for the Collection District of Kentucky
- Christian Feigenspan, a corporation v. Joseph L. Bodine, United States Attorney for the District of New Jersey, and Charles V. Dufey, Collector of Internal Revenue of the Fifth District of New Jersey, (D.C. N.J. 1920) 264 F. 186
- Hiram A. Sawyer, as United States Attorney for the Eastern District of Wisconsin, Burt Williams, as Collector of Internal Revenue of the Second District of Wisconsin, and Thomas A. Delaney, as Federal Prohibition Enforcement Director for Wisconsin v. Manitowoc Products Company
- St. Louis Brewing Association, a corporation v. George H. Moore, Collector of Internal Revenue of the First District of Missouri, Walter L. Hensley, United States Attorney for the Eastern District of Missouri, and Frank L. Diggs, Prohibition Agent for the First Internal Revenue District of Missouri

Issue:

- That the amendment process does not extend to "the manufacture, sale, transportation, importation and exportation of intoxicating liquors for beverage purposes."
- That the Congress provide evidence of its determination that a proposed amendment is necessary.
- That the entire Congress, not just a sufficient quorum for conducting business, be present to vote on a proposed amendment.

Court Decision: 7-2, Written by Justice Willis Van Devanter. "The adoption by both houses of Congress, each by a two-thirds vote, of a joint resolution proposing an amendment to the Constitution sufficiently shows that the proposal was deemed necessary by all who voted for it. An express declaration that they regarded it as necessary is not essential." "The two-thirds vote in each house which is required in proposing an amendment is a vote of two-thirds of the members present -- assuming the presence of a quorum -- and not a vote of two-thirds of the entire membership, present and absent. *Id. Missouri Pacific Ry. Co. v. Kansas*, 248 U.S.276" It is non-essential for Congress to issue an accompanying declaration that a proposed amendment is necessary.

Specifically that:

"1. The adoption by both houses of Congress, each by a two-thirds vote, of a joint resolution proposing an amendment to the Constitution sufficiently shows that the proposal was deemed necessary by all who voted for it. An express declaration that they regarded it as necessary is not essential. None of the resolutions whereby prior amendments were proposed contained such a declaration.

2. The two-thirds vote in each house which is required in proposing an amendment is a vote of two-thirds of the members present-assuming the presence of a quorum-and not a vote of two-thirds of the entire membership, present and absent. *Missouri Pacific Ry. Co. v. Kansas*, 248 U.S. 276 39 Sup. Ct. 93, 2 A. L. R. 1589

3. The referendum provisions of state Constitutions and statutes cannot be applied, consistently with the Constitution of the United States, in the ratification or rejection of amendments to it. *Hawke v. Smith*, 253 U.S. 221 40 Sup. Ct. 495, 64 L. Ed. --, decided June 1, 1920.

4. The prohibition of the manufacture, sale, transportation, importation and exportation of intoxicating liquors for beverage purposes, as embodied in the Eighteenth Amendment, is within the power to amend reserved by article 5 of the Constitution.

5. That amendment, by lawful proposal and ratification, has become a part of the Constitution, and must be respected and given effect the same as other provisions of that instrument.

6. The first section of the amendment-the one embodying the prohibition-is operative throughout the entire territorial limits of the United States, binds all legislative bodies, courts, public officers and individuals within those limits, and of its own force invalidates every [253 U.S. 350, 387] legislative act, whether by Congress, by a state Legislature, or by a territorial assembly, which authorizes or sanctions

what the section prohibits.

7. The second section of the amendment-the one declaring 'The Congress and the several states shall have concurrent power to enforce this article by appropriate legislation'-does not enable Congress or the several states to defeat or thwart the prohibition, but only to enforce it by appropriate means.

8. The words 'concurrent power,' in that section, do not mean joint power, or require that legislation thereunder by Congress, to be effective, shall be approved or sanctioned by the several states or any of them; nor do they mean that the power to enforce is divided between Congress and the several states along the lines which separate or distinguish foreign and interstate commerce from intrastate affairs.

9. The power confided to Congress by that section, while not exclusive, is territorially coextensive with the prohibition of the first section, embraces manufacture and other intrastate transactions as well as importation, exportation and interstate traffic, and is in no wise dependent on or affected by action or inaction on the part of the several states or any of them.

10. That power may be exerted against the disposal for beverage purposes of liquors manufactured before the amendment became effective just as it may be against subsequent manufacture for those purposes. In either case it is a constitutional mandate or prohibition that is being enforced.

11. While recognizing that there are limits beyond which Congress cannot go in treating beverages as within its power of enforcement, we think those limits are not transcended by the provision of the Volstead Act (title 2, 1), wherein liquors containing as much as one-half of 1 percent of alcohol by volume and fit for use for beverage [253 U.S. 350, 388] purposes are treated as within that power. *Jacob Ruppert v. Caffey*, 251 U.S. 264, 40 Sup. Ct. 141, 64 L. Ed. "

<u>Conclusions:</u> **Congress is empowered to set the threshold of a quorum for passage of an amendment within the houses of Congress**. This ruling covered seven cases lumped together and all involved the Eighteenth Amendment and the Volstead Act. Also, the Court ruled that referendum provisions of state constitutions and statutes do not apply in

the ratification and rejection of proposed amendments.[50]

Applicability: The consistent use of a two-thirds supermajority lends to the argument that an amendatory convention should also use a two-thirds supermajority for the adoption of a proposed amendment that is recommended to Congress for promulgation to the States.

23.

John Willock Noble, Secretary of the Interior v. Union River Logging Railroad Co., 147 U.S. 165 (1893)[51]
-As *Noble v. Union River Logging Railroad*

Background: "This case involves not only the power of this court to enjoin the Head of a Department, but the power of a Secretary of the Interior to annul the action of his predecessor, when such action operates to give effect to a grant of public lands to a railroad corporation."

Issue: Do the patents for right of way lands create an obligation to the relator? Can a writ of mandamus be used to compel performance?

Court Decision: Written by Justice Henry Billings Brown. "With regard to the judicial power in cases of this kind, it was held by this court as early as 1803, in the great case of *Marbury v. Madison, 1 Cranch, 137,* that there was a distinction between acts involving the exercise of judgment or discretion and those which are purely ministerial; that, with respect to the former, there exists, and can exist, no power to control the executive discretion, however erroneous its exercise may seem to have been, but with respect to ministerial duties, an act or refusal to act is, or may become, the subject of review by the courts." It is interesting that this is so similar to the wording in *Garfield v. Goldsby*.

Conclusions: "It was held that a *mandamus* to the Secretary of the Interior to deliver the patent to the relator should be granted." Significant as the first case to give a guarantee of performance protection to corporations.

Applicability: This is another example of a public or civil servant being ordered to comply with performance of a ministerial duty.

---

[50] Lester B. Orfield & Henry M. Bates, *The Amending of the Federal Constitution* (Ann Arbor: University of Michigan Press, 1942), 17
[51] http://caselaw.findlaw.com/us-supreme-court/147/165.html

24.

Ohio ex rel. David Davis v. Charles Q. Hildebrant, Secretary of State, State Supervisor and Inspector of Elections, and State Supervisor of Elections, et al., *94 Ohio St. 154, 114 N. E. 55, 241 U. S. 565, 36 Sup. Ct. 708, 60 L. Ed. 1172, (1916)*[52,53]

-As *State ex rel. Davis v. Hildebrant or as Davis v. Ohio*

Background: In 1912, Ohio enacted a referendum law that allowed for the people to pass judgment on and potentially invalidate any act of the state legislature. The legislature passed a redistricting law after Congress had determined the new apportionment by state.

Issue: Is the referendum permissible for redistricting or does it violate Article IV of the federal constitution?

Court Decision: Written by Chief Justice Edward Douglass White. Does the state cease to have a republican form of government under the Guarantee Clause of the federal constitution if a referendum is employed? – It is a political question beyond the court's purview. "Under the referendum amendment of 1912 to the Constitution of Ohio, the people of that state having disapproved of the state redistricting law passed after Congress had enacted the Apportionment Act of 1911, and the state court having held that, under the referendum amendment, the legislative power was reserved in the people to be expressed by referendum *held* that:

"The decision of the highest court of the state that, under such amendment, the legislative power of the state is now vested not only in the General Assembly, but also in the people by referendum, and that a law disapproved by the referendum was no law, is conclusive here."

Conclusions: The US Supreme Court will not examine those areas that are the jurisdiction of the state courts. But the state may, acting with limited authority under the Elections Clause, regulate and oversee federal elections and that includes redistricting.[54]

Applicability: The selection or election of delegates to an Article V convention would be a matter of state control although it is a "federal

---

[52] https://supreme.justia.com/cases/federal/us/241/565/case.html
[53] Ralph W. Aigler, "Referendum as Applied to Proposed Amendments of the Federal Constitution," *Michigan Law Review* 18 (1919): 52-3
[54] Michael T. Morley, "The Intratextual Independent "Legislature" and the Elections Clause," *Northwestern University Law Review* 109 (2015): 132-3

act" and not a state power.

25.
___

Edward Prigg v. Commonwealth of Pennsylvania, 41 U.S. 539 (1842)[55]
   -As *Prigg v. Pennsylvania*

Background: The case itself has little to nothing to do with the amending process. It concerns the plight of Margaret Morgan, who was born a slave. In 1832, she moved from Maryland to Pennsylvania. Her owner, John Ashmore, had kept her in "virtual freedom" and in 1837 his heirs sought Morgan's return to Maryland. Slavecatcher Edward Prigg was hired to retrieve Morgan. He and three other men, Nathan S. Bemis, Jacob Forward, and Stephen Lewis, Jr., were eventually caught and tried in Pennsylvania for kidnapping. Morgan's children though born free in Pennsylvania, were also taken to Maryland and enslaved.[56]

Issue: Whether Pennsylvania law or federal law was supreme. Article IV of the federal constitution and the Fugitive Slave Act of 1793 were in conflict with the Pennsylvania laws of 1798 and 1826.

Court Decision: 8-1, Written by Justice Joseph Story. The federal court held the Pennsylvania laws unconstitutional vis-à-vis the federal constitution under the Supremacy Clause. The Court's decision sidestepped the issue through ambiguous language and created a scenario that led to further conflict in the future.

Conclusions: "The Court may not construe the Constitution so as to defeat its obvious ends when another construction, equally accordant with the words and sense thereof, will enforce and protect them. (p.612)"

Applicability: **No one is authorized to question the validity of a state's application for an Article V Convention.** To attempt to do so is an attempt to circumvent the Convention Clause and its construction and to circumvent its obvious ends.

___

[55] https://supreme.justia.com/cases/federal/us/41/539/
[56] Kermit L. Hall, ed., *The Oxford Companion to the Supreme Court of the United States* (New York: Oxford University Press, 2d ed., 2005), 774

26.

Clement Smith, Administrator of Samuel Robertson, Deceased v. The President and Directors of the Union Bank of Georgetown, 30 U.S. 518 (1831)[57]
-As *Smith v. Union Bank*

Background: Samuel Robertson was a native of Maryland and a resident of Virginia and a purser in the US Navy. He died intestate in Pennsylvania owing debts in Virginia and the District of Columbia.

Issue: In which state should his estate be administered?

Court Decision: Written by Justice William Johnson.

Conclusions: On page 528, the decision states, "Whether it would or would not be politic to establish a different rule by a **convention of the states**, under constitutional sanction, is not a question for our consideration." The subject of a convention is mentioned without regard to the case facts themselves. The case itself dealt with a probate issue but specifically referred to changing the existing law through an amendment by a convention of the states.[58]

Applicability: An Article V Convention is a "convention of the States" and is therefore endowed with the powers of an interstate **convention** as were all of its many predecessors.

27.

State of New Jersey v. A. Mitchell Palmer, Attorney General, and Daniel C. Roper, Commissioner of Internal Revenue, 252 U.S. 570, 40 Sup. Ct. 345
– A National Prohibition Case as *State of New Jersey v. Palmer*

Background: In a manner similar to the argument made by Atty. Gen. Rice of Rhode Island, Atty. Gen. Thomas McCran of New Jersey claimed that the Eighteenth Amendment is an "invasion of state sovereignty" and a violation of the Tenth Amendment. The right and power to regulate the manufacturing and consumption of liquor is not enumerated in the federal Constitution and therefore beyond the reach of the Congress.

---

[57] https://supreme.justia.com/cases/federal/us/30/518/case.html
[58] Found at p. 528 of the record in 30 U.S. (5 Pet.) 518.

Issue: The Congress had failed to make certain that it had a vote of two-thirds of all members in each chamber and that a declaration of the necessity of the amendment was produced. The ratifications by the States were not entirely lawful as some had used referendums.

Court Decision: Written by Justice Willis Van Devanter. Handed down as part of the collected National Prohibition Cases.

Conclusions: As held elsewhere previously, a state initiative designed to go around the state constitution and Article V to compel an application will not be sustained. Therefore, the Court dismissed the case.

Applicability: Compiled with the National Prohibition Cases.

28.

State of Rhode Island v. A. Mitchell Palmer, Attorney General, and Daniel C. Roper, Commissioner of Internal Revenue, 253 U.S. 320 (1920),[59] 40 Sup. Ct. 179

– *A National Prohibition Case as State of Rhode Island v. Palmer*

Background: Rhode Island Attorney General Herbert A. Rice argued that the amending article was not a "substantive power but a precautionary safeguard" for the limited purpose of the correction of "errors and oversights" and not the expansion of new powers for the federal government. Prohibiting liquor would be an expansion of federal power. Rice pronounced the amendment an invasion of state sovereignty.

Issue: Use of Article V to expand federal government power was not contemplated or intended by the Framers and is an abuse of the States.

Court Decision: Written by Justice Willis Van Devanter. Handed down as part of the collected National Prohibition Cases.

Conclusions: This is one of the *National Prohibition Cases*. The two-thirds vote required in Congress for proposing amendments is two-thirds of a quorum present and voting, not of the entire membership of the legislative body. Therefore, the Court dismissed the case.

Applicability: **The Article V Convention will require only two-thirds of the quorum present and necessary to conduct business.**

---

[59] http://caselaw.findlaw.com/us-supreme-court/253/350.html

29.

Lewis K. Uhler, et al. v. AFL-CIO, et al., 468 U.S. 1310, 105 S. Ct. 5, 82 L. Ed.2d 896, (1984),[60]

-As *Uhler v. AFL-CIO*

Background: A "balanced federal budget statutory initiative" would have required that, if voters approved, the California state legislature submit a resolution to Congress asking for a limited amendatory convention for a balanced budget amendment. Failing to do so, the California Secretary of State would then be required to apply on behalf of the voters. The AFL-CIO opposed the measure and sued to prevent action questioning the constitutionality. Lewis Uhler asked the SCOTUS to stay the California Court's decision.

Issue: The California Supreme Court had to decide, like the SCOTUS did in *Hawke* sixty-four years earlier, what was meant by the term "legislature" – did it include the voters? Also, did that definition in legislature include one that is forced to act?

Court Decision: Written by Chief Justice William Hubbs Rehnquist. The California Supreme Court held that "legislatures" meant only elected representatives and did not include the voters and did not include a legislature that was forced to act. The initiative was inconsistent with state law and denied. Similar to Montana's *State ex. rel. Harper v. Waltermire*. The Court found that the statutes in the state law were really resolutions and not valid. The AFL-CIO also claimed that the case was a "political question" as found in *Coleman* and not subject to review. That position was rejected by the Supreme Court.

Conclusions: As held elsewhere previously, a state initiative designed to go around the state constitution and Article V to compel an application will not be sustained. State legislatures are independent bodies acting under Article V and outside of their traditional function as a state assembly under state law. The power to apply for an Article V convention is a power implied by Article V and granted to the state legislatures; which when making application are acting under a federal power.

Applicability: The people have no direct role in the amendment process and cannot compel a legislature to act. The amendatory

---

[60] https://www.courtlistener.com/opinion/111276/lewis-k-uhler-et-al-v-american-federation-of/?

convention is beyond the reach of instructions or coercion.

30.

William Ludwig Ullmann v. United States, 350 U.S. 422 (1956),[61] 76 S. Ct. 497; 100 L. Ed. 511
-As *Ullmann v. US*

Background: The Immunity Act of 1954 provides for an exemption from prosecution for self-incrimination when answering questions involving the national security. Ullman, a former Treasury Department employee, was subpoenaed by a grand jury from the Southern District of New York which was investigating Communist Party activity. Ullman sought to invoke his privilege against self-incrimination under the Fifth Amendment. Successive courts held him in contempt.[62]

Issue: Does the Constitution's Fifth Amendment protection against self-incrimination make the Immunity Act unconstitutional – and if so, to what extent? Specifically, does upholding the Immunity Act amount to an amendment of the Constitution?

Court Decision: 7-2, Written by Justice Felix Frankfurter. The Court decided that sufficient constitutional safeguards existed to protect the witness from prosecution. Legal scholars of the time wrote on the other methods beyond prosecution that could be employed to damage a person and/or their reputation.[63] The Act is constitutional and the conviction sustained.

Conclusions: With respect to whether the Immunity Act rewrites the constitutional provision for protection from self-incrimination, writing on page 428, "Nothing new can be put into the Constitution except through the amendatory process, and nothing old can be taken out without the same process."

Applicability: **The amendment and ratification processes cannot be changed to circumvent the Article V Convention.**

---

[61] https://www.law.cornell.edu/supremecourt/text/350/422
[62] Kermit L. Hall, ed., *The Oxford Companion to the Supreme Court of the United States* (New York: Oxford University Press, 2d ed., 2005), 1035
[63] Generally, J. Elwood Armstrong, "The Spirit of the Fifth Amendment Privilege – A Study in Judicial Method – Ullman v. United States," *Maryland Law Review* 17, no.1 (1957) and Maxwell Brandwen, "Reflections on Ullman v. United States," *Columbia Law Review* 57, no. 4 (April 1957)

31.

United States v. Claude Chambers, et al.,
291 U.S. 217 (1934)[64], 54 S. Ct. 434, 78 L. Ed. 763

-As ***US v. Chambers***

Background: Claude Chambers and Byrum Gibson were indicted in the District Court for the Middle District of North Carolina for conspiring to violate the National Prohibition Act, and for possessing and transporting intoxicating liquor contrary to that act. Between the beginning of the case in June 1933 and the conclusion on 6 December 1933, the Twenty-first Amendment repealed the Eighteenth Amendment by its ratification on 5 December 1933. The plaintiffs argued that the prosecution should cease as the law was no longer applicable.

Issue: Whether there is a public interest in continuing to pursue prosecution for a crime committed under a law no longer in force.

Court Decision: 9-0, Written by Chief Justice Charles Evans Hughes. The prosecutions must stop when the law loses its force due to an act of the people. The indictment was dismissed.

Conclusions: If an amendment is putative, or alleged, the Court will determine its validity. In this case, the ratification of the Twenty-first Amendment was questioned and the Court settled the issue. This case serves as a counter point to *Coleman*. Additionally, in the event that the people revoke a particular congressional power, in this instance that of the power granted by the Eighteenth Amendment, then that power is returned to the people. "It is a continuing and vital principle that the people are free to withdraw authority which they have conferred, and, when withdrawn, neither Congress nor the courts can assume the right to continue to exercise it."

Applicability: **The Supreme Court considers it to the "province and duty" of the Court to determine what the Constitution is including amendments.**

---

[64] https://supreme.justia.com/cases/federal/us/291/217/

32.

United States v. William H. Sprague and William S. Howey, 282 U.S. 716 (1931)[65], 51 S. Ct. 220, 44 F.2d 967 (D.N.J. 1930)
-As *US v. Sprague*

Background: The plaintiffs were caught transporting fifty half barrels of beer. William Sprague was the clerk of Wantage Township in New Jersey and William Mowey was a farmer. They argued that the Eighteenth Amendment had not been properly ratified and therefore the Volstead Act prohibiting intoxicating liquors was invalid.

Issue: "The appellees contended in the court below, and here, that notwithstanding the plain language of Article V, conferring upon the Congress the choice of method of ratification, as between action by legislatures and by conventions, this Amendment could only be ratified by the latter. They say that it was the intent of its framers, and the Constitution must, therefore, be taken impliedly to require, that proposed amendments conferring on the United States new direct powers over individuals shall be ratified in conventions." Further, that the Framers intended for any NEW powers conveyed by the people to the federal government to be ratified ONLY by conventions. The plaintiffs' attorneys argued that the Tenth Amendment restricted the choice of the ratification method.[66]

Court Decision: 8-0, Written by Justice Owen Josephus Roberts. "The United States asserts that Article V is clear in statement and in meaning, contains no ambiguity, and calls for no resort to rules of construction." Also that "The choice, therefore, of the mode of ratification, lies in the sole discretion of Congress." Addressing the matter of the Framer's intent and verbiage, "If the framers of the instrument had any thought that amendments differing in purpose should be ratified in different ways, nothing would have been simpler than so to phrase Article V as to exclude implication or speculation. The fact that an instrument drawn with such meticulous care and by men who so well understood how to make language fit their thought does not contain any such limiting phrase affecting the exercise of discretion by the Congress in choosing one or the other alternative mode

---

[65] https://supreme.justia.com/cases/federal/us/282/716/case.html
[66] Judith L. Elder, "Article V, Justiciability, and the Equal Rights Amendment," *Oklahoma Law Review* 31 (1978): 67

of ratification is persuasive evidence that no qualification was intended." Judge Clark, at the lower court level and speculating that the case would go to the US Supreme Court, presciently forecast that "[e]ven if this opinion meets with a cold reception in the appellate courts, we hope that it will at least have the effect of focusing the country's thought upon the neglected method of considering constitutional amendments in conventions."[67]

Also, with regard to the Tenth Amendment, the Court held that the Tenth Amendment is not germane to the argument of Article V providing powers to Congress for particular functions.

Conclusions: Similarly, the power granted by Article V is to the amendatory convention. "The fifth article does not purport to delegate any governmental power to the United States…On the contrary… that article is a grant of authority by the people to the Congress, and not to the United States." It should be noted that "Sprague addressed specifically not the entirety of Article V, but only unambiguous language where no construction or supplement was necessary."[68] Also, the congressional authority over calling a convention is less than that over ratification process.

Applicability: **The power granted by Article V is to the Congress specifically and not to the federal government as a whole. The selection by Congress of the mode of ratification is unreviewable.**[69]

33.

United States Term Limits, Inc., et al. v. Ray Thornton, et al., 514 U.S. 779, 838, 115 S. Ct. 1842, 1871, 131 L.Ed.2d 881 (1995)[70]

-As *US Term Limits v. Thornton*

Background: US Term Limits sought to have term limits enacted for members of Congress through a voter referendum in Arkansas. The Arkansas Supreme Court found this action unconstitutional as a violation of Article V. Changing the amount of time that a member of Congress

---

[67] Ethan P. Davis, "Liquor Laws and Constitutional Conventions: A Legal History of the Twenty-first Amendment," *Yale Law School Student Scholarship Papers*, Paper 65, (2008): 18
[68] Robert G. Natelson, *Amending the Constitution by Convention: Practical Guidance for Citizens and Policymakers* (Part 3 of 3), Goldwater Institute Report No. 11-02, (22 Feb 2011), 29
[69] Lester B. Orfield & Henry M. Bates, *The Amending of the Federal Constitution* (Ann Arbor: University of Michigan Press, 1942), 18
[70] https://www.oyez.org/cases/1994/93-1456

may hold office is tantamount to changing the Constitution itself.

Issue: Can the States or Congress pass legislation that effectively changes the federal Constitution? That is, is there an implied or alternate amendment process which circumvents Article V's explicit process?

Court Decision: 5-4, Written by Justice John Paul Stevens. "We are ... firmly convinced that allowing the several States to adopt term limits for congressional service would effect a fundamental change in the constitutional framework. *Any such change must come not by legislation adopted either by Congress or by an individual State, but rather—as have other important changes in the electoral process—through the Amendment procedures set forth in Article V....* In the absence of a properly passed constitutional amendment, allowing individual States to craft their own qualifications for Congress would ... erode the structure envisioned by the Framers, a structure that was designed, in the words of the Preamble to our Constitution, to form a "more perfect Union."

The argument was made by the petitioners that the Tenth Amendment provided the States with reserved powers by which the States could make such a constitutional change. The Court disallowed this argument with the rationale that,

> *"Petitioners' Tenth Amendment argument misconceives the nature of the right at issue because that Amendment could only "reserve" that which existed before. As Justice Story recognized, "the states can exercise no powers whatsoever, which exclusively spring out of the existence of the national government, which the constitution does not delegate to them....No state can say, that it has reserved, what it never possessed."*

Conclusions: The constitutional processes cannot be suspended or ended without following Article V. To effectuate term limits requires a constitutional amendment.[71] States cannot impose any qualifications for prospective members of Congress which are stricter than those qualifications laid out in the Constitution. Tenth Amendment arguments to claims are limited to those rights or rights that stem from or were found after the ratification of the US Constitution.

Applicability: Article V is inviolable and the convention process must follow the amendment process explicitly. Similarly, the States

---

[71] Vikram David Amar, "The People Made Me Do It: Can the People of the States Instruct and Coerce Their State Legislatures in the Article V Constitutional Amendment Process?," *William and Mary Law Review* 41, no.3 (2000): 1038

and the people cannot alter the process except through the prescribed method.

34.

White v. Hart, 80 U.S. (13 Wall.) 646, 20 L. Ed. 685, (1871)[72]

Background: Seeking fulfillment of a slave contract worth $1,230 executed during the Civil War, the suit was challenged on the grounds that the law during the rebellion was invalid.

Issue: Does secession suspend the law – constitutional and statutory – during the rebellion and is the state able to cancel contracts?

Court Decision: Written by Justice Noah Haynes Swayne. "At no time during the rebellion were the rebellious states out of the pale of the Union. Their constitutional duties and obligations remained unaffected by the rebellion. They could not then pass a law impairing the obligation of a contract more than before the rebellion, or now, since." The constitution remained and remains in effect as long as the government stands.

Conclusions: **The constitutional processes cannot be suspended or ended without following Article V. Even the occurrence of a war does not suspend the Constitution nor any part of it without following the provisions therein.**

Applicability: There is no other alternative amendment method and a convention is the only other option to Congress.

35.

Howard Joseph Whitehill, Jr. v. Wilson Elkins, President, University of Maryland, et al., 389 U.S. 54, (1967), 258 F. Supp. 589 (D. Md. 1966), 287 F. Supp. 61 (D. Md. 1968)[73,74]

-As ***Whitehill v. Elkins***

Background: As part of obtaining a teaching position at the University of Maryland, one is required to take a loyalty oath that includes pledging that one is not part of a subversive group seeking to

---

[72] https.//www.law.cornell.edu/supremecourt/text/80/646
[73] https://supreme.justia.com/cases/federal/us/389/54/case.html
[74] https://casetext.com/case/whitehill-v-elkins-3

overthrow or alter the United States and Maryland governments.

Issue: Is the requirement of an oath unconstitutional? Is the restriction too broad as to the definition of "overthrow or alter or subversive"?

Court Decision: 6-3, Written by Justice William Orville Douglas. "If the Federal Constitution is our guide, a person who might wish to "alter" our form of government may not be cast into the outer darkness. For the Constitution prescribes the method of "alteration" by the amending process in Article V, and while the procedure for amending it is restricted, there is no restraint on the kind of amendment that may be offered."

Conclusions: The constitutional processes of Article V are themselves meant to alter government.

Applicability: **A new method of ratification or amendment could not be introduced during an amendatory convention.**

Federal District and Appeals Courts

36.

Linda K. Barker, Barbara Everist, and Roy Letellier v. Joyce Hazeltine, in her Official Capacity as Secretary of State, 3 F. Supp. 2d 1088 (D.S.D. 1998)[75]

-As *Barker v. Hazeltine*

Background: Like many other states in the 1990s, South Dakota sought to impose term limits on its congressional delegation. To do so, a ballot measure, called South Dakota Initiated Measure 1 was launched by petition and adopted by a majority (over 67%) of the eligible voters. The measure directs the secretary of state to place labels on the primary and general election ballots to identify those candidates for US Senator and US Representative that do NOT support term limits. At the time, Barker is a state representative; Everist is a state senator; and Letellier is a former state representative.

Issue: Does the ballot initiative method of South Dakota conflict

---

[75] https://casetext.com/case/barker-v-hazeltine

with the federal constitution? Will attempting to force term limit support and the introduction of a bill in Congress to create term limits be tantamount to indirectly amending the federal constitution?

<u>*Court Decision:*</u> Written by District Judge Lawrence Leroy Piersol. The Court declared the ballot measure unconstitutional. "Without doubt, Initiated Measure I brings to bear an undue influence on South Dakota's congressional candidates, and the deliberative and independent amendment process envisioned by the Framers when they drafted Article V is lost."[76] Approximately half of the states had adopted congressional term limit measures by the time the United States Supreme Court declared them unconstitutional in *United States Term Limits, Inc. v. Thornton,* 514 U.S. 779 The Federal Constitution prohibits the states from imposing congressional qualifications in addition to those enumerated in the text of the Constitution. Court found the following constitutional violations:

- Article V by forcing office holders to act and vote in a certain way
- Article I, § 6 by questioning office holders as to their position in either the House or Senate
- First Amendment free speech rights of office holders and candidates
- Fourteenth Amendment rights of candidates to equal access to the ballot
- Fifth and Fourteenth Amendment rights to due process

<u>*Conclusions:*</u> The Court ruled initiatives and referenda are not permissible (the case involved setting congressional term limits) as citizens do not possess a direct role in amending. Furthermore, the Court ruled that the use of ballot notation of either the support or non-support of term limits constituted a violation of the Speech and Debate Clause in the US Constitution.

<u>*Applicability:*</u> **Article V is the only constitutional method of amending the US Constitution.**

---

[76] At page 1094

37.

Christian Feigenspan, a corporation v. Joseph L. Bodine, United States Attorney for the District of New Jersey, and Charles V. Duffy, Collector of Internal Revenue of the Fifth District of New Jersey, *264 F. 186 (D.N.J. 1920)*[77]
– A *National Prohibition Case as Feigenspan v. Bodine*

Background: Elihu Root and William Guthrie argued that the Eighteenth Amendment exercises a direct control over the lives of individuals and no constitutional provision exists to do that. They also argue that the amendment permits the federal government to deprive individuals of the property rights without due process.

Issue: Does Article V allow for an amendment which is an exercise of any federal police power or regulation? Did the States understand at the time of ratification that they were turning over the power of intrastate regulation to the federal government along with interstate regulation? If that is indeed the situation, then the balance of federalism has been disturbed. Such an interpretation would require that the Vesting Clause in Article VI be understood to be a one way proposition with the federal government able to invade and interfere with the power of the States but not for the States to invade the power of the federal government and thus the word "concurrent" as found in the amendment is meaningless.

Court Decision: Written by Judge John Rellstab. The federal government may assume, with the approval of the States, police powers. It is understood that regulation must be accompanied by the corresponding enforcement powers.

Conclusions: The Court held that the decree refusing an injunction was affirmed. What the people choose to add to the Constitution is part of the Constitution and can only be removed or invalidated by an act of the people. Legal construction will not interfere with the will of the people expressed in the organic or fundamental law.

Applicability: The lower court's decision was affirmed.

---

[77] http://www.scribd.com/doc/271094071/Feigenspan-v-Bodine-264-Federal-Reporter-188-1920#scribd

38.

Goudyloch E. Dyer, et al., v. W. Robert Blair, Speaker of the Illinois House of Representatives, 390 F. Supp. 1291 (N.D. Ill. 1975) *(Stevens presiding)*[78]

Combined with,
Dawn Clark Netsch, et al., v. William C. Harris, President of the Illinois Senate, and W. Robert Blair, Speaker of the Illinois House of Representatives,

-As ***Dyer v. Blair***

Background: Article XIV, § 4 of the Illinois State Constitution of 1970 requires a three-fifths vote of both chambers of the state legislature to ratify a federal constitutional amendment. The defendants claim that under *Coleman*, the issue not justiciable as a political question. The proposed Equal Rights Amendment had received a majority vote in both houses of the Illinois state legislature but failed to reach the requirement of a super majority of three-fifths as prescribed by the state constitution. Various elected official sued but because the issue had not been fully resolved by the legislature, the Court passed on addressing the matter. The Senate sought to pass a new senate rule that allowed for a simple majority.

Issue: The Equal Rights Amendment received a favorable vote of more than a majority but less than three-fifths of the members of each house of the Illinois legislature. Was it legitimately ratified?

Court Decision: Stevens found the matter justiciable. By virtue of the supremacy clause in article VI, it is clear that the legislature's ratifying function may not be abridged by a state. An extraordinary majority is not required for ratification. "When the Constitution requires action to be taken by an extraordinary majority, that requirement is plainly stated." The States are not the final arbiters, but the ratifying legislatures may set their own rule for passage.

Conclusions: Per now US Supreme Court Justice John Paul Stevens, who presided over the case and wrote the opinion, "the delegation [from Article V] is not to the States but rather to the designated ratifying bodies." Stevens explicitly rejected the "political question" portion of

---

[78] http://law.justia.com/cases/federal/district-courts/FSupp/390/1287/1966618/

Coleman in this decision.[79,80] This ruling amounts to a near over-turning of *Coleman* in the sense that shortly after issuing this decision Stevens was elevated to the US Supreme Court and presumably, took his view of *Coleman* with him.[81]

<u>*Applicability:*</u> Thus, **state constitutional provisions that cover legislative supermajorities and referenda do not apply to Article V applications**; only the Article V convention itself may impose such restrictions on itself, **the convention is free to set its own rules** and limitations beyond the call.[82]

39.

Donald James Gralike and Mike Harman, et al. v. Rebecca McDowell Cook, 191 F. 3d 911 (8th Cir. 1999)[83] *affirmed on other grounds sub nom. Cook v. Gralike, 531 U.S. 510 (2001)*
As **Gralike v. Cook**

Consolidated under one case:
- *Gralike (I)* 996 F. Supp. 889 (W.D.Mo.1998)
- *Gralike (II)* 996 F. Supp. 901 (W.D.Mo.1998)
- *Gralike (III)* 996 F. Supp. 917 (W.D.Mo.1998)

<u>*Background:*</u> In response to the US Supreme Court's 1995 *U.S. Term Limits v. Thornton* decision, Missouri voters passed an amendment (§§15-22) to Article VIII of the state constitution in 1996 that would impose term limits on the state's congressional delegation to three terms in the US House and two terms in the US Senate. The amendment also orders the state's congressional delegation to seek an amendment to the federal constitution for term limits. The amendment required that any candidate who did not support term limits be noted as such on the ballot. Gralike was a candidate for Congress in 1998.

<u>*Issue:*</u> Gralike claimed that the Missouri Amendment violated Article I, Article V, and the First and Fourteenth Amendments of the

---

[79] John R. Vile, *Contemporary Questions Surrounding the Constitutional Amending Process* (Westport, CT: Praeger, 1993), 28-30

[80] Robert G. Natelson, "Proposing Constitutional Amendments By Convention: Rules Governing The Process," *Tennessee Law Review* 78 (2011): 697, n.13

[81] Grover Rees III, "Rescinding Ratification of Proposed Constitutional Amendments – A Question for the Court," *Louisiana Law Review* 37, no.4 (Spring 1977): 922

[82] Robert G. Natelson, "Proposing Constitutional Amendments by Convention: Rules Governing the Process," *Tennessee Law Review* 78 (2011): 743

[83] https://www.law.cornell.edu/supct/html/99-929.ZO.html

United States Constitution, and that §21 of the Missouri Amendment violates the Supremacy Clause of the United States Constitution.

Court Decision: Written by US Appeals 8th Circuit Judge Theodore McMillian. First Amendment: the Court found the Missouri amendment to be unconstitutional as compelled speech. Article V: "Article V specifically delegates the amendment process to legislative bodies, not the voters." Allowing the voters to determine how and who amends the federal constitution violates the process as stipulated in Article V. "Article V envisions legislatures acting as freely deliberative bodies in the amendment process and resists any attempt by the people of a state to restrict the legislatures' actions." The amendment is contrary to the Speech or Debate Clause in Art. I, §6, cl. 1, of the Federal Constitution, and the Missouri constitution's Article VIII "establishes a regime in which a state officer–the secretary of state–is permitted to judge and punish Members of Congress for their legislative actions or positions."

Conclusions: "Article V envisions legislatures acting as freely deliberative bodies in the amendment process and resists any attempt by the people of a state to restrict the legislature's actions." Thus, **Article V Conventions cannot be prohibited from deliberation and consideration of a proposed amendment and thereby limited to pre-written wording.**[84]

Applicability: Relevant to an amendatory convention as it prohibits states from imposing a limitation on the speech of their delegates as well as prohibits the States from requiring that a candidate affirm a position either for or against a particular position. The decision preserves the deliberative speech and debate aspect of the convention.

40.

Ex parte Caesar Griffin, 25 Tex. Supp. 623, S. C. Chase 364 (1869) – *for the 4th Federal Circuit Court*

Background: Griffin, a black man, was imprisoned by the sheriff of Rockbridge County, Virginia on the order of a judge, Hugh W. Sheffey, who was precluded from holding office by the Fourteenth Amendment, for shooting another man.

Issue: The judge in question was a judge before the ratification of

---

[84] Robert G. Natelson, "Proposing Constitutional Amendments by Convention: Rules Governing the Process," *Tennessee Law Review* 78 (2011): 746, n.377

the Fourteenth Amendment but is considered to fall into that category of civil servants and elected officials that are barred from serving, as they are former adherents to the Confederacy.

Court Decision: Written by Chief Justice Salmon Portland Chase. When there is more than one possible construction, and either could be a reasonable interpretation, the one that is most in harmony with the "tenor and spirit of the act" is preferred. Griffin was subject to incarceration.

Conclusions: There is no limit to the people's ability to amend the constitution.

Applicability: Article V is to be interpreted in the manner that best serves the intent of calling an amendatory convention – not impeding a convention.

41.

The State of Idaho, et al., and Claude L. Oliver, et al., v. Rear Admiral Roland G. Freeman, III, Administrator of General Services Administration and National Organization of Women, et al., 529 F. Supp. 1107 (D. Idaho 1981) *vacated as moot by Carmen v. Idaho, 459 U.S. 809 (1982)*[85]

-As ***Idaho v. Freeman***

Background: After the Idaho state legislature ratified the proposed Equal Rights Amendment, a later legislature sought to rescind that ratification in the wake of changing public opinion. The legislatures of the states of Arizona and Washington joined in the suit. They sought a declaration from the federal court that the rescission was lawful and valid and that the extension by Congress of the seven year time limit for ratification was unconstitutional.

Issue: Whether a rescission is permissible under Article V. May Congress alter the time limit for ratification once stipulated? Was a two-thirds vote required?

---

[85] http://www.leagle.com/decision/19811636529FSupp1107_11473/STATE%20OF%20IDAHO%20v.%20FREEMAN

Court Decision: Written by Federal District Judge Marion Jones Callister. All three points affirmed: rescission is permissible providing the necessary three-quarters of the States required for ratification has not been reached; Congress may not alter the time limit for ratification as it is an *ultra vires* act; and a super-majority of the state legislature was required to pass. "Furthermore, a review of article V reveals that the judiciary, while only dealing with article V in a handful of cases, has nevertheless dealt with virtually all the significant portions of that article." "Giving plenary power to Congress to control the amendment process runs completely counter to the intentions of the founding fathers in including article V with its particular structure in the Constitution." "Considering that an amendment cannot become part of the Constitution until a proper consensus of the people has been reached and it is the exclusive role of the states to determine what the local sentiment is, it logically follows that the subsequent act of rescission would promote the democratic ideal by giving a truer picture of the people's will as of the time three-fourths of the states have acted in affirming the amendment."[86]

Conclusions: Article V makes clear that there are only two methods of ratification and Congress must choose one or the other mode. The ruling is similar to that of *U.S. v. Sprague*. Congress had first set a time limit of seven years for ratification of the Equal Rights Amendment, then, failing to achieve the necessary three-quarters of the States ratifications, extended the time period. This decision to extend is extremely controversial as it flies in the face of both *Coleman v. Miller* and *Dillon v. Gloss*. Legal scholars pounced on the decision immediately.[87]

Applicability: Stayed by the US Supreme Court and mooted by the failure of the proposed amendment to secure thirty-eight states' ratification. **Congress may not manipulate or change the ratification process. Also, a state may withdraw its application any time before two-thirds of the states have applied.**

---

[86] John R. Vile, *Contemporary Questions Surrounding the Constitutional Amending Process* (Westport, CT: Praeger, 1993), 31-3
[87] For example, see generally, John F. Carroll, "Constitutional Law, Recent Cases," *Akron Law Review* 16, no. 1 (Summer 1982)

42.

League of Women Voters of Maine, Elizabeth H. Mitchell, and Philip E. Harriman v. Dan A. Gwadosky and Andrew Ketterer, U.S. Term Limits, Inc., On Our Terms – Campaign Committee, John M. Michael, and Belinda A. Gerry, 966 F. Supp. 52 (D. Me. 1997)[88]

-As *League of Women Voters of Maine v. Gwadosky*

Background: Similar to *AFL-CIO v. March Fong Eu*, this case concerns the attempt to force term limits by ballot initiative. The plaintiffs challenged the Congressional Term Limits Act of 1996. Maine voters had passed a ballot initiative indicating that they wished the position of candidates regarding term limits noted on the ballot. Like other states' initiatives, the Act also required the Maine congressional delegation, state legislature and governor to work to pass a federal constitutional amendment for term limits. Non-incumbent candidates were to be required to sign a pledge to support term limits.

Issue: The plaintiffs contended that the Act violates Article V, and the First and Fifth Amendments.

Court Decision: Written by Federal District Judge Morton Aaron Brody. "The Act effectively coerces Maine's elected officials through its ballot labeling provisions. Given this coercion, the State's legislators cannot act in the deliberative and independent manner required by Article V of the Constitution. The Act is, therefore, unconstitutional."

Conclusions: The court rejected their claim that, "**A direct role in the constitutional amendment process for "citizens" was not envisioned by the Framers**. The citizen's function is to elect competent legislators, who in turn, when necessary, can amend the Constitution pursuant to the authority granted under Article V."

Applicability: Delegates to an Article V convention may not be forced to abide by a referendum or ballot initiative to vote in a particular manner.

---

[88] https://scholar.google.com/scholar_case?case=10456412735864979117&hl=en&as_sdt=6&as_vis=1&oi=scholarr

43.

Miller v. Moore, 169 F. 3d 1119 (8th Cir. 1999)[89]

Consolidated under one case:

- *Andrew Miller and Martin R. Hoer v. Scott Moore, Secretary of State for the State of Nebraska, U.S. Term Limits Foundation, Nebraska Term Limits Coalition, and Robert D. Wright,*
- *Timothy J. Duggan, Ray L. Lineweber, ACLU Nebraska, Ron Withem, and Ernest Chambers, v. Scott Moore, Secretary of State for the State of Nebraska, and U.S. Term Limits Foundation, Nebraska Term Limits Coalition, and Robert D. Wright,*
- *Timothy J. Duggan, Ray L. Lineweber, ACLU Nebraska, and Ron Withem, v.*

Scott Moore, Secretary of State for the State of Nebraska, and U.S. Term Limits Foundation, and Nebraska Term Limits Coalition and Robert D. Wright

Background: "The plaintiffs sought to enjoin Mr. Moore from implementing and enforcing Article XVIII of the Nebraska Constitution, an amendment passed by voter initiative in the 1996 general election. The Article makes it Nebraska's "official position" that its elected officials should work to enact an amendment to the U.S. Constitution limiting congressional service to two terms in the Senate and three terms in the House of Representatives. The provision then "instructs" each of Nebraska's representatives in Congress to "use all of his or her delegated powers" to pass the specified term limits amendment. It also "instructs" members of the Nebraska legislature to apply to Congress for an Article V convention, the purpose of which is to propose a congressional term limits amendment."

Issue: The plaintiffs contend that Article XVIII violates both the First Amendment and Article V of the U.S. Constitution. "The question before us, then, is where Nebraska's Article XVIII falls on the spectrum between impermissible direct involvement of the people in the amendment process (as in *Leser* and *Hawke*) and permissible advisory and nonbinding communication between the people and their representatives (as in *Kimble*)."

Court Decision: 2-1, Written by Judge Morris Sheppard Arnold. The Court agrees with the lower court that the Article is a violation

---

[89] http://caselaw.findlaw.com/us-8th-circuit/1442218.html

of the US Constitution. The Article is not advisory as it penalizes legislators. "In 1789, the House of Representatives rejected a proposed "right to instruct Representatives" that would have been one of the rights specified in the First Amendment...They feared, in addition, that a right to instruct, whether or not legally binding on legislators, would convey to the people the idea that they had a right to control the debates of Congress, thus undermining the Federalists' scheme of representative government."

Conclusions: This is another ballot labeling case with the added twist that a First Amendment claim to the right to influence elected representatives through 'popular instructions' is made. The Court found that this issue was addressed in the Grand Convention of 1787 and it was **rejected as stifling debate and compromise**. Delegate instructions stipulated through the ballot measures amount to "scarlet letters."[90]

Applicability: **Article V convention delegates cannot be coerced as to voting for or against a proposed amendment by either the voters of the state legislatures.**

44.

William G. Petusky, Robert A. Bullough, Clinton M. Black and Farrol R. Lambert, Brian Florence v. Calvin L. Rampton, as Governor of the State of Utah, Clyde L. Miller, as Secretary of State of the State of Utah, Sharp M. Larsen, as Auditor of the State of Utah; Linn C. Baker, as Treasurer of the State of Utah; Phil L. Hansen, as Attorney General of the State of Utah; Jacob A. Weiler, as County Clerk of the County of Salt Lake, State of Utah; John Preston Creer, as County Commissioner of Salt Lake County, State of Utah; William G. Larsen, as County Commissioner of Salt Lake County, State of Utah, and Marvin G. Jenson, as County Commissioner of Salt Lake County, State of Utah,

431 F.2d 378(1970), 307 F. Supp. 235, (D. Utah 1969)[91], 243 F. Supp. 365(1965), prior as Petuskey v. Clyde, 234 F. Supp. 960(1964)

-As **Petusky v. Rampton**

---

[90] Vikram David Amar, "The People Made Me Do It: Can the People of the States Instruct and Coerce Their State Legislatures in the Article V Constitutional Amendment Process?," *William and Mary Law Review* 41, no.3 (2000): 1061

[91] http://openjurist.org/431/f2d/378 and http://law.justia.com/cases/federal/district-courts/FSupp/307/235/1428309/

Background: The state legislature of Utah applied to Congress for an Article V convention to specifically address the issue of state legislative reapportionment. Petusky has sued claiming that the malapportioned state legislature is incompetent to act on the issue of its own malapportionment and that the application for the Article V convention was invalid.

Issue: Utah state legislator Brian Florence contends that an Article V convention will deny him his voice as a state legislator and that the application is therefore invalid.[92]

Court Decision: Written by Federal Appeals Judge Jean S. Breitenstein. Initially written by Federal District Chief Judge Willis W. Ritter. "[A] malapportioned state legislature could not constitutionally adopt the 1965 resolutions (for the reapportionment proposed amendments)."

Conclusions: The 1965 requirement for reapportionment was upheld. The application for the Article V convention was not valid.

Applicability: There are congressionally stipulated requirements for a valid convention application that the Court will uphold. Although numerous SCOTUS rulings have made clear that the validity of a state's application is beyond challenge, the Court is not above taking exceptions to its own rules, in this instance, that of avoiding a malapportioned legislature applying for a convention.

45.

State of Ohio ex rel. Albert G. Erkenbrecher v. James M. Cox, Governor of Ohio,

257 F. 334 (D. Ohio 1919)[93]

-As *State of Ohio ex rel. Erkenbrecher v. Cox*

Background: Ohio citizen Erkenbrecher brought suit to restrain the Ohio governor from forwarding to the state legislature the proposed Eighteenth Amendment for consideration for ratification.

---

[92] Raymond M. Planell, "Equal Rights Amendment: Will States be Allowed to Change their Minds?," *Notre Dame Lawyer* 49, no.3 (Feb. 1974): 669
[93] https://books.google.com/books?id=UVwyAQAAMAAJ&pg=PA17&lpg=PA17&dq=state+of+ohio+ex+rel.+erkenbrecher+v.+cox&source=bl&ots=VxNelbOOxS8&sig=sfXYuxtkRuo_jCYDdlsc67Wqvzw&hl=en&sa=X&ved=0CDcQ6AEwCWoVChMIn6idw5GGyAIVCG0-Ch3NggWY#v=onepage&q=state%20of%20ohio%20ex%20rel.%20erkenbrecher%20v.%20cox&f=false

Issue: First, that there was a sufficient quorum but not the whole membership of each chamber of the Congress for the vote on the proposed amendment. Second, that the proposed amendment must be germane to the existing Constitution.

Court Decision: Written by Federal District Judge Howard C. Hollister. The governor of a state is not part of the usual process of ratification. He is under no obligation to forward or not forward a proposed amendment to the state legislature. Also, a sufficient quorum for the Congress to do business is enough to pass a proposed amendment if the requisite two-thirds in each house votes for passage. Finally, a proposed amendment does not have to be germane to the existing Constitution.

Conclusions: **There is no duty on the part of the governor of a state to forward the proposed amendment promulgated** by Congress and accompanied by the ratification method prescription on to the state legislature. It is for this reason that the Congress usually sends a copy of the Joint Resolution of Congress to the state legislatures. A proposed amendment may be attacked judicially until it is adopted.[94]

Applicability: Consistency in the amendment process is necessary to avoid such instances. It is imperative that an amendatory convention adhere to as carefully defined a procedure for proposing, adopting and forwarding a proposed amendment as is possible under the rules adopted by the convention.

46.

Hiram A. Sawyer, as United States Attorney for the Eastern District of Wisconsin, Burt Williams, as Collector of Internal Revenue of the Second District of Wisconsin, and Thomas A. Delaney, as Federal Prohibition Enforcement Director for Wisconsin v. Manitowoc Products Company[95]
  – A *National Prohibition Case as Sawyer v. Manitowoc Products Co.*

Background: Neither Congress or the States possess the power to define what is meant by "intoxicating liquor" under the Eighteenth Amendment making the amendment moot.

---

[94] Lester B. Orfield & Henry M. Bates, *The Amending of the Federal Constitution* (Ann Arbor: University of Michigan Press, 1942), 28
[95] https://law.resource.org/pub/us/case/reporter/US/253/253.US.350.29.30.696.752.788.html

Issue: "The Amendment is void because a) it is not an amendment within the meaning of Article V, b) it violates the Tenth Amendment."

Court Decision: Written by Justice Willis Van Devanter. Congress does indeed have the authority to define what constitutes "an intoxicating liquor." The ruling states, "3. The proposition is that the concurrent powers conferred upon Congress and the states are not subject to conflict because their exertion is authorized within different areas, that is, by Congress within the field of federal authority, and by the states within the sphere of state power, hence leaving the states free within their jurisdiction to determine separately for themselves what, within reasonable limits, is an intoxicating liquor, and to Congress the same right within the sphere of its jurisdiction."

Conclusions: The decree granting an injunction is reversed. Congress acted within its powers.

Applicability: With the stated exceptions found in Article V, **there is no limitation on what subject can be addressed in an amendatory convention for the proposal of an amendment.**

47.

St. Louis Brewing Association, a corporation v. George H. Moore, Collector of Internal Revenue of the First District of Missouri, Walter L. Hensley, United States Attorney for the Eastern District of Missouri, and Frank L. Diggs, Prohibition Agent for the First Internal Revenue District of Missouri
  – A *National Prohibition Case as St. Louis Brewing Ass'n v. Moore*

Background: The St. Louis Brewing Association lost capital from seized stocks and equipment, they sought compensation.

Issue: Reaffirmed the arguments made by the other six prohibition cases that the amendment is not proper and affects individually unconstitutionally; that the federal government is invading state sovereignty; that the state police powers are usurped; that the amending article does not extend to unenumerated powers; and that the amendment seizes and destroys the property of individuals unconstitutionally.

Court Decision: Written by Justice Willis Van Devanter. The amendment process does indeed extend to issues and powers beyond those that are already addressed in the Constitution and that the seizure of now-contraband although produced prior to the ratification of the amendment is legal. "10. That power may be exerted against the disposal for beverage purposes of liquors manufactured before the Amendment became effective just as it may be against subsequent manufacture for those purposes. In either case it is a constitutional mandate or prohibition that is being enforced."

Conclusions: The decree refusing an injunction is affirmed.

Applicability: There is no limit to the subject matter of a proposed amendment outside of those limits prescribed in Article V. What becomes impermissible post-ratification is not within the definition of an ex post facto law.

48.

Edward J. Trombetta, et al., v. The State of Florida, and Jerry Thomas, as President of the Florida Senate, 353 F. Supp. 675 (M.D. Fla. 1973)[96], 339 F. Supp. 1359 (M.D. Fla. 1972)

-As ***Trombetta v. Florida***

Background: The Florida state constitution requires that the state legislature cannot vote on a federal constitutional amendment unless the majority of the state legislature has been elected since the proposition of the proposed amendment. State legislators sued because the rule impeded action on the Equal Rights Amendment.

Issue: Article X, Section 1 of the Florida Constitution of 1968 is repugnant to Articles V and VI of the Constitution of the United States.

Court Decision: Written by Federal District Judge William T. Hodges. The state constitution provision is unconstitutional. This decision voided a section of the Florida Constitution prohibiting legislative action on any proposed amendment to the United States Constitution unless a majority of the legislature had been elected after the proposed amendment had been submitted for ratification. Hodges relied on a combination of the arguments in *Leser* and *Hawke*.[97]

Conclusions: **An action by a state to delay consideration of a**

---

[96] http://www.leagle.com/decision/1973928353FSupp575_1833/TROMBETTA%20v.%20STATE%20OF%20FLORIDA

[97] Raymond M. Planell, "Equal Rights Amendment: Will States be Allowed to Change their Minds?," *Notre Dame Lawyer* 49, no.3 (Feb. 1974): 663

proposed constitutional amendment until after some criterion is met by the legislature is unconstitutional.

Applicability: The States cannot impede the federal amendment process as it is a federal function and beyond the scope of the powers of the States.

49.

United States v. Eugene Dennis, et al., 183 F.2d 201 (1950)[98]
-As US v. Dennis

Background: Plaintiffs were convicted of violating the Smith Act and being communists or "willfully and knowingly" conspiring to organize the Communist Party of the United States as a group to "teach and advocate the overthrow and destruction" of the government "by force and violence," and "knowingly and willfully to advocate and teach the duty and necessity of overthrowing and destroying" the government by "force and violence." All eleven defendants were present or former Communist Party officials. Dennis was the General Secretary of the party.

Issue: Was the Smith Act constitutional and was the evidence admissible? Is the suppression of the Communist Party a violation of the First Amendment?

Court Decision: Written by Federal Appeals Court Judge Learned Hand. "If the defendants had in fact so confined their teaching and advocacy, the First Amendment would indubitably protect them, for it protects all utterances, individual or concerted, seeking constitutional changes, however revolutionary, by the processes which the Constitution provides. Any amendment to the Constitution passed in conformity with Article V is as valid as though it had been originally incorporated in it; the only exception being that no state shall be denied "its equal Suffrage in the Senate." The Smith Act is constitutional and goes to actions not just words.

Conclusions: **The Constitution – and therefore the federal government – may be changed only through the Article V process.**

Applicability: Upheld by a 7-2 decision in the US Supreme Court

---

[98] http://law.justia.com/cases/federal/appellate-courts/F2/183/201/266559/

in ***Dennis v. United States***, 341 U.S. 494-(1951), ruling later overturned in other cases.

50.

United States v. George F. Gugel, 119 F. Supp. 897 (E.D. Ky. 1954)[99]

Background: Sometimes truth really is stranger than fiction… From the 1920s through the 1950s, Newport, Kentucky was an illicit gambling hotspot fit to rival Las Vegas. Like Las Vegas, gangsters held sway in Newport. As recounted in a 1960 *Saturday Evening Post* article, the US House of Representatives' Kefauver Organized Crime Committee investigated Newport. They called in the Newport Chief of Police George F. Gugel and questioned him on the activities in his city. The committee's chief counsel, Rudolph Halley asked Chief Gugel if he was not aware of the gambling and that one could take a taxi in Newport and the cab driver would take the passenger to a number of gambling joints. Gugel stated that he had never been in a taxi before.

> *"After several equally unrewarding exchanges, Halley asked with some awe, "Would you be surprised to know there is gambling going on?"*
>
> *"For me, yes, because I've never been in there," Gugel said virtuously. "All I know is what somebody told me."*

Even after this Casablanca-esque scene, Gugel continued in his ways. A Newport police detective, Jack Theim, raided a local gambling joint, Glenn Schmidt's Playtorium, with George Bailey, a photographer from the *Louisville Courier-Journal* in tow. Chief Gugel and three detectives were gambling in the casino and when their pictures were taken, Chief Gugel arrested the photographer for trespassing and breach of the peace! Gugel then destroyed the film. Gugel's subsequent arrest led to this case in which he is alleged to have violated the photographers Fourteenth Amendment guaranteed "privileges and immunities."[100,101]

Issue: The contention was made that the Fourteenth Amendment was not properly ratified. Therefore, the states that were subject to a military government during Reconstruction did not have the benefit of

---

[99] http://law.justia.com/cases/federal/district-courts/FSupp/119/897/2147646/
[100] *Saturday Evening Post*, 26 March 1960
[101] Kentucky Governor Bert T. Combs removed Gugel from office in 1961 by executive order after reviewing evidence of payoffs.

"equal suffrage in the Senate" in contravention of Article V.

Court Decision: Written by Federal District Judge Mac Swinford. The proposal and ratification process for the Fourteenth Amendment was proper and once completed is beyond challenge. "The operation of a camera is a lawful act and a citizen's privilege to take pictures, unless made specifically unlawful by statute, is such a civil right as is protected by the Constitution of the United States."

Conclusions: "Where a legislative enactment appears on the record to conform to the mode required by law it should be, in the absence of a clear showing to the contrary, upheld by the courts."

Applicability: Adherence to the proper form of creation of a constitutional amendment ensures its validity. An amendatory convention that strictly follows the Constitution and results in an amendment proposal creates a legitimate amendment proposition.

51.

United States or America ex rel. Robert A. Widenmann v. Bainbridge Colby, as Secretary of State of the United States, 265 F. 398 (D.C. Cir. 1920), *affirmed* 257 U.S. 619, 42 S. Ct. 169 (1921)
-As *United States ex rel. Widenmann v. Colby*

Background: Widenmann had petitioned the court for a writ of mandamus against the prior Secretary of State, Robert Lansing, to cancel the proclamation that the Eighteenth Amendment had been duly ratified.

Issue: Section 205 of the Revised Statutes of the United States directs the Secretary of State (or the Acting Secretary of State as was the case in this instance) to announce the ratification whenever the last of the necessary three-fourths of the states' ratification is received.

Court Decision: Written by Chief Justice Constantine J. Smyth of the District of Columbia Supreme Court. The act of formal announcement is "purely ministerial" and there is no discretion. The State Department has no authority to "examine the matter." More to the point, the court stated that, "Moreover, even if the proclamation was cancelled by order of this court, it would not affect the validity of the amendment.

Its validity does not depend in any wise upon the proclamation."

Conclusions: As the final act of the process is the proclamation of the amendment, there is no other action required or permissible.

Applicability: **The functions of an Article V Convention are complete when the convention has fulfilled its stated purpose.** There is no requirement for any other officials to proclaim that completion or closure of the convention.

52.

United States v. George Panos, 45 F. 2d 888 (N.D. Ill. 1930)[102]

Background: This is another Eighteenth Amendment case contesting the validity of the amendment.

Issue: It is contended that the Eighteenth Amendment is of such character as to make it necessary, in order to constitute a valid amendment, that the same should have been submitted to constitutional conventions in the various states for ratification; that inasmuch as the effect of the amendment is to grant to the federal government jurisdiction over a subject-matter previously within the sole jurisdiction of the various states, it follows that, under a correct interpretation of the methods prescribed for the adoption of amendments, a valid adoption could have been achieved only through the convention system.

Court Decision: Written by Federal District Judge Walter C. Lindley. The Eighteenth Amendment's ratification is no different than other amendment in terms of validity and acceptance. It was properly processed, proposed and ratified by a sufficient number of states. There is no requirement for ratification by conventions due to the topic.

Conclusions: The Eighteenth Amendment is valid.

Applicability: Congress has the complete constitutionally committed authority to determine the method of ratification. Calling a convention is at the discretion of Congress.

---

[102] https://casetext.com/case/united-states-v-panos

53.

United States of America v. George S. Sitka, 666 F. Supp. 19 (D. Conn. 1987),[103] affirmed as 845 F.2d. 43 (2d Cir.)
-As **US v. Sitka**

Background: George Sitka was indicted on various counts of failure to file income tax returns, failure to disclose income to Social Security administrators, and conversion of property of the United States. In two different motions he seeks to have some or all of the counts against him dismissed on the grounds that the Sixteenth and Seventeenth Amendments were never properly ratified.

Issue: Sitka asserts that the statute authorizing the Secretary of State to certify the ratification of a constitutional amendment was an unconstitutional delegation of legislative power.

Court Decision: Written by Senior District Judge Mosher Joseph Blumenfeld. If a legislative document is authenticated in regular form by the appropriate officials, the court treats that document as properly adopted. The principle is equally applicable to constitutional amendments. Defendant's claim that the amendments were fraudulently certified does not allow the court to adjudicate an otherwise non-justiciable issue. Since the ultimate authority to ratify lies with the people through the States, their official declaration of ratification is conclusive on the Secretary. The administrative role of the Secretary of State in the amendment process is consistent with the constitutional powers given to the Executive Branch. Article II of the Constitution provides that the Executive Branch "shall take Care that the Laws be faithfully executed."

Conclusions: Per the *Leser* and *Coleman* decisions, the issue of whether an already accepted as ratified amendment is valid, or was obtained through the allegation of fraud, is non-justiciable. The language of Article V also demonstrates that a constitutional amendment is valid *when ratified*, and, as a result, that the act of certification is ministerial and perfunctory in nature.

---

[103] http://law.justia.com/cases/federal/district-courts/FSupp/666/19/2151313/ and http://openjurist.org/845/f2d/43

54.

United States v. Louis E. Thibault,
47 F.2d 169 (2d Cir. 1931)[104]

-As *US v. Thibault*

Applicability: The certification of ratification is immaterial as the ratification is fully made when the last of the requisite three-quarters of the States completes its ratification process.

Background: Similar in its claim to the *Panos* case, it is contended that the Eighteenth Amendment is invalid because it was not ratified by conventions. Thibault, a French Canadian living in Vermont, was arrested for and convicted of violating the National Prohibition Act through possession of and selling two pints of whiskey.

Issue: It is argued that, after ratification of the Tenth Amendment, no amendment giving the national government additional power over the people or their rights can be adopted save by the people in convention.[105]

Court Decision: Written by Circuit Judge Martin T. Manton. "The Tenth Amendment does not alter or revise the Fifth Article… The representatives of the people determine whether the amendment shall be adopted and this is entirely consonant with popular government. No authority is taken away from the people, for the people elect their representatives in the state Legislatures as well as the members of their constitutional conventions. The national government is not concerned in the control or the method whereby the elections of members of the Legislatures or members of the constitutional convention may be conducted." Continuing,

> "[I]t is impossible to maintain that, because of any undelegated power to control amendments remaining in the people, the method of adopting the Eighteenth Amendment was not within the powers delegated under article 5 of the Constitution. The Tenth Amendment could have no application to article 5, because the former only reserved "powers not delegated to the United States" and the power to choose the "method of ratification [had been] left to the choice of Congress."

---

[104] http://www.leagle.com/decision/193121647F2d169_1163/UNITED%20STATES%20v.%20THIBAULT

[105] Raymond M. Planell, "Equal Rights Amendment: Will States be Allowed to Change their Minds?," *Notre Dame Lawyer* 49, no.3 (Feb. 1974): 663

Conclusions: The federal or national government is not concerned with how an Article V Convention called by state legislatures is constituted. Therefore, **the Article V Convention is empowered to organize and conduct its business as the delegates or commissioners see fit.**

Applicability: All discussion of Congress controlling an Article V convention is pointless since 1) under this decision it is clear that the Constitution makes no provision for Congress to control an amendatory convention and 2) the precedent set by the Article V ratification conventions for the Twenty-first Amendment were not controlled by Congress but by the States.

State Supreme and Appeals Courts

State decisions cover many topics but five major themes in particular are apparent throughout the list provided. First, the use of a referendum has been tried repeatedly despite the federal courts disallowal of referendums and petitions in *Hawke v. Smith (II)* in 1920. It has been firmly held that the public has no direct role in the federal amendment process. Second, the attempt at "scarlet letter" laws in which the candidate is forced to state a position on an issue and have that position recorded on the ballot has been consistently held to be a violation of the Speech and Debate Clause and a First Amendment issue. Third, states have tried to revise their state constitutions through a sleight of hand that involves creating a list of amendments that are actually a wholesale revision of the state constitution but which bypasses the more rigorous method of state constitution replacement, typically through a state constitutional convention. Such constitutional legerdemain could result in a dangerous precedent for the federal constitution but this type of action has been consistently rejected by state supreme court decisions. Fourth, are there other methods to amend the state constitution beyond that method(s) explicitly given in the state constitutions? State supreme courts have been mixed on this question but the overwhelming majority of states have held that the constitutionally explicit methods are the only permissible methods of amendment and/or constitutional revision. This last question bears greatly on the federal amendatory convention as the "parade of horribles" has always included the warning that an Article V convention could or would go beyond its mandate and simply replace or revise the federal constitution. And finally, perhaps the most pertinent question of all is whether the constitutional convention can be limited as to its powers. That is, can it NOT be plenary? Also a mix of decisions, the majority of state supreme courts have held that a convention can indeed be limited and in some cases the state constitution requires a convention to be so limited. This list of state cases is not exhaustive; it is merely a list of the most often cited decisions. There are hundreds of state cases that involve state constitutional issues that may impact the federal legal reasoning on constitutional matters.

55.

American Federation of Labor-Congress of Industrial Organizations, et al., v. March Fong Eu, as Secretary of State, et al., Lewis K. Uhler, Real Party in Interest, 206 Cal. Rptr. 89, 686 P. 2d 609, 36 Cal. 3d 687, (1984)[106] – *California Supreme Court*

-As *AFL-CIO v. Eu*

Background: The petitioners sought to prevent the California Secretary of State, Eu, from expending public monies to place on the November 1984 ballot an initiative to compel the state legislature to submit an application to Congress for calling an Article V amendatory convention for proposing a federal balanced budget amendment. Should the legislature fail to act, the Secretary of State would file directly with the Congress and the state legislators would have their salaries docked. By 18 March 1984, the requisite number of voter signatures had been secured to force the question on the ballot.[107]

Issue: Whether the state legislature has the independence to act on its own judgment or if the electors may force the issue. As found in other states, the question includes whether the term "legislature" includes the electorate.

Court Decision: 6-1, Written by Justice Allen Broussard. "We have concluded that the initiative, to the extent that it applies for a constitutional convention or requires the Legislature to do so, does not conform to article V of the United States Constitution. Article V provides for applications by the "Legislatures of two-thirds of the several States," not by the people through the initiative; it envisions legislators free to vote their best judgment, responsible to their constituents through

---

[106] http://www.leagle.com/decision/198472336Cal3d687_1685/AMERICAN%20FEDERATION%20OF%20LABOR%20v.%20EU
[107] Generally, "States' Role in Article V Conventions: AFL-CIO v. Eu," *Cincinnati Law Review* 54 (1985)

the electoral process, not puppet legislators coerced or compelled by loss of salary or otherwise to vote in favor of a proposal they may believe unwise." Also, the initiative measure violates the initiative power of the California Constitution. The term legislature includes only the legislative body and not the electors. The Court did not treat the matter as a "political question" and appears to be rejecting that doctrine.[108]

The California Court stated conclusively that,

"The only conclusion we can draw from this fact is that the drafters wanted the amending process in the hands of a body with the power to deliberate upon a proposed amendment and, after considering not only the views of the people but the merits of the proposition, to render a considered judgment. A rubber stamp legislature could not fulfill its function under article V of the Constitution."

<u>Conclusions</u>: **Financial penalties on delegates or legislators are invalid. Article V "envisions legislators must be free to vote their best judgment."** Rejected the "political question doctrine" (see *Coleman v. Miller*). The Court also held that ballot initiatives to force an Article V Convention are not permissible. The Supreme Court of California has interpreted *Hawke* as direct authority for the proposition that a state court can remove a proposed amendment from a state election ballot on the ground that it does not conform to Article V.

<u>Applicability</u>: **An Article V amendatory convention is free from the constraints of an electorate dictating the topics for amendment consideration. Only the method defined in Article V can be used to create and submit a state legislature's application for an Article V convention.**

56.

As Alabama v. Manley, 441 So. 2d 864 (Ala. 1983)[109,110] – *Alabama Supreme Court*

Consolidated under one case,
- *The State of Alabama and Don Seigelman, as Secretary of the State of Alabama v. Richard S. Manley*

---

[108] Robert G. Natelson, "Proposing Constitutional Amendments By Convention: Rules Governing The Process," *Tennessee Law Review* 78 (2011): 697, n 13.
[109] http://home.hiwaay.net/~becraft/Manley.htm
[110] http://law.justia.com/cases/alabama/supreme-court/1983/441-so-2d-864-1.html

- *Tom Brassell, as Comptroller of the State of Alabama, v. Richard S. Manley*

Background: In 1983, the Alabama state legislature proposed a new state constitution replacing the 1901 state constitution. The people of the state would be able to vote on the proposed constitution as they would a state constitutional amendment. Manley sued to prevent the legislature from circumventing the current state constitution and employing a new method of amendment that is not included in the existing 1901 constitution. The state appealed bringing these suits which are consolidated.

Issue: Do Sections 284-287 of the 1901 constitution limit the methods of ratification? May the new constitution be submitted to the people as an amendment to the 1901 constitution? May a new ratification or amendment process be substituted?

Court Decision: 6-3, Written by Justice Oscar W. Adams, Jr.. The question of whether the current constitution is limited is affirmative. The questions of whether the proposed constitution may be an amendment and whether a new amendment/ratification method may be used are both negative.

Conclusions: The only permissible methods of constitutional amendment are those specifically spelled out in the constitution. No short cuts are allowed. Substitute methods are *ultra vires*.

Applicability: **Any attempt to replace the federal constitution by "amending" it with a new constitution that would supersede all previous parts would not be constitutional.** The legal reasoning found in *Manley* would be the foundation for arguing against any such action at the federal level.

57.

James A. Barlotti v. David B. Lyons, Registrar of Voters of County of Los Angeles, 182 Cal. 575, 189 Pac. 282 (Cal. 1920)[111] – *California Supreme Court*
-As *Barlotti V. Lyons*

Background: This case concerned the ratification of the Eighteenth Amendment prohibiting the sale of alcohol. When the California

---
[111] https://casetext.com/case/barlotti-v-lyons

Legislature ratified the amendment, Barlotti and other petitioners presented a referendum petition to the registrar of voters. The registrar refused to transmit the petition to the Secretary of State, and petitioners sought mandamus from this court.

Issue: As other cases of the period asked, what is the meaning of the word "legislature" in Article V?

Court Decision: Unanimous, Written by Chief Justice Frank M. Angelotti. Legislature means only the elected body of representatives. "If by those words was meant the *representative bodies* invested with the law-making power of the several states, which existed at the time of the adoption of the constitution ... in each of the several states, and which have ever since so existed, as distinguished from the law-making power of the respective states, there is nothing left to discuss, for with that meaning attributed to the term ... the constitutional provision is so plain and unambiguous as not to admit of different constructions."

Conclusions: A referendum on federal constitutional amendment is not permissible under the state or federal constitutions. Legislature in this regard is an independent body acting behalf of the people and not acting under the usual legislative authority.

Applicability: An amendatory convention cannot be called by the people directly and cannot be forced upon the state legislature.

58.

As Bess v. Ulmer, 985 P.2d 979 (Alaska 1999)[112] – *Alaska Supreme Court*

Consolidated under one case:
- *Howard BESS, Darlene Bess, Jay Brause, and Gene Dugan, v. Fran ULMER, Lieutenant Governor of the State of Alaska, and State of Alaska*
- *The Alaska Legislature, acting by and through the Alaska Legislative Council, Representative Pete Kelly, and Senator Loren Leman, v. Fran Ulmer, in her official capacity as the Lieutenant Governor of the State of Alaska*
- *Elizabeth A. Dodd, Victor "Vic" Fischer, Katherine T. "Katie" Hurley, Ernest E. Line, George Rogers, and Jean Rogers, v. Fran ULMER, Lieutenant Governor of the State of Alaska, Sandra Stout, Director of Division of Elections, and the State of Alaska*

Background: Citizen groups challenged three ballot propositions

---

[112] https://www.courtlistener.com/opinion/1264934/bess-v-ulmer/

to amend the Alaska Constitution because the propositions were revisions not amendments; revisions can only be accomplished through a constitutional convention.

Issue: "The objective of this opinion is to elucidate the distinction between amendatory changes and revisory changes, to provide some guidance for future endeavors to change the Constitution. The Framers of the Alaska Constitution distinguished between a revision and an amendment. Like scholars and other framers in other states, they intended this distinction to be substantive. We conclude that a revision is a change which alters the substance and integrity of our Constitution in a manner measured both qualitatively and quantitatively."

Court Decision: Written by Chief Justice Warren W. Matthews. The Court based the expedited Preliminary Opinion and Order on the fact that the Constitution of the State of Alaska can be changed in only two ways, amendment and revision, and that a separate procedure must be followed for each.

Conclusions: The Court found the first proposals to not be an amendment but a revision. The other proposals were amendments.

Applicability: The Article V amendment process covers amendments – no provision is made for revisions.

59. _____

Nancy Bramberg, et al, v. Bill Jones, as Secretary of State, 20 Cal. 4th 1045, 978 P.2d 1240 (1999)[113] – California Supreme Court

-As *Bramberg v. Jones*

Background: A taxpayer and registered voter, a candidate and two elected officials challenged the constitutional validity of Proposition 225 which advocated for congressional term limits. The measure required the Secretary of State to place notations on the ballots as to the positions of candidates on term limits and instructs elected officials to work for term limits.[114]

Issue: Is it constitutional for states to impose term limits and

---

[113] http://law.justia.com/cases/california/supreme-court/4th/20/1045.html

[114] Vikram David Amar, "The People Made Me Do It: Can the People of the States Instruct and Coerce Their State Legislatures in the Article V Constitutional Amendment Process?," *William and Mary Law Review* 41, no.3 (2000): 1037-8

instructions on their congressional delegations?

Court Decision: Written by Chief Justice Ronald M. George. The case is similar to *Kimble v. Swackhamer* except that the measure is neither non-binding nor advisory. "Because Proposition 225 both directly instructs, and indirectly attempts to coerce, California's congressional and state legislators in the exercise of their federal constitutional function of proposing and ratifying amendments to the United States Constitution, we conclude that the proposition clearly conflicts with the amendment process authorized by Article V and is therefore unconstitutional."

Conclusions: The Court found the measure unconstitutional.

Applicability: The public has no direct role in the Article V amendment process.

60.

C. C. Carson v. John L. Sullivan, Secretary of State, et al, 223 S. W. 571, 284 Mo. 353 (1920)[115] – Missouri Supreme Court

-As *Carson v. Sullivan*

Background: The US Supreme Court had ruled that the Eighteenth Amendment had become part of the US Constitution and was then in effect. Any referendum for ratification by the citizens of Missouri was without effect.

Issue: May the people of the state vote by referendum on the ratification of a proposed federal amendment?

Court Decision: Written by Chief Justice Robert F. Walker. "The framers of Article V of the Constitution had in mind to refer proposed constitutional amendments "to the body of persons in the State clothed with authority to make laws." They intended that they should go to the legislative branch of the State government for ratification or rejection, and they so intended because that branch was the sole representative of the sovereign power of all the people of the State."

Conclusions: Article V limits the options for ratification and there is no discretion or leeway on the part of the States to decide how to ratify.

Applicability: Moot per US Supreme Court decision in National

---

[115] https://casetext.com/case/carson-v-sullivan-1

Prohibition Cases, specifically citing *State of Rhode Island v. Palmer*, 40 Sup. Ct. Rep. 486

61.

William A. Chenault v. Henry H. Carter, Secretary of State, 332 S.W.2d 623 (1960)[116] – *Kentucky Court of Appeals*
-As ***Chenault v. Carter***

Background: In 1959, the Kentucky Legislature passed a bill calling for a limited constitutional convention for a new state constitution. The first step was to gain the approval of the electorate for the convention through a ballot measure.

Issue: The convention would be limited to consideration of just twelve specific items making it a limited convention.

Court Decision: Written by Judge John Palmore. The convention call is correct and the election will be held. The legislature is within its power to limit the convention topics. "The limitation of the proposed convention to the twelve subjects set forth in the successive enactments of the General Assemblies is valid and will constitute a restriction on the power and authority of the delegates to the convention." Regarding the limitation of the subject material, "The choice of whether a constitutional convention shall be called rests entirely with the electorate. The discretion of the legislature is at an end when the matter is finally proposed. The formal call issued by the General Assembly following a favorable vote by the people is but a ministerial duty enjoined upon it by the Constitution in the execution of a public mandate. Inhering in that mandate are the terms and conditions of the initial proposal. The delegates to the convention are the agents not of the legislature, but of the people themselves. As a principal may limit the authority of his agent, so may the sovereign people of this state limit the authority of their delegates."[117]

Conclusions: **An Article V Convention may be limited in purpose to a single issue or to a fixed set of issues**. Thus, the state may limit the authority of the drafting convention.

---

[116] https://casetext.com/case/chenault-v-carter
[117] Paul J. Weber & Barbara A. Perry, *Unfounded Fears, Myths and Realities of a Constitutional Convention* (New York: Praeger, 1989), 85

__Applicability:__ Limiting a constitutional convention or an amendatory convention is an established practice and practical approach.

62.

Henry W. Collier, Governor v. Samuel G. Frierson, et al., 24 Ala. 100 (1854) – *Alabama Supreme Court*
-As ***Collier v. Frierson***

__Background:__ The people of Alabama sought to enact a new state constitution.

__Issue:__ Whether the current state constitution's requirement of drafting or revising a state constitution can be accomplished solely through the stipulated convention method could be done legally.

__Court Decision:__ Written by Chief Justice George Goldthwaite. An amendment voted on without a compliance with its requirements is void.

__Conclusions:__ Failure to strictly observe and comply with the amendment procedure of the constitution is "fatal" to the proposal of the state legislature. This result is independent of the people's view and favorability of the proposed constitution or amendment.

__Applicability:__ The two procedures laid out in Article V for amendment production and introduction are the sole methods of amendment proposal. The two methods of ratification are the sole methods of ratification, no deviation is permitted. Once a method is chosen and commenced, each step must be followed and completed without modification or omission.

63.

James H. Cummings, Secretary of State, et al., v. Roy H. Beeler, Attorney General, et al. 189 Tenn. 151 (1949) – *Tennessee Supreme Court*[118]
-As ***Cummings v. Beeler***

__Background:__ This case was brought to test the constitutionality of Tennessee's Chapter 49 of the Public Acts of 1949. One act provided for calling a limited state constitutional convention to propose amendments. Tennessee created a commission in 1945 to review whether a convention

---
[118] https://casetext.com/case/cummings-secretary-of-state-v-beeler

was needed. The commission asked of the state's Attorney General for an opinion on limiting a convention. The AG's report stated that the convention could not be limited. The commission recommended a limited convention and the legislature acted upon that recommendation.

Issue: Whether the convention may be limited to the issues stipulated in the enabling act.

Court Decision: Written by Justice Hamilton S. Burnett. The legislature has the authority to choose either an open or a limited convention. "It is not the legislature who limits the scope of a convention but it is the people themselves who by their vote under the terms of this act limit the scope of the convention."[119] Although the court acknowledged that the limitation by the legislature was probably not permissible under current theory, they deferred to the people and the lack of any such prohibition in the state constitution.[120] The decision did recognize and cite the supporting ruling in Virginia's *Staples v. Gilmer*.

Conclusions: Conventions are considered to be an extension or an organ of the current government. They are invested with an authority that may not be expressly designated by the people as withheld from the convention.[121] If the people vote to accept the terms of the limited convention, then it will be limited.

Applicability: In 1975, the same state Supreme Court decided in *Snow v. City of Memphis*, 527 S.W. 2d. 55, that the convention can be restricted to only certain parts of the constitution.

64.

Arthur Decher, et al v. Coleman C. Vaughan, Secretary of State,
209 Mich. 565, 177 N. W. 388, (1920) – **Michigan Supreme Court**

-As *Decher v. Vaughan*

Background: A sufficient number of petitions were submitted to the Secretary of State to ask that the Eighteenth Amendment's ratification

---

[119] Raymond H. Moseley, "The Limited Constitutional Convention," *Tennessee Law Review* 21, no.8 (June 1951): 868
[120] Francis H. Heller, "Limiting a Constitutional Convention: The State Precedents," *Cardozo Law Review* 3 (1982): 574-5
[121] Note, "Constitutional Revision by a Restricted Convention," *Minnesota Law Review* 35 (1951): 285

be determined by a public referendum. The Michigan Secretary of State refused to do so, on the advice of the state's Attorney General.

Issue: Does a state official have the authority, or right, to refuse to carry out an action that is within their duties? What is meant by the word "legislature"?

Court Decision: Written by Chief Justice Joseph B. Moore. "[u]nder the provisions ... as to initiative and referendum, the people have no power to enact legislation until the proposal therefor has been submitted by petition to the legislature for action thereon. The right of the people to thus legislate in no way makes them a part of the legislature...." "A resolution ratifying an amendment to the federal constitution is not an "act" within the meaning of the referendum provision." Participation in the Legislature does not extend to the unelected people.

Conclusions: The Secretary of State was immune from action of submitting the ratification to a referendum as the action conflicts with Article V.

Applicability: As with many other states, the Michigan action was beyond the people and the ruling concludes that the referendum cannot be used for an Article V convention.

65.

Eugenia T. Donovan, et al, v. Sharon Priest, Secretary of State of the State of Arkansas, Arkansas Term Limits, Frank Filbert, and Spencer G. Plumley, *931 S.W. 2d 119, 326 Ark. 353, (Ark. 1996)*[122,123] *– Arkansas Supreme Court*

-As **Donovan v. Priest**

Background: Several groups and individuals sought to prevent the Secretary of State from placing on the ballot a term limits question as an amendment to the state constitution. Like many other states, Arkansas sought term limits on Congress and the measure would have required Arkansas's elected officials, state and federal, to work for a term limits amendment to the federal constitution. The measure would have included

---

[122] https://www.courtlistener.com/opinion/1777722/donovan-v-priest/
[123] http://opinions.aoc.arkansas.gov/WebLink8/docview.aspx?id=198889&dbid=0

ballot notations on the position of candidates regarding term limits.

Issue: "Petitioner asserts that the proposed Amendment 9 exceeds the legislative powers reserved to the people of this state by our Amendment 7 in that it directly contravenes the amendment process provided for in Article V of the United States Constitution."

Court Decision: Written by Justice Donald L. Corbin. "The only conclusion we can draw from this fact is that the drafters wanted the amending process in the hands of a body with the power to deliberate upon a proposed amendment and, after considering not only the views of the people but the merits of the proposition, to render a considered judgment. *A rubber stamp legislature could not fulfill its function under article V of the Constitution.*"

Conclusions: This ruling requires that any assembly be more than a rubber stamp for a pre-written amendment. **The assembly must be able to engage in "intellectual debate, deliberation, or consideration" of any proposed amendment.**[124] This can be applied to an Article V Convention. In this ruling, the court also rejected ballot labeling, a ruling similar to *AFL-CIO v. Eu* and *League of Women Voters of Maine v. Gwadosky*.

Applicability: **The effectiveness of an amendatory convention is reduced by the inability to fully debate every option.** A convention must be free from constraints that would impede full deliberation of issues and proposals.

66.

Lewis G. Ellingham, Secretary of State, et al., v. John T. Dye, 178 Ind. 336, 99 N. E. 1 (1912)[125] – **Indiana Supreme Court**

-As ***Ellingham v. Dye***

Background: The state legislature decided to act as a constitutional convention and draft a new state constitution that was actually the current constitution with 23 amendments interspersed throughout.

Issue: The legislature did not have the authority of the people – through either a constitutional provision or a referendum – to act as a convention as it had not secured the approval of the people to hold a

---

[124] Robert G. Natelson, "Proposing Constitutional Amendments by Convention: Rules Governing the Process," *Tennessee Law Review* 78 (2011): 746, n.377
[125] http://indianalawblog.com/documents/ellingham%20v%20dye.pdf

constitutional convention first.

Court Decision: Written by Chief Justice Charles E. Cox. The Court held that the legislature had acted unconstitutionally. If a convention should be illegally or improperly constituted – that is, if the delegates are appointed (self or otherwise) rather than elected if so constitutionally required, then the work of the convention would be tainted and the courts should reject it. Such a constitution should not even be presented to the people for ratification.[126]

Conclusions: The legislature did not properly draft, promulgate or ratify the proposed constitution, therefore it is invalid.

Applicability: **An amendatory convention that exceeds its mandate is acting illegally and the product of that convention is invalid and unconstitutional.**

67.

Jennie Erwin v. William Nolan, et al., 240 Mo. 401, 217 S. W. 837, (1920)[127] – *Missouri Supreme Court*

-As *Erwin v. Nolan*

Background: Erwin was born seven weeks after the State of Missouri declared slaves to be emancipated. Her parents, both slaves, had lived as much as they could, as husband and wife during the Civil War. Erwin sought to claim her inheritance of her father's land but her cousins claimed her to be illegitimate and that they were entitled to her father's land.

Issue: The convention which drafted the 1865 Missouri state constitution passed an ordinance for the rights of former slaves and their children. Married slaves would have to seek a formal registering of their marriage. Louis Nolan and his wife Mary did not do so. Was the ordinance a legitimate amendment to the constitution?

Court Decision: Unanimous concurrence. Written by Chief Justice Robert F. Walker. "A State Constitution can be amended only in the manner by it prescribed. The power thus conferred is, from the terms employed, unlimited; but the people, in their wisdom, have usually in their organic law, always of their own making, prescribed limitations

---

[126] Thomas Raeburn White, "Amendment and Revision of State Constitutions," *University of Pennsylvania Law Review* 100 (1952): 1151
[127] https://casetext.com/case/erwin-v-nolan

upon and defined the course to be pursued in the exercise of this power. Nor can it be claimed with any regard for the rules of construction that the Constitution framed by this convention and which contained an emphatic declaration abolishing slavery but nothing further in regard thereto, can be construed to have a retrospective effect and thus give operative force to the ordinance." Conventions have no ordinary legislative powers, only fundamental legislative power.[128]

Conclusions: The convention did not properly draft, promulgate or ratify the proposed amendment/ordinance, therefore it is invalid. "That the convention derived its power from the people is true, but the power thus conferred was limited by the people themselves to the terms of the legislative enactment under which the members of the convention were elected." Jennie Erwin kept her father's land.

Applicability: A convention that is limited must not go beyond that stipulated power. The enactment of the convention is not retroactive.

68.

Edward P. Foley v. Democratic Parish Committee of Parish of Orleans, 70 So. 104, 138 La. 220 (1915) – **Louisiana Supreme Court**

Background: Parochial committees are required to post a slate of candidates for a primary election by a certain date according to the new 1913 state constitution. The Democratic Party objected that their preferred date for the primary was different than that stipulated.

Issue: The requirement that was included in the new constitution was outside of the limits of the convention and was therefore invalid.

Court Decision: Written by Justice Oliver O. Provosty. The limitations on the convention were not to be changed. They were binding and operative. Any action taken outside of the parameters set is invalid.

Conclusions: The ruling echoes a prior decision in *State v. American Sugar Refining Co.,* 68 So. 742 and in *Sheridan v. Police Jury,* 145 La. 403, 82 So. 386.[129] The vote by the people for a convention is taken to be a vote for a "specific" type of convention and that establishes the

---

[128] Note, "Constitutional Revision by a Restricted Convention," *Minnesota Law Review* 35 (1951): 290
[129] Robert Gallagher, "The Powers of Conventions," *Lawyer & Banker & Southern Bench & Bar Review* 9, no.148 (1916): 148

limitations.[130]

Applicability: An Article V amendatory convention that is limited cannot exceed its stipulated powers and scope.

Note: There are other similar cases: *Wood's Appeal* 75 Pa. 59; *Louisiana Ry v. Madere* 102 La. 635; *McCready v. Hunt* 2 Hill Law (S.C.) 1; among others

69.

W. C. Gatewood, et al., v. Robert Matthews, Attorney General for the Commonwealth of Kentucky, Thelma L. Stovall, Secretary of State for the Commonwealth of Kentucky,

403 S.W. 2d. 716 (Ky. 1966)[131] – *Kentucky Court of Appeals*

-As **Gatewood v. Matthews**

Background: Gatewood sought to prevent adoption of a new state constitution by prohibiting its placement on the ballot. The proposed constitution had been drafted by an appointed commission and not a convention as required by the current state constitution.

Issue: The primary question to be considered is whether by the terms of Sections 256 and 258 of the existing Constitution the people have imposed upon themselves exclusive modes of amending or of revising their Constitution. It is the appellant's contention that those sections do represent exclusive modes of reforming the Constitution.

Court Decision: The decision specifically relied on the Alabama *Wheeler* decision of 1946 and the Rhode Island *In re Opinion to the Governor* decision of 1935. The language of the constitution is the obvious controlling issue.

Conclusions: The state constitution had not "imposed upon themselves exclusive modes of amending or of revising their Constitution" on the people.

Applicability: Gatewood is often cited as a counterfactual example for amendment procedures. The most salient point is that the ratification

---

[130] Note, "Constitutional Revision by a Restricted Convention," *Minnesota Law Review* 35 (1951): 285
[131] http://law.justia.com/cases/kentucky/court-of-appeals/1966/403-s-w-2d-716-1.html

was still performed by the people and not by decree of the constitutional commission.

70.
___

In State ex rel. John W. Halliburton v. Cornelius Roach, Secretary of State,
230 Mo. 408, 130 S.W. 689 (1910) – Missouri Supreme Court
-As *State ex rel. Halliburton v. Roach*

Background: The state sought a constitutional amendment for redistricting for senatorial districts.

Issue: Can a constitutional amendment be legislative in nature?

Court Decision: "Constitutional provisions and amendments to the Constitution relate to the fundamental law and certain fixed first principles upon which government is founded.... The purpose of constitutional provisions and amendments to the Constitution is to prescribe the permanent framework and a uniform system of government, and to assign to the different departments thereof their respective powers and duties.... "The very term `constitution' implies an instrument of a permanent and abiding nature, ...".[132] The Court noted that "[t]he mere calling it an amendment to the Constitution unless the subject-matter verifies the correctness of that name is not binding upon the respondent or upon this court."

Conclusions: The amendment may not be legislative in character. A proposal that is legislative must be designated as such.

Applicability: The application and content of the Thirteenth, Fifteenth and Eighteenth Amendments would seem to refute the conclusions in *Roach*. In recent decades *Roach* has been discounted as a reliable source.[133]

71.
___

Karl Herbring v. George M. Brown, Attorney General of the State of Oregon, 92 Or. 176, 180 P. 328, (1919)[134] – Oregon Supreme Court
-As *Herbring v. Brown*

---

[132] Lester B. Orfield & Henry M. Bates, *The Amending of the Federal Constitution* (Ann Arbor: University of Michigan Press, 1942), 102-3
[133] http://law.justia.com/cases/missouri/supreme-court/1984/66482-0.html
[134] http://initiativesamendment.org/wp-content/uploads/2015/09/Herbring-v-Brown-1919.pdf

Background: Another state case involving the ratification of the Eighteenth Amendment by public referendum.

Issue: The state Attorney General refused to provide a ballot title for a referendum on the ratification of the proposed Eighteenth Amendment to the federal constitution on the grounds that such action would violate Article V of the federal constitution and Section 1, Article IV of the Oregon constitution.

Court Decision: En banc, written by Chief Justice Thomas A. McBride. "It seems clear to us that these sections apply only to proposed laws, and not to legislative resolutions, memorials and the like."

Conclusions: The Court concluded that "these sections [establishing the initiative and referendum] apply only to proposed laws, and not to legislative resolutions, memorials, and the like." A referendum may not be used to ratify a federal constitutional amendment. The act of a state legislature that ratifies a proposed constitutional amendment is not a tradition legislative act of the state law; it is a strictly federal act through a power granted by Article V and is independent of the state legislature's usual function.

Applicability: The federal requirements for ratification are not flexible.

72.

Robert Holmes and Charles Sprague v. Howell Appling, Jr., Secretary of State, 237 Or. 546, 392 P.2d. 636 (1964)[135] – Oregon Supreme Court

-As *Holmes v. Appling*

Background: Oregon's state constitution permits citizen initiatives to propose state constitutional amendments. Two former governors, Robert D. Holmes and Charles A. Sprague, wanted to "amend" the Oregon state constitution, but the Secretary of State, Howell Appling, to provide a ballot title for their proposed new state constitution. The Commission for Constitutional Revision did not succeed in garnering the

---

[135] http://law.justia.com/cases/oregon/supreme-court/1964/237-or-546-3.html

requisite two-thirds votes in the legislature to submit a new constitution to the people. The initiative appears to have been an end-around the system.

Issue: The Oregon Attorney General, Robert Thornton, advised the Secretary of State that the "amendment" was actually a new constitution and the ballot initiative was not a legal means of enacting a new constitution. Was the proposed amendment truly an amendment and was it permissible to enact a new constitution in this way?

Court Decision: Written by Justice George Rossman. The decision specifically relied on the Alabama *Wheeler* decision of 1946 and the Rhode Island *In re Opinion to the Governor* decision of 1935. The language of the constitution is the obvious controlling issue. Revision is not the same as amendment. The Court said that "To call it an amendment is a misnomer."

Conclusions: The state constitution had not "imposed upon themselves exclusive modes of amending or of revising their Constitution" on the people. But the constitution was explicit in the methods of amendment and revision separately and these were in conflict in this instance.

Applicability: Any attempt to adapt any other provision of the federal constitution to the amendment process (such as was attempted in the 1920s with the Tenth Amendment) would not be possible. Utilizing any method other than that in Article V would not be possible either.

73.

In re Opinion of the Justices, 118 *Me.* 544, 107 *A.* 673, 5 *A.L.R.* 1412, *(1919)*[136] – *Maine Supreme Court*

Background: Governor Carl Milliken asked the Maine Supreme Court to give its opinion on the idea of using the state constitution's provision for a referendum to approve the Eighteenth Amendment.

Issue: Could the people of Maine pass binding judgment on a federal constitutional amendment?

Court Decision: Written by per curiam. The Court answered in the

---

[136] http://initiativesamendment.org/wp-content/uploads/2015/09/Maine-Opinion-the-People-Cannot-Ratify-1919.pdf

negative; the referendum and initiative mechanisms are not applicable to a federal amendment.

Conclusions: The Maine Supreme Court declared that the resolution ratifying the Eighteenth Amendment was not subject to referendum because it "was neither a public act, a private act nor a resolve having the force of law. It was in no sense legislation." The action of the state legislature and the Congress itself, are both independent of their usual activities; Article V *is* a special action.

> *"[T]he power of the people of Maine over amendments had been completely and unreservedly lodged with the bodies designated by article 5, and so long as that article remains unmodified they have no power left in themselves either to propose or to ratify federal amendments. The authority is elsewhere. "But the people, by the adoption of the initiative and referendum amendment, did not intend to assume or regain such power."*[137]

Applicability: Like many other states at the time, the legislature was seeking to pass the buck, so to say, and have the people vote thereby giving the state legislators "plausible deniability" and avoid the backlash of the "drys." This political maneuver did not hold anywhere.

74.

In re Opinions of the Justices, 226 Ala. 565, 148 So. 107, (1933)[138] – *Alabama Supreme Court*

Background: In anticipation of a state convention to consider ratification of the proposed Twenty-first Amendment, Alabama's governor, Benjamin M. Miller asked the Alabama Supreme Court for their opinion as to the constitutionality of proportioning the convention delegates in the same manner as the House of the state legislature and whether a proposed statute requiring that delegates to a convention to ratify the Twenty-first Amendment pledge to follow the result of a statewide vote was permissible.

Issue: Will a convention composed in part of delegates elected from the counties, and voted for by electors in the counties only, pledged to cast their vote according to the result of a state-wide referendum, be

---
[137] Lester B. Orfield & Henry M. Bates, *The Amending of the Federal Constitution* (Ann Arbor: University of Michigan Press, 1942), 62, n.81
[138] https://casetext.com/case/in-re-opinions-of-the-justices-16

a convention as intended and provided by Article V of the Constitution of the United States? Does the Federal Constitution forbid a state law providing for an instructed delegation to such convention, a delegation pledged to voice the consent of the governed, ascertained by the method recognized throughout our system, namely, the ballot?

Court Decision: Written by Chief Justice Jonathon C. Anderson. "The Constitution put no restrictions on the states in calling their conventions. It was left to the sovereign state to frame its own laws relating to such convention, to the end that the consent of the governed be expressed thereby." "Keeping in view the fundamental doctrine of a government of the people, by the people, and for the people, we are unable to see in the Federal Constitution any purpose to prohibit a direct and binding instruction to the members of the convention voicing the consent of the governed."

Conclusions: The court said the framers of the Constitution "assumed" that legislatures and conventions "would voice the will of the people," the Alabama court reasoned that the function of deliberative bodies in ratifying proposed amendments was merely to ascertain and carry out the popular will. A direct and binding instruction to the delegates, it concluded, would more truly and efficiently fulfill that function.[139]

Applicability: This example is counterfactual to most other opinions in that while the court determined that the convention could be organized as the state wished, it is in the minority of states in allowing for delegate instructions.

75.

In Re the Opinion of the Justices, 132 Me. 491, 167 A. 176 (1933) – Maine Supreme Court

Background: In anticipation of the state Article V ratification conventions for the Twenty-first Amendment, the Maine Supreme Court was asked for an official opinion on how to select delegates and how such a convention would operate. This case stems from the attempt to use a public referendum to bind a ratifying convention and prevent deliberation.

---

[139] Lester B. Orfield & Henry M. Bates, *The Amending of the Federal Constitution* (Ann Arbor: University of Michigan Press, 1942), 60

Issue: Is it permissible for a state to resort to tradition of long established custom to determine how to select convention delegates? May a convention determine its own rules?

Court Decision: The Court determined that the convention must be deliberative to fulfill its function. This is in direct contradiction to the concurrent finding of the Alabama Supreme Court.[140]

Conclusions: **The state may rely on custom to select delegates** to ratifying conventions. By implication, they may also rely on their own particular customs to choose how to select their delegates to Article V Conventions. Along with this power is the ability to establish the convention's rules, elect its own officers, fix the hours of sitting, judge the credentials of the members, and other housekeeping requirements. This ruling also held that the ratification convention has the power to determine questions relating to the qualifications of the delegates and to fill vacancies.

Applicability: Each state may determine its own method of delegate selection and the convention itself may specify its rules.

76.

In Re Opinion of the Justices, *204 N.C. 306, 172 S.E. 474 (1933)* – **North Carolina Supreme Court**

Background: With the state conventions for considering the ratification of the proposed Twenty-first Amendment pending, North Carolina questioned with a ratifying convention could be limited to the proposed amendment at hand or whether other issues could be raised.

Issue: May a ratifying convention be limited in the authority of the convention to consider a range of subjects?

Court Decision: The state constitution's provision for a constitutional convention to amend the state constitution does not apply to a federal constitutional convention. That power is in the hands of the Congress only. The state may dictate the authority and limits of the convention's subject matter.

Conclusions: **An Article V Convention may be limited in purpose to a single issue or to a fixed set of issues**. Thus, the state may limit the

---

[140] Ibid.

authority of the ratifying convention.

Applicability: The ratifying conventions were limited and an amendatory convention could also be limited in subject matter.

77.

In re Opinion to the Governor, 55 R.I. 56, 178 A. 433 (1935) – Rhode Island Supreme Court[141]

Background: The question was raised as to whether the state constitution allowed for modes of amendment other than those explicitly named in the state constitution. The state constitution allowed only revision by a constitutional amendment or through a constitutional convention. But an 1883 state supreme court decision[142] ruled that neither the legislature nor the people could call a convention because no mechanism existed with the state constitution to do so. The state constitution(s) had proven unamendable. In the early twentieth century, the state sought to use state limited constitutional conventions to propose amendments.

Issue: The language in the amendment section of the state constitution did not specifically state the exclusive mode of amendment or revision.

Court Decision: "It is also well settled that no other method can be legally employed for amending or revising a constitution of substituting another one for it, unless such other method is expressly provided for in the constitution itself." Also, "We entertain no doubt, that, to change the constitution in any other mode than by a convention, every requisition which is demanded by the instrument itself, must be observed, and the omission of any one is fatal to the amendment."

Conclusions: The Court recognized certain historical practices for amendment and thought these to be well established. The Court disapproved of going outside of established practices. The state legislature has a responsibility to pass laws that will enable the amendment process to proceed. This decision made the state limited constitutional convention possible.

---

[141] Patrick T. Conley & Robert G. Flanders, Jr., *The Rhode Island State Constitution: A Reference Guide* (Westport, CT: Praeger, 2007), 274
[142] *In re Constitutional Convention*, 14 R.I. 649 (1883)

Applicability: The power to call a convention is an implied power. "A legislature has the power to call a convention even though the state constitution does not specifically provide for calling a convention by the legislature."

78.

In re Initiative Petition No. 364, 930 P.2d 186 (Okla.1996)[143] – Oklahoma Supreme Court

Background: "In 1994, Oklahoma became the first state to enact term limits for its Congressional representatives. This was achieved through an amendment to the Oklahoma Constitution by way of an initiative election. This initiative measure declares that the people of Oklahoma desire that the Oklahoma Legislature apply to Congress for the calling of a Federal Constitutional Convention leading to the adoption of the specific proposed amendment which is set forth in full, and the voters should be kept informed of their legislators' efforts in this regard."

Issue: May the people force the calling of an amendatory convention through a ballot measure?

Court Decision: Written by Justice Robert D. Simms. "[P]rotestant's arguments regarding issues arising under Article V of the Constitution of the United States and Art. 5, sec. 1 of the Oklahoma Constitution are persuasive and determinative of the challenge. The measure is facially violative of both provisions and must be stricken in its entirety. Protestant contends that this proposal would allow the people to do indirectly what they cannot do directly—propose amendments to the Constitution of the United States. The law is plain that the application for a convention must come from the Legislature acting freely without restriction or limitation, not from the people through exercise of their initiative power. The legislative power in the amendment process of Article V includes only that power which has been delegated to the representative bodies of the several states, it does not include the reserved legislative power of the people."

Conclusions: The Court concluded that the term limits initiative violated Article V because it called for negative ballot designations

---

[143] https://scholar.google.com/scholar_case?case=2629631348414894265&hl=en&as_sdt=6,50&as_vis=1

designed to coerce legislators into invoking their Article V powers.

Applicability: The power to call a convention is an implied power not subject to the initiative.

79.

A. M. Johnson, Jr. v. John Craft, et al, 205 Ala. 386, 87 So. 375 (1921)[144] – Alabama Supreme Court

-As *Johnson v. Craft*

Background: The state legislature proposed an amendment to the state constitution, and allowed the governor to set the date of the election for the people to ratify the proposed amendment.

Issue: A state constitutional amendment was proposed legislatively and in circumvention of the procedure given in the state constitution. Was it constitutionally valid?

Court Decision: Written by Justice Thomas C. McClellan. The Court referred back to *Collier v. Frierson*.

Conclusions: The Court found the amendment unconstitutional.

Applicability: Violations of the amendment procedure invalidate proposed amendments.

80.

Horatio P. Livermore v. Edwin G. Waite, Secretary of State, 102 Cal. 113, 117, 36 P. 424, 25 L.R.A. 312, (1894)[145] – California Supreme Court

-As *Livermore v. Waite*

Background: The state legislature proposed an amendment to the state constitution that would relocate the state capitol from Sacramento to San Jose after the approval of the people and the governor, secretary of state and attorney general. Also, the move involved a donation of ten acres to the state and a million dollars to accommodate the move. Taxpayer and citizen Livermore objected and sued claiming that the process was a violation of the state constitution and that it placed the amendment process in the hands of a few individuals.

---

[144] https://casetext.com/case/johnson-v-craft-1
[145] Walter F. Dodd, "Judicial Control Over the Amendment of State Constitutions," *Columbia Law Review* 10, no.7 (Nov. 1910): 636-7.

Issue: The process deviated from that of the written process in the state constitution – was it valid?

Court Decision: Unanimous, written by Justice Ralph C. Harrison. Constitutional amendments must be enacted in a manner explicitly provided for by the California Constitution, while constitutional revisions only must follow the United States Constitution. No individual can hold the power to ratify or approve a constitutional amendment.

Conclusions: The Court found the amendment unconstitutional.

Applicability: The amendment process cannot be circumvented and directed by a few individuals as the amendment proposed would not become operational upon the approval of the people but by the select individuals named.

81.

Arthur James McFadden v. Frank M. Jordan, as Secretary of State, Willis Allen, et al., 32 Cal. 2d. 330, 196 P.2d. 787 (1948)[146] – California Supreme Court
-As *McFadden v. Jordan*

Background: The state legislature proposed an amendment to the state constitution that would substantially change fifteen of the twenty-five articles in the constitution.

Issue: Does the proposed amendment amount to an amendment or a revision which would require a constitutional convention? Further, the initiative method was proposed and the validity of this method was in question.

Court Decision: Unanimous, written by Justice Benjamin Rey Schauer. Such a substantial revision requires a convention and input from the people. This change amounts to a new constitution. The use of the initiative was found to be inappropriate as well.[147]

Conclusions: The Court found the amendment unconstitutional.

Applicability: The wholesale rewrite of the federal constitution through a revision or a series of revisions would not be permissible. The

---

[146] http://scocal.stanford.edu/opinion/mcfadden-v-jordan 29414
[147] Joseph R. Grodin, "Popular Sovereignty and Its Limits: Lessons for a Constitutional Convention in California," *Loyola of Los Angeles Law Review* 44 (Winter 2011): 629

difference between amendment and revision is distinct and understood even if not formally defined.

82.

Karen A. Morrissey v. State of Colorado, U.S. Term Limits, Inc., and Dennis Polhill, 951 P.2d 911 (Colo. 1998)[148] – Colorado Supreme Court
-As *Morrissey v. State*

Consolidated with:
- Richard R. GOGGIN, individually and as a duly elected and appointed Election Judge for the City and County of Denver, Colorado; Walter Cross, individually and as a previous and future candidate for the Colorado State General Assembly; Charles R. Duke, individually and as a sitting Colorado State Senator; and on behalf of all others similarly situated, v. The STATE of Colorado; Roy Romer, as Governor of the State of Colorado; Victoria Buckley, as Secretary of State of the State of Colorado; Gale Norton, as Attorney General of the State of Colorado; The Title Board of the State of Colorado; Victoria Buckley, Gale Norton, and Rebecca Lennahan, as members of said Title Board; and the General Assembly of the State of Colorado, and U.S. Term Limits, Inc., and Dennis Polhill,

Background: The state legislature proposed an amendment to the state constitution, and allowed the governor to set the date of the election for the people to ratify the proposed amendment. Following the US Supreme Court decision in *US Term Limits v. Thornton*, advocates of term limits took to pursuing a federal constitutional amendment for term limits. Colorado enacted a law, "Amendment 12", that required Colorado's elected officials, state and federal, to pursue the goal of federal term limits. It also required candidates for office to declare their position on term limits.

Issue: Whether Amendment 12 represents an impermissible attempt to interfere with this procedure under Article V of the federal constitution.

Court Decision: Written by Chief Justice Anthony Vollack. "Article V precludes state citizens from having any substantial role in amending the federal Constitution for that power rests exclusively with Congress and the state legislatures and "transcends any limitations sought to be

---

[148] http://caselaw.findlaw.com/co-supreme-court/1428727.html and https://scholar.google.com/scholar_case?case=10845080296613573089&hl=en&as_sdt=6&as_vis=1&oi=scholarr

imposed by the people of a state."

Conclusions: The effect of "term limits provisions similar to Amendment 12 is that these provisions undermine representative government. Such intrusions into the legislative realm circumvent the strict requirements of Article V and disturb the balance of our representative system."

Applicability: Similar to other term limits cases.

83.

Opinion of the Justices, 263 Ala. 158, 81 So. 2d 881 (1955)[149] – *Alabama Supreme Court*

Background: A proposed change to the state constitution included a change to an entrenched clause that is unchangeable involving representation based on population.

Issue: The proposed amendment to the state constitution prompted questions from the Alabama House of Representatives to the Alabama Supreme Court:

> "Question 1. Is it within the power of the Legislature to propose the amendments of the Constitution of 1901 as set out in said bill, or would such proposal contravene the provisions of Section 284 of the Constitution, as amended?
>
> "Question 2. Does the Legislature have the power to propose an amendment to the Constitution repealing the last sentence in Section 284, as amended?
>
> "Question 3. Do the proposed amendments change the basis of representation in the Legislature to other than a population basis contrary to the provisions of Section 284 of the Constitution, as amended?"

Court Decision: The Court held that the people may change any and all parts of a constitution regardless of entrenchment. Repealing is the same as amending.

Conclusions: The Court found that the entrenched clause could be changed at the will of the people. The same issues present in this matter

---

[149] https://casetext.com/case/opinion-of-the-justices-619

were finally resolved in the wake of the federal reapportionment drive in the next decade.

Applicability: Presented as a counterfactual example wherein the state legal reasoning differs from the federal legal reasoning.

84.

Opinion of the Justices, 673 A.2d 693 (Me.1996)[150] – Maine Supreme Court

Background: Maine's Supreme Court issued a non-binding, advisory decision on certain questions regarding an Act. Both federal and state constitutional questions about the Act were propounded to the Supreme Court by the Maine House of Representatives.

Issue: Is it within the constitutional authority of the Legislature of the State of Maine, or the electors of the State of Maine by means of initiated legislation, to direct the members of the state's congressional delegation, the Governor or members of the Maine Senate or Maine House of Representatives to use their powers to make application to the Congress of the United States for a constitutional convention?

> "The question actually poses six different issues of law: 1) may the Legislature direct the activities of the congressional delegation in this manner; 2) may the electors direct the activities of the congressional delegation in this manner; 3) may the Legislature direct the activities of the Governor in this manner; 4) may the electors direct the activities of the Governor in this manner; 5) may the Legislature direct the activities of the Legislature in this manner; and 6) may the electors direct the activities of the Legislature in this manner?"

Court Decision: With regard to the Article V issue, the Maine court stated that the electors of Maine cannot force either the congressional delegation or the state legislative delegation to take actions to amend the U.S. Constitution. After reviewing the Act, the Supreme Court determined that:

> "it is not within the power of the electors to propose a constitutional amendment. The proposed initiative, if enacted by a referendum vote, would allow the electors to do indirectly that which they are forbidden to do directly. This aspect of proposed initiative does not conform to the clearly

---

[150] https://casetext.com/case/opinion-of-the-justices-564

stated procedural requirements of article V and would not appear to be constitutional."

"neither the electors of the State of Maine nor the Legislature of the State of Maine may control the state's delegates to the United States Congress in the performance of their congressional duties."

Conclusions: The Maine court stated that neither the electors of that state nor the state's legislature may control the delegates to Congress in the performance of their duties, because "Such an exercise of control would violate the essence of federalism."

Applicability: The federal function of an Article V convention is beyond the reach of the state legislatures to dictate operations.

85.

Opinion of the Justices, 6 Cush. (Mass.) 573, (1833)[151] – **Massachusetts Supreme Court**

Background: Facing the possibility of calling a convention to amend the state constitution, the Massachusetts House of Representatives exercised their prerogative to consult with the states' Judicial Supreme Court and request an advisory opinion on the issues.

Issue: In a constitutional convention called for the express purpose of proposing an amendment to the state constitution, is there a limit on the powers of the delegates? Also, is it possible to amend by any method other than that given in the constitution?

Court Decision: The court advised that, "If, however, the people should, by the terms of their vote, decide to call a convention of delegates to consider the expediency of altering the constitution in some particular part thereof, we are of opinion that such delegates would derive their whole authority and commission from such vote; and, upon the general principles governing the delegation of power and authority, they would have no right, under such vote, to act upon and propose amendments in other parts of the constitution not so specified."

---

[151] Given in a footnote: Massachusetts Law Quarterly 2, no.1 (Oct. 1916): 274-5 https://books.google.com/books?id=1DkbAAAAYAAJ&pg=PA274&lpg=PA274&dq=6+Cush.+%28Mass.%29+573,+%281833%29&source=bl&ots=Odd8GfdxHJ&sig=v_MkYHc4rlRbGlX8u0XcqJgM3UQ&hl=en&sa=X&ved=0ahUKEwjktPy2vfXJAhWG2SYKHe1lAp4Q6AEILTAF#v=onepage&q=6%20Cush.%20%28Mass.%29%20573%2C%20%281833%29&f=false

Conclusions: The delegates to a convention are covered strictly by the limits of the provisions in the convention call.

Applicability: This is one of the earliest and most frequently cited examples of a judicial determination of the legality of limiting a state constitutional convention.

86.

Opinion of the Justices Relative to the 18th Amendment to the Constitution of the US, *160 NE 439, 262 Mass 603, (1928)*[152] – *Massachusetts Supreme Court*

Background: In 1928 the Massachusetts Supreme Court was asked to opine upon a proposed initiative requesting the state's congressional delegation to support repeal of the Eighteenth Amendment."

Issue: Is the initiative equivalent to a law and does it have the same weight and bearing on the people?

Court Decision: The court held that the measure was not a proper initiative on both state and federal grounds, stating, in connection with the latter ground, that "[t]he voters of the several States are excluded by the terms of art. 5 of the Constitution of the United States from participation in the process of its amendment."

Conclusions: The decisions conflict, with one case (*Opinion of the Justices*, 262 Mass. 603) ruling that an advisory initiative violates article V, but a later decision (*Kimble v. Swackhamer*, 584 P.2d 616) upholding such an initiative when it is advisory only.

Applicability: Initiatives for legislative instructions are not permissible as they interfere with the spirit of Article V.

87.

Opinion of the Justices to the Senate, *373 Mass. 877, 366 N.E. 2d 1226 (1977)*[153] – *Massachusetts Supreme Court*

Background: In response to a resolution pending before the state legislature, the Senate asked of the state supreme court for their opinions on the questions submitted.

---

[152] https://casetext.com/case/opinion-of-the-justices-to-the-house-of-rep-9
[153] https://casetext.com/case/opinion-of-the-justices-to-the-senate-14

Issue: Questions before the Court concerning a state application for a "constitutional convention":

"1. Does the resolution require the signature of the Governor?

"2. Would the resolution, if adopted in concert with two thirds of the other States, require Congress to call a national constitutional convention, or is it merely a request?

"3. Has the Massachusetts legislature the power to limit the agenda of the constitutional convention to the single issue proposed by the resolution?"

Court Decision: "Courts and commentators agree, however, that the term "Legislatures" bears the same meaning throughout article V. The Massachusetts Supreme Judicial Court, in holding that a governor cannot veto an application for a constitutional convention, declared that "[s]ince the word `Legislatures' in the ratification clause of Art. V does not mean the whole legislative process of the State ..., we are of the opinion that the word `Legislatures' in the application clause, likewise, does not mean the whole legislative process." The Court declined to answer the second and third questions as they are federal in nature.

Conclusions: No gubernatorial signature required.

Applicability: **The governor plays no role in the approval process of an Article V Convention application** from the state. He cannot therefore veto the application. The Article confers powers on the assemblies not the executives.

88.
___

Charles B. Prior, et al, v. James R. Noland, Secretary of State, 68 Colo. 263, 188 P. 727, (1920) – *Colorado Supreme Court*

-As ***Prior v. Noland***

Background: The Colorado legislature ratified the Eighteenth Amendment. The petitioners wanted the ratification submitted to the people via referendum.

Issue: Two questions were asked: 1) Does Article V permit ratification by referendum, and 2) does the Colorado Constitution permit a referendum on a resolution?

Court Decision: The people's referendum power is not applicable to federal issues. A resolution is not an "act" and is therefore not subject to the referendum. The state legislature is not acting in its usual sense but as a special independent body exercising a special power granted specifically in Article V.

> "[I]n the matter of the ratification of a proposed amendment to the federal Constitution, the General Assembly does not act in pursuance of any power delegated or given to it by the state Constitution, but exercises a power which it possesses by virtue of the fifth article of the Constitution of the United States. That article provides that proposed amendments "shall be valid, ... as part of this Constitution, when ratified by the Legislatures of three-fourths of the several states." A ratification by a General Assembly, of a proposed amendment to the federal Constitution, is not, therefore, lawmaking legislation for the state, subject to approval or rejection by the referendum."

Conclusions: **Referendums may not be used to ratify federal amendments.**

Applicability: **Referendums may not be used to ratify federal amendments.**

89.

Rafael A. Rivera-Cruz v. R. A. Gray, as Secretary of State of the State of Florida, 104 So. 2d 501 (1958)[154] – *Florida Supreme Court*
-As ***Rivera-Cruz v. Gray***

Consolidated with:
Verla A. Pope v. R. A. Gray, as Secretary of State of the State of Florida

Background: Rivera-Cruz and Pope each sought to have a proposed amendment to the state constitution not placed on the ballot due to the extent of the amendment. Their contention was that the method of revision of the constitution is spelled in Section 2 of Article XVII of the Florida constitution and should be followed explicitly.

Issue: Do the fourteen provisions in the proposed amendments constitute a revision of the state constitution or merely an amendment?

Court Decision: Unanimous. Written by Justice Elwyn Thomas. At issue is that the fourteen provisions are interlinked or "daisy-chained" and require that all must pass for any one of them to take effect. The

---
[154] http://law.justia.com/cases/florida/supreme-court/1958/104-so-2d-501-0.html

attempt at amendment is a thinly disguised attempt at rewriting the constitution. The proposals may not be placed on the ballot.

Conclusions: "We conclude that the manner of presenting the so-called amendments to the electorate is contrary to the spirit and intent of the Constitution and, consequently, that no public monies should be spent for the purpose."

Applicability: The process of amendment is specific and not to be construed as to permit a wholesale revision of the constitution under the guise of making amendments.

90.

Michael K. Simpson, Jerry T. Twiggs, Maynard M. Miller, Bruce Sweeney, Marguerite McLaughlin, Jim D. Kempton, Laird Noh, Wendy Jaquet, Golden C. Linford, Reed Hanson, v. Pete T. Cenarrusa, as Secretary of State, and Citizens for Federal Term Limits,

130 Idaho 609, 944 P.2d. 1372, (1997)[155] – Idaho Supreme Court

-As **Simpson v. Cenarrusa**

Background: Activists for term limits sought to use the ballot initiative to get a measure that would require candidates' positions to be placed on the ballot and that they pledge to work for congressional term limits. Ten members of the state legislature opposed the measure and sued.

Issue: Are the instructions and the ballot positions unconstitutional?

Court Decision: Written by Justice Byron Johnson. "We declare that the ballot legend and pledge portions of Proposition 4 are unconstitutional, but that the instructions to members of congress and legislators do not violate Article V of the United States Constitution and are severable." "Because the ballot legend is imposed only on those legislators who do not act in accordance with the instruction, the ballot legend is, in effect, a state-imposed consequence for certain speech in the legislature. Although private individuals have a right to engage in public debate concerning the legislative actions of legislators, the state

---

[155] https://scholar.google.com/scholar_case?case=7847502708603081228&hl=en&as_sdt=6&as_vis=1&oi=scholarr

does not have a similar right. Nor can the state subject a legislator to consequences for speech in the legislature. We conclude that the speech and debate clause of the Idaho Constitution does not allow the state to question speech and debate by Idaho legislators concerning the calling of a convention for proposing amendments to the United States Constitution."

Conclusions: The state constitution and federal constitutions protect political speech both written and spoken.

Applicability: Any infringement on the speech of an elected person diminishes the purpose of the free speech clauses. A delegate to an amendatory convention must be free from intimidation regarding his or her ability to speak their mind. Instructions are permissible but are not binding.

91.

Raymon L. Smith, et al., v. Pete T. Cenarrusa, as Secretary of State,

93 Idaho 818, 475 P.2d. 11, (1970)[156] – *Idaho Supreme Court*

-As **Smith v. Cenarrusa**

Background: The state legislature proposed a revision of the state constitution through the amendment process. The bill passed by the legislature in 1965 provided for a constitutional convention and a Commission on Constitutional Revision. No convention was called but the commission produced a draft constitution. In 1970, the legislature sought to revise the 1965 bill and remove the convention provision and then submit the draft constitution for ratification. The governor vetoed the bill.

Issue: Are the methods of constitutional amendment revision listed in the state constitution the only permissible methods?

Court Decision: Written by Justice Allan Shepard. "The legislature has by express resolution deemed the calling of a constitutional convention unnecessary. The work and the result of the work of the Commission has been widely publicized through the press and the medium of public hearings. The legislature approved the proposed new constitution and by the same vote directed that it be submitted directly

---

[156] http://www.ecases.us/case/idaho/1368063/smith-v-cenarrusa

to the people for approval or rejection."

Conclusions: The state constitution is not conclusive in listing the acceptable manners of amending or revising the constitution.

Applicability: Ruling similar to Kentucky's *Gatewood* decision; included as a counterfactual example.

92.

John J. Spriggs v. Alonzo M. Clark, Secretary of State, 45 *Wyo.* 62, 14 *P.*2d 667, 83 *A.L.R.* 1364 (*Wyo. 1932*)[157] - **Supreme Court of Wyoming**

-As *Spriggs v. Clark*

Background: The plaintiff sought to block a referendum on the question of whether the 18th Amendment should be passed. The referendum was to be advisory only in order to get the consensus of the electorate. Lawyer Spriggs felt that the action was unconstitutional and waste of taxpayer funds.

Issue: Is a strictly advisory referendum to take the "pulse of the people" permissible?

Court Decision: Written by Justice William W. Riner. The decision provides a good treatment of the right to petition for redress of grievances as outlined in the First Amendment of the federal Constitution and extends back to the Right of Petition found in the 1689 English Bill of Rights.

> "[I]t undertakes to supply the political body whose duty it is to initiate proceedings to change the National Charter with reliable information concerning the attitude of the people of this commonwealth on a question admittedly of serious interest and importance to them from both state and national standpoints."
>
> "The Constitution of Wyoming, in order to fully protect the enjoyment by our citizens of this right, declares in unmistakable terms (Art. 1, Sec. 21):
>
> "The right of petition, and of the people peaceably to assemble to consult for the common good, and to make known their opinions, shall never be denied or abridged."

---

[157] https://casetext.com/case/spriggs-v-clark-sec-of-state

The decision also referred back to a 1926 Wisconsin Supreme Court action in the case of *State ex rel. Fulton v. Zimmerman*, 191 Wis. 10, 210 N.W. 381, regarding a similar attempt to discern the public opinion on amending the Volstead Act that carried out the 18th Amendment's ban on alcohol.

Conclusions: The use of a non-binding public referendum to measure the electorate's opinion on an issue is valuable to the state legislature and permissible.

Applicability: An advisory opinion is an acceptable use of the non-binding referendum. This would be repeated a half century later in California's *Uhler v. AFL-CIO*.

93.

Abram P. Staples, Attorney General of Virginia v. Henry G. Gilmer, Comptroller of Virginia, 183 Va. 613, 33 S.E. (2d) 49, (1945)[158] – Virginia Supreme Court

-As *Staples v. Gilmer*

Background: With World War II in full force, thousands of Virginians were overseas fighting and unable to vote in the 1944 presidential election. Virginia had a poll tax that must be paid at the polls in order to get a ballot thereby ruling out absentee ballots and disenfranchising Virginia's servicemen and servicewomen serving out-of-state.[159]

Issue: Could a limited power state constitutional convention be called to remove the poll tax requirement?[160]

Court Decision: Per curiam. "On the whole we are of opinion that the Act in question (Acts 1944, Ex. sess., ch. 1) does not contravene any provision in the Constitution and is therefore valid; that in the event a majority of the electors vote in favor of the convention, the powers of the convention to consider, adopt or propose revisions or amendments to the Constitution will be legally restricted or limited, as defined in the Act, and in the informatory statement printed on the ballot to be used in the

---

[158] https://casetext.com/case/staples-v-gilmer-1
[159] Francis H. Heller, "Limiting a Constitutional Convention: The State Precedents," *Cardozo Law Review* 3 (1982): 570-2
[160] Raymond H. Moseley, "The Limited Constitutional Convention," *Tennessee Law Review* 21, no.8 (June 1951): 871

proposed referendum election; and that the mandamus prayed for in the petition in this cause should issue." "The convention does not possess all the powers of the people but it can exercise only such powers as may be conferred upon it by the people. The people may confer upon it limited powers."[161]

Conclusions: The people are empowered to limit the convention to the desired purpose through legislation that defines and calls the convention.

Applicability: **An Article V convention may be limited both by the enabling legislation and by the call for a convention.**

94.

State of North Dakota ex rel. Bonnie Askew et al., v. Ben Meier, as Secretary of State of the State of North Dakota, 231 N.W.2d 821 (1975) – North Dakota Supreme Court

-As *State Ex Rel. Askew v. Meier*

Background: Like many other states at the time, North Dakota sought to ratify the Equal Rights Amendment through a public referendum as per its state constitution. The petitioners claimed that they merely wanted a referendum as a "straw poll" on the public's sentiment.

Issue: Whether the ratification by the Legislature of the Equal Rights Amendment can be the subject of a referendum, either binding or advisory?

Court Decision: 5-0, Written by Justice Robert L. Vogel. The US Supreme Court decided in *Hawke v. Smith* (I) and (II) in 1920 that such actions are not permissible. The Court did not see a straw poll in the wording but actually an attempt to derail the ratification: "This is not language indicative of an intention to hold a straw vote or nonbinding plebiscite. It is, instead, language indicative of an intention to suspend operation of a resolution and thereby end or destroy its operative effect."

Conclusions: "We therefore hold that the petitions are ineffectual to either (1) require a referendum under the State Constitution of the Legislature's ratification of the Equal Rights Amendment; or (2) authorize a nonbinding plebiscite or straw vote as to the views of the

---

[161] 183 Va. 613 at 624 cited in: Frank Balog, "Popular Sovereignty and the Question of the Limited Constitutional Convention," *Cooley Law Review* 1 (1982): 121

electorate on such ratification."

Applicability: Petitions may not be used as part of the amendment process.

95.

State ex rel. Thomas J. Donnelly v. George S. Myers, Secretary of State, 127 *Ohio St. 104, 186 N.E. 918 (1933)*[162] – *Ohio Supreme Court*

-As ***State ex rel. Donnelly v. Myers***

Background: Ohio passed a law to provide for calling a state convention for the ratification of the proposed Twenty-first Amendment.

Issue: Several individuals sought a referendum, not on the ratification, but on the Senate bill to provide for the convention to ratify. A petition was submitted to the Secretary of State challenging the Senate bill.

Court Decision: "The mode of assembling the convention set up in Amended Senate Bill No. 204 provides for a vote by all of the electors of the state upon the selection of all of the delegates. The views of the candidates, for election as delegates to the convention, will be known in advance, so that the final action of the convention should be truly representative of the will of the people upon the one special question involved. The intent of Article V of the Constitution of the United States will therefore be effectuated by this action of the state Legislature."

Conclusions: Attempts to control the amendment process and in particular, the federal Article V process of ratification, are not accessible through the referendum method. The powers to cover the process are not incidental. A state convention is also performing a "federal function" in ratification and not subject to the state control beyond the usual facets, such as delegate selection methods and rules of operation.

Applicability: **Other enumerated powers in the Constitution have certain "incidental" authority or implied powers, likewise, so do the powers of Article V.** This is not necessarily an application of the "Necessary and Proper Clause" which grants the power requisite to carry out other duties – it is independent of the Article V Convention.

---

[162] https://casetext.com/case/state-v-myers-113

This includes, but is not limited to, the ability to set its hours, judge credentials of delegates, determine its agenda and order of business, elect its own officers and establish its own rules, among other powers.

96.

State ex rel. Warren P. Gill v. Joe S. Morris, Secretary of State,
79 Ok. 89, 191 P. 364, (1920)[163] – **Oklahoma Supreme Court**

-As ***State ex rel. Gill v. Morris***

Background: Gill filed a petition with the Secretary of State to request a referendum on the ratification of the Eighteenth Amendment. Morris refused to accept the petition or request the ballot tile from the Attorney General.

Issue: Whether ratification of the Eighteenth Amendment is subject to a referendum of the people.

Court Decision: Written by Justice Matthew J. Kane. The Attorney General's contention that the issue has been decidedly settled by the US Supreme Court in *Hawke v. Smith* is correct.

Conclusions: As with other concurrent cases, no referendum is permissible.

Applicability: No referendum permissible.

97.

State of Montana ex rel. Robin Hatch v. Frank Murray, Secretary of State of the State of Montana, 165 Mont. 90, 526 P.2d 1369 (Mont. 1974)[164] - **Montana Supreme Court**

-As ***State ex rel. Hatch v. Murray***

Background: Brought in an effort to prevent use of a referendum to ratify the proposed Equal Rights Amendment. Sufficient petition signatures had been submitted to the Secretary of State for a referendum.

Issue: Whether a referendum may be used to ratify a proposed federal constitutional amendment.

---

[163] http://law.justia.com/cases/oklahoma/supreme-court/1920/35076.html
[164] https://casetext.com/case/state-ex-rel-hatch

Court Decision: Per curiam. The Court followed the federal lead in *Hawke v. Smith*. "Montana Legislature could not constitutionally subject its ratification of the proposed Equal Rights Amendment to a referendum vote of the people."

Conclusions: Once again, a referendum is not permissible for ratification of a federal amendment.

Applicability: No referendum.

98.

State of Montana, ex rel., Steve Harper, Robert C. Waltmire, Brad Belke, and Common Cause of Montana, a State affiliate of common cause, Plaintiffs and Relators, v. Jim Waltermire, Secretary of State, State of Montana, Defendant and Respondent, and Montanans for a Balanced Federal Budget Committee, Real Party in Interest, 213 Mont. 425, 691 P. 2d 826 (1984)[165] *(Rehnquist reviewing) - Montana Supreme Court*

-As **State ex rel. Harper v. Waltermire**

Background: Constitutional Initiative No. 23 was a ballot measure to force the state legislature to submit a resolution, under Article V of the federal constitution, for an amendatory convention to Congress that would focus on a balanced budget amendment.

Issue: Whether the people can compel the state legislature to act to submit a resolution for an Article V convention through an act of direct democracy.

Court Decision: 6-1, Written by Chief Justice Frank Haswell. The Court found the constitutional amendment invalid and a violation of Article V. The Court saw the amendment as really a legislative resolution which is the domain of the state legislature.

Conclusions: **The people of the state have no power to limit the deliberative process of the convention**, therefore any limitations imposed by an initiative or referendum is invalid.

Applicability: This case is a state level companion to many other similar state cases. The overriding issue was reviewed later by the US Supreme Court in *Montanans for A Balanced Federal Budget Committee and Jim Waltermire, Secretary of State of Montana v. Steve Harper et al.* with

---

[165] http://www.leagle.com/decision/19841517691P2d826_11511.xml/STATE%20EX%20REL.%20HARPER%20v.%20WALTERMIRE

the SCOTUS supporting the decision of the Montana Supreme Court in *State ex. rel. Harper v. Waltermire.*

99.

State of North Dakota ex rel. Henry Linde, Attorney General v. Thomas Hall, Secretary of State,

35 N.D. 34, 159 N.W. 281, (1916) – *North Dakota Supreme Court*

-As *State v. Hall*

Background: The question was whether the article of the state constitution requiring the initiative and the referendum was self-executing.

Issue: Does a constitutional amendment require additional corresponding enabling legislation to make it operative?

Court Decision: Unanimous decision. The Court found the constitutional provision was not self-executing as it required the implementation of enabling acts. "The questions must be answered, if possible, from the language of the constitutional provision itself but, if the language is ambiguous or the answer doubtful, then the field of inquiry is widened and rules applicable to construction of statutes are to be resorted to. In fact, a wider field of inquiry for information is proper where needed in construing constitutional provisions than legislative enactments. It is a well-settled rule that in placing a construction on a constitutional provision, the court may look to the history of the times and examine the state of being existing when the constitutional provision in question was framed and adopted by the people in order to ascertain the prior law, the mischief, and the remedy."

Conclusions: **An unauthorized or revolutionary act of the convention cannot be ratified by the electorate**. The secretary of state is not a legislative agent, and performs only ministerial duties reviewable in court proceedings.

Applicability: Overturned in part by *State ex rel. Twitchell v. Hall*. But *State v. Hall* was cited – a lot – and is included here because of those citations and because it was an important case in its day.

100.

State of Missouri ex rel. P. A. Tate v. Nike G. Sevier,
333 Mo. 662, 62 S.W. 2d 895, 87 A.L.R. 1315, (1933) cert denied 290 U.S. 679, 54 S. Ct. 102, 78 L. Ed. 586, (1933)166 – Missouri Supreme Court

-As *State ex rel. Tate v. Sevier*

Background: Tate filed a petition with the Missouri Secretary of State requesting that a referendum be held on the House bill that authorized an election for delegates to a convention to ratify the proposed Twenty-first Amendment.

Issue: The issue is nearly identical to Ohio's concurrent *Donnelly v. Myers*. Do the people have a right to a referendum on the bill authorizing a convention?

Court Decision: Written by Justice William F. Frank. "The ratification or rejection of an amendment to the federal Constitution is a federal function derived from the federal Constitution itself. By the adoption of article 5 of the federal Constitution the people divested themselves of all authority to either propose or ratify amendments to the Constitution. By the same article they vested the power to propose amendments in the Congress and in a convention called by Congress, and designated the state Legislatures and state conventions as representatives of the people, with authority to ratify or reject proposed amendments to the Constitution. When a state Legislature performs any act looking to the ratification or rejection of an amendment to the federal Constitution, it is not acting in accordance with any power given to it by the state Constitution, but is exercising a power conferred upon it by the federal Constitution." "The intent of Article V of the Constitution of the United States will therefore be effectuated by this action of the State Legislature."

Conclusions: When Congress proposes ratification by conventions for an amendment, though it does not provide how and by whom such conventions shall be assembled, **Congress' direction necessarily implies authority to provide for assembling of such conventions.**

Applicability: Conventions are left to themselves to determine their operation and rules.

---

[166] https://casetext.com/case/state-ex-rel-tate-v-sevier

101.

Valley Paper Company v. Joint Committee on Printing of Congress, composed of Reed Smoot, Jonathan Bourne, Jr., Duncan U. Fletcher, George C. Sturgiss, Allen F. Cooper, and Daniel E. Finley, 38 Wash. L. R. 171, Case #52342 (1910)167 – District of Columbia Supreme Court

-As ***Valley Paper Co. v. Smoot, et al.***

<u>Background</u>: The Joint US Senate and House of Representatives Committee on Printing failed to consider the bid of a printer that had a prior business relationship with the Committee. Valley Paper Company sued the committee for performance of the contract.

<u>Issue</u>: Could a court issue a writ of mandamus to Congress, a committee of Congress or Congressmen/women themselves to force compliance with a court order or is the issuance of legal process a violation of constitutional privilege?

> *"This is the first time in the history of the Government that a committee of Congress has been sued. So that the question is, if the action of Congress or the action of a committee of Congress or a Member of Congress, can be called in question by any court in all the land, when a committee of Congress or a Member of Congress acts in that capacity, then the distinction that is fundamental in the law of the land, defining the three departments of the Government, the executive, the legislative, and the judicial, will be broken down."*

<u>Court Decision:</u> Written by Justice Daniel T. Wright. Although the Constitution protects members of Congress from legal process while conducting congressional business and while going to and from Congress, the dignity and esteem of Congress depend on their acting in professional manner. Neglecting the very laws that they make does not comport with that goal.

> *"Your committee has not overlooked the fact that, under the rules and precedents of the House, no Member thereof can waive the privileges of the House except by the express consent of the House, and in order to save all questions of privilege we think it would be advisable for the House to grant permission to the three Members involved to make response to the order of the court."*

---

[167] https://bulk.resource.org/gpo.gov/rules/cannon/ccxxxiii.txt

Conclusions:

"Upon consideration of the petition of the Valley Paper Company filed herein this 2d day of February, 1910, it is by the court this 2d day of February, 1910, ordered that the respondents, the said Reed Smoot, Jonathan Bourne, Jr., Duncan U. Fletcher, George C. Sturgiss, Allen F. Cooper, and David E. Finley, members of the Joint Committee on Printing of Congress, show cause, if any they may have, on or before the 11th day of February 1910, at 10 o'clock a.m., why a writ of mandamus should not be issued as prayed in said petition: provided a copy of said petition and this rule be served upon said respondents, members of the Joint Committee on Printing of Congress, on or before the 7th day of February 1910.

Wright, Justice.

And, Whereas it is prayed by the said plaintiffs or petitioners that a writ of mandamus issue directing said members of the Joint Committee on Printing of Congress, to wit, that they withdraw awards which have heretofore been made and that they award certain contracts to the plaintiffs;"

Applicability: A writ of mandamus may be conveyed to Congress to force action on an amendatory convention if it can be served on a federal official - the Sergeant-at-Arms or the Clerk of the House, for example - and not an elected member of Congress.[168]

102.

Ray L. Walker, et al., v. Winfield Dunn, et al., 498 S.W.2d. 102 (Tenn. 1972)[169] *– Tennessee Supreme Court*

-As ***Walker v. Dunn***

Background: The Tennessee legislature was called in to an extraordinary session to consider ratification of the 26th Amendment. Opponents claimed that these actions were *ultra vires* and violated the state constitution.

Issue: Article II, § 32, of the Tennessee Constitution, which provides as follows:

"No Convention or General Assembly of this State shall act upon any

---

[168] Walter K. Tuller, "A Convention to Amend the Constitution. Why Needed. How It May Be Obtained.," *North American Review* 193, no.664 (Mar. 1911): generally
[169] https://casetext.com/case/walker-v-dunn

amendment of the Constitution of the United States proposed by Congress to the several States; unless such Convention or General Assembly shall have been elected after such amendment is submitted."

Court Decision: Written by Justice George F. McCanless. Although thirty-eight states had already ratified and the issue became moot, the Court took up the case as it may have future implications. The Court decided that Article II, § 32, of the Tennessee Constitution is a limitation upon the General Assembly of Tennessee in the exercise of its federally derived power. Thus, the General Assembly cannot be controlled by the provisions of Article II, § 32.

Conclusions: The Supremacy Clause of the federal constitution overrules the state constitution and the process under Article V is a federal and not a state function of the state legislature.

Applicability: A state constitutional provision in conflict with the federal constitution is overruled by the federal constitution.

103.

Francis Wells, et al., v. James Bain, et al., and Edwin H. Fitler, et al.,

74 Pa. 39 (1874) – Pennsylvania Supreme Court Companion case is Wood's Appeal, 74 Pa. St. Rep. 71 (1874)

Background: Pennsylvania had passed an act calling for an election to determine whether to hold an amendatory convention for the state constitution. The commissioners in Philadelphia attempted to set aside the law regulating elections to the convention and institute its own law.

Issue: What method of constitutional amendment proposal was available besides the action of the state legislature?

Court Decision: The Court recognized just three methods of government replacement: 1) the mode within the current state constitution that provides for a new constitution to be made, 2) calling a constitutional convention, and 3) revolution. The Court issued injunctions to prohibit the further actions of the commissioners.

Conclusions: The convention did not possess the power to go beyond its instructions and the law governing the elections could not be replaced.

Applicability: In this example, a rare runaway state convention was held to be outside the scope of its limitations and therefore the product, i.e., the law governing the delegate selection, was unconstitutional.

104.

Wheeler v. Board of Trustees of Fargo Consolidated School District,
200 Ga. 323, 37 S.E. 2d. 322 (1946)[170] – *Georgia Supreme Court*

Background: Georgia's state legislature proposed a new state constitution but did so in a manner that was not prescribed by the existing state constitution. In a manner similar to Alabama's *Manley* case, the new constitution was being added as an amendment to the existing constitution.

Issue: Was a new state constitution that was ratified by the people through a general election valid?

Court Decision: The constitution was valid. The vote of the people gave legitimacy to the constitution and the method of proposal. The Court did not see the new constitution as an amendment but a new constitution nonetheless.

Conclusions: Like many other states, Georgia decided that the ratification/adoption by amendment move was not permissible, but in this instance sided with the reservation of the sovereignty of the people and allowed the adoption of the constitution of 1945.

Applicability: The federal constitution may not be replaced through adoption of an amendment designed to install a new constitution.

105.

C. H. Whittemore, et al., v. Thomas J. Terral, Secretary of State, 140 Ark. 493, 215 S.W. 686, (1919)[171] – *Arkansas Supreme Court*
-As *Whittemore v. Terral*

Background: In response to the promulgation of the proposed Eighteenth Amendment to the federal constitution, plaintiffs sought to use a referendum for ratification.

---

[170] https://casetext.com/case/wheeler-v-trustees-of-fargo-school-dist
[171] http://opinions.aoc.arkansas.gov/WebLink8/docview.aspx?id=172375&dbid=0

Issue: Does Article V permit a referendum for ratification of a federal constitutional amendment?

Court Decision: Written by Chief Justice McCulloch. The Fifth Article does not reserve or imply a referendum power for ratification. The Court held that the word "acts" in the Arkansas Constitution (the same word as in the pre-1966 Cal. Const.) "means an enacted law — a statute." The ratification of a proposed constitutional amendment, the court said, is but a step in the enactment of a law; it does not in itself enact a law and is thus not subject to referendum.

Conclusions: The referendum is not permissible.

Applicability: No referendum for the purpose of ratification.

Court Decisions Listed by Year of Rendering

- *Hollingsworth v. Virginia*, 3 U.S. (3 Dall.) 378 (1798)
- *Smith v. Union Bank of Georgetown*, 30 U.S. 518 (1831)
- *Opinion of the Justices*, 6 Cush. (Mass.) 573, (1833)
- *Kendall v. US*, 37 U.S. (12 Pet.) 524 (1838)
- *Prigg v. Commonwealth of Pennsylvania*, 41 U.S. 539 (1842)
- *Collier v. Frierson*, 24 Ala. 100 (1854)
- *Dodge v. Woolsey*, 59 U.S. 331 (1855)
- *Ex parte Caesar Griffin*, 25 Tex. Supp. 623, S. C. Chase 364 (1869)
- *White v. Hart*, 80 U.S. (13 Wall.) 646, 20 L. Ed. 685, (1871)
- *Wells v. Bain*, 74 Pa. 39 (1874)
- *Wood's Appeal*, 74 Pa. St. Rep. 71 (1874)
- *Board of Liquidation v. McComb* 92 U.S. 531 (1875)
- *Jarrolt v. Moberly*, 103 U.S. 580 (1880)
- *Noble v. Union River Logging Railroad* 147 U.S. 165 (1893)
- *Livermore v. Waite*, 102 Cal. 113, 117, 36 P. 424, 25 L.R.A. 312, (1894)
- *Maxwell v. Dow*, 176 U.S. 581, 20 Sup. Ct. Rep. 448, 44 L. Ed. 597 (1900)
- *Garfield v. US ex rel. Goldsby*, 211 U.S. 249 (1908)

- *In State ex rel. Halliburton v. Roach,* 230 Mo. 408, 130 S.W. 689 (1910)

- *Valley Paper Co. v. Smoot,* 38 Wash. L. R. 171, Case #52342 (1910)

- *Ellingham v. Dye,* 178 Ind. 336, 99 N. E. 1 (1912)

- *Foley v. Democratic Parish Committee,* 70 So. 104, 138 La. 220 (1915)

- *State ex rel. David v. Hildebrant,* 94 Ohio St. 154, 114 N. E. 55, 241 U. S. 565, 36 Sup. Ct. 708, 60 L. Ed. 1172, (1916)

- *State v. Hall,* 35 N.D. 34, 159 N.W. 281, (1916)

- *Herbring v. Brown,* 92 Or. 176, 180 P. 328, (1919)

- *In re Opinion of the Justices,* 118 Me. 544, 107 A. 673, 5 A.L.R. 1412, (1919)

- *Missouri Pacific Railway v. Kansas,* 248 U.S. 276 (1919)

- *Ohio v. Cox,* 257 F. 334 (W.D. Ohio 1919)

- *State of Ohio ex rel. Erkenbrecher v. Cox,* 257 F. 334 (D. Ohio 1919)

- *Whittemore v. Terral,* 140 Ark. 493, 215 S.W. 686, (1919)

- *Barlotti v. Lyons,* 182 Cal. 575, 189 Pac. 282 (Cal. 1920)

- *Carson v. Sullivan,* 223 S. W. 571, 28 Mo. 353 (1920)

- *Christian Feigenspan, Inc. v. Bodine,* 264 F. 186 (D.N.J. 1920)

- *Decher v. Vaughan,* 209 Mich. 565, 576, 177 N. W. 388, 392 (1920)

- *Dempsey v. Boynton,* 253 U. S. 350, 40 Sup. Ct. Rep. 486 (1920)

- *Erwin v. Nolan,* 240 Mo. 401, 217 S. W. 837, (1920)

- *Hawke v. Smith,* (I) 253 U.S. 221 (1920), (II) 253 U.S. 231 (1920)

- *National Prohibition Cases,* 253 U.S. 350, 40 S. Ct. 486, 64 L. Ed. 946 (1920)

- *Opinion of the Justices Relative to the 18th Amendment to the Constitution of the US,* 160 NE 439, 262 Mass 603, (1920)

- *Prior v. Noland,* 68 Colo. 263, 188 P. 727 (1920)

- *State v. Morris*, 191 P. 364, 79 Okl. 89 (1920)
- *State of Rhode Island v. Palmer*, 253 U.S. 320 (1920)
- *State ex rel. Gill v. Morris*, 79 Ok. 89, 191 P. 364, (1920)
- *Dillon v. Gloss*, 256 U.S. 368 (1921)
- *Johnson v. Craft*, 205 Ala. 386, 87 So. 375 (1921)
- *United States ex rel. Widenmann v. Colby*, 265 F. 398 (D.C. Cir. 1920) affirmed 257 U.S. 619 (1921)
- *Fairchild v. Hughes*, 258 U.S. 126 (1922)
- *Leser v. Garnett*, 258 U.S. 130 (1922)
- *Druggan v. Anderson*, 269 U.S. 36, 46 S. Ct. 14, 70 L. Ed. 151 (1925)
- *Opinion of the Justices Relative to the 18th Amendment to the Constitution of the US*, 160 NE 439, 262 Mass 603, (1928)
- *United States v. Panos*, 45 F. 2d 888 (N.D. Ill. 1930)
- *United States v. Sprague*, 282 U.S. 716 (1931)
- *United States v. Thibault*, 47 F.2d 169 (2d Cir. 1931)
- *Spriggs v. Clark*, 45 Wyo. 62, 14 P.2d 667, 83 A.L.R. 1364 (Wyo. 1932)
- *In re Opinions of the Justices*, 226 Ala. 565, 148 So. 107, (1933)
- *In Re Opinion of the Justices*, 204 N.C. 306, 172 S.E. 474 (1933)
- *In Re the Opinion of the Justices*, 132 Me. 491, 167 A. 176 (1933)
- *State ex rel. Donnelly v. Myers*, 127 Ohio St. 104, 186 N.E. 918 (1933)
- *State ex rel. Tate v. Sevier*, 333 Mo. 662, 62 S.W. 2d 895 (1933) cert denied 290 U.S. 679 (1933)
- *United State v. Chambers*, 291 U.S. 217 (1934)
- *In re Opinion to the Governor*, 55 R.I. 56, 178 A. 433 (1935)
- *Wise v. Chandler*, 270 Ky. 1, 108 S.W. 1024 (1937)
- *Chandler v. Wise*, 307 U.S. 474, 59 S. Ct. 992 (1939)
- *Coleman v. Miller*, 307 U.S. 433 (1939)

- *Staples v. Gilmer*, 183 Va. 613, 33 S.E. (2d) 49, (1945)
- *Wheeler v. Board of Trustees of Fargo School District*, 200 Ga. 323, 37 S.E. 2d. 322 (1946)
- *McFadden v. Jordan*, 32 Cal. 2d. 330, 196 P.2d. 787 (1948)
- *Cummings v. Beeler*, 189 Tenn. 151 (1949)
- *United States v. Dennis*, 183 F.2d 201 (1950)
- *United States v. Gugel*, 119 F.Supp. 897 (E.D. Ky. 1954)
- *Opinion of the Justices*, 263 Ala. 158, 81 So. 2d 881 (1955)
- *Ullmann v. United States*, 350 U.S. 422 (1956)
- *Rivera-Cruz v. Gray*, 104 So. 2d 501 (1958)
- *Chenault v. Carter*, 332 S.W.2d 623 (1960)
- *Holmes v. Appling*, 237 Or. 546, 392 P.2d. 636 (1964)
- *Gatewood v. Matthews*, 403 S.W. 2d. 716 (Ky. 1966)
- *Whitehill v. Elkins*, 389 U.S. 54, (1967), 258 F. Supp. 589 (D. Md. 1966), 287 F. Supp. 61 (D. Md. 1968)
- *Petosky v. Rampton*, 431 F.2d 378(1970), 307 F. Supp. 235, (D. Utah 1969)
- *Smith v. Cenarussa*, 93 Idaho 818, 475 P.2d. 11, (1970)
- *Walker v. Dunn*, 498 S.W.2d. 102 (Tenn. 1972)
- *Trombetta v. State of Florida*, 353 F. Supp. 675 (M.D. Fla. 1973)
- *State ex rel. Hatch v. Murray*, 526 P.2d 1369 (Mont. 1974)
- *Dyer v. Blair*, 390 F. Supp. 1291 (N.D. Ill. 1975) (Stevens presiding)
- *State ex rel. Askew v. Meier*, 231 N.W.2d 821 (1975)
- *Opinion of the Justices to the Senate*, 373 Mass. 877, 366 N.E. 2d 1226 (1977)
- *Kimble v. Swackhamer*, 439 U.S. 1385, appeal dismissed 439 U.S. 1041 (1978)
- *Idaho v. Freeman*, 529 F. Supp. 1107 (D. Idaho 1981) vacated as moot by *Carmen v. Idaho*, 459 U.S. 809 (1982)
- *Alabama v. Manley*, 441 So. 2d 864 (Ala. 1983)

EXCURSUS 1

- *AFL-CIO v. March Fong Eu*, 686 P. 2d 609 (Cal. 1984)

- *Montanans for Balanced Budget v. Harper*, 469 U.S. 1301 (1984)

- *State ex rel. Harper v. Waltermire*, 213 Mont. 425, 691 P. 2d 826 (1984) (Rehnquist presiding)

- *Uhler v. AFL-CIO*, 468 U.S. 1310, 105 S. Ct. 5, 82 L. Ed.2d 896, (1984)

- *US v. Sitka*, 666 F. Supp. 19 (D. Conn. 1987)

- *US Term Limits v. Thornton*, 514 U.S. 779, 838, 115 S. Ct. 1842, 1871, 131 L.Ed.2d 881 (1995)

- *Donovan v. Priest*, 931 S.W. 2d 119 (Ark. 1996)

- *In re Initiative Petition No. 364*, 930 P.2d 186 (Okla.1996)

- *Opinion of the Justices*, 673 A.2d 693 (Me.1996)

- *League of Women Voters of Maine v. Gwadosky*, 966 F. Supp. 52 (D. Me. 1997)

- *Simpson v. Cenarussa*, 130 Idaho 609, 944 P.2d. 1372, (1997)

- *Barker v. Hazeltine*, 3 F. Supp. 2d 1088 (D.S.D. 1998)

- *Morrisey v. State*, 951 P.2d 911 (Colo. 1998)

- *Bess v. Ulmer*, 985 P.2d 979 (Alaska 1999)

- *Bramberg v. Jones*, 20 Cal. 4th 1045, 978 P.2d 1240 (1999)

- *Gralike v. Cooke*, 191 F. 3d 911 (8th Cir. 1999) affirmed on other grounds sub nom. *Cook v. Gralike*, 531 U.S. 510 (2001)

- *Miller v. Moore*, 169 F. 3d 1119 (8th Cir. 1999)

SIX
SEEKING AND ESTABLISHING THE RULES OF AN ARTICLE V CONVENTION

> *"Certum est quod certum reddi potest (It is certain, whatever can be rendered certain)."*
> -Latin proverb

It has now become clear that every convention needs rules to operate. Likewise, it has been established that past conventions have had very similar rules and practices. Confidence comes from certainty. As expected, we can turn to history and see the development of the rules of a convention. The variation in rules is noticeable but not too divergent and that is critical to the development of rules for a modern amendatory convention. During the movement of the frontier in the Colonial Era, meetings between colonies and the Native American tribes often functioned like conventions. There were, even in the rough-hewn execution of these backwoods "conventions," standard practices that had to be observed. James Merrell described in his *"Into The American Woods"* how colonial negotiators and Indians carried out certain rituals that had to be performed before the business of the meeting could be transacted. The northeastern tribes observed the "At the Woods' Edge Ceremony" which was carried out according to a time-honored script.[1] There were "Condolence Ceremonies," singing of prescribed songs and the obligatory exchanges of presents. All of which was done to get everyone into the correct, positive frame of mind for

---
[1] James H. Merrell, *Into The American Woods* (New York: W. W. Norton, 1999), 20

successful negotiations.[2] These actions are reminiscent of the opening steps of a constitutional or an amendatory or a ratificatory convention.

One of the foremost topics of discussion over the last several decades in the academic literature involving Article V has been the pre-establishment of rules to operate an amendatory convention. It is a matter of crushing urgency in the minds of many that we develop and codify rules before proceeding any further. This seems a prudent course of action. The real problem arises when we begin to argue about where to start. Whether the point of initiation lies with the Congress, the States, the convention left to its own devices, or the actions of grassroots or ad hoc legislator groups, to go about creating proposed rules could determine, in large part, the outcome before even beginning. There are many groups currently at work doing exactly that, trying to establish rules to be adopted by the participants beforehand or at the beginning of the convention in order to prevent a runaway convention, or to limit the convention to a single subject, or to determine how best to circumvent Congress. A careful analysis of Article V history shows that the overwhelming majority of the questions raised already have answers and the balance, with a few exceptions, are answerable with some thought. Former Michigan Supreme Court Chief Justice Thomas Brennan summarizes,

> "All of the procedural questions can be answered by reference to the words of Article V, the nature of the convention and the historical precedent of the constitutional convention in Philadelphia in 1787. There is no need for any new rules to guide the convention. The convention can organize itself, and perform its historic function just as its predecessors at both the state and national levels have done."[3]

As previously noted, Laurence Tribe has stated that there are just three facts that are "known or knowable" with regard to the convention process: 1) The president has no role; 2) Congress shall call a convention; and 3) amendments ratified become part of the Constitution.[4] This rather rudimentary view is based on the text, but there are other knowns or knowables as well. We know from history that many conventions have taken place between colonies and states and that the practice has been

---

[2] Ibid., 265
[3] Thomas E. Brennan, "The Last Prerogative," *Harvard Journal of Law & Public Policy* 6 (1982): 69
[4] Laurence Tribe, "Issue Raised by Requesting Congress to Call a Constitutional Convention to Propose a Balanced Budget Amendment," *Pacific Law Journal* 10 (1979): 634

generally and overwhelmingly the same providing us with a procedural precedent. We know a convention can be limited as there have been many limited conventions between the States and within the States. We know that certain topics may be excluded from consideration. We know that Congress plays a minimal role in the convention process. We know that the ratification process cannot be changed. We know that the widespread tradition of unit voting among the States will be the most likely method of operation. We know that the explicit practices of amendment may not be deviated from or that replacement or revision may not be attempted under the guise of amendment. Finally, we know that the political downside to a runaway convention is far greater and of more detriment to the instigators of a runaway than the potential benefit that they may receive from such a convention. The last and most important known is that despite all claims to the contrary, the amendatory convention is powerless to replace or even change the Constitution – it can only propose and nothing more. The greatest safeguard is that the States – three-quarters of the States at the very least – must ratify any change before it can take effect.

The Congress Acts

It is a necessity to begin by establishing the "why" of endeavoring to create convention rules <u>before</u> any convention is called or even before a convention is on the horizon. There is as much danger in having rules as in not having rules. This view has been wisely recognized by the same people seeking to establish rules. For example, when Sen. Sam Ervin, Jr. of North Carolina introduced his first convention rules bill in 1967, *S. 2307*,[5] he wrote an article for the *Michigan Law Review* that explained his rationale for the bill and for getting involved in the process at all.[6]

Previously in Chapter 4, the details of the state legislature reapportionment battle were given which prompted Sen. Ervin to act. Ervin took upon himself the drafting and introduction of the bill to lay down rules. Sam Ervin liked to portray himself as a "country lawyer" but those who knew him in Congress knew better. He was a brilliant legal mind and considered a constitutional expert within Congress. He thought long and hard before doing anything and never acted rashly. This can be seen in the time that it

---

[5] "Federal Constitutional Convention Amendment Act" - Introduced 17 August 1967 in the US Senate.
[6] Sam J. Ervin, Jr., "Proposed Legislation to Implement the Convention Method of Amending the Constitution," *Michigan Law Review* 66, no.5 (Mar.1968)

took him to respond to the introduction of the thirty-two petitions from the States for a convention to address reapportionment. The first petitions came in during 1963. The number of thirty-two petitions was reached in 1966 and Ervin introduced his bill in mid-1967. Ervin explained in his paper why he felt the bill necessary,

> "In drafting the bill I was mainly concerned with limiting the power of the Congress to frustrate the initiative of the states, particularly since the debate on the Senate floor at that time indicated that some Senators were inclined to seize on any slight irregularity in a petition as a basis for not counting it."[7]

Ervin then provided greater detail as to his concerns. He found, in his opinion, that the average congressman or senator lacked the necessary constitutional comprehension to adequately judge the appropriateness of an action on an Article V petition,

> "The scant information and considerable misinformation and even outright ignorance displayed on the subject of constitutional amendment, both within the congress and outside of it – and particularly the dangerous precedents threatened by acceptance of some of the constitutional misconceptions put forth – prompted me to introduce in the Senate a legislative proposal designed to implement the convention amendment provision in article V."[8]

Ervin went on to address the utilization of the amendment convention petitions as political footballs and exhibited his disappointment in the lack of constitutional knowledge of his peers. He had realized that the motivation of many of the people in Congress was not what was in the best interest of the nation but instead for misusing a constitutional provision to score political points. This tactic was a long used and, in Ervin's view, inappropriate tact. His reverence for the Constitution led Ervin to seek a better method of employing the long neglected convention provision and remove it from the realm of political gamesmanship. Ervin summarized the competing views within Congress on the reapportionment decision, [emphasis of the author in bold],

> "Those senators who agreed with the Supreme Court's ruling were now contending that some or all of the petitions were invalid for a variety of

---

[7] Ibid., 887
[8] Ibid., 875

reasons and should be discounted, and that, in any case, Congress did not have to call a convention if it did not wish to. Most distressing of all was the apparent readiness of everyone to concede that any convention, once convened, would be unlimited in the scope of its authority and empowered to run rampant over the Constitution, proposing any amendment or amendments that happened to strike its fancy. **That interpretation, supported neither by logic nor constitutional history, served the convenience of both sides in the apportionment controversy."**[9]

While Ervin has clearly identified the problem, he does not escape falling into the congressional trap of thinking that more governmental regulation or oversight is the answer. Where the text of Article V does not commit such regulation or oversight to Congress, and the record of the Framers' views, as found in the 1787 delegates' notes, shows that the point of the convention method was to ensure the States a work-around an obstinate Congress, Ervin makes an erroneous interpretation,

> *"The Congress is made the agency for calling the convention, and it is hard to see why the Congress should have been involved in this alternative method of proposal at all unless it was expected to determine such questions as when sufficient appropriate applications had been received and procedures of the convention and for review and ratification of its proposals."*[10]

The answer to Ervin is that Congress was involved to provide a central repository of the applications and to put Congress on notice of existence of the issues which the States consider to be pressing. Ever vigilant in providing checks and balances, the Framers instituted the practice of Congress making the call to convention as a method of restraining the States from conducting a perpetual convention for every little thing under the sun. They clearly foresaw that events could not always be predicted and that flexibility in responding to those events was necessary. This view is found in Ervin's own paper, wherein he quotes Chief Justice John Marshall from *McCulloch v. Maryland*,[11]

> *"I think the Congress should be extremely careful to close as few doors as possible...When dealing with such a measure, it is wise to bear in mind Marshall's well-worn aphorism that it is a Constitution that we are*

---

[9] Ibid., 878
[10] Ibid., 879
[11] 17 U.S. (4 Wheat.) 316 at 407, 415 (1819)

expounding and not get involved in 'an unwise attempt to provide, by immutable rules, for exigencies which, if foreseen at all, must [be] seen dimly, and which can best be provided for as they occur.'"[12]

Examination of Ervin's [first] bill for constitutional convention practices shows some surprising elements. He invests Congress with a near total discretion over the process although it was clear in the writings of the Framers that it was not their intent to allow Congress any discretion beyond issuing the call to convention and setting the date and place of convening. Not only did Ervin assign the discretionary power to Congress, he made it unassailable in the courts. He imposed a narrow limitation of only four years lifespan on applications. But the two worst provisions were that the delegates were to be apportioned unequally and that the voting would not be by one vote per state.[13] Delegates would be apportioned by one per congressional district and by the number of US senators with each state having an additional two at large delegates.[14] These two provisions would have destroyed the protection of the smaller states as well as the rural interests. Such a proportionality would leave only a handful of states with any real influence or power in the convention. Moreover, the protection of using a supermajority was not given.[15] Lastly, the ability of the States to rescind their ratification of an amendment was proposed for the first time.[16]

Senator Orrin Hatch of Utah picked up where Senator Ervin left off and proposed a constitutional convention procedures bill in each Congress from 1979 through 1991. He wasn't alone, Senator Jesse Helms of North Carolina also proposed such bills at the same time, but Hatch was the recognized ring leader. A number of congressmen presented parallel bills in the House. Between the time of Ervin's bills and later Hatch's and Helm's bills, a number of hearings had been held and lessons learned by the Congress that resulted in changes to the procedures outlined in Ervin's bills. Clearly the States had been heard as the control of the application procedure was returned to the States in Hatch's bills.[17] The period in which

---

[12] Sam J. Ervin, Jr., "Proposed Legislation to Implement the Convention Method of Amending the Constitution," *Michigan Law Review* 66, no.5 (Mar.1968), 880

[13] S.2307, 90th Cong., 1st sess. (1967), Sec. 9

[14] Ibid., Sec. 7

[15] Ibid., Sec.10

[16] Ibid., Sec.13

[17] S.1710, 96th Cong., 1st sess. (1979), Sec.3

the application remained "live" went from four years to seven.[18] Significantly, the delegate composition changed to disallow the at-large delegates of Ervin's bills and congressmen and federal officials were barred from serving as delegates.[19] Where Ervin had the Vice-President open the convention and administer the oath, Hatch designated the most senior Chief Justice of the state supreme courts. Surprisingly, Hatch prohibited the use of federal funds where Ervin had included such financial support.[20] Finally, Hatch allowed for the States to sue in the US Supreme Court for the failure to act by Congress.[21]

By the mid-1980s, Hatch had also made some modifications to his bills. Most were insignificant but a couple were important: The Speaker of the US House and the President Pro Tempore of the US Senate opened the convention and administered the oath of office in lieu of the US Vice-President; federal funds were not only allocated to cover convention costs, but to pay the delegates as well at the same rate as congressmen; and the transmittal process for ratification was modified.[22]

A number of lessons can be learned from the first two decades of trying to establish congressional control of the Article V convention process. First, federal legislators tend to assume that the only entity capable of operating the convention is the federal government despite the extensive history of conventions extending back to the earliest colonists. Second, they operate under the naiveté that future federal governments will be able to resist the urge to meddle in or obstruct the operation of the convention. Third, the federal government instinctively tends toward ideas and actions that thwart, if not outright destroy, the equality and power of the States under federalism. Fourth, constitutional interpretation will always be predominantly in the interest of an expanded and protected federal government – by the federal government – and if that means rendering the convention amendment alternative toothless, then all the better for the federal government. Fifth, and finally, the rules proposed by congressional bills will generally be complicated and convoluted enough in operation to make the convention method unworkable. To be fair, the proposed rules of

---

[18] Ibid., Sec.5
[19] Ibid., Sec.7
[20] Ibid., Sec.8
[21] Ibid., Sec.15
[22] S.40, 99th Cong., 1st sess. (1985)

both Ervin and Hatch do make a runaway near impossible and to afford the States the additional guarantee of judicial review.

It is to avoid the uncertainty of a runaway convention or even just the unknowns of a federal amendatory convention that so many have turned to attempting to codify rules for an Article V convention. We have a half-century history, albeit sporadic, of such attempts at written convention rules. The compilation of court decisions takes us most of the way, but then only so far, toward surety in the operation of the convention. Traditions and customs, although persuasive and hard to ignore, do not possess the legal weight and force of written rules.

In all the time that these many drives to secure an amendatory convention have been occurring, one problem has persisted. That is the issue of Congress' inaction equating to refusing to recognize the petitions and provide a count of the pending petitions per topic. Many Article V activists have sought to get an official count from Congress without success. The Friends of the Article V Convention (FOAVC) group have pursued numerous avenues in Congress, perhaps more arduously, aggressively and adroitly than anyone else, and for longer than any other pro-AVC group, yet they have not been able to get any more than polite letters declining to provide an answer despite FOAVC's careful research and citation of the appropriate federal law.[23] While the Congress has had a rule since 5 May 1789,[24] in the wake of the first submitted application from Virginia,[25] requiring that all applications from the States for an amendatory convention be counted and kept pending before the Congress, that body has never kept to its duty to do so. The US House has long had Rule XII (3)[26] for the disposition of petitions, memorials, [and by implication, state resolutions] and private bills. The result of this situation has been that Congress, speaking through the Legal Counsel in the Office of the Clerk, has steadfastly refused to supply a current count – as the National Archives and Records Administration has similarly refused to do. But, on 6 January

---

[23] http://www.foavc.org/reference/house_reply.pdf
[24] http://www.foavc.org/reference/05051789.pdf
[25] http://consource.org/document/virginias-application-for-a-second-convention-1789-5-5/
[26] "Petitions, memorials, and private bills
   3. If a Member, Delegate, or Resident Commissioner has a petition, memorial, or private bill to present, the Member, Delegate, or Resident Commissioner shall sign it, deliver it to the Clerk, and may specify the reference or disposition to be made thereof. Such petition, memorial, or private bill (except when judged by the Speaker to be obscene or insulting) shall be entered on the Journal with the name of the Member, Delegate, or Resident Commissioner presenting it and shall be printed in the Congressional Record."

2015, the US House adopted an amendment to Section (3)[27] to Rule XII for "Providing For Transparency With Respect To Memorials Submitted Pursuant To Article V Of The Constitution Of The United States" that requires the chair of the House Committee on the Judiciary to maintain and make publicly available such memorials and petitions. For the first time, Congress will now need to be able to count and produce the petitions. The Office of the Clerk of the House of Representatives has begun to place select petitions on their website.[28]

The Ervin, Hatch and Helms bills were attempts to legislatively construct and define the rules for an Article V convention. The problem with these efforts is simply that the organization attempting to create the rules – Congress, contrary to its assertions – has no business working to regulate a convention designed to circumvent the Congress itself.

After those efforts to create rules died out, a respite of sorts took place in which the idea was continued to be discussed but little to no activity occurred. Then shortly after the turn of the millennium, a new campaign to secure a balanced budget amendment began and it was joined by the drive to reform campaign finances. Together, these two grassroots movements provided the impetus for a new focus and effort for amendatory convention rules.

The Grassroots Act

Three groups in recent times have introduced proposals for rules for an Article V amendatory convention outside of governmental bodies. The Convention of States project[29] (COS) by the Citizens for Self-Governance[30] is seeking to call a convention to consider a number of proposals. They partnered with Professor Natelson to generate a set of rules that the States could consider and adopt. The COS is not looking to pass a singular amendment but to address three subjects that would force the "limiting of the power and the jurisdiction of the federal government" itself.[31] They propose an extensive series of amendments that would effectively curtail the authority of the federal government across all branches. It is an ambitious

---

[27] http://www.foavc.org/reference/Resolution_5.pdf
[28] http://clerk.house.gov/legislative/memorials.aspx
[29] http://www.conventionofstates.com/
[30] https://selfgovern.com/
[31] http://www.cosaction.com/strategy

proposition that is being conducted at two levels – through grassroots organizing and through a concerted national effort to push for state level action in the state legislatures.

The COS got a clean jump on everyone else in July of 2015 by releasing its proposal for rules to govern an amendatory convention.[32] The seven pages of rules were streamlined as the bulk pertained to the basic operation of the convention and the designated committees. For the balance of the requisite rules, deference to *Mason's Manual of Legislative Procedure* was made to cover all other aspects of the convention's operations. This decision was expected as most state legislatures use *Mason's* and those delegates that are state legislature members would already be familiar and comfortable with it.[33] Much of the material found in the draft contains rules or revisions to rules employed by intercolonial and interstate conventions both preceding the 1787 Philadelphia Convention and other conventions that followed the 1787 convention and are the product of the research of Professor Natelson. The proposed rules are, it would appear, a final draft.

Concurrent with the COS campaign, several state legislators began to undertake the drafting of rules for an amendatory convention through formation of The Assembly of State Legislatures (ASL) in 2013.[34] Just prior to the fourth meeting of this body in November of 2015, the ASL released its draft of proposed rules that were taken up in the November meeting in Salt Lake City. The eighteen page ASL draft contained a more comprehensive set of rules than that of the COS.[35] Having been drafted by sitting state legislators from forty-five states, one might therefore expect that the rules would be as parliamentarian and complete as possible. The ASL describes itself as bipartisan and inclusive. At the June 2016 ASL meeting in Philadelphia, representatives from a supermajority of states debated, modified and adopted a finalized set of rules. Like the COS, the ASL uses *Mason's* to resolve questions of parliamentary procedure.

The ASL is, by their own definition, a predecessor to a convention of the States, and is called to address issues of developing rules and procedures

---

[32] http://www.conventionofstates.com/proposed_rules
[33] http://www.ncsl.org/research/about-state-legislatures/masons-manual-for-legislative-bodies.aspx "Seventy of the 99 legislative chambers in the United States use Mason's Manual" – accessed 12/26/15
[34] http://www.assemblystatelegislatures.com/ - originally constituted as The Mount Vernon Assembly.
[35] The Assembly of State Legislatures draft rules: http://nebula.wsimg.com/d8e4dd1a8bbf4902263115a7f21a48ee?AccessKeyId=08BE2CBF692A30D3DD75&disposition=0&alloworigin=1

to be shared by the States. The underlying premise is that the gravitas of the state legislators as "currently serving" elected officials acting to prepare the way for a Convention of the States which will write and adopt the rules after each state passes a resolution authorizing the delegates to act on the state's behalf give more weight to their proposed rules. The ASL itself is intended to be a permanent _legislative_ body and is equivalent to an Article V convention although it will NOT draft amendments or "trigger Article V authority."[36] In comparison, the COS project is simply that, a project intended to promote and prompt the calling of an Article V Convention of States. In the planning documents that the ASL created to generate discussion among its state legislator delegates, there is an exploration of consideration of other bodies, such as for creating an interstate compact, that are NOT equivalent to the Convention of the States. The distinction among the various described bodies is based on whether the convention is acting on a federal or national issue, such as a proposal for an amendment, or on an interstate issue, such as proportioning the responsibility for keeping a bordering river clear of debris that might hinder river ship traffic.[37] In fact, the ASL deliberately set out to avoid any conflation with an interstate compact.[38]

Both the COS and the ASL show strong evidence of having turned to historical practice to determine how best to proceed. One point where there is a substantial divergence is in the issue of convention secrecy for the proceedings. Whereas the Philadelphia 1787 convention sought to restrict public intrusion that would inevitably lead to gossip and wild speculation, the modern convention rules drafting efforts are committed to public oversight. The ASL's documentation for developing the rules speaks of recording the proceedings for posterity while still preventing "showboating for the cameras for their [the delegates'] own personal gain."[39]

Finally, although not a grassroots group, the American Legislative Exchange Council (ALEC) proposed a very short set of rules in early 2016. Comprising less than two printed pages, the rules hit only the highlights of the issue, including unit voting, delegate selection and punishment, limitation of topic, and quorum composition. Surprisingly, the ALEC rules

---

[36] The Assembly of State Legislatures "Purpose Flowchart"
[37] The Assembly of State Legislatures "Committee Responsibility Form," 3
[38] Ibid., 5
[39] Ibid., 4

do not require a supermajority for amendment proposal approval by the convention. The proposed rules include a pre-worded resolution for the adoption of the rules by a state.[40]

A Comparison of the Rules Proposals

There are significant differences between the COS and ASL sets of rules proposals. Where the COS proposes officers to include a President and Vice-President, the ASL proposal has a temporary president preside over election of a President, Vice-President, who in turn name a Parliamentarian, Secretary, and Sergeant-at-Arms. Under the COS rules, the Sergeant-at-Arms maintains order at the direction of the convention President whereas under the ASL rules the President has that responsibility. Acting in bipartisanship, the ASL President and Vice-President cannot be of the same political party and no two officers can be from the same state.

Each proposal has a number of standing committees but the staffing of the committees differs in that the COS elects members to the rules, credentials and administration committees by secret ballot, the convention president appoints members to the ad hoc committees, and the remainder of the standing committees is staffed by one delegate per state selected by the state delegation. The ASL committee chairs appoint the members of their committees.

While both sets of rules require the presence of all delegates unless specifically excused with reason, the COS allows five delegates per state delegation on the floor at one time and the ASL allows ten per state with speaking privilege. Under the COS rules, a delegate may speak twice on a question and for no more than ten minutes but only once and for no more than twelve minutes under the ASL rules. The COS calculates a sufficient quorum for conducting business to be "not less than 26 member states" which agrees with the "qualified simple majority" for the ASL.

The order of business differs slightly in terms of the sequence although the individual items of business are virtually the same. The administration of the committees differs by the proposal as the COS proposal focuses on committee details governing subcommittees but the ASL committee details focus on the distinction between the Committee of the Whole versus the

---

[40] https://www.alec.org/model-policy/rules-for-an-article-v-convention-for-proposing-amendments/

individual standing and ad hoc committees' operations. The ASL had devoted greater attention to the need for standing committees and the operation of each. For both sets of proposed rules, the secrecy requirement has been relinquished as modern technology and sensibilities make public observation of the convention expected. Both proposals have exceptions to the secrecy abolition.

The COS rules are the result of research into the intercolonial conventions and draw heavily on the rules of the 1787 Philadelphia Federal Convention and the 1861 Washington Peace Conference. The ASL rules are the product of the committees of the ASL comprised of state legislators experienced at parliamentary operations. A number of issues were addressed by the ASL that the COS did not tackle. Of primary importance are the early opportunities for getting off topic prior to the formal adoption of convention rules. The ASL directly speaks to rules formulation, adoption, amendment, suspension and continuity.

Details within the ASL rules but not covered by the COS rules go to the certification of acts; record keeping and preservation; calendar maintenance; credential details; delegate recall; handling of resolutions and amendment proposals; fine points of committee operations; and the minutiae of funding, extra-conventional communications and secrecy. Of note is that the ASL devotes significant attention to the Article V applications themselves. The ASL formulates the lifespan of an application to be endless pending either a convention - actually a ratification of the amendment according to the proposed rules - for the stated topic or rescission by the issuing state legislature. The ASL assigns the validation and counting of the applications to the state legislatures – although how this is to be accomplished both physically and legally is not defined. These features may contain the elements of the rules rejection as they would appear to conflict with the constitutionally delegated ability of Congress to determine when a convention has been called.

The ASL rules make some bold assertions. They seek to include in the count for a specific topic all of the applications for an Open Convention. This would mean that the state(s) with such applications for an Open Convention would see their application discharged upon calling a limited convention forcing those states to once again apply for the balance of the issues that they deem worthy of a convention. Clearly, this is not the intent of those states applying for an Open Convention. Perhaps most perplexing is the last rules concerning the call of the convention. The ASL claims the authority to make the decision as to when the requisite number of states has submitted applications for a particular subject matter, and to then set the date and place of the convention, which is an action that is constitutionally committed to Congress to perform.

Despite the admirable work of the current crop of grassroots and state legislators, there are still issues that need to be addressed to make certain that an amendatory convention will operate smoothly and without problems. Within the last decade, the most recent efforts have identified new problems that were previously not considered. The focus has been on the reduction of the potential for a runaway and this has drawn attention to the use of a continuity clause and also on drafting a pre-written amendment. These two ideas have very different impacts on a convention. Finally, critics have asked, who are these organizations to assume that that they have the authority to attempt to draft and impose rules on a convention?

Can a Convention be Called that Merely Approves a Pre-written Amendment?

There are efforts underway to take exactly this action. Doing so removes one of the most important aspects of the amendatory convention, that of deliberation. The idea that the academic world can discuss and debate the relative merits of the various proposals and select the correct, most efficacious proposal independent of the political bodies and the electorate seems implausible.

The writing of a pre-drafted amendment proposal by a select group, be they grassroots, party members or political elite, academic experts, government bureaucrats, legal or judicial professionals, or any other segment of society that does not represent the overwhelming majority of the electorate, smacks of the influence of a special interest. The notes of the Federal Convention of 1787 are clear that the Framers intended for the present and future generations to always, without exception, act in a deliberative fashion. We must remember that many of the most controversial issues of the 1787 convention were solved through rigorous debate and compromise. The Constitution was ratified through often contentious ratificatory state conventions. The States have held hundreds of statehood, constitutional drafting, amendatory, ratificatory and policy related conventions that were all, with the notable exception of the ratification conventions for the Twenty-first Amendment, deliberative. In 1957, the Harvard Law Review noted, that "meaningful debate" was intended to be part of the process for the purpose of determining if there is indeed consensus among the States as to both the nature of the problem and the appropriateness of the proposed solution,

> "Therefore it may also be assumed that each step in the amending process was intended by the framers as a method of determining through meaningful debate whether significant agreement exists among the states on the desirability of particular changes in the fundamental law."[41]

The democratic back and forth, point-by-point debate of every seemingly esoteric detail is the point. In this exchange, the devil in the details, as the cliché goes, is exposed and the future is presumably saved from unforeseen problems. As the Harvard Law Review article states, the requisite consensus of the states is proven in the process. To ascribe to an "amendatory" convention the ability to vote only in an up or down manner on a pre-drafted amendment proposal is to deny the people their voice and to potentially hand over the shape of the Constitution to a special interest group.

This concept was demonstrated in the early 1960s with the "Confederating Proposals" that would have reduced the amendatory convention to a ratificatory convention only. Any debate over the amendment proposals was reserved to the state legislatures which prepared and adopted the resolutions calling for the convention. The people possessed no real input unless the state legislatures first held hearings on the bills. At the time, the issue of whether these proposals were "constitutionally" proposed and legitimate was debated in the literature. Professor Arthur Bonfield argued that the national nature of a convention precluded the state or local perspective of the proposals and necessitated the deliberative function of an amendatory convention,

> "Common sense alone suggests that Article V contemplates a deliberative convention that would itself undertake fully to evaluate a problem, and propose those particular solutions that it deems desirable. The reason for

---

[41] Republished with permission of the Harvard Law Review Association, from "Proposing Amendments to the United States Constitution by Convention," *Harvard Law Review* 70, no.6 (Apr.1957): 1071-2; permission conveyed through Copyright Clearance Center, Inc.

> *this is that amendments to our National Constitution are chiefly matters of national concern. Consequently, all the alternatives should be carefully explored and debated on a national level, and the details of any proposed amendments fully worked out on a national level, before they are sent to the states for their more locally oriented action of ratification."*[42]

A pre-written, pre-approved amendment wording negates the most important aspect of an amendatory convention, that of the brainstorming and scrutiny of possible solutions. In 1993, the House Committee on the Judiciary published a report that stated that "an application requesting an up-or-down vote on a specifically worded amendment cannot be considered valid."[43] It is the preferred option of the special interests.

Can a Continuity Clause be Applied to a Convention?

To prevent the taking of advantage of the window for potential mayhem between the opening gavel of a convention and the formal adoption of the convention rules requires that some provision be made for order within that period. Traditionally, a "continuity clause" is employed by parliamentary or legislative bodies that have regular sessions with regular recesses or reconstitution after an election.

There are several ways to approach this issue. Viewed according to a perceived order of descending power:

- Examining the 1787 Grand Federal Convention and all subsequent national conventions for continuity clauses or discussions of continuity to determine if the rules of the 1787 convention could be extended to cover the opening of the amendatory convention.

- Might the Congress stipulate in the call to convention that the rules of the 1787 convention are continued until the current convention adopts its own rules?

- Examining the continuity clauses of the rules of past Congresses to ascertain whether an "umbrella" of the power and the rules of Congress could be extended to the amendatory

---

[42] Arthur Earl Bonfield, "Proposing Constitutional Amendment by Convention: Some Problems," *Notre Dame Lawyer* 39, no.6 (9-1-1964): 662

[43] Thomas N. Neale, Library of Congress, Congressional Research Service Report R42592, *The Article V Convention to Propose Constitutional Amendments: Historical Perspectives for Congress*, at 17-8 (22 October 2012) – citing the committee's report titled, *Is There a Constitutional Convention in America's Future?*

convention as a body equivalent in power and on the same level of authority.

- Examining continuity clauses of the state and territorial constitutions for the wording and application of those clauses to determine whether there is a basis for extension of that power to the amendatory convention.

- Might the "implied and inherent powers" principle be applied to the amendatory convention to cover the opening?

- Might the legal principle of "custom and traditional usage" apply to the initial moments of the amendatory convention and limit actions until the formal rules are adopted?

A thorough review of the debates and discussion of the notes of the twelve known delegates to the 1787 convention that compiled and published notes reveals nothing that begins to come close to a continuity clause or a provision for order until the formal rules were adopted.[44] Although it was common for one convention to call another to address unfinished business, no trace of a continuity clause is found. The Annapolis convention of 1786 actually made the initial call for the 1787 Philadelphia convention. An argument might be made by legal scholars that the rules of the 1786 Annapolis convention could have been assumed to continue in effect at Philadelphia until that convention adopted its own rules. In turn, then, the 1787 Philadelphia rules might also extend to cover the opening of any Article V convention as an extension of the 1787 convention. Should this theory hold, it is possible that the custom of the eighteenth century that the rules of a prior convention that calls a later convention could then apply to the second convention until such time as the later convention adopts its own rules. This will require the confirmation of a constitutional attorney or a parliamentarian.

The 1787 Grand Convention had deliberately adopted the rules of the Confederation Congress for its operation.[45] It had other choices. The

---

[44] The notes of 1787 Constitutional Convention delegates Gunning Bedford, Jr. of Delaware, Maj. Pierce Butler of South Carolina, Lt. Col. Alexander Hamilton of New York, Maj. Rufus King of Massachusetts, John Lansing, Jr. of New York, Col. James Madison of Virginia, Luther Martin of Maryland, Col. George Mason of Virginia, Dr. James McHenry of Maryland, William Paterson of New Jersey, Capt. William Pierce of South Carolina and Judge Robert Yates of New York were all surveyed. Additionally, the 1787 Constitutional Convention Secretary, Maj. William Jackson, kept some notes and these were also surveyed.

[45] James Schouler, *History of the United States: 1783-1801, Rule of Federalism* (New York: Dodd, Mead & Co., 1880, 1908 ed.), 39-40

options available to it were to use the English forms of parliamentary order or the printed materials for many of the procedural practices employed.[46] Using the Confederation Congress' rules was a practical solution since so many members of the 1787 convention were already state legislature and Continental Congress members and would already be familiar with the procedures used in those bodies.

An examination of the roots and evolution of the state legislatures provides some support for the idea of extending the prior convention's rules to the succeeding convention. Dr. Peverill Squire's research on state legislature development gives some clues,

> *"What about continuity with standing committees? As discussed in Chapter 2, by the time of the revolution, most assemblies had standing committees. Like rules of procedure, standing committees carried over to the new state legislatures from their predecessors."*[47]

Squire continues that the rules were deliberately carried over, "The evidence here strongly supports a claim that the new state legislatures inherited almost all of their rules and structures directly from their colonial predecessors."[48] From this we can conclude – tentatively – that the use of continuity, whether by clause or impliedly, is as old as the Republic itself. There is some additional proof in Squire's research that shows that more than just the rules were carried over. Procedures and practices were also carried over and foremost among these are, as always, the fiscal practices. He notes,

> *"Concerns over the costs of territorial legislatures were not confined to Florida and Michigan. A Wisconsin newspaper wondered, 'The appropriation to defray the expense of the next session of the Territorial Legislature is $17,250. Will the next session of the Legislature do Wisconsin as much good as the above amount would do, if expended in improving roads? (Milwaukee Sentinel, 1844)'"*[49]

The adoption of legislative rules by the thirty-one states that

---

[46] Mary Sarah Bilder, "How Bad Were the Official Records of the Federal Convention?," George Washington Law Review 80, no.6 (Oct. 2012): 1633-4
[47] Peverill Squire, *The Evolution of American Legislatures, Colonies, Territories, and States, 1619-2009* (Ann Arbor: University of Michigan Press, 2014), 92
[48] Ibid., 93
[49] Ibid., 107

developed out of territories, as opposed to the original thirteen states and their subsequent split-off states, were typically predicated on the rules of the territorial legislature which had adopted, generally, the rules of the U.S. House of Representatives.[50] The "institutionalization" of the state legislatures in the nineteenth century, particularly the second half, led to the formal rules that are employed today and include the ubiquitous continuity clauses.

Finally, Judge Jameson offers some encouragement on this issue,

> *"Pending on the preparation of this report, in about half the cases, a resolution has been carried to adopt for their government, for the time being, the rules of the last House of Representatives of the State, so far as applicable. In a few instances, the rules of the last Convention have been temporarily put in force, and in one case, that of California, in 1849, those laid down in Jefferson's 'Manual of Parliamentary Law.'"*[51]

The second of our listed options is less favorable. If the rules of the Congress allow for the extension of its rules to the amendatory convention, then Congress will have a disproportionate influence on the convention and will exert a measure of power over the convening of the convention. This precedent could engender too much danger for co-option of the convention by Congress. Most delegates to an Article V convention will be state legislators and not congressmen; patterning the rules after the states and not adopting the rules of Congress – even for the interim until formal rules are established – would be less confusing and problematic.

The Article V conventions, both amendatory and ratificatory, are considered to be equivalent in stature to the Congress – it is co-equal. The amendatory convention is a "virtual fourth branch" of government. If Congress were able to define the rules and the procedures of the convention, its function would be severely curtailed. Remember that the convention method was included, in large part, to provide a method of circumventing a recalcitrant Congress.[52] The convention option was included in the Constitution in response to the perception of the potential for congressional unresponsiveness to the public demands for a constitutional amendment.[53]

---

[50] Ibid., 221-5
[51] John Alexander Jameson, *A Treatise on Constitutional Conventions, Their History, Powers, and Modes of Proceeding*, (New York: Scribner, 1867, 4th ed., 1887), § 284, 283, reprint by The Lawbook Exchange, (2013)
[52] Patricia A. Brannan, David L. Lillehaug, Robert P. Reznick, "Critical Details: Amending the United States Constitution," *Harvard Journal on Legislation* 16 (1979): 802
[53] Ibid.

The third option is less desirable than the previous options. This idea is a mere extension of the second option. The congressional rules, Senate and House, provide no mechanism to preserve the independence of the convention without possibly yielding to congressional control. If there is an attribute that is paramount to an amendatory convention, it is independence from Congress.

The fourth option is problematic only to the extent that it considers the input of the respective legislatures of fifty states and six territories. It differs little from the third option.

Some potential exists in the application of the "implied and inherent powers" principle to the question. Since all conventions are acknowledged to possess implied and inherent powers, it can be surmised that the extension of the rules of a preceding convention to a subsequent convention is reasonable under certain circumstances. It is a fundamental principle of political science that governments must possess powers beyond those enumerated in a charter and as a corollary, it is nigh impossible to list all powers that are implied. The reason for the inability for enumeration is that powers yet to be either needed or defined will eventually be found to be among the implied and inherent powers.

Historically, the discussion of implied powers – and implied limitations – has been directed toward the federal government.[54] In this instance, that is an appropriate point as an Article V convention is considered to be an extension of the federal power, that is, the States are performing a "federal function" while operating the convention. In *Leser v. Garnett*, the US Supreme Court held that the States are carrying out a federal function and that state limitations do not apply.[55]

We discover the existence of these powers often through the decisions of courts that need to declare the responsibility or power of government to resolve an issue and also through the declaration of the possession of a previously unknown power when government seeks to establish the need to

---

[54] Walter F. Dodd, "Implied Powers and Implied Limitations in Constitutional Law," *Yale Law Journal* XXIX, no.2 (Dec. 1919): 137
[55] *Leser v. Garnett*, 258 U.S. 130 (1920)

assert power to resolve a problem.⁵⁶ Conventions are no less than a subset of government in terms of Article V. Judge Jameson stated in 1867 in his treatise on constitutional conventions that, (author's emphasis added in bold),

> "The general rule is undoubtedly this: – as Conventions are commonly numerous assemblies,….they are possessed of such powers as are requisite to secure their own comfort, to protect and preserve their dignity and efficiency, and **to insure orderly procedure in their business.**"⁵⁷

What more could be expected from the opening of the convention than to establish order? Clearly Jameson recognized this point and assigned it a primacy of priority. He devoted an entire section of the treatise to this point, recreating the first part herein, (author's emphasis added in bold and underline),

> "§459. A Convention having provided itself with the officers needed to do or to expedite its work, its attention **would be next directed to the subject of maintaining order** in the transaction of its business, and in the conduct of its members. For this purpose, rules of order are necessary. There is **sometimes inserted in the Act calling the Convention**, a power to establish such rules as should be deemed requisite; but, **without such a clause, a Convention would be clearly authorized so to do**. <u>It is usual, before rules have been reported by the special committee for that purpose, to adopt temporarily those of the last Convention, or of the last State House of Representatives.</u> In the absence of such a vote, it has been said, that the lex parliamentaria, as laid down in the best writers, is in force. If by this is meant, that the maxims of common sense, having reference to the protection of the rights of minorities, to the preservation of order, and to the speedy transaction of the business in hand, as the same are determined by the experience of public bodies, are to be taken as a guide, the proposition may be accepted, since the lex parliamentaria is but a body of practical rules founded on those very maxims."⁵⁸

Jameson has provided the needed direction as to future conventions

---

⁵⁶ As a counter-argument, it could be said that implied powers are not real because they would expand the Constitution beyond its limits – and this argument was made for the first century or so in the use of Justice Marshall's insistence upon implied powers, often derided as his "the-means-to-an-end theory." Today, it is accepted as a judicial *fait accompli*. For detail see, generally, Margaret C. Klingelsmith, "Two Theories in Regard to the Implied Powers of the Constitution," *University of Pennsylvania Law Review* 54, no.4 (Apr.1906)

⁵⁷ John Alexander Jameson, *A Treatise on Constitutional Conventions, Their History, Powers, and Modes of Proceeding* (New York: Scribner, 1867, 4ᵗʰ ed., 1887), § 453, 455, reprint by The Lawbook Exchange, (2013)

⁵⁸ Ibid., § 459, 460-1

possessing the ability to adopt the rules of a previous convention – or legislature as the situation warrants – and therein lays the foundation on which the argument may be made that an Article V convention could theoretically proceed initially under the aegis of the Philadelphia Convention's rules until the current convention adopts its own rules.

Roger Sherman Hoar echoes Jameson in his 1917 work on constitutional conventions. He quotes the above passage of Jameson and then adds his own clarifying codicil,

> "Legislative acts, under which conventions have been assembled, have usually not attempted to determine in any detail how conventions should proceed. A constitutional convention should have freedom to determine its own organization and procedure."[59]

It is clear that an Article V convention is entitled and empowered to assume the rules of order from a previous convention and may be able to go as far as stating which convention it recognizes itself to be the successor to in a chain of conventions. A future Article V convention could open with a statement before any other business is transacted that declares itself to be operating under the rules of the 1787 Philadelphia Constitutional convention and that it is authorized to do so by:

1. historical convention practice,
2. academic consensus,
3. the body of constitutional law that concerns both conventions and the implied powers doctrine,
4. and in particular Article V itself.

Both academic scholars and the decisions of the courts substantiate this position, in their works acknowledging implied and incidental powers exist under Article V,

> "A legislature or convention exercising authority under Article V may be called an Article V assembly. The grant under Article V, together with their incidental powers, are the sole source of authority for amending the

---

[59] Roger Sherman Hoar, *Constitutional Conventions – Their Nature, Powers, and Limitations* (Boston: Little, Brown and Co., 1917), 174

Constitution."⁶⁰,⁶¹

That such powers are customary and historically accepted and recognized is established to at least the time of Jameson a full century and a half ago. It has been cited a century ago by Hoar and now today by Natelson. A future Article V convention therefore already enjoys considerable leeway in terms of the adoption of continuity of previous conventions. Natelson notes that,

> "a grant of power to an assembly operating under Article V carries with it subordinate powers that, at the time the Constitution was adopted, customarily accompanied such a grant, or are otherwise reasonably necessary to carrying out the grant."⁶²

In preparing this research, academic and legal scholars were contacted to determine if the issue of continuity was a potential problem for a future convention. Dr. Peverill Squire of the University of Missouri, graciously responded that,

> "You raise an interesting question. As I understand it, legislative chambers where rules are adopted each session—that is those that do not see themselves as continuing bodies—operate under the assumption that the old rules obtain until the new rules are adopted. Usually this happens without much fuss, but occasionally, as in the California Assembly in late 1994 and early 1995, it does become something of an issue.
>
> The constitutional conventions I have examined (but not on this question) usually adopt rules early (often the rules of one of their legislative chambers). But the question of what happens before those rules are adopted is left open. I suppose the call for the convention could contain the rules under which the convention operates."⁶³

Dr. Squire has produced the standard work on the evolution of state legislatures from the Provincial Conventions and Provincial Congresses of the early Revolutionary War period to the professional legislatures of today. His suggestion that the call could include the (temporary) rules

---

⁶⁰ Robert G. Natelson, *A Compendium for Lawyers and Legislative Drafters* (Purcellville, VA: Convention of States, 2014), 35
⁶¹ *Prior v. Norland*, 188 P. 729 (Colo. 1920)
⁶² Robert G. Natelson, *A Compendium for Lawyers and Legislative Drafters* (Purcellville, VA: Convention of States, 2014), 34
⁶³ Email of 27 May 2015 from Peverill Squire to Timothy Dake in response to Dake's 24 May 2015 email query

for a convention reiterates one of the ideas discussed in this research. His statement that the rules of a non-continuing body may carry over is helpful in answering this open issue.

Similarly, Dr. Mary Sarah Bilder of Boston College is an expert on the quality and extent of the early colonial and state records of the Revolutionary War Period. She was not aware of any continuity clauses in the early legislative or convention records that she has surveyed. This could possibly be interpreted to mean that there may be also no (known to date) exclusionary rules dating to the early conventions.[64]

Based on the evidence examined, it would appear that the "customary and traditional usage" of the early extension of convention rules to a subsequent convention could be appropriate when used in conjunction with the implied and inherent powers doctrine. This facet of law is used for everything from preserving aboriginal natives fishing and hunting rights to easements across property by non-owners for "non-commercial, long-term and consistent use."

From all this discussion, we putatively draw the following conclusions:

1. An argument can be made that the Article V convention can use temporary rules or a continuity of rules of a previous convention.
2. Conventions possess implied and inherent powers – and they are the appropriate arbiters of what those powers may be.
3. More than the law is on the side of the convention; history, custom, practice and scholarly consensus supports continuity as well.

Can the Content of the Convention Call be Controlled, and by Whom?

A newer topic is that of who takes control of the call to convention. This sounds like a small matter but in actuality it defines the course of the convention. The topic is defined, the place and date of commencement is set, and the possibility of going beyond the constitutionally decreed parameters exists. Should Congress act unilaterally, they are without bounds should they decide that their constitutional mandate to call a convention is at their discretion. The States have a limitation on input in the form of the information included in their applications. The ASL proposal includes

---

[64] Email of 18 May 2015 from Mary Sarah Bilder to Timothy Dake in response to Dake's 17 May 2015 email query

the States controlling the content of the call to convention. This step is taken in order to remove the ability of Congress to set the parameters of the convention according to the whims of Congress.

The potential for Congress to manipulate the amendatory convention is at its greatest with the determination of the content of the call to convention. Allowing Congress to set the content of the call would establish a dangerous precedent that would inevitably mitigate the purpose of the convention. Article V grants no discretion to Congress beyond the implied power to set the date and place of convening. These two points, the determination of the date and place, are **_inferred_** from Article V as **_implied and inherent powers_** and not actually stipulated in the Constitution.[65] Setting the date and place are more of a convenience to the participants as these would be the first questions asked and some singular authority must make the initial decision. In comparison, the date and place of the 1787 Philadelphia Convention were set by the delegates to the 1786 Annapolis Convention and then seconded by the Virginia legislature's formal call to convention.

Historically, the purpose, agenda, delegate qualification and selection, internal rules and other matters of a convention are the province of the participants, in this instance the delegates of the States. Review of more than thirty inter-colonial and interstate conventions by Professor Natelson has shown that the States have always made these determinations. In the majority of cases, the conventions were called, planned, convened and conducted by the colonies themselves and the later conventions by their successor states. Natelson notes that,

> "the call never attempted to dictate a particular outcome or to limit the convention to answering a prescribed question affirmatively or negatively. The call also specified the initial time and place of meeting and whether the convention resolutions would bind the participating states or serve merely as recommendations or proposals. The call did not determine how the colonies or states were to select their delegates, nor did it establish convention rules or choose convention officers. An invited government was always free to ignore a call."[66]

---

[65] Robert G. Natelson, "Proposing Constitutional Amendments by Convention: Rules Governing the Process," *Tennessee Law Review* 78 (2011): 706
[66] Generally, Robert G. Natelson, "Founding-Era Conventions and the Meaning of the Constitution's "Convention For Proposing Amendments," *Florida Law Review* 65 (2013): 15

Professor Herman Ames stated more than four score years ago, and is echoed today by Natelson, that it is American tradition that the States possess and exercise the powers to conduct these conventions. Looking to the closest possible legal and historical precedent for a federal amendatory convention, that of the 1787 Grand Convention in Philadelphia, shows that the Confederation Congress played no role in the convention other to issue a resolution for the convention to meet – and then, only after seven states had already pledged to attend. That congressional resolution of 21 February 1787 carried no legal force – it was more of an afterthought. With bolding added for clarification, the resolution in part reading,

> *"Resolved that in the **opinion** of Congress it is expedient that on the second Monday in May next a Convention of delegates who shall have been appointed by the several states be held at Philadelphia for the sole and express purpose of revising the Articles of Confederation and reporting to Congress and the several legislatures such alterations and provisions therein as shall when agreed to in Congress and confirmed by the states render the federal constitution adequate to the exigencies of Government & the preservation of the Union."*[67]

The proceedings of the Confederation Congress for that same day concur, stating,

> *"That it be **recommended** to the States composing the Union that a convention of representatives from the said States respectively be held at on for the purpose of revising the Articles of Confederation and perpetual Union between the United States of America and reporting to the United States in Congress assembled and to the States respectively such alterations and amendments of the said Articles of Confederation as the representatives met in such convention shall judge proper and necessary to render them adequate to the preservation and support of the Union"*[68]

These passages demonstrate that the Confederation Congress recognized that it possessed no power under the Articles to call a convention and had settled for expressing an opinion and making a recommendation only. The rest of the resolution wording reiterated the phrasing of the report of the Annapolis commissioners dated 11 September 1786. The

---

[67] Resolution of the Confederation Congress (Wednesday, 21 February 1787)
[68] Proceedings of the Confederation Congress (Wednesday, 21 February 1787) – the lack of appropriate wording stating where and when the convention was to be held is recorded in the proceedings as written here.

commissioners in Annapolis had prepared a convention report and forwarded it to all the state legislatures for action, and also to the Confederation Congress, but only as a courtesy. For both the Annapolis and Philadelphia conventions, the States had initiated the call to convention. Virginia played a major role in each of these conventions but with the States now sharing an equality of status and the new federal government holding supremacy in national issues, it made sense to designate the Congress as the point of reference for issuing the call to any future amendatory convention. So, this constitutional empowerment of Congress for calling an amendatory convention was both for convenience and deliberate.

Similarly, the only other occurrence of the Congress calling a convention pursuant to Article V is for the ratification of the Twenty-first Amendment in 1933. In US Senate Joint Resolution 211, Section 3, it states nothing beyond the call to the convention itself without particulars, that,

> *"This article shall be inoperative unless it shall have been ratified as an amendment to the Constitution by conventions in the several States, as provided in the Constitution, within seven years from the date of the submission hereof to the States by the Congress."*[69]

In Chapter 3, the story of the debate over the state ratification convention calls between former Attorney General A. Mitchell Palmer and former Solicitor General and then Congressman James Beck was highlighted to demonstrate the need to assign the power to make the convention call to one body and one body only. Another contemporaneous take on the debate in 1933 comes from Norman Ball,

> *"Former Attorney-General Palmer argued that, inasmuch as the amending of the Federal Constitution was a purely federal question, Congress must specify all of the details on the conventions. Congress apparently declined to decide this question, and the Amendment as finally proposed states only that ratification shall be by "convention in the several States."*[70]

The opportunity for the Congress to consider and take action to secure the power to determine the content of the call was before the 72nd Congress and they did not act. The reason is now immaterial as the political and

---

[69] US Senate Joint Resolution 211, (21 February 1933), upon ratification became the Twenty-first Amendment.
[70] Norman T. Ball, "Ratification of Constitutional Amendments by State Conventions," *George Washington Law Review* 2 (1933): 218

(potentially) legal precedent is now firmly established. Of course, it must be conceded that although these examples are both of Article V designated conventions, ratificatory and amendatory conventions are not necessarily the same thing. The comparison will have limitations but as to the calling of a generic Article V convention – be it for ratification or amendment proposal – the requirements of the call should be the same on the part of the Congress. As the Article V wording is not specific to either a ratificatory or an amendatory convention and provides only one phrasing for calling a convention, then there can be but one interpretation of the wording. Since the precedents exist for the 1780s ratification conventions and the 1933-34 conventions then that singular established interpretation could and should also hold today for amendatory conventions.

Thus, there is conclusively but a single precedent for the formal calling of a convention under Article V of the Constitution. The instance of the ratification conventions of 1787-91 is technically not under the Constitution as it was not yet ratified. Nonetheless, the recommendations of both the 1787 Grand Convention and the Confederation Congress were obeyed and the proposed Constitution was submitted to ratification conventions in the several states as stipulated in Article VII. These early ratification conventions were also not under Article V. An examination finds no evidence of the Congress assuming any powers beyond calling the ratification conventions. The 28 September 1787 resolution of the Congress reads, in part,

> *"Congress having received the report of the Convention lately assembled in Philadelphia.*
>
> *Resolved Unanimously that the said Report with the resolutions and letter accompanying the same be transmitted to the several legislatures in Order to be submitted to a convention of Delegates chosen in each state by the people thereof in conformity to the resolves of the Convention made and provided in that case."*[71]

In these two precedents of Congress exercising the power to call a convention, under Article V and Article VII, both examples exhibit a failing to exert any power beyond calling the conventions. They did not assume the authority to state the dates of convening or any other matter. For Congress to attempt to exert influence today in determining the agenda or procedures

---

[71] Resolution of the Confederation Congress (Friday, 28 September 1787)

of an Article V convention of any type, would be completely without legal or historical precedent for a multi-state convention or for individual conventions in all the states.

Most sources tell us that the limitation of the powers is on the part of the Congress. The amendatory convention needs to be able to carry out its duties without infringement or restriction by Congress. As one of the purposes of an amendatory convention is to modify the powers of a recalcitrant or obstructive Congress when necessary, the amendatory convention must be unencumbered to carry out this action. William Platz affirms,

> "Nor is Congress empowered to limit the authority of the convention, for the latter ought to be independent of a body whose powers it may find it necessary to alter. It should be remembered that provision for conventions was made intentionally to avoid complete Congressional control over the amending process."[72]

Grover Rees declares that the convention must be free of the control of Congress, even a bare minimum of control, to work properly. If Congress can control any aspect of the convention, then Congress' role is no longer ministerial and the convention is no longer truly independent and a work-around to the obstinacy of Congress. Rees asserts,

> "The central purpose of the convention method was to make it possible to amend the constitution over the opposition of Congress, this purpose would be defeated by the concession to Congress of absolute power to regulate, which is effectively the power to destroy."[73]

In anticipation of the complaints that will undoubtedly ensue that the States have no experience with organizing and conducting a federal amendatory convention, it must be stressed repeatedly that the States have held at least 236 state constitutional conventions over the last 227 years extending back to the earliest post-ratification state constitutional conventions in 1789.[74] Among these were no less than eighty limited-

---

[72] William A. Platz, "Article Five of the Federal Constitution," *George Washington Law Review* 3 (1934): 46
[73] Grover Rees III, "The Amendment Process and Limited Constitutional Conventions," *Benchmark* II, no.2 (March-April 1986). 84
[74] John J. Dinan, *The American State Constitutional Tradition* (Lawrence: University Press of Kansas, 2006), 7-9 – Dinan lists 233, but records show that he missed 3 more.

power, state amendatory conventions.⁷⁵ While the federal government has exactly zero experience calling, conducting and concluding an amendatory convention, the States are well versed at it and have refined the process. We can safely conclude that the States know precisely what to do and that includes all steps beginning with the call to convention. In considering the Twenty-first Amendment ratification conventions, although the States may have had no experience with organizing and operating a federal ratification convention, they had extensive experience with their own state constitutional and amendatory conventions, which they drew upon to draft their enabling acts. The States acted so quickly that Congress was unable to pass a template or general law for the States to follow. These state laws stipulated the delegate qualifications, election procedures, place and date at which to convene, the number of delegates and their compensation, the ballot design, oaths of office, officers of the convention, etc.⁷⁶

Alexander Hamilton famously declared in *The Federalist, No. 85* that,

*"The words of this article are peremptory. The Congress 'shall' call a convention. Nothing in this particular is left to the discretion of that body. And of consequence all the declamation about their disinclination to change, vanishes in air."*⁷⁷

Although he was the author of the majority of over forty attempts to federalize the convention process, and repeating from earlier, Senator Sam Ervin, Jr. wrote, "To concede to the Congress any discretion to consider the wisdom and necessity of a particular convention call would in effect destroy the role of the states."⁷⁸

In regard to the content itself, several points must be made. Foremost in importance and in the point of greatest contention is the limitability of the convention to a single purpose or agenda item. Exploration of this topic has previously taken dozens of pages and it suffices to say that the States simply must assert the right to limit the convention in their applications. The

---

[75] Henry D. Levine, "Limited Federal Constitutional Conventions: Implications of the State Experience," *Harvard Journal on Legislation* 11 (1973): 133, n.32

[76] Ethan P. Davis, "Liquor Laws and Constitutional Conventions: A Legal History of the Twenty-first Amendment," *Yale Law School Student Scholarship Repository*, (April 9, 2008): 23

[77] James Madison, "Federalist Paper No.85," in *The Federalist Papers: Hamilton, Madison, Jay*, ed., Clinton Rossiter (New York: Mentor, 1961), 526

[78] Sen. Sam Ervin, Jr., "Proposed Legislation to Implement the Convention Method of Amending the Constitution," *Michigan Law Review* 66, no.5 (Mar. 1968): 885

call should then specify:

- Subject matter, purpose or topic for the convention (based on the States' applications and reiterating the States' desired topic).

- Type of convention (amendatory, ratificatory, open, limited – again based on the States' requirements).

- Date of commencement.

- Place of convening.

- ASSUMING that the Assembly of State Legislatures' proposed rules for the convention operation have been adopted prior to the calling of the Article V convention, the call could reference the temporary application of a continuity clause that assures the restriction of any potential mayhem in the interim between the opening gavel and the adoption of the official rules by the convention.

Nothing more should be required so as to limit the possibility of congressional tampering and obstruction of the States' intent. We can then conclude in summary:

1. Congress must not be allowed to take control of the content of the call – ever. Doing so will lead to the inevitable sabotage of any convention by severely restricting the operations and scope of the powers of the convention resulting in an outcome favorable to Congress or the federal government but not necessarily to the States and the people. The professional parliamentarians in Congress could out maneuver the States with the establishment of congressional rules for convention procedures. Such concession by the States will allow Congress to change the interpretation of Article V from a mandatory obligation to call a convention to a discretionary power.

2. Since the obligation of Congress to call a convention is not discretionary, no action on the part of Congress to debate or vote on calling a convention should be tolerated on the part of the States. The action required by Congress is ministerial and not legislative. Allowing Congress to vote on whether to call a convention opens up the issue to the discretion of Congress. The States need to be ready and willing to act in a unified, concerted legal capacity to force the calling of the convention and to limit the ability of Congress to dictate the content of the call.

3. The States must rely on and publicly tout their experience and ability to operate conventions. They have to make a public display of resisting any and all federal encroachment on the convention process.

4. Congress may stipulate the place and the commencement date of the convention – nothing more. It should restate the States' desired purpose for the convention and the type of convention.

A Summary of the Rules as Gleaned from Article V, Court Decisions, Traditions and Customs

Having surveyed the rulings over two hundred years of constitutional jurisprudence and made examination of the body of academic literature, and harking back to Professor Tribe's three "knowns," then adding what the courts have told us, and surveying the proceedings of the hundreds of state and territorial conventions held to date for the rules contained therein, we can now compile a list of the anticipated rules for operation and limitations of an amendatory convention under Article V. The purpose of Part II is to provide evidence of the existence of rules for an Article V convention and to give a legal reasoning and understanding of the rules of an amendatory convention. Of course, the list is incomplete, but it is a formidable body nonetheless.

The National Executive

- The President plays no part in the amendment process.

The National Legislature

- The Congress issues the call to a convention including setting the date of commencement and the location of the convention when the count of applying states reaches two-thirds of the States – Congress has no discretion in the call other than the place and date and the conveyance of the specification of the States' choice of subject matter.

- The Congress receives, tallies and publishes the applications from the States.

- The Congress has the discretion of determining whether a proposed amendment is to be ratified by either the state legislatures or state ratification conventions.

- The Congress has the constitutionally delegated duty to promulgate to the States any proposed amendment from the convention without interference or consideration of the amendment proposal.

- By US House of Representatives rules, the Congress must maintain an accurate record and count of the pending applications and continually publish the same.

<u>The National Judiciary</u>

- The US Supreme Court will not entertain issues of a "political question" except that the Supreme Court alone determines what is, and what is not, a political question.

- The Supreme Court and lower federal district courts have, in the past, used the mandamus power to compel only members of the executive branch, but not Congress itself, to perform their "ministerial" duty, and they retain this power today.

<u>The States</u>

- The States individually make an application or petition for a convention in the nature of a formal legislative resolution and in that petition may [should] state the reason(s) or topic(s) for the convention. By implication, the States, through their applications aggregated together, may limit the subject matter of a convention.

- The wording of the States' applications does not need to be identical – consensus among the States is determined by the intent and not the verbiage.

- By legal precedent, tradition and custom, the States define the criteria for the qualifications and numbers for their respective delegates.

- By legal precedent, tradition and custom, the States determine the method of selection of their respective delegates.

- By legal precedent, tradition and custom, the States fund their own delegations.

- By both tradition and Supreme Court rulings, the validity of a state's application is beyond question. Although Congress has historically acted to judge the validity and quality of a state application, there is no constitutionally enumerated or implied power of Congress to do so.

- There is no expiration on the life of an application.
- A State may rescind its application at will.
- Only the States may participate in an Article V convention, the insular territories do not possess the legal standing to participate.
- The States have the power to recall, suspend the credentials of or discipline their delegates.

The Convention

- The convention is performing a federal function and not a state legislative action – state rules do not apply.
- By legal precedent, the convention must be free to conduct deliberation and debate – a pre-written amendment proposal is not permissible.
- By legal precedent, tradition and custom, the convention selects its own officers.
- By legal precedent, tradition and custom, the convention drafts its own rules.
- By legal precedent, tradition and custom, the convention maintains its own order and discipline.
- By legal precedent, tradition and custom, each state is entitled to one equal vote.
- By legal precedent, tradition and custom, a convention is the sole arbiter of the acceptance of the credentials of state delegates.
- Historically, a convention sets its own agenda and order of business, although in modern practice, legislatures and conventions often turn to formal parliamentary guides.
- Conventions have historically established both standing and ad hoc committees to partition the workload and the composition of each is entirely up to the discretion of the convention.
- Historically, both open and limited conventions have implied and incidental powers that allow them to call witnesses and

experts for advice and counsel.

• A convention should establish a continuity clause to cover the operations of the convention until such time as the convention establishes formal rules.

• A convention may name a temporary presiding officer to maintain order and progress until the formal slate of officers is elected.

• By legal precedent, it is necessary to have two-thirds of the delegations present to constitute a quorum to conduct business.

• Only a "constitutional" [drafting] convention possesses plenary powers; conversely, any type of limited power convention is NOT plenary.

• An open or general amendatory convention may take up any topic but it still limited to only the proposal of amendments.

• No convention convened under Article V on the United States Constitution is endowed with the power to write a new federal constitution, rewrite the existing federal constitution, or alter the method of ratification of an amendment as defined under Article V.

• No amendatory convention convened under Article V may do anything other than PROPOSE amendments – the power of ratification is reserved to either the state legislatures or state ratification conventions, as stipulated by Congress according to the Constitution.

• The convention has the discretion to determine whether the convention will observe secrecy or permit public observation of the proceedings.

• The convention can demand of any federal office or department the use of its archives and documents.

The People

• By legal precedents, the people have no <u>direct</u> role in the amendment process – this includes attempting either to call an Article V convention or to ratify a proposed amendment through the initiative or the referendum processes.

It would be remissive to fail to include the list of actions that an

Article V amendatory convention <u>cannot</u> do:

Powers Prohibited to the Amendatory Convention

- Wholesale rewriting of the Constitution
- Drafting and proposal of a new constitution
- Ratification of a proposed amendment
- Promulgation of a proposed amendment
- Passing ordinary statutory legislation
- Ascribe to itself any expansion of its powers

History has shown that the colonies and their successor states have a long, detailed and varied experience in calling conventions and developing rules for those conventions. Similarly, the past conventions have shown that the rules developed are very similar in content and formulation across all conventions. The conduct and execution of past conventions by the States have been relatively uniform and predictable. The rules developed to date have served well with few modifications from the general template. The model created has worked for conventions of varying composition implying that the partisanship of a given convention is not a factor. The evolved standardization of convention rules has resulted in the last century of a form that has prevented runaway conventions. From these developments, we can take confidence in a future amendatory convention that it will, more than likely, adopt appropriate rules and operate accordingly without complications.

Part III - Questioning Everything

The FAQs

Addressing the premise: "We just don't know what will happen…"

SEVEN
SO MANY QUESTIONS AND THE SEARCH FOR ANSWERS

"What distrust it shows today both in the wisdom of the founding fathers who gave us Article V and in ourselves to predict that we cannot safely use the second great mode of amendment offered by our Constitution."[1]

-John T. Noonan, Jr., Senior Judge, US Court of Appeals, Ninth Circuit

To address the last premise, that we just don't know what will happen in an amendatory convention and that is what makes it so dangerous [allegedly], requires that we review the questions usually asked. We also look at the scholarly history of the academic thinking regarding a convention as it is heavily question dependent, the roots of the opposition to the convention which raise many, if not most of the questions, and the basis of the opinions held by both sides. The controversy over an amendatory convention is of fairly recent vintage and like so many other issues in politics, is founded on misinformation, misinterpretation and money. In this third part of the book, we look at the issues that comprise the questions most often asked and review the earliest sources as to the interpretation of Article V.

The opposition to an Article V convention is driven primarily by the questions associated with the process of the convention. Many commentators say that we can place much of the concern on the shoulders of the Framers for their omission of a set of rules to govern the process. Or can we? As we

---

[1] John T. Noonan, Jr., "The Convention Method of Constitutional Amendment – Its Meaning, Usefulness, and Wisdom," *Pacific Law Journal* 10 (1979): 642

have seen, it is a reasonable assumption that the Framers believed that the process was already understood – at least in their time! Since intercolonial and then interstate conventions had been a common occurrence, the Framers undoubtedly expected that such conventions would continue throughout our history and as a consequence, the rules would continue to be known and practiced. This argument can be somewhat refuted by citing Madison's concerns, briefly stated during the 1787 convention, as detailed by Farrand,

> "Mr. Madison remarked on the vagueness of the terms, 'call a Convention for the purpose' as sufficient reason for reconsidering the article. How was a Convention to be formed? by what rule decided? what the force of its acts?"[2]

But Madison approved and accepted the proposed process so there is little here with which to be concerned. We can theorize that Madison was more focused on determining by <u>which</u> set of rules would future Article V convention operate – should the rules be standardized then and there or allowed to develop on their own as necessity and the times would dictate? The multiple efforts underway today give credence to Madison's concern and underscore the need to re-ask *who* makes the rules? Perhaps the lack of a provision of rules was a deliberate deference to the future and the perception that the people who call and convene an Article V convention were entitled to determine what would work best for them. More likely, is that time would prove which practices are the most efficient and the most practical through the operation of past and future conventions, not just amendatory but other conventions of the States such as those held for the ratification of the Constitution and amendments. The Framers probably expected that future generations would prudently take the time to examine and profit from the experience of the past generations before proceeding.

Madison's concern in the preceding quote may be taken another way, perhaps he was pointing out that the future may find itself in the position which we are in today where the answers are debated because they were originally left unaddressed. Madison was certainly not a novice at conventions. He was a member of the Virginia Provincial Convention that drafted the first state constitution in 1776. He served in the Annapolis convention just months prior to his central role in the Philadelphia convention. He took part in conventions throughout his political career

---

[2] Max Farrand, *The Records of the Federal Convention of 1787, Vol. II* (New Haven, CT: Yale University Press, 1911 rev. 1937), 558 – Monday September 10, 1787

including closing out his career as a delegate to the Virginia convention to draft a new state constitution in 1830.³

Perpetuating Uncertainty

The persistence of unanswered questions has driven the opposition to Article V conventions since the first applications were submitted by states. Over time, these questions have been answered one-by-one by either the courts, or by practice or through academic research. We can look back just a couple of decades to demonstrate how the questions have been conclusively answered. As recently as 1993, John Vile was posing these questions which are now, for the most part, answered,

> *"Although questions involving the convention are legion, a number of basic issues appear responsible for most of the controversy. These include the length of time that petitions for a convention should remain valid, how similar these petitions must be for them to be aggregated together as a single call for a convention, and whether state may call a limited convention or whether a convention would necessarily be at liberty to consider and propose anything. This last question is linked, in turn, to the key question as to whether a convention would be a safe option or not. Specifically, could a convention be limited by one or another institution of government, or would it be sovereign?"*⁴

Today, we can definitively answer how to aggregate the petitions, whether the convention can be limited, if the convention is safe and we know how to deal with the time limit for validity. This leaves the issue of the sovereignty of the convention – and that appears to be resolved as well. Article V has been called "tantalizingly vague" and the operation of a convention has been labeled a "constitutional curiosity."⁵ What has driven the opposition to a convention and has also created the apprehension that people have towards an amendatory convention is attributable to one and the same thing: uncertainty as to the rules, and therefore the outcome of

---

³ Jack N. Rakove, *Original Meanings, Politics and Ideas in the Making of the Constitution* (New York: Vintage Books, 1996), 36-7
⁴ Republished with permission of ABC-CLIO Inc., from John R. Vile, *Contemporary Questions Surrounding the Constitutional Amending Process* (Westport, CT: Praeger, 1993), 55; permission conveyed through Copyright Clearance Center, Inc.
⁵ Michael A. Almond, "Amendment by Convention: Our Next Constitutional Crisis?," *North Carolina Law Review* 53 (1975): 492

the convention.[6] This uncertainty has been used as a tool by opponents of the amendatory convention to frighten people on both sides of the political spectrum to not just fear but to actively oppose a convention.[7] Prior to Vile by just a few years, we find attorney William Barker scrutinizing the process in a paper on the status of the balanced budget amendment campaign,

> *"1. Does Article V permit the calling of a 'limited' convention to propose amendments only with regard to a particular subject or does it authorize only a 'general' convention authorized to propose whatever amendments the convention may deem appropriate to remedy what it perceives to be defects in the existing provisions of the constitution?*
>
> *2. If a 'limited' convention is constitutionally authorized, must the limits on such a convention permit it to function as a fully deliberative body called to consider a broad problem and to propose corrective measures or may the terms of the call narrowly limit the function of the convention (e.g. to proposing or rejecting a specified amendment)?*
>
> *3. If a 'limited' convention is constitutionally authorized, how closely must the applications for such a convention agree with one another in specifying the scope of the convention's mandate?*
>
> *4. For how long a period after passage of a state legislative resolution applying for a constitutional convention does that resolution remain effective as a basis for the calling of such a convention (if joined by a sufficient number of other applications for such a convention)?*
>
> *5. What procedural requirement must be satisfied to produce a valid application (e.g. is such an application subject to gubernatorial veto; may the lieutenant governor vote to break a tie if authorized by state law to do so; what majority is required to act)?*
>
> *6. Once a legislature has made application for a convention, may it rescind that application?*
>
> *7. If a convention is to be called, how should its members be selected?*
>
> *8. Ought the delegates to a convention vote individually or by states?*

---

[6] Michael B. Rappaport, "Reforming Article V: The Problems Created by the National Convention Amendment Method and How to Fix Them," *Virginia Law Review* 96, no.7 (Nov. 2010): 1526-7

[7] Robert G. Natelson, "Proposing Constitutional Amendments by Convention: Rules Governing the Process," *Tennessee Law Review* 78 (2011): 697

9. What vote of the convention should be necessary to propose an amendment?

10. Should Congress or the convention resolve the questions regarding the manner of voting and the vote necessary to propose an amendment?

11. When and in what manner should Congress specify the method of ratification (by legislatures or state conventions) for any amendments proposed by the convention?

12. Are the actions of Congress in calling the convention, defining its composition, etc. subject to presidential veto?

13. If the convention is 'limited,' who should determine whether the amendments proposed by the convention fall within its mandate and what effect would proposals have which fall outside that mandate?"[8]

These questions posed by Barker are really no different than those asked later by Vile and by many of the commenters that are writing before both of them. Every question on Barker's list has been fully answered today. Preceding Vile and Barker, we have Kenneth Ripple of Notre Dame asking a series of questions in 1982 that are today, for the most part, a repetition of others' question and also considered as now answered,

"[W]hat constitutes a valid application by a state legislature for a national convention? What procedures must a state follow in submitting an application? Must the precise language of the proposed amendment be included within the application? How similar must the language be in the applications of various states in order to permit Congress to count them? How long does an application by a state remain valid? May a state rescind its application? If so, under what conditions? What is the extent of Congress' power to review state applications? What institution of government controls the agenda of the convention – the state legislatures, Congress, the convention itself? May Congress refuse to submit the work product of the convention to the state for ratification and, if so, under what circumstances? How will delegates to the convention be selected? How will votes at the convention be counted? How will other procedures for the conduct of the convention be established? How will the convention be financed? If Congress assumes the power to answer some or all of these questions, are its determinations subject to review by any other institution of government,

---

[8] William T. Barker, "A Status Report on the 'Balanced Budget' Constitutional Convention," *John Marshall Law Review* 20 (1986): 72-3.

such as the courts?"[9]

Shortly before Ripple's queries, Laurence Tribe asked more than twenty questions in a paper from 1979. Each of these is treated in the excursus of FAQs following this chapter. He wanted to know not only the answers to his questions, but WHO may "authoritatively" answer the questions.[10] That point has become ever more pertinent today with the ALEC, the Assembly of State Legislatures and the Convention of States all proposing rules for an amendatory convention; people are rightly asking, "who are you to say what the rules are to be?" In the end, as we now know, it is the convention itself that determines its rules.

We can turn the clock back further and see examples of the concerns, and sometimes the fears, of those who saw an amendatory convention as the beginning of the end. In 1967, during the drive for an amendatory convention to address the reapportionment issue in the state legislatures, Carl Swisher and Patricia Nelson posed a number of questions concurrent with the Ervin bill,

> "What, for example, would constitute a valid application? Should the signature of the governor be required? In what manner should the application be submitted to Congress? Would the application retain its potency only during the life of a particular legislature or of a particular session of Congress or would it remain alive indefinitely with respect to the issue with which it dealt? Could a subsequent legislature recall or nullify the application previously filed, so that it would no longer contribute toward the total of two-thirds of the states, or did it take on life independent of the legislature? Within what period was Congress obligated to call a convention? What should be done about a meeting place, compensation, length of session? How should the membership be allocated as among the states? Should voting be done state by state or should each delegate be authorized to vote independently? Could or should the convention be limited to the subject dealt with in the applications from the states, or could it in any event follow the example of the convention of 1787 and deal with other subject matter and perhaps present an entirely new Constitution? By what method should the proposals of the convention be submitted for ratification

---

[9] Kenneth Ripple, "Article V and the Proposed Federal Constitutional Convention Procedures Bills," *Cardozo Law Review* 3 (1982): 531

[10] Laurence Tribe, "Issues Raised by Requesting Congress to Call a Constitutional Convention to Propose a Balanced Budget Amendment," *Pacific Law Journal* 10 (1979): 638-40

by three-fourths of the states? Might Congress in any way intervene so as to influence either procedure or content? Could and should the judiciary be permitted to play any part at all in these matters, or would it in any event regard the questions as 'political' – as non-justiciable, to be resolved only be the 'political' branches of the government?"[11]

Once again, the questions are not new, but merely restatements of earlier questions and will undoubtedly be asked yet again. Now when we look at these questions, we might be somewhat amused that these questions were ever posed, knowing what we now know. The older questions are even more basic. Prior to the reapportionment campaign, during the effort to secure a convention to address the income tax limit in the 1950s, Judge William L. Martin asked,

"When and where would the convention meet? How would the delegates be selected? Would Congress leave their selection to the states? Would they represent the states or the people in the aggregate? Would the call be addressed to the states, as in 1786 and 1787? Would the vote be by states, as in 1787? To what nature of control would the convention be subject, if any? Would Congress regulate all these matters? Would the convention be justified in writing a new Constitution superseding the present one?"[12]

The gravity of these questions in their day was great, but now, we are comfortable with the answers and a reflection on these questions shows how far we have come in addressing the concerns over a convention in the past half century. Two decades earlier in 1934, William A. Platz posed similar questions of the amendatory convention process, stoking the fires,

"What would be the size of the convention? Shall representation be by states or according to population? Shall it have forty-eight delegates, or shall it be a huge body, like a party nominating convention? Would the convention be bound to consider only amendments applied for by the states? If the new convention could propose a new constitution and not merely amendments, would not Article V so state, without leaving the matter to inference?"[13]

Before that, the Harvard Law Review was asking about limits on the

---

[11] Carl Brent Swisher & Patricia Nelson, "In Convention Assembled," *Villanova Law Review* 13, no.4 (1968): 719-20

[12] William Logan Martin, "The Amending Power: The Background of the Income Tax Amendment," *American Bar Association Journal* 39, no.1 (Jan. 1953): 78

[13] Generally, as quoted by Martin in note *supra*, William A. Platz, "Article Five of the Federal Constitution," *George Washington Law Review* 3 (1934): 17-49

convention and the ability of the courts to enforce those limits in 1916.¹⁴ As we can see, over more than a century of academic examination and debate on the questions, as one question is answered, another takes its place in the discussion. The lack of attention to the convention process in the Constitutional Convention of 1787 creates problems but then so does the sparse wording that does appear in Article V. As previously discussed, one of the more debated questions as focused on the ability to limit the subject matter of a convention. Opponents have claimed that the wording of Article V itself proves that the convention must be unlimited. For this assertion, they rely on this passage, "on the Application of the Legislatures of two thirds of the several States, [Congress] shall call a Convention for proposing Amendments,"

And it is that last letter "s" on "Amendment<u>s</u>" that stirs up the waters. Here again, Professor Vile dispatches the opponents' argument pointing out that,

> *"Textually, this provision might seem to require that a convention propose more than one amendment, but this is clearly a case where historical practice has firmly established that the grammatical plural is designed to include singular amendments as well – otherwise Congress would also have to propose more than one amendment at a time, which it clearly has not always done."*¹⁵

Congress is faced with similar wording in the preceding clauses of Article V where it states, "The Congress, whenever two thirds of both Houses shall deem it necessary, shall propose Amendments to this Constitution,.."

It is an historical fact that Congress has proposed singular amendments almost exclusively with the exception of the Bill of Rights. Remembering that the power of the States to convene a convention for proposing amendments is equivalent in power to Congress proposing amendments, we can safely conclude that the ability to limit an amendatory convention to a single proposal is an answered question. The text of the Constitution does not answer many questions on the Article V convention

---

14 "The Powers of Constitutional Conventions," *Harvard Law Review* 29, no.5 (Mar. 1916): 528
15 Republished with permission of ABC-CLIO Inc., from John R. Vile, *Contemporary Questions Surrounding the Constitutional Amending Process* (Westport, CT: Praeger, 1993), 56; permission conveyed through Copyright Clearance Center, Inc.

process, so we have to move on to historical precedents, court findings and academic debate to find our answers.

We can take the context to its (il)logical conclusion and point out many examples of where the Constitution uses the plural but in practice the singular has been the norm. This explanation is demonstrable across all of the branches of the federal government. When we examine the Constitution in detail and consider all of the plural references, the "s" on the end of Amendments in Article V appears innocuous. For example, in Article I, Section 2, Clause 4, it reads, "When vacancies happen in the Representation from any State, the Executive Authority thereof shall issue Writs of Election to fill such Vacancies."

Do we need to interpret this clause as only applicable when a state experiences two or more simultaneous vacancies in its congressional delegation? Will the clause not apply when, say, a singular congressman resigns or dies? It we take this clause as literally as the opponents to an amendatory convention take Article V's "Convention for proposing Amendments" language, then we could argue that if the Great State of East Somewhere's congresswoman from the Third District resigns, that the Governor must refuse to issue a Writ of Election to replace the honorable congresswoman until a second congressman from the delegation of East Somewhere either dies or resigns. The absurdity of this position becomes self-evident.

Similarly, Article 1, Section 3 which covers the US Senate uses plural language to also describe the filling of vacancies in Clause 2 wherein "the Executive thereof may make temporary Appointments until the next Meeting of the Legislature, which shall then fill such Vacancies."[16] Do we presume that the Framers meant only to address multiple vacancies in the Senate and not the instance of a single Senator leaving their position? Also in Section 3, "The Senate shall have the sole Power to try all Impeachments." Plural, not singular. If this indeed be the case, then the Senate acted unconstitutionally both times when it tried Presidents Andrew Johnson and Bill Clinton individually. Should the Senate have waited until it also had a federal judge or a congressman to impeach concurrently with the President?

Article I, Section 5 addresses the power of the US House to judge the

---

[16] Changed by the Seventeenth Amendment

"Elections, Returns and Qualifications of its own Members" and to "compel the Attendance of absent Members" – what of the situation of a singular absent Member or of the judging of the qualifications of a single Member? If the plural is held to be the rule, then the constitutionality of the US Supreme Court taking up the *Powell v. McCormack*[17] decision in 1969 is in doubt! The very next sentence discusses the punishment of its Members. Plural.

Section 8 speaks to the "Power to lay and collect Taxes, Duties, Imposts and Excises"; do these actions need to always be in the plural or may Congress pass but a single tax at a given time? Can it establish a singular Post Office in a specific city or must it always build two or more at a time? In a most analogous situation to proposing a single amendment, the Necessary and Proper Clause begins with, "To make all Laws which shall be necessary and proper..." What if the necessity is for a single, solitary law? Must Congress create another, parallel, accompanying law that is without merit or necessity just to fulfill the plural requirement?

With respect to the Executive, Article II, Section 2 assigns to the President the power "to make Treaties" – must he make several treaties at once or is the making of just one treaty permissible?[18] In the same section he or she is given the ability to "appoint Ambassadors, other public Ministers and Consuls, judges of the supreme Court, and all other Officers of the United States." If the interpretation of the amendatory convention opponents is correct, then every time that the President has named a new Supreme Court Justice, he has violated the Constitution.

The judiciary is covered by Article III and in Section 2 notes that "such Trial shall be held in the State where the said Crimes shall have been committed", and in the instance where a solitary crime may have been committed, can the trial be held anywhere? Article IV proclaims that "New States may be admitted by the Congress into this Union" and that begs the question of whether they must be admitted in multiples as the Dakotas were. If so, then almost every other state outside of the original thirteen is not really a legitimate state. Only the Dakotas, admitted simultaneously, would be legitimate.

Clearly, the semantical argument of the opponents as to the

---

[17] 395 U.S. 486 (1969)

[18] US Department of Justice, Office of Legal Policy, "Report to the Attorney General, Limited Constitutional Conventions under Article V of the United States Constitution" at 25 (10 September 1987)

illegitimacy of single amendment proposals of an amendatory convention is meritless as all of the articles preceding Article V use the same type of language and historically have been recognized as legal acts when done in the singular. The use of the plural is simply the style of the Framers.

While the questions and concerns have persisted for over two centuries, the answers to the questions have been coming rather steadily. The courts and the constitutional scholars have been turning out decisions and academic books and papers in response to the questions since shortly after the Constitution was written. What is perplexing is how the accumulated body of legal knowledge on Article V can still be so obscure to so many, especially within the legal community. As an example, in a paper published in a professional journal in 1955, Henry Nichols queried,

> *"Who shall decide that the steps taken are sufficient as to number, form, subject matter and time? Are the actions of some of the States, taken some years before the required number have acted, still timely and in effect or have some of them been rescinded? Is it legally possible to rescind such action? Is it proper for the Governors of the States to join or veto actions of the legislatures?"*[19]

One can point to the last question and positively answer that the question had been put to rest more than a century and a half before in 1798 – so why then is this question still being posed? Even Congress is still wrestling with the same old questions about a convention. Every few years, the Congressional Research Service updates its reports to Congress, among these is Report R42589, *"The Article V Convention to Propose Constitutional Amendments: Contemporary Issues for Congress"* which poses these questions,

> *"What constitutes a legitimate state application? Does Congress have discretion as to whether it must call a convention? What vehicle does it use to call a convention? Could a convention consider any issue, or must it be limited to a specific issue? Could a "runaway" convention propose amendments outside its mandate? Could Congress choose not to propose a convention-approved amendment to the states? What role would Congress have in defining a convention, including issues such as rules of procedure and voting, number and apportionment of delegates, funding and duration, service by Members of Congress, and other questions."*[20]

---

[19] Henry W. Nichols, "Amending the United States Constitution," *Insurance Counsel Journal* 22 (Jan.1955). 102
[20] Congressional Research Service, Report R42589, *The Article V Convention to Propose Constitutional Amendments: Contemporary Issues for Congress*, (11 April 2014), Summary page

The Evolution of Scholarly Thought on Article V

To better understand where scholars and legal thinkers are today with respect to Article V and, of course, amendatory conventions, it is always worthwhile to review the development of those positions. We can look at the genesis of the thoughts and concerns over the "unanswered questions" through an examination of the articles in law reviews since the late 1800s. There are, as cited earlier, according to Natelson, three distinct waves of scholarship.[21] To reiterate for convenience,

- First Wave: the 1960s - 1978
- Second Wave: 1979 - 2000
- Third Wave: 2010 – present

The first wave could have been extended back to a date of 1940 in recognition of the change wrought by the US Supreme Court with the *Coleman v. Miller* decision of 1939. That decision impacted the thinking and the scholarship, although in academia the change was gradual, whereas in the legal sphere, the impact was immediate. In each of these waves there are not just two opposing viewpoints to consider but also key points that remain to be resolved and are addressed in each wave:

- How will we know/define when the requisite two-thirds of the States has actually been reached validly?
- How will Congress respond?
- What can be done if Congress fails to follow the Constitution?
- How will the convention be operated and who sets the rules?
- What are the powers and the attendant limitations of those powers?
- Are the applications and ratifications final?

These questions are the crux of the debate and these points have been carried through all of the waves of scholarship. But we can see a previous wave preceding the three Natelson waves. To distinguish this period, and consensus, from Natelson's clarification system and to adapt to Natelson, this

---

[21] Robert G. Natelson, *A Compendium for Lawyers and Legislative Drafters* (Purcellville, VA: Convention of States, 2014): 13

book calls it the "0th wave."[22]

From the earliest papers through the 1950s, the consensus of opinion of scholars and writers of the 0th wave was that the convention process was a very plausible alternative. We can follow a trail of papers that, like this book, seek to organize and define the questions. Since most of the important questions were based on the experience of the early conventions and the on-going state conventions the consensus was fairly clear. This period could be termed the "Wave of Discovery" in regard to the use of Article V and amendatory conventions. It was not until the *Coleman* decision in 1939 that the picture became less clear. The most authoritative works of the period have been the published books of Jameson and Hoar – who differed in their views on a number of issues – and these were somewhat reconciled by Orfield just after *Coleman* was handed down. Their influence would carry over into the 1st wave modified only by the then extreme weight of the *Coleman* decision. As we have seen, *Coleman* created a mess for lawyers and scholars since it went, in part, against the previous decisions. We can theorize that *Coleman* forced the change that creates the distinction between the 0th and the 1st waves.

Several critical ideas came out of the 0th wave, chief among those is that the prodding effect works and can be exploited at will. The crude manner of using it would be well refined by the 1960s but a half century earlier its unquestionable effectiveness was established by the passage of the Progressive Amendments. The use of judicial review that was common before *Coleman* meant that the Prohibition Era cases were all disposed of as one would expect – without much fanfare. The great bulk of Article V cases occur during the latter part of this 0th wave. The boundaries or limits of Article V were found in this period including the exclusion of the public's participation through such Progressive Era direct democracy innovations as the initiative and the referendum. The definition of a convention and its implied and inherent powers were discussed. The earliest comparisons to the state constitutions and their powers were debated.

In the 1st wave, the extent of Congress's authority to define, regulate and limit the convention was explored. The main debate focused on whether the convention could be limited and if so, how much power does Congress

---

[22] The author's education and professional background are in thermodynamics making the use of a "0th" designation as something of an inside joke for engineers and scientists.

have to impose limits. A number of writers have summarized the debate of that period well including Michael Almond.[23] The consensus in that period was that, 1) the Court could not be successfully forced to act and that the only recourse was to the ballot box, 2) a limited convention was not possible, 3) Congress can, and should, set the rules for the convention, 4) the applications would need to be nearly identical and 5) rescission was not possible. These positions are a near complete deference to Congress. In contrast the issue of federalism and its current definition were also academic matters in that time.

But the 1st wave's focus on the perceived inability to call a convention and to secure amendments coupled with the failure of several convention drives during that wave leads one to conclude that it was the "Wave of Pessimism." Reading through the law review articles of the period of the 1960s and 1970s forces one to ask "why bother" to try to change the Constitution and improve the situation. Natelson described this wave as "agenda driven" and "sparse on research" and the little research conducted was limited to the 1787 convention primarily.[24] It is somewhat baffling that this wave coincides and culminates with the nation's Bicentennial when the United States was reaffirming its roots, values and philosophy in a positive perspective. The work of Dellinger, Gunther, Tribe and Ackerman exemplify the pessimistic assessment of Article V.

The period covering the 2nd wave was punctuated more by a sense of scholarly possibility prompting its consideration as the "Wave of Rediscovery" in terms of the ability of the American public as an electorate to steer a course of correction. The launch of the 2nd wave was possibly attributable to the issuance of a legal opinion on the amendatory convention by a lawyer in the Justice Department. The *Memorandum Opinion for the Attorney General*," No. 79-4, written by Acting Assistant Attorney General Larry A. Hammond, kicked off the research. Hammond's conclusions and recommendations included that, echoing previous writers and apparently not having dug too deep, "because no amending convention has ever been called, there is little history or law on the subject. Much of our discussion here is thus necessarily predicated not on history or judicial decisions, but on the

---

[23] See specifically, Michael A. Almond, "Amendment by Convention: Our Next Constitutional Crisis?," *North Carolina Law Review* 53 (1975)

[24] Robert G. Natelson, *A Compendium for Lawyers and Legislative Drafters* (Purcellville, VA: Convention of States, 2014): 13-4

view of legal scholars."²⁵

Hammond found that "Congress is generally thought to be obliged to call a convention," that "it is the general view that Congress may establish the convention's 'ground rules'," that "the States applications must be reasonably contemporaneous," applications must be on the same topic, that "applications need not be identical," and that "Congress may not limit the convention's deliberations." The key conclusion of Hammond is that judicial review is possible.²⁶ These findings are interesting as they were written during the Carter Administration which vehemently opposed a convention in general, but in particular, for a balanced budget amendment for which a drive was well underway.

The response to this document came from within the Office of Legal Counsel itself in another opinion issued 10 October 1979 by Assistant Attorney General John M. Harmon. Harmon differed from Hammond on several points. First, that Congress could establish the rules of the convention. Harmon saw that matter as part of the tact of limiting the convention. Second, that the convention could be limited. He stated that the convention would be limited by the call to convention and that for any product of the convention that digressed from the call,

> *"Congress would have no power to provide for the ratification of any proposal propounded by a constitutional convention unless that proposal were responsive to the application that justified the gathering of the convention in the first instance."*²⁷

Harmon firmly supported the ability to limit the convention's subject matter and argued as much in great detail including citation of the intercolonial convention practice. Harmon put into words and in a manner that few had previously done,

> *"The Annapolis Convention and its successor in Philadelphia demonstrate clearly and concretely that under the Articles of Confederation a convention could be convened for the purpose of considering constitutional problems*

---

[25] Larry A. Hammond, "Memorandum Opinion for the Attorney General, Constitutional Law – Constitution – Article V – The Amending Process – The Convention Method," Department of Justice, Office of Legal Counsel, No. 79-4, at 16 (16 Jan 1979).

[26] Ibid.

[27] John M. Harmon, "Memorandum Opinion for the Attorney General, Constitutional Convention – Limitation of Power to Propose Amendments to the Constitution," Department of Justice, Office of Legal Counsel, No. 79-75, at 394 (10 Oct 1979).

> and formulating proposals for changes; and it could be given narrow or broad powers depending on the nature of the task assigned to it. The Articles did not spell this out. They did not establish procedures for the formulation of constitutional proposals. But they were permissive. They permitted the States and Congress to establish such procedures; and when the States and Congress exerted that power, the result was first a limited convention in Annapolis and then a general convention in Philadelphia one year later."[28]

Harmon is mistaken about the Articles making allowance for a convention but he is correct about the procedure of a limited and then a general convention being used. That was an action by the States and not Congress, but the ability to tailor the convention to the needs of the people is the true point. By assailing the issue of limiting the convention, Harmon had gone for the central matter that needed to be resolved first. Therefore, the first real discussion of the limitability of the amendatory convention occurred during this phase of research. The researchers had also begun to return to the early history and rediscover the practices and customs of the ante-revolutionary conventions.[29] Of course, these opinions have some inaccuracies and errors in them. These include citations to the Necessary and Proper Clause, arguing for the application of the Presentment Clause, claiming that the Confederation Congress called the 1787 convention, and a few others.

The governmental discussion and pontification on the subject of Article V conventions continued throughout the 2nd Wave and reached its peak in 1987 with a report from the Department of Justice's Office of Legal Policy in a Report to the Attorney General. It is imperative to note that this opinion was generated during the late Reagan Administration which, unlike its predecessor, openly and solidly supported an Article V amendatory convention. That report concluded that 1) a limited convention was permissible, 2) there were methods to enforce the limitations, 3) Congress must call a convention, and 4) Congress may pass legislation to enforce the limitations on the convention subject matter.[30] At this juncture in history, the campaign to obtain an amendatory convention was just two states short

---

[28] Ibid.
[29] Robert G. Natelson, *A Compendium for Lawyers and Legislative Drafters* (Purcellville, VA: Convention of States, 2014): 14
[30] US Department of Justice, Office of Legal Policy, "Report to the Attorney General, Limited Constitutional Conventions under Article V of the United States Constitution" (10 September 1987), Executive Summary.

of the necessary two-thirds. The States themselves were beginning to look at the requirements for calling a convention.

The ability of a state to rescind its convention application is another major question that appears to have been settled during the 2nd wave despite the constant revisitation of the issue. Scholars have sought to equate the convention application to a ratification resolution. But this is erroneous since the ratification has an aura of finality to it that the application does not possess. The ratification act is more permanent and has far greater impact than the mere application. But the idea that an action is permitted in one direction only by Article V in the case of ratification and is analogous to a bidirectional action in the instance of rescission can be argued as logical when one considers the confusion that can result from trying to keep track of which applications are active and which are now dead. Some scholars have claimed that until the requisite two-thirds of the States threshold is met, states should have the ability to rescind at will. The other side of the debate is that in doing so, the States will hold applications to a lower level of scrutiny when they know that they can rescind.

There is another interesting view to allowing rescission; if the States may rescind, then they will be able to act in a more contemporaneous manner with the other states. This perspective has a counterpoint as well; the timing and temper of the nation may indeed change and rescission allows the States to act with new information. The question of whether the legal precedents which apply to ratification rescission would apply to application rescission as well will probably depend on how close the States are close to reaching the two-thirds count.[31] A last point to consider is that leaving the decision of accepting rescission in the hands of Congress may very well violate the separation of powers doctrine since this is the very basis of the political question prohibition.[32]

A key facet of the argument over rescission of a state application is the effect that such a rescission has on the process more than on the specific application. The decision of whether to pass an application resolution is not one to be taken lightly by a state legislature. If the point of such an application is merely to "send a message" to Congress, it can be considered

---

[31] Raymond M. Planell, "Equal Rights Amendment: Will States be Allowed to Change Their Minds?," *Notre Dame Lawyer* 49, no.3 (Feb. 1974): 661-2
[32] Ibid., 664

an irresponsible act since it is also a flippant action. Because there is little in the way of oversight such as a governor to review and potentially veto such an application, and that there can be a misinterpretation of the application, it behooves a state legislature to carefully explore the need for the resolution. In a comment article in a law review, it was argued that,

> *"It is probable that decision-makers tend to make more informed, responsible decisions when they act with the knowledge that those decisions, once made, are irrevocable. Opponents of extension and rescission have accordingly asserted that rescission fosters irresponsible decision-making by state legislatures and, by implication, by the Congress."*[33]

The writer was referring to the rescission of ratification of a proposed amendment, but the thinking here may be equally applicable to a state application resolution.

Academics have entertained a number of interesting theories on constitutionality and constitutional amendment over the years. In addition to the theories of limitations that were popular in the early twentieth century, there have been theories that have moved into the realm of the unusual and sometimes contrarian and counterintuitive. Akhil Reed Amar's theory of the "non-exclusive" amendability has gone beyond that of the "informal" amendment method theories of the judicial and societal moré processes.[34] These have provided some interesting and often amusing discussions on constitutionality.[35] Natelson's 2nd wave has produced much of these exploratory articles. Concurrent with Amar and Vile's response to Amar was R. George Wright's look at whether a constitutional amendment could be unconstitutional.[36]

Brendon Ishikawa addressed Amar's theory rather succinctly. He went to the heart of Amar's contentions that the Constitution may be directly amended and that the process applied to federal officials only. Ishikawa asked the question that if this were indeed the case, then why did the people need

---

[33] Republished with permission of the University of Pennsylvania Law School, from "The Equal Rights Amendment and Article V: A Framework for Analysis of the Extension and Rescission Issues," *University of Pennsylvania Law Review* 127 (1978): 512; permission conveyed through Copyright Clearance Center, Inc.
[34] Akhil Reed Amar, "Philadelphia Revisited: Amending the Constitution Outside Article V," *University of Chicago Law Review* 55, no.4 (Fall 1988)
[35] John R. Vile, "Legally Amending the United States Constitution: The Exclusivity of Article V's Mechanisms," *Cumberland Law Review* 21 (1991)
[36] R. George Wright, "Could a Constitutional Amendment Be Unconstitutional?," *Loyola University Law Review* 22, no.4 (Summer 1991)

to pass the Seventeenth Amendment – why did they not just start voting directly for US Senators without an amendment?[37] Each of these papers had the effect of moving the amendment process further into the grey areas of constitutional law. A process that has been taken to be fairly straight-forward and procedural is slowly turning into a vague and unstructured mess while the responding papers have fought to drag the process back into the light.

Another theory of "alternative amendment" was detailed in a law journal article by Kris Kobach in 1994. He studied the successes of the drives for the Seventeenth and Nineteenth Amendments and showed how the term limits drive is employing a method of working through direct popular action, or "incremental amendment process," in the States to create an inevitable demand for a constitutional amendment at the national level.[38] This method follows a state-by-state process of securing the desired objective and then pressuring the Congress to force the rest of the States to adopt it through a constitutional amendment. There is an analogy for this strategy in the balanced budget amendment campaign. Forty-nine of the fifty states have a balanced budget requirement yet the federal government still lacks such a constraint. There is a distinct difference between the approaches that Amar and Kobach promote. Amar appears to be in open defiance of the text of the federal Constitution and the usual rules of law and governance. Kobach is pointing to a novel exploitation of the existing provisions that eventually results in a formal amendment.

Perhaps the weirdest and most disturbing of the theories of the 2nd Wave is that of Frederick Schauer and "*Grundnorm.*"[39] This is the notion that if public consensus is applied to a particular viewpoint, then that view results in an informal change in the Constitution. This can be a change in social thinking that either adds or detracts to the constitutional law. Schauer's argument is that if a viewpoint has a majority social acceptance, then an extraconstitutional amendment has been made because we all agree to act and think like it has been done on the basis of shifting social morés. He uses the example of the Second Amendment to prove his point. He posits that if we all agree that it is a legal nullity, then it is and no court is obligated to

---

[37] Brendon Troy Ishikawa, "Amending the Constitution: Just Not Every November," *Cleveland State Law Review* 44 (1996): 312

[38] Generally, Kris W. Kobach, "Rethinking Article V: Term Limits and the Seventeenth and Nineteenth Amendments," *Yale Law Journal* 103, no.7 (May 1994)

[39] Schauer seems to have potentially gotten the idea from Hans Kelsen.

support it. He calls these, quoting Madison, "parchment barriers."[40]

We can see this theory being applied today in other aspects of law. Recently, there have been several stories in the media of parents arrested for neglecting their children for allowing them to play unsupervised in a neighborhood park. While there is no law on the statute books that covers a parent disallowing an eleven-year-old to play basketball in the driveway without parental supervision, the Florida Child Protective Services caseworkers acted "out of concern for the welfare of the child who might be abducted."[41] Or we have the similar case of two children walking home without parental escort in Maryland.[42] People called the police and reported the child playing alone in the park and the parent was detained and then charged while the child was then placed in protective care – the result being that the child had been abducted...by the state![43] A slippery slope indeed. Without the formality of a lawmaking process or an amending process, how does one begin to sort out the mess? Contrary to its stated purpose, *Grundnorm* simply restates the reason why we have written laws to begin with in the first place.

Part of the 2nd Wave scholarship focused on the competing theories that had developed to explain the amendment process and how the Supreme Court looked at the process. These were summarized by Michael Stokes Paulsen in 1993 as the "contemporaneous consensus" theory that the Supreme Court began to utilize in 1921 beginning with the *Dillon* decision; the "congressional power/political question" theory that the Supreme Court promoted in 1939 in the *Coleman* ruling; the "contract" model advanced by Grover Rees in the 1980s; and Paulsen's own "concurrent legislation" theory rolled out in 1993.[44]

The contemporaneous consensus theory seeks to assure that the applications for a convention or the ratifications of a proposed amendment

---

[40] Brannon P. Denning, "Means to Amend: Theories of Constitutional Change," *Tennessee Law Review* 65 (1997): 206-7
[41] http://www.parenting.com/news-break/11-year-old-boy-taken-custody-playing-alone-his-driveway
[42] http://www.usatoday.com/story/news/nation/2015/04/13/parents-investigated-letting-children-walk-alone/25700823/
[43] http://www.cnn.com/2015/04/13/living/feat-maryland-free-range-parenting-family-under-investigation-again/
[44] Republished with permission of the Yale Law Journal Company, from Michael Stokes Paulsen, "A General Theory of Article V: The Constitutional Lessons of the Twenty-seventh Amendment," *Yale Law Journal* 103, no.3 (Dec. 1993): 681-2; permission conveyed through Copyright Clearance Center, Inc.

are all within a given time period so that the nation shares a consensus that the convention or the amendment is truly what the majority of the public desire. The congressional power/political question theory holds that the Congress, and the Congress alone, has the power to determine the validity of both convention applications and amendment ratifications as the Supreme Court has decided to be a bystander and watch the show. The contract model is, according to Paulsen, a variation on the contemporaneous consensus theory that incorporates aspects of contract law that treats the step of the amendment process, such as an application, as an "offer and acceptance" transaction. Paulsen's theory posits that as long as there is a series of enacted and in force legislation among the States, Congress, etc., the amendment – and he used the Twenty-seventh Amendment as his example – is viable. This theory is not as simple as it sounds as he allows for rescissions of applications and ratifications under specific constraints. It also requires that the specialized legislation that exemplifies the amendment process be looked at and treated as ordinary legislation.[45]

While many of these theories have amounted to little more than mental fodder for academic debate, the drift over time is disconcerting. The idea of extra-constitutional amendment being taken seriously, to the point of superseding the two formalistic methods written in Article V, gives one pause for worry, extreme worry. The essence of such an idea is that *majority whim* rules over all – and this is the very thing that the Federal Convention of 1787 rejected and sought to prevent. The saving grace, to date, is that the Supreme Court and the Congress have not taken these theories to heart and incorporated them into the political process – they remain "more provocative than persuasive."[46]

The last period, that of the 3rd wave, could then be labeled, in contrast to that pessimism of the 1st wave as the "Wave of Optimism" with the full force of academic power and grassroots efforts focused on no longer thinking about the problems as the nation did during the late 2nd wave but acting affirmatively. Natelson points to the rediscovery of Article V case law and the exploration of the role of Congress in the process as significant features of this wave. The *convention rules* have become the focus of this

---

[45] Ibid., 721-32.
[46] Thomas E. Baker, "Towards A "More Perfect Union": Some Thoughts on Amending the Constitution," *Widener Journal of Public Law* 10, no.1 (2000): 3

most recent of scholarly waves.[47] In an effort to close the gap chronologically between Natelson's 2nd and 3rd waves – which leaves the decade of the 2000s unassigned, that period has been, for the purposes of this book, allocated to the 3rd wave based on the topics of the papers collected. The roles of *The Federalist* essays and other early writings were once again surveyed. The early commenters on the Constitution were reevaluated. The value of the early records as valid and factual sources were reexamined.[48] The study of originalism drove much of this revisiting of the earlier records and interpretations.

In the currently underway 3rd Wave, Natelson has predominated in both the terms of written scholarship and research. His fiduciary theory of delegate responsibility, or public trust doctrine,[49] has drawn some criticism but his overwhelming depth of research into the history of prior intercolonial and interstate conventions has been the basis of a new understanding of the operation and limitations of conventions. The historical record of the dozens and dozens of intercolonial and interstate conventions has provided the much needed answers to many of the still pending questions. More than anything else, the scholarship of this present wave is being typified by the application of the academic results to the activist push for a convention.

The Issues of the Article V Convention Academic Debate

Analysis shows that the debate, and therefore the questions, over the safety, operation, functioning and procedure of an Article V Amendatory Convention can be segregated into thirteen distinct topics. These thirteen may then be separated into major and minor topics. The six major issues are ones that deal with the roles of the Congress and the Supreme Court, that is, the secondary controlling interests. The six minor issues are all of a nature involving either the state applications or the operational characteristics of the convention.

There is one very minor issue that stands alone. It is due to the already settled nature of the topic that it stands apart but it continues to be an issue because some scholars just cannot leave it alone. That singular topic

---

[47] Robert G. Natelson, *A Compendium for Lawyers and Legislative Drafters* (Purcellville, VA: Convention of States, 2014): 15

[48] William Baude & Jud Campbell, "Early American Constitutional History: A Source Guide," a work-in-progress, dated 19 January 2016, http://papers.ssrn.com/sol3/papers.cfm?abstract_id=2718777

[49] Robert G. Natelson, "The Constitution and the Public Trust," *Buffalo Law Review* 52 (2004), generally

is **Presentment**. This is the concern of applying Article I, Section 7, Clauses 2 and 3 to the amendment proposal. Under Article I, which spells out the powers and limitations of the Executive branch, the president is given the responsibility of considering and then either approving or vetoing all laws presented for his or her signature. Article I serves as a check and balance and a corollary to the separation of powers. The application of the presentment clauses to Article V would be problematic in that it would involve the executive in a function that is divided between the national legislature and the States. The Executive and the Judiciary are supposed to sit this out as much as possible.[50]

As previously covered, to date, the matter has resulted in a number of court cases, most at the state level, but one at the federal level is important because it is the first Article V related case to come before the US Supreme Court. 1798's *Hollingsworth v. Virginia* concerned the validity of the Eleventh Amendment turning on the lack of the signature of President Washington. The Court reached the conclusion that Article V did not require the executive's approbation as Article V is a separate and distinct power from those of Article I. But to this day, legal and constitutional scholars still seek to argue that the president should approve all amendments and a call to convention. The counter argument is that such a concentration of power would lead to a destruction of the separation of powers. Kalfus refers us back to Madison in *The Federalist*, No.47, warning that, "accumulation of all powers, legislative, executive, and judiciary, in the same hands, whether of one, a few, or many, and whether hereditary, self-appointed, or elective, may justly be pronounced the very definition of tyranny."[51]

Major Issues:

For the major issues, foremost among those is the issue of **Limitability** of the convention agenda. This issue has been addressed previously. Until the turn of the twenty-first century, the issue remained hot for nearly the entire twentieth century. With the 3rd Wave of research, it appears that the limitability issue may be close to being deemed as settled.

---

[50] Mason Kalfus, "Why Time Limits on the Ratification of Constitutional Amendments Violate Article V," *University of Chicago Law Review* 66, no.2 (Spring 1999): 459-60.
[51] James Madison, "Federalist Paper No.47" in *The Federalist Papers, Hamilton, Madison, Jay*, ed. Clinton Rossiter (New York: Mentor, 1961), 301.

States have taken to devising legislation to control their delegates and to devise the rules of a potential convention through the Assembly of State Legislatures. With the recognition of the US Attorney General in 1979, one would think that the matter had been conclusively settled.

Second in the intensity of debate among the major issues is the issue of *Justiciability* addressed in Chapter 5. Nothing will move this issue except a revisitation and revision of *Coleman* by the US Supreme Court. The issue remains unresolved.

Next in importance among the major issues is that of **Congressional Control** of the convention procedures. Despite all of the historical evidence to the contrary, there are still convention opponents that believe that Congress can and will impose its control on the convention. Academic consensus is that the Congress has only a few issues to control – the convention is its own master.

Following in importance in the major issues is that of **Rescission**. With the pro-convention grassroots beating on the doors of state legislators to pass resolutions calling for a convention now matched by the efforts of the anti-convention grassroots to rescind those very same resolutions, the battle has heated up. This back and forth leaves one wondering about the status of a convention drive. The matter of rescission could be considered as close to resolution if we accept that a rescission is possible as long as the two-thirds mark has not been reached.

The ability to **Compel Congress** to act to call a convention is also a major issue. Perhaps no issue is more nebulous than this one. Despite historical proof of previous cases in which federal officials of the executive and legislative branches were compelled by the judicial branch to act according to their duty, the myriad changes in law over the last century leaves some doubt as to the efficacy of the compulsion of Congress to act. This topic remains definitively unresolved.

The last of the major issues is one that, like Presentment, should be considered settled law but somehow continues to defy resolution. The obligation of Congress to **Call a Convention** is obvious. The Constitution is textually clear but some scholars continue to claim that there is no obligation on the part of Congress. Worse, some scholars claim that Congress has some measure of discretion in the matter. Statements over the decades by members of Congress indicate that they understand their constitutional duty to call a convention, but they differ on the steps involved and the amount of discretion that they believe Congress to possess.

Minor Issues:

The minor issues focus in on the applications themselves and on the operation of a convention that by now should be obvious. The foremost among the minor issues is that of **Contemporaneity** of the applications. We have addressed this issue already. It suffices to say that the debate is unsupported by the text of Article V and the ratification of the Twenty-seventh Amendment. The most persuasive argument is that a state maintains the right to reissue a resolution for a convention at any time as proof of its contemporaneous support of a convention topic.

Similar to contemporaneity is the issue of **Homogeneity**. Also previously addressed, the States are wise to simply sidestep the issue by acting to prevent any pretext for opposition on the matter. Adopting a standard language among the States is a prudent manner of preventing congressional stalling.

The **Validity of the Time Length**, or staleness, for application shares the same situation as contemporaneity. The States are the only rightful arbiters of whether their respective applications are valid.

The issue of **Unit Voting** is historically shown to be the norm. The exceptions are, well, exceptional.

Like unit voting, **Delegate Selection** by the States is a matter of historical tradition and in the context of the separation of powers, an infringement on the province of the States if left to Congress. Where this issue becomes interesting is in the exercise of the state legislature's trust of its own people. Do they send state legislators or do they leave it up to the citizens to determine their own delegates? It is assumed that the state would be acquainted with the best and brightest of its own citizens. Then again, so may be the people themselves.[52] Most scholars anticipate that the States will opt to elect their delegates.[53]

---

[52] Sara R. Ellis, Yusuf Z. Malik, Heather G. Parker, Benjamin C. Signer & Al'Reco L. Yancy, "Article V Constitutional Conventions: A Primer," *Tennessee Law Review* 78 (2011), 688

[53] Gerald Gunther, "The Convention Method of Amending the United States Constitution," *Georgia Law Review* 14, no.1 (Fall 1979): 8, n.20

Lastly, the ***Convention Sovereignty*** is still argued although the limitations and extent of the matter were settled in the nineteenth century. The sovereignty of a convention is found in its operational decisions and in its stature as a temporary, but co-equal, branch of the federal government. There are obvious limits on the powers of a convention and an amendatory convention is by definition severely limited in its discretion.

The Origins of the Opposition

The internecine battles that Article V convention proposals can cause have been chronicled in the press. In particular, the July 1979 gathering of President Carter's staff at Camp David is useful in demonstrating the in-fighting. The meeting was held to plan the goals of the administration. Carter's pollster, Pat Caddell, has issued a memo suggesting calling an amendatory convention for idea generation and Caddell predicted that little would come of it but ideas. Reporter Elizabeth Drew of *The New Yorker* wrote that Vice-President Walter Mondale "was fairly apoplectic about the proposal for a Constitutional Convention, and called it the worst idea he had ever heard." Just seven months previous to that meeting, President Carter himself had said in a news conference that a convention was "extremely dangerous" and could be "completely uncontrollable." Incongruously, Carter's own Attorney General, Griffin Bell, had said shortly thereafter that "I absolutely do think limits can be set."[54]

Democrats and liberals were not alone in this regard; conservative icon Senator Barry Goldwater called an amendatory convention "very foolhardy" and "a tragic mistake."[55] Article V convention opposition is one of the few truly bipartisan political issues.

Much of the opposition to an amendatory convention arose during the late 1970s and early 1980s as a backlash against the campaign to secure a balanced budget amendment. A coalition of primarily liberal groups initially formed the opposition out of fear for changes to the Bill of Rights and the Fourteenth Amendment. Later, predominantly conservative groups began to take up the standard against a convention due to the effective propaganda

---

[54] James Stasny, "The Constitutional Convention Provision of Article V: Historical Perspective," *Cooley Law Review* 1 (1982): 73, n.1
[55] 125 Cong. Rec. 3159 (1979)

campaign that had been waged against the balance budget amendment.⁵⁶ One academic paper noted that the idea of changing the Constitution, state or federal, so frightens some people that it can temporarily change their political inclinations,

> *"Groups that have won protections in the past may fear losing them in new political circumstances, however remote the threat. Indeed, the prospects of a convention often induces traditionally liberal interests to take conservative stances."*⁵⁷

Part of the foundation of the view of an all-powerful convention that can do as it pleases goes back to the mid-nineteenth century, as chronicled by Russell Caplan, at the recorded speeches of state constitutional convention delegates claiming the power to do as they saw fit. These utterances are known because of the unusual character of the speeches and not because they were expository of the prevailing opinion or understanding of the people. The position for the plenary convention is the example of the sovereign convention stand. We can thank the secessionists and nullifiers for spreading the sovereign convention view that today manifests itself in the potential runaway convention fear.⁵⁸ It was never a concern for the Founders and Framers.⁵⁹

Caplan noted that the first strains of opposition were evident with the opposition to the direct election of US senators in the late 1890s through 1913. Progressives led the drive for the direct election and the stalwarts in the Senate led the opposition. The sides might have changed but the tactics did not by the time that the opposition to the income tax was in full force.⁶⁰

Natelson wrote on this topic in 2015 and documented the genesis of the opposition to an amendatory convention. He attributes the anti-convention movement to the post-war rise of liberalism and the desire to preserve the expansion of government. The Article V convention is seen as a threat to entrenched government and an unnecessary check and balance. The

---

⁵⁶ John A. Eidsmoe, "A New Constitutional Convention? A Critical Look at Questions Answered, and Not Answered, by Article Five of the United States Constitution," *USAF Academy Journal of Legal Studies* 3 (1992): 3-4

⁵⁷ Gerald Benjamin & Thomas Gais, "Constitutional Conventionphobia," *Hofstra Law & Policy Symposium* 1 (1996): 70

⁵⁸ Russell L. Caplan, *Constitutional Brinkmanship* (New York: Oxford University Press, 1988), 44-7

⁵⁹ Robert G. Natelson, "Proposing Constitutional Amendments By Convention: Rules Governing The Process," *Tennessee Law Review* 78 (2011): 715

⁶⁰ Russell L. Caplan, *Constitutional Brinkmanship* (New York: Oxford University Press, 1988), 78-89

push to repeal the Sixteenth Amendment kicked off the backlash and the opposition was championed by Rep. Wright Patman of Texas, who called the repeal movement "fascist" and "reactionary." Natelson then details the effort to discredit and stop the Council of State Governments' "Confederating Amendments" campaign. This effort drew in the academic elites as well as the support of numerous judges and US Supreme Court Chief Justice Earl Warren. As the battle heated up, several US senators joined the fight. Eventually, the media began to take an active part. By the 1970s, the Ervin bills had become a rallying point.[61]

The organized aspect of the opposition really began in earnest with the fight against the drive for a balanced budget amendment. The impact and power of such an amendment required that the game be changed for the opposition. It required a higher level of propaganda. At that time, around 1980, the notion of calling an amendatory convention as a constitutional convention was conceived. To this is added the use of the alliterative and pejorative term of "con-con" to coin a colloquialism. The claims that became the famous parade of horribles were formulated and spread. To combat the amendment concept, groups on the left and the right sides of political spectrum came together and collaborated. Groups that had previously supported an amendatory convention, such as the John Birch Society (JBS) which agitated for a convention from its founding in the late 1950s to the mid-1970s, now opposed the convention and today disavow having ever supported a convention. In 1963, JBS founder Robert Welch advocated for a convention to press for the "Liberty Amendment" that was designed to repeal income taxes, going so far as to lobby state legislators. In 1983, then JBS chairman Larry McDonald also supported a convention although he would later claim that he never had supported a convention.[62]

Other groups, such as the Eagle Forum, began a campaign to call into question the feasibility and constitutionality of the convention through their lists of "unanswerable questions."[63] These questions were, according to Natelson, variants of Professor Laurence Tribe's concerns raised in a 1979

---

[61] Robert G. Natelson, "The Liberal Establishment's Disinformation Campaign Against Article V – and How It Misled Conservatives," (2015): 6-9 – published on http://constitution.i2i.org/files/2015/03/Campaign-Against-Article-V.pdf

[62] Cong. Rec., 122, 94th Cong. sess.1, at 32634-6 (9 Oct 1975)

[63] http://www.tneagleforum.org/custpage.cfm/frm/155482/sec_id/155482

paper.[64,65] It is somewhat astonishing that Eagle Forum considers, or labels, these questions as "unanswerable" when they are contemplated. Even if one generously concedes that these questions have been in circulation for years, the age of the questions is still less than many of the US Supreme Court and federal court decisions that answer these very queries. For some of the questions, the answers have been commonly known for, without the slightest exaggeration, hundreds of years. Most of the pro-convention national groups have countered by publishing their detailed and documented answers to the Eagle Forum questions. For the sake of completeness, the Eagle Forum questions are reproduced herein,

> "1. Convention?
> 2. What authority would be responsible for determining the number of Delegates from each state?
> 3. What authority would be responsible for electing or selecting the Delegates to the convention?
> 4. Would Delegates be selected based on Population, number of Registered Voters, or along Party lines?
> 5. Would Delegates, if selected, have to meet some race, ethnicity, or gender requirements?
> 6. What authority would be responsible for organizing the convention, such as committee selection, committee chairs and members, etc.?
> 7. How would the number of Delegates serving on any committee be selected and limited?
> 8. How would the Chair of the Convention be selected or elected?
> 9. What authority will establish the Rules of the Convention, such as setting a quorum, how to proceed if a state wishes to withdraw its delegation, etc.?
> 10. What authority would be responsible for selecting the venue for the Convention?
> 11. Would proposed amendments require a two-thirds majority vote for passage?
> 12. How would the number of votes required to pass a Constitutional Amendment be determined?

---

[64] Lawrence H. Tribe, "Issues Raised by Requesting Congress to Call a Constitutional Convention to Propose a Balanced Budget Amendment," *Pacific Law Journal* 10 (1979)

[65] Robert G. Natelson, "The Liberal Establishment's Disinformation Campaign Against Article V – and How It Misled Conservatives," (2015): 11-2 – published on http://constitution.i2i.org/files/2015/03/Campaign-Against-Article-V.pdf

13. What would happen if the Con Con decided to write its own rules so that two-thirds of the states need not be present to get amendments passed?
14. Could a state delegation be recalled by its legislature and its call for a convention be rescinded during the convention?
15. Would non-Delegates be permitted inside the convention hall?
16. Will demonstrators be allowed and/or controlled outside the convention hall?
17. Would congress decide to submit Con Con amendments for ratification to the state legislatures or to a state constitutional convention as permitted under Article V of the constitution?
18. Where would the Convention be held?
19. Who will fund this Convention?
20. With all these questions unanswered, is it really wise to move forward into completely uncharted territory?"

An initially temporary alliance was born between the left and right over the opposition to the balanced budget, but that alliance has become, on this issue, a permanent bond. The threat of a limitation on gorging in the public trough led the special interests of both sides to oppose the amendment. Joining the JBS and Eagle Forum were the American Civil Liberties Union and Common Cause among others.[66] Today, these organizations have been joined by many of the remaining Tea Party groups that have embraced the anti-convention banner. There is an intriguing incongruity in that many of the groups fighting against an amendatory convention are strongly aligned with national organizations that staunchly advocate for a convention. Also, some of these right-leaning grassroots groups end up finding themselves in an uncomfortable alliance with left-leaning groups also opposed to a convention.

For many of these national groups the long time commitment of opposition to a convention became so engrained in the organization's DNA that they cannot now change even if they want to do so. For many of these groups, it is a "Chicken-Little-screaming-that-the-sky-is-falling" fundraising strategy. As long as the threat of a runaway convention remains ominously hanging over our heads, the calls for $5, $10, $20 to "save the Constitution"

---

[66] Russell L. Caplan, *Constitutional Brinkmanship* (New York: Oxford University Press, 1988), 87

will remain a steady, omnipresent chant in the monthly e-mail message.[67] In the case of the JBS, opposition to an Article V convention has become their most recognized position. Now, their opposition to the convention has been transformed into a raison d'etre to oppose the formation of rules for a convention.

As previously stated herein, Article V also includes state conventions for the ratification of proposed amendments. The rules governing the state ratification conventions as laid out in Article V are identical for those rules laid out in Article V for amendatory conventions – that is, there are none. Yet, when the States held state ratificatory conventions for the Twenty-first Amendment in 1933-34, a search of the literature of the period turns up no flood of warnings or cries of panic over the ratificatory conventions possibly re-writing the federal Constitution or removing the Bill of Rights or reinstituting slavery. If the same lack of prescribed rules applies to the ratificatory conventions as applies to the amendatory conventions in Article V, it would seem entirely plausible that the same potential for abuse and violation of those rules must be applicable.[68]

Now that we have examined the source of the questions and the genesis of the opposition to an amendatory convention, we can turn to answering the Eagle Forum questions along with all of the other frequently asked questions posed in regard to an Article V convention. The list is not, nor ever could be, exhaustive as the opponents are working tirelessly to generate new "unanswerable" questions and points of contention.

---

[67] Robert G. Natelson, "The Liberal Establishment's Disinformation Campaign Against Article V – and How It Misled Conservatives," (2015): 3 – published on http://constitution.i2i.org/files/2015/03/Campaign-Against-Article-V.pdf

[68] Robert G. Natelson, "Proposing Constitutional Amendments by Convention: Rules Governing the Process," *Tennessee Law Review* 78 (2011): 724

EXCURSUS 2
ARTICLE V CONVENTION FAQS

> *"A constitutional convention is the last bastion of public sovereignty. It is perhaps the sole remaining device by which the people of the states can act together as the people of the United States; not as citizens or subjects of a supreme national government, but as the sovereign ultimate political authority from which springs the consent of the governed and the constitutional legitimacy of all public institutions and officers."*[1]
>
> –Thomas E. Brennan, former Chief Justice of the Michigan Supreme Court

Frequently Asked Questions (FAQs) regarding the details, powers, limitations and history of an Article V convention (AVC) for amending the US Constitution with primary and secondary source citations follow. These questions were collected from the scholarly literature, websites both in favor and in opposition to an amendatory convention, books, articles in popular media, and from activists and especially state legislators. The answers are drawn from the material and sources previously given in the book but are presented here in a manner that is expected to be most helpful to legislators and activists. Many of the questions appear to be a rewording of another question; that is deliberate as people will differ in their manner of thinking. Each question is designed to be a stand-alone question so it may repeat information that a prior question may already state.

Much of this FAQ material has been published previously by the Wisconsin Grand*Sons of Liberty*.

---

[1] Thomas E. Brennan, "Return To Philadelphia," *Cooley Law Review* I (1982): 10

Defining an Article V Convention (AVC)

1. Is an Article V convention the same as a constitutional convention (a con-con)?
2. Can an AVC amend-con be turned into a con-con?
3. Can the AVC become a "runaway convention?"
4. Wasn't the 1787 Philadelphia Convention a runaway?
5. Why did the 1787 convention give this amendment power to the States; doesn't Congress already have the power to amend the Constitution?
6. Did the Delegates at the 1787 Constitutional Convention change the rules for ratification meaning that the same thing could happen today in an AVC?
7. What safeguards exist to prevent a runaway convention?
8. Have any other American constitutional conventions "ran away?"
9. How is an AVC different from Congress proposing amendments?
10. What kind of convention does Article V authorize for amending?
11. Does Article V authorize any other type of convention?
12. Is an Article V convention considered to be part of the federal government or the state governments?
13. If the prodding effect works to get amendments passed in Congress, then why bother to have an AVC?
14. Wasn't Article V a last minute addition to the Constitution and isn't well thought out or defined?

Powers of the Convention and Delegates

15. Could a convention, once assembled, impute to itself sovereignty?
16. Who has a role in the amendment process?
17. What powers are granted by Article V to the Congress, state legislatures, state ratifying conventions and Article V conventions?
18. Can the delegates just replace the current Constitution of 1787?
19. Who picks the delegates to the AVC and how?
20. Can delegates be bound by their states?
21. How many delegates are chosen from each state?

22. On what basis are the delegates chosen?
23. Could delegates be selected by quotas for race, gender, ethnicity, political party, sexual orientation or other designation?
24. Would members of Congress or the state legislatures be eligible to be delegates?
25. Could the delegates be elected, and if so, would they be able to collect campaign donations?
26. Would the delegates be paid for their service?
27. Who selects the officers of the AVC?
28. How is the Chair of the AVC determined?
29. Can the AVC pass/ratify amendments?
30. Once the subject matter specified in the "call" from Congress has been addressed by the convention, may the AVC take up other business not mentioned in the applications of the States?
31. Can an AVC be limited to a single topic or proposed amendment subject?
32. Is the topic specified in the States' applications binding on the convention?
33. What happens if a delegate proposes an amendment addressing an unauthorized issue or topic?

Congress's Role in an AVC

34. What role, if any, does Congress play in an AVC?
35. Does Congress control an AVC?
36. Can Congress prevent or refuse an AVC amend-con?
37. Even if an AVC is convened, can Congress just bypass the convention by passing its own proposed amendment and sending it to the States?
38. Who decides where and when the AVC meets?
39. Does Congress have to call an AVC if the applications are received from two-thirds of the States?
40. When does Congress have to call an AVC?
41. Is the Congress required to forward the proposed amendments from the AVC to the States for consideration of ratification?

42. What compels the Congress to act on setting the method of ratification and promulgating the amendment(s) to the States?
43. Could Congress delay promulgating the proposed amendment(s) indefinitely?
44. Does the Congress have the power to veto or reject the proposed amendments?
45. Does Congress have to choose either method of ratification or give a reason for preferring one method over the other?
46. Could Congress decide to call an AVC without sufficient (or any) applications from the States?
47. Could Congress pass legislation to take control of an AVC?
48. How does Congress count the applications toward the necessary two-thirds of the States required for calling a convention?
49. Can the Congress force the States to act on a proposed amendment?

States' Role in an AVC

50. What exactly is an "application"?
51. How specific must the state legislatures be in the wording of the application?
52. Do the applications from all the States have to be worded identically?
53. Is there a finite time period within which all the state applications must be made?
54. How is the validity of the state applications determined?
55. Who determines whether the applications are valid?
56. Can the States limit the actions of their respective delegates through binding instructions?
57. Can the States rescind their call for an AVC?
58. To whom are the state applications sent?
59. Does the state application to Congress have to specify the purpose of the AVC?
60. Can state applications dictate the exact wording of proposed amendments?
61. Could a state delegation be recalled by its state legislature?

62. How do the States pass their bills for an application?
63. Can the States submit 'conditional' applications to Congress?
64. Could the States propose amendments ahead of the convention with defined wording and then instruct their delegates to accept only that specific wording?
65. Would non-states such as the District of Columbia or the U.S. territories and protectorates have a vote or a delegation in the AVC?
66. Could a state refuse to participate in an AVC?
67. Can the States be forced to participate in an Article V convention?

Operation of the AVC

68. Does each state have just one vote or do they get more votes based on population?
69. How many votes are required to pass a proposed amendment on to the States?
70. Who funds the AVC?
71. Who is responsible for organizing and running the AVC?
72. Who determines the rules of the AVC?
73. How would the AVC create and staff committees?
74. Do all states need to be physically represented at the Article V convention to consider the business of the AVC?
75. If an AVC is its own authority, could the delegates do whatever they want?
76. If there is an agenda for the AVC determined ahead of the convention, then will there be no debate of the issue or the particulars of the proposed amendment(s) considered?
77. What if the AVC cannot reach an agreement on an amendment?
78. Could items be added to the agenda after Congress issues the call?
79. How long does an AVC last?
80. Will the public and the media be allowed to attend an AVC?

Legal Aspects of an AVC

81. What role does the Supreme Court play in the process?

82. Are there any legal guidelines for an AVC?
83. Could the AVC open up ratification to the people by referendum?
84. Could an outside third party set the rules of the AVC?
85. Are there any exceptions to the amendment process?
86. Are the actions of the AVC subject to judicial review?
87. Does the state law of the hosting state prevail over the AVC or does federal law?
88. What happens if the AVC proposes amendment(s) that are unconstitutional?
89. Could the AVC create and prescribe an entirely new ratification method that allows them to amend the Constitution and go around the States?
90. Can an amendment be proposed that "clarifies" other, already existing parts of the Constitution?
91. Could an amendment be proposed that repeals other amendments or sections of the Constitution?
92. Could an amendment be proposed that would overturn a US Supreme Court decision?

Views of Founding Fathers on a Second General Convention

93. Did James Madison fear a second constitutional convention?
94. Did any of the other Framers fear a second convention?
95. Can the States or Congress call a second plenary constitutional convention?

Miscellaneous Questions

96. What role does the executive branch play in the process?
97. How much time after the AVC occurs will the States have to ratify any proposed amendment?
98. How close have we come in the past to calling an AVC?
99. Why hasn't an AVC occurred before?
100. If the federal government does not follow our Constitution now, how will new amendments help – won't the federal government just ignore those too?
101. How can amending our Constitution address the specific problems

102. Why do we need an AVC, don't we just need to enforce the Constitution?

103. If an AVC is so safe, then why do so many reputable people and organizations oppose holding one?

104. If there has never been an AVC, how can we know what will happen?

105. If an AVC is as bad an idea as opponents say, then why would the Framers put a "self-destruct" mechanism in the Constitution?

106. Why take the risks?

Defining an Article V Convention (AVC)

1.

Is an Article V convention the same as a constitutional convention (a con-con)?

The notion that an Article V convention is the same thing as a constitutional convention is probably the greatest misconception about the ***amendatory*** convention, or, if one prefers, "amend-con." A constitutional convention, or "con-con" as it is colloquially called, is a ***plenipotentiary***, or more commonly called a ***plenary***, convention, meaning that it is full-powered.[2] Usually, full-powered conventions are usually called for the purpose of drafting a new political charter. A limited-power convention is called to ***propose*** amending or changing a small part of the charter thereby preserving the greater part of the political charter unchanged. It is simply incorrect to refer to an amendatory Article V convention as a constitutional convention or a con-con since an amend-con is deliberately designed to be of strictly limited power.[3] During the 1787 Grand Convention in Philadelphia[4] which drafted the United States Constitution, discussion was held on whether to make a provision for future plenipotentiary constitutional conventions – the idea

---

[2] http://www.merriam-webster.com/dictionary/plenipotentiary On-line dictionary definition of plenipotentiary: "invested with full power."

[3] Robert Natelson, "Amending the Constitution by Convention: A More Complete View of the Founders' Plan," Independence Institute Report IP-7-2010. (Golden, CO: Independence Institute, Dec. 2010), 1

[4] The 1787 Convention is known by several names: the Constitutional Convention, the Philadelphia Convention, the Federal Convention, the General Convention of the States, and the Grand Convention at Philadelphia as it was referred to at the time in 1787.

was soundly and firmly rejected by the delegates.[5] The 1787 delegates chose, instead, to make a provision for a limited power convention which can only propose amendments to the Constitution. The Framers recognized that the Constitution must be able to adapt to changing times and circumstances and that those situations may require adding or changing some constitutional provisions. The AVC is <u>amendatory only</u> and therefore of <u>limited</u> power.[6]

To be complete, the Framers also included in Article V a provision for conventions solely to ratify amendments, but in this question we are dealing with just the subject of the amendatory convention.

The power granted by Article V to the Congress to <u>*propose, debate and refer*</u> proposed constitutional amendments is no different than the power granted to the States via an Article V convention to <u>*propose, debate and refer*</u> a proposed constitutional amendment to Congress for promulgation to the States.[7] Both the Congress and the Article V convention have exactly the same limited power of proposal and debate but neither body has the power of ratification of proposed amendments. Each of the two prescribed methods of proposing an amendment starts with the Constitution as an existing document as opposed to starting with a blank sheet of paper and drafting a new national charter. A constitutional convention, as was held in Philadelphia in 1787, works OUTSIDE of the Constitution, whereas an Article V convention works WITHIN the Constitution according to the powers granted in Article V.

There is much fear-mongering by opponents of an AVC that an amendatory convention could "write its own rules and do whatever it wants" and that such a convention will runaway leading to a wholesale rewriting of the US Constitution. There are a number of problems with this assertion. First, an AVC does not have the power to draft a new constitution. Second, an AVC does not have the power to propose a new constitution. Third, an AVC does not have the power to refer a new constitution to the States. Fourth, an AVC does not have the power to ratify a new constitution. Fifth, an AVC does not have the power to change the ratification process. The wording of Article V is quite clear; an AVC has only the power to **PROPOSE** new amendments - and

---

[5] Notes of 1787 Grand Convention delegate Dr. James McHenry of Maryland taken from the *American Historical Review*, XI (Washington, 1905-6): 596-618.

[6] Robert Natelson, "A Response to the 'Runaway Scenario'," 4 http://constitution.i2i.org/2013/02/15/a-response-to-the-%E2%80%9Crunaway-scenario%E2%80%9D/

[7] United States Constitution, Article V

nothing more.

A second frequent objection is that the AVC will "force bad amendments on the people." This claim also has a number of problems. First, an AVC can be limited to a single issue or just a few limited issues thereby controlling what amendments are proposed and referred. Second, an AVC cannot ratify an amendment, instead it may merely propose an amendment; the States retain the right and power to ratify any amendments – not the convention and not Congress. The AVC merely produces the wording for any proposed amendment - and nothing more.

Had the Framers intended for the AVC to be empowered to draft a new constitution, they would have included the necessary phrasing for that purpose. Every word in the Constitution was vigorously debated and argued over. The records of the 1787 convention show that the possibility of another general (or constitutional) convention was proposed, discussed and rejected by the delegates no less than three times! There can never be another "con-con" under the 1787 Constitution.

2.

Can an AVC amend-con be turned into a con-con?

Because the Framers of our Constitution chose only to allow for amendatory conventions that are limited in power, the delegates of any modern or future amend-con are not empowered to change the limitations of the convention to a plenary, or full-powered, convention. Such an action is unconstitutional. All conventions have a stated purpose and/or agenda. The delegates, or commissioners, have credentials or commissions issued by their respective state legislatures that detail their limited powers, instructions and grants of authority and these credentials, like the convention agenda, may be revoked by their respective state legislatures.[8]

There are many types of political conventions; constitutional, amendatory, ratifying, nominating, to name just a few – they are all different in purpose and in the power granted to them by the people, though they are all political conventions. We cannot lump all political conventions together and say that they are all the same thing just because they share the word "convention" in their names.

---

[8] Robert Natelson, "Amending the Constitution by Convention: A More Complete View of the Founders' Plan," Independence Institute Report IP-7-2010. (Golden, CO: Independence Institute, Dec. 2010), 8-9

Throughout the history of the United States, there has been just one, single, national, plenary, constitutional convention – the Grand Convention at Philadelphia in 1787 – and there have been hundreds of state constitutional conventions.[9] Each and every one of these conventions has had a purpose defined and stated prior to the convention. The process of operating a constitutional convention is well known and very well understood.[10] The process has been perfected over the centuries. Additionally, the States have conducted dozens of ratifying conventions[11] and these specific duty ratification conventions have never once deviated from their stipulated purpose or agenda and attempted to re-write the federal or state constitutions. There are regular nominating conventions – every year or two in some states – and not one has ever tried to move into the territory of re-writing the national or state constitutions or attempting anything other than nominating candidates and drafting and adopting party platforms. To be accurate, in the **hundreds**[12] of state constitutional conventions held since 1789, there have been a total of six state constitutional conventions that can be considered as a "runaway," that is, they exceeded their limits of granted power. Not one of those six conventions attempted to rewrite or replace the federal constitution. All six of these "runaway conventions" occurred before 1909. Since that time, states have routinely enacted legislation that controls the powers of the delegates and the limits of the conventions.[13]

It is important to note that the state and federal conventions are not entirely identical. Federal conventions must be mindful of the role of federalism and the associated limitations placed upon the federal government whereas the state conventions have much less need to be

---

[9] Augustus Hunt Shearer, *A List of Official Publications of American State Constitutional Conventions, 1776-1916*, Bulletin 6 (Chicago: Newberry Library, 1917): The Newberry Library in Chicago compiled a list in 1917 of all known state constitutional conventions to date. The study canvassed 679 conventions to that point in time – September 1917. Many more state constitutional conventions have occurred since the publication of the Newberry report.

[10] Paul Weber & Barbara Perry, *Unfounded Fears: Myths and Realities of a Constitutional Convention* (New York: Praeger, 1989), 81-100

[11] At least fifteen state ratification conventions were held for the federal Constitution in 1787-91 under Article VII and 39 for the Twenty-first Amendment in 1933-34 under Article V totaling a minimum of 54 federal ratifying conventions conducted by the States. The States have also held ratifying conventions for state constitutions. See Appendix B.

[12] Estimates by some scholars are that over 233 such conventions have been held. This author has found that many more were held – see Appendix B.

[13] Roger S. Hoar, *Constitutional Conventions: Their Nature, Powers, and Limitations* (Boston: Little, Brown, 1917), 111-5

concerned beyond the interaction between the state and federal roles.[14] The American federal government is one of limited and enumerated powers[15] whereas the States' governments are plenary and limited only by what the federal and state constitutions prohibit to the States. Although some constitutional scholars may disagree with comparing the state and federal conventions as a whole, some issues do provide a comparison and therefore a precedent. A discussion of the limitability of the subject matter for a convention does allow for a comparison.

So sure are the States that their state constitutional conventions will not "runaway," that several states **require**, constitutionally or statutorily, that a state constitutional convention be held <u>regularly</u>. Alaska,[16] Hawaii,[17] Iowa,[18] New Hampshire[19] and Rhode Island[20] require a state constitutional convention be called every ten years. Michigan requires a state constitutional convention every 16 years.[21] Connecticut,[22] Illinois,[23] Maryland,[24] Missouri,[25] Montana,[26] New York,[27] Ohio[28] and Oklahoma[29] mandate a state constitutional convention every 20 years through a question being automatically placed on the ballot. Only seven states make no provision or permission for a state constitutional convention: Arizona, Arkansas, Indiana, Mississippi, New Jersey, Texas and Vermont although Arizona's state constitution makes mention of a

---

[14] Francis Heller, "Limiting a Constitutional Convention: The State Precedents," *Cardozo Law Review* 3 (1982), 576-9

[15] James Madison, *The Federalist*, No. 45: "The powers delegated by the proposed Constitution to the federal government are few and defined. Those which are to remain in the State governments are numerous and indefinite."

[16] Alaska state constitution, Article 13, § 3

[17] Hawaii state constitution, - If they don't hold a constitutional convention every ten years, the state's Lieutenant Governor orders the question, "Shall there be a convention to propose a revision of, or amendments to, the Constitution?" to be placed on a statewide ballot.

[18] Iowa state constitution, Article X, § 3

[19] New Hampshire state constitution, question automatically placed on ballot.

[20] Rhode Island state constitution, question automatically placed on ballot.

[21] Michigan state constitution, Article XII, § 3

[22] Connecticut state constitution

[23] Illinois state constitution

[24] Maryland state constitution, Article 14, § 2

[25] Missouri state constitution, Article XII, § 3a

[26] Montana state constitution, Article XIV, § 3

[27] New York state constitution, Article XIX, § 2

[28] Ohio state constitution, Article XVI, § 3

[29] Oklahoma state constitution, Article XXIV, § 2

state constitutional convention being permissible[30] and Vermont[31] has included an advisory question on a referendum in the past.

Four states are so confident that their state constitutional conventions will not runaway that they constitutionally bypass their state legislatures and permit the people to directly call a state constitutional convention through a ballot initiative: Florida,[32] Montana,[33] North Dakota[34] and South Dakota.[35]

Since the establishment of the Republic, groups of states have met in interstate conventions and conferences for the purpose of addressing specific issues that those states share. An example includes conventions held concerning water rights,[36] and no such meeting has degenerated into a proposal to re-write a constitution, state or federal. The stated purpose of all such conventions has been firmly observed without exception.

Based on the history of interstate conventions and conferences, state constitutional conventions, ratifications conventions and other political conventions, we can safely and firmly conclude that the possibility of an amendatory convention being turned into a plenipotentiary constitutional convention is virtually non-existent. In an age of instantaneous communications and widespread media coverage, any convention sleight-of-hand would be immediately broadcast and the public backlash could be swift and merciless.

3. _____

Can the AVC become a "runaway convention"?

For an AVC to runaway would require that the delegates "go rogue" and violate their oaths of office. While this is indeed possible, their action would be moot as the proposed amendment(s) adopted

---

[30] Arizona state constitution, Article 21
[31] Vermont Secretary of State Archives: 1969 referendum question: "Shall a Vermont Constitutional Convention be convened at the state house in Montpelier on October 6, 1969 to consider the following topics which shall receive a majority of the votes cast upon it in this election, and no others?"
[32] Florida state constitution, Article XI, § 4
[33] Montana state constitution, Article XIV, § 2
[34] North Dakota state constitution, Article III, § 1
[35] South Dakota state constitution, Article XXIII, § 2
[36] The "Santa Fe Conventions" of the Colorado River Commission are an example. Citing Robert G. Natelson's blog post of 17 January 2014: "In 1922, seven southwestern states sent commissioners to negotiate the Colorado River Compact. Although the assembly was called the Colorado River Commission, it was in all respects a convention of states, and it may be called the "Santa Fe Convention," after the city where its most important sessions were held. The group convened 27 times over the course of a single year." http://constitution.i2i.org/2014/01/17/the-santa-fe-convention-a-20th-century-convention-of-states/

and forwarded to the States would still require the approval of three-quarters, or presently thirty-eight, of the States. This ratification requirement is stated in the Constitution in Article V and cannot be changed without approval of at least three-quarters of the States in the form of a constitutional amendment. Such an event would require that the delegates be part of either a pre-planned conspiracy or able to find a way to circumvent the cautious, deliberative, multi-step procedure for proposal, debate, referral and ratification that has been in place for over two centuries.[37] One would expect that the rogue delegates would find that they have mortally wounded their political careers by just proposing or promoting, let alone carrying out, such an unconstitutional action.

James Madison noted that the diversity of the nation, as represented by the makeup of the Congress, points to an example of why such a conspiracy would be unlikely and that the AVC overall would tend toward being moderate.[38] Congress itself, in studying the Article V process in 1984, found that "...the notion of a 'runaway' convention, succeeding in amending the Constitution in a manner opposed by the American people, is not merely remote, it is impossible."[39]

For an AVC to turn into an extra-constitutional runaway, several things would have to occur. Some of the delegates would have to collude to rewrite the rules and then successfully convince a majority of the other delegates to take part in the violation of their oaths. The delegates would have to accept that they would be committing political suicide as this would be the last act of their political careers. They would have to change the ratification process – something that will never happen as too many other societal institutions would not permit that action to take place. They would need to hide what they were doing from the media and the public as they carried out their scheme. Constitutional scholar Robert Natelson describes this scenario as amounting to a coup d'etat.[40] In a reasoned opinion, former U.S. Attorney General Edwin Meese, speaking for the Department of Justice, in a 1987 Department of Justice tract on the subject, stated "we believe that fears of a 'runaway' convention are not

---

[37] Joseph Story, *Commentaries on the Constitution of the United States, Vol. 3* (Boston: Hilliard, Gray, 1833), 688
[38] James Madison, *The Federalist*, No. 10, "The Size and Variety of the Union as a Check on Faction," from the Clinton Rossiter, Mentor Books version of 1961, 77-84, specifically, "Hence, the number of representatives in the two cases not being in proportion to that of the constituents, and being proportionally greatest in the small republic, it follows that if the proportion of fit characters be not less in the large than in the small republic, the former will present a greater option, and consequently a greater probability of a fit choice."
[39] *Constitutional Convention Implementation Act of 1984*, 98th Cong., 2nd sess., S. Rept. 98-594, at 29
[40] Robert Natelson, *Proposing Constitutional Amendments by a Convention of the States: A Handbook for State Lawmakers* (Washington, D.C.: American Legislative Exchange Council, 2013), p17

well founded."⁴¹

In order to be able to radically change the Constitution, any conspirators would have to first...radically change the Constitution. The Framers intended to make modification of the Constitution as difficult as possible – but still practical – to prevent that it be changed, to use a familiar phrase, for "light and transient causes." The inherent difficulty in amending our Constitution is meant to generate considerable and lengthy debate of not just the subject but the need to modify the Constitution. This intentional debate is the foremost safeguard against a runaway as the public discourse would have already led to a thorough understanding of what needed to be done in the convention. The topics and agenda would be clearly formed so that a runaway convention would not have the support of the public.

4.

Wasn't the 1787 Philadelphia Convention a runaway?

This question is the second greatest misconception concerning the AVC and its history. Forty-eight of the fifty-five delegates to the 1787 Philadelphia Convention were given ***plenary*** power by their states to do as they felt necessary to improve the national government.⁴² For the remaining seven delegates, they were still able to attend, debate and make suggestions for the new proposed Constitution – and many did contribute to the writing of our Constitution, some quite significantly.⁴³ The finalized Constitution required adoption by three-quarters, or nine, of the twelve attending states (Rhode Island did not attend) to be adopted.⁴⁴ The ratification by ten states was required if Rhode Island was to be included. The Philadelphia Convention, according to the call from the Continental Congress, issued after six states had already positively responded to the actual convention call from Virginia, was called with the intent of either modifying the Articles of Confederation or to "render the federal Constitution adequate to the exigencies of Government and

---

⁴¹ U.S. Dept. of Justice, "Report to the Attorney General: Limited Constitutional Conventions Under Article V of the United States Constitution," Office of Legal Policy at 3 (Sept. 10, 1987)
⁴² *The Documentary History of the Ratification of the Constitution, Digital Edition*, eds. John P. Kaminski, Gaspare J. Saladino, Richard Leffler, Charles H. Schoenleber and Margaret A. Hogan (Charlottesville: University of Virginia Press, 2009)
⁴³ Ratification of the Constitution ("Bankson's Journal"), 1786-91, National Archives, NARA M322, 301686
⁴⁴ Robert Natelson, "Proposing Constitutional Amendments by Conventions: Rules Governing the Process," *Tennessee Law Review* 78 (2011): 719-23

the preservation of the Union."[45] An examination of the commissions of the delegates shows that ten of the twelve states that attended granted sufficient powers to their delegates to do exactly as they did. [See Appendix C.] New York and Massachusetts were the exceptions.[46] Despite their limited instructions, Nathaniel Gorham and Rufus King of Massachusetts signed on behalf of their state and Alexander Hamilton of New York signed on his own personal behalf.[47]

As early as the end of 1780, the States were beginning to see the deficiencies in the Articles of Confederation and had begun to press for changes. Some of the political leaders of the time recognized that the real issue was a weak national government resulting from deficiencies in the Articles. They began to lobby for a national constitutional convention for the explicit purpose of creating a stronger central government. Their pleas for reform can be found in the newspapers, pamphlets and letters of the period.[48]

No less respectable an authority (and 1787 convention delegate and chairman) than George Washington wrote to Thomas Jefferson on 30 May 1787, just after the start of the Philadelphia Convention, stating,

"The business of this convention is as yet very much in embryo to form any opinion of the conclusion. Much is expected from it by some; not much by others; and nothing by a few. That something is necessary, none will deny; for the situation of the general government, if it can be called a government, is shaken to its foundation, and liable to be overturned by every blast. In a word, it is at an end; and unless a remedy is soon applied, anarchy and confusion will inevitably ensue."[49]

The 1787 Grand Convention in Philadelphia operated OUTSIDE of the Articles of Confederation as there was no provision in the Articles to hold such a convention. The Commonwealth of Virginia formally called the convention, and the Continental Congress belatedly agreed by issuing the 21 February 1787 resolution. The attending States selected

---

[45] Resolution of the Continental Congress, dated 21 February 1787 – issued in response to the report of the Annapolis Convention which had recommended the calling of the Philadelphia Convention.

[46] Max Farrand, *The Records of the Federal Convention of 1787, Vol. I* (New Haven: Yale University Press, 1911 rev. 1937), 560, 563, 565-7, 572, 574, 577, 581, 585-6

[47] United States Constitution, signatories

[48] *The Documentary History of the Ratification of the Constitution, Digital Edition*, eds. John P. Kaminski, Gaspare J. Saladino, Richard Leffler, Charles H. Schoenleber and Margaret A. Hogan (Charlottesville: University of Virginia Press, 2009)

[49] Max Farrand, *The Records of the Federal Convention of 1787, Vol. I* (New Haven: Yale University Press, 1911 rev. 1937), 14

the delegates, passed acts authorizing their delegates' commissions, issued instructions to their delegates and sent their delegates to Philadelphia. The States then considered, debated and ratified the Constitution without, as a state, alleging any impropriety in calling the convention. It can be concluded that the ratifying States neither viewed the Philadelphia Convention as a runaway nor believed that the delegates had exceeded their grants of authority. James Madison, writing in *The Federalist No. 40* as "Publius," concluded that,

> "...*the charge against the Convention of exceeding their powers, except in one instance little urged by the objectors, has no foundation to support it; that if they had exceeded their powers, they were not only warranted but required, as the confidential servants of their country, by the circumstances in which they were placed, to exercise the liberty which they assumed, and that finally, if they had violated both their powers, and their obligations in proposing a Constitution, this ought nevertheless to be embraced, if it be calculated to accomplish the views and happiness of the people of America.*"[50]

When the 1787 Convention finished their work, they conveyed the new proposed constitution to the Confederation Congress, which then considered the document for two days, deciding to promulgate it to the States without a vote and then passed the proposed constitution on to the state legislatures for the establishment of conventions for ratification. If the Philadelphia Convention had indeed overstepped their authority, would not the Confederation Congress have rejected the proposed constitution as invalid and illegal and, if voting at all, voted NOT to forward the proposed constitution on to the States for ratification? The action of the Confederation Congress in forwarding the proposed constitution on the States broadly implies the Congress' acceptance and concurrence with the work done by the Grand Convention as well as recognizes that the deficiencies of the Article of Confederation were of such severity that the pressing need for reform necessitated that the States be given the opportunity to pass judgment on the proposed constitution.

Alexander Hamilton concluded, somewhat oddly, that the Philadelphia Convention was limited and had done only what it could to forestall a national disaster, leaving the final decision to the States, the same as an AVC would today, remarking, "We can only propose and

---

[50] James Madison, "Federalist Paper No. 40," in *The Federalist Papers: Hamilton, Madison, Jay*, ed. Clinton Rossiter (New York: Mentor, 1961), 254-5

recommend – the power of ratifying or rejecting is still in the States."[51] As it still is today.

Another way of looking at the 1787 Convention as becoming a runaway is to consider the purpose of the convention and how the proposed plans compared with that stated intention of Congress – and Virginia – in calling the Convention. Since the "call" from the Congress stated the intent as to "render the federal Constitution adequate to the exigencies of Government and the preservation of the Union," the emphasis must be placed on the words "federal" and "preservation of the Union." Anti-Federalist John Taylor, of Caroline, Virginia took this idea to great lengths in his classic 1823 work *"New Views of the Constitution."* Taylor explored the idea that, initially, the delegates did go rogue in that Madison and Randolph were proposing, in their Virginia Plan, a **national** government and not a *federal* government. Similarly, Hamilton was supposedly seeking a monarchy for which he knew there was insufficient support. Others were proposing a **consolidated** government with a national legislature and judiciary yet preserving the key features of federalism. Of greatest concern to Taylor was the deliberate "annihilation of the states" that these plans all exhibited.[52]

Taylor noted all of his objections to the various plans and detailed the slow but accelerating response of the delegates to move toward a federal government to replace the confederacy under the Articles of Confederation. Viewing the events of 1787 through Taylor's eyes, one would say that the Convention did start out with a deliberate effort by some delegates to go rogue but eventually returned to fulfill its mandate to "render the *federal* government adequate."[53,54]

A final important comment on this question is necessary. The 1787 Grand Convention merely PROPOSED a new constitution for the United States; it did NOT impose a new government. The proposed constitution was sent to the Congress for debate, which it did for two days, and then was sent to the States for debate in ratification

---

[51] Max Farrand, *The Records of the Federal Convention of 1787*, Vol. I (New Haven: Yale University Press, 1911 rev. 1937), 295

[52] John Taylor, of Caroline, Virginia, *New Views of the Constitution of the United States* (Washington City: Way and Gideon, 1823), 42-53

[53] Ibid.

[54] Taylor is asking, as the preservation of the federal union was secured, but at what price to the States? This question remains pertinent today.

conventions. Some states, such as North Carolina, rejected the proposed constitution initially. All during the debate and ratification process, the Articles of Confederation remained the governing charter of national government and was in effect. Even after the Constitution was ratified by nine states and therefore considered valid by those nine states, it was not in effect until the Congress set a "sunset" date for the new constitution to begin functioning – and then, only in those states that had ratified the new constitution. In those states which had not yet ratified, the Articles of Confederation remained the governing charter. Thus, for a brief period, two constitutions were ratified and in effect operating in the United States.[55]

5. ───────────────────────────────────

Why did the 1787 convention give this amendment power to the States; doesn't Congress already have the power to amend the Constitution?

Article V provides the power of initiating amendments to both the Congress and the States.[56] Historically, only Congress has exercised this power and introduced amendments.

The Framers of our Constitution had just gone through a Revolution and a separation from a national government that had become, in the eyes of the Founding Fathers and the former colonists, oppressive and unresponsive to the people that it had governed. The Framers recognized that a future American federal government, principally Congress, could become equally oppressive and unresponsive to the citizenry. Leaving the amending of the Constitution to the Congress alone left the people with no method of going around the unresponsive or oppressive Congress while staying <u>within</u> the Constitution. Records of the Federal Convention in Philadelphia show that Framer George Mason of Virginia thought that, "no amendments of the proper kind would ever be obtained by the people, if the Government should become oppressive, as [he] verily believed would be the case."[57] Framers Elbridge Gerry of Massachusetts and Gouverneur Morris

───────────────────────────────────

[55] As North Carolina and Rhode Island remained outside of the newly reformed United States under the Constitution of 1787, they ostensibly remained joined as the Confederation under the Articles of Confederation.

[56] United States Constitution, Article V

[57] Max Farrand, *The Records Of The Federal Convention of 1787, Vol. 2* (New Haven: Yale University Press, 1911 rev. 1937), 629, n.8

of New York agreed and proposed the States convention method of amending. The motion was adopted unanimously.[58] By extending the power to amend to the States, a peaceful, constitutional method of restraining the federal government was provided to the people.[59] It is a last line of peaceful defense.

History has proven that Congress, like all of the governments throughout history which preceded it, is very reluctant to give up any power once it has been granted or once Congress has assumed that particular power. Over the last two centuries, more than 11,600 amendments to the Constitution have been proposed through 2014.[60] Many of those proposed amendments were intended to curtail the power of the federal government. Congress has not acted constitutionally and significantly to curb its own power since passing the Bill of Rights in 1789[61] with the sole exception of passing the Twenty-first Amendment in 1933.[62] The Framers wisely drew upon the history of human government and placed in the Constitution a method of curtailing governmental power without relying on the goodwill of the very politicians that would see their power diminished by any such proposed amendments. Article V is another of the "checks and balances" established to prevent consolidation of too much power in the hands of any one branch of government.[63]

The Framers also expected that the people would be quicker than the politicians to recognize when Congress had become too oppressive or unresponsive to the needs of the nation. Providing the States with an amendment method which circumvents Congress can be thought of a "reset button" or a "safety valve" for the populace that is preferable to a violent revolution. Giving the States the ability to initiate – and

---

[58] Ibid.

[59] James Madison, *The Debates in the Federal Convention of 1787 Which Framed the Constitution of the United States of America* (Westport, CT: Greenwood Press, 1970, c.1920, Oxford University Press), generally

[60] https://www.senate.gov/reference/measures_proposed_to_amend_constitution.htm 11,623 proposed amendments, to be exact, through 16 December 2014 according to the Senate website. See also, John R. Vile, *Encyclopedia of Constitutional Amendments, Proposed Amendments and Amending Issues, 1789-2015*, Vol. 1, A-M (Santa Barbara, CA: ABC-CLIO, 4th ed., 2015), 333

[61] Richard E. Labunski, *James Madison and the Struggle for the Bill of Rights* (New York: Oxford University Press, 2006), 192 - The Bill of Rights was introduced in Congress by James Madison on 8 June 1789; they were proposed to the States by Congress on 25 September 1789 and formally declared ratified on 15 December 1791.

[62] Passing the Twenty-First Amendment merely reset the powers of Congress back by fourteen years to delete the power of Congress to regulate alcohol use and production.

[63] The four major ideas shaping the US Constitution are: federalism, checks and balances, separation of powers, and limited government.

to conclude - the amendment process is a key feature of federalism. It reaffirms that the States are equal partners to the federal government in the governing of the nation.

6.

Did the Delegates at the 1787 Constitutional Convention change the rules for ratification meaning that the same thing could happen today in an AVC?

The short answer is yes...and no. With regard to the conditional "yes": amending the Articles of Confederation was covered in Article XIII. It required that all amendments to the Articles be made by <u>unanimous</u> approval of the States.[64] If we consider just the requirement of unanimity, then the rules were indeed changed, but then, the Grand Convention of 1787 was NOT held under the authority of the Articles of Confederation. Nothing in the Articles described such interstate conventions. If the Articles did not have authority over the convention then the Articles' ratification method found in Article XIII obviously could not and did not apply. The 21 February 1787 Resolution issued by the Congress gave explicit approval to the powers and acts of the Convention. This is expressly shown by the action of Congress to forward the proposed Constitution to the state legislatures without any commentary. Lastly, since every one of the thirteen States had to individually ratify the Constitution, an argument could be made that the unanimity requirement for amendment of the Articles of Confederation was indeed met, though indirectly.[65]

With regard to the conditional "no": once again, the 1787 Philadelphia Convention was not held under the authority of the Articles of Confederation whereas an Article V amendatory convention held in current time would, most definitely, be convened under the authority of the Constitution, and therefore, the ratification process of the Constitution as defined in Article V would indeed apply. An amendatory convention really has very little to do with ratification; Article V provides for two methods of ratification independent of the amendatory

---

[64] Articles of Confederation, Article XIII – Note: No amendment was ever successfully made to the Articles of Confederation.

[65] Of course, a counter-argument can also be made that because only three-quarters of the States were needed to ratify the Constitution in order to bring the Constitution into force and to replace the Articles of Confederation, that the Article XIII provision was violated – had the Convention been operated under the authority of the Articles.

convention. An amendatory convention is designed to only consider and recommend a proposed amendment; the ratification process is separate in order to induce a slow process that promotes deliberation. To change the current constitutionally stipulated ratification process requires that an amendment first be made to Article V changing the process and that the ratification change amendment be approved by three-quarters, or presently thirty-eight, States to take effect. So, no, the same change to the ratification procedure could not happen within an amendatory convention today.

The purpose of an Article V convention is to put forth, debate and forward a proposed amendment to the Constitution to Congress and then on to the States. All of these actions are done under the aegis of the United States Constitution and all provisions of the Constitution apply to the Article V convention's activities. Because the Constitution is considered to be in full effect, the ratification process of Article V is also in full effect. Thus, a supermajority of three-quarters, or thirty-eight, of the States would have to ratify any proposed amendment before it took effect – and that would include any proposed change to the ratification process itself.

At best, an AVC would have to have an agenda that includes debating a proposed amendment to change the ratification process, drafting and proposing the amendment, approving the amendment and then forwarding the proposed amendment to Congress for promulgation to the States for ratification. The final decision to change the ratification process would then rest in the hands of the States – as it should.

7.

What safeguards exist to prevent a runaway convention?

The States retain the power to instruct their delegations. Since Congress does not make the rules for the AVC, the States are free to restrain their respective delegates as they see fit. This power includes recalling the delegate(s) as needed or limiting their capabilities. The States and the convention itself can limit the agenda of the AVC to a single issue prohibiting introduction, or even discussion, of any other issue or proposed amendment.[66] In the event that an unpopular proposal was made and adopted by the convention, it would still require

---

[66] U.S. Dept. of Justice, "Report to the Attorney General: Limited Constitutional Conventions Under Article V of the United States Constitution," Office of Legal Policy, at 34 (10 Sept. 1987)

ratification by three-quarters, or currently thirty-eight, of the States.[67] A <u>supermajority</u> of two-thirds, or currently thirty-four, of the States is needed to call a convention; a <u>supermajority</u> of two-thirds of the States is needed to adopt a proposed amendment in Congress and that will most likely be the same requirement in the convention (a simple majority can propose an amendment for debate); a <u>supermajority</u> of three-quarters of the States is needed to ratify a proposed amendment by the States.[68] Only a proposed amendment that enjoys wide popular support is going to receive the necessary votes to propose, adopt, and ratify it. If an unusual amendment is indeed ratified by the States, then one can safely say that the new amendment is truly a reflection of the political will of the American people.

In 1990, during the last great push for an AVC, Sen. Orrin Hatch of Utah penned a public defense of the AVC in response to the effort to stop the drive for a Balanced Budget Amendment. He listed seven safeguards against a runaway convention:

> "*1) the States limit the scope of the convention by limiting the application;*
>
> *2) Congress can refuse to call a convention unless the States agree on a limited purpose (this is questionable in the instance where the States may demand an open convention);*
>
> *3) the States could appoint delegates for a limited purpose and recall those delegates that exceed their authority;*
>
> *4) the US Supreme Court could invalidate the results of a runaway convention;*
>
> *5) Congress could refuse to submit to the States the product of a runaway convention (again, this is of dubious legality);*
>
> *6) Article V itself contemplates changes to part of the Constitution, rather than wholesale changes; and*
>
> *7) Any proposed amendment would require ratification by three-quarters*

---

[67] Congressional Research Service Report R42592, *The Article V Convention for Proposing Constitutional Amendments: Historical Perspectives for Congress,* (10 July 2012): 15
[68] U.S. Dept. of Justice, "Report to the Attorney General: Limited Constitutional Conventions Under Article V of the United States Constitution," Office of Legal Policy, at 20 (10 Sept. 1987)

of the States."⁶⁹

Constitutional scholarship has advanced greatly in the roughly quarter century since Sen. Hatch wrote his defense of an AVC, but his reasoning essentially remains strong.

Should a convention runaway and propose an amendment that is unusual and contrary to the public opinion and political will, it will fail in the ratification stage. The passage of time between the proposal and the ratification allows for a rigorous debate as to the merits of the proposed amendment; public sentiment against a bad amendment would likely increase and lead to the States' rejection of the proposed amendment. The slow, deliberative process of debate, proposal and ratification is the surest safeguard against getting a "bad" amendment.

8.

Have any other American constitutional conventions "runaway?"

To answer this question requires that we have to better understand what is meant by a "constitutional convention." Many opponents of an AVC claim that any convention called to address anything in connection with a constitution is, by definition, a constitutional convention. But such a convention is plenary, and therefore unlimited, in scope and purpose. It is for that reason that the opponents insist that an AVC called for the explicit purpose of proposing and debating amendments is, by their definition, a constitutional convention. To date, no national or federal Article V amendatory convention has occurred, so we cannot look to a prior amendatory AVC as an historical example of an AVC, let alone of a runaway convention. Since we have already established that a constitutional convention is defined as a plenary convention called to draft a *new* constitution, we should limit our analysis to those other "constitutional" conventions that have occurred.

First, let us consider the extensive history of ratification conventions. When we look at the proceedings of the state ratification conventions held after the 1787 Grand Convention, we can find no

---

[69] US Senator Orrin Hatch (R-UT), "Fear of a Runaway Convention Endangers Constitutional Right," (1 February 1990), published in several Utah newspapers, including Deseret News.

instance where any of the fifteen state ratification conventions[70] veered off the issue of ratification and took upon themselves the task of re-writing the Constitution or of writing a new constitution. Many states did attempt to *conditionally* ratify the Constitution with the stipulation that a Bill of Rights be added in the first Congress, but none sought to substantially modify or replace the Constitution by themselves.[71] The fifteen ratification conventions remained limited in scope and purpose, unlike a true, fully-powered constitutional convention.

If we consider the state ratification conventions called by thirty-nine states[72] in 1933 and 1934 for considering ratification of the Twenty-first Amendment, history shows that not one ratification convention exceeded the scope and purpose of the ratification convention and undertook re-writing the Constitution or writing an entirely new constitution.[73] Combined in both the cases of 1787-91 and 1933-34, fifty-four ratification conventions were held dealing with the express purpose of ratifying either the Constitution or an amendment to the Constitution and not a single one of those fifty-four conventions exceeded the limits placed upon its purpose and power and ran away.[74]

Second, let us consider the history of state constitutional conventions. The States have conducted <u>hundreds</u> of state constitutional conventions which are plenary, unlimited in purpose and power, at

---

[70] In addition to the thirteen original colonies that became the original states, Vermont had, during the Revolutionary War, formed the Vermont Republic, and on 10 January 1791, in convention, Vermont elected to ratify the Constitution and apply for admission to the United States as the fourteenth state. Charles S. Forbes, "Vermont's Admission to the Union," *The Vermonter: A State Magazine* VII, no.8 (March 1902): 102. Website accessed on 29 August 2014. Also, North Carolina held two ratification conventions.

[71] The original, proposed Bill of Rights contained twelve proposed amendments. These were sent to the States for consideration in 1789. Ultimately, ten of the twelve proposed amendments were approved by the States and incorporated into the Constitution as the first ten amendments. Of the two proposed amendments not approved, one eventually became the Twenty-seventh Amendment in 1992 – that amendment had been approved by only seven states between 1789 and 1792. Seven states requested that alterations be made to the Constitution as part of their ratification. The number of alterations varied widely: (in order of ratification) Massachusetts 19 alterations; South Carolina 2 alts.; New Hampshire 12 alts.; Virginia 40 alts.; New York 33 alts.; North Carolina 26 alts.; Rhode Island 21 alts. Of the seven states requesting modification, four states ratified after the Constitution had reached the nine-state threshold for ratification. Source: *Eliot's Debates* (1836)

[72] Not all states held a ratification convention for the Twenty-first Amendment. 36 states held conventions in 1933 and ratified the amendment. Following the reaching of the requisite 36 states, two more states ratified in 1933 and in 1934. South Carolina had rejected the amendment in convention and voters in North Carolina rejected holding a convention. The eight remaining states declined to hold conventions after the amendment had been duly ratified.

[73] Everett S. Brown, Ratification of the Twenty-First Amendment to the Constitution of the United States: State Convention Records and Laws (Ann Arbor: University of Michigan Press, 1938), generally.

[74] Fifteen Constitution ratification conventions in 1787-91 and 39 Amendment ratification conventions in 1933-34

the state level. Roger S. Hoar examined in depth the history of state constitutional conventions in his benchmark work "*Constitutional Conventions*" in 1917; he found six examples of state constitutional conventions that had run away – all before 1909 when the States began to impose limits on the powers of their state constitutional conventions.[75] Yet, not one of the more than two hundred state conventions held up to that time ever attempted to re-write the federal constitution or to draft a new federal constitution. It may seem a ridiculous stretch to cite that a state constitutional convention did not run away by attempting to re-write the federal constitution, but the main point being made by opponents of an Article V convention is that "anything could happen"[76] in an AVC, therefore we present the case of state constitutional conventions – which are unlimited in power – to demonstrate that <u>not</u> anything can happen – or it most likely already would have happened at some point in the last two centuries.

An extensive study of the Constitution and of the seemingly endless number of books and papers written on the Constitution shows that there are just four types of federally, constitutionally related conventions: 1) a plenary convention as was held in 1787 and not repeated since (nor, more importantly, permitted since); 2) state ratification conventions (an Article VII convention) for the Constitution held in 1787-91 and not held since; 3) state amendment ratification conventions (an Article V convention) held only in 1933-34;[77] and 4) a convention of the States for proposing amendments (an Article V convention) that has never been held. No convention – of any type - held since the 1787 Grand Convention at Philadelphia has ever runaway and tried to re-write the United States Constitution. Of the hundreds of state constitutionally related conventions held since 1787, including the hundreds of plenary state constitution drafting conventions, not one convention has ever tried to re-write the United States Constitution. Not one, ever.

---

[75] Roger S. Hoar, *Constitutional Conventions: Their Nature, Powers, and Limitations* (Boston: Little, Brown, 1917), 111-115: Georgia (1789), Minnesota (1857), Pennsylvania (1872), Alabama (1901), Virginia (1901) and Michigan (1908).

[76] http://www.eagleforum.org/publications/alerts/michigan-vote-hjr-cc.html. Quoting from the Eagle Forum website urging people to testify against a bill in the Michigan legislature: "Nobody really knows what will happen. We cannot rely on the idea that states would not support harmful amendments passed by the convention, especially in chaotic times."

[77] Everett S. Brown, Ratification of the Twenty-First Amendment to the Constitution of the United States: State Convention Records and Laws (Ann Arbor: University of Michigan Press, 1938), Appendices.

9.

How is an AVC different from Congress proposing amendments?

When Congress proposes an amendment, the process is controlled by Congress until it reaches the ratification stage, at which point the States take over. Congress drafts, debates and votes on the proposed amendment with a two-thirds vote in favor required of each chamber for passage.[78] Congress also stipulates whether the state legislatures or state ratification conventions vote on the proposed amendment(s). In this method, Congress acts as the Article V convention. When the requisite number of two-thirds, or currently thirty-four, of the States apply for an Article V convention, Congress' role is limited to issuing the "call" to a convention, including setting the date and place of the convention and to selecting the ratification method. The States perform almost all of the rest of the process. The States set the rules of the convention, select the delegates, propose and debate the amendment(s), and then the AVC sends the proposed amendment(s) back to the Congress. Congress then refers the proposed amendment(s) to each of the fifty state legislatures with a concurrent resolution detailing whether the fifty state legislatures or fifty state ratification conventions consider ratification. In the case of an AVC, the role of proposing and debating by the Congress is assumed by the States' delegates. An Article V convention differs from the congressional method of amending by including one additional body in the process – the Article V convention. And that body is merely replacing Congress in the proposal stage of the process.

The power to propose amendments is the same between Congress and the States. It is an important principle of federalism that this power be shared. If Congress can suggest, debate and then propose single amendments for ratification, then the States should share the same ability. The States could not logically be refused this ability on the grounds that an amendatory convention must be open and able to propose only multiple amendments. The same principle holds for the States' ability to propose multiple amendments at a convention.[79]

---

[78] Technically, it is two-thirds of those legislators present in the chambers for the votes. A quorum must be present but not all members of the chamber are required to vote. - Senate Journal, 1st Cong., 1st sess., at 77 (9 Sept. 1789)

[79] James E. Bond, David E. Engdahl and Henry N. Butler, *A Constitutional Convention* (Washington, D.C.: National Legal Center for the Public Interest, 1987), 6

10.

What kind of convention does Article V authorize for amending?

There are two types of recognized amendatory conventions: a general or open convention in which the agenda is not strictly limited and any type and number of amendments may be proposed; and a limited convention which may be restricted to a single-issue or a set number of issues that comprise the agenda and nothing else may be added. Some scholars have said that the runaway convention is a third type, but that version is not a planned or permitted event let alone a desirable outcome. A runaway was never the intention of the Framers. The choice of the type of convention is dictated by the subject matter of the applications of the state legislatures.[80]

The issue most often debated today by advocates of holding an AVC is whether to hold an open or limited convention. An open convention can entertain debate on any proposed amendment. The upside is that an open convention can garner widespread support from all sides of the political spectrum as everyone is guaranteed an opportunity to present their proposal and get a chance to promote it. The limited convention is much harder to promote and to secure the support of the necessary two-thirds of the States to prompt Congress to make the convention call. There is some reassurance in that the topic will be narrowly limited and more focused. Proponents of a limited convention believe that restricting the topic is another strong safeguard against a potential runaway convention.

The question of which type of convention Article V authorizes has been debated sharply for several decades since the last great push for an AVC in the 1980s. Because the wording of the Constitution states in Article V that, "The Congress,"…"shall propose Amendments to this Constitution" and "shall call a Convention for proposing Amendments" open convention advocates have claimed that the plural status of the word "Amendments" must indicate that all AVCs must be open in nature. But US Supreme Court decisions have shown that the Framers allowed for limited conventions as well. As early as 1855, the Court ruled in favor of single issue conventions.[81] A state Supreme Court reaffirmed this

---

[80] Congressional Research Service Report R42592, *The Article V Convention for Proposing Constitutional Amendments. Historical Perspectives for Congress*, (10 July 2012). 10

[81] http://caselaw.lp.findlaw.com/scripts/getcase.pl?court=US&vol=59&invol=331 Dodge v. Woolsey 59 U.S. 331 (1855)

position and ruled again for limited issue conventions in 1933.[82]

11.

Does Article V authorize any other type of convention?

Yes, Article V also mentions the state ratifying conventions but these are for the express purpose of approving, that is, <u>ratifying</u> or rejecting proposed amendments by the States. They are NOT the same type of convention as the Article V convention for proposing amendments to the Constitution. The ratifying convention is even more limited in power than the amendatory convention – the output is a simple "yea" or "nay" vote. A ratifying convention is as different from an Article V amendatory [proposing] convention as an Article V [proposing] convention is different from a plenipotentiary constitutional convention. The ratifying convention is also as different from a constitutional convention as an Article V proposing convention is different from a constitutional convention. Our Constitution then describes and prescribes three different types of conventions: amendatory (proposing),[83] Constitution ratification[84] and amendment ratification.[85]

What is missing from this list is the plenary convention similar to that held in 1787 – our Constitution simply makes no provision whatsoever for another plenary convention.

12.

Is an Article V convention considered to be part of the federal government or the state governments?

Neither, an AVC is more of a hybrid. It is considered a "federal function" carried out by the States as represented by their delegates.[86] An AVC has been characterized as a "fourth branch of the federal government" due to the federal nature of its work on amending the federal constitution.[87] Of course, this "branch" is only temporary. Once

---

[82] *In Re Opinion of the Justices* 204 N.C. 306, 172 S.E. 474 (1933)
[83] United States Constitution, Article V
[84] United States Constitution, Article VII
[85] United States Constitution, Article V
[86] http://supreme.justia.com/cases/federal/us/258/130/case.html Leser v. Garnett 258 U.S. 130 (1922)
[87] Roger S. Hoar, *Constitutional Conventions: Their Nature, Powers, and Limitations* (Boston: Little, Brown, 1917), 91, 225

the convention completes its agenda, it must close.[88] The body of law that applies to an AVC is predominantly federal – excepting those state laws that cover the delegate selection, instruction and recall processes and those state actions, usually resolutions, that petition Congress for an AVC. It is a hybrid in the sense that the purpose of the AVC is to propose modifications to the federal constitution, but it is carried out by the States' delegates during the proposal and debate stage of the amendment process. The delegates could be considered state officials carrying out a federal function.

13.

If the prodding effect works to get amendments passed in Congress, then why bother to have an AVC?

Congress has not given up any power since passing the Bill of Rights, other than the power to regulate alcohol production and consumption that it held briefly for fourteen years under Prohibition. Holding an AVC is the only method by which the States can wrest power from Congress and impose restraints on the federal government. With the passage of over two centuries and not a single AVC having occurred, it emboldens Congress to believe that the States will not be able to exercise federalism and restrain Congress or the federal government. Holding an AVC will permit that first re-balancing of the power between the States and the federal government on the States' terms.

14.

Wasn't Article V a last minute addition to the Constitution and isn't well thought out or defined?

No, Article V is the direct descendant of Article XIII in the Articles of Confederation and the amending processes found in many state constitutions that had preceded the federal constitution. The Virginia Plan that James Madison prepared and Edmund Randolph presented included an amendment provision. The difficulty in amending the Articles of Confederation was just one of the many reasons that the delegates in 1787 felt that the government needed an overhaul in design.

---

[88] *United States ex rel. Widenmann v. Colby* 265 F. 998 (D.C. Cir. 1920) affirmed as 257 U.S. 619 (1921)

The inability to successfully amend the Articles of Confederation was a significant reason to reform the government. As no proposed amendment was ever successful, the delegates knew that a less restrictive method was necessary. Extensive thought went into the crafting of Article V by many delegates. James Madison was the principal author of the Virginia Plan and had spent the year prior to the Annapolis and Philadelphia conventions studying the history of republics and the constitutions of the States in preparation for arguing for an amendment to the Articles of Confederation to obtain the power to tax for the national government. Much of his research contributed to his paper titled "*Of Ancient and Modern Confederacies.*"[89]

It is true that Article V was the last piece of business before the final vote on the Constitution as a whole document. The idea behind the article was discussed and debated several times throughout the convention of 1787.[90]

Powers of the Convention and Delegates

15.

Could a convention, once assembled, impute to itself sovereignty?

This is perhaps the most crucial of all questions that deal with the power and limitations of an amendatory convention. By definition, a limited power convention is just that – *limited* – to the power and scope that is defined in the call to convention. The agenda is set by the requested subject in the aggregated States' applications for the convention. This question is, of course, a restatement of the question of whether a convention could run away.

Each state stipulates the extent and the limitations of the power and authority of its delegates through their credentials. With some States enacting faithful delegate legislation, each state is undertaking a form of runaway convention prevention. Specification of the convention as limited and not plenary creates a legal roadblock to the delegates' assumption of unintended power.

---

[89] Ralph Ketcham, *James Madison, a Biography* (Charlottesville: University of Virginia Press, 1990), 183-4
[90] Madison's Notes, generally and in Farrand's compilation.

16.

Who has a role in the amendment process?

Congress, possibly the state legislatures, possibly state ratifying conventions and potentially Article V conventions for proposing amendments can each have a specific duty in the Article V amendment process depending on the method of congressionally specified ratification.[91] The congressional method of amending involves, first, the Congress proposing an amendment and then debating and voting on it. If it passes, then Congress selects either the state legislatures or state ratifying conventions to next consider ratification. Under the state application and convention method, the state legislatures first apply to Congress for an AVC, then the Congress verifies the subject and the count of the applications and issues the "call" to an AVC, then the AVC convenes, proposes, debates, and refers a proposed amendment(s) to Congress. Finally, Congress selects the ratification method and forwards the proposed amendment(s) to either the state legislatures or the state ratification conventions.[92]

Thus, only US Senators and US Representatives, state senators and state representatives, and state AVC delegates and state ratification convention delegates could actually play a <u>direct</u> role in the proposal, drafting, debate, adoption, voting, referral, promulgation, and ratification of a new amendment – depending on the methods of proposal and ratification. Indirectly, many more people could play a supporting role in providing the facilities, information, and logistics of the Congress, state legislatures, amendatory and ratification conventions.

17.

What powers are granted by Article V to the Congress, state legislatures, state ratifying conventions and Article V conventions?

Per constitutional scholar Professor Robert Natelson, succinctly, there are <u>eight</u> enumerated powers granted. Four powers are granted at the proposal stage and four more powers are granted to the ratification

---

[91] Robert G. Natelson, *Amending the Constitution by Convention: Practical Guidance for Citizens and Policymakers*, Goldwater Institute Policy Report No. 11-02 (Phoenix, AZ: Goldwater Institute, Feb. 2011), 6
[92] United States Constitution, Article V

stage.

> In the proposal stage, "the Constitution grants
> 1. To two-thirds of each house of Congress authority to propose amendments;
> 2. To two-thirds of the state legislatures power to require Congress to call a convention for proposing amendments;
> 3. To Congress power to call that convention (and requires it to do so); and
> 4. To the [Article V] convention authority to propose amendments.
>
> At the ratification stage, the Constitution
> 1. Authorizes Congress to select whether ratification shall be by state legislatures or state conventions;
> 2. (if Congress selects the former method) authorizes three-fourths of state legislatures to ratify;
> 3. (if Congress selects the latter method) empowers (and requires) each state to call a ratifying convention; and
> 4. Further empowers three-fourths of the [ratifying] conventions to ratify."[93]

18.

Can the delegates just replace the current Constitution of 1787?

This is the question that many people ask first. It is the greatest fear of people that appreciate the Constitution and the present form of American government. This concern is driven by the oft repeated oversimplification that the 1787 Convention was a runaway.

No, delegates cannot simply replace the Constitution; Article V of our Constitution limits the power of the Article V amendatory convention to proposing, and not passing, or ratifying, amendments.[94] Ultimately, the States, through either the state legislatures or state ratification conventions, vote to pass or reject any proposed amendment.

---

[93] Robert G. Natelson, *Amending the Constitution by Convention: Practical Guidance for Citizens and Policymakers*, Goldwater Institute Policy Report No. 11-02, (Phoenix, AZ: Goldwater Institute, Feb. 2011), 6-7
[94] United States Constitution, Article V

Writing and proposing a new constitution would be a *plenary* act, which is not a measure of power granted in the current constitution. Such an act would be unconstitutional and perhaps treasonous! The delegates are bound by the existing constitution and supporting statutes.[95] This issue was once taken up by the Supreme Court and they ruled that such an act would be "extra-constitutional and revolutionary."[96,97]

The AVC is designed to operate within the Constitution, whereas drafting and ratifying a new constitution would be going outside of the current constitution. Even the current constitution was not ratified by the 1787 Grand Convention – that was left to the States through state ratification conventions.[98] For the sake of argument, assume that an AVC did draft and forward a new proposed constitution to the States for ratification, the most likely response would be a mass rejection of the document, first by the Congress, which would undoubtedly refuse to promulgate the new charter, then by the States as a usurpation of authority and power not granted. The States would probably refuse to consider its ratification. A specified number of the States would be required to ratify the new constitution and even then, only those states which actually ratify the new constitution would presumably be bound by the new charter. Finally, the Supreme Court would most likely hear a challenge to the new charter and reject the process of drafting and ratification as unconstitutional.

Opponents of an AVC have long claimed that the scenario of an AVC writing, adopting and perhaps even ratifying a new constitution is not that far off from the events of 1787 in Philadelphia. They contend that the Congress's rules of recommending amendments to the Articles of Confederation in the 21 February 1787 Resolution were ignored and that the amendment process of Article XIII was also ignored. These actions created a precedent in the view of modern opponents. But there are significant differences between 1787 and now.

First, the central government under the Articles of Confederation was near collapse and without fiscal resources as Congress possessed no

---

[95] Russell L. Caplan, *Constitutional Brinkmanship, Amending the Constitution by National Convention* (New York: Oxford University Press, 1988), 147
[96] Lester B. Orfield, "The Procedure of the Federal Amending Power," *Illinois Law Review* 25 (1930): 418
[97] *Maxwell v. Dow* 176 U.S. 581 (1900), 20 Sup. Ct. Rep. 448, 44 L. Ed. 597
[98] United States Constitution, Article VII

power to tax. The federal government of today is deeply in debt but not on the verge of immediate financial collapse. Resources are available today and the machinery of government continues to function. Second, the central government of 1787 was new and barely established. They had few processes and practices on which to rely whereas the federal government of today is well established and relies on long engrained practices and contingency plans. Third, the Constitution holds a deep and abiding reverence among the American people who will not willingly abandon the national charter without a long, premeditated consideration of the need to do so. Fourth, the States held an expectation that something substantial must be done to rectify the problems of government in 1787 and according to the instructions issued by the States to their delegates, the drafting of a new charter was a reasonable act. Today, that expectation does not exist and no state would support such an action without first advising their delegation to undertake such a course of action. Fifth, the perspective of the American people, and their respective state legislatures and delegates, was anchored by their viewing themselves as Virginians, New Yorkers and South Carolinians, to name just a few, first and foremost before considering themselves Americans. This parochial view does not dominate today. By definition, to be American politically means to identify with the Constitution as the cornerstone of the American political system.

19.

Who picks the delegates to the AVC and how?

The States are empowered to select their own delegates according to their own respective criteria.[99] The individual state legislatures will develop, or already have developed, their own rules for selecting their delegates.[100] This method is based on the practice of selecting international diplomats that developed over centuries. Remember that the States are just that – States, which is what all countries are called. Until the American States adopted the Constitution, the States were considered as independent nations – even under the Articles of Confederation, to an extent. It makes sense that some vestiges of

---

[99] Congressional Research Service Report CRS 95-589 A (1995) *Amending the U.S. Constitution: by Congress or Constitutional Convention*, CRS-5
[100] http://www.leagle.com/decision/19751681390FSupp1291_11480.xml/DYER%20v.%20BLAIR Dyer v. Blair 390 F. Supp. 1291 (N.D. Ill. 1975 –written by later US Supreme Court Justice Stevens)

international diplomatic protocol have become engrained in our internal parliamentary procedures. Additionally, as States and as colonies, the States participated in, and continue to participate in, many conventions of an inter-colonial or interstate nature. The rules that have governed these conventions extend back, without exaggeration, for hundreds of years and are well known and often documented in the proceedings of those prior conventions.

One of the frequent objections to an AVC is that the Congress will select either the delegates or the method of selecting the delegates. The AVC opponents often state that there is no precedent for an AVC therefore no one knows what will happen, or they will state that the only precedent is the 1787 Convention. In either case, the answer is the same; the States will select their own delegates. Since there is no federal law to govern this aspect of an AVC, and if the precedent of 1787 is cited, then the States select their delegates as that is exactly what was done in 1787. Custom and tradition dictate that the States set their own criteria for the selection of delegates.

Once, scholars argued that the Congress could set the criteria, number and process for selecting the delegates under the implied powers doctrine.[101] But this has been refuted over time. Since an Article V convention is not an Article I, or legislative, function, Congress' legislative powers do not apply to any aspect of an Article V convention. Today, we recognize this as an infringement on the powers and rights of the States.

The state legislatures will deliberate on the attributes and talents that they believe necessary to best convey and represent their respective state's values and desires. It will be up to each state to decide who and how many delegates should serve in their delegation. Some states have already passed legislation that spells out how that state's delegates will be chosen. In some cases, the state will select state legislators to represent their state.[102] Other states may select prominent citizens such as attorneys or jurists. A few states will hold elections for their AVC delegates.

---

[101] Wayne B. Wheeler, "Is a Constitutional Convention Impending?," *Illinois Law Review* 21 (1927): 798-9

[102] As an example, in 2014, the Wisconsin Legislature considered bill AB635 that stipulated that five legislators in total be selected from both chambers of the state legislature to represent Wisconsin as delegates in an Article V Convention.

20.

Can delegates be bound by their states?

This is very much a current point of contention. Many scholars assert that the States have the power to instruct their delegates and to make the instructions binding. The States may, and some probably will, require their delegates to take an oath to pledge fidelity to their instructions as issued by the state legislature.[103] The delegates are the direct representatives of the people of their respective states and not directly of the state legislatures. However, it is the state legislatures which issue the commissions, or credentials, of the delegates and also the instructions by which the delegates are bound. In some states, act(s) have been passed by the state legislatures which criminally or civilly punish a delegate who disobeys or deviates from the state legislature's instructions.[104] To be fair, this is of questionable legality as it would interfere with the performance of the delegate to do what he or she thinks best. This situation is no different from that of the delegates[105] to the Grand Convention of 1787 in Philadelphia. The 1787 delegates were given explicit instructions from their respective state legislatures.[106] For the Massachusetts and New York delegates, their instructions were much narrower than the instructions of their colleagues from the other ten attending states forcing the Massachusetts and New York delegates to limit their activities. Delaware's delegates were prohibited in their instructions from voting in favor of any reduction in Delaware's stature through elimination of the unit voting, or single vote per state.

Prior to the establishment of the Republic, the colonies held numerous and frequent intercolonial conventions and conferences. A process developed whereby the colonies and their successor states selected and instructed delegates. Even today, the States regularly hold interstate conventions requiring the selection of representatives for compacts and specific issue authorities.

---

[103] U.S. Dept. of Justice, "Report to the Attorney General: Limited Constitutional Conventions Under Article V of the United States Constitution," Office of Legal Policy, at 48 (10 Sept. 1987)

[104] As an example, in 2013, Indiana passed Acts 224 and 225 that criminalized deviation from the instructions of the Indiana state legislature by Article V Convention delegates representing Indiana.

[105] Delegates to the 1787 Grand Convention were typically called "deputies" or "commissioners."

[106] For a complete list and text of all the delegate instructions from the twelve attending states and the documentary explanation of non-attendance by Rhode Island, go to the University of Wisconsin-Madison Department of History, Center for the Study of the American Constitution website located at: http://history.wisc.edu/csac/documentary_resources/delegate_instructions.htm

21.

How many delegates are chosen from each state?

The States choose their own delegations, including the number of delegates. During the many debates in Congress in the 1970s and 1980s on AVC procedures and rules, the subject of delegate apportionment was discussed. The suggestion was made to apportion the delegates equivalently to each state's Electoral College representation.[107] This formula failed to respect that at the 1787 Philadelphia Convention, each state had a singular vote despite variation in the number of delegates in their respective delegations.[108] Article V gives equal weight to each state regardless of the number of delegates in that state's delegation. Federalism is the exercise of an equality among the States.

The representation of the States participating in the 1787 Philadelphia convention varied in number although each state enjoyed a single collective vote per state delegation. New Hampshire sent the least number of just two delegates while Pennsylvania sent the most with eight delegates.[109] Equal representation in the form of the one-state, one-vote formulation is the only measure by which the large states cannot dominate the smaller states. In an AVC, the States are coming together to meet as equals; proportional representation among the States would destabilize the convention. This principle of equality among the States was so important to the Framers that it was carried over into the design of the US Senate.

During the 1850 interstate Nashville Convention, Tennessee sent 101 delegates whereas the rest of the nine attending states sent only seventy-five in total. The convention's officers wisely decided to uphold the time-honored convention rule of one-state, one-vote lest Tennessee dominate the convention. In most cases, the state legislatures had selected the delegates to the Nashville Convention.[110]

---

[107] For example: S.1272, Section 7, 93rd Congress, Federal Constitutional Convention Procedures Act of 1973 (not passed) and S.2812, Section 7, 98th Congress, Federal Constitutional Convention Procedures Act of 1984 (not passed) and others not listed here. These bills, all reintroductions of the previous session's bill, are often referred to as "the Ervin Bill." See: Sam Ervin, Jr., "Proposed Legislation to Implement the Convention Method of Amending the Constitution," *Michigan Law Review* 66, no.5 (March 1967-8)

[108] Congressional Research Service Report R42592, *The Article V Convention for Proposing Constitutional Amendments: Historical Perspectives for Congress,* (10 July 2012): 30

[109] Max Farrand, *The Records of the Federal Convention of 1787, Vol. III* (New Haven: Yale University Press, 1911 rev. 1937), 255

[110] http://tennesseeencyclopedia.net/entry.php?rec=968 Accessed 29 August 2014

If the States provide delegations in proportion to their populations or to the size of their congressional delegations, then the larger states are the only ones that need bother to send a delegation as the dozen or so smallest states will have virtually no voice in the convention. Once the larger states become aware of the disproportionate power that they would possess in just such a structured convention, we would genuinely be treated to a display of an actual runaway convention.

22.

On what basis are the delegates chosen?

Each state sets its own requirements for delegates. The pattern set by the Philadelphia Convention of 1787 would probably be followed by the modern state legislatures.[111] It is conceivable that the States will select their delegates according to criteria that the individual state legislature judges to be critical to representing the state. Such criteria may include a legal, judicial or parliamentary background, business experience, an academic or scholarly background or even an activist background. The most likely scenario is that non-legislator delegates would be elected for their familiarity with the specific issue(s) slated to be addressed in the AVC.

In some instances, states have already addressed the selection or election of delegates and codified it. Professors Paul Weber and Barbara Perry contrasted the experience of the States in their 1989 book, *Unfounded Fears: Myths and Realities of a Constitutional Convention:* The Illinois state constitution spells out the qualifications and limitations for a delegate to a state constitutional convention,[112] including a prohibition on a delegate holding any elected office at any level of government.[113] Arkansas took the opposite position and allows for elected officials at all levels to be delegates.[114] The position of Arkansas would appear to mirror that of the 1787 Philadelphia Convention as twenty-one of the fifty-five

---

[111] James K. Rogers, "The Other Way To Amend The Constitution: The Article V Constitutional Convention Amendment Process," *Harvard Journal of Law & Public Policy* 30, no.3 (2007): 1015

[112] Illinois state constitution, Article XIV, § 1

[113] Paul J. Weber & Barbara A. Perry, *Unfounded Fears: Myths and Realities of a Constitutional Convention* (New York: Praeger, 1989), 89

[114] Testimony of US Senator David Pryor of Arkansas before the Senate Judiciary Committee's Subcommittee on the Constitution: U.S. Congress, Senate Committee on the Judiciary, *Constitutional Convention Procedures, Hearing before the Subcommittee on the Constitution on S.3, S.520, and S.1710.* 96th Cong., 1st sess., at 43 (1979)

attending delegates were past or current members of the Continental and Confederation Congresses.[115] Today, this may run afoul of the prohibition in the Constitution on federal officials serving in more than one federal role.[116] The distinction lay in the definition of an "Office under the Authority of the United States." An office created under the authority granted in Article II for appointive positions may not be applicable to the Article I prohibition.[117] A pair of nineteenth century Supreme Court decisions might apply in this instance.[118]

23.

Could delegates be selected by quotas for race, gender, ethnicity, political party, sexual orientation or other designation?

No, the Equal Protection Clause of the Fourteenth Amendment would probably be construed to prohibit such discrimination. The States would determine the method of selecting their respective delegates without consideration of such physical or ideological attributes.[119] Selecting delegates on any basis of physical or ideological attributes would endow too much power in special interest groups. However, it is highly probable that the majority party holding power in any given state will exercise some degree of influence to ensure that they are given the lion's share of representation on a convention delegation.

24.

Would members of Congress or the state legislatures be eligible to be delegates?

Whether members of Congress may be delegates of the AVC has been a point of debate for decades. The Constitution contains a prohibition in Article I, Section 6, Clause 2 on Senators and Representatives holding any other federal office while serving in the Congress.[120] The US Supreme Court's 1922 decision in *Leser v. Garnett*

---

[115] Paul J. Weber & Barbara A. Perry, *Unfounded Fears: Myths and Realities of a Constitutional Convention* (New York: Praeger, 1989), 90

[116] United States Constitution, Article I, § 6, Cl. 2

[117] Douglas G. Voegler, "Amending the Constitution by the Article V Convention Method," *North Dakota Law Review* 55 (1979): 383

[118] *United States v. Smith*, 124 U.S. 525 (1888) and *United States v. Germaine*, 99 U.S. 508 (1878)

[119] United States Constitution, Amendment XIV

[120] United States Constitution, Article I, § 6, Cl. 2

held that an AVC is a "federal function" although carried out by the States.[121] This finding means that the Article I, Section 6 prohibition on congressional members serving as delegates will probably be observed and could be sustained in a possible court challenge. This prohibition was cited as a potential source of conflict during the 1993 US House Judiciary Committee's hearings on the AVC.[122] Others have made the case that members of Congress would bring a unique perspective to the debate and discussion of proposed amendments.[123] State legislators would be eligible and would be well versed in the parliamentary procedure that would govern the operation of the convention. Inevitably, the rules and procedures formulated by the AVC Rules Committee, such as have been discussed at the Assembly of State Legislatures[124] and in the future scheduled meetings, would determine the eligibility of elected officials. In some states, the legislatures are passing bills which require that state legislators serve as delegates for their state.[125]

There is a discernible downside to the involvement of elected officials at both the state and federal levels. Their knowledge of political strategy and their political acumen could prove decisive in steering the convention toward predetermined goals that may not necessarily concur with the objectives of the people. As an example, in 1967, the State of New York conducted a state constitutional convention; all of the majority and minority positions were held by, at that time, current state legislators. The convention failed to meet its goals. The problem may be one of experience vs. influence.[126]

25.

Could the delegates be elected, and if so, would they be able to collect campaign donations?

Some states have made provisions for electing delegates. Most

---

[121] http://supreme.justia.com/cases/federal/us/258/130/case.html Leser v. Garnett 258 U.S. 130 (1922)
[122] U.S. Congress, House Committee on the Judiciary, *Is There a Constitutional Convention in Our Future?* 103rd Cong., 1st sess., committee print, serial no. 1, at 20 (Washington, D.C.: GPO, 1993)
[123] Morris B. Forkosch, "The Alternative Amending Clause in Article V: Reflections and Suggestions," *Minnesota Law Review* 51, no.6 (1967): 1073 - Forkosch suggests that federal judges would also be eligible but he recommends against it.
[124] In June of 2014, the Mount Vernon Assembly changed its name to The Assembly of State Legislatures.
[125] In 2014, the Wisconsin Legislature took up AB635 that concerned the selection and powers of delegates to an AVC, the bill required that any delegates be members of the Wisconsin state legislature.
[126] Morris B. Forkosch, "The Alternative Amending Clause in Article V: Reflections and Suggestions," *Minnesota Law Review* 51, no.6 (1967): 1073, n.81

likely, the answer to this question will vary by state. It would seem reasonable that candidates for the position of an AVC delegate would need funds to run for the office. At least three possibilities exist for potential financing of the candidates' races: first, the candidates could self-fund, second, they could collect campaign donations within the existing campaign finance laws of their respective state, and third, the state provides fixed funding for the candidates' campaigns.

Undoubtedly, the candidates would be subject to the same stringent rules as other candidates for elected office. They would need to report their contributions and expenses so that the public can monitor if the candidates for convention delegate are under the influence of any special interests.

26.

Would the delegates be paid for their service?

That issue would most likely be left to the States unless Congress were to pass specific legislation prior to the AVC taking place. This also prompts the question of whether the States or the federal government would be responsible for the payment of the delegates' wages or stipends. As a corollary, the expenses of the delegates would need to be paid and the responsibility for that payment is still an open issue. The legislator members of the Assembly of State Legislatures have personally funded their own expenses treating the Assembly as an extra-curricular activity.[127] The Assembly also collects donations for self-financing through its website.[128]

A strong argument can be made for avoiding federal funding of the States' delegates as they would possibly be exposed to undue economic influence from federal special interests. Optimally, individual, independent funding would be preferred but the cost may prove difficult to absorb for many delegates and the shortfall would leave them looking for assistance that may only come from questionable special interest sources. That leaves the States as the best, most acceptable source of compensation for the expenses of the delegates.

---

[127] http://www.abc2news.com/homepage-showcase/state-delegates-meet-at-washingtons home to explore article-v-convention

[128] http://www.theassemblyofstatelegislatures.org/contribute.html

27.

Who selects the officers of the AVC?

The delegates historically select from among themselves who will be the officers of the convention as well as the positions and duties of the officers. This practice extends back through the hundreds of state and national conventions held since the Colonial Era.[129] During the congressional hearings in the 1990s on the bills to regulate an AVC, the suggestion was made that the US Vice-President should chair the convention – this is problematic, as any Article V convention would be most likely called due to a lack of response by Congress and the administration to the needs of the people and the nation. Placing a member of the executive branch in charge would probably be viewed as the proverbial "fox guarding the hen house" even temporarily.

28.

How is the Chair of the AVC determined?

Like any other convention, the chair is typically elected by the delegates very early in the process. Most likely is that a temporary chair, whose sole responsibility is the oversight of the election of the convention officers, would be selected, perhaps from the hosting state, and that chair would then conduct the election process for the permanent officers.

29.

Can the AVC pass/ratify amendments?

No, the convention is strictly for the purpose of proposing, debating and forwarding the proposed amendments to the Congress for referral to the States for ratification. The function of the convention is analogous to that of Congress proposing and considering an amendment. Article V grants the power of ratification to either the state legislatures or state ratifying conventions as stipulated by Congress. The States are always the final arbiters of whether to amend our Constitution.[130]

---

[129] Roger Sherman Hoar, *Constitutional Conventions – Their Nature, Powers, and Limitations* (Boston: Little, Brown, 1917), 184

[130] Michael Almond, "Amendment by Convention: Our Next Constitutional Crisis?," *North Carolina Law Review* 53, no.3 (February 1975): 507

30.

Once the subject matter specified in the "call" from Congress has been addressed by the convention, may the AVC take up other business not mentioned in the applications of the States?

No, the call issued by Congress will reflect the subject matter of the applications of the States and thereby set the agenda (and the limitations thereof) for the convention. When the convention does convene, the Rules Committee will be established and they will set the formal agenda and rules for conducting the convention. When the agenda is fulfilled, the convention will end and no further actions may be undertaken – the Supreme Court addressed this particular issue in *United States ex rel. Widenmann v. Colby* in 1920.[131] It is for exactly this reason that many states are passing legislation to control their delegates to prevent a "runaway." As yet another safeguard, the States are acting to limit the authority of the delegates to only the business named in the call issued from Congress.

31.

Can an AVC be limited to a single topic or proposed amendment subject?

Yes. Each state submits an application to Congress for the Article V convention. When two-thirds of the States (currently thirty-four states) submit applications, Congress must call a convention for the express purpose of the applications. If thirty-four states submit applications calling for a convention for the explicit purpose of proposing and debating, for example, a balanced budget amendment, then the convention's business is limited to that particular business.[132] The North Carolina Supreme Court ruled in the *In Re Opinion of the Justices* decision in 1933 that an amendatory convention may be limited.[133] The Philadelphia Convention of 1787 discussed and concluded that a "single proposition" was acceptable.[134]

This particular subject has been debated by scholars and pundits

---

[131] *United States ex rel. Widenmann v. Colby* 265 F. 998 (D.C. Cir. 1920) affirmed as 257 U.S. 619 (1921).
[132] Robert G. Natelson, *Amending the Constitution by Convention: A Complete View of the Founders' Plan*, Goldwater Institute Policy Report No. 241, (Phoenix, AZ: Goldwater Institute, Sept. 2010)
[133] *In Re Opinion of the Justices* 204 N.C. 306, 172 S.E. 474 (1933)
[134] Alexander Hamilton, "Federalist Paper No. 85," in *The Federalist Papers: Hamilton, Madison, Jay*, ed. Clinton Rossiter (New York: Mentor, 1961), 525

for some time and remains a major point of contention even today as opponents of an AVC frequently claim that an AVC is "uncontrollable" and will runaway because there is no control over the agenda. They claim that all AVCs are open conventions. This position ignores over a century and a half of jurisprudence dating to the first case dealing with a single issue convention going back to 1855 and the US Supreme Court's *Dodge v. Woolsey* decision.[135]

One must remember that every single amendment added to the Constitution after the Bill of Rights was a "single proposition" and "brought forward singly" by Congress.[136] Every amendment after the Bill of Rights that was not successfully ratified was also "brought forward singly."

32.

Is the topic specified in the States' applications binding on the convention?

To a certain point, the convention is limited to the topic(s) specified by the States, but to be more precise, the convention is limited by the topic(s) in the call issued by the Congress. The States set the scope of the convention and Congress administers the call and the setting of the date and the place of the convention. The Senate Judiciary Committee examined this question in 1972 and concluded that failing to establish limits on the subject topic of a convention "would be inconsistent with the purpose of Article V and, indeed, would destroy the possibility of the use of the convention method of proposing amendments." Since the Committee had already found that the convention could be either for a specific topic or open, and the States must be able to select either at will, the inability to bind the convention to a specific requested topic(s) would expose the convention to the risk of a general open convention. If any off-topic proposals for amendments were suggested, the Committee believed these would be unconstitutional and that the convention would be under no obligation to consider the proposal.[137]

---

[135] http://caselaw.lp.findlaw.com/scripts/getcase.pl?court=US&vol=59&invol=331 Dodge v. Woolsey 59 U.S. 331 (1855)

[136] Alexander Hamilton, "Federalist Paper No. 85," in *The Federalist Papers: Hamilton, Madison, Jay*, ed. Clinton Rossiter (New York: Mentor, 1961), 525

[137] Wilbur Edel, *A Constitutional Convention – Threat or Challenge?* (New York: Praeger, 1981), 131

33.

What happens if a delegate proposes an amendment addressing an unauthorized issue or topic?

The AVC's officers would be within their authority to prohibit further discussion on the issue and could ban any additional mention of the issue. Since the AVC creates its own rules and regulates its own members, it will be up to the AVC to police itself. It is highly probable that the officers will be very cognizant of their duties and of the impact of their actions. They would be well aware that the outcome will be heavily scrutinized by the media and the public as well as the state and federal governments. Doing the right thing would be paramount as the reputations and careers of the officers and delegates will be on the line. In our day and age of instantaneous electronic communications by multiple methods of media, it has become nearly impossible to hide a politician's transgressions from the public that they have taken an oath to serve.

A pseudo historical example can be given: during the 1861 Peace Conference in Washington, D.C., - our closest historical approximation to an actual federal AVC - a delegate attempted to introduce a new debate topic and proposed amendment to the conference. The other 132 delegates shouted down the offender and threatened him with expulsion from the conference. The topic was not breached again and the conference returned to focusing exclusively on the matter with which they were tasked.[138]

Congress' Role in an AVC

34.

What role, if any, does Congress play in an AVC?

Congress was given a very limited role. They collect the applications from the States and compile them. Until 2015, there was no official rule as to who must tally the count of applications. Until that time, the applications accumulated without anyone maintaining a count.[139] The President of the US Senate and the Speaker of the US House of Representatives had typically received the applications and

---

[138] Robert Gunderson, *The Old Gentlemen's Convention* (Madison: University of Wisconsin Press, 1961), generally
[139] U.S. Congress, House, Committee on the Judiciary, *Is There a Constitutional Convention in Our Future?* 103rd Cong., 1st sess., committee print, serial no. 1, at 12 (Washington, D.C.: GPO, 1993)

would have advised the leadership when the requisite thirty-four states had applied for a convention.[140] The Speaker of the House and the Senate President then forwarded the applications to the Clerk of the House of Representatives and/or the Secretary of the Senate respectively for recording and publication. Beginning in 2015, the rules have changed and the States' applications are now forwarded to the chairman of the House Judiciary Committee which maintains an internet webpage that displays the pending the applications.[141]

The applications are called "memorials" in the Congress.[142] These memorials are assigned a number and the full text is printed in the Senate *Record*[143] and the House *Congressional Record*.[144] Congress MUST issue a "call" to a convention when the two-thirds of the States number is reached – they have no discretion on this point. Congress selects the date on which the convention begins and the location of the convention. Finally, Congress stipulates the method of ratification of any proposed amendments.[145] Per Article V of the Constitution, either state legislatures or state ratification conventions are held to vote on the ratification of the proposed amendments. Congress has, over the years, claimed powers and responsibilities that include: receiving, judging and recording applications; establishing procedures to summon a convention; setting the time allotted to deliberations; determining the number and selection of delegates; setting internal convention procedures and the transmission

---

[140] A congressional attempt to set rules for an AVC included the establishment of which Congressional officers are to receive and tally the memorials. Senate bill S.40, introduced by Senator Orrin Hatch of Utah in the 99th Congress in 1985 as the "Constitutional Convention Implementation Act of 1985", included in Section 6 the requirement that the Secretary of the Senate and the Clerk of the House of Representatives be the official recipients and maintainers of the records of memorials for state applications for an Article V convention. The bill was read twice and the referred to the Senate Judiciary Committee where hearings were held and then the bill died. The bill stipulated that any state which made an application for an AVC was to submit two copies of the state resolution, one to the Speaker of the US House of Representatives and one to the President of the US Senate. A number of requirements were enumerated as to what was to be included in the state submittal package including, for example, a complete listing of all prior other states' applications currently in effect with regard to the same specific subject matter to be addressed in the AVC so that the submitting state's application would be correctly counted toward to official tally. Although S.40 did not pass, the practice of listing, within a given state's application, all other states' applications on the same subject matter has been taken up by the States as a standard practice to assure a correct on-going tally.

[141] US House Rule 12 (3)(c)

[142] Congressional Research Service Report R42592, *The Article V Convention for Proposing Constitutional Amendments: Historical Perspectives for Congress*, (10 July 2012): 28

[143] http://rules.senate.gov/public/index.cfm?=RuleVII Standing Rules of the United States Senate, Rule VII, paragraph 1

[144] http://www.rules.house.gov/singlepages.aspx?NewsID=133&rsbd=165 Rules of the House of Representatives, Rule XII, clause 3

[145] Congressional Research Service Report R42592, *The Article V Convention for Proposing Constitutional Amendments: Historical Perspectives for Congress*, (10 July 2012): 22

of proposed amendments to the state legislatures. The validity of these congressional claims to power remains very much in question.[146]

During the late 1970s and into the 1990s, forty-one separate bills were introduced in Congress for the purpose of defining and codifying the AVC process.[147,148] Many of these bills were sponsored by Sen. Sam Ervin of North Carolina and then Sen. Orrin Hatch of Utah. Hearings were held on the bills which generated much testimony that is useful today as a method of cataloging the debate among academics regarding the role of the Congress and the federal government in controlling and directing an AVC. Not one of the forty-one bills was passed. To change the process of an AVC, as it was understood from the writings of the period of drafting and ratification of the US Constitution in the 1780s, would require amending Article V of the US Constitution.

35.

Does Congress control an AVC?

No, Congress is more of a "processor" of the applications. Its role is "ministerial" and not legislative.[149] They have no input on the material discussed. They do not set the rules or the agenda except to specify in the call that subject which the States have selected for the AVC in their applications to Congress.[150] The duty of Congress to call a convention is similar to that of an elections board having to call an election to put a measure on a ballot or of Congress to reapportion after the census.[151] Constitutional scholar James Kenneth Rogers put it best, "The original purpose of Article V was to give states the power to circumvent a recalcitrant or corrupt Congress. It thus makes little sense for it to give Congress broad power to control a convention."[152] Further, some aspects of the process have been claimed by Congress through the Supreme Court's establishment of the "political question doctrine" but as Rogers

---

[146] Ibid., 1
[147] Search for bills including the words "constitutional convention procedures" at: http://beta.congress.gov/
[148] Congressional Research Service Report R42589, *The Article V Convention to Propose Constitutional Amendments: Contemporary Issues for Congress,* (11 April 2014): 36
[149] Bruce M. Van Sickle & Lynn M. Boughey, "A Lawful and Peaceful Revolution, Article V and Congress's Present Duty to Call a Convention for Proposing Amendments," *Hamline Law Review* 1 (1990): 41
[150] Congressional Research Service Report R42592, *The Article V Convention for Proposing Constitutional Amendments: Historical Perspectives for Congress,* (11 April 2014): 20
[151] Wayne B. Wheeler, "Is a Constitutional Convention Impending?," *Illinois Law Review* 21 (1927): 790-2
[152] James K. Rogers, "The Other Way To Amend The Constitution: The Article V Constitutional Convention Amendment Process," *Harvard Journal of Law & Public Policy* 30, no.3 (2007): 1011

notes, "Even assuming the validity of the political question doctrine, however, Congress still lacks authority over the convention process [Citing the SCOTUS six part test for the political question doctrine].[153] But, the political question doctrine does not apply to congressional control of a convention because it fails the first part of the test: the issue has not been constitutionally committed to Congress, but to the States [to make the application and to supply the delegates.]"[154]

36.

Can Congress prevent or refuse an AVC amend-con?

No, the Supreme Court has ruled in four separate cases that Congress cannot refuse the States' demand for a convention.[155] In the event that Congress refuses to call the amendatory convention, the States have at least one, and possibly two, options: they can sue in the Federal Courts, and if necessary, the US Supreme Court as the court of original jurisdiction[156] using a number of legal means, or they may try to simply convene the convention on their own. The problem lies in enforcement; what mechanism is there for compelling the Congress to act to call a convention? This point has been debated by constitutional scholars.[157,158] The debate in the Philadelphia Convention included discussion on whether the Congress could refuse to call an AVC. Professor James Kenneth Rogers states that, "In the face of congressional inaction, the States could circumvent the national legislature to propose needed amendments."[159] The Supreme Court has the power to issue a declaratory judgment, uphold a writ of mandamus to an officer of Congress or an

---

[153] http://www.law.cornell.edu/wex/baker_v._carr_1962 Baker v. Carr 369 U.S. 186, 82 S. Ct. 691, 7 L. Ed. 2d 663 (1962)

[154] James K. Rogers, "The Other Way To Amend The Constitution: The Article V Constitutional Convention Amendment Process," *Harvard Journal of Law & Public Policy* 30, no.3 (2007): 1014

[155] See http://supreme.justia.com/cases/federal/us/282/716/ United States v. Sprague 282 U.S. 716 (1931); http://supreme.justia.com/cases/federal/us/256/368/case.html Dillon v. Gloss 256 U.S. 368 375 (1921); http://supreme.justia.com/cases/federal/us/253/221/ Hawke v. Smith No. 1 253 U.S. 221 (1920) and http://caselaw.lp.findlaw.com/scripts/getcase.pl?court=US&vol=59&invol=331 Dodge v. Woolsey 59 U.S. 331 (1855)

[156] United States Constitution, Article III, § 2: If a state is a party to a suit, then the Supreme Court may have original jurisdiction under the Constitution. The States may elect to begin pursuit in the U.S. district courts under 28 U.S.C. § 1331 and 28 U.S.C. § 1361

[157] Wayne B. Wheeler, "Is a Constitutional Convention Impending?," *Illinois Law Review* 21 (1927): 790-2

[158] Cyril Brickfield, House, Committee on Judiciary, 85th Cong. 1st sess., *Problems Relating to a Federal Constitutional Convention* (Washington, D.C.: Government Printing Office, 1957): 27

[159] James K. Rogers, "The Other Way To Amend The Constitution: The Article V Constitutional Convention Amendment Process," *Harvard Journal of Law & Public Policy* 30, no.3 (2007): 1015

injunction from a lower court among other options.[160]

Should Congress refuse to call a convention, an appropriate course of action could be to file a suit in the District of Columbia Court asking the Court to issue a writ of mandamus to one of the non-elected officers of Congress to compel the Congress to fulfill its positive duty to call the Article V amendatory convention.[161] There are numerous federal and Supreme Court precedents to justify such an action. Whether or not the D.C. Court issues the writ, the resulting decision could be appealed directly to the US Supreme Court for enforcement.[162]

There are also precedents for forcing Congress to fulfill its duties when they are reluctant to do so. In 1910, the D.C. Court ordered the Congress' *Joint Committee on Printing* to perform its duty in the case of *Valley Paper Company v. Smoot, et al.*[163] when the committee refused to carry out its duty according to the law.[164] This is significant as we have a firm precedent of a part of Congress being ordered to carry out a legal, <u>ministerial</u> duty in the same manner as they must call a convention.

> *"The major difference is that Congress has discretionary power over its own initiation of amendments but only a ministerial duty with respect to calling a convention when two-thirds of the States apply. While a court might understandably refrain from second guessing Congress' exercise of its discretionary power, it might feel obliged to review Congress' performance or non-performance of a ministerial duty."*[165]

37.

Even if an AVC is convened, can Congress just bypass the convention by passing its own proposed amendment and sending it to the States?

In a way, this has happened. As the States got within one state

---

[160] *Powell v. McCormick*, 395 U.S. 486 (1969); *Roberts v. U.S. ex rel. Valentine*, 176 U.S. 221, 232 (1900); *Cooper v. Aaron*, 358 U.S. 1 (1958)

[161] It has been settled law since the *Kendall v. US*, 12 Peters 524, decision in 1838 that those courts have jurisdiction to issue the writ of mandamus.

[162] Additional precedents are found in: *Board of Liquidation v. McComb*, 92 U.S. 531 (1875); *Garfield v. Goldsby*, 211 U.S. 249 (1908); *Noble v. Union River Logging R.R.*, 147 U.S. 165 (1893)

[163] *Valley Paper Company v. Smoot, et al.*, 38 Wash. L. R. 171 or D.C. Sup. Ct. (28 Feb. 1910); Congressional Edition, Vol. 5834

[164] Walter K. Tuller, "A Convention to Amend the Constitution. Why Needed. How It May Be Obtained.," *North American Review* 193, no. 664 (1911), generally and specifically, 380-3

[165] James E. Bond, David E. Engdahl and Henry N. Butler, *The Constitutional Convention* (Washington, D.C.: National Legal Center for the Public Interest, 1987), 5-6

of having enough to call an AVC, the Senate decided to pass the bill that eventually became the Seventeenth Amendment in 1912. With the convention looming, the bill posed a threat to the Senate's power and after refusing to take up the bill – which the House of Representatives had passed at least five times – the Senate successfully circumvented a convention by passing an amendment bill. When the balanced budget amendment campaign got within two states of calling a convention in the 1980s, Congress once again reacted due to the prodding effect and passed the Gramm-Hollings-Rudman bill.

The most likely scenario is that Congress would recognize that the convention is inevitable and quickly pass a proposed amendment resolution before taking up the response to the States' petitions. If however, the Congress had already made the convention call but the AVC had not yet convened, the Congress might still pass and promulgate a proposed amendment.[166]

It is conceivable that a convention, once convened, may be faced with just such a scenario. In that event, the reasonable assumption is that each proposal could be considered by the States. In all of these situations, it would appear that the States would still make the final decision as to which amendment, if either, to accept.

38.

Who decides where and when the AVC meets?

Congress is granted the power to call an Article V convention. It is considered an implied power that Congress may then determine the location and starting date of the convention.[167] This cannot be considered a version of the Necessary and Proper Clause for Article V.[168] To successfully call an AVC, and to avoid argument over the "where and when" of a convention, which would unnecessarily delay and potentially derail the AVC, some singular authority must set the events in motion by announcing the location and starting date. It is logical that since Congress is constitutionally required to call the convention, it must be able to specify the place and date of the convention as part of the call.

---

[166] Wilbur Edel, *A Constitutional Convention – Threat or Challenge?* (New York: Praeger, 1981), 55

[167] United States Constitution, Article V

[168] http://www.law.cornell.edu/supremecourt/text/17/316 McCulloch v. Maryland 17 U.S. 316, 4 Wheat. 316, 4 L. Ed. 579 (1819), specifically on p. 319: "Any means which tend directly to the execution of constitutional powers of the government are in themselves constitutional."

39.

Does Congress have to call an AVC if the applications are received from two-thirds of the States?

Yes, the wording of Article V makes clear it that the call is **mandatory**; Congress has a duty to call an AVC and therefore has no choice in the matter. The article reads, "...on the Application of the Legislatures of two thirds of the several States, [Congress] *shall* call a Convention for proposing Amendments..."[169] Alexander Hamilton noted that, "the Congress will be obliged... to call a convention for proposing amendments...The words of this article are *peremptory*...Nothing in this particular is left to discretion."[170]

The Congress conceded this point during the 1972 Senate Judiciary hearings on the proposed rules bill. The Committee acknowledged that although they believed that neither the courts nor legislation could compel Congress to act, it was "inconceivable that Congress would refuse to perform its duty" since that duty was required by their oaths of office.[171] We must hope that today's Congress would recognize the same commitment to duty.

40.

When does Congress have to call an AVC?

Traditionally, as soon as the chairman of the House of Representatives Judiciary Committee notifies the House leadership that the States have met the two-thirds, or thirty-four, of the States threshold, Congress is obligated to set a date and a location and to notify the state legislatures.[172] The question of how long into the future the date may be set is unknown. If Congress is resistant, the issue may be settled by the US Supreme Court. Due to the lack of a precedent, the AVC process has never reached the stage where Congress has had to call a convention and therefore consider how far into the future to set the date. Several factors will influence this decision.

---

[169] United States Constitution, Article V

[170] Alexander Hamilton, "The Federalist No. 85," in *The Federalist Papers: Hamilton, Madison, Jay*, ed., Clinton Rossiter (New York: Mentor, 1961), 526

[171] Wilbur Edel, *A Constitutional Convention - Threat or Challenge?* (New York: Praeger, 1981), 102-3

[172] Congressional Research Service Report R42589, *The Article V Convention to Propose Constitutional Amendments: Contemporary Issues for Congress*, (11 April 2014): 18-20

First, Congress will probably want to determine if the requisite number of applications has truly been received, that is, that all thirty-four are valid. They may seek to verify that each is asking for the same thing, i.e., a limited convention to deal with topic X. While this process is going on, Congress may be proceeding with the debate and proposal of their own amendment. But that will not stop the convention from progressing as Congress is obligated to call the convention.[173]

A location must be selected and booked. Accommodations for the delegates and support staff must be secured. A budget must be developed and overseen. The convention delegates will need to reference numerous government documents and resources in order to complete their business.[174] The Library of Congress, the National Archives and Records Administration, the Congressional Research Service, the Federal Judicial Center and many other government repositories will be called upon to produce necessary documentation in the form of charters, court records, congressional records, convention histories and other sources of information. The various federal agencies, bureaus, commissions, administrations, departments and offices will need to be directed to provide timely and accurate information to the AVC. These actions may require either an executive order or the passage by Congress of an enabling act to direct federal agencies to place their respective resources to be at the disposal of the AVC. Federal lawyers (especially constitutional lawyers) will need to be dispatched to the convention to be available for consultation by the delegates.

Much of the "housekeeping" duties can be performed by the General Services Administration. These actions were discussed and recommendations made during the 1972 Senate hearings on the proposed convention bills.[175]

Several of the States will need to pass legislation for the selection of their delegates and for specifying the delegates' instructions. The state legislatures will need to convene to discuss and settle on their instructions to their delegates. The delegates will need to be chosen. The location venue will need preparation. All of these actions, and more,

---

[173] William T. Barker, "A Status Report on the 'Balanced Budget' Constitutional Convention," *John Marshall Law Review* 20 (1986): 35

[174] Paul J. Weber & Barbara A. Perry, *Unfounded Fears: Myths and Realities of a Constitutional Convention* (New York: Praeger, 1989), 98-9

[175] Wilbur Edel, *A Constitutional Convention - Threat or Challenge?* (New York: Praeger, 1981), 111

will require time to prepare, meaning that the convention may not be scheduled for at least a year between the congressional call and the actual convening of the AVC delegates. During the hearings on the proposed rules bills in the 1970s, it was acceded that Congress has an obligation to call a convention and that it should do so as quickly as is possible. The bills that Sen. Sam Ervin submitted allowed for "not later than one year after adoption of the [concurrent] resolution" for the date of convening the convention.[176]

41.

Is the Congress required to forward the proposed amendments from the AVC to the States for consideration of ratification?

Between the 1970s and the 1990s, Congress considered many bills that were introduced for the purpose of establishing the procedures of an AVC.[177] Included in the debate of these bills, was discussion as to whether Congress was obligated to forward any or all proposed amendments to the States. Initially, Congress claimed the right to reject any amendment that Congress believed was outside of the scope of the limited AVC.[178] Subsequent legislation included verbiage that recognized that Congress did not have discretion to reject an amendment for any reason beyond that of confirming that a proposed amendment was within the mandate of the convention. Also, it is acknowledged that the States could bring suit on the Congress for failing to refer the proposed amendments to the States for ratification consideration. Lastly, the legislation proposed the added timeframe of thirty days by Congress to call a convention or to forward the proposed amendments.[179] None of this legislation was successful…leaving the questions unanswered.

One of the issues that Congress believed should be under its purview was the determination of whether a proposed amendment was constitutional. The US Supreme Court holds that the Court alone has the authority and duty to evaluate the constitutionality of any

---

[176] Ibid., 104

[177] Congressional Research Service Report R42589, *The Article V Convention to Propose Constitutional Amendments: Contemporary Issues for Congress,* (11 April 2014): 36

[178] Sam Ervin, Jr., "Proposed Legislation to Implement the Convention Method of Amending the Constitution," *Michigan Law Review* 66, no.5 (March 1967-8). 882

[179] See S. 119, Section 15, 98th Cong., Constitutional Convention Implementation Act of 1984 or S. 214, Section 11(c), 102nd Cong., Constitutional Convention Implementation Act of 1991

amendment.[180]

42.

What compels the Congress to act on setting the method of ratification and promulgating the amendment(s) to the States?

The Supreme Court has ruled in the past that Congress has no choice in the matter of Article V conventions.[181] The debates in the 1787 convention covered this possibility and concluded that Congress, like the call upon receiving sufficient applications from the States, "shall" promulgate the proposed amendments on to the States.[182] As the fundamental law of the land, the Constitution ranks highest in the legal hierarchy; when the Constitution says "shall," it means "must."

43.

Could Congress delay promulgating the proposed amendment(s) indefinitely?

No, although it appears that there is no legal precedent to cite, the US Supreme Court would probably find this issue outside the political question doctrine and therefore justiciable. The Court would undoubtedly view such congressional obstruction as an unconstitutional violation of Article V and an infringement on the rights of the States.

44.

Does the Congress have the power to veto or reject the proposed amendments?

Not necessarily, if it did, then the AVC would become nothing more than an auxiliary debating forum and an advisory council to the Congress. This type of arrangement was rejected in the 1787 Philadelphia Convention.[183] Ultimately, the purpose of the Article V convention is to go around the Congress when it is not being responsive

---

[180] http://supreme.justia.com/cases/federal/us/291/217/ United States v. Chambers 291 U.S. 217 (1934)
[181] http://supreme.justia.com/cases/federal/us/282/716/ United States v. Sprague 282 U.S. 716 (1931)
[182] Merrill Jensen, et al., *The Documentary History of the Ratification of the Constitution, Vol. 5* (Madison: Wisconsin Historical Society Press, 1976), 678, 682
[183] Morris Forkosch, "The Alternative Amending Clause in Article V: Reflections and Suggestions," *Minnesota Law Review* 51, no.6 (1967): 1079

to the people and the States. All amendments must be ratified by the States – Congress does not get to choose what proposed amendments are acceptable from the AVC.[184] Constitutional scholars have argued that Congress should have the ability to reject unconstitutional proposed amendments. The issue lies in who determines that a proposed amendment is unconstitutional? Similarly, it has been suggested that any proposed amendment that was outside of the agenda of the AVC should also be rejected by Congress. If such an action should occur, it is a safe bet that an immediate challenge will be made in the US Supreme Court.

45.

Does Congress have to choose either method of ratification or give a reason for preferring one method over the other?

No, Congress has complete freedom to choose either method and no justification is required for the choice. The alternative state ratification convention method has been used only once – to ratify the Twenty-first Amendment to repeal the Eighteenth Amendment. Ironically, Congress chose the state ratification convention method for the Twenty-first Amendment because it feared that the state legislatures were too much "in the pocket" of the temperance/prohibition movement due to the movement's history of funding state legislature candidate campaigns. By using the ratification convention method, the will of the people was better reflected as the convention delegates were drawn from the general public more than from the state legislatures. In that instance, Congress went around the state legislatures! The choice of the two methods was included in Article V as a measure of checks and balances.[185]

46.

Could Congress decide to call an AVC without sufficient (or any) applications from the States?

It is highly improbable. Perhaps this could happen if Congress

---

[184] Gerald Gunther, "The Convention Method of Amending the United States Constitution," *Georgia Law Review* 14, no.1 (Fall 1979): 23

[185] http://www.gpo.gov/fdsys/pkg/GPO-CONAN-2002/pdf/GPO-CONAN-2002-8-6.pdf. U.S. Congress The Constitution of the United States, Analysis and Interpretation, (Washington, D.C.: Government Printing Office, 2004): 952

collectively sensed that it was best if the States handled a particular issue instead of the Congress and if there were enough applications for an open convention that could be applied to the count. It is highly improbable that Congress will ever take such an action as it would clearly diminish the authority and power of Congress. Congress might call an AVC if it wanted to hand off a political "hot potato" and not be held responsible for the result.

This scenario is not impossible, but is actually more likely than the scenario of Congress being forced into calling a convention. Under this scenario, Congress may choose to overlook imperfections or mistakes in applications from the States. Or Congress may choose to aggregate applications that it believes to be similar enough in a general way to group together. A realistic example could be that Congress decides after receiving, say twenty, applications from states that wish to address the issues of limiting corporate donations to candidates, regulation of superPACs, disclosure of donors to candidates, and activities of 501C3 and 501C4 organizations in issue advocacy, to aggregate these all together as "campaign finance reform." Realizing that no matter what tack Congress takes on this issue, no matter what legislation it proposes, some sizable segment of society will be enraged and call foul, Congress decides to "punt" and leave the issue to the States. Congress could then call an amendatory convention and stipulate the topic as a limited convention and thereby wash their hands of the messiness that always accompanies, as Bismarck noted, law and sausage making.[186]

Under this scenario, Congress could ignore the age and wording of the States' applications, could even ignore the rescissions of past applications. The wording of Article V makes this notion suspect in a textualist sense, but then would the States object to this opportunity?

There are constitutional scholars who disagree and state that what Article V says, Article V means, so no congressionally called convention without a request from two-thirds of the States is permissible.[187] They argue that the decision to call a convention is so important that it cannot and should not be left to a disinterested and minimally involved Congress. They make the point that the Framers intended the two-thirds requirement to foster careful deliberation and discussion on

---

[186] James E. Bond, David E. Engdahl and Henry N. Butler, *The Constitutional Convention* (Washington, D.C.: National Legal Center for the Public Interest, 1987), 8-10

[187] Charles L. Black, Jr., "The Proposed Amendment of Article V: A Threatened Disaster," *Yale Law Journal* 72 (1963): 963-4

the matter.[188] Another reason for the inability of Congress to call a convention lacking the requisite applications is that the ability to *decide* to call the convention is not an enumerated power but is an explicit power based on a conditional situation, that of the applications being submitted. Both Gouverneur Morris and Alexander Hamilton suggested at the 1787 convention that the Congress be allowed to call a convention at its pleasure, neither motion was adopted.[189]

47.

Could Congress pass legislation to take control of an AVC?

Congress attempted to do just that in between 1967 and the present. More than forty bills were introduced into Congress but none were passed. Hearings were held and testimony gathered. The academic view of today is much changed from the 1960s and 1970s; it is considered beyond the power of Congress to regulate a convention now by most legal scholars.

48.

How does Congress count the applications toward the necessary two-thirds of the States required for calling a convention?

If the goal of the States is to call a convention for addressing a single topic, then Congress will examine each state's application as to the topic. Congress will be looking for "consensus" in the subject matter. For example, if ten states submit applications for the topic of "limiting a senator to a maximum of two terms"; and twenty-one states submit applications for the purpose of discussing a proposed amendment to "restrict all elected congressional members, Senate and House to a maximum time of cumulative service to no more than twelve years" and three other states request in their applications that a convention be held to discuss "congressional term limits," then there is some room for debate as to whether the applications are all for the same subject matter. A strict view would be that there are at least two and possibly three topics among the thirty-four applications. A looser view would say that all thirty-four

---

[188] Arthur Earl Bonfield, "Proposing Constitutional Amendments by Convention: Some Problems," *Notre Dame Lawyer* 39, no.6 (Sept. 1964): 660-1

[189] Douglas G. Voegler, "Amending the Constitution by the Article V Convention Method," *North Dakota Law Review* 55 (1979): 366-7

applications deal with the issue of restricting time in Congress.[190]

If the States had the goal of securing an <u>open</u> convention, then they could simply ask for an open convention or not specify any topic. They run the risk of Congress refusing the request if no topic is given or of Congress insisting that *some* subject be given, even if that is just the phrase "open convention."

49.

Can the Congress force the States to act on a proposed amendment?

No, the States are free to decide whether they wish to take up the matter. Few amendments have been approved, or even voted on, by all states. Usually, once the requisite number of three-quarters of the States are reached, the rest do not take up the issue except as a matter of symbolism.[191]

States' Role in an AVC

50.

What exactly is an "application"?

The formal notice to the Congress by a state of the union of that state's desire for an amendatory convention is called an application. It has other names: memorial, memorialization, resolution and petition. The application should include phrasing that specifically states that the State of X is "applying" to the Congress to call a "convention for proposing Amendments" as that is the wording used in Article V. That wording makes explicit that the state wants a convention and is not just asking Congress to propose an amendment – as some states have done. The application should be directed to the attention of Congress and, in particular, the Clerk of the House and of the Senate. A copy should go to the Administrator of the General Services Administration and the Archivist of the United States and it must also be sent to the chairman of the House Judiciary Committee per statute.[192]

---

[190] James E. Bond, David E. Engdahl and Henry N. Butler, *A Constitutional Convention* (Washington, D.C.: National Legal Center for the Public Interest, 1987), 5

[191] Lester B. Orfield, "The Procedure of the Federal Amending Power," *Illinois Law Review* 25 (1930): 430

[192] 1 U.S.C. §106b (1985)

Ideally, the application should make clear whether the state is asking for a limited subject convention or an open, unlimited, general convention. If a limited subject convention is requested, it is highly advisable to state exactly what subject the state prefers to address in the convention. It is now considered a standard practice to name all other states that have a pending application for the same subject and to ask that the currently applying state's application be counted and aggregated with those named states. For example, if Kentucky is applying for a convention to address the subject of amending the Constitution with regard to establishing term limits for both houses of Congress, and the states of Idaho, Hawaii and Louisiana have already done so, then is it beneficial to name those three states as having already applied for a convention to amend the Constitution to term limit Congress and to count the Kentucky application with those three states.[193]

For the application to be valid, it must be signed by the proper leader of each chamber of the state legislature, typically the Speaker of the House and the Senate President. The Governor is not required to sign. Most often, the Secretary of State for the applying state would then formally submit the application to Congress. The vote must be recorded so that there is evidence of compliance with the state's own legislative rules – a voice vote will not normally suffice.[194]

51.

How specific must the state legislatures be in the wording of the application?

In order to assure that the chairman of the House of Representatives Judiciary Committee counts the States' applications correctly, it is recommended, but not required, that the applications share common wording. By using very specific language, the States get an exact count as to the number of applicants and no application can be ignored or discounted by the chairman.[195] Constitutionally, there is no mandate

---

[193] William T. Barker, "A Status Report on the "Balanced Budget" Constitutional Convention," *John Marshall Law Review* 20 (1986): 31-3

[194] In 1975, North Dakota applied for a convention regarding a balanced budget amendment. In their application the state legislature did not specifically state that they were applying for an amendatory convention or any other type of application. Instead they said that the state legislature "respectfully propose an amendment to the Constitution of the United States and call upon the people of the several states for a convention for such purpose." It gave the appearance that North Dakota wanted the OTHER states to make the call and that they merely supported the idea.

[195] S. 214, 102nd Cong., 1st sess.,"Constitutional Convention Implementation Act of 1991", Section 3(a)

for identical wording; the impetus on identical wording is intended to counter opposition.[196] With the current drive to convene an AVC for a Balanced Budget Amendment, the States are citing in their applications the previously submitted AVC applications from the preceding states by specifically naming those states and insisting that their application be counted with those which had preceded it.

52.

Do the applications from all the States have to be worded identically?

It is not required that the language of multiple applications from the several States be identical but it would help to make sure that the count is achieved as soon as possible and that all applications are counted properly.[197] This tactic mirrors that of the States who passed resolutions in 1787 for the instructions of their delegates to the Grand Convention in Philadelphia – six states used identical wording to state the purpose of the convention and 4 more used a variation on the wording of the six identical resolutions.[198]

53.

Is there a finite time period within which all the state applications must be made?

It is unknown how long an application remains active before it becomes "stale," if it even becomes stale at all. Many constitutional scholars recommend that the validity of the application should have a limited life commensurate with the length of time usually given to secure ratification of a proposed amendment sent to the States – that of seven years.[199] A better argument is that an identically worded application from decades past should be counted as valid if the issuing state has not rescinded the application. The States are always free to rescind their

---

[196] U.S. Congress, House, Committee on the Judiciary, *Is There a Constitutional Convention in Our Future?* 103rd Cong., 1st sess., committee print, serial no. 1, at 7 (Washington, D.C.: Government Printing Office, 1993)
[197] Ibid.
[198] *The Documentary History of the Ratification of the Constitution, Digital Edition*, eds. John P. Kaminski, Gaspare J. Saladino, Richard Leffler, Charles H. Schoenleber and Margaret A. Hogan (Charlottesville: University of Virginia Press, 2009)
[199] U.S. Congress, House, Committee on the Judiciary, *Is There a Constitutional Convention in Our Future?* 103rd Cong., 1st sess., committee print, serial no. 1, at 10 (Washington, D.C.: Government Printing Office, 1993)

applications so the notion that an application becomes stale with time and without the intention of the issuing state is nonsense. It is the state's application and that state legislature alone knows its own mind.

The issue of "contemporaneity" needs resolution. Much discussion has been made of how long Congress should let an application stand before considering it stale. The debate centers on whether the passage of time and the every-changing nature of politics render the original issue now changed or perhaps even moot. A corollary to the contemporaneity is the issue of consensus among the States. Do the earliest applying states share the same concerns on, say limiting federal spending, and wish to restrict it through a balanced budget amendment, as the latest applying states who may wish instead to create a rigid spending cap? Are these the same issue and therefore go to the heart of the "similarity and specificity" that Congress will seek?[200]

The experience of the Twenty-seventh Amendment demonstrates that the sense of the States as to their preference for the resolution of a problem remains on the table as long as the States say. It is the States' prerogative to issue, rescind or let lay an application.

54.

How is the validity of the state applications determined?

The US Supreme Court ruled in *Prigg v. Commonwealth of Pennsylvania* in 1842 that the validity of a state's application cannot be questioned. Congress must accept the application. The only question unresolved is how to classify the application, that is, does the application contain such specificity to a single issue that the application is included in the count of all state applications for a convention on a specific issue?[201] Any congressional decision or rejection would probably be subject to judicial review.

55.

Who determines whether the applications are valid?

In the *Jarrolt v. Moberly* decision of 1880, the US Supreme Court

---

[200] James E. Bond, David E. Engdahl and Henry N. Butler, *The Constitutional Convention* (Washington, D.C.: National Legal Center for the Public Interest, 1987), 4-5

[201] http://supreme.justia.com/cases/federal/us/41/539/case.html Prigg v. Commonwealth of Pennsylvania 41 U.S. 539 (1842)

held that the application is always valid by virtue of its origin in the state legislature.²⁰² Congress would expect to at least look over the application resolutions to make certain that the States are indeed requesting a convention and not something else, such as merely requesting that Congress draft and submit a proposed amendment – some states have done exactly this in the past.

56.

Can the States limit the actions of their respective delegates through binding instructions?

Yes, the States are empowered to limit the actions of the delegates through instructions from the legislature. This has been the situation throughout dozens of interstate conventions and compact conventions extending back through the Colonial Era.²⁰³ How much limitation is now a modern issue as the States' experiment with what are termed "faithful delegate" statutes.

57.

Can the States rescind their call for an AVC?

This answer has been heavily debated but many states have rescinded one or more of their applications over the years. It is logical that a state could rescind their application if they feel that the need for the convention no longer existed or if the state disliked the anticipated agenda. Constitutional scholars have debated that if a state may rescind at will, then when the state would rescind is the critical point. The current consensus seems to be that a state could rescind either before the thirty-four states count is reached or after the application effort has failed but not once the thirty-four states count threshold is reached and Congress is committed to calling or has already called the AVC.²⁰⁴ The Supreme Court included in its *Coleman v. Miller* decision that the ability of the States to rescind a ratification came under the "political question

---

[202] http://supreme.justia.com/cases/federal/us/103/580/ Jarrolt v. Moberly 103 U.S. 580 (1880)

[203] Robert G. Natelson, *Amending the Constitution by Convention: A More Complete View of the Founders' Plan*, Independence Institute Report IP-7-2010, (Golden, CO: Independence Institute, Dec. 2010): 4

[204] Dwight Connely, "Amending the Constitution: Is This Any Way to Call for a Constitutional Convention?," *Arizona Law Review* 22, no.4, (1980): 1033-4

doctrine" and therefore was beyond the Court's purview.[205] Analogously, the argument can then made for the rescission of an application being beyond the Court's purview.

If a state were to rescind when there is just one state still needed to reach the two-thirds requirement and concurrent to that rescission another state passed its resolution for an application, then a constitutional crisis is initiated wherein, it is unknown whether the two-thirds quantity has been successfully met. The other side of this argument is that allowing for rescission at will reduces the seriousness of the action on the part of the state legislature. If a state can easily rescind its application then not much forethought is required in making the application. The most important argument is that the state legislature knows the temper of the state and if it should decide that the will of the people of the state is no longer behind the application, then the legislature has an obligation to rescind.

Historically, the opinion of constitutional scholars was that rescission of an application was not permissible. The argument was made that an application is similar to Congress proposing an amendment to the States for ratification – "proposal and ratification are not treated as unrelated acts, but as succeeding steps in a single endeavor."[206] If Congress were to rescind the proposed amendment before ratification[207] was complete, it might be construed as denying the States – and therefore, the people – their say on the matter. In this view, proposal by Congress, ratification by the States and application by the States were all part of the same amending process and "possessed equal effect with the other."[208] No state would know, definitively, where the proposed amendment, or application campaign, stood if rescissions where being made at the same time as applications or ratifications depending on the process underway and there would be "great confusion."[209] States are not allowed to rescind their ratifications.[210]

Of course, once the convention is called or convened, the States

---

[205] http://supreme.justia.com/cases/federal/us/307/433/case.html Coleman v. Miller 307 U.S. 433 (1939)
[206] *Dillon v. Gloss*, 256 U.S. 368 at 374, 41 S. Ct. 510 at 512, 65 L. Ed. 994 at 997 (1921)
[207] Lester B. Orfield, *The Amending of the Federal Constitution* (Ann Arbor: University of Michigan Press, 1942), 51-2 - For an historical example, Orfield looked to the "Corwin Amendment" proposed during the Civil War. Rescission was attempted during 1864 as the proposed amendment appeared moot.
[208] Frank E. Packard, "Notes and Comments – Rescinding Memorialization Resolutions," *Chicago-Kent Law Review* 30, no.4 (Jan. 1952): 339-42
[209] Walter F. Dodd, "Amending the Federal Constitution," *Yale Law Journal* 30, no.4 (1921): 346
[210] 15 Stat. L. 706 (1868)

may not rescind their applications as the convention is then a fait accompli.

58.

To whom are the state applications sent?

Since 1985 the General Services Administrator has been the designated recipient of the state applications. The received applications are then printed in the House and Senate official records under section 2102 of Title 44.[211] Since 2015, the count is performed and maintained by the chairman of the US House of Representatives Judiciary Committee.[212]

59.

Does the state application to Congress have to specify the purpose of the AVC?

No. A state may make an application for a general or open convention for the purpose of addressing a multitude of issues. This has been done many times by almost every state.[213] Research has shown that the States have made over seven hundred applications for an AVC covering dozens of potential subjects.[214]

60.

Can state applications dictate the exact wording of proposed amendments?

No. The purpose of the convention is to discuss, debate and write the proposed amendment. Determining the wording before the convention defeats the purpose of the convention.[215] The idea of

---

[211] 1 U.S.C. §106b, Pub. L. 98–497 (1985)
[212] US House Rule XII, (3)(c)
[213] http://supreme-court-cases.findthebest.com/l/1013/Ullmann-v-United-States Ullmann v. United States 350 U.S. 422 (1956)
[214] Paul Weber & Barbara Perry, *Unfounded Fears: Myths and Realities of a Constitutional Convention* (New York: Praeger, 1989), 168-9
[215] Walter E. Dellinger, "The Recurring Question of the 'Limited' Constitutional Convention," *Yale Law Journal* 88, no.8 (July 1979): 1632

requiring exact wording has been proposed several times in Congress.[216] Constitutional scholars have argued that determining the exact wording before the convention makes the convention moot and the convention then takes on the purpose of a ratifying convention.[217] If the wording is dictated before the convention, then the delegates do not really have control over the convention; the control is in the hands of whomever is specifying the amendment wording.[218] This situation creates a scenario in which a special interest group writing the pre-worded amendment proposal holds influence over the convention.

61.

Could a state delegation be recalled by its state legislature?

Yes, since the States determine their own rules for their delegations, the States may recall their delegations or individual delegates at any time. There are some constitutional scholars that argue delegates cannot be recalled or even limited due to the Speech and Debate Clause of the Constitution.[219] But this clause appears to apply to members of Congress and not AVC delegates.[220] An argument has been made both ways by constitutional and legal scholars. These scholars make the case that by limiting the actions of their delegates, the States are restricting the convention from being a truly "deliberative assemblage" as the Supreme Court has ruled that it must be.[221] The reality is that the States will most likely place limitations on the *subject matter* and not on the details of the unwritten amendment proposal. During the 1787 Philadelphia convention, the state of New York restricted the authority of its delegation to the convention. When it appeared to the delegates that the convention was exceeding the permissible limits of the New York delegation's authority, delegates Robert Yates and John Lansing withdrew from the convention and returned home.

---

[216] Congressional Research Service Report R42589, *The Article V Convention to Propose Constitutional Amendments: Contemporary Issues for Congress,* (11 April 2014), 36

[217] Walter Dellinger, "The Recurring Question of the 'Limited' Constitution Convention," *Yale Law Journal* 88, no.8 (July 1979): 1632

[218] Frank E. Shanahan, "Proposed Constitutional Amendments: They Will Strengthen Federal-State Relations," *American Bar Association Journal* 49, no., (July 1963): 633

[219] Douglas G. Voegler, "Amending the Constitution by the Article V Convention Method," *North Dakota Law Review* 55 (1979). 385

[220] United States Constitution, Article I, § 6, Cl. 1

[221] *Hawke v. Smith, No.1,* 253 U.S. 221 (1920)

62.

How do the States pass their bills for an application?

Each state sets its own criteria for passage, but typically, the same margin for passage of a statute is used for an AVC application bill. The margin varies by state.[222] Lately, some of the States have passed resolutions with accompanying enabling statutes that cover the selection, powers and duties of the delegates.[223] Both chambers of a state legislature must concur not only in their intent to make an application for a convention, but also in the wording. They must agree to exactly what they are saying in the resolution and the presiding officer of each chamber must sign the resolution. This is not always law, but sometimes simply custom.[224] In some states, legislative rules have been enacted to cover the signing of the resolution.

63.

Can the States submit "conditional" applications to Congress?

Yes, in the 1980s, an effort to pass a Balanced Budget Amendment (BBA) through Congress was failing so several states proposed an AVC to address the issue. Many of those states issued applications that specifically stated that if Congress passed a BBA, their applications would immediately and automatically be rescinded.[225] Other states included wording that made clear that the application was for a single-issue AVC.[226] Still other states issued resolutions that called for a BBA, stating that if Congress failed to pass a BBA by a certain date, then the resolution should be considered an application for an AVC.[227,228] Self-cancelling provisions are a method of avoiding rescission campaigns for a time-sensitive issue.

---

[222] S. 1272, 93rd Cong., 2nd sess., "Federal Constitutional Procedures Act", Section 3(a)

[223] As an example, in 2014, Wisconsin considered AJR81 – a resolution for making the application to Congress for an AVC, and AB635 – a proposed statute covering the process for the selection of delegates to an AVC.

[224] Dwight Connely, "Amending the Constitution: Is This Any Way to Call for a Constitutional Convention?," *Arizona Law Review* 22, no.4 (1980): 1024-45

[225] U.S. Congress, House, Committee on the Judiciary, *Is There a Constitutional Convention in Our Future?* 103rd Cong., 1st Sess., committee print, serial no. 1, at 6 (Washington, D.C.: Government Printing Office, 1993)

[226] Ibid.

[227] Gerald Gunther, "The Convention Method of Amending the United States Constitution," *Georgia Law Review.* 14, no.1 (Fall 1979): 3

[228] William T. Barker, "A Status Report on the "Balanced Budget" Constitutional Convention," *John Marshall Law Review* 20 (1986): 33-4

64.

Could the States propose amendments ahead of the convention with defined wording and then instruct their delegates to accept only that specific wording?

To do so would circumvent the purpose of the deliberative aspect of the convention. If the wording is already set, then the convention does not, and cannot, perform its function of debating the proposed amendment and instead becomes part of the ratification process. In 1993, the Senate Judiciary Committee studied the Article V convention process and rejected this approach.[229] Constitutional scholars have argued that delegates coming to the convention with a pre-written amendment would make the convention pointless and would violate the intended checks and balances that the Framers put into Article V.[230] The Courts have addressed this several times in cases such as *State ex rel. Harper v. Waltermire*;[231] *AFL-CIO v. Eu*;[232] *Miller v. Moore*;[233] *Gralike v. Cook*;[234] *Barker v. Hazeltine*;[235] *League of Women Voters of Maine v. Gwadosky*[236] and *Donovan v. Priest*.[237]

65.

Would non-states such as the District of Columbia or the U.S. territories and protectorates have a vote or a delegation in the AVC?

Since Article V discusses only the States and makes no mention of territories or protectorates, the text makes clear that the States only have

---

[229] U.S. Congress, House, Committee on the Judiciary, *Is There a Constitutional Convention in Our Future?* 103rd Cong., 1st sess., committee print, serial no. 1, at 6 (Washington, D.C.: Government Printing Office, 1993)

[230] Walter Dellinger, "The Recurring Question of the 'Limited' Constitution Convention," *Yale Law Journal* 88, no.8 (July 1979): 1632

[231] https://www.courtlistener.com/mont/5v6F/state-ex-rel-harper-v-waltermire/ State ex rel. Harper v. Waltermire 691 P.2d 826 (1984)

[232] *AFL-CIO v. Eu* 686 P.2d 609 (Cal. 1984)

[233] *Miller v. Moore* 169 F.3d 1119 (8th Cir. 1999)

[234] http://www.oyez.org/cases/2000-2009/2000/2000_99_929 Gralike v. Cook 191 F.3d 911 at 924-25 (8th Cir. 1999) affirmed as Cook v. Gralike 531 U.S. 510 (2001)

[235] http://www.sdbar.org/Federal/1998/1998dsd037.htm Barker v. Hazeltine 3 F. Supp. 2d 1088, at 1094 (D.S.D. 1998)

[236] *League of Women Voters of Maine v. Gwadosky* 966 F. Supp. 52 (D. Me 1997)

[237] http://opinions.aoc.arkansas.gov/WebLink8/docview.aspx?id=198889&dbid=0 Donovan v. Priest 931 S.W. 2d 119 (Ark. 1996)

a say in the process.²³⁸ The status of being a State is elevated over that of a territory or protectorate and therefore has additional benefits not afforded to a territory or protectorate.²³⁹

66.

Could a state refuse to participate in an AVC?

Of course a state could refuse; Rhode Island chose not to attend the Grand Federal Convention of 1787. Any state could sit out the AVC but it does so at the cost of it having no input on any proposed amendment in the crucial drafting and debate stage. It is left with merely voicing its opinion at the very late ratification stage. States may also decide to send a delegation for the sole purpose of observing the proceedings. During the 1933-34 effort to ratify the Twenty-first Amendment, the state of North Carolina voted to not hold a ratification convention. Eight other states declined to hold a ratification convention after the amendment surpassed the requisite three-quarters threshold.

67.

Can the States be forced to participate in an Article V convention?

No, any state can choose to sit out the convention. Rhode Island did exactly that in 1787. Of course, that state loses its opportunity to have a say in the proceedings of the convention.

Operation of the AVC

68.

Does each state have just one vote or do they get more votes based on population?

Traditionally, since the 1787 convention, the rule has been "one State, one vote" and the rules of the convention will, most likely, not change that tradition of unit voting.²⁴⁰ The Rules Committee established by the AVC delegates could choose to change the weighting of the

---

²³⁸ United States Constitution, Article V

²³⁹ Congressional Research Service Report R42589, *The Article V Convention to Propose Constitutional Amendments: Contemporary Issues for Congress,* (11 April 2014): 40

²⁴⁰ Robert Natelson, *Amending the Constitution by Convention: A More Complete View of the Founders' Plan,* Goldwater Institute Policy Report No. 241 (Phoenix, AZ: Goldwater Institute, Sept. 2010), 26

votes of each state to reflect some other criterion such as population. Doing so would most likely provoke a court challenge. In the 1970s, the issue of apportionment for representation in state legislatures led to a number of court cases. Some states had widely divergent representation, particularly between rural and urban districts. The imbalance led to an effort to call an AVC to address the "one-person, one-vote" doctrine that has traditionally been followed and which had been codified by the US Supreme Court in the *Baker v. Carr* decision in 1962.[241] The principle of equal representation is firmly engrained in our political culture and the policy of equal representation among the States is a long established corollary.

The application process is made state-by-state; the ratification is done state-by-state; the 1787 Constitutional Convention operated on a state-by-state basis; the Constitution was ratified and therefore adopted state-by-state; so it stands to reason that we would adhere to this circumscription of a state-by-state unit vote within the amendatory convention itself. The process is not an exercise of democracy but one of exercising federalism.[242]

69.

How many votes are required to pass a proposed amendment on to the States?

A simple majority could suffice to propose an amendment, but the convention may adopt rules that require a greater majority. It was decided by the Supreme Court in *National Prohibition Cases* in 1920 that a quorum of delegates present and voting would suffice for Congress and constitutional scholars have argued that the same would hold for an AVC.[243,244] There has been much discussion over the last three decades as to whether the AVC would need a supermajority of two-thirds of the quorum's votes to adopt a proposed amendment, but no legislation has been successfully passed in Congress and thus it remains up to the

---

[241] http://supreme.justia.com/cases/federal/us/377/533/case.html Reynolds v. Sims 377 U.S. 533 (1964) and http://www.law.cornell.edu/supremecourt/text/376/1 Wesberry v. Sanders 376 U.S. 1 (1964), both in the wake of http://supreme.justia.com/cases/federal/us/369/186/case.html Baker v. Carr 369 U.S. 186 (1962)

[242] James E. Bond, David E. Engdahl and Henry n. Butler, *A Constitutional Convention* (Washington, D.C.: National Legal Center for the Public Interest, 1987), 16

[243] http://supreme.justia.com/cases/federal/us/253/350/ National Prohibition Cases 253 U.S. 350 (1920)

[244] Also, only two-thirds of a quorum of each house is necessary for Congress to propose an amendment – Senate Journal, 1st Cong., 1st sess., at 77 (9 Sept. 1789)

convention to set its own rules.[245]

70.

Who funds the AVC?

The States may generally fund the convention as it is a convention of the States and not of the federal government. The federal government is permitted to fund the convention and past convention procedure bills presented in Congress called for federal funding.[246] Federal agencies are also directed to provide assistance and funding as requested.[247] It is in the States' best interest to fund the operation of the AVC themselves and avoid the undue financial influence of the federal government. If the convention were called to address an issue that may involve limiting the power of the federal government, Congress may be unsympathetic to the issue and choose to exercise the "power of the purse" and refuse to financially support the convention. Some writers have suggested that Congress be responsible for the costs of the convention itself, i.e., the facility, office supplies, printing, etc., and that the States bear the expenses of their respective delegates.[248,249]

71.

Who is responsible for organizing and running the AVC?

The States are responsible for the initial organization acting through the convention delegates but once convened and operating under the adopted convention rules, the convention runs itself. The Rules Committee established by the AVC will determine the structure and operation of the convention. The courts have decided that there are implied powers granted to a convention.[250]

---

[245] Congressional Research Service Report R42589, *The Article V Convention to Propose Constitutional Amendments: Contemporary Issues for Congress,* (11 April 2014): 37

[246] Congressional Research Service Report R42589, *The Article V Convention to Propose Constitutional Amendments: Contemporary Issues for Congress,* (11 April 2014): 37

[247] Ibid., 32

[248] Morris B. Forkosch, "The Alternative Amending Clause in Article V: Reflections and Suggestions," *Minnesota Law Review* 51, no.6 (1967): 1072-3

[249] Douglas G. Voegler, "Amending the Constitution by the Article V Convention Method", *North Dakota Law Review* 55 (1979): 383

[250] *State ex rel. Donnelly v. Myers* 127 Ohio St. 104, 186 N.E. 918 (1933)

72.

Who determines the rules of the AVC?

A committee of the delegates chosen by the delegates from among their own members will draw up the convention rules. The Assembly of State Legislatures have, at the Mount Vernon, Indianapolis, Washington Naval Heritage Center, Salt Lake City and Philadelphia meetings, worked to propose the rules ahead of time so that they can be presented to the delegates for their approval at the beginning of the convention. Federal Courts have ruled in *United States v. Thibault* that the Article V convention is controlled by the States and the convention itself and not the federal government and therefore the federal government has no control or interest in the operation of the convention.[251] This opinion was backed up by later Supreme Court Justice Stevens in a federal district court case in *Dyer v. Blair* in 1975.[252]

73.

How would the AVC create and staff working committees?

An AVC has the power to create whatever committees it decides that it may need. It is entirely within the authority of any convention to create both standing and ad hoc committees. The number of delegates composing the committee, the responsibilities of the committee and committee members are determined by the convention and the Rules Committee. To a certain degree, the committee has authority to create its own rules. This practice would be in agreement to those practices observed in the 1787 Philadelphia Convention.

74.

Do all states need to be physically represented at the Article V convention to consider the business of the AVC?

No, a quorum of the AVC is analogous to a quorum in Congress, therefore a quorum of two-thirds, or thirty-four, of the States is necessary to convene the convention, according to a Supreme Court decision in *State of Rhode Island v. Palmer*, one of the *National Prohibition*

---

[251] http://www.leagle.com/decision/193121647F2d169_1163 United States v. Thibault 47 F. 2d 169 (2d Cir. 1931)

[252] http://www.leagle.com/decision/19751681390FSupp1291_11480.xml/DYER%20v.%20BLAIR Dyer v. Blair 390 F. Supp. 1291 (N.D. Ill. 1975 – Justice Stevens)

Cases of 1920 regarding a congressional quorum for an amendment.[253] In 1787, Rhode Island did not attend the Grand Convention.

75.

If an AVC is its own authority, could the delegates do whatever they want?

This is the possibly third greatest issue of concern with the AVC and the root of the idea that the convention can go rogue and become a "runaway." Since the delegates are issued instructions by their respective states, and the States retain the ability to recall any and all of their delegates, the impact of a delegation going rogue is negligible. Several states to date have passed legislation that restricts the discretion of its delegates.[254,255] As a last resort, whatever output in the form of proposed amendments is generated can be stopped by just thirteen states rejecting a proposed amendment.[256] The amendatory convention is an agent of the people as designated by the selection criteria of the state legislatures; it must remain within its stated scope. Anything done outside of the prescribed purpose is not binding and is considered a mere "recommendation."[257]

76.

If there is an agenda for the AVC determined ahead of the convention, then will there be no debate of the issue(s) or the particulars of the proposed amendment(s) considered?

The agenda is necessary to set limits on the operation of the AVC and to keep the focus of the delegates within the instructions of their respective states and the call from Congress. The agenda outlines the topic(s) to be considered, not the particulars of the topic. As an example, a Balanced Budget Amendment could very well be the issue discussed at the AVC. There are many possible variations of a Balanced Budget

---

[253] http://caselaw.lp.findlaw.com/scripts/getcase.pl?court=us&vol=253&invol=350 State of Rhode Island v. Palmer 253 U.S. 320 (1920)

[254] State Sen. David Long, *Amending the U.S. Constitution by State-Led Convention: Indiana's Model Legislation*: 7

[255] Senate Enrolled Act No. 224, Indiana (2013); Senate Enrolled Act No. 225, Indiana (2013)

[256] Since there are currently 50 states and ¾, or 38, of the States are required to ratify, mathematically it stands to reason that the balance of the remaining states plus one – in this case (50-38=12)+1=13 are all that is necessary to stop ratification.

[257] Robert Natelson, *Amending the Constitution by Convention: A Complete View of the Founders' Plan*, Goldwater Institute Policy Report No. 241, (Sept. 2010): 26

Amendment and the AVC would be focused on discussing and debating the details and ramifications of the various versions. Eventually, a consensus would be, hopefully, reached and the wording would be refined resulting in a proposed amendment sent to the Congress to be referred to the States. Undoubtedly, this complex issue would be a passionately and heatedly debated – the idea that a boilerplate amendment would be adopted without debate is both worrisome and unlikely as every state has a vested interest in the outcome and will, assuredly, seek to voice their concerns and obtain assurances as to the impact on their state. A deliberative convention is guaranteed by court decisions.[258]

77.

What if the AVC cannot reach an agreement on an amendment?

If an AVC becomes deadlocked and unable to develop an amendment, then it might be able to simply vote to dissolve itself. If a long period of time passes with no progress, the state legislatures could recall their delegations and declare the AVC closed. Since no AVC has occurred to date, no one can predict if this would happen and how it would be resolved. In all likelihood, the convention officers would report to Congress that no further progress is expected and that they have voted to end the AVC. Perhaps Congress might decide to call another AVC and direct the States to select new delegates?

78.

Could items be added to the agenda after Congress issues the call?

No, once the call is made, the agenda is set and the AVC is limited to the business that is specified. The States, through their applications to Congress have taken great pains to be very specific as to their intent to meet and to the issue(s) that they want to discuss. Deviation from the agenda is indicative to an attempt to derail, deter, or runaway with the convention. As a safeguard, many states have already passed legislation that prohibits their delegates from deviating from the agenda.

79.

---

[258] Roger Sherman Hoar, *Constitutional Conventions: Their Nature, Powers, and Limitations* (Boston: Little, Brown, 1917), 128-9

How long does an AVC last?

The length of time that the AVC meets depends on the nature of the business that the AVC takes up. Using the example of a Balanced Budget Amendment, it is reasonable to expect that the AVC will take several weeks. Each state may bring their own proposal to the AVC and will want to have their proposal heard and debated. Committees will be formed to work out the particulars of certain aspects of the proposed amendment, such as, limitations on raising taxes and making cuts to social programs, or protecting the military funding, or setting a schedule for the enactment of a budget each year. All of these actions will take time to work out the details. The work of the committees will need review by the whole of the AVC prior to voting on the proposed amendment.

80.

Will the public and the media be allowed to attend an AVC?

Most likely. But the convention rules will control the operation of the convention and the delegates may decide to restrict or even prohibit observers. There is both precedent and reason to do so. The 1787 Grand Convention was conducted in secret for good reason. To have an open and free debate of ideas, it was necessary that the delegates be guaranteed that the ideas put forth be immune to scrutiny and interpretation of the news media of 1787. News traveled slowly at that time. An idea that was not fully formed or fleshed out could have been taken out of context and the public may have been incensed by the suggestion of something unpopular and not understood, such as taxation. In today's world of instant communications and pundit analysis, a question raised by a delegate can be turned quickly into a statement or proposition, rather than the question as it was posed. If the delegates are keeping up with the newscasts, they might be unduly influenced by the public and media reactions to ideas presented, thus stifling debate. As all sides of an issue must be examined, it is in the best interest of the nation that the debates be held in confidence. With respect to the importance of historical analysis, it is likely that the proceedings would be recorded for posterity but not broadcast at the time of the convention. Such recordings could be sealed for a number of years to allow the proposal, debate, reference, and ratification processes to proceed unimpaired. It is more likely that the pressure to allow the public to observe the process – it is historical and all citizens have a stake in the outcome – will result in the convention rules permitting some observation during certain parts of the convention. The meetings of the whole body of delegates might be permissibly observed and broadcast while the committee meetings may not.

Legal Aspects of the AVC

81.

What role does the Supreme Court play in the process?

Constitutionally, the Supreme Court of the United States (SCOTUS) plays no role in the process. However, several times in the past, the States moved toward an AVC on certain issues and the Congress, sensing a threat to their power, responded by passing the very amendment that the States sought to discuss in an AVC.[259] This is known as "prodding."[260] Several times that this action occurred, some point or another was brought up that had no known answer and the result was a lawsuit brought in the courts that often found its way to the SCOTUS to address and resolve the point. On all issues of the Constitution and constitutionality, the SCOTUS can be the court of original jurisdiction according to Article III, Section 2 of the United States Constitution.[261] There is a significant body of law which has developed regarding the AVC despite the lack of an actual AVC having ever taken place.

82.

Are there any legal guidelines for an AVC?

Several cases have been adjudicated by the SCOTUS to cover such points as ratification, delegate selection, delegate positions, referendums, petition validity, conclusion of the AVC, limitations on the power of the AVC, permanence of the ratification process and holding that an AVC is not plenary. While not all issues are resolved, the basic structure of the

---

[259] Examples include the Seventeenth, Twenty-first, Twenty-second and Twenty-fifth Amendments.
[260] The Balanced Budget Amendment movement came within two states of forcing a convention in the early 1980s; Congress responded by passing an amendment in the Senate but was unable to get passage in the House.
[261] United States Constitution, Article III, § 2

convention exists in law. Many more issues have been dealt with by the federal district and appeals courts. The Congressional Research Service has published several tracts on the issue.[262] Additionally, the various notes from the Philadelphia Convention of 1787 provide guidelines for how the AVC could be structured. The notes of delegates Gunning Bedford, Jr., Pierce Butler, Alexander Hamilton, Rufus King, John Lansing, James Madison, Luther Martin, George Mason, James McHenry, William Paterson, William Pierce, Edmund Randolph, Robert Yates and historian Max Farrand's three volume *Record of the Federal Convention of 1787* provide much detail on the minutiae of the 1787 Philadelphia convention. These notes can serve as a guide on how to conduct an AVC.

83.

Could the AVC open up ratification to the people by referendum?

The Supreme Court has been clear since 1920 in *Hawke v. Smith (1)* that the issues addressed and the amendment(s) proposed are subject to ratification by only two methods as detailed in Article V. State legislatures or state ratification conventions are the only permissible methods of ratification. Referendum by the people is not legally permissible as the people, through the adoption of the Constitution "… have excluded themselves from any direct or immediate agency in making amendments to it, and have directed that amendments should be made representatively for them,…"[263]

84.

Could an outside third party set the rules of the AVC?

No. The AVC is considered a "federal function" performed by the States.[264] The States, and the States alone, have the power, through their legislatures to apply for, conduct, set the rules for and conclude the AVC. The Supreme Court addressed the issue in both *Leser v. Garnett*[265]

---

[262] Congressional Research Service, Report R42589, *The Article V Convention to Propose Constitutional Amendments: Contemporary Issues for Congress;* Congressional Research Service Report R42592, *The Article V Convention for Proposing Constitutional Amendments: Historical Perspectives for Congress;* and Congressional Research Service Report CRS 95-589 A (1995) *Amending the U.S. Constitution: by Congress or Constitutional Convention*

[263] http://supreme.justia.com/cases/federal/us/253/221/ Hawke v. Smith No. 1 253 U.S. 221 (1920)

[264] http://supreme.justia.com/cases/federal/us/258/130/case.html Leser v. Garnett 258 U.S. 130 (1922)

[265] http://supreme.justia.com/cases/federal/us/258/130/case.html Leser v. Garnett 258 U.S. 130 (1922)

and in *Dyer v. Blair*²⁶⁶ and in lower courts.²⁶⁷ There have been, and are currently, third party organizations that are proposing draft versions of amendments and even draft rules for an AVC.²⁶⁸ The potential for influence and meddling is suspect enough that such organizations will most likely be excluded from the convention as will be all other non-participants. A search of the internet turns up dozens of organizations that are working to promote their version of the "Twenty-eighth Amendment."

85.

Are there any exceptions to the amendment process?

Yes, there are three. The Equal Suffrage of the States in the Senate cannot be changed,²⁶⁹ a direct tax could not be levied²⁷⁰ and the prohibition on altering the status of slavery before 1808 could not be changed.²⁷¹ The passage of time has made obsolete the alteration of slavery before 1808. The Sixteenth Amendment negated the prohibition on a direct tax. Thus, there is currently but one issue that the AVC cannot propose amending, that of equal suffrage in the US Senate.²⁷²

86.

Are the actions of the AVC subject to judicial review?

This question is extremely important. In today's legal environment, it is highly probable that some party will challenge the work of the AVC by waging "lawfare" to stop the ratification of the proposed amendment(s). Such was the response to the Eighteenth and Nineteenth Amendments. The SCOTUS will have jurisdiction over the challenge.²⁷³ They may decide that the particular issue falls under the "political question doctrine" and thereby decline to consider the case. If the

---

²⁶⁶ http://www.leagle.com/decision/19751681390FSupp1291_11480.xml/DYER%20v.%20BLAIR Dyer v. Blair 390 F. Supp. 1291 (N.D. Ill. 1975 – written by later Justice Stevens)

²⁶⁷ *Opinion of the Justices to the Senate*, 366 N.E.2d 1226 (Mass. 1977); *State ex rel. Donnelly v. Myers*, 186 N.E. 918 (Ohio 1933); and *Prior v. Noland*, 188 P. 727 (Colo. 1920)

²⁶⁸ For example, the Convention of States proposed rules in 2015.

²⁶⁹ United States Constitution, Article V

²⁷⁰ Now moot due to the passage of the Sixteenth Amendment.

²⁷¹ United States Constitution, Article I, § 9, Cl. 1 (now moot due to the passage of time)

²⁷² United States Constitution, Article V

²⁷³ United States Constitution, Article III, § 2

challenge appears to be technical in nature, then the court may take up the case and add to the body of law covering the AVC by settling the issue. Bear in mind that many of the questions regarding an AVC are considered settled in the eyes of the US Supreme Court based on the large body of law that has already been adjudicated pertaining to an AVC. As the US Supreme Court has done so many times before, it may choose to reverse itself and take up the case setting aside part of the political question doctrine.

87.

Does the state law of the hosting state prevail over the AVC?

No, the SCOTUS has ruled in *Leser v. Garnett*[274] that the AVC is a "federal function" by the States, and as such, the hosting state has no authority to rule or overrule the convention or any particular aspect of its operation. The AVC operates under the authority granted by Article V and is therefore a federal action with supremacy to state law.

88.

What happens if the AVC proposes amendment(s) that are unconstitutional?

Several results will probably occur. First, the Congress will most likely refuse to select a mode of ratification nor will it promulgate the proposed amendment to the States although technically, they cannot do so. Second, there will be, in all likelihood, a judicial challenge in the Supreme Court. Third, the States will presumably reject such an amendment out of hand by either a down vote or by refusing to take up a debate and a vote on the amendment. Fourth, Congress may take up the issue and move quickly to draft, debate and pass either a cleaner version of the amendment or a different amendment to prevent the AVC amendment being proposed.[275] A theoretical example of an unconstitutional amendment proposal would be one that seeks to deprive smaller states of two senators and allow only for one senator because of a smaller population.

---

[274] http://supreme.justia.com/cases/federal/us/258/130/case.html Leser v. Garnett 258 U.S. 130 (1922)
[275] Robert Natelson, *Proposing Constitutional Amendments by a Convention of the States* (Washington, D.C.: American Legislative Exchange Council, 2011): 18

89.

Could the AVC create and prescribe an entirely new ratification method that allows them to amend the Constitution and go around the States?

No. To create a new amendment process that bypasses the current method and "hijacks" the AVC would require amending Article V itself. This cannot be done in the AVC – it would have to first be accepted and ratified by the States. No matter what anyone tries to do to amend the Constitution, it ultimately requires the States to approve the action – just thirteen states can stop any such action cold. The Supreme Court dealt with the issue of changing the ratification process in *United States v. Sprague*[276] and *Hawke v. Smith (1)*[277] and ruled it impermissible except through Article V.

90.

Can an amendment be proposed that "clarifies" already existing parts of the Constitution?

Yes, for example, the Twelfth, Twentieth, Twenty-second and Twenty-fifth Amendments all clarify the sections dealing with the election and succession of the President.

91.

Could an amendment be proposed that repeals other amendments or sections of the Constitution?

Yes, the Twenty-first Amendment repealed the Eighteenth Amendment ending the prohibition of possessing and consuming alcohol.[278] The Thirteenth Amendment, ratified in 1865, which outlawed slavery and involuntary servitude, negated the Three-fifths Clause[279] and the Fugitive Slave Clause.[280] The Sixteenth Amendment removed the prohibition on a direct tax.

92.

---

[276] http://supreme.justia.com/cases/federal/us/282/716/case.html United States v. Sprague, 282 U.S. 716 (1931)
[277] http://supreme.justia.com/cases/federal/us/253/221/ Hawke v. Smith No. 1, 253 U.S. 221 (1920)
[270] United States Constitution, Amendment XXI
[279] United States Constitution, Article I, § 2
[280] United States Constitution, Article IV, § 2

Could an amendment be proposed that would overturn a US Supreme Court decision?

Yes, this has happened more than once previously. The Eleventh Amendment,[281] ratified in 1795, which involves a state's sovereign immunity and prohibits a citizen(s) of one state from suing another state without the defendant state's consent is the result of a backlash against the Supreme Court's holding in the *Chisholm v. Georgia*[282] decision of 1793.[283] The Thirteenth Amendment,[284] ratified in 1865, overturned the *Dred Scott v. Sandford*[285] decision of 1857, which held that a black person had no legal or civil rights. The Sixteenth Amendment[286] was ratified in 1913 and overturned the *Pollock v. Farmers' Loan & Trust Co.*[287] decision of 1895 and granted Congress the power to levy and collect income taxes. The Nineteenth Amendment,[288] ratified in 1920, which guarantees women the right to vote, overturned the US Supreme Court's 1875 unanimous decision in *Minor v. Happersett*,[289] that had interpreted the Privileges and Immunities Clause of the Fourteenth Amendment[290] to deny women the right to vote. In 1971, the Twenty-sixth Amendment[291] was adopted which overturned the *Oregon v. Mitchell*[292] ruling of 1970 holding that Congress lacked the power to lower the voting age to eighteen.

Views of the Founding Fathers on a Second General Convention

93.

Did James Madison fear a second constitutional convention?

Respect for the opinion of James Madison is well deserved; he is frequently called "the Father of the Constitution" – rightly or wrongly.

---

[281] United States Constitution, Amendment XI
[282] http://supreme.justia.com/cases/federal/us/2/419/case.html Chisholm v. Georgia 2 U.S. (2 Dall.) 419 (1793)
[283] Bradford Clark, "The Eleventh Amendment and the Nature of the Union," *Harvard Law Review* 123, no.8 (June 2010), generally
[284] United States Constitution, Amendment XIII
[285] https://www.law.cornell.edu/supremecourt/text/60/393 Dred Scott v. Sandford 60 U.S. 393 (1857)
[286] United States Constitution, Amendment XVI
[287] https://supreme.justia.com/cases/federal/us/157/429/case.html Pollock v. Farmers' Loan & Trust Co. 157 U.S. 429 (1895)
[288] United States Constitution, Amendment XIX
[289] http://supreme.justia.com/cases/federal/us/88/162/case.html Minor v. Happersett 88 U.S. 162 (1875)
[290] United States Constitution, Amendment XIV
[291] United States Constitution, Amendment XXVI
[292] https://www.law.cornell.edu/supremecourt/text/400/112 Oregon v. Mitchell 400 U.S. 112 (1970)

As the author of the Virginia Plan which laid the foundation for the Constitution, few understood the Constitution better. This claim of Madison fearing a second runaway convention stems from a quote of James Madison taken from a private letter that he wrote to George Lee Turberville in 1788 and the quote is most often both abbreviated and taken out of context.

The usual <u>partial</u> quotation is given as: **"Having witnessed the difficulties and dangers experienced by the first Convention which assembled under every propitious circumstance, I should tremble for the result of a Second,"** and there it ends after a comma – without explanation or context, the comma leaves us fearful of another constitutional convention, or an AVC, and justifiably so.

But the contemporary context of the quote means everything. In 1788, the nation was wrestling with the ratification conventions in the States, experiencing inflation, weak money, crippled by national debt and reeling from the inability of the national government to resolve the issues effectively. The Anti-Federalists were waging an aggressive campaign to discredit the proposed Constitution and prevent its adoption. These facts framed Madison's perspective when he wrote the Turberville letter.

The complete quote is: *"**You wish to know my sentiments on the project of another general Convention** as suggested by New York. I shall give them to you with great frankness ....3. If a General Convention were to take place for the avowed and sole purpose of revising the Constitution, it would naturally **consider itself as having a greater latitude than the Congress** appointed to administer and support as well as to amend the system; it would consequently **give greater agitation to the public mind; an election into it would be courted by the most violent partisans on both sides**; it wd. probably consist of the most heterogeneous characters; would be the very focus of that flame which has **already too much heated men of all parties**; would no doubt contain individuals of insidious views, who under the mask of seeking alterations popular in some parts but inadmissible in other parts of the Union might have **a dangerous opportunity of sapping the very foundations of the fabric. Under all these circumstances** it seems scarcely to be presumable that the deliberations of the body could be conducted in harmony, or terminate in the general good. Having witnessed the difficulties and dangers experienced by the first Convention which assembled under every propitious circumstance, I should tremble for the result of a Second, **meeting in the present temper of***

America, *and under all the disadvantages I have mentioned".*²⁹³

The meaning changes considerably when put in proper context. Madison was speaking of the people who were already scheming to find an advantage under the newly proposed system. He is referencing slavery and the Three-fifths Clause, he is referencing the monarchists who wanted to establish an American monarchy; he is referencing the previously landed nobility that wished to have their privileges re-established. In writing the letter, Madison was firstly concerned about the deterioration of the national government and the fear that it would eventually lead to the formation of several, independent, regional governments who may war with each other. Secondly, he was aware of the limited temperament of the people. The public had endured the four-month-long 1787 Convention that was held in secret and may not tolerate another secretive convention. Between the Annapolis Convention held in September of 1786 and the Philadelphia Convention opening in May of 1787, Massachusetts experienced Shays' Rebellion²⁹⁴ which dramatically proved the weaknesses of the Articles of Confederation.²⁹⁵ Northeastern Pennsylvania was suffering the third Pennamite-Yankee War between Pennsylvania on one side and Connecticut and Vermont on the other. The public's patience with ineffective government had worn thin. Thirdly, he was anticipating the actions of the Anti-Federalists whom Madison believed were spoiling for another convention in order to tear apart the new Constitution and replace it with one of their own design. At the time, the Federalists were in the minority making such a result of a second convention very likely.²⁹⁶ Madison was NOT opposed to constitutional conventions, amendatory or plenary, but he was opposed to dragging out the solution to a time sensitive and volatile problem and starting over at that particular, crucial point in time.

Madison's objection was to a 1788 plenary constitutional convention, not a twenty-first century Article V amendatory convention. He believed that the new Constitution should be given a chance with the public and then evaluated before being tampered with.²⁹⁷ Madison's

---

[293] Robert Rutland & Charles Hobson, eds., *The Papers of James Madison, Vol. 11* (Charlottesville: University Press of Virginia, 1977), 330-2, letter to G.L. Turberville of 2 November 1788
[294] Christopher Collier & James Collier, *Decision at Philadelphia* (New York: Ballantine, 1986), 17 – The Colliers argue that Madison and Washington saw the rebellion as a crucial point, describing it as a "shadow" hanging over the Confederation Congress and forcing the Philadelphia convention.
[295] Paul Weber & Barbara Perry, *Unfounded Fears: Myths and Realities of a Constitutional Convention* (New York: Praeger, 1989), 20
[296] Ibid., 41
[297] Ibid., 32

reticence was due to the difficulties in securing agreement during the first convention, not due to the results. Madison knew what the other delegates knew: First, only the delegates appreciated the difficulties of having produced the Constitution. Second, they had created a charter with "no prospect of getting a better." Third, rejection or delay in ratification would inevitably lead to disunion and the collapse of the nation.[298]

The Turberville letter contained three other objections stated by Madison. That a convention would lead to a dispute among the States as to the proposed amendments; that the convention amendment method would take much longer than a set of congressional amendments; and that the reaction of Europe to the delay imposed by a convention would send the wrong signal as to the viability of the new Constitution as well as to the stability of the fledgling Republic.[299] The nation's foreign creditors, primarily the Dutch, had expressed concern that a recent loan had been made on the assurances of the swift ratification of the Constitution.[300] Madison did not want conventions to be called with any frequency lest they become too commonplace and ineffective. It wasn't that Madison did not ever want another convention; it was that under the prevailing circumstances, he just didn't want another plenary one right then. Time has proven James Madison right. For a deeper discussion on this topic, see Chapter 3.

94.

Did any of the other Framers fear a second convention?

The issue of holding a second constitutional convention was repeatedly raised by the Anti-Federalists both during and after the 1787 Philadelphia Convention. Discussion of holding a second convention was begun soon after the Virginia Plan was introduced. A formal motion was made by Edmund Randolph to hold a second *plenary* convention on 31 August, 10 September and 15 September 1787, all less than two weeks before the conclusion of the Philadelphia convention. The motion was

---

[298] Clinton Rossiter, *1787: The Grand Convention* (New York: Macmillan, 1986), 241
[299] Madison's letter to George Lee Turberville, 2 November 1788
[300] Paul Weber & Barbara Perry, *Unfounded Fears: Myths and Realities of a Constitutional Convention* (New York: Praeger, 1989), 47-8

unanimously rejected.³⁰¹ A total of three motions were made to include a provision for future "general conventions" in the Constitution. All were rejected.

95.

Can the States or Congress call a second plenary constitutional convention?

No, the records of the 1787 Grand Convention make clear that the Framers of the Constitution considered such an option and rejected it. During the Philadelphia Convention, several motions were made to either provide for a future constitutional convention (or general convention as it was called then) or for a second general convention to discuss changes to the proposed constitution as submitted by the States after they had a chance to review the proposed document. On 31 August 1787, George Mason of Virginia suggested another general convention. Governor Edmund Randolph of Virginia seconded the motion and asked that the States be allowed "to propose amendments to be submitted to another General Convention."³⁰²

On 15 September 1787, Gov. Randolph proposed again that the States allow the ratification conventions to suggest proposed amendments which would be submitted to a second constitutional convention. The motion was seconded by George Mason and affirmed by Elbridge Gerry of Massachusetts. Charles Pinckney of South Carolina spoke against the motion, stating that, "Nothing but confusion and contrariety could spring from the experiment. The States will never agree in their plans, and their Deputies to a second Convention coming together under the discordant impressions, of their Constituents, will never agree. Conventions are serious things, and ought not to be repeated." This motion was rejected unanimously by the state delegations, as noted by Madison: *"On the question on the proposition of Mr. Randolph. All the States answered - no."*³⁰³,³⁰⁴

---

[301] Notes of 1787 Grand Convention delegate Dr. James McHenry of Maryland taken from the *American Historical Review*, Vol. XI (Washington, D.C. 1905-6): 596-618.

[302] Max Farrand, ed., *The Records of the Federal Convention of 1787, Vol. II* (New Haven: Yale University Press, 1911 rev. 1937), 479

[303] *The Documentary History of the Ratification of the Constitution, Digital Edition*, eds. John P. Kaminski, Gaspare J. Saladino, Richard Leffler, Charles H. Schoenleber and Margaret A. Hogan (Charlottesville: University of Virginia Press, 2009), (accessed 16 October 2014)

[304] Max Farrand, ed., *The Records of the Federal Convention of 1787, Vol. II* (New Haven: Yale University Press, 1911 rev. 1937), 631-3

Not only can Congress not call a second, plenary constitutional convention, they lack the authority to call an amendatory convention without the initiative of the States. Congress may only respond to the States' applications for an amendatory convention. It is theorized however that the Congress can pass a resolution to invite the States to apply for an amendatory convention.[305]

Miscellaneous Questions

96.

What role does the executive branch play in the process?

None. In the earliest SCOTUS case involving Article V, *Hollingsworth v. Virginia*, the Court ruled in 1798 that the Presentment Clause[306] does not apply to amendments as there is no mention anywhere in the Constitution of the President being involved in the process.[307] This is analogous to the lack of a role for Congress is approving an amendment. The Framers were concerned that at some point, a future Congress or president may become dictatorial and could thwart a needed amendment from ratification.[308] The lack of a role for the executive is carried over to many of the states where the governor has no role in the application process.[309] It has been explained that if the executive had a role in the process then the President could possibly find some point of contention on which to base a veto of the amendment. In that event, Congress may not be able to muster the necessary two-thirds votes in both chambers to override the veto. This executive action would be interfering with the will of the people and of the States.[310,311]

It appears that the Supreme Court might have based their

---

[305] Lester B. Orfield, "The Procedure of the Federal Amending Power," *Illinois Law Review* 25 (1930): 421
[306] Article I, § 7, Cl. 2 and 3
[307] http://supreme.justia.com/cases/federal/us/3/378/case.html Hollingsworth v. Virginia 3 U.S. (3 Dall.) 378 (1798)
[308] Congressional Research Service, Report R42589, *The Article V Convention to Propose Constitutional Amendments: Contemporary Issues for Congress*, (11 April 2014): 30-3
[309] As an aside, President Lincoln did "inadvertently" sign the Thirteenth Amendment. Once he realized what he had done, he immediately notified Congress and the Senate passed a motion to ignore Lincoln's signature as unnecessary and not a precedent.
[310] S. Rep. No. 336, 92nd Cong., 1st sess., at 13 (1971)
[311] "Proposed Legislation on the Convention Method of Amending the United States Constitution," *Harvard Law Review* 85, no.8 (June 1972): 1623

analysis on the ratification of the Bill of Rights. The twelve proposed amendments were sent to the States for consideration and ratification without the signature of President Washington. A constitutional amendment is considered a change to the fundamental or organic law and not a piece of ordinary legislation. The approval of an amendment lies then with the States and not the executive.[312]

97.

How much time after the AVC occurs will the States have to ratify any proposed amendment?

Since the proposal of the Eighteenth Amendment, Congress has allotted seven years for ratification by the States. This was confirmed by the Supreme Court in two cases, *Dillon v. Gloss* in 1921[313] and *Coleman v. Miller* in 1939.[314] This seven year allotment of time became a standard practice starting with the Twenty-third Amendment and did not appear in the wording of proposed amendments after the Twenty-third Amendment.[315] When Congress promulgates the proposed amendment to the States, it will be through a "concurrent resolution" which most likely will have attached a statement that includes a limitation on the ratification time period.[316]

98.

How close have we come in the past to calling an AVC?

The nation has come within a couple of states submitting applications several times. During the 1960s, the issue of equal representation in the state legislatures led to a movement to call an AVC that managed to achieve a record thirty-three states submitting applications to Congress by 1967.[317] That was just one state short of

---

[312] Thomas A. Gilliam, "Constitutional Conventions: Precedents, Problems, and Proposals," *St. Louis University Law Journal* 16 (1971): 48

[313] http://supreme.justia.com/cases/federal/us/256/368/case.html Dillon v. Gloss 256 U.S. 368 375 (1921)

[314] http://supreme.justia.com/cases/federal/us/307/433/case.html Coleman v. Miller 307 U.S. 433 (1939)

[315] http://www.gpoaccess.gov/constitution/pdf2002/015.pdf "Article V: Ratification" in The Constitution of the United States, Analysis and Interpretation, 108th Congress, Senate Document 108-17 (Washington, D.C.: Government Printing Office, 2004): generally

[316] http://www.gpo.gov/fdsys/pkg/GPO-CONAN-2002/pdf/GPO-CONAN-2002-8-6.pdf U.S. Congress The Constitution of the United States, Analysis and Interpretation, at 950 (Washington, D.C.: Government Printing Office, 2004)

[317] Nevada Legislature Background Paper 79-12: 2

the number needed to call a convention. The previous attempt to call an AVC for the Balanced Budget Amendment fell just two states short in the mid-1980s.

In the early twentieth century, the States came just two state applications short of an AVC to change the selection of US senator – this prodded the Congress to pass the Seventeenth Amendment.[318]

The problem with the math on the count of the number of submitting states' application is that many of those proponents pushing for an AVC are discounting the rescissions of prior applications by states that no longer supported an AVC for that particular issue. The legality of rescinding an application by a state has been hotly debated since the 1970s. Strong proponents believe that, like secession, the States may not rescind a prior application whereas, opponents of an AVC believe that a state may rescind at will. Currently constitutional scholars believe that a state may rescind at any time before the count reaches the requisite two-thirds, or thirty-four, of the States. Rescission is similar to ratification of an amendment in this regard. The Court has consistently held that once ratification is given, the state may not rescind that ratification.[319] There is a long running debate as to whether the same can be held of rescission of convention applications.

99.

Why hasn't an AVC occurred before?

The answer to this question is very time dependent. Prior to about 1900, there were very few applications made by the States for an AVC. With the exceptions of the 1832-33 Nullification Crisis and the 1861 Peace Conference, no issue has stirred enough of the states to take an interest in calling a convention of the States. With the rise, first of the Populist Movement in the 1870s and 1880s and then, second, of the Progressive Movement beginning in the 1890s, the social and constitutional issues excited the people to look at amending our Constitution for elements of direct democracy. It took decades of work to force the passage of the Sixteenth, Seventeenth, Eighteenth and Nineteenth Amendments. These amendments are credited to the

---

[318] Ibid.
[319] Lynn Andretta Fishel, "Reversals in the Federal Constitutional Amendment Process: Efficacy of State Ratifications of the Equal Rights Amendment," *Indiana Law Journal* 49, no.1 (Oct. 1973): 164

Progressives and their allies in the Women's Suffrage and Temperance/Prohibition Movements.

The Seventeenth Amendment was the result of what is known as the "prodding effect." That means that the pressure by the States that almost led to an AVC prodded the Congress to pass the Seventeenth Amendment to prevent an AVC and the States from assuming powers traditionally exercised by the Congress. The prodding effect also led to the Twenty-first, Twenty-second and Twenty-fifth Amendments.

It is significant to note that each of the Progressive Era amendments did not restrict the power of Congress but rather, added to its power either directly or indirectly. The Sixteenth Amendment granted greater taxing powers to Congress. The Seventeenth Amendment removed the power of the States to select federal senators thereby freeing US Senators from allegiance and accountability to their respective states. The Eighteenth Amendment granted Congress the power to regulate and control alcohol – for personal consumption and industrial use.[320] The Nineteenth Amendment granted women the right to vote and although this did not grant Congress additional power, it did give them new constituencies.

After the Progressive Era, the scope of the proposed amendments increased and efforts were made to restrain spending and to limit Supreme Court decisions. The number of proposed amendments grew dramatically. With the increase in states requesting an AVC, the attention on the push grew and the resistance to the threat to federal power grew in proportion. It was not until the 1960s that organizations

---

[320] Daniel Okrent, *Last Call, The Rise and Fall of Prohibition* (New York: Simon & Schuster, 2010), 53-8, - Across several chapters of Daniel Okrent's masterful "Last Call, The Rise and Fall of Prohibition," the incestuous relationship between the Progressive and Temperance movements is laid out. Okrent cites the United States Brewers Association's claim that alcohol excise taxes had provided more than $200 million per year by 1910 – for a staggering 30% of the federal revenue overall. Excise taxes on alcohol paid over 40% of the cost of the Spanish-American War. The federal government, from the founding up through the early twentieth century, could not be operated without a liquor tax, therefore liquor could not be prohibited without some other means of funding the government – hence, the Sixteenth Amendment. The passage of the Sixteenth Amendment made Prohibition under the Eighteenth Amendment possible. Of course, once the Twenty-first Amendment was passed making alcohol legal once again by repealing the Eighteenth Amendment, the Sixteenth Amendment, theoretically no longer necessary, was not repealed as well. This political sleight of hand yielded a revenue windfall for the federal government and made all of the Progressives' dreams of massive social welfare and social engineering programs fiscally possible after the Great Depression ended. The stage was set for the New Deal, the Great Society and the "fundamental transformation of America." Also, the Nineteenth Amendment was made possible by the alliance of the Women's Suffrage movement with the Progressive and Temperance movements. For greater detail, see, generally, Ethel B. Jones, "The Economics of Women's Suffrage," *Journal of Legal Studies* 20 (1991) and specifically, Donald J. Boudreaux & A. C. Pritchard, "Rewriting the Constitution: An Economic Analysis of the Constitutional Amendment Process," *Fordham Law Review* 62, no.1 (1993): 147-50

on both sides of the political spectrum began to fight against an AVC. It was then that the idea of a "runaway convention" was first introduced. The Eagle Forum published its list of "20 Unanswerable Questions" to prove why an AVC was a bad idea and have continued to push this list despite repeated refutations from proponents of an AVC. The alt-right John Birch Society has steadfastly held that the convention cannot be limited and will run away, hijacked by liberals.

An AVC has not yet occurred more because of fear-mongering than anything else except perhaps the "prodding effect." The historically low amount of information in circulation with regard to the existing legal precedents and the established customs and rules of "constitutional" conventions has deterred people from exercising this constitutional right to alter and repair their federal government.

100.

If the federal government does not follow our Constitution now, how will new amendments help – won't the federal government just ignore those too?

This is the most pertinent question that can be asked at this time. If the answer is that the Congress and the President will simply ignore the new amendment – and that the new amendment has no "teeth" for enforcement – then the AVC is indeed moot. The solution is that any new amendment must not be worded to say, using the example of the Balanced Budget Amendment, something like "Congress shall not pass a budget that is not balanced." Enforcement mechanisms must be built into the amendment that includes consequences and provisions for actions by the States in response to the failure of Congress to balance the budget. Continuing the example of the BBA, the amendment might read as, "Congress shall pass no budget that is not balanced, OR the States shall be empowered to do any or all of the following:

- Reject the proposed federal budget and impose a budget as constructed by a simple majority vote of a Convention of the States, and/or,
- Revert to the last balanced federal budget, and/or,
- Withhold funds collected on behalf of the federal government by the States and the States use the funds for their ultimate purpose (an example being highway maintenance taxes

collected on gasoline), and/or,

- The States will assume and exercise control of certain functions of the federal government in the interim occurring during the period without a federal budget (an example being education, veterans' affairs, insurance regulation and oversight, health care or any other non-defense related activity)."

Additionally, we can show that the Constitution is still followed by pointing out that the people are still voting for their federal senators, meaning that the Seventeenth Amendment is still being observed. We are still voting for the president, meaning that Article II and the amendments are still being observed. We are still looking to the Supreme Court for disposition of cases, meaning that Article III is still being observed. And so on. The Constitution remains in in effect as long as we are all still arguing about it.

101.

How can amending our Constitution address the specific problems of today?

The Constitution is not perfect; it has flaws that are becoming more apparent and more problematic as time goes on. The types of problems that an AVC is best suited to address are structural problems in the Constitution, and therefore, in the government. Federal spending has become an intergenerational issue as we load future generations down with debt incurred from funding today's government expenditures. Controlling spending and reducing the ability of today's federal politicians to use taxpayer money to buy votes and grant largesse is necessary to maintain our economic stability and national security. The federal government imposes unfunded mandates on the States which cause the States to, in turn, have to take on excessive debt thereby unbalancing state government budgets. Campaign finance has grown to be an issue that troubles many Americans as the entrenched politicians find new and creative ways to extend and project their power. Proponents of campaign finance reform view average Americans as having lost not only their political voice but their franchise in the political system.

The failure of the Constitution to explicitly cite who is charged with the determination of constitutionality has led to a centuries-long battle over the ability and right of the States to refuse to comply with federal laws that they deem unconstitutional. Congress, as the legislative branch, is one of the three defined branches of the federal government. It is improper that Congress would be able to determine whether its own acts are constitutional. The same can be said for the executive branch. Thus, we have been left with the Supreme Court, as the highest level within the judicial branch, to determine constitutionality. The results have not always been correct. These breaches of federalism led, in part, to the Nullification Crisis, the Civil War, and now, the current debates over such issues as Obamacare and the growing surveillance state.

Some problems are so large that they are of a national character and require a federal solution. Federal spending, as an example, is a problem that bears heavily on the States. The federal government, acting through the Federal Reserve, has the ability to print money whereas the States do not. Printing additional money typically leads to inflation and the destruction of the value of savings such as in retirement funds. The States are burdened with higher costs for both purchasing and interest on borrowing due to inflation. The federal government can theoretically print its way out of an recessionary period but the States cannot. The money collected in federal taxes comes from the private and corporate citizens of the States. Federal spending has a discernible impact on the economies of the several states. It is apparent that the Congress has little to no interest in reining in its own spending despite the damage that profligate spending has on the nation and on the States individually. If fiscal responsibility is ever to be returned to the finances of the federal government, it will probably have to be forced upon the leviathan of the federal government by the States.

The peaceable method of restraining federal spending is through either the courts or the amendment process. A constitutional amendment that limits the ability of the federal government to spend beyond its means creates the force of law necessary to restrain the out-of-control federal spending. The States will then be obligated to enforce the provision.

102.

Why do we need an AVC, don't we just need to enforce the Constitution?

The argument has been made repeatedly that the federal government is not acting entirely within the Constitution; it is not respecting the Constitution as law; it is not confining its activities to constitutionally limited areas; it is not respecting civil rights or the States' rights; and it is encroaching on the States' traditional powers. The only constitutional mechanism for reining in the federal government, short of revolution or insurrection, is the Article V convention. Other proposed enforcement methods, such as nullification or interposition do not work, have not worked and are not supported by the courts at any level. AVCs were included by the Framers as our "nuclear option" for an out-of-control, unresponsive federal government – it is there to be used in an emergency.[321] The balance of power between the States and the federal government has been greatly disturbed. The only societal institutions with the size and power to resist the growth and dominance of the federal government are the state legislatures. The States have the requisite power to enact amendments with enforcement provisions and to duly exercise that power to enforce the entire Constitution. Many of the proposed solutions to our national problems involve measures that limit or reduce the power of Congress or the courts, such as a balanced budget, term limits, or curbing judicial activism. Congress will not act to take away even a small measure of its own power. An AVC is the only way to go around Congress and enact these changes.[322]

Constitutional scholar James Kenneth Rogers argues that, "A balanced budget amendment would make it more difficult for members of Congress to use government spending to benefit their constituents in exchange for political support. Term limits would limit the tenure of members of Congress and force many of them out of office. An amendment prohibiting unfunded mandates that affect the States would limit Congress's power to control the States."[323] All of these goals can be met – and enforced - through a constitutional amendment.

The problem with any type of enforcement on the limitation of government power can be distilled to three issues: *constitutionality, precedence and acceptance*. First, whatever enforcement mechanism is chosen must be recognized as constitutional by all sides of the political spectrum. Many of the political actions called for recently are not considered "legal" or even simply good law. If the political establishment

---

[321] Congressional Research Service, Report R42589, *The Article V Convention to Propose Constitutional Amendments: Contemporary Issues for Congress*, (11 April 2014): 43

[322] Arthur H. Taylor, "Fear of an Article V Convention," *Brigham Young University Journal of Public Law* 20, no.2 (2006): 124-31

[323] James K. Rogers, "The Other Way To Amend The Constitution: The Article V Constitutional Convention Amendment Process," *Harvard Journal of Law & Public Policy* 30, no.3 (2007): 1020-1

– and that means in particular, the federal government and the courts – does not acknowledge that the action is legitimate, then no change will occur. It is a dead end. An AVC is defined in the Constitution so it is unquestionably constitutional. The US Supreme Court has repeatedly ruled on the topic and decided many key issues.

Second, although there has never been an AVC, the precedent of amending the Constitution exists and the precedent of the States coming together to debate and resolve issues exists. We have a deep history of the States cooperating to create and adopt law extending back to before the Republic was formed by the States. The body of law created by rulings of both the state and federal courts establishes a firm foundation for the States to limit the powers of the federal government through constitutional amendment.

Third, over more than two centuries, the federal government has come to accept the power of the States to amend our Constitution and to enforce its provisions through the courts. Where the problems have arisen is in the interpretation of the meaning of the clauses of the Constitution and in the abuse of the intent of the Framers of the original Constitution and of the subsequent amendments. Clarifying the intent and the limitations of the more problematic clauses[324] and including enforcement mechanisms will indeed enforce the Constitution on the federal government. This can be done through an amendment that clarifies the purpose and language of the Constitution.

The alternative to an AVC is through litigation in the Supreme Court – this can be hit or miss. For the States to seek enforcement of the Constitution, all ambiguity must be removed from the Constitution. The weight of the law is the only force sufficient to move the federal government.

103.

If an AVC is so safe, then why do so many reputable people and organizations oppose holding one?

During the two major drives for an AVC in the 1960s and 1970s, several national organizations led the effort to stop the AVC. Their reasons were the same as we hear today; the convention will be

---

[324] Specifically, the General Welfare Clause, the Commerce Clause, the Tax and Spending Clause, the Necessary and Proper (or Elastic) Clause, and the Due Process Clauses (of the Fifth and Fourteenth Amendments).

a runaway, it is uncontrollable, no one knows what the rules are so it will be hijacked. Much of the effort to call an AVC was in response to the perceived judicial activism of the Earl Warren-led Supreme Court.[325] Reapportionment, school prayer, balanced budget, busing, abortion, the Equal Rights Amendment and other issues galvanized groups to call for an AVC. Other groups rose up in opposition and remain opposed to this day. Once the opponents started down the path of opposition, they have had to remain in opposition to be consistent in their messages.[326] For many of these groups, opposition to an AVC is the cornerstone of their fundraising efforts.

Much of the academic scholarship concerning an AVC over the last couple of decades has focused on addressing the concerns and objections raised during the previous efforts to call an AVC. Clearly it is prudent to be cautious when considering a change to anything as important as our Constitution. The debate has been healthy for the Republic and has led to a better understanding of both the process of an AVC and the potential outcomes. It has also led to debunking most of the objections raised by opponents. The usual evidence cited to support their contention that an AVC will lead to scrapping our Constitution is the citation of the 1787 Convention as a runaway and quotation – often out of context – of Framers such as James Madison that would appear to advise against an AVC. Both of these claims have been addressed herein and disproven.

104.

If there has never been an AVC, how can we know what will happen?

A pseudo-precedent exists in the form of the 1861 Peace Conference in Washington D.C. With the Civil War looming, Virginia made an application for an AVC in late 1860. Events moved quickly and other states, sensing that time was short, replied directly to Virginia that they would attend. In February of 1861, twenty-one of the twenty-eight remaining states (six had already seceded) sent representatives to attend the conference held at the Willard Hotel in Washington, D.C. For three weeks, they followed the rules used in the 1787 Philadelphia Conference and stuck to the singular issue of proposing an amendment that they

---

[325] Paul Weber & Barbara Perry, *Unfounded Fears: Myths and Realities of a Constitutional Convention* (New York: Praeger, 1989), 7
[326] Ibid., 7-9

hoped would resolve the slavery issue. When a delegate attempted to introduce a new subject, the body threatened expulsion and returned to the agenda. The conference concluded with a proposed amendment that it forwarded to Congress. The Senate voted on the amendment, rejecting it. The House never took up the matter as Lincoln had been inaugurated and Fort Sumter besieged. The example shows that with a set agenda and rules, the fear of a runaway convention or of unusual or unplanned activities is unfounded.[327]

Additionally, the Mount Vernon Assembly, now the Assembly of State Legislatures, which convened its first meeting on 7 December 2013 at George Washington's home was designed for the express purpose of addressing all of the open issues and to develop a set of rules and operational procedures for an AVC. The state legislators who have been taking part in the Assembly have identified a lengthy list of questions to answer – these are spelled out in the Resolution issued by the Assembly on 7 December 2013.

Lastly, it is important to note that many of the same objections voiced today concerning holding an AVC could have been expressed in the early 1930s with regard to using the state ratification convention method to ratify the Twenty-first Amendment. The States held their first-ever ratification conventions and all went as planned without a single, solitary problem.

105.

If an AVC is as bad an idea as opponents say, then why would the Framers put a "self-destruct" mechanism in the Constitution?

This is the question which proponents of an AVC have frequently put to those in opposition. It is a curious notion that the Framers could so wisely craft six articles in the Constitution that are considered brilliant but the remaining article is considered to be a disastrous poison-pill. This alleged anomaly is often explained away as having been an afterthought.

The Framers were designing a government for the ages – and they knew it. They had no intention of including anything in the Constitution meant to destroy it. It was for that reason they worked so hard to

---

[327] Robert Gunderson, *The Old Gentlemen's Convention* (Madison: University of Wisconsin Press, 1961), generally

minimize the impact of slavery on the new nation. The Framers were very cognizant that the seeds of future destruction most likely lay in the issue of slavery. Other problems, unknown at the time, would arise that might require modification to the national charter in order to preserve the nation. Including a mechanism for the address and resolution of those problems in a civil manner was a necessity. Article V was included as a "safety valve" meant to provide a means of saving the Constitution and the Republic from a government that is not responsive to the people or the issues.

Several of the Framers left written evidence of their intent to provide a method of rectifying the divisive issues through constitutional change. From their diaries, books, journals, pamphlets, letters, public statements and speeches we can understand their intentions. Jurists and legal scholars of the Federal Era wrote extensively on the Constitution often basing their work on their communications with the Framers and Ratifiers concerning the intent of those Framers and Ratifiers.

One of the leading and most prolific legal scholars of the Federal Era, St. George Tucker[328], described the purpose and application of Article V:

> *"Lastly, the fifth article provides the mode by which future amendments to the constitution may be proposed, discussed, and carried into effect, without hazarding a dissolution of the confederacy, or suspending the operations of the existing government. And this may be effected in two different modes: the first on recommendation from congress, whenever two thirds of both houses shall concur in the expediency of any amendment. The second, which secures to the states an influence in case congress shall neglect to recommend such amendments, provides, that congress shall, on application from the legislatures of two thirds of the states, call a convention for proposing amendments; which in either case shall be valid to all intents and purposes as part of the constitution, when ratified by the legislatures of three fourths of the several states, or by conventions in three fourths thereof, as the one or the*

---

[328] St. George Tucker was a prominent attorney, jurist and legal scholar during the Federal Era serving on the Virginia Supreme Court of Appeals (now the Virginia Supreme Court) and later the US District Court. He was a professor of law at the College of William & Mary and he produced the most widely used American legal texts of the day. He recognized that the abolition of slavery was an issue of "the first importance, not only to moral character and domestic peace, but even to our political salvation." He proposed a plan in 1796 that would have gradually ended the practice. The plan was denounced in its time and outright rejected. In our time, it is denounced as racist. He served in the Revolution, being wounded in battle several times.

other mode, of the ratification may be proposed by the congress. Both of these provisions appear excellent. Of the utility and practicability of the former, we have already had most satisfactory experience. **The latter will probably never be resorted to, unless the federal government should betray symptoms of corruption, which may render it expedient for the states to exert themselves in order to the application of some radical and effectual remedy.**[329] *Nor can we too much applaud a constitution, which thus provides a safe, and peaceable remedy for its own defects, as they may from time to time be discovered. A change of government in other countries is almost always attended with convulsions which threaten its entire dissolution; and with scenes of horror, which deter mankind from any attempt to correct abuses, or remove oppressions until they have become altogether intolerable. In America we may reasonably hope, that neither of these evils need be apprehended;* **nor is there any reason to fear that this provision in the constitution will produce any degree of instability in the government;**[330] *the mode of both originating and ratifying amendments, in either mode which the constitution directs, must necessarily be attended with such obstacles, and delays, as must prove a sufficient bar against light, or frequent innovations."*[331]

Tucker recognized that change in the Constitution is both necessary and inevitable. He had no fear of applying an Article V convention to produce the requisite changes; rather he saw such a move as the safest method of preserving the peace while correcting the federal government that has become either corrupt or incompetent. Tucker noted that this responsibility to redirect an errant federal government is in the hands of the States. He expressed no concern for either a runaway convention or that the Constitution was flawed and doomed to failure. As a jurist, Tucker would have been acutely aware of the intent of the wording and of the consequences of using an Article V convention. If the Constitution contained a weakness that would lead to its own replacement, Tucker would have most assuredly found and noted that weakness in his extensive commentaries.

---

[329] Author's emphasis added to quotation. Tucker has been proven correct with the passage of time as to the utilization of Article V. His prognostication of governmental corruption seems to be accurate as well.

[330] Author's emphasis added to quotation. Tucker had forecast that the employment of Article V will not produce the upheavals that modern critics of the AVC are predicting.

[331] St. George Tucker, *View of the Constitution of the United States* (Indianapolis: Liberty Fund, 1999, originally published in Philadelphia, 1803), 306-7 - It was originally published as an appendix in *"Tucker's Blackstone."*

106.

Why take the risks?

The best answer is that if the political situation is already so bad that people are considering an AVC, then one must ask if an AVC can make it any worse? With the federal government ignoring many provisions and requirements of the Constitution and the power of the States diminishing, time is of the essence to restore federalism, state sovereignty, the checks and balances of federal power vis-à-vis the States and the Rule of Law. If the States do not act within the Constitution to restrain and limit the federal government, we will progress through a post-constitutional republic to a tyranny. Inaction is the least effective option – and the most dangerous.

EIGHT
ARGUING *THE FEDERALIST* ESSAYS, "PUBLIUS" SPEAKS

> *"Through their state legislatures and without regard to the federal government, the people can demand a convention to propose amendments that can and will reverse any trends they see as fatal to true representative government."*
> – President Dwight D. Eisenhower, May 26, 1963

People can rarely discuss any aspect of the Constitution for very long without someone making reference to *The Federalist*. The proposition of an amendatory convention is no less of a subject for reference to *The Federalist* for those activists both for and against a convention. Current antagonists in the struggle over holding a convention are turning on both sides to *The Federalist* for support; thereby necessitating a discussion in this work. This chapter examines the eighty-five essays of *The Federalist* for its mention of both the amendment process and, chiefly, an amendatory convention.

The Impact of the Essays

The Federalist, or *The Federalist Papers*, or *The Federalist* essays depending on your inclination, are reputed to be the most authoritative source of the meaning or intent of the Framers as to the federal constitution. They are recognized for not just their insight on the framing of the Constitution, but also for their erudition on the basis of government and late eighteenth century political philosophy. It has been said of *The Federalist* that "nothing equals it in analytical breadth and conceptual power."[1] Written predominantly by two of the most active delegates to the 1787 Federal Convention, James Madison and Alexander Hamilton, and with a few more by John Jay,[2] they are the closest written source that we have been able to use to come to understand the thought process and rationale behind those who drafted the Constitution.[3] The essays are not perfect, having a number of inconsistencies in their arguments – spread across three authors working independently, and this is to be expected under the crush of the time constraint of a looming deadline of a convention vote - which has annoyed commentators for over two hundred years.[4] Of course, we must be fair and admit that the point of the essays was to influence the outcome of the ratification convention in the State of New York.[5] We know this not only from the heading of each essay as "To the People of the State of New York" but also from a letter that Madison sent to James Paulding in 1818 defining the purpose of the essays as, "The immediate object of them was to vindicate & recommend the new Constitution to the State of [New York] whose ratification of the instrument, was doubtful, as well as important."[6]

Even so, by the time that the team had completed the work on seventy-seven of the essays in May of 1788, New York's ratification was not a certainty.[7] The contemporary influence of the essays signed by *"Publius"* was arguably limited.[8] The publication dates are spaced out from 27 October 1787 through 16 August 1788 appearing initially in four of the then seven New York City newspapers.[9] This wide sharing of publication was due in part to the fact that New York had no daily papers at the time; if the authors were

---

[1] Jack N. Rakove, *Original Meanings, Politics and Ideas in the Making of the Constitution* (New York: Vintage Books, 1996), xv
[2] Gouverneur Morris was asked to draft some essays but declined. William Duer submitted material that was not to Hamilton's liking. The project was Hamilton and Jay's to begin with and they invited Madison to join them.
[3] Jay excluded as he was not a delegate to the Philadelphia convention.
[4] Seth Barrett Tillman, "*The Federalist Papers* as Reliable Historical Source Material for Constitutional Interpretation," *West Virginia Law Review* 105 (2003), generally
[5] William N. Eskridge, Jr., "Should the Supreme Court Read The Federalist But Not Statutory Legislative History?," *George Washington Law Review* 66 (1998), 1309
[6] Letter from James Madison to James K. Paulding, of 23 July 1818
[7] Dan T. Coenen, "A Rhetoric for Ratification: The Argument of The Federalist and Its Impact On Constitutional Interpretation," *University of Georgia School of Law Research Paper Series* XX, Paper No. 06-010, (Nov. 2006): 12
[8] Nom de plume used in homage to Publius Valerius Poplicola.
[9] Referring to those newspapers that had an inclination toward what would soon be called the Federalist Party.

to reach the largest audience and reach it on a more regular basis, they had to publish in multiple papers.[10] Other, perhaps edited, versions appeared in sixteen newspapers and a magazine elsewhere around the nation.[11] Five states had already ratified by the time that the 35th essay was published – leaving fifty essays to go.[12] Pennsylvania was one of the first, fast ratifying five and did so after only twenty essays had been published. The essays appeared in the newspapers of only six states: Massachusetts, New Hampshire, New York, Pennsylvania, Rhode Island and Virginia.[13] The impact on those first five ratifying states, excepting Virginia, was clearly negligible.[14] New Hampshire adjourned her convention early and decided to take a "wait and see" approach eventually becoming the pivotal ninth ratifying state just four days ahead of Virginia. The Commonwealth of Virginia had the advantage of Madison serving as a delegate in her ratification convention. He prepared for the convention by bringing bound copies of *The Federalist* for distribution to the Virginia delegates.[15] Ten of the States had already voted before New York, making the Constitution and the new federal government a *fait accompli*. Only North Carolina and Rhode Island remained to be influenced by the essays after New York ratified. Clearly, one could argue that if influencing the outcome in other states was part of the intention of the authors, they did not succeed as well as they may have liked. North Carolina first rejected ratification and Rhode Island initially refused to take up the matter. It would be another year and a half before North Carolina said "yes" and two and a half years before Rhode Island acquiesced to ratification. More telling is that historian Gregory Maggs states that his research found no mention or citation of *The Federalist* in any of the state ratification convention records.[16] On both accounts, a stronger argument could be made that economic

---

[10] Ralph Ketcham, *James Madison, A Biography* (Charlottesville: University of Virginia Press, 1990), 240-1
[11] Gregory E. Maggs, "A Concise Guide To The Federalist Papers As A Source Of The Original Meaning Of The United States Constitution," *Boston University Law Review* 87 (2007): 812-6 – and citing Elaine F. Crane, "Publius in the Provinces: Where Was *The Federalist* Reprinted Outside New York City?," *William & Mary Quarterly* 21 (1964): 590
[12] Delaware (12/7/1787), Pennsylvania (12/12/1787), New Jersey (12/18/1787), Georgia (12/31/1787) and Connecticut (1/9/1788).
[13] Gregory E. Maggs, "A Concise Guide To The Federalist Papers As A Source Of The Original Meaning Of The United States Constitution," *Boston University Law Review* 87 (2007): 812-6 – and citing Elaine F. Crane, "Publius in the Provinces: Where Was *The Federalist* Reprinted Outside New York City?," *William & Mary Quarterly* 21 (1964): 591
[14] Pauline Maier, *Ratification, The People Debate the Constitution, 1787-1788* (New York: Simon & Schuster, 2010), 257
[15] Ralph Ketcham, *James Madison, A Biography* (Charlottesville: University of Virginia Press, 1990), 253
[16] Gregory E. Maggs, "A Concise Guide To The Federalist Papers As A Source Of The Original Meaning Of The United States Constitution," *Boston University Law Review* 87 (2007): 816-7

forces played a much bigger hand in the last two ratifications than did the persuasive qualities of *The Federalist*.

The issue of interpretation of the intent of the Framers is central to the discussion. The disagreement lies in whether to place the emphasis on the intent of the Framers or on the understanding of the Ratifiers. One camp argued that the Framers' intention should hold sway while another camp believed that what the Ratifiers understood to be the meaning, and that they subsequently ratified, should be the controlling constitutional interpretation. How we judge the supposed intention of the ascribed powers and operation of an amendatory convention derives from one or the other of these viewpoints. Some expound against the view of *The Federalist* essays as authoritative; William Eskridge explains,

> *"Justice Scalia argues that* **The Federalist** *can inform constitutional interpretation by enabling judges to understand the context in which the Constitution was adopted.* **The Federalist,** *however, may not be taken as authoritative statements of the Framers' intent. Because received meaning (the original understanding, which in Justice Scalia's view is appropriate) is hard to distinguish in practice from intended meaning (intent, which Justice Scalia views as inappropriate), this distinction is not practically useful."*[17]

Note that Justice Scalia is arguing for using the essays for determining the context in which the Constitution was adopted and not for divining the intent of the authors. The motivation of the essayists was too strong to be simply an expository on good government.

The further argument is made that additional materials, such as the ratification debates, and the legislative debates of statutes must be brought into consideration. This compromise can be accepted but for the immediate purpose of arguing for or against an amendatory convention, we limit our discussion here to the views of the authors of *The Federalist* on that topic as evidenced in the eighty-five published essays themselves. Hamilton and Madison differed in their perspectives on the amending process. The *Harvard Law Review* noted in 1972 that this difference was discernible in their respective writings for *The Federalist*, with Madison viewing the amendment process as a method of correcting errors whereas Hamilton saw

---

[17] William N. Eskridge, Jr., "Should the Supreme Court Read The Federalist But Not Statutory Legislative History?," *George Washington Law Review* 66 (1998): 1302

the process as the States' vehicle for change,

> *"Even the specific intent of the framers lends support to the conclusion that the convention need not be unlimited in scope. Madison conceived of the amendment process as the amendment of specific "errors," [citing No.43] and Hamilton viewed article V as requiring that whenever the requisite number of states are "united in the desire of a particular amendment, that amendment must infallibly take place. [citing No.85]"*"[18]

Those who make the argument in favor of the positions of *The Federalist* are citing Hamilton and Madison indirectly as the source of authority on the topic of an amendatory convention. The weight of Madison's role is obvious and the value of his written position, propaganda or otherwise, is inestimable as to the constitutionality and the expectations of a convention. The impact of *The Federalist* is not to be underestimated, writing in the *Printz v. United States* decision in 1997, US Supreme Court Justice David Souter stated in his dissent that, "In deciding these cases ... it is *The Federalist* that finally determines my position."[19] He cited essays, *Nos. 27, 36, 44* and *45*. In the same decision, Justice Scalia turned to *The Federalist* as well to support his majority opinion and cited essays *Nos. 15, 18-20, 27, 28, 33, 36, 39, 44, 45, 51* and *70*. Both Justices Souter and Scalia are citing essays *Nos. 27, 36, 44* and *45*! This dual citation of even the same essay both for and against has become commonplace.[20] The farther removed from the Framing of the Constitution we become, the more authoritative the citation of *The Federalist*.[21]

Opponents and proponents of an amendatory convention alike turn to *The Federalist* for support of their arguments and reasoning. Paired with Madison's "Notes from the Convention," these comprise the longest, most detailed and contemporary resources that we have for the deliberate intent of the Framers. It seems that as much attention has been devoted to refutation of the essays as to interpretation of them. Critics have a number of standard objections – Gregory Maggs lists nine in his *"A Concise Guide to the Federalist*

---

[18] Republished with permission of the Harvard Law Review Association, from "Proposed Legislation on the Convention Method of Amending the United States Constitution," *Harvard Law Review* 85, no.8 (Jun., 1972): 1629; permission conveyed through Copyright Clearance Center, Inc.

[19] *Printz v. United States*, 521 U.S. 898 (1997) at 971 (Souter, dissenting).

[20] Matthew J. Festa, "Dueling Federalists: Supreme Court Decisions with Multiple Opinions Citing *The Federalist*, 1986-2007," *Seattle University Law Review* 31 (2007): 75

[21] Melvyn R. Durchslag, "The Supreme Court and the Federalist Papers: Is There Less Here Than Meets The Eye?," *William and Mary Bill of Rights Journal* 14, no.1 (2005): 312-5

Papers As A Source Of The Original Meaning Of The United States Constitution." Maggs notes that each has merit and none are straw men but he stresses that none succeed in discounting the value of the essays. Reliance on the essays remains a safe bet – politically and legally.[22] In the end, the essays are most valuable as an expository on the political thought of the times as well as the "true principles of Government."[23] Whether a specific point of the theory was actually incorporated into the Constitution is another point of contention altogether.

The influence that the essays enjoy had come later, much later. They were first cited by the US Supreme Court in 1798 in Justice Samuel Chase's decision for *Calder v. Bull*.[24] In 1821, US Supreme Court Chief Justice John Marshall wrote of *The Federalist* in the *Cohens v. Virginia* decision that,

> "*The opinion of* **the Federalist** *has always been considered as of great authority. It is a complete commentary on our constitution: and is appealed to by all parties in the questions to which that instrument has given birth. Its intrinsic merit entitles it to this high rank, and the part two of its authors [i.e., Hamilton and Madison] performed in framing the constitution, put it very much in their power to explain the view which it was framed.*"[25]

Justice Marshall is correct; who knew the minds – and intent - of the key players better than those same key players? Hamilton and Madison are unquestionable authorities on both the framing of the Constitution and on the principles of Federal Era nation-making, although we have to admit that they had their differences on each topic which grew farther apart over time. But, they also had an objective and putting a spin on the events and speeches made served to further their common goal of ratification.

The Federalist was, in part, created through Madison's reference to his notes from the convention.[26] The questioning of the veracity and therefore the value of the notes from the 1787 convention is not a new action. We can find in 1938, Abraham Weinfeld pointing out that the method of creating

---

[22] Gregory E. Maggs, "A Concise Guide To The Federalist Papers As A Source Of The Original Meaning Of The United States Constitution," *Boston University Law Review* 87 (2007): 804

[23] Referencing the phrasing of US Supreme Court Justice Samuel Chase.

[24] 3 U.S. (3 Dall.) 386 (1798)

[25] *Cohens v. Virginia* 19 U.S. (6 Wheat.) 264 (1821) at 418

[26] Elizabeth Fleet, "Madison's "Detached Memorandum"," *William & Mary Quarterly* 3 (1946): 565 – cited by Gregory E. Maggs, ""A Concise Guide To The Federalist Papers As A Source Of The Original Meaning Of The United States Constitution," *Boston University Law Review* 87 (2007): 821

Madison's Notes was the cause of the inaccuracies found therein, that the majority of the convention records were either Madison's notes or the various Committee of Detail drafts. Weinfeld believed that these were unreliable despite being good,

> "The records that we go by, in tracing the proceedings of the federal convention, consist mainly of Madison's notes on those proceedings and of various drafts prepared by the Committee of Detail. Viewed as a source for discovering the intention of the majority of the members of the convention, those records must be considerably discounted. The notes, though undoubtedly good, were not stenographic notes."[27]

The lesson learned here is that turning to *The Federalist* works best if done in conjunction with the citation of other contemporary works stating a similar or concurring viewpoint. Leaving *The Federalist* essays to stand on their own as the justification for a specific position could prove somewhat precarious.

Professor Charles Black took the quotations of *The Federalist* to task in his 1972 "Letter to a Congressman" directed to US Representative Emanuel Celler. He focused on the two quotations most often cited in support of a limited convention, *No. 43* (by Madison) and *No. 85* (by Hamilton), and attempted to prove them as misunderstood. Black argues that neither of the two readings has anything to do with the ability to limit an amendatory convention. *No. 43* merely states that the States initiate the process and *No. 85* that specific proposals are the result of the convention. But Black argues that neither essay addresses limitability and the contention that *No. 85* says that a proposal is to be "brought forward singly" refers to ratification.[28]

Black is employing an either-or fallacy that ignores the choice inherent in use of the plural. Had the wording been such that it referred to amendment in the singular, then some would argue that multiple amendments would not have been permissible – making the Bill of Rights an unconstitutional proposition!

Seth Barrett Tillman sums up the value and impact of *The Federalist* as

---

[27] Republished with permission of the Harvard Law Review Association, from Abraham C. Weinfeld, "Power of Congress Over State Ratifying Conventions," *Harvard Law Review* 51, no.3 (Jan. 1938): 496; permission conveyed through Copyright Clearance Center, Inc.

[28] Charles L. Black, Jr., "Amending the Constitution: A Letter to a Congressman," *Yale Law Journal* 82, no.2 (Dec. 1972): 197

source of justification for a constitutional interpretation argument, and more to our interest here, either in favor or disfavor of an amendatory convention,

> "Beyond that **The Federalist Papers** *fails as a clause by clause* **detailed** *defense or explication of the Constitution of 1787. And that is as it should be. The purpose of its publication was not to furnish a resource in the legal wrangling and law review nitpicking of our generation, but rather to encourage ratification in theirs.*
>
> *Undoubtedly, the authors brought substantial knowledge and erudition to the public's attention. Undoubtedly,* **The Federalist Papers** *should inform our sensibilities with regard to the* **larger purposes** *of the constitutional structure. But, with regard to the Constitution's details, the document they produced was by no means infallible, inerrant, or even wholly internally consistent and coherent.* **The Federalist Papers** *is not holy writ."*[29]

This is all true, but it is also necessary to point out that with *The Federalist* and the notes of the dozen delegates discovered to date, this is all we have got of an original, contemporaneous nature for interpretation of the actual Framers' intent – and that is what really makes them important. The fact that the essays were written so close on the heels of the 1787 convention makes their claim to accuracy much stronger than the memoirs of delegates written years and even decades later.

The Federalist Essays by the Numbers

Having gone to sufficient lengths to establish that even *The Federalist* is suspect as justification of a position for or against an amendatory convention, we now turn to the essays themselves. For the citations provided, all come from the 1961 Mentor Books edition by Clinton Rossiter.[30]

Although not referring directly to an amendatory convention, a passage from *No. 3* by Jay discussing the delegates to the early Congresses could shine some light on the view of the Philadelphia delegates in regard to the delegates to any future Article V convention,

> "They considered that the Congress was composed of many wise and experienced men. That, being convened from different parts of the country, they brought with them and communicated to each other a variety of

---

[29] Seth Barrett Tillman, "*The Federalist Papers* as Reliable Historical Source Material for Constitutional Interpretation," *West Virginia Law Review* 105 (2003): 617

[30] Clinton Rossiter, ed., *The Federalist Papers: Hamilton, Madison, Jay* (New York: Mentor, 1961)

useful information. That, in the course of the time they passed together in inquiring into and discussing the true interests of their country, they must have acquired very accurate knowledge on that head. That they were individually interested in the public liberty and prosperity, and therefore that it was not less their inclination than their duty to recommend only such measures as, after the most mature deliberation, they really thought prudent and advisable."[31]

Could we not expect the same from delegates to an amendatory convention? The historical record shows that the delegates to the Article VII conventions to consider ratification of the Constitution itself in 1787-91 performed their duties without violating their oaths or their instructions. Those delegates to the 1933-34 Article V ratificatory conventions for the Twenty-first Amendment were people of solid character who did not stray from their mandates. The solemnity of an event of such importance as an amendatory convention would, undoubtedly, elicit the most serious attitude and dedication of any delegate, knowing that the nation, and the world, is paying rapt attention "in a spirit of interested and suspicious scrutiny"[32] to the actions and words of each and every person involved. For many, it is the apex of their public life and the foundation of their permanent reputation. We can also note that those delegates took their duty seriously enough that neither was a pro forma or rubber stamp event. For ratification of the Constitution, New Hampshire set aside its deliberation and considered the matter before reconvening the Article VII convention at another date to finish the work. North Carolina rejected the Constitution in its first Article VII convention. Although not even a state, Vermont took up the Article VII convention and deliberated upon and then ratified the Constitution while seeking admission to the Union. In the consideration of the Twenty-first Amendment, South Carolina's delegates debated and rejected the amendment. This does not sound like the work of unserious delegates gathering to have a good time on the taxpayers' dime. It is altogether reasonable to expect any future delegates to an Article V amendatory convention will display the same dedication to their work as their predecessors.

The purpose of the convention was explained in *No. 22*, where the

---

[31] *The Federalist, No. 3,* Jay
[32] *The Federalist, No. 15,* Hamilton

expression of the sovereignty of the people is found only in the convention.[33] Any future amendatory convention would be staffed by delegates of the people, from the States for sure, but representing the people assembled. Although the delegates come together and meet as equal states and vote as states, an amendment proposal is made on behalf of the people and not necessarily the States. Hamilton concluded the essay with,

> "*The fabric of American empire ought to rest on the solid basis of THE CONSENT OF THE PEOPLE. The streams of national power ought to flow immediately from that pure, original fountain of all legitimate authority.*"[34]

This belief was shared and echoed later by Madison in *No. 42*, "the express authority of the people alone could give due validity to the Constitution."[35] That extends, naturally, to an amendatory convention and its product. Any proposed amendment is valid due to the expressed sovereign authority of the people.

In reference to the security of the small states from a tyranny of the majority, Hamilton notes in *No. 22* that the principle of unit voting is observed to protect the "right of equal suffrage" among the States. A supermajority is used to protect the minority by requiring that any proposed constitutional amendment would be overwhelmingly supported.

> "*It may be objected to this that not seven but nine States, or two thirds of the whole number, must consent to the most important resolutions; and it may be thence inferred that nine States would always comprehend a majority of the Union.*"[36]

The 1787 delegates, and the authors of *The Federalist*, assured the people that the States would remain a bulwark against any attempts at federal usurpation of their rights of the people and the States. No simple majority would suffice; it had to be a supermajority to carry. The checks and balances installed would be vigilant to federal overreach and possess the means of not just resistance but of correction as well. And that means would include the amendatory convention. Hamilton assures us in *No. 28* that,

---

[33] Herman V. Ames, "Recent Development of the Amending Power as Applied to the Federal Constitution," *Proceedings of the American Philosophical Society* 72, no.2 (Apr., 1933): 92
[34] *The Federalist, No. 22*, Hamilton
[35] *The Federalist, No. 42*, Madison
[36] *The Federalist, No. 22*, Hamilton

EIGHT 581

> "It may safely be received as an axiom in our political system that the State governments will, in all possible contingencies, afford complete security against invasions of the public liberty by the national authority. Projects of usurpation cannot be masked under pretenses so likely to escape the penetration of select bodies of men, as of the people at large. The legislatures will have better means of information. They can discover the danger at a distance; and possessing all the organs of civil power and the confidence of the people, then can combine all the resources of the community. They can readily communicate with each other in the different States, and unite their common forces for the protection of the common liberty."[37]

The "select bodies of men" clearly mean the state legislatures but would also include the amendatory conventions as they are "of the people at large." In such a convention, the States and their people "can readily communicate with each other in the different States, and unite their common forces for the protection of the common liberty." How else could the States and the people come together outside of the Congress unless it be in a convention of the States? Such a convention could be formal, as in an Article V amendatory convention, or it may be informal in such as setting as called by a singular state. This, as we have seen, was done in 1814 in Hartford, in 1850 in Nashville, in 1861 in Washington and in the innumerable trade, commerce, riverine, locust, drought and every other type and subject of interstate convention held over the last two and a third centuries since the ratification of the federal Constitution.

We see these acts of state level resistance today in the States refusal to take part in federal programs ranging from Obamacare exchanges to observance of federal marijuana law enforcement. The States file lawsuits, enact state laws that encumber actions by federal law enforcement personnel, deny use of state resources and personnel, and pursue compacts that remove federal actions from the States. As the seriousness of the matter escalates so does the appropriateness of the States' response(s). Hamilton clarifies the condition of the States in *No. 33*,

> "If the federal government should overpass the just bounds of its authority and make a tyrannical use of its powers, the people, whose creature it is, must appeal to the standard they have formed, and take such measures to redress the injury done to the Constitution as the exigency may suggest and

---

[37] *The Federalist, No. 28*, Hamilton

prudence justify."[38]

The referenced standard in the passage is the Constitution and one measure included for the redress of the injury is to amend the Constitution through a convention when the Constitution proves inadequate to restraining the power of the federal government. We can speculate that the prudence that is justified in the passage refers to the amendatory convention acting in a limited power manner to rectify the problem and not to create a wholesale reordering of the federal government in response to a singular infraction or exigency.

While not contending directly with the convention method, the amendment process itself is first given some discussion in *No. 39*. The nature of the amendment process as a hybrid of national and federal processes is the theme.

> *"If we try the Constitution by its last relation to the authority by which amendments are to be made, we find it neither wholly national nor wholly* **federal***. Were it wholly national, the supreme and ultimate authority would reside in the* **majority** *of the people of the Union; and this authority would be competent at all times, like that of a majority of every national society to alter or abolish its established government. Were it wholly federal, on the other hand, the concurrence of each State in the Union would be essential to every alteration that would be binding on all. The mode provided by the plan of the convention is not founded on either of these principles. In requiring more than a majority, and particularly in computing the proportion by* **States**, *not by* **citizens**, *it departs from the national and advances towards the* **federal** *character; in rendering the concurrence of less than the whole number of State sufficient, it loses again the* **federal** *and partakes of the* **national** *character."*[39]

We find in *No. 39* the guarantee of the federal character of the government that diminishes the impact of the larger states and reduces the tendency towards domination over the smaller sized and the less populated states. If the federal construction was not there then the States would no longer have a purpose and the amendatory convention would not work nearly as well. Indulging the notion for the moment of the elimination of the States, an idea argued for during the 1787 Convention, then such an

---

[38] *The Federalist, No. 33*, Hamilton
[39] *The Federalist, No. 39*, Madison

amendatory convention would most likely have to elect by congressional House districts. In that event, the sentiments of the large urban areas would predominate and the rural populace would hold little sway. The individual characters of the individual states are preserved in the federal mode and the States remain viable politically. We could perceive an amendatory convention as an act of federalism done in response to an act of nationalism.

In *No. 40*, Madison addresses the complaint that the Philadelphia Convention exceeded the limits of its delegated powers. He speaks to the propriety of Philadelphia and not to an amendatory convention at some future time. But the argument that he makes is easily applicable to an amendatory convention as the sense of the public that the Articles of Confederation were not working as designed will undoubtedly mirror that of the public who believes that it is time for an amendatory convention. He also makes a point, as noted more explicitly by Brannon Denning, about the morality of the amending process,[40]

> "*The* **second** *point to be examined is whether the convention were authorized to frame and propose this mixed Constitution.*
>
> *The powers of the convention ought, in strictness, to be determined by an inspection of the commissions given to the members by their respective constituents.*"[41]

In our modern parlance, Madison is saying that the call to convention generated by the resolutions of two-thirds of the States will form the limits of the convention. The commissions issued by the States to their delegations will contain the limits of their personal delegate authority. The notion that the convention will run away due to the actions of overzealous or ambitious delegates will be constrained by the fidelity to the state which sent that delegate to the amendatory convention. As each state gave varying instructions in 1787, we might expect the same to happen today, however, we see much the opposite occurring today as states collaborate to craft faithful delegate legislation and to ensure that the rules of the convention are understood beforehand as far as they may be discussed.

One of the most famous, and oft quoted, of *The Federalist* essays is *No.*

---

[40] Brannon P. Denning, "Means to Amend: Theories of Constitutional Change," *Tennessee Law Review* 65 (1997): 169

[41] *The Federalist, No. 40*, Madison

43, wherein the subject of amendment is taken up for the first time <u>directly</u>. This essay continues a string of papers discussing the "miscellaneous powers" granted to the federal government. Point number 8 in the paper states,

> "8. 'To provide for amendments to be ratified by three fourths of the States under two exceptions only.'
>
> *That useful alterations will be suggested by experience could not but be foreseen. It was requisite, therefore, that a mode for introducing them should be provided. The mode preferred by the convention seems to be stamped with every mark of propriety. It guards equally against that extreme facility, which would render the Constitution too mutable; and that extreme difficulty, which might perpetuate its discovered faults. It, moreover, equally enables the general and the State governments to originate the amendment of errors, as they may be pointed out by the experience on one side, or on the other."*[42]

Our Mr. Madison has both justified the rigor of the amendment process and the slow pace of amendment along with clarifying that the congressional and the convention methods are to be seen as equivalent in use and initiation. He is seeking and finding a balance with which the people can be contented to make the necessary amendments while not doing so too often so that the reverence that Madison thinks a national constitution should have is not denied. There is a deliberate intent to make the process hard enough to force a national discussion of the proposed amendment and to be certain that once made, the people are truly comfortable with the new amendment. Madison makes no distinction between when the congressional and the convention methods of amendment should be employed. He sees both as proper and neither as a last resort. For that, we would have to return to Madison's Notes and the discussion within the 1787 convention.

Professor Elizabeth Price Foley notes that in *No. 45*, Madison is reassuring the people that the new federal government has not taken their state's sovereignty and deposited it in a new government which they cannot control and which will run amok. The "vigorous system of dual sovereignty" of federalism is another check and balance. She says that in issuing *No. 45*, "Madison could not be any clearer in his message to the American people who ratified the Constitution: state sovereignty not only exists, but it exists

---

[42] *The Federalist, No. 43*, Madison

for the benefit of 'We the People.'"⁴³ Calling and conducting an amendatory convention is an exercise of that retained state sovereignty. The States launch the enterprise and the people execute it through the convention. It is in *No. 45* that we find the so frequently quoted passage,

> "The powers delegated by the proposed Constitution to the federal government are few and defined. Those which are to remain in the State governments are numerous and indefinite."⁴⁴

There is perhaps no greater statement of political philosophy found in the essays than this statement for it justifies not just the formation of the federal government at the time of the essay's writing but also it justifies the calling of an amendatory convention when that act is done to restore the balance of powers.

Opponents of an Article V amendatory convention often turn to *The Federalist* for supporting citations. In doing so, they frequently go to essays *No. 49* and *No. 50* quoting Madison. They will claim that Madison was opposed to "frequent recurrence" to a convention. Actually, Madison was opposed to Jefferson's ideas of a regular rewriting or revision of the Constitution on a generational basis and the collaboration of any two branches of the federal government against the third. Madison prophesied that resorting to regular conventions for such actions would take from the government and the Constitution "that veneration which time bestows on everything."⁴⁵ It is reasonable to conclude that Madison opposed proposing every little thing to solve a problem, be it small or large, as a constitutional amendment.

In *No. 49*, Madison goes on to discuss the necessity of having an amendment process but not to use it too often; there is no small irony here as James Madison is personally responsible for writing eleven of the twenty-seven amendments to the Constitution. In this essay, Madison opens with a discussion on Jefferson's *Notes on the State of Virginia*. He points out Jefferson's proposition that when two of the three branches of the federal government concur, an amendatory convention should be called. Madison responds,

---

[43] Elizabeth Price Foley, "Sovereignty, Rebalanced: The Tea Party & Constitutional Amendments," *Tennessee Law Review* 78 (2011): 753,

[44] *The Federalist, No. 45*, Madison

[45] Thomas E. Brennan, "Return to Philadelphia," *Cooley Law Review* 1 (1982): 58-9

> "There is certainly great force in this reasoning, and it must be allowed to prove that a constitutional road to the decision of the people out to be marked out and kept open, for certain great and extraordinary occasions. But there appear to be insuperable objections against the proposed recurrence to the people, as a provision in all cases for keeping the several departments of power within their constitutional limits."
>
> "In the next place, it may be considered as an objection inherent in the principle that as every appeal to the people would carry an implication of some defect in the government, frequent appeals would, in great measure, deprive the government of that veneration which time bestows on everything, and without which perhaps the wisest and freest governments would not possess the requisite stability."
>
> "The danger of disturbing the public tranquility by interesting too strongly the public passions is a still more serous objection against a frequent reference of constitutional questions to the decision of the whole society. Notwithstanding the success which has attended the revisions of our established forms of government and which does so much honor to the virtue and intelligence of the people of America, it must be confessed that the experiments are of too ticklish a nature to be unnecessarily multiplied."
>
> "But the greatest objection of all is that the decisions which would probably result from such appeals would not answer the purpose of maintaining the constitutional equilibrium of the government."[46]

These cautions from Madison are thought-provoking but are not necessarily ground for abandoning the amendatory convention method. Instead, they are evidence of the need for a truly deliberative convention and not a mere rubber stamp of a pre-worded amendment proposal. Time has tempered the validity of these warnings in the example of the Eighteenth and Twenty-first Amendments. An experiment was tried, approved by the majority of Americans who thought that the nation was taking the right path and doing the right thing. A short period of time proved otherwise and the amendment process was used to "undo" the experiment. So Article V has proven far safer than Madison anticipated. While the example of Prohibition may not meet the criteria "for certain great and extraordinary occasions" it

---

[46] *The Federalist, No. 49*, Madison – The authorship of *No. 49* is still in dispute to this day. Madison provided a list of who had written which essay to a Washington, D.C. printer years later during his retirement. That list is now considered authoritative. See Ketcham, *James Madison, A Biography*, 660-1

can be easily argued that the experiment, albeit a failure in the larger scope, was worth the effort and expense when compared to the potential damage to society through any other attempted means to invoke change.

But Madison softens his objections by *No. 50*. He explains that,

> *"It may be contended, perhaps, that instead of occasional appeals to the people, which are liable to the objections urged against them,* **periodical appeals are the proper and adequate means of preventing and correcting infractions of the Constitution.**
>
> *It will be attended to that in the examination of these expedients I confine myself to their aptitude for* **enforcing** *the Constitution, by keeping the several departments of power within their due bounds without particularly considering them as provisions for altering the Constitution itself."*

The idea of a periodic review of a constitution is not unusual; many of the States do exactly that through a state constitutional requirement for the periodic calling of a convention, or a constitutional commission. The concern that Madison was really exhibiting is that of a temporal problem, something that is a calamity in its brief day but passes. Once again we are brought to consider that constitutions should include statements of principle and not of policy.

Hamilton remarks in *No. 70* on the basis of the opposition to the Constitution and his observations may be equally applied to some of those who dissent against an amendatory convention.

> *"Men often oppose a thing merely because they had no agency in planning it, or because it may have been planned by those whom they dislike. But if they have been consulted, and have happened to disapprove, opposition then becomes, in their estimation, an indispensable duty of self-love."*[47]

This is simply a restatement of a fact of human nature. Bearing in mind the attempt to call a second, general convention after the 1787 convention, it was expected by most that those who became known as the Anti-Federalists would seek to dominate the second convention and bend it to their will. Remember that seventy-four men were chosen by their states to participate in the Philadelphia Convention and only fifty-five actually took part. Some of the selected delegates, Patrick Henry and Samuel Adams for

---

[47] *The Federalist, No. 70*, Hamilton

example, chose to sit out the convention for various reasons. Once the Grand Convention finished and published their product, those who had declined to participate were now incensed at the work produced. Henry led the battle against the Constitution's ratification in the Virginia ratification convention and pressed for a second general convention. Henry argued that,

> "To encourage us to adopt it, they tell us, that there is a plain easy way of getting amendments: When I come to contemplate this part, I suppose that I am mad, or, that my countrymen are so: The way to amendment, is, in my conception, shut."[48]

Henry then recites Article V verbatim and begins to logically lay out his objections,

> "Hence it appears that three-fourths of the States must ultimately agree to any amendments that may be necessary. Let us consider the consequence of this: However uncharitable it may appear, yet I must tell my opinion, that the most unworthy character may get into power, and prevent the introduction of amendments: Let us suppose (for the case is supposable, possible, and probable) that you happen to deal those powers to unworthy hands; will they relinquish powers already in their possession, or agree to amendments? Two-thirds of the Congress, or, of the State Legislatures, are necessary even to propose amendments: If one-third of these be unworthy men, they may prevent the application for amendments; but what is destructive and mischievous, is, that three-fourths of the State Legislatures, or of the State Conventions, must concur in the amendments when proposed: In such numerous bodies, there must necessarily be some designing bad men: To suppose that so large a number as three-fourths of the States will concur, is to suppose that they will possess genius, intelligence, and integrity, approaching to miraculous. It would indeed be miraculous that they should concur in the same amendments, or even in such as would bear some likeness to one another. For four of the smallest States, that do not collectively contain one-tenth part of the population of the United States, may obstruct the most salutary and necessary amendments: Nay, in these four States, six tenths of the people may reject these amendments; and suppose, that amendments shall be opposed to amendments (which is highly probable) is it possible, that three-fourths can ever agree to the same amendments? A bare majority in these four small States may hinder the adoption of amendments; so that we

---

[48] Speech of Patrick Henry to the Virginia Ratification Convention, 5 June 1788, as reproduced in, Ralph Ketcham, *The Anti-Federalist Papers and the Constitutional Convention Debates* (New York: Mentor, 1986), 204-5

may fairly and justly conclude, that one-twentieth part of the American people, may prevent the removal of the most grievous inconveniences and oppression, by refusing to accede to amendments. A trifling minority may reject the most salutary amendments. Is this an easy mode of securing the public liberty?"[49]

What makes Henry's objections so interesting is that they have often come true and that they are also the objections voiced today, in not so exact the wording, of the opponents of an amendatory convention. The necessity of a supermajority hindering adoption of a proposal, the "most unworthy characters" and "designing bad men" impeding progress, the refusal of Congress to relinquish powers, are his impediments to necessary amendments. Ironically, it is the ability of the few states to stop an amendment from ratification that also worried Henry. Today, this last point is used to reassure convention opponents that "bad" amendments will not be ratified. Although Henry, brilliant orator and principled statesman that he was, was proven wrong by history as to the impossibility of amendments – and quickly, as just three and half years later the Bill of Rights was ratified.

The real substance of the amendatory convention is given its due in the final essay, *No. 85*. Hamilton treats this essay as the second half of the cleanup of all the outstanding and unresolved issues and says as much in the beginning of *No. 84*.

> *"There is, however, one point of light in which the subject of amendments still remains to be considered, and in which it has not yet been exhibited to public view. I cannot resolve to conclude without first taking a survey of it in this aspect.*
>
> *It appears to me susceptible of absolute demonstration that it will be far more easy to obtain subsequent than previous amendments to the Constitution. The moment an alteration is made in the present plan it becomes, to the purpose of adoption, a new one, and must undergo a new decision of each State. To its complete establishment throughout the Union it will therefore require the concurrence of thirteen States."*[50]

Hamilton is stressing that any complete change to the government at the time prior to ratification by the requisite nine states would have forced

---

[49] Ibid.
[50] *The Federalist, No.85*, Hamilton

the whole exercise to be started over as the previously ratifying states would need to pass judgment on the new proposition. For those in opposition to an amendatory convention because they fear a new constitution will be produced, they can look to Hamilton to be reminded that any (albeit far-fetched or fanciful) new constitution would be applicable only to those states which would ratify it under that new proposal. An amendatory convention could not runaway and unilaterally impose a new constitution on the States and the people without their approval. That prophesy is a hallow threat.

Opponents have turned to the mention of a single proposition that Hamilton discusses and sought to refute that he meant to assure the people that each amendment proposal would get its own consideration. Proponents of an amendatory convention turn to this passage to provide proof that an amendatory convention could indeed be limited to a single topic and therefore be a limited and not an open convention. Before considering Hamilton's words on that point, it is key to remember that in the preceding paragraph, Hamilton spoke on the variety of opinions present in the convention and the need to compromise in creating the Constitution.

> *"Every Constitution for the United States must inevitably consist of a great variety or particulars in which thirteen independent States are to be accommodated in their interests or opinions of interest. We may of course expect to see, in any body of men charged with its original formation, very different combinations of the parts upon different points."*[51]

Mr. Hamilton is acknowledging the difficulty in forging the Constitution and sets up the argument that any single amendment will, in comparison, be easier to craft and pass than a new constitution. The difference between the drafting convention of 1787 and an amendatory convention is, in Hamilton's view, incomparably simpler in the amendatory case.

> *"But every amendment to the Constitution, if once established, would be a single proposition, and might be brought forward singly. There would then be no necessity for management or compromise in relation to any other point – no giving and taking. The will of the requisite number would at once bring the matter to a decisive issue. And consequently, whenever nine, or rather ten States, were united in the desire of a particular amendment, that amendment must infallibly take place. There can, therefore, be no*

---

[51] *The Federalist, No. 85*, Hamilton

comparison between the facility of affecting an amendment and that of establishing, in the first instance, a complete Constitution."[52]

With the exception of the Bill of Rights, Hamilton called it correctly – in terms of the congressional method. But it would seem that Hamilton might be making reference to the convention method here as well. As he references nine states – necessary to call a convention – and then ten states – necessary to ratify an amendment – and then, in the next paragraph specifically states that "persons delegated to the administration of the national government will always be disinclined to yield up any portion of the authority of which they were once possessed." He also uses the very specific wording of "united in desire of a particular amendment" – singular.[53] That scenario will most likely happen only in an amendatory convention. Hamilton then proceeds to prove this point directly,

> *"[T]hat the national rulers, whenever nine States concur, will have no option upon the subject. By the fifth article of the plan, the Congress will be* **obliged** *"on the application of the legislatures of two thirds of the States [which at present amount to nine]. To call a convention for proposing amendments which* **shall be valid**, *to all intents and purposes, as part of the Constitution, when ratified by the legislatures of three fourths of the states, or by conventions in three fourths thereof. The words of this article are peremptory. The Congress* **"shall** *call a convention." Nothing in this particular is left to the discretion of that body. And of consequence all the declamation about the disinclination to a change vanishes in air. Nor however difficult it may be supposed to unite two thirds or three fourths of the State legislatures in amendment which may affect local interests can there be any room to apprehend any such difficulty in a union on points which are merely relative to the general liberty or security of the people. We may safely rely on the disposition of the State legislatures to erect barriers against the encroachments of the national authority."*[54]

Hamilton has made the point quoted so many times that the Congress, and by implication the Executive, have no room to move when it comes to calling the convention. Hamilton was present in the convention; he knows the intentions of the Framers, having been one. Key words used are "no option," "peremptory", and "Nothing…is left to the discretion." The role of

---
[52] *The Federalist, No. 85*, Hamilton
[53] John R. Vile, *Conventional Wisdom* (Athens, GA: University of Georgia Press, 2016) 33
[54] *The Federalist, No. 85*, Hamilton

Congress is defined by these remarks; it is ministerial. The reference to the "general liberty…of the people" makes a most relevant and striking point. In a convention, the likelihood of the topic being a matter of limiting the power of the national government is clearly much greater than an amendment by the congressional method. The only limitations imposed constitutionally on the federal government AFTER ratification were the Bill of Rights and those were part of the gentlemen's agreement with a number of the States to ratify in exchange for the introduction of amendments. Without the amendatory convention, how would the people or the States pursue such an amendment to completion? Would it even be possible? The "disposition of the State legislatures to erect barriers" proves the need of the state legislatures to support and involve themselves in seeing that a convention comes to pass in those situations where the "national authority" has become obstructive and uncooperative.

It is then apparent that only a few of *The Federalist* essays touch directly on the amendment process, *Nos. 43, 49, 50* and *85*. The rest are indirectly making reference to or can be interpreted as applying to an amendatory convention. The reason that so little has been said on the amendment process in *The Federalist* and in the literature since is that the process is so simple and easily understood, especially in the days during which *The Federalist* were written.

The Prelude and Postscript to The Federalist

The creation of *The Federalist* did not happen in a vacuum. Alexander Hamilton was an incredibly brilliant individual. Historians have ranked Hamilton alongside Jefferson for supreme brilliance in a time of brilliant men. We can spot a trend at work with Hamilton, one that indicates his patience for a project. Writing articles for public consumption and persuasion was an old tactic for Hamilton long before he started *The Federalist* series. In 1778, he wrote a series of open letters published in the New York newspapers addressed to and attacking Declaration of Independence signer and future US Supreme Court Justice Samuel Chase for his war profiteering.[55] He signed the letters "Publius,"[56] a name that he got from Plutarch's "*Lives of the Noble Greeks and Romans.*" He used this nom de plume several times

---

[55] Richard Brookhiser, *Alexander Hamilton, American* (New York: Touchstone Books, 1999), 40
[56] Publius Valerius helped to establish the Roman Republic after the overthrow of the Tarquin kings of Rome.

including for *The Federalist* essays.⁵⁷ Hamilton employed the tool of the open public letter often and for varied purposes. It was said of Hamilton that he was a "manipulator of public opinion" and,

> *"The most prolific pamphleteer among the leading statesmen of the young republic, he almost always wrote under nom de plumes. And almost always the nom de plume seems to have been carefully picked to match the thrust of the argument in the pamphlet."*⁵⁸

In 1779, Hamilton proposed a constitutional convention to rectify the problems perceived in the Articles of Confederation. He wanted the national government to have taxing authority, a national bank and a strong "proper" executive.⁵⁹ In 1783, while serving in Congress in Philadelphia, Hamilton again planned to call for a constitutional convention to respond to the problems facing the nascent nation but he held back when it was apparent that the Congress was too dysfunctional to solve any problem.⁶⁰ Exhibiting that tenacity and persistence for which he was so well known, Hamilton once again called for a constitutional convention at the Annapolis Convention in 1786. He had made up his mind that the only way to correct the Articles' deficiencies was to redo the national charter. But by this time, he had an ally in Madison who wisely advised him on how to get the convention through issuing a spotless report on the Annapolis Convention that would be sent to all the States.⁶¹ Historian Richard Brookhiser noted that "Hamilton was driven by problems; Madison by theories."⁶² This complementary relationship served them well in writing *The Federalist* essay series. Madison promoted the political theories of the Constitution and sold the dream. Hamilton tackled the nation's problems and demonstrated the solutions offered, clinching the deal.

After *The Federalist Papers*, Hamilton continued his serial writings penning the thirty-eight articles called "*The Defence*" in 1795. This time he was defending the Washington administration's "Jay Treaty" designed to put to rest the unresolved issues lingering from the end of the Revolutionary

---

⁵⁷ Carl J. Richard, *The Founders and the Classics, Greece, Rome, and the American Enlightenment* (Cambridge, MA: Harvard University Press, 1994), 41
⁵⁸ "A Note on Certain of Hamilton's Pseudonyms," *William and Mary Quarterly* 12, no.2 (Apr.1955): 283
⁵⁹ Richard Brookhiser, *Alexander Hamilton, American* (New York: Touchstone Books, 1999), 44
⁶⁰ Ibid., 55
⁶¹ Ibid., 60
⁶² Ibid., 53

War and the unaddressed matters not covered by the Treaty of Paris in 1783. Hamilton signed the essays as "Camillus," for the Roman general that saved the Roman Republic from an invasion.[63] Other pseudonyms utilized by Hamilton include Americanus, Caesar, Catullus, Horatius, Metellus, Pericles, Phocion, Titus Manlius, and Tully. Brookhiser points out that between *The Federalist* and *The Defence*, Hamilton generated about 170,000 words. Hamilton's wordsmithing was so prodigious that other serial works were incorrectly attributed to him. To paraphrase the old television commercial of a stockbrokerage firm, when Hamilton wrote, people listened.

Madison's contributions to the Constitution, and to Article V in particular, speak for themselves. Amendatory convention opponents have seized on Madison's words in the Virginia Resolutions of 1798 and used those to claim the validity of nullification as a preferred option to Madison. This position goes against Madison's arguments late in life much to the contrary. Madison's opposition during the ratification campaign to an amendatory convention was predicated on the time to complete the addition of a Bill of Rights and not a rejection of the convention method.

Even among some of the Anti-Federalists, Article V was recognized for its utility during the ratification campaigns.[64] Elbridge Gerry worked hard during the Philadelphia Convention to refine the amendment process and to include the convention method. Other delegates such as George Mason, William Paca, John Lansing, Luther Martin, and Robert Yates worked against ratification without a Bill of Rights. In the ratification conventions in the States, many cited Article V as a plus to obtain the desired amendments for a Bill of Rights.[65] It has been argued that the Federalists deliberately used Article V and the promise of future amendments as an incentive to ratification without prior changes to the Constitution.[66] In the end, Article V worked, as the Bill of Rights was added as amendments proving that the process worked and that the promises made in *The Federalist* were genuine. Ultimately, the process proved to be bipartisan with the Anti-Federalists joining the Federalists in drafting and

---

[63] Ibid., 123-4
[64] Ralph Ketcham, *The Anti-Federalist Papers and the Constitutional Convention Debates* (New York: Mentor, 1986), 188, 195
[65] Ibid., 217-26, 239-40
[66] David E. Kyvig, *Explicit & Authentic Acts, Amending the U.S. Constitution, 1776-1995* (Lawrence: University Press of Kansas, 1996), Chapter 4, 66-86

then securing the amendments.

The value of *The Federalist* essays today with regard to an amendatory convention lay in the insight as to the intent of whether an amendatory convention could be limited in powers, independent of the federal government's control, and that Congress would be restrained in its involvement. From the pens of the Framers these worries appear to have been put to rest nearly two and a half centuries ago.

Part IV: Constitutional Déjà Vu

The Fears and Facts

Examining the fight over an Article V Convention

NINE
THE ARGUMENT AGAINST AN ARTICLE V CONVENTION

> *"Nor is it surprising to find that such questions have been pressed most insistently by those who are opposed to the substantive goals being sought by amendment – discouraging action by dwelling on real or exaggerated difficulties is a time-honored tradition in American political discourse."*[1]
> –*Clifton McCleskey, Professor of Government, University of Texas*

It is no surprise that the first applications for an Article V amendatory convention were submitted so quickly to Congress in 1788 by New York and in 1789 by Virginia and followed those states' notices of ratification of the Constitution.[2,3] Many of the States were concerned about the lack of a Bill of Rights and New York and Virginia genuinely seemed willing to work within the new constitutional system, in part to make certain that the issues and complaints of the States raised during the ratification process were not ignored, and perhaps in part to see how well it worked. As a result of the state ratification conventions, a total of 189 proposals for changes were submitted[4] by seven of the ratifying states to the

---

[1] Clifton McCleskey, "Along the Midway: Some Thoughts on Democratic Constitution-Amending," *Michigan Law Review* 66, no.5 (Mar. 1968): 1004. Quoted by permission of the author.
[2] Ralph R. Martig, "Amending the Constitution Article V: The Keystone of the Arch," *Michigan Law Review* 35, no.8 (1937): 1267
[3] H. Jour., 1ˢᵗ Cong., at 28-30, (May 5-6, 1789)
[4] Robert J. Sprague, "Shall We Have a Federal Convention, and What Shall It Do?," *Maine Law Review* III, no.4 (1910): 116

First United States Congress.⁵ Almost immediately, a clamor arose over the problems of an amendatory convention. It takes too long; the required two-thirds of the States is an unreachable goal; it is an expensive process; it is unworkable.

With each attempt to call an amendatory convention, the same concerns were raised and occasionally new ones added to the list of fears until we reached the state where we find ourselves today with the hyperbolic parade of horribles trotted out every time that an Article V convention is mentioned. We are now dealing with an almost untouchable canon of fears that are treated as a form of gospel in which questioning the validity of those fears is sacrilege. But, in fairness, there are some legitimate concerns and we should examine them closely and wherever possible, provide a logic-based and historically accurate refutation. Herein, an effort is made, as Alexander Hamilton promised in the first of *The Federalist* essays, "to give a satisfactory answer to all the objections which shall have made their appearance."⁶ If we are to call an Article V amendatory convention, it is in all likelihood due to a perceived breakdown in the constitutional order and that the States feel the need to assert themselves. They would be wise to act prudently and research the matter fully before committing. After all, the Declaration of Independence warns that, "Prudence, indeed, will dictate that Governments long established should not be changed for light and transient causes." The same may be said, equally prudently, of the constitutions which form those same governments.

Caution versus Constitutionalism

In regard to constitutional conventions, and more specifically amendatory conventions, opponents look to the counsel of 1787 Convention delegate Charles Cotesworth Pinckney of South Carolina, who opined, "Conventions are serious things, and ought not to be repeated."⁷ The rhetoric of opposition to an Article V convention is sometimes extreme and occasionally prophetic. One writer characterized such a convention in terms of this result,

---

⁵ Joseph R. Long, "Tinkering with the Constitution," *Yale Law Journal* 24, no.7 (1915): 574
⁶ Alexander Hamilton, "Federalist Paper, No.1," in *The Federalist Papers: Hamilton, Madison, Jay*, ed. Clinton Rossiter (New York: Mentor, 1961), 36
⁷ Max Farrand, *The Records of the Federal Convention of 1787*, Vol. II (New Haven: Yale University Press, 1911 and rev. 1937), 632

> *"A general and unlimited federal constitutional convention would at least be a futility and might be a disaster... The body which would be called into being by the action of Congress under article V would have revolutionary potentialities... it would seem obvious that limitations of subject matter can be of no avail. Once convened, the body of delegates to propose amendments in accordance with article V could, if they wished, raise the most fundamental question by proposing a complete reorganization of the government. They could take the revolutionary step which the States-General of France took in 1789 in reconstituting themselves as the National Assembly."*[8]

It is incumbent upon us to perceive that the writer speaks not of a limited amendatory convention, but of a general and unlimited convention – this is a valid citation as is the comparison made so often by the opponents of an Article V convention. In their view, and in their words, the two convention types are indistinguishable and inseparable. The truth is that they are describing a revolutionary convention which is neither a constitutional convention nor an amendatory convention.

The American Enterprise Institute (AEI) held a forum on Article V conventions in May of 1979 and produced a booklet on the results. The moderator recounted the prediction of a writer that such a convention could, "reinstate segregation and even slavery, throw out much or all of the Bill of Rights, eliminate the Fourteenth Amendment's due process clause, reverse any Supreme Court decision the members didn't like, including the one-man-one-vote rule, and perhaps, for good measure, eliminate the Supreme Court itself."[9] Robert Natelson wonders how the convention could do any of these things without the support of the military.[10] Present at the forum as a panelist was future US Supreme Court Justice Antonin Scalia,[11] who responded that,

> *"'All those things are possible,' but he had, 'no fear that such extreme proposals would come out of a constitutional convention.' He continued that, 'I am willing to take a chance in having a convention despite some doubts that now exist. I am not sure how much longer we have. I am not sure how long*

---

[8] Ralph M. Carson, "Disadvantages of a Federal Constitutional Convention," *Michigan Law Review* 66, no.5 (Mar.1968): 922-3.
[9] Richard Rovere, cited in Russell B. Caplan, *Constitutional Brinkmanship* (New York: Oxford University Press, 1988), viii – from Rovere's *New Yorker* article.
[10] Robert G. Natelson, "Proposing Constitutional Amendments by Convention: Rules Governing the Process," *Tennessee Law Review* 78 (2011): 715
[11] Then a University of Chicago Law School professor.

> *a people can accommodate to directives from a [national] legislature that it feels is no longer responsive, and to directives from a life-tenured judiciary that was never meant to be responsive, without ultimately losing its will to control its own destiny.*"[12]

It seems somewhat ironic, and even satirical, that Antonin Scalia was the longest serving (i.e., life-tenured, in his own words above) justice on the US Supreme Court at the time of his passing in 2016. Today, many opponents of the amendatory convention will cite the first five words of Justice Scalia's quote, but conveniently forget the remainder of the quotation. At the 1979 AEI conference, Scalia also stated, "There is no reason not to interpret [Article V] to allow a limited call, if that is what the states desire." In another twist, Scalia also said, again in 1979, that he "would favor a convention on abortion."[13] Contrast these sentiments of Justice Scalia with a comment that he made 8 May 2015 to the Federalist Society in New Jersey, "A constitutional convention is a horrible idea. This is not a good century to write a constitution."[14] In early 2014, Justices Scalia and Ruth Bader Ginsburg appeared on *The Kalb Report* broadcast series at the National Press Club where both were asked by journalist Marvin Kalb about the amendment process. Scalia exclaiming, "I would certainly not want a constitutional convention. Whoa! Who knows what would come out of it?"[15] Of course, in both instances, Scalia was referring to a CONSTITUTIONAL convention and not an AMENDATORY convention. Context is everything.

Other US Supreme Court justices have weighed in with their warnings as well. Former Chief Justice Earl Warren cautioned that Article V "used unwisely by an uninformed public…could soon destroy the foundations of the Constitution."[16] Former Justice Arthur Goldberg warned that "it is my firm belief that no single issue or combination of issues is so important as to warrant jeopardizing our entire constitutional system of governance."[17] Former Justice William Brennan pronounced a convention, "the most awful

---

[12] American Enterprise Institute for Public Policy Research, *A Constitutional Convention: How Well Would It Work?* (Washington, D.C.: 1979): 5
[13] Russell B. Caplan, *Constitutional Brinkmanship* (New York: Oxford University Press, 1988), 71
[14] http://dailysignal.com/2015/05/11/supreme-court-justice-scalia-constitution-not-bill-of-rights-makes-us-free/
[15] https://www.youtube.com/watch?v=z0utJAu_iG4
[16] Caplan quoting a *New York Times* article dated 23 May 1963, 74
[17] Arthur J. Goldberg, "The Proposed Constitutional Convention," *Hastings Constitutional Law Quarterly* 11 (Fall 1983): 4 - published in the *Chicago Tribune*, 16 October 1983 and the *Miami Herald*, Sunday, 14 September 1986

thing in the world."¹⁸ How then do we reconcile the differences in opinion on the matter among the various justices, past and present?

Of late, no one has done a better job of summarizing the concerns of those in opposition to an amendatory convention than perhaps, the then President of the Arizona State Senate, Andy Biggs.¹⁹ He produced a book in 2015 that outlines his concerns and details why those concerns might be valid. It is worth a look. He lists a number of both unanswered questions and issues that raise alarm:²⁰

- Length of the convention
- No control over the convention
- The influence of lobbyists and special interests
- The role of Congress
- The role of the federal judiciary
- That "settled events" will be reopened
- A media circus will ensue which will influence the convention
- The convention process is unclear
- The inability to limit the convention
- Convention is open to hijacking
- The potential harm of a convention outweighs the benefits
- Many conventions are required to fix the nation
- Lack of a precedent

State Senator Biggs' concerns are legitimate; he forecasts some unnerving outcomes. He sees that the results of an amendatory convention are possibly nothing like the results anticipated by proponents. He stresses that Congress cannot be "gotten around."²¹ The convention may lack legitimacy in the eyes of the public.²² He believes that the convention will be most comparable to a political party's nominating convention instead of a

---

[18] Gerald Benjamin and Thomas Gais, "Constitutional Conventionphobia," *Hofstra Law & Policy Symposium* 1 (1996): 54

[19] Biggs was elected to Congress in November 2016.

[20] Andy Biggs, *The Con of the Con-Con, The Case Against the States Amending the U. S. Constitution* (Gilbert, AZ: Freeman Press, 2015), generally

[21] Ibid., 73

[22] Ibid., 97

legislative body.²³ The other branches of the federal government are part of the problem and a convention simply ignores their culpability.²⁴ Sen. Biggs concludes that the amendatory convention is an appropriate solution for a different problem and one that has yet to arise. He advocates for other solutions at this time.

The litany of problems that opponents expect from a convention is long. The top concerns merit consideration and rebuttal. In no order of apparent apprehension, opponents expect:

- A runaway convention in which the agenda is ignored
- The Constitution and/or the Bill of Rights will be replaced or simply eliminated
- No rules will be in place to govern the operation of the convention
- An unlimited or open convention in which any topic taken up
- Could the convention be controlled?
- Congress will control the convention
- The delegates will be controlled by special interests
- There is no way to restrain or reverse the actions of such a convention
- The tradition of unit-voting by states will be changed to electoral voting
- The convention may choose a new ratification process
- There is no Washington, Madison, Franklin, etc., today
- An amendatory convention would cause confrontations between the branches of the federal government, the States and the convention

There is almost no end to the number of predicted potential problems that may occur and as soon as one threat is definitively dispatched, a new predicted threat takes its place in the pantheon of potential problems. Group after group has produced their position statement on the anticipated threats

---

²³ Ibid., 4
²⁴ Ibid., 30

but they are generally condensed down to those listed here.²⁵ Professor Gerald Gunther laid out his view of a convention without congressional oversight and controls:

> *"And those delegates could make a plausible case that a convention is entitled to set its own agenda. They could, for example, claim that the limitation in the congressional 'call' was to be taken as a moral exhortation, but not as a binding restriction on the convention's discussion. They could argue that they were charged with considering all those constitutional issues perceived as major concerns by the American people who elected them."*²⁶

The hue and cry against the perceived dangers of an amendatory convention has been met with (usually) patient and articulate reasoning meant to assuage the fears of the opponents. Writers seeking to refute the remonstrations of the worried have turned to a long list of state and federal court decisions and academic clarifications of the limits of power. Occasionally the frustration and impatience of the writers in law review journals come through and they can appear humorous today. One writer in 1952 produced a list of court opinions dating back to the 1830s to support his contention as to the safety of the amendatory convention. He ended the first paragraph of the article with this sentence: "It is the singular purpose of this paper to prove conclusively and for all time that the calling of such a convention is not analogous to the opening of a Pandora's box."²⁷

Compare that frustration laden declaration with this opposing, and equally frustrated viewpoint from Gerald Gunther again,

> *"But the present campaign [balanced budget amendment campaign of the 1970s and 1980s] has in fact largely been an exercise in constitutional irresponsibility – constitutional roulette, or brinkmanship if you will, a stumbling toward a constitutional convention that more resembles blindman's bluff than serious attention to deliberate revision of our basic*

---

[25] As a representative example, see Michael Leachman and David Super, "*States Likely Could Not Control Constitutional Convention on Balanced Budget Amendment or Other Issues,*" (Washington, D.C.: Center on Budget and Policy Priorities, 16 July 2014)

[26] Gerald Gunther, "The Convention Method of Amending the United States Constitution," *Georgia Law Review* 14, no.1 (Fall 1979): 9. This Article was originally published at 14 Ga. L. Rev. 1 (1979) and is reprinted with permission.

[27] Frank E. Packard, "The Inherent Safety in Calling a Convention for the Purpose of Proposing Amendments to the Constitution of the United States," *Dickinson Law Review* 56 (1952): 373

law."²⁸

The Pandora's Box comparison is as old as the efforts to call a limited convention.²⁹ In 1909, when a number of states had submitted applications for a convention for the direct election of federal senators growing, the media of the day took note that, "a convention, called for the purpose of securing a new method of electing United States Senators, would open a Pandora's Box."³⁰

It is exactly the opening of an unlimited Pandora's Box that opponents of an amendatory convention fear. That the history of government, especially American government, is rife with examples of government – at all levels – ignoring the law that constrains government and doing as it sees fit, provides a justification for the fears and apprehensions of opponents and requires that those same concerns be thoroughly addressed and, hopefully, mitigated. One must admit that there are few things in politics, law and particularly constitutional law that are absolute or that are entirely known and the potential for disaster looms ever-present. While this book seeks to assuage those fears and establish with some degree of certainty of the safety of an amendatory convention, it is simply wise to acknowledge that nothing can be predicted with absolute certainty and that to provide for contingencies is the best policy. Where provision of contingency is not possible, then being forewarned and vigilant is next best.

We can define the issue of the calling of a convention, for good or bad, by quoting Gordon S. Wood on his view of conventions,

> *"The convention was thus a political weapon in 1787-1788, and it has remained one ever since. But because it has never been used at the national level, it has a kind of doomsday machine quality about it: no one can be quite sure what invoking a convention would mean."³¹*

The potential for a convention that produces unpopular, unconstitutional, unreasonable or unnecessary amendment proposals is

---

[28] Gerald Gunther, "The Convention Method of Amending the United States Constitution," *Georgia Law Review* 14, no.1 (Fall 1979): 3 . This Article was originally published at 14 Ga. L. Rev. 1 (1979) and is reprinted with permission.
[29] It was repeated after West (*infra*) by Packard, Benjamin & Gais, Williams and more.
[30] Henry Litchfield West, "Shall United States Senators be Elected by the People," *Forum* 42 (Oct. 1909): 298 – as cited by Stasny, 84
[31] Gordon S. Wood, "The Origins of Article V of the Constitution," *The Constitution and the Budget*, American Enterprise Institute (1980), 22

paramount to the opposition to an Article V convention. Avoiding placing the constitutional health of the nation in the hands of those who may lack a sufficient understanding of the purpose and function of a constitution is the frequent motivation of opponents. An overwhelmingly vast number of amendment proposals have been for issues that are not of a constitutional nature. They were more a matter of policy than a matter of principle. Principle is separated from policy by the test of time. Principle does not change and should not. Policy is often the expedient whim of the moment. Our constitutions should contain matters of principle only and not of policy.[32] Interestingly, Harvard Law Professor Laurence Tribe made the same point, but to argue against the amendatory convention for a federal balanced budget amendment, in his testimony before the California State Assembly in 1979. He posited that constitutions should contain only fundamental law and not social or economic policies.[33] Professor Tribe did not see fiscal responsibility as a fundamental principle of government in 1979 when the accumulated federal debt was just under $826 BILLION. His view is interesting in 2016 when the accumulated federal debt has grown to nearly $20 TRILLION, or roughly twenty-four times the federal debt of 1979 and seemingly all fiduciary and fiscal responsibility has been abandoned by the federal government, most especially by the elected officials charged with its oversight.[34] In 2015, the ratio of the accumulated federal debt of $18.1 trillion relative to the GDP of $17.197 trillion amounted to 105.3%.[35]

Looking to unconstitutional or potentially damaging amendments, Pennsylvania Supreme Court Chief Justice Robert von Moschzisker said in 1925,

> *"But there never has been, and never will be, any subject of more vital importance for constant consideration by those who aspire to leadership in American thought than that of the Constitution; to preserve its blessings for future generations, we of to-day must be eternally vigilant in keeping alive a real comprehension of its basic principles and in safeguarding it from disintegrating amendments....The people must be educated to understand not only the broad conceptions on which our fundamental law rests, but*

---

[32] Credit for the argument for the expressed sentiment is attributed to then-Wisconsin State Representative Chris Kapenga – from a series of discussions between the representative and the author.

[33] Laurence Tribe, "Issues Raised by Requesting Congress to Call a Constitutional Convention to Propose a Balanced Budget Amendment," *Pacific Law Journal* 10 (1979): 628-30

[34] http://www.treasurydirect.gov/govt/reports/pd/histdebt/histdebt.htm Year-by-year federal debt

[35] Ibid., 9, Table 1.1

also the practical value of guarding against any necessary disturbance of the balance of those ideas, – so carefully worked out and reduced to principles by the founders of our national government."[36]

Chief Justice von Moschzisker took great pains to examine the body of amendment proposals in the then-recent (69th) Congress. He highlighted those proposals that did not meet the requisite quality of principle and, additionally, that infringed upon the traditional sovereignty and province of the States as dictated by American federalism. He was concerned with the apparent failure to fully think through the impact and consequences of some of the amendment proposals.

"In the desire for quick results and ease of accomplishment, the advocates of particular measures too often forget that merely writing law into the Constitution does not necessarily cure the evil aimed at."[37]

The lesson that he was trying to impart is that not everything was worthy of a constitutional amendment and that the temporal majority of the special interests must be kept in check. Although von Moschzisker was not speaking directly on the issue of an Article V convention, his concerns about the propriety of an amendment proposal's subject matter comes through when he quotes James, Viscount Bryce,[38]

"The Constitution embodied these fundamental concepts and aimed thereby to protect 'not only the states against the central power, not only each branch of the federal government against the other branches, but the people against themselves; that is, the people as a whole against the impulses of a transient majority.'"[39]

This caution raises the question of what then is appropriate subject matter for an amendatory convention? Clearly, the subject matter can be limited to one or just a few subjects but can a particular subject – other than a state's constitutionally protected equal suffrage in the US Senate – be

---

[36] Robert von Moschzisker, "Dangers in Disregarding Fundamental Conceptions when Amending the Federal Constitution," *Cornell Law Quarterly* XI, no.1 (1925): 1 – transcribed from an address before the Cornell University College of Law, Irvine lecture.
[37] Ibid., 5
[38] Viscount Bryce is an interesting figure historically. He was an historian who, while serving in the United States as the British ambassador, attempted to retrace Alexis de Tocqueville's steps and assess the political change since Tocqueville wrote "Democracy in America."
[39] Robert von Moschzisker, "Dangers in Disregarding Fundamental Conceptions when Amending the Federal Constitution," *Cornell Law Quarterly* XI, no.1 (1925): 3 - quoting Bryce from "The American Commonwealth," 406

placed off-limits to an amendatory convention? Since the States stipulate the convention topic in their applications to Congress, a single subject or a limited subject convention would have the ability to avoid a topic that could be considered inappropriate. An open convention, in contrast, would then NOT be so limited since, by definition, it is open to any proposal. It is this specific concern that provokes most opponents of an Article V convention. The most commonly expressed scenario is that of special interest groups coming to dominate the delegations of a number of key states and working in concert to propose and adopt an amendment proposition that is in the opponents' view, dangerous.

But what constitutes a constitutionally acceptable amendment topic? How do we define that which is mere policy as distinct from that which is principle and, therefore, to stand the test of time and warrant inclusion in the Constitution? Four categories for acceptable amendment proposal were suggested by von Moschzisker,

> "*They may be grouped in four classes: (a) Those relating to the structure and machinery of government, such as the method of amending the Constitution, the election of the President, the organization and power of the Supreme Court, and the treaty-making power; (b) those modifying or enlarging the exercise of power Congress already possesses, such as those relating to war and taxation; (c) those directly affecting personal rights; (d) those concerning the distribution of powers between the national and state governments. The proposals in the last-mentioned group represent, in practically every case, attempts to augment the powers of the central government, and to grant it either direct control or the right to assume control over matters connected in an intimate way with the lives of the people.*"[40]

The objections expressed by opponents of an amendatory convention over the last two centuries have been well-established and can be categorized. With the advent of law review journals in the nineteenth century, there has grown a significant body of professional and academic literature on the subject of amendatory conventions.[41] Through these journals, and the few books written on the subject, we are able to travel back in time and study the reasoning both for and against amendatory conventions. We are fortunate that the rise in the number of amendatory convention drives lags only a

---

[40] Ibid., 5
[41] The *University of Pennsylvania Law Review* was the first to publish in 1852; the *Albany Law Review* was the first student edited journal in 1875.

couple of decades behind the establishment of the law journals giving us a chronicle of these movements from a legal perspective. As far back as the first volume of *The Yale Law Journal*, published in 1892, we find an article on the public's worry about amendatory conventions. The author, John Hoober, drawing on newspaper articles of the time, speculates on the causes of the public's concern,

> *"What is there in the history, power, or mode of procedure of constitutional conventions which should deservedly make them contend against popularity? Have they in times past met in response to arbitrary calls, invested with powers of annihilation to the state; have they acted unofficially, disregarding law and custom, supplanting existing organization through revolutionary methods; or have they when charged with definite powers disregarded the purposes of assembling, seemingly acting as if they were above the law and its limitations and violating state interests to promote selfish ends? If such facts mark their genesis and development no plea can be interposed on their behalf. But their history, from the earliest original to the latest amendatory convention, warrants no such conclusion."*[42]

Hoober speaks to the issues which are, in his era in the century before last, already time-worn questions and concerns, but he concludes that history has shown these worries to be unwarranted. He goes on to segregate the opponents of an amendatory convention into three divisions: those who prefer to trust the legislature; those who want no change at any time; and those who believe that a convention is all powerful and uncontrollable. These divisions continue to exist today with the last one still very dominant. It is this last group that raises the important questions of the legal aspect of the convention,

> *"Can a convention once assembled impute to itself sovereignty? The question has suggested itself to honest minds. Can we be reasonably certain that the powers we, as electors delegate to the convention, will be honestly executed? If we commission them with a determinate function can they gather to themselves greater attributions of power? Can they supplant our wishes, treading under foot public policy and private right? Must we accept the fruit of violated instructions? Can they change our express mandate and make it of no obligatory force?"*[43]

---

[42] John A. Hoober, "Popular Prejudice and Constitutional Amendatory Conventions," *Yale Law Journal* 1, no.5 (1892): 207
[43] Ibid., 211

All of these questions are again brought up today each time that an Article V convention is proposed. Due diligence requires that we consider and answer each in their turn. They are reworded and repackaged over time but are the core of the objections that we still find ourselves contending with today.

The greatest fear expressed is that of the perceived power of an Article V convention to entirely change the Constitution. It is often said that the delegates could draft, adopt and ratify a new constitution at will. Whether it is done by an outright proposal of a new constitution or the amending of the existing law with a new constitution that as an amendment replaces the entire document, this is the foremost reason for avoiding an amendatory convention.

The fears expressed concerning the potential of an amendatory convention had been projected equally on potential ratification conventions prior to the first actual Article V ratification conventions in 1933. During the debates in the Senate over the passage of the Fifteenth Amendment in 1869, Senator Orris Ferry of Connecticut opposed the suggestion of ratification by convention that had been proposed by his fellow Connecticut Senator James Dixon, saying,

> *"If a [ratification] convention is once assembled you cannot limit its power to the simple amendment which you are proposing to it. It may go on and amend your State constitution and to subvert the whole machinery of your State government, and there is no power in your State to stop it."*[44]

We can now safely state that such a concern is unwarranted due to the historical record. Bearing in mind that the amendatory and the ratificatory conventions are both Article V conventions subject to the same requirements and limitations provides some measure of assurance that neither will run amok.

The Potential for a "Runaway" Convention

There is no greater fear or argument made against an amendatory convention than that of the potential for the convention to runaway based on the experience of the 1787 Grand Convention. One of the best summations of the runaway fear is found in the preface to *"The Constitutional Convention*

---

[44] Cong. Globe, 40th Cong., 3d sess., at 542, 828, 1040, and 1314 (1869)

as an Amending Device," and reads, "In short, the expressed fear is that democracy will generate a runaway national constitutional convention unlike anything known in American governing processes."⁴⁵

The great unknown fear of what might happen is overwhelming for many who look backward to Philadelphia and see a barely contained disaster in 1787. A close examination of the wording of the resolution from Congress recommending the convention in Philadelphia shows that the "mandate" and the instructions given by the States appear to have been exceeded. How much so and why are very different and important questions. Former US Supreme Court Justice Arthur Goldberg laid out his fear,

> *"One of the most serious problems Article V proposes is a runaway convention. There is no enforceable mechanism to prevent a convention from reporting out wholesale changes to our Constitution and Bill of Rights."*⁴⁶

Justice Goldberg's caution makes sense when one looks at the Philadelphia Convention as having "reported out wholesale changes to the Articles of Confederation" without the authority to do so. When one does examines the wording of the 1787 convention call from the Confederation Congress and sees the phrasing that stipulates the purpose of the convention to be for,

> *"the* **sole and express purpose of revising** *the Articles of Confederation and reporting to Congress and the several legislatures such* **alterations** *and provisions therein as shall, when* **agreed to in Congress** *and confirmed by the States, render the federal constitution adequate to the exigencies of government and the preservation of the union."*⁴⁷

it is a reasonable reaction to conclude that the delegates exceeded their mandate and their commissions if one focuses on the words "sole and express purpose of revising." Further evidence may be found in the words "alterations" and "agreed to in Congress." Based on these specific instructions from the Congress, it is obvious that the textual interpretation is correct that clearly the 1787 convention did take action that was more than "solely and expressly" for "revising" and creating "alterations" that were "agreed to in

---

⁴⁵ Kermit Hall, Harold Hyman, Leon Sigal, *The Constitutional Convention as an Amending Device* (Washington, D.C.: American Historical Association and American Political Science Association, 1981), vi

⁴⁶ Published in the *Chicago Tribune*, 16 October 1983 and the *Miami Herald*, Sunday, 14 September 1986

⁴⁷ Max Farrand, *The Records of the Federal Convention of 1787, Vol. I* (New Haven: Yale University Press, 1911 and rev. 1937), 14

Congress." It certainly appears, using these facts alone, that the convention was without limits, or that it exceeded the limits. Opponents today say that all constitutional conventions are without limits and they have a number of scholars to back up their contention.

Stanford Law Professor Gerald Gunther lays out the progression of a runaway convention not as a deliberate storming of the castle style of assault on the Constitution but more of a mission scope creep type of event where no one individual in particular is responsible for the deviation. It is a situation where competing interests and factions assert themselves and the mix yields a convention that no one saw coming,

> *"What we risk is a process which starts with a state focus on the balanced budget, leads to a congressional call of a convention to consider fiscal problems, develops into delegate election campaigns where amendments dealing with discrimination and health are also debated, and culminates in a constitutional convention considering amendments on a wide range of other issues as well."*[48]

A counterpoint to Gunther is given by US Supreme Court Justice Joseph Story in 1833; he rejected the runaway theory by detailing the particulars of the ratification process, emphasizing the passage of time and providing for careful inspection and consideration,

> *"Time is thus allowed, and ample time, for deliberation, both in proposing and ratifying amendments. They cannot be carried by surprise, or intrigue, or artifice. Indeed, years may elapse before a deliberate judgment may be passed upon them, unless some pressing emergency calls for instant action."*[49]

This same view was espoused exactly a century later as the nation prepared for the ratifications for the Twenty-first Amendment. The *Journal of the Florida Bar Association* ran an article that succinctly presented the argument for the slow pace and deliberative nature of the ratification convention scheme. Author Herbert Phillips refers to the Framers and the idea then being proposed in numerous states of using a referendum, and of Congress regulating the convention rules, for ratification and points out that,

---

[48] Gerald Gunther, "The Convention Method of Amending the United States Constitution," *Georgia Law Review* 14, no.1 (Fall 1979): 11. This Article was originally published at 14 Ga. L. Rev. 1 (1979) and is reprinted with permission.

[49] Joseph Story, *Commentaries on the Constitution of the United States, Vol.3* (Boston: Hillard, Gray and Co., 1833), §1824, 688

> "They did not deem it safe and wise to provide short cuts for immediate ratification of proposed amendments. They realized that, owing to the limitations of human minds and the impossibility to fully comprehend so important a matter upon first consideration, ample time should be given for discussion, deliberation, and thought, before action should be taken on proposed amendments."[50]

One would have to work extremely hard to find a more suitable caricature of the stereotypical cigar-chomping, blowhard, elitist, politician carousing with late nineteenth-century, early twentieth-century robber barons than Senator Weldon Heyburn of Idaho. Like many of his peers facing the prospect of an amendatory convention for the purpose of proposing an amendment for the direct election of US senators in 1910, he went on a rant in which he predicts the outcome of such a convention. He prophesized that the senators would lose their state's equal suffrage representation in the Senate. He warned that there would be "crystallized in the organic law of the land every vicious piece of proposed legislation we have had to fight down all these years to maintain our civilization." He saw the worst coming in the form that,

> "A constitutional convention is without limit as to its powers; when the people of the United States meet again for the purpose of making an organic law, the prohibition that no amendment can be made to the Constitution until it has been ratified by three fourths of the states, is at an end. The government is being reborn."[51]

Senator Heyburn's consistent tirade was vigorously repeated whenever and wherever he could preach it, extolling that,

> "[Article V] does not contemplate that any constitutional convention shall assemble with a limitation on it to deal with a particular question. When the constitutional convention meets it is the people, and it is the same people who made the original Constitution, and no limitation in the original Constitution controls the people when they meet again to consider the

---

[50] Herbert S. Phillips, "Has the Congress the Power Under Article V of the Constitution to Call and Regulate the Holding of Ratifying Conventions Independent of State Legislatures?," *Florida State Bar Association Law Journal* 6 (1933): 574

[51] William L. Martin, "The Amending Power: The Background of the Income Tax Amendment," *American Bar Association Journal* 39, no.1 (Jan.1953): 79-80

Constitution."[52,53]

Senator Heyburn's later histrionics were recorded in the *Congressional Record* for posterity and ended with this ominous warning, "When the States are calling for a constitutional convention they know not what they are doing. They know not the dangers that would confront them under such circumstances."[54]

The fear of the runaway convention potential has a long history. It was among the first of the fears expressed about Article V. Pre-dating Sen. Heyburn's shrieks, we can see the precautions taken by the Confederate States constitutional convention in their drafting of the Confederate Constitution in 1861 wherein they allowed only for the consideration of specific amendments proposed by the confederating states. In Article V, Section 1, the Confederate Constitution stated that a convention shall "take into consideration such amendments to the Constitution as the said States shall concur in suggesting at the time the said demand is made."[55] Were they thinking of a runaway convention or merely being thorough? It has been reported that the fear of the runaway is a late nineteenth-century creation and does not pre-date the Civil War era. This fear was created either at the same time or a short time before the notion that all Article V conventions are plenary and thus they have the possibility of being a runaway.[56] The widespread and wide scale use of the runaway prophesy was a predominantly post-WWII action. Natelson wrote that it was,

> *"first widely popularized in the 1960s and 1970s by liberal politicians, judges, and activists eager to block suggested amendments that would have overruled some liberal Supreme Court decisions. In one of the ironies of history, a handful of deeply conservative groups subsequently decided to promote the scenario to block the process from being used for any purpose."*[57]

The lack of a textual limitation on the power and extent of an

---

[52] Gerard N. Magliocca, "State Calls for an Article V Convention: Mobilization and Interpretation," *Cardozo Law Review De Novo* (2009): 80. Reprinted with permission.
[53] Cong. Rec., Vol.46, at 2769(1911)
[54] Cong. Rec., Vol.47, at 1741(1911):
[55] *Confederate States of America Constitution*, Article V as cited by Magliocca, 80-1, n.29
[56] Robert G. Natelson, "Proposing Constitutional Amendments by Convention: Rules Governing the Process," *Tennessee Law Review* 78 (2011): 715
[57] Robert G. Natelson, "A Response to the "Runaway Scenario"," (2013): 1 - independently published on the website of the Independence Institute at http://constitution.i2i.org/2013/02/15/a-response-to-the-"runaway-scenario"/

amendatory convention initially makes for a compelling argument against a convention. But Professors Weber and Perry aptly address this issue in the opening chapter of their book and point out that these claims are from people arguing for the Confederation Congress's power to control the convention and who are discounting context and the Framers' intentions.[58]

Just as easily one can make a counter-argument that the same lack of text to limit the convention also denies powers to the convention. William Platz said that, "But if the convention were to have such power (for proposing a new Constitution), would not Article V so state, without leaving the matter to inference?"[59]

The potential of a runaway convention is now being dismissed by scholars after decades of initially supporting the notion. The ability of the States and then Congress to limit the convention subject material has provided an additional safeguard against the runaway model. Arthur Bonfield explained, and quoting Cyril Brickfield of the US House Committee on the Judiciary,

> "In the end, it seems clear that an article V convention may be limited to the same general subject matter as that contained in the state applications. A runaway convention is no real danger since the power of the states and Congress in this regard is based on a sound legal and practical basis. "[T]ogether, the Congress and the State legislatures...not only initiate but also finally approve the work of any convention. With this ultimate power at their commend [sic], they may fence off the boundaries of power within which a convention must operate."[60]

There is a subtle undertone to the apprehension of the Congress to comply with a convention call. They speak of the fear of a runaway convention perhaps to mask the real fear of watching the States and the people circumvent the Congress and solve the problems that Congress seems either incapable or unwilling to take up. It is the inability of Congress to maintain any control over a body that is empowered to change the Congress and its rules that really drives their objections. The real runaway convention, from the perspective of Congress, not that they will ever admit to it, is the

---

[58] Paul J. Weber & Barbara A. Perry, *Unfounded Fears, The Myths and Realities of a Constitutional Convention* (New York: Praeger, 1989), 4
[59] William A. Platz, "Article V of the Federal Constitution," *George Washington Law Review* 3 (1934): 46
[60] Arthur Earl Bonfield, "The Dirksen Amendment and the Article V Convention Process," *Michigan Law Review* 66, no.5 (Mar.1968): 998

convention that acts to curtail the power(s) of Congress or to restore the balance of powers in federalism. Michael Stokes Paulsen lays it all out, speaking of a general convention and not a limited convention, but the same commentary could easily apply to a limited convention,

> *"The power of the convention delegates to limit their own agenda at the convention (a power over which the applying states might well exercise considerable control by selecting delegates committed to enforcing a limitation on the agenda), combined with the power of the states to decline to ratify any unwanted amendment the convention proposes, should be regarded as a complete answer to fears that the convention will generate popularly unacceptable results. In the end, the fear of what a general convention might do (and three fourths of the states ratify) is a fear of what might happen when the People act even in part without the filter of their representatives. It is, in short, an elitist fear of popular sovereignty, as applied to the most fundamental of "political questions": according to what principles are the people to govern themselves? It may be an understandable fear, but it is unworthy of our Constitution and of We the People who adopted it."*[61]

If we return to the objections initially raised concerning the deviation from the Confederation Congress call to a convention, we find other words and phrases that shed new light on their 21 February 1787 resolution. Reconsidering the resolution with a changed emphasis,

> *"the sole and express purpose of revising the Articles of Confederation and reporting to Congress and the several legislatures such alterations and* **provisions therein** *as shall, when* **agreed to in Congress and confirmed by the States, render the federal constitution adequate to the exigencies of government and the preservation of the union.**"[62]

When this passage is considered from the perspective of the last clause, that is, to "render the federal constitution adequate to the exigencies of government," the actions of the delegates begin to make sense. The situation of the national government was dismal in 1787. The States were competing with each other and economically harming one another. The economy was in a shambles and the rest of the world had little to no respect for the United

---

[61] Republished with permission of the Yale Law Journal Company, from Michael Stokes Paulsen, "A General Theory of Article V: The Constitutional Lessons of the Twenty-seventh Amendment," *Yale Law Journal* 103, no.3 (Dec. 1993): 761; permission conveyed through Copyright Clearance Center, Inc.

[62] Max Farrand, *The Records of the Federal Convention of 1787, Vol. I* (New Haven: Yale University Press, 1911 and rev. 1937), 14

States. The last few words are for "the preservation of the union" and that was the true focus of the convention. The Articles had been a failure and the government was ineffective; time was running short for the nation as a whole political unit. The delegates did not make alterations as much as they made "provisions therein" for the preservation of the union. Put in this light, the 1787 Philadelphia federal convention did its duty and fulfilled its true mandate.

Many have noted that the resolution from Congress calling the convention was an afterthought in the wake of the actions taken by seven of the States. More than that, the Articles of Confederation lack of a provision of power to Congress to call a convention rendered the resolution moot. The Congress did not possess the authority to limit the scope of the convention or the authority of the delegates acting on behalf of their respective states. Taken another step, Natelson points out that the resolution states that the call is a mere recommendation and made "in the opinion of Congress." Placing any emphasis on the view, actions or dictates of the Confederation Congress is pointless; it wasn't their business but it was the business of the States. The product of the convention, that is, the proposed Constitution, was simply a recommendation from the delegates to the Congress which retained the liberty to propose or to not propose it to the States, as per the letter of transmittal from George Washington to the Confederation Congress. As a proposal it was "non-binding and utterly without legal force." The States were not bound to consider the proposal or even to pay it cursory attention. Natelson stresses Pennsylvania delegate and future Supreme Court Justice James Wilson's view that the delegates were "authorized to conclude nothing, but…at liberty to propose anything."[63,64] Alexander Hamilton had a similar comment, "We can only propose and recommend—the power of ratifying or rejecting is still in the States."[65] Finally, James Madison summarized the authority of the Philadelphia Convention as, "[The convention was] merely advisory and recommendatory."[66]

Moreover, the proposed constitution was submitted to Congress first before they sent it on to the state legislatures urging the calling of state

---

[63] Robert G. Natelson, "Proposing Constitutional Amendments by Convention: Rules Governing the Process," *Tennessee Law Review* 78 (2011): 720-1

[64] Max Farrand, *The Records of the Federal Convention of 1787, Vol. I* (New Haven: Yale University Press, 1911 and rev. 1937), 253

[65] Ibid., 295

[66] *The Federalist*, No. 40

ratification conventions. The Congress deliberated for two days before sending it to the States. Therefore, the convention did indeed obey in "reporting to Congress" and the proposed Constitution was, in a manner, "agreed to in Congress" as required.[67] One other aspect often challenged is that the amending provision in the Articles of Confederation required unanimity for the adoption of any amendments. Although Article VII of the Constitution required only nine states to ratify to put the Constitution into effect, eventually all thirteen states did ratify the Constitution and thereby, in a roundabout way, complied with the Articles of Confederation's unanimity requirement.

Historian Forrest McDonald looks at the 1787 convention in a different light: he discusses in his *Novus Ordo Seclorum* that the delegates at Philadelphia came to the convention with their ideas – and instructions from their home states – already formed. He points out that the convention voted early on May 30 to consider a radical replacement of the Articles of Confederation, and all but three delegates were in favor.[68,69] The pre-convention views of the delegates are informative as to the intentions of those who were planning to attend and we can get a sense of their views by considering the expressed view of George Washington just six weeks prior to the convention,

> *"I am glad to find that Congress have recommended to the States to appear in the Convention proposed to be holden in Philadelphia in May. I think the reasons in favor, have the preponderancy of those against the measure. It is idle in my opinion to suppose that the Sovereign can be insensible of the inadequacy of the powers under which it acts – and that seeing, it should not recommend a revision of the Federal system, when it is considered by many as the **only** Constitutional mode by which the defects can be remedied."[70]*

The foremost citizen of the Confederation is clearly saying that the system as configured is defective to the point of needing wholesale revision.

---

[67] Collier & Collier dissect this point and show how the Congress debated the public's perception of the action of Congress in forwarding the proposed constitution on to the States. If Congress voted and approved, it is an endorsement; if Congress voted and declined to forward, it is a usurpation of the people's sovereignty. Congress astutely chose to forward without recommendation.

[68] Forrest McDonald, *Novus Ordo Seclorum, The Intellectual Origins of the Constitution* (Lawrence: University of Kansas Press, 1985), 185

[69] Roger Sherman, Robert Yates and Oliver Ellsworth

[70] Letter of George Washington to James Madison, 31 March 1787 – as presented in *The U.S. Constitution – A Reader* (Hillsdale, MI: Hillsdale College Press, 2012), 185

He stresses that Congress must be aware that the Articles of Confederation are a failure and have to be overhauled and that the overhaul has to be done officially. Later, in the same letter, he tells Madison that,

> *"as my wish is, that the Convention may adopt no temporizing expedient, but probe the defects of the Constitution to the bottom, and provide radical cures, whether they are agreed to or not – a conduct like this, will stamp wisdom and dignity on the proceedings, and be looked to as a luminary.."*[71]

In General Washington's opinion, mere patching of the national charter will not do. The whole structure requires removal and replacement of its foundation. This letter alone would suffice to show that the political leaders of the nascent nation were already of the opinion that change was necessary but we have more. Madison had contemporaneously written his *"Vices of the Political System of the United States"* and his *"Vices of the Constitution"* to outline his objections to the Articles and their deficiencies.[72] From our vantage point today, much more than two centuries removed, we do not see or feel the widespread sense of urgency to rectify the national government under the Articles.

Remember that Gouverneur Morris said that the convention was "unknown to the Confederation."[73] If we are to argue that the delegates went rogue and violated their oaths, must we not initially accept that the Confederation Congress had first gone equally rogue in issuing the call to the convention without the power to do so?[74] We can better understand the actions of both the convention delegates and the Congress by beginning with examining the situation in the young nation.[75] Both groups were acting on the same belief: that the circumstances warranted boldness – the Convention delegates saw the need to start over and the Congress saw the need to take the unprecedented step of amending, albeit drastically, the Articles of Confederation. South Carolina delegate Charles Pinckney had also submitted a plan for reorganization of the confederation government. Kyvig argues that Pinckney saw the reality of the situation advocating paying "no

---

[71] Ibid., 185

[72] James Madison, "Vices of the Political System of the United States" – as presented in *The U.S. Constitution – A Reader* (Hillsdale, MI: Hillsdale College Press, 2012), 197

[73] Max Farrand, *The Records of the Federal Convention of 1787, Vol. II* (New Haven: Yale University Press, 1911 and rev. 1937), 92

[74] Seven states first made the call and Congress then formalized it.

[75] The topic of the distressed situation in the United States in the middle 1780s has been treated elsewhere fully. For a thorough coverage of the matter, Chapter 1 of Weber & Perry's *Unfounded Fears* is recommended.

further attention to the Confederation" and beginning "*do novo*" as opposed to repairing a deficient system that could "prove absurd and oppressive."[76]

Weber and Perry use an apt analogy in their "*Unfounded Fears*" to explain the actions of the 1787 delegates, they describe an individual under house arrest for thirty days who must escape a house fire mid-sentence. That person turns himself in to the police and explains the circumstances. Technically, he broke the law but did he have justification? Weber and Perry claim he did and that the Founders were in a similar situation.[77]

Looked at in the view that the delegates did not runaway, then the quotation at the beginning of this section of the chapter rings true – a runaway convention would be unlike anything known in American governing processes. There is still another point to be made for the 1787 convention that can be compared to a modern amendatory convention. The Philadelphia Convention only <u>proposed</u> a new constitution; it did not enact or ratify one. The scenario remains the same today, an amendatory convention may propose its heart out on any number of potential amendments, assuming that it is an open convention, but it may not enact or ratify anything. Both the 1787 convention and any modern Article V convention are merely advisory.[78]

A last point to be expounded on in the issue of whether the Philadelphia Convention violated the call from Congress, and perhaps did not understand the intent of Congress, can be refuted by acknowledging the fact that about one third of the fifty-five Convention delegates were sitting members of the Confederation Congress. Eighteen of the thirty-nine signers were congressmen at the time of the 1787 convention.[79,80] They had to have known the intent of Congress in drafting the call to the convention; it was THEIR call and THEIR intent. When the Philadelphia Convention finally adjourned for good, those same congressmen promptly returned to New York to receive and debate the proposed constitution that they themselves had

---

[76] David E. Kyvig, *Explicit and Authentic Acts, Amending the U.S. Constitution 1776-1995* (Lawrence: University Press of Kansas, 1996), 45

[77] Paul J. Weber & Barbara A. Perry, *Unfounded Fears, The Myths and Realities of a Constitutional Convention* (New York: Praeger, 1989), 14

[78] Ibid., 26

[79] Paul J. Weber, "Madison's Opposition to a Second Convention," *Polity* 20, no.3 (Spring 1988): 500

[80] Forrest McDonald, *E Pluribus Unum, The Formation of the American Republic 1776-1790* (Indianapolis: Liberty Fund, 2d ed., 1979), 334

created.⁸¹

Let us place this point in context: First, the 8ᵗʰ Confederation Congress recommended the convention in its 21 February 1787 resolution – among those that voted on the resolution for the convention were eighteen members of the Confederation Congress that would later be delegates to the Philadelphia Convention.⁸² Second, the convention meeting in Philadelphia included those eighteen sitting members of Congress who were fully capable of arguing that the convention was violating the resolution of 21 February 1787 and exceeding its mandate. Third, those same eighteen sitting members of Congress that were delegates to the convention returned to Congress and debated on accepting the proposed Constitution and promulgated it to the States when they could have rejected it on the grounds of the convention exceeding its mandate.⁸³ Fourth, many of those same sitting members of Congress were then delegates to their respective state's ratification conventions to consider ratification of a Constitution that they had personally 1) recommended a convention to draft, 2) helped to draft, 3) debated in Congress to send to the States and were now 4) voting on ratification!

As an example, James Madison represented Virginia in the state legislature and in the Confederation Congress, served as a delegate from Virginia in the Philadelphia Convention, and served in the Virginia ratification convention. He also had attended the Mount Vernon Convention and the Annapolis Convention that suggested the Philadelphia Convention. If the 1787 convention was indeed a runaway convention, then it was first authorized by the same Congressmen that would perform the runaway convention, then it was accepted and sent to the States by the same Congressmen and then ratified by the same Congressmen. If they had indeed ran away, then they ran away from themselves.

Arthur Taylor presented a fascinating application of the probability theory of mathematics in his 2005 paper. He looked at the factors that would lead to the ultimate ratification of an unacceptable or "adverse amendment."

---

[81] Paul J. Weber & Barbara A. Perry, *Unfounded Fears, The Myths and Realities of a Constitutional Convention* (New York: Praeger, 1989), 33

[82] James Schouler, *History of the United States of America, Under the Constitution, 1783-1801, Vol. I, Rule of Federalism* (New York: Dodd, Mead & Co., 1880, 1908 ed.), 41

[83] http://works.bepress.com/robert_natelson/32 Robert G. Natelson, "Appendix – Delegates to Founding-Era Conventions," SelectWorks (Jan. 2013)

He identified the amendment proposal and the States as the variables. In the instance of a runaway convention, the amendment proposal value goes to "1" or a surety, but the States as ratifiers are not a surety and the value of the probability is dependent on the proposal itself. But both events must occur for the risk of an adverse amendment to happen; the amendment must be adverse and the States must ratify. This means that the probability is entirely in the hands of the ratifying states – and conversely, the prevention is also entirely in the hands of the ratifying states. Taylor presented a hypothetical case, very much in the news just nine years later,

> *"What if we take a hypothetical that has not yet been decided? What of a U.S. Constitutional amendment ensuring gays and lesbians the right to marry? Which seems greater, the risk that the Supreme Court would approve such an amendment proposed by litigants, $P(e_a)_{(gay\ and\ lesbian\ marriage\ protected)}$, or the risk that three-fourths of state legislatures would approve such an amendment proposed by a runaway convention $P(Ratf)_{(gay\ and\ lesbian\ marriage\ protected)}$?*[84]
>
> *In both cases one would probably conclude that the current risk of an adverse judicial amendment is much higher than the risk of an adverse democratic amendment, even with a runaway convention that filters no amendments of any kind."*[85]

Taylor argues that the existence of the runaway convention is proof that one of the filters, that of the amendment proposal filtering out adverse amendments, has failed. As bad as that seems, he says that this is EXACTLY the same situation of the Supreme Court ruling in favor of such a case with the same result as an act of judicial activism. He contends that the real question that the American public should ask itself is which body does it trust more to avoid such unpopular amending, that is, who should be ratifying such constitutional changes – the States or the Supreme Court? Here, Taylor concludes, the answer is obvious; the "fear of an Article V convention inadvertently *strengthens* the power of the Supreme Court, and *lessens* the power of the States."[86]

In regard to the risks of a convention and the impact of the convention – perceived versus reality – on the political balance, Gerald Magliocca deftly

---

[84] $P(e_a)$ = Probability of US Supreme Court approval
[85] Arthur H. Taylor, "Fear of an Article V Convention,", *Brigham Young University Journal of Public Law* 20 (2005): 409-14.
[86] Ibid., 415-6.

likened the situation to the Cold War standoff,

> "The trepidation about using the convention threat parallels the criticism about mutually assured destruction (MAD) during the Cold War. Nuclear deterrence was great at keeping the peace, but what if the bluff of retaliation was actually called? While this was a valid point, the reality was that the uncertainly surrounding the outcome of a nuclear war was so great that no rational (or irrational) leader ever wanted to take that risk. A constitutional convention is the ultimate political weapon, and in that context one must ask whether policymakers would really allow a convention to happen or would blink (as they have on every previous occasion when the two-thirds threshold was near). Put another way, the numerous advantages of invoking the Article V process outweigh the risks posed by the tiny probability that a convention would be summoned."[87]

Michael Rappaport argues vociferously in his 2012 paper on the constitutionality of limited conventions that the structure of the Constitution and the wording of Article V and the history of our nation's experience with conventions make clear that the only permissible conventions are for 1) the ratification of the Constitution – now moot – and for 2) ratification of any new amendment proposal – in which deliberation resulting in an up or down vote is the only option – and for 3) a convention for the debate and proposal of an amendment – which carries no other authority than to PROPOSE an amendment. No other action is provided for, and therefore is not allowed. Outside of these conventions, no branch of government is obligated to consider or respect the product of a convention. It is Rappaport's assertion that "The Constitution therefore forbids runaway conventions."[88]

There is a final safeguard against the runaway convention: the ratification process itself. Should an unpopular amendment manage to get through the convention, get past Congress and get to the States for consideration, the States have two options. They may choose to vote it down or they may choose to ratify it. Should the latter prevail, one can assume that the amendment was not as unpopular as expected. In the former instance, the States are exercising their own form of self-control and enforcing the subject

---

[87] Gerard N. Magliocca, "State Calls for an Article V Convention: Mobilization and Interpretation," *Cardozo Law Review De Novo* (2009): 90. Reprinted with permission.

[88] Michael B. Rappaport, "The Constitutionality of a Limited Convention: An Originalist Analysis," *Constitutional Commentary* 81 (2012): 56

matter limitation.[89] Both cases have occurred: the former with the rejected Equal Rights Amendment and the latter with the ratified Eighteenth Amendment.

To close out this argument, we can shorten the debate with citing a list that Professor Natelson compiled as to the checks and balances against the runaway scenario:

- Political factors: the damage that a disregard of clear limits can do to a commissioner's reputation;
- Popular opinion;
- State applications defining the scope;
- The limit on the scope of the call;
- The potential for lawsuits to enforce the foregoing;
- State instructions of commissioners;
- State power to recall commissioners;
- The need to garner a majority of state commissioners (delegations) at the convention;
- Congress' ability (and duty) to refuse to choose a mode of ratification for an ultra vires proposal;
- The requirement that the proposals be ratified by 38 states;
- The potential for more judicial challenge, at every stage of the process.[90]

For a convention to successfully [sic] "runaway," a perfect political storm must arise to overcome every single one of the checks and balances listed.

Could a Convention be Controlled?

The question of whether a convention can be controlled, by either Congress or the convention itself, depends on the precautions taken before the convention is ever called. The focus of the control is the convention agenda. US Supreme Court Chief Justice Warren Burger claimed in 1988

---

[89] James Kenneth Rogers, "The Other Way to Amend the Constitution: The Article V Constitutional Convention Amendment Process," *Harvard Journal of Law & Public Policy* 30, no.3 (Summer 2007): 1020

[90] Robert G. Natelson, "A Response to the 'Runaway Scenario'," (2013): 8-9 - independently published on the website of the Independence Institute at http://constitution.i2i.org/2013/02/15/a-response-to-the-"runaway-scenario"/

that,

> "…there is no effective way to limit or muzzle the actions of a Constitutional Convention. The convention could make its own rules and set its own agenda. Congress might try to limit the convention to one amendment or to one issue, but there is no way to assure that the convention would obey. After a convention is convened, it will be too late to stop the convention if we don't like its agenda."[91]

As a corollary, the claim is made that the agenda is at the whim of the delegates who may adopt any topic for debate that they desire.[92] Arizona State Sen. Biggs has argued that the "delegates to the convention… may attempt to take over the process" of the convention and that "it isn't the process that will produce a runaway convention, it will be the personnel attending."[93] Another corollary is that the opposite may be done, that is, a predetermined wording for an amendment may be agreed to by the states in their applications and the convention is nothing more than an up or down vote. But this would violate the spirit of debate and deliberation of the convention and make the amendatory convention into a ratifying convention. But the same argument can be made that Congress will assume too much control over the convention if they are given the power to determine the agenda.[94]

One of the tactics that the States have begun to employ of late is to draft and pass state legislation that governs the behavior and positions of their delegates. At first blush these "Faithful Delegate Acts" sound like a problematic solution as it would appear to clearly violate the Speech and Debate Clause of the Constitution. In such legislation, the topics that a delegate may discuss and may not discuss are specifically detailed. The position of the state legislature with regard to a given subject is often clarified. In 2015 alone, at least sixteen states introduced and in some cases passed bills that constrain delegate behavior.[95]

---

[91] Letter of 22 June 1988 from US Supreme Court Chief Justice Warren Burger to Phyllis Schlafly.
[92] Republished with permission of the Yale Law Journal Company, from Walter Dellinger, "The Recurring Question of the "Limited" Constitutional Convention," Yale Law Journal 88 (1979): 1624; permission conveyed through the Copyright Clearance Center, Inc.
[93] Andy Biggs, *The Con of the Con-Con, The Case Against the States Amending the U. S. Constitution* (Gilbert, AZ: Freeman Press, 2015), 21-2
[94] Walter Dellinger, "The Recurring Question of the "Limited" Constitutional Convention," *Yale Law Journal* 88 (1979): 1634
[95] AK, AL, AZ, KS, KY, MS, ND, NH, NV, NY, OK, SC, SD, TX, WV, WY,

This is not at all a new idea. In fact, legislative instructions have been the norm for, without exaggeration, thousands of years extending back into the Roman Era in Europe. In 1999, Kris Kobach published an invaluable law review article that went into great detail on the practice and, in particular, the history of delegate instruction at the revolutionary conventions and provincial congresses held during the American Revolution.[96,97] Promoting an almost opposite conclusion is a 2009 paper by Christopher Terranova that argues that legislative instructions from the States died with the Confederacy in 1865.[98] These legislative instructions played a major role in the development of the Constitution; Terranova wrote,

> *"Recognizing that the Articles [of Confederation] needed to be, at the very least, revised, states instructed their congressional delegates to recommend a general convention. And later, when the state sent delegates to the Philadelphia Constitutional Convention, the states made sure to instruct their delegates on which changes to support and which to prevent."*[99]

The idea would seem to run counter to the overturning of the "instruct-and-inform" laws that many states passed in the late 1990s that were quickly declared unconstitutional. The difference is that those laws were for regular legislative topics and for congressional action – not an amendatory convention operating under its own special circumstances. Kobach states, "The instruction of representatives had been treated as a natural law or common law right during the colonial period and was viewed the same way in most states after independence." Many of the revolutionary era state constitutions contained provisions for the instruction of state legislators by their constituents.[100] In fact, of the eleven state constitutions in effect at the close of the Revolutionary War, three specifically guaranteed

---

[96] Kris W. Kobach, "May "We the People" Speak?: The Forgotten Role of Constituent Instructions in Amending the Constitution," *University of California-Davis Law Review* 33, no.1 (Fall 1999), generally. This work, copyright 1999 by Kris W. Kobach, was originally published in the *UC Davis Law Review*, vol. 33, pp. 1-94, copyright 1999 by The Regents of the University of California. All rights reserved. Reprinted with permission.

[97] Vikram D. Amar, "The People Made Me Do It: Can the People of the States Instruct and Coerce Their State Legislatures in the Article V Constitutional Amendment Process?," *William and Mary Law Review* 41, no.3 (2000), generally

[98] Christopher Terranova, "The Constitutional Life of Legislative Instructions in America," *New York University Law Review* 84 (Nov.2009), generally

[99] Ibid., 1340

[100] Kris W. Kobach, "May "We the People" Speak?: The Forgotten Role of Constituent Instructions in Amending the Constitution," *University of California-Davis Law Review* 33, no.1 (Fall 1999): 49-50. This work, copyright 1999 by Kris W. Kobach, was originally published in the *UC Davis Law Review*, vol. 33, pp. 1-94, copyright 1999 by The Regents of the University of California. All rights reserved. Reprinted with permission.

the right to instruct representatives.[101]

Kobach cites the analogy to an amendatory convention in the form of the ratifying conventions for the Twenty-first Amendment. In his analysis, the convention delegates were given instructions from their constituents through the ballot wording. Delegates pledged to vote one way or the other and then did exactly that. The state ratifying conventions did not runaway or take up any other topics. The Article V ratifying conventions went precisely as planned and the delegate instructions were honored explicitly.[102,103] The ratification convention provided the opportunity – and the prime time socially and politically – for a runaway convention. With so many out of work and eager for a social and political restructuring, as evidenced by the public clamor for government intervention, the conventions could easily have expanded their purview, assuming that a runaway was indeed possible. But that did not happen – anywhere in any of the thirty-nine conventions held nationwide.[104] It is incongruous that today there is such fear of an Article V convention when we consider that the ratification conventions of 1933-34 were also Article V conventions, albeit ratificatory and not amendatory, but nonetheless Article V conventions. The Democrat and Republican parties both included in their 1932 platforms a call to use Article V ratification conventions for the proposed Twenty-first Amendment.[105]

Natelson emphasizes that the other federal conventions, which would include such meetings as those for federal interstate compacts and the Founding Era conventions, all were structured such that the delegates were subject to state legislative instructions.[106] He points to case law that

---

[101] Willi Paul Adams, *The First American Constitutions, Republican Ideology and the Making of the State Constitutions in the Revolutionary Era* (Lanham, MD: Rowman & Littlefield, 2001), 246

[102] Kris W. Kobach, "May "We the People" Speak?: The Forgotten Role of Constituent Instructions in Amending the Constitution," *University of California-Davis Law Review* 33, no.1 (Fall 1999): 87. This work, copyright 1999 by Kris W. Kobach, was originally published in the *UC Davis Law Review*, vol. 33, pp. 1-94, copyright 1999 by The Regents of the University of California. All rights reserved. Reprinted with permission.

[103] Robert G. Natelson, "Proposing Constitutional Amendments by Convention: Rules Governing the Process," *Tennessee Law Review* 78 (2011): 747

[104] Ethan P. Davis, "Liquor Laws and Constitutional Conventions: A Legal History of the Twenty-first Amendment," *Yale Law School Student Scholarship Repository* (April 9, 2008): 4

[105] Ibid., 19 - per n.78: "See *Republican Party Platform of 1932* ("Such an amendment should be promptly submitted to the States by Congress, to be acted upon by State conventions called for that sole purpose in accordance with Article V of the Constitution and adequately safeguarded so as to be truly representative..."); and *Democratic Party Platform of 1932* ("To effect such repeal we demand that the Congress immediately propose a Constitutional Amendment to truly represent [sic] the conventions in the states called to act solely on that proposal...")."

[106] Robert G. Natelson, "Proposing Constitutional Amendments by Convention: Rules Governing the Process," *Tennessee Law Review* 78 (2011): 747

legislative instructions have been the norm for centuries although popular instructions have not. The instructions from the state's legislature to its commissioners were often secret and written.[107] Marc Kruman stated that the "framers expected representatives to express the views of their constituents." He pointed out that the Continental Congress "called upon the people to instruct their representatives."[108]

> The same questions of who would operate the ratification conventions for the Twenty-first Amendment, who would pay for them, how would the delegates be selected, when and where would the convention be called, how long would it take to convene them, were all bandied about as they are today. The whole process took less than ten months to complete the ratification.[109] When the suggestion was raised that the Congress should and must take control of the process, the US House of Representatives was not amused. In fact, the sole action that the Congress took was for individual congressmen to take to the floor and rail against the idea.[110]

The States had experience with organizing and operating a federal ratification convention in the eighteenth century only, although they had extensive recent experience with their own state constitutional and amendatory conventions, which they drew upon to draft their enabling acts. The States acted so quickly that Congress was unable to pass a template or general law for the States to follow. These state laws stipulated the delegate qualifications, election procedures, place and date at which to convene, the number of delegates and their compensation, the ballot design, oaths of office, officers of the convention, etc.[111] Thus both tradition and history are on the side of an Article V convention being controllable.

The type of the convention provides further assurance of control. A limited amendatory convention is prohibited from any activity more than the debate and proposal of amendments. The body of law and federal and state legal decisions give more support to the claim that a convention can be controlled. The rules developed by the Assembly of State Legislatures are

---

[107] Robert G. Natelson, "A Compendium for Lawyers and Legislative Drafters," Convention of States (2014): 49-50

[108] Marc W. Kruman, *Between Authority and Liberty* (Chapel Hill: University of North Carolina Press, 2006), 76-81

[109] Ethan P. Davis, "Liquor Laws and Constitutional Conventions: A Legal History of the Twenty-first Amendment," *Yale Law School Student Scholarship Repository* (April 9, 2008): 21

[110] Ibid., 22

[111] Ibid., 23

designed for the specific purpose of controlling the convention. Finally, the two part proposal and ratification process provides the greatest surety that the convention can be controlled through the division of the process. The ratification stage allows for cooler heads to prevail after due deliberation on the outcome of the first part of the process.

Lastly, the US Department of Justice's 1987 Report to the Attorney General on the limitability of constitutional conventions laid out clearly that the convention limitation can be enforced. They recognized at least four methods of restraining the actions of the delegates,

> "We also conclude that there are four possible methods of enforcing the subject matter limitation on the convention. First, and foremost, the states, who exercise ultimate control over the ratification of all constitutional amendments, may withhold ratification of a proposed amendment which is outside the scope of the subject matter limitation. Second, the Congress may enact legislation providing for such limitations as the states request and it may be that the Congress may decline to designate the mode of ratification for those proposed amendments that it determines are outside the scope of the subject matter limitation and therefore beyond the authority of the convention to propose. Third, the courts may review the validity of the constitutional amendment procedure, including whether a proposed amendment was within the subject matter limitation. Fourth, the delegates to a convention may be bound by oath to refrain from proposing amendments on topics other than those authorized under the charter of the convention."[112]

For these restraints and for the limitation permitted by the applications and the call from the Congress, the US Department of Justice concluded that, "we believe fears of a 'run-away' convention are not well founded."[113]

Congress Will Take Control of the Convention

The individuals that are concerned that the convention cannot be controlled go on to postulate that in the absence of any self-imposed controls, the Congress must of necessity step in and direct the convention. The attempts in the 1960s and 1970s and then in again in the 1980s to pass

---

[112] U.S. Department of Justice, Office of Legal Policy, *Report to the Attorney General, Limited Constitutional Conventions under Article V of the United States Constitution*, (10 Sept. 1987): 1-2
[113] Ibid., 3

legislation in Congress doing exactly that are held up in support of this concern. And rightly so. Congress can never resist extending its influence and authority and it is expected that lacking any resistance they will do the same if it appears that a convention is imminent.

Should Congress turn its attention to the convention procedures and attempt to control the convention, undoubtedly the backlash and legal response will be swift and widespread. The states will unleash their armies of attorneys-general and their underlings to fight off the federal government.

In 1986, David Castro took a different tack and proposed that the limitability of Congress's role in a convention is judged not by the words and intent of the Framers alone but also by the understanding pronounced by the Ratifiers in their debates. Citing Ratifiers and Delegates James Iredell, James Wilson, Alexander Hamilton and John Dickinson, among others, Castro showed that the debates over the amending process in the ratification conventions produced a consensus that the States retained ultimate control of the convention and amendment processes. The Anti-Federalists as well, took up the same position and argued along the same line of thought.[114]

In 1933, instead of choosing the method of selection of the delegates, Congress left the issue to the States to resolve individually as they saw fit. With half of the States at that time having state constitutional provisions for delegate selection, they chose to apply the state rules to the federal convention. The other half of the States varied their selection methodology. The result was a smooth operation of the state conventions without congressional interference.[115] One half of the States had a plan – and it went well. One half of the States did not have a plan but they devised one – and it went well. The conclusion is that the people can be trusted to sort out the details and execute a plan. We must in fairness concede that a set of separate state ratification conventions is markedly different than a single federal amendatory convention just by virtue of the plural conventions versus a singular convention. But when we remember that we are discussing the rules of a convention, we are forced to admit that the variance between plural conventions is miniscule.

---

[114] David Castro, "A Constitutional Convention: Scouting Article Five's Undiscovered Country," *University of Pennsylvania Law Review* 134 (1986). 947-58

[115] Ronald D. Rotunda & Stephen J. Safranek, "An Essay on Term Limits and a Call for a Constitutional Convention," *Marquette Law Review* 80, no.1 (Fall 1996): 242-3

Previously mentioned are the Ervin bills; the entire purpose of the bills was to establish procedures and eliminate uncertainty and difficulties associated with the convention process. Opponents of the convention option have used these bills to argue both that, first, Congress is hell-bent on controlling the convention and second, that there are laws in place to allow congressional control of the convention [sic].

Michael Stokes Paulsen has concluded that since Congress and the convention are to be on an equal footing, it would not make any sense to have Congress supervising the convention. The limitations on the convention must flow from Article V alone and not from the Congress. The discretionary power of Congress is limited to selecting the date and place of convening and the choice of the ratification method; everything else is off the table.[116]

If the Congress was meant to have the power to control and dictate the course of Article V conventions, then the Framers would have very clearly specified as much in Article V. More contemporaneous to the Philadelphia Convention were the ratification conventions for the Constitution stipulated in Article VII. These ratification conventions were also left to the States to devise and operate. They received the mention of a single sentence in the Constitution and that included no discussion of their operation or control.[117] It is possible that the Framers viewed the operation and control of the Article V and Article VII amendatory and ratificatory conventions as a reserved power of the States.

Congress Cannot Take Control of the Convention

Ironically, other opponents vehemently argue that a convention can NOT be controlled – by Congress, the States or anyone other than the delegates! This claim is an extension of the objection that there are no rules for the convention and that Congress does not possess oversight authority for the convention. What is getting lost here is that there is no real difference between the Congress and the convention in terms of the operational aspect of the amendment process. Congress, like the convention, sets its own rules. Congress, like the convention, has no oversight. Congress,

---

[116] Michael Stokes Paulsen, "How to Count to Thirty-four: The Constitutional Case for a Constitutional Convention," *Harvard Journal of Law & Public Policy* 34, no.3 (2011): 843

[117] "The Ratification of the Conventions of nine States, shall be sufficient for the Establishment of this Constitution between the States so ratifying the Same."

like the convention, does not have any written direction provided by the Constitution.

Convention opponents point to the body of law to demonstrate the inherent lack of control. The same eight US Supreme Court decisions that have been rendered can be equally parsed to support this claim. One of the more curious examples is the frequently found reference to the *Corpus Juris Secundum*, which is a compilation of the findings of the federal and state courts' decisions. Used less frequently than in the past, such secondary, persuasive legal encyclopedias contain summaries of cases. Reference is most often made to specific findings covering the powers and duties of delegates, stating that,

> *"The members of a Constitutional Convention are the direct representatives of the people and, as such, they may exercise all sovereign powers that are vesting in the people of the state. They may derive their powers not from the legislature, but from the people. And, hence, their power may not in any respect be limited or restrained by the legislature. Under this view, it is a Legislative Body of the Highest Order and may not only frame, but may also enact and promulgate, Constitution."*[118]

This reference, oft cited and with attendant state court case citations, refers not to the powers of delegates to a federal Article V amendatory convention but to delegates to a state plenary constitutional convention. Apples and oranges in this instance.

Could the Constitution and/or Bill of Rights be Eliminated?

At the top of the list of the anticipated disasters that are forecast to happen in the wake of an Article V convention is that of re-writing the Constitution or removing the Bill of Rights. Nothing, absolutely nothing, generates more angst in convention opponents than this idea. This specific worry is more than a century old. The argument made is that because the 1787 Constitutional Convention ran away we have precedent for any new amendatory convention to do the same. Thousands of books exist that detail the actions of the delegates in 1787 and how they defied the instructions of the Confederation Congress and their respective states and took it upon themselves to draft and impose on the nation a new, unexpected and even unwanted Constitution. Well, the description just given is extreme – and

---
[118] 16 Corpus Juris Secundum 9

distorted — but it is a fair representation of both the arguments made over the history of the nation and of the fears exhibited today by convention opponents.

We can appreciate the concerns of those who espouse this view; they are looking desperately to preserve the Constitution and not destroy it. Their caution and reticence are justifiable in an age of constant constitutional reinterpretation. The flux and fluidity of judicial re-evaluation of the Constitution has left constitutional limitations of federal power turned into new (often unlimited) grants of federal power. It is not unreasonable to listen to their prognostications of constitutional destruction and carefully consider the outcome of each step in the process. What better surety do the proponents of a convention have than to have consciously, deliberately and thoroughly reviewed and then reviewed again the entire process for weaknesses?

The list of leaders that exhort the fears of an amendatory convention includes US Supreme Court justices. For example, former Associate Justice Arthur Goldberg:

> "*Article V of the Constitution does not limit the agenda of such a convention to specific amendments proposed by the states in their petitions to Congress. There is nothing in Article V that prevents a convention from making wholesale changes to our Constitution and Bill of Rights.*"[119]

And former Associate Justice William Brennan: "I honestly doubt there's any prospect we want to go through the trauma of redoing the Constitution," as a convention would be "the most awful thing in the world."[120]

There are multiple paths to refuting the fear of a constitutional replacement. If we take a textual approach, the limited words of Article V itself provide some measure or reassurance. "Shall call a Convention for proposing Amendments" is clear that the purpose is limited to the proposition only and not the complete drafting of a new charter, let alone the adoption and ratification of a new constitution.[121] But wait, say the opponents, the 1787 delegates also dispensed with the established ratification

---

[119] Quoted in Russell B. Caplan, *Constitutional Brinkmanship* (New York: Oxford University Press, 1988), vii
[120] Ibid., viii
[121] Lester B. Orfield, *The Amending of the Federal Constitution* (Ann Arbor: University of Michigan Press, 1942), 44

method of the Articles of Confederation. It is true that the delegates did revamp the ratification method as part of the new constitution but then the 1787 delegates also had the stamp of authority in the form of their commissions as delegates. The States had already reconciled themselves to the view that the Articles of Confederation were not working and that a massive overhaul was needed – so much so, that replacement of the Articles was potentially needed, and therefore, permissible for ten of the States' delegations. For the amendatory convention of today, the congressional call that is based on the applications of the States will dictate the scope and limits of the powers and agenda of the modern delegates.

Frank Packard took up this important question in a paper in 1959. He sought to assuage the fears of people that might oppose what he hoped was an impending convention to address the federal income tax rate. He included a detailed list of state Supreme Court decisions going back to the 1830s which cover the limitations of constitutional convention powers. It would be remiss to note that the state and federal court decisions are not the same but the underlying legal principle for the state and federal constitutional conventions would be the same.[122] Packard points out that the Pennsylvania Supreme Court declared in 1873 that,

> *"The convention is not a coordinate branch of government. It exercises no governmental power, but is a body raised by law, in aid of the popular desire to discuss and propose amendments, which have no governing force so long as they remain propositions."*[123]

The New Hampshire Supreme Court weighs in stating, "…the authority of the delegates is not set forth. They are not endowed with the entire sovereignty of the state."[124] And finally the Michigan Supreme Court contributes this advice, "Should the convention attempt to exercise authority not conferred upon it, its action can be restrained the same as can any other body acting illegally."[125] Packard then cites several decisions wherein state courts held that the conventions could not go beyond the instructions and agenda provided by the legislatures and take up other matters.

---

[122] Frank E. Packard, "Constitutional Law: The States and the Amending Process," *American Bar Association Journal* 45, no.2 (Feb.1959): 196-7
[123] *Wells v. Bain*, 75 Pa. 39 at 57 (1874)
[124] *Opinion of the Justices*, 76 N.H. 612 at 613, 85 A. 78(1889)
[125] *Carton v. Secretary of State*, 151 Mich. 337 at 346, 115 N.W. 429 at 432 (1908)

The response to Mr. Packard was not lacking, in fact the literature shows that he elicited numerous responses. Of note, the title of one asked, "*Cannot a State Change Its Mind?*"[126] In Part II we took up the question in detail but for now let us consider that a distressing amount of confusion as to the situation of a proposed amendment or an effort to call a convention would ensue if we had states rescinding and repassing ratification or applications at will without much forethought. If the States are free to change their minds at their leisure, what would force a state to take up a resolution with any degree of seriousness? Under such circumstances, there would seem to be little in the way of consequences if the resolution was passed without much thought and could be just as quickly and easily be rescinded. The more cogent response to Packard outlined the problems with attempting to force Congress's hand through the judiciary and with how the applications are counted.[127]

If the concern is truly that a convention will somehow become dominated by people with strange ideas and goals that are widely divergent from that of the American society as a whole and that the delegates will gain, proverbially by hook or by crook, the ability to sway enough convention votes to pass their radical amendment proposals then we must rely on the safety of the ratification process to prevent such a calamity. Once again, the convention does not possess the ability to alter the ratification process without the States first approving. This hypothetical situation of a proposed amendment that differs from the nation as a whole is not unprecedented: the Congress proposed the Corwin Amendment that would have guaranteed the continuation of slavery perpetually unabetted in the days just preceding the Civil War. The States in some instances rejected the proposal, in others they simply refused to take up the discussion. We can expect the same result today.

> *"It is no more likely today that three-quarters of the states will ratify a bizarre constitutional amendment than it was likely in 1861 that three-quarters of states would ratify an amendment to protect the immoral practice of slavery. The framers' fail-safe system in Article V of the Constitution worked in 1861, and it will work today."*[128]

---

[126] Frank W. Grinnell, "Petitioning Congress for a Convention: Cannot a State Change Its Mind?," *American Bar Association Journal* 45, no.11 (Nov.1959)

[127] Bernard Fensterwald, Jr., "Constitutional Law: The States and the Amending Power – A Reply," *American Bar Association Journal* 46, no.7 (July 1960)

[128] Ronald D. Rotunda & Stephen J. Safranek, "An Essay on Term Limits and a Call for a Constitutional Convention," *Marquette Law Review* 80, no.1 (Fall 1996): 230-1

Should a convention find some unknown way to effectively propose the replacement of either the Constitution or the Bills of Rights – or both – it would still need to garner the support of the States and people to ratify the change. In today's digital age with hundreds of cable channels and satellite radio, the ability to carry off a scheme to subvert the Constitution is implausible, if not impossible.

Lastly, the Philadelphia Convention itself dealt with the issue of a future convention which might seek to replace the Constitution. On September 15, during the course of the next to the last day's work, Roger Sherman "moved to strike out of art. V after 'legislatures' the words 'of three fourths' and so after the word 'Conventions' leaving future Conventions to act in this matter, like the present Conventions according to circumstances." He sought to empower any future Article V convention with plenary power enabling them to rewrite the Constitution. The motion was defeated by a vote of seven "noes" to three "ayes" and one divided.

In support of Sherman's defeated motion, Elbridge Gerry made a second motion to "strike out the words 'or by Conventions in three fourths thereof'" and this motion was also defeated by a vote of one in favor and ten against. A short time later, Edmund Randolph made a motion "that amendments to the plan might be offered by the State Conventions, which should be submitted to and finally decided on by another General Convention." George Mason seconded the motion and Randolph argued that a second convention would be better acquainted with the sentiments of the people. It was at this point that Charles Pinckney made his famous comment about the seriousness of conventions and issued his warning of repeating the convention stating that "nothing but confusion and contrariety could spring from the experiment." Madison's notes from the convention indicate that "On the question on the proposition of Mr. Randolph. All the States answered – no." With at least three attempts to empower a future plenary convention, the subject was closed for all time.[129] No future convention would be able to take up the replacement or rewriting of the Constitution.

There are No Rules to Govern the Convention

When considering the text of the Constitution, it is evident

---

[129] Max Farrand, *The Records of the Federal Convention of 1787, Vol. II* (New Haven: Yale University Press, 1911 and rev. 1937), 630-3

that the Framers made no provision for the operating principles of the amendatory convention. The text is so brief, at twenty-two words for the convention clause,[130] that we are at a loss to begin to determine not just how the convention was intended to function but the process of how to call the convention, select the delegates, choose the officers, set the agenda, determine the voting rules, the extent of Congress's involvement, and to maintain order. The lack of a precedent in the form of a previous federal <u>amendatory</u> convention causes great distress to opponents of an amendatory convention. Without a rigid example to follow, they contend that we cannot predict the behavior or operation of the convention and therefore, we must assume the worst.

The gray area that marks the delineation between the state and federal spheres of influence and responsibility is wide enough to dissuade many from considering a convention. Operation of the convention is a fundamental concern – so much depends on the maintaining of the agenda. If we cannot adequately predict the selection of delegates, for example, we cannot ascertain whether special interests will predominate. If we cannot prescribe ahead of time whether the states vote as a unit or the delegates as individuals, then we cannot be sure of the fairness of representation in the delegations. If we cannot specify what system of parliamentary rules will govern, we cannot be assured of the discipline to avoid prohibited topics or unconstitutional proposals.

While nearly all constitutional scholars will quickly agree that the issue of whether Congress has any discretion in calling a convention when the requisite two-thirds of the States have applied is settled, they cannot reach a consensus as to whether the Congress is permitted, or even required, to vote on the recognition or acknowledgment of the threshold having been reached. Does the Congress automatically take up the debate of the location and date of commencement of the convention or does Congress first formally vote to make the call? Opponents of the convention see the opportunity for constitutional mayhem in every step of the process.

Opponents rightly sense that the possibility for Congress to either derail or take control of the convention is created when Congress is presented with the option of voting on proceeding with the convention.

---

[130] "The Congress,…on the Application of the Legislatures of two thirds of the several States, shall call a Convention for proposing Amendments,…"

Conditions may be applied by Congress which could favor a special interest group or that so severely inhibit the operation of the convention as to make it worthless or unworkable. The worst case scenario has Congress creating a set of operational rules and limitations which will force the convention to come to the result that Congress prefers as opposed to reaching the States' objectives. In this scenario, Congress could further expand its own power and erode federalism.

The inability to ascertain who has the option of setting the rules for the convention operation gives convention opponents pause; they often voice concern that some cabal will rise up to deliberately hijack the convention for its own purposes. They claim that by way of parliamentary tricks and manipulation created through the unknown and as of yet undetermined rules, the entire Constitution is imperiled. They fear equally, the lack of rules and the imposition of rules by Congress, or by the convention itself. It is for this reason that so many were in favor of the Ervin bills.

We can, however, look to the ample precedents of the more than thirty inter-colonial and interstate conventions that preceded the 1787 convention to study the rules applied and learn from these conventions. Some were successful and others were not; the large body of experience gives us a good grounding for determining what has worked, and might just very well work again. History has shown that the conventions themselves set their own internal operational rules, selected their own officers, maintained their own order and judged credentials, meted out discipline, and most importantly, accomplished these action independent of both the national and state governments, regardless of whether they operated under the Crown of England, the Crown of the United Kingdom, the colonial charters, the Articles of Confederation or, for post-1787 interstate conventions, the United States Constitution.

There is an historical precedent to follow. When the First United States Congress met under the authority of the Constitution in 1789, an argument could easily have been made that the Constitution did not make a provision for the rules governing the operation of Congress, therefore chaos would ensue! People could have objected to the convening of Congress with the admonition that "there are no rules; we don't know what will happen!" But then, like now, the people could have looked backward and cited the operation of the First and Second Continental Congresses and the eight

Confederation Congresses as examples of the rules. One could have with a justification equivalent to that of the Article V convention opponents of today claimed that Congress would runaway. This is all the more analogous when one considers that Congress is really a sitting, permanent constitutional convention. The Constitution provides for the US Supreme Court but lacks any rules for its operation. Yet, somehow, the people of the early Republic figured it out.

Of course, there is another significant example in the Electoral College. There are no constitutionally prescribed rules of procedures, and yet, for over two hundred years it has functioned without incident.

The actions of the Assembly of State Legislatures should reassure and calm convention opponents. Without the pressing timeline of an impending convention, the state legislators have the opportunity to resolve all the issues through a deliberative process. Current academic scholarship is regularly turning up new examples of past intercolonial and interstate conventions and their operational rules, all of which adds to the body of knowledge of convention operation and creates options.

The Limited versus Unlimited Convention Debate

Almost a precursor or a foundational argument to the runaway convention concern is that of whether a convention can be limited in subject matter. The text of Article V itself is the cause of this debate. Since the text reads *"shall call a Convention for proposing Amendments"* some have interpreted this to mean that only a convention which takes up multiple amendment propositions would be allowed. Under this theory, there is no limit to what can be proposed and considered. In this scenario, the convention would continue indefinitely until all proposals have been given their day and then voted upon. Professor Morris Forkosch of the Brooklyn Law School insists,

> *"Thus, there can be little doubt that the Constitution's draftsmen never intended that article V be so narrowly construed as to limit the power of the Constitutional Convention to propose more than one amendment."*[131]

Professor Forkosch's pronouncement is backed by the view of former US Supreme Court Justice Arthur Goldberg,

---

[131] Morris B. Forkosch, "The Alternative Amending Clause in Article V: Reflections and Suggestions," *Minnesota Law Review* 51, no.6 (1967): 1076

> "History has established that the Philadelphia Convention was a success, but it cannot be denied that it broke every restraint intended to limit its power and agenda. Logic therefore compels one conclusion: Any claim that the Congress could, by statute, limit a convention's agenda is pure speculation, and any attempt at limiting the agenda would almost certainly be unenforceable. It would create a sense of security where none exists, and it would project a false image of unity."[132]

Driving the concern of illimitability is the observance that there is no confirmation that Congress – or the States – may restrict the scope or powers of the convention and that the convention will "attain the plenary authority" to propose amendments or take on any other activities that are not expressly listed in the either the States' applications or the Congress' call to convention.[133] Paulsen insisted that, "There can be no such thing as a 'limited' convention. A constitutional convention, once called, is a free agency."[134]

The assumption that the Framers intended for the convention to entertain multiple amendment proposals has other supporters. They go a step further and contend that not only must the convention treat all proposals equally and give them their moment, but that this is evidence of the illimitability of the convention. In this view, any convention application that tries to suggest that the convention be limited is invalid and can be ignored by Congress. The alternative is to treat all applications as being intended for a general or open convention.[135]

During what Natelson termed the first wave of scholarship, the question of whether Congress was obligated to make a convention call was hotly debated and, more than that, elevated to a status of near unquestionability by preeminent scholars such as Charles L. Black, Jr. of Yale University. In a pair of papers that were published interestingly as open letters to a Congressman[136] and then a Senator,[137] Black lays out one side of

---

[132] Published in the *Chicago Tribune*, 16 October 1983 and the *Miami Herald*, Sunday, 14 September 1986
[133] Sara R. Ellis, Yusuf Z. Malik, Heather G. Parker, Benjamin C. Signer & Al'Reco L. Yancy, "Article V Constitutional Conventions: A Primer," *Tennessee Law Review* 78 (2011): 671
[134] Republished with permission of the Yale Law Journal Company, from Michael Stokes Paulsen, "A General Theory of Article V: The Constitutional Lessons of the Twenty-seventh Amendment," *Yale Law Journal* 103, no.3 (Dec. 1993): 738; permission conveyed through Copyright Clearance Center, Inc.
[135] Harold Babbit, "Article V and Constitutional Conventions," *Cleveland Bar Journal* 50 (April 1979): 144
[136] Rep. Emanuel Celler, Chair of the Judiciary Committee in the US House of Representatives in 1972.
[137] Sen. Edward "Ted" Kennedy, Chair of the Committee on the Judiciary of the US Senate in 1979.

the debate. Black asked whether Congress has a duty under the Constitution to call a convention and terms it a question of the "first magnitude." Black places this question alongside but not necessarily dependent on whether there are "valid" applications and if they "are in effect." Black insists that the single-issue applications are not valid and as such, Congress has no obligation to respond to the applications.[138] Contrary to Black's claim, there is no "genuinely controverted" question here as to the duty of Congress to call a convention – that was established by the Framers themselves and has been previously cited herein with reference to Alexander Hamilton among others.[139]

Black then turned the issue by saying that the Ervin bill, on which the paper was based, could not place on future congresses the obligation of making such a call without debate and a vote. While Black is correct that a present Congress cannot bind a future Congress; that is in regard to the legislative or statutory sense. The purpose of a Constitution is to bind everyone, Congresses included, to the fundamental law. This is particularly true with regard to a co-equal branch of the federal government. Referring to the Ervin bill is but a side-step from the true binder that is Article V. The text is clear in Article V; where does Black find room for Congress to question its duty or even the possibility of a vote?

But all this is only a preliminary to the meat of his paper: the inadmissibility of a limited convention. Black contends that, echoing Orfield a generation earlier, as so many others have done but not nearly as verbosely, that the plural in "for proposing Amendments" can only mean that an unlimited number of amendments for any purpose or reason that the convention may choose to be the only logical interpretation. Black takes to task the *Report of the Senate Committee on the Judiciary*[140] for their mistake which develops its own argument and pays no attention to other claims. He then gives us a new interpretation of both Madison and Hamilton's comments from *The Federalist* from which it would appear that there is now "*The Living Federalist*" version. But this claim is firmly and succinctly refuted by the Department of Justice in their 1987 report,

---

[138] Charles L. Black, Jr., Amendment by National Constitutional Convention: A Letter to a Senator," *Yale Law Journal* 32 (1979): 627

[139] Charles L. Black, Jr., "Amending the Constitution: A Letter to a Congressman," *Yale Law Journal* 82, no.2 (1972): 191-4

[140] Senate Judiciary Committee, *Federal Constitutional Convention Procedures Act*, S. Rep. No.92-336, 92nd Cong., 1st sess., (1971)

> "In the Constitution (as in everyday discourse), plural nouns are used to denote both the singular and plural meaning of those nouns. For example, the executive authority "to make Treaties" clearly includes the power to make a single treaty."[141]

Black makes a point that he believes that Article V "*implies*" – his word, used frequently – that the text "a Convention for proposing Amendments" actually means:

- "a convention for proposing such amendments as to that convention seem suitable for being proposed"
- "a convention for proposing amendments as that convention decides to propose"
- "a convention with power to propose such amendments as it thinks wise"
- "a convention for proposing such amendments as to it seem wise"
- "a convention for proposing such amendments it decides to propose"

In each case, Black says that these are his interpretations of what he thinks Article V means and that the Framers meant.[142] But why would any convention propose any amendments that do NOT seem suitable to propose? Or why would they propose any amendments that they decide NOT to propose? Or that do NOT seem wise to propose? The only way that his argument against a limited convention and for an unlimited convention works, is if we adopt his phrasing – and that would change the meaning of Article V.

Black dismisses the lengthy argument for a limited convention with the caveat that "the full-blown theory of the convention limited by the tenor of the state petitions is nothing but a child of the twentieth century." It is Black's pervasive influence throughout the first Natelson wave of scholarship that prompts this treatment of Black's views. Black is representative of the academic views in that period from about 1960 to 1978. The overwhelming

---

[141] U.S. Department of Justice, Office of Legal Policy, *Report to the Attorney General, Limited Constitutional Conventions under Article V of the United States Constitution*, (10 Sept. 1987): 25

[142] Republished with permission of the Yale Law Journal, from Charles L. Black, Jr., "Amending the Constitution: A Letter to a Congressman," *Yale Law Journal* 82, no.2 (1972): 196-204; permission conveyed through Copyright Clearance Center, Inc.

pessimism and negativity toward the convention method coalesced to successfully stop a number of convention drives. The academic emphasis was less on research and factual analysis and more on support of an ideology that sought expansion of the federal government's power.

Black continues his analysis in the second paper addressed to Sen. Kennedy. He contends that, one has to begin with the idea that Article V has "one plain meaning" and that meaning is that a "Convention for proposing Amendments" can only mean a general, unlimited convention.[143]

As a condition of proving this point, Black states that he can think of no logical reason to doubt his conclusion, so he considers it to be obvious.[144] So now it appears that we are using logical fallacies to support ONE interpretation of the text of the Article and insisting that no other meaning is possible – simply because it is, in one man's opinion, obvious?

If this is the case, and the Framers intended for us to have only unlimited, or open, conventions then we have a solid reason to avoid Article V amendatory conventions as we cannot, as opponents predict, know what will happen – or is this not the case? We know that ultimately, all proposed amendments must find ratification with three-fourths of the States. So a convention can propose anything that it wants, no matter how ridiculous some may see the proposition, and rest secure in the knowledge that only the proposals that truly represent the will of the people are going to make the final cut.

That reassurance aside, we must still contend with the expense, effort and disruption to the political system of an on-going convention. Assuming, for the moment, that this is the situation as the Framers intended, then we must face that by the same reasoning, the Framers intended for us to NOT have the ability to call a convention for a single subject. Imagine that the Constitution was written without that significant "s" on the end of "amendments" in the alternative amending clause and that the text read "for proposing amendment" instead. Would we not then have to conclude that we could only have a convention for a single topic and that no convention to consider two or three or ten subjects would be legally permissible? Under such logic, we would have to hold multiple conventions – one for each topic.

---

[143] Charles L. Black, Jr., Amendment by National Constitutional Convention: A Letter to a Senator," *Yale Law Journal* 32 (1979): 629
[144] Ibid.

Here, grammatical convenience is trumped by procedural rigidity. It is more reasonable that the Framers were exhibiting brevity and that they considered such phrasing as both acceptable and understandable. In the *Report to the Attorney General* of 1987, the Department of Justice writer assesses Black's tracking argument on illimitability. He summarizes Black's position as,

> "Black had proven that Article V **permits** unlimited conventions, but he has not shown that Article V also **prohibits** limited conventions. His hypothetical application may well be one valid possibility, but his argument does nothing to show that it is the only possibility."[145]

Grover Rees takes the claim that a convention must not be limited, and therefore, has to consider any and all amendment proposals to task and refutes the semantics argument, "But Article V also provides that Congress may 'propose Amendments' on its own initiative, and no one has suggested that Congress must propose more than one amendment at a time."[146]

Twenty-seven amendments later and no one has said to Congress, or in Congress, just once, "Wait, where are the other amendment proposals? There have to be more than one at a time because the Constitution says 'Amendments' - plural!"[147,148] We can see why the issue of plural or singular amendment proposals is miniscule. It is the States' province to determine both the subject(s) of the potential convention and the necessity of addressing the given subjects at all. Rees declares that the "syntactical ambiguity" of Article V "seems to have been an accident" and that the intent, as deduced from a reading of the delegate's aggregated notes, was indeed to allow the States to propose "particular amendments."[149] Rees points us to *The Federalist, No. 43* wherein Madison stressed that Article V "equally enables the General and the State Governments to originate the amendment of errors as they may be pointed out by the experience on one side or the other."

---

[145] U.S. Department of Justice, Office of Legal Policy, *Report to the Attorney General, Limited Constitutional Conventions under Article V of the United States Constitution*, (10 Sept. 1987): 24

[146] Grover Rees III, "Constitutional Conventions and Constitutional Arguments: Some Thoughts on Limits," *Harvard Journal of Law and Public Policy* 6 (1982): 84

[147] Grover Rees III, "The Amendment Process and Limited Constitutional Conventions," *Benchmark* II, no.2 (March-April 1986): 75

[148] It must be conceded that Congress generates about 200 amendment proposals per Congress but this does not mean that the proposed amendments are all proposed at the same exact time and in conjunction with each other. Individual congressmen typically propose their amendments as they draft them without consultation or dependence on other proposals. Congress is, in effect, a permanent, sitting, on-going amendatory convention.

[149] Grover Rees III, "The Amendment Process and Limited Constitutional Conventions," *Benchmark* II, no.2 (March-April 1986): 78

Note, "equally" as in there is no difference between the proposal power of either the Congress (General or Federal Government) and the convention (State Governments).[150] Of course, there is that other essay in *The Federalist*, this one by Hamilton, that answers conclusively that,

> *"Every amendment to the constitution...would be a single proposition, and might be brought forward singly. There would then be no necessity for management or compromise in relation to any other point – no giving or taking. The will of the requisite number would at once bring the matter to a decisive issue."*[151]

Paulsen seeks to argue that the convention must be unlimited and plenary. But in making his argument, he makes a point that supports the refutation of the separate intentions for the Congress versus the convention, when he says that the two methods are "worded in parallel," giving the implication that the two methods are equivalent in powers.[152] Paulsen goes on to argue that the ability of Congress to proposed unlimited amendments proves that the convention must also be unlimited. He finds that the text of Article V lacks anything to imply a limitation.[153] However, Michael Stern rebuts Paulsen by pointing out that "It is true that the text is silent as to what amendments the convention may propose. It is not at all obvious, however, that this silence means that the convention is unlimited in what it may propose."[154] But in retrospect, we can see that Congress always proposes amendments singly, so then would we be surprised to see a convention do the same? Paulsen then contends that the placement of a limitation in the call for a convention by Congress would expand the role of Congress beyond that prescribed in Article V and thereby proves that a limited convention is not possible or permissible. Again, we can refute this by pointing out that it is the States that have made the restriction through their applications which stipulate the purpose and limitation of the convention and the role of Congress is, once again, merely ministerial in that Congress is simply

---

[150] Ibid., 79

[151] Alexander Hamilton, *The Federalist*, No. 85

[152] Michael Stokes Paulsen, "A General Theory of Article V: The Constitutional Lessons of the Twenty-seventh Amendment," *Yale Law Journal* 103, no.3 (Dec. 1993): 739

[153] Michael Stokes Paulsen, "A General Theory of Article V: The Constitutional Lessons of the Twenty-seventh Amendment," *Yale Law Journal* 103, no.3 (Dec. 1993): 738, and Michael Stokes Paulsen, "How to Count to Thirty-four: The Constitutional Case for a Constitutional Convention," *Harvard Journal of Law & Public Policy* 34, no.3 (2011): 842-3

[154] Michael Stern, "Reopening the Constitutional Road to Reform: Toward a Safeguarded Article V Convention," *Tennessee Law Review* 78 (2011): 772

passing on the word of the restricted agenda. Stern again counters Paulsen and suggests that the "triggering clauses" for each method are the same – two-thirds of both houses for the congressional method and two-thirds of the state legislatures for the convention method – and that this equivalence demonstrates that if Congress may propose singular amendment proposals, then so must the States be able to propose singular amendment proposals.[155]

The alternative view is that the convention can be limited by the applications of the States. The subject matter contained in the applications defines and limits the purpose an agenda of the convention. The limited convention model was intended by the Framers and each method of amending – by Congress or by amendatory convention – was co-equal in terms of utility. The Framers did not expect, or desire, a reworking or replacement of the Constitution and had made no such provision.

> *"It is clear that neither of the two methods of amendment was expected by the Framers to be superior to the other or easier of accomplishment. There is certainly no indication that the national legislature was intended to promote individual amendments while the state legislatures were to be concerned with more extensive revisions. On the contrary, there is strong evidence that what the members of the convention were concerned with in both cases was the power to make specific amendments. They did not appear to anticipate a need for a general revision of the Constitution. ...Provision in article V for two exceptions to the amendment power underlines the notion that the convention anticipated specific amendment or amendments rather than general revision."*[156]

This raises the question of, if the Framers did not want a comprehensive or wholesale future revision of the Constitution, then why would they, as opponents of an Article V convention today so vociferously contend, make allowance for it in the Constitution, assuming that the Framers did do so? Looked at another way, if the Framers did not want a second constitutional convention in 1787 or 1788, as many were then very vocal in rejecting, and omitting the Anti-Federalists, why would they have included the option in the Constitution? We can safely conclude that the limited convention provision was intentional. Some researchers have pointed to the records of the ratification debates and concluded that the

---

[155] Ibid., 772-3
[156] Sen. Sam J. Ervin, Jr., "Proposed Legislation to Implement the Convention Method of Amending the Constitution," *Michigan Law Review* 66, no.5 (Mar. 1968): 882

Ratifiers understood and accepted that the amendatory convention would not have plenary powers and that the States would naturally limit the agenda and topics through their applications.[157] Further examination of the ante-revolutionary and revolutionary convention records shows that it was a common practice to "limit in advance the topic and scope of multi-government conventions."[158]

Van Alstyne aptly condenses the argument into a single paragraph wherein he addresses both the unlimited and the limited conventions' rationale:

> "If the purpose of article V is by one mode to permit Congress to propose whatever amendments it deems appropriate from time to time (whether one or several, whether narrow or very broad), and by a different mode to enable the states to gain specific recourse against **particular** usurpations that Congress may have no interest in correcting, then it might not be unreasonable for Congress to reject state legislative applications that seek a convention of unlimited revisory power over the entire Constitution. **That kind of 'second Philadelphia' (or new Armageddon), one might argue, so far outstrips the rationale for an independent state mode of securing particular kinds of amendments that Congress would be warranted in turning back such applications.** In brief, a modest case can be made that article V presupposes that when state legislatures wish to secure constitutional amendment, they will identify the particular proposal adequately to enable Congress to determine whether that felt need is sufficiently well shared by thirty-three other states to require calling a convention. Subject-matter consensus among the applications is implicitly required because state-initiated conventions are inappropriate forums for merely generalized grievances, for less for revolutionary purposes, but entirely appropriate for the thoughtful review of more particularized proposals."[159]

The States, of course, retain the option of applying for an open or unlimited convention. Congress would be equally obligated to call an open convention. If Congress tried to force an open convention, then the States will be leery of it should it lead to unintended consequences; if Congress denies the option of an open convention, the States will be refused the

---

[157] Robert G. Natelson, "Proposing Constitutional Amendments by Convention: Rules Governing the Process," *Tennessee Law Review* 78 (2011): 728-9.
[158] Robert G. Natelson, "A Compendium for Lawyers and Legislative Drafters," Convention of States (2014), 42
[159] William Van Alstyne, "The Limited Constitutional Convention – The Recurring Answer," *Duke Law Journal* 1979 (1979): 991

option to reform the government as they think is best when needed. The only course of action left to Congress it to observe the request of the States and not interfere with the States' prerogative. Congress must make no restriction on the type, subject, or extent of the convention save what the States request.[160] Any convention called to address particular problems has to be allowed to explore any and all potential solutions.

> *"A convention called to propose amendments to remedy particular grievances must be free to formulate the best solutions to those grievances... Congress should merely restate the problem in the concurrent resolution by which it calls the convention."*[161]

There are two types of limitations of a convention: procedural, which deals with housekeeping issues, and substantive, which involve what topics the convention may address.[162] It is usually the procedural limitations that provoke the most debate. The substantive issue of the topic(s) of the convention is typically presented in the form of the procedural context of the amendment focused on the "subject-matter validity" of the amendment(s) proposed.[163]

Opposition to a limited convention has been theorized to be just a ruse by opponents of all conventions as a backdoor way to prevent any convention. The opponents are trading on the fear that people have for an unlimited convention by claiming that no convention can be actually limited so that the public sentiment will assume the worst and stop all conventions.[164]

Another theory advanced as to the distinction between the limited and unlimited conventions is that of the "Dual Purpose Theory." This is the idea that the limited convention is the province of Congress as it has the sole ability to propose specific amendments. Conversely, the unlimited

---

[160] "Proposed Legislation on the Convention Method of Amending the United States Constitution," *Harvard Law Review* 85, no.8 (June 1972): 1628-9

[161] Republished with permission of the Harvard Law Review Association, from "Proposed Legislation on the Convention Method of Amending the United States Constitution," *Harvard Law Review* 85, no.8 (June 1972): 1631-2; permission conveyed through Copyright Clearance Center, Inc.

[162] Henry D. Levine, "Limited Federal Constitutional Conventions: Implications of the State Experience," *Harvard Journal on Legislation* 11 (1973): 133-4

[163] Michael A. Almond. "Amendment by Convention: Our Next Constitutional Crisis?," *North Carolina Law Review* 53 (1975): 504, n.67

[164] Henry D. Levine, "Limited Federal Constitutional Conventions: Implications of the State Experience," *Harvard Journal on Legislation* 11 (1973): 138

convention is the territory of the States' convention.¹⁶⁵ In this way, there is parity between the Congress and the States on amendment initiation. This idea is easily refuted by questioning why the Framers, if this was their intent, did not explicitly say so instead of waiting 185 years for someone to finally figure out their intentions. Additionally, if the spirit of federalism is to be faithfully observed, then one can claim, with vigor, that if Congress can propose a singular amendment, then the States can also propose singular amendments.¹⁶⁶ James Kenneth Rogers addressed the same subject and concluded that,

> *"Thus, a convention may propose multiple amendments just as Congress can, but it may also propose single amendments. This language should be read as expanding the possible roles of a convention, rather than limiting them."*[167]

Van Alstyne pointed out the implausibility of calling a convention in lieu of leaving the matter to Congress to resolve and in the process limiting the convention to less power than Congress enjoys in its ability to propose amendments.[168] But it is precisely this situation that many claim will exist. They make the claim that Article V grants to the States only the power to petition for a convention, but none to operate the convention, thus, it remains a federal function, and therefore, in the hands of Congress.[169,170]

A final argument can be made against the illimitability of the amendatory convention by the US Department of Justice. In 1987 in its Report to the Attorney General on the topic, the Department of Justice stated that,

> *"We conclude that Article V does permit a limited convention. This conclusion is premised on three arguments. First, Article V provides for equality between the Congress and the states in the power to initiate constitutional change.*

---

[165] Robert M. Rhodes, "A Limited Federal Constitutional Convention," *University of Florida Law Review* XXVI, no.1 (Fall 1973): 8-11 – Rhodes ascribes the Dual Purpose Theory to Charles Black, Jr.

[166] John T. Noonan, Jr., "The Convention Method of Constitutional Amendment – Its Meaning, Usefulness, and Wisdom," *Pacific Law Journal* 10 (1979): 643

[167] James Kenneth Rogers, "The Other Way to Amend the Constitution: The Article V Constitutional Convention Amendment Process," *Harvard Journal of Law & Public Policy* 30, no.3 (Summer 2007): 1017

[168] William Van Alstyne, "Does Article V Restrict the States to Calling Unlimited Conventions Only? – A Letter to a Colleague," *Duke Law Journal* 1978 (1978): 1297

[169] Dwight W. Connely, "Amending the Constitution: Is This Any Way to Call for a Constitutional Convention?," *Arizona Law Review* 22 (1980): 1021

[170] James Kenneth Rogers, "The Other Way to Amend the Constitution: The Article V Constitutional Convention Amendment Process," *Harvard Journal of Law & Public Policy* 30, no.3 (Summer 2007): 1016

> *Since the Congress may limit its attention to single issues in considering constitutional amendments, the state also have the constitutional authority to limit a convention to a single issue. Second, consensus about the need for constitutional change is a prerequisite to initiating the amendment process. The consensus requirement is better met by the view that Article V permits limited constitutional conventions than by the view that it does not. Third, history and the practice of both the states and the Congress show a common understanding that the Constitution can be amended issue by issue, regardless of the method by which the amendment process is initiated."[171]*

In that paper, the Department of Justice argued that not only is a limited convention permissible, but also that the limitations on a convention may be enforced.

The Delegates May Be Controlled by Special Interests

This concern should be one of the lesser concerns as the selection of delegates historically has been carried out by the States. The two major contending options are popular election by the people and appointment by either the Governor or the state legislature. Either option makes opponents nervous as they see the potential for special interest groups, in the first case funding a delegate's campaign, and in the second case the state selecting a delegate based on his or her fealty to the donors of the prevailing political party in the state. Former Justice Arthur Goldberg states his concerns,

> *"Moreover, the absence of any mechanism ensuring representative selection of delegates could put a 'runaway convention' in the hands of single-issue groups whose self-interest may be contrary to our national well-being."[172]*

Convention opponents see a limited convention as opening the door to the special interest groups. Their solution is for either the open convention so that the competing interests will "balance out" each other or to open the convention to the special interest groups and provide some measure of control in the diverse representation of the groups. The typical legislative bargaining for votes over the issues would engender a deeper discussion and examination of the issues according to their view. The goal is to create an

---

[171] U.S. Department of Justice, Office of Legal Policy, *Report to the Attorney General, Limited Constitutional Conventions under Article V of the United States Constitution*, (10 Sept. 1987): 1

[172] Arthur J. Goldberg, "The Proposed Constitutional Convention," *Hastings Constitutional Law Quarterly* 11 (Fall 1983): 2 - Published in the *Chicago Tribune*, 16 October 1983 and the *Miami Herald*, Sunday, 14 September 1986

"offset" of pressures and interests. More realistic is that each state will be fully cognizant of the makeup of its constituent interests and accordingly adjust within their respective delegation. Even more realistic is that special interests and competing factions are a normal, long standing facet of American political life and should be factored into the equation. Suppressing their views and influence is counter to the usual methodology of working through sticking points in politics. Even in the modern era of instantaneous communications and the seemingly endless number of publications, cable channels and ease of establishing a political action committee, the number of special interest groups may be increasing, but each one does so at the expense of diluting the political power of the others through increased factionalization. There will probably be more special interest groups in existence than delegates for a convention.

During the push for a Balanced Budget Amendment in the 1970s and 1980s, a number of academics spoke out against the effort as short-sighted and misinformed. One of the more vociferous opponents was Gerald Gunther of Stanford's law school who saw that either manner of selecting delegates would lead to special interests asserting themselves in the convention. He was especially worried about popularly elected delegates,

> *"The convention delegates would probably be chosen in popular elections, elections where the platforms and debates would be outside of congressional control, where interest groups would surely seek to raise issues other than the budget, and where some successful candidates would probably respond to those pressures."*[173]

An appropriate response might be to remind the opponents that all politicians are exposed to the same special interests and that, most likely, the same percentage of politicians as delegates would prove susceptible to the 'charms' of such lobbyists. Although it may actually be the case that fewer delegates would be unfaithful to their oaths due to the narrower focus of the amendment issue considered and the short term of office. Any special interest would need to secure a MAJORITY of the delegates, and in particular the convention officers, to carry out their scheme. With the intense media scrutiny that the delegates will endure before, during and after

---

[173] Gerald Gunther, "The Convention Method of Amending the United States Constitution," *Georgia Law Review* 14, no.1 (Fall 1979): 8. This Article was originally published at 14 Ga. L. Rev. 1 (1979) and is reprinted with permission.

their service in the convention, it would be inadvisable, if not downright foolish, to compromise oneself as a delegate – there would be simply nowhere to hide.

A related, although different, take on the ability of the convention to be controlled by a special interest comes in the form of state-wide interests exerting influence in the convention. Neal Manne summarizes the view, shared by Ackerman and Black, that this is possible as, "limited conventions would make constitutional amendment too easy: they could permit minority control of the amendment process, allowing parochial, state-centered interests to prevail."[174]

Manne admits that the same overt influence may be possible in an open or unlimited, general convention as well. He notes that the notion of minority control is based on a worst case scenario that not only is highly unlikely to happen but is also easily avoided. In fact, Manne concludes that the convention method may be precisely what is needed when Congress decides that some amendment desired by the public is too "narrow or parochial" to be justified. He reaches the conclusion that the problem is that both sides of the debate over a convention are claiming the same thing in this argument: the proponents argue for restraints and the opponents argue against the convention because there are not enough constraints possible – in the end they are both arguing that "the people, ultimately, cannot be trusted."[175]

Along a more partisan line of thinking, many have come to expect that the convention will be dominated by delegates that have distinctly sharp leanings politically to either the left or the right. The right prophesizes that the convention will "become a tool of leftist or internationalist groups" with the intention of either undermining the current Constitution or creating a new one and they will somehow ratify it without following the current ratification process.[176] Those convention opponents on the left fear that right-wing groups will strip out civil liberties and subjugate minorities.[177]

---

[174] Neal S. Manne, "Good Intentions, New Inventions and Article V Constitutional Conventions," *Texas Law Review* 58 (1979): 165. Reprinted with permission.

[175] Ibid., 166

[176] Andy Biggs, *The Con of the Con-Con, The Case Against the States Amending the U. S. Constitution* (Gilbert, AZ: Freeman Press, 2015), 16

[177] John A. Eidsmoe, "A New Constitutional Convention? Critical Look at Questions Answered, and Not Answered, by Article Five of the United States Constitution," *United States Air Force Academy Journal of Legal Studies* 3 (1992): 4

The inclusion of both groups tempers out their concerns by putting them upfront in the store windows for all to see.

No Restraining or Reversing of the Actions of a Convention is Possible

As a companion to the runaway convention fear, it is often proclaimed that there is no way, short of regulation by Congress, to keep the convention within the limits set by the call or to repeal the actions of the convention. Opponents, recognizing that if a convention will happen, seek a method of firmly restricting the convention from exceeding its mandate and also to veto its actions before the States consider the ratification of the convention's output. These opponents have no faith in the States' ability to control their delegates or of the delegates themselves to observe their oaths of office. Without some form of either incentive or disincentive to self-regulate their behavior, the delegates might succumb to the influence of donors, special interests, lobbyists or extortionists.

The problem is one of recognizing that a debate or discussion will have to, of necessity, go off on a tangent every now and then to fully explore the options of a proposed amendment. The consequences of the proposal must be explored in their entirety. Once the discourse is "in the weeds" how do the delegates reel it in and at what point is it exceeding its mandate? Professor Gunther uses the balanced budget as an example,

> *"But I would add that even a convention limited to a subject as narrow as the 'budget' could still be a quite far-ranging one; as any legislator who has sat on a budget committee knows, discussion of a budget can readily include consideration of particular items in a budget. If a convention cannot be limited to simply voting 'yes' or 'no' on a particular balanced budget scheme, what is to prevent it from considering such questions as permissible or impermissible expenditures for, say, abortions or health insurance or nuclear power?"*[178]

Opponents will frequently cite the lack of restraints as evidence of the danger of such a convention positing that once a convention starts, all outside restraint is ended. They claim that neither Congress nor the States can impose any limitations on the actions of the convention

---

[178] Gerald Gunther, "The Convention Method of Amending the United States Constitution," *Georgia Law Review* 14, no.1 (Fall 1979): 18. This Article was originally published at 14 Ga. L. Rev. 1 (1979) and is reprinted with permission.

that the convention itself cannot either ignore or remove under its own authority. The 1787 convention is given as the foremost example of a convention that exceeded its authority. They point to the redefining of the ratification requirements from a unanimous ratification under the Articles of Confederation to a much reduced three-fourths of the States under the Constitution for any amendments. If the Constitution had been ratified according to Article XIII of the Articles, then ALL states would have had to agree to the Constitution as an "amendment" of the Articles before it took effect.

The separate ratification process is the safeguard against an amendatory convention product that exceeds the limits of its mandate. Once the amendatory convention completes its work and disbands, there is no threat posed by the output; should the people feel that the product is defective, they have the ability to press either their state legislators or ratification convention delegates to refuse acceptance of ratification. The amendatory convention is merely a proposition and not an enactment.

The States Will Not Have an Equal Vote

One of the most persistent arguments made is that the equal suffrage of the smaller states will be eliminated with the onset of an amendatory convention leaving the convention on the hands of a few large states. Special interest groups may be able to target the delegations of the larger states and exert influence on those states while ignoring the smaller states. In this manner, they can redirect the efforts and focus of the convention.

The adherence to unit voting is the best method – and the most time-honored method – of assuring that each state had an equal say in the amendment proposal process. As covered in Chapter 1, the unit voting process has been observed and perfected over time. Electoral voting would relegate the small states to the sidelines as the larger states work out voting blocks and manipulate the process. The adoption of a supermajority requirement in the passage of any proposal or motion would guarantee that the smaller states have a role in the convention.

The Convention Can Enact a New Ratification Process

Opponents point to the 1787 convention and the substitution of Article VII of the Constitution in place of Article XIII of the Articles of

656 Far From Unworkable

Confederation as an example of the power of an amendatory convention to change standing law. This point is particularly egregious since the act of replacing the Articles with the Constitution is often considered a breach of the mandate and instructions given to the delegates to Philadelphia. The change in the ratification method is deemed to be the icing on the cake as if the rewriting of the Articles was not enough, the delegates had to go a step farther and disenfranchise entire states of their vote in the demise of the Confederation.

It is theorized that delegates to a modern convention would follow the historical precedent and rewrite part or all of the Constitution, or at the least, draft a controversial amendment that they expect would not pass muster with three-fourths of the States and then redraft the ratification process to make acceptance of the proposed amendment possible. They might change the ratification standard to a mere majority of the States – requiring just twenty-six in lieu of the currently requisite thirty-eight. They might go to a public referendum and accept a majority of the public nationwide and disregard the vote within the states. They might change the process to a majority of the votes in Congress. They might leave it to the decision of the President alone. They might start by scrapping Article V altogether. Without fixed and immutable rules, the delegates could do whatever they want.

As terrifying as that sounds to constitutionalists, it is a false fear. Under the scrutiny of a rigorous analysis, we find that a much different story took place in 1787. Let's establish the facts of the Philadelphia convention's actions, as laid out by Arthur Taylor in 2005:

- The convention wrote Article V of the Constitution that replaced Article XIII of the Articles of Confederation. It was a proposal only.

- The delegates did NOT change the ratification procedure – Congress and the States did, technically. The convention merely PROPOSED a change in Article VII but Congress approved the change when they debated the Constitution on 26-27 September 1787. The States then ratified that change in the ratification conventions.

- The ratification was not a *fait accompli*; the States debated the Constitution and in the case of North Carolina, they rejected the Constitution in the first convention and in the case of Rhode Island, they refused to take up the question initially. Those states were free to continue under the Articles of Confederation or go their own separate ways.

- Ultimately, all thirteen states ratified and accepted the Constitution so that Article XIII of the Articles of Confederation was eventually complied with by the States.

- Article V retains congressional control over the process even when employing the convention method as Congress still validates the applications, calls the convention and sets the date and place of convening. Congress also specifies the method of ratification.

- There is no judicial precedent, Supreme Court or otherwise, that demonstrates that the States can violate or circumvent the Constitution and change the ratification process. Congress must be involved; it was in 1787 and would need to be involved today.[179]

In Congress, during the consideration of the Constitution and whether it should be sent to the States for ratification, Richard Henry Lee of Virginia and Melancton Smith of New York rose to ask whether the convention had the authority to do as it had done to change the ratification requirements. Taylor takes an interesting and thought provoking stance that changes the picture. When Lee and Smith asked from whence came the authority and approval for the action of Congress to approve the deviation from the Articles, they appealed to the highest legal authority in the land. According to Article XIII, that highest court was the Congress itself as it read, "Every State shall abide by the determination of the United States in Congress assembled, on all questions which by this confederation are submitted to them."

The Congressional Court was posed the question by Lee and Smith to,

"find that the said Constitution in the thirteenth article thereof limits the power of Congress to the amendment of the present Confederacy of thirteen states, but does not extend it to the creation of a new confederacy of nine states."[180]

---

[179] Arthur H. Taylor, "Fear of an Article V Convention," *Brigham Young University Journal of Public Law* 20 (2005): 421-4

[180] Kenneth E. Harris & Steven D. Tilley, eds., *Index: Journals of the Continental Congress, 1774-1789* (Washington, D.C.: National Archives and Record Service, General Services Administration, US Government Printing Office, 1976) - citing *Papers of the Continental Congress* III, no.36,377 – notes of Richard Henry Lee, 26 September 1787

The Court debated and voted to dismiss the case by indefinite postponement. Taylor concludes with noting that Congress exercised its "plenary judicial authority" that was bestowed on it by the Articles of Confederation and that settles the issue as simply a misreading of history. He finishes his explanation of the ratification circumstances with,

> "In review, the Convention merely proposed the ratification change – they did nothing more. Congress, who had the authority to reject it, with either its legislative or judicial authority, instead enabled and ultimately endorsed it as an exercise of both."[181]

Paulsen notes that the method of ratification and even the number of ratifying states are fixed by Article V and therefore cannot be modified. Congress retains the power to specify the ratification method and it is highly doubtful that they might willingly cede their power.[182] In the extremely unlikely case where an Article V convention did go rogue and propose a new constitution, every state would possess the authority to refuse to consider or adopt such a charter. Introducing a new constitution introduces a new government and a new nation; no state can be forced short of at the point of arms to join such a union. North Carolina and Rhode Island demonstrated this in 1787. Although Rhode Island did face the threat of economic boycott, she had the choice to go it alone without threat of war.

No Washington, Franklin, Jefferson or Madison, etc., Exists Today

An intriguing point of concern for opponents of a convention is the assumption of the lack of statesmen in our age who would lead such an amendatory convention. It has been said, first by Jefferson, that the 1787 Convention was a "collection of demi-gods."[183] People today claim that there is no present political leader of the caliber of the Founders or Framers and that the partisanship of today is so pervasive that such a statesman could not long survive in today's political environment. While the Patriots had many talented and forward thinking leaders, we think ourselves hard-pressed to name a single one of our time. Columnist George Will wrote in 1981 near the height of the last drive for a convention to consider a balanced

---

[181] Arthur H. Taylor, "Fear of an Article V Convention," *Brigham Young University Journal of Public Law* 20 (2005): 426

[182] Michael Stokes Paulsen, "How to Count to Thirty-four: The Constitutional Case for a Constitutional Convention," *Harvard Journal of Law & Public Policy* 34, no.3 (2011): 842-3

[183] Letter of Thomas Jefferson to John Adams, 30 August 1787.

budget amendment that he wanted someone to explain who would be acting as Madison, Hamilton and Franklin.[184]

The same concern was expressed by conservative icon Phyllis Schlafly of the Eagle Forum in her testimony before the Montana legislature in 1987 as they considered passage of a resolution to call an Article V amendatory convention,

> *"We haven't noticed that we have any George Washingtons, Alexander Hamiltons, James Madisons, and Ben Franklins around today, and we are very leery of the people who think they are George Washingtons, Alexander Hamiltons, and all the rest."*[185]

This sentiment goes back at least as far as the Great Depression when former Solicitor General and US Representative James Beck of Pennsylvania stated that he feared a convention because "we could not repeat the success of the convention of 1787" since "we have not public statesmen who are comparable with the statesmen of 1787, but also because we could no longer make any successful attempt to embody the needs of a highly complex age in a written form of government." As Caplan explains, he continued that "thoughtful Americans" who understand that "changes are needed" would most likely oppose a convention because "it might prove a 'witches' Sabbath' of socialistic demagoguery."[186]

The men who forged our nation are considered to have been the most educated, most professional, most read, most widely traveled, most financially successful, most industrious, most well-spoken, most able men in the small nation of less than four million people. The notion that a nation which has grown to nearly one hundred times that size and yet cannot produce a single person – man or woman, young or old – worthy of the company of such illustrious men is utterly preposterous. We have the inestimable benefit of not only being able to read the same works of political science and philosophy as the Founders and Framers, but also the works produced over two centuries of scholarly study of the actions of those same Founders and

---

[184] George F. Will, "The Folly of a Constitutional Convention," Washington Post, 21 May 1981, at A27, Col. C – Contrast this 1981 view of Will with his 2014 view in "Amend the Constitution to Control Spending," Washington Post, 9 April 2014

[185] Phyllis Schlafy testimony before the Montana State Senate Committee on State Administration, 26 March 1987

[186] Russell B. Caplan, *Constitutional Brinkmanship* (New York: Oxford University Press, 1988), 67 - quoting the *New York Times* of 24 May 1932

Framers. We have instantaneous access through the internet to the analysis of the actions of those men. We have the benefit of history to prove or disprove the theories of the Framers.

We have the advances made in political science and in the understanding of human nature on which to build. We have a political system that has been "perfected" of sorts. General Washington wrote to his nephew, future US Supreme Court Justice Bushrod Washington, that,

> "...I think the People (for it is with them to Judge) can as they will have the advantage of experience on their Side, decide with as much propriety on the alterations and amendment [to the Constitution] which shall be found necessary, as ourselves, or I do not conceive that we are more inspired, have more wisdom or possess more virtue than those who will come after us. The power under the Constitution will always be in the People."[187]

We also have nearly two and a half centuries under the Constitution upon which we can draw for inspiration and examples. A more modern reference may be found in the words of Justice Scalia,

> "[W]e will not have Madison and Hamilton – the caliber of people will not match them. But, on the other hand, they will be people who can examine 200 years' worth of experience under the existing Constitution. You trade a little bit of smarts for a little bit of experience. I think it's likely to come out almost as well."[188]

Justice Scalia was correct; it is not just the intelligence of the Framers but their experience and education added to that intelligence. This we can match today and then some. The idea that we as a nation can no longer produce statesmen but only politicians is logically ludicrous. The issue of perspective also comes into play. The topics that might be taken up in a convention will draw the experts. Those same people may today be, as the saying goes, "toiling in obscurity," but if called to serve in a convention, they may prove to be as wise and up to the task as our eighteenth century forefathers. Yale's Professor E. Donald Elliott addressed this issue with regard to a convention and the federal deficit,

> "One need not believe that our generation is particularly blessed with an

---

[187] Letter from George Washington to Bushrod Washington, 10 November 1787.
[188] American Enterprise Institute for Public Policy Research, *A Constitutional Convention: How Well Would it Work?*, (Washington, D.C.: 1979), 20

abundance of 'Madisons' and 'Jeffersons' in order to believe that we should welcome a convention to consider ways to deal with the deficit...Rather, the key to understanding why a convention might be able to solve a problem that Congress cannot solve is recognizing that a convention would address the issues surrounding the deficit in a setting vastly different from that in which Congress functions."[189]

Elliott is arguing that in a convention setting, the usual criteria may be replaced by something else. Instead of making budget decisions as to which items to cut and therefore which group/constituency to offend/hurt as Congress would do, the convention would be looking at restructuring the political institutions that drive our federal budget battles every two years. Institutional change would take precedence over patronage and spoils.[190]

Throughout American history, we have seen that whenever a crisis occurs, the events themselves often "make the man" – or woman as the case may be. We entered a civil war without a large standing army or navy and found thousands of capable leaders both in the government and the military. The same can be said of the Second World War. During the Cold War America put men on the moon – six times.

Professor Sanford Levinson puts the whole debate into perspective. He does not buy the argument that modern Americans are unable to act with the same statesmanship and dedication to purpose that our forefathers did over two centuries past. He does not lament the lack of a Washington, Madison or Franklin easily named among us today. Instead, he asks the pertinent question,

"One gains immense pride in the sagacity even of relatively unknown Americans from reading the debates surrounding the adoption of the Constitution. 'We the people' had acted with courage and cogency once. Why not again in the future?"[191]

A final point is worth making, if we truly cannot and do not want to rewrite the Constitution, do we need a Washington, Franklin, Jefferson or Madison just to amend it?

---

[189] E. Donald Elliott, "Constitutional Conventions and the Deficit," *Duke Law Journal* 1985, no.6 (Dec. 1985): 1106

[190] Ibid., 1108

[191] Sanford Levinson, ""Veneration" and Constitutional Change: James Madison Confronts the Possibility of Constitutional Amendment," *Texas Tech Law Review* 21 (1990): 2452

A Convention Would Cause a Confrontation Between the Branches of the Federal Government, the States and the Convention

Professor Laurence Tribe raised these concerns during his testimony before the California State Assembly and later in his law review articles. He foresaw that the separation of powers would lead to conflict as each branch tried to figure out what exactly it was required and empowered to do with regard to the convention.

Tribe predicted that in a conflict between the Congress and the Convention, the two bodies would spar over who has the greater authority and sovereignty. The Supreme Court would inevitably be drawn into the fight. Control of the convention and constitutional power would be the desired prizes. Tribe thought that this battle would damage the nation. He does not say how it would damage the nation or what the end results might be. It would seem that any conflict would be brief and minimal as the procedural questions are in the hands of the convention to determine and the limitations on topics are to be spelled out in the call from Congress. As Congress is limited to setting the date and place of convening, there is little left to debate.[192]

The professor next considered the potential of a confrontation between the Congress and the Supreme Court. Here, some angst may be justified. With the *Coleman* decision looming over the heads of the Court, it is possible that Congress may very well have a point with regard to the ability of the Court to direct events and make decisions. Tribe states that the Court would be "obliged to protect the interests of the states" and this would be the justification for dismissing any discussion of justiciability. In this scenario, Tribe described the Court facing such possibilities of deciding whether the convention would use unit voting or electoral voting. Congress would, conceivably respond by legislating to limit the authority of the convention.[193]

It is of a greater likelihood that the Court, taking the full measure of history into its calculation, would see the need and value of a carefully constructed precedent. For once the first Article V Convention occurs, the next is sure to follow with a much smaller interval between conventions. The Court would ignore the lamentations of the Congress and focus on the

---

[192] Laurence Tribe, "Issues Raised by Requesting Congress to Call a Constitutional Convention to Propose a Balanced Budget Amendment," *Pacific Law Journal* 10 (1979): 635
[193] Ibid., 636-7

extraordinary occasion of the convention and the shepherding of its course.

The third case that Professor Tribe detailed is that of a conflict between the Supreme Court and the States. Tribe makes a most important point in restating that "the convention device was, after all, meant to *evade* control by Congress." Here again, we can expect that the unusual political drama being played out is one that will garner the interest and close attention of the Court and everyone else on the political stage. It is, after all, the States' play.[194]

Backing Tribe is Jeffery Mitchell, who claimed in the early 1990s that the convention could not be controlled and that it was inevitable that the Congress and the States clash over a convention. He believed that the uncontrollability of the convention by the States will force the Congress to intervene – much to the ire of the States. He also forecast that the States would seek to use the power of rescission at some point and this would force another clash with Congress. Mitchell predicted that the Congress will recognize and be uncomfortably mindful of its diminished stature with a convention solving the problems that Congress could not successfully or would not address.

Any attempt by Congress to assert control over the convention would face an enormous public backlash. Mitchell could see the disapprobation of the Supreme Court towards Congress' actions. He cites quotations from Justices Scalia and Souter that Congress has no authority to attempt control of the convention.[195] Mitchell tempers his concerns with this *bon mot*, "while some predict an uncontrollable convention, others suggest that the convention delegates could do no worse than has the Congress."[196,197] It is a very safe bet that the overwhelming majority of Americans would express this same sentiment when asked.

Besides the worries that opponents have with the convention operation itself, they have other objections external to the operations of the convention. Opponents in large national organizations have conducted campaigns against Article V conventions since the 1960s. These campaigns have used the same

---

[194] Ibid., 637
[195] Jeffery K. Mitchell, "The Threat of a Second Constitutional Convention: Patrick Henry's Lasting Legacy," *University of Richmond Law Review* 25 (1991): 532-7
[196] Walter Berns, "Comment: The Forms of Article V," *Harvard Journal of Law and Public Policy* 6 (1982): 76
[197] Jeffery K. Mitchell, "The Threat of a Second Constitutional Convention: Patrick Henry's Lasting Legacy," *University of Richmond Law Review* 25 (1991): 538

alternative methods of resolving the nation's constitutional issues throughout their half century of amendatory convention opposition.

- The argument is made that the Constitution is fine the way that it is and that we need not change it; what is needed is constitutional adherence
- An another argument is that we need only to elect "more constitutional candidates"
- The answer is to better educate people
- Nullification and/or interposition are the appropriate methods of resolution

The first point made is a curious redirection of the problem. No one is making the claim that the Constitution, as written, is defective. Rather, the argument is being made that it is *lacking* in some respects. Specifically in one case, the ability to restrain the out-of-control deficit spending and fiscal irresponsibility of Congress is not addressed in the Constitution. This is an addition to the Constitution and not a change. It is not a defect, just an omission. The major clauses often cited as all-encompassing grants of federal power, that is, the General Welfare, Commerce, Tax and Spending and Necessary and Proper Clauses, were often intended also as limitations of federal power. These clauses are often cited as ripe for clarification. Again, this is an addition and not a change. The original meaning is to be reaffirmed according to proponents. But it is never been claimed that the Constitution is the problem – the issue has been that there are omissions or ambiguities that need correction. This problem of virtual unamendability pre-dates the Constitution as it was one of the major problems with the Articles of Confederation and Perpetual Union and the 1787 delegates knew that they were tasked with correcting that deficiency first and foremost.

Electing more constitutionally minded candidates is often professed to be the answer to our problems. The issue here is two-fold: there is a paucity of constitutionally minded candidates as opposed to party minded candidates, and those that are elected are often quickly co-opted to work within the party-dominated establishment structure else their effectiveness and advancement are limited, if not stopped altogether. After a half century or more of professing this solution, there has been little, if any, noticeable change.

Educating Americans has not proven to be a solution. Constitution courses are held regularly all across the nation but few people are taken with the constitutional fervor. Adults cannot be forced to learn something of which they have no apparent interest.

The remaining point has been covered elsewhere to a great extent, there is no need to expand on it here other to say that it has no legal recognition or promise.

The Past is Not Necessarily Prologue

In 1986, as the nation was on the eve of celebrating the two-hundredth anniversary of the Philadelphia Constitutional Convention, New Jersey Governor Thomas Kean offered his view on the possibility of a potential amendatory convention to propose a balanced budget amendment. He summarized his interpretation of the events of 1787,

> *"Although Congress granted permission for the convention, it was not without its suspicions and attempted to control the convention. The resolution permitting the convention expressly limited the agenda and Congress instructed the convention delegates to not only submit proposals to it, but to the state legislatures as well. Other qualms were quieted by the knowledge that the Confederation required unanimous approval for change.*
>
> *But as the delegates toiled behind the locked doors of Independence Hall, the convention was quickly transformed from a discussion of commerce to a runaway that decided the Confederation government must be replaced. Not only did the delegates remake the national government, but they rewrote the rules for ratifying their changes. Every protection the Confederation Congress believed it had installed failed. And by later packing the ratifying convention(s) with pro-constitution people, the Constitution writers succeeded in carrying the day."*[198]

These are pretty heady charges from a sitting United States governor, particularly a governor from one of the original thirteen states. Governor Kean further stated that, "Many of the criticisms leveled in 1787 are leveled in 1987: The government cannot govern. It is too unwieldy. The political process has broken down."[199]

---

[198] Thomas Kean, "A Constitutional Convention Would Threaten the Rights We Have Cherished for 200 Years," *Detroit College of Law Review* 4 (1986): 1089
[199] Ibid., 1090

To an extent the governor is correct, but on the whole he has misconstrued the situation. To begin with, Congress did not grant permission for the 1787 convention – the States had already taken it upon themselves to call and organize the Philadelphia convention beginning their work after the September 1786 convention in Annapolis. The Confederation Congress did not involve itself in the process until 21 February 1787 when it issued its resolution calling the States to the convention. On that date, Congress first rejected a New York motion to have Congress call its own convention separate from, including date and place, the Philadelphia convention. Instead, they adopted a Massachusetts motion that was more in line with the Annapolis call to convention.[200] By that time, Congress was the proverbial, day late and a dollar short, as the work was already underway and unstoppable; seven states (a majority) had already announced their plans to attend.[201] Congress' situation is reminiscent of the famous, although probably apocryphal, quote attributed to one of the leaders of France's 1848 February Revolution, Alexandre-Auguste Rollin-Ledru. As he was being interviewed in a Paris café, a crowd of protesters passed by and he told the reporter, "There go the people. I must follow them, for I am their leader."[202] Congress too saw the States metaphorically marching down the street and did not want to be left behind sitting on its rear in a New York City café. Undoubtedly, that scene will replay itself when the inevitable amendatory convention eventually looms near.

Kean said that the Congress gave limited instructions and attempted to control the convention. The resolution and the *Report of Proceedings of the Confederation Congress* for 21 February 1787 tell a different story. The author's emphasis is added in bold.

> "Whereas there is provision in the Articles of Confederation & perpetual Union for making alterations therein by the assent of a Congress of the United States and of the legislatures of the several States; And whereas **experience hath evinced that there are defects in the present Confederation,** as a mean to remedy which several of the States and particularly the State of New York by express instructions to their delegates in Congress have suggested a convention for the purposes expressed in the following resolution

---

[200] John R. Vile, *The Constitutional Convention of 1787: A Comprehensive Encyclopedia of America's Founding, Vol. I* (Santa Barbara, CA: ABC-CLIO, 2005), 177

[201] Virginia announced its delegation to attend on 23 November 1786 and circulated a call to convention.

[202] Alvin Calman, "Ledru-Rollin and the Second French Republic," *Studies in History, Economics and Public Law* 103, no.2 (1922): 374

and such convention appearing to be the most probable means of establishing in these states a firm national government.

Resolved that in the opinion of Congress it is expedient that on the second Monday in May next a Convention of delegates who shall have been appointed by the several states be held at Philadelphia for the **sole and express purpose of revising the Articles of Confederation** and reporting to Congress and the several legislatures such alterations and provisions therein as shall when agreed to in Congress and confirmed by the states **render the federal constitution adequate to the exigencies of Government & the preservation of the Union.**"[203]

While the "sole and express purpose" was the revision of the Articles, the true congressional mandate was the establishment of a "firm national government" and the "preservation of the Union." As to the convention transforming from a discussion of commerce to a runway convention, that is a matter of taking liberties with the historical record. The intent to create a firm national government was underway before the convention began to convene. Edmund Randolph came with his (and Madison's) Virginia Plan firmly in hand;[204] William Paterson showed up with his New Jersey Plan;[205] Charles Pinckney was prepared with his South Carolina Plan;[206] the ever-cunning Alexander Hamilton waited as these plans submitted at the outset of the conventions were tore apart and then submitted his personal plan in June.[207] Thus, a full third of the states attending came prepared with plans to significantly revamp the national government before the convention even began.

Considering the claim that the delegates rewrote the ratification process, it must be remembered that the Articles of Confederation did in fact have a requirement for a unanimous ratification of amendments, but it made no provision for conventions – if there was a deviation from the Articles, then the first deviation was the calling of the convention itself by the Congress as Governor Kean as asserted. As noted previously, Gouverneur Morris had reminded all in the convention that, "This Convention is

---

[203] http://avalon.law.yale.edu/18th_century/const04.asp Journals of the Continental Congress, at 38 (manuscript), Library of Congress.
[204] http://avalon.law.yale.edu/18th_century/vatexta.asp
[205] http://avalon.law.yale.edu/18th_century/patexta.asp
[206] http://avalon.law.yale.edu/18th_century/pinckney.asp
[207] http://avalon.law.yale.edu/18th_century/hamtexta.asp

unknown to the Confederation."²⁰⁸ Once Congress issued the February 21 resolution, then all bets were off and the rules of the Articles no longer applied.

For Governor Kean's last point that the ratification conventions were packed with "pro-constitution people," it needs to be reiterated that the majority of the delegates to the States' ratification conventions were elected popularly.²⁰⁹ In many states, in particular, the large states of Virginia and New York, ratification was not a sure thing, in fact, it was greatly in doubt. North Carolina rejected the Constitution in its first convention. Rhode Island refused to consider the question until it found itself standing alone in 1790.

Governor Kean has actually made the case for a modern convention. He says that the political process has broken down. That is exactly the situation that the Framers anticipated and provided for in 1787. The governor states that, "The best way to look at the convention power is as the framers of the document intended: as yet another check on national government."²¹⁰ That is true, but of what good is a check that the national government knows will never be utilized? – it is then just an empty and meaningless threat. It is the dire nature of the current situation that justifies something as radical as the people, acting through their state legislatures, calling a convention to resolve a long-standing and seemingly intractable issue that the federal government has either bungled or refused to address. Ultimately, every problem is the people's to resolve; if the national government enacted and elected to resolve problems in the people's stead fails to do so for whatever reason, the people are obligated to act. A convention is the predictable and historical method of fulfilling that obligation.

Professor John Vile takes all of the concerns into account and concludes that the fears are unwarranted. He reaches the conclusion that even in a general convention, not a limited convention, that the possibility of the convention to go constitutionally crazy is remote and indicative of a

---

²⁰⁸ Max Farrand, *The Records of the Federal Convention of 1787*, Vol. II (New Haven: Yale University Press, 1911 and rev. 1937), 92

²⁰⁹ http://avalon.law.yale.edu/18th_century/ratva.asp Note the wording of the ratification notice from Virginia – "We the Delegates of the People of Virginia duly elected…"

²¹⁰ Thomas Kean, "A Constitutional Convention Would Threaten the Rights We Have Cherished for 200 Years," *Detroit College of Law Review* 4 (1986): 1091

larger problem,

> *"The people, acting in a general convention, would have the power to do all these things just as they currently have the power to propose such amendments to the Congress. Moreover, opponents of a new convention (although in this respect too, they resemble earlier thinkers) argue not so much against popular sovereignty as they do about the possibility that a convention could thwart or distort such sovereignty. Still, to suggest that slavery might be reinstated or the Bill of Rights repealed reveals a fear that the people and their elected representatives are incapable of self-government."*[211]

As for the fears of Charles Pinckney, mentioned in the beginning of this chapter, we should, as we have found with many of the quotations of the Framers, look into the full quote and context of the cited passage. The preceding sentence provides the context, "The States will never agree in their plans – And the Deputies to a second Convention coming together under the discordant impressions of their Constituents, will never agree." Paul Weber dissects the whole quotation and observes that Pinckney's fear is that a second convention would not reach an agreement whereas the present opponents to an amendatory convention fear that a convention would indeed reach a new agreement![212]

The reluctance, or maybe it should be termed the refusal, of the people to call a limited amendatory convention may be traced to past experience with state constitutional conventions, and in particular those six conventions that ran away prior to 1909 and to another facet of society's view of conventions. Robert F. Williams notes that voters have taken a negative view of conventions over the last few decades. He points to the defeat of calls for a convention at the polls by "wide margins." He states, citing the research of Gerald Benjamin and Thomas Gais,[213]

> *"The rejection of convention calls has been occurring at the same time that dissatisfaction with state government has been increasing. The public seems to view a constitutional convention as political business as usual by the 'government industry.' Constitutional conventions seem to have lost their*

---

[211] John R. Vile, "The Amending Process: The Alternative to Revolution," Southeastern Political Review 11, no.2 (Sept. 1983): 73; Permission to republish from John Wiley and Sons, conveyed through Copyright Clearance Center, Inc.

[212] Paul J. Weber, "Madison's Opposition to a Second Convention," Polity 20, no.3 (Spring 1988): 506, n.24

[213] Gerald Benjamin & Thomas Gais, "Constitutional Conventionphobia," Hofstra Law & Policy Symposium 1 (1996): 71

legitimacy in the public mind. At the time many states' original constitutions were drafted, the politicians and special interests were afraid of the people acting through constitutional conventions. Now, by contrast, the people are afraid of politicians and special interests acting through constitutional conventions."[214]

Historian Ann Stuart Diamond summed up the value of using the term "constitutional convention" to describe an amendatory convention,

"An Article V convention could propose one or many amendments, but it is not for the purpose of 'an unconditional reappraisal of constitutional foundations.' Persisting to read Article V in this way, so that it contemplates a constitutional convention that writes – not amends – a constitution, is often a rhetorical ploy to terrify sensible people."[215]

The last of the major predictions are that amendments to the Constitution will not work. The Constitution is not being followed now so why would the federal government follow any new amendments? This is perhaps the most easily refuted claim of all. Following a rebuttal style found in many articles and sites on-line, the Socratic method of response asks, among many other questions,

- Are the Supreme Court, the Congress and the Executive branch still operating?
- Are regular elections still being held?
- Does the American military still answer to civilian control?
- Are US senators being selected by the people?

Proof that amendments do work can be found in the Bill of Rights with the adjudication of the steady stream of lawsuits alleging First Amendment violations; or the fact that people have not been held in slavery in the United States for a century and a half; or that minorities, women and eighteen-year-olds can vote. Clearly, this list is not exhaustive.

Among the minor claims against the amendatory convention are

---

[214] Robert F. Williams, *The Law of American State Constitutions* (New York: Oxford University Press, 2009), 388 – Williams does suggest that the use of initiatives and constitutional commissions may be contributing significantly to this trend.
[215] Republished with permission of Oxford University Press – Journals, from Ann Stuart Diamond, "A Convention for Proposing Amendments: The Constitution's Other Method," Publius, The State of American Federalism, 1980 11, no.3 (Summer 1981): 137; permission conveyed through Copyright Clearance Center, Inc.

that the length of the convention is uncertain and that this will lead to a permanent convention. The appropriate control of the convention finances will solve that little issue. The argument has been made that "settled issues" will be reopened. With the agenda fixed, this is a non-starter. The media is predicted to attempt to influence the convention. With the convention closed to the media that will prove difficult. It is alleged that many conventions may be needed to correct the course of the nation and to restrict the federal government. Multiple conventions would be a good thing as the control of the direction of the nation would then be more easily managed in an incremental fashion thereby preventing special interests from gaining a foothold with the delegates.

All of these small issues aside, the real problem, according to convention proponents, is that Congress does not listen or respond to the people or the States. It seeks only to protect and expand its own power, privileges and patronages. The executive branch is guilty of the same. The Supreme Court has simply become too politicized to operate effectively. The collection of fears and phobias that people possess in regard to an amendatory convention is out of scale with the intent and the potential of the convention tool.

TEN
AND THE ARGUMENT IN FAVOR...

> *"I will venture to add that to me the convention mode seems preferable, in that it allows amendments to originate with the people themselves, instead of only permitting them to take or reject propositions originated by others not especially chosen for the purpose, and which might not be precisely such as they would wish either to refuse or accept."*
> -Abraham Lincoln, First Inaugural Speech, March 4, 1861

No greater argument can be made for an Article V amendatory convention than to cite the guarantee of a peaceable solution to government gone bad or just simply government gone unresponsive to the people. In the American system, we rely not on the force of arms to ensure the continuation of responsible government but on the continuation of the favorable support of the people. When the trust and consent of the governed is lost, there is still, fortunately, more than a singular, *ultima ratio* solution.

To adequately and respectively consider the arguments both for and against an amendatory convention, we need to be able to understand both the perspective as well as the basis of the argument. Lawyers have, usually, five types of legal arguments to which they turn in making their case: text, intent, precedent, tradition and policy.[1,2] For those arguing in favor of an

---

[1] Generally, Wilson R. Huhn, *The Five Types of Legal Arguments* (Durham, NC: Carolina Academic Press, 2d ed., 2007)

[2] Tradition and precedent are bequeathed to us by our legal forebears, the Romans. These were the usual sources of Roman public law – Andrew Lintott, *The Constitution of the Roman Republic* (New York: Oxford University Press, 1999), 4

amendatory convention from a legalistic viewpoint, we can take these one at a time and see where they lead. For *textual* arguments, there is little to go on; the Constitution is succinct in terms of the content of Article V racking up a mere 143 words with a third of those going to the entrenchment clauses.[3] A paltry twenty-two words address the convention method. Within the category of text, there are three methods of textual interpretation. First, is the plain meaning of the words as written and their definition at the time of drafting. There is not much to work with in terms of a deeper understanding of the purpose. As an example, it is clear from the wording that the purpose of the amendatory convention is for proposing amendments. It is in this regard that Supreme Court Justice Joseph Story wrote nearly two centuries ago that, "Every word in the Constitution is to be expounded in its plain, obvious, and common-sense meaning, unless the context furnishes some ground to control, qualify or enlarge it."[4]

Second, are the canons of construction that make inferences from the context. An example of a canon of construction is the recent emphasis on superfluity, or "ordinary meaning" of the wording. In this instance, any superfluous wording is ignored to find the meaning or intent. Here, we can point to the wording of "shall be valid to all Intents and Purposes" as the superfluous portion and the "shall call a Convention for proposing Amendments" as the operative, or most germane, portion. Third, are intra-textual arguments that rely on another part of the document to explain the portion under consideration. In this instance, the clause that covers calling a convention for proposing amendments is preceded by mention of the applications from two thirds of the States implying that the convention is for and operated by and on behalf of the States.

For arguments from *intention*, we have little latitude for speculation but some scholars have very successfully made the most of what is there. As an example, Van Alstyne says this of the Framers intent for a convention,

> *"The first point is that securing a way to propose and to submit for ratification amendments other than those that might originate in or be congenial to extraordinary majorities in Congress was a steadfast determination in the Philadelphia Convention. The second point is that the most expected use*

---

[3] The last two clauses that prohibit interfering with slavery before 1808 and the protection of the States' equal suffrage in the Senate.
[4] Joseph Story, *Commentaries on the Constitution of the United States, Vol. I* (Boston: Hillard, Gray & Co., 1833), §436

of that authority would be in response to alleged usurpations, whether of states' rights or of personal liberties, by the national government itself."[5]

This is, of course, a matter of record but the extent of the motivation of all of the 1787 delegates is an issue of scholarly debate. Intent can be found by examination of sources other than the Constitution, such as the notes of the delegates or the ratification debates or even discarded, previous versions of the article (in this form, the reason for discarding may shed light on why the adopted version was preferred). This aspect is particularly relevant as the delegates debated the pros and cons extensively after first preferring a convention method, then rejecting it in favor of a congressional method of proposal and then rejecting that method in favor of the adopted method since it promoted federalism and the circumvention of Congress when needed.

For arguments made from the view of *precedent*, we have the prior court decisions to turn to that are detailed in Part II; this is probably the most extensive source of information as to the process of Article V conventions. Precedents are based, more often than not, in the case of Article V on two things: historical tradition and judicial interpretation. This topic is covered more in depth in Part II of the book.

Tradition plays a growing role in Article V interpretation. As historians and legal scholars unearth more of the history of prior intercolonial and interstate conventions, the procedures and processes employed have been documented and explored giving us a view of the methodology of past generations' efforts to address issues. We can fill in some of the blanks of how to operate the first Article V amendatory convention through study of how other interstate conventions have handled similar operations. Alongside these sources are the practices and methods of the post-1787 interstate conventions such as those for the river commissions and the interstate compacts. Perhaps no aspect of interpretation is as voluminous or extensive as this area. Since the turn of the century, more evidence and anecdotal material has been uncovered than maybe all of the prior material since the turn of the previous century. Historians have only recently begun to mine the motherlode of material available on the convention methods of the last few hundred years and then seek to interpret their applicability to the

---

[5] William Van Alstyne, "The Limited Constitutional Convention – The Recurring Answer," *Duke Law Journal* 1979 (1979): 990

present needs. Finding a consensus among the dozens, if not hundreds, of previous intercolonial and interstate conventions as to the operations and rules is probably the most important breakthrough that could be achieved in discerning how an Article V convention could and should operate. While any modern convention is entitled to set its own rules and procedures, it is wise to consider that the widespread and most common practices used in the past are most often the result of trial and error and a natural selection of practicality and effectiveness.

The last type of argument is that of *policy*. Whereas the four types discussed thus far have dealt with after-the-fact methods of analyzing legal issues, and specifically, the amending process, policy takes a different perspective. Policy is intended to affect a certain future outcome. Attempts to establish policy have been tried repeatedly by Congress. The problems with the 1970s and 1980s era Ervin bills were rooted in the potential usurpation of the States' power to control the convention. Policy will undoubtedly be the most problematic aspect of the planning of a convention's operation. Competing interests will jockey to assure that their particular concerns are protected from the outset of the convention. It is at this juncture that either the careful selection of the members of the Rules Committee must pay off to avoid any contamination by the special interests or that pre-convention efforts, such as that of the Assembly of State Legislatures, must prevail to establish permanent, unbiased rules for all future conventions.

To look at the effects of an Article V convention proposal, we needed this background to understand that the arguments for – or against – a convention are limited by text, based on the opinions of scholars, historians and opponents and proponents as to the intent, and not secured by future policy. They are based mostly on historical precedent and tradition. There must be a balance between the "tried and true" practices of the past and the uncertain predictions of the actions of the future.

Circumvention of Congress

The most attractive and most powerful aspect of the amendatory convention is the ability of the people and the States to circumvent an obstructive and defiant Congress. If the Congress were allowed to control an amendatory convention, the conclusion would be known before the convention had even occurred. The national legislature's ability to set the national political agenda and also to deny a place on the agenda gives a disproportionate measure of power to Congress that allows it to preserve the status quo. Congress may, as it has in the past, ignore or suppress the people's desire for constitutional change. Exercise of that power has contributed to the misconception of Congress knowing best and the promotion of a pervasive elitism throughout government at all levels. Providing the people and the States with the ability to obviate the actions or plans of Congress is the strongest check and balance on Congress after that of periodic elections. A convention is the equal of Congress and not only independent of Congress but can be perhaps also effectively competitive with and productively antagonistic toward Congress. The threat of an amendatory convention constantly serves to force Congress to "remember its place." A looming convention serves to remind Congress and the Executive of the power of the public opinion and the system of checks and balances. Little can compare in terms of the ability to modify the behavior of Congress to the impending forced change in its powers. The threat of a convention is the ever-present nudge of the federal government back ***towards*** the Constitution.

Another way to look at this question is consider what would justify the action of the States to circumvent Congress. By what measure do we judge Congress to be out of the bounds of acceptable behavior and deserving of a reaction? St. George Tucker remarked nearly two centuries ago that such a convention "will probably never be resorted to, unless the federal government should betray symptoms of corruption."[6] Today, Vincent Pulignano rephrases Tucker and states, "the question is whether the government is so corrupt that the states must take matters into their own hands."[7] The fact that the question is being posed, probably provides its own answer.

There is an inherent fear of a convention that is so charged with reining in Congress. Where does a convention's power end? Even a limited convention is still equipped to take up a singular, albeit powerful, measure that could result in a major constitutional shift. In the end, what everyone is concerned about is whether the convention will be "safe." But what does that mean exactly? One definition that addresses most, if not all, of the concerns of the public, academia and the political class is that of Professor Paul Weber,

---

[6] St. George Tucker, *Blackstone's Commentaries*, (Philadelphia: William Young Birch and Abraham Small, 1803), App., 371-2
[7] Vincent Pulignano, "A Known Unknown: The Call For An Article V Convention," *Florida Law Review Forum* 67 (2016): 158-9

> "[S]afe means that the procedure allows input into the amending process by a variety of political forces at various points and over an extended period of time such that a consensus within the nation is reached; that procedures are established to resolve potential impasses in the process; and that the process retains the aura of legitimacy that is necessary for political stability and voluntary compliance with the law."[8]

Weber appears to point out that the perception of safety is the search for certainty and that is hard to procure in a charged political environment. We have to remember that the convention is meant for times when certainty is in short supply and there is a need for radical action outside of the political norm. The fear of the convention lay in it being "unsettled law." Weber stated that, "Those who argue that a constitutional convention is risky assume that unsettled law is unsafe law."[9] Without the unsettled law, all that remains is violence.

Limitability of the Convention

The safety and security of an amendatory convention which is limited provides an advantage over other methods of societal change. The other method of constitutional change, the path through the Congress, has removed the people until the final ratification stage. At that point, it becomes a "take it or leave it" proposition. Congress is free to do as it sees fit devoid of the influence of the people or the States with the notable exception of the testimony of congressional hearings. The rationale that the Article V convention is limited in powers and unable to runaway through the exercise of wide ranging powers was supported early in court decisions, such as that frequently cited opinion of Pennsylvania Chief Justice Daniel Agnew in "Wood's Appeal" in 1874,[10]

> *"A convention has no inherent rights; it exercises powers only. Delegated power defines itself."*
>
> *"To impute absolute power to a convention of mere delegates is to assume a*

---

[8] Paul J. Weber, "The Constitutional Convention: A Safe Political Option," *Journal of Law and Politics* 3 (1986): 52

[9] Ibid., 52

[10] Herein Justice Agnew is referring to the calling of a state constitutional convention for the Commonwealth of Pennsylvania, but the sentiments expressed in the passages cited are equally relevant to the federal situation. Wood's Appeal dealt with the outcome of the Pennsylvania state constitutional convention of 1872-73 that was considered a runaway.

grant by the people without terms, without the means of limitations, and without any clearly evinced intent. It is an assumption without a just basis against the security, the interest and the welfare of the people which no body of men have a right to make and no judicial reason or rule can justify."

"The people have the same right to limit the power of their delegates that they have to bind their representatives. Each are representatives but only in a different sphere. The right of the people to restrain their delegates by law cannot be denied unless the power to call a convention by law and the right of self-protection be also denied."[11]

Chief Justice Agnew argues that limitations on conventions are not only permissible but normal and to be expected and certainly not to be overlooked.

"A limit must be set to power. No people can be safe in the presence of a divine right to rule or of self-imputed sovereignty in their servants to bind them without ratification. Let a convention in such seasons possess by mere imputation all the powers of the people, and what security is there for their fundamental rights?"[12]

In the same period, Jameson astutely noted that limitations are a fundamental part of <u>any</u> convention,

"What is a convention that it should assume to be exempt from obedience to that department of the government which is charged with sovereign attributes – is more nearly sovereign – than any other in it? Does it claim to be above the legislature?"[13]

The limitability of an Article V convention is perhaps the second greatest feature after the ability to circumvent Congress. The question of whether an amendatory convention can indeed be limited in scope and purpose is both old and settled. The earliest court decision to that effect came in 1831 in the *Smith v. Directors of Union Bank of Georgetown* decision.[14] Therein, the US Supreme Court held that an Article V convention was a "convention of the States" and implied that it could be limited in purpose.

---

[11] Wood's Appeal, Pa. State Reports, Vol. 75, 71
[12] Ibid., 74
[13] John Alexander Jameson, *Treatise on Constitutional Conventions, Their History, Powers and Modes of Proceeding* (New York: Scribner, 1867, 4th ed., 1887), 493 - reprint by The Lawbook Exchange, (2013)
[14] 30 U.S. (5 Pet.) 518, at 528 (1831)

Defining the limitability of a convention was covered by Walter Dellinger in three assumptions,

> *"1) Congress may limit in advance the subject matter authority of any convention called for proposing amendments;*
>
> *2) it is valid for states to specify in their applications that the convention may be formally limited; and*
>
> *3) Congress, in response to these requests for a "limited subject matter" convention, must call a limited convention, define the scope of the matters that may be considered in accordance with the state applications, and require that the convention stay within those limits."*[15]

But there are two ways to look at the limitability of an amendatory convention. If the opponents of a limited convention prevail in their assertion of illimitability, then we get an open convention which could, with some serious and strenuous stretching of the definition of a convention, theoretically rewrite the Constitution by proposing an enormous amount of amendments that cover much of the existing Constitution. This ability is offset by the requirement that Congress would then have to aggregate all applications together irrespective of stated purpose. Proponents of this illimited view also argue that, historically, there was but one exception to the rule of all applications being for an open convention until the last century, therefore the idea of a limited convention is a recent innovation, but the cited exception cancels the rule.[16] It has become the practice of the States to make applications for a limited only convention. The history of state applications shows this with examination of some of the earlier applications. Take for example that of a California statute of 1903,

> *"And the request of and consent to, the calling and holding of such a convention as hereby made and given, is limited to the consideration and adoption of such amendments to said Constitution as herein mentioned and no other."*[17]

Much of the argument for an unlimited power of a convention is

---

[15] Walter Dellinger, "The Recurring Question of the "Limited" Constitutional Convention," *Yale Law Journal* 88 (1979): 1624

[16] Alabama made an application for a limited convention in 1833 for addressing the issue of the tariff.

[17] Cal. Stat. 683 (1903) – quoted from Lester B. Orfield, *The Amending of the Federal Constitution* (Ann Arbor: University of Michigan Press, 1942), 45, n.18

meant simply as a scare tactic to induce state legislators to vote against any convention application out of the fear that the convention will be uncontrollable and that they will be held responsible for opening Pandora's Box.[18]

A number of scholars have hypothesized that the runaway aspect can be managed through a set of congressional actions. These include refusing to promulgate any unconstitutional amendment proposals from a runaway convention; including a recommendation from Congress not to ratify a particular amendment proposal; assigning an extremely short ratification period; Congress could pass its own proposed amendment that would compete in the ratification process with that of the convention; or Congress could pronounce the proposed amendment as outside of the limitations in the call and refuse to receive it from the convention.[19]

The counterviews are that any involvement by Congress in calling a convention beyond the stipulated setting of the date and place is too much of a temptation by Congress to take over the convention as well as setting a dangerous precedent for congressional intervention and usurpation of the convention. Another counterview is that the potential of a runaway is too high to take the risk since there is no method of containment. But these viewpoints are not substantiated by established facts. Limitability of conventions is proven and can be protected at the state and federal levels.

Cooling Effect of the Convention

There is a long-recognized "cooling effect" in conventions that are permitted to deliberate on an issue without public scrutiny. When the political pressure of party politics that runs rampant in legislatures is absent in a non-partisan convention, solutions that are policy-based are most often the result. Hoober noted as long ago as 1892 that, "This is the recorded experience of past conventions. Policy – individual, party or public, - is forceful and restraining when the expediency of a movement – individual, party, or public – is in question."[20]

---

[18] John R. Vile, *Contemporary Questions Surrounding the Constitutional Amending Process* (Westport, CT: Praeger, 1993), 58-63

[19] Gerald Gunther, "The Convention Method of Amending the United States Constitution," *Georgia Law Review* 14, no.1 (Fall 1979): 9

[20] John A. Hoober, "Popular Prejudice and Constitutional Amendatory Conventions," *Yale Law Journal* 1, no.5 (1892): 214

This limitation is the product of selecting the correct delegates; ones who are "selected for one determinate purpose ensuring a concentration of energies."[21] The normal partisanship ever present in Congress is tempered in a limited convention by the extreme focus on the matter of consideration. The federal and state legislatures are permanently subject to a contest for securing and retention of long term power by one party over the other. Every issue considered is weighed against the effect of the vote on the ability of the party in power to remain in power. A convention is divorced from that dynamic due to its temporary nature.

In comparison, congressional deliberation is subject to less scrutiny. Putting a particular topic in front of delegates and allowing them unfettered deliberation encourages idea generation and exploration. The radicalism of the fringe political elements is tempered and dampened by the convention discussion with an eye toward finding a consensus that will result in an acceptable amendment proposal. Within Congress, consensus is what will pass a vote. For those instances, and an example being the late and post-Civil War years, when a party overwhelmingly controls the national legislature, poorly written or excessively biased amendments may pass without appropriate or complete deliberation. A non-partisan convention outside of the usual congressional environment "cools" the ardor of political passions and facilitates an equitable resolution in the form of an amendment proposal.

Prodding Effect of the Convention

The "prodding effect" has proven very effective in forcing Congress to take up issues that the public wants resolved. The earliest instance is that, obviously, of the Bill of Rights. As detailed previously, the ratification conventions yielded both the list of the 189 proposed amendments coupled with the demand of a Bill of Rights in return for ratification and the two Article V convention applications from Virginia and New York setting the precedent for Congress to offer amendments. The prodding effect alone makes the amendatory convention a valuable and also viable tool for constitutional change. In addition to the Bill of Rights, we can point directly to the Seventeenth, Twenty-first, Twenty-second and Twenty-fifth

---

[21] Ibid., 209

Amendments as the results of convention campaigns.[22,23]

The most famous example of the prodding effect is that of the aforementioned Seventeenth Amendment which permitted the direct election of US senators in lieu of the constitutionally stipulated selection by the state legislatures. It is the most fitting example of Congress refusing to do anything that might even remotely compromise the power of Congress. Drafted in response to what was perceived as the "selling" of Senate seats, the proposed amendment was introduced in the usual manner in Congress. Although the bill passed the House of Representatives FIVE times – including twice without a single opposing vote – the Senate refused to take up the bill for a vote even once.[24,25] The States reached an application count of thirty out of the requisite thirty-one before the Senate acquiesced and voted to pass the bill and promulgate the proposed amendment on to the States.[26] Many of the state applications for an Article V convention stated outright that the reason for the application was due to the "failure of Congress to submit such amendment;"[27] "the Senate of the United States has so far neglected to take any action whatever upon the matter;"[28] "Whereas the national House of Representatives has on four separate occasions, within recent years, adopted resolutions in favor of this proposed change in the method of electing United States Senators, which were not adopted by the Senate;"[29] "Whereas the United States Senate has each time refused to consider or vote upon said resolution, thereby denying to the people of the several States a change to secure this much-desired change."[30] Each state was expressing their displeasure at the US Senate for refusing to take up the people's business in a clear attempt to preserve unchanged the Senate's power. This is the lesson that we must remember in attempting to call an

---

[22] Paul J. Weber & Barbara A. Perry, *Unfounded Fears, The Myths and Realities of a Constitutional Convention* (New York: Praeger, 1989), 75

[23] Charles W. Hucker, "Constitutional Convention Poses Questions," *Congressional Quarterly* 37, no.7 (17 Feb. 1979): 273

[24] Walter K. Tuller, "A Convention to Amend the Constitution. Why Needed. How It May Be Obtained.," *North American Review* 193, no.664 (1911): 370

[25] Wayne B. Wheeler, "Is a Constitutional Convention Impending?," *Illinois Law Review* 21 (1927): 786 - July 21, 1894 (Cong. Rec., 26, 7783); May 11, 1898 (Cong. Rec., 31, 4825); April 13, 1900 (Cong. Rec., 33, 4128); February 13, 1902 (Cong. Rec., 35, 1722).

[26] At the time of the passage of the Seventeenth Amendment, there were 46 states.

[27] Louisiana application (1907)

[28] Kansas application (1907)

[29] Pennsylvania application (1901)

[30] Wisconsin application (1908)

amendatory convention. The Congress will fight tooth and nail against it and the people and the States must fight even harder to secure the convention. One scholar posits that,

> "[E]ven though an article V convention was never called, the possibility, or rather the apparent inevitability, of a national convention eventually compelled Congress to take action favored by the people. In this manner, then, the alternative amendment process served precisely the function intended by the Framers."[31]

The Senate itself publicly recognized the prodding effect of the convention method, especially with regard to the passage of the amendment for the direct election of US senators,

> "The history of the Seventeenth Amendment illustrates the usefulness of having a method by which a recalcitrant Congress can be bypassed when it stands in the way of the desires of the country for constitutional change."[32]

For the prodding effect to work, it must be believed by both the public and the Congress that the drive is real and bears a significant probability of success. Weber and Perry sum it up as that the threats must credible, and for a convention that means it has to be a "safe political option."[33] The effort in the late 1970s and early 1980s for obtaining a balanced budget amendment was so successful in prodding Congress that in the 96th Congress eighty balanced budget amendment proposals were introduced in the US House and fifteen in the US Senate in the first session alone![34]

The potential refusal of Congress to carry out its duty has been expounded on by many scholars over the last couple of centuries. On the specific issue of calling an Article V amendatory convention, one legal writer in particular stands out; Walter K. Tuller, an attorney in Los Angeles a century ago, studied the notes of Jonathan Elliott on the *Debates of the Ratification Conventions*. Writing in 1911, he argued that Congress must call

---

[31] Michael A. Almond, "Amendment by Convention: Out Next Constitutional Crisis?," North Carolina Law Review 53 (1975): 500. Reprinted with permission of the North Carolina Law Review.

[32] S. Rep. No. 92-293, "Report of the Committee on the Judiciary, United States Senate, Together With Additional Views to Accompany S. 1272", 93rd Cong., 1st sess., at 6 (1973)

[33] Paul J. Weber & Barbara A. Perry, *Unfounded Fears, Myths and Realities of a Constitutional Convention* (New York: Praeger, 1989), 3

[34] Dwight Connely, "Amending the Constitution: Is This Any Way to Call for a Constitutional Convention?," *Arizona Law Review* 22 (1980): 1016, n.52

a convention, laying out his reasoning:[35]

- Every member of the national legislature has sworn an oath to uphold the federal Constitution.

- The Constitution is the Supreme Law of the Land and, as thus, cannot be denied.

- The word "shall," as used in Article V, is a legal term and there is, as often decided by competent courts of law, no discretion on the part of Congress as to what "shall" means or what it requires.

- The Framers prescribed two methods of proposing amendments in order to circumvent an obstructionist Congress.

- It was the will of the Framers to make certain that the people and the States could amend the Constitution without the consent of Congress.

- A refusal to act by Congress is a refusal to do its duty and a refusal to obey the Constitution.

- If there is no legal remedy to Congress's refusal, then the Constitution is a nullity and Congress is above the law – this has been shown repeatedly to not be the case.

- The power to force the compulsion of Congress lay in the judiciary of the federal court and, ultimately, the US Supreme Court.

- The argument that the executive, legislative and judicial branches are co-equal and co-ordinate and each supreme within its sphere of influence is voided by the system of check and balances.

- That when considering the applications of the States to call an Article V amendatory convention, the Congress is NOT acting in its usual legislative capacity, but is acting in a "purely ministerial" role. "Congress is simply the agent appointed and commanded by the Constitution to perform a specific act when certain specific conditions have been fulfilled. That Congress is commanded to do the act, regardless of its discretion, demonstrates beyond the necessity of argument that it is a

---

[35] Walter K. Tuller, "A Convention to Amend the Constitution. Why Needed. How It May Be Obtained.," *North American Review* 193, no.664 (1911): 374-83

ministerial duty."

- Where the law imposes a legal duty upon a person or body, it is clearly within the jurisdiction of the judiciary as well as its duty to compel and enforce the action. This is why courts are created. When performing this function, the judiciary is not invading, limiting or infringing on the rights, powers or province of the other branches of government – it is simply fulfilling its obligation to the Constitution.

- The branches are acting <u>under</u> the authority of the Constitution and are therefore subservient to the Constitution. The supremacy of Congress is NOT independent of the Constitution.

- The right and duty of the judiciary to compel performance is "simply the converse of the principle" of the judiciary to nullify any act of Congress which violates the Constitution.[36]

Thus, Article V remains the ever present "sword of Damocles" hanging over the head of Congress. The threat of a convention remains a constant reminder of the responsibilities and limits of federal power. Phillip Kurland remarked that "the primary importance of Article V may be found in the *in terrorem* effect of an ultimate appeal to the people for the correction of the abuses of their government."[37]

In fairness, one must admit that the prodding effect does not always work. If the stakes are too high, even for Congress, they will not acquiesce and write a bill. There are some situations where Congress simply has too much to lose to cave in. The convention method will not only be rejected but actively fought. Yale's Professor E. Donald Elliott succinctly summarizes the problem,

> *"The essential reason why we cannot expect Congress to initiate the kind of changes that will be necessary to deal with the deficit is that incumbents are the prime beneficiaries of the present system. The present system allows incumbents to enhance their prospects for reelection by catering to well-organized interest groups and imposing costs on future generations. There is*

---

[36] The use of the word "nullify" in this instance is in the strict judicial sense and not in the theoretical legislative sense.
[37] Philip B. Kurland, "Article V and the Amending Process," in *An American Primer*, ed., Daniel Boorstin (New York: Meridian, 1966), 132-4 quoted in US Senate Report No. 92-293, 92nd Cong., 1st sess., (1971) by the Subcommittee on Separation of Powers, (119 Cong. Rec. 22732-36)

no reason to assume that Congress will volunteer to the part of the solution, because Congress is part of the problem."[38]

As Elliott has demonstrated, there comes a time where the proverbial line in the sand must be drawn and then disrespected. The people and/or the States must step over that line and carry out the threat to its conclusion to resolve the constitutional crisis. For the prodding effect to be actually effective requires that it be the lesser, in Congress's view, of two evils.

Difficulty of the Amendment Process

We hear the oft-repeated refrain that the Constitution is too hard to amend, the process is too cumbersome and that Article V itself needs to be amended. The proof provided is to point to the time elapsed since the last amendment was added in 1992 – more than two decades ago. This claim is all too easily refuted. The initial amendments of the first twelve were accomplished in a mere fourteen years.[39] No amendment was made again until the three Civil War Amendments were added the late 1860s.[40] The period between amendments stretched more than sixty-one years between the Twelfth and Thirteenth Amendments.

Similarly, another amendment drought occurred during the last half of the nineteenth century with exactly forty-three years – to the day – between the Fifteenth and the Sixteenth Amendments.[41] In short order, four amendments were added over the next seven years.[42] The next amendment drought lasted only for a little over twelve years and ended with the addition of the Twentieth and Twenty-first Amendments in 1933.[43] From that point on, the addition of amendments to the Constitution became a fairly regular event. The Twenty-second Amendment was added in 1951; the Twenty-third Amendment in 1961; the Twenty-fourth Amendment in 1964; the Twenty-fifth Amendment in 1967 and the Twenty-sixth Amendment in 1971. The Twenty-seventh and last amendment was "unexpectedly" added in 1992.

---

[38] E. Donald Elliott, "Constitutional Conventions and the Deficit," *Duke Law Journal* 1985, no.6 (Dec.1985): 1098

[39] The Bill of Rights was proposed in September of 1789 and the Twelfth Amendment was ratified June 15, 1804.

[40] The Thirteenth Amendment was ratified 6 December 1865; the Fourteenth Amendment was ratified 9 July 1868 and the Fifteenth Amendment was ratified on 3 February 1870.

[41] The Sixteenth Amendment was ratified February 3, 1913.

[42] The Sixteenth Amendment; the Seventeenth Amendment on 8 April 1913; the Eighteenth Amendment on 16 January 1919; and the Nineteenth Amendment on 18 August 1920.

[43] Ratified 28 January 1933 and 5 December 1933 respectively.

We can conclude from this examination that the frequency of amendments actually <u>increased</u> in the last century rather than became more difficult.

The complaint of extreme difficulty in the amendment process would have clearly been more accurate in the nineteenth rather than the twentieth century. It is somewhat comical today, to read the accounts given in the law journals of a century ago wherein the writers complain that the amendment process has broken down and needs to be changed. An example is provided from 1909, just four years short of adding two amendments in the same year, "To say that, however, is to say that it shall not be changed at all, for we are taught by a century of our history that the Constitution can no longer be thus amended."[44]

The dissatisfaction with the amending process is older than a mere century. In 1833, Chief Justice John Marshall wrote in his opinion on *Barron v. Baltimore* of the process as being "unwieldy and cumbrous."[45] But the first attempt to amend Article V to make it easier to amend the Constitution was not proposed until 1864 – seventy-five years and twelve amendments after the Constitution's ratification.[46] Interestingly, the very first proposal to change the amending process came from Rhode Island when it voted to ratify the Constitution in 1790. They recommended making the process MORE difficult![47] Amusingly, after the passage and ratification in rapid succession of the Eighteenth and Nineteenth Amendments, some political pundits of the day complained that the process was too easy and sought changes to make it harder.[48]

The pre-eminent progressive history professor Charles A. Beard criticized the Constitution's amendment process, saying,

> *"The extraordinary majorities required for the initiation and ratification of amendments have resulted in making it practically impossible to amend the Constitution under ordinary circumstances, and it must be admitted that only the war power in the hands of the federal government secured the*

---

[44] William P. Potter, "The Method of Amending the Federal Constitution," *University of Pennsylvania Law Review and American Law Register* 48, no. 9 (1909): 590 - quoting an unnamed speaker at the American Bar Association meeting of 1907. The speaker was most likely US District Court Judge Charles F. Amidon.
[45] Ibid., 604
[46] Michael A. Musmanno, "Is the Amendment Process Too Difficult?," *American Law Review* 57 (1923): 698
[47] Joseph R. Long, "Tinkering with the Constitution," *Yale Law Journal* 24, no.7 (1915): 586
[48] Herman V. Ames, "The Amending Provision of the Federal Constitution in Practice," *Proceedings of the American Philosophical Society* 63, no.1 (1924): 69

passage of the great clauses relating to slavery and civil rights."⁴⁹

Of course, Beard, like many of the prognosticators of his time, was proven wrong by the amending frenzy of the 1910s. Not only did they get the probability of amendment wrong, they did not grasp the short period of time that it was now taking between promulgation and ratification. The Sixteenth Amendment took forty-three months to complete but the Seventeenth Amendment, completed in the same year, took "four days less than one year from the day on which it was proposed."[50] The Eighteenth Amendment took thirteen months and the Nineteenth Amendment needed fourteen months to ratify after being passed by Congress.[51] The process was becoming more streamlined as the political organizations of the day began to work together to achieve their mutual goals. When an idea's time has come, the amendment effort is ultimately successful.[52] There is a lesson here to be learned by modern activists seeking to amend the Constitution. The preparation for an amendment drive is the most crucial phase. If the public is not educated on the issue and convinced of the need, the legislature will not follow, but once the public is ready, the amendment will pass with minimal resistance.

Eventually, the historians and legal pundits of the time came to realize that the Progressive Amendments were not as difficult to secure as they have complained about prior to 1913. One writer noted that "the pendulum has swung in swift vibration from the theory of the rigidity and unamendability of the Constitution to the perception of a danger from too great ease" of amending. The saving grace, the writer observed, was that "matters not of paramount importance to every state of the union have not yet been injected into" the Constitution. The same writer comically theorized that prior to the amending rush of the 1910s, that "the irresponsible proposing of amendments to please their constituents may have been merely a pleasing pastime for Congressmen."[53]

---

[49] Joseph R. Long, "Tinkering with the Constitution," *Yale Law Journal* 24, no.7 (1915): 576
[50] Ibid., 577
[51] Michael A. Musmanno, "Is the Amendment Process Too Difficult?," *American Law Review* 57 (1923): 697
[52] Musmanno notes that the first bill to do what the Seventeenth Amendment accomplished was introduced in 1826. Between that first bill and the final passage in 1912, the idea was proposed 198 times. *Supra*, 702
[53] Republished with permission of the University of Pennsylvania Law School, from Margaret C. Klingelsmith, "Amending the Constitution of the United States," *University of Pennsylvania Law Review* 73 (1925): 367; permission conveyed through Copyright Clearance Center, Inc.

This new sentiment was reflected in the attempts of Congressmen to make the amending process harder following the rapid amendment of four proposals in less than a decade. In referring to one particular bill before Congress, the Bar of the City of New York said,

> "[I]t will avoid the danger of hasty, uninformed, popular action. Finally it will lessen the danger of the passage of amendments through pressure on state legislatures by propaganda, organized lobbyists and other more discreditable means."[54]

Compare these results to the potential outcome of an Article V convention. With all, or perhaps almost all, of the States participating in the drafting of a new amendment, each having their say on the content and wording, the likelihood is that once the proposed amendment is completed and promulgated to the State legislatures or ratification conventions, the ratification process will go very quickly. The States will come away from the convention with a sense of "ownership" in the proposed amendment. A substantial majority of the States, and therefore of the people, is needed just to call an amendatory convention

Time has shown that the difficulty of the amending process has actually proven to be one of its "chief virtues." The deliberative nature and the effect of forcing second consideration and clear articulation are strengths. The lack of patience on the part of those seeking an amendment demonstrates an incomplete understanding of the purpose of the process.[55]

Another justification given for changing the amending process is to lessen the tendency of the executive branch to attempt to "informally" amend the Constitution through extra-constitutional means. In our time, we have the right and the left – depending on the party of the current president - complaining of an abuse of executive orders. This is not, however, a recent development. In 1909, Pennsylvania Supreme Court Justice William Potter, in a law journal article, advocated for making the amendment process easier, pointing to the problem of executive order abuse,

> "A well-grounded fear has been felt and expressed, that the difficulty of amendment is considered a sufficient excuse for seeking, through executive

---

[54] Special Report of Committee on Constitutional Amendments of the Association of the Bar of the City of New York, Year Book 1924, at 236, - referring to the proposed Wadsworth-Garrett Amendment.
[55] Thomas E. Baker, "Towards A "More Perfect Union": Some Thoughts on Amending the Constitution," *Widener Journal of Public Law* 10, no.1 (2000): 2

action and forced construction, the exercise of powers not clearly bestowed by the Constitution."[56]

Potter backed up his expression of concern with a recent anecdote. He cited a speech by then president Theodore Roosevelt given in Harrisburg, "He frankly declared that, in his opinion, the Federal powers should be increased 'through executive action and through judicial interpretation and construction of law.'"[57] Today we are living with exactly that situation.

Presidents acting unconstitutionally is no strictly modern dilemma. Potter pointed to examples of both Lincoln and Jefferson admitting their constitutional infidelities. Lincoln dismissed his actions as wartime measures. Jefferson took a different approach. In describing Jefferson's own executive action with regard to the Louisiana Purchase, the president wrote to John C. Breckenridge stating,

> "The Constitution has made no provision for our holding foreign territory, still less for incorporating foreign nations into our union. The executive in seizing the fugitive occurrence which so much advances the good of the country, has done an act beyond the Constitution."[58]

But Jefferson was anxious about the action that he had taken and drew up a proposed amendment that would cover any future actions that were similar. He looked for someone in Congress to introduce the bill but was not able to find anyone that was concerned about the unconstitutionality of Jefferson's actions![59] The process of calling an amendatory convention is heavily predicated on the making of a clear argument in favor of calling a convention. If the need cannot be both sufficiently articulated and perceived as pressing, then the convention will not happen. The process does a remarkable job of screening out the passionate, intemperate effort from the logical, rational drive.

Leveling Effect of a Convention

What is often overlooked in a review of the nearly 12,000 proposed

---

[56] William P. Potter, "The Method of Amending the Federal Constitution," *University of Pennsylvania Law Review and American Law Register* 48, no.9 (1909): 592
[57] Ibid., 595
[58] Letter of Thomas Jefferson to John C. Breckenridge, 12 August 1804.
[59] William P. Potter, "The Method of Amending the Federal Constitution," *University of Pennsylvania Law Review and American Law Register* 48, no.9 (1909): 598-9

amendments in the last 227 years is that there have been "waves" of amendment proposals. This makes sense as the rate of proposal numbers increases during times of perceived political distress due to social, economic or political conditions. Congressmen and women will introduce more proposed amendments during these times of supposed greater need. The reason that the number of amendments completed is low and are relatively equally spaced out over the last century is that the conditions prompted the introduction of the proposals are temporary. Once the upheaval or distress has passed, the proposals lose any support and momentum. This has a "leveling effect" of sorting out the truly necessary and significant proposals from the merely "fashionable" proposals. Over time, the Constitution has proven to be very adequate to the nation's needs.[60] The difficulty in amending the Constitution has turned out to be a beneficial feature that prevents the more emotional part of our society from running rampant. Nineteenth-century newspaperman Carl Schurz put it well, describing, "the dangerous tendency of that impulsive statesmanship which will resort to permanent changes in the Constitution of the state in order to accomplish temporary objects."[61]

This sentiment is echoed by Professor Joseph Long in 1915, when he stated that "[a] constitution to be respected as fundamental law must possess in a reasonable degree the quality of permanence."[62] Long felt that amending too often for too light a reason would "impair the dignity" of and create a "distinct injury" to the Constitution. He argued that if the objective could be accomplished by a lesser legal means, such as a statute or an ordinance, then that was preferable to amendment. Madison thought along the same lines, believing that Article V "guarded against that extreme facility which would render the Constitution too mutable; and that extreme difficulty which might perpetuate discovered faults."[63]

Any effort to call a convention will encounter a seemingly endless list of obstacles. Assuming that the articulation of the need is credible, the next step will require concerted action on the part of the States. Meeting the list of reasons for the leadership of Congress refusing to call a convention is a final litmus test as that list is long and old. During the early twentieth-

---

[60] Joseph R. Long, "Tinkering with the Constitution," *Yale Law Journal* 24, no.7 (1915): 579
[61] Ibid., 580
[62] Joseph R. Long, "Tinkering with the Constitution," *Yale Law Journal* 24, no.7 (1915): 581
[63] James Madison, *The Federalist, No. 42*

century effort to pass the Seventeenth Amendment, the reasons were that,[64]

- The applications were not received in a "reasonable" timeframe.

- The applications were not all for the EXACT SAME reason – there was variation in the wording of the reasons, even though the general idea was obviously the same.

- The applications were not all for a limited subject convention.

Any modern campaign for a convention would need to surpass these hurdles. We are assured that the convention campaign that reaches this level is publicly supported and has passed muster for a sincere necessity of amendment. The amendment proposals introduced in Congress do not always possess this surety. With several past drives for a convention having gotten to within one, two or three states short of the requisite number of applications, we can look at the positive and say with conviction that when the need and the desire were present, the prodding effect worked and delivered the amendment. Of course, the amendment may not always have been exactly what the people wanted, but the process has indeed worked. With Congress now attuned to the prodding effect, it is necessary for amendment proponents to look toward the convention method and secure a more acceptable and effective amendment through the convention method. The leveling effect will continue to screen out the inferior proposals and drives.

Difficulty in Obtaining a Convention

One of the finer attributes of the Article V convention method is the degree of difficulty in securing the convention. History has shown that the enthusiasm for a convention is high at the beginning of the drive and then tapers off precipitously after the thirty state threshold is reached. It should. As Charles Pinckney famously noted in Philadelphia in 1787, "conventions are serious things." When a state legislature contemplates an amendatory convention application resolution, it is taking the constitutional health of the nation in hand and it is a grave and heavy responsibility. The closer to the magic two-thirds of the States number, the more weighty the proposition

---

[64] Robert J. Sprague, "Shall We Have a Federal Convention, and What Shall It Do?," *Maine Law Review* III, no.4 (1910): 123

becomes. In 1979, at the height of the last balanced budget amendment campaign, Professor Gerald Gunther, no advocate of an amendatory convention, recounted the story of how the Montana legislature was weighing passage of its bill, which would have made Montana the thirtieth state to pass such a resolution. One of the legislature's leaders asked the legislators to consider if the bill were for the thirty-fourth state and not the thirtieth. They did not pass the bill.[65] Weber and Perry referred to this slowing down of the campaign momentum as "fourth quarter cautiousness."[66] Whether or not this was the correct action is not the point; the lesson to be learned is that such action must be taken seriously since so much is at stake. The process of thirty-four states carefully reaching the same conclusion that "something must be done" about a given problem is one of the safety nets of the system. The radical and fringe proposals are weeded out by the process and as the magic number is approached, the process becomes more focused and sober. Another more forceful example is that of the Wisconsin legislature in 1969 during the push for a convention to address the reapportionment issue. Wisconsin declined to pass its Assembly Joint Resolution 55 or Senate Joint Resolution 69 and become that all-important thirty-fourth state.[67]

Public Scrutiny

One of the most recurrent arguments against an amendatory convention is that of the potential for abuse of the process leading to excesses and violations of civil liberties and long standing institutions. A laundry list of imagined abuses is usually presented. The potential for abuse ranges from the probable to the possible to the preposterous to the pitiful.

We should acknowledge that nothing is completely safe and all the planning and theorizing will not eliminate every possibility because we cannot imagine every possibility. All that we can do is trust in ourselves and our descendants to remain vigilant and focused as to the objectives and the value of the institutions with which we – or they – are tinkering. We must, of necessity, teach our children to respect and value our Constitution and our civil liberties if we wish to see them passed down from one generation to

---

[65] Gerald Gunther, "The Convention Method of Amending the United States Constitution," *Georgia Law Review* 14, no.1 (Fall 1979): 19
[66] Paul J. Weber & Barbara A. Perry, *Unfounded Fears, Myths and Realities of a Constitutional Convention* (New York: Praeger, 1989), 109
[67] 1970 State of Wisconsin Blue Book (Madison, WI: Legislative Reference Bureau, 1970), 165-7

another. Abuses result from the hubris of our egos and the greed associated with the lust for power. The amending power is sufficiently checked to prevent most abuses. One will have to be very clever to circumvent the checks and balances of the amending process. The amount of time and the necessity of interaction between delegates will probably expose those who are not adequately and correctly motivated.

There are both legal and political remedies to any convention shenanigans. Orfield lays out the situation succinctly,

> "[I]t should be pointed out in the first place that the fact that a power may be abused does not necessarily militate against the existence of the power. The Supreme Court has declared over and over again that the possibility of abuse is not to be used as a test of the existence or extent of a power."[68]

The combined leveling and cooling effects work to prevent abuses and mischiefs. The amendatory convention has the benefit of greater public scrutiny and control. Congress appears to operate on autopilot in comparison to the media and public oversight that we could expect for an amendatory convention. The rarity of an amendatory convention draws the public scrutiny and with it, an extra measure of validation for proposal, discussion and ratification.

Ratification Threshold

One of the central arguments of convention proponents in disproving the probability of a runaway convention is that the requirement for three-quarters of the States to ratify places a high bar to clear in the path of any "radical" or "fringe" amendment proposal. As the last step in the process, the States and the people once again retain the control of the amendment process and the convention method. Whether Congress specifies the ratifying convention or the state legislature as the ratifying body, the public has the upper hand in both cases. If the convention is selected, the people will have both the opportunity to run to be delegates or, assuming that no intervening election of the state legislature takes place, to bring public pressure on the state legislators. In both instances, the public's voice will be loud and clear. This was evident in the ratification of the Twenty-first Amendment in 1933

---

[68] Lester B. Orfield, "The Scope of the Federal Amending Power," *Michigan Law Review* 28, no.5 (1930): 580

and 1934.[69]

No amount of pressure on Congress or a convention will matter as long as the States are still in control of the ratification process. The natural antagonism between the state and federal levels of government and the contention over the division of power creates a safeguard in the process. It would take an extraordinary amount of political power to persuade, cajole or threaten three-quarters of the States to approve ratification of a proposed amendment that they find unacceptable. American history points to examples of proposed amendments that supposedly enjoyed widespread public support yet failed to achieve ratification. The Equal Rights Amendment, the Child Labor Amendment, the Nobility Amendment, and the Congressional Representation Amendment which was first proposed by James Madison along with his other eleven amendment proposals that were indeed ratified, come to mind.[70] While each exhibited public support in its day, they each failed to reach the necessary number of ratifying states and remain footnotes in constitutional history. The ratification process is the ultimate validation and confirmation of the States' consensus. Thousands more of amendment proposals have been introduced in Congress, never to see the light of day.

Delegate Scrutiny

In any potential convention delegates' campaigns, their positions will be publicly dissected and examined with intense scrutiny. The public attention paid to the campaigns would greatly heighten the public's interest in the subject amendment topic as well as to inform and educate the public and prompt much needed debate. Delegates would undoubtedly be pressed on their view of the potential – and the assurance against – a runaway convention. Even those state legislators already ensconced in office will face the wrath of the disproving public should they ratify an unpopular amendment proposal. It was for that reason that the ratifying conventions were chosen in the 1933 – state legislators feared the power of the "drys" at the voting booth.[71]

---

[69] Ronald D. Rotunda & Stephen J. Safranek, "An Essay on Term Limits and a Call for a Constitutional Convention," *Marquette Law Review* 80, no.1 (Fall 1996): 230-1
[70] Michael J. Lynch, "The Other Amendments: Constitutional Amendments That Failed*," *Law Library Journal* 93, no.2 (2001), generally
[71] Ronald D. Rotunda & Stephen J. Safranek, "An Essay on Term Limits and a Call for a Constitutional Convention," *Marquette Law Review* 80, no.1, (Fall 1996): 241-3

Congressional and presidential candidates are evaluated and elected on multiple issues and virtually no candidate is 100% acceptable to any given individual voter. But convention delegates, specifically those for a limited convention, are to be chosen for their avowed stand on typically one or two issues. Voters are rarely faced with so clear of a choice.

Restoring Federalism

One of the strongest arguments for an amendatory convention is that of restoring or strengthening federalism. An exercise of power in the hands of the States and the people serves to offset that of actions by the federal government. Over time, the balance between the States and the federal government has become severely disproportionate with a decided advantage to the federal government. There has, in an era of large grants and unfunded mandates, been a shift in the attitude of the States from viewing the federal government as an equal partner to that of the States as subservient minions unwilling to risk the federal munificence. The prophetic predictions of several of the Framers at the Philadelphia Convention that the States would slowly whither away and succumb to the federal government are coming slowly but painfully true. The price of this seismic shift is the loss of cultural diversity among the States and a growing political homogeneity in the States. A convention offers the opportunity to restore the balance of power and re-establish the boundaries between the States and the federal government according to constitutional principles and provisions.

The constitutional order has been dislodged as the federal government, often acting through the US Supreme Court, has assumed powers and responsibilities for areas traditionally considered the provinces of the States. There is too little in the way of a national conversation on the limits of federal power and the surrender of state powers. A convention is the perfect and natural setting for this conversation to occur as the States and the people express their concerns and ideas for the reset of these divisions. As an equivalent, although temporary, branch of the federal government, the convention is the appropriate forum for airing the grievances of the States and for a reassessment of the federal role in societal matters. The emphasis on constitutional issues in lieu of the mundane legislative issues of the Congress or state legislatures makes the convention serve as yet another check and balance on the federal government.

The amendatory convention is then an alternative method for oversight of federal actions. As Congress has sought to use the amendment process on at least four occasions to correct what it perceived as the mistakes of the Supreme Court, it is fitting that the States and the people use the convention method of amendment to correct congressional and executive misdeeds. The authoritative review must lie outside the federal bubble to be unbiased. With many of the current problems originating within the federal government and spread across more than one branch, it is essential that we find and use a method of review and discussion that is independent of the federal government and those dependent on its largesse. The more effective and prominent voice is that of the States expressed in the amendatory convention. While the Supreme Court may hear and rule within a year or even within a half year, the States and the people have little to no input and their rulings are not always consistent with the Constitution. The debate is extremely one-sided.

The federal government's scope of power and responsibility has grown in fits and starts, but today the rate of change is fairly constant. Outside of the federal government, those who are suffering from the loss, that is, the States and the people, can often find no venue for reclaiming their purloined powers and rights. An Article V convention holds the potential for a dramatic and sudden jolt to restore the balance. It is a methodology beyond the reach of the federal government in all its branches. A convention holds the possibility of setting a permanent constitutionally based threshold beyond which the federal government's powers may not expand. While the federal government may have gotten away with acting outside of constitutional boundaries to date, the mechanism and ability to force the federal government to stay within the lines constitutionally is still found in the Article V amendatory convention.

The States are empowered through the convention method to address those issues which the Congress, the executive or the courts refuse or are fearful to take up. The unwillingness of the US Senate to act on the issue of direct election of federal senators can be extended to the state level as well. The reluctance of the state legislatures to vote on the repeal of Prohibition forced the use of the Article V ratification conventions. Pursuing a convention can have the impact of compelling state and federal actors to publicly declare their positions and be firmly held to those declarations.

The Necessity of Action

Actually an argument against rather than for a convention is that of the claim by opponents that there is an unreasonable cry from proponents that "we need to do something." Opponents view the call to action as considered and presented as rash and unwarranted. They respond that something does NOT need to be done, that the situation is fine and any action is dangerous and fraught with unintended consequences. We are best served to let a sleeping dog lie.

But this is an unsupportable argument when we look at the constant incremental infringement upon the powers and limitations of the Constitution. The status quo is steadily degenerating and things will not simply remain the same. Change is the order and will always prevail. This dynamic was clearly understood and accounted for by the Framers in Article V. Recognizing that times, mores and standards will change, the drafters of our Constitution sought to institutionalize the change through a managed process that would elicit the proper amount and type of change. We have an amendment process because something must be done. When the discussion of an amendment proposal's content becomes commonplace, we have reached that critical mass of public opinion and dissatisfaction that requires change. Something must be done.

The question is only what must be done, not how – which has already been answered. Other suggested methodologies are neither sufficient nor constitutional for our purposes. We have been provided more than a singular method of amendment to our fundamental law. If any other road were to be open to us, it can be argued that after an estimated 10,000 years of recorded human history, the efficient, peaceful method(s) would have been added by the erudite and scholarly inclined Framers alongside the two methods prescribed. Technically, we could term it the three prescribed methods as the prodding effect has created a third method in practice. More to the point, if we find ourselves debating a point or issue and the suggestion of amendment is made more than once, then we should seriously concede that indeed, something must be done. Inaction or hesitation has now been disqualified as a reasonable course of action. We can look to our history and see that the record shows that by the time that some topic has reached the stage of the consideration of amendment, all other more expeditious political solutions have failed to resolve the issue.

As contemporaneous examples, let us look at the previously used examples of the balanced budget and campaign finance reform. Proponents have long argued for a balanced budget amendment. Opponents have argued that it is not only dangerous but unnecessary. If we focus on the argument of the lack of necessity, we can see that all other options have been tried. The Congress was prodded into passing the *Gramm-Rudman-Hollings Balanced Budget and Emergency Deficit Control Act of 1985*[72] and its subsequent *Balanced Budget and Emergency Deficit Control Reaffirmation Act of 1987*[73] but these laws were found to be both failures in practice and unconstitutional in design in *Bowsher v. Synar*.[74] What recourse is left outside of constitutional amendment?

The issue of campaign finance reform also received congressional action with the *Bipartisan Campaign Reform Act of 2002* or McCain-Feingold Act.[75] Like the budget control laws, the campaign finance reform law found itself under attack as unconstitutional and led to a flurry of lawsuits. In *McConnell v. Federal Election Commission*,[76] and *Federal Election Commission v. Wisconsin Right to Life*,[77] *Inc.*, and *Davis v. Federal Election Commission*,[78] and *Citizens United v. Federal Election Commission*,[79] various sections of the law were found by the US Supreme Court to be unconstitutional. Today, proponents of campaign finance reform have agreed that any change will need to be achieved through a modification to the organic law.

In both of these cited instances, the normal legislative process was tried and then adjudicated. The failures of the statutes were such that only a change to the fundamental law of the nation will resolve the underlying issues. In both instances, it is concluded that "something needs to be done" and that particular something is constitutional. All other avenues have been tried and yet the problems persist. What remains is whether the desired change is reached through congressional action and the prodding effect or the States exercising their prerogative under Article V's application and convention method.

---

[72] 99th Congress, S.1702, Pub. L. 99–177, Title II, December 12, 1985, 99 Stat. 1038
[73] Pub. L. 100–119, Title I, Sept. 29, 1987, 101 Stat. 754, 2 U.S.C. § 900
[74] 478 U.S. 714 (1986)
[75] Pub. L. 107–155, 116 Stat. 81
[76] 540 U.S. 93 (2003)
[77] 551 U.S. 449 (2007)
[78] 554 U.S. 724 (2008)
[79] 558 U.S. 310 (2010)

The Necessity of Change

A final argument in response to the opponents of an amendatory convention involves the claim that there is nothing wrong with the Constitution. This is a recent and fervent claim. The argument begins with a premise that the Constitution is perfect and needs no modification. A twisted bit of logic is applied that goes like this: If the Constitution is flawed and is not heeded now, how will changing it lead to the Constitution being followed? If we tinker with the Constitution, we risk the whole thing being changed. It is best to leave it alone and change nothing (although this will, admittedly, not resolve a thing).

The claim is made that changing the Constitution does not fix anything or end any problem, it merely creates a new problem or a new opportunity for creating a problem. History is not on the opponent's side here. The ADDITION of the Bill of Rights solved many problems including that foremost problem, the acceptability of the Constitution to those who wanted a Bill of Rights. Imagine the America of today without the First Amendment. Or the Second, Fourth, Fifth, etc... Yes, new problems were introduced, such as defining what is meant by "free speech" or the "freedom of religion" or the extent to which reports may reveal the government's dirty laundry. But no one today would seriously argue that the cost has been too high for maintaining these liberties.

Similarly, the Thirteenth Amendment's prohibition of slavery has drastically changed America for the better and the nation could not have achieved the goal secured by that amendment without an amendment. Those who argued at the time in the 1860s against the Thirteenth Amendment have been conclusively proven wrong by the passage of time as to whether the Constitution should be left alone and not amended. We can make the same conclusion about the Nineteenth Amendment's provision for women to vote or the Twenty-First Amendment's repeal of the Eighteenth Amendment. Had we heeded the words of their opponents what would today's United States look like?

Whether we amend for addition or correction, the result is the same. We improve the Constitution, and when we do not, as with the Eighteenth Amendment, we repeal – by amendment. The accumulation of judicial precedent has, in fact, substantially altered the original meaning and spirit of the Constitution. An amendment can mean a restoration of the original meaning.

A corollary to the argument against the amendment convention necessity is that of enforcement over amendment. We see this styled as "defend, not amend." While stylistically charming, it lacks the understanding of the need for amendment and a recognition of the times in which amendment is applied. To enforce the Constitution requires some method or mechanism to enforce it. That would usually be the courts, typically the federal courts. If the federal courts are not inclined to support the Constitution or to ignore its provisions, how exactly does one "defend, not amend?" If the courts are not persuaded of the righteousness of the cause or of the utility of the chosen mechanism for defense, what recourse do these opponents suggest? Most often, that answer is a matter of applied constitutionality.

The Familiarity of Convention Practices

The long and varied national and state experiences with convention prove that our traditional method of wide-ranging problem solution is the best method of creating consensus and action amongst diverse groups and political ideologies. Although critics may decry the lack of federal amendatory convention experience, this is a false flag. The national experience is more than just the numerous attempts to call an Article V amendatory convention. It is also exemplified in the countless interstate conventions on every imaginable topic from railroads to riverine management to immigration to utility regulation to commercial issues to beyond. It is a little recognized fact that there are, without a hint of exaggeration, dozens of interstate conventions held every year.

One can sort through the offerings on Amazon.com to find the reprints of reports of conventions held on all these topics and more over the last two centuries. Some conventions are organized by industry associations, some by local and state governments, and some by federal agencies. Examples found in a cursory search include proceedings and reports found on Amazon.com:

- Southern Interstate Immigration Convention, Montgomery, Alabama, December 12-13, 1888
- National Convention of Railroad Commissioners, 1890 – sponsored by the federal government's Interstate Commerce

Commission

- Interstate Commerce Law Convention, Chicago, October 26-27, 1905
- Annual Convention of Regulatory Utility Commissions, sponsored by the federal government's Interstate Commerce Commission
- Inter-state Mississippi River Improvement and Levee Convention, Vicksburg, Mississippi, May 1, 1890
- Convention on the Improvement of Rivers and Harbors, Chicago, July 5, 1897

These examples are but a few of the types of conventions that have occurred and continue to occur every year in which the States send representatives to foster cooperation on interstate issues. We typically think of Congress as handling interstate matters but the states have acted in concert through interstate conventions and interstate compacts since before the Revolution. The States aggressively and routinely employ federalism to work out issues and solve problems without the intervention of the federal government.

The example of the riverine conventions is perhaps one of the best demonstrations of the interstate convention in action. These conventions started as local and state conventions among landowners and elected officials in the 1840s and then grew into interstate and regional conventions sometimes encompassing entire river valleys.[80] The conventions were at first for advocacy and education, then they became vehicles for economic development and the lobbying of federal officials. The post-Civil War conventions attracted the who's who of government and business.[81] They organized levee building projects and eventually became the interface to the federal government's river control projects. In Karen O'Neill's exemplary work in the subject, *Rivers By Design, State Power and the Origins of U.S. Flood Control*, she highlights the annual convention as the place to discuss and debate policy among "congressional representatives, senators, [Army] Corps [of Engineers] officials, governors and cabinet members" as well as businessmen, local and state elected officials, "shipping companies, regional

---

[80] Karen M. O'Neill, *Rivers By Design, State Power and the Origins of U.S. Flood Control* (Durham, NC: Duke University Press, 2006), vxii
[81] Ibid., 44-5

trade and river development organizations, chambers of commerce, farming organizations and levee districts, and commercial associations." The conventions drew thousands of attendees. O'Neill includes an appendix that details the nearly annual conventions between 1842 and 1927.[82] These conventions epitomize the exertion of federalism in that the States often organize and operate the conventions inviting federal officials to learn of the States' issues and actions. Other times, an agency of the federal government organizes and operates a convention for the States acting merely to facilitate federalism. We can find proceedings of conventions called by the Interstate Commerce Commission, the Department of Agriculture, and the Railroad Administration.

Similarly, the States participate in over two hundred interstate compacts and on average, each state belongs to twenty-five compacts. There are at least three types of compacts: border, advisory and regulatory, or administrative. According to the National Center for Interstate Compacts, the most prevalent are the regulatory compacts that cover such issues as: regional planning and development, crime control, agriculture, flood control, water resource management, child support collection and more. In this category, permanent agencies or commissions with interstate authority are created to administer an issue. Regulatory compacts require congressional approval but typically do not have congressional oversight. Topics are usually selected for policy issues that are in the traditional province of the states and outside of federal control. Thus a compact is an on-going interstate convention with rules, regulations and committees.[83]

In his comprehensive works on interstate cooperation, Professor Joseph Zimmerman has examined the extent and impact of the States; interactions outside the federal sphere. The agreements cover issues ranging from "combating organized crime, hot pursuit by police across state boundary lines, mutual assistance in extinguishing forest fires, prevention of environmental pollution" and more.[84] Zimmerman astutely notes that the Constitutional Convention of 1787 grew out of the 1785 Mount Vernon Compact meeting of Virginia and Maryland to discuss cooperation on the

---

[82] Ibid., 109 – and Appendix I, 187-95
[83] National Center for Interstate Compacts, "10 Frequently Asked Questions" (Lexington, KY: The Council of State Governments, 2015)
[84] Joseph F. Zimmerman, *Interstate Cooperation, Compacts & Administrative Agreements* (Albany, NY: SUNY Press, 2012), 3

Potomac River and Chesapeake Bay Navigation and Trade Agreement which led to the Maryland General Assembly inviting Delaware and Pennsylvania to join the compact. In turn, the Virginia General Assembly extended an invitation to all states to meet in Annapolis in September 1786 to develop a system of nation trade and commerce.[85] The Constitution was born of interstate cooperation and both sustains such cooperation and wisely ignores it as not all compacts require congressional approval – only those that encroach upon federal powers.[86]

The interstate compact process, like Article V conventions, is not detailed in the federal Constitution. It is left to the States to work out following the long established rules that predate the Constitution itself. In fact, the Confederation Congress granted its approval to three boundary compacts and the regulatory compact of the aforementioned Potomac River and Chesapeake Bay Navigation and Trade Agreement.[87] In two appendices, Zimmerman lists 190 selected interstate compacts out of an estimated over two hundred in operation.[88]

Citing compacts and formal interstate agreements approved by Congress does not limit or exhaust the list of examples of interstate cooperation. The topics covered range from the mundane and trivial to the nationally catastrophic. As an example, in the mid-1870s, the plains states were subjected to annual locust storms that destroyed entire national crops. In response to the 1875 swarm that measured an estimated 1800 miles long by 110 miles wide and covered sixteen states and territories, Minnesota Governor John S. Pillsbury called a convention held 25-26 October 1876 in Omaha that was attended by six governors, two state entomologists and numerous scientists to map out a strategy to fight the locust plagues. Without federal government input, the convention determined the appropriate methods of combating the grasshoppers and produced, among other solutions, 10,000 pamphlets to be distributed to farmers detailing methods of saving their crops.[89,90]

---

[85] Ibid., 7-8
[86] Ibid., 33
[87] Ibid., 41-4
[88] Ibid., 237-49
[89] Jeffery A. Lockwood, *Locust: The Devastating Rise and Mysterious Disappearance of the Insect that Shaped the American Midwest* (New York: Basic Books, 2004), 85
[90] Weston Arthur Goodspeed, *The Province and the States: Minnesota, Montana, North Dakota and South Dakota*, Vol. VI (Madison, WI: Western Historical Association, 1904), 109

Interstate conventions and compacts are extensions of federalism operating outside of the federal government's domain.

Constitutionality of Article V

The unquestionable constitutionality of the convention method means that the actions taken are not of dubious judicial quality. The courts will find that the public spotlight casts a harsh glare on the decisions of courts which may consider failing to enforce the Constitution. There is no question on the appropriateness of the convention as a political solution as compared to other more legally suspect solutions. Actions such as nullification or secession may stop a federal action, albeit temporarily, but do not provide actual fixes in the manner of an amendatory convention. These other political notions must first successfully garner support and acceptance and this may be years or decades or centuries in the making, if at all.

Nullification is cited often as the "rightful remedy" and its proponents will acquiesce to the undetermined constitutional quality of nullification. They will argue that it is *implied* in the Constitution and that alone makes it constitutional. They point to the Tenth Amendment as the source of nullification's constitutionality. They also conveniently ignore or look away from the lack of any other constitutional source and the plethora of court decisions rejecting nullification. The conclusive argument of nullification proponents is that we must accept their claim of IMPLICIT constitutionality of this "method" of resolution, but we must reject the EXPLICIT constitutionality of Article V's amendatory convention. In 2014, during a hearing of an Assembly Committee in the Wisconsin Legislature, then State Representative David Craig responded to the assertion of one individual who had argued instead for nullification while testifying against AJR81, a resolution for an Article V convention application for a balanced budget amendment, with the laconic question, "How do you propose to nullify the federal budget?"

The amendatory convention refocuses the national debate on the principles of the fundamental law and the concurrence of the policies of the executive, the actions of the legislature and the decisions of the judiciary with the time tested fundamentals absent the minutiae of partisan politics. All branches of the federal government are then adhering to the same long game of power. Finally, the convention is the only constitutional mechanism for staying the heavy hand of federal regulation and intervention. The convention method is that long sought constitutional remedy for federal overreach and bad behavior that has been hiding in plain sight.

CONCLUSION
THE FRAMERS' EMINENTLY WORKABLE SOLUTION

> *"Although the amending process which Article V provides may not be perfect, we have reason to be grateful to the Framers for having produced, through compromise, an amendatory provision which is **far from unworkable**."*[1]
>
> –Professor Paul J. Scheips, Historian, U.S. Army Center of Military History

In 1981, Wilbur Edel observed in his *A Constitutional Convention – Threat or Challenge?* that there has been a pattern to the amending of the Constitution. After the Constitutional Convention of 1787, the Bill of Rights was added with the intent, mainly, of guaranteeing personal liberties, and secondarily, to secure the support and ratification of some of the more hesitant states. Following the Civil War, in a second wave of amending activity, three more amendments were added to protect the individual from the state. And, Edel explained, that in the twentieth century eleven amendments were ratified and that all but three dealt with either the extension of the voting franchise or improving the effectiveness of government. The three outliers focused on issues of "dissatisfaction" in the forms of moral outrage and fiscal policy.[2]

This analysis still holds today as a third of a century later we are still wrestling with out of control federal spending on the fiscal policy side and

---

[1] Paul J. Scheips, "Significance and Adoption of Article V of the Constitution," *Notre Dame Lawyer* 26, no. 1 (1950): 67

[2] Wilbur Edel, *A Constitutional Convention – Threat or Challenge?* (New York: Praeger, 1981), 59

issues such as campaign finance reform on the moral outrage side. The fact that these issues remain in the forefront of the public political discourse demonstrates the problem of an unresponsive Congress which has decided that it has no real interest in these issues – or that, more than likely, resolution of the issues poses too great a threat to the Congress's power.

Orfield observed that "the Constitution was proposed by a Convention, was ratified by conventions, and was considered as established between the ratifying states."[3] He continued,

> *"Unless the view be adopted that the people of the United States are not sovereign and that they are not to be trusted to alter their fundamental institutions but are to be carefully safeguarded by a small groups of men who know or think they know what is best for the people, it seems necessary to conclude that they have a full power to amend free from any implicit limits no matter what abuses may result."*[4]

The on-going nature of these problems underscores that we, that is, the people, need to implement a constitutional solution as quickly as is practicable. Two centuries of government which has grown and run unrestrained pose a greater threat within than any foreign power without. The cute, precocious, independent two-year-old has grown into the unruly and mouthy eleven-year-old who is rapidly growing into the uncontrollable and occasionally violent seventeen-year-old. We are approaching tipping points for such matters as out of control spending, expansion of unrestrained regulatory power, political elitism, and widespread corruption.

In his paper based on his letter to a Congressman to persuade against any future Article V convention, Professor Charles L. Black, Jr., inadvertently made the argument against his own position. He states with regard to calling a convention, notwithstanding a general unlimited convention and not a limited amendatory convention, in lieu of the usually utilized manner of congressionally proposing amendments,

> *"Common sense would advise me that where one method is entirely satisfactory, has always been used, and fully registers the requisite consensus of the people of the States, the alternative method ought to be construed to cover* **extraordinary occasions**,*[5] which may have been feared at first,*

---

[3] Lester B. Orfield, "Sovereignty and the Federal Amending Power," *Iowa Law Review* 16 (1931): 508
[4] Lester B. Orfield, "The Scope of the Federal Amending Power," *Michigan Law Review* 28, no.5 (1930): 581
[5] Author's emphasis added. Black is actually quoting Madison from *The Federalist, No. 49.*

but which now are quite unlikely to arise – occasions where, by some unforeseeable mischance, there may be urgently needed the very thing the text seems most certainly to refer to – the general convention."[6]

We now find ourselves with a Congress, an Executive and a Supreme Court that have chosen to repeatedly act unconstitutionally. Congress will take no steps to curb the abuse of the constitutional clauses in question. The executive will not willingly restrain itself from excessive executive orders and presidential memoranda. The Supreme Court will not uphold the long established understanding of the Constitution and deems it a living, evolving document whose meaning is unclear from day-to-day. Does that situation not qualify as, if not exemplify, an *"extraordinary occasion?"* If we are unable to secure a permanent and clear understanding of the meaning of key parts of the Constitution, and efforts, by the "always been used" method, to amend the Constitution to provide that needed clarity are unsuccessful due to the reticence of Congress to propose such a bill, is that not evidence of an "extraordinary occasion?"

What is the recourse if the Congress will not honor its duty to call a convention and the US Supreme Court will argue that it has no duty to compel the Congress to act? If all legal means are unsuccessfully exhausted and the "extraordinary occasion" continues unabated, what path remains open to the people and the States? Dismissing the horrible and unthinkable resort to the right of revolution, there is but a single road to take. Of course, here we are not seeking the "general," plenary convention to which Black makes reference, but the limited-power amendatory convention. The people and the States must then seek to peacefully convene and draft their own proposed amendments - and then undertake to ratify the proposed amendments by legal means. This idea is not new although for some reason it has been seen as radical. During the 1787-91 ratification debates, Edmund Pendleton, President of the Virginia Ratifying Convention, rose to address this very scenario. He was speaking to the question of what may happen if the

---

[6] Republished with permission of the *Yale Law Journal*, from Charles L. Black, Jr., "Amending the Constitution: A Letter to a Congressman," *Yale Law Journal* 82, no.2 (1972): 203; permission conveyed through Copyright Clearance Center, Inc.

Congress refused to assent to introducing amendments and queried,[7]

> "Where is the cause of alarm? We, the people, possessing all power, form a government, such as we think will secure happiness: and suppose, in adopting this plan, we should be mistaken in the end; where is the cause of alarm on that quarter? In the same plan we point out an easy and quiet method of reforming what may be found amiss. No, but, say gentlemen, we have put the introduction of that method in the hands of our servants, who will interrupt it from motives of self-interest. What then? We will resist, did my friend say? conveying an idea of force. Who shall dare to resist the people? No, we will assemble in Convention; wholly recall our delegated powers, or reform them so as to prevent such abuse; and punish those servants who have perverted powers, designed for our happiness, to their own emolument."[8]

Of all the questions presented herein, perhaps none is so important as that which asks what will the States do if Congress will not fulfill its duty? For all Congress's claims of supporting their oaths of office and of their strict observance of constitutionality, we have from the *Congressional Record* in May of 1979, regarding holding hearings on the convention rules bills, Rep. Henry Hyde claiming that, "hearings were not held because the Democratic leadership did not want to provide momentum to the proliferating convention calls." Subcommittee chairman [Rep. Don] Edwards explained, "We have never felt it was significant enough to hold hearings," and cautioned that "anything that encourages this sort of utilization of Article V is unwise."[9]

Over a half century ago, the debate was over what to do in a Congress which did not fulfill its mandatory duty to call a convention and was raging with nearly the same dialogue that we hear today.

> "Some people feel that under the present Article V the States will never be able to act with sufficient concert and within a reasonable time to satisfy Congress that a convention is necessary…On the other hand there are

---

[7] John R. Vile discussed this quote as used by Akhil Amar in Amar's "Philadelphia Revisited" in Vile's "Contemporary Questions Surrounding the Constitutional Amending Process." Vile questioned the applicability of the quote to Amar's hypothesis. Henry Monaghan thought that Pendleton may have been talking about secession. The author of this work is confident of the usage here as appropriate to discussing the amending process and the inability to get an amendment through the congressional method.

[8] Jonathan Elliot, *The Debates in the Several Conventions on the Adoption of the Federal Constitution, Vol.3* (Philadelphia: J.B. Lippincott, 1836), 37 – Virginia debates, Thursday, 5 June 1788

[9] Wilbur Edel, *A Constitutional Convention – Threat or Challenge?* (New York: Praeger, 1981), 114 and referencing the *Cong. Rec.* at E819 (daily), 1 March 1979

those who feel that if there is sufficient urgency, not only will the States act promptly and in concert but such public pressure will be brought upon Congress that it in turn will have to call a Convention and promptly establish such rules and appropriations for its formation as may be necessary.

If Congress cannot be expected to initiate cures for its own evils, then you ask is it not possible for two thirds of the States, acting in sufficient concert and within a reasonable time, to force Congress to call a convention for the purpose? It is possible but is it probable?"[10]

For all this consideration, there is a most salient point to be taken: no campaign will ever work without the pressure of public opinion firmly and agitatedly behind it. The people will not take the time out of their lives to get involved and contact their elected officials at the state and federal levels or become grassroots activists unless they sense that all other options have already been fully exercised and are now off the table. It is a modern version of the Olive Branch Petition scenario.

As time goes on, the attitude of the federal government – in all branches – becomes an elitist one of knowing what is best for the people and excluding the people from government for their own good. It is this same undemocratic attitude that leads the federal government to reinterpret the Constitution in terms of what will most effectively accomplish the desired ends of the prevailing powers. The power to affect constitutional, and therefore true political, change still remains in the hands of the people providing that they can rouse themselves and refocus on their long-term needs.

A perfect example of the power of the public to quickly bring to bear its displeasure with the federal government was amply demonstrated in 1992. A series of congressional scandals led to the culmination of a drive to amend the Constitution. The public was angry and disgusted by Congress voting itself a 47% pay raise; a corresponding 47% increase in pension pay; an almost immediate cost-of-living pay increase; 20,000 kited checks through the Congressional bank; $647,000 in unpaid lunches; campaign fund mismanagement; the savings and loan scandal; and much of this done on an unrecorded voice vote.[11] The vote for the pay raise was taken at night and the

---

[10] Henry W. Nichols, "Amending the United States Constitution," *Insurance Counsel Journal* 22 (Jan.1955): 103
[11] Christopher M. Kennedy, "Is There a Twenty-Seventh Amendment? The Unconstitutionality of a "New" 203-Year-Old Amendment," *John Marshall Law Review* 26, no.4 (Summer 1993): 977, n.6

Congress recessed and went home the next day.[12] The public ire was raised and the timing for Congress could not have been worse. The long forgotten, but still pending proposed Congressional Pay Amendment covering pay raises for Congress had been slowly getting some traction mostly at the hands of a college student/state legislative aide that had written a college paper on the topic in 1982.[13] Five states voted within a week in early May of 1992 to put the count over the top and make the proposal the Twenty-seventh Amendment to the United States Constitution.[14]

In 1963, Fred Graham, a former Chief Counsel of the US Senate Subcommittee on Constitutional Amendments, made clear that,

> *"Congress can ignore or block an amendment campaign unless the proposal is so popular that the voters would be aroused to retaliate at the polls. The result is that Article V is misleading, to the extent that it appears to offer the state legislatures legal leverage in the amending process, divorced from any political consideration. In practice, a state application under Article V has no more effect than a simple memorial petition to Congress – both are judged by the political force behind them."*[15]

But if the public's opinion and willingness to force change can be harnessed, then a convention may be secured and succeed. The Congress and the Supreme Court will have to carefully weigh the costs of both opposing and thwarting the public's demand for change through an amendatory convention. The extent of the public dissatisfaction is the only barometer of the predicted success of the convention and the predicted response of the government. In the wake of the unanticipated ratification of the Twenty-seventh Amendment in 1992, there was considerable debate as to whether the amendment and its ratification were even legal due to the amendment's over two hundred year old proposal. In an editorial for the *Miami Herald* following the ratification, and reflecting the power of the public's opinion, Jim Hampton wrote, "Congress itself could challenge the amendment's ratification. But in today's mood of public contempt for Congress, it would

---

[12] Michael Stokes Paulsen, "A General Theory of Article V: The Constitutional Lessons of the Twenty-seventh Amendment," *Yale Law Journal* 103, no.3 (Dec. 1993): 678-9

[13] Gregory Watson got a "C" on his paper at the University of Texas and then he went on a mission.

[14] 5 May 1992: Alabama and Missouri; 7 May 1992: Michigan and New Jersey; 12 May 1992: Illinois

[15] Fred P. Graham, "The Role of the States in Proposing Constitutional Amendments," *American Bar Association Journal* 29, no.12 (Dec. 1963): 1177

be rash indeed to step in front of this juggernaut."[16]

One scholar describes Article V as having "become, therefore, only a 'protest clause' – a device for venting popular protest against congressional refusal to initiate a given amendment."[17] Short of the critical mass of the public ire raised in unison, it is merely a protest clause, but when the public can be educated on the issue and the need to carry through on the sole remaining option, then the convention campaign can and will succeed – either is securing the convention or the amendment through the usual manner.

Justice Scalia has made clear that he sees some risks but that the advantages outweigh any possible disadvantages,

> *"I am willing to run the risk of an open convention to get the changes that are wanted...even with respect to the limited proposal of financial responsibility at the federal level. I think that risk is worth taking. It is not much of a risk. Three-quarters of the states would have to ratify whatever came out of the convention."*[18]

About that risk, for an opponent of an amendatory convention, one must ask themselves honestly, why would the Framers place a self-destruct mechanism within the Constitution? The truth is simply that it is not a self-destruct mechanism, but a self-preservation mechanism and somewhat of a last resort. The wording of the Framers was intentional and, in its time, very specific. A "convention for proposing amendments" is not a general convention, or an unlimited convention, or an open convention, or more importantly, a constitutional convention. It is not plenary.

For some people, politicians included, any tampering with the Constitution is tantamount to treason. They see the addition or modification of some passage as no less than setting fire to a sacred text. The value of the antiquity is presumably greater than the wisdom that it holds. As an example, we turn to former Speaker of the US House, Thomas Foley, "I'm a real fiery defender of the Constitution…On my watch, I'm not going to have

---

[16] Jim Hampton, "Mr. Madison, We Thank You," *Miami Herald*, 10 May 1992, at 2C – quoted in Christopher M. Kennedy, "Is There a Twenty-Seventh Amendment – The Unconstitutionality of a New 203-Year-Old Amendment," *John Marshall Law Review* 26, no.4, (Summer 1993): 977, n.7

[17] Robert G. Dixon, Jr., "Article V: The Comatose Article in Our Living Constitution," *Michigan Law Review* 66, no.5 (Mar.1968): 944

[18] American Enterprise Institute, *A Constitutional Convention: How Well Would It Work?*(Washington, D.C.: 1979), 22-3

the Constitution amended, if I can avoid it."[19]

This sentiment of Speaker Foley is widespread. It is also misplaced. By now, one should have reached the conclusion that an Article V convention is just the beginning of the amendment process. We have informal methods, not addressed herein, that are superseding the formal process of Article V. The most prolific of these informal processes is that of judicial amendment by reinterpretation of the Constitution to allow for either a new meaning of a given provision of the discovery of a new right or power within the existing provisions. It is important to distinguish that this method, typically by the US Supreme Court, does not require any previous action, just a "case or controversy" to address. Compare this to the effort to have an amendment introduced into the Congress; that requires a groundswell of activity to bring the subject to the attention of the Congress. This method has a distinct advantage over the congressional, or the convention, method. Any pronouncement by the Supreme Court is given immediate authority – even one that does not possess public support.[20] And there is no ratification process – why do the American people accept this constitutional usurpation?

What the philosophers are getting at is that we need to be periodically reminded of why we are an American nation and no longer part of the British Empire. That we have certain fundamental principles on which we have built this nation and that when the institutions of this nation are threatened or imperiled, we must return to our first principles and reaffirm them to set right the ship of state. Gordon S. Wood cites Niccolo Machiavelli and Algernon Sidney and asks if it is not true that all constitutions are susceptible to corruption unless they are "timely renewed" through a return to the first principles on which their foundations rest. While Wood sees constitutions as "eventually correctable by the people" he also cautions that it is impossible if the people themselves "become corrupted and sunk in vice."[21] That is, if the people no longer value the Constitution because they no longer endorse its foundation. Wood makes the comparison

---

[19] David Rogers, "After Years of Gridlock and Scandals, Foley Appears Poised to Fulfill Potential as Speaker," *Wall Street Journal*, 4 December 1992, at A10 - quoted in Donald J. Boudreaux & A. C. Pritchard, "Rewriting the Constitution: An Economic Analysis of the Constitutional Amendment Process," *Fordham Law Review* 62, no.1 (1993): 161, n.253

[20] Arthur H. Taylor, "Fear of an Article V Convention," *Brigham Young University Journal of Public Law* 20 (2005): 408-9

[21] Gordon S. Wood, *The Creation of the American Republic, 1776-1787* (Chapel Hill: University of North Carolina Press, 1998), 34-5. Published for the Omohundro Institute of Early American History and Culture. Used by permission of the publisher.

to the decay and fall of the Roman Republic. He cites Thomas Paine's later writing, *The Rights of Man*, about the post-Revolution America and how the American people had embraced and quickly come to revere their constitution. He called it "a political bible" that was "possessed by every family and every member of the government."[22] Today we have politicians that openly proclaim not only their socialism, but their antipathy to the premises of our form of government and their disdain for the Constitution. How can the government of a republic function with such leaders? How can a free people select and accept such leaders?

We have addressed the three premises of the opponents to an amendatory convention, that "we have never done this before," that "there are no rules," and that "we don't know what will happen" in a convention. We have examined in turn proof that each premise is incorrect and that the opposite is true in each case.

To say that "we have never done this before" is superficial. If the one making the claim is referring strictly to the matter of a federal amendatory convention, the comment is of little value in that the particulars of the rules, the processes, the output and the fine details are all known quantities – little here is new ground. If the matter is specifically one of having never held an amendatory convention, then we can dismiss this claim out of hand as we have seen that the States have done precisely that repeatedly – nearly one hundred times over the last two centuries.

To claim that the experience of the States is without merit because those conventions were intrastate and not interstate is also of next to no value. We can recognize the differences between state and federal are consequential, but not so much so that to the uninitiated a state convention and a federal convention would appear different. Rather, to the uninformed observer, one would conclude that although they are two separate conventions, they would appear to be the same type of convention with the same procedures. The state experience would be highly valuable and informative as to the manner in which the federal convention, when held, would be conducted. The potential for solving federal problems or answering federal questions with state answers or state solutions is immediately obvious.

To complain that the pre-Revolutionary War conventions are of no

---

[22] Ibid., 259

help due to their intercolonial nature disregards the fact that the rules employed then are the basis or genesis of the rules applied now. The continuity is not just present but ever-present in all the various types of conventions today. The activity and rules of the intercolonial conventions are actually more germane as they were rules for separate and sovereign nations in the wake of Independence – clearly a greater order of magnitude then, than today of the interaction of separate but interdependent states in a federal republic. Michael Pierce summarized this debate and pointed to Natelson's work on the early intercolonial and interstate conventions and asked whether these conventions are relevant to the modern amendatory convention discussion,

> *"Natelson's analysis asks the right question with regard to the relevance of pre-Constitution multi-state convention practices: 'was the [Article V] convention to be the same sort of entity that prior multi-government conventions had been?'"*[23]

Pierce answers affirmatively although he is not convinced that there is a "universally established model" of convention. Between his argument and Natelson's argument we can conclude that the Article V convention is still open to some debate and the process and form have room for modification, perhaps we should call it improvement or perfection. Pierce finds that "Americans are suffering a crisis of trust," but that the lack of trust is in their politicians – and by extension we can surmise that will include convention delegates if those delegates are chosen or elected from among the current crop of politicians and not from non-politician Americans – and not in their Constitution.[24] The distrust of politicians occurs for many reasons, but among these are the seemingly greater interest on the part of the politicians in fundraising[25] and in the aggregation of power than in "perfecting the union."

Holding that today's states are not accustomed to the formal etiquette of a "constitutional convention" due to the passage of time since the last one occurred in 1787 is erroneous as well. Today's states interact many times a year through the meetings of the numerous interstate compacts and regional

---

[23] Michael Pierce, "The Anti-Corruption Force of Article V's Convention Clause," *Dartmouth Law Journal* XIII (Spring 2015): 84
[24] Ibid., 59
[25] Ibid., 84

riverine, trade and other conventions that are little different in output and operation than an amendatory convention would be. The protocols of such conventions are well established and perfunctory. In all actuality, today's states are better equipped, better staffed and better acquainted with the workings and protocols of interstate conventions and relations than the governments of the states in 1787. The States interact through conventions, interstate compacts,[26] formal interstate administrative agreements and other reciprocity statutes.[27]

We found that the hundreds of conventions have not runaway with but six state exceptions and those were more than a century past and could not happen again. We found that the Article V conventions held for the Twenty-first Amendment were regular and without incident, each formed and operated without the influence or interference of Congress.

When we considered the premise of there has never been an amendatory convention, we found that the roots of political conventions run long and deep. The amendatory convention has developed over the last four centuries in America although elements can be found over the last several millennia. If a twenty-first-century American went back in time to the first-century B.C., late Roman Republic and witnessed a *contio* and was asked "was this a convention?," he or she would emphatically answer "no." But if asked whether there were elements present of a modern political convention, our American observer would point to the deliberative aspect and the formal rules governing the *contio* and conclude that, yes, the elements are there that have been passed down through the ages.

Should we bring a Roman citizen of the late Republic forward in time to witness a modern political convention, perhaps a nominating or a constitutional convention, maybe an interstate compact meeting, but specifically an amendatory convention, would he see the *contio* present in our practices? He would most assuredly answer that while the process had understandably changed with time, all Roman citizens would recognize the formal leadership leading the convention, the people speaking on the issue by turns and according to rules, as elements of a *contio*.

Should we travel backward in time to some intermediate point

---

[26] United States Constitution, Article I, §10
[27] Joseph F. Zimmerman, *Interstate Cooperation, Compacts & Administrative Agreements* (Albany, NY: SUNY Press, 2012), ix

equidistant between the late Roman Republic and the modern American Republic, perhaps to the Convention of the Barons at Runnymede, we may find the nobles gathered on the banks of the Thames. We could ask if they, after traversing time and witnessing both the Roman *contio* and the American amendatory convention, could see in those events any of the familiar practices prevalent in the Middle Age English conventions. They may well agree that both exhibit some similarity to the English event in 1215. The English nobles would strike a chord with the *contio* in the formal communication with the people at large, and both would be seen as familiar with the representatives speaking on the behalf of their constituents and the American convention would be recognizable in the issuance of the formal document.

The thirteenth-century English convention is then an anchoring, midstream pillar of the political, cultural bridge spanning between the Roman Republic and the American Republic. The history of western civilization is cluttered with conventions and as time has marched on, the political convention has morphed and specialized. The convention mechanism made federalism possible and practical. We have never done this before? – Rather, we have <u>always</u> done this! We convene, we draft, we propose, we amend, and we do so with an astonishing regularity.

In considering the second premise of the opponents of an amendatory convention, that "there are no rules," we found that the rules are many, they are detailed, they are comprehensive and they are fairly standardized. The argument that the rules do not exist is meant to frighten and fear-monger. The people are expected to recoil at the idea of the Constitution attacking itself with Article V being used to destroy the other articles. The Constitution is presented as a fragile and endangered artwork that must be sequestered from the people.

Arthur Taylor summarized the situation of how people have come to view an Article V amendatory convention,

> *"How can a system of constitutional government 'by the people, for the people, and of the people' remain democratic when constitutional action taken by the States and the people, such as an Article V Convention, is not only restrained, but also loathed? Is a democracy that appeals to the government to protect the Constitution from the people safer than one that*

appeals to the people to protect the Constitution from the government?"[28]

From our examination of the legal aspects of an Article V convention and the case law built up around the convention, we can distill the issues down to two major points. First, are there rules to govern the convention and prevent it from running away? The answer is whole-heartedly affirmative. There are rules found in the proceedings of the hundreds of past conventions at the federal, state, territorial, interstate and provisional levels. There are rules found in the immense body of case law generated over more than two centuries. There are rules found in the numerous published works of parliamentary practice. There are indeed rules.

Second, can the Congress be forced to act? This answer will depend on the skill and fervor of the lawyers and activists that resolve to force the moment to its crisis. The answer is at best a qualified "maybe." Our judicial history appears to say "yes," but that is, most unfortunately, a matter of interpretation. The offsetting of the separation of powers from the application of coercion to comply with constitutional mandates will need to be played out. We can contrast the matter of the congressional duty to call a convention with the congressional power of impeachment. In one situation, the Congress exercises a constitutional power to coerce another co-equal branch to act in a certain way. In the other situation, the separate but co-equal Supreme Court is called upon to coerce the Congress to act in a certain way. How is it that we can argue for and accept the action where a branch can punish, but not compel or provide for an incentive to act in a constitutional and ministerial manner? It is strange that we can see clear to punishing a prior unconstitutional act, but not to compel a future constitutional act.

To selectively support parts of the Constitution and to equally selectively reject other parts treats our Constitution as an *a la carte* menu. The system will not work if this group observes that section and ignores another and that group or special interest accepts and observes this Article but refuse to acknowledge that one. It is an all or nothing proposition. Resolving the people's displeasure with any specific portion thereof is the point and purpose of Article V. In his farewell address, President George Washington spoke to the obligation of all to abide by the provisions of

---

[28] Arthur H. Taylor, "Fear of an Article V Convention," *Brigham Young University Journal of Public Law* 20 (2005): 416

the Constitution and to adhere to its provisions, including that of the amendment process,

> "This Government, the offspring of our own choice, uninfluenced and unawed, adopted upon full investigation and mature deliberation, completely free in its principles, in the distribution of its powers, uniting security with energy, and containing within itself a provision for its own amendment, has a just claim to your confidence and your support. Respect for its authority, compliance with its laws, acquiescence in its measures, are duties enjoined by the fundamental maxims of true Liberty. The basis of our political systems is the right of the people to make and to alter their Constitutions of Government. But the Constitution which at any time exists, till changed by an explicit and authentic act of the whole people, is sacredly obligatory upon all."[29]

In a 1979 opinion of the Office of Legal Counsel for the Attorney General, Assistant Attorney General John Harmon made the case that,

> "[T]he people and their officers execute the law; and when enough of them choose to disregard it, law is ineffective. Whatever Article V of the Constitution may require or permit in the way of legal limitation on the process of amendment by convention, it can be no more effective than was its predecessor, Article XIII of the Articles of Confederation, if the citizens and their representatives undertake to disregard it."[30]

The *a la carte* constitutionalists heaping derision on Article V and claiming that it is a danger to the rest of the document are lending support to the indictment of and cries for a loose interpretation of other parts of the Constitution. The real danger lies in their choice to disregard Article V and not to undertake to repair the constitutional crises before them. Maintaining the status quo only maintains, and most probably enlarges, the problems. The compulsion of Congress to call a convention is then one of those questions cited in the Introduction that we do not yet have an answer for, but still we must not shy away from.

We address the last premise of not knowing what will happen in a convention, and therefore a convention is just too dangerous, by looking to the combination of the answers to the history of past conventions and the

---

[29] Farewell Address of President George Washington, composed 17 September 1796 and published 19 October 1796 in numerous newspapers nationwide.
[30] Opinion 79-75 of the Office of Legal Counsel, at 393 (10 Oct 1979).

compilation of the rules. We have found that conventions are predictable creatures, even more so today with the advent of the instructed delegate statutes of many states, the limited call to convention, the formalization of rules before the convention, and the failsafe of the ratification supermajority requirement. The evolution of conventions due to social pressures during crises has repeatedly led to new types of conventions as the need arose and the existing body of convention types proved insufficient.

In the seventeenth-century settlement period, the amendatory convention was conceived in response to the need to accommodate changes to the composition of the societies in the colonies. During the Revolutionary War period, the ratification convention became a necessary innovation when the sovereignty of the people was recognized and needed to confirm the acceptance of a new constitution. When the Civil War started, the secessionary convention was the answer to how best to preserve as much of the existing state constitutions while making limited change. Post-Civil War, the need for the hybridized reconstruction conventions sought to undo the changes of the secessionary conventions, while again preserving the parts still functioning properly. In the present, the highly specialized planning convention of States allow for compromise and exploration before the stress and strain of the formal convention. The trend is then towards a regimented, limited, more specialized "lower energy" convention. We see this trend in the off shoot of the constitutional commissions that some states have adopted to debate and propose constitutional revisions and amendments. These commissions are cheaper to operate however they lack the democratic element of being elected by the people. This development introduces an undercurrent of elitism that potentially disenfranchises the people.

One last set of questions present themselves for consideration. How do we know when it is time to consider unresponsive government as having gone too far? How do we know when we are oppressed? What do we do when we believe, as a people, or when we are fractured as a people, that the government is no longer on the side of the people? There are many, many books on the market advocating a convention; there are many websites and many organizations working to bring about an amendatory convention. This book is concerned only with the procedure and process of securing and operating the convention and not with the content of proposed amendments. Those issues will all be worked out in the inevitable convention. The avoidance of "light and transient causes" forces the study of the process and procedures as being as important as the proposed amendments. The point is to preserve constitutionality above all.

The convention method is not broken, as so many writers and scholars have claimed,[31] it is merely unfulfilled. The process has not been pursued to completion. The current situation in this nation is such that we have a federal government which is often acting not only in opposition to the will of the people but also in deliberate spite of the people. The elitist mindset of the governing knowing better than the people has led to a scenario where the nation is failing in nearly every category. This is the extraordinary occasion that the Framers foresaw and for which they planned. They could not foresee or predict every possible scenario or provide for every contingency, but the Article V convention is a broad enough brush to cover many of the constitutional issues. Napoleon Bonaparte observed that, "Forethought we may have, undoubtedly, but not foresight."

Launching an amendatory convention – even one that has a singular topic – will have additional benefits beyond just the proposed amendment. It will draw the attention of the American public and kick off a long-running discussion about all things constitutional. It will generate interest in and grassroots activity over the constitutional issues. Solving the nation's political problems may become *en vogue*. Professor Elizabeth Price Foley incisively stated in 2011,

> *"This is the gift the Tea Party movement has given us: It has made it acceptable and fashionable again to talk about the Constitution. While some elitists may whine that these pesky Americans do not know what they are talking about and should not have any input, my own experience is that they know more than many lawyers do, and are hungry to learn more. This cannot, by any stretch of the imagination, be a bad thing for America."*[32]

Senator Orrin Hatch of Utah astutely and succinctly remarked at the National Conference on a Balanced Budget Amendment in Salt Lake City in 1988 that,

> *"If you don't believe in calling a constitutional [amendatory] convention,*

---

[31] Michael B. Rappaport, "Reforming Article V: The Problems Created By The National Convention Amendment Method And How To Fix Them," *Virginia Law Review* 96, no.7 (Nov. 2010): 1512

[32] Elizabeth Price Foley, "Sovereignty, Rebalanced: The Tea Party & Constitutional Amendments," *Tennessee Law Review* 78 (2011): 763. . The full text of this Article was published originally by the Tennessee Law Review Association, Inc. at 78 Tenn. L. Rev. 751 (2011), and this version, approved by the Author, appears by their permission.

you don't believe in the Constitution."[33]

We contemplate the anxiety induced by the amendatory convention by returning to reflect upon the purpose of a constitution and as a corollary, constitutional and amendatory conventions, which is to provide for the security, the ordered liberty and the happiness of the people. A free people cannot preserve any of these values if they are in trepidation of any part of the very charter that exists for the explicit purpose of the preservation of the people and their liberties and values. To act firmly to preserve our representative, constitutional Republic demands that we set aside the unfounded fears and illegitimate apprehensions of the very tool that the Framers provided for these extraordinary occasions. Constitutional preservation and restoration requires that the people embrace with confidence and courage that method handed down for the express function of exercising the power of the citizenry to restrain and control its own government. Former US Attorney General Griffin Bell indicted the criticism of an amendatory convention by pointing out that, "Those who wring their hands over the prospects of a[n Article V] convention run the risk of exposing their elitism, implying that the average citizen cannot be trusted."[34]

Griffin is not alone in seeing the class division of elitism raising its head in objection to the idea of an Article V Convention which is designed to upset the established – and corrupted - order. Michael Stokes Paulsen recognized this fear and its true cause, and chastised that,

> *"It is, in short, an elitist fear of popular sovereignty, as applied to the most fundamental of 'political questions': according to what principles are the people to govern themselves? It may be an understandable fear, but it is unworthy of our Constitution and of We the People who adopted it."*[35]

We began this work with a quote from an ancient Greek; we will conclude in the same manner. In his funeral oration for the Athenian war dead, Pericles wisely counseled to,

> *"Make up your minds that happiness depends on being free, and freedom

---

[33] Orrin Hatch, speech at the National Conference on a Balanced Budget Amendment, Symphony Hall, Salt Lake City, UT, 26 March 1988
[34] Griffin Bell, 14 April 1984
[35] Michael Stokes Paulsen, "A General Theory of Article V: The Constitutional Lessons of the Twenty-Seventh Amendment," *Yale Law Journal* 103, no.3 (Dec. 1993): 760-1

depends on being courageous."[36]

Article V requires, it demands, that the people act courageously to face the issues confronting them constitutionally and to resolve their problems of an ineffective, unresponsive or potentially oppressive government. It expects of a new generation of Americans, who are determined to remain free, to muster their courage and choose their place to stand to once again move the world politically.

---

[36] Thucydides, "Pericles Funeral Oration," *History of the Peloponnesian War* (New York: Penguin, 1954 translation, 1972 ed.) Translated by Rex Warner, 149-150

Appendices

Appendix A
RELATION OF ALL POWERS

Chapter 1 explored the relationship between the plethora of powers distributed among governments at all levels, and the People. We can graphically depict those relationships of the individual powers on a chart to make the distribution clearer.

If we think of a large, metal wall and imagine that every conceivable political power is written on a magnet with the name of one power on it in very small letters, then that wall might be covered with magnets representing every conceivable power that we may name. It would be difficult to determine which powers were granted to the federal government, which powers were assigned to the state governments, which powers were given to the municipal governments, and which powers were considered off limits to all governments and thereby reserved strictly to the People.

Imagine now that in the middle of the wall we draw a circle. We place inside that circle every type of power that the federal government possesses courtesy of the United States Constitution. If we were to draw a line that separates those types of powers from each other within the circle, we would get what is depicted in the graphic of Appendix A.1. There would be three separate areas within the circle, one each for the Inherent, Enumerated and the Implied powers. We would then place all of the magnets for the Inherent, Implied and Enumerated Powers within their respective areas.

The Inherent powers are those that all governments possess by virtue of being a government. The Enumerated powers are those powers that are specifically stated in the federal constitution. These include the eighteen powers found in Article I, Section 8 and it includes the powers granted in other parts of the original constitution and in the subsequent amendments. The Implied powers are those that must be granted in order to do the things that governments must do to fulfill their mandates.

Now we draw another, larger circle around the first circle. We label that circle as the FEDERAL GOVERNMENT to denote that all powers within the circle are the powers of the federal government. Next we draw another, even larger circle around the two previous circles. Inside that circle we place the label CONCURRENT powers. It is within this circle that we place the magnets with the names of the powers that both the federal and state governments possess jointly, or share.

Next we draw a horizontal line above the concentric circles that we have already drawn and labeled. Below this line, and outside of the circles, we place the magnets with the names of all the powers that the federal government has not been granted but that the state governments and the People jointly possess. These are the Reserved powers. Remember that the People are the sovereign and they are the actual owners of the powers and they merely loan those powers to the governments that they construct. These powers that are outside of the circles are far numerous, perhaps too numerous to count, since the state governments are plenary, or relatively unlimited in their delegation of powers.

Finally, we place the magnets with the names of the powers which the People have granted to no government and that they have reserved strictly to themselves in the space above the line. These are the Prohibited powers. Over time, many new magnets naming new powers are placed on the wall. Some are placed directly inside one of the federal circles; some are placed in the space for the Reserved powers allocated to the States and some are placed in the Prohibited space and thereby retained by the People.

The goal of federalism is keep the size of the concentric circles containing the powers of the federal government as small as possible. The goal of libertarianism is to keep the position of the line separating the Reserved and the Prohibited powers as low on the wall as possible. The goal of authoritarianism is to make the circles as large as possible and to move the position of the line as far up on the wall as possible. The goal of constitutionalism is to fix the lines and circles as much as possible permanently in place with as few moves as possible.

On Appendix A.2, we add another circle to represent the Amendatory Convention. This new circle overlaps the federal, state and people's domains. The convention is a temporary body endowed with certain, limited powers. Some of these powers are analogous to powers of the federal and state governments and some are temporary grants from the People. The power to propose an amendment is a power that the federal government holds as well as the People assembled in a convention. The States do not possess the power to directly propose an amendment.

Finally, the plenary convention is not depicted on a graph because a plenipotentiary convention would possess, potentially, ALL of the powers – federal and state government powers as well as that of the People. The entire wall and every magnet on it would fall within the domain of the plenary convention. It is for that reason, in part, that the Framers made no provision for another plenary convention.

Appendix A.1- Relation of All Powers

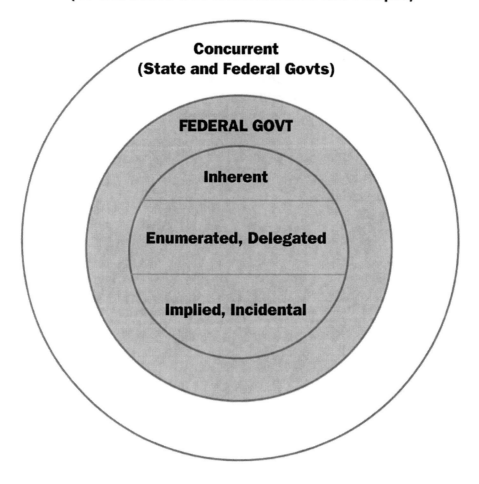

Appendix A.2- Relation of All Powers

Prohibited
(From Government, only for the People)

Amendatory Convention

Inherent

Enumerated, Delegated

Implied, Incidental

FEDERAL GOVT

Concurrent
(State and Federal Govts)

Reserved
(To the State Government and the People)

Appendix B
TABLES OF INTERCOLONIAL, INTERSTATE AND CONSTITUTION RELATED CONVENTIONS

As preparation for this work and to respond to the assertion that we have never held an Article V convention before, it was necessary to catalogue as many constitutional conventions as possible. Such an endeavor required searching the archives of all the States and Territories as well as thinking outside of the traditional venues. As we saw in Chapter 2, the colonies met quite frequently to discuss many issues as did the States during the Revolutionary War. Since then, the States have continued to meet to discuss problems of a mutual concern, and on occasion, to form compacts and to develop policies for shared matters.

While such authoritative sources such as Albert Sturm and John Dinan have compiled extensive lists of the state constitutional conventions and put their count at, respectively, 233 or 236 such conventions,[1] research shows that the States have held many more. These conventions are listed in Appendix B.1. It is worthy to note that since the admission of Kentucky in 1792, the process has been refined and has evolved. Kentucky held ten conventions in preparation for applying for statehood.[2] This attention to detail and development of the process was emulated – but streamlined – in all states to follow. These "statehood" and "planning" conventions were instrumental in working out the great difficulties that faced a given territory in its quest for statehood before the requisite constitutional convention. It didn't always work; some states required multiple constitutional conventions before successfully crafting a state constitution. The greater the impediments,

---

[1] John J. Dinan, *The American State Constitutional Tradition* (Lawrence: University Press of Kansas, 2009), 1
[2] George L. Willis, Sr., "History Kentucky Constitutions and Constitutional Conventions," *Register of Kentucky State Historical Society* 28, no.85 (Oct. 1930): generally

the more numerous the conventions to resolve the issues – case in point is the separation of the Dakotas into two states.[3] Another example is the effort to turn the Indian Territory into the State of Oklahoma.[4]

Of interest is that in some cases, multiple conventions were needed just to arrive at a single constitution for a state or territory. In 1857, Minnesota was so divided politically that the Republicans and the Democrats refused to meet together to draft a constitution for statehood. Instead they each took one chamber of the territorial capitol and held separate, but concurrent conventions. When they were done, a committee was selected to reconcile the two documents into a single constitution, which still serves Minnesota today.[5] At almost the same time, in the Indian Territory, the Choctaw Nation was experiencing the same political division.[6] The Choctaw resolved their differences by holding two competing conventions in two Oklahoma towns, Skullyville and Doaksville, and then took two years for combining the documents.[7] The conventions required to achieve these goals are found in Appendix B.2.

Similarly, the insular territories of the United States have worked arduously to secure a territorial or commonwealth constitution. It is timely to note that much of the work being done recently in terms of constitutional development has been occurring in the territories. Appendix B.3 shows the convention history of the current six insular territories. Note the number of amendatory conventions undertaken by the territories within the last half century. While the States have begun to move away from the more costly and slower constitutional convention practice and in its place adopt the constitutional commission model, the territories have embraced the convention model and exercised it with a gusto. American Samoa had held constitutional conventions, amendatory conventions and constitutional referendums every few years since the 1960s.[8]

Even the attainment of territorial status could be a struggle. Appendix B.4 shows that many provisional states and territories sought to join the

---

[3] http://ndstudies.gov/content/moving-toward-statehood
[4] http://www.okhistory.org/publications/enc/entry.php?entry=ST025
[5] William Anderson, "Minnesota Frames a Constitution," *Minnesota History* (March 1958): 1-12
[6] Arrell Morgan Gibson, *Oklahoma: A History of Five Centuries* (Norman: University of Oklahoma Press, 1981), 74
[7] Angie Debo, *The Rise and Fall of the Choctaw Republic* (Norman: University of Oklahoma Press, 1961), 75
[8] Office of Archives and Records Management. American Samoa Government.

union unsuccessfully despite following the pattern and practice of the statehood and state constitutional convention model. It is amusing to scan the list of provisional "states" that did not succeed in becoming states particularly when one looks to the history of these political entities and finds that many functioned as de facto states or territories for several years before being displaced by another political entity. Deseret evolved into the State of Utah. Frankland (Franklin) formed the nucleus of Tennessee.[9] Jefferson became Colorado.[10] Nataqua was succeeded by Nevada.[11] Those listed in the Appendix are only those failed states and territories that actually held at least one constitutional convention.

Of even greater interest are those political entities found in Appendix B.5 – the constitutional conventions for other nations that occurred within the present day borders of the United States within territory that either is, or was at the time, United States controlled territory. Besides the obvious Confederate States of America, we find the lesser known nations of the Republic of East Florida[12] and the Republic of West Florida,[13] the Republic of Indian Stream in present day New Hampshire, the Republic of the Rio Grande[14] whose capital was situated in present day Laredo, Texas, the Republic of Watauga Association[15] which was superseded by the "State of Frankland." Within the United States were the foreign nations that became American states: Hawaii,[16] Texas[17] and Vermont[18] – which all held constitutional conventions.[19]

Lastly, just to give an idea of the extent of the use of both constitutional drafting and amendatory conventions, only a few of the Native

---

[9] Edwin R. Keedy, "The Constitutions of the State of Franklin, the Indian Stream Republic and the State of Deseret," *University of Pennsylvania Law Review* 101 (1953): generally
[10] "Colorado Government History," Colorado State Archives (2001), "pa7122g743internet-2.pdf"
[11] William Newell Davis, Jr., "The Territory of Nataqua: An Episode in Pioneer Government East of the Sierra," *California Historical Society Quarterly* 21, no.3 (Sep. 1942): generally
[12] http://www.floridamemory.com/blog/2014/01/09/patriot-constitution/
[13] http://www.exploresouthernhistory.com/westflorida.html
[14] http://www.historynet.com/the-republic-of-the-rio-grande.htm
[15] Max Dixon, *The Wataugans* (Johnson City, TN: The Overmountain Press, 1989), 18-9, original copyright by The Tennessee American Revolution Bicentennial Commission (1976)
[16] Richard H. Kosaki, "Constitutions and Constitutional Conventions of Hawaii," *Hawaiian Journal of History* 12 (1978): generally
[17] https://dlc.dcccd.edu/txgov1-2/texas-constitutional-history
[18] Paul S. Gillies and D. Gregory Sanford, Editors, *Records of the Council of Censors of the State of Vermont* (Montpelier: Office of the Secretary of State, 1991)
[19] California was for a very short period the Bear Flag Republic but did not hold a constitutional convention until it was a United States territory.

Appendix B.1 - All State Constitutional Conventions

American constitutional conventions are listed. In this instance, the "Five Civilized Tribes" are listed with just a few of their constitutional conventions to demonstrate that they have held and continue to hold both constitutional drafting and amendatory conventions.[20] Unfortunately, it would require another volume to analyze the extent and diversity of the Native American experience with constitutional conventions. Today, there are 567 federally recognized tribes or nations in primarily the lower forty-eight states.[21] There are over ninety federally recognized Alaskan native communities and the currently on-going discussion of the status of the Hawaiian natives today is in flux (at the time of this writing in 2016, a constitutional convention restricted to the native Hawaiians was scheduled to begin in February 2016, but was stopped by federal court action prior to convening).[22]

Appendix B.6 lists all of the Article V conventions held to date, which is to say the conventions held to ratify the Twenty-first Amendment in 1933-34. Similarly, Appendix B.7 lists all of the Article VII conventions held to ratify the Constitution between 1787 and 1791. That list also includes a Pennsylvania convention convened under the call for a convention to ratify the Constitution, but which was subsequently called to consider and propose amendments to the federal constitution as part of the Pennsylvania ratification.[23]

There have been so many intercolonial and interstate conventions that it is probably impossible to compile a complete and detailed list of every one of those conventions. Some have been lost to history as no record was made of their proceedings or their call to convene. We must remember that a couple of centuries ago, an intercolonial or an interstate convention was a pretty commonplace event and the common people took little notice of the call to convention. A list of the dozens of interstate commercial and regulatory conventions that take place every year would fill an entire volume. Appendix B.8 gives just some of the major intercolonial and interstate conventions of note with a focus on the colonial and Revolutionary War eras.

Finally, Appendix B.9 lists nearly all of the <u>amendatory</u> conventions of the States, territories and federally oriented conventions since the

---

[20] Arrell Morgan Gibson, "The Constitutional Experiences of the Five Civilized Tribes," *American Indian Law Review* 2, no.2 (Winter 1974): generally

[21] http://www.indianaffairs.gov/WhatWeDo/index.htm

[22] http://www.huffingtonpost.com/entry/supreme-court-hawaii-election_us_565f6849e4b079b2818d1767

[23] http://teachingamericanhistory.org/ratification/mcmasterstone/chapteri/

Appendix B.1 - All State Constitutional Conventions

Constitution was ratified. More than eighty amendatory conventions were counted during the research for this work. The count does not include those held by the Native American nations.

For all of the conventions compiled in the tables, there are seventeen types of convention noted. A straightforward convention for drafting a constitution is termed a "drafting" convention. A convention to draft an amendment is termed an "amendatory" convention. A convention to ratify a new constitution or an amendment is called a "ratification" or ratificatory convention. These are the most common and best known types of conventions. There are also the five types of conventions in the former Confederate states arc of conventions: "secessionary, restoration, reconstruction, redeemer and disenfranchisement." An early corollary to those conventions were the "anti-secessionary" conventions. Another type is the "legislative" convention that passed laws in place of the actual legislature and its southern relative the "nullification" convention. Occasionally, the States would hold a "limited" convention for addressing a specific topic for either amendment or just discussion of policy. There is also the arc of conventions that territories followed to gain statehood before convening a state constitutional convention. These include: "planning, statehood and separation" conventions. These also have their opposing corollary in the "anti-division" convention. Finally, there are the "commission" conventions that are typically appointed rather than elected and have a limited slate of powers even when drafting a proposed state constitution.

The sources of the material in the tables are most frequently the proceedings of the conventions when they can be found, the state and territorial archives, or the typical academic writings on the topic.

Appendix B.1 - All State Constitutional Conventions

State	Start Date	Dates Convened	End Date	Type	Location	Product
Alabama	1819	7/5-8/2	1819	Drafting	Huntsville	1st state
Alabama	1861	1/7/-3/21	1861	Secessionary	Montgomery	2nd state
Alabama	1865	9/12-9/30	1865	Restoration	Montgomery	3rd state
Alabama	1867	11/5-12/6	1867	Reconstruction	Montgomery	4th state
Alabama	1875	9/6-10/12	1875	Redeemer	Montgomery	5th state
Alabama	1901	5/21-9/3	1901	Disenfranchisement	Montgomery	6th state
Alaska	1955	11/8-2/6	1956	Drafting	Fairbanks	1st state
Arizona	1860	4/2-4/5	1860	Drafting	Presido, Tucson	Territorial
Arizona	1861	3/16/1861	1861	Secessionary	Mesilla	Drafting
Arizona	1861	3/28/1861	1861	Secessionary	Tucson	Ratification
Arizona	1861	8/28/1861	1861	Drafting	Tucson	Confederate
Arizona	1891	9/7-10/3	1891	Drafting	Phoenix	Ignored by DC
Arizona	1910	10/10-12/10	1910	Drafting	Phoenix	1st state
Arkansas	1836	1/4-1/30	1836	Drafting	Little Rock	1st state
Arkansas	1861	3/4-5/6	1861	Secessionary	Little Rock	2nd state
Arkansas	1864	1/4-1/23	1864	Restoration	Little Rock	3rd state
Arkansas	1868	1/7-2/14	1868	Reconstruction	Little Rock	4th state
Arkansas	1874	7/14-9/7	1874	Redeemer	Little Rock	5th state
Arkansas	1917	11/19-11/21, 7/1-8/23, 9/18-9/20	1918	Drafting	Little Rock	Rejected
Arkansas	1969	1/6-1/7, 5/27-8/21, 1/12-2/10	1970	Drafting	Little Rock	Rejected
Arkansas	1979	5/14-6/30	1980	Drafting	Little Rock	Rejected
California	1849	9/1-10/13	1849	Drafting	Monterey	1st state
California	1878	9/28-3/3	1879	Drafting	Sacramento	2nd state
Colorado	1864	7/1-7/20	1864	Drafting	Golden/Denver City	Rejected
Colorado	1865	8/8-8/12	1865	Drafting	Denver	Rejected
Colorado	1875	12/20-3/15	1876	Drafting	Denver	1st state
Connecticut	1818	8/26-9/18	1818	Drafting	Hartford	1st state

Appendix B.1 - All State Constitutional Conventions

State	Start Date	Dates Convened	End Date	Type	Location	Product
Connecticut	1902	1/1–5/15	1902	Drafting	Hartford	Rejected
Connecticut	1965	7/1–10/28	1965	Drafting	Hartford	2nd state
Delaware	1776	8/27–9/20	1776	Drafting	New Castle	1st state
Delaware	1791	11/29–6/1	1792	Drafting	Dover	2nd state
Delaware	1831	11/8–5/29	1831	Drafting	Dover	3rd state
Delaware	1852	12/8–4/30	1853	Drafting	Dover	Rejected
Delaware	1896	12/1–6/4	1897	Drafting	Dover	4th state
Florida	1838	12/3–1/11	1839	Drafting	St. Joseph	1st state
Florida	1861	1/3 – 4/27	1861	Secessionary	Tallahasee	2nd state
Florida	1862	1/14-1/27	1862	Amendatory	Tallahasee	
Florida	1865	10/25–11/7	1865	Restoration	Tallahasee	Failed
Florida	1868	1/20–2/25	1868	Reconstruction	Tallahasee	3rd state
Florida	1885	6/9–8/3	1885	Redeemer	Tallahasee	4th state
Florida	1966	11/28–12/16, January	1967	Commission	Tallahasee	
Georgia	1776	10/1–April	1777	Legislative	Savannah	1st state
Georgia	1788	11/4–11/24	1788	Drafting	Augusta	
Georgia	1789	1/4–1/20	1789	Amendatory	Augusta	
Georgia	1789	5/4–5/6	1789	Ratification	Augusta	2nd state
Georgia	1795	5/3–5/16	1795	Amendatory	Louisville	
Georgia	1798	5/8–5/16, 5/30	1798	Drafting	Louisville	3rd state
Georgia	1833	5/6–5/15	1833	Amendatory	Milledgeville	
Georgia	1839	5/6–5/15	1839	Amendatory	Milledgeville	
Georgia	1861	1/16-1/29, 3/7–3/23	1861	Secessionary	Milledgeville/Savannah	4th state
Georgia	1865	10/25–11/8	1865	Restoration	Milledgeville	5th state
Georgia	1867	12/9–3/11	1868	Reconstruction	Augusta	6th state
Georgia	1877	7/11–8/25	1877	Redeemer	Atlanta	7th state
Hawaii (Kingdom)	1852	?–6/14	1852	Drafting/Legislative	Honolulu	National

Appendix B.1 - All State Constitutional Conventions

State	Start Date	Dates Convened	End Date	Type	Location	Product
Hawaii (Kingdom)	1864	7/7-8/13	1864	Drafting/Legislative	Kawaiaha'o (Honolulu)	National
Hawaii (Republic)	1894	5/30-7/3	1894	Drafting	Honolulu	National
Hawaii	1950	4/4-7/22	1950	Drafting	Honolulu	1st state
Hawaii	1968	7/15-10/21	1968	Amendatory	Honolulu	
Hawaii	1978	7/5-12/2	1978	Amendatory	Honolulu	
Idaho	1889	7/4-7/25	1889	Drafting	Boise City	1st state
Illinois	1818	8/3-8/26	1818	Drafting	Kaskaskia	1st state
Illinois	1847	6/7-8/31	1848	Drafting	Springfield	2nd state
Illinois	1862	1/7-3/24	1862	Drafting	Springfield	Rejected
Illinois	1869	12/13-5/13	1870	Drafting	Springfield	3rd state
Illinois	1920	1/6-7/7, -9/21, 11/8-12/9, 9/6-10/10	1922	Drafting	Springfield	Rejected
Illinois	1969	12/8-9/3	1970	Drafting	Springfield	4th state
Indiana	1816	6/10-6/29	1816	Drafting	Corydon	1st state
Indiana	1850	10/7-2/10	1851	Drafting	Indianapolis	2nd state
Iowa	1844	10/7-11/1	1844	Drafting	Iowa City	Rejected
Iowa	1846	5/4-5/15	1846	Drafting	Iowa City	1st state
Iowa	1857	1/19-3/5	1857	Drafting	Iowa City	2nd state
Kansas	1855	9/19, 10/23-11/11	1855	Drafting	Topeka	Rejected
Kansas	1857	9/7-11/7	1857	Drafting	Lecompton	Rejected
Kansas	1858	3/23-4/3	1858	Drafting	Minneola/Leavenworth	Rejected
Kansas	1859	7/5-7/29	1859	Drafting	Wyandotte (KC)	1st state
Kentucky	1784	11/7-11/8	1784	Statehood	Danville	
Kentucky	1784	12/27-1/5	1785	Statehood	Danville	
Kentucky	1785	5/23	1785	Statehood	Danville	
Kentucky	1785	8/8	1785	Statehood	Danville	
Kentucky	1786	9/25	1786	Statehood	Danville	
Kentucky	1787	9/17	1787	Statehood	Danville	

Appendix B.1 - All State Constitutional Conventions

State	Start Date	Dates Convened	End Date	Type	Location	Product
Kentucky	1788	7/28	1788	Statehood	Danville	
Kentucky	1788	11/3	1788	Statehood	Danville	
Kentucky	1789	7/20	1789	Statehood	Danville	
Kentucky	1790	7/26-7/30	1790	Statehood	Danville	
Kentucky	1792	4/2-4/19	1792	Drafting	Danville	1st state
Kentucky	1799	7/22-8/17	1799	Drafting	Frankfort	2nd state
Kentucky	1849	10/1-6/11	1850	Drafting	Frankfort	3rd state
Kentucky	1861	11/18-11/20	1861	Secessionary	Russellville	
Kentucky	1890	9/8-9/28	1891	Drafting	Frankfort	4th state
Louisiana	1812	11/4-1/22	1812	Drafting	New Orleans	1st state
Louisiana	1844	8/5-8/24, 1/14-5/26	1845	Drafting	Jackson; New Orleans	2nd state
Louisiana	1852	1/17-7/31	1852	Drafting	Baton Rouge	3rd state
Louisiana	1861	1/23-1/26, 1/29-3/26	1861	Secessionary	Baton Rouge; New Orleans	4th state
Louisiana	1864	4/6-7/25	1864	Restoration	New Orleans	5th state
Louisiana	1867	11/23-3/11	1868	Reconstruction	New Orleans	6th state
Louisiana	1879	4/21-7/23	1879	Redeemer	New Orleans	7th state
Louisiana	1898	2/8-5/12	1898	Disenfranchisement	New Orleans	8th state
Louisiana	1913	11/10-11/22	1913	Revisory	Baton Rouge	
Louisiana	1921	3/1-6/18	1921	Drafting	Baton Rouge	9th state
Louisiana	1973	1/5-1/19	1974	Amendatory	Baton Rouge	10th state
Louisiana	1992	8/23-9/22	1992	Legislative	Baton Rouge	Rejected
Maine	1816	9/30	1816	Drafting	Brunswick	Rejected
Maine	1819	10/11-10/29, 1/5-1/7	1820	Drafting	Portland	1st state
Maryland	1776	8/14-11/11	1776	Drafting	Annapolis	1st state
Maryland	1792		1792	Legislative	Annapolis	Rejected
Maryland	1850	11/4-5/13	1851	Drafting	Annapolis	2nd state
Maryland	1864	4/27-9/6	1864	Reconstruction	Annapolis	3rd state

Appendix B.1 - All State Constitutional Conventions

State	Start Date	Dates Convened	End Date	Type	Location	Product
Maryland	1867	5/8-8/17	1867	Redeemer	Annapolis	4th state
Maryland	1967	9/12-1/10	1968	Drafting	Annapolis	Rejected
Massachusetts	1778	6/17-2/28	1778	Drafting	Ipswich	Rejected
Massachusetts	1779	9/1, 10/28-11/5, 1/5-3/2, 6/7-6/16	1780	Drafting	Cambridge:Boston	1st state
Massachusetts	1820	11/15-6/9	1821	Amendatory	Boston	
Massachusetts	1853	5/4-8/2	1853	Amendatory	Boston	Rejected
Massachusetts	1917	6/6-8/21,	1919	Amendatory	Boston	
Michigan	1835	5/11-6/24	1835	Drafting	Detroit	1st state
Michigan	1850	6/3-8/15	1850	Drafting	Lansing	2nd state
Michigan	1867	5/15-8/22	1867	Drafting	Lansing	Rejected
Michigan	1873	8/27-10/16	1873	Drafting	Lansing	Rejected
Michigan	1907	10/22-3/3	1908	Drafting	Lansing	3rd state
Michigan	1961	10/3-8/1	1962	Drafting	Lansing	4th state
Minnesota	1857	7/13-8/29	1857	Drafting	St. Paul	1st state
Minnesota	1857	7/13-8/29	1857	Drafting	St. Paul	1st state
Mississippi	1817	7/7-8/15	1817	Drafting	Washington	1st state
Mississippi	1832	9/10-10/26	1832	Drafting	Jackson	2nd state
Mississippi	1849	10/1-10/3	1849	Planning	Jackson	
Mississippi	1851	11/10-11/17	1851	Planning	Jackson	
Mississippi	1861	1/7-1/26, 3/25-3/30	1861	Secessionary	Jackson	
Mississippi	1865	8/14-8/24	1865	Restoration	Jackson	
Mississippi	1868	1/7-5/18	1868	Reconstruction	Jackson	
Mississippi	1890	8/12-11/1	1890	Disenfranchisement	Jackson	
Missouri	1820	6/12-7/19	1820	Drafting	St. Louis	1st state
Missouri	1845	11/17-1/13	1846	Drafting	Jefferson City	Rejected
Missouri	1861	2/28-3/22	1861	Secessionary	Jefferson City: St. Louis	failed
Missouri	1861	7/22-7/31	1861	Secessionary	Jefferson City	

Appendix B.1 - All State Constitutional Conventions

State	Start Date	Dates Convened	End Date	Type	Location	Product
Missouri	1861	10/10-10/18	1861	Secessionary	Neosho: St. Louis	
Missouri	1862	6/2-6/14	1862	Legislative	Jefferson City	
Missouri	1863	6/15-7/1	1863	Legislative	Jefferson City	
Missouri	1865	1/6-4/10	1865	Reconstruction	St. Louis	2nd state
Missouri	1868		1868			
Missouri	1875	5/5-8/2	1875	Redeemer	Jefferson City	3rd state
Missouri	1922	5/15-11/6	1923	Amendatory	Jefferson City	rejected
Missouri	1943	9/21-9/29	1944	Drafting	Jefferson City	4th state
Montana	1866	4/9-4/14	1866	Drafting	Helena	lost
Montana	1884	1/14-2/9	1884	Drafting	Helena	not ratified
Montana	1889	7/4-8/17	1889	Drafting	Helena	1st state
Montana	1972	1/17-3/22	1972	Drafting	Helena	2nd state
Nebraska	1860	Never held	1860			
Nebraska	1864	7/4/1864	1864	Drafting	Omaha	no doc
Nebraska	1866	2/9/1866	1866	Drafting/Legislative	Omaha	1st state
Nebraska	1871	6/13-8/19	1871	Drafting	Lincoln	Rejected
Nebraska	1875	5/11-6/12	1875	Drafting	Lincoln	2nd state
Nebraska	1919	12/2-3/25, 10/19	1920	Amendatory	Lincoln	
Nevada	1863	11/2-12/3	1863	Drafting	Carson City	Rejected
Nevada	1864	7/4-7/28	1864	Drafting	Carson City	1st state
New Hampshire	1775	12/21-1/5	1776	Drafting	Exeter	1st state
New Hampshire	1778	6/10, 10/13, 6/5, 9/21	1779	Drafting	Concord	Rejected
New Hampshire	1781	6/5-9/14	1781	Drafting	Concord	Rejected
New Hampshire	1782	1/23, 8/21, 12/31	1782	Revisory	Concord	Rejected
New Hampshire	1783	6/3-10/31	1783	Revisory	Concord	2nd state
New Hampshire	1791	9/7-9/16, 2/8-2/24, 5/30-8/27, 9/5-9/6	1792	Amendatory	Concord	3rd state

Appendix B.1 - All State Constitutional Conventions

State	Start Date	Dates Convened	End Date	Type	Location	Product
New Hampshire	1850	11/6-11/22, 12/3-1/3, 4/16-4/17	1851	Drafting	Concord	Rejected
New Hampshire	1876	12/6-12/15	1876	Amendatory	Concord	
New Hampshire	1889	1/2-1/12	1889	Amendatory	Concord	
New Hampshire	1902	12/2-12/19	1902	Amendatory	Concord	
New Hampshire	1912	6/5-6/22	1912	Amendatory	Concord	
New Hampshire	1918	6/7-6/7/1918, 1/13-1/29/1920, 1/28/1921, 2/16/1923	1923	Amendatory	Concord	Rejected
New Hampshire	1930	6/4-6/13	1930	Amendatory	Concord	
New Hampshire	1938	5/11-6/1/1938, 11/8/1938, 9/23-9/26/1941	1941	Amendatory	Concord	
New Hampshire	1948	5/12-6/4	1948	Amendatory	Concord	
New Hampshire	1956	5/15-6/13/1956, 12/2-12/4/1959	1959	Amendatory	Concord	
New Hampshire	1964	5/13-6/10, 7/8	1964	Amendatory	Concord	
New Hampshire	1974	5/8-6/26	1974	Amendatory	Concord	
New Hampshire	1984	5/9-6/28	1984	Amendatory	Concord	
New Jersey	1776	5/26-7/2	1776	Drafting	Burlington	1st state
New Jersey	1844	5/14-6/29	1844	Drafting	Trenton	2nd state
New Jersey	1942		1942	Commission	Trenton	
New Jersey	1944		1944	Legislative	Trenton	Rejected
New Jersey	1947	6/12-9/10	1947	Drafting	New Brunswick	2nd state
New Jersey	1966	3/21-6/14	1966	Limited	New Brunswick	
New Mexico	1848	10/10-10/14	1848	Drafting	Santa Fe	
New Mexico	1849	9/24-9/26	1849	Drafting	Santa Fe	
New Mexico	1850	5/15-5/25	1850	Drafting	Santa Fe	Rejected
New Mexico	1866	called but had no quorum	1866		Santa Fe	no quorum
New Mexico	1872	2/3/1870	1872	Legislative	Santa Fe	

Appendix B.1 - All State Constitutional Conventions

State	Start Date	Dates Convened	End Date	Type	Location	Product
New Mexico	1889	9/3-9/21	1889	Drafting	Santa Fe	Adopted
New Mexico	1890	8/18-8/20	1890	Amendatory	Santa Fe	rejected
New Mexico	1901		1901	Drafting	Albuquerque	Ignored by DC
New Mexico	1907	1/7	1907	Drafting	Santa Fe	failed
New Mexico	1910	10/3-11/21	1910	Drafting	Santa Fe	1st state
New Mexico	1969	8/5-10/20	1969	Drafting	Santa Fe	Rejected
New York	1776	7/10-4/20, 5/13	1777	Drafting/Legislative	White Plains:Kingston	1st state
New York	1801	10/13-10/27	1801	Amendatory	Albany	
New York	1821	8/28-11/10	1821	Drafting	Albany	2nd state
New York	1846	6/1-10/9	1846	Drafting	Albany	3rd state
New York	1867	6/4-2/28	1868	Drafting	Albany	Rejected
New York	1894	5/8-9/29	1894	Drafting	Albany	4th state
New York	1915	4/6-9/10	1915	Amendatory	Albany	
New York	1938	4/5-8/26	1938	Amendatory	Albany	
New York	1967	4/4-9/26	1967	Amendatory	Albany	Rejected
North Carolina	1776	11/12-12/18	1776	Drafting	New Bern	1st state
North Carolina	1823	11/10-11/15	1823	Amendatory	Raleigh	Rejected
North Carolina	1835	6/4-7/11	1835	Amendatory	Raleigh	
North Carolina	1861	5/20-6/28, 11/18-12/13, 1/20- 2/26, 4/21-5/13	1862	Secessionary	Raleigh	
North Carolina	1865	10/2-10/19	1866	Restoration	Raleigh	
North Carolina	1868	1/14-3/16, 6/14	1868	Reconstruction	Raleigh	
North Carolina	1875	9/6-10/11	1875	Redeemer	Raleigh	
North Dakota	1889	7/4-8/17	1889	Drafting	Bismark	1st state
North Dakota	1971	4/6-4/9, 1/3-2/17	1972	Drafting	Bismark	Rejected
Ohio	1802	11/1-11/29	1802	Drafting	Chilicothe	1st state
Ohio	1850	5/6-3/10	1851	Drafting	Columbus	2nd state

748 Far From Unworkable

Appendix B.1 - All State Constitutional Conventions

State	Start Date	Dates Convened	End Date	Type	Location	Product
Ohio	1873	5/13–8/8; 12/2–5/15	1874	Drafting	Columbus: Cinncinnati	Rejected
Ohio	1912	1/9–8/26	1912	Amendatory	Columbus	
Oklahoma	1905	7/12	1905	Drafting	Oklahoma City	
Oklahoma	1906	11/20–3/5, 4/16–7/6, 7/10–8/16	1907	Drafting	Guthrie	1st state
Oregon	1843	5/2, 5/15, 7/4–7/5	1843	Drafting	Champoeg	Provisional
Oregon	1845	6/25–7/2	1845	Drafting/Legislative	Oregon City	
Oregon	1857	8/17–9/18	1857	Drafting	Salem	1st state
Pennsylvania	1776	7/15–9/28	1776	Drafting	Philadelphia	1st state
Pennsylvania	1789	11/24–2/26, 8/9–9/2	1790	Amendatory	Philadelphia	2nd state
Pennsylvania	1837	5/2–2/22	1838	Amendatory	Harrisburg	3rd state
Pennsylvania	1872	11/12–11/27: 1/7–11/3	1873	Amendatory	Harrisburg; Philadelphia	
Pennsylvania	1967	12/1–2/29	1968	Drafting	Harrisburg	
Rhode Island	1824	6/21–7/3	1824	Drafting	Newport	Rejected
Rhode Island	1834	2/22, 3/12, 9/1–9/13, 11/10, 2/9, 6/29	1835	Drafting	Providence	no doc
Rhode Island	1841	10/4–10/9,11/16–11/18, 1/13, 2/19	1842	Drafting	Providence	Rejected
Rhode Island	1841	5/5: 7/5, 11/1–2/19, 1/12	1842	Drafting/Legislative	Newport: Providence	Rejected
Rhode Island	1842	9/12–11/5, 1/13	1843	Drafting/Legislative	Newport: East Greenwich	1st state
Rhode Island	1944	3/28	1944	Amendatory	Providence	
Rhode Island	1951	6/1–6/3	1951	Amendatory	Providence	
Rhode Island	1955	6/20	1955	Amendatory	Providence	
Rhode Island	1958	1/31–2/7	1958	Amendatory	Providence	
Rhode Island	1964	12/8/1964–2/17/1969	1969		Providence	Rejected
Rhode Island	1973	9/4–10/4	1973	Amendatory	Providence	
Rhode Island	1986	1/6–6/26	1986	Drafting	Providence	2nd state
South Carolina	1776	2/11–3/26	1776	Drafting/Legislative	Charles Town	1st state
South Carolina	1776	10/12–10/21	1776	Drafting/Legislative	Charles Town	not implemented
South Carolina	1778	3/19	1778	Drafting/Legislative	Charles Town	2nd state

Appendix B.1 - All State Constitutional Conventions

State	Start Date	Dates Convened	End Date	Type	Location	Product
South Carolina	1790	5/10-6/3	1790	Drafting	Columbia	3rd state
South Carolina	1852	4/26-4/30	1852	Secessionary	Columbia	
South Carolina	1860	12/17, 12/20-1/5, 12/26-1/8, 9/9-9/17	1862	Secessionary	Columbia: Charleston	
South Carolina	1861	3/26-4/10	1861	Secessionary	Charleston	4th state
South Carolina	1865	9/13-9/27	1865	Restoration	Columbia	5th state
South Carolina	1868	1/14-3/17	1868	Reconstruction	Charleston	6th state
South Carolina	1895	9/10-12/4	1895	Disenfranchisement	Columbia	7th state
South Dakota	1883	9/4-9/18	1883	Drafting	Sioux Falls	
South Dakota	1885	9/8-9/24	1885	Drafting	Sioux Falls	
South Dakota	1885	9/8-9/24	1885	Drafting	Huron	
South Dakota	1886	7/13	1886	Drafting	Sioux Falls	
South Dakota	1886	12/15-12/17	1886	Drafting	Huron	
South Dakota	1889	7/4-8/5	1889	Drafting	Sioux Falls	1st state
South Dakota	1889	3/3	1889	Amendatory	Huron	
South Dakota	1889	4/2	1889	Amendatory	Huron	
Tennessee	1796	1/11-2/6	1796	Drafting	Knoxville	1st state
Tennessee	1834	5/19-8/30	1834	Drafting	Nashville	2nd state
Tennessee	1861	4/30-5/6	1861	Secessionary/Legislative	Jackson	
Tennessee	1865	1/9-1/16	1865	Restoration	Nashville	
Tennessee	1870	1/10-3/23	1870	Reconstruction	Nashville	3rd state
Tennessee	1953	4/21-6/5, 7/14	1953	Amendatory	Nashville	
Tennessee	1959	7/21-7/31	1959	Amendatory	Nashville	
Tennessee	1965	7/1-10/28	1965	Amendatory	Nashville	
Tennessee	1971	8/2-9/15	1971	Amendatory	Nashville	
Tennessee	1977	8/1-12/21	1977	Amendatory	Nashville	
Texas (Republic)	1832	10/1-10/6, 4/1-4/13	1833	Secessionary/Drafting	San Felipe de Austin	Rejected
Texas (Republic)	1835	10/16, 11/3-11/14	1835	Drafting	Columbia: San Felipe de Austin	National

Appendix B.1 - All State Constitutional Conventions

State	Start Date	Dates Convened	End Date	Type	Location	Product
Texas (Republic)	1836	3/1-3/17	1836	Drafting	Washington-on-the-Brazos	National
Texas	1845	7/4-7/27	1845	Drafting	Austin	1st state
Texas	1861	1/28-2/24, 3/2-3/25	1861	Secessionary	Austin	2nd state
Texas	1866	2/7-4/2	1866	Restoration	Austin	3rd state
Texas	1868	7/1-8/31, 12/1-2/8	1869	Reconstruction	Austin	4th state
Texas	1875	9/6-11/24	1876	Redeemer	Austin	5th state
Texas	1974	1/8-7/30	1974	Legislative	Austin	Rejected
Utah	1856	3/17-3/27	1856		Salt Lake City	
Utah	1862	1/20-1/23	1862		Salt Lake City	
Utah	1872	2/19-4/2	1872		Salt Lake City	ratified
Utah	1882	4/10-4/27	1882		Salt Lake City	ratified
Utah	1887	6/30-7/7	1887		Salt Lake City	ratified
Utah	1895	3/4-5/8	1895	Drafting	Salt Lake City	1st state
Vermont (Republic)	1777	7/2-7/8,12/25	1777	Drafting	Windsor	1st state
Vermont (Republic)	1785	6/2-6/8, 9/29-10/21, 2/2-2/14	1786	Drafting	Windsor	2nd state
Vermont	1792	6/6-6/7, 10/8-11/30	1793	Drafting	Rutland	3rd state
Vermont	1799	Oct 1799: Feb 1800	1800		Bennington:Windsor	Council
Vermont	1806	June, Oct: Middlebury; Dec: Woodstock	1806		Bennington	Council
Vermont	1813	6/4, 10/14-11/2, 1/19-1/24	1814		Middlebury	Council
Vermont	1814	1st Thursday July -7/9	1814	Amendatory	Montpelier	
Vermont	1820	6/7-6/8, 10/16-10/27, 3/15-3/26	1821		Montpelier	Council
Vermont	1822	2/21-2/23	1822	Amendatory	Montpelier	
Vermont	1827	6/6-6/8, 10/15-10/25, 11/26-11/30	1827		Montpelier:Burlington	Council
Vermont	1828	6/26-6/28	1828	Amendatory	Montpelier	Council
Vermont	1834	6/4-6/6, 10/15-10/24; 1/7-1/16	1835		Montpelier:Middlebury	Council
Vermont	1836	1/6-1/14	1836	Amendatory	Montpelier	Council
Vermont	1841	6/2-6/3, 10/20-10/29, 2/9-2/15	1842		Montpelier:Burlington	Council

Appendix B.1 - All State Constitutional Conventions

State	Start Date	Dates Convened	End Date	Type	Location	Product
Vermont	1843	1/4	1843		Montpelier	
Vermont	1848	6/7-6/9, 10/4-10/19; 2/16-2/27	1849		Montpelier;Burlington	Council
Vermont	1850	1/2-1/11	1850	Amendatory	Montpelier	
Vermont	1855	6/6-6/8, 10/2-10/18; 2/12-2/26	1856		Montpelier;Middlebury	Council
Vermont	1857	1/7-1/12	1857	Amendatory	Montpelier	
Vermont	1862	6/4-6/6, 10/21-10/25	1862		Montpelier	Council
Vermont	1869	2/24,6/2-6/4, 7/27-8/6, 10/19-10/22	1869		Montpelier	Council
Vermont	1870	6/8-6/15	1870	Amendatory	Montpelier	
Virginia	1776	5/15-6/29	1776	Drafting	Williamsburg	1st state
Virginia	1829	10/5-1/15	1830	Drafting	Richmond/Winchester	2nd state
Virginia	1850	10/14-8/1	1851	Drafting	Richmond	3rd state
Virginia	1861	2/13-2/18	1861	Secessionary	Richmond	
Virginia	1864	2/13-, 3/14-4/7, 4/11	1864	Restoration	Alexandria	
Virginia	1867	7/, 12/3-1/29, 4/7	1868	Reconstruction	Richmond	
Virginia	1901	6/12-6/26	1902	Disenfranchisement	Richmond	
Virginia	1945	4/30-5/2	1945	Amendatory	Richmond	Limited
Virginia	1956	3/5-3/7	1956	Amendatory	Richmond	Limited
Washington	1878	6/11-7/27	1878	Drafting	Walla Walla	Ignored by DC
Washington	1889	7/4-8/23	1889	Drafting	Olympia	1st state
West Virginia	1861	4/22	1861	Anti-secessionary	Clarksburg	Planning
West Virginia	1861	5/13-5/15	1861	Anti-secessionary	Wheeling	Ordinance
West Virginia	1861	6/11-6/25, 8/6-8/21	1861	Separation	Wheeling	1st state
West Virginia	1861	11/26-2/18	1862	Drafting	Wheeling	
West Virginia	1863	2/12-2/20	1863	Ratification	Wheeling	
West Virginia	1872	1/16-4/9	1872	Redemption	Charleston	2nd state
Wisconsin	1846	10/5-12/15	1846	Drafting	Madison	Rejected
Wisconsin	1847	12/15-2/1	1848	Drafting	Madison	1st state
Wyoming	1889	9/2-9/30	1889	Drafting	Cheyenne	1st state

Appendix B.2 - All State Non-constitutional Conventions

State	Start Date	Dates Convened	End Date	Type	Location	Product
Arizona	1856	8/29	1856	Statehood	Tucson	Territorial
Arizona	1893	11/27-11/28	1893	Statehood	Phoenix	
Arizona	1901	10/26	1901	Statehood	Phoenix	
Arizona	1905	5/27	1905	Statehood	Phoenix	
Arizona	1905	12/14	1905	Statehood	Tucson	
Georgia	1850	12/10-12/14	1850	Planning	Milledgeville	
Kentucky	1784	11/7-11/8	1784	Statehood	Danville	
Kentucky	1784	12/27-1/5	1785	Statehood	Danville	
Kentucky	1785	5/23	1785	Statehood	Danville	
Kentucky	1785	8/8	1785	Statehood	Danville	
Kentucky	1786	9/25	1786	Statehood	Danville	
Kentucky	1787	9/17	1787	Statehood	Danville	
Kentucky	1788	7/28	1788	Statehood	Danville	
Kentucky	1788	11/3	1788	Statehood	Danville	
Kentucky	1789	7/20	1789	Statehood	Danville	
Kentucky	1790	7/26-7/30?	1790	Statehood	Danville	
Maine	1785	10/5, 1/4	1786	Statehood	Falmouth	
Maine	1786	9/6, 1/13	1787	Statehood	Portland	
Michigan	1836	9/26-9/30	1836	Planning	Ann Arbor/Pontiac	Rejected
Michigan	1836	12/14-12/15	1836	Planning	Ann Arbor	Accepted
Minnesota	1848	8/26	1848	Statehood	Stillwater	
Mississippi	1849	10/1-10/3	1849	Planning	Jackson	
Mississippi	1851	11/10-11/17	1851	Planning	Jackson	
Nevada	1859	6/6	1859	Planning	Carson City	Territorial
New Mexico	1846		1846			
New Mexico	1848	2/10-2/14	1848	Statehood	Santa Fe	
New Mexico	1905	11/25	1905	Statehood	Albuquerque	

Appendix B.2 - All State Non-constitutional Conventions

State	Start Date	Dates Convened	End Date	Type	Location	Product
North Dakota	1882	1/4	1882	Statehood	Fargo	
North Dakota	1882	6/21	1882	Statehood	Canton	
North Dakota	1883	9/12	1883	Statehood	Fargo	
North Dakota	1887	7/23	1887	Statehood	Fargo	
North Dakota	1888	12/5-12/6	1888	Planning	Jamestown/Watertown	
Oklahoma	1891	12/15	1891	Statehood	Oklahoma City	
Oklahoma	1893	9/30	1893	Statehood	Purcell	
Oklahoma	1893	11/28	1893	Statehood	Kingfisher	
Oklahoma	1896	1/8	1896	Statehood	Oklahoma City	
Oklahoma	1901	11/12	1902	Statehood	Muskogee	
Oklahoma	1902	January	1902	Statehood	Oklahoma City	
Oklahoma	1902	11/28	1902	Statehood	Eufala	
Oklahoma	1903	6/24	1903	Statehood	Shawnee	
Oregon	1841	2/17-2/18, 6/1, 8/1, 10/5	1841	Statehood	Champoeg	
Oregon	1842	9/22	1842	Statehood	Champoeg	
South Carolina	1832	11/19-11/24, 3/11-3/18	1833	Nullification	Columbia	
South Dakota	1882	6/21	1882	Planning	Canton	
South Dakota	1883	6/19-6/20	1883	Statehood	Huron	
South Dakota	1887	7/13-7/18	1887	Statehood	Huron	
South Dakota	1887	12/15	1887	Anti-division	Aberdeen	
South Dakota	1888	7/10-7/11	1888	Statehood	Huron	
Utah	1850		1850			
Virginia	1816	8/19-8/24	1816	Planning	Staunton	Reform
Virginia	1825	7/25-7/31	1825	Planning	Staunton	Reform
Virginia	1842	May	1842	Planning	Clarksburg	
Virginia	1842	8/1-8/3	1842	Planning	Lewisburg	

Appendix B.2 - All State Non-constitutional Conventions

State	Start Date	Dates Convened	End Date	Type	Location	Product
Washington	1889	1/3	1889	Statehood	Ellensburgh	
West Virginia	1861	4/22	1861	Anti-secessionary	Clarksburg	
West Virginia	1861	5/13-5/15	1861	Anti-secessionary	Wheeling	Planning
West Virginia	1861	6/11-6/25, 8/6-8/21	1861	Separation	Wheeling	Ordinance
West Virginia	1863	2/12-2/20	1863	Ratification	Wheeling	

Appendix B.3 - All Territorial Constitutional Conventions

State	Start Date	Dates Convened	End Date	Type	Location	Product
Amer. Samoa	1960	4/20-4/26	1960	Drafting	Fagatogo	1st Const.
Amer. Samoa	1963		1963	Amendatory	Fagatogo	
Amer. Samoa	1965	11/4 & 11/10	1965	Amendatory	Fagatogo	
Amer. Samoa	1966	9/26	1966	Amendatory	Fagatogo	2nd Const.
Amer. Samoa	1971	8/18-October 1972	1972	Amendatory	Fagatogo	Rejected
Amer. Samoa	1972	7/30-October 1973	1973	Amendatory	Fagatogo	Rejected
Amer. Samoa	1982	2/16	1984	Amendatory	Utulei	
Amer. Samoa	1984		1986	Amendatory		Rejected
Amer. Samoa	2010	6/21-7/3	2010	Amendatory	Utulei	Rejected
District of Columbia	1982	1/31-5/29	1982	Drafting	Washington, D.C.	Ratified
Guam	1969	6/1-6/29	1970	Drafting	Hagatña	Rejected
Guam	1977	5/4, 7/1-10/31	1977	Drafting	Hagatña	Rejected
North. Mar.	1976	10/18-12/6	1976	Drafting	Saipan	1st Const.
North. Mar.	1985	6/18-7/21	1985	Amendatory	Saipan	
North. Mar.	1995	6/5-8/3	1995	Amendatory	Saipan	
Puerto Rico	1952	9/17-2/6	1952	Drafting	San Juan	1st Const.
USVI	1964		1965	Drafting		Rejected
USVI	1971	Sept-Sept	1972	Drafting		Rejected
USVI	1977	10/3-	1978	Drafting		Rejected
USVI	1980	3/4-	1980	Drafting		Rejected
USVI	2007	10/29-	2012	Drafting	Charlotte Amalie	Rejected

Appendix B.4 - Provisional State and Territory Conventions

State	Start Date	Dates Convened	End Date	Type	Location	Product
Columbia	1851	8/29	1851	Statehood	Cowlitz Landing, WA	
Deseret	1849	3/5-3/10, 7/1-7/18	1849		Salt Lake City	Rejected
Deseret	1856	3/17-3/27	1856		Salt Lake City	Rejected
Deseret	1862	1/20-4/17	1862		Salt Lake City	
Deseret	1872	2/16-2/28?	1872		Salt Lake City	
East Tennessee	1861	5/30	1861	Drafting	Knoxville	
East Tennessee	1861	6/17	1861	Drafting	Greeneville	
Frankland	1772	Spring	1772		Tennessee	
Frankland	1782	April	1782		Tennessee	
Frankland	1784	8/23	1784		Jonesboro, Tennessee	
Frankland	1784	12/14	1784		Greeneville, Tennessee	Failed
Frankland	1785	11/14	1785		Greeneville, Tennessee	Failed
Frankland	1787	May	1787	Amendatory	Tennessee	
Jackson	1873	7/29-7/30	1873	Statehood	Jackson, Mississippi	Failed
Jefferson	1858	November	1858	Statehood	Denver	
Jefferson	1859	4/11, 4/15, 5/7	1859	Statehood	Auraria, Colorado	
Jefferson	1859	6/6, 8/1	1859	Drafting	Denver, Colorado	
Jefferson	1859	10/3-10/5, 10/10	1859	Drafting	Denver, Colorado	
Denver	1860	September -9/21	1860	Drafting	Denver	
Nataqua	1856	4/1	1856	Planning	Honey Lake, California	
Nataqua/Nevada	1857	8/8	1857	Planning	Genoa, Nevada	
Nataqua/Nevada	1859	7/18-7/28	1859	Drafting	Genoa, Nevada	
Sequoyah	1905	8/21-8/22, 9/5-9/8, 10/14	1905	Drafting	Muskogee: South McAlester OK	Ignored by DC
South Alaska Terr.	1923	11/15-11/20	1923	Planning	Juneau, Alaska	
Superior	1858	8/25	1858	Drafting	Ontonagon, Michigan	
Transylvania	1775	5/23-5/26	1775	Drafting	Boonesborough, Kentucky	
West Kansas	1992	3/17	1992	Planning	Garden City, Kansas	
West Kansas	1992	9/11	1992	Drafting	Ulysses, Kansas	No document

Appendix B.5 - All National Constitutional Conventions (Non-US Govt)

State	Start Date	Dates Convened	End Date	Type	Location	Product
Cherokee Nation	1827	7/26	1827	Drafting	New Echota, GA	1st Const.
Cherokee Nation	1839	6/19, 7/12, 9/6	1839	Drafting	Tah-le-quah, OK	2nd Const.
Cherokee Nation	1866	11/26	1866	Amendatory	Tah-le-quah, OK	
Cherokee Nation	1948		1948	Drafting	Tah-le-quah, OK	
Cherokee Nation	1975		1975	Drafting	Tah-le-quah, OK	
Cherokee Nation	1999	02/26	1999	Drafting	Tah-le-quah, OK	
Chickasaw Nation	1846		1846	Drafting	Boiling Springs	1st Const.
Chickasaw Nation	1848		1848	Drafting	Boiling Springs	2nd Const.
Chickasaw Nation	1856	August & December	1856	Drafting	Tishomingo, OK	3rd Const.
Choctaw Nation	1826		1826	Drafting	Mississippi	1st Const.
Choctaw Nation	1834		1834	Drafting	Kiamichi, Oklahoma	2nd Const.
Choctaw Nation	1838	10/03	1838	Drafting	Nanih-waiya, OK	
Choctaw Nation	1842	11/10	1842	Amendatory	Nanih-waiya, OK	
Choctaw Nation	1850		1850	Amendatory	Nanih-waiya, OK	
Choctaw Nation	1856		1856	Drafting	Skullyville, OK	
Choctaw Nation	1858		1858	Drafting	Doaksville, OK	
Choctaw Nation	1860		1860	Drafting	Nanih-waiya, OK	
Creek Nation	1859		1859	Drafting	Oklahoma	1st Const.
Creek Nation	1867	October	1867	Drafting	Oklahoma	2nd Const.
Seminole Nation	1856		1856	Drafting	Oklahoma	1st Const.
Confederate States of America	1861	2/4	1861	Drafting	Montgomery, AL	National
Federated States of Micronesia	1975	7/12-11/8	1975	Drafting	Saipan	National
Hawaii (Kingdom)	1840		1840	Drafting/Legislative	Honolulu	National
Hawaii (Kingdom)	1852	?-6/14	1852	Drafting/Legislative	Honolulu	National
Hawaii (Kingdom)	1864	7/7-8/13	1864	Drafting/Legislative	Honolulu	National
Indian Nation	1870		1870	Drafting	Okmulgee, OK	
Republic of East Florida	1812	March	1812	Drafting	Fernandina, FL	National

Appendix B.5 - All National Constitutional Conventions (Non-US Govt)

State	Start Date	Dates Convened	End Date	Type	Location	Product
Republic of Indian Stream	1832	6/11-7/9	1832	Drafting	NH	Approved
Rep. of the Marshall Islands	1977	Aug - Nov (3 sessions)	1978	Drafting	Kwajalein, Pac. Trust Terr.	National
Republic of Palau	1978	1/28-4/2	1979	Drafting	Koror, Pac. Trust Terr.	National
Republic of the Rio Grande	1840	1/7	1840	Drafting	Oreveña, Laredo, TX	National
Republic of West Florida	1810	9/22-10/28	1810	Drafting	St. Francisville, LA	National
Republic of Watauga Assoc.	1772		1772	Drafting	Elizabethton, Tennessee	
Texas (Republic)	1832	10/1-10/6, 4/1-4/13	1833	Secessionary/Drafting	San Felipe de Austin	Rejected
Texas (Republic)	1835	10/16; 11/3-11/14	1835	Drafting	Columbia: San Felipe de Austin	National
Texas (Republic)	1836	3/1-3/17	1836	Drafting	Washington-on-the-Brazos	National
Vermont (Republic)	1777	7/2-7/8, 12/25-	1777	Drafting	Windsor	1st state
Vermont (Republic)	1785	6/2-6/8, 9/29-10/21, 2/2-2/14	1786	Drafting	Windsor	2nd state

Appendix B.6 - All Article V Federal Conventions

State	Start Date	Convened	End Date	Type	Location	Product
Alabama	1933	8/8	1933	Ratification	Montgomery	21st Amendment
Arizona	1933	9/5	1933	Ratification	Phoenix	21st Amendment
Arkansas	1933	8/1	1933	Ratification	Little Rock	21st Amendment
California	1933	7/24	1933	Ratification	Sacramento	21st Amendment
Colorado	1933	9/26	1933	Ratification	Denver	21st Amendment
Connecticut	1933	7/11	1933	Ratification	Hartford	21st Amendment
Delaware	1933	6/24	1933	Ratification	Dover	21st Amendment
Florida	1933	11/14	1933	Ratification	Tallahasee	21st Amendment
Idaho	1933	10/17	1933	Ratification	Boise	21st Amendment
Illinois	1933	7/10	1933	Ratification	Springfield	21st Amendment
Indiana	1933	6/26	1933	Ratification	Indianapolis	21st Amendment
Iowa	1933	7/10	1933	Ratification	Des Moines	21st Amendment
Kentucky	1933	11/27	1933	Ratification	Frankfort	21st Amendment
Maine	1933	12/6	1933	Ratification	Augusta	21st Amendment
Maryland	1933	10/18	1933	Ratification	Annapolis	21st Amendment
Massachusetts	1933	6/14	1933	Ratification	Boston	21st Amendment
Michigan	1933	4/10	1933	Ratification	Lansing	21st Amendment
Minnesota	1933	10/10	1933	Ratification	St. Paul	21st Amendment
Missouri	1933	8/29	1933	Ratification	Jefferson City	21st Amendment
Montana	1934	8/6	1934	Ratification	Helena	21st Amendment
New Hampshire	1933	7/11	1933	Ratification	Concord	21st Amendment
New Jersey	1933	6/1	1933	Ratification	Trenton	21st Amendment
New Mexico	1933	11/2	1933	Ratification	Santa Fe	21st Amendment
New York	1933	6/27	1933	Ratification	Albany	21st Amendment
Nevada	1933	9/5	1933	Ratification	Carson City	21st Amendment
Ohio	1933	12/5	1933	Ratification	Columbus	21st Amendment

Appendix B.6 - All Article V Federal Conventions

State	Start Date	Convened	End Date	Type	Location	Product
Oregon	1933	8/7	1933	Ratification	Salem	21st Amendment
Pennsylvania	1933	12/5	1933	Ratification	Harrisburg	21st Amendment
Rhode Island	1933	5/8	1933	Ratification	Providence	21st Amendment
South Carolina	1933	12/4	1933	Ratification	Columbia	Rejected
Tennessee	1933	8/11	1933	Ratification	Nashville	21st Amendment
Texas	1933	11/24	1933	Ratification	Austin	21st Amendment
Utah	1933	12/5	1933	Ratification	Salt Lake City	21st Amendment
Vermont	1933	9/23	1933	Ratification	Montpelier	21st Amendment
Virginia	1933	10/25	1933	Ratification	Richmond	21st Amendment
Washington	1933	10/3	1933	Ratification	Olympia	21st Amendment
West Virginia	1933	7/25	1933	Ratification	Charleston	21st Amendment
Wisconsin	1933	4/25	1933	Ratification	Madison	21st Amendment
Wyoming	1933	5/25	1933	Ratification	Casper	21st Amendment

Appendix B.7 - All Article VII Federal Conventions

State	Start Date	Dates Convened	End Date	Type	Location	Product	Comment
Connecticut	1788	1/3-1/9	1788	Ratification	Hartford	US Constitution	ratified
Delaware	1787	12/4-12/7	1787	Ratification	Dover	US Constitution	ratified
Georgia	1788	12/25-12/31	1788	Ratification	Augusta	US Constitution	ratified
Maryland	1788	4/21-4/26	1788	Ratification	Annapolis	US Constitution	ratified
Massachusetts	1788	1/9-2/6	1788	Ratification	Boston	US Constitution	ratified
New Hampshire	1788	2/13-2/22; 6/18-6/21	1788	Ratification	Exeter; Concord	US Constitution	ratified
New Jersey	1787	12/11-12/20	1787	Ratification	Trenton	US Constitution	ratified
New York	1788	6/17-7/26	1788	Ratification	Poughkeepsie	US Constitution	ratified
North Carolina	1788	7/21-8/4	1788	Ratification	Hillsborough	US Constitution	rejected
North Carolina	1789	11/16-11/21, 1/1	1790	Ratification	Fayetteville	US Constitution	ratified
Pennsylvania	1787	11/20-12/15	1787	Ratification	Philadelphia	US Constitution	ratified
Pennsylvania	1788	9/3	1788	Amendatory	Harrisburg	Amendments	no impact
Rhode Island	1790	3/1-3/6; 5/24-5/29	1790	Ratification	South Kingston; Newport	US Constitution	ratified
South Carolina	1788	5/12-5/23	1788	Ratification	Charleston	US Constitution	ratified
Vermont	1791	1/6-1/10	1791	Ratification	Bennington	US Constitution	ratified
Virginia	1788	6/2-6/25	1788	Ratification	Richmond	US Constitution	ratified

Appendix B.8 - Select Intercolonial and Interstate Conventions

Purpose/Convention	Start Date	Dates Convened	End Date	Type	Location	Product	Comment
United Colonies of New England	1643	5/9	1643		Boston		MA, CT, New Haven and Plymouth
Indian Negotiations	1671	November	1671		Albany		NY, CT, 4 tribes
Indian Negotiations	1677	April	1677		Albany	Silver Covenant	VA, MD, 6 tribes
Indian Negotiations	1684	7/30-8/6	1684		Albany		4 colonies, 5 tribes
Defense	1689		1689		Boston		
Indian Negotiations	1689	7/31	1689		Albany		5 tribes
Defense	1690	5/1	1690		New York		NY, MA, MD, Ply, CT
Defense	1693		1693		New York		
Indian Negotiations	1694		1694	Drafting	Albany	treaty	4 colonies, 5 tribes
Defense	1704		1704		New York		
Defense	1711		1711		Boston		
Indian Negotiations	1722		1722		Albany		
Defense	1744		1744		Albany		
Indian Negotiations	1744		1744		Lancaster, PA		
Defense	1745		1745		Albany		
Indian Negotiations	1745		1745		Albany		
Defense	1747		1747		New York		
Indian Negotiations	1751		1751		Albany		all colonies, 6 tribes
Iroquois diplomacy	1754	6/19-7/11	1754	Limited	Albany		8 colonies
Defense	1757		1757		Boston		
Stamp Act	1765	10/7-10/25	1765		New York		9 colonies
Indian Negotiations	1768		1768		Fort Stanwyx, NY		
British Acts	1774		1774		New York		
1st Continental Congress	1774	9/5-10/26	1774	Drafting	Philadelphia	Cont. Association	Ratified, 12 colonies
2nd Continental Congress	1776	6/12-11/15	1777	Drafting	Philadelphia	Articles of Confed.	Ratified, 13 states

Appendix B.8 - Select Intercolonial and Interstate Conventions

Purpose/Convention	Start Date	Dates Convened	End Date	Type	Location	Product	Comment
Paper Currency/Public Credit	1776	12/25-1/2	1777		Providence		4 states
Prices	1777	3/26-4/3	1777		York Town, PA		6 states
Military Matters	1777	6/26-6/27	1777		Providence		4 states
Paper Money/Trade	1777	7/30-8/5	1777		Springfield, MA		5 states
Prices	1778	1/15-2/1	1778		New Haven, CT		7 states
Trade	1779	10/20-10/28	1779		Hartford		5 states
Prices	1780	1/29-2/8	1780		Philadelphia		7 states
Military Matters	1780	8/3-8/9	1780		Boston		3 states
Military Matters	1780	11/8-11/22	1780		Hartford		5 states
Military Matters	1781	4/12-4/17	1781		Providence		3 states
Annapolis Commerce Conv.	1786	9/11	1786	Planning	Annapolis	National	Failed, 5 states
Federal Convention	1787	5/24-9/17	1787	Drafting	Philadelphia	US Constitution	Ratified, 12 states
Hartford Convention	1814	12/15-1/5	1815		Hartford, CT		5 states
Nashville Convention	1850	6/3-6/12	1850	Planning	Nashville	National	Failed, 9 states
Nashville Convention	1850	11/11-11/18	1850	Planning	Nashville	National	Failed, 5 states
Washington Peace Conv.	1861	2/4-2/27	1861	Amendatory	Washington	National	Failed, 23 states
Grasshopper/Locust Conv.	1876	10/25-10/26	1876	Planning	Omaha	Regional	6 states
Colorado River Compact	1922		1922		Santa Fe	Regional	

Appendix B.9 - All Amendatory Conventions

State	Start Date	Dates Convened	End Date	Location	Product
Florida	1862 1/14-1/27		1862	Tallahasee	
Georgia	1789 1/4-1/20		1789	Augusta	
Georgia	1795 5/3-5/16		1795	Louisville	
Georgia	1833 5/6-5/15		1833	Milledgeville	
Georgia	1839 5/6-5/15		1839	Milledgeville	
Hawaii	1968 7/15-10/21		1968	Honolulu	
Hawaii	1978 7/5-12/2		1978	Honolulu	
Louisiana	1992 8/23-9/22		1992	Baton Rouge	Rejected
Maryland	1792		1792	Annapolis	Rejected
Massachusetts	1820 11/15-6/9		1821	Boston	
Massachusetts	1853 5/4-8/2		1853	Boston	Rejected
Massachusetts	1917 6/6-8/21,		1919	Boston	
Missouri	1922 5/15-11/6		1923	Jefferson City	Rejected
Nebraska	1919 12/2-3/25, 10/19		1920	Lincoln	
Nevada	1863 11/2-12/3		1863	Carson City	Rejected
Nevada	1864 7/4-7/28		1864	Carson City	1st state
New Hampshire	1791 9/7-9/16, 2/8-2/24, 5/30-8/27, 9/5-9/6		1792	Concord	3rd state
New Hampshire	1850 11/6-11/22, 12/3-1/3, 4/16-4/17		1851	Concord	Rejected
New Hampshire	1876 12/6-12/15		1876	Concord	
New Hampshire	1889 1/2-1/12		1889	Concord	
New Hampshire	1902 12/2-12/19		1902	Concord	
New Hampshire	1912 6/5-6/22		1912	Concord	
New Hampshire	1918 6/7-6/7/1918, 1/13-1/29/1920, 1/28/1921, 2/16/1923		1923	Concord	Rejected
New Hampshire	1930 6/4-6/13		1930	Concord	
New Hampshire	1938 5/11-6/1/1938, 11/8/1938, 9/23-9/26/1941		1941	Concord	
New Hampshire	1948 5/12-6/4		1948	Concord	
New Hampshire	1956 5/15-6/13/1956, 12/2-12/4/1959		1959	Concord	
New Hampshire	1964 5/13-6/10, 7/8		1964	Concord	

Appendix B.9 - All Amendatory Conventions

State	Start Date	Dates Convened	End Date	Location	Product
New Hampshire	1974 5/8-6/26		1974	Concord	
New Hampshire	1984 5/9-6/28		1984	Concord	
New Jersey	1942		1942	Trenton	
New Mexico	1890 8/18-8/20		1890	Santa Fe	Rejected
New York	1801 10/13-10/27		1801	Albany	
New York	1915 4/6-9/10		1915	Albany	
New York	1938 4/5-8/26		1938	Albany	
New York	1967 4/4-9/26		1967	Albany	Rejected
North Carolina	1823 11/10-11/15		1823	Raleigh	Rejected
North Carolina	1835 6/4-7/11		1835	Raleigh	
North Carolina	1861 5/20-6/28, 11/18-12/13, 1/20-2/26, 4/21-5/13		1862	Raleigh	
North Carolina	1875 9/6-10/11		1875	Raleigh	
Ohio	1912 1/9-8/26		1912	Columbus	
Pennsylvania	1789 11/24-2/26, 8/9-9/2		1790	Philadelphia	2nd state
Pennsylvania	1837 5/2-2/22		1838	Harrisburg	3rd state
Pennsylvania	1872 11/12-11/27; 1/7-11/3		1873	Harrisburg; Philadelphia	
Rhode Island	1944 3/28		1944	Providence	
Rhode Island	1951 6/1-6/3		1951	Providence	
Rhode Island	1955 6/20		1955	Providence	
Rhode Island	1958 1/31-2/7		1958	Providence	
Rhode Island	1973 9/4-10/4		1973	Providence	
South Dakota	1889 3/3		1889	Huron	
South Dakota	1889 4/2		1889	Huron	
Tennessee	1865 1/9-1/16		1865	Nashville	
Tennessee	1953 4/21-6/5, 7/14		1953	Nashville	
Tennessee	1959 7/21-7/31		1959	Nashville	
Tennessee	1965 7/1-10/28		1965	Nashville	
Tennessee	1971 8/2-9/15		1971	Nashville	

Appendix B.9 - All Amendatory Conventions

State	Start Date	Dates Convened	End Date	Location	Product
Tennessee	1977	8/1-12/21	1977	Nashville	
Texas	1974	1/8-7/30	1974	Austin	Rejected
Vermont	1814	1st Thursday July -7/9	1814	Montpelier	
Vermont	1822	2/21-2/23	1822	Montpelier	
Vermont	1828	6/26-6/28	1828	Montpelier	Council
Vermont	1836	1/6-1/14	1836	Montpelier	
Vermont	1850	1/2-1/11	1850	Montpelier	
Vermont	1857	1/7-1/12	1857	Montpelier	
Vermont	1870	6/8-6/15	1870	Montpelier	
Virginia	1945	4/30-5/2	1945	Richmond	Limited
Virginia	1956	3/5-3/7	1956	Richmond	Limited
Amer. Samoa	1963		1963	Fagatogo	
Amer. Samoa	1965	11/4 & 11/10	1965	Fagatogo	2nd Const.
Amer. Samoa	1966	9/26	1966	Fagatogo	Rejected
Amer. Samoa	1971	8/18-October 1972	1972	Fagatogo	Rejected
Amer. Samoa	1972	7/30-October 1973	1973	Fagatogo	
Amer. Samoa	1982	2/16	1984	Utulei	
Amer. Samoa	1984		1986		Rejected
Amer. Samoa	2010	6/21-7/3	2010	Utulei	Rejected
North. Mar.	1985	6/18-7/21	1985	Saipan	
North. Mar.	1995	6/5-8/3	1995	Saipan	
Frankland	1787	May	1787	Tennessee	
Pennsylvania - Fed. Const.	1788	9/3	1788	Harrisburg	Amendments
Nashville Convention	1850	6/3-6/12	1850	Nashville	National
Washington Peace Conv.	1861	2/4-2/27	1861	Washington	National

Appendix C
1787 DELEGATE COMMISSIONS

It is often the contention of opponents of an Article V amendatory convention that the 1787 Philadelphia convention ran away and, therefore, we can expect any future amendatory convention to do the same. Their claim is that the limits of the 21 February 1787 call to convention from the Confederation Congress spelled out the extent of the delegates' powers and that these limits were exceeded. An examination of the commissions of the 1787 delegates shows that this assertion is untrue. When compared to the report of the 1786 Annapolis Convention, the wording of the resultant state delegate commissions becomes apparent as to the States' intentions. The 14 September 1786 report of the Annapolis Convention directly provided some of the wording cited in the delegate commissions of the States. Using selected sections of the Annapolis Convention proceedings,

> "*That the State of New Jersey had enlarged the object of their appointment, empowering their Commissioners, 'to consider how far an uniform system in their commercial regulations and other important matters, might be necessary to the common interest and permanent harmony of the several States,' and to report such an Act on the subject, as when ratified by them 'would enable the United States in Congress assembled,* **effectually to provide for the exigencies of the Union.**'"

> "*In this persuasion, your Commissioners submit an opinion,* **that the Idea of extending the powers of their Deputies, to other objects, than those of Commerce, which has been adopted by the State of New Jersey, was an improvement on the original plan, and will deserve to be incorporated into that of a future Convention;** *they are the more naturally led to this conclusion, as in the course of their reflections on the subject, they have been induced to think, that the power of regulating trade*

is of such comprehensive extent, and **will enter so far into the general System of the federal government, that to give it efficacy, and to obviate questions and doubts concerning its precise nature and limits, may require a correspondent adjustment of other parts of the Federal System.**"

"That there are important defects in the system of the Federal Government is acknowledged by the Acts of all those States, which have concurred in the present Meeting; That the defects, upon a closer examination, may be found greater and more numerous, than even these acts imply, *is at least so far probable, from the embarrassments which characterize the present State of our national affairs, foreign and domestic, as may reasonably be supposed to merit a deliberate and candid discussion, in some mode, which will unite the Sentiments and Council's of all the States. In the choice of the mode, your Commissioners are of opinion,* **that a Convention of Deputies from the different States, for the special and sole purpose of entering into this investigation, and digesting a plan for supplying such defects as may be discovered to exist,** *will be entitled to a preference from considerations, which will occur, without being particularized."*

"*Under this impression, Your Commissioners, with the most respectful deference, beg leave to suggest their unanimous conviction, that it may essentially tend to advance the interests of the union, if the States, by whom they have been respectively delegated, would themselves concur, and use their endeavours to procure the concurrence of the other States, in the appointment of Commissioners, to meet at Philadelphia on the second Monday in May next,* **to take into consideration the situation of the United States, to devise such further provisions as shall appear to them necessary to render the constitution of the Federal Government <u>adequate to the exigencies of the Union</u>;** *and to report such an Act for that purpose to the United States in Congress assembled, as when agreed to, by them, and afterwards confirmed by the Legislatures of every State, will effectually provide for the same.*"[1]

The States produced commissions which vary in the wording but adhere to generally the same sentiment. The exceptions being the commissions of the resolution amendments made in the Massachusetts Senate and those of New Hampshire and North Carolina. The original

---

[1] http://avalon.law.yale.edu/18th_century/annapoli.asp

resolution passed by the Massachusetts House contained language in line with the Annapolis report and the commissions from the other States.

Connecticut: [17 May 1787] "...and to discuss upon *such Alterations and Provisions,* agreeable to the general Principles of Republican Government, as they shall think proper, *to render the federal Constitution adequate to the Exigencies of Government, and the Preservation of the Union,*..."[2]

Delaware: [3 Feb 1787] "...and to join with then devising, deliberating on, and discussing, *such Alterations and further Provisions, as may be necessary to render the Foederal Constitution adequate to the Exigencies of the Union,*..."[3]

Georgia: [10 Feb 1787] "...and to join with then in devising and discussing all *such alterations and farther provisions, as may be necessary to render the federal constitution adequate to the exigencies of the union,* ..."[4]

Maryland: [26 May 1787] "...to assemble in convention at Philadelphia, for the purpose of revising the federal system, and to join with them in considering *such alterations, and further provisions, as may be necessary to render the federal constitution adequate to the exigencies of the union*, and in reporting such an act for that purpose to the United States in congress assembled,..."[5]

Massachusetts House: [22 Feb 1878] "...for the sole & express purpose of revising the articles of Confederation, and reporting to Congress & the several Legislatures, *such alterations & provisions* therein, as shall when agreed to in Congress, and confirmed by the States, *render the federal Constitution adequate to the exigencies of Government, & the preservation of the Union-*"

Massachusetts Senate: [9 Mar 1787] "And it is further Resolved, that the Said Delegates on the part of this Commonwealth be, and they are hereby instructed not to accede to any alterations or additions that may be proposed to be made in the present Articles of Confederation, which may appear to them, not to consist with the true republican Spirit

---

[2] http://csac.history.wisc.edu/delegate_inst13.pdf
[3] http://csac.history.wisc.edu/delegate_inst6.pdf
[4] http://csac.history.wisc.edu/delegate_inst7.pdf
[5] http://csac.history.wisc.edu/delegate_inst14.pdf

and Genius of the Said Confederation: and particularly that they by no means interfere with the fifth of the Said Articles which provides, 'for the annual election of Delegates in Congress, with a power reserved to each State to recall its Delegates, or any of them within the Year & to send others in the stead for the remainder of the year-"[6]

New Hampshire: [27 Jun 1787] "...it was not possible in the infant state of our republic to devise a system which in the course of time and experience, would not manifest imperfections, that it would be necessary to reform. And Whereas, the limited powers, which by the articles of confederation are vested in the Congress of the united states, have been found inadequate to the *enlarged purposes* which they were intended to produce."

Continuing later, "...and with them to discuss and decide upon the effectual means to remedy the defects of our federal union; and to procure, and secure, the *enlarged purposes* which it was intended to effect, and to report such an act, to the United States, will effectually provide for the same-"[7]

New Jersey: [24 Nov 1786] "...for the purpose of taking into consideration the state of the Union as to trade and other important objects, and of devising *such further provisions as shall appear necessary to render the Constitution of the federal government adequate to the exigencies* thereof."[8]

New York: [26 Feb 1787] "...for the sole and express purpose of revising the Articles of Confederation and reporting to Congress, and to the several legislatures, *such alterations and provisions* therein, as shall, when agreed to in Congress, and confirmed by the several state, *render the federal constitution adequate to the exigencies of government and the preservation of the Union,*..."[9]

North Carolina: [6 Jan 1787] "...and with them to discuss and decide upon the most effectual means to remove the defects of our federal union, and to procure the *enlarged purposes* which it was intended to effect,..."[10]

Pennsylvania: [30 Dec 1787] "...and to join with the in devising,

---

[6] http://csac.history.wisc.edu/delegate_inst11.pdf
[7] http://csac.history.wisc.edu/delegate_inst15.pdf
[8] http://csac.history.wisc.edu/delegate_inst3.pdf
[9] http://csac.history.wisc.edu/delegate_inst10.pdf
[10] http://csac.history.wisc.edu/delegate_inst5.pdf

deliberating on, and discussing *such alterations and further provisions as may be necessary to render the federal constitution fully adequate to the exigencies of the Union,...*"[11]

South Carolina: [8 Mar 1787] "...they being duly authorized and impowered in devising and discussing all *such alterations, clauses, articles and provisions as may be thought necessary to render the federal constitution entirely adequate* to the actual situation and future good government of the confederated states, and that the said deputies or commissioners, or a majority of those who shall be present, provided the state be not represented by less than two, do join in reporting such an act to the united states in congress assembled, as when approved and agreed to by them, and duly ratified and confirmed by the several states, will *effectually provide for the exigencies of the union.*"[12]

Virginia: [23 Nov 1786] "...and to join with them in devising and discussing *all such alterations and further provisions, as may be necessary to render the Federal Constitution [the Articles] adequate to the exigencies of the Union,...*"[13]

Note a few issues that are involved here:

First, Virginia, New Jersey, Pennsylvania, North Carolina, Delaware, and Georgia had [chronologically] issued their convention delegate commissions BEFORE the 21 Feb 1787[14] call to convention issued by the Confederation Congress. Additionally, New York had already made their decision to attend before the Congress's call to convention and then issued delegate commissions on 26 Feb 1787 – five days after Congress's call to convention. Therefore, fully half the States had already committed to attending the Philadelphia Grand Federal Convention before Congress had acted. Congress was acting in response to the States, and not in leading them.

Second, note the similarity in the wording of the commissions to Virginia's call to convention and their delegate commissions. The same phrasing is present in variations of "...all such alterations and further provisions, as may be necessary to render the federal government adequate to the exigencies of the Union..." This wording directly reflected the report of the Annapolis commissioners. The New Hampshire and North

---

[11] http://csac.history.wisc.edu/delegate_inst4.pdf
[12] http://csac.history.wisc.edu/delegate_inst12.pdf
[13] http://csac.history.wisc.edu/delegate_inst2.pdf
[14] http://csac.history.wisc.edu/delegate_inst8.pdf

Carolina commissions use nearly identical wording and refer to the "enlarged purposes" of the government thereby granting their delegates the authority to remodel the federal government.

Third, only Massachusetts and New York restricted their delegates from addressing <u>all</u> problems. New York utilized the same language implying that the state acceded to the changes and granted the powers to remodel the federal government.

Lastly, in James Madison's notes from Congress for 21 Feb 1787, the day that Congress issued the call of convention, he noted that, "The reserve of many members made it difficult to decide their real wishes and expectations from the present crisis of our affairs. All agreed and owned that the federal government in its existing shape was inefficient and could not last long."[15]

We can firmly conclude that the state legislatures knew exactly what they were doing in sending their delegations to Philadelphia to reform the federal government. The States had all expressed their desires for a more centralized government and had recognized the issues and problems prevalent nationwide. The fact that four states out of twelve, that is one-third, presented plans for redesigning the federal government and no state presented a plan that was restricted to a modification of the Articles of Confederation shows that the notion of the convention running away is not contemporary to the convention but is a modern claim.[16] The convention did not runaway, rather the States had every intention of doing exactly as they did prior to sending their delegates to Philadelphia.

---

[15] http://csac.history.wisc.edu/delegate_inst9.pdf
[16] Gov. Edmund Randolph and James Madison presented the Virginia Plan; Charles Pinckney presented the South Carolina Plan; William Paterson presented the New Jersey Plan; and Alexander Hamilton presented his own plan.

Appendix D
GLOSSARY OF TERMS

Throughout this work a number of terms are used that refer to specific concepts in the amendment process. For the sake of clarity, those terms are formally defined herein. Since so much of the discussion in this book is of a legal nature, it is necessary to turn to sources of a legal nature in order to provide those definitions. The passage of time has changed some definitions making it difficult to determine which is the proper explanation of a given term. To better meet the need for a definition, several sources were consulted and the definitions are then explained here.

The Framers were very concerned about the choice of wording and the records of the convention show that debate including making reference to individual books and to the careful selection of wording.[1] They were meticulous in their writing and editing being fully aware, as so many of them were lawyers, that their work would be considered and argued in the courts endlessly making every word, and its definition, vitally important.

At the time of the 1787 Philadelphia Convention, the legal terminology would have been accessed through a number of law dictionaries. The most prominent of the time was Timothy Cunningham's *A New and Complete Law-Dictionary*, specifically the 3rd Edition published in 1783. A second commonly used dictionary was that of Thomas Blount, *A Law-Dictionary and Glossary* published in its 3rd Edition in 1717. Another was the extremely popular *A New Law-Dictionary* published by Giles Jacob; the most used edition being the 8th issued in 1762 although a 9th Edition was issued in

---

[1] Gregory E. Maggs, "A Concise Guide to Using Dictionaries from the Founding Era to Determine the Original Meaning of the Constitution," *George Washington Law Review* 82 (2014): 370

1772 and a 10th Edition in 1782.² Jacob's is potentially the more frequently turned to dictionary as he was "heavily influence by John Locke" as were the Framers.³ Some of the 1787 delegates may have brought along references works of their own to the convention but most likely they turned to the Library Company of Philadelphia which is known, thanks to their service to the 1787 convention and to the Continental Congresses,⁴ as the "Delegates' Library." All of these law dictionaries were, and are still, in the possession of the Library Company of Philadelphia.⁵ Any record of the delegates' use of the library that may have once existed has, sadly, been lost to history.⁶

We can turn to these works to understand what the delegates thought that were meaning when they used a particular word or phrase in the Constitution. But restricting ourselves to a singular definition or even to a few definitions set in a narrow timeframe may not always give the correct answer. Because "dictionaries tend to lag behind linguistic realities" a certain word or phrase may be popular in use at the time but not included in the dictionaries of the day until they are updated later, sometimes even decades later.⁷ For this reason, some entries include a definition from John Bouvier's *A Law Dictionary*, the 1st Edition printed in 1839. Finally, the modern definitions are extracted and paraphrased from *Black's Law Dictionary*, 10th Edition, as it is the pre-eminent modern law dictionary. The *Black's* definitions are modified to focus on the amendatory convention subject. For the verbatim, explicit and accepted definition, please see *Black's*. To differentiate the sources used in the glossary listings, this convention is provided:

Cunningham = (1783); Bouvier = (1856); and Black = (Modern).

Agenda: (n.) Modern: A list of topics, items or issues for consideration and discussion in a convention. These are usually ordered for consideration.

---

[2] Robert G. Natelson, "A Bibliography for Originalist Research," (2007), available at: https://www.fed-soc.org/publications/detail/a-bibliography-for-originalist-research

[3] Gregory E. Maggs, "A Concise Guide to Using Dictionaries from the Founding Era to Determine the Original Meaning of the Constitution," *George Washington Law Review* 82 (2014): 391

[4] Ralph Ketcham, *James Madison, A Biography* (Charlottesville, VA: University of Virginia Press, 1990), 61

[5] http://www.librarycompany.org/

[6] Jack P. Greene, *The Intellectual Heritage of the Constitutional Era, The Delegates' Library* (Philadelphia: Library Company of Philadelphia, 1986), 5

[7] Antonin Scalia & Bryan A. Garner, "A Note on the Use of Dictionaries," *Green Bag*, 2d Series, 16, no.4 (Summer 2013), 423 – reprinted as Appendix A of: Antonin Scalia and Bryan A. Garner, *Reading Law: The Interpretation of Legal Text*, (St. Paul, MN: Thomson/West, 2012)

Amend: (v., 13th cent.) Modern: 1) To correct or make minor changes in or to something; to rectify or set right; to address omissions. 2) To change the wording of a constitution, statute, ordinance, regulation or motion by the addition, insertion or the striking out of words intended to alter or add powers or limitations to the instrument.

Amendatory: (adj., 1859) Modern: Intended or employed to be for amending or in relation to the process or act of amending.

Amendatory convention: (n.) Modern: A convention limited in power and purpose to the discussion, debate, proposal and recommendation solely of amendments to a constitution of some other work.

Amendment: (n., 17th cent.) 1783: Cunningham does not directly address constitutional amendment, instead the dictionary addresses statutory amendment of Common Law. 1856: An alteration or change of something proposed in a bill. Modern:1) A formal and typically minor addition or revision (in proportion to the total document) formally suggested or done to a constitution, statute, pleading, motion, order or other instrument; often a change created through the addition, correction or deletion in the wording. 2) The formal process or pursuance of a change or revision.

Anti-federalist: (n., 1787) Modern: Historically, a person who opposed the increasing of the powers of the federal government and/or the ratification of the United States Constitution. The usage is generally limited to the period covering the time of the drafting and ratification of the United States Constitution of 1787.

Application: (n., 15th cent.) 1856: The act of making a request for something. Modern: In relation to the United States Constitution, a formal request, petition or demand for the convocation of an Article V convention.

Call: (n., 13th cent.) Modern: 1) A command, demand or request, specifically to come or to assemble in a formal body; an invitation or summons to a convention, in this particular scenario, to an amendatory convention. 2) (18th cent. Parliamentary Law) A formal written notice of a meeting which states the date, time, place and the agenda or issue of a convention, sent in advance to the prospective members.

Comitia: (n., Latin for "assembly," Roman Law) An assembly of the Roman people called together in a specific location for a legislative, judicial or electoral purpose. There were two, the Comitia Tributa for the civilians and the Comitia Centuriata for the soldiers.

Commission: (n., 14th cent.) 1783: Is for the most part in the understanding of the law, as much as *delegatio* with the civilians, and is taken for the warrant, or letters patent, that all men exercising jurisdiction, either ordinary or extraordinary, have for their power to hear or determine any cause or action. 1856: A person authorized to act in a certain matter. Letters-patent granted by the government, under the public seal, to a person appointed to an office. Modern: 1) A warrant of authority issued by the government, court or otherwise body endowed with the requisite authority which grants power to a person to carry out official acts for one of more other persons, as in the formal naming of a delegate to a convention. 2) The formal, usually documented authority by which one person acts for another or a group.

Commissioner: (n., 15th cent.) 1783: Is he that hath commission, as letters patent, or other lawful warrant to execute any public office. 1856: One has a lawful commission to execute a public office. Modern: One who either directs a commission (body of delegates or commissioners); is a member of a commission or other authorized body, or acts on behalf of others in a convention.

Concurrent power: (n., 1812) Modern: A political power that is exercised independently by (usually) both state and federal governments within the same area of law. It may also be a power concurrent to a state and a county depending on the state law, or concurrent to a city and county.

Constitution: (n., 18th cent., from the Latin "constitutio" meaning an imperial decree and later, a collection of laws complied from orations, edicta, mandata, dicreta and rescripta.) 1856: The fundamental law of the state, containing the principles upon which the government is founded, and regulating the divisions of the sovereign powers, directing to what persons each of these powers is to be confided, and the, manner it is to be exercised as, the Constitution of the United States. Modern: 1) The plan or philosophy of the construction of an idea, 2) The fundamental or organic law of a nation or state which details the institutions, and structures of the government and defines the limitations and powers of the government and guarantees the liberties of the people, 3) the formal (usually, but not necessarily) written document along with any amendments.

Constitutional: (adj., 18th cent.) 1856: That which is consonant to, and agrees with the constitution. Modern: Relating to or involving a constitution, or the quality of being in concordance with a constitution.

Contio: (n., Latin for "public meeting" Roman Law) A public meeting in which a magistrate summons the people to hear a speech or hear a judicial, electoral or magisterial decree.

Convene: (v., 15th cent.) To call together or to cause people to assemble for a meeting or a convention.

Conventio: (n., Latin for "to come together" from the word "convenire") 1783: Is a word much used both in ancient and modern law-pleadings for an agreement of convenant. Modern: Historically, an agreement between two or more persons and used to describe the formal meetings of people for specific business.

Convention: (n., 15th cent.) 1783: Is properly where a parliament is assembled, but no act is passed, or bill signed. 1856: This term is applied to a selecting of the delegates elected by the people for other purposes than usual legislation. It is mostly used to denote all assembly to make or amend the constitution of, a state, but it sometimes indicates an assembly of the delegates of the people to nominate officers to be supported at an election. Modern: A specific, elected and deliberative assembly brought together for the purpose of drafting, framing, revising or amending a constitution. Similarly, 1783: convention parliament: On the abdication of King James II, an. 1689. The assembly of the states of the kingdom to take care to their rights and liberties, and who settled King William and Queen Mary on the throne, was called the convention: and the lords and commons thus convened were declared the two houses of parliament, notwithstanding the want of any writ of summons, etc.

Delegate: (n., 15th cent.) 1856: A delegate is also a person elected to some deliberative assembly, usually one for the nomination of officers. Modern: 1) One who, as a representative, acts on the behalf of another person or group, particularly, one who is elected or appointed to speak for, vote on behalf of, or make decisions for a group. 2) (Parliamentary Law) One who is a voting member of a convention.

Delegated power: (n., 17th cent.) A political power that has been ascribed to another lower authority, often temporarily.

Deputy: (n., 5th cent.) 1783: Is he that exercises in another man's right, either office or other things. 1856: One authorized by an officer to exercise the office or right which the officer possesses, for and in place of the latter. Modern: A person appointed or delegated to act on behalf of others. Usually not an elected position.

Enumerated power: (n., 1805) A power expressly delegated to a government by a constitution. Also called an expressed or explicit power.

Implied power: (n., 1807) A power that is not enumerated in a constitution but is necessary to execute an expressed power.

Incidental power: (n., 17th cent.) Although not an expressed power, a power that is part of and necessary in order to execute an expressed power.

Instructed delegate: (n., 1899) A delegate who has been elected or appointed to act on behalf of others but has been bound to vote in accordance with the expressed wishes of their constituency. Such a delegate may have been supplied with written instructions or parameters of their power.

Justiciability: (n., 15th cent.) The condition, quality or state of an issue to be appropriate for adjudication.

Plenary: (adj., 15th cent.) 1856: Full, complete. Modern: 1) Complete, entire, unlimited or full powered, 2) (Of an assembly) To possess the attendance of all members or participants.

Plenary power: (n., 16th cent.) Broadly construed, or virtually unlimited powers.

Plenipotentiary: (n., 17th cent.) 1856: Possessing full powers. Modern: One who has the full powers of government to act for a government, i.e., a representative to another country.

Promulgate: (v., 16th cent.) 1783: Is first to make a law, and then to declare, publish, and proclaim the same to public view. Modern: 1) To announce, declare or proclaim. 2) To place in effect or in force, a law or decree. 3) To publish a proposed rule, regulation, amendment, constitution or other public notice.

Prorogue: (v., 15th cent.) 1783: To prolong, or put off to another day. The difference between a prorogation and an adjournment, or continuance of the parliament, is, that by the prorogation in open court there is a session, and then such bills as passed in either house, or both houses, and had not the royal assent to them, must at the next assembly begin again. Modern: To postpone or defer. To discontinue or suspend a session of a legislative body. Often done to forestall (undesired) legislative action.

Ratification: (n., 15th cent.) 1783: A ratifying or confirming. Modern: The enactment or adoption of an act, specifically, the last step in the formal process of amending.

Refer: (v., 17th cent. Parliamentary Law) To send to a committee or body for consideration or investigation. Often used to kill a bill or amendment.

Rescission: (n., 17th cent. Civil Law) Annulment of avoidance of a judicial or legislative act. The retraction of a convention application or the ratification of a pending amendment.

Reserved power: (n., 1831) A power denied to a government as it is not enumerated or is prohibited by a constitution. It is retained by the people or by another level of government.

Ultra vires: (adj., Latin for "beyond the powers") Unauthorized power beyond the scope of the granted powers of an assembly or law.

Uninstructed delegate: (n., 1962) A delegate who has been elected or appointed to act on behalf of others but is free to vote according to their own conscience.

Validity: (adj., 16th cent.) The quality of being legally sufficient or binding. In terms of a state application for a convention, the quality of being beyond the question of the Congress.

Bibliography
CITED MATERIALS

Books

Adams, Willi Paul. *The First American Constitutions, Republican Ideology and the Making of the State Constitutions in the Revolutionary Era.* Lanham, MD: Rowman & Littlefield, 2001.

Biggs, Andy. *The Con of the Con-Con, The Case Against the States Amending the U. S. Constitution.* Gilbert, AZ: Freeman Press, 2015.

Bilder, Mary Sarah. *Madison's Hand, Revising the Constitutional Convention.* Cambridge, MA: Harvard University Press, 2015.

Bond, James E., David E. Engdahl, and Henry N. Butler. *A Constitutional Convention.* Washington, D.C.: National Legal Center for the Public Interest, 1987.

Botsford, George Willis. *The Roman Assemblies From Their Origin to the End of the Republic.* New York: Macmillan, 1909.

Bouvier, John. *A Law Dictionary, Adapted to the Constitution and Laws of the United States of America and to the Several States of the American Union.* 6th Ed., Philadelphia: Childs and Peterson, 1856.

Brennan, Thomas E. *The Article V Amendatory Constitutional Convention.* Lanham, MD: Lexington Books, 2014.

Brookhiser, Richard. *Alexander Hamilton, American.* New York: Touchstone Books, 1999.

Brown, Everett S. *Ratification of the Twenty-First Amendment to the Constitution of the United States: State Convention Records and Laws.* Ann Arbor: University of Michigan Press, 1938.

Caplan, Russell B. *Constitutional Brinkmanship.* New York: Oxford University Press, 1988.

Carroll, Bartholomew. *Historical Collections of South Carolina, Vol. 2.* New York: Harper and Brothers, 1836.

Chaput, Eric J. *The People's Martyr: Thomas Wilson Dorr and His 1842 Rhode Island Rebellion.* Lawrence: University Press of Kansas, 2013.

Chester, Alden & Edwin Melvin Williams. *Courts and Lawyers of New York: A History 1609-1925, Vol. I.* New York: American Historical Society, 1925.

Collier, Christopher & James S. Collier. *Decision at Philadelphia*. New York: Ballantine Books, 1986, 2007 ed.

Conley, Patrick T. & Robert G. Flanders, Jr. *The Rhode Island State Constitution: A Reference Guide*. Westport, CT: Praeger, 2007.

Corbett, William, John Wright, & Thomas Curson Hansard. *The Parliamentary History of England, from the Earliest Period to the Year 1803*. London: R. Bagshaw, Oct. 1806.

Cruger, Lewis. *Journal of the First Congress of the American Colonies*. New York: E. Winchester, 1845.

Cunningham, Timothy. *A New and Complete Law-Dictionary, or, General Abridgment of the Law*. London: J.F. and C. Rivington, et al, 1783. Reprinted by the LawBook Exchange, 2003.

Davies, Norman. *The Isles – A History*. New York: Oxford University Press, 1999.

De Grazia, Sebastian. *A County With No Name, Tales From The Constitution*. New York: Vintage Books, 1997.

Debo, Angie. *The Rise and Fall of the Choctaw Republic*. Norman: University of Oklahoma Press, 1961.

Dinan, John J. *The American State Constitutional Tradition*. Lawrence: University Press of Kansas, 2006.

Dixon, Max. *The Wataugans*. Johnson City, TN: The Overmountain Press, 1989.

Dodd, Walter Fairleigh. *The Revision and Amendment of State Constitutions*. Baltimore: Johns Hopkins Press, 1910.

Doyle, John Andrew. *English Colonies in America – The Puritan Colonies, Vol. 2*. New York: Henry Holt, 1886.

Edel, Wilbur. *A Constitutional Convention – Threat or Challenge?*. New York: Praeger, 1981.

Edgar, Walter. *Partisans & Redcoats, The Southern Conflict That Turned the Tide of the American Revolution*. New York: Perennial, 2003.

Elliot, Jonathan. *The Debates in the Several State Conventions on the Adoption of the Federal Constitution*. Philadelphia: J.B. Lippincott, 2d ed., 1836.

Farrand, Max. *The Records of the Federal Convention of 1787, Vols. I, II, III and IV*. New Haven: Yale University Press, 1911 rev. 1937.

Flint, Martha Bockée. *Early Long Island: A Colonial Study*. New Rochelle, NY: Knickerbocker Press, 1896.

Foner, Eric. *A Short History of Reconstruction, 1863-1877*. New York: Harper & Row, 1990.

Freedman, Samuel S. & Pamela J. Naughton. *ERA, May A State Change Its Vote?*. Detroit, MI: Wayne State University Press, 1978

Galvin, John R. *The Minute Men, The First Fight: Myths and Realities of the American Revolution*. Washington, D.C.: Brassey's, 1989, 1996 ed.

Garner, Bryan A., ed. *Black's Law Dictionary*. 10th Ed. Eagan, MN: West/Thomson Reuters, 2014.

Gibson, Arrell Morgan. *Oklahoma: A History of Five Centuries.* Norman: University of Oklahoma Press, 1981.

Gold, David M. *The Great Tea Party in the Old Northwest, State Constitutional Conventions, 1847-1851.* New Orleans: Quid Pro Books, 2015.

Goodspeed, Weston Arthur. *The Province and the States: Minnesota, Montana, North Dakota and South Dakota.* Madison, WI: Western Historical Association, 1904. In multiple volumes.

Grasso, Christopher. *A Speaking Aristocracy: Public Discourse in Eighteenth Century Connecticut.* Chapel Hill: University of North Carolina Press, 1999.

Greene, Jack P. *The Intellectual Heritage of the Constitutional Era, The Delegates' Library.* Philadelphia: Library Company of Philadelphia, 1986.

Gross, Robert A. *The Minutemen and Their World.* New York: Hill and Wang, 1976

Guerra, Darren Patrick. *Perfecting the Constitution, The Case for the Article V Amendment Process.* Lanham, MD: Lexington Books, 2013.

Gunderson, Robert Gray. *Old Gentlemen's Convention.* Madison: University of Wisconsin Press, 1961.

Gutzman, Kevin R. C. *James Madison and the Making of America.* New York: St. Martin's Press, 2012.

Hall, Kermit, Harold Hyman, Leon Sigal. *The Constitutional Convention as an Amending Device.* Washington, D.C.: American Historical Association and American Political Science Association, 1981.

Hall, Kermit L., ed. *The Oxford Companion to the Supreme Court of the United States.* New York: Oxford University Press, 2d ed., 2005.

Hoar, Roger Sherman. *Constitutional Conventions – Their Nature, Powers, and Limitations.* Boston: Little, Brown, 1917.

Hoebeke, Christopher Henry. *The Road to Mass Democracy: Original Intent and the Seventeenth Amendment.* Piscataway, NJ: Transaction Publishers, 1995.

Huhn, Wilson R. *The Five Types of Legal Arguments.* Durham, NC: Carolina Academic Press, 2d ed., 2007.

Hunt, Agnes. *The Provincial Committees of Safety of the American Revolution.* Cleveland: Winn & Judson, 1904. Republished contemporarily by the University of Michigan Libraries.

Hunt, Galliard, ed. *James Madison, The Writings of James Madison, Vol. 9.* New York: G.P. Putnam's Sons, 1900.

Hutchins, Stephen C. & Edgar Albert Varner. *Civil List and Constitutional History of the Colony and State of New York.* Albany: Weed, Parsons, 1891 ed.

Jameson, John Alexander. *A Treatise on Constitutional Conventions – Their History, Powers, and Modes of Proceeding.* New York: Scribner, 1867. 4th ed., 1887. Reprint by The Lawbook Exchange, 2013.

Jefferson, Thomas. *Notes on the State of Virginia.* Paris, 1785.

Jennings, Thelma. *The Nashville Convention: Southern Movement for Unity, 1848-1850.* Memphis, TN: Memphis State University Press, 1980.

Jensen, Merrill, et al. *The Documentary History of the Ratification of the Constitution.*

Madison: Wisconsin Historical Society Press, 1976.

Jones, Dan. *Magna Carta, The Birth of Liberty.* New York: Viking, 2015

Kaminski, John P., Gaspare J. Saladino, Richard Leffler, Charles H. Schoenleber and Margaret A. Hogan, eds. *The Documentary History of the Ratification of the Constitution, Digital Edition.* Charlottesville: University of Virginia Press, 2009.

Kaminski, John P. *Secrecy and the Constitutional Convention.* Madison: The Center for the Study of the American Constitution, University of Wisconsin-Madison 2005.

Kammen, Michael. *People of Paradox, An Inquiry Concerning the Origins of American Civilization.* Ithaca, NY: Cornell University Press, 1972, 1990 ed.

Keller, Morton. *The Constitutional Convention as an Amending Device.* Washington, D.C.: American Historical Association and American Political Science Association, 1981.

Ketcham, Ralph. *James Madison, A Biography.* Charlottesville, VA: University of Virginia Press, 1990.

Ketcham, Ralph. *The Anti-Federalist Papers and the Constitutional Convention Debates.* New York: Mentor, 1986.

Koch, Adrienne & William Peden. *The Life and Selected Writings of Thomas Jefferson.* New York: Random House, 1944.

Kurland, Philip B. and Ralph Lerner. *The Founders' Constitution, Vol.4.* Indianapolis: Liberty Fund, 1987.

Kurland, Philip B., "Article V and the Amending Process," in *An American Primer*, ed., Daniel Boorstin. New York: Meridian, 1966. at 994

Kruman, Marc W. *Between Authority and Liberty.* Chapel Hill: University of North Carolina Press, 2006.

Kyvig, David E. *Explicit and Authentic Acts, Amending the U.S. Constitution 1776-1995.* Lawrence: University Press of Kansas, 1996.

Kyvig, David E. *Unintended Consequences of Constitutional Amendment.* Athens: University of Georgia Press, 2000

Labunski, Richard. *James Madison and the Struggle for the Bill of Rights.* New York: Oxford University Press, 2006.

Larson, Edward and Michael Winship. *The Constitutional Convention, A Narrative History from the Notes of James Madison.* New York: The Modern Library, 2005.

Leachman, Michael and David Super. *States Likely Could Not Control Constitutional Convention on Balanced Budget Amendment or Other Issues.* Washington, D.C.: Center on Budget and Policy Priorities, 16 July 2014.

Lefer, David. *The Founding Conservatives.* New York: Sentinel, 2013.

Levy, Leonard. *Origins of the Bill of Rights.* New Haven, CT: Yale University Press, 1999

Lincoln, William. *The Journals of Each Provincial Congress of Massachusetts in 1774 and 1775 and of the Committee of Safety.* Boston: Dutton & Wentworth, Printers to the State, 1838.

Lintott, Andrew. *The Constitution of the Roman Republic.* New York: Clarendon Press, 1999.

Lockwood, Jeffery A. *Locust: The Devastating Rise and Mysterious Disappearance of the Insect that Shaped the American Midwest.* New York: Basic Books, 2004.

Lutz, Donald. *A Preface to American Political Theory.* Lawrence: University of Kansas Press, 1992.

Lutz, Donald S. *Colonial Origins of the American Constitution: A Documentary History.* Indianapolis: Liberty Fund, 1998.

Mackie, J. D. *A History of Scotland.* London: Penguin Books, 1964.

Madison, James. *The Debates in the Federal Convention of 1787 Which Framed the Constitution of the United States of America.* Westport, CT: Greenwood Press, 1970, c.1920, Oxford University Press.

Maier, Pauline. *American Scripture: Making the Declaration of Independence.* New York: Vintage Books, 1997.

Maier, Pauline. *From Resistance to Revolution.* New York: W. W. Norton, 1972, 1991 ed.

Maier, Pauline. *Ratification, The People Debate the Constitution, 1787-1788.* New York: Simon & Schuster, 2010.

McCoy, Drew R. *The Last of the Fathers, James Madison & The Republican Legacy.* New York: Cambridge University Press, 1989.

McCrady, Edward. *The History of South Carolina Under the Proprietary Government 1670-1719.* New York: MacMillan, 1897.

McDonald, Forrest. *E Pluribus Unum, The Formation of the American Republic 1776-1790.* Indianapolis: Liberty Fund, 1979, 2d ed.

McDonald, Forrest. *Novus Ordo Seclorum, The Intellectual Origins of the Constitution.* Lawrence: University of Kansas Press, 1985.

McSherry, James. *History of Maryland.* Baltimore: Baltimore Book, 1904.

Meigs, William Montgomery. *The Growth of the Constitution in the Federal Convention of 1787: An Effort to Trace the Origin and Development of Each Separate Clause from Its First Suggestion in That Body to the Form Finally Approved – Primary Source Edition.* Philadelphia: J. P. Lippincott, 1900.

Merrell, James H. *Into The American Woods.* New York: W. W. Norton, 1999

Morstein-Marx, Robert. *Mass Oratory and Political Power in the Late Roman Republic.* New York: Cambridge Press, 2004.

Mouritsen, Henrik. *Plebes and Politics in the Late Roman Republic.* New York: Cambridge University Press, 2004.

Natelson, Robert G. *A Compendium for Lawyers and Legislative Drafters.* Purcellville, VA: Convention of States, 2014.

Natelson, Robert G. *Amending the Constitution by Convention: A Complete View of the Founders' Plan* (Part 1 of 3). Goldwater Institute Policy Report No. 241. Phoenix, AZ: Goldwater Institute, Sept. 2010.

Natelson, Robert G. *Learning from Experience: How the States Used Article V Applications in America's First Century* (Part 2 of 3). Goldwater Institute Report No. 11-06. Phoenix, AZ: Goldwater Institute, Nov. 2010.

Natelson, Robert G. *Amending the Constitution by Convention: Practical Guidance for Citizens and Policymakers* (Part 3 of 3). Goldwater Institute Report No. 11-02. Phoenix, AZ: Goldwater Institute, Feb. 2011.

Natelson, Robert G. *Amending the Constitution by Convention: A More Complete View of the Founders' Plan.* Independence Institute Report IP-7-2010. Golden, CO: Independence Institute, Dec. 2010.

Natelson, Robert G. *Amending the Constitution by Convention: Lessons for Today from the Constitution's First Century.* Independence Institute Report IP-5-2011. Golden, CO: Independence Institute, Jul. 2011.

Natelson, Robert G. *Amending the Constitution by Convention: Practical Guide for Citizens and Policymakers.* Independence Institute Report IP-6-2012. Golden, CO: Independence Institute, May 2012.

Natelson, Robert G. *Proposing Constitutional Amendments by a Convention of the States: A Handbook for State Lawmakers.* Washington, D.C.: American Legislative Exchange Council, 2013.

Okrent, Daniel. *Last Call, The Rise and Fall of Prohibition.* New York: Simon & Schuster, 2010.

O'Neill, Karen M. *Rivers By Design, State Power and the Origins of U.S. Flood Control.* Durham, NC: Duke University Press, 2006.

Orfield, Lester Bernhardt, *The Amending of the Federal Constitution.* Ann Arbor: The University of Michigan Press, 1942.

Palgrave, Francis. *The Rise and Progress of the English Commonwealth, Vol. I.* London: John Murray, 1832.

Perman, Michael. *The Road to Redemption, Southern Politics, 1869-1879.* Chapel Hill: University of North Carolina Press, 1984.

Peterson, Merrill D., ed. *Democracy, Liberty, and Property – The State Constitutional Conventions of the 1820s.* Indianapolis: The Liberty Fund, 2010. Originally published by Bobbs-Merrill Company, 1966

Poole, W. Scott. *Never Surrender: Confederate Memory and Conservatism in the South Carolina Upcountry.* Athens: University of Georgia Press, 2004.

Rakove, Jack N., *Original Meanings, Politics and Ideas in the Making of the Constitution.* New York: Vintage Books, 1996.

Ranney, Joseph A. *In the Wake of Slavery, Civil War, Civil Rights, and the Reconstruction of Southern Law.* Westport, CT: Praeger, 2006.

Raphael, Ray. *The First American Revolution: Before Lexington and Concord.* New York: New Press, 2003.

Rhodes, P. J. *A Commentary on the Aristotelian Athenaion Politeia.* New York: Oxford University Press, 1993.

Richard, Carl J. *The Founders and the Classics, Greece, Rome, and the American Enlightenment.* Cambridge, MA: Harvard University Press, 1994.

Ridpath, John Clark. *The New Complete History of the United States of America.* Chicago: Elliot, Madison, 1912.

Rossiter, Clinton, ed. *The Federalist Papers: Hamilton, Madison, Jay.* New York: Mentor, 1961.

Rossiter, Clinton. *1787: The Grand Convention.* New York: Macmillan, 1986.

Rossum, Ralph A. *Federalism, The Supreme Court, and the Seventeenth Amendment: The Irony of Constitutional Democracy.* Lanham, MD: Lexington Books, 2001.

Rutland, Robert & Charles Hobson, eds. *The Papers of James Madison.* Charlottesville: University Press of Virginia, 1977. In multiple volumes.

Scalia, Antonin & Bryan A. Garner. *Reading Law: The Interpretation of Legal Texts.* St. Paul, Minnesota: Thomson/West, 2012.

Schouler, James. *History of the United States of America, Under the Constitution, 1783-1801, Vol. I, Rule of Federalism.* New York: Dodd, Mead & Co., 1880, 1908 ed.

Shearer, Augustus Hunt, *A List of Official Publications of American State Constitutional Conventions, 1776-1916,* Bulletin 6. Chicago: Newberry Library, 1917.

Solberg, Winton U. *The Constitutional Convention and the Formation of the Union.* Urbana: University of Illinois Press, 2d ed., 1990.

Sorauf, Frank J. *The Constitutional Convention as an Amending Device.* Washington, D.C.: American Historical Association and American Political Science Association, 1981.

Squire, Peverill. *The Evolution of American Legislatures, Colonies, Territories, and States, 1619-2009.* Ann Arbor: University of Michigan Press, 2014.

Staples, William Read. *Rhode Island in the Continental Congress, Council of War to President of Congress, 26 April 1779.* Providence, RI: Providence Press, 1870.

Stimson, Frederick J. *The American Constitution As It Protects Private Rights.* New York: Scribner, 1923.

Story, Joseph. *Commentaries on the Constitution of the United States, Vol. 3.* Boston: Hilliard, Gray, 1833.

Strayer, Joseph Reese. *The Delegate from New York or Proceedings from the Federal Convention of 1787 from the Notes of John Lansing, Jr.* Princeton, NJ: Princeton University Press, 1939. Reprint by The Lawbook Exchange, 2002.

Sturm, Albert L. *Thirty Years of State Constitution-Making: 1938-68.* New York: National Municipal League, 1970.

Tarr, G. Alan. *Understanding State Constitutions.* Princeton, NJ: Princeton University Press, 1998.

Taylor, Alan. *American Colonies: The Settling of North America.* New York: Penguin Books, 2001.

Taylor, John, of Caroline, Virginia. *New Views of the Constitution of the United States.* Washington City: Way and Gideon, 1823.

Temple, Oliver Perry. *East Tennessee and the Civil War.* Cincinnati: Robert Clarke Company, 1899.

Tourtellot, Arthur B. *Lexington and Concord.* New York: W. W. Norton, 1959, 2000 ed.

Trumbull, James Hammond. *Historical Notes on the Constitutions of Connecticut, 1639-1818.* Hartford, CT: Hartford Press, 1901.

Tucker, St. George. *View of the Constitution of the United States.* Indianapolis: Liberty Fund, 1999, originally published in Philadelphia, 1803.

Vile, John R. *Contemporary Questions Surrounding the Constitutional Amending Process.* Westport, CT: Praeger, 1993.

Vile, John R. *Conventional Wisdom.* Athens, GA: University of Georgia Press, 2016

Vile, John R. *Encyclopedia of Constitutional Amendments, Proposed Amendments and Amending Issues, 1789-2015.* Santa Barbara, CA: ABC-CLIO, 4th ed., 2015. In two volumes.

Vile, John R. *Essential Supreme Court Decisions, Summaries of Leading Cases in U.S. Constitutional Law.* Lanham, MD: Rowman & Littlefield, 15th ed., 2010.

Weber, Paul J. & Barbara A. Perry. *Unfounded Fears, The Myths and Realities of a Constitutional Convention.* New York: Praeger, 1989.

Weslager, Clinton Alfred. *The Stamp Act Congress.* Newark: University of Delaware Press, 1976.

Williams, Robert F. *The Law of American State Constitutions.* New York: Oxford University Press, 2009.

Williams, Samuel Cole. *History of the Lost State of Franklin.* New York: Press of the Pioneers, 1933.

Wood, Gordon S. *The Creation of the American Republic, 1776-1787.* Chapel Hill: University of North Carolina Press, 1998. Published for the Omohundro Institute of Early American History and Culture. Used by permission of the publisher.

Wood, Gordon S. *The Idea of America, Reflections on the Birth of the United States.* New York: Penguin Books, 2011. Any third party use of this material, outside of this publication, is prohibited, parties must apply directly to Penguin Random House LLC for permission.

Zimmerman, Joseph F. *Interstate Cooperation, Compacts & Administrative Agreements.* Albany, NY: SUNY Press, 2012.

A Constitutional Convention: How Well Would It Work? Washington, D.C.: American Enterprise Institute for Public Policy Research, 1979.

American Historical Review. Washington, D.C. 1905-6. In multiple volumes.

The Parliamentary or Constitutional History of England, From the Earliest Times, to the Restoration of King Charles II. London: J. & R. Tonson, April 1751.

The U.S. Constitution – A Reader. Hillsdale, MI: Hillsdale College Press, 2012.

Government Documents

Annals of Congress (1789-1824)

Congressional Globe (1833-1873)

Congressional Record (1873-present)

Federal Register (1936-present)

House Bills and Resolutions (1799–present)

House Committee Hearings (1909–present)

House Documents (1795-present)

House Journal (1789-present)

House of Representatives Journal (1789-present)

House Reports (1795–Present)

Register of Debates (1824-1837)

Senate Documents (1817-present)

Senate Journal (1789-present)

Senate Reports (1847–present)

United States Statutes at Large (1789-present)

Bankson's Journal, 1786-91, National Archives, NARA M322, 301686.

Brickfield, Cyril, *Problems Relating To A Federal Constitutional Convention*, Staff of the House Committee on the Judiciary, 85th Cong., 1st sess., (Comm. Print 1957).

Cole, Jared P., Library of Congress, Congressional Research Service Report R43834, *The Political Question Doctrine: Justiciability and the Separation of Powers*, (23 December 2014)

Durbin, Thomas M., Library of Congress, Congressional Research Service Report CRS 95-589A, *Amending the U.S. Constitution: by Congress or by Constitutional Convention*, (10 May 1995).

Gillies, Paul S. and D. Gregory Sanford, eds., *Records of the Council of Censors of the State of Vermont* (Montpelier: Office of the Secretary of State, 1991).

Hammond, Larry A., "Memorandum Opinion for the Attorney General, Constitutional Law – Constitution – Article V – The Amending Process – The Convention Method," Department of Justice, Office of Legal Counsel, No. 79-4, (16 Jan 1979).

Harmon, John M., "Memorandum Opinion for the Attorney General, Constitutional Convention – Limitation of Power to Propose Amendments to the Constitution," Department of Justice, Office of Legal Counsel, No. 79-75, (10 Oct 1979).

Harris, Kenneth E. & Steven D. Tilley, eds. *Index: Journals of the Continental Congress, 1774-1789*. Washington, D.C.: National Archives and Records Service, 1976.

Hoadly, Charles J. *The Public Records of the State of Connecticut, From October 1776 to February 1778, Inclusive.* Hartford, CT: Case, Lockwood & Brainard, 1894.

Huckabee, David C., *Constitutional Convention Applications of States Relating To Federal Spending*. Library of Congress. Congressional Research Service Report, at CRS-2 (22 April 1980).

Hutton, E. Jeremy, Library of Congress, Congressional Research Service Report, *Calling a Constitutional Convention*, (1974)

Moneyhon, Carl H., "TAX-PAYERS' CONVENTION," *Handbook of Texas Online*

Neale, Thomas N., Library of Congress, Congressional Research Service Report R42589, *The Article V Convention to Propose Constitutional Amendments: Contemporary Issues for Congress*, (11 April 2014).

Neale, Thomas N., Library of Congress, Congressional Research Service Report R42592, *The Article V Convention to Propose Constitutional Amendments: Historical Perspectives for Congress* (22 October 2012).

Neale, Thomas N., Library of Congress, Congressional Research Service Report R44435, *The Article V Convention to Propose Constitutional Amendments: Current Developments* (29 March 2016).

Poore, Benjamin. *The Federal and State Constitutions.* Washington, D.C.: Government Printing Office, 2d ed., 1878.

Small, Norman J., "Procedures for Amending the United States Constitution," *Library of Congress Legislative Reference Service* 283/77 (1965).

Sorenson, Theodore, "A New Federal Constitutional Convention?," Cong. Rec., 113 (June 12, 1967).

Congressional Budget Office, *An Update to the Budget and Economic Outlook: 2014 to 2024.*

Congressional Research Service Report CRS 95-589 A (1995) *Amending the U.S. Constitution: by Congress or Constitutional Convention.*

Constitutional Convention Implementation Act of 1984, 98th Cong., 2nd sess., S. Rept. 98-594

Hawaii Legislative Drafting Manual, 10th ed., Legislative Reference Bureau, 2012.

House Committee on the Judiciary, *Problems Relating to State Applications for a Convention to Propose Constitutional Limitations on Federal Tax Rates*, 82nd Cong., 2d sess., (1952).

Montana Constitutional Convention Memorandums, Montana Constitutional Convention Commission (1971).

Nevada Legislature Background Paper 79-12

The Nomination of Robert H. Bork to Be Associate Justice of the Supreme Court of the United States, Hearing before the Committee on the Judiciary, 100th Cong., 1st sess. (1987) (statement of Robert H. Bork).

Opinion 79-75 of the Office of Legal Counsel, (10 Oct 1979)

Pub. L. 79-404, 60 Stat. 237 (1946)

Pub. L. 87-748, 76 Stat. 744 (1962)

Pub. L. No. 92-512

Pub. L. 98–497 (1985), 1 U.S.C. §106b,

Pub. L. 99-177, 99 Stat. 1038, Balanced Budget and Emergency Deficit Control Act of 1985, 99th Congress, S.1702, Title II, December 12, 1985

Pub. L. 100–119, Title I, Sept. 29, 1987, 101 Stat. 754, 2 U.S.C. § 900

Pub. L. 107–155, 116 Stat. 81

Rules of the House of Representatives

S.40, 99th Cong., 1st sess. (1985)

S. 119, Section 15, 98th Cong., Constitutional Convention Implementation Act of 1984

S. 214, Section 11(c), 102nd Cong., Constitutional Convention Implementation Act of 1991

S.817, 97th Cong. 1st sess., "The Constitutional Implementation Act of 1981"

S.1272, Section 7, 93rd Congress, Federal Constitutional Convention Procedures Act of 1973

S.1710, 96th Cong., 1st sess. (1979)

S.2307, 90th Cong., 1st sess. (1967)

S.2812, Section 7, 98th Congress, Federal Constitutional Convention Procedures Act of 1984

S. Rep. No. 92-293, "Report of the Committee on the Judiciary, United States Senate, Together With Additional Views to Accompany S. 1272", 93rd Cong., 1st sess., (1973).

S. Rep. No. 336, 92nd Cong., 1st sess., (1971)

Senate Judiciary Committee, *Federal Constitutional Convention Procedures Act*, S. Rep. No.92-336, 92nd Cong., 1st sess., (1971)

Standing Rules of the United States Senate

Staff of House Comm. on the Judiciary, 82nd Cong., 2d sess., "Problems Relating to State Applications for a Convention to Propose Constitutional Limitations of Federal Tax Rates" (Comm. Print 1952).

Testimony of US Senator David Pryor of Arkansas before the Senate Judiciary Committee's Subcommittee on the Constitution: U.S. Congress, Senate Committee on the Judiciary, *Constitutional Convention Procedures, Hearing before the Subcommittee on the Constitution on S.3, S.520, and S.1710.* 96th Cong., 1st sess., at 43 (1979).

U.S. Congress, Senate Committee on the Judiciary, *Constitutional Convention Procedures, Hearing before the Subcommittee on the Constitution on S.3, S.520, and S.1710.* 96th Cong., 1st sess., (1979).

U.S. Congress, House Committee on the Judiciary, *Is There a Constitutional Convention in Our Future?* 103rd Cong., 1st sess., committee print, serial no. 1, (Washington, D.C.: GPO, 1993).

U.S. Congress *The Constitution of the United States, Analysis and Interpretation*, 108th Congress, Senate Document 108-17 (Washington, D.C.: Government Printing Office, 2004).

US Department of Justice, Office of Legal Policy, "Report to the Attorney General, Limited Constitutional Conventions under Article V of the United States Constitution" (10 September 1987).

Works Progress Administration and Robert S. McElvaine. *Mississippi: The WPA Guide to the Magnolia State.* New York: Viking Press 1938, republished by the University of Mississippi Press, Jackson, Mississippi, 1988.

15 Stat. L. 706 (1868)

1970 State of Wisconsin Blue Book (Madison: Legislative Reference Bureau, 1970).

Articles

Aigler, Ralph W., "Referendum as Applied to Proposed Amendments of the Federal Constitution," *Michigan Law Review* 18 (1919): 51-4

Albert, Richard, "The Next Constitutional Revolution," *University of Detroit Mercy Law Review* 88, no.4 (Sum. 2011): 707-35

Almond, Michael A., "Amendment by Convention: Our Next Constitutional Crisis?," *North Carolina Law Review* 53 (1975): 491-533

Amar, Akhil Reed, "Philadelphia Revisited: Amending the Constitution Outside Article V," *University of Chicago Law Review* 55, no.4 (Fall 1988): 1043-1104

Amar, Vikram David, "The People Made Me Do It: Can the People of the States Instruct and Coerce Their State Legislatures in the Article V Constitutional Amendment Process?," *William and Mary Law Review* 41, no.3 (2000): 1037-92

Ames, Herman V., "Recent Development of the Amending Power as Applied to the Federal Constitution," *Proceedings of the American Philosophical Society* 72, no.2 (Apr. 1933): 87-100

Anderson, William, "Minnesota Frames a Constitution," *Minnesota History* (Mar. 1958): 1-12

Armstrong, J. Elwood, "The Spirit of the Fifth Amendment Privilege – A Study in Judicial Method – Ullman v. United States," *Maryland Law Review* 17, no.1 (1957): 75-83

Babbit, Harold, "Article V and Constitutional Conventions," *Cleveland Bar Journal* 50 (April 1979): 143-6

Bacon, Selden, "How the 10th Amendment Affected the Fifth Article of the Constitution," *Virginia Law Review* 16, no.8 (1930): 771-91

Baker, Thomas E., "Towards A "More Perfect Union": Some Thoughts on Amending the Constitution," *Widener Journal of Public Law* 10, no.1 (2000): 1-19

Ball, Norman T., "Ratification of Constitutional Amendments by State Conventions," *George Washington Law Review* 2 (1933): 216-21

Balog, Frank, "Popular Sovereignty and the Question of the Limited Constitutional Convention," *Cooley Law Review* 1 (1982): 109-31

Barker, William T., "A Status Report on the "Balanced Budget" Constitutional Convention," *John Marshall Law Review* 20 (1986): 29-96

Baude, William, "Sharing the Necessary and Proper Clause," *Harvard Law Review Forum* 128 (2014): 39-48

Baude, William & Jud Campbell, "Early American Constitutional History: A Source Guide," a work-in-progress available on the SSRN

Beck, J. Randy, "The New Jurisprudence of the Necessary and Proper Clause," *University of Illinois Law Review* 2002, no.3 (2002): 581-650

Benjamin, Gerald & Thomas Gais, "Constitutional Conventionphobia," *Hofstra Law & Policy Symposium* 1 (1996): 53-77

Berns, Walter, "Comment: The Forms of Article V," *Harvard Journal of Law and Public Policy* 6 (1982): 73-7

Biber, Eric, "The Price of Admission: Causes, Effects, and Patterns of Conditions Imposed on States Entering the Union," *American Journal of Legal History* XLVI (2004): 119-208

Bilder, Mary Sarah, "How Bad Were the Official Records of the Federal Convention?," *The George Washington Law Review* 80, no. 6 (2012): 1620-82

Black, Jr., Charles L., "Amending the Constitution: A Letter to a Congressman," *Yale*

Law Journal 82, no.2 (Dec. 1972): 189-215

Black, Jr., Charles L., "Amendment by National Constitutional Convention: A Letter to a Senator," *Yale Law Journal* 32 (1979): 626-44

Black, Jr., Charles L., "The Proposed Amendment of Article V: A Threatened Disaster," *Yale Law Journal* 72 (1963): 957-66

Bonfield, Arthur Earl, "Proposing Constitutional Amendments by Convention: Some Problems," *Notre Dame Lawyer* 39, no.6 (Sept. 1964): 659-79 – Now *Notre Dame Law Review*

Bonfield, Arthur Earl, "The Dirksen Amendment and the Article V Convention Process," *Michigan Law Review* 66, no.5 (Mar. 1968): 949-1000

Borgeaud, Charles, "The Origin and Development of Written Constitutions," *Political Science Quarterly* 7, no.4, (Dec. 1892): 613-32

Boudreaux, Donald J. & A. C. Pritchard, "Rewriting the Constitution: An Economic Analysis of the Constitutional Amendment Process," *Fordham Law Review* 62, no.1 (1993): 111-62

Bowman, Larry. "The Virginia County Committees of Safety, 1774-1776," *Virginia Magazine of History and Biography* 79, no.3 (Jul. 1971): 322-37

Brandwen, Maxwell, "Reflections on Ullman v. United States," *Columbia Law Review* 57, no. 4 (Apr. 1957): 500-17

Brannan, Patricia A., David L. Lillehaug, Robert P. Reznick, "Critical Details: Amending the United States Constitution," *Harvard Journal on Legislation* 16 (1979):763-809

Braxton, Allen Caperton, "Powers of Conventions," *Virginia Law Register* 7, no.2 (Jun. 1901): 79-99

Brennan, Thomas E., "Return To Philadelphia," *Cooley Law Review* I (1982): 1-72

Brennan, Thomas E., "The Last Prerogative," *Harvard Journal of Law & Public Policy* 6 (1982)

Brill, Howard W., "The Citizen's Relief Against Inactive Federal Officials: Case Studies In Mandamus, Actions 'In The Nature Of Mandamus,' And Mandatory Injunctions," *Akron Law Review* 16 (Win. 1983): 339-96

Brown, Richard D., "The Massachusetts Convention of Towns of 1768," *William and Mary Quarterly*, 3d ser., 26, no.1 (Jan. 1969): 94-104

Bryan, Charles F., "A Gathering of Tories: The East Tennessee Convention of 1861," *Tennessee Historical Quarterly* 39, no. 1 (Spr. 1980): 27-48

Buckwalter, Doyle W., "Constitutional Conventions and State Legislators," *Chicago-Kent Law Review* 48, no.1 (Jan. 1971): 20-37

Bybee, Jay S., "Ulysses at the Mast: Democracy, Federalism, and the Sirens' Song of the Seventeenth Amendment," *Northwestern University Law Review* 91, no.2 (1997): 500-72

Calman, Alvin, "Ledru-Rollin and the Second French Republic," *Studies in History, Economics and Public Law* 103, no.2 (1922)

Cannon, Henry L., "The Character and Antecedents of the Charter of Liberties of Henry I," *American Historical Review* 15, no.1 (Oct. 1909): 37-46

Carroll, John F., "Constitutional Law, Recent Cases," *Akron Law Review* 16, no. 1 (Sum. 1982): 151-61

Carson, Ralph M., "Disadvantages of a Federal Constitutional Convention," *Michigan Law Review* 66, no.5 (Mar. 1968): 921-30

Castro, David, "A Constitutional Convention: Scouting Article Five's Undiscovered Country," *University of Pennsylvania Law Review* 134 (1986): 939-66

Catterall, Ralph C. H., "The Failure of the Humble Petition and Advice," *American Historical Review* 9, no.1 (Oct. 1903): 36-65

Clark, Bradford, "The Eleventh Amendment and the Nature of the Union," *Harvard Law Review* 123, no.8 (Jun. 2010): 1817-1918

Clark, Homer, "The Supreme Court and the Amending Process," *Virginia Law Review* 39, no. 5 (Jun. 1953): 621-52

Clark, Walter, "The Next Constitutional Convention of the United States," *Yale Law Journal* 16, no.2 (Dec. 1906): 65-83

Coenen, Dan T., "A Rhetoric for Ratification: The Argument of *The Federalist* and Its Impact On Constitutional Interpretation," *University of Georgia School of Law Research Paper Series* XX, Paper No. 06-010, (Nov. 2006): 1-71

Connely, Dwight, "Amending the Constitution: Is This Any Way to Call for a Constitutional Convention?," *Arizona Law Review* 22 (1980): 1011-36

Cooley, Thomas M., "The Power to Amend the Federal Constitution," *Michigan Law Journal* 2, no.4 (Apr. 1893): 109-20

Corwin, Edwin S. & Mary Louise Ramsey, "The Constitutional Law of Constitutional Amendment," *Notre Dame Lawyer* XXVI, no.2 (1951): 185-213

Crane, Elaine F., "Publius in the Provinces: Where Was *The Federalist* Reprinted Outside New York City?," *William & Mary Quarterly* 21 (1964): 589-92

Davis, Ethan P., "Liquor Laws and Constitutional Conventions: A Legal History of the Twenty-first Amendment," *Yale Law School Student Scholarship Papers*, Paper 65 (2008): 1-40

Davis, William Newell, "The Territory of Nataqua: An Episode in Pioneer Government East of the Sierra," *California Historical Society Quarterly* 21, no.3 (Sep. 1942): 225-38

Dellinger, Walter, "The Legitimacy of Constitutional Change: Rethinking the Amendment Process," *Harvard Law Review* 97 (1983): 386-432

Dellinger, Walter, "The Recurring Question of the "Limited" Constitutional Convention," *Yale Law Journal* 88 (1979): 1623-40

Denning, Brannon P., "Means to Amend: Theories of Constitutional Change," *Tennessee Law Review* 65 (1997): 155-244

Diamond, Ann Stuart, "A Convention for Proposing Amendments: The Constitution's Other Method," *The State of American Federalism, 1980* 11, no.3 (1981): 113-46

Dinan, John, "The Political Dynamics of Mandatory State Constitutional Convention Referendums: Lessons from the 2000s Regarding Obstacles and Pathways to their Passage", *Montana Law Review* 71, no.2 (Sum. 2010): 395-432

Dixon, Jr., Robert G., "Article V: The Comatose Article of Our Living Constitution," *Michigan Law Review* 66, no.5 (Mar. 1968): 931-48

Dodd, Walter F., "Amending the Federal Constitution," *Yale Law Journal* 30, no.4 (Feb. 1921): 321-54

Dodd, Walter F., "Implied Powers and Implied Limitations in Constitutional Law," *Yale Law Journal* 29, no.2 (Dec. 1919): 137-62

Dodd, Walter F., "Judicial Control Over the Amendment of State Constitutions," *Columbia Law Review* 10, no.7 (Nov. 1910): 618-38

Dodd, Walter F., "Judicially Non-Enforcible Provisions of Constitutions," *University of Pennsylvania Law Review* 80 (Nov. 1931): 54-93

Dunaway, Jr., Wayland F., "The Virginia Conventions of the Revolution," *Virginia Law Register* 10, no.7 (Nov. 1904): 567-86

Durchslag, Melvyn R., "The Supreme Court and the Federalist Papers: Is There Less Here Than Meets The Eye?," *William and Mary Bill of Rights Journal* 14, no.1 (2005): 243-349

Eidsmoe, John A., "A New Constitutional Convention? Critical Look at Questions Answered, and Not Answered, by Article Five of the United States Constitution," *United States Air Force Academy Journal of Legal Studies* 3 (1992): 1-25

Elder, Judith L., "Article V, Justiciability, and the Equal Rights Amendment," *Oklahoma Law Review* 31 (1978): 63-109

Elliott, E. Donald, "Constitutional Conventions and the Deficit," *Duke Law Journal* 1985, no.6 (Dec. 1985): 1077-1110

Ellis, Sara R., Yusuf Z. Malik, Heather G. Parker, Benjamin C. Signer & Al'Reco L. Yancy, "Article V Constitutional Conventions: A Primer," *Tennessee Law Review* 78 (2011): 663-92

Ervin, Jr., Sen. Sam, "Proposed Legislation to Implement the Convention Method of Amending the Constitution," *Michigan Law Review* 66, no.5 (Mar. 1968): 875-902

Eskridge, Jr., William N., "Should the Supreme Court Read The Federalist But Not Statutory Legislative History?," *George Washington Law Review* 66 (1998): 1301-23

Feer, Robert A., "Shays's Rebellion and the Constitution: A Study in Causation," *New England Quarterly* 42, no.3 (Sep. 1969): 388-410

Fensterwald, Jr., Bernard, "Constitutional Law: The States and the Amending Power – A Reply," *American Bar Association Journal* 46, no.7 (Jul. 1960): 717-21

Festa, Matthew J., "Dueling Federalists: Supreme Court Decisions with Multiple Opinions Citing *The Federalist*, 1986-2007," *Seattle University Law Review* 31 (2007): 75-106

Fishel, Lynn Andretta, "Reversals in the Federal Constitutional Amendment Process: Efficacy of State Ratifications of the Equal Rights Amendment," *Indiana Law Journal* 49, no.1 (Oct. 1973): 147-66

Fleet, Elizabeth, "Madison's 'Detached Memoranda'," *William & Mary Quarterly* 3d ser., 3, no.4 (Oct. 1946): 534-68

Flynt, Wayne, "Alabama's Shame: The Historical Origins of the 1901 Constitution," *Alabama Law Review* 53, no.1 (2001): 67-76

Foley, Elizabeth Price, "Sovereignty, Rebalanced: The Tea Party & Constitutional Amendments," *Tennessee Law Review* 78 (2011): 751-64. The full text of this Article was published originally by the Tennessee Law Review Association, Inc. at 78 **Tenn. L. Rev.** 751 (2011), and this version, approved by the Author, appears by their permission.

Forbes, Charles S., "Vermont's Admission to the Union," *The Vermonter: A State Magazine* VII, no.8 (Mar. 1902): 101-2

Forkosch, Morris B., "The Alternative Amending Clause in Article V: Reflections and Suggestions," *Minnesota Law Review* 51 (1967): 1053-85

Frierson, William L., "Amending the Constitution of the United States: A Reply to Mr. Marbury," *Harvard Law Review* 33, no.5 (1920): 659-66

Fritz, Christian G., "Recovering the Lost Worlds of America's Written Constitutions," *Albany Law Review* 68, no.2 (2005): 261-93

Frolov, Roman M., "Public Meetings in Ancient Rome: Definitions of the *Contiones* in the Sources," *Graeco-Latina Brunensia* 18 (2013): 75-84

Gallagher, Robert, "The Powers of Constitutional Conventions," *Lawyer & Banker & Southern Bench & Bar Review* 9, no.148 (1916): 148-52

Gaugush, Bill, "Principles Governing the Interpretation and Exercise of Article V Powers," *Western Political Quarterly* 35, no.2 (Jun. 1982): 212-21

Gibson, Arrell Morgan, "The Constitutional Experiences of the Five Civilized Tribes," *American Indian Law Review* 2, no.2 (Win. 1974): 17-45

Gilliam, Thomas A., "Constitutional Conventions: Precedents, Problems, and Proposals," *St. Louis University Law Review* 16 (1971): 46-62

Glow, Lotte, "The Committee of Safety," *English Historical Review* 80, no.315 (Apr. 1965): 289-313

Goldberg, Arthur J., "The Proposed Constitutional Convention," *Hastings Constitutional Law Quarterly* 11 (Fall 1983): 1-4

Gough, Robert J., "The Myth of the "Middle Colonies," An Analysis of Regionalization in Early America," *Pennsylvania Magazine of History and Biography* 107, no.3 (Jul. 1983): 393-419

Graham, Fred P., "The Role of the States in Proposing Constitutional Amendments," *American Bar Association Journal* 49, no.12 (Dec. 1963): 1175-83

Grinnell, Frank W., "Petitioning Congress for a Convention: Cannot a State Change Its Mind?," *American Bar Association Journal* 45, no.11 (Nov. 1959): 1164-6

Grodin, Joseph R., "Popular Sovereignty and Its Limits: Lessons for a Constitutional Convention in California," *Loyola of Los Angeles Law Review* 44 (Winter 2011): 623-36

Guida, Anthony James, "States' Role in Article V Conventions: AFL-CIO vs. Eu," *Cincinnati Law Review* 54 (1985): 317-32

Gunther, Gerald, "The Convention Method of Amending the United States Constitution," *Georgia Law Review* 14, no.1 (Fall 1979): 1-25

Hanson, Walker, "The States' Power to Effectuate Constitutional Change: Is Congress Currently Required to Convene a National Convention for the Proposing of Amendments to the United States Constitution?," *Georgetown Journal of Law & Public Policy* 9 (2011): 245-59

Heath III, George D., "Making the Instrument of Government" *Journal of British Studies* 6, no.2 (May 1967): 15-34

Heller, Francis H., "Article V: Changing Dimensions In Constitutional Change," *University of Michigan Journal of Law Reform* 7 (Fall 1973): 71-89

Heller, Francis H., "Limiting a Constitutional Convention: The State Precedents," *Cardozo Law Review* 3 (1982): 563-79

Hemstad, Richard W., "Constitutional Amendment by Convention – a Risky Business," *Washington State Bar News* 36 (Feb. 1982): 16-21

Hendricks, Homer, "Some Legal Aspects of Constitutional Conventions," *Texas Law Review* 2 (1924): 195-207

Hoober, John A., "Popular Prejudice and Constitutional Amendatory Conventions," *Yale Law Journal* 1, no.5 (May 1892): 207-15

Hucker, Charles W., "Constitutional Convention Poses Questions," *Congressional Quarterly* 37, no.7 (Feb. 1979): 123-4

Hutson, James H., "John Dickinson at the Federal Constitutional Convention," *William and Mary Quarterly* 40, no.2 (Apr. 1983): 256-282

Hutson, James H., "Riddles of the Federal Constitutional Convention," *William and Mary Quarterly* 3d ser., 44, no.3 (Jul. 1987): 411-23

Ishikawa, Brendon Troy, "Amending the Constitution: Just Not Every November," *Cleveland State Law Review* 44 (1996): 303-43

Ishikawa, Brendon Troy, "Everything You Always Wanted to Know About How Amendments Are Made, but Were Afraid to Ask*," *Hastings Constitutional Law Quarterly* 24 (Win. 1997): 545-97

Jameson, John Franklin, "The Early Political Uses of the Word Convention," *American Historical Review* 3, no.3 (Apr. 1898): 477-87

Jones, Ethel B., "The Economics of Women's Suffrage," *Journal of Legal Studies* 20 (1991): 423-37

Kalfus, Mason, "Why Time Limits on the Ratification of Constitutional Amendments Violate Article V," *University of Chicago Law Review* 66, no.2 (Spr. 1999): 437-67

Kanowitz, Leo & Marilyn Klinger, "Can a State Rescind Its Equal Rights Amendment Ratification: Who Decides and How?," *Hastings Law Journal* 28 (Mar. 1977): 979-1009

Kauper, Paul G., "The Alternative Amendment Process: Some Observations," *Michigan Law Review* 66, no.5 (Mar. 1968): 903-20

Kay, Richard S., "The Illegality of the Constitution," *Constitutional Commentary* 4 (1987): 57-80

Kean, Thomas, "A Constitutional Convention Would Threaten the Rights We Have Cherished for 200 Years," *Detroit College of Law Review* 4 (1986): 1087-91

Keedy, Edwin R., "The Constitutions of the State of Franklin, the Indian Stream Republic and the State of Deseret," *University of Pennsylvania Law Review* 101

(1953): 516-28

Kennedy, Christopher M., "Is There a Twenty-Seventh Amendment? The Unconstitutionality of a "New" 203-Year-Old Amendment," *John Marshall Law Review* 26, no.4 (Sum. 1993): 977-1019

Kimball, Dale A., "The Constitutional Convention, Its Nature and Powers – And the Amending Procedure," *Utah Law Review* (Sept. 1966): 390-415

Klingelsmith, Margaret C., "Amending the Constitution of the United States," *University of Pennsylvania Law Review* 73 (1925): 355-79

Klingelsmith, Margaret C., "Two Theories in Regard to the Implied Powers of the Constitution," *University of Pennsylvania Law Review* 54, no.4 (Apr.1906): 214-29

Kobach, Kris W., "May 'We the People' Speak?: The Forgotten Role of Constituent Instructions in Amending the Constitution," *University of California-Davis Law Review* 33, no.1 (Fall 1999): 1-94

Kobach, Kris W., "Rethinking Article V: Term Limits and the Seventeenth and Nineteenth Amendments," *Yale Law Journal* 103, no.7 (May 1994): 1971-2007

Kogan, Vladimir, "Lessons from Recent State Constitutional Conventions," *California Journal of Politics & Policy* 2, no.2 (2010): 1-13

Kosaki, Richard H., "Constitutions and Constitutional Conventions of Hawaii," *Hawaiian Journal of History* 12 (1978): 120-38

Kyvig, David E., "Everett Dirksen's Constitutional Crusades," *Journal of the Illinois State Historical Society* 95 (Spr. 2002): 68-85

Lash, Kurt T., "Inkblot: The Ninth Amendment as Textual Justification for Judicial Enforcement of the Right to Privacy," *University of Chicago Law Review Dialogue* 80 (2013): 219-33

Lash, Kurt T., "Rejecting Conventional Wisdom: Federalist Ambivalence in the Framing and Implementation of Article V," *American Journal of Legal History* 38, no.2 (Apr. 1994): 197-231

Lemont, Eric, "Developing Effective Processes of American Indian Constitutional and Governmental Reform: Lessons from the Cherokee Nation of Oklahoma, Hualapai Nation, Navajo Nation and Northern Cheyenne Tribe," *American Indian Law Review* 26, no.2 (2002): 147-76

Levi, Edward, "Some Aspects of Separation of Powers," *Columbia Law Review* 76, no.3 (Apr. 1976): 371-91

Levine, Henry D., "Limited Federal Constitutional Conventions: Implications of the State Experience," *Harvard Journal on Legislation* 11 (1973): 127-59

Levinson, Sanford, "'Veneration' and Constitutional Change: James Madison Confronts the Possibility of Constitutional Amendment," *Texas Tech Law Review* 21 (1990): 2443-61

Long, Joseph R., "Tinkering with the Constitution," *Yale Law Journal* 24, no.7 (May 1915): 573-89

Lucas, James W., "To Originate The Amendment Of Errors: Reforming Article V to Facilitate State and Popular Engagement in Constitutional Amendment," (2013): 1-45

Lynch, Michael J., "The Other Amendments: Constitutional Amendments That

Failed*," *Law Library Journal* 93, no.2 (2001): 303-10

Magliocca, Gerard N., "State Calls for an Article V Convention: Mobilization and Interpretation," *Cardozo Law Review De Novo* (2009): 74-95

Maggs, Gregory E., "A Concise Guide to the Federalist Papers as a Source of the Original Meaning of the United States Constitution," *Boston University Law Review* 87 (2007): 801-47

Maggs, Gregory E., "A Concise Guide to the Records of the Federal Constitutional Convention of 1787 as a Source of the Original Meaning of the U.S. Constitution," *George Washington Law Review* 81 (2012): 1-43

Maggs, Gregory E., "A Concise Guide to the Records of the State Ratifying Conventions as a Source of the Original Meaning of the U.S. Constitution," *University of Illinois Law Review* 2009, no.2 (2009): 457-96

Maggs, Gregory E., "A Concise Guide to Using Dictionaries from the Founding Era to Determine the Original Meaning of the Constitution," *George Washington Law Review* 82 (2014): 358-93

Manne, Neal S., "Good Intentions, New Inventions and Article V Constitutional Conventions," *Texas Law Review* 58 (1979): 131-70

Marbury, William L., "The Limitations Upon the Amending Power," *Harvard Law Review* 33, no.2 (Dec. 1919): 223-35

Martig, Ralph R., "Amending the Constitution Article V: The Keystone of the Arch," *Michigan Law Review* 35, no.8 (1937): 1253-85

Martin, Philip L., "The Application Clause of Article Five," *Political Science Quarterly* 85, no.4 (Dec. 1970): 616-28

Martin, William Logan, "The Amending Power: The Background of the Income Tax Amendment," *American Bar Association Journal* 39, no.1 (Jan. 1953): 77-80

McCleskey, Clifton. "Along the Midway: Some Thoughts on Democratic Constitution-Amending," *Michigan Law Review* 66, no.5 (Mar. 1968): 1001-16

Metaxaki-Mitrou, Fotini, "Violence in the *Contio* During the Ciceronian Age," *L'Antiquité Classique* 54 (1985): 180-7

Miller, Robert J., "Tribal Constitutions and Native Sovereignty," SSRN-id1802890, (2011): 1-23

Millet, Thomas, "The Supreme Court, Political Questions, and Article V – A Case for Judicial Restraint," *Santa Clara Law Review* 23, no.3 (Jan. 1983): 745-68

Mitchell, Jeffery K., "The Threat of a Second Constitutional Convention: Patrick Henry's Lasting Legacy," *University of Richmond Law Review* 25 (1991): 519-42

Molloy, Michael J., "Confusion and a Constitutional Convention," *Western State University Law Review* 12 (1985): 793-800

Monaghan, Henry Paul, "We the People[s], Original Understanding, and Constitutional Amendment," *Columbia Law Review* 96, no.1 (Jan. 1996): 121-77

Morey, William C., "The Genesis of the Written Constitution," *The Annals of the American Academy of Political and Social Science* 1 (Apr. 1891): 529-557

Morison, Samuel Eliot, "Our Most Unpopular War," *Massachusetts Historical Society Proceedings* 80 (1968): 38-54

Morley, Michael T., "The Intratextual Independent "Legislature" and the Elections Clause," *Northwestern University Law Review* 109 (2015): 131-51

Moseley, Raymond H., "The Limited Constitutional Convention," *Tennessee Law Review* 21, no.8 (Jun. 1951): 867-74

Mussmanno, Michael A., "Is the Amendment Process Too Difficult?," *American Law Review* 57 (1923): 694-705

Natelson, Robert G., "A Response to the "Runaway Scenario"," (2013)

Natelson, Robert G., "A Bibliography for Originalist Research," (2007)

Natelson, Robert G., "Appendix - Delegates to Founding-Era Conventions," *Florida Law Review* (2013)

Natelson, Robert G., "Founding-Era Conventions and the Meaning of the Constitution's "Convention For Proposing Amendments," *Florida Law Review* 65 (2013): 1-76

Natelson, Robert G., "James Madison and the Constitution's "Convention For Proposing Amendments"," *Akron Law Review* 45 (2012): 431-48

Natelson, Robert G., "Proposing Constitutional Amendments by Convention: Rules Governing the Process," *Tennessee Law Review*, 78 (2011): 693-750

Natelson, Robert G., "The Constitution and the Public Trust," *Buffalo Law Review* 52 (2004): 1077-1178

Natelson, Robert G., "The Liberal Establishment's Disinformation Campaign Against Article V – and How It Misled Conservatives," (2015)

Nichols, Henry W., "Amending the United States Constitution," *Insurance Counsel Journal* 22 (Jan. 1955): 99-111

Noonan, Jr., John T., "The Convention Method of Constitutional Amendment – Its Meaning, Usefulness, and Wisdom," *Pacific Law Journal* 10 (1979): 641-6

Oberst, Paul, "Genesis of the Three States-Rights Amendments of 1963," *Notre Dame Lawyer* 39, no.6 (Sept. 1963): 644-58

Orfield, Lester B., "Sovereignty and the Federal Amendment Power," *Iowa Law Review* 16 (1930): 504-22

Orfield, Lester B., "The Federal Amending Power: Genesis and Justiciability," *Minnesota Law Review* 14 (1930): 369-84

Orfield, Lester B., "The Procedure of the Federal Amending Power," *Illinois Law Review* 25 (1930): 418-45

Orfield, Lester B., "The Scope of the Federal Amending Power," *Michigan Law Review* 28, no.5 (1930): 550-85

Packard, Frank E., "Constitutional Law: The States and the Amending Process," *American Bar Association Journal* 45, no.2 (Feb.1959): 161-4, 196-8

Packard, Frank E., "Notes and Comments – Rescinding Memorialization Resolutions," *Chicago-Kent Law Review* 30, no.4 (Jan. 1952): 339-49

Packard, Frank E., "The Inherent Safety in Calling a Convention for the Purpose of Proposing Amendments to the Constitution of the United States," *Dickinson Law Review* 56 (1952): 373-6

Paulsen, Michael Stokes, "A General Theory of Article V: The Constitutional

Lessons of the Twenty-seventh Amendment," *Yale Law Journal* 103, no.3 (Dec. 1993): 677-789

Paulsen, Michael Stokes, "How to Count to Thirty-four: The Constitutional Case for a Constitutional Convention," *Harvard Journal of Law & Public Policy* 34, no.3 (2011): 837-72

Penrose, Mary Margaret, "Conventional Wisdom: Acknowledging Uncertainty in the Unknown," *Tennessee Law Review* 78 (2011): 789-805

Phillips, Herbert S., "Has the Congress the Power Under Article V of the Constitution to Call and Regulate the Holding of Ratifying Conventions Independent of State Legislatures?," *Florida State Bar Association Law Journal* 6 (1933): 573-8

Pierce, Michael, "The Anti-Corruption Force of Article V's Convention Clause," *Dartmouth Law Journal* XIII (Spring 2015): 58-85

Planell, Raymond M., "Equal Rights Amendment: Will States be Allowed to Change their Minds?," *Notre Dame Lawyer* 49, no.3 (Feb. 1974): 657-70

Platz, William A., "Article Five of the Federal Constitution," *George Washington Law Review* 3 (1934): 17-49

Posner, Eric A., "The Constitution of the Roman Republic: A Political Economy Perspective," *University of Chicago Law School*, Working Paper No. 540, (Nov. 2010): 2-33

Potter, William P., "The Method of Amending the Federal Constitution," *University of Pennsylvania Law Review and American Law Register* 48, no. 9 (1909): 589-610

Presser, Stephen B., "Constitutional Amendments: Dangerous Threat or Democracy in Action," *Texas Review of Law & Policy* 5, no.1 (2000): 209-25

Pritchett, C. Herman, "Congress and Article V Conventions," *Western Political Quarterly* 35, no.2 (Jun. 1982): 222-7

Pulignano, Vincent, "A Known Unknown: The Call for An Article V Convention," *Florida Law Review Forum* 67 (2016): 151-160

Rackoff, Maryanne R., "The Monster Approaching the Capital: The Effort to Write Economic Policy Into the United States Constitution," *Akron Law Review* 15 (Spr. 1982): 733-51

Rappaport, Michael B., "Reforming Article V: The Problems Created By The National Convention Amendment Method And How To Fix Them," *Virginia Law Review* 96, no.7 (Nov. 2010): 1509-81

Rappaport, Michael B., "The Constitutionality of a Limited Convention: An Originalist Analysis," *Constitutional Commentary* 81 (2012): 53-109

Rees, Charles A., "Remarkable Evolution: The Early Constitutional History of Maryland," *Baltimore Law Review* 3, no.2 (2007)

Rees III, Grover, "Constitutional Conventions and Constitutional Arguments: Some Thoughts on Limits," *Harvard Journal of Law and Public Policy* 6 (1982): 79-91

Rees III, Grover, "Rescinding Ratification of Proposed Constitutional Amendments A Question for the Court," *Louisiana Law Review* 37, no.4 (Spr. 1977): 896-925

Rees III, Grover, "The Amendment Process and Limited Constitutional Conventions," *Benchmark* II, no.2 (Mar.-Apr. 1986): 63-108

Rhodes, Robert M., "A Limited Federal Constitutional Convention," *University of Florida Law Review* XXVI, no.1 (Fall 1973): 1-18

Ripple, Kenneth, "Article V and the Proposed Federal Constitutional Convention Procedures Bills," *Cardozo Law Review* 3 (1982): 529-62

Rogers, James Kenneth, "The Other Way to Amend the Constitution: The Article V Constitutional Convention Amendment Process," *Harvard Journal of Law & Public Policy* 30, no.3 (Sum. 2007): 1005-22

Rotunda, Ronald D. & Stephen J. Safranek, "An Essay on Term Limits and a Call for a Constitutional Convention," *Marquette Law Review* 80, no.1 (Fall 1996): 227-44

Scalia, Antonin & Bryan A. Garner, "A Note on the Use of Dictionaries," *Green Bag*, 2d Series, 16, no.4 (Sum. 2013): 419-28

Scheips, Paul J., "Significance and Adoption of Article V of the Constitution," *Notre Dame Lawyer* 26, no.1 (1950): 46-67

Shanahan, Jr., Frank E., "Proposed Constitutional Amendments: They Will Strengthen Federal- State Relations," *American Bar Association Journal* 49, no.7 (Jul. 1963): 631-6

Shields, David S., "'We declare you independent whether you wish it or not': The Print Culture of Early Filibusterism," paper delivered at the 24th Annual James Russel Wiggins Lecture in the History of the American Culture, 16 June 2006, *American Antiquarian Society*, 233-59

Sioussat, St. George L., "Tennessee, the Compromise of 1850, and the Nashville Convention," *Mississippi Valley Historical Review* 2, no. 3 (Dec. 1915): 313-47

Skinner, George D., "Intrinsic Limitations on the Power of Constitutional Amendment," *Michigan Law Review* 18, no.3 (Jan. 1920): 213-25

Sprague, Robert J., "Shall We Have a Federal Convention, and What Shall It Do?," *Maine Law Review* III, no.4 (1910): 115-25

Stasny, James, "The Constitutional Convention Provision of Article V: Historical Perspective," *Cooley Law Review*, I (1982): 73-108

Stern, Michael, "A Brief Reply to Professor Penrose," *Tennessee Law Review* 78 (2011): 807-11

Stern, Michael, "Reopening the Constitutional Road to Reform: Toward a Safeguarded Article V Convention," *Tennessee Law Review* 78 (2011): 765-88

Swindler, William F., "Current Challenge to Federalism: The Confederating Proposals," *The Georgetown Law Journal* 52, no. 1 (Fall 1963): 1-41

Swisher, Carl Brent & Patricia Nelson, "In Convention Assembled," *Villanova Law Review* 13, no.4 (Sum. 1968): 711-31

Taft, Henry W., "Amendment of the Federal Constitution. Is the Power Conferred by Article V Limited by the 10th Amendment?," *Virginia Law Review* 16, no.7 (1930): 647-58

Tan, James, "*Contiones* in the Age of Cicero," *Classical Antiquity* 27, no.1 (Apr. 2008): 163-201

Taylor, Arthur H., "Fear of an Article V Convention," *Brigham Young University Journal of Public Law* 20, no.2 (2006): 407-38

Terranova, Christopher, "The Constitutional Life of Legislative Instructions in America," *New York University Law Review* 84 (Nov. 2009): 1331-74

Tillman, Seth Barrett, "*The Federalist Papers* as Reliable Historical Source Material for Constitutional Interpretation," *West Virginia Law Review* 105 (2003): 601-19

Tribe, Laurence, "Issues Raised by Requesting Congress to Call a Constitutional Convention to Propose a Balanced Budget Amendment," *Pacific Law Journal* 10 (1979): 627-40

Tuller, Walter K., "A Convention to Amend the Constitution - Why Needed - How It May Be Obtained," *North American Review* 193, no.664 (Mar. 1911): 369-87

Turner, Frederick Jackson, "Western State-Making in the Revolutionary Era," *American Historical Review* 1, no.1 (Oct. 1895): 70-87

Turner, Frederick Jackson, "Western State-Making in the Revolutionary Era II," *American Historical Review* 1, no.2 (Jan. 1896): 251-69

Uhl, Raymond, "Sovereignty and the Fifth Article," *Southwestern Social Science Quarterly* XVI, no.4 (Mar. 1936): 1-20

Van Alstyne, William, "Does Article V Restrict the States to Calling Unlimited Conventions Only? – A Letter to a Colleague," *Duke Law Journal* 1978 (1978): 1295-1306

Van Alstyne, William, "The Limited Constitutional Convention – The Recurring Answer," *Duke Law Journal* 1979, (1979): 985-98

Van Sickle, Bruce M. and Lynn M. Boughey, "Lawful and Peaceful Revolution: Article V and Congress' Present Duty to Call a Convention for Proposing Amendments," *Hamline Law Review* 14, no.1 (Fall 1990): 1-35

Vile, John R., "American Views of the Constitutional Amending Process: An Intellectual History of Article V," *American Journal of Legal History* 35, no.1 (Jan. 1991): 44-69

Vile, John R., "Legally Amending the United States Constitution: The Exclusivity of Article V's Mechanisms," *Cumberland Law Review* 21 (1991): 271-307

Vile, John R., "Three Kinds of Constitutional Founding and Change: The Convention Model and Its Alternatives," *Political Research Quarterly* 46, no.4 (Dec. 1993): 881-895

Voegler, Douglas G., "Amending the Constitution by the Article V Convention Method," *North Dakota Law Review* 55 (1979): 355-408

von Moschzisker, Robert, "Dangers in Disregarding Fundamental Conceptions when Amending the Federal Constitution," *Cornell Law Quarterly* XI, no.1 (1925): 1-19

Weber, Paul J., "Madison's Opposition to a Second Convention," *Polity* 20, no.3 (Spr. 1988): 498-517

Weber, Paul J., "The Constitutional Convention: A Safe Political Option," *Journal of Law and Politics* 3 (1986): 51-70

Webster, W.C., "Comparative Study of the State Constitutions of the American Revolution," *Annals American Academy Politics & Social Science* 9 (1897): 380-420

Weinfeld, Abraham C., "Power of Congress Over State Ratifying Conventions," *Harvard Law Review* 51, no.3 (Jan. 1938): 473-506

West, Henry Litchfield, "Shall United States Senators be Elected by the People," *Forum* 42 (Oct. 1909): 291-8

Wheeler, Everett P., "Limit of Power to Amend Constitution," *American Bar Association Journal* 7, no.2 (Feb. 1921): 75-9

Wheeler, Wayne B., "Is a Constitutional Convention Impending?," *Illinois Law Review* 21 (1927): 784-803

White, Thomas Raeburn, "Amendment and Revision of State Constitutions," *University of Pennsylvania Law Review* 100 (1952): 1132-52

White, William H., "Article V: Political Questions and Sensible Answers," *Texas Law Review* 57 (1979): 1259-82

Willis, Sr., George L., "History Kentucky Constitutions and Constitutional Conventions," *Register of the Kentucky State Historical Society* 28, no.85 (Oct. 1930): 305-29

Willis, Hugh Evander, "The Doctrine of the Amendability of the United States Constitution," *Indiana Law Journal* 7, no.8 (1932): 457-69

Wood, Gordon S., "The Origins of Article V of the Constitution," *The Constitution and the Budget*, American Enterprise Institute (1980)

Wright, R. George, "Could a Constitutional Amendment Be Unconstitutional?," *Loyola University Law Review* 22, no.4 (Sum. 1991): 741-64

Yawitz, Milton, "The Legal Effect Under American Decisions of an Alleged Irregularity in the Adoption of a Constitution or Constitutional Amendment," *St. Louis Law Review* 10, no.4 (1925): 279-98

"A Note on Certain of Hamilton's Pseudonyms," *William and Mary Quarterly* 12, no.2 (Apr.1955): 282-97

"The Equal Rights Amendment and Article V: A Framework for Analysis of the Extension and Rescission Issues," *University of Pennsylvania Law Review* 127 (1978): 494-532

Note, "Constitutional Revision by a Restricted Convention," *Minnesota Law Review* 35 (1951): 283-97

Note, "Sawing a Justice in Half," *Yale Law Review* 48, no. 8 (June 1939): 1455-8

"The Powers of Constitutional Conventions," *Harvard Law Review* 29, no.5 (Mar. 1916): 528-33

"Proposed Legislation on the Convention Method of Amending the United States Constitution," *Harvard Law Review* 85, no.8 (Jun. 1972): 1612-48

"Proposing Amendments to the United States Constitution by Convention," *Harvard Law Review* 70, no.6 (Apr. 1957): 1067-76

Reports

Amendment of the Constitution by the Convention Method Under Article V (Special Committee Report), American Bar Association, (1974)

National Center for Interstate Compacts, "10 Frequently Asked Questions" (Lexington, KY: The Council of State Governments, 2015)

Special Report of Committee on Constitutional Amendments of the Association of the Bar of the City of New York, Year Book 1924

SURVEYED MATERIALS

Books

Anthony, Elliott. *The Constitutional History of Illinois*. Chicago: Chicago Legal News, 1891, reprint by Forgotten Books, 2012.

Berger, Raoul. *Federalism – The Founders' Design*. Norman, OK: University of Oklahoma Press, 1987.

Braden, George D. and Rubin C. Cohn. *The Illinois Constitution: An Annotated and Comparative Analysis*. Champaign: University of Illinois Press, 1969.

Bradford, M. E. *Original Intentions - On the Making and Ratification of the United States Constitution*. Athens, GA: University of Georgia Press, 1993.

Cooley, Thomas M. *A Treatise on the Constitutional Limitations Which Rest Upon the Legislative Power of the States of the American Union*. Boston: Little, Brown, 1868.

D'Alemberte, Talbot. *The Florida State Constitution: a Reference Guide*. Westport, CT: Praeger, 1991.

Dinan, John D. *The Virginia State Constitution: A Reference Guide*. Westport, CT: Praeger, 2006.

Galie, Peter J. *Ordered Liberty: A Constitutional History of New York*. New York: Fordham University Press, 1996.

Gardner, James A. *Interpreting State Constitutions – A Jurisprudence of Function in a Federal System*. Chicago: University of Chicago Press, 2005.

Hill, William C. *The Vermont State Constitution: A Reference Guide*. Westport, CT: Greenwood Press, 1992.

Howard, A. E. Dick. *Commentaries on the Constitution of Virginia*. Charlottesville: University of Virginia Press, 1974.

Laska, Lewis L. *The Tennessee State Constitution*. Westport, CT: Greenwood Press, 1990.

Levy, Leonard W. *Origins of the Bill of Rights*. New Haven, CT: Yale University Press, 2001.

Lydecker, Robert C. *Roster Legislatures of Hawaii, 1841-1918*. Honolulu: Hawaiian Gazette, 1918.

Marshall, Susan E. *The New Hampshire Constitution - A Reference Guide*. Westport, CT: Praeger, 2004.

McMillan, Malcom C. *Constitutional Development in Alabama, 1798-1901*. Chapel Hill, NC: University of North Carolina Press, 1955.

Peterson, Merrill D., *The Portable Thomas Jefferson*. New York: Penguin, 1975.

Saye, Albert Berry. *A Constitutional History of Georgia, 1732-1968*. Athens, GA: University of Georgia Press, 1970.

The Heritage Guide to the Constitution. Washington, D.C.: Regnery, 2005.

Secret Proceedings and Debates of the Constitutional Convention 1787. Hawthorne, CA: reprint by Omni, 1986.

Articles

Albert, Richard, "Constitutional Amendment by Constitutional Desuetude," *American Journal of Comparative Law* 62 (2014): 1-39

Albert, Richard, "Constitutional Disuse or Desuetude: The Case of Article V," *Boston University Law Review* 94 (2014): 1029-80

Almand, Bond, "The States Should Call a Constitutional Convention," *Georgia Bar Journal* 10 (1947): 437-46

Amar, Akhil Reed, "The Consent of the Governed: Constitutional Amendment Outside Article V," *Columbia Law Review* 94 (1994): 457-508

Ames, Herman V., "The Amending Provision of the Federal Constitution in Practice," *Proceedings of the American Philosophical Society* 63, no.1 (1924): 62-75

Baker, Thomas E., "Exercising the Amendment Power to Disapprove of Supreme Court Decisions: A Proposal for a "Republican Veto"*," *Hastings Constitutional Law Quarterly* 22 (Win. 1995): 325-57

Berns, Walter, "Comment: The Forms of Article V," *Harvard Journal of Law and Public Policy* 6 (1982): 73-7

Bernstein, David, "The Constitutional Convention: Facts and Figures," *History Teacher* 21, no.1 (Nov. 1987): 11-19

Black, Charles L., "The Proposed Amendment of Article V: A Threatened Disaster," *Yale Law Journal* 72 (1963): 957-66

Brennan, Thomas E., "You Were There," *Thomas M. Cooley Law Review* 28 (2011): 3-8

Call, Joseph L., "Federalism and Constitutional Amendment," *Los Angeles Bar Bulletin* 39 (Mar. 1964): 144-8

Carrington, Paul D., "The Case for Calling an Article V Convention," *Thomas M. Cooley Law Review* 28 (2011): 57-60

Dalotto, Juliana Gisela, "American State Constitutions of 1776-1787: The Antecedents of the Necessary [and Proper] Clause," *Journal of Constitutional Law* 14, no.5 (Apr. 2012): 1315-50

Dellinger, Walter E., "Constitutional Politics: A Rejoinder," *Harvard Law Review* 97 (1983): 446-50

Dellinger, Walter E., "Who Controls a Constitutional Convention? – A Response," *Duke Law Journal* 1979 (1979): 999-1001

Denning, Brannon P. and John R. Vile, "The Relevance of Constitutional Amendments: A Response to David Strauss," *Tulsa Law Review* 77 (2002): 247-82

Dow, David R., "When Words Mean What We Believe They Say: The Case of Article V," *Iowa Law Review* 76 (1990): 1-66

Dowling, Noel T., "Clarifying the Amending Process," *Washington and Lee Law Review* 1, no.2 (Mar. 1939): 215-30

Dunker, William L., "Constitutional Amendments – The Justiciability of

Ratification and Retraction," *Tennessee Law Review* 41 (1973): 93-112

Eiselen, Malcolm R., "Dare We Call a Federal Convention?," *North American Review* 244, no.1 (Aut. 1937): 27-38

Eldridge, Seba, "Need for a More Democratic Procedure of Amending the Constitution," *American Political Science Review* 10, no.4 (Nov. 1916): 683-8

Eliot, Edward C., "Changing the Constitution," *Yale Law Journal* 24, no.8 (Jun. 1915): 649-60

Feibelman, Herbert U., "The Evolution of Article V," *Commercial Law Journal* 38 (1933): 197-200

Feerick, John d., "Amending the Constitution Through a Convention," *American Bar Association Journal* 60, no.3 (Mar. 1973): 285-8

Fisch, William B., "Constitutional Referendum in the United States of America," *American Journal of Comparative Law* 54 (Fall 2006): 485-504

Gaither, Bruce Darrow, "Amendment Of The Constitution Through Convention Under Article V – May A Constitutional Convention Be Limited In Its Function Under Existing Law?," *Oklahoma Bar Journal* 58, no.39 (Oct. 1987): 3013-6

Garrett, Finis J., "Amending the Federal Constitution," *Tennessee Law Review* 7 (1928-29): 286-309

Garver, Frank Harmon, "Some Misconceptions Relative to the Constitutional Convention," *The Historian* (1938): 24-32

Garver, Frank Harmon, "Some Propositions Rejected by the Constitutional Convention of 1787," *The Historian* (1944): 113-27

Griffin, Stephen M., "The Nominee Is...Article V," *Constitutional Commentary* 12 (1995): 171-173

Guida, Anthony James, "States' Role in Article V Conventions: AFL-CIO vs. Eu," *Cincinnati Law Review* 54 (1985): 317-32

Gunther, Gerald, "Constitutional Brinkmanship, Stumbling toward a Convention," *American Bar Association* 65 (Jul. 1979): 1046-9

Hadju, Robert and Bruce E. Rosenblum, "The Process of Constitutional Amendment," *Columbia Law Review* 79, no.1 (Jan. 1979): 106-72

Haskins, George L., "The Legal Heritage of Plymouth Colony," *University of Pennsylvania Law Review* 110 (1962): 847-59

Heckman, J. William, "Ratification of a Constitutional Amendment: Can a State Change Its Mind?," *Connecticut Law Review* 6 (1973): 28-35

Hoar, Roger Sherman, "Legislative Notes and Reviews: Constitutional Conventions," *American Political Science Review* (1916): 519-28

Holding, Archibald McCall, "Perils to be Apprehended from Amending the Constitution," *American Law Review* 57 (Jul-Aug 1923): 481-97

Huq, Aziz Z., "The Function of Article V," *University of Pennsylvania Law Review* 162 (2014): 1166-1236

Ireland, Gordon, "Constitutional Amendments – Powers of Conventions," *Tulane Law Review* 6 (1931): 75-82

Ishikawa, Brendon Troy, "Amending the Constitution: Just Not Every November," *Cleveland State Law Review* 44 (1996): 303-43

Ishikawa, Brendon Troy, "The Stealth Amendment: The Impending Ratification and Repeal of a Federal Budget Amendment," *Tulsa Law Journal* 35, no. (1999): 353-82

Jenner, Albert E., "Observations on the Proposed Alteration of the Constitutional Amendatory Procedure," *Notre Dame Lawyer* 39, no.6 (1964): 625-27

Jennings, Thelma, "Tennessee and the Nashville Conventions of 1850," *Tennessee Historical Quarterly* 30, no. 1 (Spr. 1971): 70-82

Jones, Eugene W., "A New Look at Constitutional Amendment," *Southwestern Social Science Quarterly* 46, no.2 (Sept. 1965): 122-9

Joshi, Sopan, "The Presidential Role in the Constitutional Amendment Process," *Northwestern University Law Review* 107, no.2 (2013): 963-98

Ku, Raymond, "Consensus of the Governed: The Legitimacy of Constitutional Change," *Fordham Law Review* 64, no.2 (1995): 535-86

Lacy, Donald P. and Philip L. Martin, "Amending the Constitution: The Bottleneck in the Judiciary Committees," *Harvard Journal on Legislation* 9 (1972): 666-93

Lanier, Alexander Sidney, "Amending the Federal Constitution," *Virginia Law Register* 9, no.2 (Jun. 1923): 81-4

Lash, Kurt T., "The Constitutional Convention of 1937: The Original Meaning of the New Jurisprudential Deal," *Fordham Law Review* 70, no.2 (2001): 459-526

Laska, Lewis L., "A Legal and Constitutional History of Tennessee," *Memphis State University Law Review* 6 (1976): 563-672

Lass, William E., "The Birth of Minnesota," *Minnesota History* (Sum. 1997): 267-79

Latham, Darren R., "The Historical Amendability of the American Constitution: Speculations on an Empirical Problematic," *American University Law Review* 55, no.1 (Oct. 2005): 145-258

Levinson, Sanford, "The Political Implications of Amending Clauses," *Constitutional Commentary* 13 (1996): 107-23

Lousin, Ann M., "How to Hold a State Constitutional Convention in the Twenty-first Century," *Loyola of Los Angeles Law Review* 44 (2011): 603-22

Lutz, Donald S., "Toward a Theory of Constitutional Amendment," *American Political Science Review* 88, no.2 (Jun. 1994): 355-70

Lynch, Timothy, "Amending Article V to Make the Constitutional Amendment Process Itself Less Onerous," *Tennessee Law Review* 78 (2011): 823-30

Markman, Stephen, "The Amendment Process of Article V: A Microcosm of the Constitution," *Harvard Journal of Law & Public Policy* 12, no.1 (1989): 113-21

Martin, William Logan, "The Amending Power: The Ebinger Proposal," *American Bar Association Journal* 40, no.9 (Sept. 1954): 767-71, 802-3

Mathias, Charles, "What's the Constitution Among Friends?," *American Bar Association Journal* 67, no.7 (Jul. 1981): 861-3

McCormick, Peter J., "The 1992 Secession Movement in Southwest Kansas," *Great Plains Quarterly*. Paper 994, 15 (Fall 1995): 247-258

Mikhail, John, "The Necessary and Proper Clauses," *Georgetown Law Journal* 102

(2014): 1045-1132

Miller, Justin, "Amendment of the Federal Constitution: Should It Be Made More Difficult?," *American Law Review* 60 (1926): 181-205

Natelson, Robert G., "The Article V Convention Process and the Restoration of Federalism," *Harvard Journal of Law & Public Policy* 36, no.3 (2013): 957-60

Natelson, Robert G., "The Enumerated Powers of States," *Nevada Law Journal* 3 (Spr. 2003): 469-94

Natelson, Robert G., "The State-Application-and-Convention Method of Amending the Constitution: The Founding Era Vision," *Thomas M. Cooley Law Review* 28 (2011): 9-19

Needham, Charles Willis, "Changing the Fundamental Law," *University of Pennsylvania Law Review and American Law Register* 69, no.3 (Mar. 1921): 223-36

Neuborne, Burt, "One-State/Two-Votes: Do Supermajority Senate Voting Rules Violate the Article V Guaranty of Equal State Suffrage," *Stanford Journal of Civil Rights & Civil Liberties* X (Jan. 2014): 27-54

Oberst, Paul, "Genesis of the Three States-Rights Amendments of 1963," *Notre Dame Lawyer* 39, no.6 (1964): 644-58

Paxson, Frederick L., "The Territory of Colorado," *American Historical Review* 12, no.1 (Oct. 1906): 53-65

Quarles, James, "Amendments to the Federal Constitution," *American Bar Association Journal* 26 (Jul, 1940): 617-20

Robbins, Caroline, "Laws and Governments proposed for West New Jersey and Pennsylvania, 1676-1683," *The Pennsylvania Magazine of History and Biography* 105, No. 4 (Oct. 1981): 373-92

Rocha, Guy Louis, "Nevada's Emergence in the American Great Basin; Territory and State," *Nevada Historical Society Quarterly* (Win. 1995): 255-80

Rogers-Kingsbury, Linda, "The Dangers of a Second Constitutional Convention," *Judges' Journal* 26 (Sum. 1987): 35-7, 62-3

Roslof, Charles M., "Should We Fear A "Runaway Convention"?: Lessons From State Constitutional Conventions," SSRN-1d2626158, (2014), 1-23

Schaefer, George J., "Amendments to Constitution: Ratification by State Convention," *St. John's Law Review* 2, no.7 (May 1933): 375-8

Schaller, Thomas F., "Consent for Change: Article V and the Constitutional Amendment Process," *Constitutional Political Economy* 8 (1997): 195-213

Sears, Kenneth C., "Voting on Constitutional Conventions and Amendments," *University of Chicago Law Review* 2, no.4 (Jun. 1935): 612-8

Segall, Eric J., "Constitutional Change and the Supreme Court: The Article V Problem," *Journal of Constitutional Law* 16, no.2 (Nov. 2013): 443-51

Seidman, Louis Michael, "The Secret Life of the Political Question Doctrine," *John Marshall Law Review* 37 (2004): 441-80

Sheldon, Addison E. "Nebraska Constitutions of 1866, 1871 & 1875," *Nebraska Legislative Reference Bureau and Nebraska State Historical Society*, Bulletin No. 13 (Sept. 1920)

Strauss, David A., "The Irrelevance of Constitutional Amendments," *Harvard Law Review* 114 (2001): 1457-1505

Taft, William Howard, "Can Ratification of an Amendment to the Constitution Be Made to Depend on a Referendum?" *Yale Law Journal* XXIX, no.8 (Jun. 1920): 821-5

Tanger, Jacob, "Amending Procedure of the Federal Constitution," *American Political Science Review* (1915): 689-99

Taylor, Rod, "A New Look at Article V and the Bill of Rights," *Indiana Law Review* 6 (1973): 699-709

Thill, David W., "Federalism and Supreme Court Review: Is Article V an Exception to the Independent and Adequate State Grounds Doctrine?," *Hastings Constitutional Law Quarterly* 13 (Win. 1986): 389-414

Van Alstyne, William W., "A Response to Justice Thomas Brennan's Remarks at the Thomas M. Colley Law School Article V Symposium," *Thomas M. Cooley Law Review* 28 (2011): 51-6

Vile, John R., "The Amending Process: The Alternative to Revolution," *Southeastern Political Review* 11, no.2 (Sept. 1983): 49-95

Vile, John R., "Judicial Review of the Amending Process: The Dellinger-Tribe Debate," *Journal of Law & Politics* 3 (1986): 21-50

Vile, John R., "Limitations on the Amending Process," *Constitutional Commentary* 2 (1985): 373-88

Vile, John R., "The Supreme Court and the Amending Process," (1980): 33-66

Walcoff, Jonathan L., "The Unconstitutionality of Voter Initiative Applications for Federal Constitutional Conventions," *Columbia Law Review* 85, no.7 (Nov. 1985): 1525-45

Weclew, Robert G., "The Constitution's Amending Article: Illusion or Necessity," *De Paul Law Review* 18, no.1 (1968): 167-87

White, Alexander, "Keep 'Em Separated: Article I, Article V, and Congress's Limited and Defined Role in the Process of Amending the Constitution," *Columbia Review* 113 (2013): 1051-96

Williams, George Washington, "What, If Any, Limitations Are There Upon the Power to Amend the Constitution of the United States?," *Virginia Law Register* 6, no.3 (Jul. 1920): 161-74

Williams, Robert F., "State Constitutional Law Processes," *William and Mary Law Review* 24, no.2 (Win. 1983): 169-228

Ziegler, Mary, "Ways to Change: A Reevaluation of Article V Campaigns and Legislative Constitutionalism," *Brigham Young University Law Review* (2009): 969-1010

"Constitutional Law: Referendum as to Amendments of Federal Constitution," *Michigan Law Review* 18, no.7 (May 1920): 698-9

"Constitutional Law: Constitutional Conventions – Legislature's Power to Call," *Yale Law Journal* (1917):132-3

"Constitutional Revision by a Restricted Convention," *Minnesota Law Review* 35 (1951): 283-97

Index

1787 Grand Federal Constitutional Convention in Philadelphia: —
  1787 Philadelphia Convention delegate instructions: Appendix C, 767
  Committee of Detail: 142, 144-147, 577
  Philadelphia Convention: 16, 35, 42, 60-61, 69, 74, 120, 123, 127-138, 143, 153-157, 162, 165, 174, 231, 271-277, 338, 410-417, 422-428, 442, 461, 474-497, 505-510, 515, 520, 526, 532, 537, 540-548, 554-556, 572, 577, 583-588, 594, 611-622, 627, 631-632, 637, 641, 656, 665-666, 674, 697, 717, 767-773

Adams, Samuel: 91-94, 156, 587

AFL-CIO: 308, 312, 321, 336, 350, 360, 384, 399, 539

Aggregation in resolutions: 193, 531

Agnew, Daniel: 678-679

Alabama: 43, 186-187, 193, 351-352, 357, 363-369, 372-375, 394, 398, 702
  Alabama Supreme Court: 351, 357, 367, 369, 372, 375

Alaska: 353-354, 399, 483, 738

Amar, Akhil Reed: xxxv, 458

Amending: -
  amending clause: 205, 644
  amending power: 23, 31, 36, 41, 49-51, 53-58, 136, 140, 231, 258-260, 276, 297, 695
  amending procedure: xviii
  amending process: xxxiv, 14, 38, 43, 56, 73, 101-103, 119, 138-140, 154, 174, 191, 209, 219, 222-228, 231-235, 240, 257, 298, 318, 328, 351, 360, 415, 429, 460, 535, 574, 583, 631, 676-678, 688-690, 695, 709, 714
  constitutional amendment: 4, 23-25, 47, 52, 69-70, 113, 118, 155, 162, 197, 200-201, 210, 227, 233, 247, 260, 263, 268, 292-294, 299-304, 310-311, 325-326, 331, 336, 342-347, 352-355, 364-366, 370-376, 382, 387-389, 393-395, 404, 419, 451, 458-459, 469, 480, 485, 558, 563-565, 580, 585, 608, 623, 630, 636, 648, 651-653, 700, 714, 775

Amendments of the Federal Constitution:-
  Eighteenth Amendment: 52, 159, 162, 194, 288, 295-301, 307, 311-315, 319, 323-324, 330, 339-340, 345-348, 352, 355, 358, 365-367, 378-379, 387, 394, 527, 551, 558-560, 625, 689, 701
  Eleventh Amendment: 224, 275, 289, 303, 463, 552

Fifteenth Amendment: 114, 309, 611
Fifth Amendment: 322
First Amendment: 19, 294, 329, 333, 337-338, 343, 349, 383, 670, 701
Fourteenth Amendment: 196, 310, 329, 333-334, 344-345, 466, 511, 552, 601
Nineteenth Amendment: 288, 299, 302, 308-309, 552, 560, 689, 701
Ninth Amendment: 54
Second Amendment: 459
Seventeenth Amendment: 161, 189-194, 198, 249, 459, 522, 559-562, 683-684, 689, 693
Sixteenth Amendment: 159, 194, 468, 549-552, 560, 689
Tenth Amendment: 31, 54-57, 71, 161, 261-262, 267, 294, 319, 324-326, 341, 348, 366, 706
Thirteenth Amendment: 276, 551-552, 701
Twenty-eighth Amendment: 549
Twenty-fifth Amendment: 687
Twenty-first Amendment: 27, 41, 64, 160-162, 178, 263, 272, 323, 349, 367-369, 386, 390, 415, 427, 430, 471, 491, 496, 527, 540, 551, 567, 579, 613, 628-629, 695, 701, 719, 738
Twenty-fourth Amendment: 687
Twenty-seventh Amendment: 255, 293, 296, 461, 465, 533, 714
Twenty-sixth Amendment: 552, 687
Twenty-third Amendment: 558, 687

American Bar Association: 266, 274, 277-278

American Civil Liberties Union: 206, 337, 470

American Civil War: 9, 16, 23-24, 44, 102, 111, 185-188, 327, 361, 563-566, 615, 636, 661, 687, 709, 723

American Constitution: 4, 9, 13-16, 19, 21, 24-28, 31, 43, 69, 102, 106, 113-114, 118, 126-128, 158, 178, 183-184, 192-194, 201, 231, 241, 271-272, 276-288, 294-297, 301-302, 309, 317-319, 326-329, 332-333, 342, 349-352, 355, 359-360, 365-368, 373-374, 380-383, 388-394, 426-427, 435, 459, 471, 479, 482, 486, 489, 493, 497, 500-501, 547, 576, 581, 612, 617, 639, 667, 685, 705, 714, 729, 738, 769-771, 775
   Case or Controversy Clause: 299
   Commerce Clause: 664
   Contracts Clause: 297
   Elections Clause: 317
   Establishment Clause: 299
   General Welfare Clause: 664
   Guarantee Clause: 44, 317
   Immunities Clause: 310, 552
   Necessary and Proper Clause: 29, 35-36, 161, 258-262, 296, 386, 450, 456, 522, 664
   Presentment Clause: 303, 456, 557
   Speech and Debate Clause: 33, 237, 294, 329, 333, 349, 382, 537, 626
   Supremacy Clause: 15, 264-265, 318, 331-333, 393
   Tax and Spending Clause: 664
   Three-fifths Clause: 185, 551, 554
   Vesting Clause: 330

American Enterprise Institute forum: 601-602

American Revolution: 8, 75, 85-87, 95, 108, 125, 627

Ames, Herman: xxxvi, 41-42, 161-162, 426

Index **813**

Andros, Edmund: 83-85

Annapolis Convention of 1786: 65, 88, 127-133, 151, 417, 425, 442, 455, 554, 593, 622, 767

Anti-Federalists: 117, 143, 162, 166, 169, 183-184, 261, 553-555, 587, 594, 631, 647

Anti-polygamy campaign: 193-194

Aristotle: 124, 244

Arizona: 334, 483, 603, 626

Arkansas: 186, 193, 325, 359, 394-395, 483, 510
    Arkansas Constitution: 395
    Arkansas Supreme Court: 325, 359, 394

Articles of Confederation: 16-17, 24, 43, 46, 65, 68, 83, 125, 128-129, 133, 139-144, 156, 163-164, 170, 175, 183, 268, 426, 455, 486-492, 501-502, 505-506, 554, 583, 593, 612, 617-620, 635, 639, 655-658, 664-667, 722, 769-770, 772
    Inability to amend the Articles of Confederation: 46, 133-136

Articles of the Constitution (during development):
    Article II: 68, 251, 347, 392-393, 450, 511, 562
    Article III: 299, 450, 547, 562
    Article IV: 317-318, 365, 450
    Article IX: 143
    Article VI: 330-331
    Article VII: 42, 153, 271-272, 428, 497, 579, 619, 632, 655-656, 738, 761
    Article VIII: 332-333
    Article V's: 27, 58, 67, 136-152, 325, 348, 380, 395, 568, 591
    Article XIII: 46, 133, 136, 143, 492, 501, 505, 655-657, 722
    Article XIV: 331
    Article XIX: 146-149
    Article XVI: 138
    Article XVII: 380
    Article XVIII: 337
    Article XXIII: 102

Article V (US Constitution): 27, 58, 67, 136-152, 325, 348, 380, 395, 568, 591

Article V amendatory convention: 4, 10-11, 17, 20, 28, 33-34, 39-41, 49, 56, 60, 62, 71, 105, 169, 176, 179-182, 185, 209-210, 222, 233, 241, 282, 310, 350-351, 363, 409, 436, 456, 462, 492, 495, 504, 521, 554, 579, 581, 585, 599-600, 633, 659, 673, 675, 684-685, 698, 702, 720, 767

Article VII ratification conventions: 42
    Amendment proposals by the ratification conventions: 599-600

Article V ratificatory convention: xxiv-xxv, 27

Assembly of State Legislatures: xxv (n), 20, 71, 190, 199, 410-414, 431, 446, 464, 512-513, 543, 567, 629-630, 640, 676

Authorized convention: 17, 20, 115

B

Balanced Budget Amendment campaigns: 201-204, 212, 251, 254-256, 265, 270, 311-312, 321,

350, 388, 399, 409, 444, 455, 459, 466-470, 494, 515, 522, 532-533, 538, 544-546, 559-561, 564-566, 605-607, 613, 652, 654, 658, 665, 684, 694, 700, 706, 724

Balanced Budget and Emergency Control Act of 1985 (Gramm-Rudman-Hollings): 203, 700

Barker, William: 234-235, 442

Beard, Charles A.: 688-689

Beck, James: 161, 427, 659

Bedford, Jr., Gunning: xxx, 548

Bell, Griffin: 466, 725

Benjamin, Gerald: 669-670

Biggs, Andy: xxviii, 603-604, 626

Bilder, Mary Sarah: xxxi, 35, 424

Black and Tan Convention: 113

Black Jr., Charles L.: xxxv, 577, 641-645, 710-711

Black, Hugo: 219, 226

Bond, James E.: xxvii, 35-36, 257-259, 262

Bones and Banjo convention: 113

Bonfield, Arthur: 47, 210, 253, 415, 616

Boston: 85, 92, 128

Bourbon Era Redemption convention: 114

Bourne, Jonathan: 391-392

Brandeis, Louis Dembitz: 281, 299, 309

Braxton, Allen: 12, 17, 59

Brennan, Thomas E.: xxviii, 69, 402, 472

Brennan, William: 602, 634

Brickfield, Cyril: 616

Brill, Howard: 236-237

Budget Committee: 311, 388, 654

Burger, Warren: 625-626

Butler, Henry N.: xx, xxvii

Butler, Pierce: xxx, xxxii, 276, 548

C

California: 64, 117, 193, 201, 321, 350-355, 372-373, 384, 419, 423, 607, 662, 680
    California Constitution: 351, 373
    California Supreme Court: 321, 350, 352, 354, 372-373
    Los Angeles: 352, 684

Caplan, Russell: xxvii, 74, 88, 158, 170, 190, 467, 659

Index **815**

Carter, Jimmy: 203, 455, 466

Chase, Samuel Portland: 275, 303, 334, 576, 592

Checks and balances: xx-xxii, 155, 405, 491, 527, 539, 570, 580, 625, 677, 695

Child Labor Amendment: 200, 226, 275, 290-291, 696

Citizens United: 700

Civil rights: 124, 552, 564, 689

Cold War: 624, 661

Colonial Era: xxxvi, 12, 25, 85-86, 252, 401, 514, 534

Colorado: 193, 195, 374, 379, 737
    Colorado Constitution: 379
    Colorado Supreme Court: 374, 379

Comitia (Roman): 3-5, 775-776

Committees of Correspondence: 87, 92-93

Committees of Safety: 87-90, 97

Common Cause: 388, 470

Communist Party: 322, 343

Commutation conventions 1783-84: 117

Concurrent powers: 30, 341, Appendix A

Confederate States: 109, 113, 187, 615, 737, 739
    Confederate Constitution: 187, 615

Confederating Amendments: 208, 468

Confederation Congress (under Articles of Confederation): 1, 17, 35, 63-65, 117, 128-129, 133-134, 156, 417-418, 426-428, 456, 488, 511, 612, 616-618, 620-622, 633, 640, 665-666, 705, 767, 771

Congress (US): 1, 33-35, 40, 42-43, 48, 70, 209, 247-250, 258, 260, 262, 264-265, 269-270, 272, 284-285, 517-530, 630-633, 676-678

Congressional Pay Amendment: 714

Congressional Research Service: xvii, 251, 451, 524, 548

Connecticut: 77-80, 83, 91, 94, 117, 120, 125, 128, 143, 148, 156, 185, 279, 297, 309, 483, 554, 611, 769
    Connecticut Resolutions: 91
    New Haven: 78, 83, 120

Contemporaneity: 180, 205, 253-256, 259, 277, 465, 533

Continental Association: 68, 98

Continental Congress: 1, 16, 22, 65, 87-88, 94, 97-99, 101-104, 108, 119-120, 128-129, 285, 418, 486-487, 629, 639, 774
    First Continental Congress: 88, 94, 119-120
    Second Continental Congress: 99

Continuity Clause: 414, 416-417, 431, 435

Contio (Roman): 3-5, 115, 719-720, 777

Contracts Clause: 297

Case or Controversy Clause: 299

Convention limitations: 48-62
  Alterations Only theory: 56-59
  Implied Limitations theory: 50-54
  Tenth Amendment Modifies Article V theory: 55-56

Convention of States project: 409-414, 446

Convention of the Barons, 1215: 2, 12, 720

Convention Parliaments, 1660 and 1689: 8, 12

Convention powers: 18, 28-43, 635, Appendix A

Convention procedures: 62-70, 211, 246, 406, 431, 464, 518, 631

Convention process: 14, 56, 63, 101, 105-108, 111-112, 118, 161, 199, 219-220, 231, 234, 246, 253, 262-265, 274, 277, 283, 326, 402-403, 407, 430, 432, 447-448, 453, 520, 539, 603, 632

Conventions:-
  Amendatory convention: 4, 9-11, 17-28, 32-42, 45-50, 56, 59-63, 67, 70-73, 78, 97, 105-106, 113-115, 118, 121, 131, 146-148, 157-158, 169-170, 173-191, 195-202, 205-213, 218-219, 222-223, 231-233, 237, 241-252, 256, 258, 263-265, 268-270, 273-274, 277-278, 281-282, 285, 288, 294, 300, 305, 310-312, 316, 321, 325, 328, 333-334, 340-341, 345, 349-353, 357, 360-363, 370-371, 382, 388, 392-393, 401-403, 408-410, 414-420, 425-432, 435-436, 441-444, 446-451, 454-456, 462, 466-468, 470-473, 479-480, 484, 492-495, 498-504, 515, 520-521, 528, 530, 541, 544, 554, 557, 571, 574-575, 577-587, 589-595, 599-611, 614, 616, 621, 626-635, 638, 647-650, 655-659, 664-666, 669-685, 690-698, 701-702, 706, 710-711, 714-720, 723-725, 731, 767, 774-775
  Anti-revolutionary Convention: 18
  Article V amendatory convention: 4, 10-11, 17, 20, 28, 33-34, 39, 41, 49, 56, 60-62, 71, 105, 169, 176, 179-182, 185, 209-210, 222, 233, 241, 282, 310, 350-351, 363, 409, 436, 456, 462, 492, 495, 504, 521, 554, 579, 581, 585, 599-600, 633, 659, 673, 675, 684-685, 698, 702, 720, 767
  Article VII ratification conventions: 42
  Banjo Conventions: 113
  Black and Tan Convention: 113
  Commutation Conventions: 117
  Constitutional convention(s): xxxvi, 9, 11-21, 24-28, 34-39, 44-49, 59-60, 63, 66, 76, 80, 96, 99, 101, 106-108, 110-115, 117-120, 129, 136, 148, 152, 154-157, 160, 162-163, 168-170, 175-178, 183-184, 187, 191-192, 195-196, 199, 203-211, 219, 247, 251-252, 271, 274, 278-281, 346-350, 354-357, 360-361, 369-371, 373, 376-379, 382-384, 393, 402, 406, 421-423, 429, 444, 448, 455, 466-470, 473-474, 478-484, 487, 492, 495-497, 500, 510-512, 541, 552-557, 593, 600-602, 605, 610-615, 624-627, 630, 633-635, 640-641, 647, 651, 665, 669-670, 678, 704, 709, 715, 718-719, 735-751, 755-758
  Convention of the Estates: 6-7
  Convention of the Nobles: 6
  Convention Parliament: 8, 96, 777
  Convention powers: 18, 28-43, 635, Appendix A
  Convention practices: 47, 74, 80, 406, 702, 718
  Founding-Era Conventions: 66, 86-87, 119-120, 639, Appendix B
  General convention: 25, 82, 144, 152, 157, 162-174, 189, 193, 249, 252, 274, 456, 478, 531, 552-553, 556, 587-588, 617, 627, 637, 653, 668-669, 711, 715

Index **817**

    Hartford Convention of 1814: 22, 66, 77, 185
    Hempstead Convention: 82
    Interstate conventions: 62, 66, 73, 119-121, 151, 231, 263, 319, 410, 425, 442, 462, 484, 492, 508, 534, 581, 639-640, 675-676, 702-706, 718-719, 738, 762-763
    Legislative convention: 17, 20, 25, 28, 86, 99, 113
    Levee Convention: 703
    Limited convention: 23-25, 33, 128, 146, 149-150, 154, 204, 212, 251, 264, 277, 356, 358, 413, 443, 454-456, 499, 524, 528, 577, 606, 617, 642-643, 646-651, 668, 677, 680-682, 697
    Nashville Convention of 1850: 66, 509
    Nominating convention: 9, 22, 26, 447, 603
    Open convention: 212, 413-414, 494, 499, 516, 528-530, 536, 590, 604, 609, 621, 641, 648, 651, 680, 715
    Old Gentlemen's Convention: 187
    People's Convention: 24, 44
    Provincial convention: 87-88, 93, 423, 442
    Ratification convention: 4, 20-21, 63, 101, 106-107, 154, 157-161, 165, 169, 183, 249, 301-302, 369, 427, 430, 496, 503, 527, 540, 567, 572-573, 588, 613, 622, 628-629, 655, 723
    Reconstruction conventions: 16, 114, 723
    Revolutionary convention: 1, 7, 12, 16-22, 25, 28, 49, 76, 84-85, 95-99, 601, 627, 648
    Runaway convention: 23, 28, 198, 204, 210, 402-403, 408, 467, 470, 474, 484-486, 493-495, 499, 502, 510, 553, 561, 567-569, 604, 612-616, 621-628, 640, 651, 654, 681, 695-696
    Secessionary convention: 20-22, 26, 723
    Second general convention: 152, 162, 164, 166, 169, 174, 478, 552, 556, 588
    Specialized conventions: 16, 21-22, 25-26, 28
    Spontaneous convention: 17-19, 25, 28, 45
    State-application-and-convention method: 137, 282
    State conventions: xxxvi, 15, 26-27, 35-38, 41, 60-63, 97, 101, 136, 152, 155-157, 160-161, 187, 245, 274-278, 291, 304, 367-369, 386, 390, 394, 414, 445, 453, 471, 482, 497, 504, 588, 631, 637, 703, 717
    Tax-Payers' Convention: 115-117
    Types: 25-26
    Unlimited convention: 25, 192, 601, 640, 643-644, 648-649, 710, 715
    Wheeling Conventions: 111

Convention sovereignty: 37-38, 60, 466, 502

Convention threat as a tactic: 179, 606

Coode's Rebellion of 1689: 85

Cooley, Thomas McIntyre: 125-126

Cooling effect: 681-682

Copperhead Convention (1862 Illinois): xxix

Corwin Amendment: 187, 636

Corwin, Thomas: 187

Councils of Safety: 87

Crittenden Compromise: 187

D

Day, William Rufus: 300-302
Declaration of Independence: 8, 68, 87-88, 94, 99-100, 102, 119, 592, 600
Delaware: 67, 119, 186, 193, 254, 289, 508, 705, 769, 771
Delegate commissions: 767, 771, Appendix C
Delegated powers: 50, 337, 583, 712, Appendix A
Delegate selection: 12, 270-272, 369, 386, 394, 411, 465, 501, 547, 631, 651-654
Dellinger, Walter: xv, xxiii, xxxv, 45, 140, 154, 680
Democrat Party: 114, 117
Dickinson, John: xxx, 631
Dinan, John: 118, 278, 738
Dirksen, Everett: 195, 197-198, 205, 207, 210
Discretionary theory: 181
Dodd, Walter Fairleigh: xxviii, xxxvi, 38, 59, 240
Dominion of New England: 65, 83
    United Colonies of New England: 64, 83, 100
Dorr's Rebellion: 44
Douglas, William Orville: 328
Dual Purpose Theory: 649-650
Due process: 310, 329-330, 601
Dutch conventions: 81-83
Dutch Wars: 81

E

Eagle Forum: xxxvii (n), 468-471, 561, 659
Edel, Wilbur: xxvii, 709
Elections Clause: 317
Electoral College: 4, 68, 260-261, 509, 640
Electoral or popular voting: 64-69
Elliot, Jonathan: xxix, xxxii
Elliott, E. Donald: 660-661, 686-687
Ellsworth, Oliver: 143-144, 157
Engdahl, David E.: xxvii, 35-36, 257-259, 262
English Bill of Rights: 8, 383
    English Civil Wars: 8, 81, 89, 95
    English Commonwealth: 81, 124

Index **819**

English Bill of Rights: 8, 383

English Civil Wars: 8, 81, 89, 95

English Kings-
- Charles I: 80-81
- Charles II: 8, 125
- Henry I: 124
- Henry II: 6
- Henry III: 7
- Henry IV: 8
- Canute: 6
- Edgar: 6
- George I: 75, 85
- George III: 155
- Ine: 6
- James: 777
- John: 2
- William: 75, 777
- Richard I: 6

Enumerated powers: 29-30, 231, 259-260, 263, 386, 483, 503, 729, Appendix A

Equal Protection: 511

Equal Rights Amendment: 161, 200, 229, 267, 297, 307-308, 331, 334-335, 342, 385-388, 566, 625, 696

Ervin Jr., Sam: 71, 73, 207, 210-212, 249, 403-408, 430, 519

Establishment Clause: 299

Eu, March Fong: 308, 336, 350, 399

F

Factional convention: 19

Faithful Delegate Acts: 626

Failed and provisional states (Deseret, Franklin, Jefferson, Nataqua): Appendix B

Farrand, Max: xxix, xxxii, 137, 144-145, 442, 548

Federal constitution: 9, 13-16, 19-21, 24-28, 31, 43, 69, 113-114, 118, 128, 158, 178, 183-184, 192-194, 201, 231, 241, 271-272, 276-284, 288, 294, 297, 301-302, 309, 317-319, 326-329, 332-333, 349, 352, 359, 365-368, 373-374, 380, 383, 388-390, 393-394, 426-427, 435, 459, 471, 482, 486, 489, 497, 500-501, 571, 581, 612, 617, 667, 685, 705, 729, 738, 769-771

Federal Era: xxxvi, 25, 75, 252, 568, 576

Federal function: 36-38, 161, 231-233, 262, 267, 276, 302-303, 309, 343, 377, 386, 390, 420, 434, 500-501, 512, 548, 550, 650

Federalism: 14, 29, 36, 47, 52, 121, 205, 229, 262, 330, 377, 407, 454, 482, 489, 492, 498, 501, 509, 541, 563, 570, 583-584, 608, 617, 639, 650, 675, 697-699, 703-704, 706, 720, 730

Federalists:
- *Federalist Papers*: 462, 571, 574-575, 577-578, 583, 592-593, 595, 600

Federalist Party: 185-186
Federalist Society: 602
The Federalist Papers: xxix, 249, 430, 462, 571, 575, 578, 593, 645-646
Feigenspan, Christian: 313, 330, 396
First Congress (under the Constitution): 90, 172, 184, 294, 311, 496
Florida: 109-110, 342, 380, 398, 418, 460, 484, 613, 737
    Florida Constitution: 342, 380
    Florida Supreme Court: 380
    Republic of East Florida: 109, 739
    Republic of West Florida: 109-110, 739
Foley, Elizabeth Price: 584, 724
Foley, Thomas: 715-716
Founding Era: 119, 154, 628
Founding Fathers: 335, 441, 478, 490, 552
France: 5, 109-110, 168, 175-176, 601, 666
Franklin, Benjamin: 65, 87, 174
Friends of the Article V Convention: 181, 408
Fugitive Slave Act: 318
Fundamental Orders of Connecticut: 77

G

General Assembly: 6, 44-46, 187, 205, 228, 290, 317, 356, 374, 380, 392-393, 705
General Welfare Clause: 664
George Eve letter: 172
George Lee Turberville letter: 166-168
Georgia: 105-112, 119, 183, 186, 193, 394, 552, 769, 771
    Georgia constitution: 105
    Georgia Supreme Court: 394
Gerry, Elbridge: xxiii, 139, 143-144, 147, 150, 152, 490, 556, 594, 637
Ginsburg, Ruth Bader: 602
Glorious Revolution of 1688: 10, 85
Goldberg, Arthur: 602, 612, 634, 640-641, 651
Goldwater, Barry: 203-204, 466
Gorham, Nathaniel: 144, 487
Graham, Fred: 191, 714
Gramm-Rudman-Hollings: 203, 522, 700
Great Britain *see also England*: 5, 102, 104, 109-110, 177
    British Constitution: 102-103, 123-125

Index **821**

British Crown: 22, 76
British Empire: 94, 104, 716
British Isles: 12, 74, 80-81, 103
United Kingdom: 123, 639

Great Migration: 80-81

Griffin, Caesar: 333, 395

Grundnorm: 459-460

GSA: 47-48, 524, 530, 536

Guarantee Clause: 44, 317

Guerra, Darren Patrick: xxvii, 103

Gunther, Gerald: 605, 613, 652, 694

H

Hamilton, Alexander: xxx, 128, 143, 147, 155, 248, 262, 268, 430, 487-488, 523, 529, 548, 572, 592, 600, 618, 631, 642, 667

Hamilton, Elwood: 307, 313

Hamilton's Pseudonyms: 592-594

Hammond, Larry A.: 454-455

Hancock, John: 156

Harmon, John M.: 455-456, 722

Hartford Convention of 1814-15: 22

Hatch, Orrin: 71, 212, 406-408, 494, 519, 724

Hawaii: 35, 483, 531, 737-738

Levine, Henry: 273, 281

Hatch, Orrin: 71, 212, 406, 494, 519, 724

Henry, Patrick: 99, 135, 156, 165, 174, 177, 295, 587-589

Heyburn, Weldon: 614-615

Hoar, Roger Sherman: xxviii-xxix, xxxvi, 11, 20, 24, 32-33, 37-39, 59-60, 95-96, 422-423, 497

Holmes, Oliver Wendell: 298

Homogeneity: 80, 180, 250-252, 272, 465, 697

Hughes, Charles Evans: 291-292, 299, 323

Humble Petition and Advice: 125

I

Idaho: 193, 229, 246, 291, 334, 381-382, 398-399, 531, 614
    Idaho Constitution: 382
    Idaho Supreme Court: 381-382

Illinois: xxix, 186, 193-197, 228-229, 331, 483, 510
    Illinois Constitution: xxix

Illinois Copperhead Convention: xxix

Immunity Act: 322

Immunities Clause: 310, 552

Implied powers: 29, 32, 161, 261, 264, 386, 420-422, 507, 542, Appendix A

Indiana: 186, 193, 201, 303, 360, 483
    Indiana Supreme Court: 360

Indian Territory: 736

Inherent powers: 30-32, 417, 420, 424-425, 453, Appendix A

Inter-Colonial Committee of Correspondence: 98

Internal Revenue Service: 295, 307, 313, 319-320, 330, 340-341

Interstate Commerce Commission: 315, 702-704

Interstate compacts: 66, 628, 675, 703-705, 718-719

Interstate Conventions *see Conventions*

Interstate cooperation: 704-705

Intolerable Acts: 92, 285

Iowa: 189, 198, 483

Ishikawa, Brendon Troy: xxxv, 458

J

Jackson, William: xxx-xxxi, 156

Jacob, Giles: 773, Appendix D

Jacob Leisler's Rebellion of 1689: 85

Gralike, Donald James: 294, 332

Jameson, John Alexander: xxviii-xxix, xxxvi, 2, 17-20, 23, 33-34, 37-40, 59-60, 96, 118-119, 253-254, 267-268, 419-423

Jameson, John Franklin: 13

Jay, John: 132, 183, 572

Jefferson, Thomas: xxii, 35, 74, 132-133, 136-137, 158, 165, 171, 201, 487
    Jefferson's Notes: 175, 585

Jim Crow laws: 114

John Birch Society: 195, 468, 561

Johnson, Andrew: 112, 276

Judicial restraint: 246

Judicial review: 15, 223, 228, 236, 240, 258, 277, 408, 453-455, 478, 533, 549

Justiciability: 221-224, 229-232, 238-239, 245, 267, 283, 464, 662, 778

K

The Kalb Report: 602

Kalfus, Mason: 28-29, 255, 463

Kansas: 118, 193, 226-227, 275, 291-292, 310-311, 314, 396
    Kansas Supreme Court: 292

Kean, Thomas: 665-668

Kentucky: 106-107, 111-112, 185-186, 193, 290, 307, 313, 344, 356, 363, 383, 531, 735
    Kentucky Distilleries: 307, 313
    Kentucky Legislature: 356
    Kentucky Resolution: 185

Ketcham, Ralph: xxx, 92

King, Rufus: xxx, 139-140, 487, 548

Kobach, Kris: 14, 459, 627-628

Kurland, Phillip B.: xxix, 686

Kyvig, David E.: xxviii, xxx, 64, 184, 195-196, 620-621

L

Labunski, Richard: xxx, 153

Landholder's Constitution: 44

Lansing, Jr., John: xxx, xxxii, 139, 537, 548, 594

Lee, George: 166, 553

Legal arguments: 50, 673-676

Leges Statutae Republicae Sancti Marini: 124

Legislative Commission: 307

Legislative convention: 17, 20, 25, 28, 86, 99, 113

Legislative instructions: 39, 177, 378, 627-629

Legislative Procedure: 35, 410

Leveling effect: 691-693

Levine, Henry: 273-274, 281

Levy, Leonard: 126, 261

Lexington and Concord: 88, 92

Lex Parliamentaria: 35, 421

Liberty Amendment: 195, 468

Limitability: 430, 456, 463, 483, 577, 630-631, 678-681

Limited convention: 23-25, 33, 128, 146, 149-150, 154, 204, 212, 251, 264, 277, 356, 358, 413, 443, 454-456, 499, 524, 528, 577, 606, 617, 642-643, 646-651, 668, 677, 680, 682, 697

Lincoln, Abraham: 112, 187, 213, 276, 673

Lord Dunmore: 98-99

Louisiana: 110, 116, 177, 193, 289, 362-363, 531, 691
    Louisiana Supreme Court: 362
    New Orleans: 109

Louisiana Purchase: 110, 691

M

Madison, James: xxx-xxxi, 28, 41, 110, 133, 137, 140, 149, 153-154, 162-177, 182-184, 259, 262, 268, 442-443, 478, 485, 488, 501-502, 548, 552-555, 566, 572, 585, 618, 622, 696, 772
    Madison Administration: 185
    Madison's Notes on the Convention: 66-68, 577, 584, 637, 772

Maggs, Gregory: 573, 575

Magliocca, Gerald: 623-624

Magna Carta Libertatum: 2, 124

Maier, Pauline: xxx, 22, 63, 90, 94

Maine: 13, 79, 193, 336, 360, 366-368, 376-377, 399, 539
    Maine Supreme Court: 13, 366-368, 376

Mandamus action: 225, 236, 289-290, 300-301, 305-306, 316

Mandatory theory: 180

Marshall, John: 51, 53, 405, 576, 688

Martin, Luther: xxx, 548, 594

Marbury, William L.: 50-52

Maryland: 45-46, 51, 85, 88-89, 119, 128, 194, 198, 308-309, 318-319, 327-328, 405, 460, 483, 704-705, 769

Maryland Assembly of Freemen: 88

Mason, George: xxiii, xxx, 123, 140, 150, 152, 162, 490, 548, 556, 594, 637

Mason's Manual: 35, 410

Massachusetts: 76-77, 80, 83-96, 101-104, 117-120, 129-131, 139, 144, 158, 177, 194, 198, 295, 313, 377-379, 487, 490, 508, 554-556, 573, 666, 769, 772
    Massachusetts Colony: 76-77
    Massachusetts Constitution: xxii
    Massachusetts House: 377, 769
    Massachusetts Provincial Congress meeting: 94
    Massachusetts Supreme Court: 377-378

Mayflower Compact: 75-77, 79

McCain-Feingold Act: 700

McCoy, Drew: xxx, 176

McDonald, Forrest: xxxi, 619

McHenry, James: xxx, 548

Michigan: 69, 193, 207, 358-359, 402-403, 418, 473, 483, 635
    Michigan Supreme Court: 69, 358, 402, 473, 635

Millionaire's Amendment: 195

Minnesota: 193, 705, 736

Mississippi: 112-113, 116, 243, 483, 703

Missouri: 187, 193, 294, 304, 309-310, 313-314, 332-333, 341, 355, 361, 364, 390, 396, 423, 483
    Missouri constitution: 333
    Missouri Supreme Court: 355, 361, 364, 390

Missouri Amendment: 332-333

Mondale, Walter: 203, 466

Montana: 193, 311-312, 321, 387-389, 483-484, 659, 694
    Montana Constitution: 312
    Montana Legislature: 311, 388, 659, 694
    Montana Supreme Court: 311-312, 387-389

Morris, Gouverneur: 144, 147, 150, 152, 169, 490, 529, 620, 667

Mount Vernon Compact meeting: 622, 704

N

Nashville Convention of 1850: 66

Natelson, Robert G.: xxxv, 36, 42, 63, 71, 86, 119, 255-256, 409-410, 423-425, 467, 485, 503, 601, 615, 618, 625, 628-629

Natelson's Research Wave Designation: xxxv, 452-462, 641-643

National Archives: 408, 524

National Press Club: 602

Native American: 82, 279-280, 401, Appendix B

Native American constitutions and conventions: Appendix B

Native Americans: 75, 83, 279-280
    Cherokee: 186, 279
    Chickasaw: 300
    Choctaw: 279, 736, 738
    Creek: 186

Nebraska: 188, 193, 197, 217, 337
    Nebraska Constitution: 337

Necessary and Proper Clause: 29, 35-36, 161, 258-262, 296, 386, 450, 456, 522

Nevada: 193-194, 307-308, 737

Las Vegas: 344

Nevada Supreme Court: 307-308

New Amsterdam: 81-83

New Hampshire: 79-80, 83, 94-97, 119, 159, 166, 483, 509, 573, 579, 635, 737, 769-772
    New Hampshire constitution: 96
    New Hampshire Supreme Court: 635

New Jersey: 83, 87, 91, 104, 119, 128-130, 142, 152, 186, 193-194, 274, 313, 319, 324, 330, 483, 602, 665-667, 767, 770-771

New Jersey Plan: 142, 667

New York: 52-54, 65, 81-87, 90-91, 96-97, 108, 116-119, 128-130, 134, 139, 143, 155, 166, 172, 181-183, 193-194, 198, 206-207, 279, 322, 483, 487, 491, 508, 512, 537, 553, 572-573, 592, 599, 621, 657, 666-668, 682, 690, 770-772
    Albany: 85, 90
    Albany Congress: 65, 87
    Albany Plan of Union: 65
    Long Island: 83

Nobility Amendment: 696

Nominating convention: 22, 447, 603

Non-delegation Doctrine: 61

North Carolina: 22, 89, 107-109, 117-119, 157-159, 193, 207, 323, 369, 403, 406, 490, 515, 519, 540, 573, 579, 656-658, 668, 769-772
    North Carolina Supreme Court: 369, 515

North Dakota: 385, 389, 484
    North Dakota Supreme Court: 385, 389

Nullification: 176, 185-186, 559, 563-564, 594, 664, 706, 739

Nullification Crisis: 186, 559, 563

O'Neill, Karen: 703-704

Occupy Movement: 19

Of Ancient and Modern Confederacies: 137, 502

Ohio: 177, 186-187, 193, 203, 297, 301-302, 317, 339, 386, 390, 396-397, 483
    Ohio Supreme Court: 386

Oklahoma: 193, 371, 387, 483, 736
    Oklahoma Constitution: 371
    Oklahoma Legislature: 371
    Oklahoma Supreme Court: 371, 387

One person, one vote: 197

Open convention: 212, 413-414, 494, 499, 516, 528-530, 536, 590, 604, 609, 621, 641, 648, 651, 680, 715

Oregon: 188, 193, 364-366, 552
    Oregon constitution: 365
    Oregon Supreme Court: 364-365

Orfield, Lester B.: xxviii, xxxv-xxxvi, 22-23, 39-40, 53-54, 56, 212, 216, 224-225, 240, 453, 642,

695, 710

P

Packard, Frank: 635-636

Paine, Thomas: 125, 717

Palmer, A. Mitchell: 161, 312-313, 319-320, 427

Parliament: 6-12, 16, 81, 91, 96, 103, 777-778
  Parliamentary Law: 419, 775, 777
  Parliamentary Practice: 35, 74, 721

Parliamentary Law: 419, 775, 777

Paterson, William: xxx, 142, 548, 667

Paulsen, Michael Stokes: xxxv, 255, 261, 460, 617, 632, 646, 658, 725

Pendleton, Edmund: 711-712

Penn, William: 102

Pennsylvania: 63, 85-87, 93, 102, 118-120, 140, 156, 175, 183, 189, 193, 318-319, 393-395, 509, 533, 554, 573, 607, 618, 635, 659, 678, 690, 705, 738, 771
  Pennsylvania constitution: 102
  Pennsylvania Supreme Court: 393, 607, 635, 690
  Philadelphia: 1, 4, 16, 35, 42, 46, 66, 69, 74, 78, 93-94, 120, 123, 127-133, 135-138, 143, 153-155, 162-165, 174-175, 187, 231, 263, 271, 276, 393, 402, 410-413, 417, 422, 425-428, 442, 455-456, 474, 479-482, 486-492, 497, 502, 505, 508-510, 515, 520, 526, 532, 537, 543, 548, 554-556, 566, 578, 583, 587, 593-594, 612, 618-622, 627, 632, 637, 641, 648, 656, 665-667, 674, 693, 697, 767-769, 771-774
  Philadelphia Conference: 566

People's Constitution: 44

Perry, Barbara: xxvii, 60-62, 194, 274-275, 510, 615, 621, 684, 694

Pierce, William: xxx, 548

Pilgrim Code: 77

Pinckney, Charles: 46, 130, 136, 138, 154, 556, 620, 637, 667, 669, 693

Pinckney, Charles Cotesworth: 600

Pinckney's Plan: 138

Piscataqua: 79-80

Planning convention: 723, Appendix B

Platz, William: 56, 429, 447, 615

Plimouth Combination: 75

Plymouth Agreement: 77

Plymouth Colony: 76-77

Political Question Doctrine: 223-231, 236, 246, 291-293, 351, 520, 526, 534, 550

Polygamy: 193-194

Popular convention: 21

Populist Movement: xxxiv, 559

Potter, William: 690-691

Powers Prohibited: 436

Presentment: 275, 303-304, 456, 463-464, 557

Presentment Clause: 303, 456, 557

Presidential Reconstruction: 112-113

Pre-written amendment proposal: 434

Procedures Act: 211, 236

Prodding effect: 174, 184-190, 193-195, 198-202, 209, 213, 283, 453, 474, 501, 522, 560-561, 682-687, 693, 699-700

Progressive Movement: xxxiv, 453, 559, 688-689

Prohibited powers: 31, 33, Appendix A

Prohibition: 31-33, 39, 52-54, 60, 118, 162, 193, 282, 295, 298, 304, 307, 311-315, 319-320, 323, 330, 340-342, 348, 356-358, 396, 453, 457, 501, 510-512, 527, 541, 544, 549, 551, 560, 586, 614, 698, 701
    Federal Prohibition: 313, 340
    National Prohibition: 282, 295, 307, 311-312, 319-320, 323, 330, 340-341, 348, 355, 396, 541, 543
    Prohibition Act: 298, 323, 348
    Prohibition Agent: 313, 341
    Prohibition Era: 453
    Prohibition Movements: 560

Providence: 44, 78-79, 98, 120

Provincial Congress: 9, 87-89, 94, 96, 423, 627

Provincial Conventions: 87, 423

Public debt: 111, 135

Publius: 488, 571-572, 592

R

Radical Republicans: 112, 115

Randolph, Edmund: xxx, 137-138, 152, 163-164, 170, 174, 501, 548, 555-556, 637, 667

Rappaport, Michael: xxxv, 624

Ratification conventions: 4, 20-21, 63, 101, 106-107, 154, 157-161, 165, 169, 183, 249, 301-302, 369, 427, 430, 496, 503, 527, 540, 567, 572-573, 588, 613, 622, 628-629, 655-658, 723

Ratifiers: xxxii-xxxiv, 568, 574, 623, 631, 648

Reagan Administration: 204, 456

Reapportionment: 197-199, 202, 205-211, 259, 274, 339, 376, 403-404, 446-447, 566, 694

Reapportionment Revolution: 197, 208

Reconstruction: 16, 20, 26, 112-118, 268, 344, 723, 739

Reconstruction Acts: 114

Reconstruction Amendments: 268

Reconstruction conventions: 16, 114, 723

Redeemer or Redemption convention: 112-115, 117

Reed-Dirksen Amendment: 239, 249

Rees III, Grover: 43, 429, 460, 645

Rehnquist, William Hubbs: 308, 312, 321

Republic of East Florida: 109, 737

Republic of Indian Stream: 109, 737

Republic of the Rio Grande: 109, 737

Republic of West Florida: 109-110, 737

Republic of Watauga Association 737

Rescission: 200-201, 211, 229, 254, 266-270, 334-335, 413, 454, 457-458, 464, 535-538, 559, 663

Reserved powers: 30, 261-262, 326, Appendix A

Revenue sharing campaign: 199-200

Revolutionary convention: 1, 7, 12, 16-18, 22, 25, 28, 49, 76, 97-99, 601, 648

Revolutionary War: 65, 74-75, 90, 102-103, 119, 184, 423-424, 593, 627, 723, 735

Rhode Island: 22-24, 44-46, 78-79, 83, 94, 98, 111, 120, 133-136, 156, 184, 309, 312, 319-320, 356, 363, 366, 370, 397, 483, 486, 540, 543-544, 573, 656-658, 668, 688
    Rhode Island constitution: 44
    Rhode Island Supreme Court: 370

Rhodes, Robert: 146-147

Right of revolution: xxiii, 7, 12

Ripeness: 232, 244

Roberts, Owen Josephus: xxxv (n), 324

Rogers, James Kenneth: 231, 519-520, 564, 650

Roman Era: 627
    Roman Empire: 2
    Roman Law: 775, 777
    Roman Republic: 2-3, 5, 124, 594, 717, 719-720
    Romans: 2, 5, 12, 124, 592
    Roman Republic: 2-5, 124, 594, 717-720

Roosevelt, Franklin Delano: 195
    New Deal: 195, 238

Rules Committee: 69-71, 512, 515, 542-543, 676

Rule XII (US House): 408-409

Runaway scenario: 484-486, 611-625

Rutledge, John: 145, 149

S

Salt Lake: 338, 410, 543, 724

Saxons: 2, 5, 123

Scalia, Antonin: 174, 574-575, 601-602, 660, 663, 715

Schauer, Frederick: 459-460

Scheips, Paul: 709

Scobell, Henry: 35

Scottish Parliament: 11

Secession: 16, 21-22, 111-115, 185, 327, 559, 706

Secessionary convention: 20-22, 26, 723

Second general convention: 152-155, 162-166, 169, 174, 183, 478, 552-556, 588

Senate Journal: 311

Senate Record: 518

Separation of powers: 14, 29, 47, 224-225, 229, 235-236, 240, 457, 463-465, 662, 721

Shays' Rebellion: 131-132, 554

Sherman, Roger: xxiii, 11, 20, 95, 148-152, 422, 637

Slaughter-House Cases: 310

Smith, Melancton: 183, 657

Social Security: 347

Sons of Liberty: 87, 90-91, 94

Souter, David: 575, 663

South Carolina: 13, 22, 46, 85, 89, 104-105, 116-119, 130, 136-138, 186, 276, 556, 579, 600, 620, 667, 771

South Dakota: 193, 328-329, 484

Southern convention arc: 111-115, Appendix B

Special interest groups: 204, 511, 609, 651-652, 655

Specialized conventions: 16, 21-22, 25, 28

Specificity: 180, 250, 259, 533

Speech and Debate Clause: 33, 237, 294, 329, 333, 349, 382, 537, 626

Spontaneous convention: 17-19, 25, 28, 45

Squire, Peverill: 418, 425

Staleness: 255-256, 293, 465

Stamp Act: 65, 87, 90-91, 97

Stamp Act Congress of 1765: 65

Standing: 38, 66, 89, 97, 100, 189, 197, 226, 232-234, 238-239, 243-244, 299-300, 412-413, 418, 434, 543, 652, 656, 661, 668, 694

State of Franklin: 107, 111

States' Rights: 196, 205, 210, 564, 675

Stern, Michael: 71, 223, 229, 275, 646-647

Stevens, John Paul: 228, 294, 326, 331, 543

Story, Joseph: 318, 613, 674

Story, Joseph: xxxiv, 318, 326, 613, 674

Straight-Out Era Disenfranchisement convention: 114

Sturm, Albert: 63, 735

Suffolk Resolves: 93

Suffrage Amendment: 299

Supremacy Clause: 15, 264-265, 318, 331-333, 393

T

Taft, Henry: 55-56

Taxpayer Convention: 117

Taylor, Arthur: 622-623, 656-658, 720-721

Taylor, John of Caroline: xxxiv, 489

Tea Party: 19, 92, 110, 470, 724

Tea Party movement: 110, 724

Tennessee: 66, 107-112, 118, 186, 193, 309, 357, 392-393, 509, 737
    Tennessee Constitution: 392-393
    Tennessee Supreme Court: 357, 392

Term limits: 175, 288, 294, 325-329, 332, 336-337, 354, 359-360, 371, 374-375, 381, 399, 459, 529, 531, 564

Territorial Legislature: 418-419

Territories: 34, 109, 118, 177, 279, 419-420, 434, 477, 539, 705, 735-737

Texas: 115-117, 193-195, 309, 468, 483, 599, 737
    Texas Supreme Court: 116

Three-fifths Clause: 185, 551, 554

Three-Fifths Compromise: 165

Tribe, Laurence: 220, 402, 432, 446, 468, 607, 662-663

Tucker, St. George: xxxiv, 568, 677

Tuller, Walter: 235-236, 684-686

Turner, Frederick Jackson: 86, 108

U

United Colonies of New England: 64, 83, 100

United Kingdom: 123, 639

United States Constitution: 4, 31, 106, 287, 333, 342, 350, 355, 360, 373, 381-382, 435, 479, 493, 497, 547, 576, 639, 714, 729, 775

Unit voting: 24, 64-69, 83, 212, 403, 411, 465, 508, 540, 580, 655, 662

Utah: 193, 199, 212, 310, 338-339, 398, 406, 494, 519, 724, 737

V

Validity: 26, 162, 197, 210, 221-226, 245, 256-258, 261, 275-277, 292, 298-299, 309, 312, 318, 323, 339, 345-346, 354, 373, 433, 443, 461-463, 465, 476, 519-520, 532-533, 547, 580, 586, 594, 600, 630, 649

Valley Paper: 391-392, 396, 521

Van Alstyne, William: xxxv, 140, 648-650, 674-675

Van Devanter, Willis: 295-296, 307, 313, 320, 341

Vermont: 96-97, 102, 106, 111, 119, 177, 193, 309, 348, 483-484, 554, 579, 737

Vesting Clause: 330

Vile, John R.: xxvii-xxviii, xxxvi, 18, 23-24, 184, 223-224, 227

Virginia: 24, 35, 98-99, 107-108, 111, 119, 123, 128-142, 153-154, 165-166, 169-170, 174-177, 181-188, 193, 224, 238, 254, 275, 282, 287, 303, 309, 319, 333, 358, 384, 395, 408, 425-427, 442-443, 463, 486-490, 501-502, 553-557, 566, 573, 576, 585, 588, 594, 599, 622, 657, 667-668, 682, 704-705, 711, 771

    Virginia Resolution(s): 185, 594

    Virginia Supreme Court: 384

Virginia Plan: 136-138, 142, 175, 489, 501-502, 553-555, 667

Voegler, Douglas: 245, 254

Volstead Act: 312, 315, 324, 384

Voluntary Committee of Lawyers: 64

von Moschzisker, Robert: 607-609

W

Walker, Robert F.: 355, 361

Warren, Earl: 468, 566, 602

Washington: 66, 69, 132, 138, 185-188, 193, 224, 241-242, 275-276, 303, 334, 413, 463, 487, 517, 543, 558, 566-567, 581, 593, 604, 618-620, 658, 660-661, 722

Washington, George: 69, 132, 138, 224, 275-276, 303, 463, 487, 558, 567, 618-620, 660, 721

Washington Peace Conference of 1861: 66, 187-188, 413, 517, 559, 566-567

Watauga Association: 109, 737

Weber, Paul J.: xxvii, 60-62, 170, 194-196, 274-275, 510, 615, 621, 669, 678, 684, 694

West Virginia: 24, 108, 111, 238, 254, 303, 309

White, Edward Douglass: 311, 317

Wild beasts theory: 204

William, Robert F.: 118, 274, 280, 669

Willis, Hugh Evander: 49-50, 56

Wilson, James: 140, 144-148, 618, 631

Wisconsin: 192-194, 198, 279, 288, 313, 340, 384, 418, 473, 694, 700, 706
    Wisconsin Legislature: 192, 198, 694, 706
    Wisconsin Supreme Court: 384

Women's Suffrage: 560

Wood, Gordon S.: xxxi, 97, 125, 129, 606, 716

Worcester: 93-94

Wyoming: 64, 194, 383

Y

Yates, Robert: xxx, xxxii, 67, 537, 548, 594

Z

Zimmerman, Joseph: 704-705

CPSIA information can be obtained
at www.ICGtesting.com
Printed in the USA
LVOW11*0759190617
538591LV00007B/57/P